MW00667482

The publisher gratefully acknowledges
the generous support of the Humanities Endowment Fund
of the University of California Press Foundation.

THE THIRD REICH SOURCEBOOK

Weimar and Now: German Cultural Criticism

EDWARD DIMENDBERG, MARTIN JAY, AND ANTON KAES, GENERAL EDITORS

THE THIRD REICH SOURCEBOOK

Edited by

ANSON RABINBACH AND SANDER L. GILMAN

University of California Press
Berkeley Los Angeles London

University of California Press, one of the most distinguished university presses in the United States, enriches lives around the world by advancing scholarship in the humanities, social sciences, and natural sciences. Its activities are supported by the UC Press Foundation and by philanthropic contributions from individuals and institutions. For more information, visit www.ucpress.edu.

University of California Press
Berkeley and Los Angeles, California

University of California Press, Ltd.
London, England

© 2013 by The Regents of the University of California

LIBRARY OF CONGRESS CATALOGING-IN-PUBLICATION DATA

The Third Reich sourcebook / edited by Anson Rabinbach and Sander Gilman.
p. cm.—(Weimar and now : German cultural criticism ; 47)
Includes bibliographical references and index.
ISBN 978-0-520-20867-4 (cloth : alk. paper)
ISBN 978-0-520-27683-3 (pbk : alk. paper)
ISBN 978-0-520-95514-1 (ebook)
1. National socialism—Germany—History—Sources. 2. Germany—History—1933–1945—Sources. I. Rabinbach, Anson. II. Gilman, Sander L.
DD256.5.T5245 2013
943.086—dc23 2012050019

Manufactured in the United States of America

21 20 19 18 17 16 15 14 13
10 9 8 7 6 5 4 3 2 1

The paper used in this publication meets the minimum requirements of ANSI/NISO Z39.48–1992 (R 2002) (*Permanence of Paper*).

Contents

PART TWELVE. DEFEAT

Illustrations

Preface

The Third Reich Sourcebook offers English-language readers a broad range of texts, written or published during the twelve years that the National Socialist (Nazi) regime held sway in Germany, from its rise after World War I to the time it took power on 30 January 1933. This book is a companion volume to *The Weimar Republic Sourcebook* edited by Anton Kaes, Martin Jay, and Edward Dimendberg and published by the University of California Press in 1994. We have sought to provide a comprehensive collection of newly translated documents that offer insights into Nazi ideology, economics, politics, society, cultural policy, and influence in the fine arts and popular culture. Any responsible documentation of National Socialism must include explicit recognition that the "German Renaissance" promised by the Nazis culminated in unprecedented horror—World War II and the annihilation of European Jewry. This volume considers Nazi politics, ideology, and culture from that vantage point.

Like *The Weimar Republic Sourcebook,* this collection seeks to present English-speaking undergraduates, graduate students, and general readers with a wide selection of primary sources that reflect the complex and often contradictory nature of German politics, society, and culture during this period of history. While some of the documents in this volume are well known and often cited, many of the texts have been recently excavated by historians and are translated and published here for the first time. In addition, many of those already in translation have been revised for a contemporary audience. To avoid replicating what has become a "canon" of Nazi texts, we were compelled to rethink what pieces would be most useful to scholars and students in the twenty-first century. The result is an archaeology of National Socialism emphasizing many arenas of thought and action in Nazi Germany hitherto underexamined. This volume thus contains speeches and texts of political leaders such as Adolf Hitler, Joseph Goebbels, and Heinrich Himmler, as well as texts by lesser-known commentators who contributed to the admittedly limited public dialogue about pivotal historical figures, such as the philosopher Friedrich Nietzsche and the composer Richard Wagner, or who wrote about major issues of the time, such as the meaning of sex, the soul, "social fitness," suicide, or modern art.

The Third Reich Sourcebook documents how the Nazi leadership used ideas of racial purity, the German people—the *Volk*—and the nation to judge not only works of art but individual human beings, whose fate often depended on an intertwined political and aesthetic vision. National Socialism relied heavily on visual imagery for its success, and the *Sourcebook* attempts to demonstrate how the visual culture (film, photography, newsreels, posters, advertisements, commercial art, illustrated magazines) of National Socialism reinforced its ideological and racial assumptions.

Most difficult to understand in light of the ultimate crimes of the regime is the reality that Nazism's racial utopia was a plausible and compelling idea for a great many contemporaries. The embrace of Nazi ideology and practice for countless ordinary Germans did not result merely from political propaganda but also from the more subtle mixture of commercial entertainment and "soft" ideology purveyed by the propaganda machine created by Joseph Goebbels. Goebbels frequently noted that the most successful propaganda worked through stealth, concealing a subliminal message in the supposed normality and conventionality of the stereotypes and concepts promoted by the Nazis. Even commercial culture adopted the style of the regime by promoting tanning creams and blond hair dye for women, as well as politically "correct" fashions. In many respects, Nazi ideology was a mélange borrowed from a variety of sources. The much-displayed concept of degeneration, for example, did not originate with the Nazis but began in the mid-nineteenth century as a French medical term that equated hereditary mental illness with crime, madness, "nervousness," and social decline. The history of this concept and others raises important questions that these documents aid in answering: How did political language create myths or concepts of normalcy that ultimately became their own reality? How did an aesthetic of purity and degeneration become acceptable—indeed "normal"—during the first years after the Nazi seizure of power? How did National Socialism integrate concepts appropriated from the textbooks of biology and natural history into a politically motivated aesthetic doctrine and practice? How did the elaboration of a biosocial metaphor evolve from the natural to the normative to create a new kind of body politics? How did this metaphor of purity and degeneration not only become official policy but also take hold as a widely shared and acceptable ideal? The fact that these ideas belonged to the standard mental equipment of educated Europeans and Americans long after the end of the nineteenth century only increased their destructive potential.

Of course, no "German Renaissance" was possible under such cultural tyranny. In the end, the assault on culture merely anticipated the eventual criminal policies of a racial state. Nazism was responsible for the greatest cultural diaspora of modern times, sending artists and writers into exile around the globe. The cultural resistance of these exiles is therefore an integral part of the story of Nazi policy, so we have included some of their voices in this volume.

Our intent, like that of the editors of *The Weimar Republic Sourcebook,* is to allow a teacher or researcher to examine a slice of German cultural and political history using primary sources. We have not aimed for an exhaustive treatment of the period but have sought to offer an evocative mosaic of the German experience between 1933 and 1945. We have focused on the key personalities, debates, and events in Germany, an ever-changing geographic area at the time, but we have also looked at how German and non-German Jews were victimized and how the genocide unfolded as the "total war" of the German military machine took control of the occupied lands of Central Europe and Eastern Europe. Limited space is also given to the voices of the internal German opposition and of German exiles in various lands of refuge. This mosaic reveals how complex the experience of Nazi Germany was for the widest range of its inhabitants.

In using *The Weimar Republic Sourcebook* as our model and guide, we soon came to a striking realization that sets *The Third Reich Sourcebook* apart from that volume. With few exceptions, the texts of the 1919–33 period in the earlier volume are intellectually and linguistically engaging. With the exception of a few Nazi texts, they represent some of the most creative and intellectually gifted German writers and thinkers throughout the political spectrum. To earn a place in the Weimar volume, the texts had to be readable and stimulating. In contrast, texts after 1933 are often turgid, self-aggrandizing, and intellectually vacuous, testifying to the nature of the events that took place in Germany during the Nazi period. Whereas the Weimar period offers major texts by such extraordinary figures as Theodor W. Adorno, Walter Benjamin, Albert Einstein, Joseph Roth, Kurt Weill, and Paul Tillich, we were condemned to reprint anti-Semitic laws, polemics, and diatribes and to document the specious undertakings of party functionaries posing as university professors (or university professors posing as party functionaries), artists suddenly raised from marginal to official status, and sycophantic writers and playwrights whose goal was to herald the "New Revolution" in language touted as "simple" and "direct," which today can be read only with the greatest effort. Even when the material reflects the behavior of some major figures of the Weimar era after 1933—such as Gottfried Benn and Carl Schmitt—these texts are exceptional only for the perversity of their authors' attachment to the regime. This shift, as the German Jewish literary scholar Victor Klemperer observed in his diaries from the period, is not accidental but intrinsic to the alterations in the German language initiated by Nazism. The documents assembled here remind us that ruthlessness and terror can result from very conventional notions and that evil, as the theologian Dietrich Bonhoeffer, who was murdered in April 1945, remarked, "can appear in the shape of light." Perhaps these disturbing historical images can also provoke reflection about the contemporary world, even when—as the German-Jewish political philosopher Hannah Arendt observed—such reflection strains the limits of the imagination.

If there is a disjuncture between the Weimar and Nazi sourcebooks, it is that the Nazi regime drained life from the intellectual and political spheres of Germany, not merely by forcing the flight of Jews and left-wing (and some right-wing) intellectuals from Germany, but also by inflicting the most moribund and crass use of what Klemperer called the *Lingua Tertii Imperii,* the language of the Third Reich, on the minds and actions of those remaining in Germany. There should be exceptions, but it is hardly possible to see the "brilliance" of Hitler's or Joseph Goebbels's public utterances today. The words and ideas of these "masters" of propaganda seem flat and narrow, which, of course, they were. Reading the philosophers, philologists, physicians, and historians of the day reveals their intellectual blindness, which was clothed in language that can be described only as execrable. (Only in the articulate responses of critical voices such as Klaus Mann, Clemens August Count von Galen, or Thomas Mann can one see an effort to expose the innate bloody-mindedness of the majority of the so-called intelligentsia of the Third Reich.) This, then, is the core undertaking of our volume: to show that the politics and culture of the Third Reich were bound by narrow and parochial concerns; that the debates within National Socialism, while present, never took on an intellectual edge or dared to express true conflicts of belief; and that the "masters" of the German language during this period were the pedants of Nazi culture. Consequently, National Socialist ideology never reached the intellectual level even of Italian Fascism or Soviet Communism. No effort was made to offer a coherent doctrine, apart from the incoherent ramblings of Hitler's *Mein Kampf.* For the most part, Nazi ideology was an unpalatable potpourri, creating realities as they were needed and generating seeming conflicts that were "resolved" through the cult of personality surrounding the Nazi leadership and that furthered the political exigencies of the moment. All of this is revealed in the words of regime leaders, just as the flow of history destroys their arguments.

To show this dynamic, we needed translations that capture the surface dullness of Nazi language while revealing the inner tensions of this shifting ideological morass. Lilian Friedberg has supplied new translations for the bulk of the texts and has redone older ones, some of them contemporaneous to the original texts. (A number of texts, such as the Nuremberg trial documents, first appeared in English.) Unless otherwise noted, she is the translator of all German texts. We have adapted some translations from more recent English sources, in which cases we note the translator in the source citation at the beginning of the text. These translations have been reedited and partially retranslated with an eye to providing the most accessible language for our readers. The endnotes and bracketed comments in the texts, whether newly translated or previously published in English, are those of the translator (or the editor of an English edition) unless otherwise noted. (However, we felt free to add first names in brackets without comment.) Ellipses in square brackets indicate omissions from a text; we do not use them either at the beginning or end of excerpted texts. When we present texts of laws and policies, the order and the nature of the outline follow the originals rather than common usage. Italics reflect emphasis in the originals unless otherwise noted.

Working on this volume has been a revelation. Reading ever more broadly in the primary texts of the period, we realized, of course, that the Third Reich was bankrupt from its origin. We found no "jewels" in the head of this toad, only ever-increasing circles of the banal, the trivial, the destructive, the hateful, and the inane. This deadly mix deformed the experiences of those living in Europe from 1933 to 1945 and caused the suffering and deaths of millions. If the mosaic offered here has value, it is to show that the leveling of diverse intellectual and emotional positions to a single doctrine acceptable to a cadre of individuals poses a serious threat to any society by destroying people's ability to think (and act) critically, which contributes to tearing down the moral underpinnings of a culture.

The Princeton University Committee on Research in the Humanities and Social Sciences has generously supported our work on this project, and we gratefully acknowledge the support of the National Endowment for the Humanities. We thank Daniel Magilow, Andres McConnon, Charles Melby-Thompson, Timothy Nunan, Clara Oberle, Martin Ruehl, Robyn Schiffman, and Susanne Schmid for their indispensable work as researchers for this project. We are especially grateful to Kenny Chumbley for his careful work on the permissions and on the manuscript. The late Peggy Reilly's administrative assistance must be here acknowledged; we remember her for her efficiency and cheerfulness. We are especially thankful for the support and encouragement of the editors of the Weimar and Now series at the University of California Press, Edward Dimendberg, Martin Jay, and Anton Kaes. At the press, we are indebted to Adrienne Harris for her attentive, patient, and above all cheerful work on this grim volume. Mary Frances and Suzanne Knott oversaw the project and offered the direction and guidance it needed in the final stage.

Key Abbreviations

BDM	Bund Deutscher Mädel	League of German Girls
DAP	Deutsche Arbeiterpartei	German Workers' Party
HJ	Hitler Jugend	Hitler Youth
KdF	Kraft durch Freude	Strength through Joy
KPD	Kommunistische Partei Deutschlands	German Communist Party
NSDAP	Nationalsozialistische Deutsche Arbeiterpartei	National Socialist German Workers' Party
SA	Sturm Abteilung	Storm Troopers
SD	Sicherheitsdienst	Security Service
SPD	Sozialdemokratische Partei Deutschlands	Social Democratic Party of Germany
SS	Schutzstaffel	National Socialist Defense Force

PART ONE

. . .

THE BEGINNINGS OF NATIONAL SOCIALISM

1
The Munich Years and the Legacy of the War

NO EVENT IS MORE CRUCIAL to understanding the emergence of Nazism than Germany's surrender to the Allies at 11 o'clock on 11 November 1918. Until the very end of World War I, wartime propaganda portrayed the undefeated Imperial German Army as invincible, giving no hint of the coming disaster on the Western Front. The anti-Hitler journalist Sebastian Haffner recalled that when he was eleven years old and saw the newspaper headline "Armistice Signed," his "entire inner world . . . collapsed."[1] Adolf Hitler, recuperating from partial blindness in a military hospital in Pasewalk, also recalled the trauma of defeat, later describing in *Mein Kampf* the moment when an elderly pastor told the stunned patients that the royal House of Hohenzollern had fallen, the Kaiser had gone into exile, and the German Empire had become a republic. For Hitler, as for many of his generation, his personal suffering vanished, as he wrote in *Mein Kampf,* "in comparison with the tragedy of the fatherland." During the 1930s, much of the literature produced in National Socialist Germany mythologized the experience at the front and lauded war veterans. For example, Heinrich Lersch's war poems presented a redemptive vision of death and destruction, and Otto Gmelin portrayed a simple but war-wise German in his saga *Prohn Fights for His People* (1938). Though the account in *Mein Kampf,* composed during Hitler's brief fourteen-month imprisonment in the Landsberg Fortress for an abortive coup in Munich on 9 November 1923, may be questioned, Hitler claimed that on the day of Germany's humiliation—9 November—he had vowed "to go into politics."[2]

When Hitler joined the Deutsche Arbeiterpartei (German Workers' Party, DAP) in Munich in September 1919, he was still by his own description a "nameless" political neophyte. His pan-German sympathies did not begin to emerge until the summer of 1919 after he received political training as a military informer in an anti-Bolshevik instruction course, courtesy of the Reichswehr (Armed Services). In his first written statement on the "Jewish Question," a letter dated 16 September 1919, written at the behest of Captain Karl Mayr, head of the Army Intelligence and Propaganda Unit, to a soldier, Adolf Gemlich, Hitler proposed a "rational" rather than "emotional" anti-Semitism in order to be all the more effective "in the irrevocable removal of the Jews."

Hitler was greatly influenced by the economic theorist Gottfried Feder (1883–1941), whom he had heard speak and whose *Manifesto for Breaking the Bondage of Interest* had just appeared. Feder was a central figure in the DAP, which had been organized in 1919 and was one of many political groups that emerged on the fringes of Munich's turbulent political scene. The DAP's founding statement, published on 5 January 1919, addressed its appeal to the working class, promoted antipathy to the "socialization" of the German economy put forward by the parties of the Left, called for wage stabilization and profit sharing, and passionately demanded government by Germans rather than by "foreigners and Jews." From its inception, the DAP embraced an ideological cluster of antiliberalism, pan-Germanic nationalism, antimodernism, racial anti-Semitism, and a mystical ideal of Germanic or Nordic spirituality derived from a variety of pre-1914 "*völkisch*" sources. It blamed Germany's defeat on the "November criminals"—Marxists and Jews—whom it held responsible for any and all of Germany's misfortunes. The fourth point of the party's twenty-five-point program, adopted on 24 February 1920, explicitly excluded Jews from citizenship, defining citizens as "members of the nation" who are "of German blood." Along with Feder, who focused largely on economic issues like Germany's debt and the need to nationalize the credit system, the main ideologues of the DAP were the poet Dietrich Eckart (1868–1923), who saw all life as a world-historical battle between the worldly Jew and the spiritual non-Jew, and Alfred Rosenberg (1893–1946, executed at Nuremberg), whose writings were marked by biological and racial anti-Semitism and a radical hatred of Bolshevism.

When the Nazis came to power in 1933, they rewrote their early history to put Hitler at center stage from the beginning, publishing a highly fictionalized account of the founding of the DAP and of Hitler's 1924 trial in a collector's album illustrated with stick-on photographs that was offered with cigarette purchases. Though the official version of how Hitler joined the movement was fanciful, the miniscule size of the party at its inception, his discovery of his ability to mesmerize audiences, and the resulting mushrooming of membership were not exaggerated. After seizing control of the party in July 1921, Hitler revamped it, calling it the Nationalsozialistische Deutsche Arbeiterpartei (National Socialist German Workers' Party, usually referred to in English as the Nazi Party and in German abbreviated as NSDAP); designing its red, white, and black swastika flag; creating the uniformed paramilitary Sturm Abteilung (Storm Troopers, SA); starting a daily newspaper (*Völkischer Beobachter*); staging countless mass meetings featuring speakers trained to create political fireworks; and adopting new propaganda techniques, some of which are described in Hans Hinkel's *One of a Hundred Thousand* (1933).[3] One of the greatest successes of the Nazi Party in the 1920s was in recruiting young activists and mobilizing the Hitler Jugend (Hitler Youth, HJ) and the Bund Deutscher Mädel (League of German Girls, BDM), which by 1930 had twenty-five thousand members under eighteen. Hans Johst's (1890–1978) play *Schlageter,* based on the life of a young Nazi martyr executed by the French in 1923, depicts party members as dynamic and idealistic, the mirror opposite of the cynical and exhausted older generation. Also typical of propaganda in the earlier years were the books by Wilfrid Bade. Combining his writer's activity with his role as press chief (*Reichsamtsleiter der Reichspressestelle*) of the Nazi Party, Bade was an able popularizer of the history of the party and an advocate of its technological triumphs, especially the putative expansion of mass automobile ownership.

In the late 1920s, under the leadership of Joseph Goebbels, the Nazi Party focused on winning the battle for the traditionally Social Democratic stronghold of Berlin by staging barroom brawls, disrupting meetings, and provoking street battles with Socialist and Communist opponents. Midlevel party organizers such as Fritz Oertner exhorted speakers to be drilled in effective anti-Marxist rhetoric. Though the party was already a formidable presence, not until its breakthrough in the elections of 14 September 1930, described here by Herman Führbach, did it become a force in German politics and a threat to the Weimar Republic.

NOTES

1. Sebastian Haffner, *Defying Hitler: A Memoir,* translated by Oliver Pretzel (New York: Farrar, Strauss and Giroux, 2002), 26.

2. Adolf Hitler, *Mein Kampf,* translated by Ralph Manheim (New York: Houghton Mifflin, 1943), 204, 206.

3. The use of the term *Nazi* is a well-established convention in English. It emerged around 1924 among opponents of National Socialism, who borrowed it from the nickname Nazi (from the masculine proper name Ignatz, the German form of Ignatius), meaning "a foolish, clumsy, or awkward person." The NSDAP briefly adopted the Nazi designation as what the Germans call a "spite word," but they soon gave this up and generally avoided the term, considering it derogatory. Before 1930, English speakers had called the party members National Socialists, a term that dates from 1923. The use of "Nazi Germany," "Nazi regime," and so on was popularized by German exiles abroad. From them, the term spread into other languages and eventually was brought back to Germany after the war.

1

Guidelines of the German Workers' Party

Announced on 5 January 1919. Published in *Dokumente der Zeitgeschichte,* edited by Fritz Maier-Hartmann and Adolf Dresler (Munich: Verlag Franz Eher Nachfolger GmbH, 1938), 85. Translated by Barbara Miller Lane and Leila J. Rupp.

What is the German Workers' Party?

The German Workers' Party is a socialist organization, composed of all folk comrades engaged in mental and physical work. It may only be guided by German leaders who put aside all personal goals and allow national needs to be the highest concern of the party program.

What does the German Workers' Party offer the worker?

The DAP seeks the ennoblement of the German worker. Skilled resident workers have the right to be considered members of the middle class. A sharp distinction between workers and proletarians should be made. An international agreement with the trade unions of other countries must stabilize wages, making it impossible for the working class of a particular country to engage in sharp bargaining. In the future, the competitive position of an individual country shall be determined not by the lowest wages but by the diligence and efficiency of its workers. In this way, the causes of friction among various countries will be avoided. Big business provides food and employment and is therefore to be protected, as long as it does not relentlessly exploit the worker and make it impossible for him to lead a worthwhile life. The DAP believes that the socialization of German economic life signals the collapse of the German economy. By controlling socialized businesses, our enemies would be in the best possible position to efficiently collect the war indemnities which have been imposed on us, and to do so at the expense of the German workers. Therefore, the German worker should not have socialization but profit sharing. Profit sharing can be facilitated by establishing labor cooperatives in the cities and farming cooperatives among agricultural workers in the country, to protect land and soil.

Who is the DAP fighting against?

The DAP is fighting with all its might against usury and inflation. Against all who create no values, who make high profits without any mental or physical work. We fight against the drones in the state, most of whom are Jews; they live the good life and reap what they have not sown. They control and rule us with their money. For these drones Germany and her entire *Volk* are but objects of speculation; their party slogans are much the same. All talk, no action. The DAP honors the principle that he who shall not work shall not eat. Our fight is for justice, true freedom, and happiness. No dictatorship of the proletariat! Equal justice for all. No rule of bayonets. Everyone shall feel himself free to be a free German. There is no happiness to be found in platitudes and hollow speeches at meetings, demonstrations, and election campaigns. Our striving is toward the free happiness of good work, the full pot, and prospering children.

To what extent is the DAP politically active?

The DAP opposes any threat to the unity of the Reich, but excludes the predominance of one single state. We want to be governed solely by Germans; foreigners and Jews govern us only in their own interest or in the interest of foreign countries. With the people and the government they make deals, not politics. The Foreign Office shall consist of German representatives from all the states participating in the federation, representatives elected by citizens of the federated states. The party advocates an international law for the press of all countries. By punishing the intentional reporting of false news, this law will prevent the kind of incitement of violence within the populace that occurred during the World War. The highest principles of justice and truth must again be made valid in today's world.

How does the DAP think the costs of the war can be paid?

Our guiding star is this: war is a disaster for a country, and disaster means suffering. For this reason, no one had any right to gather riches at home while our soldiers fought abroad.

Regardless of earnings before the war, we consider 10,000 marks to be the highest permissible annual earnings during the war; the rest is to be delivered to the central government, which will use it to pay war costs. Furthermore, property owners must be called upon to help cover the war costs, and any estates which are little encumbered are to be forced to take up compulsory mortgages.

2

ADOLF HITLER

Letter to Adolf Gemlich

Written on 16 September 1919. Published in *Hitler: Sämtliche Aufzeichnungen 1905–1924*, edited by Eberhard Jäckel and Axel Kuhn (Stuttgart: Deutsche Verlags-Anstalt, 1980), 88–90.

Dear Herr Gemlich,

If the danger posed by Jewry for our *Volk* today finds expression in the undeniable aversion among broad sectors of our population, the cause of this aversion is not to be sought, for the most part, in a clear recognition of the consciously or unconsciously systematic and pernicious effect of the Jews as a whole upon our nation. Rather, it arises largely from personal contact, from the personal impression left by the individual Jew—almost always an unfavorable one. For this reason, anti-Semitism is too easily characterized as a mere emotional phenomenon. And yet this is incorrect. Anti-Semitism as a political movement may not and cannot be defined by emotional impulses, but by recognition of the facts. These are the facts: First, Jewry is absolutely a race and not a religious association. Even a Jew never designates himself as a Jewish German, a Jewish Pole, or a Jewish American but always as a German, Polish, or American Jew. The Jew has never yet adopted much beyond the language of the foreign peoples in whose midst he lives. A German who is forced to avail himself of the French language in France, Italian in Italy, Chinese in China does not thereby become a Frenchman, Italian, or Chinaman anymore than the Jew who lives among us and is forced to avail himself of the German language becomes a German. Neither does the Mosaic faith, as essential as it is to the survival of this race, unequivocally settle the question of whether someone is a Jew or non-Jew. There is scarcely a race whose members belong exclusively to any one specific religion.

Throughout thousands of years of inbreeding, often restricted to a very limited group, the Jew has in general preserved his race and its peculiarities far more distinctly than many of the peoples amongst whom he has lived. And this is the reason that we have a non-German, alien race in our midst, which is neither willing nor able to sacrifice its racial character nor to deny its sentiments, thoughts, and aims, and yet still possesses all the political rights we do. If the Jew's sentiments are restricted to the purely material realm, his thoughts and aims all the more so. His dance around the golden calf is becoming a ruthless struggle for all those earthly possessions that, in our heart of hearts, we know should not be the most highly prized and sought after on earth.

The value of the individual is no longer determined by his character or by the significance of his achievements on behalf of the whole, but exclusively by the size of his fortune, by his money.

A nation's esteem is no longer to be measured by the sum of its moral and spiritual prowess, but rather by the wealth of its material possessions.

These sentiments are the basis for those thoughts and aims centering on money and power, both of which protect and preserve those very sentiments that render the Jew unscrupulous in his choice of methods and means and ruthless in their employment to these ends. In autocratically ruled states, he wheedles his way into the favor of "His Majesty," then abuses that power like a leech to bleed the nation's people. In democracies, he vies for the favor of the masses, bows down before the "majesty of the people," and recognizes only the majesty of money.

He destroys the character of princes with Byzantine flattery, national pride (the strength of a *Volk*), with ridicule and the shameless cultivation of depravity. His weapon of war is public opinion that is never expressed in the press, but which is nonetheless orchestrated and falsified by it. His power is the power of money, which multiplies in his hands effortlessly and endlessly by way of accrued interest, and which forces the *Volk* under the most dangerous of yokes whose ultimately tragic consequences are concealed by the initial attraction of gold and glitter. Everything men strive after as a higher goal—be it religion, socialism, or democracy—is to the Jew but a means to an end, a way for him to satisfy his lust for money and domination.

In his effects and consequences, he is like a racial tuberculosis of nations and peoples.

And this leads to the following conclusions: an anti-Semitism grounded solely on emotion will find its ultimate expression in the form of pogroms. An anti-Semitism grounded in reason, however, must lead to systematic legal eradication and elimination of those privileges that distinguish the Jew from the other aliens who live among us (through Legislation Concerning National Aliens). The ultimate objective [of such legislation] must, however, be the irrevocable removal of the Jews in general.

Only a government of national strength, never one of national impotence, is capable of achieving both these ends.

The Republic in Germany owes its birth not to the uniform national will of our *Volk*, but the clever exploitation of a series of circumstances which found general expression in a deep, widespread sense of dissatisfaction. These circumstances, however, were independent of the form of the state structure and are still operative today. Indeed, now more than before. Thus, a great portion of our *Volk* recognizes that altering the form of state cannot in itself alter and improve our situation—this, rather, will require a rebirth of the nation's moral and spiritual powers.

And this rebirth cannot be initiated by a state leadership of irresponsible majorities, influenced by certain party dogmas, an irresponsible press, or platitudes and slogans generated by the international community. [It requires] instead the relentless installation of nationally minded leadership personalities [*Führerpersönlichkeiten*] possessed of an inner sense of responsibility.

This fact, though, robs the Republic of the essential inner support of the nation's spiritual forces. And thus today's state leaders are compelled to seek support among those who have used and continue to use the new reconstruction of Germany exclusively to their own advantage, and who for this reason were ultimately the driving force behind the revolution—the Jews. Even though today's leaders fully realize the danger of Jewry (as various statements from leading personalities attest), they are forced, in their own self-interest, to accept the readily proffered support of the Jews and to return the favor. And this payoff consists not only in favoring the Jews in every possible way, but, above all, in hindering the struggle of a deceived *Volk* against its deceivers, that is—in repressing the anti-Semitic movement.

Respectfully,
Adolf Hitler

3

WILFRID BADE

The Founding of the Party in 1920

First published as "Die Gründung der Partei 1920," *Deutschland erwacht: Werden, Kampf, und Sieg der NSDAP,* edited by Wilfrid Bade (Altona-Bahrenfeld: Cigaretten Bilderdienst, 1933), 12–13.

When the officer training instructor Hitler was charged with the task of attending a meeting of the "German Workers' Party," he had no idea that this evening would become a decisive one, not only for him. In a small back room—the "Leiberzimmer" of the Sterneckbräu beer hall in Munich—he met with between twenty and twenty-five people who were listening to a lecture given by Gottfried Feder.

You couldn't speak in terms of a "party." It was a club, a political debate club, in which all the overall uncertainty, and the dubitable nature of everything—every form of existence and every idea that had left its mark on the time around 1919—became utterly apparent. At any rate, a brochure that a young worker placed in Hitler the soldier's hand as he was leaving the "meeting" offered more than the evening he'd just frittered away there. The brochure was titled "My Political Awakening" and penned by a certain Anton Drexler, head of said Workers' Party in Munich. In this brochure were reflected soul-searching struggles such as Hitler had himself wrestled with intensively during his time in Vienna.

Another day, he received word that he had been accepted into the party, an announcement that elicited from him as much laughter as annoyance.

But he nevertheless pursued this most recent invitation calling him to the "Altes Rosenbad," an obscure locale where Hitler thus encountered the whole listless, hapless clique of six people who had joined forces in the cause of rescuing the German worker. And yet, from somewhere in the midst of their flailing, apolitical, nonpropagandistic manner, something shined through to captivate Hitler: the sincere, honest belief that the German worker must succeed in winning back the fatherland from Marxism and the Red Revolution.

After two days' deliberation, Hitler decided to join the German Workers' Party.

He received provisional membership certificate number seven.

No one in Munich was familiar with the "party" whose members were thrilled just to receive a few letters from who knows where, which they spent hours debating how to respond.

Every Wednesday, there was a so-called committee meeting at Café Gasteig, and once a week an "evening discussion forum" [*Sprechabend*].

But since the whole movement was comprised of but seven men, the same people always met in rarefied seclusion—and isolation.

Shattering that seclusion seemed to be Hitler's primary goal. If anything were to come of this whole thing, the party would have to emerge from anonymity.

Invitations to the meetings were written by hand. Hitler delivered eighty of them personally. But when the evening of the meeting arrived, again only the same old seven people gathered, and no one else.

So Hitler began having the invitations typed up—and the results were thus improved. The number of listeners increased to eleven, to thirteen, to seventeen, to twenty-three, to thirty-four.

Taking up a collection of money at one of these meetings afforded party members the opportunity for placing an announcement for the next one in the *Münchener Beobachter.* Lo and behold: 111 attended. It was a tremendous success.

For the first time, Hitler had the sense that he possessed the talent to speak before a greater circle—a fact that the party president could not bring himself to believe. Hitler's appeal to the willingness to sacrifice on the part of attendees even succeeded in coaxing 300 marks from their pockets.

To the party, that was a fortune.

What is more, after this assembly, a number of young men made themselves available with whom it was possible to start thinking about working on a much more extravagant scale. Because the very moment that an anti-Marxist party first made a public appearance in the year 1919–20, there would be blood on the carpet and heads would begin to roll. The party leadership was afraid of such clashes. Hitler didn't go out in search of them, nor did he go out of his way to avoid them and thought it better to let it come down to public clashes than to hide in the dark. So it was that on October 19, a new meeting was called to order. This time, 130 people were in attendance. An attempt to break up the meeting was nipped in the bud. Two weeks later, 170 men showed up at yet another demonstration. The numbers increased steadily. Before long, there were two hundred, three hundred people listening to the orator Adolf Hitler.

At the same time, the National Socialist German Workers' Party (NSDAP) was formed from a smaller circle within the German Workers' Party. The nascent organization began formulating the twenty-five points. The process wasn't without fierce disputes, but ultimately the superior spirit of the party's propaganda leader prevailed—it was Adolf Hitler.

The Marxist press had already begun covering the new party. The first articles dripping with malice appeared. Hitler's supporters began speaking at other meetings. The movement was no longer unknown.

Even though the speakers of the German Workers' Party were constantly being shouted down at the meetings of other parties, they were nevertheless becoming known, and even the most die-hard Marxist had to see that the Social Democrats and Communists were not the only ones running around out there who were not intimidated by a balled fist and were anything but bourgeois.

In the party, a conflict arose between the national party chairmen, Herr [Karl] Harrer and Hitler.

To Harrer, the tempo Hitler had set seemed too tempestuous, and when Hitler managed to call a truly mass meeting to order in the big banquet hall of the Hofbräuhaus, Harrer resigned from his post. He was afraid the party would collapse.

Hitler threw himself full throttle into preparations for the assembly. Impetuously, he ran roughshod over all the reservations held by the far too timid clubhouse politician.

Flyers and posters were printed. The color of the posters was a blood red that would be sure to attract attention whatever the occasion or purpose. What is more, these red posters must have especially provoked the Marxists, who believed themselves in possession of a hereditary lease on this color—and reaching Marxists was precisely what Hitler deemed most important; his most urgent task was to wrench precisely those indoctrinated, inveigled workers on the left from the clutches of the Jewish leaders. Before the demonstration took place, Hitler saw to it that the party program that had long been in the works was available. And then came that memorable February 24th, when, from the clatter of the movement's first great beer-hall brawl and from the elation of two thousand people, when the program was announced, the National Socialist German Workers' Party was born.

4

DIETRICH ECKART

Jewishness in and around Us

First published as "Das Judentum in und außer uns," parts IV and V, *Auf gut Deutsch,* nos. 1–7, January–April 1919, 28–31, 79–80, 95–96, 109–12. Translated by Barbara Miller Lane and Leila J. Rupp.

IV

To repeat once again, and yet again, the most important thing up to now: *in the Jewish religion, the belief in a spiritual life after death is completely lacking.* One even gets the almost certain impression that in the course of time everything which could remind one even slightly of an incorporeal existence after death has been systematically eliminated and the Jews stand alone in the world with their purely earthly religion! Do not forget this for a *moment:* it is so significant. For in this exceptional position lies the reason that a "crypto-nation" like the Jews survived the greatest and most glorious peoples and will continue to survive until the end of time, until the hour of salvation for mankind strikes. Sooner will the Jewish people *not* perish. The world is preserved, as we shall see, only through its affirmation. In the Jewish people this affirmation of the world is completely pure, without any admixture of negation of the world. All other peoples of the past or present had or have this admixture, characterized by the idea of the next world, if even only by a trace of it. Even this mere trace would have been or would be sufficient to give the necessary balance to the unmixed affirmation of the world embodied in the Jewish people. For the inner light—and the belief in immortality *is* the inner light—does not need to shine with the brightest glow all the time in order to be effective: but it must be there, it must not be extinguished, otherwise mankind would be lost forever to this world. Everything must have its appropriate moment, however—a fact that is often overlooked. The negation of the world still needs a long time in which to grow before it will gain lasting predominance over affirmation of the world. At the present time, negation of the world seems to have again fallen back to zero; its opposite, symbolized in the Jewish people, triumphs as never before; it looks as if the inner light had entirely disappeared from the earth. But to anticipate a little, it only looks that way. Negation of the world *cannot* perish because it belongs to the essence of the soul of mankind, and this is *immortal.* Where immortality dwells, longing for the eternal and renunciation of the temporal must continually reemerge; that is, the negation of the world must continually reappear. And that is the meaning of the non-Jewish peoples: they are the *preservers* of the negation of the world, of the idea of an existence after death, even if they preserve it ever so meagerly. Therefore one or the other of these peoples can perfectly well be destroyed; what is important will live on in the heirs. But if the Jewish people were to perish, there would no longer be a nation that cherished affirmation of the world: the end of time would have come.

But this would also be the case if the *Zionist* ideal were realized—that is, if all of Jewry came together in a national union, in Palestine or elsewhere. There has *never* been such a union of Jews; this fact must be emphasized here twice and three times, since it is so little known. *Long before the destruction of the temple in Jerusalem,* a good part of the Jews lived in the Diaspora—that is, scattered among the "heathen" peoples—just as every school child knows that at the very beginning of their history, they played the "guests" among the Egyptians. What arose later in Palestine was not a state: at best, it was an attempt at a state; at worst, the training ground for the exploitation or destruction of foreign peoples. To the Jew Weininger, his own nation appears to be an invisibly connected web of slimy fungus, always existing and spread over the wide earth; and precisely this spreading, he rightly remarks (without, however, giving reasons for it), lies in the *idea,* in the *essence* of Jewishness.[1] That becomes immediately clear if we again view the Jewish people as the embodiment of the *affirmation of the world.* Without this, nothing earthly is imaginable, no people either; and thus the Jew, the only consistent and therefore the only effective affirmer of the world, must be present everywhere as the ever-necessary counterweight, even where the other men have only the slightest impulse to overcome the world. For otherwise the former impulse would immediately reach fulfillment, and the world would not be redeemed (for the Jewish people would still remain) but would be destroyed in another way, by the elimination of the spiritual force without which it cannot exist. This, however, I shall explain later. Here it was only important to show that the world could not exist if the Jews lived by themselves, for which reason an old prophecy announces the destruction of the world on the day on which the Jews found a state in Palestine.

V

It follows from all of this that Jewishness belongs to the organism of mankind as, let us say, certain bacteria belong to the human body, and just as necessarily as these. As we know, the body contains a lot of small organisms without which it would be destroyed, although these organisms feed on it; and similarly mankind needs the Jewish presence in order to remain vigorous until the fulfillment of its earthly mission. In other words, the affirmation of the world, pernicious in itself, which is present in the purest form in Jewishness, is the condition of worldly existence as long as there are men and cannot be imagined away; only with the salvation of all mankind will it collapse.

Thus we must accept the Jews among us as a necessary evil for who knows how many centuries to come. But as our body would atrophy if those bacteria developed to more than a healthy extent, so also, to make an analogy, would our people gradually succumb to a permanent spiritual infirmity if the Jew got to be too much for it. That which Zionism wants or at least pretends to want, to leave completely, would be just as fatal as the Jew ruling us. The mission of the German people ends, it is my firm conviction, with the last hour of mankind, but we cannot get there if before that time we lose the affirmation of the world—the Jew among us; because without affirmation of the world no existence is possible. But on the other hand, if the Jew constantly stifled us, we would never be in a position to fulfill our destiny, which consists of the salvation of the world, but would, to put it bluntly, succumb to insanity, for pure affirmation of the world, as the unchecked desire for transitory existence, leads to no other end. It would literally amount to nothingness, to the *annihilation* not only of earthly appearances but also of what truly exists, the *spiritual.* Viewed in himself, the Jew represents nothing but this blind desire for annihilation, the madness of mankind. It is known that the Jewish people suffer to an exceptional degree from mental illness; we have already discovered the reason. "Governed by madness," Schopenhauer too says of the Jew.

Some time ago the Jew *Martin Buber* gave a lecture *in* Munich in which he vividly dealt with the future state in Palestine.[2] Very vividly. The most important of his statements was the following hint, expressed unintentionally but with great sullenness: if this state should be founded and there should creep into it *even the slightest trace of* a *supernatural tendency, then it also would have* to *be destroyed!*

The secret of Jewishness could not have been revealed more plainly. It wants the *despiritualization of the world* and nothing else; but this would be the same as its *annihilation.* While the Jews still live among us, everything they do comes to this, and *must* come to this.

Their goal is the despiritualization of mankind. Therefore, they attempt to destroy every form behind which the living soul operates; because, as archmaterialists, they are of the insane opinion that the spiritual—only vaguely suspected by them—is connected as a matter of life and death with the form and must be destroyed together with it. Therefore they are all without exception *anarchists,* consciously or unconsciously; indeed, they *cannot* be anything but opponents of *law* and *order* because these two bear in incomparable fashion the shining stamp of a purer world. Schiller calls order the *daughter of heaven,* and in Schiller, but especially in Goethe, there are innumerable proofs of the divine origin of law.

But no idea of state can be realized without law and order; they are the indispensable basis for it. Therefore the Jew, their deadly enemy, can never create a viable state in Palestine. Instead, the *Chaos* would come again, for this word means, correctly translated: the infinite emptiness; in German, *nothingness.*

Here again Weininger approaches the truth, but here again he falls short of full understanding. First of all, he thinks the (pure) idea of state has never been even approximately realized in any historic form, which is true, but only because mankind has until now lacked the necessary profundity; but then he adds that, in spite of this, there is in every historic attempt to form a state something, perhaps only that minimum of a pure idea of state, which lifts the structure above a mere union of business and power interests. This is true in the *Aryan* attempts at forming a *state,* but Weininger did not know that previously this minimum *could* not become a maximum because until the present day the Aryans had not attained the corresponding maximum of *spiritual force.* But even the minimum sufficed to help the Aryan formation of states to prosper, at least for a while, often for centuries.

Notes

1. Otto Weininger (1880–1903) was an Austrian critic and philosopher and the author of *Geschlecht und Charakter* (*Sex and Character*), 1903.—Eds.
2. Martin Buber (1878–1965), Jewish philosopher and religious scholar active in the Zionist movement.

5

The Program of the German Workers' Party

The Twenty-Five Points

Announced on 24 February 1920 in Munich. Published in *Das Programm der NSDAP und seine weltanschaulichen Grundgedanken* (Munich: Verlag Franz Eher Nachfolger GmbH, 1932), 15–19.

The program of the German Workers' Party is of limited duration.[1] The leaders have no intention, once the aims announced in it have been achieved, of setting up fresh ones, merely in order artificially to increase the discontent of the masses, and so ensure the continued existence of the party.

1. We demand the union of all Germans to form a Great Germany on the basis of the right of self-determination enjoyed by nations.
2. We demand equality of rights for the German people in its dealings with other nations and abolition of the peace treaties of Versailles and Saint Germain.
3. We demand land and territory (colonies) for the nourishment of our people and for settling our excess population.
4. None but members of the nation may be citizens of the state. None but those of German blood, whatever their creed, may be members of the nation. No Jew therefore may be a member of the nation.
5. Anyone who is not a citizen of the state may live in Germany only as a guest and must be regarded as being subject to foreign laws.
6. The right of voting on the leadership and legislation is to be enjoyed by the state alone. We demand therefore that all official appointments, of whatever kind, whether in the Reich, in the country, or in the smaller localities, shall be granted

to citizens of the state alone. We oppose Parliament's corrupting custom of filling posts merely with a view to party considerations and without reference to character or capacity.

7. We demand that the state shall make it its first duty to promote the industry and livelihood of citizens of the state. If it is not possible to nourish the entire population of the state, foreign nationals (noncitizens of the state) must be excluded from the Reich.
8. All non-German immigration must be prevented.
9. All citizens of the state shall be equal in rights and duties.
10. It must be the first duty of each citizen of the state to work with his mind or with his body. The activities of the individual may not clash with the interests of the whole, but must proceed within the frame of the community and be for the general good.

We demand therefore:

11. Abolition of incomes unearned by work.

Breaking the Bonds of Interest

12. In view of the enormous sacrifice of life and property demanded of a nation by every war, personal enrichment due to a war must be regarded as a crime against the nation. We demand therefore ruthless confiscation of all war gains.
13. We demand nationalization of all businesses (trusts)
14. We demand that the profits from wholesale trade shall be shared.
15. We demand extensive development of security for old age.
16. We demand creation and maintenance of a healthy middle class, immediate communalization of wholesale business premises, and their lease at a cheap rate to small traders, and that extreme consideration shall be shown to all small purveyors to the state, district authorities, and smaller localities.
17. We demand land reform suitable to our national requirements.
18. We demand ruthless prosecution of those whose activities are injurious to the common interest. Sordid criminals against the nation, usurers, profiteers, etc., must be punished with death, whatever their creed or race.
19. We demand that the Roman Law, which serves the materialistic world order, shall be replaced by a legal system for all Germany.
20. With the aim of opening to every capable and industrious German the possibility of higher education and of thus obtaining advancement, the state must consider a thorough reconstruction of our national system of education.
21. The state must see to raising the standard of health in the nation by protecting mothers and infants, prohibiting child labor, increasing bodily efficiency by obligatory gymnastics and sports laid down by law, and by extensive support of clubs engaged in the bodily development of the young.
22. We demand abolition of a paid army and formation of a national army.
23. We demand legal warfare against conscious political lying and its dissemination in the press. In order to facilitate creation of a German national press, we demand:
    (a) that all editors and their assistants of newspapers employing the German language must be members of the nation;
    (b) that special permission from the state shall be necessary before non-German newspapers may appear. These are not necessarily printed in the German language;
    (c) that non-Germans shall be prohibited by law from participation financially in or influencing German newspapers, and that the penalty for violating this law shall be the suppression of any such newspaper and the immediate deportation of the non-Germans involved.

It must be forbidden to publish papers that do not promote the national welfare. We demand legal prosecution of all tendencies in art and literature that exert a corrupting influence on our life as a nation, and the closing of institutions that contravene the requirements mentioned above.

24. We demand liberty for all religious denominations in the state, so far as they are not a danger to it and do not militate against the moral feelings of the German race. The party as such stands for positive Christianity, but does not bind itself in the matter of creed to any particular denomination. It combats the Jewish-materialist spirit within us and outside of us.

The Common Interest over Individual Interest

25. That all the foregoing may be put into effect, we demand the creation of a strong central power of the Reich. Unconditional authority of the politically centralized parliament over the entire Reich and its organizations. The formation of chambers for classes and occupations for the purpose of carrying out the general laws promulgated by the Reich in the various federal states.

The leaders of the party swear with the utmost determination to bring about and—if necessary, to sacrifice their lives—to fulfill the foregoing points.

Note

1. The name of the German Workers' Party was changed to the National Socialist German Workers' Party (NSDAP) in August 1920.

6

GOTTFRIED FEDER

Manifesto for Breaking the Bondage of Interest

First published as "Das Manifest zur Brechung der Zinsknechtschaft des Geldes," in *Kritische Rundschau* 2 (Summer 1919), 14–15. Translated by Barbara Miller Lane and Leila J. Rupp.

Mammonism is the heavy, pervasive, stifling disease from which our present culture, and indeed all humanity, is suffering. It is like a devastating plague, like a devouring poison that has seized the peoples of the world.

By Mammonism we must understand:

On the one hand, the international financial superpowers, the supranational financial force that rules over all the rights of self-determination of individual peoples, the golden international;

And on the other hand, a frame of mind that has overcome the broadest segments of the population; the insatiable greed for gain, the view of life that is focused solely on worldly goods, [a view] that has already led to a frightening decline in moral values, and must continue to do so.

This frame of mind is embodied and carried to its extreme in the international plutocracy.

The source of Mammonism's power is the effortless and infinite multiplication of wealth that is created by interest.

The golden international was born out of the thoroughly immoral idea of loan interest. Greed for loan interest produces a mental and moral outlook in the individual that has led to a frightening dissolution within one part of the bourgeoisie.

The ideal of loan interest is the diabolical invention of big capital. It alone makes possible the lazy drone life of a minority of financially powerful people at the cost of the productive peoples and their labor. It has led to deep insurmountable differences, to class hatred, out of which civil war and fratricide have been born.

The only remedy, the *radical means* to cure suffering humanity, is:

Breaking the bondage of interest.

Breaking the bondage of interest means the only possible and effective emancipation of productive labor from the secret financial superpowers.

Breaking the bondage of interest means the restoration of personal freedom, the redemption of mankind from slavery, from the magic spell in which his soul is ensnared by Mammonism. Whoever wants to do battle with capitalism must break the bondage of interest.

Where must breaking the bondage of interest begin? *With loan capital!*

Why?

Because loan capital is so overpowering in comparison to all industrial capital that the great monetary powers can be successfully combated only by breaking the bondage of interest to loan capital. Twenty to one is the ratio of loan capital to industrial capital. Every year the German *Volk* must raise more than 12 billion [marks] in interest for loan capital, in the form of direct and indirect taxes, rents and increasing cost of living, while even in the years of the war boom the total sum of all dividends paid by German corporations amounted to only 1 billion.

The avalanche-like growth of loan capital by the constant, endless, and effortless multiplication of wealth [caused by] interest and compound interest is beyond human comprehension.

What benefits will be brought by breaking the bondage of interest, for the working people of Germany, for the proletarians of all countries of the earth?

Breaking the bondage of interest allows us to undertake the abolition of all direct and indirect taxes. Hear this, you people of all lands, states, and continents, you who create value: all revenue from direct and indirect sources flows into the pockets of big loan capital.

The profits of commercial state enterprises, such as mail, telegraph, telephone, railroads, mining, foresting, and power, suffice completely to pay for the necessary outlays of the state for education, culture, administration, and social welfare.

This means that all true socialism will bring no benefits to humanity as long as economic enterprises of the community owe their profits to big loan capital.

We demand, therefore, first as a constitutional law for the various German peoples, then as basic law for all those brother peoples who want to enter with us into the cultural community of a league of peoples, the following:

1. That, by abolition of the obligation to pay interest, the shares of war loans, all other debt instruments of the German Reich, all other debt instruments of the German federal states, especially railroad loans, and further the bonds of all legally constituted governments, be declared legal tender at face value.
2. That, in the case of all other papers bearing a fixed rate of interest, mortgage bonds, industrial obligations, mortgages and the like, the obligation to pay interest be superseded by the obligation to repay principal. After twenty or twenty-five years, according to the rate of interest, the loan shall be repaid and the debt dissolved.
3. That all debts on real estate, mortgages, and the like be repaid in installments as before, according to the charges entered in the property register. Real estate properties—house or land—disencumbered in this way shall become partially owned by the state

or legally constituted government. This will enable the state to determine and lower rents.

4. The entire monetary system is to be subordinated to a central state treasury. All private banks and bankers, as well as postal banks and savings and loan associations, shall be affiliated as branch establishments.
5. All real credit is only to be given out by the central state bank. Personal credit and credit on goods is given to private bankers by state license. This license is to be given according to need and will prohibit the establishment of branches in certain districts. The scale of fees is to be set by the state.
6. Dividends shall be redeemed in the same way as papers bearing a fixed rate of interest—in annual installments of five percent. Surplus profits shall be paid out in part to the stockholder as compensation for "risked" capital (in contrast to papers at a fixed rate of interest and gilt-edged securities). The remaining surplus reverts by independent right to the workers and is either to be distributed for social purposes or applied to the lowering of consumer prices.
7. All persons who, for physical reasons (old age, physical or mental inability to work, extreme youth) are not able to earn their living shall continue to receive the previous interest on securities paid out of existing capital funds as an annuity in return for depositing their bonds or securities.
8. In the interest of reducing existing inflation by substituting legal tender, a general, sharply graduated confiscation of property shall be undertaken. The property thus confiscated will take the form of war bonds or other debt instruments of the Reich or the states. These papers will be destroyed.
9. It must be made clear to the *Volk* by a most intensive popular enlightenment campaign that money is not and must not be anything but an *exchange for labor;* that any highly developed economy certainly does need money as a medium of exchange, but that this exhausts the function of money and can under no circumstances endow money, through interest, with the supernatural power to reproduce itself at the cost of productive labor.

Why have we not yet achieved all this, this perfect solution that seems as self-evident as the discovery of America, the ideal remedy for the social question?

Because in our *mammonistic delusion we have forgotten how to see that the theory of the sacredness of interest is a monstrous self-deception,* that the gospel of salvation by interest has entangled our entire thinking in the golden nets of the international plutocracy. Because we have forgotten, and the omnipotent money powers work industriously to foster this illusion, that, for all but a few financially well-endowed people, interest—supposedly so beloved and sweet, so dear to the thoughtless—is eaten up by taxes. Our whole tax law is and shall remain a tribute paid to big capital, and not, as we sometimes imagine, [a] voluntary sacrifice for the benefit of the community until we are freed from the bondage of interest.

Therefore, emancipation from the bondage of interest is the clear solution for the world revolution, for the emancipation of productive labor from the fetters of the international money powers.

7

OTTO GMELIN

Prohn Fights for His People

First published in *Prohn kämpft für sein Volk* (Jena: Eugen Diedrichs Verlag, 1933), 5–10.

When, in August of the year 1914, war broke out over the German people, a war that the great majority of Germans, after such a long and happy period of peace, never seriously thought possible, everyone was forced to pause for reflection and ask himself where he belongs now. For the strong, able-bodied men, everyone agreed, nothing was more urgent and important than taking up arms and defending against the enemy; everything else was secondary for the moment. For this reason, hundreds of thousands left their peacetime jobs and pursuits at the time and registered with the voluntary regiments, because it seemed to them—rightly so—pointless to sit bent over books or at typewriters as long as the fate of their people and thus their own fate would be decided by gunfire and cannons.

It was easy for all these men to find their place in those days because they knew exactly where they belonged. It was much more difficult for those whose physical condition prevented them from following that natural path. For these people in particular, the less they were able to intervene and actively participate themselves, the more acutely and with much more consternation they experienced events.

Even though I belonged to this latter group, none of this became apparent until I met Prohn. That was in November 1914. After I'd been relieved of my post as a volunteer enlisted man on medical grounds shortly after I signed up, I was transferred by the office of civil service to the beautiful town of T. in the Black Forest. I took up residence, with meals included, in the clean and modest Gasthof zum Hirschen because I liked its location near the forest and thus spared myself the burdensome search for a room. After several days, the proprietress, whose husband was on the battlefield, told me that all the seats at the table were taken for the afternoon meal and, if I didn't mind, she'd like to seat me at the table with two gentlemen who were high school teachers. I had nothing against it. The next day, though, I was not very happy about the company at my table. The one named Spieß was a young, redheaded fellow with only one arm; one might have felt sorry for him on account of that had he not been the worst kind of flag-waving hoorah patriot who compensated for his inability to carry a weapon and march against the enemy with his comrades by boastfully shooting off at the mouth. The other was Prohn. My first impression of Prohn was not good. He was a small weakling of a man with disheveled dirty blond hair and a contorted face, which, despite his youth, was covered in wrinkles that assumed a certain contrived masculinity on account of his sizeable mustache. Behind the round lenses of his gold-rimmed glasses, a pair of small dark blue eyes peered out. But what stood out on this gnome-like little man already the first time I sat down to lunch with him and to this day, nearly twenty years after the events I am about to relate, what I can still see before me with unwavering clarity, were his hands. I saw—though I didn't know it myself at the time because it didn't dawn on me until much later, not until I began reminiscing about him—I watched these hands during the meal; they were small, slender, and delicate. His fingers were thin, lean on flesh and muscle—they almost looked like little twigs—[with] blue veins protruding all across the surface of the backs of his hands, and brownish ones leading to his wrist and forearms thick with hair, and flabby skin hanging in creases and wrinkles all over. His hand truly resembled a gorilla hand, even in its movements, which were abrupt and jerky. But, of course, as I would soon learn, a comparison of this nature was utterly superficial because this hand, in its very impracticability, expressed something else altogether.

But this was not something I was aware of immediately. Above all, what disgusted me was the way he ate—bent over his plate, shoving overstuffed spoons and forks into his mouth beneath the drooping moustache—the way he chewed, the way he wiped his mouth; all that seemed at first like a disregard for form that bordered on rudeness. In conversation, he was the opposite of his colleague, who simply couldn't be grandiose enough in his talk; Prohn, on the other hand, with his curt, gruff responses, resisted all my efforts to strike up a conversation with him. Of course, I don't know anymore exactly what I discussed with him, or tried to discuss with him, but what I do know for certain is that the way he responded to my question about whether he was a teacher of modern languages like his colleague was only to grumble:

"Latin and Greek mean zilch to me!"

All in all, I was not exactly happy with this less than stimulating and scarcely entertaining company at the table, but I nevertheless failed to do anything to try and find another table to sit at for lunch. That was probably because, at a time when others were lying in the mire of the trenches facing the enemy, it didn't seem worth worrying about being selective in my choice of company at the table. Back in those days, one began attaching less significance to things that might have otherwise seemed important. Ultimately all the rules of etiquette stemming from my bourgeois upbringing were ridiculous trivialities compared to what friends and comrades were going through out there. When Germany's fate was at stake, it seemed more than irrelevant to worry about the table manners of the men seated beside you at the table. These were the considerations and sentiments that prevented me from doing anything to change the situation and, on the contrary, to attempt to enter into a relationship that approached human understanding with my fellow men at the table. But, as far as the one-armed man is concerned, I did not succeed in this endeavor. He was one of those people who took refuge in empty words simply to avoid having to admit to himself his own inadequacy. But the more I kept my distance from him, in fact the more I developed a sort of antagonistic position toward him, the more I got to know the rest of the men at the table, and that was something I'd never live to regret.

It's hard to say how I came to get so well acquainted with Prohn. At first, we sat together every day at lunch for a mere half hour, now and then perhaps an hour. I believe that people, even when they have nothing to say, whether they want to or not, always exude something of their character. If the person you're with has a character that resembles your own, a bond gradually begins to form that is at first imperceptible.

If my recollection is correct, this first visible sign of commonality became apparent when I explained that I had tried in vain to register as a volunteer soldier in various regiments and that, once I'd finally secured a place, quickly had a physical collapse and was relieved of my duties.

Then Prohn peered at me through his glasses, indicating, for the first time, a sign of a certain attentiveness and scrutiny, and said,

"So, so. So you're another one of those men they don't need." And then he added, in a tone rife with annoyance and self-irony, "I didn't even bother trying."

I responded by saying something like you had to figure out where you stood and from there, do everything in your power. But he seemed to take little fancy in this consolation that seemed shallow even to me.

"Yeah, yeah, that's easy for you to say," he answered, wiping his mouth and the bushy moustache and immersing himself again in the newspaper he was holding in his left hand while spooning soup with his right.

His curt "that's easy for you to say" kept going through my head, though, and at any rate, from then on he was no longer just anyone to me. Perhaps, though it wasn't something I was consciously aware of, this statement of his may have been what caused me to go sit down next to him one night in the Wirtstube zum Hirschen, where he was sitting alone in a corner with a glass of beer smoking a Swiss stogie. At first we talked about the daily news reports of triumphant advances in the East under General von Mackensen. A happy smile came over Prohn's unsightly facial features as he said,

"They're putting the screws to the Russians! You can be glad for that! Glad for that!" But then he immediately turned serious again and added, "But you know, that won't be without its costs. Many a man is going to bite the dust over there!"

He simply put in words much of what I had thought and felt many a time. But I said, "These are the bitter necessities." He fell silent, took another drink of his beer, sucked on his stogie, blew out the smoke in front of him, his elbows propped on the table top, and only after a long pause, while I was skimming the paper, he said,

"You know what I think, those of us who are sitting here at home really don't have anything to say about it. There's much too much nonsense being said."

I had to concede that he was right.

8

HEINRICH LERSCH

The German Soldier

First published in *Volk im Kriege. Gedichte* (Jena: Eugen Diederichs Verlag, 1939), 13, 45.

There's a line of troops rushing along the railroad tracks
A proud roaring of the train locomotives:
Our rail is headed straight to battle and victory.
"To the slaughter, to the slaughter" the young throats screamed.
The slogans on the walls stared at me;
My blood climbed from all the depths of my heart
when I saw the half-erased inscription:
"Hail! From our homeland into death. Hurray!"

Who are you, brother, that you should write this?
I would like to kiss your hands in reverence,
The way you give your life in blissful pride
and smile happily while performing this sacred obligation.
You forged onward into a foreign land,
you saw yourself, mortally wounded, face down, kissing the soil—
Your heart, in death, near to the fatherland:
"Hail! From our homeland into death. Hurray!"

You were already a hero before the battle ensnared you
The gruesome song of death and red blood
you mastered death before it became your master
you stormed death's door in your heroic mien
Come what may! Nothing can defeat you
Death is your victory, not the shaft of fate.
May immortality be yours after death.
"Hail! From our homeland into death. Hurray!"

And if you someday return as victor,
new life will surround you in air.

Teach, brothers, teach life as you teach death,
Teach them to love as you teach to hate.
When you return, riding the German rail to your homeland,
I'll change the lyrics to your song
In sickness and in death, reign as victors supreme.
In sickness and in death for the homeland. Hail. Hurray.

IN THE MILITARY HOSPITAL

Those nights, millions of hearts turned eavesdropping ears to the west, where masses of peoples charged our army.
That forces us, the soldiers, in the military hospitals to again take up arms.
We feel our energies swell in the wounded arms and legs, stormy breath in gasping lungs,
We feel ourselves growing stronger by the hour. Our brothers' need stills the ailments we suffer.
All through the night salvos of grenades shake us from sleep and from dreams.
The darkness of walls: clouds of smoke. Our ceiling is a split tree trunk.
Hunger and thirst.—The wounds ache.—We have awoken: the nurses glide over the beds.
The view from the window: Silent night. Moonlit night . . . And—yesterday's news report:
Attack after 70 hours of artillery preparation, cavalry in the Champagne.—That is our home! In a grave shot to pieces they lie,
Friend and foe torn apart, bleeding. Forests and apartment buildings ablaze—
You brothers, those of you who are still alive—stand up—stand and let yourselves be charged by the storming mobs on our behalf.
The moon passes by the window, land lies in peace, bathed in blue light,
Full of mothers and women. On silver strings, the soul has strung high praises to the heavens,
longing harps in their strings, songs of anguish glide on the moon's rays to the heavenly thrones
Faith and hope sing a lullaby, to be sung when the guns and cannons fall off to sleep.

9

HANNS JOHST

Schlageter

First published in *Schlageter* (Munich: Albert-Langen—Georg Müller, 1933), 82–85.

AUGUST: You won't believe it, Papa, but that's how it is: young people don't put much stock in these old slogans anymore . . . they're dying out . . . the class struggle is dying out.

SCHNEIDER: So . . . and what is left to live for then?

AUGUST: The *Volk* community!

SCHNEIDER: And that's *not* a slogan . . . ?

AUGUST: No!! It's an experience!

SCHNEIDER: My God! . . . Our class struggle, our strikes, they weren't an experience, or what . . . ? Socialism, the International, were they perhaps fantasies . . . ?

AUGUST: They were necessary, but they *were* . . . they are things that they *have been* . . . with respect to the future, that is, they are historical experiences.

SCHNEIDER: So . . . and the future belongs to your *Volk* community? Tell me, how do you actually envision it? Differences between the rich and the poor, the healthy and the sick, upper class, lower class, all that ceases to exist with your generation, eh? A socially conscious land of Cockaine, or what . . . ?

AUGUST: Look, Papa . . . upper class, lower class, poor, rich, that will always exist: What is decisive is the way these questions are framed.

To us life is not chopped up into working hours and furnished with price charts. Rather, we believe in human existence as a whole. None of us regards making money as the most important thing; we want to serve. The individual is a corpuscle in the bloodstream of his *Volk*.

SCHNEIDER: That's just adolescent romanticism! Juveniles as saviors of the *Volk!* Rub your nose in reality first!

World views aside for now . . . Let's talk about something concrete: What *is* the attitude of your corps and your "*Volk* community" toward passive resistance?

AUGUST: We want to turn it into a putsch, into a national uprising.

SCHNEIDER: Turn it into a putsch . . . ?

AUGUST: You, as an old revolutionary, I must say, stress the word "putsch" rather oddly. The government either will march with us or it will vanish!

SCHNEIDER: You are talking to a high-ranking government official and he is telling you: the government will raise hell with putschists!

AUGUST: I'm just having a casual conversation with my dear old father.

SCHNEIDER: Your dear old father happens to be a state official who considers passive resistance a good thing!

AUGUST: And your son is a revolutionary!!

SCHNEIDER: My son is a lout who is about to get a box on the ears.

. . . Now fall in line!

AUGUST [*moves back, laughing]:* You may be a high-ranking government official, but you still manage things like an old taskmaster. That's all right for teaching children good manners! But . . .

SCHNEIDER: But . . . but . . . We old fogies aren't as stupid as you young whippersnappers might think. To you, Schlageter and his cronies are national heroes . . . to us here, they are just putting on a show!

Schlageter will be a dead man if he doesn't fall in line! The governments of Europe all agree that the last adventurers and fanatics and firebrands and bandits of the World War must be exterminated with fire and sword!

We want peace. That's what I'm telling you, young man, and I stood four years under fire for Germany as it is today and as it shall remain for as long as I'm still standing!

AUGUST: No!!

And I'm telling you that as someone who doesn't have a clue about a war of materiel, about the barrages, about flame-throwers, and tanks.

We young people who stand by Schlageter do not stand by him because he is the last soldier of the World War, but because he is the first soldier of the Third Reich!!!

(Curtain)

10

HANS HINKEL

One of a Hundred Thousand

Published in *Einer unter Hunderttausend* (Munich: Knorr & Hirth, 1942), 53–56. [The book was originally published in 1937.] Translated by Randall Bytwerk. Calvin College, German Propaganda Archive.

The Fight against Daily Lies

The number of party members who, already in those days, were traveling through regions of the fatherland or even through all of Germany to preach or speak of the Führer's idea was still small. But those who a few years later were named Reich speakers by the party leadership, but who had already been crossing the country from one end to the other, have a tale or two to tell about the tremendous resistance they had to overcome, about the prejudices that they had to fight against for months or even years, about the web of lies woven from the evil consciousness of the united front of our opponents to enshroud our Führer and his movement. Faster than a bolt of lightning, a lie about us spread like wildfire throughout the country; it was thrust into every attic room where poor people lived by newspapers that had sold out or were sympathetic to the opponent. Every three-line lie in an opposing newspaper cost us National Socialists a week's work in combating it. No sooner had we exposed one lie, a hundred more new lies reared their ugly heads. Like a Hydra, the opponent's horror stories about National Socialism and its supporters spread like a plague. There was not a speech by the Führer or his associates that was not immediately twisted and tastefully served up to the average German at breakfast or dinner. From the story that Adolf Hitler had "spat out the communion wafer," to the one about Hermann Göring smuggling opium or morphine, to the one about the "missing 'v' " in Robert Ley's name, to the tale about Pastor Münchmeyer's "moral crimes" in Borkum.[1] We might have oft laughed our heads off were it not for the fact that we witnessed, by the hour, the amazing gullibility of millions of German citizens ensnared by the enemy's web of lies. The only thing to do was for all of us to get out amongst the people, campaigning and fighting everywhere, speaking and educating. Sooner or later the opponents would have to face us and be revealed as liars to the public.

In this attempt to offer a brief summary of these days, I turn to some letters written to my friends at the time, relating the great difficulties we faced. In December 1926, I wrote, among other things:

> Today I worked out the schedule for public meetings with *Gauleiter* Schultz. A week from this Wednesday, I will be speaking in Homburg; on Thursday, in Melsungen; Friday, in Kassel (a discussion evening); Saturday, in Altmorschen; Sunday afternoon, in Oder-Ellenbach; Sunday evening, in Bisförth. Monday, there is an SA [Storm Troopers] propaganda march in Kassel; Tuesday, in Eschwege; Wednesday, in Spangenberg; Thursday, in Arossen; Friday, in Malsfeld; Saturday, in Korbach; and Sunday in Massenhausen. The following Monday I finally have a day off in Kassel. Tuesday I leave again for two days in the Marburg area.

That is the pace at which we speakers had to work and the way cities and villages alternated in our calendars. This went on for months at a time, week after week. Monday was usually the only day we weren't scheduled to speak anywhere. We fought tirelessly for each individual. We read today in our reports of those days when "at a large mass meeting" in Melsungen—with seven hundred participants!—eight new members joined and we gained four new readers for our few party newspapers. In Arossen, it was nine and six; in Massenhausen, only three; in Marburg, seven and eleven; and in Eschwege, two new members and three new newspaper readers. In some villages and cities, we considered recruiting even a single new man a success. Sooner or later, the same thing that happened in the *Gau* [district] of Hessen-Nassau took place in every nook and cranny of Germany. All too often we had to make three, four, or six attempts at holding a meeting in a city before we finally succeeded. Often our first attempt at a meeting was forcibly disrupted by an opponent a hundred times stronger than us, or thwarted by ruthless efforts to forbid their followers from attending our meetings. We had to keep our nerve and avoid being driven to distraction and doing something stupid: the state's attorney was always ready to spring on us with the "Law for the Defense of the Republic!"—and always prepared to try the same thing again and again. This struggle made us National Socialists tough—tougher than our opponents thought and tougher than any outsider thought possible, or could even understand. We were forged like steel from the inside out and quickly shed the last vestiges of any reconciliation complexes we may have had. No degree of mockery and no measure of disdainful ridicule could shake us from the conviction that we National Socialists were, as one of our old guard once said, Germany's last hope.

Moscow or Us

The misery of unemployment was particularly acute that winter in Kassel. The city council, its majority loyal to the system, tried to keep the victims of the Dawes Plan in check with empty platitudes and police violence.[2] The few National Socialists, headed by Roland Freisler, waged a desperate battle.[3] And then it happened—just before Christmas of that year, the city council met shortly after the Weimar majority had voted down emergency Christmas assistance for the unemployed!—thousands upon thousands of citizens who had been robbed of their right to work surrounded the sprawling, splendid city hall and berated the System Republicans meeting inside. They were about ready to storm the building. Every available police unit was called in to protect those Novemberlings.[4] Those who had still been celebrating "their" Mayor [Philipp] Scheidemann just a few years earlier had since realized that they'd been betrayed. And it was on that very cold winter night, when the city was teeming with the frenzy of an upturned anthill to the sound of display windows of major businesses shattering, that Roland Freisler burst out of the chattering council meeting and trudged along with us to the nearby Friedrich Square, where we addressed the starving masses. We forgot the middle-class niceties! We had to stop Moscow from winning over these citizens driven crazy by hunger, making them willing subjects of the insane ideas of Bolshevism [. . .]

If the city of Kassel was spared mass plundering and hard, bloody fighting, it is thanks to a few hundred SA men who stood at our side as speakers and demonstrated the national socialism of our movement!—Only a few weeks later, I needed an escort to leave or return to my apartment morning or night. Several loyal SA men had to be with me all the time, since Communist unemployed men, unscrupulously incited against us National Socialists, wanted to attack me now that they knew who I was. Every day I joined the unemployed who demonstrated in the large courtyard of the labor office on Giesberg Street. More than once, I had to be met by party members at the Kassel train station to protect me from lurking Communist terror troops. It was the same or worse for all of our prominent Kassel party members and SA men, just as for the Storm Troopers of our movement who put their lives on the line every hour of every day in every city and every village in Germany. As public speakers, of course, we were prime targets for the enemy. And the attending laws mandated that we remain unarmed. We would have been in deep trouble had any kind of weapon turned up during a body search! Even a nail file could be considered a weapon. Later, even a party badge with a long pin passed for a weapon!

The System officials had faith in the notion that we would never make any progress when hindered by this array of chicanery—that "faith" was our good fortune. The gentlemen miscalculated.

The Old Guard

The party office in Westphalia asked me to come there for eight to ten meetings at least every other month. Those cities that were not Red fortresses were entirely in the hands of the Center Party.[5] A bitter battle had begun here and elsewhere in the West. Here, one's full efforts were necessary to win over every single heart. Manual laborers in particular needed to hear our thinking. The attempts of our party comrades to hold a National Socialist meeting failed half a dozen times or more. Most meetings were made impossible by the thousandfold numerical superiority of the opponent, or else broken up before they could finish. Our protective service, to which every party member of each local group belonged, was still too weak in most areas to stand up against the Red avalanche, which is increasingly driven by Communists. One National Socialist against five hundred or even a thousand citizens—that is how it always is there!

In the middle of the month I got sent to Dortmund. Our meeting is in the Red north of the city, at the "Fedenbaum." As many as two-thirds of those present may have been Marxists. On that November day, nine years after the stock exchange revolt and four years after Adolf Hitler's act, allow me to speak from my own experience. I attempt to do so by describing my experiences in 1918 and 1923. Based on those experiences, I predict a Marxist betrayal of the German population. The disruptive heckling swelled to a pitch; somewhere, in one corner of the room, a fight had already broken out and lasted several minutes, but our comrades quickly succeeded in throwing the troublemaker out. During the discussion period five Marxists were scheduled to speak—two Communists, two Social Democrats, and a so-called Syndicalist. After a flood of phrases from one of the Social Democrats, one of the Communists launched a perfidious attack against us, describing Adolf Hitler as a "fool" and the "leader of the organization that slaughters workers!" Well, that was the last straw for us! Ten minutes later, and after a hard fight, our comrades, with many an Oberlander [*Oberländler*] amongst them, succeed in ousting the far more numerous Communists from the hall. About half the audience is left, and I come to my conclusion faster than expected. After I had spoken about twenty minutes, a worker jumped up on a table and called upon the "comrades" to leave the meeting of the "Fascist band of brothers." Several dozen start singing the "Internationale," and we were left with no choice but to try and overpower the bawdry strains of these comrades with our "Deutschland, Deutschland über alles." Another several hundred leave the hall. The singing match quieted down and peace was gradually restored. I finished my speech before an audience of several hundred, all that was left of the more than a thousand who were there to start.

Afterwards we sat for a few hours in the back room of a small party office. The local group leader, old Kämpen König, told me that the meeting gained seven new members and perhaps a half dozen subscribers for the *Völkischer Beobachter.* König, a worker from the Hoesch iron and steel works, was very satisfied. The SA leader Franz Bauer, an old veteran, and his comrade Arthur Heimmich thought it could have been worse, since we were able to end the meeting as planned. Neither had believed that their "Sturm 68" could "hold down the fort" in that place.

That evening, I learned that as early as October 1920 a man had raised Adolf Hitler's flag in the fight for Dortmund: Wilhelm Ohnesorge, a Nazi postal official. I had met Ohnesorge the previous week in Hagen, where he was now working. He founded the first party outpost here in Dortmund at a time when only a few places in the entire Reich had heard of Adolf

Hitler. A loyal comrade, the old Free Corps fighter Wilhelm Kolm, was at his side. Kolm, along with a troop of Oberlanders from Bavaria, had occupied the central post office in Dortmund a few months prior to keep it out of the hands of the boys from Moscow. The two men met then and formed a lifelong fighting comradeship. Kolm placed his Oberlanders at Ohnesorge's disposal as the first small protective force for the local group Ohnesorge had founded. And since Kolm had become one of a "roving band of foot soldiers" made homeless by the November Republic, postal official Ohnesorge put him up with his family for the time being. In the columns of that dog-eared, detestable rag the *Dortmunder Generalanzeiger,* that was seen as a declaration of war by a straggler against an enemy a hundred thousand times as numerous. König told me that one of the first comrades who spoke publicly during the party's early years was Hermann Esser, whose speaking ability helped firm up small National Socialist outposts in the middle of these Red fortresses. Over the years, in tireless labor and constant battle that spared no comrade from the worst and most foul, postal official, Ohnesorge won over one man after another for the cause. I learned during my visit in Hagen what Wilhelm Ohnesorge meant to the numerically tiny group of National Socialists. I could compare this man only with my fatherly friend in Lower Bavaria: they were the kind of men each of us wished our fathers had been!

Novel Propaganda

For years now, we speakers have been traveling the country up and down, through every *Gau* in Germany. I speak primarily in Saxony, Brandenburg, Hessen-Nassau, and in the West. We see that even Red Saxony is streaming increasingly toward National Socialism. The meetings are difficult, but always successful.

For weeks, I travel through the Erzgebirge, just as I did some months before. Things were happening in Annaberg. The meeting there was a great success. Splendid chaps work for the movement in this city. When I speak in the tiny and tiniest villages of the Erzgebirge, I sense not only the dreadful poverty of the inhabitants, but also the terrible fatalism with which they bear their lot. Those families who do their work at home are particularly miserable. If these people do not learn to believe in National Socialism, they will all fall into Bolshevism. I spent a while in Neuhausen in the Erzgebirge and had time to study the situation. Wages in the toy-manufacturing industry are shamefully paltry; the firms are themselves at the end of their resources because exports have dried up. Everyone is fighting with everyone else.

How delighted we were when, a few weeks later, a lovely package of hand-carved toys arrived just before Christmas. A loving gesture that was doubly appreciated.

At many meetings, the Marxists unleash bloody terror. Our valiant SA men put up one hell of a fight! Things got particularly nasty in Chemnitz. Nearly half the people gathered at this big meeting were Red Front Fighters. Seeing the innocent young lads and men in their ranks nearly brought tears to your eyes! We have to win these betrayed citizens back. It's more about them than it is about the middle class, which, for the most part, has no will to fight and "takes things as they come" from one situation to the next.

I spent a few days in Lehnitz working out a new kind of propaganda. I want to test it out on my next speaking tour in the Lower Rhine area, party comrade Florian's *Gau.* I do not know why or how it happened, but several years ago, I began collecting pictures from newspapers and illustrated magazines of every shade on the political spectrum from the *Roter Stern* to *Woche.* I have pictures of all the leading System politicians, court reports, pictures from the society pages. I had the feeling that they might come in handy some day. While reading them as part of my editorial duties, I often wondered why the lords of the System press were so stupid and so confident as to photograph their party's saints in the worst situations and then present them to the starving public. What is more, those newspaper Jews were intent on paving the way for Communism, even when they were working for "nationalist" papers. In fact, that opened up even more opportunities to do so!

A school friend, now a starving engineer in Berlin, told me about a projection device that enlarged everything. I had to have it, even if it cost a lot of money. No sooner said than done. The ever-practical Hansl Hornauer made me a huge packing crate, since the big thing and all its parts had to be carted from meeting to meeting. I pasted the newspaper and magazine photographs on cardboard and added amusing or serious captions. I made sure to include the source of each picture. I also prepared title sheets with text on a white background, particularly figures from the "Decree of Anti-Peace" of Versailles, the Young Plan, or the emergency decrees of the System government. I arranged them all in the proper order and was ready for action. The big crate came along in the baggage car. An acquaintance was kind enough to bring us to the North Station with his car. As we hauled it through the Anhalter Station, Hansl Hornauer commented, "Well, the lads in Düsseldorf will be delighted to see this!"

The "premiere" was in a large hall. It was all so new that the crowd was interested in it for that reason alone. Now there was something to see. I did not need to say much. After a brief introduction, I got going. "Pictures without words," I said. Then they saw Berlin from every angle: miserable housing in Wedding and the East, Mrs. Representative X in the latest society outfit, the leaders of this "Free Republic," pictures of our "banned" SA, Jews in the black-red-gold of the Nationalist party, priests as parliamentarians, "colleagues" in the Reichstag restaurant, Isidor in a riding outfit, Soviet Jews, this and that, and much, much more, all mixed in with the figures from Versailles and Dawes.[6] It was effective. The pictures from the November Revolt and Russia were particularly effective, as were the pictures of the past and of the "Dessau" Bauhaus buildings. I was pleased that Jewish film pictures were greeted with laughter. In the conclusion, I spoke strongly. I stressed that all the pictures came from newspapers and magazines that were our enemies, even the caricatures of Comrade Scheidemann with and without his goatee, the pictures of Bernhard Weiss dancing with film star Y, or Reich minister the Jew Rudolf Hilferding, M.D., in conversation with Reichsbanner General Hörsing. All these were taken not by a National Socialist, but rather a Jew for the society pages of the "Berliner Tageblatt." And the signatures at the bottom of the "Treaty" of Versailles were those of Dr. Bell and Herman Müller. [. . .]

My new propaganda method worked particularly well in smaller towns. Every photo from a so-called big-city newspaper hit the mark. The descriptions of the latest fashions in the Jewish papers, which praised "socialism" on their other pages and railed against the bourgeoisie and capitalism, found excited readers. They saw the original material on the screen before them. None of the opponents present could doubt that.

I traveled though many districts with my crate for months. Then it was taken from me by government order. "Slandering the Republic!"—"Insulting the representatives of the present state!"—"Incitement to violence!"

I could no longer use the crate if I did not want to face constant fines of a thousand marks. There was a fine for noncompliance of RM 20—or 10—or two days in jail!

So I got along without the crate. Meeting followed meeting. We propagandists of Adolf Hitler traveled throughout Germany. To the smallest village.

For how long? When would this hard battle end? When would more Germans wake up? When would hundreds of thousands finally be ready to march into battle behind the banner of National Socialism?!

None of us thinks about the "when." Forward!—Only forward! Each heart won over is a victory! The day will come . . . !

Notes

1. Ley had been accused of changing his name from Levy to Ley—that is, of concealing his Jewish ancestry. Pastor Ludwig Münchmeyer was a prominent early Nazi speaker and fanatical anti-Semite who had been defrocked for scandalous misconduct.—Eds.
2. The Dawes Plan was a 1924 international agreement on German World War I reparations payments.—Eds.
3. Roland Freisler later became a notorious Nazi jurist.—Eds.
4. Nazi term for leaders of the Weimar Republic.
5. Zentrum, the conservative Catholic party.
6. "Isidor" was the derisive Nazi name for Bernhard Weiss, the Jewish vice chief of police in Berlin.—Eds.

11

WILFRID BADE

The Hitler Trial

First published as "Hitler Prozess," in *Deutschland erwacht: Werden, Kampf, und Sieg der NSDAP,* edited by Wilfrid Bade (Altona-Bahrenfeld: Cigaretten Bilderdienst, 1933), 29–30.

Foggy gray. The day: 26 February 1924.

On Blutenburg Street, uniformed throngs fan out in swarms, forming formidable cordons to block the streets.

Trial in the People's Court of Munich. In the building that once housed the military academy. Hitler and comrades on trial. For high treason.

Chevaux-de-frise [Spanish horsemen], barbed wire in the approach road. Passport checks, weapons checks, admissions checks. Green police, blue police, yet another roadblock.

The press surges into the somber courtroom; all the seats for observers are occupied.

A hot wave rises as the defendants appear. No one pays any attention to the Court.

There they are: the defendants, smiling. They are standing tall and broad, and it is plain to see from looking at them that they have no fear.

Hitler is wearing the Iron Cross on his chest. Beside him, Frick, stretched to his full height, Böhmer, Kriebel. And all the others.

It is a strikingly exclusive dock. One head after another brimming with character.

Finally, the presiding judge calls the court to order.

"Herr Adolf Hitler?"

The Führer bows slightly.

"I would like to first request that you provide us a detailed description of your life history."

Very good. This is exactly what Hitler wants, too. The presiding judge's request is like a catchword that sets him off.

And Hitler speaks. Speaks for four and a half hours. The courtroom sinks, the court sinks, the walls sink—only one man is left standing and hundreds of thousands listening—millions—this man is not the accused, by God, he is an inexorable accuser, and his sentences burn like flames.

Hitler portrays his life. Vienna, hunger, work, Marxism, the so-called labor leader, terror, ancient Austria, the international Jew.

"I left Vienna a confirmed anti-Semite, a deadly foe of Marxism." The statement sweeps through the room like a peal of thunder.

Quietly, Hitler continues. Speaking of war, speaking of the 1918 revolution.

He does not need to waste much breath on this period. Everyone in the room remembers, the gentlemen with rifles slung backwards over their shoulders, the plunderers and marauders, the rucksack-Spartacists and the [Munich] Soviet republicans, the spurious "sailors" who defiled the honor of the fleet, the hostage killers, and sadists.

And he speaks of the struggle of the first seven, the struggle of the Storm Troopers, of the beer-hall brawl in the Hofbräuhaus and of that day in Coburg. His voice rises again, turns stringent and severe. "The terror of the Left can only be confronted with even more drastic terror."

A veritable hailstorm of applause is unleashed. All those people sitting in the courtroom can no longer contain themselves. This is a brave man speaking and he has earned our praises. Does it matter whether this is the proper court etiquette? What is at issue here is not etiquette; what is at issue is that someone is standing there speaking the truth and that this valiant truth speaks from the heart and soul of the *Volk*.

But he has only just begun to speak. All this was but a prelude, the cornerstone. Now he's coming to the politics of the last few months, to the national revolution, the betrayal on the part of Herr von Kahr, the shots fired at the Field Marshall's Hall.[1]

What was it about Kahr's government? Was the oath made by Bavarian troops to Munich instead of to the Reich an act of sedition or was it not? The statement hurls through the air like an axe to hit Herr von Kahr: "If someone is in control of one division in an army of seven and rebels against the army chief of staff, then he must either dare to finish the job or he is but a wretched mutineer." Again, thunderous applause ensues. The judge abandons any futile attempt to squelch it.

"Two days before the putsch," Hitler cries, "I issued orders that there would be a change of national government on November 8th at 8:30 A.M. Would I have made the same decision if I hadn't been certain that [Otto von] Lossow, Kahr, and [Hans Ritter von] Seißer were also seeking to alleviate the current situation? It would have been sheer madness to have done the one thing without being assured of the other."

"If I have committed high treason—in my opinion, there is no such thing as high treason against the traitors of 1918—but if I have committed high treason, then Herr von Kahr and Herr von Lossow and Herr Colonel Seißer have done the same, and I am surprised not to find them seated here at my side."

Hitler is showered in thunders of applause.

But he is not finished yet. The decisive statement is yet to come: that proud, virile word to summon the future and the past against the present wretched state of affairs. "The judges of this state may as well convict us for our deeds. History, the Goddess of a higher truth and greater justice, will someday nevertheless smile as she tears this verdict to shreds, only to exonerate us from sin and exempt us from atonement."

With this statement, the jubilation climbs to tremendous heights. Never before has a traitor spoken thus before his judges.

And now for his comrades. Dr. Weber addresses the court, speaking of Kahr's political policies, reporting that he sought to create a separate Bavarian currency. The forked tongue of his politics is witness to this chief state commissioner and belies the dubious nature of his plans. On 6 November, Kahr explains, he was in complete agreement with Hitler. On 9 November . . . . The name of the Bavarian chairman of the people's party and separatist Dr. Heim is mentioned. His negotiations with the French in Wiesbaden are revealed. Even the specter of that circus from Parma-Bourbon makes its rounds among the ranks of these Donau confederates.

The indictments keep piling up—but certainly not on the shoulders of the accused.

On March 3 the prosecutor posted to the court his infamous petition for the immediate remand of Kahr, Lussow, and Seißer on charges of murder and high treason.

Fierce verbal assaults ensue.

The phrase "November criminals" is dropped.

Hitler springs to his feet at the mere mention of it: "I took charge of the political actions taken against the November criminals; that was my mandate and shall forever remain my mandate, if not now, then at some time in the future."

History electrifies the courtroom like sheet lightning.

And then came time for Kahr to testify.

The defense counsel makes haste:

"Why did you fail to enforce federal law in Bavaria?"

"Why didn't the Bavarian troops declare their allegiance to the state?"

"Why did you have the gold confiscated from the federal bank in Nuremberg?"

"Why did you think it necessary to strike in Thuringia? Things in Thuringia had, after all, already settled down by November 6. Who were you going after there?

Why did you tell a publisher in Stuttgart that you couldn't wait any longer?

Why? . . .

Why? . . .

Why? . . .

Kahr does not answer.

He doesn't so much as dare to defend himself.

The only question he bothers to answer is an incidental one—and his answer is immediately exposed as a lie.

As he is leaving the courtroom, a narrow path opens before him. The people avoid him like the plague. Many of them turn their heads away as Kahr passes by. They don't want to touch this man with so much as a glance.

They can't bear even to look at him.

Day by day, Hitler becomes less a defendant and more a public prosecutor.

The fact that Kahr had every intention of staging a putsch—just not the Hitler putsch, but rather a truly seditious putsch that would blast Bavaria into secession from Germany—was apparent, and not only to the court. And Hitler's reason for intervening, indeed, for placing the Party itself at risk, was equally apparent.

On 31 March, the day the verdict was scheduled to be announced, the city of Munich resembled a military camp.

The police don't trust the public. The lawyers for the defense, wherever they go, are showered with resounding cheers. They can barely clear a path for themselves through the crowds.

They are celebrated by the crowds, whose praise is due those men inside the cells of the people's court.

And Herr von Kahr's police force is well aware of that.

No one can say who brought the news that the defense counsel would be riding in an open car if Hitler were acquitted or received the minimum sentence of "fortress arrest." They would be riding in a closed car if—and only if . . .

Munich clenched its fists in its pockets.

And waited for the scales of justice.

Then came the verdict:

Hitler, Weber, Böhmer, Kriebel—all sentenced to the minimum term of five years' "fortress arrest" with eligibility for parole after six months.

Röhm, Wagner, Frick, Brückner—three months.

Ludendorff was acquitted.

The courtroom bursts into tremendous applause. The cheers veritably swoop down on the court.

Ludendorff anxiously protests his acquittal.

And then came the opinion of the court.

It is a complete vindication of Hitler. "The court, under the provisions of the Law for the Protection of the People, is authorized to deport . . . but for a man who is as German as Hitler in his thinking and his emotions, a man who voluntarily stood at the front for four and a half years."

The courtroom punctuates every sentence with incredible applause.

Munich celebrates Hitler.

The Kahr police force is left standing sullen beside the glowing profession of faith from the *Volk*.

Note

1. Gustav Ritter von Kahr (1862–1934) was a German conservative politician and state commissioner (*Staatskommissar*) of the state of Bavaria. He was one of the key figures to oppose and ultimately thwart Adolf Hitler's Beer Hall Putsch in 1923. He was murdered more than ten years later in the Night of the Long Knives.

12

WILFRID BADE

The SA Conquers Berlin

A Documentary Report

First published in *Die S.A. erobert Berlin. Ein Tatsachenbericht* (Munich: Knorr & Hirth, 1933), 18–21.

The worker Schulz, who had an infinite amount of time on his hands, slowly let himself drift homeward, through Potsdamer Street toward Schöneberg, through Bülow and North Streets until he landed in a tavern on Zossener Street.

He's not a big fan of taverns, but how else should he spend the long evening? Besides, here in this locale, he always finds interesting people.

KPD [Kommunistische Partei Deutschlands, German Communist Party] is written above the door.

Inside, there is a Soviet star hanging above a round corner table.

Schulz steps up to the bar, orders a beer, and listens to what the interesting people at the corner table are discussing amongst themselves. Their talk is all very candid, and they don't seem to have anything to hide.

"Number 23 registered it," one of them says, and the others nod and grin.

"What's his name?" one of them asks.

"Goebbels," another one answers, and the worker Schulz perks his ears. He's heard this name once before, while standing outside the window of the NSDAP headquarters.

And since Schulz knows one of the men seated at the corner table, he walks over and joins them with a brief greeting. He's always curious about what's going on in the world.

"Goebbels?" he asks. "What about him? Who is he?"

His acquaintance laughs. "Who he is? He's the new Herr *Gauleiter* [regional district leader] of Berlin under the Nazi gentlemen. He raised quite a ruckus in the Ruhr region, and now he's expected to put the screws on here. Well, we'll see whether he doesn't get screwed himself! Berlin is and shall forever remain Red. And whoever attempts to take a stand against the commune will be toppled. Even Herr Goebbels."

"So, so," says the worker Schulz, pensively. "You all seem to have already eaten him alive."

"Indeed, we have. And we will. He won't be hosting any rallies here! Not here! Maybe in Spandau, where there are a few Nazis. But here, not on your life!"

"But don't they have an office in the Potsdamer Street?" asks Schulz, cautiously. "I suppose you don't dare go there, huh?"

The men at the table look around and guffaw.

"That dive?" one of them says, dismissively. "Naw, ain't worth the bother. Naw, we got better things to do. Ain't that right, Gustav?"

They exchange telling looks and wink at each other.

And then they continue telling their old stories about the glory of the Soviets and all the things that have to change in this German state and what needs to be turned around and stood on its head to make the bottom rise to the top, and the worker Schulz started to feel rather glum.

It's all just one big pile of crap, he thinks, embittered, as he gets up to leave—all just one big pile of crap.

He rushes to get out in the fresh air, nearly stumbling out of the tavern and bumping into a fat man on the street who nearly loses his balance.

"Oh," Schulz says, shaken, as he grabs the fat man by the arm in order to help him stay on his feet.

But the fat man, a well-dressed man with a conspicuous smell of beer on his breath, angrily tears himself free. He looks at the worker Schulz from head to toe in his wretched slacks, his cheap green shirt, and his threadbare leather jacket. And screams at him: "Watch where you're going, you dirty little prole!"

And this despicable word cuts through the worker Schulz like a single, burning flame. He can't bear to hear this dreadful word anymore.

13

FRITZ OERTER

Our Speakers in the Anti-Marxist Struggle

The Balance of an Election Year

First published as "Unsere Redner im antimarxistischen Kampf. Die Bilanz eines Wahljahrs," *Unser Wille und Weg* 2 (1932), 350–56.

As we review the Reichstag, provincial parliament, and city elections of 1932, we must conclude that the day of huge mass meetings and mass marches is over, at least when it comes to winning new supporters for the National Socialist movement.

Those citizens whom we could interest in our worldview through marches and mass meetings, the sensible members of the middle class, have been reached. The "middle-class" reactionary front has been ground down—despite their election "victory" of 6 November. Nationalist circles are the ones that increasingly visited our mass meetings, that saw our marches with growing enthusiasm, and that remain today about 95 percent of the attendees at our meetings, though they have long since been won over to National Socialism.

But this loyal core of National Socialist supporters will surely grow weary of filling our mass meetings. In some *Gaue,* it is already true that only the most familiar leaders of our party, like Hitler, Strasser, Goebbels, Göring, Frick, etc., are able to bring out crowds in the tens of thousands. The high point of this form of propaganda is over, and we must now reach those circles that our propaganda so far has unfortunately been unable to reach in sufficient numbers.

Let us be honest with ourselves. The road is free and open, but our main enemy has done unexpectedly well in resisting the National Socialist advance. We have certainly succeeded in fragmenting the Marxist front and in winning a large number of former Marxists for our worldview. The Social Democrats are fighting desperately for their survival, and thanks to National Socialist educational work, hundreds of thousands, even millions of people, who once were firm supporters of the Marxist nonsense are beginning to waver. They are looking into the National Socialist movement, naturally, against the wishes of their "leaders." Still, Marxist propaganda, and especially its press, regularly succeeds in leading people who have seen the light back into error and bringing them back under the control of Marxist party leaders.

Why? In opposing Marxism, we oppose a deeply rooted worldview that is based on over sixty years of intensive work. It is in turn founded on the still older liberal worldview and economic order. It enjoys not only the protection of tradition, but also the strength that an older movement can bring to bear against a younger one. Liberalism was not able to resist Marxism. The liberal parties and ideologies could only fight defensively against a worldview with greater strength and clarity of purpose. Even the Marxist worker, who long doubted and sought for something better, eventually had to conclude that Marxism is the only worldview that can bring a new and better society and economic order. Who can hold it against him that he rejected the forces that denied him equality and a share in the results of his labor? The German worker absorbed Marxism in his parents' home and was surrounded by people who thought the same in the workplace. In what remained of his sound understanding, he knew that there was a flaw somewhere in the worldview. He realized that there was a catch somewhere to the lovely teachings of "expropriating the expropriators," of "the equality of everyone with a human face," of "international brotherhood," of "international solidarity," but he did not know where, and there was no one to show him the contradictions, the weak points in the thinking of Karl Marx and his followers.

Thanks to our ten years of educational work, he is suspicious. He became a seeker, a doubter, but unfortunately only a few of his comrades have found their way to us. The 1932 election results prove this. We have made inroads into the ranks of the SPD [Sozialdemokratische Partei Deutschlands, Social Democratic Party of Germany] and the KPD [Kommunistische Partei Deutschlands, German Communist Party], but not to the extent that the "leaders" of the Marxist parties have deserved as a result of their inability, incompetence, and contradictory policies.

Every National Socialist fighter who speaks to meetings of Marxist workers must recognize this and draw the necessary conclusions. The Marxist party "leaders" have made mistake after mistake. They have promised everything since 1918 and delivered nothing. They have worked a hundred times with Jewish racketeers and a thousand times with capitalism. They are responsible for all the need and misery of the German people and of German workers. Yet, if our Reich, *Gau,* and county speakers do not succeed in reducing the Marxist nonsense propounded by the Socialists and Communists to absurdity, their sacrificial work will not succeed in widening the breach in the Marxist front. Without that, the deceptive Marxist worldview will fail to collapse in the manner of those organizations that supported calcified liberalism.

We should not take Marxism lightly! To defeat the enemy, we must know its weapons. If its weapons are good, we must have better ones if we are to survive. Only when we know, and know precisely, what Marxism teaches can we succeed in convincing the Social Democratic and Communist workers of the unfruitfulness of this doctrine, thereby making National Socialists of them. Of course, it remains necessary to show German workers who are still excited by the doctrines of Marx, Engels, Lassalle, or Lenin what kind of "leaders" they have. However, revealing the nature of their "leaders" and policies shakes only their confidence in their party, rarely their attitudes about the worldview.

Our propaganda, our intensive educational work, must make clear to the German worker that the aims of the *Communist Manifesto* and the "Erfurt," "Görlitz," and "Heidelberg" programs, proclaimed for decades, are impossible and utopian and that the materialist philosophy and economic system of *Das Kapital* are erroneous and lead in the wrong direction. We must show them that this is the reason for the behavior of many Social Democratic and Communist "leaders." They have no choice but to play such a treasonous role. Only if we do this will Marxism's supporters give up all hope of a future Marxist state and become willing to consider true German socialism.

The conclusion is simple: *Training, untiring and thorough training, is necessary!* It is necessary not only for the members, whom some functionaries and speakers handle as if they were a bit stupid, but for everyone at the political front. For officials and speakers, anti-Marxist training is of the greatest importance. Unfortunately, many of our speakers—and often not the worst ones either—have completely avoided training about Marxism. True, they understand National Socialist thinking, but not Marxist views and theses. They are like army officers who have good soldiers but do not know how strong the enemy is or where he is located.

That is why there are complaints about this or that speaker in nearly every *Gau*. Party members want better education, better speakers, to enable them to hold their own against opponents, even if a question comes up that goes beyond current events. Marxist meeting visitors have been worked on through the lies of an unscrupulous press. They are especially critical. A single ill-chosen phrase or the least sign of uncertainly drives these citizens away, and some who were making their way toward us are lost forever. Our work has made them distrust their own leaders, but the long rabble-rousing of their "leaders" has also left them suspicious about National Socialist thinking.

It is nonsense to think that a popular style of speaking (which often turns out to be vulgar) is enough to win sympathy for the speaker in a meeting of workers. The opposite! The Marxist worker can tell what is genuine and what is artificial. When he sees that a speaker has taken on a "popular" style of speaking, or that he wears a shirt without a collar or rolled-up sleeves or other things like that, he becomes reserved and critical. Obviously, a workers' meeting is not a university auditorium. The speech must be simple and clear. But coarse language and shabby clothing generally harm the overall impression, just as do an elevated lecturing style and elegant dress.

There is too much of this going on, in part due to a lack of thorough training, which is replaced by outward appearances. Unnecessary exaggeration is also harmful. For example, a speaker at a meeting of workers before the 6 November election announced that our vote total would rise significantly and that we would win 250 seats. The half-won Marxists lost faith in this prophet and the worldview he preached. Even worse, some National Socialist speakers who fail to understand Marxism's idea of class struggle said that the NSDAP might call for a general strike if Herr von Papen dared to dissolve the newly elected Reichstag. Similar exaggerations, of which there were unfortunately many, destroy everything that the speaker thinks he accomplished in his speech.

One mistake is particularly common. When National Socialist speakers who were formerly Marxists speak in workers' areas, the publicity often says, "The former Marxist union secretary so-and-so will speak on the theme, 'Marxism or German workers.'" The Marxist worker attends such a meeting to hear a discussion of worldviews. He is deeply disappointed when he gets only a normal discussion of current events, which does not in any way make it easier for him to decide which worldview to support.

What good does such a meeting do the Marxist worker? He knows that his "leaders" have betrayed the "goals of the revolution." He knows they supported the Young Plan [Allied plan for German war reparations in 1929]. He knows that Soviet Russia is not a land of milk and honey. He knows that National Socialism is fighting [Franz] von Papen. He knows that [President Paul von] Hindenburg was supported by the Social Democrats and some in the KPD. He did not come to listen to a former Marxist speaker to hear these things again. He wants to hear something different. He wants to know why this former Marxist left the red flag and now fights for the swastika. He is a seeker. He has lost faith in Marx and his doctrines. His world is threatening to collapse, and he wants a new and better worldview.

The former Marxist who found a new worldview in National Socialism should help his former party members to make a final break with Marxism. He should make it easier for them to become National Socialists. The Marxist worker wants to hear why the speaker today opposes that which he once honestly fought for, perhaps for more than a generation. He wants to know why the speaker chose National Socialism and how it is superior to Marxist thinking.

The attitude of a large part of the Marxists who come to our meetings can be summarized in this way: they no longer believe their "leaders"; they doubt Marxist doctrine; they look to the worker-speakers of the National Socialist people's movement to find a justification to bring them from Marxism to National Socialism.

They want a plausible justification and good reasons for doing what they instinctively feel. For decades, the materialist worldview has been pumped into them. They have learned to evaluate everything from a materialistic and rational perspective. As convinced Marxists, they have been ruled by cold, clear reason, not by feelings. Mind and stomach, not heart and soul, have been the driving forces behind events. In their hearts and souls, many of these former Marxist workers are already National Socialists; only their materialism keeps them from breaking with the false gods of the past.

The movement's speaker has the task of making it easier for Marxist workers to break with the past. He must be ready and able to give these citizens a logical basis for their emotional longing for National Socialism. He can do that only by knowing the Marxist worldview as well as he knows his own. He must be able to deal directly with the ideas of Marxists in the audience. He must be able to handle even the best Marxist discussion speakers.

Can every National Socialist speaker do that? No. The news from the *Gaue* proves it. The order of the day is thus training and more training. Some good National Socialist literature already deals with the fundamentals of Marxism. The National Socialist who has read these materials and understood them is capable of dealing with the average Marxist speaker, but not with well-trained Marxist speakers who have a solid understanding of the writings of Marx and Engels and who have mastered them. Therefore, the training should be conducted by party comrades who have studied Marxist doctrine in depth and are able to cross swords with even the best opponents from the Marxist camp.

Unfortunately, many diligent speakers have the incorrect belief that they do not need to learn anything further, that it is enough if they keep up with current events. They will know better once they have participated in a well-organized training course in which Marxist workers with better than average political education defend their worldview against the attacks of National Socialism. In such a course, the National Socialist speaker learns what he is lacking in order to be able to win the German worker to National Socialism. In fair and factual ways, but also in compelling and precise form, these training courses discuss the worldviews of National Socialism and Marxism. These discussions prove that the National Socialist worldview is far superior to Marxist ideology, but also that Marxist spokesmen, including minor functionaries and speakers, enjoy training that could be of great value to some of our speakers in workers' meetings. The lack of such training is the reason that many of them lack the success they desire.

When our Führer determines Germany's fate, such training will be of particular importance. Hand in hand with the practical refutation of Marxist theories that will come by realizing National Socialism, we need an intensive theoretical education of the working masses in order to free the last German worker from internationalism and materialism. They need to be persuaded of German idealism, of the principle that "the common good goes before the individual's good."

This is hard work, but the goal is worth it. *Millions of German citizens will once again believe in their race, fatherland,* and social justice. To work, then, you National Socialist fighters against Marxism and Reaction! Prepare yourselves for the final battle against Marx and his followers! Then victory will no longer be denied us!

14

HERMANN FÜHRBACH

How I Became a National Socialist

Written in 1934. From Theodore Fred Abel Papers, 1930–1986, Hoover Institution, Stanford University, Stanford, California.

I, Hermann Führbach, was born on 9 December 1907, in Mühlheim-Ruhr, the son of the building contractor Carl Führbach, and attended the Catholic primary school until I was fourteen. When the war broke out—I was seven years old—my eldest brother, Carl, received his call to join the 135th Infantry Regiment; my brother Wilhelm, even though he had not yet finished his apprenticeship, volunteered for the navy. Their patriotic enthusiasm had its effects on me too. Thus, even as a boy, I carried the guns of departing soldiers to the railway station for them. Every time that the army communiqué reported a new German victory, I enthusiastically ran to the church and helped ring the victory bells. When my brothers came back from the front on leave and told their stories, I was thrilled. I was very deeply stricken by the news that my eldest brother, shortly before the end of the war, was killed in Flanders; even before that, two cousins, second lieutenants both, had given their lives for the fatherland. The end of the war and the revolution are events that I can still remember vividly. What I felt to be a particular disgrace was an incident in which Red revolutionaries stopped some officers and right in front of our eyes in the schoolyard ripped off their epaulets.

After finishing school, I was apprenticed to the Thyssen Company as a die worker. On my very first day there, I got to know the class struggle, as taught by Marxism: people tore the black, white, and red rosette off my windbreaker and tried to force me to join a Syndicalist union. Since I saw no other way out, I applied for an apprentice membership in the German Metal Workers' Union.

It was in 1923 that I first heard about the Hitler movement. I quit the Metal Workers' Union and joined the defense league "German Eagle." Now everybody at the plant hated me. During every wildcat strike, I, as a German-minded boy, took my lumps from all sides. But I did not allow myself to be deterred from my path. When the French marched in, during the so-called Ruhr invasions, I got a lot of work from the defense league German Eagle. Whenever possible, we got the facts on French troop strength and precise information on their equipment—guns, trucks, etc. At the end of 1925, we took a night march to Kettwig, from which we did not return until seven the next morning because of the detours we were forced to make on account of the French. It was on the day the French departed from Mühlheim, on that day of all days, that I was fired from my apprentice's job for my *völkisch* convictions. On the evening of that same day, we showed the black, white, and red flag and performed the stage play *Tauroggen.*[1] Marxists and Communists on this occasion wanted to tear the uniforms off us. For two weeks we performed the play, and for two weeks we had to guard our uniforms, which, after all, we needed for our performance, day and night.

From this time on, the number of our adherents increased. At the end of 1925, Dr. Goebbels founded the local group Mühlheim-Ruhr of the National Socialist German Workers' Party, which I joined immediately. From that point on, I fought untiringly against Communists, Marxists, Center Party people, and fellow travelers. On 4 July 1926, at the second Reich Party Rally, I took the oath on the flag before the Führer, the first man from Mühlheim to do so, a member of Storm Trooper Detachment No. 26. It was only now that I knew that Germany had a leader again. Our work never ended, even if it was only a matter of providing protection for meetings, or distributing leaflets, or other such things. We were persecuted day and night. We were called daydreamers, and the Center Party people insulted us with names like Nazi kids and pagans.

September 1930 was the most difficult of the election battles for us. We kept going day and night. During the day we distributed leaflets; at night we hung up our posters; in the evening we were ordered to duty at meetings. If we slept much, it was for two hours on the bare floor of the Lion's Inn. On the evening of 14 September, our reward came—our great victory—our slogan, "Awaken, Germany!" had had its effect. One hundred and seven National Socialist deputies were elected to the Reichstag. Enthusiasm was high. The Jews were packing their bags, many were already running away, but they came back a short time later.

So we had to fight on, without flinching. But people were beginning to be afraid of us. The party organization was banned, and we had to take off our brown shirts. If we put on white ones instead, as we turned up to protect a meeting, the police beat us out of the hall with rubber truncheons. If we all wore blue caps, or black ties, we were subversive elements too. The Communists bludgeoned us down, the police put us in prison, comrades were shot in the back. None of this could stop us; it could only strengthen us in our resolve to bring about the breakthrough of Adolf Hitler's idea among the German *Volk*. We were firm in our faith that one fine day we would have won our battle for the unity of the German *Volk*. We pushed ever deeper into the ranks of the Communists and the Marxists and brought the best of them over to us. The Center Party people fought us with particular bitterness; Catholic priests refused church funerals to dead comrades. We were not allowed to enter church in uniform, even though, as National Socialists, our basis is a Christian one.

Yet in spite of all hostility, we advanced slowly but all the more surely. On January 30th, 1933, Adolf Hitler created a united German *Volk*. The great point of his program, to give work again to eight million unemployed, is being fulfilled more quickly than expected. Just in this first year alone, millions went back to work. I, too, am to be counted among those fortunate people. Untiringly now, we are working and helping to construct the National Socialist state, until every German will understand the National Socialist ideology, faithful to our oath:

For our *Führer* and his idea we shall fight unto death.

Hermann Führbach
Mühlheim-Ruhr

Note

1. Maximilian Böttcher's 1920's "Führerdrama" about the Prussian resistance to Napoleon.—Eds.

2
Nazism in Power: 1933

THOUGH HITLER'S FOLLOWERS CLAIMED that his appointment as chancellor on 30 January 1933 was "a national revolution," his opponents, like the exiled writer Heinrich Mann (1871–1950), countered that "it was the violent suppression of a people that no longer dared to resist."[1] Hermann Rauschning (1887–1982), former mayor of Danzig and one of the most influential defectors from Nazism in the 1930s, called it a "revolution of nihilism."[2] Historians have been reluctant to apply the term *revolution* to the National Socialist regime since no social revolution occurred and because they view the National Socialists as "counterrevolutionaries" who were opposed to the Marxists—Social Democrats and Communists—that comprised almost 15 percent of the voters in the Weimar Republic. But insofar as National Socialism was largely an "anti" movement in its antisocialist, anticommunist, antiliberal, and anticapitalist rhetoric, it was undoubtedly first and foremost an anti-Jewish revolution, as the first legal measures demonstrated.

After the fiasco of his coup attempt in 1923, Hitler pursued a legal road to power through the crisis-ridden Weimar democracy. Though the Nazis despised constitutional government, they were adept at mobilizing a mass electorate that regarded them as a people's protest party, and after 1930, they used their 107 seats in parliament to perpetuate a climate of crisis and political paralysis. As party historian Walter Frank observed, Hitler's aim was to topple Weimar democracy by legal means and then "to destroy democracy using democratic methods."

Despite Chancellor Heinrich Brüning's (1885–1970) efforts to control spiraling unemployment by public austerity, he had little support from fellow conservatives and had to rely on the Social Democrats to ignore parliament and rule by presidential decree, as was permitted by Article 48 of the Weimar Constitution.[3] When street violence became endemic in April 1932, Brüning banned both the Rotfrontkämpferbund (Communist Red Front Battle League) and the Nazi Storm Troopers, a move that led President Paul von Hindenburg (1847–1934) to replace him with a new Reich chancellor, Franz von Papen (1879–1969). Papen, with the support of the leader of the nationalist Stahlhelm (Steel Helmets), Kurt von Schleicher (1882–1934), and backed by the army, promised to create "a new state"—which he did in July 1932 when he took control of the government of the state of Prussia by a coup d'état. Attempting to "box Hitler in," conservative elites like Alfred Hugenberg (1865–1951) pressured Hindenburg to appoint Hitler chancellor at the head of a coalition, with Papen as vice chancellor. That night, as Hermann Göring addressed the *Volk* on the radio, Joseph Goebbels organized a huge torchlight parade in Berlin, with more than fifty thousand brownshirts passing through the Brandenburg Gate.

To be sure, not all Germans cheered Hitler's ascent to power, but even skeptics had their own authoritarian solutions, such as Oswald Spengler's (1880–1936) vision of a strong-willed Prussian socialism that would save the white race from the "colored menace." As Spengler observed of his Weimar compatriots, "[The] absence of any form of authority manifested itself in the way everyone screamed for his own form of dictatorship without so much as knowing any dictator or being able to recognize one."

On 21 March 1933, Hitler and Hindenburg participated in a ritual at the old Prussian Garrison Church in Potsdam to symbolically enact the marriage of the old conservative elites and the new plebeian radicals: the elderly president, in full field marshal's dress uniform, laid a wreath at the tomb of the Prussian kings, and Hitler, dressed in a cutaway, bowed as he clasped the president's hand, flanked by representatives of the army, the SA, the blackshirted Schutzstaffel (Defense Force, SS), and the Steel Helmets. Goebbels hailed the spectacle as the restoration of German honor. Even the writer Erich Ebermayer, who later that day was "ashamed and distressed" by his own emotions, noted in his diary that the "Day of Potsdam" signified the "preservation of the great tradition of our *Volk*" and the "stability of government instead of constant vacillation."

On 1 May 1933, the traditional Labor Day celebration, the Nazis staged an even grander spectacle at Tempelhof airfield with the flagship *Graf Zeppelin* overhead. The party carefully choreographed a media spectacle that expressed the unity of the worker, the artisan, and the farmer, characterizing them as equal members of the *völkisch* community—the "end to the splintering of our *Volk*," as Hitler said in his Labor Day speech. The "young" National Socialist movement was in fact the most socially diverse and multiclass political party in Germany, but its political advent did not please its most devout followers. The party ranks suddenly swelled with the influx of new joiners who came on board after March—"March violets." The SS weekly, *Das Schwarze Korps,* ever the guardian of Nazi purity, demeaned these new converts as arrogant and lacking in conviction, complaining that the newcomers looked down on nonparty members as "second-class citizens." Yet, despite the grumbling, the party's new theater state, the redemptive rhetoric of the leaders, and, above all, the growing dominance of the party in every corner of German life put the "average man in the street," as *Das Schwarze Korps* put it in a political frame—though not one of his or her own making.

The fire that destroyed the Reichstag building on the night of 27 February 1933, an act of arson by the Dutch anarcho-communist Marinus van der Lubbe, gave the regime the pretext to be done with democracy and take revenge on political enemies, especially the Communists, who were immediately blamed for the fire. Claiming that the conflagration was a "signal" for an insurrection, on the following day the regime promulgated a decree "for the protection of *Volk* and state," suspended civil liberties, declared martial law, expanded the power of the federal government, and gave the police license to imprison any person who committed an act "detrimental to public welfare." Within a few weeks, the first concentration camp was established in Dachau, near Munich, and on 23 March, Hitler sealed the demise of the Weimar Republic with a law (the Law to Remedy the State of Emergency of *Volk* and Reich, known as the Enabling Act) that ended parliamentary government and gave him and his cabinet full dictatorial power. Just before the law passed, the chairman of the Sozialdemokratische Partei Deutschlands (Social Democratic Party of Germany, SPD), Otto Wels (1873–1939), delivered an eloquent final speech in defense of democracy and the Weimar Republic. By that time, thousands of Communists and Social Democrats had been arrested and hounded out of Germany. A few weeks later, on 7 April, the Law for the Restoration of Professional Civil Service removed all Jews from public life.

Still, the complex interplay of the Rechtsstaat (the old constitutional judiciary), the police, the party, and the SA made the legal basis of the Nazi state unclear, at least for a time. A variety of interpretations were put forward by some of Germany's leading constitutional theorists in order to give the new regime juridical legitimacy. One of the first to comment was the constitutional specialist Carl Schmitt (1888–1985), who put forward a corporatist view in a book titled *State, Movement, Volk*. Schmitt proposed a tripartite foundation in which each element would carry equal weight. Ernst Forsthoff, while acknowledging the importance of the *Volk* community and hierarchy and the unity of state and party, argued that "with the takeover of power, the party leader Adolf Hitler accrued the transpersonal justification of state leadership." But chief party ideologue Alfred Rosenberg stepped in and rejected the idea of the "total state" as a liberal residue, since the state was ultimately only a "tool" of the Nazi worldview. After Hitler had SA leader Ernst Röhm and a number of other key figures in the movement murdered on 30 June 1934, Schmitt altered his earlier view, declaring the Führer to be "the supreme judicial authority of the *Volk*," a position that Hans Frank (1890–1946, executed at Nuremberg), president of the Nationalsozialistische Rechtswahrerbund (National Socialist Jurists Association), considered too limited, in contrast to his authoritative 1936 declaration that the Führer was the ultimate source of the law.

NOTES

1. Heinrich Mann, *Der Hass: Deutsche Zeitgeschichte* (Amsterdam: Querido Verlag, 1933), 107.
2. Hermann Rauschning, *The Revolution of Nihilism; Warning to the West* (New York: Longmans, Green & Co., 1939).
3. Dr. Heinrich Brüning (1885—1970) was the leader of the Center Party and chancellor of Germany from 1930 to 1932.

15

WALTER FRANK

On the History of National Socialism

First published in *Zur Geschichte des Nationalsozialismus* (Hamburg: Hanseatische Verlagsanstalt, 1939), 20–22.

New Year's Day 1934, Chancellor Adolf Hitler addressed a letter to the Prussian prime minister, Hermann Göring. In it, with reference to November 1923, he said, "It was bitter necessity that forced us to act, and divine Providence that foiled our success."

A big statement and a deep insight. Because today we can see what he means: if the attempt on 9 November 1923 had succeeded, it would have become less a National Socialist revolution and more a national change of government. It was only the catastrophe of the year 1923 that forced the National Socialist movement to sink its roots so deep in the soil of the German empire that it could survive even the severest storm.

In that tempestuous year of 1923, Hitler had hoped to create the Reich of his dreams in one fell swoop, much in the manner of Mussolini's "March on Rome."

Even though the army's chief of staff at the time was named Ebert and Hitler's ally was General Ludendorff, the discipline of the troops was not shaken by the national revolution. This experience and this insight would prove decisive for the second phase of Adolf Hitler's struggle.

In the year 1925, General Field Marshall von Hindenburg became president of the republic. With this imperial soldier, who personified for the great masses of *Volk* the experience of the Great War, the democracy of Weimar garnered its first pillar of moral authority. With it also disappeared, however, the last possibility for toppling the state of Weimar illegally and by force. The only possibility left was to overpower it by legal means.

The big question in the second phase of the National Socialist movement was thus whether or not it is possible to destroy democracy using democratic methods.

In principle, it was conceivable that a party that had employed the method of mass democracy might itself fall prey to mass hysteria.

If this did not happen, then it was as a result of the Führer principle as embodied by Adolf Hitler.

A demagogue lets himself be led by the masses. Hitler led the masses and reforged them into a *Volk*. [. . .]

The struggle of the National Socialist movement from its inception through to the seizure of power can be divided into three major periods. The first period, from its inception to 14 September 1932, is the period of internal growth and formation. The second period, from the September elections through [Chancellor Heinrich] Brüning's capitulation in May 1932, encompasses the decisive dispute over the NSDAP state as opposed to a parliamentary state structure. The third period, from summer 1932 to January 1933, is characterized by the confrontation between National Socialism and the old form of imperial conservatism.

In the first stage of its development, the movement was relatively free of dramatic events but rich in quiet, contemplative work. In the years between 1925 and 1929, the party's first accomplishment was to rebuild its organizational infrastructure. But then party members' agitation took hold and spread. In 1923, the party had been restricted primarily to Bavaria. But now it was becoming what it had always been in ideological terms: a German party with a nationwide presence.

National Socialism drew new recruits from all the German *Gaue,* from all walks of life and all generations. And it forged from them a new type of man. Personally, I don't think

I've ever experienced such a tangible expression of this power for unifying people as I felt at the 1929 Reichsparteitag (Reich Party Rally) in Nuremberg, where I saw General von Epp and Dr. Joseph Goebbels seated side by side at the Führer's table. The thirty-two-year old tribune, who was then just beginning to take over Berlin and making his name as a man to be detested and feared by his enemies—and the sixty-one-year-old famous soldier who had given his name to the vilified movement at a very young age. The younger, a leader of the urban masses; the elder, a leader of soldiers. Joseph Goebbels in an aura of machines droning on the factory floor and of the dull thud of the minions' feet somewhere in Wedding or Neukölln as he drives through in his car. Franz von Epp in the aura of fresh forest air, in the woods he, as a hunter, loved so much, and of the whiz and hum of the imperial standards clanking from their poles carried by the bodyguard regiment of men he is leading to battle or of the crisp marching steps of the "white garden" on Munich's streets . . .

Ten steps in front of the two men, at the center of the podium, you could see where the man was seated who was responsible for the union of these two opposites to a higher unity—the man who tamed German anarchy: Adolf Hitler.

In May 1928, the NSDAP entered German parliament with twelve representatives in the Reichstag. At the time, they were still just an insignificant splinter group. But only one year later, by fall 1929, the NSDAP would make its first broad foray into domestic politics in Germany.

The group joined with the German Nationalist Party, which, led by [Alfred] Hugenberg's secret council, had assumed a staunchly oppositional stance against Weimar democracy, and with the "Steel Helmet" Corps [of Franz] Seldte to prevent ratification of the Young Plan through a people's referendum.[1]

But the referendum failed. It got only 13.8 percent of the votes. Nevertheless, it wasn't without positive effects for the NSDAP. For the first time, the party expressed its opposition to all of Germany and all of Europe. For the first time, the Weimar democracy was put on the political defensive.

In 1930, influenced by appeasement policies and economic crisis, the masses began flocking to the party in droves. In the same year, the NSDAP formed the SA—an instrument of power that was rare both in its force and its precision. And it was the same year that the party set out to demonstrate its capacity for governance in the daring and dangerous attempt to participate in a coalition government in Weimar in the person of Dr. Frick.

These advances occurred at a time when the parliamentary crisis in Germany entered a decisive phase.

Early in 1930, the Reich president charged Brüning's cabinet with the task of bringing the financial crisis under control. He was explicit in stating that this could not be accomplished by any of the customary cabinet coalitions, but rather only by a cabinet of his choosing, and one that he granted special powers.

But Brüning's cabinet was, of course, one that was substantially controlled by the Center [Party] and a cabinet consisting of the bourgeois middle, hence a cabinet of parliamentarians. But it was with Brüning's cabinet that the parliamentarians were forced for the first time to concede that it was impossible to overcome the crisis using parliamentary means alone. They had to take recourse to the extraordinary executive powers of the office of Reich president. And they were forced to think about how they might secure yet another nonparliamentarian force, the bayonets of the German army, which was supposedly under the secret control of General von Schleicher.

They decided to address Dr. Heinrich Brüning, Germany's last parliamentary chancellor, as the best parliamentarian Germany had to offer, which he probably was. But perhaps it was characteristic of this political system itself that its best man was utterly estranged from the people and their passions. That he, as a cold calculator of the tides of change, either knew nothing or knew too little about the elementary events that took place or lay dormant in the depths of the people's souls.

This is why Brüning was wrong in his calculations about National Socialism. He saw in the movement little more than a radical wave that would quickly pass through and recede.

His first decisive act of governance already reflected his drastic underestimation of National Socialism. He dissolved the Reichstag, which had rejected all emergency ordinances. His reason for doing so was that he hoped to shatter Hugenberg's opposition party with the intention of replacing it with a loyalist group from the Conservative People's Party [Konservative Volkspartei].[2]

Brüning was counting on [the leader of that party, Gottfried] Treviranus's victory.

And so it came to 14 September 1930. When 107 National Socialists entered the German parliament representing 6.5 million voters, the Weimar Republic and the entire public sentiment in Europe for a time had the feeling that a volcano was erupting beneath their feet.

Notes

1. Franz Seldte (1882–1947) was cofounder of the conservative authoritarian Stahlhelm and, later, a member of the Nazi Party.—Eds.

2. The Konservative Volkspartei (Conservative People's Party, KVP) was a numerically insignificant party led by Gottfried Treviranus (1891–1971) that split from the Deutschnationalen Volkspartei (German National People's Party, DNVP) in July 1930 and entered the government of Chancellor Heinrich Brüning. The KVP differed from the DNVP in its loyalty to the state and the Weimar Constitution.—Eds.

16

OSWALD SPENGLER

The White World Revolution

First published as "Die weiße Weltrevolution," in his *Jahre der Entscheidung* (Munich: C.H. Beck, 1933), 141–43, 145–46. Translated by Charles Francis Atkinson.

Like everything that is associated with parties and programs, socialism of every kind is today as antiquated as the liberal forms from which it stems. The century of the workers' cult, 1840 to 1940, has come to an irrevocable end. Whoever would sing "the worker's" praises today has no grasp of the times. The manual laborer is fading into the whole fabric of the nation, no longer as its pampered lapdog but as the lowest rung on the ladder of an urban society. The social antagonisms that were resolved by the class struggle will again become permanent fixtures separating the upper and lower classes and will be accepted as a matter of course. It is the resignation of the imperial period in Rome, in which there were no economic problems of this nature left. But how much can be destroyed and leveled down in the final stages of world anarchy? Indeed, so much that in certain white nations there will be nothing left upon which a Caesar might build his creation, his *army*—for armies will supplant political parties in the future—and his state.

In all the white countries that were party to the Great War, is there any shred of a viable foundation from which such men and such future-oriented tasks might emerge amongst what, vaguely enough, goes by the name of "youth" and the "front generation"? The profound shock of the Great War, which jolted everyone from the sluggish illusions of security and progress as the purpose of history, is nowhere more apparent than in the psychological chaos it left in its wake. The fact that we are not in the least aware of this and believe ourselves to be the bearers of a new order is the most tangible evidence of its existence. To those born around 1890, the sight of a genuinely commanding leadership figure has been utterly lacking. By that time, the figures of [Otto von] Bismarck and [Helmuth Karl von] Moltke, not to mention those of other countries, had already vanished in the mists of a historical literature. They might have set a standard for true greatness, but not without a living present, and the war did not produce a single important monarch, a single prominent statesman, or one successful military strategist in a crucial position. All the monuments and street names in the world cannot gloss over that fact. The result was the complete lack of any sense of authority among the millions who returned home from the trenches on both sides. This was evident in the unrestrained sophomoric criticism of everything at hand, of men and of things, without a trace of *self-criticism* anywhere. People scoffed at yesterday without any inkling of its ongoing power. Above all, this absence of any form of authority manifested itself in the way everyone screamed for his own form of dictatorship without so much as knowing any dictator or being able to recognize one, in the way leaders were elected and worshipped one day and rejected the next—[the Spanish dictator Miguel] Primo de Rivera, [the Italian poet-politician Gabriele] d'Annunzio, [the German general and political leader Erich] Ludendorff—and the way leadership became a problem to be discussed, but no one was prepared to acknowledge and accept it were it ever to emerge. Political dilettantism took the upper hand. Everyone set his own prescriptions for what his future dictator ought to do. Everyone demanded discipline from others, because he was incapable of self-discipline. Because people had forgotten what it meant to be a good steward of state, men fell prey to a hysteria of programs and ideals and indulged in dissolute verbal and written rants and raves about what absolutely had to change—assuming all the while that such changes were even possible. The lack of respect for history was never greater than in these years. Everyone failed to acknowledge or admit that history had its *own* logic by which all programmatic solutions are destined to fail. But Bismarck attained his end because he understood the course of history in his century and adapted himself to it. That was political policy at its finest, the art of the *possible.*

In their lack of understanding, the "youth" in all the white countries sought to "put an end" to two centuries of world change from the bottom up—and this in the form of Bolshevism, something they were amply endowed with themselves—and, typically, they raised a revolutionary hue and cry against "individualism" in Germany, in England, in Spain, everywhere. But they were themselves little individualists—very little—lacking talent, lacking depth, and, for that very reason, obsessed by the frantic need to be right, which is why they despised the superiority of people greater than themselves, men for whom at least a tinge of self-skepticism was not entirely alien. All revolutionaries are humorless—and this is the cause of their demise. Petty obstinacy and no sense of humor: that is the very definition of fanaticism. They were utterly oblivious to the fact that leadership, authority, and respect precluded the very notion of "socialism." This anti-individualism is as much the theoretical fashion of the moment among the intellectuals, in spite of themselves, in all white countries today as was the individualism that was fashionable yesterday; and, as a matter of fact, there is not much difference between the two. Feeble as this type of *Geist* is, it is the only one they have. It is the reign of metropolitan literati, nothing more, and anything but novel, for the Jacobins had already talked themselves to sleep over it. Lack of intelligence can hardly be considered a victory over rationalism.

And just what does it consist of, the "socialism" of these heroes who take the field against the freedom of personality? It is the impersonal Asiatic collectivism of the East, the spirit of the Great Plains coupled with the Western *levée en masse* of 1792. [. . .]

The Celtic Germanic is the strongest-willed "race" the world has ever seen. But this "I will—I will!" that fills the Faustian soul to the brim, that constitutes the ultimate purpose of its existence, and dominates every expression of the Faustian culture in thought, in deed, in education, and in comportment, is also what awakened the "I's" awareness of its own utter solitude in endless space. Will and solitude are ultimately one in the same thing. Hence, on the one hand, Moltke's silence and on the other hand, [Johann Wolfgang von] Goethe's softer and more feminine compulsion toward perpetual confessions before an audience of elective affinities that pervades all his works. It was the yearning for an echo from the universe, the sufferings of a tender soul at the hands of the monologue of its existence. One may take pride in this solitude or suffer from it, but one cannot escape it. The religious man of "eternal truths," such as Luther, longs for grace and salvation from this fate, fights it, even defies it. But the political man of the North gleans from it a gigantic *defiance of reality:* "Thy trust is in thy sword more than in Thor," says an Icelandic saga. If there is any such thing as individualism in the world, then it is this individual defiance of the whole universe, the individual's knowledge of his own unbending will, his delight in ultimate decisions, and his love of destiny itself even at the moment he is crushed by it. And being "Prussian" consists in the bending of one's own *free* will. The value of sacrifice lies in the fact that it is *hard.* If a man has no "I" to sacrifice, he has no business speaking of loyalty. He simply runs along behind someone whom he has burdened with responsibility. If we should be astonished by anything today, it is the poverty of the socialist ideal that is supposed to be the world's salvation. This cannot redeem us from the forces of the past; it merely serves to perpetuate the worst tendencies of those forces. It is *cowardice* in the face of life.

Authentic—authentically Prussian—loyalty is what the world most needs in this age of great catastrophes. We can only lean on what offers resistance. And the test of a great leader is whether or not he acknowledges this fact. Anyone who has risen from the masses must know, better than most, that masses, majorities, parties are no genuine liegemen. They are only after their own advantage. They would leave their leader in the lurch as soon as he demands sacrifices. Whoever thinks and feels as a product of the masses will never succeed in leaving a historical legacy other than that of a mere demagogue. And this is where there is a parting of ways to the left and right: the demagogue is at home with the masses as one of them; the born ruler may use them, but he disdains them. His most difficult battle is not against the enemy, but against the minions of his all-too-devoted friends.

This is why *armies,* and not parties, are the future form of power—unselfish, devoted armies, such as Napoleon never possessed after Wagram. His old soldiers were reliable; not so his senior officers—and the value of any army is measured first and foremost by its officers. They came to regard him not as their commander in chief but as their perpetual provider. As soon as the necessary sacrifices outweighed the advantages, it was all over for the Grand Army.

It is high time that the "white" world, first and foremost Germany, begins to reflect seriously on these facts. For behind the world wars and the as-yet-unfinished proletarian world revolution there looms the greatest of all dangers, the *colored* menace—and it will require every bit of "race" still present in the white nations to confront it. Germany, of all countries, is not an island, as the political ideologues who seek to execute their programs with Germany as their object seem to assume. It is but a small spot in the great, fermenting world, though undoubtedly a spot in a decisive position. But Prussianism is intrinsic to Germany alone. With this treasure of exemplary Being, it may become the "educator" of the "white" world, and perhaps its savior.

17

HERMANN GÖRING

Radio Address: 30 January 1933

First published as "Rundfunkansprache des Ministers Göring," in *Die nationalsozialistische Revolution,* edited by Walther Gehl (Breslau: Ferdinand Hirst, 1933), 69–70.

As I stand here at the microphone, hundred of thousands of people are thronging outside in front of the windows of the Reich Chancellery in a mood that can only be compared with that in August of 1914 when a nation again set out to defend everything in its possession. The 30th of January 1933 will similarly go down in German history as the day the nation found its way back to itself, because a new nation emerged and made short work of all the agony, humiliation, and treachery of the past fourteen years. Today will be the day we close the book of German history on the recent years of hardship and treason and start a new chapter, and freedom and honor will rest on this chapter as the foundation of the emerging nation. It is not only the Führer we have to thank for this great movement today. Our thanks also go to the wise old General Field Marshall von Hindenburg, who has consecrated a bond with the younger generation today . . .

May the German *Volk* welcome this day with joy in their hearts, just as the hundreds of thousands gathered outside the windows do, inspired by new hope and renewed faith in the prospect of a brighter future. Then we will all put our hands to the plow, our confidence will be restored, and so it is that we can and ought hope that the future will bring that for which we have been struggling in vain: bread and work for the national comrades, freedom and honor for the nation.

18

JOSEPH GOEBBELS

Day of Potsdam
22 March 1933

First published as "*Vom Kaiserhof zu Reichskanzlei. Eine historische Darstellung in Tagebuchblättern (vom 1. Januar 1932 bis zum 1. Mai 1933)*" (Munich: Zentralverlag der NSDAP Franz Eher Nachfolger GmbH, 1940), 285, 286. Translated by Kurt Fielder.

The great day of Potsdam will be unforgettable in its historical significance.

In the morning I drove with the Führer to the Luisenstädtische Cemetery. We did not attend the church service, but instead visited the graves of our fallen comrades.

On the way from Berlin to Potsdam, we passed through infinite crowds of cheering people. Potsdam was smothered in flags and green garlands. It was almost impossible to keep the road clear for the cabinet and the members of parliament to pass. We were nearly suffocated by the multitudes. Hindenburg entered the Garnisonkirche (Garrison Church) together with the Führer. A solemn silence fell over everyone present. Succinctly and somberly, the president of the Reich delivered his message to the members of the Reichstag and the German *Volk*. His voice was clear and firm. In our midst stands a man who unites whole generations.

Then the Führer speaks. His words are harsh with a penetrating urgency. By the time he is finished, everyone is profoundly shaken. Sitting near Hindenburg, I can see the tears swelling in his eyes. Everyone rises from their seats to offer enthusiastic praise to the aging field marshal as he shakes hands with the young chancellor.

A historical moment! Germany's shield of honor has been washed clean once again.

The banners bearing eagles are rising once more.

Hindenburg places laurel wreaths at the tombs of the great Prussian kings, amidst the salvos of the guns.

Now the trumpets sound, the president of the Reich stands on an elevated platform, the field marshal's staff in hand, and salutes the Reichswehr, SA, SS, and Steel Helmets, who march in review.

He stands and salutes them; the whole scene is bathed in infinite sunshine; the hand of God is held in invisible benediction over the gray town of Prussian grandeur and duty.

That afternoon, the cabinet sits in session at the Ministry of the Interior. An emergency bill prescribing severe penalties for the unauthorized wearing of uniforms is passed. Then the plenary session sits in council. Since there are no facilities available in the burned-out Reichstag, we have moved into the Kroll Opera House.

It is a solemn moment when the Führer enters the Kroll Opera House. All the formalities that used to take nearly a week are settled in half an hour. Göring is reelected president and introduces himself with a staunch and manly speech.

That evening, we are barely able to get through the huge crowds of people marching beneath the linden trees in an endless torchlight procession. Trams and buses are filled with singing and cheering men, women, and children. A fantastic spectacle such as has never before been seen.

19

ERICH EBERMAYER

My Day of Potsdam

Diary Entry

Written 21 March 1933. First published in *Denn heute gehört uns Deutschland. Persönliches und politisches Tagebuch* (Hamburg: Zsolnay, 1959), 45. Translated by Rodney Stackelberg and Sally Winkle.

In the morning, broadcast of festivities in Potsdam on the radio. Everything is smooth, impressive, even exciting, at least for the masses. But we cannot and must not close our eyes to what's happening here. Here today the marriage was successful, if not forever, then at least for a time, between the masses led by Hitler and the "Spirit of Potsdam," the Prussian tradition, represented by Hindenburg.

What magnificent staging by the master director Goebbels! Hindenburg, the cabinet, and members of parliament ride from Berlin to Potsdam through a single, solid cordon of cheering millions. All of Berlin seems to be in the streets. The cabinet and members of parliament walk from the Nikolai Church to the Garrison Church. Bells pealing and cannons firing.

Hindenburg and Hitler enter the Garrison Church. The radio announcer is moved almost to tears.

Then Hindenburg reads his message aloud. Simple, powerful, coming from an unpretentious soul and therefore likely to appeal to unpretentious souls. Merely the fact that here is a man who unites generations of German history, who fought in 1866, who was present at the Kaiser's coronation in 1871, at Versailles, who rose up to become a national hero from 1914 to 1918, whose popularity among our peculiar *Volk* could be diminished neither by lost battles nor by the lost World War; a man whose defeat, on the contrary, actually elevated him to mythical proportions; who then as an old man once again and finally a second time assumed leadership of the Reich, not out of vanity or lust for power but undoubtedly out of a Prussian sense of duty. He has achieved now, with one foot in the grave, the marriage of his world with the newly ascendant world represented by the Austrian corporal Hitler.

Then Hitler speaks. It cannot be denied: he has matured. Surprisingly enough for his opponents, the demagogue and party leader, the fanatic and rabble-rouser seems to be developing into a real statesman. So he is a genius after all, in whose enigmatic soul unsuspected and unprecedented possibilities lie dormant? The government declaration stands out in its striking moderation. Not a word of hatred against opponents, not a word of racial ideology, no threats directed inside or outside of the country. Hitler speaks only about what they want. Preservation of the great tradition of our *Volk*, stability of the government instead of constant vacillation, taking into consideration all the experiences in the life of the individual and the community that have proven to be useful for the well-being of the people throughout the millennia.

Hindenburg lays wreaths on the graves of the Prussian kings. The aging field marshal offers his hand to his corporal from the World War. The corporal bows low over the field marshal's hand. Cannons thunder over Potsdam—over Germany.

No one can escape the emotion. Father is deeply impressed as well. Mother has tears in her eyes.

Silently, I leave the room, then the house, and go out into the woods. I must be alone.

That evening, a quiet hour with M. He is completely unmoved by the events of the day, as if wrapped in a thick protective skin. He thinks it is all merely a rigged theatrical act; he does not for a moment waver in his instinctive aversion. "You'll see what I mean soon enough!" says the twenty-one-year-old.

I say nothing, ashamed and distressed.

20

Decree of the Reich President for the Protection of *Volk* and State

Announced on 28 February 1933 as "Verordnung des Reichspräsidenten zum Schutz von Volk und Staat," in *Reichsgesetzblatt* (Berlin: Reichsverlagsamt, 1933), 1:85–87.

Pursuant to Article 48, Section 2, of the Reich Constitution, the following is decreed as a defensive measure against Communist acts of violence endangering the state:

1. Suspension of Basic Rights

Articles 114, 115, 117, 118, 123, 124, and 153 of the Constitution of the German Reich are suspended until further notice. Thus, restrictions to personal liberty, on the right of free expression of opinion, including freedom of the press, on the right of assembly and the right of association, and violations of the privacy of postal, telegraphic, and telephonic communications, and warrants for house searches, orders for confiscations of as well as restrictions on property, are also permissible beyond the legal limits otherwise prescribed.

2. Reich Government as Executive State Authority

If in a state the measures necessary for the restoration of public security and order are not taken, the Reich government may temporarily assume the powers of the executive state authority.

3. Decrees of the Reich Government

According to orders decreed by the Reich government pursuant to Article 2, the authorities of the states and provinces, inasmuch as their jurisdiction is involved, are required to abide by these regulations.

4. Violations

Anyone who violates or who provokes, appeals to, or incites to violation of the orders issued by the executive state authorities or the authorities subject to them for the execution of this decree, or the orders issued by the Reich government pursuant to Article 2, is subject to punishment—insofar as the act is not subject to harsher sentencing pursuant to other decrees—of imprisonment no less than one month, or with a fine between 150 and 15,000 Reichsmarks.

Anyone who endangers human life by violating Article 1 is subject to a prison term, under mitigating circumstances, of not less than six months, and, if the violation causes the death of an individual, shall be sentenced to death. Sentencing may also include confiscation of property.

Anyone who provokes or incites to an act that is detrimental to the public welfare is subject to a prison term, under mitigating circumstances, of not less than three months.

5. Imposition of the Death Penalty

The crimes which under the Criminal Code are punishable by life imprisonment are to be punishable by death: i.e., in Sections 81 (high treason), 229 (poisoning), 306 (arson), 311 (explosion), 312 (flooding), 315, Paragraph 2 (damage to railway facilities), 324 (public endangerment through poison).

Insofar as a more severe sentence has not been previously handed down, the following crimes are punishable with death or life imprisonment or a prison term of up to fifteen years:

1. Anyone who undertakes to assassinate the Reich president or any member or commissioner of the Reich government of a state government, or who provokes to such assassination, or agrees to commit it, or accepts such an offer, or conspires with another to commit such a murder;
2. Anyone who, under Section 115, Paragraph 2, of the Criminal Code (aggravated rioting) or of Section 125, Paragraph 2, of the Criminal Code (aggravated disturbance of the peace) commits these crimes using weapons or cooperates deliberately and intentionally with an armed person;
3. Anyone who commits a kidnapping under Section 239 of the Criminal Code with the intention of holding the kidnapped individual hostage in a political struggle.

6. Enters into Force

This decree enters in force on the day of its promulgation.
Berlin, 28 February 1933

Reich President: von Hindenburg
Reich Chancellor: Adolf Hitler
Reich Minister of the Interior: Frick
Reich Minister of Justice: Dr. Gürtner

21

ANONYMOUS

The Reichstag Fire

Declaration of Martial Law?

First published as "Reichstagsbrand—Verhängung des Ausnahmezustandes?" in *Inprekorr,* no. 26 (28 February 1933): 849.

Berlin, 28 February 1933

Last night, just after 9:00 P.M., a blaze broke out in the Reichstag that did extensive damage. The fire broke out in several places and destroyed the plenary hall, the rostrum, and large sections of the structure. The entire Berlin fire department was called to the scene. By around 11:00 P.M., the fire department had the fire under control. The cause of the fire was arson.

The bourgeois press is publishing notices and articles explaining that the arson was initiated by Communists. According to the accounts in these papers, the police are said to have arrested a twenty-five-year-old man as he sought to exit the building. The man was wearing nothing but a pair of trousers. A Dutch passport bearing the name Van der Lubbe was found on his person. According to a report in the *Völkischer Beobachter,* his name was said to be Van Dergen. According to various additional versions of the story, he is said to be a "known radical Communist." The man is said to have confessed to participating in the arson attack and to have performed the arson single-handedly.

The bourgeois *Berliner Tageblatt* had the following to say about the whole affair: "In the official report disseminated by Wolff's office concerning the fire in the Reichstag, you can find the statement that we can 'obviously reckon with additional acts of terror committed by Communists.' No information has been provided regarding the basis for this speculation."[1]

The official Prussian press agency published a memorandum stating, among other things, that "the arsonist from the Reichstag admitted in his confession to being affiliated with the Social Democratic Party."

Protective custody for the entire Communist faction in Parliament—a complete ban on the Social Democratic and Communist press in Prussia.

The memorandum issued by the official press agency furthermore states that:

> . . . This arson attack is the most abominable act of terrorism ever known in Germany. Among the hundred centers of seditious writings confiscated, instructions on how to carry out terrorist acts in the Bolshevist way were found. According to these documents, government buildings, castles, museums, and essential businesses are to be set ablaze. In addition, instructions are given for women and children to be sent to the front of terrorist groups at riots and clashes, wherever possible the wives and children of police officials.
>
> The discovery of these materials has disrupted plans to stage a Bolshevist revolution. Nevertheless, the fire in the Reichstag was supposed to be seen as a beacon signaling a call to bloody uprising and to civil war. Rampant pillage was already in preparation for Tuesday at 4:00 A.M. in Berlin. It is clear that today is the day that marks the onset of terrorist attacks against individual personalities, against private property, against the life and limb of the peaceful population throughout Germany, and the day that should unleash all-out civil war.
>
> The commissioner of the Prussian Department of the Interior, Reich Minister Göring, has countered these horrendous threats with the most drastic measures. He

is determined to maintain state authority under any and all circumstances and by any means necessary. It is clear that this first attack on the part of the criminal elements has, for the moment, been put down.

In the interest of securing public safety, all public buildings and essential businesses have been placed under police protection since Monday evening. Special police units are patrolling those areas of the city most likely to be targeted around the clock. All units of uniformed police and plainclothes detectives in Prussia were immediately placed at the highest level of alert. The auxiliary police force has been called up.

A warrant has been issued for the arrest of two Communist members of the Reich parliament under strong suspicion. The remaining Communist members of parliament and functionaries of the Communist Party are being taken into protective custody. Communist newspapers, magazines, leaflets, and posters have been banned for four weeks throughout Prussia.

All newspapers, magazines, and flyers printed by the Social Democratic Party have been banned for two weeks because the Reichstag arsonist admitted in his confession to having affiliations with the Social Democratic Party.

This confession clearly establishes the fact that the Communists and Social Democrats quite obviously built a united front. This mandates that those responsible for securing the safety of Prussia take drastic measures as outlined by the duties of their office in order to maintain state authority in this time of danger. The need for those measures already in place (the "fire at will" order, the auxiliary police, etc.) has been fully substantiated by these most recent developments. These measures guarantee that the state powers are sufficiently armed to prevent any further assault on peace in Germany, and thus in Europe, and to extinguish the fires of rebellion before they even start.

In this dire hour, Reich Minister Göring demands of the nation utmost discipline; he expects the undying support of the civilian population whose safety and protection he has personally guaranteed.

Note

1. Wolffs Telegraphisches Bureau, founded by Bernhard Wolff (1811–79), was one of Europe's first news agencies.—Eds.

22

OTTO WELS

Speech against the Passage of the Enabling Act

Delivered 23 March 1933. First published in *Die nationalsozialistische Revolution 1933,* vol. 1 of *Das Reich Adolf Hitlers; Dokumente der deutschen Politik,* edited by Paul Meier-Benneckenstein and F. A. Six (Berlin: Junker u. Dünnhaupt, 1933), 36–38. Translated by Thomas Dunlap.

Ladies and gentlemen! We Social Democrats agree with the foreign policy demand raised by the Reich chancellor of equal treatment for Germany, [and do so] all the more emphatically since we have always fundamentally championed it. In this context, I may be permitted the personal remark that I was the first German who stood up to the untruth of Germany's guilt for the outbreak of the world war before an international forum, at the Bern Conference on 3 February 1919. Never was a principle of our party able to, or did in fact, prevent us from representing the just demands of the German nation to the other peoples of the world.

The day before yesterday, as well, the Reich chancellor made a statement in Potsdam to which we subscribe. It says, "From the lunacy of the theory of eternal winners and losers came the madness of reparations and, in their wake, the catastrophe of the world economy." This statement is true for foreign politics; it is no less true for domestic politics. Here, too, the theory of eternal winners and losers is, as the Reich chancellor says, lunacy.

But the words of the Reich chancellor remind us of others that were spoken in the National Assembly on 23 July 1919. At that time it was said, "We are defenseless; defenseless but not without honor. To be sure, the enemies are after our honor, there is no doubt. However, that this attempt at defamation will one day redound back upon the instigators, that it is not our honor that is being destroyed by this global catastrophe, that is our belief to the last breath."

(Interjection from the National Socialists: "Who said that?")

This appears in a declaration that a Social Democratic–led government issued at the time in the name of the German people before the whole world, four hours before the truce expired, in order to prevent the enemies from marching further. That declaration is a valuable supplement to the statement by the Reich chancellor.

A dictated peace is followed by few blessings, least of all at home. A real national community cannot be based on it. Its first prerequisite is equal law. The government may protect itself against raw excesses of polemics; it may rigorously prevent incitements to acts of violence and acts of violence in and of themselves. This may happen, if it is done toward all sides evenly and impartially, and if one forgoes treating defeated opponents as though they were proscribed. Freedom and life can be taken from us, but not our honor.

After the persecutions that the Social Democratic Party has suffered recently, no one will reasonably demand or expect that it vote for the Enabling Act proposed here. The elections of 5 March have given the governing parties the majority and thus the possibility of governing in strict adherence to the words and meaning of the constitution. Where such a possibility exists, there is also an obligation to take it. Criticism is salutary and necessary. Never before, since there has been a German Reichstag, has the control of public affairs by the elected representatives of the people been eliminated to such an extent as is happening now and is supposed to happen even more through the new Enabling Act. Such omnipotence of the government must have all the more serious repercussions inasmuch as the press, too, lacks any freedom of expression.

Ladies and gentlemen! The situation that prevails in Germany today is often described in glaring colors. But as always in such cases, there is no lack of exaggeration. As far as my party is concerned, I declare here: we have neither asked for intervention in Paris, nor moved millions to Prague, nor spread exaggerated news abroad. It would be easier to stand up to such exaggerations if the kind of reporting that separates truth from falsehood were possible at home. It would be even better if we could attest in good conscience that full protection in justice has been restored for all. That, gentlemen, is up to you.

The gentlemen of the National Socialist Party call the movement they have unleashed a national revolution, not a National Socialist one. So far, the relationship of their revolution to socialism has been limited to the attempt to destroy the Social Democratic movement, which for more than two generations has been the bearer of socialist ideas and will remain so. If the gentlemen of the National Socialist Party wanted to perform socialist acts, they would not need an Enabling Law. They would be assured of an overwhelming majority in this house. Every motion submitted by them in the interest of workers, farmers, white-collar employees, civil servants, or the middle class could expect to be approved, if not unanimously, then certainly with an enormous majority.

And yet, they first want to eliminate the Reichstag in order to continue their revolution. But the destruction of that which exists does not make a revolution. The people are expecting positive accomplishments. They are waiting for effective measures against the terrible economic misery that exists not only in Germany but in the whole world. We Social Democrats bore the responsibility in the most difficult of times, and for that we had stones cast at us. Our accomplishments for the reconstruction of the state and the economy, for the liberation of occupied territories, will stand the test of history. We have established equal justice for all and a social labor law. We have helped to create a Germany in which the path to leadership of the state is open not only to princes and barons but also to men from the working class. You cannot back away from that without relinquishing your own leader. The attempt to turn back the wheel of history will be futile. We Social Democrats know that one cannot undo the facts of power politics with mere legal protests. We see the power-political fact of your present rule. But the people's sense of justice is also a political power, and we shall not cease to appeal to this sense of justice.

The Weimar Constitution is not a socialist constitution. But we stand by the principles enshrined in it—the principles of a state based on the rule of law, of equal rights, of social justice. In this historic hour, we German Social Democrats solemnly pledge ourselves to the principles of humanity and justice, of freedom and socialism. No Enabling Act gives you the power to destroy ideas that are eternal and indestructible. After all, you yourselves have professed your adherence to socialism. The socialist law has not destroyed social democracy. German social democracy will draw new strength also from the latest persecutions.

We greet the persecuted and the oppressed. We greet our friends in the Reich. Your steadfastness and loyalty deserve admiration. The courage of your convictions and your unbroken optimism guarantee a brighter future.

23

Law to Remedy the State of Emergency of *Volk* and Reich

Announced on 24 March 1933 as "Gesetz zur Behebung der Not von Volk und Reich." First published in *Reichsgesetzblatt* (Berlin: Reichsverlagsamt, 1933), 1:141.

The Reichstag has enacted the following law, which is hereby promulgated with the approval of the Reichsrat upon determining that all requirements have been met for legislation involving changes to constitutional law.

Article 1

Laws for the Reich can be enacted by the Reich government not only in compliance with, but also outside the procedures established by the Reich Constitution. This also applies to the laws outlined by Article 85, Paragraph 2, and Article 87 of the constitution.

Article 2

Laws for the Reich enacted by the Reich government may deviate from the Reich Constitution so long as they do not directly affect the institution of the Reichstag and the Reichsrat as such. The executive powers of the Reich president shall remain intact.

Article 3

Laws for the Reich enacted by the Reich government shall be executed by the Reich chancellor and published in the *Reichsgesetzblatt* (Reich Law Gazette). Unless otherwise specified, these laws shall enter in force the day following their publication. Laws enacted by the Reich government are exempt from the provisions outlined in Articles 68 through 77 of the Reich Constitution.

Article 4

Treaties of the Reich with foreign countries pertaining to matters of Reich legislation shall not, for as long as these laws shall remain in effect, require the approval of bodies participating in this legislation. The Reich government is invested with the power to issue such provisions as are required for the execution of said treaties.

Article 5

This law shall take effect the day of its promulgation. It shall become invalid on 1 April 1937, or at such a time as the current Reich government is succeeded by another.

Reich President: von Hindenburg
Reich Chancellor: Adolf Hitler
Reich Minister of the Interior: Frick
Reich Minister of Foreign Affairs: Freiherr von Neurath
Reich Minister of Finance: Count Schwerin von Krosigk

24

Law for the Restoration of the Professional Civil Service

Announced on 7 April 1933 as "Gesetz zur Wiederherstellung des Berufsbeamtentums." First published in *Reichsgesetzblatt* (Berlin: Reichsverlagsamt, 1933), 1:175.

Article 3

1. Civil service officials of non-Aryan descent are to be retired; in the case of officials active on a volunteer basis, they are to be relieved of their status as officials.
2. Section 1 does not apply to officials who have been in office since 1 August 1914 or who served for the German Reich or for her allies at the front in the World War, or whose fathers or sons died in the World War. Additional exceptions may be made by the Reich minister of the interior in accordance with approval of the appropriate ministry or with the executive state authorities for civil service officials abroad.

Article 4

Civil service officials whose previous political activities provide no guarantee for the notion that they are prepared to act in the interest of the national state at all times and without any reservations can be dismissed from their service. They shall be entitled to severance pay in the amount of their current salary for a period of three months following their dismissal. At the end of that period, they shall receive three-quarters of their pension and the attendant survivor's benefits.

Reich Chancellor: Adolf Hitler
Reich Minister of the Interior: Wilhelm Frick
Reich Minister of Finance: Count Schwerin von Krosigk

25

ADOLF HITLER

Speech to Commemorate National Labor Day

Delivered on 1 May 1933. First published in *Die Reden Hitlers als Kanzler* (Munich: Verlag Franz Eher Nachfolger GmbH, 1934), 29–30, 35.

My German Comrades, Men and Women alike!

May has come, so the German folk song says. And over many centuries, the first day of May was not only symbolic of spring's advent upon the land, it was also the day of joy, of exuberant spirit and sentiment. Then came a time that laid claim to this day for itself and transformed the day of coming life and hopeful exuberance into a day of conflict and internal struggle. A teaching that took our *Volk* in its grip sought to transform the day of nature's waking, of spring's visible grand entrance, into a day of hatred, of fratricide, of intrigue, and suffering. Decades have descended upon the German lands in which this day repeatedly seemed to document the separation and splintering of our *Volk*. Then, finally, after our *Volk* was stricken by the profoundest suffering, the time of deep contemplation arrived, a time of inner reflection and of finding a renewed sense of togetherness among the German people.

And today we can once again sing along with the old folks' song: May has come, our *Volk*'s awakening has arrived. The symbol of the class struggle, of eternal strife and quarrel, is thus in turn transformed into the great symbol of the nation's unification and its rise to ascendancy. And that is why we have chosen, now and for all time, this day of nature's waking as a day to commemorate the recovery of our energy and our strength, and with it, that creative work that knows no constraints, that is not tied to the unions, to the factories and the offices, a job that we wish to acknowledge and support wherever it is performed in good faith in the interest of our *Volk*'s existence and its life.

The German *Volk* has survived a period of dreadful hardship. It is not as though this could possibly be attributed to a lack of diligence, no! Millions of our people are now back at work; millions of our farmers now step behind the plow the same as ever; millions of workers are again stationed at the vise, at the droning anvil. Millions of our people are employed, and millions more would like to be, but alas, are not able. Tens of thousands have voluntarily put an end to a worldly existence that seemed to promise them only heartache and misery. They have traded in their lives for an afterlife that they hope will provide bigger and better things. Horrible suffering and misfortune have caused us to take stock, and this has left despondency, even desperation in its wake. And now we must ask ourselves, to what end?

It is a matter of political hardship. The German *Volk*, now fallen to ruin, is sapped of every ounce of vitality by its inner struggle. It must build on the force of its own will, for its inner strength has been weakened. Millions look to the rest of the world, hoping that good fortune and salvation shall befall them. The *Volk* is falling to ruin, and in this ruin, its vitality dwindles, it is losing the will to live. We see the results of this class struggle all around and amongst us, and we want to learn from it. Because we have recognized that this is the first prerequisite to recovery for our *Volk*:

The German *Volk* must get to know itself again.

The millions of people who have been divided into professional groups and kept apart in artificial class categories, who have so fallen prey to class conceit and class hysteria that they can no longer understand one another, they must find a way to unite once more! An enormous, formidable task—this we know! When over a seventy-year period hysteria has been promulgated and promoted as a political ideal, when for seventy years the destruction of the national community has reigned as the political mandate, then it becomes very difficult to turn the tide of people's thinking in one fell swoop. And yet, we cannot be driven to despair or desperation in this task. What human hands have built can be torn asunder by human hands; what was devised by human folly can again be overcome by clever insight.

We know that this process of finding our way back to one another and reaching mutual understanding is not something that will involve a matter of weeks or months, even of a few years. But we alone have the unshakable will to fulfill this great task in Germany history; we have the resolve to lead the German people back to themselves, and, if need be, to force them back.

This is the spirit of the First of May that shall henceforth be celebrated in Germany for centuries to come, that, on this day, all those who have joined the cadre of workers actively involved in the creative task of our nation might join forces and, once a year, join hands in recognition of the fact that nothing can be accomplished unless everyone carries his full weight in terms of performance and work. And so we have decided that this sentence should serve as the motto for this day:

Honor the work and respect the workers!

For millions, it will be hard to reunite after all the hatred and misunderstanding that has been artificially cultivated in the past. But there is one thought that will allow us to embark upon this path with ease. *Regardless of where or what any individual is doing, he should not and cannot forget that his comrade, who is fulfilling his obligations in his turn, is indispensable, that the nation does not exist as the result of the government's doing, or that of a certain class or by dint of its intelligence, rather that it exists only through the combined and harmonious efforts of all!* [. . .]

We are being persecuted by the whole world; the world has turned against us, it does not want to acknowledge our right to live, does not want to believe that we have the right to protect our homeland.

My German comrades! With the world poised against us like this, it is all the more important that we join together as one, that we become all the more inexorable in assuring them: You can do as you will, but you will never bring us to bend, never force us to acknowledge your yoke! You will never again eliminate the call for equal rights from our *Volk!* The German *Volk* has come to its senses. The German people will not tolerate the presence of anyone who is not on the side of Germany! *We are determined to earn our nation's return to greatness honestly, through our diligence, our tenacity, and our unshakable will!* We are not beseeching the Almighty, "Lord, set us free!" We want to be active, working, together as brothers, wrangling together toward the day we may appear before the Lord and pray: *"Lord, you see that we have changed. The German* Volk *is no longer the* Volk *of infamy, of disgrace, of self-destruction, of despondency and little faith. No, Lord, the German* Volk *has regained the strength of its will, the strength of its tenacity, the strength of its willingness to bear the brunt of every sacrifice. Lord, we will not leave your side! Now, bless us in our struggle for freedom, bless our German* Volk *and our fatherland!"*

26

DAS SCHWARZE KORPS

Second-Class Comrades?

First published as "Volksgenosse zweiter Klasse?" in *Das Schwarze Korps* (28 May 1936), 22.

The conditions prevailing in Germany during the Wilhelmine Era, the collapse of 1918, the profound disparities among us in the postwar years—all this was possible only because the German *Volk* essentially remained utterly *apolitical* in the second half of the nineteenth century.

From the perspective of the then-dominant class, politics was not an affair that concerned *"the average man on the street"*—a notion that was as comprehensive and all-inclusive as can be. Our whole education and upbringing revolved around elevating this "man on the street" to a "good citizen and productive member of bourgeois society." Anyone who disagreed with this "ideal," who saw in it the seeds of destruction and demise, anyone who dared have his own opinion, was immediately branded as an "enemy of the state" or a "social democrat," even if he had absolutely nothing to do with Marxism. This attitude on the part of the state is precisely what drove many a fine upstanding German straight into the arms of Marxism.

The Politicization of the German

A catastrophe as devastating as the World War and the collapse of the mighty imperial empire necessarily ushered in a politicization of the Germans. Nevertheless, in that unbelievable political turmoil in the years immediately following the war, in that clashing of political passions that was only intensified by the fact that the fundamental concepts that had thus far guided our lives became ever less stable, in the host of platforms, programs, and perspectives this period produced, there is no evidence to indicate that even a hint of political will was waking in the German *Volk*. On the contrary, these developments were little more than the last unsettling shred of evidence that a virtually apolitical *Volk* had fallen into complete confusion.

The real politicization of the German will to live found expression in the young, slowly emerging National Socialist movement and not in the mumbo jumbo of the parliamentary democracy Germany had since become. This is where the political experience of the frontline soldier returning home from the battlefields and trenches of the Great War took shape. It was here that the front generation and the youth joined together to form a truly political battle squadron.

Those brave men who, with unprecedented tenacity and strength of conviction, faithfully pledged allegiance to that unknown soldier of the Great War, Adolf Hitler, from those first difficult years onward, have done a great deed: *they have authored the unified, undeniably political will of an entire nation.*

It goes without saying that Wilhelmine Germany, which, with its flawed approach, drove all those Germans sincerely striving for healthy socialism straight into the arms of Marxism, also prevented many fine upstanding Germans from finding their way to National Socialism after the war.

Seasoned National Socialists like us know from the period of struggle exactly what sort of valuable energies and how much truly healthy intent were oft to be found among the working-class masses who had been so contaminated by Marxism at the time. And it was precisely because we knew this that we struggled so passionately to reach these people. The object of our struggle wasn't the bourgeois citizen but rather *the German workers,* and the fact that they were so hard to vanquish is what made them so valuable to us as comrades in arms once they'd joined our ranks for good.

Conviction Is All That Counts

The year 1933 brought home to us Germans, for the first time, the overwhelming experience of a truly socialist community of Germans. Especially after that first national Labor Day brought with it the overwhelming pledge of allegiance to socialism and to the German worker, especially after the first great socialist measures of the Third Reich were implemented, it was no longer possible to support the National Socialist movement at the superficial level of merely joining the party, the support had to come *from deep within.*

No National Socialist has ever weighed a person's worth solely on the basis of whether or not he was in possession of the NSDAP membership manual. Conviction and allegiance to Adolf Hitler can find expression at any given time and in any situation in life. And precisely this allegiance in the daily struggle for life is much more sincere and significant than mere possession of a membership card.

The year 1932 brought to the National Socialist movement an overwhelming influx from what had thus far been bourgeois circles. The Reich chancellor at the time, Papen, for example, lifted the ban on membership in the NSDAP for civil servants. And they came running, real ones and phonies alike; there is no profile or stereotype to fit their numbers. There was thus no longer any personal risk attached to being a National Socialist, unless, of course, one was fighting the Red murderers in the streets alongside the SA and the SS. The majority of these newcomers, though, remained wary of that level of participation and, when the "great crisis" or "reprisal" arrived under Schleicher's term, many retreated from the ranks they had so enthusiastically joined, but not without consternation.

The Revolution Profiteer

There was a certain breed of people who, after the takeover of power, sought to create a new prototype: the revolution profiteers. They were there on the spot at every opportunity. They spoke up wherever there was any sort of post to be filled. They had just come to the party in 1932–33 and sought to profit from their party membership cards. There was only one thing that upset them: the introduction of cuff titles, chevrons, and the newly designed golden NSDAP badge of honor. *Why insist on making these distinctions?* All it does is create discrepancies in the movement. But this disaffection was quickly overcome. They gave the old soldiers a fatherly pat on the back and concealed their discontent over the fact that such people exist. They just tried their best to make sure none of these suspicious characters were allowed into their *Arbeitskreis* (working circle). They were not welcome there.

The word *gleichschalten* (Nazify) was for these characters the perfect catchword. Whoever had first discovered his National Socialism in March 1933 was already in a position to apply his newfound spirit to obtaining major enterprises, civil service assignments, etc. by April—for a corresponding fee, of course. One can just imagine the consequences, and, unfortunately, one often had to live with them. But ultimately, these people unmask themselves because the [illegible] party membership card is no substitute for conviction.

The second thing these kind sirs attempt is this: just that they secretly loathe the old National Socialist; they take malicious public offense at anyone who is not a party member. They hope to brand everyone who is not in possession of a party membership card as a second-class comrade, to mark him as an abhorrent individual, and especially if the poor soul perhaps at some time in his life was once a Marxist.

They don't even bother to make the effort to ascertain whether the victim of their indignant anger was perhaps an unknown assistant to the air force, the workers front, or the National Socialist League of University Assistants [Nationalsozialistischer Deutscher Dozentenbund], serving quietly and humbly but fulfilling his obligation as National Socialist far better than they, even in the absence of a party membership card.

The kinds of class differences that these gentlemen desire have no place in National Socialist Germany, where judgments are not made according to superficial affiliations, but rather according to whether or not the individual proves himself a National Socialist in his daily work and deed.

27

CARL SCHMITT

State, Movement, *Volk*

The Tripartite Division of Political Unity

First published in *Staat, Bewegung, Volk: Die Dreigliederung der politischen Einheit* (Hamburg: Hanseatische Verlagsanstalt, 1933), 11–14. Translated by Timothy Nunan.

The political unity of the current state is a tripartite aggregation of state, movement, *Volk*. This unity differentiates itself from the ground up from the liberal democratic state schema handed down from the nineteenth century, and indeed not only with respect to its ideological assumptions and its common principles but also in all the fundamental lines of construction and organization of the concrete constitution of the state. Every fundamental concept and every meaningful feature is affected by this difference.

The new structure of state is distinguished by the fact that the political unity of the *Volk*, and with it the entire ordering of its public life, is presented in three differentiated tiers of order. The three traces of order stand not coordinated, nor next to one another; rather, one of them, namely the movement, carrying both the state and the *Volk*, pervades and leads the other two. Three tiers of order run next to one another, each itself internally ordered. They meet one another at certain decisive points, especially at the pinnacle; they have certain proprietary, mutual contacts and crossovers that nonetheless do not cancel out the differentiation between the three, and in their totality—a totality effected by the borne-along tiers of order—they form the constitution of the political unity. They are each formed through different points of view and—if I may say so—different materials, and yet they are all, if all in different ways, included in the public legal order.

Each of the three words *state, movement, Volk* can be used for the entirety of the political unity. Each word, however, at the same time designates as well a *particular side* and a *specific* element of this system. Let the state be regarded more exactly as the political-stately part, the movement as the political-dynamic element, and the *Volk* as the *unpolitical* side, growing in the protection and shade of political decisions. Indeed, it would be false and sophistic to make the tripartite division of the state out to be alternatively dividing and mutually excluding oppositions, to pit the state against the movement or the movement against the state, the *Volk* against the state or the state against the *Volk*, the *Volk* against the movement or the movement against the *Volk*. That would correspond to the liberal disruptions to be handled later whose political mentality calls for the abolition, or at least the relativization, of the political whole. The movement in particular is both state and *Volk*, and neither the current state (in the sense of the political unity) nor the current German *Volk* (as the subject of the political unity "the German Reich") would be imaginable without the movement.

In accordance with this, there unfold the following three tiers of order.

(a) The stately entity of authorities and offices, consisting of the army and the stately bureaucracy; this entity is often still (in the sense of a handed-down linguistic use) designated as the state, but it is so only as the commanding, administrative, and judicial organization, therefore, only in a limited sense, while the word *state*, as has been said, is still used as the handed-down designation for the whole of the political unity of a *Volk*.

(b) A party, bearing in it both state and *Volk*, recruiting from all strata of the *Volk* but self-contained and hierarchically led, as the political body in which the movement finds its particular form. The party has been designated as an "order," an "elite," or the like by sociologists in order to distinguish it from the (fundamentally not tightly organized, but rather based on "free solicitation") political party of the liberal state. Indeed, because there is hardly still a threat of misunderstanding, the prevailing name *party* can be retained here. This corresponds to the text of the law of 14 June 1933 (*Reichsgesetzesblatt* [vol.] I, page 479) against the reformation of parties: "In Germany there exists as the only political party the National Socialist German Workers' Party."

(c) A sphere of the *Volk* given its own self-administration, a sphere that encompasses the professional economic and social order as well as (as concerns the local vicinity) communal self-administration. Even a corporate state (*stato corporativo*) of the fascist state that fundamentally rejects any territorial self-administration and permits only professional and "functional" forms of self-administration, a system of unions and guilds, a "demotic social order" (this phrase is a formulation from Werner Sombart). These spheres could fill out a nonstately yet public-judicial self-administration and insert any possible autonomy, camaraderie, or even different styles of federations into the public life of the *Volk* within the total framework of the political leadership.

In the state of the German National Socialist movement, just as in the Fascist state of Italy—if in a different manner—is this new threefold total picture of the political unity to be recognized. It is distinctive for the state of the twentieth century. Even in the Bolshevik state of the Soviet Union, a tripartite construction of state, party, and soviet as the total collection of the political and social reality has been attempted. The tripartite construction is, however, not only visible wherever one seeks to overcome the dead ends of the liberal democratic state and to tackle a new state suitable to the social and political reality of the twentieth century; the tripartite construction also corresponds to the great traditions of German thinking about the state as founded by Hegel. German thinking about the state was first displaced from the consciousness of the German *Volk* in the second half of the nineteenth century under the influence of liberal and alien theoreticians and writers. The outline of the tripartite structure could therefore be commonly understood today as the first vivid sketch of the present state structure; it is by no means affected by the objection that it amounts to only an idealization of the Italian Fascist situation.

28

ERNST FORSTHOFF

The Total State

First published in *Der totale Staat* (Hamburg: Hanseatische Verlagsanstalt, 1933), 34–39. Translated by Timothy Nunan.

The Order of Rule

In the final years of the disintegration of the Weimar Constitution, the governments tried with increasing clarity to claim an authoritarian character for themselves. In every case, this occurred with reference to the fact that the Reich president had appointed the government and that the government had largely disengaged itself from the interplay of parliamentary forces; the claim to authority fundamentally occurred in order to establish the independence of the government from parliament. The real authority these governments held in the *Volk* was minimal. The *Volk* manifested a subtle understanding of the fact that a mere disengagement from an ineffective parliament does not ground authority, because this authority does not prove any rank. For authority cannot be conferred but only seized. Authority is the effect of a rank that is not awarded but rather recognized by the *Volk*.

Every order of rule is an order of rank and presupposes a disposition of the spirit, one accessible to the essence of rank. For rank is a spiritual phenomenon that becomes visible only as a symbol and, even in such cases, only for he who has spiritual access to the essence of rank. Genuine rank grows directly out of the elementary presuppositions of blood and race. It eludes all learnable abilities of the spirit and body. Orders of rank exist only in communities that rest on the total mobilization of the community's members, for only total mobilization brings the elementary factor into the community. Only such a community has honor and genuine symbols. Only in such a community is there an order of rank and, with it, leadership in the political and authentic sense of the word.

Leadership of state and leadership of a group are not the same. A *Freikorps* leader, the leader of a youth league, can gather his band of comrades around himself and maintain his identity through violence. Adolf Hitler began as such a leader. But by becoming leader of the state, Hitler became subject to a new law. He became the ruler of the millennium of the ancient tradition of the German state. The responsibility for the historic existence of the German *Volk* fell to him. In this process, there changed not only his right to leadership—a right to leadership that henceforth encompassed the entire German *Volk*—but also the movement as led by him, which henceforth, drawn into the sphere of direct historical responsibility, became the authentic bearer of the German state and gained the prestige of all associated with the state. With the takeover of power, the party leader Adolf Hitler accrued the transpersonal justification of state leadership.

As a result of the National Socialist revolution, the order of leadership of the National Socialist movement from the time of struggle has become a fundamental part of the state's order of rule. The order of rule of the National Socialist state is distinguished through the connection of the National Socialist order of leadership with the bureaucratic administrative organizations and how these organizations, without any sort of penetrating personal and organizational reforms, were lifted from the earlier orders of state. The connection of these two elements of the current order of rule becomes most evident through the assumption of the leading functions of the state by the leader of the movement, in the culling of the upper stratum of leadership of the movement into the most important state positions, as well as in the creation of organizational connections between state offices and the corresponding party bureaus, bringing into being the best possible unity of direction and conflict-free cooperation through individual laws and decrees. The unity of state and party was practically already realized when it was declared through the law of 1 December 1933.

The unity of state and party is first and foremost a spiritual-political one and signifies the obligation of the National Socialist ideology and objectives for the state in all its modes of existence. Only under the presupposition that this unity is perfect can the unification of obsolete administrative organizations with the order of leadership of the party be realized into a homogenous order of rule.

This unification is the creation of the preeminent statecraft that was capable of binding both of these elements, so essentially different in their structures and laws of life. In order to fully grasp the current order of rule, it is necessary to recognize political leadership and the subordination of official-hierarchical offices as such and to dissociate the one from the other.

With the elevation of leadership to a constitutional principle, a form of government has been realized in Germany that cannot be fully grasped because of its novelty with respect to the obsolete categories and criteria according to which one normally distinguishes forms of government, according to which one designates democracies, monarchies, aristocracies, etc. Leadership does not mean the same as the monarchical right to rule, nor is it the same as the power of government granted to the head of state elevated to or confirmed in his position by the *Volk*. Nor does it mean the same as the authority of the military superior or the leading figure in a hierarchical bureaucracy. The democratic doctrine made the following into the criterion by which constitutions are distinguished: was there an identity between ruler and ruled or not? The goal of this doctrine was the constitution of identity; its opponent, monarchy. Recent constitutional theory has stood under the mark of this doctrine and is forced to continue to stand on the basis of the objects that surround it. Leadership, however, cannot be grasped on the basis of this distinction. For it does not apply that the Führer is so different from the *Volk* on the basis of a qualitative otherness or a rank granted to him that he is no longer a racial comrade. Nor does he belong "to the *Volk*" per se without any reservation, for leadership is neither a transcendentally grounded claim to rule without consideration for the will of the *Volk,* nor is it a mere duty of the *Volk* granted through plebiscite.

It is not possible to give leadership an abstract expression as an activity imprisoned by the realm of political experience. This is why it is so unusually different to clarify the constitution of the National Socialist state to foreigners. The word *leadership* resists translation just as much as other words claiming to represent specifically German sensations: *Volk*dom [*Volkstum*], homeland [*Heimat*], blood and soil [*Blut und Boden*], disposition [*Gemüt*]). Therefore, only the following can be said about leadership as a demarcation of the idea from obsolete concepts and political schemata of thinking.

Leadership is an encompassing political event of life that unifies a multitude of political men ready for action into the person of the Führer: on the one hand, through his making them into his following, on the other hand, the Führer being elevated out of this following without allowing him to become superior and in such a way to separate him from the following. Führer and following form a unity that cannot be formally or logically grasped but that rather can be experienced. One will not give just consideration to leadership as an encompassing event if one only characterizes the obvious preeminence of the will of the leader as the feature of leadership. It is just as mistaken to prevailingly regard the leader as the exponent of the following and, in doing so, to come closer to the doctrines of democratic legitimacy of the state's use of force. It is much more the novelty and decisive factor of the constitution of leadership that it overcomes the democratic distinction between the rulers and the ruled in a unity in which the leader and following are fused. This unity is formed by and maintains itself through a perpetual interaction between leader and following.

Leadership, as a total event of life, is possible only under the precondition of existential equality of type as this grows out of the community of race, of history, and of *völkisch* destiny. Should this prerequisite be lacking, then the ordered community must necessarily restrict itself to another discipline. The authority of a soldierly or bureaucratic superior, too, comprises only the outer discipline—in other words, one that becomes visible. It is for this reason that the officer is not a leader in the full political sense of the word; he is, in any event, not leader by virtue of the force granted to him by an institutional rank structure. However, in those instances of most extreme danger, when in the face of death all matters of discipline lose their meaning and effect, then it resolves itself whether or not the officer is also leader whose call is heard and followed by his squad. For in the moment of most extreme danger, the institutional order of rank collapses. In those moments, the only thing that asserts itself is the existential test of leadership.

It is necessary to hold fast to this narrow and strict sense of leadership, for every uncritical application of the leadership principle to power relations to inferior levels of order of any kind devalues leadership and, with it, the core of our constitution. It is to be especially maintained that the bureaucratic-hierarchical lesser order of the bureaucrat subordinated to his superior may not be brought into connection with leadership. If, in the most recent reforms of the bureaucracy, the one individual office holder is given precedence before his collegial authorities, this has nothing to do with an introduction of the leadership principle; rather, the situation ought be regarded as the establishment of clear responsibilities.[1] Even less so does leadership allow itself to be carried over to unpolitical communities, such as private organizations.

The order of leadership of the National Socialist state is the order of leadership of the National Socialist movement. This order of leadership is born through the authority of the Führer, an authority that communicates itself to the Führer's subordinates with its call to a function within the party. This does not exclude the fact that inside of this order of leadership there exist connections of leadership that bind the subordinate leaders to their following. This is especially true of the SA and SS, which are differentiated from military units in that they are *led* and not *ordered* by virtue of any order of command or rank. The fact that leadership does not exclude command and order goes without saying. Yet the unity and clout of these groups are based not only on discipline in a superficial sense, but rather on the total outer and inner mobilization that makes up the essence of the following.

Leadership and the civil service system are mutually exclusive. The bureaucratic administrators of the National Socialist Party are not career civil servants. Their decline into mere offices, their bureaucratization, would transform the order of leadership into an administrative organization that would no longer be fundamentally different from state bureaucracy. This decay would constrict the disposition of leadership in favor of a bureaucratic disposition, if not placing the entire disposition of leadership in question. The bureaucratic administrator of the NSDAP is, in fact, a type of the public functionary who by his very embodiment is adapted to the requirements of an order of leadership and who in this respect is an exemplar as has never existed in the history of German disposition or administrative history. Without the protection of hard-earned rights, without any kind of guarantees, the bureaucratic administrator is placed in service of the faith of the Führer and his subordinates. He is the aide of the Führer and his subordinate in the ascertaining and gathering of the German *Volk*.

Note

1. The Prussian Municipal Constitution Law of 15 December 1933 correctly designates the superior bureaucrat responsible for the administration of a municipality as the *head* (*Leiter*) and not *leader* (*Führer*) of the municipality.

29

ALFRED ROSENBERG

The Total State?

First published as "Totaler Staat?" in *Völkischer Beobachter,* 9 January 1934.

In recent months, many speeches and essays have managed to lend expression to the viewpoint that a so-called total state is now slated to replace the party state, to replace the liberalist fragmentation of the state structure. This "total state" is allegedly bent on seizing control of virtually all aspects of the nation's political, economic, and cultural life and is supposedly to be appointed guardian, director, and commandant over every manifestation of life in order to secure the national unity Germany needs in all spheres of life. What is overlooked in these pronouncements is the fact that the abstract state is a notion that clearly originates from a liberalist era in which it was taken for granted as an already extant technological instrument of power to be placed on a par with economics and culture and idolized accordingly or that was ardently opposed by alternate currents in society. [. . .]

The revolution of 30 January 1933 is by no means to be confused with a mere extension of the absolute state under a new rubric; rather, it establishes a relationship to the *Volk* and *Volkstum* that differs not only from that established in 1918 but which is also distinct from that of 1871. What has come to pass in this past year and what is yet to come on a much broader scale is not the so-called totality of the state but rather the totality of the National Socialist movement. The state—whether as a mechanized apparatus or as an instrument of domination—is no longer something that should exist independent of the *Volk* and of the movement; it is rather a tool of the prevailing National Socialist worldview. [. . .] Should we continue to speak in terms of a "total state," gradually today's young National Socialists, as well as future generations, would again seek to focus primarily on the notion of the state and on the actions of government officials. However, if we are unequivocal now in stressing that it is a specific political worldview and movement that lays claim to the right of totality, then future generations will concentrate on this movement and will come to view the relationship between the state and the NSDAP in an entirely different light than they would as long as the concept of "nationhood" or "statehood" per se is assigned primacy. The National Socialist movement is the tangible expression of twentieth-century thought regarding the safeguarding of the greater German *Volk,* its blood and its character. The state is the most potent, the manliest instrument of power that the movement has at its disposal, and the seeds of the state's vigor and motive forces are to be sown by the movement, that it might remain supple and unyielding and circumvent the dangers of bureaucratization, of ossification, and of alienation from the *Volk*. It is only in this context that the lifeblood of the National Socialist conception of state and nationhood comes to the fore, and we believe that this context is also what properly consecrates the state, its inner strength and its greater authority, far more so than if it were to be transformed, possibly through the efforts of energetic individuals, into a means to an end and ossify as a result.

For all these reasons, all National Socialists should henceforth refrain from speaking in terms of a total state and speak instead of the totality of the National Socialist movement, of the National Socialist German Workers' Party as the physical embodiment of this worldview, and of the National Socialist state as the instrument for securing the soul, the mind, and spirit, and the blood of National Socialism as the epochal manifestation that has its beginnings in the twentieth century.

30

CARL SCHMITT

The Führer Protects the Law

On Adolf Hitler's Reichstag Address of 13 July 1934

First published as "Der Führer schützt das Recht: zur Reichstagsrede Adolf Hitlers vom 13. Juli 1934," in his *Positionen und Begriffe im Kampf mit Weimar—Genf—Versailles 1923–1939* (Hamburg: Hanseatische Verlagsanstalt, 1940), 198–201. Translated by Timothy Nunan

I

At the German Jurists' Annual Convention held in Leipzig on 3 October 1933, the Führer spoke on the subject of the state and the law. He elaborated the distinction between substantive *law,* inseparable from neither morality nor justice, and the empty *legality* of a false neutrality, and he elaborated on the inner contradictions of the Weimar system, which destroyed itself by this neutral legality and turned itself over to its enemies. To this he added, "This must be a warning to us."

In his Reichstag address of 13 July 1934, directed to the entire German *Volk,* the Führer recalled another historical warning. The powerful German Empire, founded by Bismarck, collapsed during the World War, because at the decisive moment it did not have the strength "to avail itself of its articles pertaining to war." Paralyzed by the logic of a liberal "constitutional state," the civil bureaucracy lacked all political instinct and could not find the courage to handle mutineers and enemies of the state according to the law entrusted it. Whoever reads today in volume 310 of the Reichstag official record the report about the public plenary session of 9 October 1917 will be appalled and will understand the Führer's warning. The Reich government reported that the ringleaders of the mutinying sailors had carried on negotiations with Reichstag representatives of the Independent Socialist Party.

The German Reichstag responded with loud indignation to the fact that one was not allowed to curtail a party's constitutional right to disseminate propaganda among the army and argued that in this case there was no conclusive proof of high treason. And just a year later, the Independent Socialists spat this hard proof right back into our faces. With exemplary bravery and with dreadful sacrifices, the German *Volk* held the onslaught of an entire world at bay for four years. But the political leadership failed woefully in this struggle against the poisoning of the German *Volk* and the undermining of the German law and its sense of honor. To this very day we still atone for the hesitations and paralyzed state of the German governments during the World War.

All moral outrage over the shame of such a collapse has coalesced in Adolf Hitler and has become in him the driving force of a political act. The experiences and warnings of the history of the German misfortune are alive in him. Most people are frightened by the severity of such warnings and would rather flee into an evasive and compensatory superficiality. The Führer, however, takes the warnings of German history quite seriously. This gives him the right and the power to found a new state and a new order.

II

The Führer protects the law from its worst abuse when in the moment of danger he, by virtue of his domain as Führer and as the supreme judicial authority, directly creates law: "In this hour, I was responsible for the destiny of the German nation and thereby became the *supreme judicial authority of the German* Volk." The true Führer is always a judge as well. From his domain as Führer flows his domain as judge. Whoever wants to separate, or even to juxtapose, these two domains makes the judge into an anti-Führer or into the tool of an anti-Führer and seeks to unhinge the state with the help of the judicial system. It was characteristic of the legal blindness of liberal legal thought that it sought to make out of criminal law a general amnesty, the "Magna Carta of the criminal" (Fr. von Liszt). Constitutional law thus became the Magna Carta of the high traitor and the treasonous. The judiciary is transformed into a calculating machine through whose predictable and calculable functioning the criminal has won his well-earned subjective right. Yet, in this respect, the state and the *Volk* are fettered to a supposedly all-encompassing legality. In the most extreme emergencies, however, some liberal jurists may secretly permit some underhanded apocryphal emergency loopholes depending on the nature of the circumstances but that are denied by others in the name of the constitutional state and regarded as "juridically nonexistent." This manner of jurisprudence, however, does not grasp the word of the Führer that he has acted as "the supreme judicial authority of the *Volk*." This manner of jurisprudence can only reinterpret the act of the Führer as an ex post facto measure justified by the clear and present danger of the state of siege. Through this reinterpretation, a fundamental principle of our present constitutional law, the principle of the primacy of political leadership, would become a juridically meaningless phrase and the gratitude that the Reichstag expressed to the Führer in the name of the German *Volk* would be contorted into an indemnity or even an acquittal.

In truth, the Führer's deed was an exercise of real legal jurisdiction. It was not subordinate to the judiciary; it was rather itself the supreme judiciary. It was not the action of a republican dictator, who in extralegality creates a fait accompli while the law shuts its eyes for a moment so that the fictions of all-encompassing legality can find traction. The judicial domain of the Führer springs from the same source of law from which springs the law of every *Volk*. The supreme law proves itself in extreme necessity, when there appears the highest degree of judicially administered revenge as the realization of this supreme law. All law stems from the *Volk*'s *right to exist.* Every legal statute, every judicial decision only contains justice insofar as it flows from this source of law. What remains is not law but rather a "positive network of coercive norms," which every clever criminal scoffs at.

III

The Führer has emphasized the difference and sharp contrast between his government and his state against the state and government of the Weimar system: "I did not want to hand the young Reich over to the same fate as the old one. . . . A new government was not formed for the umpteenth time on 30 January 1933; rather, a new rule has done away with an old and diseased era." When the Führer demands the liquidation of a sad chapter of German history with such words, then his words must also have juridical consequences for our legal thinking, legal practice, and interpretation of laws. We must examine anew our usual methods and trains of thought, as well as the heretofore-prevailing theories and preliminary decisions of the highest courts in all areas of the law. We cannot blindly be permitted to adhere to the juridical concepts, arguments, and prejudices brought forth by a sick and diseased era. Many a sentence in the grounds for decisions of our courts can be understood from the perspective of justified resistance against the corruption of the previous system. If perpetuated thoughtlessly today, this practice would have the opposite significance and would turn the judiciary into the enemy of the current state. When the Reichsgericht (Imperial Court of Justice) in June 1932 (RGSt. 66, 386) regarded the meaning of judicial independence in terms of its duty "to protect the citizen of the state in accordance with his legally recognized rights from the potential arbitrariness of a government prejudiced against him," this was expressed from a liberal-individualistic position.[1] "We understand the judiciary as being in an adversarial position against not only the head of state and the government, but also the administrative organs in general." Such a statement is comprehensible from the perspective of those times. Today, however, we have incumbent on us the responsibility to assert the *new sense of meaning in all public legal institutions,* including the judiciary, with the greatest decisiveness.

At the end of the eighteenth century, the aged [Karl Friedrich] *Häberlin,* pondering the question of state emergency law in connection with the problem of the separation of *judicial affairs and government affairs,* came to the conclusion that in the event of danger or great damage to the state, a government could interpret every judicial affair as a government affair. In the nineteenth century, [Gabriel Michel] *Dufour,* one of the fathers of French administrative law, defined the act of government (*acte de gouvernement*) immune to ex post judicial review as that act whose goal was the defense of society—indeed, the *defense of society* from *enemies* within and without, open or hidden, present or future. Whatever one thinks of these determinations, they exhibit at any rate a juridically significant particularity of political "acts of government" that has even procured legal recognition in liberal constitutional states. In a Führer state, however, in which legislation, government, and judiciary do not coercively and distrustfully control one another, as in a liberal constitutional state, then what is legitimate for a "government act" must be valid to an incomparably higher degree for an act through which the Führer has stood the test of his highest domain as Führer and judicial authority.[2]

The Führer himself determines the content and scope of his course of action. Once again: the Führer's speech has assured us of the fact that since early in the morning on Sunday 1 July, the situation of "normal law" has been restored. The law on measures of state self-defense of 3 July 1934 (RGBl. I, 529) [. . .] designates the temporal and substantive scope of the Führer's immediate action in the form of a government decree.[3] "Special operations" not empowered by the Führer, not standing in any connection to the dealings of the Führer, or falling outside or inside of the time frame of these three days, are unjust; the higher and purer is the justice of the Führer, the more direly unjust are such actions. According to the statements of the Prussian prime minister, *Göring,* on 12 July and the statements of the Reich justice minister, *Gürtner,* on 20 July 1934, especially strict prosecution is to be employed against such impermissible special courses of action.[4] The fact that determining the distinction between authorized and unauthorized acts cannot be in the competency of a court in such cases of doubt goes without saying following the previous indication about the particularity of the government act and the acts of the Führer.

IV

Within the period of those three days, the judicial acts of the Führer through which he, as leader of the movement, punished the *breach of loyalty committed against him,* the highest leader of the movement, *by his subordinate* (*Unterführer*), has a special significance. The Führer of the movement has a particular judicial duty whose inner justice cannot be realized by any other actor. The Führer explicitly accentuated the fact in his Reichstag address that there is only one carrier of the political will in our country, the National Socialist Party. Yet in such a collective entity, one that is structured and divided into state, movement, and *Volk,* there exists the proprietary inner right of those state-supporting life as well as communal institutions that are especially based on their sworn loyalty to the Führer, secured through the oath. And today no less than the fate of the political unity of the German *Volk* depends on the party fulfilling its tasks. "This mighty task, in which is concentrated the entire danger of the political, cannot be taken away from the party or the SA by any other institution, least of all by a juridically proceeding civilian court. Here this task stands by itself."[5] Therefore, the political Führer became the supreme judge, as a result of the special qualifications of the crime.

V

The Führer reminds us again and again of the collapse of 1918. Our situation today can be determined only from the perspective of that date. Whoever wants to correctly judge the serious events of the 30th of July may not take the individual events of that and the two following days out of the context of our political situation. They may not, as is procedurally done in certain punitive cases, isolate and seclude those discrete events until they have been emptied of their political substance and only the "purely juridical facts of the matter" and "facts not pertaining to the matter" remain. Such methods do not deal justly with a matter of high politics. To depict this procedural of isolation as the one and only practice fit for a liberal constitutional state was one aspect of the poisoning of the *Volk* over the past decade and is a long-used trick of anti-German propaganda. In the fall of 1917, all the confused German parliamentarians—capitalists as well as Communists, clerical politicians as well as atheists—remarkably demanded in their perverse unanimity that Germany's political fate be handed over to such procedural fictions and distortions. The spiritually hapless bureaucracy never emotionally grasped the political sense of those "juridical" demands. In the face of Adolf Hitler's deed, many of Germany's enemies will come forth with similar demands. But they will be shocked to find that today's German state has the power and will to distinguish between friend and enemy. They will promise us the praise and applause of the entire world, if only we would once more, as in 1919, lie down and sacrifice our political existence to the false idols of liberalism. Whoever sees the daunting background of our political situation will understand the admonitions and warnings of the Führer and arm themselves for the great spiritual struggle in which we have to preserve our own righteous law.

Notes

1. Compare the recent writings of Heinrich Henkel, *Die Unabhängigkeit des Richters in ihrem neuen Sinngehalt* (Hamburg: Hanseatische Verlagsanstalt, 1934), 10f.

2. Compare to the essay by E. R. Huber, "Die Einheit der Staatsgewalt" in *Deutsche Juristen-Zeitung* (August 1934), 950.

3. RGBl. I, 529 is a reference to the Gesetz über Maßnahmen der Staatsnotwehr of 3 July 1934, justifying the state-sanctioned murders committed during the Röhm purge on 30 June 1934.—Eds.

4. *Völkischer Beobachter* (13 July 1934 and 22/23 July 1934); *Deutsche Justiz* (1934), 925, 983.

5. Carl Schmitt, *Staat, Bewegung, Volk* (Hamburg: Hanseatische Verlagsanstalt Hamburg, 1933), 22.

31

HANS FRANK

On the Position of the Judge before National Socialist Law and in the National Socialist State

Delivered on 14 January 1936. First published as "Leitsätze des Reichsrechtsminister Hans Frank über die Stellung des Richters in dem nationalsozialistichen Staat und vor dem nationalsozialistichen Recht" (14 January 1936), in *Dokumente der deutschen Politik,* edited by Franz Alfred Six (Berlin: Junker und Dünnhaupt, 1942), 337.

1. The judge is not placed over the citizen as a government authority. Instead, he stands in the ranks of the living community of the German *Volk.* It is not his task to help apply a legal order that is higher than the racial community or to enforce some system of universal values; far more, he is charged with the task of safeguarding the concrete order of the racial community, exterminating pestilential elements, punishing behaviors that are detrimental to the community, and arbitrating quarrels among members of the community.
2. The basis for interpreting all legal sources is the National Socialist *Weltanschauung,* especially as expressed in the party program and in statements made by our Führer.
3. A judge has no right to examine a decision of the Führer that has been issued in the form of a law or a decree. The judge is bound, too, by other decisions of the Führer that clearly express a desire to establish law.
4. Legal regulations issued prior to the National Socialist revolution may not be applied if such application should violate today's healthy sentiment of the people. If a judge should suspend some legal regulation with this in mind, it will be possible to obtain the decision of the highest court on the matter.
5. To fulfill his task in the racial community, the judge must be independent. He is not bound by instructions. The independence and dignity of the judge make it essential to protect him properly against efforts to influence him and against unjustified attacks.

3

The Political Religion

Führer Cult, Ceremonies, and Symbols

FASHIONING HITLER'S PUBLIC IMAGE was a preoccupation of the Nazi Party from the early 1920s. He was one of the first politicians to make public use of the airplane, and he always traveled with his personal photographer, Heinrich Hoffmann, who documented him in a variety of flattering poses. Hoffmann shaped his subject's image to fit the circumstances: in the 1920s, Hitler was the fervent, brown-shirted party leader with a resolute gaze; to appeal to voters in the 1930s, he was a man of the people; after 1933, he was most often the statesman; and during the war, he was the resolute military leader. During his feverish electoral campaigning, he was, according to a press aide, like a musical celebrity on a concert tour: traveling, performing, having his bags packed, and leaving for the next town. His rhetorical skill was legendary, and he was much in demand as a speaker, especially among the regional *Gauleiters* (party leaders) who relied on him to fill their halls—and their coffers. As part of this publicity push, Hoffmann designed a photo album that was published in 1932 as *Hitler as No One Knows Him*. Hoffmann (who shared his royalties with Hitler) also depicted him in his less official moments: playing with his dog, quietly reflecting in idyllic rural settings, or relaxing in his airplane. But Hitler's well-managed public persona was often at odds with the shenanigans of his entourage—"nobodies in their shirt-sleeves playing at being Metternich"—and the brutal violence of his street fighters.[1]

By mid-1933, Hitler's popularity had soared and the newly established Reichsministerium für Volksaufklärung und Propaganda (Ministry for Popular Enlightenment and Propaganda) under Joseph Goebbels was entrusted with shaping the media representation of the new regime and its leader. Controlling Hitler's image became a matter of state. But much of the adulation was spontaneous, or, more precisely, designed to anticipate Hitler's approval. Towns and cities renamed streets and squares after him, poems were composed in his honor (such as the ode by the head of the Hitler Youth, Baldur von Schirach), and the "German greeting" of "Heil Hitler!" became so common that *Das Schwarze Korps* poked fun at the awkward "German Protestant" and "German Catholic" greetings. Tailors were instructed in how to cut men's suits to ease the outstretched arm, bakers designed cakes bearing the Führer's name, cafés were renamed after him, and shops overflowed with chocolates, picture postcards, china plates, tin horns, and photographs bearing his image. Apart from the latter merchandise, which was sold and distributed by the party, the commercial use of Hitler's likeness and name was banned by Goebbels in May 1933 as "national Kitsch."

One serious problem with Hitler's public image was that he was manifestly not a German but an Austrian—a situation legally rectified in 1932 when he was hastily granted German citizenship by the city of Braunschweig so that he could become a candidate for Reich president. For publicity purposes, however, his somewhat insecure German identity was more firmly established in the photo album *Adolf Hitler's Homeland,* one of the first such publications to depict his "solid German peasant ancestry."

Ironically, in many respects, National Socialism's success before 1933 can be attributed to the self-conscious ability of the party to copy and outdo the images, practices, and style of its opponents, especially the Communists. The public face of National Socialism was the SA,

SS, and party rhetoric (such as the use of "party comrade"). The party's careful attention to uniforms, decorations, insignia, and, above all, the red flag was designed to contest the hegemony of its adversaries by directly appropriating and imitating the imagery of the movement it set out to destroy. As Franz Alfred Six, a university-trained economist—and a faculty member, until he became a member of the SA and later the Sicherheitsdienst (Security Service, SD)—noted in his dissertation on National Socialist propaganda (accepted at the University of Heidelberg), it was the direct challenge to the hegemony of "Marxists" in the streets through mass rallies and demonstrations, and not their parliamentary tactics, that accounted for the triumph of the "political soldiers" of the SA and the SS. But even the swastika, the prime symbol of the movement since 1921, could not be considered something uniquely National Socialist or even Germanic, as overenthusiastic Nazis sometimes claimed. Its origins were, as its own propagandists admitted, obscure. One of the most precise observers of the Nazi corruption of the German language, the Romance-language scholar Victor Klemperer, noted that the positive meaning given to the word *fanaticism* was one of the most disturbing examples of National Socialism's ability to elevate a term despised by the thinkers of the Enlightenment into a virtue—a point underscored by Six's disquisition on oratorical technique and the power of public persuasion. Another area of serious concern was the visual representation of the movement and its leader. Erwin Schockel's comparison of one of the most successful electoral posters, which featured the stark image of Hitler's face on a black background, with a less successful poster is noteworthy not only for its praise of the "harmonious coherence evoked by the poster as a whole" but also for its recognition that political propaganda had to compete with commercial advertising for the viewer's attention.

Orchestrating mass meetings and developing sophisticated propaganda campaigns in public spaces were highly developed tools of the Nazi movement both before and after 1933. As Frank Leberecht's "Call to the Fire" demonstrates, no detail of the rituals and chants performed by the Hitler Youth was too unimportant to prescribe. In "New Meanings for 'Inherited' Customs," Hannes Kremer noted that the new regime understood that it had to create new holidays and rituals to deepen the experience of community and bridge a fragmented society. But even if Christmas could be given a national interpretation, Kremer warned against obscuring its traditional significance by turning it into a "versified dissertation" about nebulous Germanic customs. The 27 February 1934 Law Concerning Holidays put in place a new calendar punctuated by dates synchronized to the mythical history of the Nazi movement (30 January, the assumption of power; 1 May, celebration of the German *Volk;* and 1 November, the commemoration of the Munich putsch), but the traditional Christian holidays were retained, including Good Friday, Easter, and Christmas. Another important new holiday was 24 February, the anniversary of the proclamation of the party program, a ceremonial occasion that combined quasi-sacred ritual and a new liturgy scripted by the party around the "Oath to Adolf Hitler," taken by the Hitler Youth, the League of German Girls, and other organized groups each year. The ceremony rhetorically linked the public affirmation of unconditional loyalty to Hitler to the memory of "all those who fought, sacrificed, suffered, risked or gave their lives for Germany's resurrection under National Socialism." After 1939, Hitler's birthday, 20 April, also became a national holiday when public buildings were festooned with swastika flags and streamers, culminating in a massive celebration in Berlin as the *Völkischer Beobachter* reported on 29 April 1939. During the war, Memorial Day was refashioned to honor the increasing number of German men who did not return from the front, with the party providing detailed instructions on how to avoid cheapening the ceremony with poetry and music.

For the party, the most important event was the Reichsparteitag, the Reich Party Rally, which met annually in Nuremberg until 1938 (the 1939 meeting was canceled because of the war). Over time, the organization of this enormous event evolved, with Rudolf Hess dubbing the 1933 meeting "the Victory Rally" and with the 1934 rally reaching still greater heights through worldwide dissemination of the famous film commissioned by Hitler and directed by Leni Riefenstahl, *Triumph of the Will.* As the mayor of Nuremberg, Willy Liebel, proudly wrote in a souvenir brochure for participants, not only the sheer size of the undertaking—with the associated problems of providing sufficient capacity, transportation, and provisions—but also the huge construction projects necessary to stage these events made the rally the centerpiece of the year for the party faithful. In addition to many admiring Germans, visiting dignitaries, like former British prime minister David Lloyd George, were favorably impressed with Hitler's "marvelous transformation in the spirit of the people"—remarks George later regretted when he allied with Winston Churchill in his fight against the government's pro-appeasement policies in the late 1930s. But what did the majority of Germans outside of the parade grounds and stadiums think of the speeches, banners, and marches? It is very hard to know, but a clue is provided by Victor Klemperer's account of his experience at a truck stop: the locals paid no attention; the only one listening to Göring's speech on the radio was Klemperer, a Jewish professor who had been dismissed from the university and was terrified of his future under the new regime.

NOTE

1. This observation is from Hitler's press aide, Ernst Hanfstaengl, in *The Unknown Hitler* (London: Gibson Square Books, 2005), 233.

32

ALBERT REICH

Adolf Hitler's Homeland

First published as *Aus Adolf Hitlers Heimat* (Munich: Verlag Franz Eher Nachfolger GmbH, 1933), 5–7.

The question of Adolf Hitler's nationality has been raised so often in politics—more often than not, maliciously falsified—that it seems appropriate to provide a comprehensive overview for the broader public here.

For this reason, images and words have been joined in this book to present a unified whole, presented here for the entire world to see.

For anyone familiar with history, there is no question as to whether Adolf Hitler is to be regarded as a German, even though he was born under the sign of Austria's double-headed eagle. It is a well-known fact that, unlike the subsequent Bismarck Empire, the Holy Roman Empire encompassed all German-speaking territories. The subsequent destruction of this Greater German Empire was certainly not the fault of those fragments of the empire that were shuffled around like bounty in the horse trading that went on back then! But the struggle to regain the German diaspora that has emerged along the various borders of the old empire is far from over, even though it cannot, under the currently prevailing momentary political powerlessness, be conducted with the same fervor deemed necessary. Gottlieb Johann Fichte once said, in his "Addresses to the German Nation," "Just as it is undoubtedly true that everywhere where a special language is to be found, there is a special nation that has a right to conduct its affairs independently and to govern itself; well, that can be turned around to say that a *Volk* which has ceased to govern itself deserves to lose its language and merge with the conquerors. You would be jerked around from every angle until your *Volk* perished!"

But because since time immortal the authentic Austrian has spoken German as his mother tongue, Fichte's notion of the alien conqueror is inapplicable here because Austrians have been Germans since the beginning of time and, as brothers of the Reich, legitimate sons of the *Volk!* This cleavage has been introduced to the natural unified national fabric in the myopic pursuit of power politics in the House of Habsburg and strictly dynastic interests. The complete elimination of, or the bridging of, this divisive rift is a supremely natural exigency and is thus also one of the core issues addressed in the policies advanced by Adolf Hitler himself. To persist in the attempt to list the reasons for considering Adolf Hitler a German would be like chasing windmills! Far more, it would seem the thing to do is to spit in the face of the ever more prevalent backbiting calumny that would stigmatize him as a "Czech, Slovakian, or Bohemian."

In this context it is utterly irrelevant whether Adolf Hitler was actually born on the left or the right bank of the Inn River. He could just as easily have come into the world in Passau by circumstance of birth—that is to say, on German imperial soil, where his father, Alois Hitler, a midlevel customs official, had been transferred shortly after the birth of his son Adolf. In that case, his German ancestry would have been more plausibly substantiated in the minds of that broad circle of shortsighted individuals, even though, as the son of an Austrian father, he would have nevertheless remained a citizen of Austria in the eyes of both national law and of politics. At any rate, if the stars had been more felicitous and he had been born under different circumstances, he might have at least been lucky enough to spare himself the demeaning farce surrounding his German nationality that was only clarified through the circuitous route of the governing council in Braunschweig.

We have no desire to exhaust ourselves in the attempt to prove a foregone conclusion and shall hence restrict ourselves to providing incontrovertible evidence defending our Führer Adolf Hitler from the malicious charge of "foreign ancestry" that has been leveled against him often enough by certain elements of society against their better knowledge.

A documented family tree is and remains the most reliable and surest way to determine the bloodlines [*Stammreihe*] and racial belonging [*rassische Zugehörigkeit*] of any individual. Research into Adolf Hitler's ancestry traced almost seamlessly back six generations, through approximately seventy known paternal and maternal ancestors, dating back to the year 1670, and not a single name was found that was not of purely Germanic origin! The Hitler family—or Hiedler, as the name was often spelled in older documents—is of solid German peasant ancestry and has been residing in the ancient German forest area around the Kamp River, in the former "East Mark"—an area that was settled and opened up by Bajuvarian settlers many centuries ago—as we will provide substantial evidence to indicate.

Hitler's ancestors all resided in an area encompassed by no more than a seventy-mile radius. Here, firmly rooted at the center of a Germanic tribal population, his male ancestors—even by virtue of their association by geographic proximity—could have selected their wives only from this German-blooded stock of women in the German tribal population living there, and for this simple reason alone, we can preclude any possibility of interbreeding with alien bloodlines.

What is more, the inhabitants of the Kamp Valley, as we learn from a large number of contemporary accounts by writers and genealogists across many epochs, strictly avoided any sort of contact or association with the Wendish or Czech elements of the population, to the extent that they sought to ostentatiously distinguish themselves in their customs and cultural practices, even in their national dress, and above all insisted on stridently nationalistic distinctions between them. Marriages between the German elements and members of foreign nations, as well as any form of kinship ties "between nations," were rendered virtually nonexistent, particularly in these border regions, by the ostracism that accompanies the instinctive racial consciousness. Where racial intermarriages nevertheless did occur—and this is particularly well documented in the Kamp region—there followed almost inevitably a total boycott of the spouses in a mixed-race marriage, which almost always resulted in that couple leaving the community.

Ever since the earliest studies were conducted, incontrovertible evidence of the racial purity of the lower Austrian East Mark region has been confirmed again and again, based on the careful examination of a large number of bloodlines in families that have been indigenous to the area for centuries, families who are the ancestors of Adolf Hitler.

33

BALDUR VON SCHIRACH

Hitler as No One Knows Him

First published as *Hitler wie ihn keiner kennt,* edited by Heinrich Hoffmann (Berlin: Zeitgeschichte Verlag, 1933), xii–xiv. Translated by Randall Bytwerk. Calvin College, German Propaganda Archive.

Whoever has ever had the good fortune of working close beside the Führer of young Germany has always been and remains impressed by the sides of Adolf Hitler that the public does not see. This book will make Hitler clearer to a circle broader than just his friends.

What Adolf Hitler the Führer means to his *Volk* is known or felt by millions today. It will be the task of historians to put these feelings and knowledge into words, for their task is to present Hitler as a historic figure to posterity. But that book about the Führer cannot be written for many years, for those with greater distance also have the greater ability to judge.

This book is different.

A German (for this corresponds to his nature and inner laws) rightly expects his leader to display some degree of synthesis between ability and personality. He expects his leader to be a role model and exemplary man, even in his private life. This explains the love and esteem that two great sons of our *Volk*, Goethe and Frederick the Great, have earned from our people. It also explains the fanatic love for and belief in Adolf Hitler, for whom National Socialists are willing to bleed and die, for whom we have all faced great danger or prison time.

I wish to emphasize the two traits I think are strongest in Adolf Hitler's character: his strength and his goodness. These are the characteristics that the images in this book display. Whether Hitler is motoring through Germany, surrounded by cheering crowds of construction workers, or standing beside the grave of a murdered comrade, deeply moved and shaken, his nobility and profound humanity often render speechless those who meet him for the first time, be they young or old. May this book of largely unpublished photographs spread the experience of Adolf Hitler far beyond the circles of the National Socialist movement, so that those who do not know him may share the feelings of those who have worked with him for many years and learned to honor and love him. The shadow of this man is over Germany today. Many are astonished at the miracle that, after the absolute dominance of Marxism, a single face is able to transform the nation.

Whoever views these photographs with an open heart as their witness will have an inkling of the enigma behind this unique personality. And he will understand: this is not only the revelation of a charismatic Führer but that of a great human being and a good man.

To be popular means to be photographed often. Adolf Hitler always tried to avoid being photographed. Twelve years ago, as his name for the first time began to become known, he was a declared opponent of the camera. Even then, the world's illustrated press tried to secure a picture of the Führer, although without success. Despite substantial offers, Hitler rejected every request to be photographed.

A major satirical magazine back then published an article titled "What Does Hitler Look Like?" with a series of caricatures of people's outrageous "suggestions" for how they might imagine Hitler to appear. The article illustrated the state of affairs: people talked about Hitler, whether to praise or blame him, but did not know what he looked like.

In those days, a leading American newspaper asked the Munich photographer Heinrich Hoffmann to secure a picture of the chairman of the National Socialist German Workers' Party. With the help of his friend Dietrich Eckart, Hoffmann tried to find a good opportunity to take a picture. His attempt failed. He did get a glimpse of the Führer as he was stepping into his car, but just as he was ready to take the picture, three of Hitler's Herculean companions tackled him and held him down as Hitler raced away. Later, Hoffmann had better luck. He did take a picture, but Hitler asked him not to publish it. Hoffmann followed the Führer's wishes, and later, when his followers began pressing him for images, Hitler rewarded Hoffmann with exclusive rights to produce pictures for the National Socialist movement. The Führer soon recognized the enormous propaganda value of photography for the National Socialist movement. While the newspapers blathered on about the "colossal failure" of National Socialist meetings, Hoffmann produced panoramas of large Hitler meetings and refuted the lies of the enemy with his photography.

The close friendship between Adolf Hitler and his old fellow combatant Hoffmann soon made them constant travel companions and gave Hoffmann the opportunity to take pictures that could only be made by someone close to the Führer.

This is the real power of this book: its task is not a literary treatment of the Führer's life, but rather a vivid portrayal of what someone saw with his own eyes.

Hitler is a universal spirit. It would be impossible for one hundred photographs selected from thousands to do justice to the multiplicity of his being. These pictures show only some aspects of this unique personality. It is almost unknown that Hitler does not drink alcohol or smoke or that he is a vegetarian. Without insisting that anyone follow his example, even in his closest circle, he holds like iron to his self-established principles. He works amazingly hard. Not only does he head the enormous apparatus of the National Socialist movement, he also makes strenuous speaking tours. Today he is in Königsberg, tomorrow in Berlin, the next day in Munich, all this with a minimum of sleep, since the Führer usually works into the early hours of the morning.

So many lies and gossip have been spread about his private life that a few words on the topic are in order here. Hitler's greatest joy is his library of about six thousand volumes. He has read them all, not just paged through them. The larger share consists of books on architecture and history. In both areas, Hitler has masterful authority. For him, art is essential, music above all. As he says, "If the artists only knew what I would do for German art, none of them would oppose me."

Naive people believe that Adolf Hitler lives a life of ease, working an eight-hour day and then visiting a café. Few have any idea of the enormous burdens on his shoulders.

Our age will perhaps honor and love this outstanding man but will not be able to understand his true greatness. It does not need to.

We need only look respectfully on the powerful personality of the Führer and thank God in heaven that he has not forsaken us this time either.

34

RUDOLF HESS

The Oath to Adolf Hitler

Delivered on 25 February 1934. First published as "Der Eid auf Adolf Hitler," in *Reden* (Munich: Zentralverlag der NSDAP, 1938), 10–14. Translated by Randall Bytwerk. Calvin College, German Propaganda Archive.

German men, German women, German boys, German girls, over a million of you are gathered in many places in all of Germany!

On this the anniversary of the proclamation of the party's program, you will together swear an oath of loyalty and obedience to Adolf Hitler. You will display to the world what has long been self-evident to you and what you have expressed for many years, often unconsciously.

You are swearing your oath on a holiday that Germany celebrates for the first time: Heroes' Memorial Day. We lower our flags today, first and foremost and now more than ever, in remembrance of those who lived as heroes and who died as heroes. The flags bow down today before the giants of our past, before those who fought for Germany, before the millions who fought in the world war, before those who died paving the way for the new Reich. I cite Horst Wessel because his name has become a symbol for us, and commemorate, through him, all those "shot and killed by the Red Front and Reaction."

Woe to the people that fails to honor its heroes! Some day, it will cease to produce them—it will know no heroes. Heroes spring from the essence of their people. But a people without heroes is a people without leaders, for only a heroic leader is a true leader able to withstand the challenge of difficult times. The rise or fall of a people can be determined by the presence or absence of a leader.

We do not want to forget the mothers, women, and children who gave their dearest, often their husband or father, and bear their fate with quiet heroism.

The battle-ready manly heroes and the quiet sacrifices of mothers and women are sacred examples of loyalty for us Germans. The flags that we now raise once more are symbols of this loyalty, which for Nordic man is closely bound to heroism!

The hero of Germanic origin is loyal to the point of self-sacrifice. Do not forget that as you swear your loyalty on this day of heroes' remembrance!

Loyalty not only in deed but also in character is demanded of you. Loyalty of character often demands no less heroic virtue than does loyalty in deed. Loyalty in character is unshakable loyalty, a loyalty that knows no ifs, ands, or buts, that knows no weakness. Loyalty in character means absolute obedience that questions neither the results of the order nor its reasons and instead obeys for the sake of obedience itself. Such obedience is an expression of heroic character when following the order leads to personal disadvantage or seems even to contradict one's personal convictions. Adolf Hitler's strength as a leader is that he almost always works through the power of his persuasion; rarely does he command. He must know, however, that when he *does* issue a command, or allows one to be issued, that it will be obeyed absolutely, down to the last block warden.

The power and effectiveness of a good organization is even greater when discipline prevails. The greater its obedience to even the smallest details, the more clearly it marches to the right or the left depending on the command of the leader, the more exactly the command to march in short or long steps is followed, the more surely the Führer can take the steps necessary to realize the National Socialist program.

All we National Socialists work for the realization of this program, just as we once worked to gain control of the state. We fought for the souls of the farmers, for the souls of the workers, for the souls of the middle class, for the souls of men, for the souls of women, for the souls of the old, for the souls of the young—we the members of the main organization of the NSDAP, as well as the men of the Labor Service, the leaders of the affiliated organizations of the party such as the National Socialist women. With the same will, young men and women strive toward the same goal, to become those who will replace us as the masters of Germany's fate.

Hitler Youth! You have given the same absolute loyalty to the Führer that Germany's young volunteers gave twenty years ago at Langemarck, which demanded their heroic deaths for our *Volk* and our Reich. You have made the youth of Langemarck your model. You have the good fortune to live in a Reich that the best warriors of 1914 could only dream of—a Reich that for all eternity will remain united if you do your duty. For you, doing your duty means: obey the Führer's orders without question! The best way for you to honor your dead comrades of the first years of the war is for you to maintain discipline in your ranks.

The more a Hitler Youth leader demands discipline from his boys, the more he must display it himself. He must demand discipline from them above all when his boys, in their entirely natural drive for freedom, engage in wild behavior. It should be easier for the youth of today to accept discipline and subordination—combined with an appreciation of the accomplishments of the older generation—since the older generation is the generation of the world war. I know how you were persecuted, maligned, hated, and mocked because of your faith in the Führer. I know how many of your comrades sacrificed their young lives! I know it well!

But I also know that all the dangers and sorrows that a Hitler Youth suffered, even in the most Communist neighborhood in the years before the seizure of power, are not comparable to the dangers and sorrows that a front soldier experienced in a single day! Never forget that when your leader, who endured the battleground for us, demands self-discipline of you.

I say to the political leaders what I said to your comrades in *Gau* Thuringia as they were sworn in last year: be true to Hitler's spirit! Ask in all that you do: What would the Führer do? If you act accordingly, you will not go wrong!

Being true to Hitler's spirit means knowing that a leader has not only rights but also responsibilities. Being true to Hitler's spirit means always being a role model. "To be a leader is to set an example," just as Hitler and his work set an example for you. Being true to Hitler's spirit means being modest and unassuming. Being true to Hitler's spirit means remaining a thorough National Socialist in good times and bad. Being a National Socialist through and through means thinking ever and only of the whole National Socialist German people. It means, no matter what, always being a servant of the total National Socialism of Adolf Hitler, being above all else a fully conscious, heartfelt follower of the Führer.

Be ever a servant of the whole, within the movement as well, and never forget that only the whole movement, not a part of it, can guarantee victory and the conquest of the future.

Be ever aware that, wherever you are, you owe thanks to the Führer, for it was his leadership that secured our victory. Wherever you are, be it high or low, work for his movement and, therefore, for Germany. Remember what Adolf Hitler says: it makes no difference if one is a street cleaner or a professor, as long as he works for the whole and does his duty.

The reward for your labors is the feeling of having done one's duty for the movement, for Adolf Hitler, for Germany.

All of you, whether political leader, SA, SS, or Hitler Youth, share a common pride: being a member of Adolf Hitler's NSDAP!

You are all the scouts and the defenders of the National Socialist army of the movement. You are each indispensable and equal. Each of you is as unique in history as National Socialism itself. You are typical National Socialists.

SA, SS, and political leaders have a common tradition, embodied in the "Old Guard." It includes all who fought, sacrificed, suffered, risked or gave their lives for Germany's resurrection under National Socialism. It has the honor to have bled and sacrificed for our people's future. You have earned the thanks of all who enjoy the blessings of life in a new Reich. It is a Reich led by men who share a desire for national freedom, socialist community, and peace in dignity and honor.

Political leaders! Leaders of the Labor Service, the forces of labor! Women's leaders! Hitler Youth leaders! Leaders of the League of German Girls! You will now take an oath to Adolf Hitler!

Your oath is not a mere formality; you do not swear this oath to some stranger. You do not swear in hope but with certainty. Fate has made it easy for you to take this oath unconditionally and without reservation. Never in history has a people taken an oath to a leader with such absolute confidence as the German people have in Adolf Hitler. You have the enormous joy of taking an oath to a man who is the embodiment of a leader. You take an oath to the fighter who demonstrated his leadership over a decade, who always acts correctly, and who always followed the right path, even when at times the larger part of his movement failed to understand why.

You take an oath to a man whom you know follows the laws of providence, which he obeys independently of the influence of earthly powers, who leads the German people rightly, and who will guide Germany's fate. Through your oath, you bind yourselves to a man who—this is what we firmly believe—was sent to us by higher powers. Do not seek Adolf Hitler with your mind. You will find him through the strength of your hearts!

Adolf Hitler is Germany, and Germany is Adolf Hitler. Whoever takes an oath to Hitler takes an oath to Germany!

Swear to Greater Germany, to whose sons and daughters throughout the world I send our best wishes.

[Throughout Germany, people take the oath].[1]

This has been the greatest common taking of an oath in history!

We greet the Führer!

Note

1. The oath: "I swear eternal allegiance to Adolf Hitler and to those designated by him unbroken obedience."—Eds.

35

BALDUR VON SCHIRACH

To the Führer; Hitler

First published in *Die Fahne der Verfolgten* (Berlin: Zeitgeschichte Verlag, 1935), 40, 41.

TO THE FÜHRER

This is the truth that led me to your hand,
While looking for you, I found my fatherland.
I was but a leaf in unlimited space blowing free,
Till you came along, became my home and tree.
How far gone I'd have been, lost to whims of the wind
but for your strength that seeks the root for its origin.
I believe in you, for you are the nation,
I believe in Germany because you are Germany's son.

HITLER

Behind me, there are many thousands of you,
and you are me and I am you.
I have yet to entertain one single thought
that was not in your hearts wrought.
Nary a word that springs from my lips
is not wholly one with your will.
For I am you and you are me
and Germany, we all believe in Thee.

36

DAVID LLOYD GEORGE

I Talked To Hitler

First published in *Daily Express* (London, 17 November 1936).

I have just returned from a visit to Germany.[1] In so short time, one can only form impressions or at least check impressions that years of distant observation through the telescope of the Press and constant inquiry from those who have seen things at a closer range had already made on one's mind.

I have now seen the famous German Leader and also something of the great change he has effected. Whatever one may think of his methods—and they are certainly not those of a parliamentary country—there can be no doubt that he has achieved a marvelous transformation in the spirit of the people, in their attitude towards each other, and in their social and economic outlook.

He rightly claimed at Nuremberg that in four years his movement has made a new Germany.

It is not the Germany of the first decade that followed the war—broken, dejected, and bowed down with a sense of apprehension and importance. It is now full of hope and confidence, and of a renewed sense of determination to lead its own life without interference from any influence outside its own frontiers.

There is, for the first time since the war, a general sense of security. The people are more cheerful. There is a greater sense of general gaiety of spirit throughout the land. It is a happier Germany. I saw it everywhere and Englishmen I met during my trip and who knew Germany well were very impressed with the change.

One man has accomplished this miracle. He is a born leader of men, a magnetic, dynamic personality with a single-minded purpose, a resolute will and a dauntless heart. He is, not merely in name but also in fact, the national Leader. He has made them safe against potential enemies by whom they were surrounded. He is also securing them against that constant dread of starvation, which is one of the poignant memories of the last years of the War and the first years of the Peace.

Over 700,000 died of sheer hunger in those dark years. You can still see the effect in the physique of those who were born into that bleak world. The fact that Hitler has rescued his country from the fear of a repeat of that period of despair, penury and humiliation has given him unchallenged authority in modern Germany.

As to his popularity, especially among the youth of Germany, there can be no manner of doubt. The old trust him; the young idolize him. It is not the admiration accorded to a popular Leader. It is the worship of a national hero who has saved his country from utter despondency and degradation.

It is true that public criticism of the Government is forbidden in every form. That does not mean that criticism is absent. I have heard the speeches of prominent Nazi orators freely condemned. But not a word of criticism or of disapproval have I heard of Hitler. He is as immune from criticism as a king in a monarchical country. He is something more. He is the George Washington of Germany—the man who won for his country independence from all her oppressors.

To those who have not actually seen and sensed the way Hitler reigns over the heart and mind of Germany this description may appear extravagant. All the same, it is the bare truth. This great people will work better, sacrifice more, and, if necessary, fight with greater resolution because Hitler asks them to do so. Those who do not comprehend this central fact cannot judge the present possibilities of modern Germany.

On the other hand, those who imagine that Germany has swung back to its old Imperialist temper cannot have any understanding of the character of the change. The idea of a Germany intimidating Europe with a threat that its irresistible army might march across frontiers forms no part of the new vision.

What Hitler said at Nuremberg is true. The Germans will resist to the death every invader at their own country, but they have no longer the desire themselves to invade any other land. The leaders of modern Germany know too well that Europe is too formidable to be overrun and trampled down by any single nation, however powerful its armaments may be. They have learned that lesson in the war.

Hitler fought in the ranks throughout the war, and knows from personal experience what war means. He also knows too well that the odds are even heavier today against an aggressor than they were at that time. What was then Austria would now be in the main hostile to the ideals of 1914.

The Germans are under no illusions about Italy. They also are aware that the Russian Army is in every respect far more efficient than it was in 1914. The establishment of a German hegemony in Europe, which was the aim and dream of the old pre-war militarism, is not even on the horizon of Nazism.

Note

1. Lloyd George was the Liberal prime minster of Great Britain from 1916 to 1922.—Eds.

Das ist nationaler Kitsch!

Wovor uns das Kitsch-Gesetz schützen soll

Eine ganze Industrie ist in den wenigen Monaten seit dem 30. Januar emporgeblüht. Aber ihr Fundament ist ungesund, ihre Fruchtbarkeit schadet dem Volk mehr als sie der Wirtschaft nützt. Diese „Industrie der Geschmacklosigkeiten" hat das Bedürfnis zu wittern geglaubt, immer und überall die neuen Farben, Symbole und Hoheitszeichen des Reiches, die Bilder der neuen Staatsmänner und historischen Persönlichkeiten zu sehen und zu zeigen — zu Hause, auf der Straße, im Schaufenster, im Gasthaus, an der Kleidung. Sicherlich hat nur eine verschwindende Minderheit dieser Kitschfabrikanten in ehrlicher Ueberzeugung die Fabrikation solcher Gegenstände aufgenommen — in der primitiven Ueberlegung, ihrer eigenen Begeisterung und der des Publikums für den Sieg der nationalen Bewegung in dieser

Zum Kampf des Propagandaministeriums gegen nationalen Kitsch: Einige Beispiele von Erzeugnissen allzu geschäftstüchtiger Fabrikanten, gegen die sich das kommende Kitschgesetz richtet: Eine Kinder-Lärmtrompete.

Künstliche Schneeglöckchen mit Hakenkreuzen und politische Bonbons.

Allzu große Geschäftstüchtigkeit, gegen die jetzt eingeschritten wird: Herstellung von Papierbechern mit verzerrten Bildern des Reichskanzlers.

FIGURE 1. "This Is National Kitsch! Article describing a 1933 law banning Nazi kitsch such as whistles, licorice, and paper cups with the swastika or Hitler's visage. *Berliner Illustrirte Zeitung,* 23 May 1933, 753–54.

37

ANONYMOUS

"This Is National Kitsch!"

What the Ban on Führer Kitsch Is Supposed to Protect Us From

First published as "Das ist nationaler Kitsch! Wovor uns das Kitsch-Gesetz schützen soll" in *Berliner Illustrirte Zeitung,* no. 21 (1933), 753, 754.

A whole new industry has burst into bloom in the few months since 30 January. But its roots feed from fallow ground and the fruits it bears are a greater detriment to the *Volk* than they are a boon to the economy. This "industry of tastelessness" sensed a need to see and display the new colors, symbols, and national emblems of the Reich, pictures of the new statesmen and historical personalities anywhere and everywhere—at home, on the street, in shop windows, restaurants, on clothing. Certainly, a dwindling minority of these kitsch manufacturers have begun to manufacture such items out of sincere conviction—that is, in the naive consideration that this was the only way to lend expression to their own enthusiasm and the enthusiasm on the part of consumers for the victory of the national movement. The majority of kitsch manufacturers belong to that miserable pack of profiteers and moneymongers who are unashamed to profit from the desecration of national symbols as bric-a-brac. The manufacturers sent these items to the Propaganda Ministry and had no doubt that they would reap praises for their products. There was bitter disappointment when it turned out that both the official and unofficial offices were utterly dismissive in their response and the worst of the kitsch makers were enthusiastically escorted out the door. In preparing the kitsch ban, a number of offices in Berlin have gone to the trouble of collecting documents and information about particularly excessive expressions of loyalty to the state from all over the Reich. A miniature museum of these "tasteless trinkets" has come into being as a result.

38

ANONYMOUS

City and Countryside Shine in Celebratory Splendor

First published as "Stadt und Land erstrahlen in festlichem Glanz," in *Völkischer Beobachter,* 20 April 1939, 2.

The German *Volk* is preparing to celebrate the Führer's fiftieth birthday. The nominal consecration of the date, 20 April, was conferred when it was declared a national holiday in 1939. But the hearts of millions of national comrades in all the German districts and everywhere in the rest of the world where Germans live and work will exalt the Führer with jubilation and awe as never before. Thanks heaped upon [a] thousand heartfelt thanks are due to the great deeds of Adolf Hitler. Every German sees in him the only man in the nation who has allowed Germany to rise up from humiliation and hardship to make it free, strong, and fit to defend itself.

The unshakable faith of the Führer has taken root in the *Volk*. A *Volk* that pays him highest tribute on his fiftieth birthday, expressed in love, in honor, but also in its utmost and unconditional declaration of devotion to him.

All of Greater Germany, city and countryside, glisten with the splendor of festive decorations. The Reich capital is bustling with activity today just as it would on any similar occasion. Streets and buildings are lavishly adorned with flags and garlands. Expansive, customized banners inscribed with birthday greetings for the Führer express the population's birthday wishes. Hardly a single display window is not gay with fresh flowers, framing pictures or busts of Adolf Hitler. Public buildings are draped in the customary holiday decorations—hung with the long swastika flags and golden streamers, freshly cut greenery, golden laurel leaves, and garlands. To the north and the south, to the east and to the west ends of Berlin, it is the same: flag upon flag, flowers and garlands, and, in their midst, the Führer's image.

Thousands of national comrades from throughout the Reich have come to Berlin to experience this day of celebration. In front of the new Reich Chancellery, at Wilhelmsplatz and the East-West Axis, throngs of people crowd the streets. Traffic ebbs to and fro like a wave with no end in sight. Men, women, and children are animated with glee, imbued with hopeful anticipation that they might offer their heartfelt greetings, that they might exalt him as he passes by at the end of the parade.

Festivities on the eve of his birthday reached their climax with the Führer's ride along the East-West Axis, which was subsequently reopened to traffic. At 10:00 P.M., the German army performed its "Great Tattoo" and concluded with a march-in-review before the Führer. As in years past, the ranks of the NSDAP marched in formation to conduct a torchlight procession in which honorary award holders from the district of Berlin, as well as fifty honorary award holders from each of the remaining districts, participated.

These events were preceded that afternoon by the presentation of candidates of the SS-officer candidate school in Braunschweig who were being promoted; an address by the director of Reich propaganda, Reich Minister Dr. Goebbels, broadcast live by all German radio stations; as well as the birthday wishes addressed to the Führer by the NSDAP Führerkorps under the direction of the Führer's deputy shock troops [*Stoßtrupp*], "Adolf Hitler," as well as by all bearers of the Blood Order Award registered as residents of Berlin.

As the midnight hour approached, the evening's festivities drew to a close with the national broadcast [*Reichsringsendung*] "Germany's Youth Salutes the Führer," at which a chorus of SS bodyguards sang "Adolf Hitler" in the honor court of the Reich Chancellery.

39

ENGELBERT HUBER

The Swastika

Originally published in *Das ist Nationalsozialimus: Organisation und Weltanschauung der NSDAP* (Stuttgart: Union Deutsche Verlagsgesellschaft, 1933), 69–71.

The swastika stands for National Socialism and is also a *völkisch,* Nordic symbol denoting unequivocal opposition to all that is un-German, corrupting, and generally Jewish. But this anti-Semitic meaning has been associated with the swastika only since it was adopted by the *völkisch* leagues as a symbol of their struggle. History does not provide any grounds for the anti-Semitic interpretation of this symbol.

The swastika is one of the oldest symbols in human history. There is hardly an ancient culture that has not employed it as a symbolic ornament. It serves as a pattern for etchings on clay pots; embellishes decorative objects carved from wood, bone, and metal; and sanctifies weapons of stone and bronze. We encounter it in the characters of the archaic Chinese alphabet; it consecrates the oath of witness on ancient Sumerian contracts, and we find it in the rock carvings and the paltry remnants of the earliest Atlantic-Arctic cultures. The symbol is known in the high North, with its ancient memories of collective existence; in sites of ancient civilization along the Euphrates and the Tigris; in Persia, India, China, and Japan; in Egypt and prehistoric Africa, as well as in pre-Columbian America, not only among the North American Indians but also in the empires of the Aztecs and the Incas to the south. [. . .]

In the first half of the nineteenth century, it was presumed to have originated in India because the hooked cross, or "Suastika," was so widespread as a good luck charm in the symbolism of ancient Indian culture. From its presumed primeval origin in India, which was the only area then known to have been host to widespread symbolic use of the swastika, it was associated with the primordial religious imagination of the Aryan race. From there, it was then unceremoniously transformed into a symbol of struggle under which the blood heirs of the Aryan race should gather for their cultural or economic struggle for existence.

But the point of departure for this interpretation of the war symbol was deceptive because later, in research conducted at additional sites of ancient human civilization, swastikas were found that were thousands of years older than those known from India.

The decisive factor determining the anti-Semitic interpretation of the swastika was obviously the intention of the earliest fighters in the *völkisch* liberation movement, who took it upon themselves to render this sign the symbol of their battle for rejuvenation. This anti-

Semitic interpretation is not historically based, for history still owes us an answer to the question of the purpose and meaning of this sacred sign. [. . .]

All attempts at clarifying the original purpose of the swastika's symbolic meaning are pure speculation. But they are unanimous in associating the swastika symbol with the sun and solar cults. The ball of the sun traversing the heavens, the wheel of the charging chariot of the sun, its axle and spokes—all of these imaginary images can be traced to the same conceptual world. When the arms of the cross run in a clockwise direction, this indicates the rising of the sun, waking, growing, maturing. When the arms, however, run counterclockwise, this signifies demise and death.

40

FRANZ ALFRED SIX

The Propaganda of the Street and the Masses

First published in *Die politische Propaganda der NSDAP im Kampf um die Macht* (Heidelberg: Druckerei Winger, 1936), 32–38.

Not one among the parties in that criminal "November State" has managed to assign the proper respect due the propaganda campaign, the mass rally, the press, and all the tools of menial work, nor to deploy them as instruments to roil the masses to the heights of frenzy as extensively as the National Socialists. [. . .] The fight for the streets is an expression of the modern political struggle in the party state. As the masses enter the halls of history, the aim of every revolutionary organization has become to herald its stewardship of state by taking possession of the street. Marxism, as the first political organization of the great masses in recent history, established possession of the street as a basis for the legal claim to take control of the state. When Marxism set the masses in motion for the first time and took them to the streets under the motto "Freedom to the Streets!," this was a declaration of war against the existing state, a weighing of forces on the balances of power. All the early successes that Marxism counted to its credit, both political and economic, were attained as the result of pressure from mass demonstrations and strikes. Every one of Marxism's significant achievements has been hard-won with the threat of the masses in the streets. In this manner, the structure of the old state has been dismantled mortar by mortar until in the end, as lords of the streets, they tore it asunder.

The National Socialist idea is the antithesis of Marxism; the National Socialist movement is thus created for the express purpose of defeating this enemy. In order for the National Socialist idea to have an impact, it had to be brought to the public: "*The young movement, from the first day, espoused the standpoint that its idea must be put forward spiritually but that the defense of this spiritual platform must, if necessary, be secured by strong-arm tactics.*"[1] When the movement was denied the opportunity to advance its ideas, when the attendant natural right to the streets was contested, it was forced to resort to using similar means as its adversary.

What is more, effecting political decisions by speaking in parliament is not among National Socialist tactics, for instead National Socialism addresses the masses directly, employing the most modern means of propaganda, demonstrations, and mass rallies. If it were ever to win over the masses by carrying out propaganda campaigns, it had to go head-to-head with the Marxist masses who were prepared to defend their dominance on the streets by any means necessary. The first prerequisite to conducting propaganda campaigns, to reaching the *Volk* and the masses of workers, was thus regaining control of the streets. The streets had to be wrested from the adversary.

"What had given Marxism its success," writes Adolf Hitler, "was its complete combination of political will and activist brutality."[2] Terror became the expression of its political activity. Prior to that, decisions relating to power had presumably been fought out on the barricades, but the bludgeoning of opponents as a political strategy was unheard of as yet. In the seventy years of its struggle against the Bismarck government, it elevated the use of terror to unprecedented pinnacles of proficiency and, with the seizure of power, even transferred it to the state. This political strategy, which originated as a display of power at mass demonstrations, became a terrorist tactic against individuals and the masses under Bolshevism, and in the Weimar Republic it assumed a form of police terror that ultimately went as far as spiritual, intellectual rape in its terrorist domination of schools and universities.

If National Socialism were to carry the struggle for power full term, it would have to form a combat force vested with the authority to tackle the confrontation with this adversary at an ideological level, but also in terms of real political power. It was to this end that Adolf Hitler established the Storm Troopers, the SA, and the SS as emissaries representing the idea of National Socialism and as protectors of its propaganda and organization and outlined their position in the notion of "political soldiers." As the human embodiment of the National Socialist idea, they were to represent the new type of man, a man of the future who promised to deliver the political decisions of the future. This type must be bursting with the character of that military tradition that has been known in Germany since time immemorial—which, in its spontaneity, discipline, and bravery, has always been at the core of the German soldier's glory. This military tradition of the "career soldier" must be accompanied by political prowess and political instinct, which are the very characteristics that endow the career soldiers with purpose and motivation in the first place.

[. . .] The SA and the SS, as bearers of this battle, were thus forced to take their fight to the streets. As members of a political organization structured along military lines, they could not appear in civilian clothing, but on the other hand, as representatives of a spiritual-intellectual revolutionary movement, they could not simply adopt or imitate the uniform and equipage of the old army. So, they designed their own *political uniform,* the brown shirt.[3] One characteristic of any revolutionary political movement is that it creates a visually recognizable sign as an expression of its internal stance in its uniforms and symbols, which in turn render its members publicly recognizable as adherents to a certain worldview. Thus, Hitler's political soldiers saw in the brown shirt a profession of faith and in the swastika flags and standards sacred symbols of supreme majesty.

Much like the uniform, the flag—as the symbol of an epoch—bears its stamp and is as much an expressive sign of a new will and a new conviction. The swastika flag emerged from the knowledge that as long as the National Socialist movement rejected the old army uniform as a model for its political dress, then the black, white, and red flag was, by the same token, "a symbol of conditions that could be overcome by Marxism only under anything but glorious circumstances and attendant effects, ill suited as a symbol under which this same Marxism would be annihilated."[4] The new flag was a mythic symbol of battle for the future of the new state. The red background with the white circle and swastika in its center, striking in its effect—worn as an armband and as the party badge—was the best provocation of [National Socialism's] adversaries and a luminous sign visible from a great distance to adherents of the movement. As Adolf Hitler writes, this symbol "was the very best embodiment of the movement's will. As National Socialists, we see our program in our flag. In red we see the social idea of the movement, in white the nationalistic idea, in the swastika the mission of the struggle for the victory of the Aryan people and, by the same token, the victory of the idea of creative work, which as such always has been and always will be anti-Semitic."[5]

This was the symbol the SA and the SS had before their eyes when they embarked upon their march to the streets. They marched into workers' quarters, into the citadels of Marxism, and there they subdued the terror. They drove from town to town in long convoys of trucks, bringing the National Socialist idea to the remotest regions of the lowlands, areas where nary a speaker would venture to go. So the SA and the SS became the guarantors of the movement, harbingers of the idea, and vehicles for its propaganda. By seeking out their opponents in their own camps, they were able to draw skeptics and adversaries to the movement in a pitched battle. Once they had subdued the terror and breached "enemy lines" so that the organization could follow in their footsteps, there was no longer any stopping the movement's victory march.

Through their conduct, appearance, and discipline, the SA man and the SS man, assigned the task of special service, were the public face of the National Socialist worldview, the embodiment of the National Socialist movement's strength. The tremendous efficacy of the SA and the SS lay in their courageous dedication and their readiness for action. The public risking of their lives, the daily state of readiness were militant expressions of the heroic conception of the National Socialist cast of mind, and the SA and SS men were bearers of the National Socialist will. The hundreds who fell to their deaths from the formations performed a sacrificial deed that could only emanate from their sheer strength of conviction and force of spirit. This anonymous martyrdom put the adversary on the moral defensive and brought the ambivalent masses under the spell of the National Socialist idea. Only those who envision the greatness of an idea can go to their death for it. Their death was propaganda in deed, testimony to the strength of the idea and the movement. Battle and sacrifice only served to fortify the will to take the world by storm in these truly great warriors of a worldview and thrust the movement forward.

It was the natural expression of the popular belief that the SA and the SS who had made the blood sacrifice of three to four hundred of their men should, of course, have earned themselves the glory of heroes, and the notion quickly set in that these soldiers had fallen not on behalf of a political party but, much like casualties of war, had given their lives for the freedom of the fatherland.

Through the efforts of the SA and the SS, the propaganda campaign became an expression of power; it was in itself will to power. These overwhelming demonstrations, in which the full force of the movement's tremendous momentum flourished, were the most powerful political weapon on the road to the idea's breakthrough. One of the conclusions to be drawn from the history of political struggle is that parades and marches are capable of exerting the profoundest influence on public sentiment and deeply affecting the souls of the *Volk*. The German has a particular affinity for and a unique understanding of public expressions of power that are only this pronounced in the German. The German *Volk* is shaken and swept up in the feeling of self inhering in the power of such public displays. It evokes in the German a sense of pride and confidence in being linked to this strength and represented by this power. National Socialism has brought it to the public in this march to confident consciousness. It brought to light the spirit and the will of a new day, of the structure of power in the future Third Reich.

[. . .] Demonstration

Inasmuch as the propaganda campaign may be said to have been the best weapon in the National Socialist arsenal, the impact of this form of propaganda attained the requisite depth and fortification though the mass rallies and demonstrations. It is a characteristic peculiar to National Socialist propaganda that it has lent its own bent to those methods long since recognized as strategies for leading the masses, and this is what determines the drastic penetrative force of its style of combat. [. . .]

National Socialism had to develop a form of assembly based on experiences it gleaned from knowledge of its opponent and that was congruent with the fundamental principles of the nature of the National Socialist struggle. It is for this reason that the National Socialist movement, from its very inception, differentiated between the evening discussion forum and the mass rally. The purpose of the evening discussion forum [*Heimatabend*] was to educate party comrades and reinforce National Socialist thought processes. The verbal articulation of the party program that took place in these forums served to clarify ambiguities in its conceptualization and to establish general guidelines. Here, the young party comrade was afforded occasion to speak and to rehearse the presentation of his ideas. The evening discussion forum also provided the opportunity to attract sympathizers and other adherents who were already familiar with the idea, in the hope of later convincing them to sign up as bona fide members of the organization. It was here that every fledgling local group assumed its organizational stability and spiritual, intellectual moorings. Even though the evening discussion forums extended far beyond the limited framework of the members' meetings, they were nevertheless convened with the aim of calling together a small circle of National Socialists or such persons who hoped to join the party.

Different standards had to be applied to the *mass rally.* The goal of these public people's assemblies was to unite large masses of people, opponents and adherents alike, in the hope of influencing or persuading them through the sheer force of oratory and of the presentation's content. Here, the main objective was to establish a direct connection between party leadership and the *Volk;* it was the ideal opportunity for clarifying to the people assembled here the movement's program and idea in the hope of winning their support for the movement. The mass assembly was thus the place ideally suited to strengthening the party's image and solidifying its powers of persuasion. Once the movement had gained a certain degree of widespread publicity, the primary task of National Socialist propaganda was to draw the masses to their assemblies. As has already been stressed, it could hardly be in the best interest of a workers' party to restrict solicitation of its organizational base to intellectual, bourgeois, and petty bourgeois circles. Just as the propaganda was tailored to the purpose of enlisting the support of the working-class population, so too was it paramount that invitations to National Socialist people's assemblies similarly addressed this grassroots level. In light of the fact that, since the advent of Marxist parties, no other party had dared to contest Marxism's claim to exclusive ownership of the "proletariat," the convening of public people's assemblies—with the attendant appeal to every individual worker—naturally came as a challenge to these opponents whose organizations responded with the old familiar charge of "provocation of the proletariat" in no time at all. Both the invitations for public attendance of the rallies printed on the red posters and the positions taken on political issues were consciously construed to provoke opponents into attending the National Socialist assemblies. Adolf Hitler describes in his work the ever-changing tactics of Marxist adversaries in contending with the mass rallies of the National Socialists—tactics that were almost uniformly directed at all the pivotal structures of the National Socialist movement.

Notes

1. Adolf Hitler, *Mein Kampf* (Munich: Verlag Franz Eher Nachfolger GmbH, 1927), 534.
2. Ibid., 532.
3. See Hans Schwarz van Berk, *Die sozialistische Auslese* (Socialist Selection) (Breslau, 1934), 25ff.

> Revolutionaries have their own uniform. They are recognizable, responsible representatives of their cause and thus must be intent on displaying a typical outward appearance. That goes without saying and need not be enforced by regulation.
>
> Nothing is better suited to illustrating this point than the history of the brownshirt. Hitler wore it for pragmatic reasons while he was under fortress arrest; a few loyal followers who visited him similarly began wearing it simply because they were inspired to thus express their devotion. These few soon became many. The first brownshirt was colored in blood, then the second, the third, the tenth was riddled with bullet holes, and so it became the martyrs' dress, and the material from which it was made assumed the same attraction as everything that is consecrated in blood.

4. Hitler, *Mein Kampf,* 494. [Translation altered slightly—Eds.].
5. Ibid.

41

FRANZ ALFRED SIX

The Power of the Spoken Word

First published in *Die politische Propaganda der NSDAP im Kampf um die Macht* (Heidelberg: Druckerei Winger, 1936), 44–47.

In [the NSDAP's] fourteen-year struggle for power, a cadre of orators emerged from the [party] who, in their political dexterity and rhetorical skill, represent an unprecedented occurrence in German history. "We did not systematically recruit these orators and train them to become brilliant rhetoricians," writes Dr. Goebbels, "they sprouted and grew from the movement itself. It was inner enthusiasm that provided them the energy and ability to have such an effective galvanizing influence on the masses."[1] The impact these speakers had, born of the sheer force of the idea, was that thousands of additional orators followed in their wake, and every political soldier thus became a successful champion of his worldview. The strength of these National Socialist orators and the success of the party's propaganda stemmed from the same source: namely, the art of simplifying the constituent facts of political issues, of unraveling complicated, seemingly indecipherable connections, and the headstrong promulgation of certain thought processes that follow from the National Socialist worldview. In their acknowledgment of the interaction between propaganda and rhetoric, these orators applied the fundamental principles of propaganda to the spoken word, and this in turn was decisive in determining the design of the propaganda itself. Speaking was to them synonymous with developing the will of the *Volk*, with developing momentum toward political resolve. "In the political struggle, the spoken word is not just a repository for conceptual knowledge, it becomes the symbol of and the vehicle for mass public sentiment; not a means of communication, but rather the watchword and weapon of political action."[2]

Adolf Hitler, in *Mein Kampf,* devoted a substantial amount of space to his discussion of the spoken word and to oratory techniques; in so doing, he provided the first systematic treatment of contemporary rhetoric.

To speak is to be capable of leading and steering the masses. The effect and force of a speech is to a large degree already placed in the offing through the generation of highly charged psychological anticipation in the audience before the speaker appears. This is generated even through the impatience of the waiting audience and is further intensified by the ceremonial National Socialist protocol for mass meetings as set forth by Dr. Goebbels. There must be receptivity on the part of the audience before the speaker even takes the floor, and it should be his first words that unleash this pent-up enthusiasm.

The power of oratory is above all a development of the individual's own forces of will; it is a spiritual-intellectual struggle that involves vanquishing the weaker will of the masses and subordinating it to the influence of one's own. The National Socialist orator, for example, never displayed any consideration for his audiences. In his audience, he placed the German *Volk* in the docket; he laid bare the *Volk*'s own weaknesses on their bodies, didn't praise them, but rather browbeat them with facts.

The mass audience is generally less impressed by the sheer scope of knowledge than it is by the persuasive power and fanaticism with which a view is presented, with the speaker's confidence in his ability to convey his opinion and assertions in apodictic sentences. By gradually layering one thought upon the next, while at the same time leaving his audience uncertain about the direction this thought will take, he intensifies their anticipation until the moment arrives in which the tension is released when his final statement is spoken like a linguistic trigger. Here, the art of "dialogue"—the ability to discern any objections still latent in every individual and defuse them from the very outset—is particularly crucial. In those days, writes Adolf Hitler, "I learned something important in a short time: *to strike the weapon of reply out of the enemy's hand myself.*"[3] Similarly, it would be erroneous to think that the speaker's effect on the crowd is one-sided. The effect of a speech is always reciprocal. "The stump orator," Adolf Hitler continues,

> will always let himself be borne by the great masses in such a way that instinctively the very words come to his lips that he needs to speak to the hearts of his audience. And if he errs, even in the slightest, he has the living corrective before him. As I have said, he can read from the facial expression of his audience whether, firstly, they understand what he is saying; whether, secondly, they can follow the speech as a whole; and to what extent, thirdly, he has convinced them of the soundness of what he has said. If—firstly—he sees that they do not understand him, he will become so primitive and clear in his explanations that even the last member of his audience must understand him; if he feels—secondly—that they cannot follow him, he will construct his ideas so cautiously and slowly that even the weakest member of the audience is not left behind, and he will—thirdly—if he suspects that they do not seem convinced of the soundness of his argument, repeat it over and over in constantly new examples. Sensing their unspoken objections, he himself will utter them, and continue to confute and explode them, until at length even the last group of an opposition, by its very bearing and facial expression, enables him to recognize its capitulation to his argument.[4]

The speaker is energized by the crowd in direct proportion to the degree to which he has enthused them. The crowd lives with him, accompanying his every gesture and movement, [and] is more overcome by emotion than convinced by dint of reason. His exertion elevates the crowd to the heights of frenzy, releases all its inner drives, and may just as easily let them crash back to the ground.

The rhetorical effect is equally subject to the influences of time and place. As I have already mentioned, according to the National Socialist methods of conducting mass meetings, one factor in determining the mood of the crowd was to never hold a workers' demonstration at a bourgeois meeting place or, in any case, to be sure that at least the surface image of flags, banners, and symbols reflected a celebratory spirit, and that this effect was drastically intensified through the presence of large masses of brownshirts. Similarly, the time of day has a defining influence on the success of a meeting. The experience of event organizers has shown that it is difficult to animate crowds in the morning and afternoon, that their mood remains stoic and that they are, on the other hand, more receptive in the evening hours. "In all these cases we have to do with an encroachment upon man's freedom of will. This applies most, of course, to meetings attended by people with a contrary attitude of will, who must now be won over to a new will. In the morning and even during the day, people's willpower seems most energetically resistant in its struggle against any attempt to foist upon them a foreign will and a foreign opinion. At night, however, they succumb more easily to the dominating force of a stronger will."[5]

The successes of the National Socialist movement's oral propaganda are, to a large degree, indebted to all these insights into mass psychology and their attendant application to the technique of the mass meeting.

Notes

1. Joseph Goebbels, *Kampf um Berlin: der Anfang* (Munich: Verlag Franz Eher Nachfolger GmbH, 1934), 211.
2. Emil Obergfell, "Die Problematik der Subjektivität in der politischen Tagespresse," (PhD diss., Donaueschingen, 1934), 44.
3. Adolf Hitler, *Mein Kampf* (Munich: Verlag Franz Eher Nachfolger GmbH, 1927), 466.
4. Ibid., 471.
5. Ibid., 474–75.

FIGURE 2. Nazi campaign poster from the 1932 German presidential election: "Give your voice to the man of power, Hitler." Nazi propagandist Erwin Schockel criticized this poster for its cluttered design. Erwin Schockel, *Das politische Plakat: Eine psychologische Betrachtung* (Munich: Zentralverlag der NSDAP, Franz Eher Nachfolger GmbH, 1939), 198.

42

ERWIN SCHOCKEL

Good and Bad Posters

First published as "Gute und schlechte Plakate," in *Das politische Plakat* (Zentralverlag der NSDAP, Franz Eher Nachfolger GmbH, 1939), 197, 198, 203, 206, 237.

One NSDAP poster deserves special attention: the one titled "Just One Man" [see figure 2]. [Translation of figure 2 text follows.]

One Man against Party Cadavers and a Stack of Special Interests!
Center (Bavarian People's Party)
Christian Unions
German People's Party
People's Conservatives
Iron Front
Social Democratic Reich Banner
Free Trade Unions
State Party of Democratic Freethinkers
Economic Parties, . . .
NSDAP Alone: 11 Million
Hindenburg Voters Combined: 18 Million
Cast your vote for the strongest man = Hitler

FIGURE 3. Nazi campaign poster from the 1932 German presidential election. Nazi propagandist Erwin Schockel praised this poster for its direct presentation. Erwin Schockel, *Das politische Plakat: Eine psychologische Betrachtung* (Munich: Zentralverlag der NSDAP Franz Eher Nachfolger GmbH, 1939), 206.

In detail, the following conclusions can be drawn: A good job has been done both in the division of space and the arrangement of text. The selection of the Führer's image as an eye-catcher is good even in that it serves as a resting point for the eye in the confusing array of details in the overall picture, and the viewer's eye automatically returns to the image again and again.

Both the content and its visual representation—with the "Stack of Special Interests" placed in opposition to "NSDAP Alone: 11 Million" and the "Hindenburg Supporters Combined: 18 Million"—is flawless.

The resulting challenge to the viewer seems logical and convincing: "Give your vote to the strongest man."

And yet, here comes the big "however."

Of all things, the primary theme of the whole poster—the Führer portrait—is simply horrendous.

Whether this is due to the photograph itself or to the touch-up or the quality of reproduction cannot be determined. The effect is that of an actor from an American film shot with a soft-focus lens. This image destroys the whole effect. "The strongest man" would have to look like the Führer who is depicted in the picture "We are taking the fate of the nation into our hands!" or in the picture showing him together with Hindenburg—in short, our Führer the way he really looks.

We might look for an explanation for the selection of this particular picture in the fact that such a photograph is likely to have special appeal to women.

Women, who comprise a considerable portion of voters, are, as we know, more easily influenced by outward appearances. [. . .]

It goes without saying that this poster [see figure 3] is infinitely more effective. Its effectiveness is already improved by the superficial effect of harmonious coherence evoked by the poster as a whole. The strength, composure, and benevolence written all over the Führer's face speak to the viewer. The impression it leaves on people whose souls remain uncorrupted must have been good. What is more, the fact that the poster was printed in white against a black background must have made it stand out as an eye-catcher amid the garish colors of the advertising pillars of the time.

43

DAS SCHWARZE KORPS

With German Protestant Catholic Greetings

First published as "Mit deutsch-evangelisch-katholischem Gruß," in *Das Schwarze Korps,* 15 May 1935, 13.

As unsettling as it must be for an old dyed-in-the-wool National Socialist to see the way this person or that who could not do enough to vilify National Socialism prior to 30 January is now screaming "Heil Hitler" at the top of his lungs, preferably with both arms raised in salute, it's just as amusing to observe the way many in Germany still seek to circumvent the use of the salute that has since become commonplace. But the real fun begins when you take a look at official documents issued by the pastorate. Some pastors have taken to signing their memos with the closing "with German greetings" (and there's really nothing wrong with that). Others seek to avoid the awkward closing by simply signing their names. Recently, though, a pastor in Goseck really took the cake by signing his letter with the closing "with German Protestant greetings."

But, lest we violate the equality of denominations, let us also cite the Catholic equivalent: the "non-Catholic" proprietor of the convent bakery Kleinbeeren in Berlin's Steglitz district uses the closing "with German Catholic greetings." In recognition of the noble sentiment motivating this moneymonger, we've reproduced his newsletter in its entirety here:

> To the honorable directors . . .
>
> The convent bakery Kleinbeeren is operated by Catholics, unlike the convent bread once owned by Franciscans that is still on the market and for which the undersigned had organized arrangements for its sale.
>
> The previous proprietor, a Franciscan monk, was a turncoat who took off to Brazil "on vacation." The current owners of this former convent bakery are not Catholics.
>
> Would you be so kind as to allow us to solicit your business, for the event that this does no damage to any master baker, or at the very least to sample the wares of the "convent bakery Kleinbeeren"?
>
> The undersigned—as he readily concedes—is seeking to recover financial damages suffered as a result of the Franciscan monk's traitorous decision to go "on vacation." He would be most grateful for any support you may lend him in this endeavor.
>
> In anticipation of your cordial assistance, I have included here a gift certificate which you may use to order a sample bread, which I would be happy to deliver personally in order to reassure you that what I contend is true.
>
> With German Catholic Greetings,
> Convent Bakery Kleinbeeren
> Hans Sieger

44

WILFRID BADE

The Party Rally Day of Victory

The Victory of Faith

First published as "Der Parteitag des Sieges—Der Sieg des Glaubens," in *Deutschland erwacht: Werden, Kampf, und Sieg der NSDAP,* edited by Wilfrid Bade (Altona Bahrenfeld: Cigaretten Bilderdienst, 1933), 144–51.

On 1 September 1933, the fifth party rally [*Parteitag*] of the NSDAP opened in Nuremberg.

[Rudolf] Hess, the sober, the clear, the man ill disposed toward all things effusive, called it "the Victory Rally." And it is by this name that it will live on—as the rally marking the victory finally won, following on the heels of the 1927 rally of breakthrough and the rally of 1929, situated as it was between slaughters, a rally of gathering strength.

It is overwhelming, the scene the old imperial city of Nuremberg has to offer in these first days of September, when we begin storing the harvest in the barns. Even those who are accustomed to the festive marches, to the enormous mass demonstrations, to hundreds of thousands of cheering people, to enthusiastic national comrades, to hours of deep solemnity and sublime devotion, even those who have participated in previous congresses are caught up in the elemental force of it!

The force of these days is overpowering!

Never before has there been such a grand march-in-review, such a confluence of masses. The heavens spread an enormous pale blue silk blanket on the skies above and bless us with a glorious day of beautiful Hitler weather as the movement gathers together. [. . .]

If you had left it up to each individual to decide whether or not to come, not a soul in all of Germany would have stayed home; you wouldn't have seen a single brownshirt anywhere else in Germany—all of them, all these millions, would have made the pilgrimage to Nuremberg to pay homage to the Führer, to cheer him, and to celebrate victory together with everyone else.

But it is impossible to cram millions upon millions of people into a city: that alone—getting these enormous crowds here, lodging, feeding, transporting them, setting them out to march back and forth and getting them home again—involved a master stroke on the part of event organizers. [. . .]

And then the rally commences, on Friday, 1 September, in the festively decorated hall in Luitpold Arena.

Deputy Führer Hess, Adolf Hitler's most loyal supporter, opens the ceremony.

Composed and stern, his eyes peer out from beneath his bushy brows, his chin chiseled to an angle: "I hereby open the fifth NSDAP rally, the first rally since the National Socialist takeover of power.

"I hereby open the Victory Rally."

And with that, the first endless roar of applause ascends from the crowd.

With a single sentence, everyone is transported headlong into the core sentiment of these days.

Hess continues, and his taut features grow sterner and more angular yet, "First and foremost, I would like to commemorate our dead." All at once, the crowd rises to its feet.

And, as the chief of staff approaches to read the list of the fallen, arms go up in the air.

Behind the chief of staff, the flag of 9 November hangs bloodred from its staff, supported by an SS man. Quietly, the drums strike up, as name upon name echoes through the hall, name upon name—well over one hundred, two hundred, three hundred—and still, the chief of staff is not through. It is a distressingly long list. [. . .]

Thunderous adulations of "Heil!" to the Führer roll through the enormous banquet hall like thunder. Then the Bavarian minister of the interior and *Gauleiter* Wagner reads the Führer's proclamation, which includes the memorable words "The National Socialist movement is not here to preserve the federal states of the past but to liquidate them in favor of the future Reich. The state is not the pillar of the Reich; it rests rather solely and exclusively on the German *Volk* and the National Socialist movement."

The city of Nuremberg honors the nation's Führer by presenting him with the famous copper engraving by Albrecht Dürer, *The Knight, Death and the Devil*—and it could not have found a more fitting gift than this beautiful old engraving, which depicts a knight in shining armor, riding fearless and beyond reproach, unscathed by death and the devil, untouched by enmity, envy, and animosity, with his gaze fixed forward, set on victory and fulfillment.

The same day, the Führer speaks at the party's big conference on culture. He is crystal clear in his delineation of the racial foundations of every form of art, and one can sense how deeply he speaks from the heart in this matter. [. . .]

The next day brings with it the big midlevel functionary's roll call on the Zeppelin Field. One hundred sixty thousand functionaries report to the call, along with one hundred thousand SA men and SS men and one hundred sixty thousand from the civilian guard of the party. There is no end to the stream of bloodred flags flooding into the gigantic field, gushing down the stairs in ever-increasing numbers, in an electrifying and, in a strange way, enchanting sight. It seems as if this bloodred stream of flags will never end, as if it symbolizes the immortality of National Socialist Germany.

There they stand—one hundred fifty thousand strong—local group leaders and regional leaders, cell leaders and neighborhood monitors, district directors, press agents, propaganda directors, officials with myriad tasks to fulfill, old fighters in the name of Adolf Hitler's idea, tested and tried a thousand times in battle.

Flags flutter above them; the eagle of the German emancipation movement looms large and luminous before them. Greenery and foliage line the boundaries of this expansive field, which, even filled as it is with this immense horde of human beings, still leaves room for more.

It is a gripping image—this brown army of heart and mind, the way it cheers its Führer in one unanimous, unified, and uniformed squall. The way the flags take wind and rise, the banners billowing boldly and big, and the glorious swastika shining victorious.

Year upon year they have struggled and fought, and they know that years upon years of struggle lie ahead before victory is theirs, before it is secure in the hearts of the German people, until no one can so much as imagine anything but a National Socialist Reich. [. . .]

In the afternoon, the Führer stands before sixty thousand members of Hitler Youth. They too have come to pitch their tents; they too have set up camp and marched as only men from the ranks of the SA and the SS are able.

And now, here they stand to pledge allegiance to the Führer and to tell him that his call to the future is not in vain, that already today, already now, as young boys and girls, they solemnly swear to continue his work, and to pass it on to their children in their turn, pure and unadulterated, as if they had received it from the hand of Adolf Hitler himself—these, the German youth of the near future.

For several minutes, the Führer is so overwhelmed by the effervescent salvos of ovation that he cannot even take the floor. Every time he raises his hand to quell the crowd, he is inundated by another springtide of "Heils!" and he has no option but to let his hand fall and humbly concede to letting these absolutely stunning outpourings of joy gush over him. And here, before the flaming passion of youth, the severity that has held his brow earnest in the last few days melts away: his face suddenly lights up in a burst of spectacularly delighted and relieved laughter. Adolf Hitler, laughing—he is so profoundly overjoyed by what he is experiencing here; and in fact, it is true—where might any statesman, any *Volksführer,* ever experience anything of the sort?

It is the grace of God, a gift of gratitude for the past fourteen years of drudgery and toil—and it is by far the best way to give thanks to the Führer.

His words to the German youth are bold and binding. He does not talk down to them; he demands that they strain themselves to the utmost in the effort to understand what he is saying. He formulates his sentences as if he were speaking to a crowd of adults. He sings the praises of camaraderie and challenges them to take the ideals of youth with them as they pass into manhood, never to be ashamed of them and never to forget them. He challenges them to practice virtue, to be loyal and brave, and to honor the sacrifices of their fathers. [. . .]

On Sunday, 3 September, the rally reaches its climax with the pageant of SA, SS, and Shock Troop Adolf Hitler [Stoßtrupp Adolf Hitler]. A hundred thousand men descend upon the Luitpold field, and their multicolored caps glisten in the sun like a gigantic blooming flowerbed. Midnight blue mingles with sulfuric yellow, bleeds into dark brown, climbs to a light green, turns black, blazing red, dark burgundy, forest green, dark ocher, light blue, white, pale grey mixed with field grey, stark white, emerald green, brick red, rich cobalt blue and the royal red of the staffs—quietly, the play of colors sways to and fro above the brown backdrop of uniforms, until finally one single commando brings the hundred thousands to a sudden standstill, frozen stiff into a single unit.

45

WILLY LIEBEL

Five Years: Nuremberg, City of Party Rallies

First published in *Fünf Jahre Stadt der Reichsparteitage Nürnberg,* edited by Willy Liebel (Nuremberg: K. Ulrich, 1938), 36–42.

"City of the National Socialist Reich Party Rally." One must imagine what it means for a big city like Nuremberg to have its population suddenly more than double in the course of a single day. While a "mere" 313,372 visitors to the Reich Party Rally of the National Socialist Party were registered in 1933, that number had already climbed to 501,822 in 1934, and by 1935 even reached 509,528. In 1936 and 1937, rallies were host to 489,265 and 497,196 people, respectively. These are overwhelming numbers, but the full scope becomes apparent only when you add to this the population of the city of Nuremberg. After Berlin, Vienna, and Hamburg, that makes the city of the Reich Party Rally, temporarily at least, the fourth largest city in the German Reich. But one has to bear in mind the fact that these other cities occupy large areas, but in Nuremberg at the time of the Reich Party Rally, approximately one million people gather in a very cramped space.

For every thousand square meters of space at the 1 September 1935 congress in Berlin, there were five people, but at the time of the 1933 rally in Nuremberg, there were nine.

It goes without saying that providing for such masses of people and regulating traffic places the highest demands on the city. One has to imagine the overwhelming amounts of bread, meat, milk, beer, etc. that must be made available and the substantial preparation involved in delivering them.

Seen from this perspective, the question of traffic assumes particular significance. During the Reich Party Rally, the German Reich Railroad and other transportation services performed overwhelming feats. In 1937, 1,213 special trains were needed. Over two million people were conveyed by the railroad. [. . .]

As overwhelming as the organizational achievements during the Reich Party Rally are, they shrink by comparison to the gigantic construction projects undertaken in the past five

FIGURE 4. Albert Speer with designs for the 1934 Reich Party Rally in Nuremberg. Collection of Foreign Records Seized, Heinrich Hoffmann (no. 242.1), box 214, item 21915–2, U.S. National Archives and Records Administration, College Park, Md.

years at the rally grounds. The point here is not to elaborate on the details of these tremendous works; it would be impossible to do so in the framework of this brief report. Here, only scant reference and overview can be provided.

The Reich Party Rally structures. At the Führer's order, powerful, monumental structures are currently under construction that have already attracted attention and great admiration the world over. This became apparent at the 1937 World Exposition in Paris, where, in addition to a model of the entire rally grounds, a large-scale model of the Märzfeld [March Field] and a model of the Congress Hall were on display. Furthermore, at the First German Exhibition of Art and Architecture in 1938 in the capital of the movement, Munich, the major focus of the exhibit was on the new structures in Nuremberg.

Overwhelming artistic and technological achievements have emerged from the countless construction sites of the Administrative Union for the National Socialist Reich Party Rally in Nuremberg in the past few years. The Luitpold Arena was built alongside the redesigned old banquet hall where Adolf Hitler spoke numerous times during the period of struggle and that is thus closely tied to the history of the National Socialist movement. Traditionally, it is here in the Luitpold Arena that the SA roll call takes place and where the SA, the SS, and the National Socialist Motor Corps [Nationalsozialistisches Kraftfahrkorps; motorized bike units] annually renew their vows of allegiance to the Führer. The Führer's architect, Albert Speer, designed these parade grounds together with the city Building Surveyor's Office and its Parks Department. The 84,000-square-meter surface of the parade area accommodates 150,000 people, and the surrounding bleachers 50,000. A processional avenue 260 meters long and 18 meters wide and paved with heavy granite slabs leads from the main bleachers to the Memorial to the Fallen Soldiers.

Next to the Luitpold Arena, the Congress Hall is under way, for which the Führer laid the cornerstone at the Reich Party Rally in 1935. In accordance with the Führer's suggestions, the Nuremberg architect Professor Ludwig Ruff, prior to his all-too-untimely death, designed the plans, which have now been entrusted to his son for their completion. The Congress Hall is the largest architectural structure currently under construction anywhere in the world. The hall will provide enough space to accommodate fifty thousand people, and the cubic capacity of the entire structure is slated to exceed 3 million cubic meters. In 1937, the overwhelming work of soil compaction at the construction site was finished. The foundation and masonry for the basement have since been completed as well. The masonry for the ground floor of the pavilion has already been erected, with the exception of the outer walls. The window breasts on the third floor of the pavilion are expected to be installed in time for the 1938 Reich Party Rally. The 95-meter-wide Grand Promenade, designed by Professor Speer to be paved with Jurassic marble, leads from the Congress Hall to the March Field and past the German Stadium situated near the grounds of the Zeppelin Field. The main and auxiliary bleachers together make up a seating capacity of forty-eight thousand. During the Reich Party Rally, overwhelming demonstrations have taken place on this field: the Labor Service roll call, the parade of midlevel functionaries, the pageants, and march-in-review ceremonies of the German army before the Führer. The German Stadium, future site of the NS-Kampfspiele (National Socialist combat games), will be erected in granite according to blueprints by Professor Speer.[1] Four hundred five thousand national comrades will be seated in this overwhelming stadium—the largest in the world. The installation is 560 meters in length, 450 in width, and 83 meters in height. Its construction will require 1.5 billion bricks.

Similarly overwhelming in its dimensions is the March Field, the future parade grounds of the army. Preparing the 170,000 cubic meters of building stone needed for its construction would require 4.2 million man-hours if completed using the old methods of masonry.

And yet, these overwhelming works do not stand alone but rather are components of an incomparably great total work of art: the National Socialist Reich Party Rally Grounds at Nuremberg.

Note

1. The NS-combat games (NS-Kampfspiele) were created by a decree of Adolf Hitler on 30 November 1936 ordering athletic and sport competitions for all branches of the NSDAP to take place at future party rallies—Eds.

46

VICTOR KLEMPERER

Listening to Göring's Speech at the 1938 Nuremberg Rally

First published in *I Will Bear Witness: A Diary of the Nazi Years 1933–1941,* translated by Martin Chalmers (New York: Modern Library, 1999), 256–57.

New truck stop in Lonnewitz. Village just before Oschatz, "Long Distance Lorry Drivers' Restaurant." The huge vehicles outside, the huge portions inside. The Party Rally was coming over the loudspeaker. Announcement. The arrival of Field Marshal Göring. Introductory march, roars of triumph, then Göring's speech, about the tremendous advances, affluence, peace, and workers' good fortune in Germany, about the absurd lies and hopes of her enemies, constantly interrupted by the well-drilled roars of applause. But the most interesting thing about it was the behavior of the customers, who all came and went, greeting and taking their leave with "Heil Hitler!" But no one was listening. I could barely understand the broadcast because a couple of people were playing cards, striking the table with loud thumps, talking very loudly. It was quieter at other tables. One man was writing a postcard, one was writing in his order book, one was reading the newspaper. And landlady and waitress were talking to each other or the card-players. Truly: not one of a dozen people paid attention to the radio even for a single second, it could just as well have been transmitting silence or a foxtrot from Leipzig.

47

Law Concerning Holidays

Announced on 27 February 1934 as "Gesetz über die Feiertage." First published in *Reichsgesetzblatt* (Berlin: Reichsverlagsamt, 1934), 1:129.

The Reich government has enacted the following regulations and hereby promulgates them into law:

Article 1

The national holiday to celebrate the German *Volk* is May 1.

Article 2

The fifth Sunday before Easter [*Reminiszere*] is Veterans' Memorial Day.

Article 3

The first Sunday after St. Michael's Holiday is Thanksgiving Harvest Day.

Article 4

In addition to the national holidays cited in paragraphs 1–3 and all Sundays, the following national holidays shall be observed:

1. New Year's Day
2. Good Friday
3. Easter Monday
4. Ascension Day
5. Whit Monday
6. Day of Atonement on the Wednesday following the last of the three Trinity Sundays
7. Christmas Eve and Christmas Day

Article 5

(1) In addition to the holidays cited in Article 4, in accordance with the respective customs previously in force, national holidays are also declared in those municipalities with predominately Protestant populations on Reformation Day, and in those municipalities with predominately Catholic populations on Corpus Christi Day.
(2) The Reich minister of the interior or the administrative agency he delegates shall determine which municipalities shall be subject to the stipulations of Clause 1.

Article 6

The holidays unequivocally outlined by this law are to be treated as feast days or holidays in the spirit of state or regional regulations concerning holidays.

Article 7

(1) The Reich minister of the interior is authorized, in consultation with the Reich minister for popular enlightenment and propaganda, to promulgate legislation concerning the protection of Sundays and holidays, even such as are strictly religious in nature.
(2) Determinations surrounding the nature and organization of holiday events (Articles 1–3) shall be made by the Reich minister for popular enlightenment and propaganda in consultation with the Reich minister of the interior.

Article 8

This law goes into effect the day it is announced. At the same time, the law of 10 April 1933 . . . concerning the introduction of National Labor Day as a national holiday becomes ineffective.

Berlin, 27 February 1934

Reich Chancellor: Adolf Hitler
Reich Minister of the Interior: Frick
Reich Minister for Popular Enlightenment and Propaganda: Dr. Goebbels

48

HANNES KREMER

New Meanings for "Inherited" Customs?

First published as "Neuwertung 'überlieferter' Brauchformen?" in *Die neue Gemeinschaft* 3 (1937), 3005. Translated by Randall Bytwerk. Calvin College, German Propaganda Archive.

In our efforts to deepen National Socialist forms of behavior in the area of rituals and ceremonies, we have two main tasks. On the one hand, we must create new customs to accommodate new ideas, and on the other hand, it is necessary to adjust those customs that have grown out of the people to the "new community of the Germans," which means giving these inherited customs a new content consistent with the people's community [*Volksgemeinschaft*].

That is clear when we look at the annual calendar. First, there are the political holidays that regularly remind the people of the political achievements of the National Socialist movement during its battle for the Third Reich, along with its great idealistic motives. (30 January, 1 May, 9 November. Themes: battle, work, sacrifice).

Here it is a question of creating new customs to suit the new political worldview governing the daily organization of our *Volk* today, customs that will also enable later generations to be reminded of those forces of instinct, emotion, and spirit that have been recognized as so critical in our struggle for existence and for the security of the people's community (to cite just a few of those forces: courage, bravery, affirmation of life, awareness of duty).

These new customs develop directly from the ideas, experiences, and traditions of the party itself. One must accept the risk that in the course of their development wrong choices will occasionally be made. This is true with anything that is new. The advantage is that a strong new spirit can develop its own forms of expression, heedless of convention. But there are also those holidays that have a long history with the people, and which still may have public value, but no longer have the significance in the popular mind they once did (solstices, Christmas, etc.).

The significance of holidays and rituals—from the political standpoint—lies in the spiritual or emotional deepening of the experience of community. Thus, these historically inherited occasions for holidays and rituals, along with their living expressions, may in no way be thought less important in their educational and political effects than those newly developed in our day. If we are to attempt to make inherited customs politically useful, we must be clear that this is possible only if we give them a fundamentally new content. Even if religious fanatics object, this is justified because it deepens the sense of belonging to the people's community. Obviously, the goal here is not to serve denominational interests, but, on the contrary, it is designed to transcend the denominational fragmentation with overarching ideas to act as bridges between denominations.

It is thus necessary to give inherited customs a meaning that reaches each member of the community in the same way (that is, a political meaning that reaches the people as a whole).

"Christmas" is an example, as we will see.

When we conduct such a holiday or ceremony, we want—as in everything else—to mobilize the spiritual or emotional forces of the community for National Socialism. Nothing makes more sense than to present this inherited holiday about a *theoretical peace for all of humanity*—one whose celebration requires no national or social exigency—as a holiday about an *actual internal national peace,* which is in fact without question a critical demand of the National Socialist people's community, to each individual German. If we make visible the blessings of this actual peace, along with its foundations and requirements, then "Christmas" doubtless can also become a high point in the course of the political year. Both according to popular custom and popular view, the Christmas holiday can justifiably be seen as the festival of the homeland.

From this perspective, it can be easily integrated into the arena of politics and worldview.

But if we do this, we must understand that the Christmas holiday or Christmas festival is more than a date on the calendar that lends itself to cheap entertainment. We cannot meet our goals in the style of pre-war clubs with their "variety evenings," raffles, or the ever so popular military farce. Not even if "Bananini the Magician" or "Bear Mouth the Sword Swallower" make a guest appearance.

In light of this, the question becomes what to do in place of such things. One may object that there are rarely the means available for an "expensive celebration" and that, ultimately, there really is no readily available political content. This is the classic point at which someone, usually someone who is ignorant of pre-history, hastily comes up with some (ostensibly "authentic ancient Germanic") custom that no one understands or is moved by.

While it is certainly necessary to educate the public in matters concerning pre-history, it is nevertheless inappropriate to turn our ceremonies into versified dissertations (particularly if they are done by dilettantes!). The ceremony should appeal not to the knowledge of the few, but to the spirit, and the life sentiment of the many. They should seek not to reconstruct the presumed needs of our ancestors of two thousand years ago, but rather to speak to the needs that are very much alive in our spiritual consciousness today. We cannot set our sights on merely imitating our ancestors in our festivities. Instead, we must strive to develop effective and understandable methods that will awaken the innately Germanic forces within each German person of our century to the National Socialist idea, and this in ever new and strengthening ways. But this cannot succeed if in a ceremony we appeal to knowledge of historical customs that may or may not be common knowledge; it can only succeed if we have the courage to express today's spiritual condition in the language of our time. Who, pray tell, would possibly be moved by dull verses about the customs of our ancestors, to whom we lack any living connection, much less any concrete knowledge of their history? This may be a regrettable state of affairs. But that does not alter the facts that we must confront in our political work.

A Christmas ceremony based on events and views that are no longer comprehensible from today's perspective does more harm than good. This only serves to arouse distrust of our goals, not confidence in our ability to lead the people spiritually (which is more than necessary!). In some places, arrangements have been made for people to participate in such museum-like tours through archaic history in events dubbed "festival of light" in which, of course, representatives of every economic and professional grouping in society carry a little candle in honor of the "people's community." And of course, the "blue-collar" worker parades hand-in-hand with the "white-collar" worker across the platform. The blue-collar worker is clad in brand spanking new overalls and holds a hammer in his hand; and the white-collar worker? The best he could do to represent his position would be to don a business suit with leather elbow patches and—depending on his profession—perhaps a briefcase, drawing instruments, or a book. On the one hand, it is entirely superfluous to present, even in this context, people according to their respective "class" if we hope to appeal directly and in a unified way to the German as German (in the name of the eternal nation); on the other hand, we may not make the movement, the community, and their symbols into "living images." Because when we conduct a ceremony or a solemn holiday, this involves a serious and genuine affirmation that should find its base in the real and the true, not in sentimental illusions. We do not want simply to stir emotions at the surface level (a movie with a "happy ending" usually can do that much better!), but rather to make people aware of their responsibility for the nation's fate. We must stress that theatrics is not the same as ceremony and that ceremony is not mere performance if we hope to avoid reducing "ceremony" to just another name for the entertainment industry, but rather to view it as a serious task affecting the worldview and political life forms of the community. One known disadvantage we face is that, in many places, we do not have the "ceremonial facilities" at our disposal, and, especially when it comes to indoor festivities, this places us a decided disadvantage from the start. However, with the necessary degree of determination, we can use simple means to overcome such obstacles to the extent that they are at least tolerable. The important point is this: that we avoid the theatrical spirit and theatrical props and stay with political reality—even when we celebrate. A Christmas "festival of lights" can be an affirmation if it is done properly (and whether this is what it should be called is open for debate; we, however, think that such a literary travesty hardly merits the name "Christmas celebration"). Simply by virtue of the fact that we take advantage of the opportune moment to make visible in a festive way those things taken for granted during the rest of the year, but which are the foundations of our national life and thinking, we elevate them to the level of symbols.

Seen in the context of fundamentally sound basic premises, there is no reason that we should neglect to lend new meaning to inherited customs, especially when, as for example in the popular custom of the Christmas tree, these customs themselves present a wealth of opportunities to have a political impact. And this is precisely why we must concern ourselves with these matters—because they do "have an impact." *And if they do not have an impact that is in line with our will and sensibilities, their impact can all too easily work without and against us!*

We have no reason to forget that not long ago, the reigning pope described German Christmas customs as "pagan," and that the German bishops worked hard to change this opinion at the time. Frankly, they apparently saw in these "pagan customs" most valuable psychological props. Since, however, the highest office of the church called them a "nonessential element" of Catholic ritual, one cannot hold it against us if we rely on this judgment and keep these customs alive for the day when they fully and finally are eliminated from the church's religious rituals.

49

FRANK LEBERECHT

Call to the Fire

First published as "Aufruf zum Feuer," in *Chöre des jungen Deutschland. Eine Sammlung von Sprechören für Fest und Feier,* edited by Hans Redlich and Karl Seidelmann (Potsdam: L. Voggenreiter, 1934), 54–56.

General Information:

The majority of our choral arrangements have already been put in practice and tested. The directions for enunciation included here have been developed from actual rehearsals and, as such, have proven themselves effective.

The directions for enunciation to the chorus are intended for all those with little or no experience directing declamatory choruses.

The directions included here have divided speakers according to high or low pitch—that is, in tenor and in bass. The direction "tenor leads" does not mean that the tenor speaks alone; rather, that the entire chorus sings but that everything is to be sung according to the pitch set by the tenor. When the "bass leads," the pitch is set by the bass. [. . .]

CALL TO THE FIRE

CALL (caller): Comrades, is it time yet?
RESPONSE (chanters): The wood has been stacked.
CALL (caller): Has the bonfire been set?
RESPONSE (chanters): It's ready to crack!
CALL (caller): Is everyone ready, have you taken the count?
RESPONSE (chanters): Many are here—
RESPONSE (antagonist) (*quietly*): —still, some are absent.
RESPONSE (chanters): We have counted a thousand comrades!
RESPONSE (antagonist) (*mockingly*): —still, some are absent.
RESPONSE (chanters): We have counted a thousand comrades!
RESPONSE (antagonist) (*shrill*): —still, some are absent.
CALL (caller): If some are still absent, then do not begin
'Till I have brought the last man in!
(*heraldic fanfare*)
CALL (caller) (*emphatically*): I'm calling, listeners, step up and be near!
I call you to come, pay heed to your ear!
From the darkness of your dens, come to the brand!
I call you now on behalf of your fatherland!
RESPONSE (antagonist) (*mockingly*): Call all you want, cry as you will.
Whoever's still absent, so be it!
CALL (caller) (*joyous*): Have ye yet worry, doubt, or despairs
Shoulder them now, all these your cares!
We're building a bonfire, brightly 'twill blaze.
Cast your sorrows into the flames!
RESPONSE (antagonist) (*mockingly*): Alas, the fire, methinks
of bygone sins doth stink.
CALL (caller) (*joyous*): All your misery be consumed,
Not a trace may be exhumed,
At this hearth your vanity
Reduced to ash eternally.
(*fanfare*)

Rise from the ashes, pure as day,
You are the phoenix, German bird of prey!

(*song of the wander boys' choir*)

SPEAKER: At this hour, from all the far corners of our fatherland,
They are streaming here in droves to converge at the blazing fire.
Droves of young men and women, who have
Set out from the cantons of smaller towns,
Set out from the din of the factories,
Set out from the classrooms and lecture halls,
Set out from their daily routine, from the fray,
From their worries, from isolation.

(*song of the wanderers*)

SPEAKER: At this hour, they stream and converge,
Bavarians, Frisians, Hessians, Silesians, Westphalians,
People march—
At this hour, the Germanic tribes
Are on the march.
The highways resound with the rumble of their feet.
Their songs echo from the cliffs and hills.
Night is warmed by their laughter.

(*marching step*)

SPEAKER (*with increasing glee*): Hundredfold professions, hundredfold districts,
All with one aim:
To get to the great fire, fanned by the winds of change,
The great fire of solidarity.

(*singing softly*)

SPEAKER: From the sounds of their step—of their songs—
Of their laughter, it rings and resounds:
A wayfaring *Volk* on its way home to itself!

(*the song crescendos forcefully*)

CALL (caller): Harkener , still standing at sideline?
Come to the fire, now is the time.
Every last man I promised to bring.
Comrade, you're the last man, now come join the ring!

50

CENTRAL CULTURAL OFFICE, REICH PROPAGANDA LEADERSHIP

Honoring Fallen Heroes

NSDAP Veterans' Memorial Day Celebrations

First published in *Die Heldenehrungsfeiern der NSDAP* (Munich: NSDAP Hauptkulturamt, 1939), 8–10, 14, 22, 24, 25.

No one in Germany has been or will ever be as profoundly and painfully affected by this struggle for the existence or nonexistence of our *Volk* that has been foisted upon us by our enemies than the survivors left behind by our fallen soldiers; accordingly, no one is thus more entitled to the emotional support of the *Volk* than these wives, parents, siblings, and children who now mourn the loss of their husbands, sons, brothers, and fathers.

FIGURE 5. Heinrich Hoffmann photographing Hitler at the "march of the old guard" of party veterans in front of the Brown House (Nazi headquarters) in Munich, 9 November 1937. Postcard, "Vorbeimarsch der alten Garde am Braunen Haus." Collection of Anson Rabinbach.

They all have a right to palpable expressions of sympathy for their fate from the national community. But the community is also obligated to express its deepest sympathy, especially in those moments when their need for emotional succor is greatest. And that is in the moment of the first and most acute pain. This is when it is most important to demonstrate that the comradeship of the *Volk* is palpable fact, not merely empty platitude.

It is paramount that we reject as superficial the attitude that we will have time and opportunity enough to honor our dead in a dignified fashion once victory has been won, that we ought to thus postpone these efforts until that time. What matters is not the scope of our efforts—however grandiose or modest they may be—the question is not whether we conduct ceremonials honoring the fallen, or how often we do; rather, it involves lending adequate expression to our debt of gratitude and our reverence for the sacrifices made by the dead—to each and every one of them. It is a matter of reminding the community again and again of the magnitude of this sacrifice and the responsibility that it brings. It is not a matter of engendering an atmosphere of mourning but of galvanizing the *Volk*'s resolve to pursue the struggle, holding up as examples those who have given us their blood and their lives and acting in their names.

Materials to Be Used

Here more than for any other special occasion, the materials used in observance ceremonies (decorations, place settings, etc.) must be dignified and authentic. Paper decorations (decorative flags, garlands, etc.) are not to be used under any circumstances. If [. . .] an iron cross is used, then it may not be constructed of cardboard. It must maintain a graphic quality and dignified effect. The appropriate material to be used is plywood. The edges of the cross should be crisp, the outer silver profile as well as the swastika and year are to be raised, and the colors kept matte (no glossy varnish). [. . .]

Concerning the ceremony's inner spirit, suffice it to say that every form of theatricality is to be avoided and that cheap sentimentalities are entirely out of place, both in the music, the song and the chorus, and in the spoken word. Whenever specially trained speakers are not available, the use of poetry and other materials that might seem appropriate should be avoided completely, and instead, the clearly recognizable simplicity of example should be adhered to.

It is especially important to guard against filling the festivities with an excess of poetry and music and running the risk of turning an event into something between a poetry recital and a concert. The point of this ceremony is not to provide a forum for the recitation of every single poem that seems remotely appropriate nor to provide an entertaining hour of music. The function of the poetic word and the music is to provide the framework for the immediate purpose and nothing else. Poetry and music are well suited to preparing or strengthening the emotional receptivity of participants.

The Speaker

It is a difficult task to speak at ceremonial festivities. Polemical excesses and catchwords are inappropriate to the ceremonial address, as is thunderous applause. Thunderous applause is an indicator that the audience has deviated from the solemn mood of the ceremony. The ceremonial address is not supposed to elicit superficial accord from the crowd; it speaks to and steers the audience's emotional reception, not its intellectual response. So, the form it assumes must differ from that of a rally speech; it must be kept solemn and austere.

This is not to imply that the tone should be pastoral. It should be a soldierly speech, as soldierly as the man who delivers it. In any case, the ceremonial speaker should adequately prepare himself for and concentrate on this form of address. Neither the thought processes nor the expression thereof should be left to coincidence. [. . .]

Only to be deployed for major events in district seats and larger cities:

The prerequisite [. . .] is that experienced speakers (no dilettantes) are available who possess the speaking skills needed to read a poem or prose piece in such a way as to produce the desired effect. Generally, this will be the case only in district seats or in larger cities.

(a) "Trumpet call in honor of the dead"
(b) Poem or a prose piece selected from reading materials included here (a short passage that speaks to the sacrifices of the heroes and our gratitude)
(c) Chorus ("nothing can rob us") and
(d) Ceremonial music
(e) Address of the keynote speaker (commanding officer of the leadership corps/bearers of sovereignty) and ceremony to honor the fallen.

The keynote speaker shall either introduce his address with a citation from the Führer or shall incorporate it into his address. If the names of the fallen are not to be presented (which, in the case of central celebration in a large city is entirely conceivable from a psychological or military perspective), then during the entire memorial service the "Song of the Good Comrade" is to be played.

PART TWO

. . .

THE NATIONAL SOCIALIST WORLDVIEW

4

Between Myth and Doctrine

NAZI IDEOLOGY HAD ITS ROOTS in a broad array of *völkisch,* anti-Semitic, and pseudoscientific ideas put forward during the nineteenth century, including social Darwinism, eugenics, pan-Germanism, Aryan mysticism, and extreme nationalism. But it never developed a consistent or officially prescribed doctrine. Unlike Soviet Marxism, which relied on canonical Marxist-Leninist texts, or liberal democracy, which was based on the rule of law, the Nazi Party was more intent on publicly affirming National Socialism's "worldview" than on putting forth a coherent statement of it. Despite Hitler's frequent claim that "National Socialism is a worldview," even the leading ideologues of the movement—like Rosenberg, Krieck, Goebbels, and Hitler himself—showed little consensus about what this worldview encompassed.

Ernst Krieck (1882–1947), for a time the party's leading academic philosopher, stressed the superiority of the "*völkisch*-political totality of life" over reason, truth, and science. Krieck's concept of national political education advocated a political conception of history and pedagogy that was capable of mobilizing followers, but he was highly critical of "racial science." Alfred Rosenberg (1893–1946) relied on Houston Stewart Chamberlain's 1899 racialist tract *The Foundations of the Nineteenth Century* to promote his obscurantist "Teutonic" religion of race in his *Myth of the Twentieth Century* (1930). In this pseudoscholarly tome, Rosenberg described the authentic "Aryan" or "Nordic" man as a person of physical beauty and a higher morality, who originated in Atlantis but ultimately made Northern Europe his natural homeland. Relying loosely on myths and esoteric doctrines explicitly borrowed from Zoroastrianism and Indian religion via the nineteenth-century German philosopher Arthur Schopenhauer, Rosenberg's myth conceived of an Aryan God descended to earth and forced to join the struggle between light and darkness, racial purity and bastardization.

Largely ignored outside a small circle of devotees before 1933, Rosenberg's position in the new Reich unleashed a storm of protest against the *Myth* among established church leaders who were affronted by his declaration of a soul war (*Seelenkrieg*) against Christianity and by his claim that the immortal racial soul did not require a transcendental deity. Catholics protested his condemnation of the pope, and Protestant theologians justifiably accused him of provoking a culture war (*Kulturkampf*). In 1935, the government assured the Vatican that it did not officially sanction Rosenberg's ideas, and Rosenberg retreated; in the third edition of his *Myth* (1941), he declared that National Socialism was "neither for nor against any given denomination." The Nazi elite dismissed his book as excessively provocative and unreadable. Goebbels once called it an ideological "hiccough."

By 1935, a few commentators outside Germany began to compare National Socialism to Soviet Communism and found the two dictatorships remarkably similar in their assaults on art, literature, a free press, and especially religion. Goebbels's *Communism with the Mask Off* (1935) was Nazism's official response, claiming that unlike international and atheistic Bolshevism "directed by the Jews," National Socialism was not for export. Contrary to Rosenberg, Goebbels affirmed Nazism's belief in God and "transcendental idealism." He also claimed that unlike the Nazis, the Bolsheviks inflicted a reign of terror on their own populace. He, of course, did not see the persecution of German Jewry as an attack on Germans.

Even the concept of race, so obviously central to Nazi ideology, was never firmly defined. Hans F. K. Günther (1891–1968), dubbed "Race Günther" (Rassen-Günther) by his colleagues after publishing the first edition of his *Racial Studies of the German Volk* in 1922, was one of the most prolific racial theorists in Weimar Germany and the Third Reich.[1] Günther believed that the Nordic race could be specified according to hereditary physical characteristics, a view that brought him into conflict with his fellow race thinker and coeditor of the journal *Race* (*Rasse*), Ludwig Claus, who believed that a Nordic soul could also inhabit bodies that were not corporeally Nordic. Despite his claim to scientifically demonstrate the physical features common to any racial group, especially the Nordic race, Günther conceded that the "Germanic race" did not exist in pure form because there were many Germans who were not tall, blond, and blue-eyed, and many "un-Germanic people" who displayed such features. Thus, he allowed that race was a combination of "endowed physical features and spiritual characteristics." Günther also contended, in contrast to Hitler, that the Jews were not a race but "a nation of mixed races."

In his *Art and Race* (1928), Paul Schultze-Naumburg (1869–1949) maintained that just as biology determined the physical and spiritual characteristics of a race, art, or any "spiritual creation," was subject to the same laws as physical reproduction.[2] Consequently, works of art exhibited the traits of racial patrimony; racial principles engendered aesthetic principles, giving rise to racial similarity (*Artgleichheit*) in a people's judgments about art. In *Nordic Beauty* (1937), Schultze-Naumburg claimed that the Nordic race was superior to the classical model because it was endowed with both a "creative will" and an "internalized standard" for the epitome of beauty that, in periods of weakness, gave rise "to racially alien dogmas." The promotion of a "sublime" ideal of racial beauty also took the more prosaic form of Wolf Willrich's vulgar and sexually delirious tirades demanding a purge of the "salacious soul-baring" commercial culture and corrupting "un-Nordic" influences of the Weimar Republic. But not all theorists accepted the primacy of the Nordic ideal. Alfred Baeumler, who became a leading party philosopher after 1933, drew on his idiosyncratic reading of Nietzsche, and what he called the Germanic renaissance after the Great War, as heralding a new unity of the *Volk* constituted through the symbols of National Socialism.[3] Baeumler, who dedicated his life to giving the National Socialist movement a philosophical foundation, regarded Nazism as "German Hellenism."

The notion that ancestral Germans were originally an intoxicated, violent, and "wild" and "raging" youth cult gained currency when the cultural anthropologist Otto Höfler (1901–87) published his *Secret Cultic Societies of the Germanic Peoples* (1934). Höfler explained that he did not mean to imply that the "ecstatic" or "cultic altered state of consciousness" of the ancestral cults of Wotan-Odin led to chaos or abandon. Rather, he claimed that the demonic leagues of the ancient Germans, which he had discovered, could still empower the "festivities of Germanic communal life." Höfler's findings that the ancient Germans were "drug-crazed" members of secret cults or "berserks" (a description derived from their fear-inspiring bearskins) set off alarm bells: he seemed to glorify youthful violence, perhaps reminiscent of the Storm Troopers, which was itself violently purged between the appearance of Höfler's two-volume treatise and the 1936 publication of Harald Spehr's dismissive review in *Race*. In the end, thinkers could not reach a consensus about what it meant to be a "German." Even some of the most enthusiastic exponents of the "German spirit," such as Eberhard Freidank, admitted that the "steady diet of 'Nordicism' is a bit overdone," and Susanna Pertz expressed the frustration of trying to find the meaning of the word *Nordic*.

In part, this confusion was inevitable. As many critics of Nazism observed at the time, the party's precepts were nebulous, incoherent, and ultimately, as the Marxist philosopher Georg Lukács argued in the 1930s, based on "the destruction of reason."[4] Yet, this lack of coherence should not be mistaken for the absence of ideology. Certain basic notions, like extreme anti-Semitism, the primacy of race, and the role of the laws of nature in human affairs, were common to all National Socialists. One of the most succinct attempts to provide the movement with a worldview was Hitler's speech to the Nuremberg Reichsparteitag (Reich Party Rally) in 1933, in which he declared that "National Socialism thus avows a heroic doctrine of valuing blood, race, and personality as well as the everlasting laws of selection."

During his nine months of imprisonment in the Landsberg Fortress, Hitler wrote his autobiography, *Mein Kampf,* a rambling account of his youthful development and the political and racial phantasms that proved to be the basis of Nazi rule. With cynical frankness, Hitler described his method of winning support: a big lie repeated "eternally" is preferable to a small one. But his book was meant to be revered more than studied or quoted. Before 1933, *Mein Kampf* sold a respectable hundred thousand copies. By 1940, sales had reached six million, in part because the tome was an obligatory gift for marriages, retirements, and other occasions. In *Mein Kampf,* Hitler described all life as a permanent struggle for existence governed by rigid biological laws. Victory or defeat, especially in the struggle of nations, would be decided by racial purity. Jews, who belonged to no nation, were the personification of evil; liberals, who promoted race mixing, produced only weakness and degeneracy. In putting the natural superiority of the Nordic race above even nationality and culture, the Nazis differed from conventional nationalists. Racial well-being and aesthetic beauty were linked, since the Nordic man and woman were supposed to be ideal types, and as Hitler observed in a 1933 speech, the "racially determined ideological tendencies of an age will also determine the characteristics and psyche of its art."

One of the characteristics of the National Socialist worldview was its flexibility and plasticity in a variety of practical domains, especially in law and medicine. Carl Schmitt, the leading legal theorist of the Third Reich, argued in 1934 that it was no longer possible to "carry forward the tearing asunder of the juridical and the political, of the juridical and the ideological, of the juridical and the moral." Referring to his correspondence with an unnamed American legal scholar, Schmitt argued that the importance of National Socialism was to "tear down this normativistic Tower of Babel and put in its place a healthy, concrete order of thought." For Schmitt, normative law, or Roman law, as opposed to National Socialist law, was the product of the Jews as a stateless people who required statutes and abstract principles—"*idées générales*"—to protect them. If there was no consensus about what National Socialism stood *for,* the same cannot be said for what it stood *against:* the Jews.

NOTES

1. Hans F. K. Günther, *Rassenkunde des deutschen Volkes* (Munich: J. F. Lehmann, 1922).
2. Paul Schultze-Naumburg, *Kunst und Rasse* (Munich: J. F. Lehmann, 1928).
3. Alfred Baeumler, *Männerbund und Wissenschaft* (Berlin: Junker und Dünnhaupt, 1934), 100.
4. Georg Lukács, "Nietzsche als Vorläufer der faschistischen Ästhetik," *Internationale Literatur,* no.8 (August 1935): 76–92.

51

ADOLF HITLER

The Aryan

First published in *Mein Kampf* (Munich: Verlag Franz Eher Nachfolger GmbH, 1925), 306–13. This translation from *Mein Kampf* (1927), trans. Ralph Manheim (New York: Houghton Mifflin, 1943): 290–96.

If we were to divide mankind into three groups, the founders of culture, the bearers of culture, the destroyers of culture, only the Aryan could be considered as the representative of the first group. From him originate the foundations and walls of all human creation, and only the outward form and color are determined by the changing traits of character of the various peoples. He provides the mightiest building stones and plans for all human progress and only the execution corresponds to the nature of the varying men and races. In a few decades, for example, the entire east of Asia will possess a culture whose ultimate foundation will be Hellenic spirit and Germanic technology, just as much as in Europe. Only the outward form—in part at least—will bear the features of Asiatic character. It is not true, as some people think, that Japan adds European technology to its culture; no, European science and technology are trimmed with Japanese characteristics. The foundation of actual life is no longer the special Japanese culture, although it determines the color of life—because outwardly, in consequence of its inner difference, it is more conspicuous to the European—but the gigantic scientific-technical achievements of Europe and America; that is, of Aryan peoples. Only on the basis of these achievements can the Orient follow general human progress. They furnish the basis of the struggle for daily bread, create weapons and implements for it, and only the outward form is gradually adapted to Japanese character.

If beginning today all further Aryan influence on Japan should stop, assuming that Europe and America should perish, Japan's present rise in science and technology might continue for a short time; but even in a few years the well would dry up, the Japanese special character would gain, but the present culture would freeze and sink back into the slumber from which it was awakened seven decades ago by the wave of Aryan culture. Therefore, just as the present Japanese development owes its life to Aryan origin, long ago in the gray past foreign influence and foreign spirit awakened the Japanese culture of that time. The best proof of this is furnished by the fact of its subsequent sclerosis and total petrifaction. This can occur in a people only when the original creative racial nucleus has been lost, or if the external influence that furnished the impetus and the material for the first development in the cultural field was later lacking. But if it is established that a people receives the most essential basic materials of its culture from foreign races, that it assimilates and adapts them, and that then, if further external influence is lacking, it rigidifies again and again, such a race may be designated as "culture-bearing," but never as "culture-founding." An examination of the various peoples from this standpoint points to the fact that practically none of them were originally culture-founding, but almost always culture-bearing.

Approximately the following picture of their development always results:

Aryan races—often absurdly small numerically—subject foreign peoples, and then, stimulated by the special living conditions of the new territory (fertility, climatic conditions, etc.) and assisted by the multitude of lower-type beings standing at their disposal as helpers, develop the intellectual and organizational capacities dormant within them. Often in a few millennia, or even centuries, they create cultures that originally bear all the inner characteristics of their nature, adapted to the above-indicated special qualities of the soil and subjected beings. In the end, however, the conquerors transgress against the principle of blood purity to which they had first adhered; they begin to mix with the subjugated inhabitants and thus end their own existence; for the fall of man in paradise has always been followed by his expulsion.

FIGURE 6. A display of National Socialist literature featuring a map showing the global distribution of *Mein Kampf*. Collection of Foreign Records Seized, Heinrich Hoffmann (no. 242.1), box 214, item 21915–2, U.S. National Archives and Records Administration, College Park, Md.

After a thousand years and more, the last visible trace of the former master people is often seen in the lighter skin color that its blood left behind in the subjugated race, and in a petrified culture that it had originally created. For once the actual and spiritual conqueror lost himself in the blood of the subjected people, the fuel for the torch of human progress was lost! Just as, through the blood of the former masters, the color preserved a feeble gleam in their memory, likewise the night of cultural life is gently illumined by the remaining creations of the former light-bringers. They shine through all the returned barbarism and too often inspire the thoughtless observer of the moment with the opinion that he beholds the picture of the present people before him, whereas he is only gazing into the mirror of the past.

It is then possible that such a people will a second time, or even more often in the course of its history, come into contact with the race of those who once brought it culture, and the memory of former encounters will not necessarily be present. Unconsciously, the remnant of the former master blood will turn toward the new arrival, and what was first possible only by compulsion can now succeed through the people's own will. A new cultural wave makes its entrance and continues until those who have brought it are again submerged in the blood of foreign peoples.

It will be the task of a future cultural and world history to carry out research in this light and not to stifle the rendition of external facts, as is so often unfortunately the case with our present historical science.

This mere sketch of the development of "culture-bearing" nations gives a picture of the growth, of the activity, and the decline of the true culture-founders of this earth, the Aryans themselves.

As in daily life the so-called genius requires a special cause, indeed, often a positive impetus, to make him shine, likewise the genius-race in the life of peoples. In the monotony of everyday life even significant men often seem insignificant, hardly rising above the average of their environment; as soon, however, as they are approached by a situation in which others lose hope or go astray, the genius rises manifestly from the inconspicuous average child, not seldom to the amazement of all those who had hitherto seen him in the pettiness of bourgeois life—and that is why the prophet seldom has any honor in his own country. Nowhere have we better occasion to observe this than in war. From apparently harmless children, in difficult hours when others lose hope, suddenly heroes shoot up with death-defying determination and an icy cool presence of minds. If this hour of trial had not come, hardly anyone would have ever guessed that a young hero was hidden in this beardless boy. It nearly always takes some stimulus to bring the genius on the scene. The hammer-stroke of Fate that throws one man to the ground suddenly strikes steel in another, and when the shell of everyday life is broken, the previously hidden kernel lies open before the eyes of the astonished world. The world then resists and does not want to believe that the type that is apparently identical with it is suddenly a very different being; a process that is repeated with every eminent son of man.

Though an inventor, for example, establishes his fame only on the day of his invention, it is a mistake to think that genius as such entered into the man only at this hour—the spark of genius exists in the brain of the truly creative man from the hour of his birth. True genius is always inborn and never cultivated, let alone learned.

As already emphasized, this applies not only to the individual man but also to the race. Creatively active peoples always have a fundamental creative gift, even if it should not be recognizable to the eyes of superficial observers. Here, too, outward recognition is possible only in consequence of accomplished deeds, since the rest of the world is not capable of recognizing genius in itself, but sees only its visible manifestations in the form of inventions, discoveries, buildings, pictures, etc.; here again, it often takes a long time before the world can fight its way through to this knowledge. Just as in the life of the outstanding individual, genius or extraordinary ability strives for practical realization only when spurred on by special occasions, likewise in the life of nations the creative forces and capacities which are present can often be exploited only when definite preconditions exist.

We see this most distinctly in connection with the race that has been and is the bearer of human cultural development—the Aryans. As soon as Fate leads them toward special conditions, their latent abilities begin to develop in a more and more rapid sequence and to mold themselves into tangible forms. The cultures that they found in such cases are nearly always decisively determined by the existing soil, the given climate, and the subjected people. This last item, to be sure, is almost the most decisive. The more primitive the technical foundations for a cultural activity, the more necessary is the presence of human helpers who, organizationally assembled and employed, must replace the force of the machine. Without this possibility of using lower human beings, the Aryan would never have been able to take his first steps toward his future culture; just as without the help of various suitable beasts which he knew how to tame, he would not have arrived at a technology which is now gradually permitting him to do without these beasts. The saying, "the Moor has worked off his debt, the Moor can go," unfortunately has only too deep a meaning. For thousands of years the horse had to serve man and help him lay the foundations of a development that now, in consequence of the motorcar, is making the horse superfluous. In a few years his activity will have ceased, but without his previous collaboration, man might have had a hard time getting where he is today.

Thus, for the formation of higher cultures the existence of lower human types was one of the most essential preconditions, since they alone were able to compensate for the lack of technical aids without which a higher development is not conceivable. It is certain that the first culture of humanity was based less on the tamed animal than on the use of lower human beings.

Only after the enslavement of subjected races did the same fate strike beasts, and not the other way around, as some people would like to think. For first the conquered warrior drew the plow—and only after him the horse. Only pacifistic fools can regard this as a sign of human depravity, failing to realize that this development had to take place in order to reach the point where today these "apostles" could force their drivel on the world.

The progress of humanity is like climbing an endless ladder; it is impossible to climb higher without first taking the lower steps. Thus, the Aryan had to take the road to which reality directed him and not the one that would appeal to the imagination of a modern pacifist. The road of reality is hard and difficult, but in the end, it leads where our friend would like to bring humanity by dreaming. And yet by their very actions to bring mankind closer to this goal, they only push him farther and farther away from it.

Hence it is no accident that the first cultures arose in places where the Aryan, in his encounters with lower peoples, subjugated them and bent them to his will. They then became the first technical instrument in the service of a developing culture.

Thus, the road which the Aryan had to take was clearly marked out. As a conqueror, he subjected the lower beings and regulated their practical activity under his command, according to his will and for his aims. But in directing them to a useful end though arduous activity, he not only spared the life of those he subjected; perhaps he gave them a fate that was better than their previous so-called "freedom." As long as he ruthlessly upheld the master attitude, not only did he really remain master, but also the preserver and increaser of culture. For culture was based exclusively on his abilities and hence on his actual survival. As soon as the subjected people began to raise themselves up and probably approached the conqueror in language, the sharp dividing wall between master and servant fell. The Aryan gave up the purity of his blood and, therefore, lost his sojourn in the paradise he had made for himself. He became submerged in the racial mixture, and gradually, more and more, lost his cultural capacity, until at last, not only mentally but also physically, he began to resemble the subjected aborigines more than his own ancestors. For a time he could live on the existing cultural benefits, but then petrifaction set in and he fell prey to oblivion.

Thus cultures and empires collapsed to make place for new formations.

Blood mixture and the resultant drop in the racial level is the sole cause of the dying out of old cultures; for men do not perish as a result of lost wars, but by the loss of that force of resistance which is contained only in pure blood.

All who are not of good race in this world are chaff.

And all occurrences in world history are only the expression of the races' instinct of self-preservation, in the good or bad sense.

52

ADOLF HITLER

Speech at the NSDAP Congress on Culture

Delivered on 3 September 1933. First published as "Adolf Hitlers Rede auf der Kulturtagung der N.S.D.A.P.," in *Die Reden Hitlers am Reichsparteitag 1933* (Munich: Verlag Franz Eher Nachfolger GmbH, 1934), 23–27.

On 30 January 1933, the National Socialist Party was entrusted with the political leadership of the Reich. By the end of March, the National Socialist revolution was—superficially—complete. Complete inasmuch as the absolute takeover of political power is concerned. Except that only those who harbor an incomplete understanding of the nature of this overwhelming struggle can believe that the struggle between worldviews came to an end in that moment. That would have been the case if the goals of the National Socialist movement were no different from those of the remaining national parties. But for these more conventional parties, the day they take over political leadership generally represents the zenith of their resolve and thus also of their existence. But for *worldviews,* attainment of political power is merely the prerequisite to setting their actual mission in motion. The solemn proclamation of a decision to make a *certain ideological premise* and, accordingly, a clearly recognizable tendency the foundation for any and all actions already inheres in the word *worldview.* Any such premise may be right or wrong: it forms the point of departure for the formulation of opinions on all phenomena and events in life, and thus becomes a binding and obligatory law governing every form of agency. The greater the overlap between this basic premise and the natural laws of organic life, the more useful its conscious application becomes for the life of a *Volk.*

It is for this reason that the most natural worldview is borne by the instincts of the unspoiled, primitive *Volk,* and it is this that enables its people to automatically assume *the most natural and hence the most expedient stance* with regard to any and all questions immediately affecting its life. Just as the individual human being in his natural, healthy, and unspoiled state of existence unconsciously draws on his inner instinct to develop an utterly natural reaction in response to all questions that move and concern him, so too does the healthy *Volk* respond to all the needs of its own untainted state of existence by drawing on its innate instinct for self-preservation to arrive at the most salutary stance concerning all the demands in life as these become apparent. The fact that all living beings belonging to the same species are the same essentially eliminates the need for formulating binding rules and obligatory laws.

It is only the physical crossbreeding of individual beings of essentially disparate natures that confounds the perspective and generates the need to draft laws and rules to facilitate the formulation of a unified expression in response to life's influences and demands on the part of such a *Volk* that would otherwise remain fragmented by disparate reactions.

Since it is the will of divine Providence that these different species of man not be created with the same life purpose in mind, what becomes decisive for directing and shaping the life of this intermixture is determining which sectors in the various areas of the existential struggle manage to assert that basic premise that is natural to them as obligatory for the general populace.

All of the worldviews in recorded history are comprehensible only when viewed in relation to the life purpose and life view of *specific races.* This makes it very difficult to form an opinion about the rightness or wrongness of such views without examining them according to the impact they have had on the men they have affected, wittingly or unwittingly.

For what seems to a certain *Volk* the most natural expression of life by virtue of the fact that it is innate and thus befitting may for a different *Volk* of an alien aboriginal nature not only pose a grave threat under certain circumstances, but also in fact imply its final *end.*

But a *Volk* that is comprised of several different lines of racial stock cannot under any circumstances allow the most relevant matters in life to be determined by, nor can it build upon, two or three different premises at the same time. Sooner or later, this necessarily leads to the dissolution of any unnatural union of this kind. If this is to be avoided, then *the decisive issue is which component of the racial stock is by nature best able to assert its worldview.* This in turn determines the direction of the further development of that *Volk.*

Every race, in asserting its existence, acts in accordance with the energies and values endowed its members by nature. Only the man who is predisposed to the *heroic* can think and act *heroically.* Providence has provided him the prerequisites for doing so. Those life forms that—even at a purely material level, for example, those that are physically *unheroic*—similarly exhibit only *unheroic* characteristics and strategies in conducting their struggle for existence. But as much as it is possible that, for example, the unheroic elements of a national community may indoctrinate those who are fundamentally inclined toward the heroic and thus divest them of their innermost nature, it is equally possible that the emphatically heroic may purposefully subordinate heroically incompatible elements to its tendency.

National Socialism is a worldview. Inasmuch as it circumscribes those people whose innermost proclivity qualifies them for membership in this worldview and brings them together in an organic community, it becomes the party of those who *by their inner constitution are to be counted as members of a certain race.* As such, National Socialism recognizes the fact that varying racial substances do exist within the racial community of our *Volk*. It is far removed from any rejection of this diversity that comprises the whole spectrum of ways of life amongst our *Volk* per se. National Socialism acknowledges that the normal span of our capacities is determined by the *inner racial structuring* of our *Volk*. But what it wishes is that the political and cultural leadership of our *Volk* reflect the face and expression of that race from which, solely by virtue of its heroism that is in turn based on innate predisposition, the *German Volk was originally created from a conglomerate of diverse components. National Socialism thus avows a heroic doctrine of valuing blood, race, and personality as well as the everlasting laws of selection* and so consciously enters into irreconcilable contradictions with the worldview of pacifist international democracy and its ramifications.

This National Socialist worldview necessarily leads to a *reorientation* in almost all sectors of *völkisch* life. The stupendous implications of this overwhelming spiritual-mental revolution cannot even begin to be estimated today.

Just as the connection between sexual reproduction and birth became apparent to man only at the end of a long course of development, *the meaning of racial and hereditary laws* is only now beginning to dawn on mankind. Lucid recognition and conscious consideration of these facts will some day serve as the foundation for future development.

Acting on the knowledge that, in the long run, the sum of our creations can be preserved only by the same forces that were themselves once the bearers of creation itself, National Socialism will foster the dominant influence and thus the visible manifestation of those elements that have inspired and facilitated the shaping of the racial body of our German *Volk* over the course of many centuries.

But if the National Socialist mission is to retain its internal justification, then it will have to *lift the German people from the morass of a strictly materialistic view of life* and elevate it to the heights of a dignified representation of that which we are to understand by the word *man*. Then, in order for this man to truly be in a class with higher life forms, he must himself stand apart from the very category of animal. Were he to have forever restricted his ambitions to the limits of fulfilling primitive needs, he would never have succeeded in rising above the realm of basic animal nature. Here, too, man must obey the dictates placed upon him by Providence. Because the fact that some species of man actually does fulfill its purpose in life by satisfying the most basic of life's necessities is for these peoples just as natural as it would be unnatural if those races predestined by Providence to rank among the higher races were to defy the admonitory voice of their conscience, the ardent compulsion of their nature, and revert to that same primitive way of life or even allow themselves to be forced by rape to do so, which amounts to the same thing.

Since nature is inclined to unleash spirited opposition to such a case, deep rifts have risen in peoples in which two fundamentally different racial elements have sought to live side by side. The man who needs nothing more than food and drink to satisfy and fulfill his life has never possessed any understanding of the man who would rather be chary of his daily bread in order to quench the thirst of his soul and satisfy the hunger of his mind. But it would be equally incorrect to assume that man will ever be capable of comprehending or grasping what Providence has not placed within reach of his nature to so much as comprehend. But just as the maintenance of every form of human society is contingent upon upholding certain principles, even though not all individuals within that society agree with them, the cultural makeup of a *Volk* must be forged *from its best elements,* and these alone must be allowed to become the sole innate bearers of culture by nature.

But for all that those who are not predestined to become bearers of culture are lacking inborn understanding, for all whose hearts and souls will never be in a position to grasp such things, they must at least be taught to display deferent respect for these things through *calculated education*. What is more, they simply must learn to acknowledge these expressions of life of one part of [the nature of the] people in the same way others must come to terms with their mentality.

It is for this reason that, throughout history, worldviews have determined not only the nature of politics but also the shape of cultural life. Poets have praised heroes whenever heroic epochs have allowed them to appear, or they have descended into the morass of everyday life in times that turned unheroic, and the people who were in step with those times set the tone.

Art can never be separated from man. The platitude that art in particular is international is vacuous and idiotic. Even if there are other precincts in life that remain subject to the instructional influence of education, *one must be born to create art*—that is to say, that the fundamental propensity and suitability that lie beyond any form of education are of crucial importance. But this propensity is a *component of hereditary racial bloodstock*. Hence, not everyone who is *racially* endowed with the ability to become a creative artist must become an artist simply because he is a member of the artistic race. But true genius will spring only from someone who is, and it will be *only this race* that is capable of understanding or feeling it.

It is a sign of the gruesome spiritual intellectual decadence of a bygone age that its people spoke in terms of style without acknowledging the underlying racial predetermination of style. The Greeks did not build in an international style but rather in a Greek style—that is to say that *every clearly defined race has left its own unique signature in the book of art* inasmuch as it is not, like the *Jewish race,* for example, completely devoid of its own artistic productive capacity. Whenever peoples begin to copy art forms that are alien to their nature, this is proof not of art's internationality but rather that it is possible to plagiarize the intuitive experiences and creations of other peoples.

One can speak in terms of a truly insightful entry of one people into the art of another only when there is one and the same *racial root between* them that transcends all boundaries of time and language. So the greater the degree of dominant influence a certain genetic stock within the *Volk* is able to exert on the external worldview as a reflection of that internal core, the greater the likelihood that kindred peoples and states will immediately adopt the same approach to life and that this will find expression not only in the political sector but also in the cultural—regardless of any temporal distances between them. Because despite any and all differences in the shape the external world assumes, the inner predisposition of the races remains unchanged. As long as the inherited characteristics of the inherited aspects remain uncorrupted, even thousands of years can have no influence.

It is for this reason that the *ideal standard of beauty* advanced by the peoples and states of antiquity shall reign immortal for as long as people displaying the same predispositions based on hereditary inheritance populate the earth. It is neither the stone itself nor the inert mass that is immortal; rather, it is the people who share the same origins by virtue of their common descent from the same root. So it is erroneous to believe that the original creative impulse that shapes the artistic and cultural expressions of any race is determined or regulated by any form of stylistic law. No: *only the* Volk *that has become instinctually insecure* because its racial unity has been undermined is in need of rules to prevent it from losing the marvelous thread once found by the uncomplicated natural representatives of a gifted race. It is ridiculous to contend that without an *ideological rejuvenation and the attendant racial cleansing,* a new "life-, cultural, and artistic style" could possibly emerge, just as it is ridiculous to assume that nature would have entrusted this prescient task to the hands of your average bungling dullard.

Not every Greek was capable of building a Pantheon. But once a Greek had created this magnificent marvel, everyone knew that it was, by virtue of its splendorous magnitude, the most overwhelming proclamation of an innately Greek intellect and character.

In this manner, the racially determined ideological tendencies of an age will also determine the tendencies and psyche of its art. The race that leaves its mark on the whole spectrum of the life of a *Volk* will also see the tasks of art through its eyes. Availing itself of all the circumstances and conditions of purpose and of material, it fashions in the most sovereign manner the work of art after its own image. However, only the most lucid human intellect is capable of finding the paths of sublime beauty. The ultimate standard of measure here rests, however, in recognizing the fulfillment of a crystal-clear utility. This has absolutely nothing to do with that putative "objectivity" that does not want to comprehend that man should not confuse animalistic primitiveness with harmonious beauty.

Not every artist will attain this height of perfection; each should, nevertheless, seek to attain it. Every *Volk* is subject to its natural limitations. Every god-gifted artist, as the human representative of his people's epitomized tenacity, will always surpass the average overall level of knowledge and will always unconsciously arrive at that form of artistic expression that is perceived to be representative of the most supreme and most sublime beauty but whose unadulterated utility can often only be proven thousands of years later.

Just as *noble man* was always mutually aware of *beauty* in both sexes but only after thousands of years recognized that the supreme beauty of the female sex lay in the utilitarian construction and perfection of her body and her nature and, on the other hand, that this was equally true of the male sex, so it is that the truly gifted artist may well succeed in solving the constructive and tectonic aspects of his respective tasks long before the so-called exact science is in a position to deliver proof that this solution is indeed empirically correct.

But what we know about ourselves is that in antiquity and in the modern period, the Aryan-Nordic man has consistently arrived at the necessary synthesis between the task at hand, its purpose, and the available materials. His lavishly creative spirit has always remained consistent and, even though over centuries certain worldviews acting as outward expressions of foreign peoples have imposed the constraints of stylistic laws upon our people—constraints that may have been ideologically appropriate to them but that were contrary to the truly constitutive nature of the Aryan—this spirit has always sought an alternative in its own world, however bygone it may have been at any given moment.

And so it is no wonder that every *politically heroic age* has immediately sought in its art to find the bridge leading to a no less heroic past. The Greeks and the Romans thus suddenly seem to resemble the ancient Germans because all of them trace their *roots to the same original race,* and this is why the immortal achievements of ancient peoples will always continue to exert an attractive effect on their racially related progeny. Since it is always better to *imitate the good* than it is to produce afresh the bad, the extant intuitive creations of these peoples are *without doubt able to fulfill their didactic and authoritative mission with regard to stylistic considerations today.* To the same extent that the Nordic spirit currently experiences its conscious resurrection, it will also have to tackle *contemporary cultural tasks* with no less pronounced clarity and, hence, aesthetic beauty than its racial predecessors mastered the problems presented to them in their time.

It would be just as ridiculous, even puerile, to seek to pusillanimously avoid those classical forms and expressions of creative artistic genius already developed by their predecessors, as it would be stupid to reject the forms of knowledge and experience pertinent to other areas in life simply because previous generations have already arrived at the same truths.

The human race would degenerate, culture would regress, if an aversion to preserving an *expeditious hereditary bloodstock* of cultural properties and earthly possessions were to gain the upper hand simply because decadent or racially alien elements that, in their spiritual-intellectual anarchy or in their hereditarily motivated interdiction, would prefer to set a torch to any and all achievements of the past.

By the same token, though, a creative race cannot elevate the sum of all past achievements of its predecessors to a tyrannical stylistic law that constrains or even rapes every further achievement of its own.

The future can be built only from the past and the present simultaneously. The given purpose, the constructive capacity of the present, and the technical materials are the elements from which and with which the truly creative spirit forms its works without fear of applying the salutary traditional assets handed down through the ancestors and with courage enough to *combine them with the new things that it has discovered on its own!*

For it would be just as trifling to seek to outwardly deny, with the construction of a new theater, for example, that we are but the rejuvenators and the contemporary purveyors of an institution whose parameters have been essentially the same for thousands of years as it would, by the same token, be unacceptable to seek to allow for an outward revival of Greek or Gothic formalistic elements in the construction of a modern machine factory or an electrical power plant. It follows then that it is entirely spurious to speak of seeking to establish a "*new* style"—rather, one can only hope that the *very best of our human racial stock* will be chosen by Providence to draw on the hereditarily inspired inner nature of their beings in attempting to resolve the tasks we are charged with today in the same sovereign fashion that, for example, the Aryan peoples of antiquity succeeded in doing. We hope to be able *to draw freely from and further develop* those things, together with any additional constructive and artistically valuable experiences of that past that is intimately related to us as a people have bequeathed us, just as the art of the ancients was itself but the result of a far-reaching development. What is singularly decisive is that, through *the conscious cultivation of the racial substance* that our *Volk* bears in its genetic makeup as well as through the sovereign proclamation of its characteristic nature and the attendant worldview, *we create a core that will be able to make its creative spirit felt for many ages to come.*

It is no coincidence that the age that was most ideologically turgid in its liberalistic permissiveness—in other words, its insecurity—was similarly insecure in the area of cultural productivity. In the course of barely a century, all the artistic achievements of the peoples and the worldviews of nearly all times were tested, one after another, and subsequently abandoned. This insecurity finally found the only appropriate form of expression in the cult of primitiveness surrounding cubism and Dadaism. *It is this that represents the cultural expression of life of the uncultured dregs of nations.*

Marxism necessarily leads not only to political but also to cultural *nihilism.* So, while the official artistic industry at the end of this age can leave behind only the most horrendous impression, *the ground has nevertheless been paved,* not only at the intellectual-political level but also at the cultural level, *for the rejuvenation of peoples.*

Just as National Socialism in Germany represents the fulfillment of countless prescient prophecies and actual scientific revelations, so too has *the preliminary work toward a new artistic renaissance of the Aryan people been under way* at a subconscious level.

Strikingly enough, it developed from tasks that could not be completed based on the existence of any previous model or precedent. Modern technology forced people to seek their own means. The utilitarian and material exigencies caused us to find and develop forms that, as for example in the aesthetics of many machines, exude an air of Greek spirit more than any poorly imitated edifice. This overwhelming new field, as a sort of uncharted territory, is sure to exhibit intellectual monuments to a creative productivity that is as modern as it is aesthetically satisfying. From there, of course, the necessary development goes beyond the use of innovative materials such as steel, iron, glass, concrete, etc. and proceeds along a course that is in line with the very purposes of their [*sic*] construction and of these materials themselves.

But here too it is not the average man who is called upon to create works of immortal proportion. Whoever pursues innovation simply for the sake of its newness all too readily wanders astray in the playgrounds of buffoonery, for here is but the height of imbecility chiseled in stone and materials, and it is, of course, all the more readily passed off as truly innovative than in bygone times when not every idiot was permitted to insult the environment with the monstrous products of his sick mind.

Since time immemorial, Providence has always assigned only the god-gifted few the mission *to create things that are truly immortally new.* But these few become the pathfinders for a long future, and it is the educational task of the nation to teach its people to demonstrate the commensurate reverence for these great figures, for they are the highest values of a *Volk* made flesh. They have created what they have not under the reign of the pathological notion of bearing forth something new at any cost but rather have created something new because *they sought to create the best and were compelled to succeed in creating the best.*

The fact that an achievement is something that has "never been before" is not proof of its superior quality; rather it can just as easily be proof of the fact that nothing as infinitely inferior in quality as this has ever existed. So, if a so-called artist sees as his sole purpose in life serving up the most convoluted and incomprehensible representation of past or even present achievements, at least we can be assured that the genuine achievements of the past remain achievements, while the artistic stammering of such a painting, music-making, sculpting, or constructing charlatan will one day be seen as little more than proof of the grandiose magnitude of a nation's demise.

Nor is it possible for a man who has stooped to such contemptuous depths to suddenly change his ways and create something better. He is worthless and shall forever remain worthless. He has failed because he lacks the inner calling of the High Almighty and thus the most natural distinction of all. To distinguish oneself with deliberate lunacies and to thus cull critical acclaim—that is not only testimony to artistic failure but also evidence of a moral defect.

Art is a majestic mission and one that demands fanaticism. Whoever has been chosen by Providence to reveal to the rest of the world the soul of a people, be it by lending voice to it in song or in stone, suffers under the force of the all-consuming compulsion that commands him, and he will continue to speak his language even if the rest of the world does not or does not want to understand him; he would rather burden himself with privations of any sort than ever betray the star that acts as his innermost guiding light.

The National Socialist movement and leadership of state cannot tolerate, even in the cultural sector, that incompetents and impostors suddenly *change their colors* and trim their sails to the wind of the new state as if nothing had gone between in order to once again start flapping at the mouth in the sector of *arts and cultural policy.* We do not know whether Providence has blessed us all with the men who are able to grace us with those forms of cultural expression that are equal to the political will of our time and its achievements. *One thing we do know, however, is that under no circumstances whatsoever shall the representatives of the degeneracy we have just put behind us suddenly become the ones to hoist the flag of the future.* Either the monstrosities they produced in their time were the genuine products of their inner experience—in which case they present a danger to the mental and spiritual health of the *Volk* and belong in the custody of medical practitioners—or their work was the product of pure speculation—in which case, they are guilty of fraud and should be institutionalized accordingly. Under no circumstances do we want to see the cultural expression of our Reich defrauded by such elements because it is *our state,* not theirs.

But this new state will devote a much greater degree of attention to the manifestation of cultural matters than the old one. Because National Socialism recognizes the right to *especially privileged treatment* on the part of those elements in the racial body politic of our *Volk* that once initiated and facilitated its formation, it must also *provide the moral justification* for so doing.

It is the nature of all human beings to satisfy their basic animal needs. There is not a single species that could derive from this alone the peculiar authority to lead, much less to dominate. The only thing that can identify men as uniquely ordained to do so is the clearly demonstrable capacity to rise above the primitive and to ennoble the base characteristics of life. However, both in spirit and in deed, *political leadership* is what must provide the prerequisite for the *efficacy of art*. Even when a *Volk* lapses into extinction and people fall silent, stones continue to speak as long as there are other peoples who possess a modicum of the same cultural capital and capacity.

So it is that every great political age in world history justifies its right to exist by exhibiting the most visible certificate of its value possible: *its cultural achievements.*

Especially in times of economic hardship and despair, it is important to make clear to everyone that a nation is in possession of even greater tasks than flourishing in the midst of mutual economic egotism. The cultural monuments of humanity have always been the altars for contemplating their greater mission and greater dignity.

If there are peoples who no longer care to acknowledge this, then they have already lost the better part of their blood, and their demise is only a matter of time. But, convinced as we are of the inner dignity of the German *Volk, we want to be sure that our political and national leadership will provide the German* Volk *the opportunity for proving this dignity.*

May *German artists* themselves now become aware of the task that the nation has placed upon them. *Since folly and injustice seem to rule the world, we beseech the artists to play their part in proudly defending the German* Volk *with their German art.*

53

ERNST KRIECK

The Racial-*Völkisch*-Political Conception of History

First published as "Das rassisch-völkisch-politische Geschichtsbild," in *Wissenschaft, Weltanschauung, Hochschulreform* (Leipzig: Armanen Verlag, 1934), 6–8, 36–39.

With the National Socialist revolution, the principle of a *völkisch*-political totality of life has made a triumphant breakthrough; it conjoins worldview and reality of life in a new coherent definition and is also applicable as an authoritative standard for religion, science, and art. Every individual human community, every function of communal life, all forms of social organization are component parts of a whole, links in the chain of a greater whole, a superordinate, autonomous, and autarchic unity of life: the totality of the *Volk*. Every link in this chain—even the individual personality—retains its autonomy, for that is what distinguishes organic life from the collectivity, but is superseded by the law of the totality from which it stems, which it serves, and in which it finds its own fulfillment.

This has brought with it a shift in emphasis in terms of worldview and of the organization of life [*Lebensordnung*]. We did not arbitrarily or capriciously select this revolutionary and constitutive principle; rather, with the onset of the *völkisch* awakening, it sought us out and, in a stroke of fate, thrust us into a new situation, presented us with a new task and a new worldview.

Science and research are thus similarly confronted with a completely altered situation and task, not only inasmuch as the objects of scientific study are changed (for example, with increasing focus on racial theory and the like), but also inasmuch as the approaches, methods, perspectives, and aims are fundamentally altered, and this in turn results in a restructuring of the order of precedence and value with respect to potential objects of scientific study.

Rationalism as the sovereign principle guiding worldview, lifestyle, and scientific research is at an end. But reverting to its opposite in any sort of "irrationalism" was at once as childish as it was an impractical reaction: one cannot refute a position simply by juxtaposing it with its negation—say, for example, reason versus lack of reason.

Far more, *ratio,* the "queen of reason," is integrated into the greater whole, in a place and fashion that is far more befitting of her nature: she becomes a servant, but, even as such, nevertheless fully retains her unique validity and dignity. The totality of our *Volk* has been charged—by fate, character, and history—with a totality of task whose fulfillment requires that reason play her part as is appropriate to her means and her manner.

This is in accord with the nature and task of future scholarship and science, the nature of which is and remains within the purview of rational science: "irrational science" would be as oxymoronic as wooden iron. In accordance with the organic reintegration of reason in the service of the totality of *völkisch* life and its history-making totality of task, science also forfeits its claim to autonomy and sovereignty in all its consequences:

1. Science neither emanates from nor exists within an epistemological truth that is independent of time and *Volk* and universally valid for all time. Rather, acting in accordance with the worldview, it proffers the rational form of a truth that is inextricably bound to the *Volk* and its times by virtue of race, character, and fate.
2. Science is not isolated from the world of events, situated on an eternal and unshakable island of pure and absolute reason; it is, rather, with all its approaches, its means and methods, all its values, aims, and tasks, integrally incorporated into life's occurrences, into the historical process of the *Volk* as it evolves, and it actively participates in and endures these occurrences and this process of evolution.
3. Science is not based on a mechanism or apparatus consisting of pure, automated forms of reason (as in Kantian forms of sensibility, categories, and regulative ideas). Rather, its rational foundations and categorical concepts are always drawn to the surface anew from the inexhaustible reservoir of human existence and of the race, always reformulated in accordance with the situation and task at hand and with the aim and the means. There is no such thing as "pure reason" and no such thing as "absolute science"; there is, rather, a form of reason, of science, and of epistemological truth that is valid for our race, our *Volk,* our historical situation, and our historical task. This is why a corresponding scientific doctrine is needed.
4. Reason, science, truth, method, category, objects of knowledge, the individual are "sublated moments" (Hegel) of our *völkisch*-political totality of life, and it is here that they receive their form, their meaning, and their determination.
5. The process of history is not the progression of humanity or of the *Volk* toward a concrete final goal. Nor does this sort of progress exist for reason, truth, and science. Far more, living and concrete history constitutes a constant reconstruction of new forms from the substrata of *völkisch* life for as long as its substrata and elemental forces have not yet been depleted. History does not transpire according to a preordained, predictable scheme; rather, it emerges from the alignments of and tensions between forces extant at any given moment in the totality of life, and in each case, new tasks, possibilities for new constellations, ever in alternating periods of rise and fall, are always given. Reason, science, and truth are integrated into the process of history with its constant variation of form and meaning and in fact emanate from it to become vital forces in the formative processes of participating human beings.

The path of German science can be traced back neither to free rationalism, and even less so to a dogmatically binding scholasticism, nor to that form of scholasticism that would have posed religious dogma as its mandate and aim, mediated by an ideological-racial-political dogma; rather, it proceeds from the hardships and necessities of life among the German *Volk,* is inherently bound to its character and its task, and yet within this framework nevertheless remains a product of unfettered creative personalities who are subject to their obligation to the whole and their service of the idea and furthermore on equal footing with all the prevailing ideas, functions, and personalities that comprise the *völkisch*-political commonwealth of the German people. If German science—together with the new rules for the organization of life—succeeds along these lines in rising to a new fulfillment of purpose in perfected form, thereby lending classical expression to the German sensibility and the German nature, then it attains a new level of precedent and sets an example for leadership among the peoples of the world that the German *Volk* has been called and chosen to lead. [. . .]

I

The new conception of history that is about to emerge is a primary component of the resurgent conception of the world built on the foundation of racial-political thought: it establishes the depth of temporal dimension intrinsic to this conception of the world. Our answer to the fundamental question of "where are we going" is congruent with the question of "from whence we have come." Peoples who are without a past have no future either. But we must first rid ourselves of a preconceived notion that has been implanted in our minds by the science of history: history is comprised first and foremost of current events, that is to say that which is happening, not that which has happened. Our lives come to fruition in the span between our present situation, with all its hardships, and the task of the whole of the people [*Volksganzen*] is to overcome these hardships. It is from this position that each of us enters into a relationship with past and future events, each of us is thus forced to formulate the nature of his questions with regard to the past and to the future, and the result is that the perspective, the context, and the stability of meaning of individual facts, events, personalities, actions, and challenges encountered or found along the way is determined in both directions. The conception of history is always a contemporary one: the present is the fulcrum at which the past and the future converge and from which they assume plasticity and receive their stability of meaning. The generation of German people living today has, since 1914, experienced a historical event of such stupendous force and magnitude as has scarcely befallen any previous generation. The enormous proportion and far-reaching consequences of the historical crises inherent in the experience of war, collapse, relapse, together with the emergence and triumph of National Socialism, determine the shape of our conception of the world and of history because they have forced us to reconfigure the questions we pose and to develop a new approach to our confrontation with the world and with history—both in the past and in the future.

Our decisions are made between religious and political poles. The experiences of war, collapse, reaction, and revolution have placed us in a different relationship to God, and it is from our questions to God that the meaning and purpose of our lives ensue, and with it, the task of reshaping our lives in accordance with that meaning and that purpose begins. But since, both in our questions and in our decisions, we do not stand as isolated individuals before God, since we do not appear before God's countenance or in His judgment on behalf of our own private interests and the salvation of our own individual souls, but rather in the foreordained nexus of race and blood, of *Volkheit* and history, it is from this final religious crisis that the primacy of the political ensues: the task of determining the political constellations in the national community and the race. This responsibility to God, to the *Volk,* and to the future is fundamental to the religious and political, the *völkisch* and racial foundational component of our conception of history as the principle guiding our confrontation with the past and with the future. All of the questions we pose and the answers we arrive at concerning the history of the German *Volk,* the rest of the peoples of the world, antiquity, Christianity, of early Germanic history and its prehistory, emanate from the contingencies of race and

Volk, of our historical situation and historical task. As the embodiment of the National Socialist idea in its totality, the Third Reich represents the meaning and spirit of our people's history and it is this that forms the foundational premise, the constructive principle of the racial-*völkisch*-political conception of history.

History is not the sum of individual things: of individual facts, circumstances, events, persons, not any more than a *Volk* is the sum of individual people. History only becomes history in the meaningful compilation of those details, with the stability of destiny in the genealogy of peoples as the super-ordinate units of life and totalities of life. [. . .]

The hour for political action, for history-making deeds, pregnant with fate, with vocation and calling are forthcoming in a movement that has burst forth from the bowels of the *Volk*'s soul, a call and a compulsion issued forth from the deepest spiritual depths—from a state of readiness. The vanguard movement itself bears the purpose, the task to be fulfilled is its very meaning. But its anonymous force cannot come into power, cannot fulfill its purpose on its own. In order to do so, it needs the chosen few, gripped by faith and fated to speak their piece at the propitious hour, to reveal the meaning of the creative act, and to lend shape to the new form. History follows from and finds its fulfillment in the space between political and metaphysical poles, in the words of the prophets and in the deeds of the *heroes.* History is manifest politics; politics is surrendered history.

II

For us, there is a political concept of race that is more significant and more critical than existing racial theories and racial science. This political concept of race encompasses the following definitional components:

1. Racial unity and racial purity are not prerequisite in the reality of a *Volk.*
2. Race is the constant fundamental composition, the fixed and enduring fundamental character, a law that encompasses mind, body, spirit, and soul in equal measure, regulates them, and determines the standard and direction of life, the hierarchy of values, attitude, and conception of the world.
3. The Teutonic race that is dominant among the German *Volk* forms the very backbone of the national community and the state, just as it determines the order of the *Volk,* religion, law, economics, science, upbringing, vocational training, and education. The processes of selection and selective breeding of the strong and masterful from the racial diversity of the *Volk* allows for the evolution of a politically, spiritually, and intellectually elite class to develop in the *völkisch*-political commonwealth of Germans.
4. The preeminent race has always been a fundamental component in the history of the German *Volk,* distinguished by the constancy of its character, of its outlook, and its worldview and thus for the nature of its outlook and its reaction to the fateful events of history.
5. Race manifests itself in the will, the outlook, and the worldview in accordance with the racial hierarchy of values. The Germanic hierarchy of racial values conforms to the heroic, soldierly, and political ideal, and places top priority on the values of honor, loyalty, camaraderie, tenacity of body and spirit, veracity, commitment to the commonwealth of the *völkisch* totality, and of social justice. It is upon these values that the state, the organization of the *Volk,* culture, and upbringing are built.
6. Upbringing (breeding and education included) can only cull to perfection that which is innately present in the race. The methods, values, lifestyles, and goods applied to this task, must, if they are to have an effective racial and purposeful impact, have their origins in and be congruent with their own racial stock.
7. What is congruent with the race is evident in the reaction of its members to the creations and products of fellow members of the race, as, for example, Hitler has demon-

strated based on the example of the Greek race's reaction to Phidias's Athenian Temple. This is a particularly salient manifestation of the living political concept of race.

8. The law of the leading Germanic race is applicable to the whole spectrum of the national community; that is, even to non-Germanic blood. In this manner, Germanic speciation will always manifest the fact that those who are its bearers are the only ones truly in a position to fulfill the law. This is how natural selection, ranking and ordering according to species and rank, according to mastery and slavery, comes to fruition in the *Volk:* a new aristocracy.

54

ALFRED ROSENBERG

The Myth of the Twentieth Century

On the Third Edition

Published in *Der Mythus des 20. Jahrhunderts: Eine Wertung der seelisch-geistigen Gestaltenkämpfe unserer Zeit,* 3rd ed. (Munich: Hoheneichen Verlag, 1941), 5–7, 81–87. First edition published in 1930.

> Oh, compatriots of my times!
> Ask not the doctors nor the priests when you fall to inner ruin.
> —*Hölderlin*

The first appearance of this volume immediately unleashed fiercely controversial debate. While intellectual disputes were to be expected based on the candor with which I posed my questions and the intentionally trenchant character of my assertions, I must admit that I was nevertheless shaken by the concentrated hatred that was hurled at me and the unscrupulous perversions undertaken, as if on command, to discredit the statements I made—shaken, but at that same time pleased. Because these savagely unrestrained polemics coming from expressly Roman Catholic circles demonstrated to me how profoundly justified I was in the assessment I bestowed upon the Roman Syrian principle in this work. In keeping with long-established methods, certain assertions and arguments were lumped together, taken out of the larger context of this capacious volume, and unfurled before the faithful readers of the Roman press that is German in word alone and in pamphlets as evidence of its author's "blasphemy," "atheism," "anti-Christianity" and "Wotanism." What the falsifiers neglected to note is that I went so far as to postulate a religious origin and foundation for the whole of Germanic art; that, citing Wagner, I explained that a work of art is the living representation of religion. What was overlooked was the great reverence for the founder of Christianity expressed in the work; what was omitted was that the observations on religion were obviously intended to reveal the greatness of His personality, absent the distorted embellishments subsequently added by various churches. Overlooked was the fact that I presented Wotanism as a *dead* religious form (though I, of course, have great respect for the Teutonic character that gave birth not only to Wotan but also to Faust), and instead I was falsely accused in the most unscrupulous fashion of advocating a return to the "pagan cult of Wotan." In short, there is nothing that has not been distorted and falsified; and what seemed to adhere to the literal rendering of the text was ripped from its context to cast it in an entirely different light. Consistently, the Roman press omitted all the historical—and hence unassailable—observations; consistently, all the thought processes behind certain views were perverted, and the arguments outlined in defense of my contentions were concealed. The prelates and cardinals mobilized the "faithful masses," and

Rome—which is itself in league with atheistic Marxism, that is, with the powerful political support of the subaltern masses, and engaged in a campaign of annihilation against Germany that includes the sacrifice of German Catholic masses—suddenly had the audacity to rant and rave about a culture war [*Kulturkampf*].[1] The arguments presented in this work, which in form and content certainly extend far beyond contemporary everyday concerns, were not subjected to an objective and thus welcome critique; rather, they were haphazardly deployed as weapons in a chaotic battle over everyday current events. Not against me alone—I couldn't have cared less about that—but against the National Socialist movement as well, a movement I have belonged to since its inception. Despite the fact that, in my introduction and in the work itself, I made explicitly clear that a political movement involving a wide array of religious creeds cannot solve questions concerning religion or the philosophy of art, that my ideological creed is thus a *personal* one, the obscurantists did everything in their power to distract from the political crimes they have committed against the German *Volk* and instead keened and complained about the "threat to religion," even though there has never been and is no greater threat to genuine religion than the systematic cultivation of Marxism by the Center Party under the direction of Roman prelates. It is not the task of the National Socialist movement to promulgate any given religious dogma, neither for nor against any given denomination; however, the fact that a man who is involved in political life is denied his right to express a religious conviction that runs contrary to Roman beliefs demonstrates the degree to which spiritual repression already runs rampant. [. . .]

The fact that the Teutons produced all the nations of the West and their creative values has long been recognized as common wisdom, but it was only with the work of Houston Stewart Chamberlain that the ineluctable implications of this fact became clear. For Chamberlain takes as a foregone conclusion the notion that the complete disappearance of this Germanic blood from Europe (and hence the gradual depletion of the nation- and prototype-building forces it produces) would bring with it the demise of the entire culture of the West. More recent studies in prehistory, combined with the insights of racial science, support and complement Chamberlain's work and have called forth an even more profound inner reflection: the dreadful realization that we are confronted with a *final* crisis today. Either we rise to purified heights through the revitalization and selective cultivation of this ancient bloodstock, coupled with an acceleration of the will to struggle, or we allow the last vestiges of the Germanic-Western values of civilization and the cultivation of nations to sink in the filthy human flood of the "great" metropolises, to be crippled by the scorching, sterile asphalt of bestialized inhumanity, or to slowly seep away, only to fester like a pestilent germ in the blood of emigrants bastardizing themselves in exile in South America, China, the Dutch East Indies, and Africa.

In addition to the emphasis on the complete re-creation of the world by Germanic peoples, yet another structural feature of Houston Stewart Chamberlain's worldview seems of particular importance today: his introduction of an epoch situated between ancient Nordic Rome and the modern-day Germanic Occident, which was characterized by rampant miscegenation—that is to say, bastardization—fomenting everything that is diseased, overinflated Syrian superstition, excessive sensual excesses, spreading a febrile delirium in the hearts and souls of human populations all over the globe. Revealing the genuine artistry of a seminal historian, Chamberlain coined the term *racial chaos* to describe this period. This term, which denotes a certain condition and defies precise temporal demarcation both in terms of its future and its past, has nevertheless entered the general consciousness and has become the self-evident intellectual asset of all those possessed of deeper insight. This new form of periodization to replace "antiquity" and "the Middle Ages" ranks, however, in the truest sense of the word, amongst the greatest discoveries of the late nineteenth century concerning the laws of human existence and the human psyche and has since come to form the foundation of the way we view history in the advancing twentieth century. Because what this knowledge implies is that if Theodoric the Great had not succeeded Caracallas, "eternal darkness" would have descended upon the whole of Europe. The roiling floods of mire flowing through the blood of mongrels in Asia, Africa, the entire Mediterranean basin and its *littorai* would have eventually recovered from the chaotic eruptions and settled. Life's eternal ebb and tide probably would have eradicated these decaying and decrepit elements, but what would have been lost for perpetuity was the creative force of a cultural soul characterized by its perpetual rebirth; what would have vanished forever was the earth-shaping genius of the Nordic race, a genius whose quest extends into the most distant reaches of the universe. All that would have remained to carry on in its vegetative state was that "breed of man" such as we see in southern Italy today—which cannot be said to live but rather to barely manage to perpetuate its survival, hobbling along, devoid of any bold physical and psychological force, devoid of genuine desire, accumulating by multitudes in profoundly servile penury of their existence on masses of volcanic rock or amidst the barren wastelands of the rock desert.

Therefore: if even today, some two thousand years after the first appearance of the Teutons, any trace of influence remains of national cultures, of their creative force and of their daring spirit of enterprise, then these forces—however much they may still seem to be at war amongst themselves—owe their existence to one thing and one thing alone: the most recent Nordic wave that has surged across the European continent and beyond, fertilizing everything in its effluvial tempest, swirling in whorls at the feet of the Caucasus, crashing in waves over the pillars of Hercules, before finally ebbing away in the deserts of North Africa.

Seen in the context of its broadest outline, the history of Europe consists of a struggle between this new breed of man and the force of mass multitudes of the Roman racial chaos stretching from the Rhine to the Danube and beyond. This dark, seething tide seemed to bear glittering values on its surface, seemed to emit scintillating desires; its waves told of bygone, once overwhelming world dominance and a world religion that answered all questions. Substantial portions of the Nordic bloodstock, in their capricious and puerile extravagance, became themselves the bearers of a nearly visionary ancient Roman grandeur and all too often took arms against the whole world in the service of sheer fantasy, and were thus reduced from the position of ancestral progenitors that was the circumstance of their birth to mere inheritors. So, until the arrival of Martin Luther, the struggle between the Teutonic race and the racial chaos assumed the form of a wrestling match between an organically grown heroic race and a heroism in the service of an artificial fantasy that often involved kindred opponents engaged in armed conflict over mortally opposed values.

Note

1. This is a reference to Otto von Bismarck's attempt to bring the Catholic Church under state control between 1871 and 1887.—Eds.

55

JOSEPH GOEBBELS

Communism with the Mask Off

Delivered on 13 September 1935. Published in English in *Communism with the Mask Off: Speech Delivered in Nürnberg on September 13th, 1935 at the Seventh National Socialist Party Congress* (Berlin: M. Müller, 1935).

In the beginning of August, this year, one of the most authoritative English newspapers published a leading article entitled "Two Dictatorships," in which a naive and misdirected attempt was made to place before the readers of the paper certain alleged similarities between

FIGURE 7. Catalog for the 1937 Great Anti-Bolshevik Exhibit in Nuremberg, 5–29 December 1937. Collection of Anson Rabinbach.

Russian Bolshevism and German National Socialism. This article gave rise to an extraordinary amount of heated discussion in international centers, which was only another proof of the fact that an astonishing misconception exists among the most prominent West European circles as to the danger which communism presents to the life of the individual and of the nation. Such people still cling to their opinion in face of the terrible and devastating experiences of the past eighteen years in Russia.

The author of the article stated that the two symbols which are today opposed to one another, namely that of Bolshevism and National Socialism, stand for regimes which "in essential structure are similar and in many of their laws—their buttresses—are identical. The similarity is moreover increasing." He went on to say:

"In both countries are the same censorships on art, literature, and of course the press, the same war on the intelligentsia, the attack on religion, and the massed display of arms, whether in the Red Square or the Tempelhofer Feld."

"The strange and terrible thing is," he declared, "that two nations, once so widely different, should have been schooled and driven into patterns so drably similar."

One sees here much verbiage and little understanding. The anonymous writer of this article has obviously not studied the essential and fundamental principles either of National Socialism or Bolshevism. He considers merely certain superficial phenomena and he has not taken cognizance of what serious journalists have had to say on the matter in question or compared his views with their objective statements. This entirely erroneous judgment of the case might be passed over with a shrug of the shoulders and considered merely as part of the daily order of things, were it not for the fact that the two problems here discussed belong in their essentials to political phenomena which are important for the future of Europe. Moreover, this strikingly cursory judgment on the problem is not merely a single case, but has to be taken in conjunction with a much wider and more influential section of West European opinion.

In contradistinction to this, I shall try here to analyze Bolshevism into its basic elements and show these as clearly as I can to the German and European public. This is not an easy task, in view of the fact that the Propagandist Institutions of the Communist International are undoubtedly well organized and have not been unsuccessful in putting before the public of the world, outside of the Russian frontiers, an entirely false picture of Bolshevism. This picture is an extraordinarily dangerous one because of the tension that it can and must naturally cause. Let us also note the profound hatred in liberal circles throughout the world in regard to National Socialism and its practical constructive work in Germany. Hence the possibility here also of mistaken judgments, such as these already mentioned. They pass by what is essential. International communism would entirely do away with all national and racial qualities that are founded in human nature itself; in property, it sees the most primary cause of the breakdown of world trade in the capitalist system. Accordingly, it exploits this through an extensive and carefully organized and brutal system of action, setting aside personal values and sacrificing the individual to a hollow mass-idol that is only a travesty of actual life itself. At the same time, it ignores and destroys all the idealistic and higher strivings of men and nations, through its own crass and empty materialist principles. On the other hand, National Socialism sees in all these things—in property, in personal values and in nation and race and the principles of idealism—these forces that carry on every human civilization and fundamentally determine its worth.

Bolshevism is explicitly determined on bringing about a revolution among all the nations. In its own essence it has an aggressive and international tendency. But National Socialism confines itself to Germany and is not a product for export, either in its abstract or practical characteristics. Bolshevism denies religion as a principle, fundamentally and entirely. It recognizes religion only as an "opium for the people." For the help and support of religious belief, however, National Socialism absolutely places in the foreground of its program a belief in God and that transcendental idealism which has been destined by Nature to bring to expression the racial soul of a nation. National Socialism would give the lead in a new concept and shaping of European civilization. But the Bolsheviks carry on a campaign, directed by the Jews, with the international underworld, against culture as such. Bolshevism is not merely anti-bourgeois; it is against human civilization itself.

In its final consequences it signifies the destruction of all the commercial, social, political and cultural achievements of Western Europe, in favor of a deracinated and nomadic international cabal that has found its representation in Judaism. This grandiose attempt to overthrow the civilized world is so much more dangerous in its effects because the Communist International, which is a past master in the art of misrepresentation, has been able to find its protectors and pioneers among a great part of these intellectual circles in Europe whose physical and spiritual destruction must be the first result of a Bolshevik world revolution.

Bolshevism, which is in reality an attack on the world of the spirit, pretends to be intellectual itself. Where circumstances demand, it comes as a wolf in sheep's clothing. But underneath the false mask that it here and there assumes, there are always the satanic forces of world destruction. And where it has had the opportunity of practicing its theories, it has created "The Paradise of the Workers and Peasants" in the shape of a fearful desert of starving and hungering people. If we are to take the word of its doctrine, then we find a terrible contradiction between its theory and its practice. Its theory is glowing and grandiose, but it carries poison in its attractive gloss. Over against this, what we have from it in reality is terrible and forbidding. This is shown in the millions of sacrifices that have been made in honor of it, through executions with the sword, the axe or the hangman's rope or hunger. Its teaching promises "the fatherland of the workers and peasants," which shall know no frontiers, and a classless social order which will be protected against exploitation through the state, and it preaches an economic principle in which "everything belongs to everybody" and that thereby a real and universal world peace will be ushered in.

Millions of workers on hunger-wages such as are not thought of in western Europe, millions of afflicted and sorrowing peasants who have been robbed of their land, which is being completely ruined by the stupid experiment of a paralyzing collectivism, famine which claims millions of victims year after year in a country of such vast extent that it might serve as a granary for the whole of Europe, the formation and equipping of an army which, according to the claims of all leading Bolshevists, is to be used for carrying out the world revolution, the brutal and merciless domination of this madly-led apparatus of State and Party at the hands of a small terrorist minority which is mostly Jewish—all this speaks another language, a language the world cannot listen to permanently because it rings with the story of nameless suffering and indescribable hardships borne by a nation of a hundred and sixty million people.

The fact that, in order to carry out its aims, Bolshevism uses propagandist methods that are perceptible only by those which have experience in such things and are entirely accepted in good faith by the average citizen makes this Terror International extraordinarily dangerous for other states and peoples. This propaganda starts out from the principle that the end sanctifies the means, that lies and slander, the terrorizing of the individual and of the mass, robbery and burnings and strikes and insurrection, espionage and sabotage of armies can and ought to be made use of, and therewith that the aim of revolutionizing the whole world must be specially and solely kept in view. This extraordinarily pernicious method of influencing the masses of the people does not stop before anything or anybody. Those alone who see into its secret driving forces are competent to deal with it and are capable of adopting the necessary contrary measures. This propaganda understands how to adopt every instrument to its purpose. It takes on an intellectual shape in intellectual circles. It is bourgeois with the bourgeoisie, and proletarian with the proletariat. It is mild and passive where that attitude suits, and it is pugnacious wherever it meets opposition that needs to be suppressed.

Bolshevism carries on its International propaganda through the Comintern.

A few weeks ago this apparatus for world destruction made public to the whole of Europe its plan of campaign for the annihilation of the nations and the states, all arranged and set forth in its tactical and strategic elements. Yet the bourgeois world, whose extirpation was announced openly and without any reserve whatsoever, failed to make any public protest of indignation and unite all the forces at its command as a definite counter-defense.

The cry of warning was raised only by those states in which Bolshevism has been finally overcome through the restoration of national principles. But this cry of warning was laughed at by the threatened bourgeois world and set aside as an exaggerated alarm.

Swept clear of internal enemies and united under the National Socialist standard, Germany placed herself at the head of the groups marshaled in the fight against the international bolshevization of the world. Herein she is quite aware that she is fulfilling a world mission that reaches out beyond all national frontiers. The fate of our civilized nations depends on the successful issue of this mission. As National Socialists, we have seen Bolshevism through and through. We recognize it beneath all its masks and camouflages. It stands before us, derobed of its trappings, bare and naked in its whole miserable imposture. We know what its teachings are, but we know also what it is in practice.

Here I shall give an unvarnished picture, which is backed up in all particulars by incontestable facts. If there is a spark of reason left in the world, and the faculty for clear thinking, then the states and peoples must be shocked at the prospect and induced to come together for their common defense against this acute danger.

I leave the methods and practices of the Communist Propaganda and theory within and without Russia to speak through examples that appear to me to be symptomatic. These examples could be replaced and supplemented by thousands of others, all of which when taken together show up the terrible aspect of this world disease.

Murder of individuals, murder of hostages and mass murder are the favorite means applied by Bolshevism to get rid of all opposition to its propaganda.

In Germany, three hundred National Socialists fell victims to the Communist terror practiced on individuals. On January 14th, 1930 Horst Wessel was shot through the half-opened door of his house by the Communist, Albrecht Höhler—called Ali—his accessories the Jews Salli Eppstein and Else Cohn. On August 9th, 1931, the police captains, Anlauf and Lenck, were shot down in the Bülowplatz in Berlin. The Communist leaders, Heinz Neumann and Kippenberger, were accused as instigators of the murder. Shortly afterwards, Heinz Neumann was arrested in Switzerland because of a passport that was invalid and a request for extradition made by Germany was not granted, on the plea that it was a "political crime." These are only some single examples of the communist terror wreaked on individuals. As further instances of the blood lust and cruelty to which they bear evidence we may turn to the hostage murders that took place in previous years.

On April 30th, 1919, in the Courtyard of the Luitpold Gymnasium in Munich, ten hostages, among them a woman, were shot through the backs, their bodies rendered unrecognizable and taken away. This act was done at the order of the Communist terrorist, Eglhofer, and under the responsibility of the Jewish Soviet Commissaries, Levien, Levien-Nissen and Axelrod. In 1919, during the Bolshevik regime of the Jew Béla Kun, whose real name was Aron Cohn, in Budapest twenty hostages were murdered. During the October Revolution in Spain eight prisoners were shot at Ovièdo, seventeen in Turon; and in the barracks at Pelàno, to protect a communist attack, thirty-eight prisoners were placed at the head of the insurgents and some of them shot. At the Comintern Congress, on July 31st, 1935, the communist leader, Carcio, expressly declared that this revolution was carried through "under the leadership of the communists."

This list of bloodshed becomes all the more fearful and horrible when we add to it the apparently incredible number of mass murders carried out by the Communists. As a classical prototype of this, we have the Paris Commune of the year 1871, which was passionately celebrated by Karl Marx and is approved today by modern Soviets as the model of the Bolshevik World Revolution. The number of victims who fell in that terrible year 1871 can no longer be ascertained. The Jewish Chekist, Bela Kun, made an experiment that rivaled the Paris Commune in bloodshed when he ordered the execution of 60,000 to 70,000 people in the Crimea. For the most part, these executions were carried out with machine-guns. At the Municipal Hospital in Alupka, 272 sick and wounded were brought out on stretchers in front of the gate of the Institution and shot there. The truth of this has been officially confirmed in the report made to the Geneva Red Cross. During the 133 days of his Terror Rule in Hungary, the Jew Bela Kun had innumerable men murdered. The names of 570 of those have been given in official documents. In November 1934, the Chinese Marshal Chiang Kai-shek made public the information that in the province of Kiangsi one million people were murdered by the communists and six millions robbed of all their possessions. All these blood-stained and horror-raising events have reached a climax in the mass murders committed throughout Soviet Russia.

According to returns given by the Soviets themselves and taking reliable sources into account, the number of persons executed within the first 5 years of Soviet rule must be placed at about 1,860,000, in round numbers. Of these, 6,000 were teachers and professors, 8,800 were doctors of medicine, 54,000 were army officers, 260,000 soldiers, 105,000 police officials, 49,000 gendarmes, 12,800 civil servants, 355,000 persons of the upper classes, 192,000 workers, 815,000 peasants.

The Soviet statistician Oganowsky estimates the number of persons who died of hunger in the years 1921/1922 at 5,200,000. The Austrian Cardinal-Archbishop, Monsignor Innitzer, said in his appeal of July 1934 that millions of people were dying of hunger throughout the Soviet Union. During his speech delivered before the House of Lords on the July 25th, 1934, the Archbishop of Canterbury, speaking on reports relative to the famine victims in Soviet Russia in 1933, said that the number was nearer to six than three millions.

We have thus before our eyes a full picture of this fearful and harrowing mass terrorization which is only approximately paralleled by even the most blood-curdling examples of war or revolution that are recorded in the history of the world. This is the actual system of bloodshed and terror and death that is carried out by hysterical and criminal political maniacs who would have it copied in every country and among every people with the same terrorizing practices, insofar as they might find the possibility of doing so.

In view of all this, it would be idle to bring forward proofs of the spirit of discipline and generous consideration that the National Socialists showed in carrying through their revolutionary aims.

Such is "the strange and terrible" resemblance between the methods followed by the two regimes which the writer of the article in the English newspaper alleges to be similar in "essential structure." But the facts to which I have referred do not fill out the picture. Revolutions cost money. Propaganda campaigns throughout the world must be financed. Bolshevism procures the means of doing so after its own fashion.

In the summer of 1907 Stalin led the notorious bomb attack at Tiflis on a money transport from the State Bank. Thirty persons fell victims to the attack. The 250,000 rubles that were robbed from the transport were sent to Lenin, who was then in Switzerland. They were to be at his disposal for revolutionary purposes. On the January 17th, 1908, the Jew Wallack-Meer, who now goes by the name of Litwinow and has been Chairman of the Council of the League of Nations, was arrested in Paris in connection with the bombing and robbing of the transport at Tiflis.

The Communist Party in Germany organized and led the plunder expeditions there and also the robbery of explosives from official depots. The list of such cases brought before the Courts of the Reich is very long. In this list are thirty crimes described as major and extreme cases. To them must be added the burnings and bombings organized and perpetrated without any consideration whatsoever for the lives of innocent persons.

On the April 16th, 1925, there was an explosion in the Cathedral of Sofia, which had been organized and carried out by the Bolsheviks. In July 1927 the Communists set the Palace of Justice at Vienna on fire. To celebrate the Lenin Feast, on January 22nd, 1930, the Simonoff Monastery at Moscow, a building dating from the 14th century, was blown up. On the night of February 27th–28th, 1933 the Reichstag in Berlin was set on fire as a signal for the armed communist rising. Through the medium of strikes, street fights and armed risings, the first preparatory stage of the Bolshevik revolution is meant to be effected. The methods used are the same in all countries. A long series of revolutionary acts that might be added on all sides furnish a striking witness of this. In one of its propagandist publications, the Comintern boasted that it had organized nearly all the strikes that have taken place during recent years. These strikes find their violent sequel in street fights. From the street fight to the armed rising is but one step. In this sequence, the following risings took place: October 1917 in Russia, January 1919 the Spartacus rising in Germany, 1920 the Max Hoelz revolt in Vogtland, and the Red Army in the Ruhr district, 1921 in Central Germany, September 1923 at Hamburg, December 1924 at Reval, on October 23rd, 1926, February 22nd, 1927 and March 21st, 1927 at

Shanghai. December 1927 in Canton, October 1934 in Spain, April 1935 in Cuba and May 1935 in the Philippines.

Bolshevik propaganda aims its chief blows against the armed forces of a country. For the Bolsheviks know that if they were to adopt the principle of trying to secure support from the majority of the people, they could never carry out their plans. Force, therefore, is the only means left to them; but in every well-ordered state this meets with the opposition of the army. The Bolsheviks accordingly feel bound to introduce their disintegrating propaganda within the ranks of the army itself. Their idea is to corrupt it from within and thus render it ineffective as a bulwark against anarchy.

Before the advent of National Socialism to power in Germany, there was the closest co-operation between the Soviet espionage and the Communist organizations here. A foreign department of the O.G.P.U. operated officially in our country. It was the special representative and directive agent of the Communist espionage. The aim of this espionage was not only to obtain military secrets in a traitorous way, but also to carry on a system of sabotage among the police and the army. Part of the program was to introduce a mutinous spirit into the *Reichswehr* and, by an increasing work of revolutionary instruction, to bring about a revolt of the soldiers and sailors in the German defense forces. From July 1931 to December 1932 one-hundred-and-eleven cases of high treason were dealt with before the German Courts.

These cases originated with the activities of the Communist Party. Furthermore, there were an extraordinary number of cases of espionage of a treasonable character in the industrial factories. The most boorish example of the interference of "Soviet Diplomats" for the purpose of creating domestic political trouble in another country is afforded by the Jewish Soviet Ambassador, Joffe, who had to leave Berlin on November 6th, 1918, because he had utilized the diplomatic courier to transport sabotage material that was to be used to undermine the German army and make the revolution possible. What were called "Revolution Funds" were used in great part by Liebknecht for the purchase of weapons for the German Communists, and partly also for the production of propaganda material to be used among the army. On December 26th, 1918, one of the Socialists members of the Reichstag, the Jew Dr. Oskar Cohn, declared that on the 5th of the previous month, he had received 4 million rubles from Joffe for the purpose of the German Revolution.

We can now see that all these activities were meant for the purpose of bringing about the downfall of the German Reich through the undermining and corruption of the German Army.

Amid all these single acts of terror, of hostage murders and mass murders, plunder and arson, strikes and armed risings, espionage and sabotage of armies, we see the Communist World Propaganda showing its forbidding and grimacing countenance. An idea and a movement that has used such dastardly and revolting means to secure power and to hold it can maintain itself only by chicanery, slander and falsehood. These are the typical methods used by Bolshevism in its propaganda; and they are applied in different ways according to the suitability of the occasion. Thus, for example, we can understand how it is that crises, catastrophes etc. which happen in other countries outside the Soviet Union are exploited by the Bolshevik Propaganda, whereas we are told that within the Soviet frontiers a work of social construction is in progress that has banished economic distress and created a State in which there is no unemployment. The real truth is that a condition of commercial disorder exists throughout the country and an industrial collapse that baffles description. The "Land without Unemployment" contains hundreds of thousands and even millions of beggars and homeless children who throng the streets of the big cities, and hundreds of thousands who are condemned to banishment and forced labor.

While in all the other countries alleged Capitalist and Fascist dictatorships are in power, Russia affords an example of freedom and democratic order. So we are told.

In reality, this land is wilting under the Jewish-Marxist rule of force, which will stop at no means to maintain itself in power. The pretended freedom and right of self-determination among the nationalities constituting the Soviet Union turns out in fact to be a process of enslavement and extirpation of those nationalities themselves. The pretended liberation of colonial and semi-colonial peoples through the international proletariat is, when looked at in its true light, a bloodstained and ruthless example of Soviet imperialism of the worst kind.

[. . .]

Therewith we may close the account.

That is Communism with the mask off. That is its theory, its practice and its propaganda. I have given a bald and staid account of facts which have been gathered mostly from official sources; but this account points to a state of affairs which is so terrible and revolting in all its effects that it must shock the average civilized human being. This gospel of "the emancipation of the proletariat from the yoke of capitalism" is the worst and most brutal kind of capitalism that can be imagined. It has been thought out, set afoot and led under the inspiration of the Mammon worship and materialist thought that is incarnated in international Jewry, scattered throughout every country of the globe. It is no social experiment. It is nothing else than a mammoth system for the expropriation and despoiling of the Aryan directive classes in all the nations, and the substitution of the Jewish underworld in their place. Those people who put themselves forward here as the apostles of a new teaching and the liberators of mankind are in reality figures that herald anarchy and chaos for the civilized world.

There is no longer any political question at issue here. This thing cannot be judged or estimated by political rules or principles. It is iniquity under a political mask. It is not something to be brought before the bar of world history, but rather something that has to be dealt with by the judicial administration of each country. It must be met with the same ruthless and even brutal means with which it strives to usurp power or hold power in its hands. Here there can be no bargaining, because the danger that threatens Europe is acute. Overnight, it might break in among the civilized nations of the world and spread universal catastrophe. Those states that make peace with it will soon learn from experience that it is not they who will tame Bolshevism, but that Bolshevism will bring them under its heel. It cannot be said that the Comintern has changed its practices. It is and remains what it always was—the propagandist and revolutionary machinery that is avowedly intended to bring about the downfall of the West.

Bolshevism is the declared enemy of all nations, all religions, and all human civilization. The World Revolution is now, as always, its acknowledged and proclaimed goal. Stalin himself has, as the organ of the War Commissariat, "The Red Star," in January 1935, triumphantly announced: "Under Lenin's banner, in the proletarian revolution, we shall triumph over the whole world." And the communist emigrant, Pieck, said at the Seventh World Congress of the Comintern, held on July 28th this year: "The triumph of Socialism in Soviet Russia proves at the same time that the triumph of Socialism throughout the whole world is inevitable." On the day before the Congress was held, "L'Humanité" (the organ of the French Communists) greeted it with the outburst: "Long live the Comintern, the General Staff of the World Revolution."

Traffic with Bolshevism is not possible either on a political basis or on the basis of general principles in life. The acknowledgment of the Soviet Union on the part of the United States has given rise to an increase in communist propaganda, innumerable strikes and general unrest throughout America. The military pact between France and the Soviet Union led shortly afterwards to an increase of communist votes at the municipal elections, in which they won 43 mandates and thus doubled the number of mandates formerly held by them, while all the other parties lost accordingly. The military alliance between Czechoslovakia and the Soviet Union led to sabotaging in the army and to an unexpected increase of communist votes at the elections that followed.

Whoever has made pacts with Bolshevism will have reason to rue his act.

Nothing could be farther from our minds than the wish to prescribe for other nations and their governments, or even to counsel them. We do not mix up in their domestic affairs. We only see the dangers that threaten Europe and raise our voices in warning, so that the magnitude of those dangers may be recognized.

As far as we ourselves are concerned, we have completely overcome this menace. Indeed, perhaps outside of his work in Germany, the greatest service that our Führer has rendered the world is that here in Germany, he has set up a barrier against world Bolshevism against which the waves of this vile Asiatic-Jewish flood break in vain. He has taught us not only to recognize Bolshevism as the world's greatest enemy, but also to meet it face to face and crush it. Instead of this teaching, he has supplied a new and better and nobler ideal for the liberation of a whole nation. In the Sign of this Idea we have fought our battles and brought our banners to victory. This ideal has enabled us to free Germany from the menace of Bolshevism and banish it once and for all from the German nation. Today we know how to cope with these insidious forces.

The nation has been rendered immune against the poison of the red anarchy. It has repudiated the false and hollow catchphrases of the communistic world propaganda. Seriously and industriously, and with patience and discipline, it has given itself to the solution of problems that arise out of its own destiny. History will one day give due credit to the *Führer* for having saved Germany from the most acute and deadly peril by overthrowing Bolshevism and thereby saving the whole civilization of the West from the abyss that yawned before it.

I hope that it will not be left to posterity to recognize the greatness of this historic mission, but that it will [be] acknowledged by our contemporaries and that they will decide to act upon the truth of its teachings. As the true and loyal Old Guard of the Führer and the Party, we rejoice that we are standing under his banners in this most decisive struggle that the history of the world has experienced.

56

CARL SCHMITT

National Socialist Legal Thought

First published as "Nationalsozialistisches Rechtsdenken," in *Deutsches Recht: Zentralorgan des Bundes Nationalsozialistischer Deutscher Juristen* 4, no. 10 (25 May 1934): 225–29. Translated by Timothy Nunan.

The great and incomparable deed of the National Socialist movement is its overcoming of the schism and shearing that stood in service of certain political tendencies for many centuries. An entire system of antitheses—body and soul, spirit and material, law and politics, law and economy, law and morality—an entire litany of dualistic shearings of matters of both life and being that were inseparable from one another presented themselves in ever-changing development in the service of a certain ideology and its attendant political tendencies and goals.

It is an error, if not worse, in light of the concrete facts of the matter of the legal situation today, to want to carry forward the tearing asunder of the juridical and the political, of the juridical and the ideological, of the juridical and the moral. The fact that every reactionary or anyone in step with the past adheres to these antitheses is not astonishing. But we may not allow a clear, strong sense of the law and sense of justice on the part of upstanding men to be erroneously depicted through the help of this artifice, namely through the antithesis of the juristic and the ideological. We may not allow young National Socialist students or junior lawyers to be taught that what they feel and think as National Socialists may well be ideologically good and worthy but juridically false.

1

These systematic shearings are associated with a past era since overcome through National Socialism. *In a higher sense, they are not scholarly, juridical, or intellectual* but rather the product of a certain time and of certain political movements and tendencies. A conversation with a world-famous, world-traveled, experienced scholar of more than seventy years of age from the United States of America belongs to the major experiences and encounters I have had as a jurist in the service of National Socialism. The scholar summarized for me in 1932 the result of his recent experiences and his diagnosis of our current condition with the following sentence: "*We are today experiencing the bankruptcy of the* idées générales." [. . .]

An entire legal and scholarly system whose particularity consists in its ability to place uncoupled general concepts in the place of concrete reality was erected in the course of a century. This system succeeded in calling upon its particularity, *the monopoly of the juridical.* We must underestimate neither the meaning of this precedent nor the monstrous task that hangs incumbent on us as German National Socialist jurists when we want to tear down this normativistic Tower of Babel and put in its place a healthy, concrete order of thought. But what that American legal scholar had to say when he spoke of the *bankruptcy of "general ideas"* is nonetheless correct. This method is internally bankrupt among all *Völker* who still have any life at all. This method has no true life to it and is no longer a real form of legal scholarship. It is the overextension of a single and often the central element of a way of juridical thinking—namely that of the rule, of the general norm, *of the law* in opposition to justice.

This normativism, which was supposed to play a secondary, marginal role in juristic thought, appointed itself within this scholarly total system as exclusive lord of intellectual and scholarly thought, and particularly of juristic thought.

2

We in Germany have succumbed to this normativistic way of thinking to a particularly high degree, particularly so as the consequent effect of a certain legal-historical event, namely the *reception of Roman law.* [. . .]

Ancient Roman law was the most reasonable thing in the world for Roman peasants, the paterfamilias, *and soldiers who created and carried this law.* But Roman law becomes the most senseless, most scandalous, most dangerous thing in the world once detached from a concrete reality, carried over to another order of a *Volk,* once the abstraction of its detached maxims is passed off as the only pure juridical and scholarly legal wisdom. For generations now, this abstract normativism has been driven into healthy German brains. The normativistic way of thinking that thus arose among us was further encouraged in the nineteenth century by the fact that the *influx of the Jewish guest* Volk [that] drove this development [even] further in the direction of a normativistic way of thinking about the law. Firstly, that is because of the unique nature of the Jewish *Volk,* which for millennia lived not as a state on its own soil but rather only in the law and in the norm, a *Volk* that is, therefore, in the truest sense of the word "existentially normative." Second, however, it goes without saying that a foreigner, a guest, a *metic,* sees the law of a *Volk* under whom he is guest normativistically and only from the point of view of legal certainty, from the point of view of the predictability of legal decisions. This foreigner certainly does not belong to the reality of the *Volk,* the reality in which he lives. The foreigner perceives this reality's law as a calculably effective norm, as a standard of the state's functioning to which he conforms, upon whose basis he can calculate outcomes and upon "whose basis he can protect himself from the state." The foreigner wants to have the timetable in order to know when and where he can get on and get off. As a result, he puts in place of justice the law in the sense of a previously determined, calculable norm.

3

Thus, it has come to the point where one declares punishable acts as unpunishable in the name of "positivism," in the name of juridical scholarship, because

in the normativistic way of thinking, punishment is defined not on the basis of the crime; rather, the crime is defined on the basis of the normative threat of punishment.

It is the mark of the normativist that he defines concepts in reverse. For example: "Crime is an activity that involves the threat of imprisonment." In truth and according to the law, the relation is the reverse: something is a crime not because it involves the threat of imprisonment; rather, because it is a crime, it involves the threat of imprisonment. But a jurist of this way of thinking cannot and does not want only to think in reverse. The state constitution is for him nothing more than a law that is more difficult to modify than other laws; marriage, a contract that can be abrogated only through a judge's verdict. *What does one truly juridically know of the constitution or of marriage when one is familiar with such definitions?* And yet it is precisely those definitions that currently stand as particularly astute, juridically speaking. And such a way of thinking is taken up year after year by young, healthy Germans. It is therefore not a legal-historical whim that we are fighting against when we struggle against Roman law; we struggle rather against a way of thinking that still rules today at the universities and in the practice of jurists. We struggle against a way of thinking that is in essence foreign to us, a way of thinking that has brought to rule in Germany a way for jurists to think that is alien to us.

If we want to demand National Socialist legal thought and, in doing so, to speak much of the struggle against Roman law, then our struggle is just as profound and as universal as every other National Socialist demand. We would make it too cheap and easy if we let the fundamentality and profundity of such a National Socialist demand out of our sight, and if instead we consider such demands as outgrowths, as superficialities.

The National Socialist struggle against Roman law is a struggle against the monopoly and rule of a certain juridical way of thinking. There are different manners of thinking about the law. They complement one another; different ones come into the foreground at different times and then later retreat. It is a question of the concrete situation, but moreover also a question of the concrete nature of a *Volk. Every* Volk *has its associated juridical type.* [. . .]

5

[. . .] *We are now coming from an abstract-normativistic type to a type of concrete order of thought.* Everywhere, National Socialism creates a different kind of order, starting from the National Socialist German Workers' Party to the numerous new orders that we see growing before us: corporate orders, the orders of factories and other concerns, camps and unions, orders of the most different kind.

All of these orders bring their inner justice with them, and when a portion of the German jurists do not understand that, it will do them no good to retreat onto the melting sheet of ice of the old forms of convulsive normativism and positivism.

This portion of German jurists will sink into the flow of history. Our effort, however, has the course of living growth on its side, and our new order comes solely from ourselves. Our new order is no alien and artificial scaffolding, devoid of any sense and connection with the situation at hand. Our new order is, moreover, in its juristic concepts a living expression of our present reality. [. . .]

The more the old, abstract statutory jurisprudence conducts itself *ad absurdum,* the more it disguises itself positivistically or purely scholarly, the freer our new order will grow. Here we have, as I already said, all of the good *Völker* of the earth and all their good intellects on our side. In all countries there are indications of a new development in legal scholarship. All countries and *Völker* seek to turn back to their own soil, to their own blood and to the natural orders that arise from blood and soil, and to liberate themselves from the artificial superstructure of the *idées générales.* Our National Socialist endeavor for German justice and German legal scholarship stands in a leading role in this magnificent process of renewal that concerns the entire world. *We are rethinking legal concepts.* This is no event that one could dismiss as merely intuitive, emotional, and irrational with the antithesis of the political and the juridical, or of the ideological and the juridical. It is an event whose totality already grasps the thoughtful and the truly *scholarly* side of legal life. It is an event that we all, we German National Socialist jurists, must be proud of having taken part in. *We are on the side of things to come!*

57

HANS F. K. GÜNTHER

A Modest Racial Study of the German People

First published in *Kleine Rassenkunde des deutschen Volkes* (Munich: J.F. Lehmann, 1933), 9–13, 21–25, 59. First edition published in 1929.

Much has already been written on the subject of race in man, on the individual races of man that were regarded as such, on the "race question" and the racial composition of nations (*Völker*); and since it all dealt with the question of man's race, this literature gave rise to a long, drawn-out controversy. The reason for such a protracted and relatively unfruitful dispute over the "race question" most often lay in the fact that both sides did not clearly understand the concept of "race." In most cases, the controversy was not even concerned with races but with racially mixed tribes, peoples of mixed racial stock, or groups of peoples belonging to the same linguistic family. The dispute raged over the recognition or importance of a "Germanic race" as opposed to a "Latin race" or a "Slavic race"; the concept of a "Jewish race" or a "Semitic race" was put forward. In the process, these writers must have completely forgotten that a human group may be designated as a race only when all of their representatives demonstrate identical physical and spiritual features in the most important points. How could anyone speak of a "Jewish race," seeing that there are tall and short, slim and stocky, light and dark Jews with thin and broad faces, Jews with "Jewish noses" and those without them, not to mention the differences in the attitudes of individual Jews?

The idea of a "Germanic race" was put forward, and the race was happily described as tall, blond, and blue-eyed, and occasionally as long or oval headed and thin faced. Its psychic essence was also more or less defined. Now, the fact that frequently very "un-Germanic" people, in both their physical and mental characteristics, could be found among the peoples of Germanic language—for example, among the English, the Dutch, the Germans, and the Danes—should have served to warn against presenting a concept of a "Germanic race"; so, too, the fact that people of typical "Germanic" appearance and comportment were often present among the peoples of the Slavic and Romance languages, and even among Caucasian tribes and Kurds. Furthermore, in view of the large variety of human types among the peoples of the Semitic languages, how could one speak of a "Semitic race"?

In short, a proper distinction was not made between the concepts of "race" and "people" [*Volk*] or "group of people" [*Völkergruppe*]. Membership in a language group was confused with membership in a racial group, and there was a desire to see racial borders where there were really only linguistic and national-ethnic [*Volkstum*] borders. It was only when the concept of "race" was strictly defined and when it found currency among at least a few educated people that a valid and fruitful discussion of the "race question" or of various "race questions" became possible. Anyone who continued to speak of a "German race," or an "English race," or a "Latin race," or a "Jewish race" betrayed an ignorance of the basic concepts of the subject he wanted to discuss.

"Race" is an anthropological concept that has been established in the same way as the sciences of zoology and botany (fauna and flora) and that, *like* them, discusses families, genera, species, and varieties. Eugen Fischer, director of the Kaiser Wilhelm Institute for the Study of Anthropology, Human Heredity and Eugenics in Berlin-Dahlem, has called the following assertion by Grosse the best definition of the concept of "race":

"By race, anthropology understands a large group of people who are related to one another through the common possession of a certain inherited complex of physical and spiritual characteristics which also distinguishes them from other similar groups."

Consequently, a race must necessarily show, in all its representatives, a uniformity of physical and spiritual features and must continue to reproduce from within itself people with the same physical and spiritual characteristics. Where there exist in a group of people essential differences in physical and spiritual endowment, where children essentially differ from their parents, or from one of them, there can be no question of a race or of parents with the same inherited set of features. I regard the following definition of the concept of "race" as useful:

A race is made up of a group of people that is distinguished from all other groups of people by a combination of endowed physical features and spiritual characteristics and that repeatedly reproduces only its own kind.

Hence, a race is a group of people possessing an identical hereditary endowment. Whoever tries in this way to visualize the nature of a race must immediately admit that it is hardly possible to find a race anywhere in the world as a self-enclosed human group. The human groups in this world that are linked by the same language, the same customs, or the same faith and thereby constitute a *Volk* are, with hardly a single exception, a mixture of races, not races. All Western peoples [*Völker*] are mixtures of races that include, in certain proportions, pure and mixed, all the races of Europe, or in which at least several European races are represented.

What varies from *Volk* to *Volk*—from the ethnological viewpoint—is not, for instance, the race as such, but the proportion in which the races are mixed. In the mixture of one people, one or more races may be more strongly represented than in the race mixture of another people. Anyone who would try to gather together the peoples of Europe who are related by race—or, rather, the people who appear to be related by race (since the inherited and the apparent image do not necessarily correspond)—in order to form uniform groups of people who appear to possess identical hereditary endowments, would have to connect these people from among all the peoples of Europe. At the same time, he would discover that these uniform groups of people are small minorities in comparison with the great mass of Europe's population, since the majority of the people of the West, as well as of the whole world, consist of a blend of two or more races.

From the standpoint of the definitions given above, the Jews, who, because of their non-European origin, will not be counted among the racial mixtures of Europe in the discussion that follows but will instead be taken up as a subject in and of themselves, cannot be viewed as a race. Rather, they constitute a people of mixed race. If popular usage is particularly reluctant to give up the term *race* in the case of the Jews, the reason lies in the fact that in the racial mixture of the Jewish people, physical and spiritual hereditary endowments of non-European peoples are predominant, and these are quite conspicuous when seen among the differently composed racial mixtures of the European population and especially that of northwestern Europe. The average European in Europe is not regarded as the bearer of racial features, but this is certainly the case with the average Jew. Therefore, popular usage will continue for a long time to speak of a "Jewish race," even though educated persons will have long since acknowledged that the Jews, like other peoples, represent a mixture of races.

For the research on the races of mankind according to their physical appearance, for the identification of different human races in a certain geographical area where various race mixtures are found (tribes, peoples, ethnic groups), anthropology avails itself of specific procedures of the measurement and description of physical features that cannot be indicated here in detail. [. . .]

The Nordic race is tall, long legged, slim, with an average height, among males, of around 1.74 meters. The limbs, the neck, the shape of the hands and feet are vigorous and slender in appearance. The Nordic race is long legged and narrow faced, with a cephalic index of around 75 and a facial index above 90. As in all races, at least in the medium- and long-headed ones, the female head, in comparison with that of the male, appears to have a higher cephalic index and a lower facial index. The back of the Nordic head characteristically projects far beyond the nape of the neck. The protruding part of the back of the head, however, is comparatively low, so that in Nordic people the head springs backward, as it were, over the part of the neck visible above the collar. The face is narrow, with a rather narrow forehead, a narrow, high-built nose, and a narrow lower jaw and prominent chin. The cut of the face of the Nordic race—at least in the male—creates the effect of a unique boldness through three striking traits in the lines of the profile: first in the flat, backward-tilting forehead; then in the straight or outwardly curved nose springing from high nasal roots; and finally in the prominent chin. The smooth parts of the face support the expression of clean-cut physiognomy. In the female, the chin is mostly arched rather than tilted backward; the nose is less sharply delineated and the chin less prominent.

The skin of the Nordic race is roseate bright and the blood shines through so that it looks especially enlivened and at the same time mostly somewhat cool or fresh. The facial complexion, at least among the youth and among the females, often looks like "milk and blood," even in middle age. The hair is smooth-straight or wavy; in childhood, also curly. The individual hairs are soft and thin. The hair color is blond; among most of the existing types it can extend from a pink undertone of light blond to golden blond up to dark blond. Nordic children are often white-blond. People who were light blond during their youth will later become dark blond or dark haired, a phenomenon that is called "darkening" and that is viewed as a sign of Nordic (or also Phalian or East Baltic) strain also among non-Nordic peoples. [. . .]

If an illustrator, painter, or sculptor wants to represent the image of a bold, goal-determined, resolute person, or of a noble, superior, and heroic human being, man or woman, he will, in most cases, create an image that more or less approximates the image of the Nordic race. He will also create a man who will be regarded as a typical representative of the upper social strata. For example, the artists for the humorous journals will endow their creations with the features of the Nordic race rather than the features of the non-Nordic races of Europe.

Actually, one could conceivably designate willpower, a definite faculty of judgment rooted in a coolly deliberating sense of reality, the impulse to truthfulness, and an inclination to knightly justice as the repeatedly striking psychical features of Nordic men. Such features can be intensified in individuals within the Nordic race to a pronouncedly heroic disposition, to a transcendent leadership in statesmanship or creativity in technology, science, and art. The relatively great number of Nordic people among the famous and outstanding men and women of Western countries is striking, as is the relatively low number of famous men and women without noticeable Nordic strain.

58

SUSANNA PERTZ

The Word *Nordic*

First published as *Das Wort "nordisch." Seine Geschichte bis zur Jahrhundertwende* (Dresden: Dittert, 1939), 6–7.

The term *Nordic race* designates a group of human beings of a certain physical, intellectual-psychological type that includes not only the major portion of ancient Germanic tribes but that also applies to certain non-Germanic peoples based on their physical constitution and their unique intellectual-psychological nature as evidenced in their cultural achievements. The outward appearance of men of the Nordic race can be precisely determined based on absolute and proportional numbers and based on physiognomic tests. But what is equally, if not more, important is recognizing the spiritual predisposition of the Nordic race, its values, and behavior with respect to every aspect of life, however great or small. But throughout the history of man, as far back as we can be trace it, there has never been an absolute, all-encompassing embodiment of *Nordic thought*—the unconditionality and profundity of which is comprehensible only to Germans. So it is perhaps most appropriate to speak in terms of the Nordic movement and the Nordic ideal. What is at issue here is the word *Nordic,* which has undergone such an overwhelming expansion and deepening of meaning in contemporary ideological debates. Even if this idiomatic usage departs to some degree from previous common usage and may seem illogical from an etymological perspective, it is nevertheless pointless, myopic, and thus erroneous to seek to counter this development based on abstract speculations. Not only the history of real events but also the history of words is made by creative agents in the world because they produce the ideas that determine events, not by historically inclined thinkers who, based on intimate knowledge of past conditions, seek to identify an absolute logical progression of events in the sequence of ideological and material events. This does not imply an attempt to dispense with the endeavor to view intellectual history from a scholarly, scientific perspective—that is to say, to provide proof of certain laws that are effective everywhere and without exception in this history. But experience should teach us that a contemplative stance with regard to the events in the lives of peoples, which form the prerequisite to every form of historical science and scholarship, must always give way to the willingness to recognize the active forces rising from the depths of man's being to give life to new impulses, which are not always evident at first glance.

59

PAUL SCHULTZE-NAUMBURG

Nordic Beauty

Portraits of Perfection in Life and in Art

First published in *Nordische Schönheit. Ihr Wunschbild im Leben und in der Kunst* (Munich: J.F. Lehmann, 1937), 34–36.

Since these races consist of such an amalgam of characteristics—indeed, since they encompass, in their posture, individual forms and movement, such a sweeping diversity of contrasts—it is impossible to arrive at a uniform standard for the epitome of beauty that might be applicable to all Germans. It is nevertheless utterly apparent that German civilization has clearly established an internalized standard for the epitome of beauty that has consistently manifested itself as generally accepted and acceptable over the past few thousand years of our history. This also finds expression in art, which at least up until the beginning of the twentieth century, has always acknowledged a particular human type as being representative of human beauty, even if it was not always able to lend vibrant expression to it. Upon closer examination of this phenomenon, we find that this standard for the epitome of beauty unmistakably follows the outline of that race that has assumed leadership in all the great epochs of German history. And that is the Nordic race. It is highly endowed with a talent for nation building, and by far the greatest percentage of cultural capital has been the product of its highly developed intellectual aptitudes. Even in light of the diverse admixture evident in the German *Volk*, it is easy to see that high-level achievements occur primarily when there is sufficient or even a surfeit of Nordic blood present in the population. The creative will to be active in the world on the part of Nordic man is perhaps the spark that triggers the release of aptitudes dormant in the remaining portions of the race. This strong quotient of Nordic blood, however, can also manifest itself among Germans whose outward appearance reveals the presence of alien blood. And this is perhaps the reason that the whole German civilization has professed its faith in the Nordic standard for the epitome of beauty. It seems entirely understandable, then, that alien races should never have hoped to adhere to the same, perhaps because they were entirely unable, because it is not a matter of a common consensus but rather of entirely instinctive professions of the emotive life. The degree to which alien races acknowledge the superiority of another race not only by dint of its power but also at the very basic emotional level is one of the most pressing questions that merits further investigation and one that we have little to go on in search of an answer. The same applies to the acceptance of standards for the epitome of beauty. The standard that Nordic man applies as a general rule of thumb to distinguish the high from the low, the beautiful from the ugly, is of course not likely to be readily accepted by the subjects of those marked with such distinctions. Nevertheless, here, too, purely empirical standards are in evidence. The superiority of the Nordic man over the Bushman and even over the Eskimo is discernible from his achievements and the role he has played throughout the globe. One can certainly concede that the Eskimo is in possession of vitally essential traits that Nordic man has perhaps never possessed in the same degree or that have since been lost to him. All this notwithstanding, the Eskimo will surely consider his wife more beautiful than a European woman, inasmuch as he is even capable of formulating any concept of a perfect portrait of "human beauty." On the other hand, it is often enough remarked that lower races are unabashed in their adulation of higher races. Particularly with regard to women, one can observe again and again the way that the Jew (and the Negro) lasciviously lusts after and seduces the Nordic woman.

Our past has been unanimous in its judgment of beauty as something that is based on a supposedly "classical" model. It has often been declared that this classical ideal is the result of adopting an alien portrait of perfection—namely, the Greek—and, based on this assumption, charged with being un-German. I have addressed this issue so exhaustively in my book *Art and Race* that it merits reference here. This "classical" model, then, did not reign supreme as the standard measure within Germanic culture because the Greeks had discovered a universal human law that would be valid as eternal truth, as if it were some sort of geometric axiom. Rather, Nordic man discovered the works created by a *Volk* of the same blood that was able to develop a racially specific art because the external exigencies were more favorable and this *Volk* was not enslaved by racially alien dogmas. Furthermore (as [Hans F. K.] Günther points out), this artistic development was able to flourish unhindered by virtue of climactic forces and natural resources that were unleashed on cultural achievements, which would have been conjoined with and consumed differently in a harsher climate associated with a more strenuous struggle for existence. It is thus entirely understandable that for the Germanic peoples, when they stumbled upon the treasures of antiquity in Italian territory, these seemed to them revelations of their own soul, as flesh of their flesh and bone of their bone. Since this was the standard for the epitome of beauty that was thus blood of their blood, they were able to adopt it without reservations, or at least to hold it up as a highly valued model. It never would have been possible to foist off a racially alien model on the Germanic *Volk* as it threw off the shackles of the Middle Ages. These sorts of influences might hold sway in periods of extreme weakness of a *Volk,* such as we experienced in the years between 1918 and 1933. But as soon as a *Volk* has liberated itself from such conditions and has again come to its senses under calculated and clear leadership, this alien crust is shed all on its own, just as a scab releases itself from a wound that has healed and is replaced by new skin.

This process is not to be confused with successes in education and upbringing, as much as this is and remains the elusive dream of educators. Man is not inclined to admit the limits of his active capacities once he has overestimated them beyond heaven's reach. One cannot contend that the German *Volk* was "educated and raised" to accept a different model in the years between 1918 and 1933. Rather, the ruling political powers employed all the tools of their tyranny to superimpose their own ideas on the *Volk* to the extent that it seemed as if the German *Volk* had itself fallen prey to these racially alien ideas. Undoubtedly, especially the young people, in the impressionable age of youth, tread on the heels of primarily alien ideals. Many of them simply buckled under the pressure, while others were happy to cash in on it. Many did not even notice, for we cannot neglect to consider the fact that leadership in the nineteenth century was oblivious to biological concerns while in the twentieth it was so antagonistic toward the principles of natural selection that the stock of inferior human beings has risen to dangerous heights. The healthy sector of the *Volk,* and we would like to hope that this group constitutes the majority, merely clenched its teeth as it watched these things grow and proliferate around it until the day finally came when its members all rose up and followed the call of the Führer.

On the other hand, nor is it possible now to *educate* the German *Volk* to a standard for the epitome of beauty that is appropriate to its nature. It may be possible to lead the *Volk* to it, but ultimately only those who already carry it in their blood will find their way to it, while others may at best be led to pay lip service to it—and that is of benefit to no one. But, from a pragmatic perspective, it is sufficient that a majority of the *Volk* is led to acknowledge this epitome of beauty because the half-hearted bystanders on the periphery are powerless to dethrone the generally recognized standard.

60

WOLF WILLRICH

The German Face

First published as "Das deutsche Antlitz," in *Das Schwarze Korps,* 6 March 1935, 11.

The typical appearance of the German face—that is, the appearance of the German face in contradistinction to alien races—assumes a genuinely Nordic form and an attendant Nordic expression.

But the typical image of men and women that has since come to dominate the film industry and the boulevard press, and even the magazine industry, tends to be anything but German in the truest sense of the word.

The industry barons are in a predicament.

The black wiry lashes of the Hollywood diva, "the vamp"—we are pretty much vamped out—why, hardly anyone still believes in their power to bring men to their knees now that they run rampant as a pack of hounds. Even the gentlemen criminals and ballroom heroes are gradually beginning to pale against the backdrop of healthy reality. What is more, a waking sense of instinct is spreading amongst the *Volk,* and the voices demanding from the film industry and the boulevard press that they produce different, more realistic character types for men and women are mounting steadily. The industry would be happy to accommodate this new tide without losing the mainstream circle of clientele they have come to rely on. What is more, the people employed by the entertainment industry are still predominantly American in typology (brand name: racial cocktail). The "Nordic" types are not generally natural-born actors; they don't much like being photographed and are more useful as instruments of *real* life than as mere representations of life, especially when such representations are tinged with the tastes of writers and directors of alien blood.

So it is that, despite all forms of censure, the film industry and boulevard press all too often continue to produce "beauties" that are *corrupt to the core* or that simply conform—but on a superficial and contrived level—to the Nordic ideal, however that may be defined. Whoever is genuinely inclined toward racial thought by virtue of inner conviction will be as embarrassed by this sensationalist opportunism as they are by Hollywood's universalist portrayals. He will be repulsed not only by the masks but by the triviality and the overall tastelessness of this whole style of filmmaking.

Nordic man is the very personification of restraint—especially when it comes to expressions of delicate matters. Any dame who displays her romantic interests from miles away is lacking in psychological sensitivity, even if her eyes are blue and her hair has been bleached "Nordic" blond. Every flagrantly broad stroke of innuendo that actors, and particularly stars of the silver screen, are so reluctant to eschew violates the sense of propriety that is intrinsic to Nordic man. He does not derive any pleasure from having "his nose" so blatantly "rubbed in the emotional affairs of his fellow men"; he would prefer to arrive at the same conclusions by way of conjecture based on *indirect* behaviors and actions.

Soul-searching snivel and salacious soul baring are both equally un-Nordic.

The artistry of a Nordic actor must reach its zenith in that which he cannot portray and does not attempt to portray, in that which he rather leaves to tasteful audiences to discern. This is the reason that Nordic man comes across as unaffected or "unsightly" in the fields of film, theater, or journalistic photodocumentary. If anything, his image is best captured in photographic snapshots. Sports photographs are proof of that. But even there, his image seems fleeting and accidental, not typical of his intrinsic nature. For the still shot captures only one split second in time and, only in exceptional cases, the typical essence of its subject.

A painter or a sculptor is still at a distinct advantage in this regard. Once he has arrived at the point in his work at which the Nordic model has finally come to grips with the fact of being put on display and thus immerses himself in empirical thought, inwardly concentrating, contemplating, planning, etc., then those traits that are not merely accidental but rather typical come to the fore untainted and undisturbed. Then all the artist has to do is capture the whole without bothering to analyze it, to provide a faithful rendering in artistic form; in this way, he succeeds in portraying the "German countenance" that transcends any sort of accidental semblances. If you take stock of the similarities found in countless images that have been cut directly from life in this manner—not from life's theater!—this is about what you come up with: daring and pride, shrewd restraint, seriousness, resoluteness, candor, loyalty—these are the virtues that can be read from the prototypically Nordic German face.

The typical faults [of the Nordic German]—which are difficult to discern clearly—are found frequently in the form of powermongering, envy, and "fervent ambition" as distortions of honorable daring and pride; as sober stringency or irascibility instead of restraint; heavy-handedness, awkwardness, and pedantry instead of inner seriousness; ruthless boorishness or rash and capricious frankness instead of due proper candor; obdurate doggedness instead of honorable and dignified loyalty.

The emotions—especially when it comes to expressions of delicate matters—are deeply buried beneath a surface mien of action and will. Whenever emotion is hauled to the surface it all too readily degenerates into sentimentality and then has the effect of being overly theatrical in comparison with the natural gracefulness of the Mediterranean race.

While the Spanish woman may be able to succeed in intentionally giving off an air of gracefulness, the young Nordic woman can only be graceful *subconsciously:* if she makes a conscious effort, she only appears affected.

But when it comes to staying the course, out of honor and loyalty, in the fight for a good cause that holds no promise of victory, no promise of glory but only the certainty of defeat, conscious self-restraint in the best interest of a task without going cross-eyed in search of admiration—the Nordic race ranks far above the rest—and that is in line with the heroic traits in the German face.

61

OTTO HÖFLER

Secret Cultic Societies of the Germanic Peoples

First published in *Kultische Geheimbünde der Germanen,* vol. 1 (Verlag Moritz Diesterweg, 1934), vii, ix, 1, 2, 322–25.

The version of the Germanic myths surrounding the phantom host presented here forms the basis for all the subsequent interpretations [in this study]. Because it stands in such stark contrast to customary renderings, I shall have to reckon with radical skepticism on the part of many colleagues. For this reason, I have not been sparing with thorough documentation and evidence and prefer to provide too much analysis rather than too little. [. . .]

Already here, I must seek to avoid a misunderstanding: for modern man, the word *ecstasy* is perhaps most immediately associated with frenzied surrender, with reckless abandonment in chaos ensuing from the dissolution of all bonds. It is a fact of unforeseeable significance, though, that the Germanic traditions of the "wild" or "raging" army and its leader reveal to us a creature of an altogether different nature: this sort of cultic altered state of consciousness does not imply sweeping sybaritic excesses; rather—and this is precisely what this book hopes to substantiate through a comprehensive investigation—it implies an obligation to the dead.

While the limits of the individual are certainly transgressed in this version of ecstasy, the individual is not released from the bounds of order for his own sake but rather as a way of allowing him to enter into a community of bonds with the dead—with "his" own dead—that transcends the individual. *This cultic altered state of consciousness does not, then, imply chaos but rather order. Not delirium but obligation, not abandon but a communal bond with the ancestors.* This is where two worlds part.

And even the word *demonology* is dangerously effulgent with multiple meaning. The context in which it is applied here should become apparent based on the historical documentation presented. In his famous conversation with Eckermann on 2 March 1831, Goethe described the demonic as "that which cannot be conjured through rationality and reason." And those bonds between the living and the dead similarly defy rational explanation, and no form of rationalism will ever be in a position to take this power seriously. And yet this power is a fundamental component of human existence. The old forms of bonding with the dead have admittedly become alien to us—so alien, in fact, that even science has completely renounced them. Our task is to discover in and through these forms the life forces that remain decisive for historically minded men, even in more recent epochs while they slowly slip away into the realms of rational atomism. This power of the past and of the ancestors that has dissipated increasingly into mere "feeling" in recent times is vitally manifest in the early cult. And it continues to live on with greater continuity than rationalistically informed research has even begun to imagine. This is what we would like to make clear here. [. . .]

Sagas Surrounding the Phantom Host as Reflections of Ecstatic Secret Cults

[. . .] Our way of clarifying this departs substantially from what is customary in this regard and leads to a realm that is apparently altogether different in nature: to the realm of religious ecstasy, the demonic cult of the dead, but at the same time—what is likely most unexpected—to the basic festivities of Germanic communal life.

These are mysterious, secret cults from which, as we hope to demonstrate, the myths of Wotan's phantom host were primarily derived. Combatant cultic associations were their representatives, and the secrecy in which they were shrouded was so seamless that the true nature of this whole set of traditions is misunderstood to this day. The fabric of communal life that we hope to render apparent against the backdrop of our mythology of death at one time formed the center of religious life and at the same time the pillar upon which social order was built.

The demonic leagues of the ancient Germans are the focal point of our investigation.

These associations came to a climax in cultic ecstasy, and they were firmly rooted in the dark depths of the irrational. But their proliferation drove them out into the open.

Their influence is by no means restricted to those aspects of life pertinent only to the religious historian. But we cannot demonstrate the way these communities of cultic associations developed historically until we have first outlined the details of their religious content and the forms of their "mythological" customs.

These cultic forms reveal themselves to be utterly primal and must extend seamlessly back into the furthest reaches of prehistory. They can only have been practiced by organized associations, and it is for this reason that these leagues must be seen historically in the context of period designations of prehistory. As long as the rituals of the leagues have not yet lost their original meaning, we can still describe these groups as being "cultic," even though the rest of their political and economic activity seems to have flourished to the extent that it seems to dominate the whole picture.

We hope to demonstrate that the social fabric of what is apparently purely "practical" in nature was fed by secret mythological sources of power over an astonishingly long period of time. Once we have directed our attention to the communal power of these secret currents, the ritual practices of, say, the guilds, the Hanseatic League, and a whole series of additional associations appear in a different light; we can view their inner structure and the play of their vital "nation-building" powers from a perspective that allows us to glean an entirely different image from that presented by historical materialism of every stripe. [. . .]

Wotan and the Ancient Germanic Men's Leagues

If the study presented here has succeeded in providing evidence that the ancient Germanic traditions of the phantom host are not merely examples of nature mythology but rather were derived for the most part from a league of demonic cults, how, then, does this conclusion bear significantly on the figure of the leader of the wild hunt, the god Wotan?

The contemporary perspective on the ancient Germanic mythology of death introduced by L[ily] Weiser's work certainly must cast the Germanic leader of the dead, Wotan, in an entirely different light.

I believe that an accurate profile of this highly controversial figure can be apprehended only by viewing him as the god of the ecstatic men's leagues. It is only in this context, then, so it seems to me, that the manifold and apparently paradoxical characteristics of this most famous of ancient Germans are manifest and united; it is only here that he takes shape.

No other Germanic deity has so enraptured the senses as this mysterious God of Gods. In Old Nordic poetry he is the most versatile of gods, and already the infinitely changing names he was given there are proof of the degree to which he captured the imagination. Modern scholarship has also concerned itself more with the enigmatic Wotan than with other mythological figures whose nature is more readily apparent. And yet it must be noted that none of these efforts has succeeded in bringing to the fore the prevailing unity in all this diversity; none has found the center that conjoins the multivalent traits of this god.

He is the God of the Storm and of the Harvest, he is at once the God of War and of Runes, God of Death, and God of "Rage," Lord of the Word and Master of Romance but also of Magic and Masks, of Deception and Human Sacrifice.

How are we to find our way out of this bewildering maze? Is Wotan-Odin but a collective name used to describe varying mythological functions, ultimately perhaps only a shapeless, reconfigured, and amalgamated product of some late religious syncretism? But what, then, was the original fount from which the figure emerged? What was he before the outlines of his profile were blurred and obscured in an aesthetic game, before his character became as nebulous as many sources would demonstrate—or seem to demonstrate? This question leads to another no less significant one: when did the nebulization of this figure begin, and to what extent is a meaningful whole yet discernible in its rich and manifold being?

It seems to me that all those attempts that sought to "derive" from the glitteringly iridescent Wotan a portrait based on only one of his character traits—on his function as the God of Storm, for example—have been hardly felicitous. How can his relationship to magic, to fertility, to war, to mummery, romantic adventure, or poetry be explained on this basis? Without doubt, any number of transitions and links can and have been constructed in the most disparate ways. But these constructs seem hardly convincing to me. It is precisely the existence of such castles in the sky that has lent mythology the reputation of being a less soundly constructed science.

62

HARALD SPEHR

Were the Ancient Germans "Ecstatics"?

A Comment on Otto Höfler's Secret Cultic Societies of the Germanic Peoples

First published as "Waren die Germanen 'Ekstatiker'?" in *Rasse: Monatsschrift der nordischen Gedanken* 3 (1936): 394–400.

Höfler [. . .] sees in Wotan-Odin not merely the God of Ecstasy but rather the "God of the League," the God of the Ecstasy of the cultic men's leagues [. . .] "who at given times transform themselves into wild demons and wander about, driven by such elemental force that it is reminiscent of a raging storm" [. . .]. Secret cultic men's leagues, whose members must endure the tests of adolescent men's initiation rites, are the representatives of the cult and, as such, were ancient Germans by culture and by state. "They ascended to the level of powers in possession of extreme endurance and thrust, and who went down in world history as warriors, history makers, and ruling forces" [. . .]. Providing documentation of the existence of these leagues and their initiation rites in Germanic antiquity is the primary aim of this scholarly but very unclear and poorly organized book by Höfler.

The significance of the initiation rites for young men among primitive peoples is well known. The men's leagues of the Knights Templar, the Hanseatic League, and the guilds have left an indelible mark on history. Village fraternities still exist today in many places, and in the Third Reich new organizations for young boys and men are forming. Surely, they also played a role in Germanic antiquity.

But are these leagues of young men secret societies? Are they cultic in nature?

Höfler borrows the notion that there were young men's initiation rites and cultic men's leagues in Germanic antiquity from Lily Weiser-Aall [. . .]. According to this account, the ancient Germans had "initiation warriors," members of a secret society who were dedicated acolytes of Odin and "who availed themselves of myriad means to work themselves into a state of ecstatic possession and, disguised as raging ghosts of the dead, left noninitiates trembling with fear" [. . .] because they portrayed demons, the dead ancestors of the *Volk* and appeared to onlookers as if they were actually the dead. Masks and costumes "waken savage instincts that inspire the intoxicants to horrifying deeds [. . .]. But the first evidence of a German antiquity is a professional warrior tribe, the Hariis, which demonstrates neither initiations rites nor secrecy nor any form of cultic activity. The only thing we hear about the Hariis is that they deliberately seek to assume as uncanny an outward appearance as possible in order to inspire fear in their enemies. Kurt Meschke sought in vain to demonstrate the cultic significance of the sword dance. There is nothing to indicate that young men's initiation rites or cultic secret societies existed in German territories in the pagan period.

Nor are they evident in the pagan North. The berserks, those raging warriors of Nordic antiquity, never appear as a closed society requiring certain rites for membership; far more, for many races, becoming a berserk is often seen to involve the hereditary predisposition of particularly strong men. Odin's devotees were not members of some private boys' clubs you could join by rite of initiation; rather, they were mature men who fell in battle. [. . .]

In conclusion, this brings us to the grave threat present for our current cultural-political situation. Both [Höfler's work and that of Martin Ninck] seek to indoctrinate us into a conception of the ancient Germans that contradicts extant scholarship; both, in their attempts to cast the ancient Germans in a different light, supplant the concept of history that has been constructed from a tedious process of conscientious work and is being disseminated amongst the *Volk* in the Third Reich and that, according to the most stringent standards of ethics still valid today, is of constitutive significance. Measured against our best and most reliable sources, the image they present is racially alien to us, borne by a Jewish spirit that is thus impressed upon our ancestors. The ancient Germans were neither slaves to demonology nor drug-crazed members of secret cults, nor ecstatics. "Willful abandon, intoxication, *ekstasis,* the sacred orgy, out-of-body experiences and willful wallowing in the psychic spheres of other men are characteristic traits of the Near Eastern racial soul; moderation, *metron, temperamantia* are characteristic traits of the Nordic racial soul and of aboriginal Indo-Germanic piety, *eusebeia* as a cognate of *sophrosyne.*" Here we have an attempt to discard the Germanic worldview built on the standards of heroic honor and propriety in favor of a magical worldview. Should this heretical doctrine be made available to the *Volk* in these works? Since they have both been published by reputable publishing houses and since they seem to have won over laypeople with their emphasis on the ideals of the men's leagues and seem to be compatible with the increasing force of struggle of today's standards, we are obligated to build a united front against them. We know which values the Germans of antiquity still and once more have to offer, if we would only properly understand their nature. Preserving the purity of this source is a *völkisch* task.

63

EBERHARD FREIDANK

Nordic Ecstasy

First published as "Nordische Ekstase," in *Reichswart,* vol. 5 (February 1933).

More than a decade has passed since the *völkisch* idea became more widespread in Germany. In the first years following the war, the ever-increasing incursions of an alien spirit generated a defensive resurgence of *völkisch* thought. In the most essential sectors of public life—in politics, economics, and culture—the Jew strove to attain power; before long, a swelling anti-Semitic movement, the expression of a healthy German drive for self-preservation, sought to rein in the raging Jewish incursion. Once it was sparked, the *völkisch* idea could not restrict itself to anti-Semitism—that is, simply to its very negation—it was urgently in need of an attendant political policy. In order to conquer the alien spirit, it had to counter it with its own, its *German* spirit. But what exactly was the German spirit? Of all the manifold cultural phenomena, which among them was a manifestation of the peculiarly German spirit? This task was anything but easy. For many years, Michel [the everyday German] was happy to be seen as cosmopolitan; the spiritual fruits borne of such breeding ground were hardly recognizable as expressions of a pure German nature, much in the same way the myriad foreign influences to which the German has been subjected since time immemorial, among other things the alien religious circle once foist upon us made it difficult to discern between what was foreign and what was ours. This is all the more reason to claim for ourselves what came *before* this time as that which is in keeping with our nature and which should thus serve as the model for a race that extricated itself from the fetters of an alien spirit. As a model to last for at least another thousand years!

But this is an account that cannot be settled squarely. Today's German is no longer the man who lived in the ancient times of the Edda and the Sagas; he is, for the most part, only about 40 percent ancient German; the remaining quotient of the hereditary bloodstock of his ancestors has been sacrificed to crossbreeding with other peoples. Well, then, a whole unanimous chorus of voices resounds to a man, telling us that if 40 percent represents the most valuable component of German blood, then we, as the *de*generated *Volk,* must "regenerate," "hyper-Nordify" ourselves. And part of that process requires that we must first intimately familiarize ourselves with the ideological world of the ancestors so that we may learn to acknowledge the fact that they were not *barbarians!* The magazine *Germanien,* which is currently convinced it must expand its scope "in light of the profound misery of the German *Volk,*" has included in its January circular an insert in which the following words, printed in bold, stand out: "Our ancestors were not barbarians!" This bombastic reassurance, which can be heard elsewhere as well, is a matter of preaching to the choir. There is hardly a serious man alive today who suffers from such delusions. Even the Roman who first graced the ancient Germans with this epithet may not have associated the term *barbarian* with the same derogatory connotations that inhere in it today. The Greeks, for example, called the Persians, who clearly ranked above them in terms of cultural development, "barbarians." So we are at least in good company!

A veritable avalanche of "Nordic" print media is emerging in pursuit of the same aims as the magazine mentioned above. With such newly established forums as the forthcoming *Nordische Welt,* the editors are apparently seeking to accommodate a "deeply felt" need. What is more, some sectors of the *völkisch* population, youth in particular, have begun forming such "Nordic" organizations as leagues, rings, and "orders." Similarly, "Nordic" conferences take place where participants seek to secure victory for "Nordic" thought and where Nordic priests and priestesses speak in lofty tones about the "revival of the Nordic soul." They hope to bless us with a "Nordic" style, demand a "Nordically oriented" cultural policy, faculty positions for "Nordic" scholarship on German universities, and heaven knows what else! It is worth pointing out one conspicuous symptom here—namely, that the boisterous appeal to the "Nordic" soul has met with limited resonance among the Scandinavians who remain to this day the most pure-blooded Germanics. The Nordic peoples are inclined to view these matters much more soberly than the German ideologues. You can read about this in the report published in the *Reichswart* (no. 32, 1932) on last year's German-Nordic student gathering in Rostock.

This steady diet of "Nordicism" is a bit overdone. Because it is predicated on the fallacious assumption that the German is completely ignorant of his forefathers, this flurry of activity is akin to chasing windmills. Do we really need these heavenly Nordic hosts to bring us in touch with the world of our ancestors? Hasn't a "*völkisch*" science—that is to say a science based on researching our own *Volkstum*—been in existence for a long time, for at least a century? Did Jacob Grimm and the countless Germanists and ethnologists who followed in his footsteps achieve nothing? How many neglected treasures are buried in our libraries, just waiting to be put to good use—the majority of which are completely unknown to those who would now presume to enlighten us about our forefathers! These treasures are worth their weight in gold and cannot even be measured in terms of the inflationary and pinchbeck change that is today's customary standard. One need only make reference to Wilhelm Wägner's splendid work *Our Prehistory* [*Unsere Vorzeit*], which is also suitable for a broader audience of laypeople and whose most recent editions take into account the latest findings in scholarship. The people who wrote these books were German idealists, altruistic in their aims, as is characteristic of the German race as a whole, and modest—they never called much attention to themselves—character traits that, unfortunately, seem to be lacking in certain "Nordic" pseudogeniuses in our times.

64

ALFRED BAEUMLER

Hellas and Germania

First published in "Hellas und Germanien," in *Studien zur deutschen Geistesgeschichte* (Berlin: Junker und Dünnhaupt Verlag, 1943), 295–96, 299–300.

The reclamation of Hellenic traditions for Western culture is the result of one of the most overwhelming efforts that the Germanic racial soul has put forth on its path back to itself. German Hellenism in particular, undertaken in the truest spirit of unparalleled historical courage, represents a triumphant crusade to conquer the most distant coastal regions and the pinnacles of the past, a veritable Alexandrian crusade into the realm of the soul, of the intellect, and of the spirit.

If this monumental event has not always been seen and interpreted in the proper light, the reason may be found in the fact that our crusade to reclaim the Hellenic world is not yet complete. At this point, it is still possible to hold a blind eye to the fact of Germanic Hellenism. One can still overlook unsettling phenomena appearing in [Friedrich] Hölderlin and [Friedrich] Nietzsche or somehow seek to interpret them out of existence. But the decisive battle has begun. Our century will be forced to provide an answer to the question as to which values of the West it will allow to shape its future. We live with the certainty that the only value system capable of wrenching Europe from the anarchy of values is one that demonstrates a great degree of intrinsic similarity to the Hellenic system. The discovery of the

Hellenic world implies no less than the presentation of a new age, an age that transcends the Gothic and the Enlightenment. For us, the Hellenic is not merely one value among others, not merely a form of greatness on a par with the Roman, the Iranian, or the Indian. Far more than this, our knowledge substantiates the intuitive certainty expressed by [Johann Joachim] Winckelmann, Hölderlin, and Nietzsche that our fate will be decided in the countenance of Hellas. [. . .]

Nietzsche is to be credited with having recognized and excoriated the danger presented by historicism. In his tragic struggle against the "New Humanism," Nietzsche resuscitated the significance of the Hellenic tradition for the life of Western culture. Ever since Nietzsche, Germanic and Hellenic traditions have stood face-to-face on equal footing. Their alliance is the guarantor of Europe's spiritual unity. This unity is derived not merely from the scientific and scholarly collaboration between them—it can only be based on the mutual belief in the same set of eschatological convictions. The peoples that comprise the spirit of Europe may not agree on everything; the significance, however, of the notion that they might be united under the emblem of a single system of values that guides their lives, that system being called Hellas, is not to be underestimated.

The New Humanism, crippled by its excessive critical historicism, has attributed to the prejudices of *classicism* the fact that the Hellenic world necessarily acts as our model and as our mandate. But it is precisely this decisive point that distinguishes the superiority of classicism over the New Humanism that followed in its wake. Historicism objected to the fact that classicism sought to establish one unconditional norm. But that is not where the error lies, rather in the fact that, in practice, this norm was understood to be purely aesthetic in nature. Racialist thought teaches us to understand the meaning of that absolute norm much more profoundly—and at the same time, as a Hellenic norm—from a physical perspective.

Let us cast aside the New Humanism—that hapless son of critical philology and historicism—and turn our attention to the only context in which creative acts may be placed, that which is sure to one day be of greater significance to the spiritual reclamation of the true Hellenic culture for the history of the Germanic West than that oft-heralded Renaissance. [. . .]

This reevaluation, which, at least in some respects, situates Athens in a place once reserved for Rome, is conjoined with a no less significant cataclysmic shift in perspective. Winckelmann is not one of those modern humanists who substitutes his admiration for the literary beauties of ancient authors for an admiration of the sculptured beauties of Greek artists but rather a revolutionary who, from the fervent depths of his soul, dares to measure his own time against the standards of an intuitive grasp of Hellenic reality. This is what distinguishes German classicism from every form of humanism: that it is not a matter of mimicking or imitating a given form but rather of discovering a world. When we read Winckelmann's words, the Hellenic world appears as if by the stroke of a magic wand before our eyes, enigmatically prescient and clearly discernible for all its rococo-like relativity. As always, the fact that he is a discoverer of the cosmos is revealed in his linguistic style. This is not about art and literature but rather about the man who creates art and literature. The Hellenic, as Winckelmann sees it, epitomizes human potential. What rises to resplendent heights here is a way of acting in and interpreting the world that is free from the shadow of the Middle Ages and entirely unobscured by the doubts of otherworldly concerns.

5
Racial Science

"RACE" HAD MULTIPLE MEANINGS in European science of the nineteenth century. On the one hand, it simply meant "all human beings," but it also reflected an older, seventeenth-century notion of deep, unbridgeable divisions among human beings, marked by external (as well as unseen) qualities: skin color, facial structure, character, and intelligence. Charles Darwin's (1809–82) mid-nineteenth-century claim to present the theoretical underpinnings of all biological development immediately had both scientific and popular resonance in Wilhelmine Germany. Ernst Haeckel (1834–1919) was Darwin's major proponent in German science. He argued that "higher" species embodied each stage of their earlier, more primitive predecessors, or "ontogeny recapitulates phylogeny."[1] Haeckel thus argued for a "biogenic theory," suggesting that the more "primitive" races needed the "supervision" and "protection" of more "mature" societies to develop fully. But the popular and political reception of the "new" biology was of equal force. If, as the biologists thought, "natural selection" formed more resilient beings, could not purposeful selection do the same? Francis Galton (1822–1911), Darwin's cousin, arrived at the notion of "eugenics" (and coined the term): a system of selective breeding that would improve the race.[2]

This view of racial improvement became a mainstay of the politics of the West, finding its way into virtually all political positions, from the ultraright to the ultraleft. Both Nazism and Communism embraced the notion that a society could breed better human beings with different ideologies but with similar qualities. Built into this view was the fear that "weak" races could biologically drag down the "superior" ones, whether in Africa or in Europe. In Germany, science, as much as military prowess, had begun to define the new imperial state as a world power. The litmus test for the biology of race was the definition of "Jews" as a racial group. Yet, as Johann Fahlbusch argued in 1935, the case of the "black bastards" of the occupied Rhineland was the first test of the acceptability of political intervention in matters of race. The offspring of German women and black French soldiers (most were actually soldiers from North Africa) were considered racially impure and therefore dangerous. The solution, already widely practiced in the United States, was to castrate those labeled "mentally defective." And this policy seems to have provoked little public outcry.

Biology was a central metaphor in Nazi thought before 1933. Thereafter, what many had seen as metaphor quickly became policy. The Nazis shifted their emphasis from "racial science" to "racial mysticism," as George Mosse has pointed out, but a mysticism of race and blood that was certainly part of the "science of race."[3] The views of those within the party apparatus appeared to be uniform, but these views were often contradictory and occasionally publicly at odds with one another. Were the Jews a "mongrel" race, as the archracist Houston Stewart Chamberlain (1855–1927), Richard Wagner's son-in-law, claimed in his *Foundations of the Nineteenth Century* (published in German in 1899), or were they a people who, as Hitler claimed in *Mein Kampf,* spent all of their energies preserving their pure blood?

After 1933, racial science became a practical political matter. In 1934, Ludolf Haase proposed creating an official policy and a Reich Office of Racial Affairs, arguing that the population's physical weakness had caused Germany to lose the war and seeking to assuage anxiety about the party's multiple views of race. Haase railed against abortion and birth control (except for "inferior peoples") in the name of "the rekindling of the maternal instinct." Yet, he believed that "ethnic cleansing" was necessary to halt the infiltration by other races that had and would continue to sap the *völkisch* (inherent) nature of the Germans. With his notions of racial hygiene, already put forth in the Wilhelmine thought of the 1890s, came an entire vocabulary of Protestant virtues, now yoked to the idea of race. Such notions "protected" women and children, who were seen as most at risk from racial impurity. But Nazi policy also stressed the need for "healthy" reproduction, as Walter Gross (1904–45), the head of the Rassenpolitisches Amt (Racial-Political Office of the NSDAP), noted in his speech to German women in October 1934.

"Official" biological and medical science in Germany after 1933 became suffused with racial science. Few exceptions to this rule can be found, and even these assume a biological imperative to improve the race. Paul Brohmer argued that such a science should be at the core of every young German's education "in organic *völkisch* thinking." On 13 September 1933, the Prussian school system made racial theory a required course in all schools. This was no mere fringe science—major figures argued for new biological thinking in schools' education for life: evolution in the service of the party. The longer the Nazis were in power, the more radical became the race concept, until the beginning of the "Final Solution of the Jewish Question" in 1941 (see document 70,"Racial Policy," in this chapter).

Race extended to the notion of a life at one with nature, which Haeckel called "ecology" and anthropologist Friedrich Ratzel (1844–1904), a follower of Haeckel and a major racial thinker of the time, saw as a geographic imperative (part of the study of geopolitics): correct races in correct places. Space and race became one, represented by the term *völkisch.* Space was an extension of biology and its core. The only way to ensure healthy people in a healthy space was to eliminate the threats from the racially different and the physically and emotionally weak. "Nature conservation," a concept developed before World War I by Hugo Conwentz (1855–1922) and subsequently extended to biology, was a principle the Nazis were happy to appropriate. Like Ratzel's views about geography, Conwentz's outlined the ideal of a healthy space to be inhabited by healthy people. By 1942, as an SS pamphlet on racial thinking emphasized, the inherent difference between Germans, who had a healthy culture and a real history, and the inferior races was that the latter "have no history; they lack the necessary prerequisite for that: the ability to master their own fate." The Nazis knew well who was healthy and who was not, who would determine the future and who must vanish.

NOTES

1. Ernst Haeckel, *The History of Creation,* 3rd ed., translated by E. Ray Lankester (London: Kegan Paul, Trench, 1883). First published in 1868.

2. Francis Galton, *Inquiries into Human Faculty and Its Development* (London: J. M. Dent, 1883).

3. George L. Mosse, "The Mystical Origins of National Socialism," *Journal of the History of Ideas* 22, no. 1 (January–March 1961): 81–96.

65

LUDOLF HAASE

We Need a Reich Office of Racial Affairs

First published as "Wir brauchen ein Reichsrasseamt," in *Weltkampf,* October 1933, 293–99.

It is only with the establishment of the Reich Bureau of Population Growth, Racial Improvement, and Nordification that the genuinely *völkisch* idea will attain its breakthrough. And yet we are dealing with the fulfillment of tasks that must be taken on as quickly as possible in light of the rapidly progressing degeneration of our *Volk* and whose effects are by no means always first recognizable after generations. Let us consider, for example, two basic truths that, if we fail to grasp them, would spell the end of our future even despite the National Socialist takeover of power: We must, in the first place, understand that our *Volk* has grown weary of life and must first regain its will to live. Second, we must recognize that the guardians and bearers of this life are women and not men.

Our will to live has died.

No amount of praise for the Third Reich, no amount of heroic bravado on the part of our SA, not a single political or economic force or agent can deny this fact. One single statistic delivers proof of that: as you know, every year, at least one million crimes are committed against unborn life. This number is not new, but only a few amongst us clearly understand what it means. Let us assume that half of these unborn, murdered children would have died or been born inferior, that still leaves a half million strong German people who are murdered in the womb each year, and that is an irretrievable loss of human potential in our *Volk*. Any soldier knows what it means to lose two hundred fifty thousand recruits year after year. Within a single decade, this adds up to a huge host of two and a half million men, an army greater in number than all the troops we had fighting on the western front in 1918. We all know that our population will shrink in number as those age groups with the greatest numbers now begin to die off. If the biological situation remains as it is, then, in a few short decades, with our population drastically reduced in number, we will face the tremendous superior force of a growing population from the east, while at the same time France, with its black army, will be able to put the screws to us from the other side.

This is the guaranteed partition of Germany!

Our enemies don't need a war. All they need to do is sit back and wait until we have exterminated ourselves to the degree that they can put an end to Germany without risking their lives. And all the parents who today are dazzled by blind faith into believing that they must safeguard their children's future by keeping their families small, these parents are beyond a shadow of doubt delivering precisely these children straight into death at the hands of a merciless enemy.

That is one fact! The other is that we have yet to recognize the full scope of women's importance to the future of our blood. And this is, incidentally, no coincidence because we've had enough of intellectual women and "girls" who in many ways still prevent us from appreciating that figure to whom the future belongs: the maternal woman. Whoever is interested in increasing the numbers of our population must address first and foremost the female of the species!

Beyond that, the work of the Office of Racial Affairs must circumscribe the totality of life in the nation. It should imbibe them not only with a renewed will to live and reproduce, which is alarmingly weak today, but, as an office that establishes direction and guidelines, should bring about the species-specific course of our lives and facilitate the aims of selection. The hierarchical organization of our *Volk* that rests on the rise of the virtuous is an attainable goal.

From the very onset, the office must allow the innately Germanic processes of life in politics, culture, and economics to flourish in a manner so genuinely suited to the species that the best of the best automatically rise to the top and, on the other hand, whatever is undesirable from a German perspective is simply unable to hold its own. Today we are a denigrated and pitifully uncultivated *Volk* without genuine stature. This is what caused the collapse of 1918.

Who can help?

But anyone who approaches this task from the perspective of a "doctor," a "jurist," or any kind of "specialist" is destined to fail. So the question of personnel becomes paramount. While science may exist to serve the Office of Racial Affairs, it should not lend a professorial character to the department. *Only a natural-born politician is equal to the task as outlined.* The only man who is in a position to win the hearts and souls of Germans and German women in particular for the divine cause of the race and for the will to improve the race and bear children is one who possesses not only the organizational skills but who is well versed in matters of the soul and its imponderable forces. The rekindling of the maternal instinct I have already emphasized is for us one of the most decisive tasks facing the nation today because it is literally a question of our life or death. But we cannot promote motherhood solely by means of laws and income supplements, as indispensable as these measures are; motherhood is a fundamental expression of the soul, and if we do not succeed in restoring this instinct to health, the female sex is bound to respond to even the most far-reaching legislation with a boycott on births.

All this demands that the leadership of the Office of Racial Affairs be highly political while, as the most important bearer and disseminator of racial thought, at the same time not only pursuing the intellectual and spiritual dissolution of opposing worldviews in Germany to the point of extermination but also indirectly affecting everyday politics at the most basic level, if only by virtue of the fact that the following objectives and guidelines will emerge and, sooner or later, will be signed into law.

1. To regulate the flow and constitution of domestic migration as well as to organize a fortress consisting of the highest-caliber men to guard our borders. We must reckon with enemy attempts to impede our efforts.
2. To regulate immigration and emigration in conjunction with large-scale "ethnic cleansing." The targeted, graduated influx of millions of Germans who are currently living abroad, whether permanently or temporarily, and who are slowly falling prey to the unalterable absorption of our people by others. Re-emigration and immigration offices! The collection and gathering of those people bearing the greatest degree of the highest-caliber ancient Germanic genetic material in the Germanic heart of Europe! The concentration of our racial strength and the fortification of *völkisch* forces against constricting borders!
3. Racial-political organization and the fortification of those members of the Germanic community living abroad.
4. Racial-political weakening and dissolution of anti-Germanic blood and spiritual communities here and abroad.
5. The absolutely essential rallying of our *Volk*'s thought around the core question of biological race is, as regards determination of the time and duration, interdependent of the international situation.

Already today we can look forward to welcoming the imminent institution of population policies in the Reich. What is more, there are countless preliminary efforts to be evaluated and a series of already existing agencies with a wealth of experience to be enlisted in the establishment of this department. And yet we must all remain very clear about the fact that it is only a complete totality, something so overwhelming that we cannot even imagine it today, something entirely unprecedented and dominating that can preserve the essential nature of our *Volk* and in fact allow it to prevail for all time.

It's going to be a difficult battle.

The struggle itself, then, requires a lucid understanding of the political exigencies of the Reich, as well as the limits that are placed upon it by necessity, but, as a matter of principle, it must be conducted with an utterly indefatigable endurance that cannot be diminished by the slightest hint of disappointment. Since history has shown us that, especially in the field of biology, it is nearly impossible to rescue a duped *Volk*, none of us can say today just how difficult it will be to lead the German people by hook or by crook to victory in the fight against selfishness, convenience, against the lack of endurance, materialism, and against waning faith. The only thing that is certain is that we National Socialists are particularly intent on avoiding half measures in this regard and that we must arrive at utterly bold decisions.

Once the project of building the *völkisch* state is complete, it will essentially overlap with the Office of Racial Affairs. Today, though, we must satisfy ourselves with the establishment and development of special offices that should rapidly grow in significance to the level of ministries, regardless of what they are called. And even if this immediate objective should at first remain but an elusive dream, it is nevertheless necessary that at least a healthy seed be sown, which will thus provide a point of departure from which everything else might naturally develop. Omissions and faulty solutions can have disastrous consequences in times of war and peace. Lest we never forget the lessons of our Battle of the Marne in 1914!

Proposal for the Office of Racial Affairs
Reich Commissioner—Secretary of State

1. Administrative Department: household affairs—administrative building—construction projects—sanitaria—acquisitions—personal data (also for the state organizations)—chancellery, etc.
2. *Volk* information gathering: card catalog, identification cards indicating health status (basis for decentralization)—*völkisch* personnel policies with special roster (to indicate whether candidates' applications are certified, deferred based on objections, or denied)—research on psychological profiles—dissemination of information concerning citizenship laws (to Reich minister of the interior)—Offices of Racial Affairs created incrementally in conjunction with the expansion of marriage-counseling agencies throughout the Reich subject to budgetary provisions (marriage counseling, mediation, marriage certificates, birth control for inferior peoples, sterilization, selection of candidates for settlement, functionaries for nature preserves, regulation of immigration and emigration, women's officers for the advancement of motherhood in family and education in families, agencies, organizations, institutions, the workplace, etc., motherhood schools, enforcement of racial thought)—statistics—correspondence with marriage license bureaus, churches, public health officials, the police (fines)—the trade press (genealogical research, etc.)—liaison to the Ministry of Agriculture, to the Office of Racial Affairs and the SS branch of the NSDAP—liaison to the Ministry of Popular Enlightenment and Propaganda.
3. Overall Health and Hygiene of the *Volk*: laws and measures in the interest of hygiene and the health of the *Volk*—women's work and female social hygiene—promotion and protection of motherhood, protection of children—specialized assistance for Offices of Racial Affairs listed in Paragraph 2 with special consideration given to the administration of the women's division—medical councils, regional physicians, midwives, asylum physicians [. . .], promotion and protection of motherhood and children—institute for the production of semen—biologically sound nutrition and holistic healing—evaluation of recent research—statistics—trade press (prevention of diseases, cures, classical medicine)—liaison with the Ministry of Culture in the interest of influencing school children

and the education of future medical professionals—liaison with the Ministry of Labor (social security, Labor Service, etc.)—liaison with the Medical Department in the Ministry of the Interior (legislation concerning contagious disease, etc.)—liaison with the Propaganda Ministry—correspondence with professional organizations—liaison with the German Labor Front.

4. The Maintenance of Genetic Health: eradication policies, National Socialist information, non-Jewish blood aliens—statistics—laws and measures—research institutes (among others, the Kaiser Wilhelm Institute for Anthropology, Eugenics Department)—specialist assistance for Offices of Racial Affairs listed in Paragraph 2 with special consideration given to the administration of the Office of Women's Affairs—trade press (genetic health, social hygiene)—liaison with the Ministry of Culture in the interest of influencing schoolchildren and the education of future medical professionals—liaison with the Ministry of Propaganda—liaison with the German Labor Front.
5. Racial Breeding: racial studies, promoting the increase in family size and reproduction of the *Volk*, racial breeding—laws and measures—economics that are beneficial and intrinsically suited to the race—statistics. Here, centralized administration—specialist assistance for Offices of Racial Affairs listed in Paragraph 2 with special consideration given to the administration of the Office of Women's Affairs—research institutes (among others, the Kaiser Wilhelm Institute for Anthropology, Department B, racial research)—oversight, support of, and opposition to literary products, film productions, etc. (Office of Cultural Oversight)—expert publications (racial hygiene, racial breeding)—[support of] of expert-press workers in all departments—bureau of fashion—Commissioner's Office for Gymnastics and Sport—involvement in foreign policy—liaison with the highest echelons of leadership in the SA, SS, the Hitler Youth, and the Ministry of Economics [*Reichswirtschaftsministerium*]—liaison with the Ministry of Culture in the interest of influencing schoolchildren and the education of future medical professionals—liaison with the Ministry of Labor (social security, Labor Service, etc.)—liaison with the Ministry of Economics (economics that are beneficial and intrinsically suited to the race)—liaison with the Ministry of Agriculture in the interest of creating the prerequisites to striving for the healthy and multitudinous reproduction of future generations of the *Volk*—liaison with the Ministry of Propaganda—liaison with the German Labor Front. Here, centralized administration of liaisons between all the departments and ministries, etc. (Office of Enlightenment and Office of Cultural Oversight).
6. Office of Women's Affairs in the Reich: education of the female sex toward maternity and motherhood (basic tenet: the path to childbearing proceeds from woman's soul). Here, centralized leadership of the tasks assigned to all departments in the Office of Women's Affairs—laws and measures—statistics—promoting the increase in family size and reproduction of the *Volk*, psychological and material protection of the family (appropriate selection of spouses, mediation, family counseling, housing policies in cities and rural areas, etc.)—specialist assistance for Offices of Racial Affairs listed in Paragraph 2 with special consideration given to the administration of the Office of Women's Affairs—gender-specific training for women in matters of psychology, life studies, and health—expert press (hereditary health, women's social hygiene, women's work, child care, protection of women and children)—correspondence with associations (Organization for Large Families, etc.)—liaison with the Youth Leagues of the NSDAP—liaison with the Syndicated Women's Associations of the Reich. There, if possible, directorship or liaison with the Ministry of Labor (making determinations for women's Labor Service that facilitate education toward maternity and motherhood, social security, etc.)—liaison with the Ministry of Culture in the interest of influencing schoolchildren and the education of future medical professionals—liaison with the Ministry of Economics

in the interest of promoting and protecting motherhood and children—liaison with the Ministry of Agriculture in the interest of creating the prerequisites to striving for the healthy and multitudinous reproduction of future generations of the *Volk*—liaison with the Ministry of Propaganda—liaison with the German Labor Front.

66

WALTER GROSS

National Socialist Racial Policy

A Speech to German Women

First published as *Nationalsozialistische Rassenpolitik. Eine Rede an die deutschen Frauen* (Dessau: C. Dünnhaupt, 1934). Translated by Randall Bytwerk. Calvin College, German Propaganda Archive.

My Dear German Women and Girls!

When Germans come together today to discuss the things that concern us both as individuals and as a nation, it is a solemn occasion, whether we wish it to be or not. During the political struggles of the past, we could speak of party programs or of civilization without any involvement of our soul.

Now we have forgotten how to approach an issue merely with our understanding, merely with our mouth, merely with our heart. We have become whole people once again. When we speak with others, we do so with our full being.

That is what made the movement strong, and great, and powerful from its first days. It is also that which the enemy on this side of the border and the other cannot understand, and which it hates with deadly strength. As this great and beautiful people's movement began, so too began a hard and bitter struggle between enemy and German forces, between an old world that is really long dead and buried and the new world that is struggling to reach the light through us. This struggle has been going on in people's hearts and souls for years and is nowhere near its end. The world finds it difficult to understand that which is at the center of our endeavors: *the value of blood and race.*

Our enemies first laughed in pity, then in hatred as we spoke of it.

Let us speak of what we National Socialists mean by that so that it will become clear why the German woman may be even more concerned about these matters than the man, his state, and his fighting organization can be.

There was a time in the past when we were untrue—untrue in the deepest sense. We were untrue not to other people, or parties, or states, or kings, but untrue to something far greater, untrue to the laws of life. As long as the world exists, as long as life grows, flourishes, and perishes, so long will this life have the urge to live on into the future and win new territory. Whether plant or animal or man—as we, or I, or you: *wherever there is life, it has the longing to bring forth new life.*

It should be unnecessary to speak of such things. We speak of them only because for a few decades a crazy era ignored, blasphemed, and mocked these greatest, most beautiful, and purest dreams of life. This was an age that made the idol of money supreme and said, "The world should be governed not by what serves life but rather by what some fool of an accountant decides is best." We know the results. The great laws of life were evaluated according to money sacks and checkbooks. When we think back on our parents, grandparents, and great-grandparents, there were many children in the house. It may have been crowded and hard financially, but we were happy, perhaps because there were so many of us in so large a family.

But the time came when people said, "As man or woman, as parents or teachers of leaders, you have the duty to show the people the way to a better future." That better future, people thought, could only be a richer future, a future in which the individual had more money. And when they were asked where this money would come from, a false teaching arose in the last century: "The fewer people there are, the more an individual child can inherit from his parents." He who loves his children and wishes a prosperous future for his nation should therefore see to it that Germany's population is small and that only a few children continue the family after he is gone. That was the terrible teaching of birth control, which Marxism preached and the bourgeois followed. No one dared stand against it. That was the doctrine that made us what we are today: *a dying people,* in which fewer children are born each year, in which today more people die each year than are born. This all was supposed to lead to a happy future. It understood happiness only in terms of possessions. It was, therefore, inherently false. But even in its own terms it was false, for it forgot something:

When a people begins to die, when a people no longer obeys the laws of life, when a people values money more than its existence and posterity, this people is on the path to disaster, both historically and politically. Within a few decades it will be dead, oppressed by other peoples who are stronger, closer to life, and who follow life's laws better than we.

If present trends continue, by the end of the century Germany will be a nation with only forty to fifty million inhabitants, and we know that on our borders other peoples are growing quickly and strongly. Sooner or later, these other peoples will come in conflict with a shrinking and dying German people, and the result of the supposed doctrine of happiness will be a hard and bitter *national death for our children.* Those who believed that they can give their children a happy and peaceful future by reducing the number of children err deeply. They give the children only the promise of a hard and bitter struggle for Germany's existence as a state and as an idea.

Today, when we work to show people that the ideas of yesterday are false, that the state and nation cannot do without the family, that the family cannot exist without children, and when we not only provide economic support to make it easier to begin families and have children but also tell people again and again of the sanctity of life and the necessity of continuing our people into the future, our enemies on both sides of the border suddenly have insults and hateful things to say about us. They wish to disturb our work. Suddenly there are voices saying, "National Socialism's doctrines are inhumane and barbaric. National Socialism's views on children turn people into breeding animals." When it says *that it is the duty of men and women to continue the eternal chain of life, a chain that begins in the distant past and continues into the future, a chain of which we are only a link leading into the distant future,* our enemies on both sides of the border claim, "You reject the dignity and value of humanity. National Socialism holds that men and women have no value other than that of breeding cattle." It is a shame that we have to respond to such words, but it is necessary because our enemies have always tried to persuade women to oppose us, even though what we say is rooted in the souls of the men and women we speak to. This is our response: "You are mistaken in accusing us of thinking that the only purpose of humanity is to continue the species by passing on our blood to future generations. We know the other values. We support them and find wherever we can those values that the individual shows in his work and selfless service. We know well enough that *each person lives a double life. The first is the one he lives between birth and death. We are to do as much as we can to make this life rich, to accomplish that which is good and beautiful, to use our strengths and gifts for others. That is the duty of the individual. But as a person you are something more: you are a link in the chain of life, a drop in the great bloodstream of your people.*"

There, too, you have duties and obligations before the eternity of the nation. You have the duty to pass on what you received from your parents and ancestors. I do not believe that such behavior, which obeys both the laws of reason and of life, is barbaric, hateful, or inhumane. I believe instead that the barbarism is to be found in the years we have left behind us, when any dirty lout could besmirch the most valuable, holy life of a man or women in their families, or drag children through the filth without anyone defending their culture against such an attack.

I believe that when we tell people once more of the great value of blood and remind them that they have duties not only for the sixty-year span in which they work and serve but also to the millennia of the past from which we come and to the millennia of the future to which we are heading, then we are giving them higher values than those of yesterday. Let me say also, however, that it is wrong if someone thinks that only those who found families and bear children are valuable to our state. We know that is not so. We know there are reasons why some people leave their people's flow of blood. We know that some are denied what the nation places great value on. We do not ignore them or think ourselves their betters. We only say this: "My friend, you and I must do our duty to our people, and when we cannot fulfill it in one way, then we must do what we can with even greater energy and devotion." *When you do your duty you are one of us—we extend our hand to you; we honor your humanity and your service for Germany. Let us work together so that in the future as many people as possible will be able to serve the nation in both ways.*

That is a piece of the thinking of blood and race that National Socialism has taught us. And there is another aspect. When we see people today, we can recognize that we are not all alike. There are differences in value—*not every person has the same value as everyone else.* In the past, people believed that these differences were superficial, the result of the environment in which one grew up. People believed that what became of a person depended primarily on the house he grew up in or on his social environment or the class he came from. They believed that a person born in a slum, surrounded by shadows, troubles, and poverty, a child lacking in love and affection, could become only a second-class human being, a physically and psychologically ill member of the society, someone failed by the society and the state. One thought that a child growing up in such a slum inevitably became sick or even criminal. It was because he grew up in such a poor environment. The Marxists claimed that if every child in Germany grew up in an environment that gave him all he needed, he would inevitably become a useful, decent, upright, proud, and honest adult. After a few years or decades, the entire German people would consist of such decent and useful people. In the past, people believed the environment was responsible even when a person failed miserably.

We recall the days of delirium when millions of unemployed were thrown on the street by a sick political and economic system, made superfluous. A single person pried the tracks apart and derailed a train in the middle of the night. Within a minute, he murdered thirty innocent people who had never done anything to him and stole their money. And what did the world of yesterday say? "He can't help himself. He is a victim of circumstances. He has Beethoven's hands and an artistic temperament. We need not put him on the gallows or in prison to protect us and our children. No, this poor Schlesinger is sick only because of his environment. Put him in a modern sanitarium, give him what he needs: radio, a library, a smoking salon, a language teacher, a pastor, a newspaper room; give him everything he needs to put him in touch with better things. In a few years, this mass murderer of thirty people will leave as an ideal human being, so pure and innocent that one can put him in charge of a kindergarten." That's what people thought in the past.

Today, that seems a bad joke to us, a crazy fantasy, but a few years ago it was government policy in Germany. Those who did well under such policies and have joined to fight us think that they can dismiss our doctrines of blood and race as barbaric.

Why do we see things differently? Because we have learned something: *in the end, you are not as important and significant as you thought yesterday;* your strength and abilities are not as great as you believed during the liberal era. Oh yes, it was a lovely dream to say, "I will do with my life what I want, and if I happen to be a teacher, I will teach what I want and do what I enjoy and what I think right." Well, that was your idea of the environment.

We are a bit more modest, a bit more humble before the laws of fate.

We have learned that what I can do for myself or what you can do for yourself, or what we can all do to each other is not as important or as deep as that which a greater power has already done to us. It is that power that even before our birth gave us a part of our nature and laid out our path in the world. Here are joined two things: the knowledge of modern science and the sensitivity and understanding of a humble person. Suddenly, we see that *what you are, what I am, and what I can be in my life are in part predetermined by that which I have inherited.*

If my inheritance is good and strong, and if I am true to it and develop what is within me, my life will be successful and perhaps of benefit and joy to others. If such an inheritance is denied me, or if for some inexplicable reason fate has given me other, perhaps weak, perhaps even bad traits, I can struggle against them for my entire life and still not be able to rid myself of that which slumbers in me because of the actions of a higher power.

We see, then, that a good part of a people's history is determined by what it has inherited. If we ask what sorts of physical or intellectual traits these may be, or what groups there are, we will see that each people has three groups. The first is a large group of people with average gifts, the most of us who are able to deal with the normal problems life presents to us. Next, there is a very small group. This group has received a better inheritance than most of us, not because of any particular virtue on its part but simply because of fate. The leaders of humanity, those who build states, lead people, or touch the soul, come from this group. And there is a third small group with particular traits, also not their fault: those who are sick or genetically defective. They are not up to the challenges of life and need outside help to survive.

As humanity or a nation goes through the centuries, the decisive fact is which of these three groups is the strongest. One might say, "That is not a question at all. The strongest will win, the group from which the leaders come. This superior group has to be the strongest in the end, it must gradually have its way." Well, that is how things would be if people with their little brains did not believe that they could change the laws of life given to the world by heaven.

Man has interfered in these matters. He has tried to change the laws of struggle and existence and selection. Those were ancient laws of life to which men too were subject; that which cannot meet the challenges dies.

That is hard, perhaps, but it is also the way that nature makes life stronger and better. Man has tried more and more to abolish these laws. He has kept life going by using artificial means in cases where, left to itself, it would have ended. He has used all his understanding, love, and sympathy to keep a person alive, even when it is no joy but only a burden and misery. We now keep thousands, even tens of thousands of unhappy creatures alive through artificial means, those to whom life itself has denied the right to life. But keeping them alive is not itself the problem. What is worse is that they have been given the opportunity to pass on their unfortunate physical and mental characteristics. That is the worst that has happened. We have taken the physically weak, the mentally ill, the genetically defective criminals and not only kept them alive and cared for them—that is our duty as human beings, which we certainly do not want to ignore in the future either—[but have] given them the ability to have children with the same deficiencies, thus doubling or multiplying their misery. The German people do not know the extent of this misery; they do not know the depressing spirit of the homes where thousands of cripples live their lives only by being fed and cared for, poor creatures who are worse than any animal. The animal at least is as it should be. These poor creatures are distortions of life, no joy either to themselves or to others. They are a burden throughout their miserable existences, but, thanks to the selfless care and devotion of those who care for them, may live sixty, seventy, or eighty years. The German people do not realize the enormous sums that have been spent for decades, money that has been taken from those who are healthy, who could do something useful, but cannot because the money is lacking.

There was a winter in which children in Bavaria did not even have wooden shoes to wear as they walked through the snow on their way to school. They had to walk for hours barefooted. At the same time, the government made sure that those unfortunate souls in a large institution had fresh bananas twice a week so that they got the necessary vitamins. But these vitamins could not give them joy or strength or health. But they were thus denied to those somewhere in the Bavarian forest, or in the Ruhr, or in a poor fishing village on the Frisian coast, where they could have reduced the poverty and need in some worker's house. At the same time, there was a case in which *a single mentally ill Negro of English citizenship lived for sixteen years in an institution in Berlin, costing 26,000 marks.*

Twenty-six thousand marks were thrown away on a life that had no meaning. Twenty-six thousand marks that could have been used to prepare a dozen strong, healthy, and gifted children for life and a job.

But I am not speaking of this as a kind of theft. Money is not an end in itself. Rather, we here committed a theft of spirit and soul, because we tried to persuade the nation and humanity that our greatness could come from sacrificing for the worst and most helpless. In the end, we went so far as *to put the sick and the dying before the young, strong, healthy, and promising.*

That is against nature and life. A nation going this way is heading for the abyss. We went so far as to preach year after year to healthy families that they should have no children, or at most one, else they sinned against the nation and the spirit of this enlightened age. But if some imbecile of a whore and a genetically ill criminal had children, they were not only a financial burden for their entire lives but also took the labor of people to whom our society gave nothing better to do than to change these poor creatures three times a day and feed them. That is a perversion of everything great and healthy and a sin against life and the spirit of Creation.

With full knowledge of our duties as human beings and the requirements of pity, we made the decision not to allow such miserable creatures to pass on their misery to the next generation, multiplied perhaps two or three or more times. That is a major accomplishment, for which our children and their children will one day thank us.

I know that there are those who will say, "You are meddling in matters that are not your concern. You are interfering in an area outside human control. Life and death are not in the hands of man but in those of a higher power. If God wants sick and genetically ill people to be born, you may not interfere with God's will through laws, operations, or any other measures. And if you do so—and you have with your Law for the Protection against Hereditarily Diseased Offspring [see document 152 in chapter 13—Eds.] then you are acting against the will of God, and you are heretics."

This is our answer: "My friend, you are wrong. It is true that we are subject to a higher power. We humans may never interfere with the great laws of the Creator. But you are wrong. See the laws the Creator has established for his world and your life. The great law is that life must be able to preserve itself and that if it cannot it will collapse. It is the hard, brutal law of the struggle for existence and of selection and extinction. It is the law we saw day by day, hour by hour, under all the clouds of heaven and all the stars of the sky, in which life seemed to find a senseless death, whether plant or animal or person, whether in distant Africa or near us.

"*That which cannot meet the challenges of life dies, no matter how much pain it causes,* and even if your small understanding or mind cannot comprehend it, these are the great laws of life and of the world that God himself gave us. These are laws, my German friend, that in our crazy fantasies we broke in the past."

With overweening human pride and false pity, we broke the great law and kept those alive who, under the laws of God, would long since have perished.

Today we are once more following these old laws, using humane methods, for they follow a more hard and brutal course in nature according to God's will. We are doing nothing more than reestablishing the laws of Creation and bowing to the heavenly order. We are thus showing piety and true humility—you are the heretics.

This applies as well to the third and last principle of our racial thinking. This third and last principle is that the people in this world, in America, Africa, or China, are different both in body and soul. They are not equal, as yesterday's lie had it.

People are different.

They not only speak different languages and look different: they are different in the depths of their hearts and natures and in their abilities for good and evil. In the past, people believed that these differences were accidental, the result of climate or civilization, and that one could overcome these differences and create a unified man in a unified state in which all would be equally happy. We have learned that such ideas are false. We have learned that the differences between the major blood groups of the world, between the major races, are not the result of human action, but of the laws of Creation. We have learned that the lines between blood and blood, race and race, are also the lines between soul and soul and spirit and spirit. We have learned that the opposite of the old phrase "What God has brought together, let no man put asunder" is also true. We have learned: *What God has separated, man should not bring together.*

Heaven thought it good not to have only one type of people on the earth but different kinds, various racially bound peoples. That is a part of Creation. We bow before this truth and respect its borders. That means that the foundation of our separation of the races is not a matter of politics or economics but rather it rests on a higher level, to which we in the end are responsible.

In our Reich, we are separating that which belongs to us, because it is blood of our blood, from that which does not belong to us, because it is foreign. We are doing that which is right not only for the moment but for eternity.

Believe me, my dear German fellow citizens, it is not true, as some say, that this doctrine is a sign of arrogance or superiority or boasting. We do not think ourselves better than the other races on the earth. No, we do not think ourselves better, nor do we believe that others are worse than we are. We insist only on one thing—a law established by the Creator himself: *man differs from man and race from race in this world.*

The others may not be better or worse, but they are different than we are, and because they are different than we are, there is a kind of wall between us that is part of the laws of life. That is the core of National Socialism's racial thinking. Our goal is not to insult others, to say, "What a great guy I am!" Rather, we hold to the humble recognition that each healthy piece of life has its corner of the world and its special tasks. This is just as true of humans as it is of plants and animals in all their multiplicity. We know that one type is no more valuable than another. But we also know that each variety of life has a right to existence only as long as it keeps itself pure and strong. Only when a tree bears the proper fruit does it have a right to live. Otherwise, it will be cut down and destroyed. We do not know why things are the way they are, and it would be foolish to ask the reason. That is just the way it is. Our task is to humbly accept the laws that govern our human existence and to accept the fact that we are born Germans in Germany, not as Chinese or Eskimos. That is not because of our virtues, nor is it our fault, nor is it our will. It is fate that came from above. We have no choice but to accept this fate and to develop the abilities that fate has given us according to necessity and law.

Others may develop in their own way in their own land. We must listen to the depths of our own people, to draw from blood and inheritance the strength we need to build our homeland. A higher power will take care of the life beyond.

I believe, my dear German fellow citizens, that everyone who is of our spirit will grant the correctness of our thinking about blood and race and will say, "I see now that you are not only on the right path but are honest and in the deepest sense true to demands that are greater than the laws of man."

Let us then together follow the path to a new worldview. Let us go the path of blood and race, which does not ignore faith and knowledge and a sense of higher powers. Let us go this path, not a path of matter, superstition, and heresy, but rather a path of deep humility and piety before the laws of God. Let us go along this path together and listen to the deepest depths where blood and soul rule. Let us draw from there the strength to build the state and, even more important, the Reich. It will be a Reich not only of politics, a Reich of organization, or the economy, but a Reich of a people. Germany today has the fortune to find a new way, led by a great Führer. German women today have the good fortune to see a strong and loyal woman at their head. Let us together go forward, hand in hand, as befits comrades building the future, and let us join the strength of men and women, rooted deep in their blood, to build what the world has never before seen:

The holy Reich of the German soul.

Heil!

67

PAUL BROHMER

Biological Studies and *Völkisch* Education

First published in *Biologieunterricht und völkische Erziehung* (Frankfurt: Verlag Moritz Diesterweg, 1933), 8–10, 68–72, 74–80. Published in English in George L. Mosse, ed. and trans., *Nazi Culture* (Madison: University of Wisconsin Press), 81–90.

The significance of emphasizing physiological ideas in the teaching of botany and zoology is also to be found in the fact that it serves to pave the way for developing the emerging field of *anthropology.* The physiological processes in plants and animals with which the student becomes acquainted create a basis for an understanding of the corresponding processes in man. In the actual teaching of anthropology, however, a strong emphasis on physiology is necessary because it prepares the way for teaching hygiene, and it certainly is a task of this branch of instruction in biology to provide a guide for a rational way of life. *Personal hygiene,* then, is in turn the prerequisite to the ever so significant *racial hygiene.* Thus the study of physiology is likewise connected with this problem. It can, however, only be successfully utilized on the basis of a totalizing perspective, which must be introduced into all branches of the teaching of biology.

The concept of the totality will come to the fore in the study of living plant or animal *communities* more than it will in any other branch of biology instruction. [. . .] Unfortunately, this idea has been understood by many methodologists in a purely external way as a principle of the organization of matter. It is more than that. Behind it stands a repudiation of an outmoded tendency in research; the aim should be to present a view of the totality, to apply methods of instruction relevant to the subject matter, to arrive at a national formulation of biology teaching and the discovery of internal interconnections in the occurrences of life. The metabolic changes in a closed biotic community reveal to the students a meaningful plan in the greater occurrences of nature, and when we come to understand that the whole world is a living space for one biotic community, we can then discover ultimate interconnections and finally arrive at a concept of nature that does not conflict with religious experience, whereas this was necessarily the case with the former purely mechanistic attitude.

Introducing the student to this mode of observation is in the spirit of a *völkisch* education. On the basis of an elaboration of biological laws we appeal to the emotional life of the student: he must come to see Germany as his "living space" and himself as a link in the German biotic community and the German destiny; and he must regard all Germans as his blood relations, his brothers. If we reach this goal, then all party and class divisions sink into nothingness and more is accomplished for education in citizenship than is done by studying governmental and administrative structures.

For the very reason that the theory of the biotic community is so important for the development of biological knowledge and for education in organic *völkisch* thinking, it would be expedient to base the school curriculum on this idea. When we go into the free, open spaces, we always come upon animals and plants in their specific living space in which they form biotic communities. It is not a mechanical system that orders the natural arrangement of organisms, but the living space. This living space not only presents an external frame of community but also links its inhabitants to each other with indissoluble bonds. Whoever, in teaching the concept of the biotic community, utilizes it only as a principle of the organization of matter has not grasped the deeper meaning of bionomics. He stands, as it were, in front of a deep well of precious water and draws nothing from it although his companions are dying of thirst. Thus it is a question of opening up *völkisch* values to the students.

At the same time, this produces effects that, from a didactic point of view, are not to be scorned. For one thing, instruction along the lines of the concept of the living community compels the teacher to take his students on frequent trips outside the classroom and to collect observations for later evaluation. Thus a true teaching of life is striven for, not just an accumulation of knowledge acquired by studying "animal skeletons and dead bones." There is little justification for "museum biology" in the instruction that we are striving to establish. Even the illustrative specimens, which in many school lessons still must serve as a substitute for nature, can be dispensed with in most cases. They may still serve as a supplement to what has been seen in a living context, but they can no longer be the source for the formation of views.

It is not enough to make one visit to a biotic community, such as a beech wood. Rather, it must be visited at least once every season. How different is the effect which a beech wood, for example, makes on us in early spring, when the ground is covered with a carpet of anemones, from that which it makes on us in midsummer, when a mysterious penumbra prevails, when it looks to us like a cathedral with high, slender columns! Anyone who absorbs the atmosphere of the landscape, its soul, begins to love his homeland, and it is precisely love of the homeland which we want to arouse and can arouse with the help of the concept of the biotic community. It is almost self-evident that educational hikes to the biotic communities in his regional environment provide the student with a knowledge that is not limited to the field of biology but includes knowledge about the homeland. [. . .]

Beyond and above this, the place of man vis-à-vis nature must constantly be discussed in the teaching of biology. This is made easy precisely by arranging the subject matter and the insights deriving from it in terms of a biotic-community approach. Since our concept of biotic community is a broad one, we would begin with the domain of "house and home." In it, man is the master; he has taken into his household the animals and plants which he keeps either for his use or for his pleasure. He gives them shelter, food, and care; he has changed them through breeding and he holds their lives in his hands. Without him, most of the organisms he keeps as domestic animals or indoor plants would perish. At this point we can discuss in an elementary way the attitude of man toward nature. In this biotic community we meet first and foremost the will to rule over nature, the viewpoint of utilitarianism, which is, however, accompanied by the joy in the beauty of the things of nature and love of nature itself. Similar discussions will come up in the study of biotic communities in the garden, field, and meadow.

It might be thought that with the "anthropological idea," as I should like to designate the emphasis on anthropology in biology teaching, our aim is to return to the anthropocentric point of view that has been justifiably attacked, or that we wish to foster a utilitarian pedagogy by discussing more thoroughly than was done in the past with regard to domestic animals, useful plants and their parasites, and eugenics from the viewpoint of individual and racial hygiene. It is anthropocentric if it is assumed that nature has been created only for man. We firmly reject this attitude. According to our conception of nature, man is a link in the chain of living nature just as any other organism. On the other hand, it is a fact that man has made himself master of nature, and that he will increasingly aim to widen this mastery. The teaching of natural history must contribute to this. Thus its task is not merely to transmit theoretical knowledge, to foster joy in nature, to arouse love of one's homeland and one's country; it has, in addition, practical aims. One may call this a *utilitarian pedagogy* if one so pleases. But in our view, any instruction in biology that does not take the problems of agriculture, forestry, gardening, and fishing into consideration is a failure; it is a form of teaching that is alien to the practical life of our people. School is not a research laboratory but an institution that aims to educate Germans, and these should stand at their posts in the life of the German *Volk*. We are as far removed from a one-sided utilitarian viewpoint as we are from pedagogy that is alien to life. [. . .]

Still more important, it seems to me, is the fact that the task of biology instruction, briefly referred to above, can be fulfilled by an orientation toward the concept of the biotic community. It must be grasped here once more on the basis of another idea. We have stated that the student must be led to the conception that Germany is his living space to which he is linked by the bond of blood. We have explained in detail that the bionomic approach teaches that the organisms within a living space are dependent on each other as well as dependent upon the whole, and that each link must perform an indispensable function in the total accomplishment. When this insight is applied to the human biotic community, when the future German racial comrade feels himself to be a link in the German biotic community, and when he is imbued with the idea of the blood relationship of all Germans, then class differences and class hatred cannot assume the extreme forms they often did in the past due to a misunderstanding of the actual bond that unites all estates together. Once every German regards Germany as his living space and feels himself to be a link in the German biotic community, he will be fully conscious of the fact that every individual within the metabolism of the biotic community into which he was born must fulfill his own important task. Thus a supra-individualistic attitude is created, which constitutes the best possible foundation for training in citizenship. Indeed, it can be said that it has achieved its deepest fulfillment once this attitude is transformed into action.

The notion of racial hygiene works in the same way, namely, to direct the education of the student toward nationalism. Although it constitutes the finishing touch of biology instruction, its concepts should from the very beginning permeate all biological instruction in all types of schools and not be left for discussion in anthropology, which concludes the study of biology. It should be repeatedly emphasized that the biological laws operative in animals and plants apply also to man; for example, that the knowledge acquired from studying the genetics of these organisms can, in a general way, be applied to man. Thus the teaching of animal breeding and plant cultivation can effectively prepare the way for conceptions of racial biology. Naturally, a more systematic discussion of these questions will first take place in the teaching of anthropology.

It is not so much a matter of making the student knowledgeable on all questions of eugenics, but of creating motives for his action. Racial hygiene is particularly valuable for school because of its educational significance. If the emphasis on the ideology of the biotic community creates a feeling of belonging to our people and state, then racial hygiene generates the will to struggle, body and soul, for the growth and health of this biotic community.

This is also the place for discussing, from a biological viewpoint, the value of family and the improvement of the sense of family, which has been sorely neglected by many modern pedagogues. The family, after all, is the smallest biotic community since it forms the germ cell of the state. When we take up these questions, matters of individual and racial hygiene, of genetics and sex education, combine to form a meaningful unit, just as, generally, the teaching of biology, which in the past was fragmented into many unrelated individual fields, will be fused into a unified whole once our efforts reach fruition. In these discussions on the family we are less concerned with the student's enlarging his knowledge and more with the aim that he be imbued with a sense of responsibility, that he begin to sense that the deepest meaning of human life is to grow beyond himself in his children, and that nothing he could leave to them would be more valuable than the German heritage that he has received from his ancestors, and that, through race mixing, he could taint and impair his progeny in a most unfavorable way.

Such ideas lead to a *racial genealogy of the German people,* which we mentioned earlier by way of a few pedagogical observations. And what remains to be discussed is at what stage it should be introduced. As we have explained, the way to it is already prepared in zoology and botany and it is concluded in the teaching of anthropology. Now, a short remark on the goal of racial genealogy: the knowledge of physical and spiritual features of the individual races has little value if it does not lead to the firm will to fight against the racial deterioration of the German nation [*Volk*] and if it does not imbue the student with the conviction that the fact of belonging to a race imposes a responsibility. [. . .]

The actual method of teaching racial hygiene necessarily varies with individual types of schools. Even the simplest village school may not pass over these problems. It can build upon the children's own radius of experience in the fields of animal breeding and plant cultivation. From this, simple rules of heredity can be deduced; these, however, do not need to involve cellular research and the theory of chromosomes. Children are familiar with symptoms of degeneration in animals and plants, and not much initiative is required to find such signs of degeneration and decline in man too. Thus a point of departure is created for introducing racial hygiene during instruction in zoology and botany. At suitable opportunities—this can also be done in the teaching of geography and history—such ideas will be elaborated further until they are most fully treated in the teaching of anthropology. Not one elementary school pupil should leave school without having internalized the iron command that he is to bear part of the responsibility for the fate of his fatherland, without the awareness that he is only a link in the chain of his ancestors and descendants and the carrier of the future generation. The higher schools can devote more time to racial hygiene: the students in the later classes are more mature than those in the elementary and intermediate schools. Here, too, the way will be prepared in zoology and botany. Further, the teaching of history can be made very meaningful through racial hygiene since we know that modern historians consider the cause of the collapse of the ancient world to lie in non-eugenic racial mixtures.

When teaching the theory of genealogy and race, as well as eugenics, it is methodologically important to stimulate independent activity on the part of the student to the greatest possible degree. It can be suggested that the student draw up a genealogical chart of his family as far back as he can go. In addition, he can be asked questions about the physical characteristics of his parents and other forebears as far as they can be determined (size, figure, shape of head and face, color of hair and eyes, form of nose, etc.), about their intellectual qualities and character, their special achievements (for example, rescues during the war, scientific or literary publications, compositions), their life span, and cause of death. In given cases, deformities and hereditary diseases should also be reported. The number of children produced by the student's ancestors should be determined. This is the kind of material in which the student will be directly interested. But when explaining hereditary diseases the teacher must take care not to arouse feelings of inferiority or fear of such diseases in students who come from families with handicaps of a hereditary character. It also goes without saying that he is duty-bound to keep certain information confidential as far as the other students are concerned. In every class, then, there will be sufficient usable material that can serve as a basis for teaching in the aforementioned fields.

68

GÜNTHER HECHT

Biology and National Socialism

First published as "Biologie und Nationalsozialismus," in *Zeitschrift für die gesamte Naturwissenschaft* 3 (1937/1938): 287–89.

Based on the knowledge that the most precious asset our *Volk* possesses is the racial inheritance of our ancestors who have thus placed in our trust an unlimited wealth of creative potential, German National Socialism is intent on securing the future of our *Volk* even beyond the systematic cultivation of German-blooded tribes that are racially fit for life. Everything else that we do acts merely as means and method for achieving this overarching aim of preserving and cultivating those tribes that are the bearers of our *Volk*.

As such, National Socialism, as a political movement, stands with its feet firmly rooted in actual reality and, in pragmatic questions, consciously rests on the decisive insights of life science that maintain the immutability of racial inheritance (wherever crossbreeding with alien races has been avoided) and the racial determination of human existence in physical constitution, intellectual performance, and psychological makeup—hence, it rests on an actual reality that has itself been formed on the basis of creative tensions.

As a political movement, National Socialism flatly rejects being equated with scholars or researchers or with any branches of research within the life sciences. It is wrong and bespeaks a profound misapprehension of the tasks of a *political* movement when the theories of any arbitrary researcher are attributed to the movement as "official" or as "party endorsed." National Socialism is a political movement, not a scientific one. It draws a strict and clear distinction between the reality established by fundamental science and the countless branches, methods, and theories of scientists. Thus, neither Lamarck, Darwin, and Ernst Haeckel (however indisputable their great, in some ways pathbreaking significance to science) nor their many adherents, some of whom are of equal significance to science, and opponents, are in any way to be seen as opponents, precursors, or even the founders of the basic political tenets of National Socialism, nor can we equate any doctrines advanced by living biologists with our movement since, as researchers, they present their doctrines as scientific problems, whereas the propositions posed by the movement serve only political-ideological tasks and became reality only through the efforts of the Führer and his political soldiers. The movement will never be in a position to officially subscribe to a theory proposed, for example, by the science of eugenics, only to then declare those theories that deviate from it, however scientifically sound and seriously discussed, as a threat to the state. The party is a *movement* and rejects all forms of official party endorsement or support of any scientific doctrine in the interest of keeping itself free from dogmatic determination and shielding itself from potential attacks against its political tasks and tenets on scientific grounds.

The great and important question of the origin of the inborn forces that build the species and races is of no interest to the party per se since this strictly scientific question has no bearing on political exigencies. In his speech before the Reichstag on 30 January 1937, the Führer said, "It is not our position as men to dispute Providence's reason for creating the races but rather to recognize the fact that Providence punishes whoever displays contempt for her creations." Here he has clearly stated that it is not our position to question the origin of all things in our political tasks; rather, that we must reckon with and work within the established reality.

As far as the evolution of man is concerned, there exists a wealth of ideas. One of the major doctrines holds that the man who stands erect on two legs descended from ape-like beings that once lived in trees and crawled on all fours. One of the major opposing doctrines sees in man a branch of mammals that has been walking on two legs since very early times and that descended as higher specialized forms from several species of ape that still live in trees today.

But the National Socialist movement does not need to take any sort of position on all these scientific questions because the answers to these questions are irrelevant to the demographic-political tasks before us. It is therefore intolerable that adherents to the first doctrine are automatically labeled "National Socialist," while adherents of the second doctrine are described as "obscurantists" from the outset simply because the confessional struggle against the "descent of man" from ape takes this doctrine as its star witness. We are dealing here with open questions that can be answered, assessed, and adjudicated only by the researchers themselves. National Socialism, as the only worldview that affirms natural law, is firmly rooted in reality and hence, empirically, in the basic assumptions of racial science, of eugenics. There is no such thing as "National Socialist biology"—that could exist only if the basic premise of National Socialism rested on purely imaginary or speculative concepts or constructs that can be substantiated only on a dialectical-theoretical basis—*there is, rather, only a form of scholarly inquiry that emanates from the spirit of the movement and is replete with responsibility for the* Volk *and the nation.* Because National Socialism is by nature undogmatic simply by virtue of the fact that its worldview is so firmly rooted in reality, indeed, it is fundamentally alien to every sort of dogmatic fixation that would in turn involve a mere construction. Hence, there is also no such thing as a National Socialist anthropology or genetics that "one" is supposed to follow; rather, in this matter, the only thing that could be National Socialist in nature is the research approach and the subject of inquiry—only a researcher's outlook and his exploitation of research resulting in the interest of his *Volk* and his nation, never his science itself, may be described as being National Socialist in nature. The logical conclusion to be drawn from this is that scientific research, in biology, for example, is an ideal worth pursuing and must remain one that any cultured people would seek to support and enable, if only for the sake of cultivating its own culture.

69

JOHANN FAHLBUSCH

Colored Blood in the Rhineland

First published as "Farbiges Blut im Rheinland," in *Volk und Welt: Das deutsche Monatssbuch,* February 1935, 8.

The decline in the number of births among younger generations in so many European countries obligates these peoples to devote increasing attention to the qualitative makeup of their progeny. The greatest threat, next to hereditary diseases, is the introduction of alien, substandard blood to the bloodlines. Many a German may never have stopped to consider the fact that, in Rhineland alone, *there are six hundred offspring of black soldiers* from the period of occupation. Siamese, Senegalese niggers, and Moroccans are the fathers of these wretched mongrel waifs, most of whom will have to be raised as wards of the state in youth homes and clinics and will thus burden the *Volk* with expenditures for their care.

And the mothers of these bastards? Capricious women who lacked any sense of propriety or nationalist consciousness, on the one hand; and their character traits may well complement the genetic inheritance of an animalistic, unrestrained savage to produce splendid results. On the other hand, there are enough hapless German women among the mothers of bastards who were raped by France's menial mercenaries and were subsequently forced by a dispassionate "liberal" legislation to give birth instead of being allowed to kill the criminally begotten life. They were thus forced to raise these brown-skins and yellow-skins, were forced to witness the horrifically alien manifestations of life of savage peoples in "their own" children. And as the children of German mothers, these Negro bastards are in possession of German citizenship.

70

REICHSFÜHRER SS CENTRAL OFFICE FOR RACIAL POLICY

Racial Policy

First published as *Der Reichsführer SS/SS-Hauptamt, Rassenpolitik* (Berlin, 1942). Translated by Randall Bytwerk. Calvin College, German Propaganda Archive.

> I speak prophetically. Just as the discovery that the earth moved around the sun led to a complete transformation of the way people looked at the world, so too the blood and racial teachings of National Socialism will change our understanding of mankind's past and its future.
>
> —*The Führer before the Reichstag on 30 January 1937*

The development of German culture has not followed a steadily rising course. Decades of no growth are followed by periods of slow but steady progress; then new ideas suddenly appear that transform our culture in fundamental ways. A new view of the world opens up, giving us entirely new ideas of our nature and our environment that can only gradually be investigated. They give our people the opportunity for new growth, new flowering, and new possibilities.

The fifteenth and sixteenth centuries during the Middle Ages were a period when the Nordic spirit found characteristic expression in Copernicus's teaching that the earth revolved around the sun. The earth, which formerly was thought to be the center of the universe, became a small planet that was just as subject to the harmony of eternal laws as the course of the stars. The former world of appearances collapsed, and the Nordic spirit opened the door to a new scientific worldview. As a result of his revolutionary discovery, the worldview that the medieval church had so successfully built to control people's minds gradually fell apart over the following centuries. Today's scientifically based worldview freed us from the spiritual domination of the priesthood. We owe to it our great advances in technology, the sciences, and economics.

Today we are in the middle of another revolutionary epoch. Revolutionary scientific understandings of genetics and race have found political expression in the National Socialist worldview. Once again, a world of appearances that had concealed from our eyes the true nature of humanity and the connections between body, soul, and spirit collapsed. The foundation of the Christian worldview is the doctrine of the separation of body and soul; the soul and spirit belong to a world independent of the physical, free of natural laws, and they are

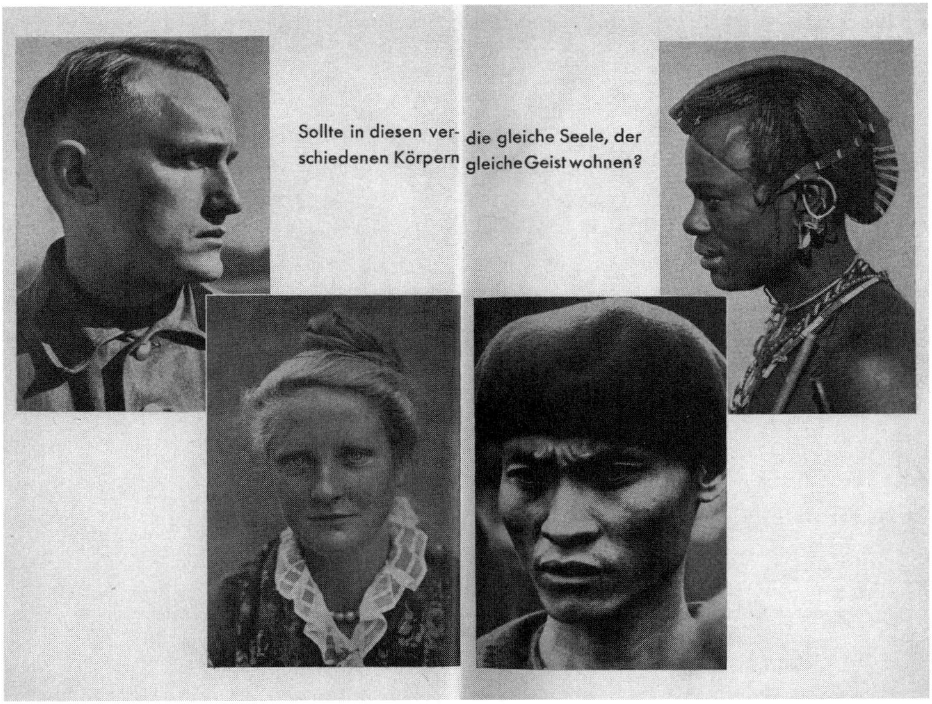

FIGURE 8. Illustrations from a 1943 SS pamphlet promoting Aryan racial superiority over Africans and Asians: "And the same soul, the same spirit, is supposed to reside in these most different of bodies?" Der Reichsführer SS/SS Hauptamt, *Rassenpolitik* (Berlin: Der Reichsführer SS/SS-Hauptamt, 1943), 33, plate 43.2.

even to a certain degree able to free the human body from its natural setting. It is a major shift when racial theory recognizes the unity of body, soul, and spirit and sees them as a whole that follows the eternal laws of nature. A new epoch is coming, one perhaps even more revolutionary than that resulting from Copernicus's work. Ideas about humanity and peoples that have endured for millennia are collapsing. The Nordic spirit is struggling to free itself from the chains that the church and the Jews have imposed on Germandom. And it is not only a spiritual battle, for it finds expression in National Socialism's struggle for power, as well as in today's battlefields to the east and west. The coming victory will bring a fundamental change in our view of the world and opens the way for Nordic mankind to a new and greater future. [. . .]

Race Is the Decisive Force in the Life of the Peoples

Race is the decisive and molding force in the life of the nations. Language, culture, customs, piety, traditions, lifestyle, but also laws, governmental forms, and economies—the whole variety of life is racially determined.

Only racially superior peoples are creators and bearers of a high culture, and they alone shape the course of events. Inferior races have no history; they lack the necessary prerequisite for that: the ability to master their own fate. Only racially superior peoples have this ability; races that are lacking in the courage to make history have no history. The life of a people does not develop mechanically, nor does it develop in a steady forward progression. It is a constant struggle with nature and the environment and, above all, with other peoples. It is an eternal battle, an eternal struggle. Hence, there is no unified, gradual development of all peoples toward a common goal. Cultures rise and fall, and peoples vanish without others being able to build on their foundation. Each people has unique racial elements that determine its life-style and culture, elements that only it can develop and fill with new life.

Peoples are culturally and historically significant and productive only as long as they preserve and maintain the purity of their superior racial inheritance. The decline of a people's culture is always the result of racial mixing and a racial degeneration. Any change in the racial makeup of a people leads to a change in its nature and its culture. If the race that gave a people its nature is debased by mixing with alien and inferior races, the people's culture will perish and can never again be restored to full life.

A philosophy of history that assumes human equality and teaches that all of humanity is part of a common, step-by-step process of development is either a mistake or a deliberate deception. There is no common development of all of humanity in which all peoples of the earth are participant, and there is no such thing as a unified human culture. The results of all serious historical investigations provide evidence against this viewpoint.

Human history is thus the history of peoples.

The history of peoples is racially determined. It is racial in nature.

It is equally false to assume that cultures, like individual organisms, are subject to the laws of growth and decline and that every culture must therefore eventually perish. History provides many examples of peoples that endure for millennia, reaching ever new levels of cultural development, as long as they maintain their racial purity. Only those peoples and cultures that act in defiance of the law of blood, and that do not maintain the purity of the leading and guiding race, perish.

Since the rise or fall of a people's culture depends above all on the maintenance, care, and purity of its valuable racial inheritance, responsible statesmanship must be concerned with racial policy and must do everything possible to maintain the purity of the racial inheritance for the future. Our Führer, Adolf Hitler, was the first statesman in history to recognize this and base his policies on it. The all-encompassing global war that the German people are currently engaged in under his leadership is the battle of the Nordic race against the forces of chaos and racial decay. It is decisive for the future of our Germanic culture, for the purity of the racial elements that make our culture, and for the fate of Europe as a whole.

The Triumph of Racial Thinking

One can hardly presume that the new scientific understanding of the importance of blood for the existence of the German people and its culture would have prevailed on its own. Our people's thinking had become far too muddled by the forces of the church, liberalism, Bolshevism, and Jewry. It was only the victory of Adolf Hitler and the National Socialist worldview that enabled the German people to think in racial terms again. This worldview appeals to the Nordic blood inheritance of each German. We have it to thank for the enormous progress of our people after 1933 and for the unprecedented triumphs of our army in building a new order in Europe and the world. Destroying Jewry will remove the final cause that led to the decline and fall of Europe and its culture.

When National Socialism seized power in Germany, most citizens did not understand the revolutionary significance of racial science and genetics. The victory of racial thinking in so short a time seems all the more astonishing in light of this. Scientific knowledge often requires decades, even centuries, to enter a people's thinking. The worldview Adolf Hitler developed, based on these incontrovertible scientific results, enabled the greater part of our people to be persuaded of the correctness and decisive significance of racial thinking.

6
Germany's Colonial Mission

IN 1919, THE SHORT-LIVED GERMAN colonial empire, begun in 1883, was dissolved by the Treaty of Versailles. German colonies in Africa, the South Seas, and Asia were given over to the victorious powers, from Japan to Great Britain. All settlers were ordered removed (except for those in German Southwest Africa). Even though Prussia had established colonies in Africa (Great Friedrichsburg, now in Ghana) as early as 1682, the Reich chancellor, Otto von Bismarck (1815–98), had always opposed "foreign" colonies and had left the "scramble for Africa" (and everywhere else) to the French and British colonial empires. In 1883, the popular mood in Germany shifted, and Germans suddenly imagined they needed "space" beyond the scope of the nation's traditional eastward expansion. Against his better judgment, Bismarck led the new German Empire into the beginnings of a colonial expansion. If the great rivals for European domination had colonies, Germany needed them too. After Bismarck left office in 1890, Wilhelm II promoted a radical expansion of the colonial German Empire. Germany acquired colonies in the Pacific in German New Guinea (1885) and Samoa (1899); in Africa, with German East Africa (1885; today Tanzania, Rwanda, and Burundi) and German Southwest Africa (1884; today Namibia and Botswana); and in China, with Kiautschou (1898).

During the Weimar Republic, members of the nationalist right saw the seizure of the German Empire as one more insult against them by the victorious powers and expressed a constant and articulate demand for the return of Germany's colonies for the sake of both economics and prestige. Hitler himself was lukewarm about colonies. He saw too much risk in Germans' "going native" or dying from the "unnatural climate," one of the themes of German colonial literature from the 1890s through the 1940s. In the face of the violent and genocidal wars of colonial expansion, such as those against the Herero in German Southwest Africa (1904), Gustav Frenssen sought to rationalize the murder of forty thousand to sixty thousand Hereros in his novel *Peter Moor's Trip to Southwest Africa* (1906). Equally influential writers such as Wilhelm Raabe in his 1890 *Stopfkuchen,* subtitled an "Ocean and Murder Tale," saw such adventures as leading to race mixing and the dissolution of the true "German" nature. After 1919, the cause of the colonies was fought more and more in the world of fiction rather than in reality.

Of all the colonial writers who had a major impact on Nazi Germany, the most important was Hans Grimm, whose father had been one of the founders of the German Colonial Organization in 1882, which precipitated Bismarck's decision to expand into the colonial world. Beginning in 1920, Grimm worked on his novel of European expansion into Africa, *People without Space,* which made him a celebrity when it appeared in 1926. It was rumored that this became one of Hitler's favorite books. True or not, its title became one of the slogans that the Nazi Party used to justify eastward expansion, though ironically not, as Grimm desired, as a serious attempt to reclaim the lost colonies. Never a Nazi, indeed excluded from the Reichsschrifttumskammer (Reich Literature Chamber) in 1935 and threatened with arrest, Grimm remained a lone ultraconservative voice against the Nazis' "forgetting" of their lost colonial inheritance, as is evident in his depiction of the German colonial experiment in his novel *Lüderitzland* (1933).

The politics of colonial expansion quickly became part of the rhetoric of Nazi Germany, though not a major thrust of German foreign policy. The Nazis centered their claims to a necessary space for expansion of the German people in Eastern Europe, in the older German settlements of Central Europe and the Baltic, and in the Soviet Union. Party ideologues argued that Germany was overpopulated and needed to displace Poles, Ukrainians, and other ethnic groups in order to export its excess population and to import food and raw materials. With the work of the "geopolitical philosopher" Major General Professor Karl Haushofer (1869–1946), the notion of a living space (*Lebensraum*), the necessary space in which a "race" could flourish, became both a buzzword and a serious political argument. The official Nazi Party program of 1920 stated, "We demand land and territory (colonies) for the nourishment of our people and for settling our excess population" (see document 5 in chapter 1). Borrowed directly from Friedrich Ratzel's ecological theory, Haushofer's notion of a "people without space" (appropriated later by Hans Grimm) became part of Nazi ideology. Hitler had been a fan of Haushofer's ideas since 1921 when the two first met. Already the largest state in Western Europe (only Russia was larger), Germany was seen to have either an exploding population (by one measure) or a vanishing one (by another). Economic growth and better public health led to smaller families, but the total population of the German states (which had been primarily agrarian) grew exponentially after the Napoleonic Wars as Germany unified and industrialized. Consequently, many Germans claimed that they required more space as a superior race and that they had to strengthen their race by encouraging healthier and larger families. For some, like Hans Simmer, the advantages of practicing eugenics and the appeal of taking colonies were part of the same argument. One could improve the health of the indigenous population so that Germans could become better workers and subjects and even improve their stamina so that they could better rule the colonies.

On 5 May 1934, General Franz Xaver Ritter von Epp (1868–1946), one of Hitler's old Bavarian political supporters, was named *Reichsleiter* of the Kolonialpolitisches Amt der NSDAP (Colonial-Political Office of the Nazi Party) and, in May 1936, the *Bundesführer* of the Reichskolonialbund (Reich Colonial Organization). On 9 September 1936, Hitler reiterated that " Germany cannot surrender its colonial demands. The right to life of the German nation is just as great as that of other nations." These developments are reflected in Ernst Gerhard Jacob's position paper titled "Colonial Policy as Cultural Mission." After 1937, any discussion of the colonies was relegated to the dustbin. Both official organizations were dissolved in 1943. Ernst Janisch's essay of that year, "The Biological-Historical Background of German Living Space," is one of the classic presentations of the theory of a living space that transmuted the colonial ideal to the notion of eastern expansion. By then, the "movement to the east" had been halted at Stalingrad.

71

KARL HAUSHOFER

National Socialist Thought in the World

First published in *Der nationalsozialistiche Gedanke in der Welt* (Munich: Georg D. W. Callwey Verlag, 1933), 19–21.

Potential for the Transmission and Dissemination of National Socialism from Its Home in the Heartland into Territories Dominated by Other Ideas: Differences in Expansion between the Old World and the New

In our assessment of the facts in the first section, we have already identified the three largest and most important seats or "hearths" of National Socialism that flared up from admittedly very disparate regions of the earth, regions that have been endowed geopolitically to varying degrees. The first hearth was situated in the sweeping, yet very cramped landscape of Central Europe north of the Alps, south of the Nordic seas—the area from which the prototype of the race once emigrated, cordoned off to the west by the crushed and crumbling wall of a language barrier that was at least uniform, with three branches and many scattered settlements scarcely separable from the Western Slavs. A second seat or "hearth" was situated in the heart of the Mediterranean world that was once the territorial center of a world empire; a third was located in the Far East, along the shore of the Pacific Ocean. Each possessed utterly disparate potential for transmission by virtue of their basic geopolitical characteristics as island crescents accessible only by sea, as a peninsula accessible only by sea or through the Alps, and as an inland territory subject to enemy attack from all sides, sheltered by scarcely a natural border, robbed of its once expansive stretches of shoreline but internally isolated. Is it any wonder, then, that, in its desire to attain the same potential for transmission and equal rights in the eyes of its fellow men, the German hearth, which nature, cruel stepmother that she is, had so poorly endowed, would have to burn more ardently and fervently—so that it would have to be more forceful in its dealings with foreign entities, to be more adamant in emphasizing the exclusivity of its racial idol—especially when it is being reproached for supposedly harboring a will to expansion that was in fact merely a necessary will to self-preservation? The notion that Italy sought to annex Trient and Triest much in the same way it had once absorbed Milan and Venice was considered justified even in the United States of America, and Italy wrested additional scraps of territory from lands that were German at their very core in the interest of its greater strategic security. The notion that Japan's sense of intuition sought not only to keep foreign powers at bay from Yezo-Hakkaido, Tshushima, the Bonin and Volcano Islands had been encroaching not only since 1807 but was also in 1905 permeated by the same feeling the Anglo-Saxon harbored toward Flanders (Antwerp in particular)—that Korea was the gun pointed at Japan and that its need to establish national security went as far as Mongolia. The rest of the world stood silently by and condoned it or satisfied itself with paper-tiger protests.

But when the German *Volk* and ancient German territories—along the Danube, for example, or at the mouth of the Weichsel River, in Austria and in Danzig—found themselves embroiled in the same surge of blood on the ancient hunting lands of the *Volk*, even that was supposed to be expansion. That is why National Socialism was decried as a "firebrand" or, as one issue of the *Economist* maliciously likened it to a childhood disease that "threatened to infect the coolest *Volk* in all of Europe, the Swiss." Indeed, echoes could be heard throughout Hungary and found resonance even in the Netherlands and in Scandinavia. On the other hand, Western Europe has always been busy building dams: and not only as far as the restraining force of England and France reached, but also, inasmuch as it was possible, to mobilize the Western Slavic system of alliances of the Little Entente after they had lessened the burden on their own backs by making pacts with the Soviets. But what wasn't taken into account was that the new southern European states were new in name alone and, by virtue of an isolation and strangulation that was truly breathtaking in international scope, were at least in one direction very similar to the German territory and nevertheless had to continue to bear the brunt of latent Russian pressure. Thus, to tell the truth, here, too, the example of Germany as well as that of Italy was more seductive than the opposing doctrines of the *Volk* in the West.

Here, too, independent of the more conscious movements in the Northeast, in Finland, Latvia, and Poland, the feeling continued to spread that old Western Europe was fighting a losing battle, despite the fact that it was better equipped with the strength and weight of its iron and its gold.

72

HANS SIMMER

German Territory and German *Volk*

First published as *Deutsches Land und Deutsches Volk. Grundzüge der Geopolitik in Anwendung auf Deutschland* (Munich: Oldenbourg, 1934), 116–18.

(a) Tasks of German Imperial Policy

The reason we pursued imperial economics is that we were forced to do so. The tremendous economic achievements of the German *Volk*, on the other hand, were the primary determining factor forcing the young Reich to develop an *imperial policy* whose foremost task was to represent the interests that had arisen throughout the world as a result of the German spirit of entrepreneurship, German industrial diligence, and commercial daring—that is, its task was to promote and to protect our imperial economics, our commerce, and our colonies.

To this end, it was essential that the two routes, especially the oceanic route, be kept open and, above all, secured in times of war. This purpose was served by the German merchant fleet that was protected by a formidable flotilla nearly half the size of the British fleet. The disadvantages of our geographic position were supposed to be compensated for by the military fleet and the army.

The acquisition of Heligoland [a small German archipelago in the North Sea] was also of great significance. It was only here that the foundation was laid for our overseas economic activity. From Heligoland the military fleet could defend Germany and keep England from the German coast, even if they were unable to hinder the blockage of the oceanic route. Hence, from the beginning of the twentieth century onward, the German government never allowed the objections of the British to thwart it in its expansion of the military fleet and it sought, unsuccessfully, to reach an alternative settlement with England on naval warfare and staunchly supported the open door policy—a matter of life and death for Germany—which most of the major powers sought to block by imposing exorbitant protective duties. Many insightful men also demanded a reinforcement of our foreign fleet so that the colonies would not be left unprotected to the enemy, demanded that more of our own cables and bases be secure so that the naval routes could be kept open in times of war, and spoke in terms of fully realizing the notion of freedom of the seas.

In the nineteenth century, from 1815 to 1870 and beyond, major international policy was strictly European, though, of course, this also included the Mediterranean and the Near East; only England and Russia practiced imperial policy above and beyond that. Even the colonialist policies of the great powers in the 1880s still hadn't changed much in this regard; and yet the partition of Africa did not transpire without political contradictions and conflicts. All that changed when, with the Sino-Japanese War [1894–95], East Asian problems were added to the flux of European focal points.

The problem thus became one of maintaining balance amongst the great powers, to which the [Soviet] Union and Japan were now added. In this manner, the European system of statehood became the world system of statehood.

But Germany couldn't afford to stand idly by and watch the way the world was once again divided up and parceled out because it had risen to such tremendous economic significance. So Germany also appeared on the map, even though its political development lagged behind that of the other world powers following its transition to imperial policy.

(b) The Difficult Situation of German Imperial Policy

Our imperial policy, though, faced from the very beginning a much more difficult situation than did the other world powers. This was related to the fact that Germany was the last of the great powers to have entered into imperial politics, at a time when the best parts of the world had already been divided up. Even Bismarck still saw his primary task in the consolidation of the hard-won unification and thus privileged continental policy over imperial policy because he was astute in recognizing the unique political situation in Germany, which, without any direct possibility for expansion, unlike the neighboring great powers, was difficult to secure against enemy alliances. It is for this reason that, in order to distract France from the Rhine and to promote a conciliatory stance, he favored French expansion in Africa and Asia and sought to be considerate of British interests when he finally began acquiring African-German possessions. Nevertheless, this represented a weakness in German imperial policy because we neglected our own colonial expansion for far too long and at the same time helped our own opponent, France, regain a position of commanding respect as a colonial and imperial power and, to a great degree, succeeded in strengthening France, fueling its ambitions and its drive to expansion, and furthermore failed to get our English cousins on our side.

The oceanic route represented yet another weakness. If the adverse effects of the disadvantages of our imperial economic policies could make themselves felt already in times of peace by revealing our dependence on the conditions prevailing in those countries with whom we stood in alliance, these became even more apparent in times of war. Many a man who recognized the degree to which our prosperity, our industry, was largely dependent on the arbitrary whims of England, on the supply of raw materials from Britain, looked with great concern toward the future as he witnessed our relationship to England deteriorate steadily once we entered the arena of colonial politics.

By 1871, the notion that divine Providence had summoned the German *Volk* "to serenely sit around thinking and writing poetry" was firmly entrenched as a basic tenet of belief for the French and the British; under no circumstances was it destined to rival England and France in a bid for power in Europe and certainly not in other parts of the world; that is, neither as a potential world or financial power, nor as a naval force, was Germany destined to have any future.

This was exacerbated by the fact that most of us did not have any comprehension of the vital necessity for a German imperial policy and imperial economics, for the unity of the will to live, the idea of and the will to power. Indeed, most of us did not even comprehend that the will to live was a unified, coherent common will.

Given our position at the heart of Europe, we could embark upon the dangerous path of imperial policy only if we were reasonably certain of our own economic independence, of the autarchy of our own country. The fact that this was accomplished at least in part against the will of the doctrinaires of free trade and those who would oppose the strengthening of the Reich on principle, and only recognize the justification for imperial policy in other countries, ranks among the primary contributions of Bismarck, whose duty tax introduced tremendous upheaval to economic life.

Following on the heels of the tariff legislation, and after 1881, the social legislation that would prove exemplary for all countries resulted in an incredible elevation of the standard of living for the entire population, not merely for the individual, as in England.

73

HANS GRIMM

My Father, My Colonies

First published in *Lüderitzland: Sieben Begebenheiten* (Munich: Albert Langen/Georg Müller, 1934), 9–11, 16, 17.

To my Father:

[. . .] My earliest memory of you as a German man—that is, beyond those first reticent glimpses of the family patriarch seated at the enormous, heavy oak kitchen table that is now the kitchen table at my monastery—begins after 1880; from then on, there was more and more talk of Bismarck and Bennigsen and his party, and the ever-more-agitated talk of exported goods and human material, of social democracy and the onset of new wealth, of a renewed sense of entitlement and the precipitous decline, brought on by poverty, in what I call good old-fashioned bourgeois etiquette—even amongst the hereditary nobility.[1]

In the year 1882, as a seven-year-old sitting at this table, I heard the word "colony" for the first time and soon understood that there was something afoot that quelled your mounting fears with hope and filled you with renewed zeal. And then the name of the Bremen merchant, Adolf Lüderitz, was mentioned.[2] Sometime in the late summer or fall or the winter of 1883, the leaves were pulled out on the oak table, it was draped in a green cloth, and a meeting took place in which, if I remember correctly, in addition to Lüderitz, some gentlemen from Frankfurt were present—a meeting devoted to the subject of colonial affairs. After the meeting, your eyes lit up as you reported the latest details from the trading post at Angra Pequena, where Heinrich Vogelsang, under contract by Lüderitz, built a factory installation and set out from there to acquire from the chief of the Bethanian-Hottentotts a broad tract of land in the south-southwest of Africa on 1 May 1883.[3] You related the story just as Lüderitz told it. The port at Angra Pequena, owing its name to some obscure confusion, had long been a point on the nautical maps but hadn't yet been renamed Lüderitz Harbor, and the stone fortress "Fort Vogelsang"—a few fragments of whose masonry foundation I have lying around here even now—wasn't even built yet, nor had the territory yet been declared a protectorate of the Reich.

You reported the way that Lüderitz had admitted that the coast, even though it was likely to yield a rich store of precious and easily accessible mineral deposits, was itself desolate and uninviting, but what mattered was taking possession of a port of entry to the hinterland, and he was setting his sights on the German Reich seizing control of all of Namaqualand and all of Damaraland—that is, of the one no-man's-land where the Hottentotts entered from the south and of the other no-man's-land where the Herero had entered from the north. You embellished a bit and at the same time spoke on behalf of your hope and Lüderitz's hope that, if Prince Bismarck were first able to place Angra Pequena under the mandate of a Reich protectorate, then the door would be flung wide open for all of young Germany to come in and do just as Lüderitz himself had done.

Only later, once I'd become a merchant myself, was I able to recognize that you pioneering

...ies of colonialism had in fact found each other by very different paths, and unwittingly ...ained worlds apart, and that these different modes of thought have continued to play a ...ole in the tragicomic debates for and against colonialism over the course of the past fifty years. [. . .]

For a *Volk* that is large in number, a *Volk* forced to live cramped shoulder to shoulder and whose members must each relinquish a portion of their own most primeval humanity, and to a no lesser degree, a mysterious portion of God's power, in the interest of the general welfare, the value of a colony will not be determined based on swift evidence and swift victory.

It all hinges, rather, on flinging the doors wide open so that young men of the same *Volk* can pass through them again and again, men seeking to preserve the nature of their *Volk;* men ill suited to being squatters illicitly housed amongst foreign peoples but who nevertheless would like to put to the ultimate test which of the forces beyond the general welfare are of divine provenance and which are not; men who, based on the notion of such divine forces, on the very awareness that they exist, preserve the youthfulness of the entire *Volk*.

It is conceivable that even a nation under good leadership can ultimately end up living in one great big garden patch, albeit under paltry, strictly regulated circumstances, and thus without anyone literally starving to death. In such a land characterized by a steady decrease in its male population, the production of the highest quality of free men in the country will eventually come to an end, and if by some miracle one should happen to appear, he would be ferociously consumed by the most dreadful envy born of confinement and of the confined soul. We Germans, poised as we are before our task in a great time, a time whose greatness and whose consequences will be determined now as never before by the scope of our numbers, have two things that are decisive: breeding for quality and the eternal eradication of envy from the souls of our *Volk* comrades.

Notes

1. Rudolf von Bennigsen (1824–1902) was a leading figure of the German National Liberal Party in Parliament (1872–91). After the annexation of his native Hanover in 1866, he defended provincial and communal self-administration and worked with Bismarck to create a liberal-conservative constitutional compromise.—Eds.

2. Adolf Lüderitz (1834–86) founded a factory in Lagos, British West Africa, in 1881 and subsequently purchased land on the coast and inland along the Orange River (today the border of Namibia and South Africa). In 1885, he sold his considerable holdings to a consortium that became the German colonial Society for Southwest Africa.—Eds.

3, Heinrich Vogelsang (1862–1914) acquired Angra Pequena, now Lüderitz, Namibia, by signing a fraudulent lease with the Bethanie community. In 1883, Angra Pequena was made into a trading station, and the following year Chancellor Otto von Bismarck declared the station and the surrounding area a protectorate under the German Reich.—Eds.

74

ERNST GERHARD JACOB

Colonial Policy as Cultural Mission

First published in *Deutsche Kolonialpolitik in Dokumenten; Gedanken und Gestalten aus den letzten fünfzig Jahren* (Leipzig: Dieterich'sche Verlagsbuchhandlung, 1938), 16–19.

The written statements of the inspector of the Barmer Mission Society, D. Fabri, in his "Does Germany Need the Colonies?" (1879), are testimony to the significant contribution the Protestant mission in particular has made to the inauguration of the German colonial movement and later to Germany's colonial policies.

Here, he outlines the following: under the influence of the doctrine of free trade, people in Germany have thus far never taken a serious look at the colonial question. They believed that colonial possessions were nothing but a burden. However, England, on the other hand, despite its interventions on behalf of the doctrine of free trade, not only kept its colonies but also only recently acquired South Africa and Cyprus. Moreover, the fact that Germany is in possession of a naval fleet readily prompts us to reexamine the question of whether or not Germany indeed has no need for colonies. It goes without saying that Germany's overseas interests have not encouraged competition with the great naval powers. But Germany's fleet is extremely popular today. Hence, the acquisition of colonies is highly advisable if only as a way to provide a practical backdrop for our aspirations as a naval power. We need trade and settler colonies. Germany's acquisition of them is not a question of power but rather of culture. In particular, central Africa should be taken into consideration. The mission could have a pioneering impact here.

The colonial question has already become a matter of life and death for Germany's development. A cautious yet vigorous grasp of this question will yield some of the most fruitful consequences for our economic situation, indeed for our entire national development. Even by virtue of the fact that this involves a new question whose manifold significance for the German *Volk* remains a relatively uncharted, virgin territory, it may prove beneficial in many ways. So much in the new Reich has already grown embittered, so much soured and poisoned by the unfruitful partisan quarrels, that the opening of a new, promising path of national development is likely to have a liberating effect inasmuch as it provides a powerful and multifaceted inspiration to the spirit of the *Volk*. That too would be felicitous and profitable. What is, of course, even more portentous is the notion that a *Volk* that has been led to the pinnacle of political power can succeed in maintaining a historical position only as long as it recognizes and proves itself as the representative of a cultural mission. At the same time, this is the only way to guarantee the continuity and continued growth of national prosperity that is in turn the necessary foundation for a permanent increase in power. The days in which Germany was almost exclusively concerned with participation in the tasks of our century through intellectual and literary contributions are gone. We have become political and powerful. But political power, when it is thrust to the forefront of a nation's ambitions as an end in itself, leads to cruelty, even to barbarism, if it is not ready and willing to serve the ideals—both moral and economic—of the cultural tasks of its time. The French nationalist economist Leroy Beaulieu concludes his work on colonization with the following words: "The best nation in the world is that which has colonized the most; if it is not the greatest today, it will be tomorrow." No one can deny the fact that England is far superior to all other states in this regard. Admittedly, there has been much talk in the course of the last decade of the "declining power of England," even in Germany. Whoever would determine the degree of a state's power based on the size of the military troops it has at its disposal and ready for war, as it has since become almost par for the course in this age of steel, might easily find justification for such views. However, whoever registers a more sweeping survey of the planet with an eye for the ever-increasing enormous scope of Great Britain's colonial possessions, whoever takes into consideration the powers that emanate from this, the dexterity with which these possessions are administered, indeed the dominant position that the Anglo-Saxon race assumes in all the overseas territories, will easily come to the conclusion that such talk seems like philistine cavil. But the fact that England is able to maintain its worldwide colonial possessions and its powerful position as a dominant worldwide naval power, with troops whose numbers amount to about a quarter of the combined army ground troops of our continental military states, is not only a great economic advantage but, at the same time, the most conclusive evidence of the solid power—that is, the cultural strength of England. It goes without saying that Great Britain will seek to shy away from any widespread military conflicts in continental ‹pe or will enter the fray only in conjunction with its allies, but this will not damage the ‹ver of the insular empire in any way. At any rate, it would be good if we Germans could ‹arn from our Anglo-Saxon cousins' knack for colonial acquisition and begin to imitate their efforts in the spirit of peaceful competition. Centuries ago, when the German Reich was the leading figure among European states, it was the foremost economic and naval power. If the new German Reich wishes to secure and maintain its newly regained position of power in the long run, it will have to embrace this as a cultural mission and will thus not hesitate to reassume its vocation as a colonial power.

75

ERNST JANISCH

The Biological-Historical Background of German Living Space

First published as "Der deutsche Lebensraum in seiner biologisch-historisch Begründung," in *Zeitschrift für die gesamte Naturwissenschaft* 9, nos. 1, 2 (January/February 1943): 1–2, 16–19.

Every human being is born from the blood of his clan, and, as the bearer of his ancestral hereditary stock, no tie is more binding for him, none ranks inherently higher, no moral obligation is greater than his obligation to his *Volk*. So the *Volk* represents a community of men joined by blood and by fate, a community of common descent that shares a common culture and a common language as expressions of its inner nature. As it becomes aware of the racial forces within it, though, a political will takes shape that is the same will as that which clearly emerged in our German *Volk* when Adolf Hitler restored to the whole of the German *Volk* its belief in itself through his own belief in the force of the essence of German nature.

But our history finds expression in the will to form a community of quintessentially Germanic Germans joined in the passionate longing to build a "Reich," which we must place at the forefront as that which expresses our bonds of blood more than any other historical perspective is capable of doing, be it based on considerations of state, dynasty, religious or economic policy, or any other consideration. Any racially oriented historical perspective must include the whole *Volk*, regardless of whether certain portions thereof have always been united in one Reich or were divided into different states or even come under the sovereignty of foreign peoples. [. . .]

As significant as leadership has been since time immemorial, ultimately decisions affecting the fate of the populace have always been made exclusively by the people themselves, especially in times of great hardship in which the leadership faltered, as has been evidenced since the beginning of time by the Germans living not only on the eastern and southeastern borders but also on the remaining borders of the Reich. Whenever the Reich was strong, its protection was also extended to include those members of the *Volk* living beyond its borders, and it was easier for them to remain true to their *Volk*. But whenever the Reich was weak, whenever push came to shove in the borderlands, the people living there were left to fend for themselves. In the east, for example, the Slavic peoples advanced and sought to dismantle or expel the Germanic populace, or, as we have recently seen with the Poles, sought to annihilate them. It is in such desperate times that the full force of the blood pulsing through the racial soul reveals itself, a force that, however, can make itself felt only when the race is able to assert itself in a space that is truly its own. [. . .]

Never have the advances of alien peoples or racially alien hordes been able to shake the German people's tenacious hold on the soil of their homeland—neither the Romans at the beginning of our current calendar, nor the Huns (fourth and fifth centuries), nor the Magyars (tenth century), the Mongolians (thirteenth century) or the Turks (sixteenth century), neither the Slavic advances, the Thirty Years' War, which substantially weakened the German *Volk*, nor the Napoleonic crusade. Regardless of whether this involved military incursions that introduced alien peoples to the Germanic territories or whether it involved a gradual infiltration, the German *Volk* has always found its way back to its own quintessential species and has always defended its living space, even if it was, as in the east, only in the form of sparse but nevertheless quantifiable settlements. It is here that the nature of a history that is not "man-made" manifests itself, instead a history that arises from the very essence of the *Volk*, a history forged solely by race and by space. It was only with Adolf Hitler's recognition of the fact that race is the primary determining factor in the life of people and nations that we were given a standard for judging the accomplishments of men who are leaders, regardless of whether they were acting in the context of the laws of race and space and thus served the evolution of the *Volk* or not. One example of the fact that both *völkisch* and political events of any given time can transpire simultaneously is Charlemagne. Even though the state that he had built on the border of the Rye Zone ultimately dissolved, his unification of a great portion of the Germanic tribes under a powerful hand is what laid the groundwork for the emergence of the Reich from Heinrich I through Bismarck and to Adolf Hitler. Charlemagne was forced to elevate the only essentially international idea available to him at the time to the defining moment of his state—Christianity, whose ideological representatives, the pope and the political church, would later staunchly oppose the representative of state power, the emperor, especially after Heinrich I created the first German state as an explicitly political entity. But it was Adolf Hitler who developed the blood-based worldview of National Socialism, which, with its claim to totality, for the first time in history conjoined ideological and political power in one hand. His political policies emanated from the history of the life of our *Volk* and now strive toward the ultimate ordering of Europe and the world according to the internal laws of life governing the *Volk*. [. . .]

The most dangerous obstacle for young National Socialist Germany on its way to a Greater German Reich was situated on the old border of the Reich, at the center of German living space, occupied by Poles from the east. This was the site of centuries-old tensions that were consciously accelerated by the Polish Versailles state. It was a tremendous political feat for Hitler to have then signed a nonaggression pact with them, if only for the sake of unifying the remaining territories that were expressly German in nature—the East Mark, the Sudetenland, the Memel—within the Reich and for excluding that branch of Czechs who were encroaching from the south. But the interest in coming to some sort of agreement with the Poles was also a necessity because, in a region where two distinct peoples have staked a claim for living space, they either come to an agreement based on absolute respect and mutual consideration of their respective concerns, as was possible with the Czechs, or there is a fight to the death. Poland has chosen to fight and has thus received a response that mandates that the eastern territory shall be returned to the German people, who own it by dint of natural law.

Understanding race and space as salient organizational forces also sheds light on why the border to France has only shifted insubstantially despite centuries of ongoing conflict. The Führer's explanation for why Germany lays no claim to France and why he has always sought to come to some form of agreement with it also becomes clearer: it is because of the natural border—a boundary that is as firmly rooted in biology as is the border to Italy in the Alps. Recognizing that border has led Adolf Hitler and Mussolini to bring an end to a centuries-old, disastrous policy that cost both sides the loss of some of their best blood.

Emanating as they do from the natural fact of race and space, the Führer's policies and the establishment of a Greater German Reich are the most powerful proof of the hold these forces have, even in the history of times past, and they demonstrate that the National Socialist worldview does not rest on some arbitrary, fictitious idea that is wholly removed from reality but is rather firmly rooted in and fully embraces the reality of life. This, however, in turn follows from the most profound belief in the eternal nature of our blood. For thousands of years, the German *Volk* inhabits its own space. The migrations of peoples succeeded in abducting the best of its forces well into the period of emigration in the last century. Wars raging in our own territory and beyond our borders have cost us streaming losses of blood. Hordes of foreign armies have threatened us from afar, have penetrated German space and, in some cases, ripped it from beneath our feet. But we German people have found our way back to ourselves and distanced ourselves from all that is alien to our nature.

PART THREE

. . .

ANTISEMITISM

The Core Doctrine

7

Jews

The Visible Enemy

European anti-Semitism is as old as the early Christian church and as new as the racial science that emerged in early twentieth-century Vienna. If ancient writers also left occasional evidence of their dislike of Jews, theirs was a resentment that was never central to their self-definition as Romans or Greeks. With the rise of Christianity, however, came a new phenomenon: a teaching of contempt that made anti-Judaism part of Christian theology, as in Paul's assertion in his letter to the Romans that Israel has to become Christian before the kingdom of God can arrive (Romans 11:25).

With the spread of Christianity into Europe, the Jews came to bear the permanent marks of physical, intellectual, and characterological differences. By the eighteenth century, a general increase in toleration meant that Jews could quit the ghettos in which they had been confined (the first was created in Venice in the fifteenth century), speak the language of the country in which they lived, enter into those professions previously closed to them, and eventually acquire full civil rights. They entered universities and became physicians, journalists, lawyers (and to an extent even bankers) as society slowly began to accept them in these professional roles. Many Jews acculturated, converted, and assimilated. Judaism as a religious practice in Germany was also reformed by thinkers such as Moses Mendelssohn (1729–86), fitting itself into the mold of liberal Protestant practice. Some (like Samson Raphael Hirsch [1808–88]) even rethought the faith to design a Jewish orthodoxy for the modern world. As Jews began to act and look and speak "like everyone else," other Germans viewed their ability to change as a "typical" Jewish skill at mimicry. The more they tried to become authentic Germans, the more others saw them as a mere simulacrum of German identity. As a result, not only did anti-Semitism increase but it became institutionalized within political parties in Germany (led by the court preacher Adolf Stöcker) and in the Austro-Hungarian Empire (led by the mayor of Vienna, Karl Lueger). During the nineteenth century, scholars regarded Jews as a "nomadic" people (Ernst Renan), a "pariah" people (Max Weber), and the carriers of capitalism (Werner Sombart). No matter the specifics, however, they were defined as a people apart.

The nineteenth century was largely a success story for German Jews as they were able to enter into the body politic, but this very act made them more vulnerable, and they offered a ready target for those attempting to define "Germanness" by what it was not. In his 1879 *The Victory of the Jews over the Germans,* the journalist Wilhelm Marr, looking for a new "scientific" label for Jew hatred, coined the term *anti-Semitism* to point out the "racial" underpinnings of the reaction to "Semites." A similar transformation of religious anti-Semitism into the secularized anti-Semitism of "racial science" and "racial mysticism" took place at every level of society during the nineteenth century. Opinions about the Jews ranged from pseudoscientific efforts to define the qualities of a Jewish race (as suggested by the anthropologist Hans F. K. Günther) to the strange beliefs of the cult of Aryan worshippers who gathered around Lanz von Liebenfels (1874–1954) in the back alleys of Vienna (with whom Hitler may have come into contact as a young man). Within the NSDAP, racial mystagogues like Alfred Rosenberg and the general of the police and head of the Reich Security Office Reinhard Heydrich (1904–42) tried to escape from the confines of modern science into a "purity of the blood."

In *Mein Kampf* (1925–27), Hitler told the probably apocryphal story of his transformation into an anti-Semite. As a boy, he did not notice Jews, for they looked like everyone else. "There were few Jews in Linz. In the course of the centuries their outward appearance had become Europeanized and had taken on a human look; in fact, I even took them for Germans. The absurdity of this idea did not dawn on me because I saw no distinguishing feature but the strange religion."[1] When he first arrived in Vienna in 1908, he suddenly saw Jews in their "true" form: "Once, as I was strolling through the Inner City, I suddenly encountered an apparition in a black caftan and black hair locks. 'Is this a Jew?' was my first thought. For, to be sure, they had not looked like that in Linz. I observed the man furtively and cautiously, but the longer I stared at this foreign face, scrutinizing feature for feature, the more my first question assumed a new form: 'Is this a German?' "[2] Jewish visibility (in this case, through Eastern European Jews' traditional clothing adapted from the Polish garb of the seventeenth century) was absolutely necessary for the anti-Semite. And Nazi ideology emphasized this visibility. In Germany, Jews from Eastern Europe—who were now part of Germany after the division of Poland between Prussia and Russia—mingled with and were disdained by acculturated German Jews. In the Austro-Hungarian Empire, too, the "east" was present in Vienna with Jews from Galicia.

The anti-Semitic racism of the Nazi era introduced no fundamentally new themes but drew on motifs that had developed over centuries. For example, as the chief of the SS Security Service, Reinhard Heydrich, noted in the SS weekly *Das Schwarze Korps,* "The corrosion of the blood, in addition to bastardizing the race, has always led to the gradual dilution of any acute sensibility for racial thought on the part of the 'guest people.' " Alfred Rosenberg the self-proclaimed philosopher of the Nazi movement, laid the anxiety about Communism at the feet of the Jews, a charge heard well beyond the boundaries of Germany. Classic Nazi propaganda films, such as *The Eternal Jew* (*Der ewige Jude,* 1940), identified two sorts of Jewish threats: the dirty, ugly, impoverished Jews of Eastern Europe, immersed in the degenerate piety of Judaism and the assimilated Jews of Western Europe, who posed an even greater danger because they were unrecognizable as Jews. Indeed, the capacity of Jews to metamorphose from their eastern brethren into the modern assimilated citizens of Western Europe was regarded as a "mimetic" deception.

To suggest that Christian civilization led ineluctably to the Shoah is far too simplistic; hatred of Jews is not a sufficient explanation for the Holocaust, for such enmity has not always led to murder. Even in Nazi Germany, there was seldom a clear-cut distinction between religious and racial anti-Semitism. The Nazi classification system required Germans to demonstrate their Aryan status by showing baptismal certificates for themselves, their parents, and their grandparents. The law, as E. H. Schulz and R. Frercks stated in 1934, had to reflect the reality of Jewish biological difference. Even *Mein Kampf,* which in general propagated a "scientific racism" in defining Jewish difference, such as later outlined by Engelbert Huber, reiterated classic theological contentions—for instance, that the Jews had no moral system because their Bible has no concept of the immortality of the soul. Huber also equated the French revolution, Freemasonry, liberalism, and capitalism with Jewish mendacity. The Jewish philosopher Martin Buber (1878–1965) attempted in 1933 to counter the religious anti-Semitism of the Lutheran theologian Gerhard Kittel by pointing out Kittel's limited understanding of the biblical texts on love of the guest. Yet, as Kittel's rejoinder shows, his argument rested not only on asserting a religious difference between Judaism and Christianity but also on defining the innate nature of the Jews themselves. Thus, theology became biology.

NOTES

1. Adolf Hitler, *Mein Kampf,* translated by Ralph Manheim (Boston: Houghton Mifflin, 1943), 52.
2. Ibid., 56.

76

ADOLF HITLER

Aryan and Jew

First published in *Mein Kampf* (Munich: Verlag Franz Eher Nachfolger GmbH, 1925), 317–29, 344–46. Published in English in *Mein Kampf* (1927), translated by Ralph Manheim (Boston: Houghton Mifflin, 1943), 300–11, 324–27.

The mightiest counterpart to the Aryan is represented by the Jew. In hardly any people in the world is the instinct of self-preservation developed more strongly than in the so-called "chosen." Of this, the mere fact of the survival of this race may be considered the best proof. Where is the people, which, in the last two thousand years, has been exposed to so slight changes of inner disposition, character, etc., as the Jewish people? What people, finally, has gone through greater upheavals than this one—and nevertheless issued from the mightiest catastrophes of mankind unchanged? What an infinitely tough will to live and preserve the species speaks from these facts!

The mental qualities of the Jew have been schooled in the course of many centuries. Today he passes as "smart," and this in a certain sense he has been at all times. But his intelligence is not the result of his own development, but of visual instruction through foreigners. [. . .]

Since the Jew—for reasons which will at once become apparent—was never in possession of a culture of his own, the foundations of his intellectual work were always provided by others. His intellect at all times developed through the cultural world surrounding him. The reverse process never took place.

For if the Jewish people's instinct of self-preservation is not smaller but larger than that of other peoples, if his intellectual faculties can easily arouse the impression that they are equal to the intellectual gifts of other races, he lacks completely the most essential requirement for a cultured people, the idealistic attitude.

In the Jewish people, the will to self-sacrifice does not go beyond the individual's naked instinct of self-preservation. Their apparently great sense of solidarity is based on the very primitive herd instinct that is seen in many other living creatures in this world. It is a noteworthy fact that the herd instinct leads to mutual support only as long as a common danger makes this seem useful or inevitable. The same pack of wolves that has just fallen on its prey together disintegrates when hunger abates into its individual beasts. The same is true of horses that try to defend themselves against an assailant in a body, but scatter again as soon as the danger is past.

It is similar with the Jew. His sense of sacrifice is only apparent. It exists only as long as the existence of the individual makes it absolutely necessary. However, as soon as the common enemy is conquered, the danger threatening all averted, and the booty hidden, the apparent harmony of the Jews among themselves ceases, again making way for their old causal tendencies. The Jew is only united when a common danger forces him to be or a common booty entices him; if these two grounds are lacking, the qualities of the crassest egoism come into their own, and in the twinkling of an eye, the united people turns into a horde of rats, fighting bloodily among themselves.

If the Jews were alone in this world, they would stifle in filth and offal; they would try to get ahead of one another in hate-filled struggle and exterminate one another, insofar as the absolute absence of all sense of self-sacrifice, expressing itself in their cowardice, did not turn battle into comedy here, too.

So it is absolutely wrong to infer any ideal sense of sacrifice in the Jews from the fact that they stand together in struggle, or, better expressed, in the plundering of their fellow men.

Here again the Jew is led by nothing but the naked egoism of the individual.

That is why the Jewish state—which should be the living organism for preserving and increasing a race—is completely unlimited as to territory. For a state formation to have a definite spatial setting always presupposes an idealistic attitude on the part of the state-race, and especially a correct interpretation of the concept of work. In the exact measure in which this attitude is lacking, any attempt at forming, even at preserving, a spatially delimited state fails. And thus the basis on which alone culture can arise is lacking.

Hence the Jewish people, despite all apparent intellectual qualities, is without any true culture, and especially without any culture of its own. For what sham culture the Jew today possesses is the property of other peoples, and for the most part it is ruined in his hands.

In judging the Jewish people's attitude on the question of human culture, the most essential characteristic we must always bear in mind is that there has never been a Jewish art and accordingly there is none today, either; that above all the two queens of all the arts, architecture and music, owe nothing original to the Jews. What they do accomplish in the field of art is either patchwork or intellectual theft. Thus, the Jew lacks those qualities that distinguish the races that are creative and hence culturally blessed.

To what an extent the Jew takes over foreign culture, imitating or rather ruining it, can be seen from the fact that he is mostly found in the art which seems to require least original invention, the art of acting. But even here, in reality, he is only a "juggler," or rather an ape; for even here he lacks the last touch that is required for real greatness; even here, he is not the creative genius, but a superficial imitator, and all the twists and tricks that he uses are powerless to conceal the inner lifelessness of his creative gift. Here the Jewish press most lovingly helps him along by raising such a roar of hosannas about even the most mediocre bungler, just so long as he is a Jew, that the rest of the world actually ends up by thinking that they have an artist before them, while in truth it is only a pitiful comedian.

No, the Jew possesses no culture-creating force of any sort, since the idealism, without which there is no true higher development of man, is not present in him and never was present. Hence his intellect will never have a constructive effect, but will be destructive, and in very rare cases perhaps will at most be stimulating, but then as the prototype of the "force which always wants evil and nevertheless creates good." Not through him does any progress of mankind occur, but in spite of him.

Since the Jew never possessed a state with definite territorial limits and therefore never called a culture his own, the conception arose that this was a people that should be reckoned among the ranks of the nomads. This is a fallacy as great as it is dangerous. The nomad does possess a definitely limited living space; only he does not cultivate it like a sedentary peasant, but lives from the yield of his herds with which he wanders about in his territory. The outward reason for this is to be found in the small fertility of a soil that simply does not permit of settlement. The deeper cause, however, lies in the disparity between the technical culture of an age or people and the natural poverty of a living space. There are territories in which even the Aryan is enabled only by his technology, developed in the course of more than a thousand years, to live in regular settlements, to master broad stretches of soil and obtain from it the requirements of life. If he did not possess this technology, either he would have to avoid these territories or likewise have to struggle along as a nomad in perpetual wandering, provided that his thousand-year-old education and habit of settled residence did not make this seem simply unbearable to him. We must bear in mind that in the time when the American continent was being opened up, numerous Aryans fought for their livelihood as trappers, hunters, etc., and often in larger troops with wife and children, always on the move, so that their existence was completely like that of the nomads. But as soon as their increasing number and better implements permitted them to clear the wild soil and make a stand against the natives, more and more settlements sprang up in the land.

Probably the Aryan was also first a nomad, settling in the course of time, but for that very reason he was never a Jew! No, the Jew is no nomad; for the nomad had also a definite attitude toward the concept of work that could serve as a basis for his later development insofar as the necessary intellectual premises were present. In him the basic idealistic view is present, even if in infinite dilution, hence in his whole being he may seem strange to the Aryan peoples, but not unattractive. In the Jew, however, this attitude is not at all present; for that reason, he was never a nomad, but only and always a parasite in the body of other peoples. That he sometimes left his previous living space has nothing to do with his own purpose, but results from the fact that from time to time he was thrown out by the host nations he had misused. His spreading is a typical phenomenon for all parasites; he always seeks a new feeding ground for his race.

This, however, has nothing to do with nomadism, for the reason that a Jew never thinks of leaving a territory that he has occupied, but remains where he is, and he sits so fast that even by force it is very hard to drive him out. His extension to ever-new countries occurs only in the moment in which certain conditions for his existence are there present, without which—unlike the nomad—he would not change his residence. He is and remains the typical parasite, a sponger who, like a noxious bacillus, keeps spreading as soon as a favorable medium invites him. And the effect of his existence is also like that of spongers: wherever he appears, the host people dies out after a shorter or longer period.

Thus, the Jew of all times has lived in the states of other peoples, and there formed his own state, which, to be sure, habitually sailed under the disguise of "religious community" as long as outward circumstances made a complete revelation of his nature seem inadvisable. But as soon as he felt strong enough to do without the protective cloak, he always dropped the veil and suddenly became what so many of the others previously did not want to believe and see: the Jew.

The Jew's life as a parasite in the body of other nations and states explains a characteristic that once caused Schopenhauer, as has already been mentioned, to call him the "great master in lying." Existence impels the Jew to lies and to lie perpetually, just as it compels the inhabitants of the northern countries to wear warm clothing.

His life within other peoples can only endure for any length of time if he succeeds in arousing the opinion that he is not a people but a "religious community," though of a special sort.

And this is the first great lie.

In order to carry on his existence as a parasite on other peoples, he is forced to deny his inner nature. The more intelligent the individual Jew is, the more he will succeed in this deception. Indeed, things can go so far that large parts of the host people will end by seriously believing that the Jew is really a Frenchman or an Englishman, a German or an Italian, though of a special religious faith. Especially state authorities, which always seem animated by the historical fraction of wisdom, most easily fall a victim to this infinite deception. Independent thinking sometimes seems to these circles a true sin against holy advancement, so that we may not be surprised if even today a Bavarian state ministry, for example, still has not the faintest idea that the Jews are members of a *people* and not of a "*religion*" though a glance at the Jew's own newspapers should indicate this even to the most modest mind. The *Jewish Echo* is not yet an official organ, of course, and consequently is unauthoritative as far as the intelligence of one of these government potentates is concerned.

The Jew has always been a people with definite racial characteristics and never a religion; only in order to get ahead he early sought for a means that could distract unpleasant attention from his person. And what would have been more expedient and at the same time more innocent than the "embezzled" concept of a religious community? For here, too, everything is borrowed or rather stolen. Due to his own original special nature, the Jew cannot possess a religious institution, if for no other reason because he lacks idealism in any form, and hence belief in a hereafter is absolutely foreign to him. And a religion in the Aryan sense cannot be imagined that lacks the conviction of survival after death in some form. Indeed, the Talmud is not a book to prepare a man for the hereafter, but only for a practical and profitable life in this world.

The Jewish religious doctrine consists primarily in prescriptions for keeping the blood of Jewry pure and for regulating the relation of Jews among themselves, but even more with the rest of the world; in other words, with non-Jews. But even here it is by no means ethical problems that are involved, but extremely modest economic ones. Concerning the moral value of Jewish religious instruction, there are today and have been at all times rather exhaustive studies (not by Jews; the drivel of the Jews themselves on the subject is, of course, adapted to its purpose) which make this kind of religion seem positively monstrous according to Aryan conceptions. The best characterization is provided by the product of this religious education, the Jew himself. His life is only of this world, and his spirit is inwardly as alien to true Christianity as his nature two thousand years previous was to the great founder of the new doctrine. Of course, the latter made no secret of his attitude toward the Jewish people, and when necessary he even took to the whip to drive from the temple of the Lord this adversary of all humanity, who then, as always, saw in religion nothing but an instrument for his business existence. In return, Christ was nailed to the cross, while our present-day party Christians debase themselves to begging for Jewish votes at elections and later try to arrange political swindles with atheistic Jewish parties—and this against their own nation.

On this first and greatest lie, that the Jews are not a race but a religion, more and more lies are based in necessary consequence. Among them is the lie with regard to the language of the Jew. For him it is not a means for expressing his thoughts, but a means for concealing them. When he speaks French, he thinks Jewish, and while he turns out German verses, in his life he only expresses the nature of his nationality. As long as the Jew has not become the master of the other peoples, he must speak their languages whether he likes it or not, but as soon as they became his slaves, they would all have to learn a universal language (Esperanto, for instance!), so that by this additional means the Jews could more easily dominate them!

To what an extent the whole existence of this people is based on a continuous lie is shown incomparably by the *Protocols of the Wise Men of Zion,* so infinitely hated by the Jews. They are based on a forgery, the *Frankfurter Zeitung* moans and screams once every week: the best proof that they are authentic. What many Jews may do unconsciously is here consciously exposed. And that is what matters. It is completely indifferent from what Jewish brain these disclosures originate; the important thing is that with positively terrifying certainty they reveal the nature and activity of the Jewish people and expose their inner contexts as well as their ultimate final aims. The best criticism applied to them, however, is reality. Anyone who examines the historical development of the last hundred years from the standpoint of this book will at once understand the screaming of the Jewish press. For once this book has become the common property of a people, the Jewish menace may be considered as broken. [. . .]

The Jew's domination in the state seems so assured that now not only can he call himself a Jew again, but he ruthlessly admits his ultimate national and political designs. A section of his race openly owns itself to be a foreign people, yet even here they lie. For while the Zionists try to make the rest of the world believe that the national consciousness of the Jew finds its satisfaction in the creation of a Palestinian state, the Jews again slyly dupe the dumb Goyim. It doesn't even enter their heads to build up a Jewish state in Palestine for the purpose of living there; all they want is a central organization for their international world swindle, endowed with its own sovereign rights and removed from the intervention of other states: a haven for convicted scoundrels and a university for budding crooks.

It is a sign of their rising confidence and sense of security that at a time when one section is still playing the German, Frenchman, or Englishman, the other with open effrontery comes out as the Jewish race.

How close they see approaching victory can be seen by the hideous aspect which their relations with the members of other peoples takes on.

With satanic joy in his face, the black-haired Jewish youth lurks in wait for the unsuspecting girl whom he defiles with his blood, thus stealing her from her people. With every means he tries to destroy the racial foundations of the people he has set out to subjugate. Just as he himself systematically ruins women and girls, he does not shrink back from pulling down the blood barriers for others, even on a large scale. It was and it is Jews who bring the Negroes into the Rhineland, always with the same secret thought and clear aim of ruining the hated white race by the necessarily resulting bastardization, throwing it down from its cultural and political height, and himself rising to be its master.

For a racially pure people that is conscious of its blood can never be enslaved by the Jew. In this world, he will forever be master over bastards and bastards alone.

And so he tries systematically to lower the racial level by a continuous poisoning of individuals.

And in politics he begins to replace the idea of democracy by the dictatorship of the proletariat.

In the organized mass of Marxism he has found the weapon that lets him dispense with democracy and in its stead allows him to subjugate and govern the peoples with a dictatorial and brutal fist.

He works systematically for revolutionization in a twofold sense: economic and political.

Around peoples who offer too violent a resistance to attack from within he weaves a net of enemies, thanks to his international influence incites them to war, and finally, if necessary, plants the flag of revolution on the very battlefields.

In economics, he undermines the states until the social enterprises that have become unprofitable are taken from the state and subjected to his financial control.

In the political field, he refuses the state the means for its self-preservation, destroys the foundations of all national self-maintenance and defense, destroys faith in the leadership, scoffs at its history and past, and drags everything that is truly great into the gutter.

Culturally, he contaminates art, literature, the theater, makes a mockery of natural feeling, overthrows all concepts of beauty and sublimity, of the noble and the good, and instead drags men down into the sphere of his own base nature.

Religion is ridiculed, ethics and morality represented as outmoded, until the last props of a nation in its struggle for existence in this world have fallen.

Now begins the great last revolution. In gaining political power, the Jew casts off the few cloaks that he still wears. The democratic people's Jew becomes the blood-Jew and tyrant over peoples. In a few years, he tries to exterminate the national intelligentsia and by robbing the peoples of their natural intellectual leadership, makes them ripe for the slave's slot of permanent subjugation.

The most frightful example of this kind is offered by Russia, where he killed or starved about thirty million people with positively fanatical savagery, in part amid inhuman tortures, in order to give a gang of Jewish journalists and stock exchange bandits domination over a great people.

The end is not only the end of the freedom of the peoples oppressed by the Jew, but also the end of this parasite upon the nations. After the death of his victim, the vampire sooner or later dies too.

77

ENGELBERT HUBER

The Anti-Semitism of the NSDAP

First published as "Der Antisemitismus der NSDAP," in his *Das ist Nationalsozialismus: Organisation und Weltanschauung der NSDAP* (Stuttgart: Union Deutsche Verlagsgesellschaft, 1933), 90–96.

Anti-Semitism in the NSDAP is ultimately founded on racial and biological *facts about race and biology,* and on its practical implementation in line with political, cultural, and economic considerations. The fact that these have found a relatively broad resonance in the NSDAP *party program* is the natural consequence of the times in which the platform was first outlined. It was the time of the Jewish-Bolshevik *Soviet rule* in Bavaria, the time of tyranny at the hands of those Jewish "Lenin's Boys" in *Hungary,* the time when Jewish criminals in Russia slaughtered all of the bourgeois intellectuals—nearly two million people—out of cruelty and revenge, the time when the corrupt *Jewish intelligentsia* staged the November revolts and, supported by Marxist bosses in the Reich and in the provinces, shouldered their way into office, when *Jewish racketeers* and *economic swindlers* descended like a pack of wolves on the downtrodden, despairing *Volk* and gorged themselves in a life of gluttony from the values and valuables plundered and pillaged from the German *Volk*. It was the time of [Kurt] Eisner, [Karl] Kautsky, Hirsch, [Georg] Sklarz, [Alexander] Parvus-Helphand, [Henry and David] Barmat, [Ivan Baruch and Alexander] Kutisker, [Johannes] Werthauer, and countless greater and lesser Jewish rogues and thieves. The fact that even the Jewish population in Germany is host to a large number of unsullied, highly competent and laudable men has no bearing on the basic position with regard to the Jewish Question.

Adolf Hitler also devoted a great degree of space to this aspect of the Jewish Question in his book, *Mein Kampf.* Presumably, while he was under fortress arrest in Landsberg, he concerned himself with historical questions surrounding the Jews and Judaism and thus found historical substantiation to fortify his instinctive aversion based on recollections of the anti-Semitic wave under [Karl] Lueger as well as his own experiences during the days of the *November crimes.* He came to the realization that the Jews, from the time they were first dispersed amongst the peoples of the world across the globe, have consistently been present as "*fermentum decompositionis,*" as Paul de Lagarde has stated—that is, as a corrosive element that destroys the essence of the *Volk*.

The NSDAP has always recognized the Jews and Judaism as the greatest enemy of the German *Volk* and the greatest obstacle to the nation's betterment.

Unity among Jews

Clinging tenaciously together, this muddle of racial mongrels—historical research proves that there are no pure Semitic bloodlines among Jews—has, despite its widespread dispersal throughout the globe, managed to sustain a close-knit sense of unity through its materialistic religion and its legally sanctioned inbreeding. Internationally, they are all the same *by nature, by blood, and by virtue of their materialist interests. For thousands of years, they have maintained dominion over the peoples of the earth;* they have subordinated them and, ever since they became associated with Freemasonry in the mid-eighteenth century, have formulated their claims to dominance in a cleverly concocted system of political, cultural, and economic demands.

Jews, Judaism, and Freemasonry

At that time, the newly established Freemasonry crossed paths with the Jews and came under their control. What was behind the Freemasons' propagandistic exhortation of *indi-*

vidualism and *liberalism* was the Jew, who saw in the doctrine of Freemasonry his free ride to economic and world supremacy. It was the doctrine of Freemasonry that engendered the *Enlightenment,* which engendered the *theories of liberalism* that paved the way for the [French] Revolution of 1789. The whole course of the revolution, the destruction of class hierarchy, the deployment of terrorist tactics—all of this was outlined in minute detail at the Freemasons Congress of Wilhelmsbad in 1784 [*sic,* 1782—Eds.]. "Me-Myself-I" is at the very center of the Jewish view of the world, and that is why *egotism, self-interest,* and *profiteering* are seen to shape a legitimate worldview. The doctrine of Freemasonry would propound the *equality of all men*—"all that bears a human face is equal"—and thus tear asunder the boundaries erected between Jews and non-Jews by the ancient Christian worldview as anchored in the blood memory of the *Volk*. It dissolved the *ghetto,* where the Jew had lived as a guest with the rights of a guest, separated from his Christian neighbors by walls and gates; it demanded equality for Jews, placing them *on a par with their hosts*—and all that in the name of *humanity.*

The *Freemason's sermon of liberalism* engendered Jewish capitalism, the consolidation of many assets in a few Jewish hands.

Capitalism

Capitalism was born around the turn of the nineteenth century, after Napoleon put an end to the revolution of 1789—and it was the brainchild of Jews. Not merely because the account holders for this consolidation of vast assets were Jews, but because the spirit that permitted and acknowledged these means of amassing millions was a Jewish spirit—taken directly from the Talmud. Even though the spirit of *egotism, self-aggrandizement,* and *ruthless greed* had already become the *driving force* behind economic activities by the time of the 1789 revolution as a result of the prevailing doctrine of Freemasonry and had dismissed the Christian doctrine of the individual's inherent *obligation to the common good* as antiquated and backward, there were still certain internal reservations non-Jews had to overcome before they could adopt without any qualms the Jewish economic methods that fed into capitalism. So non-Jewish devotees of capitalism always came in a few lengths behind their unscrupulous Jewish forerunners in the capitalist race. There were but a few Jewish families—the Rothschilds, for example, the Wormsers, Oppenheimers, Speyers, and others—who, at the beginning of the nineteenth century, controlled untold millions in liquid assets and with them, dominated a substantial portion of the Western world.

Jewish Scheme for World Domination

All this brought the ancient Jewish scheme for world domination appreciably closer to fruition. Ever since the plot for Jewish world domination was first laid out at the fifth kabbalistic Sanhedrin in Prague in 1851, it was methodically advanced throughout the nineteenth century.

According to *kabbalistic prophecies,* the year 1941 was supposed to mark the day that the Jewish throne would reign supreme over all the peoples of the earth. And the world political and economic situation today tells us that the prophecy is not far from fulfillment.

Jews at the Forefront of Marxism

Assuming leadership of the proletarian masses of workers was paramount to Jewish plans for world domination. The *Manifesto* that Karl Marx thrust upon the world in 1848 from London was merely the reiteration of the "social-anarchist program" set forth by world Freemasonry in 1843. That same year, this Freemasons' program was distributed to lodges throughout the world with the authoritarian directive to use the principles outlined there as a way of gathering, dominating, and leading the revolutionary proletarian masses in a unified movement in such a way as to prevent them from posing any detriment to capitalism. In this manner, the *Jew Karl Marx* concocted the intoxicating brew that poisoned the minions of workers into a drunken stupor to the point that they finally fell in line behind the Jews and Jewish capitalism. They allowed these Jewish leaders to strip them of their socialism and to supplant it with the surrogate that is Marxism; they let the social struggle be steered into the straits of politics and, rather than strive for that socialism which had been toppled by the Jewish economic monopoly that is capitalism, they stooped to the level of becoming sentinels for Jewish capitalism.

Liberalism and Marxism: The Bastions of Jewish World Domination

In *liberalism* and *Marxism,* then, the Jews managed to construct two powerful bastions behind which they could work unfettered and untroubled to bring their plans for world domination ever closer to perfection.

Thanks to these two mighty fortresses, from around 1918 onward, *Germany* had already become the exclusive *domain of Jewish exploitation.* Every sector of public life—justice, science, medicine, and the arts, film, and radio, and especially the press—all had become nothing more than instruments of Jewish power. The whole economic sector was indentured by debts owed the Jewish investment banks, and the whole German *Volk* was held in bondage to international world Jewry by the loans and levies imposed by the Dawes and Young plans.

Shattering Jewish Domination

There is no other way for National Socialism to rebuild the Reich and revive the German *Volk* than to *forcibly shatter this abominable reign of Jewish domination.* And since the global task of National Socialism is the *obliteration* of the world of ideas surrounding the revolution of 1789 and all its ramifications, *rescinding and nullifying* everything the Jews have accomplished since 1789 emerges as one of our most urgent concerns. It is not merely a matter of reiterating the historical and economic, political, and cultural considerations; it is, above all, a matter of stressing our solemn *responsibility,* our *concern for preserving and promoting our own race* in the interest of *protecting both Volk and land.*

The Question of the Jewish Race

National Socialism is not concerned with the biological question of whether or not Jews constitute a separate race. The Jew is seen here in his historical context. The question of race is relevant only inasmuch as it seeks to make clear that neither *religious conversion, baptism,* nor the *legal disassociation* from the community of Jewish faith shall hinder us from taking action against the Jews. The "solution" to the Jewish question that is so indispensable to the project of revitalizing the *Volk* has been clearly outlined in the National Socialist program. The Jews are no longer to be seen as citizens of this state. They are no longer permitted to vote or to occupy public office. The Jewish press has compelled us to enforce particularly stringent measures. In the new *Volksstaat,* Jews are forbidden from working as editors or collaborating in any way with German newspapers, even from exerting any form of financial influence on the newspaper industry. Violators risk deportation.

With its abrupt seizure of the state apparatus, the national revolution has been largely successful in implementing its solution to the Jewish Question as outlined in the party program, at least within the limits placed upon it by the period of transition and regard for the gradual transformation of the liberalistic economic order. While this solution may imply a tragic outcome for many directly affected by it, individual destinies must give way to the fate of the *Volk.*

78

E. H. SCHULZ AND R. FRERCKS

Why the Aryan Law? A Contribution to the Jewish Question

First published in *Warum Arierparagraph? Ein Beitrag zur Judenfrage* (Berlin: Verlag Neues Volk, 1934). Translated by Randall Bytwerk. Calvin College, German Propaganda Archive.

The basic premise for this discussion is the scientific fact that the Jew is different from the German. This is neither arrogant nor boastful. It simply is the way things are. For us, the Jewish Question is a question between two peoples. Its characteristics are determined by the racially determined differences between the two and by the unusual sociological and numerical development of Jewry in the course of its history, developments that have become particularly evident in the past decades through a constantly growing process of foreign infiltration that has reached an intolerable level for the German people.

More than once in the course of its history, the German *Volk* has absorbed foreign elements, but this involved racially identical or similar population groups, such as the Huguenots. With the Jews, things are fundamentally different. They are seen everywhere as foreigners and see themselves that way as well. Walter Rathenau said it most clearly as early as 1897: "How strange! In the middle of German life there is a separate, foreign tribe that stands out in every way with its hot-tempered behavior. An Asiatic horde has settled on the sands of Mark Brandenburg." Einstein said something similar in 1931: "I have to laugh when I hear the phrase 'German citizen of the Jewish faith.' [A leading German Jewish organization had this name.] In the first place, these citizens want nothing to do with my poor Eastern European brothers, and secondly, do not want to be sons of my (Jewish) people, but only members of the Jewish cultural community. Is that honorable? Can a non-Jew have any respect for people who engage in this form of dissimulation? I am not a German citizen. I am a Jew and am happy to belong to the Jewish people."

The most remarkable thing about Jewry is that it has not disappeared over the millennia, even though it lacks its own territory and language. Even more remarkable is that it lacks the main characteristic of a minority population, its own pockets of settlement to which it could retreat, if necessary. Only time will tell if Palestine will someday fill this gap. That question is made more difficult by the fact that the Arabs maintain their claim on Palestine. Whatever the twists of history, the Jew has always remained the same, whether as a grain speculator in ancient Rome or as a bank or stock exchange potentate in the modern era—he has always maintained control over the wealth of whole nations. The Jew has survived even when nations, peoples, and cultures in his vicinity have perished. In antiquity, we see him carrying on his business in the trading centers of the Mediterranean. In the Middle Ages, he provided money for German nobles and free cities. Today he rules the banks and stock exchanges of the whole world, forcing nations under the yoke of financial capitalism. The power of this people of fifteen million rests on these international relations. This is how they seem to fulfill the prophecy of Jehovah—the world domination of the chosen people.

The secret of the Jewish people, which has enabled them to survive through all of history's twists and turns, is that it has always recognized the laws of blood, even anchoring them in the laws of its religion. The consciousness of blood and family that believing Jews have has been stronger than all the other forces of history, giving us a unique example of a people without its own land and language that still meets the criteria for being a people and has outlasted many other peoples.

This historic manifestation of Jewry, which is unprecedented in its uniqueness, brings to the fore the question of the relationship between the host and guest peoples. It has been answered in differing ways throughout history, depending on the worldview and thinking then predominant.

Ever since the Jews were first dispersed throughout the Diaspora, they have been held together by the laws of their religion and their belief in the fact that they were the chosen people. Until the middle of the eighteenth century, Germans and Jews lived side by side but strictly segregated from one another, and the Jews were afforded no opportunity for participating in the religious or political-intellectual life of their host people. On the other hand, they could practice their own customs without interference. They had their own religion and their own laws. During the Middle Ages, the ghetto was the way Jewry could maintain itself in the midst of other peoples and fulfill its Jewish duties, which grew out of its race, origins, and laws. In this way, the values and ideals of the respective peoples remained mutually unaffected. This segregation into separate domiciles was possible only because the Jewish consciousness of race and blood was countered by an equally strong sentiment in the host people. According to the writer Grau, "There was no racial treason or baptism, no attempt to join a nation that one could never be a member of, and no attempt to intellectually silence the guest people." So it was in the ghetto of the Middle Ages that the Jew first developed his nature and characteristics that would later become significant in Western history, while maintaining the community of blood and race. The latter is particularly important, since the strict physical segregation between the host and guest peoples is what preserved the foreign, alien nature of the Jewish body that we daily see so clearly, now that the barriers between have long since fallen.

Even in the Middle Ages, the most important thing was not the religious distinction between the Christian and Mosaic faiths. Rather, there was, on the one hand, the commonly held natural sense that the Jew was of an alien race and, on the other hand, the strict laws of blood that demanded a clear separation if the Jews were to fulfill the historical mission, which they had been assigned by way of Jehovah's prophecy. Just this element of the Jewish Question has always been kept in the background by historians, who present the ghetto as a tolerated asylum for Jewish martyrs persecuted on account of their faith. There is a gap to be filled here. The task of historians writing from our new viewpoint will be to examine the portrait of the ghetto of the Middle Ages to discover its importance for the development of Jewry and the relationship between the guest and host peoples. Even the Jewish side is demanding that. O. Karbach criticizes historical writing because it "in significant ways, conceals the historical fact that the Jews in the centuries before their emancipation possessed a legal standing that was better than the greater part of the rest of the population, namely complete or partial agricultural freedom."[1]

The barriers between Germans and Jews fell as a result of the Enlightenment and the French Revolution. The prophecy of Jewish world domination would be fulfilled in a manner different from that which pious, observant Jews had expected. Emancipation made it possible for Jews to establish dominance and preeminence among all peoples through secular means. With the disappearance of racial consciousness, only religious differences seemed to remain. It seemed at the time unjust to give someone preferential legal standing within the state based solely on his religious beliefs, which are an entirely personal matter. At the time, this notion of human equality, combined with that of human freedom, was altogether revolutionary. It shattered the church dogmas that had ruled for centuries and were the foundation of liberal thinking during the past two hundred years. Since the new goal became humanity and human community, nothing stood in the way of racial mixing. Where objections surfaced, some harbored the quiet hope that assimilation would lead to the complete absorption of Jewry. Jewry itself, however, was more than willing to exploit the opportunities of religious assimilation, which opened the path to all important positions, even to political leadership. As H[einrich] Heine said, "Baptism was the ticket to European culture." Gradually, an intermixing with the German people developed, particularly in its cultural elite. Alien blood had infiltrated to a degree that we realize only today now that the Law for the Restoration of Professional Civil Service has exposed numerous sources of alien blood [see document 25 in chapter 2—Eds.]. This process of racial infiltration was greatly accelerated during the fourteen years leading up to the National Socialist seizure of power.

Today, the age of raceless thinking is being displaced by the ideals of human variability. Values are rooted in origin and territory, and each group has a historic mission based on its own unique and eternal values. The breakthrough of a renewed emphasis on racial thinking will necessarily meet with opposition by all those who, either by dint of dogma or reason, still believe in the unity of humanity in culture, social order, and organization. The Jew will, of course, resist even the mention of racial questions, since the denial of any significant differences between people is the prerequisite to his infiltration of Western European society. The Jew finds any mention of the racial question as an attack on his current existence. His leading role in every antinational area is characteristic of his mimicry and is necessary for his continued existence. That explains the phrase "German citizen of the Jewish faith."

The recognition that the Jew is of an alien and different race, along with the reawakening of German racial consciousness, must necessarily lead to a restructuring of relations between Germans and Jews.

Note

1. O. Karbach, in *Ordnung in der Judenfrage,* edited by E. Czermak (Vienna: Reinhold, 1933).

79

REINHARD HEYDRICH

The Visible Enemy
The Jews

First published in *Das Schwarze Korps,* 15 May 1935.

Since the beginning of time, the Jew has been the mortal enemy of all nations and peoples [*Völker*] joined by Nordic leadership and racial bonds. His aim has been and remains world domination at the hands of a more or less visible Jewish elite. This is a goal to be achieved by *any* means and *any* organizational form necessary, regardless of how stupid or ridiculous it may seem at first glance. *The plan has been and remains the same.*

Every *Volk* that, during times of political and racial weakness, has permitted Jewish immigration and, later, even racial interbreeding with Jews, has been systematically corroded. The corrosion of the blood, in addition to bastardizing the race, has always led to the gradual dilution of any acute sensibility for racial thought on the part of the "guest people." This in turn has allowed for an insidious penetration of every sector of *völkisch* life and an attendant systematic poisoning of the mind and spirit. So, for example, in England and here in Germany during the Middle Ages, the whole fabric of professional guilds and cottage industries was so utterly permeated by Jewish customs and Jewish components that it deteriorated into sheer Jewish Freemasonry.

Whereas in previous centuries, the Jews seized control of key positions in the royal court—as treasurers or political advisors (often in the guise of the court jester)—by the time of the Great War, the German nobility, with its roots for the most part in solid racial foundations, had been corroded. Cleverly arranged marriages for money and the rank of nobility that many princes often granted their Jewish financiers bastardized the elite classes (which were still not completely divested of power) to the degree that they were easily overpowered by the Marxist and Bolshevist revolutions, which were in turn spawned and supported by Jews.

Following the seizure of power, of course, racial legislation succeeded in at least placing substantial limits on the *direct* influence of Jews. But the Jew, in his tenacity and pertinacity, only saw in this legislation a *limitation.* For him, the only questions worth posing were, How can I regain control of my former position, and how can I work to harm Germany?

In assessing the way that Jews conduct their battles, it is important to distinguish between the *Jewish organizations* working overtly as Jews and the *auxiliary* and *special-interest* societies run by world Jewry.

There are two distinct groups of Jews living in Germany: the *Zionists* and the *assimilationists* (who, tellingly, describe themselves as German Jews). The Zionists advance a decidedly racial point of view and strive for the establishment of a Jewish state by emigrating to Palestine. The assimilationists deny their racial heritage as Jews, either by touting their many years of residence to maintain that they are *Germans,* or by having themselves baptized and claiming they are *Christians.* It is primarily these assimilationists who, with every imaginable declaration of loyalty and the obtrusiveness that is unique to their race, threaten to sap the foundations from National Socialist principles.

They have also sought to turn the introduction of compulsory military service to their advantage. Ever since the introduction of the law was announced, organizations led by former army reserve officers, the Reich Federation of Jewish Front Soldiers [Reichsbund *jüdischer* Frontsoldaten] and the League of National German Jews [Verband nationaldeutscher Juden] have stopped at nothing in their attempts to infiltrate the German army with Jews.[1]

The individual Jew, although he has no interest whatsoever in serving the German military and exhibits no particular inclination to voluntarily submit himself to the challenges of the soldier's life, is badgered into voluntary registration for military service by the politically motivated, aggressive tactics of league leaders.

And while we witness the Jew thus gesticulating in the throes of outlandish patriotism for the fatherland in order to violate the Aryan laws, the waves of Jewish bankruptcy and negative press coverage abroad spread by Jewish emigrants continue to batter at Germany unabated.

The sole purpose of the Freemasons' lodges and their affiliated organizations (such as "All Peoples' Association"), all of which are similarly dominated by Jewish directorship, is to subject people to a seemingly harmless form of social organization actually designed to serve the interests of world Jewry. They have an organization suited to serving the interests of any state structure or professional status. It doesn't matter who is doing the governing; they have some form of league to fit whatever state structure happens to be in place. In times of liberalism and democracy, the humanist lodges came to the fore, and whenever nationalist governments were in power, they had the so-called national lodges. Had Bolshevism made a successful breakthrough, then they'd have had a workers' lodge.

Oddly enough, the methods used to stupidify and dominate people are much like those used in the monastic retreat houses of the politicized priesthood. Here, a vast array of mechanisms are methodically employed in the attempt to obliterate and obviate, *one* after *the other,* certain innate traits that are quintessentially German—by blood and in spirit. These exercises serve to guarantee that by the time participants reach the higher echelons of these organizations, they act on blind subordination and are *entirely oblivious to any sense of racial instinct.*

What is more—and this is flagrantly at variance with the basic tenets of existence that are the prerequisites to a healthy life for the *Volk* and the nation—these lodges demand blind subordination in service to an *unknown* and *secret* master. This subservience is then sanctioned in the hideous spectacle of an oath-taking ceremony, saturated with the trappings of Judaic custom. Let us hope that the events of the past few years and decades are a reminder to even the most forgetful of our fellow citizens that Bolshevism is one of the most significant instruments of Jewish special interests. It hardly seems necessary in this context to elaborate on the danger it presents.

And yet, the Aryan laws are by no means sufficient to eliminate the danger that Judaism presents to Germany.

The Jewish special-interest organizations and their networks of international leadership have been and remain diligently engaged in the task of destroying our *Volk* and all of our values. All the sectors of public life—art, science, the economy, etc.—that the Jew has infiltrated almost to the point of saturation are not safe from the enemy despite whatever rudimentary groundwork has been laid in this regard. *There are surreptitious means by which he seeks to make inroads, millions of channels by which he seeks to extend his sphere of influence, step by step.*

His work is made easier by the fact that there are still national comrades (the churches in fact *promote* this position) who acknowledge the Aryanization laws only under severe duress and who do not want to embrace the basic tenets of racial thought.

Whereas there is a portion of the German *Volk* that has already begun to grow indifferent to the Jew now, only two years into the National Socialist revolution what we see in the Jew is a persistent, ever-eternal, and ongoing effort toward one aim, and it is always the same aim: *to dominate the world and to destroy the Nordic peoples.*

Note

1. The Reich Federation of Jewish Front Soldiers was founded in February 1919 by Leo Löwenstein. The League of National German Jews was founded in 1921 by Max Naumann. The organization was dissolved by the Gestapo in 1935, and Naumann was briefly incarcerated at Columbia Haus concentration camp.—Eds.

80

ALFRED ROSENBERG

Bolshevism

The Work of an Alien Race

Speech delivered at Nuremberg Party Rally, 12 September 1935. First published as "Der Bolschewismus als Aktion einer fremden Rasse," in *Europa und sein Todfeind* (Munich: Verlag Franz Eher Nachfolger GmbH, 1935), 10–11.

The form taken by the greatest threat to the peoples of the twentieth century goes by the name of Bolshevism.

For anyone possessed of deeper insight, it is no coincidence but rather a necessary consequence of nature that those who would promote and defend a movement that is anti-European to the core would not be Europeans themselves. Karl Marx is neither a German nor an assimilated Englishman but rather the rabbinical descendant of an alien Jew who, without a shred of understanding of the truly formative forces at work amongst European peoples facing the dire social crisis brought about by the advent of the Machine Age with the profoundest instinctive sense of urgency, did not conceive of a system of recovery and reconstruction, but who instead erected a social and ideological dogmatic construct designed to immortalize the fissures that have begun tearing at the social fabric and to posit this social fragmentation as indispensable and ineluctable. Marx recognized that the age of technology had descended upon the world, and that this required an attendant maturation of the social framework. He, along with his followers, an international swarm of Jewish orators and literati from the cosmopolitan centers of increasingly racially degenerate cities, got together to formulate a set of social tenets for the despairing victims of an age who are so estranged from land and landscape as to have been stripped of the standards for judging this disastrous doctrine of doom.

In order to understand the phenomenon of Bolshevism in its historical context, one must first accept the notion that parasites exist not only in the world of flora and fauna but, to put it in pedestrian scientific terms, also in the world of human beings. Furthermore, one must recognize that these parasites are not the products of external influences, they are not shaped by forces in the environment: in fact, the opposite is true—this parasitical nature is a *characteristic* trait unique to certain forms of plant, animal, and human life, which can later be cultivated to maturity in them. If, in the past, many a prince was driven by personal powermongering to employ the Jews as moneylenders and tax collectors, this came as a result of a susceptibility to exploitation that had already been ascertained by observation and experience. The Jews did not acquire this capacity for exploitation as a result of having been employed as usurers and profiteers; rather, they were chosen to adopt this role precisely because [the princes] recognized them for the *parasites* that they are. A bloodsucker does not acquire its ability to suck because someone has attributed to it this characteristic ability; rather, it is attributed the characteristic ability based on an observation of its ability to suck blood. This characteristically parasitical quality, one that is never intent on original creativity but is always intent on reaping the fruits of foreign labors, is a characteristic feature of the Jew's blood and is anchored in his so-called religious law.

81

MARTIN BUBER

An Open Letter to Gerhard Kittel

Written in July 1933. First published in *Die Stunde und die Erkenntnis. Reden und Aufsätze 1933–1935* (Berlin: Schocken, 1936), 171–77.

You have sent me your essay on the Jewish question, *werter Herr Kollege.* From the accompanying letter and from the text itself, I conclude that you believe yourself to be in agreement with me; not, to be sure, on your specific judgments about Jewry and your suggestions on how to treat it, but on the essential issue: our basic religious commitment.

However—especially since your statements were made publicly—I must contradict them publicly.

I need say nothing of your judgments and demands; they are the prevailing ones. I learned from your essay something I neither knew nor ever suspected: that you share these views; that you would maintain that "a member of a foreign people" has "no business in German literature"; that "if he wants to be a writer," he should "work in a literature that is clearly marked as Jewish and that is intended for his coreligionists and *Volksgenossen*"; that "if his book is of general literary value and transcends that particular *Volkstum,*" there would be "nothing to prevent its being read by Germans in the same way that Swedish and French literature is translated and read by us." You and the public will, hopefully, understand that I have nothing to say to this or to anything of this sort in your essay, especially since you clearly state your intention of "lending a Christian interpretation to the struggle against Jewry" in your introduction.

Yet it is incumbent upon me to object, especially since you welcome the participation of Jews in this lending of interpretation, namely those Jews who, like myself, greatly anticipate a religious renewal of Jewry. In your view, the problem is "whether it will be possible to arouse a living religion in that part of Jewry which approves of its alien status." The "authentic Jewry of the future" is, by your account, that which practices "obedience under alien status." But what you understand by "alien status" is clarified by the answer to the question of what should happen to Jewry. There you have stated that one should "resolutely and consciously preserve the historical fact" of the Jews' "alien status" among nations. And what you mean when you speak in terms of preservation becomes clear on the basis of the following: the "right of the guest" must, however, be sharply set off from that of the citizen; the Jew must relinquish "all claims to civil equality." If he proves a "decent guest," "there may then come a time" when he appears only "relatively unequal" and no longer "absolutely inferior." So, when speaking in terms of "obedience under alien status"—which, in your view, is part and parcel of a pious Jewish attitude—you mean to imply that discrimination against and defamation of Jewry must be accepted in faith; that it must therefore be viewed not only as God's just dispensation but also as the just action of men. Hence, you presuppose that your understanding of alien status is identical to God's understanding of the same; the God, to whom we owe obedience. But this is not so.

That which the God of the Bible means by alien status—more correctly, guest status (a *ger* is a man who resides as a "guest" in a land)—can be gleaned from the Pentateuch. In an extraordinary appeal, the community is admonished (Num. 15:16; cf. Lev. 24:22), "Congregation! There shall be one law for you and for the resident guest; it shall be a law for all times throughout the generations. You and the guest shall be alike before YHVH (the Lord); the same instruction and the same rule shall apply to you and to the guest who resides among you." Hence, no discrimination! But it is not only a question of law; it is a question of love. "When a guest resides with you in your land, you shall not wrong him. The guest who resides with you shall be to you as one of your citizens. You shall love him as yourself for you were guests in the land of Egypt" (Lev. 19:33ff.). In Deuteronomy, with even greater emphasis, love is not only expressed in the dative (showing love to him) case, but in the accusative (loving him) in a way at once holy and paradoxical. "For YHVH your God is the God of gods and the Lord of lords, the great, the mighty, the awesome God, who shows no favor and takes no bribe, but upholds the cause of the fatherless and the widow, who loves the guest and gives him food and clothing. You, too, must love the guest for you were guests in the land of Egypt" (Deut. 10:17ff.). Love of the guest is an aspect of biblical *imitatio Dei:* As God loves the unprotected, so also must you love him! The acceptance of this stance has consequences that extend to a redemption and a mystery that unites all. It is said of the peace offering that is offered by the community because of an "error" (Num. 15:26): "The whole Israelite community and the guest residing among them shall be forgiven, for it happened to the entire people through error."

Yet, *Herr Kollege,* although you quote a passage from Deuteronomy in which we read that one may not subvert the rights of the alien [Deut. 24:17], you quote none of those passages in which we read that this right of the alien is not separate from that of the native inhabitants of the land but that both rights are the "same right." Only if you start from this Magna Carta of biblical faith, which should be binding not only upon Israel but upon all nations where guests reside (or is it your belief that God no longer demands this justice and love from nations?), and only if you believe that this was not abrogated by the New Testament (for how could the gospel intend a diminishing of justice and love between nation and nation?), only then is it possible to speak in an *attitude of faith* of an "alien status" and of an "obedience under alien status." If, however, one does this in the seriousness of faith as a believer among nations, then surely one must first of all inquire into the obedience of the *nations.*

However, God does demand of us an obedience under alien status as you understand it, but not as God understands it. It does not become us to rebel against it, but nor does it become us to yield to the will of a *Volk* as though it were *the will of God.* Psalm after psalm of our Book, adopted by the church, utters an appeal to the liberator from oppression. Psalm after psalm would be blasphemy if God not only demanded of us that we should endure but also that we resign ourselves without appeal to whatever he has ordained. We are still praying to this day. We do not pray in opposition to others, but we do pray for our own redemption and for that of others. The "enemy" against which the psalmist inveighs, as we utter the psalm in prayer, refers not to men or human powers, but to the original tempter, who hinders redemption in history.

"Authentic Jewry," as you say, "remains faithful to the symbol of the restless and homeless alien who wanders the earth." Judaism does not know of any such symbol. The "wandering Jew" is a figment of Christian legend, not a Jewish figure. Authentic Jewry is ever aware of the fact that the promise may be fulfilled *at any given moment in time,* and its wandering may end. It does not believe that it is ordered to affirm the dispersion but believes that it must prepare itself in the dispersion for the ingathering. It knows of no "tragedy willed by God" that it must needs recognize but knows only the mercy that calls man to his work.

History is not a speech from the throne of God but rather his dialogue with humanity. Whoever does not wish to miss everything must be mindful to discern between the voices of his partners. The "historical fact" of "alien status," the reinstatement of which you, *Herr Kollege,* hold to be the "solution of the Jewish question," is partly the question itself—God's question to the nations and to Israel that he poses in history; partly, it is the lack of an answer. To be sure, emancipation as it took place was not the true answer either. But it does not follow from this that one must now take recourse to that lack of an answer.

82

GERHARD KITTEL

Response to Martin Buber

First published in *Die Judenfrage* (Stuttgart: W. Kohlhammer, 1934), 88–91.

It hardly surprises me that you see in my work a refutation of the "discrimination and defamation of Jewry." There are two kinds of defamation: one that is directed against the individual Jew, together with his own respective historical background; and another that is directed toward your people [*Volk*] per se. I have clearly reserved the right to register complaints against *certain specific individuals* among your *Volksgenossen,* and should you contend that I have defamed many of them, I would respond by stating that I stand by these complaints. Furthermore, I have registered complaints against the conditions resulting from the emancipation and assimilation processes of the nineteenth and twentieth centuries and the way they have escalated to altogether grotesque proportions since 1918. I have denounced these conditions in the most scathing terms imaginable; I certainly cannot retract my *complaints about these preposterous conditions* and about fundamentally unacceptable professional options simply by virtue of the fact (a fact that I was emphatic in stressing) that there may be and in fact are many fine upstanding and honest men working in these professions and living in these conditions, now can I?

Many serious Jews agree with me in principle up to this point. *I staunchly and flatly dispute your contention that this can all be reduced to "the defamation of Jewry."* It is not a defamation of Jewry for me to maintain that there are a substantial number of mediocre and bad writers amongst the Jewish literati, nor is it [a defamation of Jewry] to state that a Jewish-German writer may be significant in stature but that he is nevertheless not a *German* writer. It would entail a defamation of Jewry only if I were to maintain that a Jewish writer is necessarily a bad writer because he is a Jew, or, and I could arbitrarily fill in the blanks here, that he is necessarily a bad doctor because he is a Jew, or that he is just a rotten human being or an inferior individual. It seems to me that this kind of defamation of Jewry is the only one that really fits the definition. All other forms of defamation do not apply to "Jewry" but rather to some, perhaps to many, of its representatives or to historical forms of expression it has assumed. I would have liked to have believed that the reader of my essay would have been able to sense the way that my sole concern *was to remove this discrimination and defamation of the absolute and intrinsic inferiority from Jewry and to replace it with a more just and more accurate determination of a difference in nature.* And with that, I think I have identified precisely the point that must also be of concern to the Jews when it comes to the question of "defamation of Jewry"—a question that should take priority over all other questions about whether here or there any individual Jew has experienced adversity or hardship. (And, incidentally, I do believe I have clearly demonstrated, in several of my comments in my original essay, the fact that I do not take these hardships lightly.) Of course, I have little prospect for fruitful discussion with anyone who experiences even the determination of a difference in nature as a form of defamation.

It would be defamation "of Jewry" if I were to state that the Jew could not serve as one of our judges because every Jew is necessarily an unjust judge, but is it a defamation "of Jewry" if, in the first place, we ascertain that in recent years, Jewish judges and Jewish attorneys have taken it upon themselves to pervert German law and to defile any sense of German justice, and if, secondly, we believe that "justice" and "law" are not abstractions but the organic products that spring from the blood and soil and history of a *Volkstum?* Would it be a "defamation of Jewry" if, for this reason, we were to deny even the fine, upstanding, honest Jews the right to establish a German law school, to become ministers of justice, to provide the Germans with a federal constitution?

8
Eliminating the Jews
From the Nuremberg Laws to Kristallnacht

THE EFFECT OF NAZI ATTITUDES toward the half million Jews in Germany was felt almost immediately after the National Socialists came to power. Many supporters (and detractors) had assumed that anti-Semitic vitriol was simply rhetoric that the party would abandon once in power. The official organization of Jews in Germany, the Central Verein, issued a statement calling for calm and declaring, "We do not believe our German fellow citizens will let themselves be carried away into committing excesses against the Jews."[1] In March 1933, on the pretext that Jewish organizations abroad were boycotting German goods, the party organized an "anti-Jewish boycott" for 1 April exclusively aimed at German Jews and extending to Jewish shops, Jewish goods, and Jewish doctors and lawyers. The public rhetoric of the regime was nothing short of an incitement against the Jewish population. By quasi-legal and by clearly illegal means, the state began a campaign of harassment against Germany's Jewish minority. During the summer of 1935, things took an ominous turn as anti-Jewish violence spread throughout Germany. Nazi radicals assaulted Jews who used park benches or entered public swimming pools. Anyone who even "looked Jewish," a claim of visibility often made in racial science, bore the brunt of these systematic attacks. In mid-July 1935, an anti-Jewish riot occurred on the main shopping street in western Berlin, the Kurfürstendamm, when Jewish women were struck and beaten by Nazi thugs. A similar riot had taken place on the same, upper-class street on Rosh Hashanah in 1931. Then, however, a dozen Nazis belonging to the Storm Troopers had been arrested and sentenced to a year in prison. In 1935, the police offered Jews little or no succor.

On 15 September 1935, on the occasion of the Reich Party Rally of the NSDAP (labeled the "Meeting of Freedom") in Nuremberg, the Reichstag promulgated the basic anti-Semitic program of the Nazis as a set of laws. These included the Law for the Protection of German Blood and German Honor, the Reich Citizenship Law, and, of equal importance to the Nazis, the Reich Law Concerning the Display of the Flag. The latter made the swastika flag the official German standard and instituted a set of public controls governing its display. Jews were not permitted to fly or even possess a German flag (though oddly, they were permitted a flag with "Jewish colors"). The Law for the Protection of German Blood and German Honor forbade marriage and sexual contact between Jews and Germans (Aryans). Jewish men, characterized as sexual predators, were seen as the criminals in any liaison with an Aryan woman; at this point, the party did not criminalize the victims, considering women to be incapable of resisting Jewish seduction. Initially, at least, criminal charges were lodged against Jewish men under Article 5.2 of the law, and almost two thousand Jewish men were convicted between 1936 and 1940, one of whom, Lehmann "Leo" Katzenberger (1873–1942), was executed.

Jews were forbidden to hire German maids under the age of forty-five, and a complex genealogical system was elaborated to determine who was "Jewish" by the number of Jewish parents and grandparents he or she had. "Fully Jewish," "half Jewish," and "quarter Jewish" became terms of law. In 1933, there were approximately 522,000 Jews (according to Nazi racial laws) in Germany; by 1939, approximately 304,000 had emigrated. Jewish converts to

Christianity who were "fully Jewish" or "half Jewish" were simply classified as Jews under the racial laws. With these measures, the specter of anti-Semitism that had saturated the rhetoric of National Socialism became embodied in the law and became the subject of extensive legal interpretation. In their commentary on the Nuremberg Laws, Wilhelm Stuckart and Hans Globke distinguished between members of the *Volk* community who were fully Reich citizens by blood, those belonging to a racially "kindred" people who were eligible for citizenship by their service to the community, and Jews, who were "an alien body among all European peoples" and could never be citizens.

In his concluding remarks to a conference of more than a hundred legal experts held in Berlin 4–6 October 1936, the preeminent legal philosopher Carl Schmitt (1888–1985) emphasized that the elimination of the Jewish "spirit" from German jurisprudence called for removing all Jews from the practice of law. These "findings" of the conference, he assured the gathering, "*will lay the groundwork for future scholarly legal work*. In doing so, we have, as German guardians and teachers of the law, provided a contribution to meaningful fields of research for the first time, just as the body of racial knowledge has already provided to other fields." Though historians debate the extent of Schmitt's anti-Semitism before 1933, by 1936, there is no doubt that he not only opposed what he called the dominance of Jewish legal thought over all spheres of juridical life but also favored removing the writings of individual Jewish scholars from German jurisprudence so that it would reflect the sense of justice of the German people. No longer the raving of cult members in the alleys of Vienna, anti-Semitism became intellectually and legally acceptable.

The Reich Citizenship Law made it impossible for anyone who did not have "German or kindred blood" to be a citizen. All Jews lost the right to vote. They became, in the eyes of the Nazis, a separate people, who would no longer be permitted to share in the civil rights that had been slowly granted them during the nineteenth century. Jews were criminalized, their successful integration into German society denounced as a fraud, and they were denied every quality that made them German. Even their command of the language, as Karl Friedrich Euler observed, was a sham. Their "natural" tongue was Yiddish, "*a secret language of the Jews.*" Indeed, they were no longer designated German citizens (*Reichsbürger*); they were now subjects of the state (*Reichsangehöriger*). The newly designated *Reichsangehöriger* were urged to emigrate, and an agreement was signed in August 1933 with the Jewish Agency to allow sixty thousand German Jews to emigrate to Palestine by 1939. This struck a number of leading German Jewish intellectuals, such as the avant-garde novelist Alfred Döblin (1878–1957), who had never thought of himself as a Jew, as ironic. It was the Nazis who had turned him into a Jew. German Zionists, such as Gershom Scholem (1897–1982), a resident of Jerusalem since 1923, also found irony in the fact that Jews who had thought themselves more German than Jewish were suddenly confronting their Jewish identity, and he saw this as an argument for Jews to return to Zion. Scholem's older brother had been a Communist, and his younger brother had supported the German nationalist Volkspartei, but according to Scholem, would have joined even more reactionary parties had they accepted Jews as members.

The situation for Jews worsened dramatically after the annexation (*Anschluß*) of Austria in March 1938, which brought 192,000 Austrian Jews into the Reich. That year saw the forced Aryanization of Jewish businesses, sold for pennies to Germans. Most Jewish institutions were stripped of any official status (28 March 1938), and every Jew was ordered to carry a special identity card (23 July 1938). The SS collected the names of Jews in a special register, and Jews' given names were altered by a 1938 law declaring all Jewish males' middle names to be "Israel" and all Jewish females' middle names to be "Sara."

In order to legitimize the flood of new anti-Jewish laws, pseudo-academic "Jewish specialists," like the Nazi economist Peter-Heinz Seraphim (1902–79), articulated a more academically respectable version of the virulent views Germans could read in anti-Semitic tabloids like *Der Stürmer.* The role of such experts was not so much to be the "architects of annihilation" but to prepare the ground by making Jew hatred seem scientifically sanctioned and by demonstrating that Jews represented a biologically distinct race. The Jews had become, by 1938, not merely a people apart but more ominously an enemy to be combated by people such as the anthropologist and SS officer Fritz Arlt (1912–2004), later director of the Abteilung Bevölkerungswesen und Fürsorge (Office for Population Policy and Welfare), which was set up in occupied Poland to segregate the Jews.

Germans who suddenly were informed that they had sufficient Jewish ancestry (two grandparents) to be redefined as Jews under German law, no matter what their confessional identity or lack of it, had to confront accusations of cultural and biological degeneracy. Degeneracy theory, which was developed in the 1850s in Paris (by the Vienna-born B. A. Morel), held that Jews represented a biologically "morbid deviation from the norm."[2] The antithesis of the nineteenth-century product of progress, degeneracy theory was a "throwback" to earlier stages of development (following Haeckel's notion of "ontogeny recapitulating phylogeny"). The Jew might look like a "normal" German but was in fact a degenerate. Cesare Lombroso (1835–1909), professor of criminology and anthropology in Turin, developed his own theory of degeneracy and criminality in the 1870s, and his views were widely accepted throughout the early twentieth century. Lombroso, like the racial theorists of his day, based his diagnoses on theories of inheritance as well as on the appearance of the degenerate. The shape of the ear, the length of the stride, the jutting jaw, the appearance of tattoos—all signified the degenerate. For racial theorists such as Johann von Leers, however, Lombroso posed a problem, for he was an Italian Jew who, in his 1894 book *Anti-Semitism and Modern Science,* had refuted racial theory and made it clear that he in no way thought of Jews as degenerate.

Part of the politics of biological and racial mysticism after 1933 was to reinforce the popular notion that Jews, by definition, were prime movers in the world of criminality, usually defined as "white-collar" criminality. Like other degenerates who committed violent acts (men) or stealthy ones such as poisoning (women), the Jew was by nature a criminal and could not be otherwise, a view exhibited by Herwig Hartner-Hnizdo. As a "degenerate race," Jews acted out their horror of healthy races (such as the Germans) by exploiting them. The figure of the Jewish criminal, which had its roots as early as the eighteenth century in Germany, was proof of Jews' racial predisposition.

In 1933, the first "concentration camp" (already a term of opprobrium because of the British treatment of the Boers in South Africa between 1899 and 1902) was created in the idyllic artists' village of Dachau outside Munich. By 1939, five additional large concentration camps had been established throughout Germany and Austria: Sachsenhausen (1936), Buchenwald (1937), Flossenbürg (1938), Mauthausen (1938), and the camp for women and children at Ravensbrück (1939). The camps were putatively for "political reorientation" or criminal punishment. They quickly became places of death for opponents such as the journalist Carl von Ossietzky (1889–1938), who was arrested by the Nazis on 28 February 1933, the morning after the Reichstag fire. Ossietzky was first sent to a Berlin prison, then later to smaller concentration camps—first to Sonnenburg and later to Esterwegen-Papenburg, where, according to reports by fellow prisoners, he was badly mistreated. He was awarded the Nobel Peace Prize in 1936 for his vehement feuilletons in opposition to the Nazis and to all forces opposed to the idea of a democracy. He died in 1938 as a result of the injuries he had sustained in the concentration camps.

As *Das Schwarze Korps* made manifest in 1936, the SS felt no need to hide the existence of the camps, instead publicizing their utility in separating "race traitors, sexual degenerates, and common criminals" from society. The camps often served a dual purpose. The asocial and the degenerate, the alcoholic and the drug user as well as the petty criminal, could be sent to the concentration camps by eugenic clinics such as the one in Berlin-Charlottenburg for a limited time to try to change their pattern of activity. The prevailing notion was that one could not alter the nature of the degenerate but could stop his or her degenerate acts. While the "concentration camps" were not extermination camps (such as Auschwitz), the extremely high death rate through mistreatment and disease made them the pattern for the later sites of death.

The turning point in the persecution of the Jews of "Greater Germany" came at the beginning of November 1938 when the seventeen-year-old Polish Jew Herschel Grynszpan learned that because of Polish and German machinations, his entire family had been declared "stateless" and exiled to Poland. He purchased a revolver and, on 7 November 1938, assassinated the secretary of the German Embassy in Paris, Ernst Eduard vom Rath. On 8 November, as Rath lay dying, the party newspaper, the *Völkischer Beobachter,* published an ominous editorial stating,

> It is clear what conclusions the German people will draw from this latest event. We shall no longer tolerate a situation where hundreds of thousands of Jews within our territory control entire streets of shops, throng places of public entertainment, and pocket the wealth of German leaseholders as "foreign" landlords while their racial brothers incite war against Germany and shoot down German officials. [. . .] The shots fired in the German Embassy in Paris will not only mark the beginning of a new German attitude in the Jewish Question but will hopefully also provide a signal for those foreigners who up to now have not grasped that ultimately there is only one thing standing in the way of international understanding between nations—International Jewry.[3]

Upon the announcement of Rath's death, Propaganda Minister Joseph Goebbels declared at a Munich SA meeting commemorating the 1923 putsch that the "Jew" had to be taught a lesson. SS leader Reinhard Heydrich called for violence against Jews, destruction of their property, and the burning of synagogues. The message was conveyed to regional and local Nazi organizations throughout Germany. The fury and violence that followed can be described as organized spontaneity, as Betty Scholem, Gershom's mother, observed, a combination of state-sponsored terror and orchestrated "public outrage."

The synagogue in Bad Hersfeld was the first to be set afire; soon, burning buildings were seen in every German city. Jews throughout Germany were targets of systematic murder, beatings, and humiliation. Synagogues, Jewish organizations, businesses, and Jewish-owned buildings were burned; cemeteries were desecrated throughout the nation; and thirty thousand Jews were arrested and sent to concentration camps, where hundreds were murdered or beaten so badly that they died after their release. As an added insult, the Jews of Germany were ordered to pay a billion Reichsmark fine as restitution for the damages they had caused against Germany. The attack on Jewish institutions, businesses, and individual Jews, which took place on the night between 9 and 10 November 1938, was initially designated "Kristallnacht" because of the ubiquitous broken glass (soon the ironic prefix *Reichs* was added, as in *Reichskristallnacht* or *Reichspogromnacht* (State Pogrom Night). Gershom Scholem's mother, Betty Scholem, wrote a moving and frightening account of the events of that night.

Secret SS sources noted that German citizens who were horrified by the excesses of Kristallnacht were quickly quieted: were they such friends of the Jews that they wanted to suffer the same fate? There were a few notable exceptions. Wilhelm Krützfeld, the head of a police station in central Berlin (Berlin-Mitte), rescued the "New Synagogue" (1859–66) on Oranienburger Street by explaining that it was officially listed as a landmark historical building. He drove off the SA hooligans and ordered the fire department to rescue the building. Nothing happened to him. But many others, including the Jews of "Greater

Germany," realized that they had to flee if they could. Within weeks, Jews were banned from parks, gardens, beaches, and resorts. They were forbidden to attend cinemas, theaters, concerts, and exhibitions. Jews could no longer drive cars or walk in certain neighborhoods. Non-Jews learned silence. Gloating at the "free world's" lukewarm response to the flight of German (and Austrian) Jewry, an editorial entitled "What Now, Jews?" in *Das Schwarze Korps* (24 November 1938) provided a succinct description of the situation for those Jews who remained (or would come) under Nazi rule—"complete elimination, absolute segregation!"

NOTES

1. Cited in Moshe Raphael Gottlieb, *American Anti-Nazi Resistance, 1933–1941: An Historical Analysis* (Jersey City, N.J.: KTAV Publishing House, 1982), 6.

2. B. A. Morel, *Traité des dégénérescences physiques, intellectuelles et morales de l'espèce humaine et des causes qui produisent ces variétés maladives* (Paris: J. B. Baillière, 1857), 7–8.

3. *Völkischer Beobachter, 8 November 1938,* cited in Wolfgang Benz, "The Relapse into Barbarism," in *November 1938 : From "Reichskristallnacht" to Genocide,* edited by Walter H. Pehle, translated by William Templer (Oxford: Berg, 1991), 3.

83

Reich Citizenship Law

Announced on 15 September 1935 as "Reichsbürgergesetz." First published in *Reichsgesetzblatt* (Berlin: Reichsverlagsamt, 1935), 1:1146.

The Reichstag has unanimously adopted the following law, which is herewith promulgated:

Article 1: Concept of State Subject

(1) A subject of the state is a person who belongs to the protective union of the German Reich, and who therefore has particular obligations towards the Reich.
(2) The status of subject is acquired in accordance with the provisions of the Reich Citizenship Law.

Article 2: Concept of Reich Citizenship

(1) A citizen of the Reich is only that subject who is of German or kindred blood and who, through his conduct, proves that he is both willing and able to faithfully serve the German people and Reich.
(2) The right to citizenship is acquired by the granting of a certificate of Reich citizenship.
(3) Only the citizen of the Reich enjoys full political rights in accordance with the provisions of the law.

Article 3: Implementation

The Reich minister of the interior, in conjunction with the deputy to the Führer, shall issue the legal and administrative decrees necessary for the implementation and amplification of this law.

Nuremberg, 15 September 1935
at the Reich Party Rally of Freedom

Führer and Chancellor of the Reich: Adolf Hitler
Reich Minister of the Interior: [Wilhelm] Frick

84

Law for the Protection of German Blood and German Honor

Announced on 15 September 1935. First published as "Gesetz zum Schutze des deutschen Blutes und der deutschen Ehre," in *Reichsgesetzblatt* (Berlin: Reichsverlagsamt, 1935), 1:1147.

Compelled by knowledge of the fact that the purity of German blood is the prerequisite for the continued existence of the German *Volk*, and inspired by the unbending will to secure the future of the German nation in perpetuity, the Reichstag has unanimously adopted the following law, which is hereby promulgated:

Article 1: Prohibition of Marriage between Jews and Germans

(1) Marriages between Jews and state subjects of German or related blood are forbidden. Marriages concluded in defiance of this law shall be considered null and void even if, for the purpose of circumventing this law, they have been concluded abroad.
(2) Annulment proceedings may be initiated solely by the Public Prosecutor.

Article 2: Prohibition of Extramarital Relations

Extramarital affairs between Jews and state subjects of German or related blood are forbidden.

Article 3: Minimum Age for Domestic Employees

Jews shall not be permitted to employ female nationals of German or related blood under forty-five years of age in their households.

Article 4: Prohibition of the Use of the Reich Flag and Colors

(1) Jews shall be forbidden from flying the Reich or national flag or from displaying the colors of the Reich.
(2) However, Jews shall be permitted to display the Jewish colors. The exercise of this entitlement is protected by state law.

Article 5: Penalties

(1) Any person found to be in violation of Article 1 shall be subject to a term of hard labor.
(2) Any man found to be in violation of Article 2 shall be subject to imprisonment or hard labor.
(3) Any person found to be in violation of Articles 3 or 4 will be subject to either imprisonment of up to one year and a fine, or one or the other of these penalties.

Article 6: Implementation

The Reich minister of the interior, in conjunction with the deputy to the Führer, shall issue the legal and administrative decrees necessary for the implementation and amplification of this law.

Article 7: Taking Effect

The law shall enter in effect the day following its promulgation; except for Article 3, which will not enter into effect until 1 January 1936.

Nuremberg, 15 September 1935
at the Reich Party Rally of Freedom

Führer and Chancellor of the Reich: Adolf Hitler
Reich Minister of the Interior: [Wilhelm] Frick
Reich Minister of Justice: [Franz] Gürtner
Deputy to the Führer: Rudolf Hess

85

WILHELM STUCKART AND HANS GLOBKE

Civil Rights and the Natural Inequality of Man

First published in *Kommentare zur deutschen Rassengesetzgebung,* vol. 1 (Munich: 1936), 20, 26, 28, 30.

Theories of state over the past century have considered the state an entity in itself, an abstract juridical concept of the state as "person" or state personality [*Staatsperson*]. By contrast, however, the fundamental political value of National Socialism is not the state as such, but rather the *Volk*. Here, perhaps, is where the most profound differences between the Germanic world of ideas and Roman thought become apparent. In Germanic community thought, the state consists of a system of communities—family, clan, squadron, community of the *Volk*—each of which may encompass additional, more intimate communities. The entire life of each individual comrade unfolds within these communities. Outside of these communities, no human life exists in the legal sense, but only a biological, vegetative existence, which is why anyone expelled from the community for a crime becomes an outlaw. Thus, the state is not something "other," in contradistinction to the comrade, or even something "above" the comrade. Rather, the comrades of the community as a whole constitute the state.

In Roman thought, however, the state, as an abstract personality with its administrative governmental apparatus, occupies the center. In the individualistic-liberal conception of the state, heavily influenced as it is by Roman thought, the primary element was the free and independent individual and the sum of all individuals in society. For this reason, only the state was deemed worthy of protection because, through the "free play of forces," it supposedly achieved the greatest potential for happiness in the individual and in the sum of individuals, the greater good, and the state was looked upon as an apparatus that stood apart from, or even above, the individual, as an independent mechanism that, juristically, was conceived as a political personality hovering high above the *Volk*. This concept of the state was entirely congruent with the prevailing mechanistic worldview. Exercising strict control over society, this juristic political personality, entirely cut off from the people, had to promote the free development of the individual and see to it that no one's personal liberty was restricted. A strict line of distinction was drawn between state and *Volk*, between the state authority and its subjects. The lone individual was the antipode of the abstract state personality. Both entered into legal relations with each other, though not as equals. The reality of *Volk* and state dissolved into a system of legal relations between the state and each individual within it. The enduring legal nexus between the human personality and the state personality was expressed in the status of nationality viewed as a legal relationship between the two. The spirit of nationality found fertile grazing grounds in positivistic-legalistic relationships within the liberal constitutional state. With painstaking concern for the individual and his rights, one sought to precisely define and determine the parameters of citizenship. Obviously, this concern focused primarily on the rights of the state subject, on the degree of influence he exerted over the state, and his degree of independence from that state. In accordance with the individualistic mode of thought, the essence of nationality, save for some obligations of the state subjects, such as service in the armed forces, was seen as a cluster of rights, the so-called civil rights, which were essentially directed against the state. In every constitution, in particular in the Weimar Constitution, the so-called basic rights played a prominent role. Above all, the principle of equality was most scrupulously guarded. Rights and responsibilities were the same for every citizen of the state. It was not a matter of blood right. There was no genealogical [*völkisch*] foundation for citizenship. The question of *völkisch* rights to citizenship on the part of individuals within the state was never raised.

The revolution in the conception of the state has perforce changed the concept, the essence, and the definition of nationality and citizenship. National Socialism has placed the *Volk* directly into the center of thought, of faith and will, of creation and of life. As Reich Minister Frick says, [National Socialism] derives from the mightiest of all traditions on earth: from the eternity of the *Volk*, which ever renews itself. "The point of departure of National Socialist doctrine does not rest with the state but with the *Volk*. That is to say, in order to be able to test, judge, and correct the suitability and efficacy of external *völkisch* forms, we must grasp them as more than mere means to an end. Therefore, the focal point of all National Socialist thought lies in the living substance which we, according to its historical development, call the German *Volk*" (from the Führer's closing address at the 1935 Party Rally).

The community of the *Volk*, sustained by a common will and consciousness of honor of the racially homogeneous German *Volk*, constitutes political unity. This community is not only spiritual; it is real. The real bond is the common blood. This community of blood is what forms the *völkisch*-political unity of purpose in our confrontation with the surrounding world. The *völkisch*-political community is the fulcrum of our entire governmental and *völkisch* life. Accordingly, we do not look upon the state from the individualistic-liberal point of view—namely, as an abstract *Staatsperson* with its state apparatus, standing apart from and lording over the individual. The state is the *völkisch*-political organization of the living organism—the *Volk*. The state concept of National Socialism is the idea of the *völkisch*-political community. The opposition between the state idea and the state purpose, on the one side, and nation and family [*Volkstum*], on the other, which runs through history—this severance of *Volk* and state that has inflicted so much suffering on the German *Volk* in the past—has been overcome. Today we understand that the nation is to the state as content is to form, as purpose is to means. The state is the means to the end of safeguarding the *Volk*. "Its end is the preservation and promotion of a community of living beings who are physically and psychologically alike. This preservation is first and foremost concerned with the racial stock and thereby permits the free development of all the energies dormant in this race" (the Führer in *Mein Kampf*).

The Reich is the external legal structure in which the ordered community of the Germans appears to the outside world. It is the legal concept of German political unity. So when we speak in terms of a Third Reich, there is profound constitutional significance in our words. This Third Reich is the German *Volk* idea made manifest. It should, therefore, not be regarded as a special organism and as an abstract state personality lording over the *Volk*. Rather it is, and will increasingly become, the political-*völkisch* organization in total harmony with the vital laws of the organism, the *Volk*. The Reich is the political constitution of the *Volk* community within German territory. Hence we no longer look upon the Reich as a self-sufficient, abstract state, existing by and for itself. Rather, for us, the Reich is the community order governing all areas of *völkisch* life—the supreme organizational manifestation of the *Volk* community bound by ties of blood that gathers all the organizations and functions of the people into one active unit, into public power. The Reich organization as such can no longer be considered to have an existence and purpose of its own, as it does in the individualistic concept of the state. If, however, the state—not its apparatus, but the state in the *völkisch*-racial sense—derives from the nation, if it is the organization of the living organism of the *Volk*, this is thus also a clear expression of the fact that the state is not an insignificant entity. The *Volk* needs an organizational structure suitable to its character, and the organizational framework must have its content if the *Volk* is not to become an amorphous mass and the Reich a rigid, dead form. The repudiation of the abstract state personality, however, does not prevent the Reich—as the political-*völkisch* organization of the people—from being the vehicle of rights and responsibilities; in other words, the Reich has full competence in all legal proceedings. The vehicle of this competence is no longer the abstract legal figure of the state, but the community of the *Volk* in its politically informed and legally ordered structure.

This conception of *Volk* and Reich also determines the relationship of the individual to the whole. As we have already emphasized, the liberalistic conception of the state placed the individual and society in opposition to the state. It did so by emphasizing the individual's right to the greatest possible degree of unrestricted activity and by assuming that it was responsible for freeing the citizen from the fetters of an overpowerful state authority and of protecting him from state interference. The individual was not looked upon as a member of a community but as an opponent of the state. The relationship of the individual to the state was determined in terms of each individual as such and favored the individual at the expense of society as a whole.

According to the National Socialist perspective, however, it is not individual human beings, but races, peoples [*Völker*], and nations that constitute the elements of the divinely willed order of this world. The individual is rooted in his *Volkstum* by fate. The community of the *Volk* is the primary value in the life of the whole as well as of the individual. The individual human being can be conceived only as a member of a community of people to whom he is racially similar, from whom he inherits his physical and spiritual predispositions (family). National Socialism does not recognize a separate individual sphere, which, apart from the community, is to be painstakingly protected from any interference by the state. The moral personality can prove itself only within the community. Every activity of daily life has meaning and value only as a service to the whole. Thus, the life of the individual can be developed to the full only in the service of the *völkisch* community. In the legal order, therefore, the position of the individual is no longer determined in terms of each individual as such, but in terms of the community. From the standpoint of the public interest, as against that of a private person, the center of concern is no longer what the individual requires for the free development of his potentialities, or for the attainment of his personal goals, his striving for personal gain and possessions, and how much of this he can forgo for the sake of the community in times of emergency. Rather, on the basis of the greatest responsibility to *Volk* and Reich, National Socialism poses the question, How much scope does the community grant to the rights of the individual? Thus a clear order of rank is created between the needs of the community and the justifiable aspirations of any individual. This does not mean the denial of the individual's civil rights but rather his integration into a *völkisch* structure based on social justice and honor. He is evaluated as the smallest unit of the nation and as a part of the whole; he is protected by law for the sake of the whole. Civil rights and responsibilities do not flow from the unrestrained personality of the individual being and from the legal relations between him and the state personality. Instead, they derive from his own rank and position in the community. The individual is born as a member of his *Volk*. This membership generates rights and responsibilities toward the *Volk* as a whole and its other members. Hence, the rights and responsibilities of the individual do not owe their existence to a bilateral legal relationship between the individual person and the state personality. Rather, they stem directly from the individual's membership and position in the community.

Reich citizenship, the totality of all Reich citizens, is the *Volk* in its political configuration. The attainment of citizenship places the racial comrade who belongs to the state in full possession of the rights and responsibilities emanating from his membership in the *Volk*. The Reich Citizenship Law assigns the German national or citizen of kindred blood his proper place as a full member in the *völkisch* community. This membership generates full political rights and duties.

The Reich Citizenship Law actualizes the *völkisch* ordering of the German people on the political level. It has thus become the fundament that guarantees and supports the entire political *Volk* order of the Third Reich. No other legislation adopted since the National Socialist revolution has so completely rejected the intellectual attitude and the state concept of the past century. In the Reich Citizenship Law, National Socialism sets the doctrine of the equality of man and of the fundamentally restricted freedom of the individual vis-á-vis the state against the hard yet ineluctable fact of the natural inequality and disparate natures of men. From the dissimilarity of races, peoples, and men there follows a necessary differentiation in the rights and responsibilities of the individual. This dissimilarity, based on life and on unalterable natural laws, is reflected in the Reich Citizenship Law in terms of the basic political organization of the German *Volk*. Thus, it differentiates between state subjects and Reich citizens. A state subject, according to Article 1 of the law, is one who is under the protection of the German Reich and who therefore is especially obligated to it. A Reich citizen, on the other hand, is a subject of German or of related blood, who, by his attitude, proves that he is willing and able to loyally serve the German *Volk* and the Reich. The structure of *völkisch* life and the *völkisch* order, and of the leadership state based upon it, requires that state subjects be distinguished from foreigners and stateless persons and that the inner-political right of Reich citizenship be established as the qualification for the exercise of civil rights and responsibilities. It was alien to liberal legal thinking to link the exercise of political rights and responsibilities to the *völkisch* descent and membership of the individual. It follows from the National Socialist concept of the state that the National Socialist state, as a *völkisch* state, necessarily makes the exercise of civil rights dependent upon membership in the *Volk*. What is German, and what either benefits or harms the German people and the Reich, can be sensed, known, and hence determined only by those of German blood. Thus, in addition to state citizenship, membership in, or racial kinship with, the German people is a prerequisite for Reich citizenship rights.

The Reich Citizenship Law hence fulfills a basic demand of the National Socialist Party platform: only those who are racial comrades can become citizens. Only one who is of German blood, no matter what his religious faith, can be a racial comrade. Therefore, no Jew can be a racial comrade. Anyone who is not a citizen can live in Germany only as a guest and is subject to special legislation for foreigners. The right to determine leadership and legislation of the state may be granted only to citizens. We demand, therefore, that every public office, regardless of its importance, and whether in the Reich, in the province, or in the municipality, be occupied only by citizens.

The Reich Citizenship Law elevates the bearer of German or racially related blood above the rest of state subjects by according to him alone the right to assume full citizenship. All persons of alien blood—hence, especially Jews—are automatically excluded from attaining Reich citizenship.

But citizenship is not automatically granted to everyone of German or racially related blood. Rather, the Reich Citizenship Law demands from him the will and ability to loyally serve the German *Volk* and Reich. Before assuming the right of citizenship, his behavior must demonstrate that this prerequisite is met.

In principle, the subjective prerequisite for Reich citizenship—namely, the will to serve the German *Volk* and Reich—can be considered fulfilled unless there is evidence to the contrary. For the Reich Citizenship Law by no means aims to restrict the exercise of political rights to a small fraction of the German people to the exclusion of all other racial comrades. It is, however, the spirit and intent of Reich citizenship legislation not to admit indiscriminately every state subject to citizenship upon the attainment of a certain age, but to grant it only after an evaluation of his worthiness and then by an act of sovereign power—namely, the issuance of a certificate of citizenship. Consequently, the vast majority of all nationals will be granted full Reich citizenship upon attainment of a certain age. On the other hand, by denying or even withdrawing citizenship, it is possible to exclude misfits from having a voice in political matters. Felony crimes, offenses against the state, violations of civic duties, such as refusal or ineligibility to serve in the armed forces, refusal to hold public office, professional misconduct, will exclude any German national from Reich citizenship. [. . .]

A member of any minority group demonstrates his ability to serve the German Reich when, without surrendering membership in his own specific *Volk* group, he loyally carries out his civil duties to the Reich, such as service in the armed forces, etc. Reich citizenship is, therefore, open to racially related groups living in Germany, such as Poles, Danes, and others. It is an altogether different matter with German nationals of alien blood and race. They do not fulfill the blood prerequisites for Reich citizenship. The Jews, who constitute an alien body among all European peoples, are especially characterized by racial foreignness. Jews, therefore, cannot be seen as being fit for service to the German *Volk* and Reich. Hence, they must necessarily remain excluded from Reich citizenship.

According to the law, the Reich citizen is the sole bearer of political rights. Only he can participate in the Reichstag elections or be a candidate in them; only he can take part in plebiscites, occupy honorary offices in a state and municipality, or be nominated as a professional or honorary public servant. Hence, in the future, no Jew shall be permitted to hold any public office. In view of its far-reaching consequences and its supreme importance for the nation as well as for the individual, Reich citizenship can be granted only with utmost prudence and only through the specially empowered offices of the Reich and party leadership. Thus, in accordance with the will of the Führer, the certificate of Reich citizenship will be the most valuable document that the nation has to bestow and the highest honor that a German citizen can ever earn. Accordingly, it is obvious that Reich citizenship can be withdrawn if the prerequisites to it, especially conduct worthy of a citizen, ceases to be met.

A German state subject does not gain full Reich citizenship simply by virtue of his ethnic origin or through activity on behalf of the German people but only after an investigation of his worthiness and through an act of sovereign power by the grant of the certificate of Reich citizenship. The necessarily continuous examination of the German nation will lead to the exclusion of all elements unfit for the continued development of the German *Volk* and Reich from political life. Thus, for all time, it will put the fate of the German nation into the hands of the bearers of good German racial ancestry and German spirit.

In addition to Reich citizens who are the only authorized racial comrades, state subjects form a much wider circle. [. . .] Up to now, the concept of German nationality has never been anchored in law, and its definition has been largely left for jurisprudence to determine. The Reich Citizenship Law finally provides a legal definition. According to it, the material prerequisite for citizenship is membership in the protective association of the German Reich—that is, the right to the protection of the German Reich. The obligations of a state subject to the German Reich are indissolubly linked to this right. State citizenship is significant both with regard to domestic politics as well as in the sphere of foreign policy. In its relation to international law, it distinguishes between the citizen and an alien—that is, the individual who is either a citizen of another country or stateless. In terms of domestic politics, it is the protective fellowship of all who belong to the same state association. This protective fellowship embraces, in the first place, all Reich citizens, but beyond that all other racial comrades—those who have not yet become Reich citizens due to their age, those to whom Reich citizenship has been denied or from whom it has been withdrawn, and finally, all subjects of alien racial origin. The possession of state citizenship establishes the basis for the legal status of state subjects as member comrades in the protective state association. This is not a bilateral legal arrangement between the state and the single individual. Rather, the legal status of state subjects within the protective association establishes legal relationships extending in multiple directions. The public rights and responsibilities of the state subject emanate from his membership in the state protective association.

Through the separation of state citizenship from the acquisition of state civil rights by virtue of the grant of Reich citizenship, the concept of state citizenship has lost its political content. The political privileges heretofore connected with state citizenship no longer exist. The state subject as such no longer enjoys any political rights. He can, of course, utilize all public institutions according to prevailing regulations; he can, to the extent that there are no legal restrictions, be gainfully employed; and he enjoys the protection of state organs. Conversely, he is obligated to help carry all public burdens and in emergencies put everything he owns on the line in the defense of the state. He has, however, no political state rights. The possession of state citizenship does not entitle him to claim Reich citizenship.

In contrast to Reich citizenship, state membership is independent of membership in the blood or ethnic fellowship. Accordingly, even those of alien races may in the future acquire German state citizenship, provided that their overall personality fulfills prevailing requirements. However, since the law of 15 May 1935, petitions for naturalization are no longer valid. Rather, the grant of German state citizenship depends on the decision of the naturalization authorities, who are duty bound to conduct a thorough examination and evaluation of each individual applicant. In the course of time, new regulations pertaining to the acquisition and loss of state citizenship will have to be promulgated, in keeping with the concept already expressed in the law of 15 May 1935, that German state citizenship can no longer be acquired, lost, or changed arbitrarily.

86

CARL SCHMITT

German Jurisprudence and the Struggle against the Jewish Spirit

Delivered on 4 October 1936 at the conclusion of a Nationalsozialistischer Rechtswahrerbund (National Socialist Jurist's Organization) conference of university teachers. First published as "Die deutsche Rechtswissenschaft im Kampf gegen den jüdischen Geist," in *Deutsche Juristen-Zeitung* 41, no. 20 (15 October 1936), 1193–99. Translated by Timothy Nunan.

The Jewish law appears, as all of the lectures at this conference have shown, as salvation from a chaos. *The remarkable polarity of Jewish chaos and Jewish lawfulness, of anarchical nihilism and positive normativism, of crude, sensual materialism and an abstract sense of morality now stands so clearly, so vividly before our eyes that we can deem this fact the main finding of our conference, a finding that is not only scholarly, but also one that is decisive for the knowledge of the racial soul, and one that will lay the groundwork for future scholarly legal work.* In doing so, we have, as German guardians and teachers of the law, provided a contribution to meaningful fields of research for the first time, just as the body of racial knowledge has already provided to other fields. [. . .]

Further, the issue of citations is decisive. After such a conference, it is simply no longer possible to cite a Jewish author like any other author. It would be downright irresponsible to quote a Jewish author as the leading expert or as a kind of authority at all with respect to any field. For us, a Jewish author has no authority, no "purely scholarly" authority. This determination is the point of departure for the handling of the citation question. For us, a Jewish author is, if he is cited at all, a Jewish author. [. . .]

The most important finding that has presented itself during these days to us is no doubt the *clear and definitive recognition that, as concerns their intellectual content, Jewish opinions cannot be placed on the same level as the opinions of German or non-Jewish authors.* It has become clear to us all with the greatest of clarity that it amounts only to an apparent obstacle should there be Jews who have voiced views either patriotic or in support of the state, such as the famous Stahl-Jolson.[1] The recognition that the Jew is unproductive and sterile to the German spirit has pervaded our conference again and again. The Jew has nothing to say to us, regardless of how astutely he blends in or how eagerly he assimilates himself. It is a sign of a lack of schooling in racial science and thus National Socialist thought to fail to see and believe that. And it is a deep problem for such an opinion that some Jews write and speak as nationalists, others as internationalists, that they sometimes stand as representatives of liberal theories, other times as representatives of conservative theories, sometimes as representatives of subjective theories, other times as representatives of objective theories. And the much-vaunted critical endowment of the Jew results only from his perfidious relation to all that is essential and racially specific. It is a totally different concept of criticism from when a German teacher of the law reciprocally critiques and encourages others in true communal work.

And neither is it correct to refer to the Jew as especially logical, especially conceptual, constructive, or rationalistic. The Jew's "carefree logical trenchancy" is not so much that which we think of as logic, but rather a weapon aimed against us, a weapon that comes out of the faulty relation to the fact and to the object.

1. *The relation of Jewish thought to the German intellect* is the following: the Jew has a *parasitic, tactical,* and *mercantile* relation to our intellectual work. Through his proclivity for mercantile activity, the Jew often has a sharp sense of the genuine; he has a nose for it and knows how to find the genuine with his great resourcefulness. That is his instinct as a parasite and a genuine merchant. But just as little as the Jew's talent for painting is demonstrated by the fact that Jewish art dealers uncover a genuine Rembrandt more quickly than German art historians is it evidence for the talent of the Jew in the legal field that the Jew has recognized good authors and theories as such with greater speed than others. Jews notice quickly where the German substance is that draws them in. We do not need to credit them for this characteristic in order to feel awkward about the situation. This characteristic is simply grounded in the overall makeup of the Jew, grounded in his parasitic, tactical, and mercantile relation to the German intellectual character. And neither can such a harrowing and uncanny change of the mask as the one that lies at the bottom of Stahl-Jolson's entire existence mislead one. When it is claimed again and again that this man was "subjectively honest," that may be the case, but I must add that I cannot see into the soul of this Jew and that we have completely no access to the most inner essence of the Jews. We understand only their faulty relation to our kind. Whoever has ever grasped this truth also knows what race is.

2. It is further necessary to recognize *how differently the Jews have behaved in different periods of history*. Heinrich Lange has alluded to this fact in his preeminent essays.[2] The especially telling turning points of Jewish behavior in the past century are the years 1815, 1830, 1848, 1871, and 1890—Bismarck's resignation and the beginning of the Wilhelmine Era—1918, and 1933. It is therefore impermissible to compare an instance of the Jewish manner from 1830 with an instance from 1930. Here again appears the Jew Stahl-Jolson, who still today exercises his effect on the confessional-ecclesiastic opposition against the National Socialist state. It is totally false to place him as an exemplary conservative Jew in contrast to other, later Jews who could unfortunately no longer live up to his example. That would amount to a dangerous misunderstanding of the essential insight—the fact that with every change in the overall situation, with every new historical period, there also occurs a change in overall Jewish behavior, a change of the mask, which occurs with such speed, like a demonic enigma, that we can grasp it only with the greatest attentiveness. In the face of this, the question as to the subjective innocent trustworthiness of the single Jewish individual participating in the whole is totally uninteresting. The great adaptability of the Jew has grown into the realm of the monstrous throughout his millennia-long history by virtue of certain racial talents, and the virtuosity of his mimicry has been cultivated through long practice. We can recognize these traits in their consequences, but we cannot really grasp them. Indeed, we may not allow it to escape our vision that there exists this virtuosity of the Jew.

3. I repeat again and again the pressing plea to read every sentence in Adolf Hitler's *Mein Kampf* about the Jewish Question, especially his remarks on the "Jewish dialectic." What was presented by specialists in many scholarly outstanding presentations at our conference was said there, simply and totally exhaustively, in a way that is understandable to every racial comrade. Direct our students of jurisprudence again and again to these words of the Führer.

As we think about the Jewish problem, let us not forget *the German side of this question*. In direct practical application of that which Dr. Falk Ruttke laid out, one can, for example, say that the case of Karl Marx and the effect that proceeded from him is for us the case of Friedrich Engels or Bruno Bauer or Ludwig Feuerbach or perhaps Hegel, too. Here lies the grounding of a tragic problem. How was it possible that a German man from Wuppertal completely fell for the Jew Marx? How could it have been that thousands of upstanding and brave racial comrades succumbed to the Jewish spirit for long decades in such a manner? Why the susceptibility of many German-blooded men, and why in that historical moment the weakness and darkening of the German kind, why the total lack of resistance against Jewry? The test of this question belongs, too, to our scholarly reckoning with ourselves and to the armament for the new period of the struggle.

We have recognized this with the greatest scholarly clarity through this conference. In opposition to the infatuation and ignorance of earlier times, the current situation is marked more by a cataclysmic recognition. Armed with this recognition, we may enter the struggle whose newest stage has just begun. Let us not delude ourselves as to the difficulties of this struggle. The speeches of the Nuremberg Reich Party Rally allow for no doubt on this matter. Jewry is, just as the Führer says in his book *Mein Kampf,* not just enemy to all who are enemy to the Jew but rather the sworn enemy of all genuine productivity among all other *Volk*. Jewry's global power bears no national productivity; if it did, its own mode of existence would be confounded. The interest in the genuine productivity of the other *Volk* and the speed with which Jewish art dealers or intellectual merchants hurl themselves at German artists, poets, and scholars in order to get their hands on a pension are no merits and no qualities that allow us to turn our gaze from the fundamental here. The Jew concerns us not for his own sake. That for which we are searching and that for which we are fighting is our own unadulterated kind, the undamaged purity of our German *Volk*. "By fending the Jew away from me," says our Führer, Adolf Hitler, "I fight for the work of the Lord."

Notes

1. A reference to Friedrich Julius Stahl (originally Julius or Joel Jolson, 1802–61), who was one of the founders of German jurisprudence and the idea of a state defined by *Rechtstaat* (law). Schmitt's use of "Stahl-Jolson" highlights his Jewish origins.—Eds.
2. Compare to *Deutsche Juristen-Zeitung,* 1935, 406, and *Deutsche Juristen-Zeitung,* 1936, 1129.

87

HERWIG HARTNER-HNIZDO

Accident of History or Destiny of the Race?

First published as "Zufall der Geschichte oder Schicksal der Rasse?" in his *Volk der Gauner: Eine Untersuchung des jüdischen Gaunertums* (Munich: Hoheneichen Verlag, 1939), 7–8, 55–56.

The fact that these phenomena have appeared everywhere and in all times would seem to indicate that we are dealing with the effects of a racial predisposition. It is utterly impossible that the same environmental conditions have always just happened to prevail whenever and wherever Jews happened to be. And why is it that these same environmental conditions have not had the same effect on other races who are also dispersed throughout the world? That has only been the case with a part of the Armenians and the Levantines (racial mongrels from the eastern Mediterranean region), both of whom demonstrate a racial mixture similar to the Jews.

The fact that we are dealing here with racial predispositions becomes especially apparent in the so-called assimilated Jews, who represent one of the most tragic results of liberal permissiveness. *Assimilator* is a term describing those Jews who have removed themselves from all association with Jewry by religion and upbringing. They have either been baptized or declared themselves unaffiliated with any faith or are still Mosaic, but at any rate, liberal-progressive. They have attended German schools, may have scant knowledge of Hebrew gleaned strictly from religious instruction at school, and their use of Yiddish is restricted to traces found in business jargon, in jokes, and in smut; they are generally ashamed of their Jewish heritage and disdainfully look down upon the Jews of the ghetto as a dirty *Volk*; they want to be seen as "Germans" and bear witness to their Germanic elective affinities by christening themselves with "baptismal names" like Siegfried, Siegmund, and others; they discard their former German-Jewish surnames that are so uniquely apt in reflecting the dubious essence of the Jewish nature and its driving force—names like Rosenblüh, Silberblatt, Goldzieher, Goldfarbe, Siebzehner, Finkelstein, Teitelbaum, Leibdrucker!—and exchange them for names that are German to the core. They have adopted the German habit of dress, adopted German names, education, and way of life, but the whole investiture becomes something entirely different in their hands, so, for example, the tasteless, shrill palette of colors so beholden to the Jewess, or the language that always remains a Jewish German, and above all the manners—or, more correctly, the lack of manners—that are so indicative of the tendencies of this permissive Jewry. In the economic sector, the effect these assimilators have is no different from that of the merchants and profiteers in the Middle Ages or in the Polish-Galician ghettos. And the same applies to their effect on the life of the mind. So German-language literature written by Jews is markedly distinct from Aryan-German literature, even though the Jewish literati and writers in particular inevitably stem from the wealthiest strata of the assimilationist spectrum and have enjoyed the benefit of the same cultural environment as their Aryan counterparts. The unbridled moral laxity that often tests the basest limits of vulgarity, the maliciously mendacious satire unilaterally leveled at German people, the glorification of the criminal who is made into a "hero" because he breaks through the barriers set by Gentile society with regard to moral and legal customs, his whole view of life and living, the endeavors he considers worthwhile—in all these respects, the products of the Jewish assimilators are as distinct from German literary production as the Jewish Oriental-Negroid mongrel race is distinct from the races that are the bearers of the German *Volk*.

Thus, the only conclusion we can draw is that the contrast between the Jews and the other peoples of the earth must, beyond a shadow of doubt, be anchored in the race; it must be rooted in the psychological propensities deep in the Jewish soul. This specifically Jewish racial predisposition, which is so fundamentally different in nature from the Aryan, to which it is in many respects diametrically opposed, is further compounded by a perspicuous sense of *inferiority,* equally apparent in darker types and blondes, both of which are frequently found among Jewry. The incontrovertible evidence supporting *both* of these claims is the "criminal underground" or "roguery" that is largely the product of Jews. [. . .]

The biggest political fraudster of all time was Trebitsch-Lincoln, who, wherever his wheeling and dealing took him, quickly managed to climb the ladders of influence and, since he was ever wont to exploit the economic benefits of this influence, was forced, again and again, after each fleeting moment of success, to relocate and stage his efforts in another country.[1]

Born in Hungary, already in his early years his first run-ins with the law forced him to emigrate to London, where he converted to Christianity and was baptized. Shortly thereafter, he married in Hamburg, then surfaced in Canada, and from there relocated to the United States, where he transformed himself into a Baptist and became one of the most popular preachers in New York. Following a series of scandals involving fraud and sordid love affairs, he disappeared only to surface again in England—in the guise of an Anglican priest who quickly managed to become the darling of the archbishop of Canterbury. But these priestly robes he donned were but a springboard for the political career he saw as his divine calling, and in 1912, he was actually elected to the lower house of Parliament on a staunchly conservative platform. He used that position to orchestrate such massive swindles that, after just a few months, he was again forced to move to another stage. The next scene in the comic travesty of his life played itself out in Galicia and Romania, where he appeared in a leading role in the oil industry, which was actually just a cover for a far-reaching spy operation serving the interests of England, with an eye to securing himself the opportunity to return there. And, in fact, just before the outbreak of war, he did return to England and become a naturalized citizen. With the outbreak of war, he was called to service—not, of course, on the front lines, but as a military censor. But since this post did not offer the potential for business opportunities, he went to Holland as a British spy, where he assumed the role of a double agent, working for England against Germany and for Germany against England and, already by 1916, was forced to flee to America. There, he became an enthusiastic participant in the antiwar defamatory campaign against Germany and adroitly manipulated the black market, accruing mountains of debt as the result of myriad forgeries in the process. After serving a prison sentence, he was deported in 1919 and returned to Germany, where he joined the monarchist, conservative German nationalist movement. In March 1920, he was actively participant as press secretary in the Kapp Putsch in Berlin and subsequently established ties with Bavarian, Austrian, and Hungarian monarchists in the hope of conquering Austria with the aid of Italian troops, then ultimately betrayed the monarchists by selling insider information to Czechoslovakia, only to turn around once the deal had been made and sell forged documents to the same state government for an exorbitant sum before he finally disappeared from Europe. After that, he orchestrated his political and business deals on various stages in East Asia, where he quickly rose to rank of mandarin in China. And no sooner had his betrayals and swindles pulled the rug out from under him, there he became a Buddhist and, in this guise, opened a Buddhist monastery in Shanghai—under the auspices of the British, of course—and sought to educate European adherents to the Buddhist faith in the true spirit of Buddha. History has been silent on what kind of scams he was able to generate from this.

Trebitsch-Lincoln was a Wandering Jew in the truest sense of the word—an Ahasver who managed to orchestrate chaos the world over, but whose grandiose political plans somehow always degenerated into ignominious little swindles. In the end, he was little more than a fraudulent petty merchant-trader.

In comparison to the veritable cornucopia of fraudulent con men that God's Chosen People has produced, what is a handful of harmless little people of Aryan descent who rose to the top for a few fleeting moments from the fraudulent little theatrics they staged: the valet who traveled in the guise of a prince, the handmaiden who passed herself off as a princess, the ex-convict who donned the captain's uniform to play the big man for a day? Oh, but the sensationalism surrounding the captain of Köpenick, the way his capers were touted throughout the world as a disgrace to the German nation and as the bankruptcy of German militarism and how they became the stuff of stories and theater ([Carl] Zuckmayer!). These were all just little people who, after their one great prank, sank back into the obscurity from whence they'd come, but the really big con man is hard to pin down in the first place, setting up his swindles in one country today and another tomorrow as he does, and once he is apprehended and incarcerated, as soon as he's released, he's back to his old ways and then is even more difficult to nab than he was before.

Note

1. Ignatius Timothy Trebitsch-Lincoln (1879–43) was born in Hungary to an Orthodox Jewish family and led a remarkable life on three continents. He was a member of the British Parliament, an international confidence man, a spy, a Buddhist monk, and an anti-British Japanese propagandist in China. Trebitsch-Lincoln worked for the German and Japanese security services until his death in Shanghai in 1943.—Eds.

88

JOHANN VON LEERS

The Criminality of Jewry

First published as "Die Kriminalität des Judentums," in *Das Judentum in der Rechtswissenschaft* (Berlin: Deutscher Rechtsverlag, 1940), 68–72.

The first significant foray into Jewish criminal psychology was made by the prominent personality Cesare Lombroso. Lombroso hailed from a Venetian Jewish merchant family whose roots can be traced to a colony of Spanish Jews who were driven out of Spain to North Africa (in Spanish, *lumbroso* means "light, shining"). Cesare was born in 1835 as an Austrian subject in Verona. Resentment toward reactionary Austrian rule over the "Lombard-Venetian Empire" had a major influence on C. Lombroso's thinking starting in early childhood. In 1861, he wrote about his school days: "I was subjected to disciplinary force in the classroom at a time when you might say that the Middle Ages had extended into our own time in my country; not in the romantic portrayals that later became popular in novels and plays, but the way it really was in 1789 and was restored by the clash of bayonets in 1814. This brutal disciplinary force was a violation of an atavistic spirit of logic, and the mere memory of it is so traumatic that even today it disrupts my dreams with nightmarish visions." [. . .]

So what serves as the leitmotif for Lombroso's criminal psychology is not sympathy with the criminal but rather antipathy and resentment toward the immediate effect of disciplinary force exerted by the state. Crime is then displaced and presented as the necessary psychological perspective and the natural and necessary expression of life in prehistoric, archaic man. When the criminal psychological aspect is thus displaced, crime is removed from the realm of ethical and political definitions, and with it, at the same time, the driving force of the conservative penal code is shattered. In the end, Lombroso's "atavistic spirit of logic" triumphs over the "brutal disciplinary force" of the conservative state, whose efficacy is concentrated precisely in its political penal supremacy. The first assault on the state and its penal supremacy made by politicized Jewry from the perspective of criminal psychology, then, emanated straight from Lombroso's masterful hand.

Why, then, did this first foray of Lombroso's into criminal psychology so unexpectedly and quickly fall flat after its initial stunning success? Why didn't the whole cadre of Jewish intelligentsia fall in behind the battle cry of "*delinquente nato,*" or the "born criminal?" Why didn't the whole phalanx of second- and third-rate Jewish intellectual giants close ranks with him and get behind the will and the wake of this exemplary Jewish pioneer? Why is it that there is no direct line leading from Lombroso's race-based theoretical approach to the conceptual world of contemporary biogenetics and racial psychology? To ask this question in this way is at the same time to answer it!

Lombroso's foray was, of course, firmly entrenched in the highly specific tactical situation of political Jewry acting within the living space of its host peoples. Immediately following the emancipation and granting of political equality to Jews, there was no danger that, in the context of the then-prevailing ideology of equality, Lombroso's abstract constellation of a race of criminals could unwittingly direct unwanted attention to the highly concrete problem of the Jewish race and be used against it in its confrontation with the host people. It was obviously self-evident to Lombroso that the Jewish people were aligned with the racial bloc of modern cultured men, not with the atavistic criminal race of *delinquente nato!* But the construction of this racial opposition between *Homo sapiens* and *Homo delinquens* could prove disastrous for the Jews because all it would take would be for their opponents to turn it around and create an opposition between the Jewish race and the commonwealth of cultured men. So the catchphrase *delinquente nato* could at any time become the catchword to define a racially based anti-Semitism. Already the pernicious [Heinrich] Heine, in his *Travel Sketches,* clearly set forth one of the characteristics of the Jewish race that would have to be seen as a fairly close parallel between the Jewish race and an archaic race of criminals when he described the Jews as "that mummified people wandering the earth, wrapped in its swathing of prescriptive letters, *an obstinate piece of world history,* a specter that bargains for its living with bills of exchange and old trousers." Wouldn't it have seemed rather risky business, then, for Lombroso to similarly speak in terms of the criminal as an "obstinate piece of world history," a prehistoric apparition, the very picture of a living anachronism?!

Herein lies the weak spot in Lombroso's criminal psychology. His assault against the conservative state and its penal supremacy could easily turn against the Jews simply by substituting anti-Semitism for an archaic race of born criminals in Lombroso's racial scheme, thus rendering the Jews themselves an "obstinate piece of world history." When Lombroso first proposed his doctrine of an abstract race of criminals, racial consciousness was dormant in Europe. There was, at the time, hardly any danger that the analogy would be made between this abstract race of criminals and the cosmopolitan world of Jewry, so the risk that his polarized racial scheme would be misappropriated for anti-Semitic purposes was minimal. But just a few years later, the stock market crashes of the *Gründerzeit* in the late nineteenth century emphatically directed attention to the concrete racial problem involving politicized Jewry. The first wave of anti-Semitism swelled to the surface. The racial theories of [Joseph Arthur Comte de] Gobineau gradually began having an impact. [Georges Vacher de] Lapouge in France, [Otto] Ammon and [Houston Stewart] Chamberlain in Germany inaugurated a renaissance of racial ideology. The Jews were clearly cognizant of the implications of these early warning signals and adeptly ran for cover from the storm in the nick of time. At the very height of his fame, Lombroso suddenly became an anachronism himself! In light of the altered strategic situation of the Jews, recognizing inborn racial differences became a fundamentally and inherently precarious mistake. The *Homo delinquens* construct thus had to be considered a historical precedent that could be turned against the *Homo judaicus.*

89

DAS SCHWARZE KORPS

Concentration Camps and Their Inmates

First published as "K. Z. und seine Insassen," in *Das Schwarze Korps,* 13 February 1936, 10.

Whenever the foreign boulevard press runs short of sensationalist hot air to spew against Germany—and that has happened more and more in the past few months, at increasingly short intervals—then it resorts to the hackneyed old standby that still seems to have the most pull: the "horrors of the German concentration camps."

The number of concentration camps has been reduced to but a few in which, according to signed affidavits by Jewish émigrés, the intellectual elite of the Third Reich are interned. The fabricators of these horror stories make out the concentration camps to be what the gold rush towns of Sacramento and Santa Fe were for sensationalistic dime-store novelists, with all the trapdoors, back stairs, suicide shots, and mysterious Chinamen and whatever other props are part and parcel to making our hair stand on end and curling our toes while lying in bed reading at night.

Well, today we're publishing some actual photographs from the German concentration camps in order to demonstrate to readers just what those people look like with whom the emigrated "bearers of German culture" express an eternal affinity.

This is a collection of race traitors, sexual degenerates, and common criminals who have spent the better part of their lives behind bars and other individuals who have cast themselves outside the bounds of the national community with their conduct and only three years ago were still being coddled by psychoanalysts and defense attorneys as "victims of bourgeois society."

The foreign press has never hesitated to lavish coverage on the "victims of brutal random violence" and any number of other things that apparently have filtered through only to them and that no one else within the German Reich has gotten wind of. Despite their vigilance, they have studiously overlooked, and hence decided to silence in their papers, the story of how countless former political enemies were released from prison at Christmastime and received gifts of clothing, food, and money from *Gauleiter* Streicher.

But the foreign press and its readers don't want to hear about that. Nor do our neighbors abroad learn anything about what shape the minds of these loser inmates are in, these "scions of German civilization and culture," who are supposedly the sole guarantors of European peace. In the spirit of friendliness and of commitment to our word that is our innate nature, we offer these images to the foreign press for reprint free of charge and, in return, ask only that [the press] allow its readers to determine whether they would like to have these "martyrs of their dissenting views" that these émigrés hold so dear to their hearts as guests in their own homes or not.

We would be happy to send them off to any country that takes stock in having an abundant supply of notorious criminals and expressed enemies of their system of law and order in the form of this exemplary stock of specimens.

90

PETER-HEINZ SERAPHIM

Jewry in the Eastern European Space

First published in *Das Judentum im osteuropäischen Raum* (Essen: Essener Verlagsanstalt, 1938), 407–12.

In the course of the migrations during the Diasporic period, a series of additional racial admixtures entered Jewish bloodlines, especially from the dark-skinned Dinaric and Mediterranean race and the light-skinned Nordic and eastern Baltic race. Jews often try to counter this claim by pointing to the conscious segregation of Jews and non-Jews and non-Jews from the Jews not only in the Middle Ages but also in more recent times, and by stating that the Jewish ghetto must have helped maintain the racial purity of Jews and allowed for occasional, but by no means substantial, incidents of racial miscegenation with neighboring peoples. There is no doubt that the religion and traditions of the Jewish community fostered this sort of isolation and made the ghetto into a sort of racial inbreeding ground for Jews, so that they could not be assimilated as guest peoples despite their dispersion as settlers throughout the world. At the same time, we may assume that myriad possibilities existed for absorbing the influx of alien bloodlines: in times of war as the result of violent acts committed by the conquerors, in times of peace as the result of occasional connubial relations between rich Jewesses and non-Jews, more frequently in illegal relationships that are especially conceivable during the period of the general demoralization of Jewry combined with the legal dependency of Jews on the *szlachta* and of the peasantry on the Jews toward the end of the Polish-Lithuanian empire.

The various racial admixtures present in the two major areas of Jewish inbreeding in Europe, Spain, and Poland-Lithuania have gradually produced a distinct difference in types between the so-called Western and Eastern Jews. One strain was subjected to considerable influx from the Mediterranean race, whereby the weight of the already much more widespread Oriental racial factor, which has many similar character traits with the Mediterranean race, was increased. The addition of Western and Nordic blood, as well as admixtures of the Negroid race compounded this. The racial type of these Western Jews thus became relatively uniform, with the following racial characteristics: moderately tall, generally slender build; dark pigmentation, hair, and eye color; most often an elongated skull and a straight, sharply formed nose, more striking than in Eastern Jews, who adopted a greater diversity of alien racial elements that differed more fundamentally from the Near Eastern Oriental basic type.

The fact that a sizable portion of the Jews who migrated to Eastern Europe spent a considerable amount of time living in the same area with the people of the Near Eastern race who so closely resemble the Jewish basic type must have amplified this racial component in them. But since the Jews streaming into Eastern Europe through the Caucasian Pass in the context of the great migrations that made up the first seven centuries of our calendrical time came into contact with Germanic, Turko-Tatarian, Mongolian and Slavic peoples, [and] Nordic, eastern Baltic, Tatar, and Mongoloid influences, pockets of which were substantial, [. . .] presumably influences from the darker-pigmented Central European races (Dinaric and Alpine) entered through the Balkan Peninsula and southern Germany. The so-called Ashkenazi Jews then actually represent a markedly variegated racial conglomerate, especially since, in addition to the dominant races, a series of recessive racial types appear (taller built and blond races from the Near East and Dinarics). [. . .]

What is clearly apparent [here] is the broad spectrum of variety in the racial makeup of the Eastern Jewish race, which has led to the extraordinary diversity of racial types evident amongst the contemporary Jewish population of Eastern Europe. "The Ashkenazi Jews," according to one Jewish anthropologist, "unlike the Sephardic Jews, do not constitute a homogenous whole in which common features between groups substantially outnumber differences. It is in the Ashkenazi Jews that we find the greatest physical and psychological contrasts. One need not even compare an Eastern European Jew to the Jews who have adopted not only the psychological but also, in many respects, the physical characteristics of indigenous inhabitants of the region in order to ascertain an overwhelming difference. It is to be found equally amongst the Jews in various Eastern European countries as it is within the groups in each individual region."

It would be impossible to provide a comprehensive list of the various racial types amongst Eastern European Jews, especially since the already multifaceted composition of Eastern European Jews is further complicated by the number of mongrel types and recessive traits. Only the basic types can be outlined here:

1. The predominately Oriental type: This type, very similar to the Sephardic Jews, characterized by dark-pigmented skin, black head and facial hair, and dark eyes, is present in Eastern Europe not only in the purebred form with an elongated skull and slender build, but also as crossbred with Near Eastern and Alpine racial elements with a shorter skull and stocky build. Decisiveness and fanaticism have been discussed as characteristic traits in this group of Jews. According to studies conducted by Elkind, the purer "Bedouin," as well as the predominately Oriental hybrid types, are particularly widespread in Congress Kingdom of Poland but are less prevalent in Jewish areas of Lithuania, southern Russia, Galicia, and Moldavia.
2. The primarily Near Eastern type: The most striking characteristics of this, likely the most common Eastern Jewish type, are its extremely short head (hyperbrachycephaly) and its fleshy, crooked nose (the so-called Jewish nose). All the same, it is not seldom that especially the Jews of White Russia, Eastern Poland, and even Galicia demonstrate

very little fundamental difference in somatic type from the surrounding population, especially when differences in clothing, hairstyle, beard cut, and general habit of appearance are removed from consideration.

Several studies on the scope and distribution of blond Jews completed by Jewish anthropologists seem to indicate that there is a decline in the blond type in the southern Carpathian, Congress Kingdom of Poland, and southern Russian areas, and a more pronounced presence of the blond element in Galicia and White Russian Lithuanian settlements.

3. Alien Jewish types: Unmistakably Tatarian genetic influences are often found in Jews of southern Russia. These people, usually women and children, have a short, nearly square face, high protruding cheekbones, and sunken cheeks. The nose is small and thick, often with an inward bent at the root, but otherwise straight and not infrequently turned up. The eye is set at a Mongolian slant, with the outer corner placed higher than the inner and with a narrower socket than the eyes of other types. Hair is black, very thick, and straight. This type, which is also found amongst the Slavic-speaking populace of southern Russia, can be traced to the fact that the Jewish race in southern White Russia experienced an influx of Tatarian blood when the Khazarians converted to Judaism.

   An additional alien type among the Jews of Eastern Europe is of Mongoloid origin and finds its most prominent expression in women and children. This type is quite prevalent in southern Russia, where Weißenberg's study results show that of those examined, 23 percent had protruding cheekbones, 13 percent had slanted eye sockets, and 16 percent had drooping eyelids; this type is similarly prevalent among Hungarian Jews.

   Finally, there is the Negroid, or "Hamidic," type. It appears fairly frequently in Eastern European Jews with extremely dark skin, curly hair, and an elongated head protruding at the back of the skull. The mouth is set forward, its lips large and fleshy, the nose flat and wide, and the chin juts out. The anthropological explanation for the emergence of this type among the Eastern European Jews holds that it is more a manifestation of ancient Judaic racial components from Palestinian times than the result of an influx of North African Jews known to be heavily infused with Negro blood—but who only rarely migrated to Eastern Europe.

4. Cross- and half-breed types: Any attempt at classifying Eastern European types necessarily fails to do justice to the diversity of racial strains present in these groups of people. The matter is further complicated by the myriad racial crossbreeds, particularly prevalent among the Ashkenazi Jews—where one might find more traits from non-European Jewish breeds, while elsewhere the racial components of lighter- or darker-skinned European breeds may prevail or the entirely alien or recessive racial traits may come to the fore. There is an extremely high incidence of mutation, especially since the general principle of the dominance of dark pigmentation and an overall darker constitution in women as well as in men cannot by any means be seen as schematic in the sense of somatic unification, since every gene carrying hereditary material is paired up with another dominant gene, but only under the prerequisite that this other gene is not accompanied by certain specific genes that would influence the mutation. In other words, the concept of dominance, as defined by hereditary science, does not refer to a mechanical or absolute principle but rather to a variable and relative process. The "bleeding through" of certain racial traits, the crossbreeding of selective racial elements, the influx of racial components or the reappearance of others that had long since disappeared—all of this complicates matters tremendously and results not only in the creation of racial types that are clearly recognizable as such but also in countless additional mixed-race and half-breed types that serve to further obfuscate the already rather motley racial composition of the Eastern European Jews.

The overall conclusion that can be drawn from this is that the racial diversity of Eastern European Jews, brought about by racial crossbreeding and hybridization, has led to a diversity of anthropological types that precludes any reference to one specific Jewish type. Even a geographic classification of anthropological types cannot, as a rule, be made—although environmental influences on the blood have certainly played a role. The attempt at such regional anthropological classifications is rendered all the less viable by the fact that the Eastern European Jews comprise a highly transient population group and by the fact that their constant migrations within the boundaries of individual states and between various Eastern European states inevitably led to an unabated process of racial miscegenation.

91

KARL FRIEDRICH EULER

The Yiddish Language as Expression of the Jewish Mind

First published as "Die jiddische Sprache als Ausdruck jüdischer Geistesart," in *Das religiöse Gesicht des Judentums, Entstehung und Art,* edited by Karl Friedrich Euler and Walter Grundmann (Leipzig: G. Wigand, 1942), 172–73, 175.

We have already established [in the preceding pages] that Hebrew is not the language of the Jewish people. Furthermore, we stated that when Hebrew words appear in Yiddish, it is only when they are meant to express a strikingly Jewish sentiment or when there is a particular intent behind the application of Hebrew words. We must reconcile these two conclusions and can say, in this regard, that it is not the Hebrew words themselves that lend contour to the unique strain of thought that is expressed in the Yiddish language, but the use of Hebrew words is itself the defining moment; that is, it is the Yiddish strain of thought itself. The use of Hebrew words—albeit to a certain calculated degree—along with the use of English, Polish, Russian, and other words is but a symptom of the strain of thought—and the same applies to the ossification or excessive use of the Middle High German linguistic base. Here [I offer] a summary of three characteristics of this strain of thought.

We have already identified the first characteristic of this strain of thought to be the lack of linguistic intuition. Whoever concerns himself more closely with the Yiddish language is confronted with the observation that the native speaker of Yiddish is completely devoid of any tangible, firmly established sense of language. One could say that the native speaker of Yiddish merely toys with language—what we might call an awareness of the mother tongue is incomprehensible to him. The fact that the Jew can learn foreign languages quickly and easily is not a sign of talent but rather of his lack of any binding sense of language. On the other hand, a lack of this nature will always necessarily lead to the excessive alienation of any language appropriated by the Jew. The Jew can switch from one language to another without any sense of inner affinity or attendant binding obligation. The Yiddish language, with its haphazardly thrown together vocabulary, is the best evidence to substantiate these statements.

The second characteristic concerns the relationship between the Jews and the appropriated language. *This relationship is strictly analytical in nature in the Jew and not, as is the case for us, synthetic.* That is to say that the strain of thought and language do not form a coherent unity. Instead, words and concepts are reinvented as soon as the language has been appropriated by the Jew. German-language concepts are unequivocally clear from the very onset when they are used by a German or are translated in accordance with their Germanic implications into another language. The words of the Yiddish language are—from the very onset—

flamboyantly suggestive and ambiguous, even when Hebrew words are at issue. I call to mind just a few words such as *Zores, Mesimme,* etc., or, to cite German words of Yiddish origin: *Geschäft* [business], *Gelegenheit* [opportunity], *Fach* [subject], etc. And the same applies to the English language, for example, when it is spoken by the Jew and words like *business, to do,* and similar words that are more general in nature for others assume a special significance for the Jew. Whatever language is at issue, once the Jew has appropriated it, it loses its specific clarity, its concepts forfeit their stability and, as long as the Jew continues to use the language, what remains is a perpetual state of multivalent ambiguity.

The third characteristic stems from the unique role played by the Hebrew language in Jewish life. For Hebrew is also the language of the Talmud and other Judaic religious texts. And for most Jews, knowledge of Hebrew is gleaned from Jewish religious instruction in the Talmud and Judaic religious literature. But to assume that the appearance of Hebrew words was merely the result of religious influences would be to render the phenomenon more innocuous than it is. And yet this is exactly what world Jewry would have us believe when it attempts to explain the unique nature of the Yiddish language by describing Yiddish as a dialect derived exclusively from religious considerations. But then why are Hebrew words used in conjunction with the utterly profane considerations in everyday life? Why then do these so-called strictly religious concepts that are anchored in the Hebrew language persistently and repeatedly abandon the religious realm and migrate into the profane world of everyday issues and events—especially with regard to purely political issues that have absolutely nothing to do with religion? Why is it that these most ambiguous of words, be they strictly religious or strictly profane (e.g., *Zores, rachmunes, emes,* etc.), are so widespread in the Judaic vernacular? The ultimate answer to these questions can be derived from the very fact that the words are spoken by a Jew—by a Jew, we must add, for whom the Hebrew language is the language of his religion, and any Hebrew word, whatever it may be, always represents some form of religious expression. We can deduce two things from this fact: First, *the Yiddish language is a singular testament to the notion that the Judaic religion engulfs without any exception all provinces of life and without exception has an impact on any and all provinces of life.* In the province of language, this implies an excessive stock of foreign-language vocabulary and a destabilization of conceptual meanings as well as a distinct linguistic habit, even though this may be apparent based on mildly symptomatic indicators. Second, *the flamboyant application of suggestive and ambiguous Hebrew words turns the Yiddish language into a secret language of the Jews—a language understood only by those who are intimately familiar with the Jewish strain of thought—that is, only to the Jew himself. And this is the point in which the Jewish strain of thought has found its profoundest expression in the Yiddish language.* [. . .]

Is Yiddish even a language in the sense that German, Italian, Spanish, etc. are languages? Or is it a dialect, like Bavarian, Frisian, East Prussian, etc.? Based on what we have said so far, despite the fact that Yiddish demonstrates forms and formulations that may be seen as language or as dialect, we conclude that this question must be answered *in the negative.* For what is lacking in the Yiddish language is an inner life, the compelling sense of urgency that determines and shapes development. It is not even worthy of being described as a corrosive, denigrating dialect of the German language. It is a form of jargon, on a par with only one other, the thieves' cant.

Yiddish is Janus-faced. On the one hand, it faces the ghetto, which the Jews have chosen for themselves and for which they are themselves to blame. The ghetto—isolated, run-down, and contaminated—is just like Yiddish. On the other hand, it turns its face to the rest of the world. The deep-seated desire for world citizenship and world domination that is anchored in the linguistic hodgepodge of Yiddish assaults the listener from afar. Yiddish—not the language of a certain country, not the language that unifies a certain people, but rather the language of a people who live suspended somewhere between the ghetto and world citizenship.

Our sensitivity for and understanding of language always associates a given human type with any language. German can resonate only when spoken by a German; French is French only when spoken by a Frenchman. Yiddish resonates only when spoken by a man whose whole character is shaped by the experience of the ghetto and the deep-seated desire for world citizenship. Or shall we call a spade a spade here and name that character by his own name: Yiddish is the language of Ahasver—the language of the eternal Wandering Jew.

92

Second Decree Concerning Implementation of the Law on Changes to Family Names and First Names

Announced on 17 August 1938 as "Zweite Verordnung zur Durchführung des Gesetzes über die Änderung von Familiennamen und Vornamen." First published in *Reichsgesetzblatt* (Berlin: Reichsverlagsamt, 1938), 1:1044.

Pursuant to Article 13 of the Law on Changes to Family Names and First Names of 5 January 1938 (*Reichsgesetzblatt,* 1:9), the following decree is hereby ordered:

Article 1

1. Jews may be assigned first names only as are permissible according to the guidelines for regulating first names issued by the Reich minister of the interior.
2. Article 2 applies not only to Jews but also to everyone in possession of foreign citizenship.

Article 2

1. Inasmuch as Jews bear first names that may not be assigned to them pursuant to Article 1, they must, as of 1 January 1939, adopt an additional first name to supplement their own: in the case of males, the first name Israel; in the case of females, the first name Sara.
2. Whoever is required, pursuant to Article 1, must, within one month of the date on which the additional name requirement becomes effective, notify in writing the register of deeds in the town of his birth and of his marriage, as well as with the local police in the town of his residence or domicile.

93

FRITZ ARLT

The Final Struggle against Jewry

A Historical Reflection on Jewish Enmity

First published as "Der Endkampf gegen das Judentum: Eine geschichtliche Betrachtung der Judengegnerschaft," in *Der Weltkampf,* no. 1 (March 1938): 124, 126.

It is no secret—neither to the Jews (cf. Arnold Zweig, "The history of anti-Semitism is one and the same as the history of the planetary Jewish community," and Dr. Jacob, "If you understand anti-Semitism to mean a hostile attitude toward Judaism, then it is as old as the Jewish people"), nor to the non-Jews who have devoted a considerable amount of attention to this question, nor to Jews' enemies—that anti-Semitism is not merely a contemporary concern or product of our time but is rather as old as Judaism itself; that is to say, it forms a substantial component of Jewish history.

Although aversion to the Jew has been an enduring historical phenomenon, the aspects contributing to that aversion have not always been the same and in fact have varied throughout history in accordance with prevailing worldviews and the tenets of those worldviews concerning the foundations of community and teachings about what it means to be human (that is, about the relationship between body, soul, and mind, to what degree they are interdependent and with regard to their fundamental constitution). Of the many underlying reasons for aversion to the Jew, three basic aspects are discernible.

The first major anti-Judaic movements in antiquity and late antiquity (Egypt, Persia, Asia Minor, etc.) that led to pogroms and expulsion of these strangers (Jeb on the Island of Elephantine, for example, in 410 B.C., the pogroms of Alexandria, Cesarea, Damascus, Skythopolis, Antiochia) were all based on a national sentiment of enmity to the Jews. The nature of political communities at the time was that they were not built on blood ties, on a shared culture, or any other natural prerequisites, but rather on declarations of loyalty to the reigning political system: the empire. So, in those days, without any regard for the natural prerequisites to community, the Jew Saulus was as entitled to become a *cives romanus* (Roman citizen) as your average German peasant's son.

The Jews of the Galut were communally organized, culturally and politically, according to their own laws, levies, and taxes, etc., within the Kahal, because they never professed allegiance to the international religious, political, or cultural establishment but instead developed their own religion, political structure, and culture as a nation among nations. This is why we may describe the above-mentioned form of anti-Semitism that prevailed in antiquity up until about 300 A.D., when Christianity assumed religious predominance, as a national anti-Semitism. The Jewish people were opposed as a nation within nations.

The steadily increasing rise in Christianity ultimately led to a dissolution of the ecumenical religious, political, and cultural structures of the Roman Empire and, with the institution of the *una sancta catholica* in both the Eastern and Western Empires, the cultures of Rome and Byzantium introduced a new doctrine on the fundamentals of human existence and [the nature of] man. The basic prerequisite to human existence became membership in the church, and there was no salvation to be found outside the church. Man was seen as being split into two spheres: the body, which has no bearing on his immortality, and another sphere that does: the soul, which in the community of the faithful becomes a vehicle for eternal life. In this period, beginning around 300 A.D., anti-Semitism was based on a religious, confessional justification: Judaism was combatted as a church that lays as much claim to being the sole true path to salvation as the *una sancta catholica*. The fact that this opposition was by no means merciful or driven by love is evidenced by the forced expulsions of Jews that took place in periods of heightened piety: the Black Death, the Crusades, etc. The fact that it was meant to be of lasting consequence is evidenced by the canonical legislation and its regulations, which might be seen as earlier attempts at effecting laws similar to our Law for the Protection of German Blood and German Honor in the Third Reich [see document 84 in this chapter—Eds.]. The division of the church into denominations under Martin Luther led to the creation of a specifically Protestant anti-Semitism. The ensuing secularization of laws that had thus far been primarily ecclesiastical led to a decline in religious anti-Semitism. But with the incendiary impact that the French Revolution had on the Enlightenment, anti-Semitism within the church, though it remained, struck a new note. The hateful sentiment of the pogroms and expulsions was replaced by a paternalistic love of the poor Jews. Protestantism continued to indulge profusely in polemics on the inferiority of the Judaic understanding of God. The theological anti-Semitism of the church as a secondary level of justification for opposing the Jews lost its political significance.

During the period of Jewish emancipation around the turn of the century between the eighteenth and nineteenth centuries, perspectives on the fundamental principles of human existence changed. Now, community is seen as being held together by universal ethical standards, and the human individual is seen as being driven by his moral ideas. It is the advent of the age of idealism in which man is judged according to the inner workings of his mind. [. . .] The most typical justification for this form of anti-Judaism can be found in Johann Fichte's article "Contributions to the Justification of Public Opinions on the French Revolution" (1793): "But before we could ever grant them [Jews] civil rights, I think we would have to take the following drastic measure, at the very minimum: Chop off their heads in the middle of the night and replace them with heads that are completely void of Jewish ideas." Here we see a third primary justification for anti-Judaism in the notion of idealism: the Jew is opposed as the purveyor of an alien idea. This form of anti-Semitism remains in place until liberalism and historical materialism, the stepchild of Hegelian thought, take the lead in ideological debates and ultimately form the foundation for constitutional law. During this period, anti-Judaism ceases to exist as a major form of political action because materialism and liberalism do not allow for distinctions drawn between men according to their ideals, their religion, or even according to their nature, since their political doctrines acknowledge neither ideals nor religion nor nation, not even the natural *völkisch* community as the basis for individual or *völkisch* existence.

Adolf Hitler's blood revolution, which takes the blood as the basic foundation for individual and *völkisch* existence and regards blood as the foundation for all expressions of men and the human community, represents the final struggle against the Jew. Up until now, anti-Judaism has been utterly fragmentary and weak: during periods of national anti-Semitism, it was easy for the Jew to exempt himself from the opposition to Jews as a whole simply by declaring allegiance to the prevailing system of state rule and by seeking membership in the leading nation (like the Jew Paulus). During the period of religious anti-Semitism, baptism formed a bridge for the Jew to be accepted in non-Jewish circles (see [Johannes] Pfefferkorn or [Wilhelm] Marr, for example).[1] During the period of idealist anti-Semitism, the Jew simply had to adapt his natural aptitude for ideological masquerade to the spirit of the times and participate in the intellectual controversies of the day (example: the Berlin salons). So, up until now, there has always been a bridge that the Jew could cross in order to leave his community and join the community of non-Jews. The anti-Semitism of the past was by its nature profoundly fractured.

But the anti-Judaism that is based on blood firmly establishes one thing: the Jew can arbitrarily extol his beliefs and declare his national allegiance according to his inclinations. As long as his parents were Jews, he remains a Jew, and his thought, his belief, his character, and his comportment are and remain those of an alien species. There is no bridge he can cross to join the community of non-Jews. *Hence, anti-Judaism on a racial basis represents the final struggle in the history of all struggles against the Jew.*

Note

1. Johannes Pfefferkorn (1469–1523) was a Catholic polemicist who had converted from Judaism; Wilhelm Marr (1819–1904) was a non-Jewish journalist who coined the term "anti-Semitism" in the 1870s.—Eds.

94

REINHARD HEYDRICH

Instructions for Kristallnacht

Instructions delivered on 10 November 1938. First published in Office of U.S. Chief of Counsel for the Prosecution of Axis Criminality, *Nazi Conspiracy and Aggression* (Washington, DC: U.S. Government Printing Office, 1946), 3:545–47.

Secret
Copy of Most Urgent telegram from Munich of November 10th, 1938, 1:20 A.M.
To:
All Headquarters and Stations of the State Police
All Districts and Sub-districts of the SA
Urgent! For immediate attention of Chief or his deputy!
Re: Measures against Jews tonight

Following the attempt on the life of Secretary of the Legation vom Rath in Paris, demonstrations against the Jews are to be expected in all parts of the Reich in the course of the coming night, November 9th/10th, 1938. The instructions below are to be applied in dealing with these events:

1. The Chiefs of the State Police, or their deputies, must immediately upon receipt of this telegram contact, by telephone, the political leaders in their areas—*Gauleiter* or *Kreisleiter*—who have jurisdiction in their districts and arrange a joint meeting with the inspector or commander of the Order Police to discuss the arrangements for the demonstrations. At these discussions, the political leaders will be informed that the German Police has received instructions, detailed below, from the *Reichsführer-SS* and the Chief of the German Police, with which the political leadership is requested to coordinate its own measures:

(a) Only such measures are to be taken as do not endanger German lives or property (i.e. synagogues are to be burned down only where there is no danger of fire to neighboring buildings).

(b) Places of business and apartments belonging to Jews may be destroyed but not looted. The police are instructed to supervise the observance of this order and to arrest looters.

(c) In commercial streets, particular care is to be taken that non-Jewish businesses are completely protected against damage.

(d) Foreign citizens—even if they are Jews—are not to be molested.

2. On the assumption that the guidelines detailed under paragraph 1 are observed, the demonstrations are not to be prevented by the police, who are only to supervise the observance of the guidelines.

3. On receipt of this telegram, the police will seize all archives to be found in all synagogues and offices of the Jewish communities so as to prevent their destruction during the demonstrations. This refers only to material of historical value, not to contemporary tax records, etc. The archives are to be handed over to the locally responsible officers of the SD [Sicherheitsdienst, Security Service—Eds.].

4. The control of the measures of the Security Police concerning the demonstrations against the Jews is vested in the organs of the State Police, unless inspectors of the Security Police have given their own instructions. Officials of the Criminal Police, members of the SD, of the Reserves and the SS in general may be used to carry out the measures taken by the Security Police.

5. As soon as the course of events during the night permits the release of the officials required, as many Jews in all districts—especially the rich—are to be arrested as can be accom-

modated in existing prisons. For the time being, only healthy male Jews who are not too old are to be detained. After the detentions have been carried out, the appropriate concentration camps are to be contacted immediately for the prompt accommodation of the Jews in the camps. Special care is to be taken that the Jews arrested in accordance with these instructions are not ill treated.

Signed Heydrich,
SS-Gruppenführer

95

Secret Report of the Security Service of the Reichsführer SS

The Actions against the Jews on 9, 10, and 11 November 1938

First circulated as "Die Aktion gegen die Juden am. 9./10./11. 1938." First published in *Meldungen aus dem Reich 1938–1945. Die geheimen Lageberichte des Sicherheitsdienstes der SS,* edited by Heinz Boberach (Herrsching: Pawlak Verlag, 1984), 2:25–26.

Following the murder of German Legation Secretary [Ernst] vom Rath by the Jew of Polish nationality [Herschel] Feibel Grynspan, the basis for Jewish life and its organization was fully transformed by a number of successful measures taken against the Jews throughout the Reich.

measures taken

In general, these actions included the destruction or burning of synagogues and the demolition of almost all Jewish businesses, which were thus forced to close up shop. In some cases, the apartments of Jews were also affected by these actions. In some instances, valuable archival materials and works of art were destroyed as a result of carelessness or ignorance on the part of participants. A number of Jews were killed or injured while offering resistance to these actions.

At the same time, in order to increase pressure to emigrate, about twenty-five thousand male Jews were transferred to concentration camps, some of them temporarily.

purpose/outcome

Once these actions had been taken, Jewry was to be kept in check through a series of regulatory laws and ordinances. In particular, one basic principle was to be applied: that the Jew should under no circumstances be permitted to assume leadership positions, but rather should be employed only as a subordinate and that he should no longer be permitted to participate in the communal life of the *Volk*. This is the primary purpose served by the ordinance of 12 November 1938 issued by the official executor of the Four Year Plan, General Field Marschall Göring, which stipulates that Jews shall no longer be permitted to operate individual retail outlets, mail-order businesses, or contracting services, nor to serve as self-employed skilled laborers, effective as of 1 January 1938. No Jew shall be permitted to act as plant manager or chief clerk. In addition, the ordinance of 3 December 1938 concerning the utilization of Jewish assets stipulated that the proprietor of a Jewish commercial, agricultural, or forestry enterprise may be directed to either dispose of or dissolve his business within a certain time frame. Jews are not permitted to own land or title. Jews are required to deposit all their stocks, mining shares, and fixed-interest bonds and similar securities and assets into escrow accounts in an exchange bank. Access to assets deposited in said accounts or issuance of assets from such accounts requires prior approval of the Reich minister of economics. Jews are furthermore forbidden to acquire or independently sell gold, silver, and platinum objects as well as precious gems.

Additional regulations prohibited Jews from owning weapons and allowed for the ultimate exclusion of Jews from participating in German cultural life and education. What is more, the Jews were forced to pay restitution for damages incurred in the course of these actions taken against them, in the amount of 1 billion Reichsmark, to which was added 20 percent for Jews with assets valued at more than 5,000 Reichsmark.

In summary, what can be ascertained is that Jewry—at least with respect to those Jews who are state subjects and stateless Jews—has been completely excluded from communal life in Germany, so that the only option left for Jews to secure their existence is to emigrate.

96

BETTY SCHOLEM

Report on Kristallnacht

Written in March–April 1939. First published in Itta Shedletzky and Thomas Sparr, eds., *Mutter und Sohn im Briefwechsel, 1917–1946/Betty Scholem, Gershom Scholem* (Munich: C. H. Beck, 1989), 531–34.

The November action was organized right down to the smallest detail, much like a military mobilization. They were just waiting for an excuse and, even without the affair in Paris, would have created one.[1] Every member of the Hitler Youth and the SA was stationed in his place, all the instruments of destruction poised to signal the feigned outbreak of some collective national frenzy of "public outrage." But the public [*Volk*] was as taken by surprise, as were the Jews, and just stood there watching, struck speechless. As soon as news of the death came in from Paris, everyone feared the worst. That very night, all hell broke loose. Lorry trucks filled with commandos stopped at *every* Jewish shop—when the order was given, they smashed in the windows and demolished everything inside, using crowbars to topple cabinets and shelves; all the merchandise was smashed to smithereens and trampled over; in the beauty parlors, the marble washbasins and mirrors were shattered with sledgehammers, the light fixtures ripped from the ceiling; in grocery stores, even the foodstuffs that were not stolen were destroyed. The custodians [*schammes*] were forced to open the doors to the synagogues, whereupon canisters of gasoline or petroleum were poured down the central corridor of the sanctuary and ignited, setting fire to the benches and the galleries. The windows were shattered from the outside, and the roof truss set on fire—everything was fated to destruction by any means necessary. The fire department was only allowed to prevent the fires from spreading to neighboring houses and instructed to leave the synagogues to burn to the ground. Two major synagogues in the west sustained extensive damage and are beyond repair. They will likely force the Jewish congregation to demolish them. (Dr. Meyer wrote to say that the synagogue and all the gravestones in the cemetery in Emmendingen are completely obliterated!) In east Berlin around the Alexanderplatz, these animals forced their way into the apartments, too, threw the furniture out the windows and slashed open the down quilts so that the feathers were flying all around! The Nathan Israel Department Store was reduced to rubble—which cost a pretty penny because the proprietor is British and immediately reported the damage to the British consulate, which demanded that the damages be repaired within four days at the expense of the state. A whole army of contractors was busy working night and day to finish the job, and we were there as soon as it reopened, so we could see the full extent of havoc they'd wreaked upon it. They had brought the big chandelier crashing down into the light well, the glass elevator shafts had been shattered, and the smaller chandeliers were left hanging, but their arms were bent beyond repair. Makeshift lighting had been affixed throughout. As was required for all Jewish businesses, the sign that said "Aryanization of this business is under way" already hung in the windows. The proprietor, Wilfried Israel, finally gave up the fight. No one knows who took over the business. All we know is that in February 1939, we witnessed the arrival of the sign that said "Jews not welcome

FIGURE 9. Anti-Semitic advertisement for *Der Stürmer* in front of the Vienna opera house, 1938: "To be Jewish is to be criminal. Read the special edition of *Der Stürmer*." Photograph no. 11189, United States Holocaust Memorial Museum Photo Archives, Washington, D.C. Courtesy of Scherl Bilderdienst.

here," which has since become *mandatory* for all businesses. Across the street from Israel, at Grumach—a store that has been in business for just as long—there is a sign that says "We don't sell to Jews!" On the same day, the morning after that ominous night, the "laws" appeared. The Jews are to take on the expense of immediately restoring the "appearance of the streets," the insurance money shall be paid out to the state, businesses are to be transferred to Aryans by 1 January at the latest, etc. Officially, Jews were permitted to continue selling their merchandise until Christmas, but the police actually began enforcing the ban on Jewish merchants the very next day. The public was led to believe that the Jews remained in possession of their businesses. Their driver's licenses were revoked because they supposedly presented a traffic risk! Jews were forbidden, under threat of *punishment by law,* from attending the theater, the movies, visiting museums, exhibitions, sporting events, public swimming pools, etc. They were forbidden to set foot on certain streets—the Voßstraße and Wilhelmstraße—and from the monument and the Wilhelmsplatz. They were placed under curfew and not allowed to leave their homes on 3 December, the Day of National Solidarity. They were expelled from all the schools and colleges. In the two weeks immediately following Ernst vom Rath's death, approximately twenty thousand men aged fifteen and older were taken into custody in Berlin alone, some of them snatched straight off the streets. The only ones who were able to escape the raids were those who spent the night away from their own homes. We had several friends spending the night with us. Same with Phiechen. Many of them were released five to six weeks later after providing written assurances that they would emigrate *immediately.* There was a terrible cold spell during these days (with temperatures hovering below zero). People were forced to endure terrible suffering. They had to lie around on the floor in rooms with no heat, were not allowed to bathe or shower; many of them were forced to work outdoors completing construction on the concentration camps; there were so many deaths, it was simply horrific! Once the poor souls were finally released, they were herded to the remotest train stations in neighboring towns with no means of transportation to return. The Jewish community quickly set up emergency assistance centers. Individual people, and vehicles as well, left stranded in the streets, were picked up, taken to the train station, and tickets were purchased for them to return to Berlin, where they were immediately—without exception—admitted to the Jewish hospital. Their heads were shaved bald; they were so filthy dirty and frozen stiff that they were barely recognizable. We gave them the best possible care. An acquaintance who was with Werner [Scholem] wrote asking me to visit him in the hospital. I couldn't bring myself to do it, so Edith went instead and came back shocked and in tears. There were ten men lying around in the same room, all of them with badly frostbitten limbs—our friend had just had one of his toes amputated! Werner, his friend explained, was assigned to indoor detail and supervision, and in this position, was able to do a lot of good for others. He wanted me to know that he'd resigned himself to his fate and learned to live with it, but he hoped that I would be able to arrange for his emigration.

On 12 November, we were required to submit statements of assets—retroactively, as was the case with *all* these laws—and a 20 percent "Jewish levy" was slapped on our assets. In my case, that was simple. But people who had substantial properties, businesses, homes, and real estate—nonliquid, essentially fictitious assets –were required to come up with outrageously exorbitant sums of money! The pensions of retirees were counted as capital, and they were expected to remit funds that they didn't even have. Our local revenue office was plastered with posters publicizing the most offensive insults against us. "No punishment is severe enough for the Jews who are the world's misfortune! The Jews are responsible for the war of 1914 and will bring on the next war, too! No sympathy for the Jews!" And you could certainly count on that last sentence (printed in bold red letters)!! You had to wonder at the degree of integrity the agents of the revenue office actually displayed in their treatment of us, considering the fact that they were basically ordered to victimize us.

The insurance companies were really taken for a ride. They were forced to pay the state on the insurance claims that were due their Jewish clients and so turned to their foreign reinsurance companies, asking them to back them up. The response was that they would not pay out so much as a penny. The damages did not result from *force majeure,* from circumstances beyond reasonable control, nor from an accident, and certainly not from rioting (which was the kind of comical window dressing Goebbels would have put on the event!), but rather from a well-prepared and deliberate act of destruction for which the company was not obligated to render compensation.

Note

1. In [the Paris event], a German official, Ernst vom Rath, was assassinated by a seventeen-year-old Polish Jew named Herschel Grynszpan.

97

SOPADE

Reactions of the Populace to Reichskristallnacht

First published as "Reaktionen der Bevölkerung auf die Reichskristallnacht, November 1938," in *Deutschland-Berichte der Sozialdemokratischen Partei Deutschlands (Sopade)* (Frankfurt am Main: Verlag Petra Nettelbeck, 1980), 5:1205.

The brutal measures taken against the Jews have elicited outrage in the populace. People are rather open about it, and many Aryans have been arrested as a result. After it was revealed that a Jewish woman was ripped from the bed where she'd just given birth, even a police officer said that this was going too far. "What kind of direction is Germany taking with these methods?" he asked, and was subsequently arrested himself. [. . .] Who is going to be the next victim after the Jews? That's what people are asking themselves here. Will it be the Catholics? Or will there be a special confiscation of everyone's assets? [. . .] There is widespread outrage over this vandalism throughout Germany. It found expression, for example, in one incident in which the SA, while ransacking a shop after dark, was bombarded with rocks under the cover of darkness from an orchard across the way. [. . .] A lot of people took Jewish women and children in and gave them shelter in their homes. [Non-Jewish] women are going shopping for Jewish women because it is forbidden to sell them groceries. Another thing that is clear is that the intensity of the actions [on Kristallnacht] varied substantially from place to place. But the effect of these measures has been to intimidate large sectors of the population. [. . .] People are no longer willing to speak as openly. One thing has become utterly apparent: the Nazis have the power to do whatever they choose. [. . .] But it was utterly clear [that night] that the people of Berlin did not approve of the plundering and arson, the assaults on Jewish men, women, and children of every age. Their protests found expression in everything from scornful looks and contemptuous gestures to voicing disgust and unabashed profanity.

98

DAS SCHWARZE KORPS

What Now, Jews?

First published as "Juden was nun?" in *Das Schwarze Korps,* 24 November 1938, 1.

One of the characteristics of our rise to victory and the fall of the others is that we learn from our experiences and are happy to learn, whereas the *others never learn.*

Friends of the Jews—whether they are genuine friends or friendly for strategic reasons—in the democracies, whether they are in government or not, godless or good Christians, are still screaming in outcry just as they've been doing since 1933. And their slanderous insults are the same: they never get beyond the word *barbarian*—a charge that leaves us utterly cold because we know precisely which side the better people have always been on whenever the crusading Christian missionary priests or power-hungry Britons have ventured into the world to bring the blessings of their "faith" and their "culture" to the "savages."

Let Things Be!

Their threats remain the same—but ever since the days of crisis in Czechoslovakia, they carry little more weight than a paper tiger. And it is the same fine art of political extortion at work when they declare that there is no way to arrive at a peaceful compromise with Germany. Let things be, friends! Who in the world can't see that the only kind of peace you'd ever let us have is the peace we defiantly deny you?!

Up until 1933 and even beyond, we remained gullible and naive. Whenever the so-called court of international opinion got bent out of shape over the fact that our "barbarism" prevented Jews from abusing our wives and daughters, we diligently set ourselves to the task of outlining the Jewish Question from start to finish. How dumb can you be!? As if any dyed-in-the-wool democrat had placed a shred of stock in that!

So what does it boil down to in reality? Neither Mr. Roosevelt nor a British archbishop nor any other self-proclaimed democrat would so much as consider bedding his daughter with some slimy Eastern Jew; only when it comes to Germany are they suddenly utterly oblivious to the Jewish Question, concerning themselves exclusively with the "persecution of innocents based on their beliefs," as though we ever had any interest whatsoever in what a Jew believes or does not believe.

In reality and in truth, these self-proclaimed democrats know exactly what the Jewish Question is—and *one need only take a good look at their immigration laws and their fear of an influx of Jews* to recognize the practical consequences that stem from their intimate knowledge of this question. But then they feign innocence and ignorance when it looks like they may be able to use the issue to inflict damage on Germany.

Well, even a few years ago, that might have come as a surprise to us. Today, though, their hue and cry is but a steady stream of white noise that couldn't possibly get any louder. It is common knowledge that the human ear can hear only up to a certain frequency. It blocks out whatever sounds and noises resonate at a higher frequency than that. We have grown immune to the decibel level of world Jewry's screaming outcry.

And the simple *Volk* gleans from that an unshakable wisdom. At every twist and turn you can hear the same argument: if we had addressed the Jewish Question completely and in the most brutal fashion already in 1933, the outcry would have been no less bothersome than the steady stream we have heard ever since, as we have been solving the Jewish Question one step at a time with individual measures that we are forced into taking by the Jews themselves and their friends. The gist of this argument is correct. But only in theory, because, at the time, we lacked the *military* force that we *possess today.* Back then, the Jews would have perhaps succeeded in inciting the peoples [of the world] to retaliatory war against us; today, even the most vehemently vitriolic democrats would think long and hard about that.

Now, though, we will finally move toward a total solution to the Jewish Question—because we must, because we are deaf to the world outcry, and ultimately, because there's not a thing in the world that can stop us. The agenda has been set. And what it is:

Complete elimination, absolute segregation!

What does that imply?

It *not only* implies the exclusion of Jews from the German national economy, which they have wrecked with their murderous deeds and their inquisitionist war- and murder-mongering—

The implications are far greater!

There is not a German in the world who can be expected to live under the same roof as these Jews, not anymore than he could be expected to live with a branded race of murderers and criminals, mortal enemies of the German *Volk.*

The Jews, therefore, must be driven out of our apartment buildings and neighborhoods and dispatched to cattle cars or barracks where they will remain amongst themselves and have as little contact as possible with Germans. They must be clearly marked and, furthermore, stripped of the right to own homes and property or any share in the same in Germany, because not a single German can be expected to subordinate himself to the whims of Jewish land and property owners and to feed them with the fruits of his labor.

Reverting to Criminality

Left to its own devices in every respect, this parasitic people, since it has neither the will nor the capacity to work and produce on its own, will, thus isolated, be reduced to poverty and ruin. Even though the Jews today may still have billions to their name, even though there are still hundreds of millionaires amongst them, even though the occasional exception of the "poor" Jew may have embezzled and squirreled away sufficient resources, they will have soon squandered their capital once they have been cut off from the mother lode that is the lifeblood of the parasite.

And if we force the rich Jews to support their "poor" racial comrades—which we will certainly need to do—all of them will revert to criminality because this is consistent with the genetically programmed propensities that are uniquely their own.

After that, no one can possibly believe that we will sit idly by and watch these developments. The German *Volk* has no desire whatsoever to tolerate hundreds of thousands of criminals in its midst—people who not only secure their very existence by committing crimes but *who are furthermore intent on exacting revenge!*

And we have even less desire to witness the way these hundreds of thousands of wretched Jews provide a breeding ground for Bolshevism and an organizational catch basin for criminal political elements of a subhuman race that is withering away by virtue of natural selection at the perimeter of our own.

Were we to tolerate that, it would result in the development of an underground conspiracy that might be plausible in America but certainly is not possible or even conceivable in Germany.

Were we to find ourselves in that state of development, we would be faced with the grim necessity of eliminating the Jewish underground just in the same way we tend to eliminate criminals in the state of law and order in which we live: by *brandishing the fire and the sword.* The result would be the de facto complete and total end of the Jewish race in Germany, its absolute annihilation.

Whatever elements living abroad choose to think that any of these developments—and one must admit that they are logical and *inevitable*—can be prevented by the ongoing monotony of outcry, by threats and extortion, only serve to prove that they have learned nothing since 1933.

Now there must be a parting of minds between those who seriously hope to come to the Jews' aid with their sophomoric humanitarian drivel and those who merely use the Jewish Question as a front for their deep-seated aversion to all things German.

Now that it's clear that they cannot achieve anything with the clamor of empty brouhaha, the democratic statesmen who are sincerely concerned about the fate of the Jews would be advised to concede that they must render a *positive contribution to a resolution of the Jewish Question.* As for the others—those who would merely use the Jews with priestly cunning as scapegoats against Germany—let it be known that, after a certain point, *even their own people will see through them* as soon as they keep howling and hounding without cutting to the chase when it's finally time to *take action!*

At this point, there is no other conceivable alternative.

This Land Is All We Have!

The Jews may have convinced the democracies and the democracies may have convinced the Jews that it won't be long before it's all over for this Hitler Germany, and, as the saying goes, never trouble trouble before trouble troubles you. We have every reason to believe that the most recent developments will shatter any such flailing, misplaced hopes in these pathetic little blockheads. *Now it's time to do less hoping and take more action!*

Germany is in no position to solve its Jewish Question beyond its own borders because this land is all we have, and we must free it from Jews. The others, on the other hand—these glorified democracies, some of which are actually controlled by Jews and Freemasons, others merely by the friends of Jews who still represent major world powers—they have an overabundance of land.

PART FOUR

. . .

NATIONALIZING GERMAN YOUTH

9

Educating the Race

Children and Adolescents

IF THERE WAS A LEGACY of the Protestant Reformation that became a hallmark of things "German," it was the emphasis on education as a means of self-improvement. By the end of the nineteenth century, the Germans had invented everything from early childhood education (Friedrich Fröbel, 1782–1852, the creator of the kindergarten) to the modern university (Wilhelm von Humboldt, 1767–1835). Education was the path to *Bildung,* that impossible word that signified culture, knowledge, sophistication, and social status. Beginning with Johann Gottfried Herder (1744–1803), the eighteenth century saw a turn to an authoritarian notion of education as indoctrination in the service of a "people." Early twentieth-century theoreticians such as Ernst Krieck (1882–1947), who later became the *NS-Hofpädagoge* (Nazi court educator; see document 53 in chapter 4), and Herman Nohls (1897–1960) also stressed the importance of transforming the individual (*Menschenformung*) in service to the nation.

When the Nazis seized power, they saw this desire for education as a path to inculcating a new generation (those who came of age between 1933 and 1945) into a single, rigid (though never unambiguous) ideology of the Führer and German racial and cultural hegemony. The school, stripped of its liberal and Jewish (not always the same thing) teachers after 1935, became a place of indoctrination, as evidenced by the prescribed regimen for both the appearance and flow of events in the classroom. Every aspect of the school day—from gymnastics (which had a long political history in Germany) to mathematics—was designed to shape the minds of young Germans. The pedagogue Wilhelm Kirchner observed in 1939, "We will not begin and end our racial education with the study of race. Each child, in studying plants, animals, and human beings, will collect insight over the years without ever using the word race."[1] And "race" meant the Jews. Race formed the basis for the education of the youth, but the *Führerprinzip,* the primacy of Adolf Hitler, shaped every moment of each school day. Hitler was omnipresent in the classroom: in texts, images, and, as a first-grade student's notebook shows, the now-obligatory "German greeting" of "Heil Hitler."

Krieck was the first to outline an educational system rooted in Nazi notions of human biology. He prescribed the notion of society as an organic whole in which each individual was to be educated for his or her "natural" place in society, following the model of breeding animals for their appropriate functions (*Zucht*). Alfred Baeumler (1887–1968), one of the leading philosophers and theoreticians of the Nazi Party (see document 64 in chapter 4), wrote in 1942, "We desire to have the school respond to the race." Central to this goal was the exclusion of Jews and liberals from the schools and the purification of the teacher corps. Jewish students were initially limited to 1.5 percent of the student body and were eventually completely removed after Kristallnacht. Even the schools created by Jewish communities were all closed by 1942. By 1936, 95 percent of the teachers in Germany were members of the Nationalsozialistische Lehrerbund (National Socialist Teachers Association), the official Nazi teachers' organization.

Central to the education of Nazi youth was the creation of an extracurricular youth movement that would encompass every child in Germany, no matter his or her location, "appropriate natural" position, or gender. Beginning in the 1890s, Germany saw a proliferation of youth groups. Most influential was the Wandervogel (Wandering Birds), a liberal "back-to-nature" movement founded in 1896. Though initially unpolitical, the Wandervogel emphatically disavowed the patriotic paternalism of the Wilhelmine state, organizing a gathering of some two to three thousand participants at a protest rally of "free German youth" in 1913 on the Hoher Meißner mountain near Kassel. After World War I, such groups were politicized (parallel to the rise of the Boy Scouts in Great Britain), becoming the mainstay of political and religious movements (categories that often overlapped), ranging from the Zionists (Blau-Weiss [Blue-White] in 1912) to the Nazis. By 1930, the Nazis had separate organizations for young men, the Hitler Jugend, and young women, the Bund Deutscher Mädel. The Nazis believed strongly in the separation of the sexes. In their high school reform, they reinstituted single-sex education in 1937. As Erna Bohlmann notes in her essay, German women were "historically" defined by their biological destiny much more than their male compatriots were. However, they were not prudish: the BDM encouraged (though it did not advertise it) premarital sex and even multiple partners, if such behaviors served the Aryan community and prepared young girls for motherhood. This was also very much in line with attitudes toward sexuality within the original Wandervogel movement. The BDM-Werk Glaube und Schönheit (BDM Organization–Faith and Beauty) program even encouraged a healthy eroticism for older girls from seventeen to twenty-one. During wartime, the BDM sponsored hair-collection drives to demonstrate support, put on practical fashions shows, and as Jutta Rüdiger observed, even encouraged deployment to the newly occupied eastern areas to assist local "Germanic" populations with farming, child-rearing, and cultural activities.

After the Nazi seizure of power, only the Nazi groups were permitted to exist, as mandated in the Law Concerning the Hitler Youth of 1 December 1936, and all other youth groups were closed. The Nazi youth groups were among the earliest of the Nazi organizations. Only the Storm Troopers, under which the Nazi youth groups were organized, was older, although by barely a year. In 1926, Kurt Gruber, a law student, reorganized what had been a loosely structured group, the Jugendbund der NSDAP (Youth League of the NSDAP, created in 1922) into a paramilitary organization, the Großdeutsche Jugendbewegung (Greater German Youth Movement). In 1932, even before the Nazi seizure of power, Baldur von Schirach (1907–74) was made the first *Reichsjugendführer* (Reich youth leader), a position that placed him, in theory, at the same rank in the Nazi hierarchy as Heinrich Himmler. Schirach was the most visible advocate for a new German youth in the Third Reich. A published (but very bad) poet, his verses glorified the *Führerprinzip* and the "new Germany" and were sung or recited regularly at youth group meetings. (He was succeeded in 1940 by Arthur Axmann.) Together with the reconstruction of the schools to reflect the precepts of racial science, the youth groups made it possible for the Reich to dominate the youth from waking to sleeping. Membership in one of these groups became a major sign of youthful identity. Indeed, the students at the Institute for the Blind in Berlin-Steglitz appealed to Schirach to allow them to create HJ and BDM groups in their school. Much to their dismay, this appeal was rejected because of the possibility that their blindness was hereditary and that therefore they should be excluded from the race. As the Sopade (the Social Democratic Party information service) reported, in spite of the enthusiasm generated by the youth organizations, many young people tried to escape the one year of mandatory "rural civil service."

NOTE

1. Wilhelm Kirchner and G. Laub, eds., *Die Siedlung: Planungsheft der DAF* (Berlin: Verlag der Deutschen Arbeitsfront, 1939), 55.

99

UNKNOWN CHILD

Adolf Hitler Is Our Führer!

Unpublished "Schulbuch aus Wien," Fluegge Collection, Frankfurt am Main, n.d.

We are Germans: the way we say hello is, *Heil Hitler!*
Rudi is a German boy.
Lise is a German girl.
Rudi says hello: *Heil Hitler!*
Lise says hello: *Heil Hitler!*
All Germans love their Führer!

Elementary school, first grade, Hegelgasse 12

100

ANONYMOUS

Conference Minutes

Horst Wessel School in Kassel

First published in *Schule im Dritten Reich—Erziehung zum Tod? Eine Dokumentation,* edited by Geert Platner and Schüler der Gerhart-Hauptmann Schule in Kassel (Munich: Deutsche Taschenbuch Verlag, 1983), 197–203.

2 May 1933: In addition to portraits of the Reich president, pictures of the Reich chancellor may also be displayed in schools. Particularly honorable students shall be awarded the book *The Army and the Naval Fleet* [*Heer und Flotte*].

12 August 1933: The Nazi salute will be introduced as a form of greeting at this school. Jewish students will be excluded from instruction on Saturdays. The film *Sports and Soldiers* will be required viewing for all students. The Reich League of Air Security is recruiting members and will be offering a lecture series.

21 September 1933: Attempts to foster relationships with the Hitler Youth; a spokesman for the Hitler Youth will be appointed at our school. Theories of hereditary and racial science are to be promoted. We will begin commemorating Horst Wessel's birthday.[1]

1 December 1933: In the future, every student will be required to make a financial contribution to the Association of Germanic Peoples Living Abroad. Sex education in the classroom is banned by ministerial ordinance.

18 December 1933: More emphasis shall be placed on the study of genealogy.

1 February 1934: More patriotic, nationalistic texts are needed in the school libraries!

15 March 1934: Complaints registered about excessive demands placed on students by extracurricular activities. A slide series is available for teaching racial science and genetics.

8 August 1934: All teachers shall pay their respects to our deceased Reich president by wearing a black band of mourning on their left forearm for two weeks.

20 September 1934: Mandatory payments from students will be used to fund the purchase of projectors. In addition, a fee will be charged for each screening of films. The involvement of the Hitler Youth in school affairs is discussed.

19 October 1934: The number of students has risen to 1,060. Middle-school principal G. goes into retirement. The Hitler Youth, Troop 83, thanks the school for supporting it with

sales of the book *Will and Power* [*Wille und Macht*]. The gymnasium will be made available for the SA to use on Monday and Friday evenings. Non-Aryan students will not be allowed to participate in certain school-sponsored activities. Herr B. gives instructions for the next air-raid-warning drill on 25 October 1934!

20 November 1934: Conference at the Forest School [*Waldschule*].[2] Herr H. offered comments on the purpose and mission behind the Forest School. Sports activities in the schools are not as much about developing specific competencies as about developing certain capacities, not as much about our discipline as about our breeding. General principles should be drilled into our students—things like voluntary subordination, self-discipline and -control, orderliness, courage and self-confidence, willingness to sacrifice, camaraderie, patriotism, etc. It is more important that our students learn a sense of orientation and of direction, that they learn to gather information, to stay calm, to assess a situation in a flash, to act quickly and quietly, than it is for them to be able to describe a given survey of land or area. Afterward, we are given a tour of the property and allowed to observe various groups, and this is followed by a military discipline drill, a recess period, and listening exercises. The daily routine at the Forest School: 6 A.M.: rise, physical education, run through the forest, make the beds, clean the shoes, household chores; 8:00 A.M.: breakfast, garden work; 10:45 A.M.: outdoor chores; 1:00 P.M.: lunch and free time; 2:30 P.M.: roll call, followed by classroom instruction; 3:30 P.M.: target practice; 4:30 P.M.: coffee, free time until 7:00 P.M.: dinner, followed by laundry and repair of clothing; 9:30 P.M.: the Great Tattoo.[3]

Life in the Forest School is communal labor in a community that is separate from school or home life. The daily service routine becomes supreme law to the student, and it requires the complete commitment of all human faculties. The body, still drunk with sleep, is strengthened in the fresh forest air of the morning; the lungs are purified. Refreshed and alive, it enjoys its first bite of bread in the morning. For many of our students, this is the first time they've ever worked the soil of their homeland with spade and hoe. There is a constant back-and-forth between physical and mental training. The art of firing weapons is practiced with a steady hand and an iron will; the recruit can take pride in reviewing his accomplishments in the art of throwing grenades—by distance and accuracy. The field exercises present the most strenuous challenges to body, mind, and spirit. The student participates with heart and soul. It is here that the written lessons of the Great War are put into practice and made flesh. Even a late-night air-raid alarm cannot squelch interest in the field exercises. There are excellent training opportunities for the troops and intermediary leaders. Successful external and internal strengthening of all our young men—this is required of us in these times. In terms of the field sports, the Forest School is able to provide an extension and development of the material that cannot currently be offered by the Hitler Youth to all of our young men as it should be, due to a shortage of trained leaders.

14 December 1934: Ordinance concerning ceremonial flag raising at the start and end of the school day. The literary works that have been donated to the school (for example, Hindenburg's testament) are to be used accordingly in classroom instruction.

11 March 1935: Allowing students to take a leave of absence in order to attend Hitler Youth seminars during the school year is not something that can be avoided altogether. The national director of sports for the Reich will be able to attend physical education classes at all schools. Parents are obligated to pay fees for films—if need be, measures must be undertaken to force them to do so. In general, we can say that very difficult work is being performed here at the Horst Wessel School despite the small, overcrowded classrooms and poor ventilation.

7 May 1935: Hitler Youth duty rosters will allow us to monitor the transfer of duty on the National Day of Youth through the schools. Failures to report for duty will henceforth be

addressed using the same policies and procedures as school absences. In the coming weeks, leaders of youth groups in the classes will recruit youth for enrollment in the Hitler Youth. The names of Jewish students who shall be dismissed from instruction on the National Day of Youth were announced.

4 September 1935: A curriculum for hereditary and racial science will be developed. A series of lectures will be offered by the Office of Racial Affairs.

19 August 1936: The whole teaching colloquium will facilitate an ideological training camp in Bad-Sooden-Allendorf. In the beginning of February, the school will sponsor an event to benefit the Winter Relief Works; the event will consist of gymnastic presentations by all the classes.

25 November 1936: The Wehrmacht requests that we concentrate particularly on those areas that will be required of youth later in their army training and that we thus take a substantial load off their work. We have already put together the materials and should immediately incorporate them into the curriculum.

1 September 1937: Germans living abroad are to be remembered in a special school-wide celebration. We need to stress the importance of having proof-of-ancestry cards [*Ahnenpass*] for all students (if need be, filling out the genealogies together in classroom instruction). Dissolution of all civil service associations is mandated.

26 January 1938: We are reminded of the obligation of any civil servant who intends to marry to provide documentation of German ancestry and blood for the future spouse.

1 March 1938: The mayor of the city has determined that gymnasiums and classrooms must be abandoned during air-raid alarms since it is impossible to turn out the lights in them.

21 April 1938: The Municipal Audiovisual Archive [Stadtbildstelle] will monitor showings of mandatory-viewing films.

6 September 1938: Ministerial edict: students in their final classes will be required to fill out genealogical charts [*Ahnentafel*]. Any changes in curriculum made to support the aims of the Third Reich shall be outlined and registered in departmental meetings in various subjects. These must then be made available for classroom use.

25 January 1939: A high-ranking government official spoke to the teachers' colloquium about the Law for the Restoration of Professional Civil Service. The legislation considers the core of civil servants a pillar of our entire state and bestows upon them the obligation to maintain the racial purity of the entire body of German civil servants—keeping its bloodline free from alien, genetically unrelated elements. Every *völkisch* ordinance we pass is necessary for securing the apparatus of power. Holding an office is something that is impersonal, but that is why this office must be occupied by those national comrades who are German in flesh and blood. The office is an organ of state, the executor of the national estate. The constitutional law of the Third Reich rests on the following foundations: We do not live in tyranny, not in a dictatorship, but rather in a Führer nation. Hitler is the Führer of the *Volk*, the state, and the party. He is at the same time the Supreme Lawmaker. The reason we don't have a written constitution is that the *völkisch* state cannot so much as imagine constricting its thought by anchoring it in specific forms that may be valid for the next ten years but not for the long run. And yet, the following principles are clearly definitive: (1) The sovereignty of the *Volk*. (2) The totality of the state's mandate. (3) The *Führerprinzip*. (4) The unity of party and state. (5) The Reich is a uniform state. (6) The *völkisch* order is our foundation (maintaining racial purity of German blood).

27 November 1939: We have been directed to introduce colonialist thought into instruction. Colonies are, for a great and powerful *Volk* like the Germans, a matter of honor and provide the youth of such a people with a lesson in character building.

14 December 1939: Current curricular offerings and materials are to be adapted to pro-

mote the military mind-set. This way, military training is not merely a consideration of the mind; instead, it already assumes concrete form. The military mind-set cannot be but an empty challenge written on the page; it should be the foundational principle for action in every individual.

3 May 1940: Ministerial directive: Instructors must file reports concerning what they are doing to promote air flight in class: building model airplanes in shop class; teaching principles of aviation in math class; promoting the notion of flight in physics and chemistry classes, in geography, and in biology; using foreign-language instruction to spark enthusiasm for flying; and fostering that enthusiasm in art classes.

23 January 1942: School library: translations from American, British, and French literature shall be removed from circulation. The ban on Russian literature remains in place.

10 November 1942: Directive concerning mixed bloods mandates that all first-degree mixed bloods shall be barred from enrolling in any public educational facility. Songs that are considered mandatory in the classroom (1) "Do You See the Red Sun Rising in the East?" (2) "Rise, Raise the Flags of the Reich!" (3) "Our Lives Belong to One Thing Alone: Freedom," (4) "Forward, March! To the East!"

14 December 1942: In a confidential memorandum, the school council requires all instructors to remind their students in the first week of class that they should not show any kindness toward prisoners of war. Any signs of violations of this rule, especially those that appear politically motivated, must be reported immediately.

5 March 1943: It is the task and the duty of each individual educator to elicit and sustain the endurance, conviction, and the will to see this through to the final victory in our students.

9 August 1944: Indefatigable commitment to the war effort is demanded of everyone.

15 September 1944: A conference had to be called to address a single point on the agenda. School superintendent announces that any changes in the class schedule must receive prior approval from the superintendent's office due to the exigencies of wartime operation (air-raid alarms, etc.).

24 November 1944: The rector, Mr. Z., reports on negotiations with school council member B. over the relocation of our school from Gersfeld to Großenlüder.[4] A petition filed by school administration to stop the relocation to Großenlüder based on the argument that the move will place students at risk of air raids has been rejected. A meeting with party representatives confirmed that the rejection came as a result of the current situation in general. At the moment, the most important concern is not the safety of the youth but rather their training! Teachers have been instructed to refrain from agitating against the relocation with the students and with their parents.

27 March 1945 (still in Gersfeld): Middle-school teacher K. reads aloud the order of the *Bannführer* in Fulda outlining the mandate to immediately move the camp compound at Gersfeld to the barracks compound at Waldkappel. The school will not comply with this ridiculous order because: (1) Under current highly dangerous conditions, it would be impossible to determine whether the Waldkappel fulfills the technical requirements for housing the youth there. It is furthermore likely that the enemy will penetrate the vicinity of Waldkappel even before the transport arrives there. (2) The school director points out that we cannot fulfill our obligation to the parents given the tremendous danger involved in the transport and the risk of air raids. Therefore, we have decided that all students shall be dismissed and sent home tomorrow after third period. Middle-school teachers W. and H. will escort the students in their departure.

Notes

1. Horst Wessel (1907–30) was a Nazi Party activist and member of the SA who was murdered in dubious circumstances in 1930. He was later turned into a martyr by the Goebbels propaganda machine, and

a national holiday was established in his honor. A song bearing his name became the anthem of the Nazi Party.—Eds.

2. The *Waldschule* was a European-wide open-air boarding school movement created by Karl Triebold in the 1920s and appropriated by the Nazis as a means of physical and mental training for pupils. There were many such campuses throughout Germany, including one in Kassel.—Eds.

3. The Great Tattoo was a ceremony for the lowering of the flag before the massed faculty and student body.—Eds.

4. The Horst Wessel School had been relocated to Gersfeld after the bombing of Kassel.—Eds.

101

PAUL GARZ AND OTTO HARTMANN

German Grammar

Active/Passive Voice

First published in *Deutschkundliches Arbeitsbuch für die Volksschule,* 50th ed., vol. 2 (Frankfurt am Main: M. Diesterweg, 1937), 40.

Exercises:

Before Hitler came to power:
Attacks people on the streets.
Houses set on fire
The Reichstag building set on fire
Railroad tracks torn up
Telegraph lines destroyed
Businesses plundered
Transport put at risk
Riots incited
Railroad cars blown up
Banks robbed
Compounds burglarized
Money embezzled
News reports falsified
Fraudulent information disseminated
Discord sown
Dissent fomented
The fatherland decried

Example:

Active:
People attacked others on the streets in broad daylight.
People set houses. . . .
Passive:
People were attacked on the streets in broad daylight.
Houses were set. . . .

102

PAUL HABERMANN, ARTHUR LAUDIEN, AND RUDOLF TOBLER

Heritage and Mission

A German Primer for Young Readers

First published in *Erbe und Auftrag: Deutsches Lesebuch für Jungen,* Fifth-Grade Edition (Bielefeld: Velhagen & Klasing, 1941), 275.

Reading for German Class:
The order comes from the top, from the head of the line where the major is mounted on his prancing sorrel steed: Now sing! And the whole *Freikorps* company bursts into song, buckling over with laughter in a singular display of derision:

Killer Corps Company Schulz, so they said:
With a swastika sealed to each steel-helmed head,
Wearing the armbands in black, white, and red!

We may have been duped and double-crossed
By tricks and taunts of traitors' dross
But faith in the fatherland never we lost!

With that flatfoot shuffle, down at the heel,
Flabby hook nose worn like a seal—
Judah and sons, prepare your last meal!

103

BALDUR VON SCHIRACH

To the Flag

First published as "An die Fahne," in *Deutsches Lesewerk für Mittelschulen, Gedichtband,* edited by Heinrich Dreyer, Rudolf Fiedler, and Paul Skriewe, Third- to Sixth-Grade Edition (Frankfurt am Main: Otto Salle, 1942), 42.

You are the finest flag e'er to have flown,
The strength that beckons the soldier to war,
You bring salvation even to sinners who die in your name,
The almighty hand of the hero's last prayer.
You are the source of our fervor and our flame.
All who have fallen, in your furls live on.
You are the bridge between this world and yon'.
Hail to the men, full of grace,
To all who have fallen in the shade of your face.

104

DIETRICH KLAGGES

Volk and Führer

German History for Schools

First published in *Volk und Führer: Deutsche Geschichte für Schulen,* edited by Dietrich Klagges, Middle-School Edition (Frankfurt am Main: Diesterweg, 1942), 187–88.

Western liberals abandoned the nationalist goals of the freedom fighters as these were first pronounced by [Friedrich] Jahn and [Johann] Fichte. These liberals were not concerned with nationalist ideals but rather with fulfilling their liberal ideal: individual freedom no matter what the cost; they wanted freedom from the constraints of the state and the right to sow their wild oats. They wanted to rule themselves, not to be ruled. So they advocated freedom of the press, free trade, equality for all, and the principle of majority rule (democracy). No wonder, then, that the democratic egalitarian mania that completely elided any consideration of the unique character and rights of Germans soon erupted into unbridled admiration of everything foreign—indeed, into visions of a brotherhood of man in a world in which all men and races were considered equal.

The Hambach Festival. The festival at the castle ruins of Hambach (in the Pfalz in 1832) marked the advent of Western liberalism with its ignominious dabbling adulation of all things foreign, with its blather about the brotherhood of man.[1] It was another mountaintop pilgrimage festival [*Bergfest*] but worlds apart from the one fifteen years ago! There were Frenchmen, Poles, and Italians present among the thousands of participants. One of the speakers addressed his audience with a lengthy speech praising the festival as the most magnificent and meaningful pilgrimage to be celebrated in Germany in centuries: Long live the Poles, Germany's allies! Long live the Franks, our German brothers, who hold our national sovereignty and self-sufficiency in such high esteem! Long live every *Volk* that breaks free of its shackles and joins us in declaring allegiance to liberty: Fatherland—*Volk*-over-Land—Fraternity! Long may they live!

This should have been seen as a prelude to goals that would be set by Marxism just a few decades later. [. . .]

International forces threatening Volk *and state.*
The Jewish people as destroyers of national life.
Jews as outsiders to the national community of the Volk.

Under the influence of liberalism, the corrosive influence of the Jewish people has begun affecting the German *Volk*. Up until the time of the Enlightenment, the Jews had been viewed as an alien body of people by all peoples and treated accordingly. They were forced to live in their own neighborhoods (in the ghetto) and to dress in a fashion that rendered them recognizable as Jews on sight. Since the church forbade Christians from loaning money for interest, the Jews were able to seize control of loan-sharking and usury, things they had long since mastered anyway. They became a significant economic power; but their ruthless, insatiable greed made them so detestable that they were driven out of many German cities during the Middle Ages. But before long, their financial power secured for them access and influence in the royal courts. The court Jews served the princes as weapons suppliers and war-loot launderers, moneylenders, and mint masters; many a state became heavily indebted to the Jews. The princes even went so far as to bestow the rank of nobility on their court Jews. Rothschild took advantage of the battle [of Waterloo] fought at la Belle-Alliance to orchestrate a clever stock market maneuver and thus managed to amass a sizable fortune, and this marked the beginning of Jewish dominance on the international market.

Note

1. The festival, held from 27 to 30 May 1838 near Neustadt an der Weinstrasse, was the first popular expression of German national identity. It had wide-ranging representation from across the classes and regions of the various German states, as well as from France and from occupied Poland.—Eds.

105

GERHARD KÖLLING AND EUGEN LÖFFLER

Math Lessons

First published in *Mathematisches Unterrichtswerk für höhere Lehranstalten,* Third- to Fifth-Grade Edition, (Leipzig: Teubner, 1942), 2:131.

1. A convoy of military vehicles traveling at a speed of 85 km/h departs from a location 6 km farther back on the same street 24 minutes on the heels of an infantry battalion marching at a speed of 5 km/h.
   (a) At which distance from its point of origin will the battalion be passed by the convoy?
   (b) How long will the battalion have been on the march?
2. A tank division leaves its headquarters at 6:00 in the morning traveling at a speed of 45 km/h. At the same time, 22 km from the same location, on the same street, a motorcycle infantry unit departs at a speed of 65 km/h.
   (a) How far will the motorcycle unit have to travel before it passes the tank division?
   (b) At what time will this occur?

106

OTTO STECHE, ERICH STENGEL, AND MAXIM WAGNER

School Subject: Biology

First published in *Lehrbuch der Biologie für Oberschulen und Gymnasien,* Fifth-Grade Edition (Leipzig: Quelle Und Meyer, 1942), 3:32.

The psychological qualities of the Jewish soul. The features of Near East Asian and Oriental races that are so repulsive to us as Germans have increased substantially among the Jewish population. This is the result of miscegenation, on the one hand, but on the other hand, the result of the fact that the Jew has incorporated stringent laws for breeding and natural selection as components of his religion. These vainglorious people, who call themselves the "chosen ones," are audacious enough to openly admit to their hatred of all things non-Jewish and their religious intolerance. That's why the Jew is the "world public enemy" and why he is pitted against National Socialist Germany in particular, because National Socialist Germany is what called to life the potent racial forces of the Nordic peoples so that they became manifest in their successful achievements. The Jews' antagonistic relationship with all other peoples will never change. The history of the Jews demonstrates that they serve no purpose in the building of a nation, for they are incapable of voluntarily subordinating themselves as individuals to the interests of the whole. Their most potent weapon is their cold, soberly calculating intellect. This is what turns them into clever traders and merchants who have mastered the fine art of availing themselves of every auspicious opportunity with absolutely no regard

FIGURE 10. Hitler Youth waving from the windows of a passing train. Photograph no. 09683, United States Holocaust Memorial Museum Photo Archives, Washington, D.C.

or consideration for their fellow humans or human decency; because according to their laws, any means necessary may be employed in dealings with non-Jews. This is how they were able to exploit the works of others to amass great wealth and power, even though they are completely devoid of any capacity for creative achievement of their own. The spirit of their thought is critical, corrupt, and corrosive, never constructive. The heroic ideal has never found a place in the ranks of Jews. There is scarcely a blatantly heroic deed to be found in Old Testament tales of Jewish history—but there is plenty of murder, treachery, cowardly betrayal, and boundless cruelty. So it is no wonder that the Jews have always been the number one criminals in all times and amongst all peoples.

107

Law Concerning the Hitler Youth

Announced on 1 December 1936 as the "Gesetz über die Hitlerjugend." First published in *Reichsgesetzblatt* (Berlin: Reichsverlagsamt, 1936), 1:993. Office of U.S. Chief of Counsel for the Prosecution of Axis Criminality, *Nazi Conspiracy and Aggression* (Washington, D.C.: U.S. Government Printing Office, 1946), 3:972, 973.

The future of the German *Volk* is dependent on its youth. All of Germany's youth must therefore be prepared for fulfilling their future obligations. The Reich government has thus enacted the following law, which is hereby promulgated.

Article 1

All of the German youth within the territory of the Reich shall be members of the Hitler Youth.

Article 2

All of the German youth shall be subject to education not only through family and school but also to physical, mental, and moral training to serve the *Volk* and the *Volk* community in the spirit of National Socialism through the Hitler Youth.

Article 3

The task of education of the German youth in the Hitler Youth is assigned to the NSDAP youth leader of the Reich, who thus becomes the youth leader of the German Reich [*Reichsjugendführer*]. He assumes the rank of a higher Reich authority, seated in Berlin and directly subordinate to the Führer and Reich chancellor.

Article 4

All of the administrative ordinances and legislative decrees required for the implementation and amplification of this law shall be issued by the Führer and Reich chancellor.

108

SOPADE

Reports on German Youth

First published in *Deutschland-Berichte der Sozialdemokratischen Partei Deutschlands, 1938 (Sopade)* (Frankfurt am Main: Verlag Petra Nettelbeck, 1980), 5:1390.

It is easier to influence the opinions and sentiments of youth than it is of adults. This fact has made it easier for the regime to win over the youth in the first few years following the collapse. It seems as though the same thing is now making it difficult for the regime to keep the youth in its clutches. The sentiments of youth are by nature influenced by popular opinion within the community overall, and whatever can be reported from the perspective of youth is likely to reflect the same measure and nature of discontent and disenchantment also found in reports from the general populace. But this is further complicated by the fact that the youth have been particularly disappointed by the current regime. They were made big promises, and only a very few of them have been fulfilled. The greater majority of youth now finds that the most lucrative posts in public administration and in the party apparatus are being taken by comrades who were lucky enough to have been a few years older than they were. The grim prospects for these youth are compounded by increased demands placed on them in every sector of life. In the long run, young people are starting to feel particularly burdened by the lack of freedom and the mindless drills practiced by National Socialist organizations. So it is no wonder that the signs of fatigue would be particularly prominent in their ranks. The following reports can be explained against this backdrop: [. . .]

Fourth Report: The youth are becoming a great cause for consternation amongst the governing party officials. Male and female alike, young people are attempting to avoid the year of rural civil service by any means necessary. In May 1938, in the greater metropolitan area of Berlin, 918 young men and 268 young women were sought after they had secretly run away from home in an attempt to avoid the mandatory year of service. Police paddy wagons in the areas of Grunewald, Tegel Forest, and Wannsee have been known to round up youth by the wagonload, some of them from Berlin, others from the surrounding province. There is a certain sector of youth that seeks a romantic life. Bundles of trashy literature have been found squirreled away in nooks and crannies. More often than before, apprentices are beginning not to come home and instead simply fritter away their days in the hustle and bustle of the city.

109

Song of the Hitler Youth
Devotion to the Fatherland

First published as Hans Baumann, "Und haben wir die Treue," in *Unser Liederbuch: Lieder der Hitler-Jugend,* edited by Der Reichsjugendbewegung (Munich: Verlag Franz Eher Nachfolger GmbH, 1939), 66.

Devotion to the fatherland, this we hold dear,
Devotion will suffice, we have no one to fear,
We have no one to fear!

Our faith shall not be tainted, our foes shall not preside,
Our faith shall not be trampled by death's relentless stride,
By death's relentless stride.

Our devotion comes to life in you and me, in all of thee, by night and by day,
And wherever we may perish, the seeds of faith are sown in the clay,
Are sown in the clay.

Devotion, this we hold dear
Devotion will suffice, we have no one to fear
We have no one to fear!

110

BALDUR VON SCHIRACH

The National Socialist Youth Movement

First published as "Die nationalsozialistische Jugendbewegung," in *Deutschland erwacht: Werden, Kampf, und Sieg der NSDAP,* edited by Wilfrid Bade (Altona Bahrenfeld: Cigaretten Bilderdienst, 1933), 58–64.

How many battles had to be fought out before politics hit home with individual families, driving rifts between father and son, brother and sister, mother and her sons and daughters, detonating entire families like bombs, leaving them shell-shocked and shattered?

How many a young man has been cast from his home and his homeland for pledging allegiance to Adolf Hitler because his father was a Communist, or a reactionary, perhaps a Marxist, or a democrat, or a member of the Center Party?

How many have not been beaten and badgered, how many have had to withstand the daily barrage of threats and mother's tears, how many have not come home to be punished and beaten for having been at a *Heimabend* meeting, how many came home to doors slammed in their faces when they returned from an outing simply because at these *Heimabend* meetings and these outings the banner with the swastika was hoisted high above these events? Who can even begin to estimate the implications of having to sit in a classroom together with the browbeaten fellow students of Communist parents, ruled by the command of a Marxist teacher, to be vilified, spat at, beaten, persecuted, and pursued and still to remain steadfast and true to Hitler, to suffer any injury, to risk it all, rather than to lose faith in the Führer? Can anyone so much as begin to fathom the serene heroic valor in these young men's struggles as they fight in solitary, each man for himself, on a daily, an hourly basis, on a different battlefield—one that is no less strenuous than the front?

And yet, what ultimately emerged triumphant over all else was the defiance, the tenacity, the love, the level of devotion unique to the sanctity of youth.

When the flag fluttered before them, when the songs resounded through the air, then everything was fine, all the tears and sorrows thrown to the wind.

That's when the only thing left was the burning heart's desire: to march for Germany, for Hitler!

Let the flags flutter far and wide,
We want to join this great storm tide,
Tried and true in the old peasant's way.

Whatever man fails to join this race,
Can hold his breath till he's blue in the face,
But we will meet again on Judgment Day.

And with that, victory is won, and the youth are on the march, on the march, on the march; they skirt the edges of the streets and squares, jubilantly cheering the Führer who has liberated them and thanked them for their struggle.

There they are—Germany's youth, gathered at the Lustgarten to celebrate the first of May, the day that commemorates an end to the class struggle; the day that transformed a day of internationalism, treachery, deception, and deceit into a German day; a day for celebrating national productivity and work; a day that swept away class differences and class conceits to fulfill the deepest yearnings of the German youth . . . a German youth that gathers to solemnly celebrate mutual allegiance, from one boy to another, one young man to another, to the grand old men, the general commanding forces in battle on the fields where their fathers fought and the beloved Führer, the corporal in the Great War, forever and ever, for now and for eternity—and the field marshal's words graze over their blond heads—at once solemn and happy with anticipation. Their arms stretch upward—their faces grow taut, the flags are hoisted high and flutter in the fresh air of spring: Hail to the Führer! Hail to Germany!

Your youth will not forsake you.
Führer, you can place your trust in us!

A great, exquisite educational feat has been accomplished with these youth, a feat they have themselves brought to fruition. Camaraderie, loyalty, simplicity, pride, patriotism, propriety, willingness to serve, obligation, discipline, self-sufficiency, diligence, strength, reliability, and faith: all these things they have learned, these young men in the brown shirts.

Here they have been given a glimpse of the future—but they have also been trained to become the future.

Just as it has done for all time, the nation has trained its young men for battle. And in the coming years these young men will put that training to good use. Driven and directed by the notion of patriotism and loyalty, they will be all the more earnest, all the more intense in their struggle to eliminate and overcome even the contradictions between generations in their mutual service to the *Volk* and the Reich, in their mutual commitment to the swastika.

When we march side by side
Singing the songs of old
We can feel it in our souls
We must bring the changing times!

111

REIMUND SCHNABEL

Leadership Training Program of the Hitler Youth

First published as *Das Führerschulungswerk der Hitler-Jugend* (Berlin: Junker und Dünnhaupt, 1938), 5.

The leadership training project of the Hitler Youth consists of voluntary committees made up of leaders of the Hitler Youth and the German Boys Club as well as leaders of the League of German Girls and the German Girls Club.[1]

In the larger locations of the Reich, local leaders of the Hitler Youth form committees consisting of an average of twenty male and female leaders, ever contingent on available resources and exigencies of each respective locale. Party comrades, Hitler Youth leaders, scientists, and scholars who have been called as specialists for certain subjects based on their previous experience and rank are obliged to preside over these committees. [. . .] As is the case with the general training offered by the Hitler Youth, the primary aim of the Leadership Training Program is not to present future leaders with facts and knowledge. Far more, the aim is to encourage individual thought and independent work. Leaders are to become politically active and should learn to place the individual events of any given day into a larger political framework. [. . .]

The goal of these committees, then, is to expand the horizons of each of these future leaders, to provide them with an overview that encompasses the bigger picture, and to develop in them the capacity for evaluating and classifying everyday experiences and events around them on the basis of a National Socialist worldview.

Each of these committees will remain in active service throughout the winter semester—from 1 October to 31 March. Participants meet on a weekly or biweekly basis. [. . .]

By the end of the first semester in winter 1937–38, the Leadership Training Program had been introduced with convincing results. Originally, the plan initiated by the directors of the Reich Youth Education Leadership [Reichsjugendführung] was scheduled to include only designated urban sites, but committees were also established with a great measure of success in smaller towns, where participants often had to cover long distances by bus or bicycle to reach the site. Throughout the Reich, twelve thousand leaders, male and female, voluntarily participated in five hundred committees in this first Leadership Training Program, in spite of the fact that, at this time, substantial areas were completely barred from participation as the result of the hoof-and-mouth disease outbreak. But following the successes of this first Leadership Training Program, this initiative promises to expand and become increasingly popular. Today it has become a permanent feature of the training offered to the future leaders among Germany's young men and women.

The subjects to be addressed by each committee in the Leadership Training Program are listed here. Each subject is outlined briefly in the effort to provide an overview of what subjects merit consideration. A succinct list of educational topics has been provided for use by committee chairs and participants. [. . .]

Racial Politics and Demographics
    The Primary Task of the National Socialist State Is the Preservation of the Species
Strengthening Germany [. . .]
    The German *Volk* Fights for Its Daily Bread, Its Jobs, and Its Future
    Volk, Movement, and State in the Endeavor to Strengthen the Third Reich
The Work of the Hitler Youth Leader [. . .]
    Youth in the Legal Sector
    The Hitler Youth Leader in Action

Prehistory and History[. . .]
The Ancient Germans—Barbarians or Bearers of Culture?
What Our Homeland Can Tell Us about the Coming of the Reich
The East: Destined to Be German
German Sacrifices on Behalf of Unity in the Reich
The *Volk* Takes a Stand against Rome
The Career Soldier: Germany's Eternal Strength
Two Thousand Years of German Sentry Duty against Asia
International Politics [. . .]
World Politics Faces New Challenges
Moscow Threatens Peace in Europe
National Socialist Foreign Policy and the Great Powers of Europe
Fourteen Nations Border the Reich
Power Plays in the Danube Region
Struggle for Control of the World's Natural Resources
Ways and Means of National Socialist Foreign Policy
Völker Fight for Living Space
Is England Still a World Power?
The Mediterranean: A Space Designated by Destiny
The Jewish Question as a Problem of World Politics
The World in Weapons
Japan's Struggle for World Recognition

Note

1. These youth clubs were founded in 1926. The Hitler Youth (Hitler Jugend) was for boys aged fourteen to eighteen, and the League of German Girls (Bund Deutscher Mädel) for girls aged ten to eighteen. The German Boys Club (Deutsches Jungvolk) and the German Girls Club (Jungmädelbund) were for children between ten and fourteen.—Eds.

112

ANONYMOUS

A Hitler Youth Scout Is Loyal and True!

First published as "Pimpfe sind Treu," in *Sommerlager und Heimabendmaterial für die Schulungs- und Kulturarbeit* (Berlin: Reichsjugendführung der NSDAP, Summer 1941), 24–26.

> We must not only be true to the fatherland, we must also be true to ourselves.
>
> —*Carl von Clausewitz*

"We pledge allegiance to Adolf Hitler." This statement is not to be taken lightly; it is one we must live with the very fiber of our young hearts, souls, and minds—with our very being. Now and then we must take a few moments to reflect solemnly on the degree of confidence the Führer has vested in us simply by allowing us to pledge allegiance to him and his flag. The very act is one of devoting oneself, body and soul, to him and to our German *Volk*. Our commitment must be unconditional, and we must be prepared to serve without asking about advantages and disadvantages. And our loyalty is something we can demonstrate in many small ways in our daily lives. When a Hitler Youth scout perseveres, even when the going gets rough, when he has a task to fulfill, he grits his teeth and doesn't give up; when he remains true to his task, he demonstrates that he has properly understood the meaning of the sword oath [*Schwertwort*].

In the following story, you will learn about a Hitler Youth scout named Kalle, who stayed loyal to his comrades even when it put him in danger. You can see from it that genuine camaraderie is based on loyalty. The real scout shows his loyalty by staying true to his brother through thick and thin.

Late one Sunday afternoon, Hitler Youth Scout Troop 6 was returning to the campsite, in a rather tired and sluggish march. It was an oppressively hot day. The sun hadn't scorched the earth with a heat this hot in ages. Sweat was trickling down the boys' faces.

The blistering heat had hung over them for a week already. The grass on the meadows was turning yellow, and many a leaf drooped its drowsy crown. The sun flickered in a harsh glare on the sandy dirt roads, and the air trembled in the heat.

The boys were barely moving, shuffling along more than they were actually marching. They choked the songs they tried to strike up and sing before they got through the first few measures. There wasn't much talk—each scout was lost in his own thoughts—and they were all looking forward to a cool dip in Lake Selpiner.

But at various points along the way, they stopped suddenly for a moment. What was that? A siren wailing on Sunday, the day of rest? And was that the chiming of church bells from the village steeple? But the boys paid no mind to it; they simply registered it in their minds and trudged on in the heat.

Finally, they reached their campsite.

But wait a minute! Where the heck is Hanne?

"Hanne! Hanne!" He was supposed to be here doing guard duty.

Uli hollered loudly.

Where the heck is he? He was supposed to be here guarding the tent, wasn't he? He can't just pack up and leave like that without so much as a word.

"Hanne!"

No one answered.

The surface of Forest Lake lay shimmering and still before them. But lo and behold—there, near the shoreline, was a strange bundle floating in the water.

"Dang! Where the heck can he be?" And that was a question that immediately jolted all of the boys' from their fatigue.

But then one of the scouts suddenly held up a slip of paper in his hand that he'd found at the entrance to the tent. Hastily scratched out in sloppy letters was a note that read,

"Lutziner Forest on fire! Went to help put out! Hanne."

What on earth?!

The Lutziner Forest is on fire?

That's why the sirens went off. That's why the bells were chiming. That's what that strange smell was that kept getting stronger the farther they went into the forest.

"Help put it out," Uli said in a flash.—But.—Lutziner Forest, where is Lutziner Forest?

Get out the map. Quick, hurry up!

Aha! There it is! Uli measured the distance. The scale was 1:25,000. Six centimeters. That makes a kilometer and a half.

Uli sniffed the air one more time, stood there thinking for a moment, then in a split-second decision started giving orders: "Come on, let's go! We've got to help! The forest is on fire! We've got to get to the Lutziner Forest right now! About face! On the double! March! March!"

The boys took off, and their feet fell in dull thuds on the flat, pine-covered forest floor: Left, two, three, four. Left, two, three, four.

"Stick it out! Stick it out! Now, show us you've got the endurance!"

Clip-clop, clip-clop, clip-clop!

They were streaming in sweat.

And leading the pack: Kalle. The forest was on fire, Hanne had gone to help put it out, his best friend was in danger! Faster, faster. Kalle wanted to help, too, wanted to be there!

Finally, they reached the main road.

A fire engine from the city overtook them. Beep-beep! Ding-dong, ding-dong!

It looked as though they might run out of breath. But they kept going: endurance! The forest—their forest, the playground for their games, the place that was home to their campsite—was on fire, and they had to help put it out.

The smell of fire grew stronger by the meter. Suddenly it appeared: a billowing cloud of smoke!

They'd finally reached the Lutziner Forest.

Now, one last stretch. One last sprint.

The din of crackling and cracking limbs announced its approach.

Finally, there it was, the point of origin.

The fire lashed viciously and loudly at the majestic slender trunks of the trees. The blazing trees threw off a hellish heat.

At this point, the blaze was still confined to the ground, the ground cover was scorched raven black, but the raging flames hadn't yet engulfed the treetops. All you could see were the glowing red-yellow drops of sap seeping from the opposite end of the tree trunks with a hiss.

Help was sorely needed here. A few, maybe twenty or thirty men from the local volunteer fire department and a couple of Sunday strollers who happened to come along, were doing their best to put up a fight, hoisting pickax and spade against the flames. Uli reported his men to the captain of the fire brigade.

"We're here to help. What do you want us to do?"

The old captain gave them brief instructions.

And the boys from Hitler Youth Scout Troop 6 were off to fetch big spruce branches from the timber forest. Before long, they were busy threshing, thrashing, and pounding at the voracious flames. Tirelessly, they persisted in their fierce battle against the blaze.

If they didn't nip this fire in the bud now, it would soon spread to the treetops, and the fire's head would get bigger and bigger and would ravish the forest like raging floodwaters.

Thank God there was only a light breeze blowing, because the wind is always the blaze's best ally.

The boys, covered from head to toe in sweat from heat and exhaustion and sometimes on the verge of collapse, dug in and worked the site. Flaming sparks swirled around them, and before long, they were covered in black soot and ash. But that was nothing. They were fighting here with a bitter vengeance against a gargantuan opponent. And they absolutely had to conquer it!

A column of Labor Service men had since arrived. They immediately began digging deep trenches in the earth and building a wall to act as a dam to guard against the heat emitted by the flames. Some additional pine trees were felled in order to increase the distance.

Kalle was swinging his spruce branch and working right there alongside the rest of these men and boys who'd taken up the embittered battle against the treacherous flames.

Where on earth could Hanne be? The question kept going through his mind. He paused for a moment to survey the ranks of men and boys, but Hanne was nowhere to be seen.

Kalle started getting anxious.

Once he'd put out the last remnant of the voracious flames in the area that he'd been assigned, he ran over to Uli, who was covered from head to toe with filthy ash and soot, shoveling like an ox. He asked for permission to go look for Hanne.

Then he took off running along the head of the fire.

There was no sign of Hanne anywhere.

More and more people arrived to help. A technical emergency crew arrived, armed with axes, hatchets, hoes, shovels, and saws.

Kalle penetrated ever deeper into the woods, boldly thrashing with his spruce branch at the ravishing tongues of flame in his path.

He wanted to call for Hanne, but his throat was so parched from the indescribable heat that all he could do was utter a few muted syllables. His lips were cracked, his face burned, and he could feel an occasional singeing in his hair. His hands, bulging with blisters, ached. But Kalle suppressed any sense of pain. He worked his way forward, tireless, tenacious, battling the insatiable flames. But where, oh where, was his comrade Hanne?

"Hanne, Hanne, where are you?" he croaked with his hoarse throat.

Suddenly, there!

Who is that staggering out from the underbrush, over there to the left?

Raven black, barely dragging himself along, his clothing tattered and burned?

Isn't that Hanne?

Boom! He stumbled one more time, then fell to the ground! What's wrong with him? It looks like he really can't go on.

Kalle charged through the flames. He grabbed Hanne and, half-carrying him, half-dragging him along the ground, hauled him out of the danger zone. Hanne's clothes were on fire, and Kalle had to quickly throw himself to the ground to extinguish the flames.

He ripped Hanne's clothes off his body.

But what was Hanne carrying in his arms?

"Hanne, Hanne, answer me, will you? What you got there?"

Despite the burns all over his body, Hanne struggled, and I mean struggled, to crack a smile, and at the same time—in a singular stroke of tenderness—petted the soft brown-and-white-specked fur.

"Kalle," he whispered, his voice reduced to a faint gasp, "I just had to rescue this little fawn. You're such an animal lover yourself—let's take care of it together."

And Kalle thought to himself, "Hanne, you're such a great guy. From now on, I'll go through the fires of hell for you any time!"

113

OBERBANNFÜHRER STEPHAN

The League of German Girls Organization in the Hitler Youth

First published as "Die Organisation des Bundes Deutscher Mädel in der Hitler-Jugend," in *1935: Wir schaffen, Jahrbuch des BDM,* edited by Hilde Munske (Munich: Zentralverlag der NSDAP, 1935), 11.

The totalizing approach of the Hitler Youth (HJ) certainly could not and may not ever fail to include German girls in its embrace. So today, in addition to the HJ's organization for boys and the German Boys Club, we are proud to host the largest girls' movement in the world, the League of German Girls (BDM) in the Hitler Youth and the HJ German Girls Club.

Long before our seizure of power, a small number of girls had already made their way into the ranks and had formed the League of German Girls. In the struggle to gain power,

FIGURE 11. Members of the League of German Girls chatting with SS men affiliated with the Lebensborn (Fountain of Life) organization. Photograph no. 89435, United States Holocaust Memorial Museum Photo Archives, Washington, D.C. Courtesy of Bildarchiv Preussischer Kulturbesitz.

the German girls have endured with the same degree of sacrifice, effort, and persecution as the boys in the Hitler Youth have uncompromisingly championed the cause of National Socialism, often in defiance of their parents, their schools, and their teachers.

The League of German Girls, then, grew as a natural offshoot of the organization, just like all the other divisions—it is not something that was created and established by the HJ leadership. It is for this reason that the organization, just like the HJ and the German Boys Club, is structured from the bottom up and is equal to the exigencies any struggle may present to it. In the beginning, the administration of the BDM fell under the auspices of smaller units of the HJ, but over time, it became an independent organization with its own administrative structure.

Today, we have four core groups of National Socialist youth: the Hitler Youth, the German Boys Club, the League of German Girls, and the German Girls Club, which was first formed after the seizure of power. All of these units are run by the central Reich Youth Education Leadership and together comprise the Hitler Youth. [. . .]

There are a total of two million girls enrolled in the BDM and the German Girls Club. A corps of division leaders numbering 125,000 girls has been charged with performing bigger tasks and with leading the girls; they receive training at three Reich Leadership Training schools and at thirty-five Regional Training schools, where they receive uniform instruction in leadership.

With the formal organization of the BDM and German Girls Club, the girls also received new uniforms. The brown dress was discarded and replaced by a more modern outfit: a white blouse, blue skirt, and black neckerchief. A special blouse was designed for outings and campouts. The brown climber's vest is also part of the BDM uniform.

And so it is that today, the National Socialist youth also has a strictly disciplined, but not masculinized, organization for girls. Surely there is many an error yet to be overcome and much that will still need to be ironed out within the organization, but, in light of the fact that there is not a single precedent in the past for a girls' organization of the size and significance of the League of German Girls, we must acknowledge the incredible contribution the National Socialist youth has made in organizing the League of German Girls and the German Girls Club within the Hitler Youth.

114

ERNA BOHLMANN

The Position of the Ancient Germanic Woman

First published as "Die Stellung der germanischen Frau," in *Wille und Macht* 2, no. 20 (1934): 17–23.

> Indeed, they even believe that a certain holiness and power of prophecy resides in women, nor do the Germans scorn their council or ignore their answers. . . . They also formerly revered Albruna and many others, but not with pandering flattery, nor as if making them goddesses.
>
> —*Tacitus,* Germania

As the first generation of German girls ever to have been organized into a league that is part of a concrete educational and training program, we are charged with particularly important tasks because we have virtually no models to draw on for direction. We are thus left to our own devices: the ideal for German girls and German women that we seek to establish is one we will have to shape based on our knowledge of our own inner nature and the exigencies of our times.

In our search for this ideal, we are confronted with the astonishing and enormous fact that *the ancient Germanic woman in particular* has, to a very large extent, *clearly and largely embodied precisely those features that are innately characteristic of our race.*

But this is not the only reason we focus on the position and perspective of women in our ancient Germanic prehistory, rather, more importantly, because *the position of women in any culture is generally taken as a measure of the people's level of development.* If we apply this measure to our own history, German prehistory emerges with a clarity and magnitude that has yet to be seen since as a new ideal to guide us. [. . .]

The first thing we need to know as we delve deeper into the *life of the Nordic woman* is what Dr. Bernhard Kummer has written:

> The pagan woman was revered and sheltered by unwritten laws. She was better endowed with power, in spirit, and in sanctity than man. Even as a housewife, she was much closer to the center of moral life, and, accordingly, she was seen as "heaven's mediator," as Tannhäuser describes Elisabeth in Wagner's opera. This explains women being given the role to make mead. It explains her gift of prophecy, her inviolability, her active participation in blood revenge, her drive to action [. . .].
>
> We can see that women here are *equal to men* in every regard: the way they ride to council meetings, the way they manage their own business affairs with farm products,

the way they disburse land holdings to freedmen, the way they dissolve animosities and disseminate peace. Even Iceland's highest public office, the *Gode,* or Chieftain, is open to them. At the same time, they do also have their own specific domain. But their role as housewives is parallel to man's role as breadwinner and demands—as the mistress of any household even today can tell you—just as much intelligence as this.

Seems to me woman could not hope to assume a higher position than this. [. . .] Much in the same way that the woman was respected and stood on equal footing as an independent mate to man, so too were *girls* raised to participate as equals in the same athletic training as their brothers. Caesar is astonished to report the way that boys and girls swim together in the nude and simply cannot comprehend the way the clear, unadulterated Nordic air made it possible before the sultry and sensuous notion of romantic love blew in from the south and destroyed it. There was something of a girls' community even in the Dark Ages. It existed in the form of shared working, spinning, and weaving rooms.

We can only view the broad range of activities these women and girls engaged in during those times with amazement. The home offered them infinitely more tasks to complete than it does today: handiwork and household repairs, artistic work, pottery, weaving, the economic management of the entire farm, and, of course, the athletic activity that was taken as a given for girls in this period [. . .].

The goal of the women's movement cannot offer us any guidance unless we also see a decidedly German work ethic in this drive to engage in meaningful activity that provided the impetus for talented women to excel as industrialization robbed them of the last of their creative outlets for labor in skilled trade. But this work ethic, influenced by the liberalist spirit of the times, soon became just a problematic effort to attain equality with men. The blessings of women's suffrage and the international women's movement were as powerless in satisfying our needs as they were problematic to us as a burden. We wholly support the right of women and girls to employment, especially when the challenges of labor respect our unique, complementary nature, but above all, we wholly support woman's role as housewife and mother—and our understanding of this role is as extensive and as significant as is imaginable, and we think this is how this role must be seen, if the family is ever to truly become the central unit of the National Socialist state. Because any race of *Volk* that hopes to find its way back to itself must also define woman's role in accordance with the laws of its own race. And as a *Volk* surrounded on all sides [*Volk der Mitte*] that is always subject to the most strenuous demands, as the war has demonstrated to us in so many ways, we cannot afford to fail in our attempt to forge a concept of womanhood that is heroic and recognizes all of women's innate strengths and allows her to have the same impact as a complement to man and his accomplishments, according to the same supreme laws of honor and of the national community of *Volk*.

115

GÜNTER KAUFMANN

Faith and Beauty

First published as "Glaube und Schönheit," in *Wille und Macht* 6, no. 3 (February 1938): 1.

"The enthusiastic female athletic type, when she surrounds herself with feminine charm, with a carefully cultivated sense of women's vanity combined with the attendant degree of uniquely feminine pride and posture—this represents an expression of what we conceive of as the ideal portrait of women, love, and propriety"—that is what we wrote on this subject in our Christmas issue. But since then, we have come closer to realizing that ideal on a very pragmatic level *as a result of Baldur von Schirach's successful efforts to lend concrete manifestation to the matters that have concerned him in the past few years as a conscientious educator.* As we now know, the ban on campouts for girls was issued in 1937, and the institution of all-girl youth hostels merely marked the beginning of a cataclysmic overhaul in the way the generation of girls ages seventeen to twenty-one are educated. The things that proved successful for educating young teenage girls could not in the long run also be applied to girls seventeen and older. Just as the education of boys is tailored to suit the characteristics and tendencies of their age group, so, too, shall the new BDM program Faith and Beauty introduce a new form of education for girls appropriate to their age group. The camping trips and campsites cannot accommodate the goals that have been set by the new BDM program for girls in this age group: Faith and Beauty. *What we are seeking to avoid is any sort of discrepancy between political service and the everyday lives of girls in the seventeen to twenty-one age group,* and the way we seek to avoid it is by making that service conform to the natural changes the girls experience as they pass into womanhood. Once a pattern of discipline and order has been instilled in the girls between the ages of ten and sixteen in the BDM service, we can concentrate on their subsequent personality development, so that a genuine dynamism and lust for life can develop in them, so that they develop enthusiasm for the value of all things beautiful, an awareness of what it is that truly enriches and brings meaning to our lives, and an inkling of what it means to be guided by the higher power of a vocation or calling in the individual. And inasmuch as a Reich youth leader is endowed with this knowledge of education, he will see his primary task where it grips the human being most profoundly, where it is most deeply rooted in the individual: at the place where it grows naturally from the development of a sense of belonging and thus builds character and shapes perspectives on life, faith, and sensibilities for what is beautiful.

People in Germany have become more beautiful now that they have liberated themselves from the inferior status assigned to the body by the church and, with an expressed preference for the Greek ideal standard of beauty, the *Volk* has enthusiastically begun participating in more sports activities. Taking pleasure in human beauty must emanate from feminine vanity and must be accompanied by a rigorous culture of physical hygiene and a certain elegance. But participating in athletics and the desire to maintain a strong and well-trained body are part and parcel of the well-groomed appearance. In this way, it is impossible for any of our girls to develop into helpless female weaklings or into sloppy but physically fit athletic types. *In the context of our new educational institutions, dance and athletic games, socializing, and participation in cultural life are of paramount importance,* and they are what shape the ideal type of young German women. We know that the pretty girls will be particularly enthusiastic about signing up for this program. Inasmuch as these girls have thus far remained unassociated with the BDM, inasmuch as their personal development in life was not compatible with the demands of political service in the BDM, this new emphasis on explicitly feminine ideals, on cultivating them and highlighting them, is sure to bring those girls who have been going their own way back into the community. For many of them, this will be the first place they are able to experience *the ideal standard of feminine beauty in its depths and inner core*—here, where it becomes one with faith in the prophetic mission of the *Volk* and with the task of each individual.

Faith and beauty! What more could it be if not a profession of belief in the Eternal and at the same time an affirmation of His world? What more could it be if not the commitment to an idea and service to that idea in the form of a genuine lust for life? This is the way great works come into the world, transported by the healthy forces in life. Its triumphant flags will unfurl and hurl it beyond the horizon of tension and ideology, beyond self-righteousness and philistinism, beyond abstractions and dogma.

116

Collecting Women's Hair

Reich Directive 36/K

First published as *Reichsbefehl* 36/K, "Sammlung von Frauenhaar" 12 April 1940.

Pursuant to Reich Directive 18/III of 13 May 1938, we hereby direct attention to the ordinance regarding the collection of women's hair. This collection shall forthwith be intensified in the following municipalities: Berlin, Hamburg, Leipzig, Breslau, Dresden, Zwickau, Plauen, Braunschweig, Dessau, Glogau, Halle, Hanover, Frankfurt/Main, Freistadt, Görlitz, Hirschberg, Leignitz.

Units deployed in these municipalities should be explicitly reminded of the importance of completing this task.

Every girl is expected to collect the hair in her own household and deliver it to a hairdresser. The hairdressers have been instructed in what to do with it. (The hair will be used to manufacture felt fabric.)

At present, this renewal of the order to collect hair is to be distributed only to those units deployed in the municipalities listed because, according to statements issued by the office handling the collection and recycling of materials in the Reich Commissary, the organizational infrastructure for the collection of women's hair is not in place at this time.

The *Obergaue* affected by this are to print this ordinance in the *Obergau* directive.[1]

Note

1. The *Obergau,* or upper region, was a grouping of five districts of the League of German Girls, which equaled approximately twenty *Untergaue.* Each *Obergau* had approximately seventy thousand members.—Eds.

117

JUTTA RÜDIGER

The "Eastern Deployment" of the BDM

First published as "'Osteinsatz' des BDM," in *Das junge Deutschland,* 36 (1942), 3.

The Girls' Eastern Mission

Once Germany's eastern territory had been liberated and the Reich districts of Wartheland and Danzig-West Prussia were established, a very large and wonderful territory was opened up for the work of the German girls. [. . .] Their task was to contribute to the military conflict by leading a successful campaign in the hearts and minds of the *Volk*. [. . .]

In the coming year, in accordance with the annual theme declared by the Reich youth leader, the "eastern deployment" that has since become the most popular form of service for our girls is to be expanded. [. . .] We are calling all girls who are over fifteen years of age who have not yet fulfilled their obligatory year of service to complete this service amongst the German peasants in the east. They will live in camps supervised by BDM unit leaders. What is decisive is that professions for women are created in the east that will provide an attractive calling for young women there. These professions are that of farmer's wife and educator. Directors of the Rural Civil Service Program [*Landdienst*] of the Hitler Youth are beginning to prepare the girls for settling in to live with the *Wehrbauer* [soldiers designated as colonizers in the east] in the east in the near future. These young women and girls who act as troop leaders are preparing to become the future teachers, school assistants, kindergarten assistants, and kindergarten teachers. The biggest task of our girls, which will go far beyond wartime activity, is simply to fill those eastern territories with the pulse of German life that the Führer has wrenched back into our possession by force.

118

KRISTEL PAUN

Wartime Fashion Show

First published as "Modeschau im Krieg, 1942," in *Wir Schaffen. Jahrbuch des BDM* (Munich: Verlag Franz Eher Nachfolger GmbH, 1942), 156.

Upcoming Fashion
Fashion Show in Zoppot

The BDM is sponsoring a fashion show!

In general, the event is being viewed with skepticism—people aren't exactly inclined to expect much from the BDM in this regard. People are turning out for this fashion show, just like they did for the last one, only because they don't want to miss it, because they want to be in the know and have something to talk about at the beach, in the cafés, and during the evenings at the casino.

The event kicks off with lighthearted strains of music: dressed in their white gym suits, the girls in the BDM project Faith and Beauty blithely weave through the rows of spectators until they reach the freestanding platform, where they stage a cheerful display of gymnastics, working with hoops, balls, and batons. They exude an aura of youthfulness and joy, health and natural radiance. The pennants flutter playfully from the masts on the bridge, the sand sparkles in the sun. [. . .] There is not a single spectator who can resist the gleeful atmosphere and the splendid display.

The first girl walks down the runway to the tune of Mozart music; featherlight in her step, she wheels around, takes a few steps back, and shows off the little jacket as she saunters gleefully back down the runway [. . .]; one splendid image follows the next.

When it was over, a BDM unit leader stated that the BDM, and in particular the BDM program Faith and Beauty, sees an obligation not to simply ignore various trends in fashion but rather to actively participate in designing fashions that are appropriate for our times and to thus allow the outer appearance to clearly reflect the inner workings of human beings. [. . .]

"I have many amends to make with regard to the BDM!" I overhear someone near me say.

That makes us really happy to hear: people are trying to understand us; even people who've been at odds with us are beginning to recognize our goals and tasks as valid.

10

Higher Education

Science, History, and Philosophy Revised

IN 1933, JEWISH SCHOLARS and political opponents of the Nazis suffered an unprecedented loss of positions and livelihood at Germany's universities. Of the 1,700 faculty members and 313 full professors who lost their jobs, 80 percent were removed on "racial" grounds. The rest were pacifists or had left-wing sympathies. The remaining members of the academic elite by and large uttered no word of protest when their Jewish and liberal colleagues were dismissed or when Jewish students were barred from admission to their universities.

The new regime had no coherent academic policy apart from a few slogans and did not appoint a minister of education until 1934. (The new minister, Bernhard Rust [1883–1945], was a schoolteacher who had been dismissed for sexual harassment.) A party stalwart since 1922, Rust's official title was Reich minister of science, education, and national culture. Though most student organizations were already in the hands of the Nazis by then, before 1933 there were few Nazi Party members among the professorate. The philosopher Ernst Krieck (1882–1947), who became rector of the University of Frankfurt am Main in May 1933, promoted a "renewal of the university" to produce the "new man," whom he imagined as "the spiritual soldier" of the Third Reich. But party ideologues frequently expressed frustration at their inability to penetrate the academic fortress—evidenced, for example, in Alfred Rosenberg's efforts to bypass the universities entirely and establish his own "higher schools" to inculcate the party elite with his version of the National Socialist worldview. Many in the party expressed contempt for the "desktop intellectuals," whose "wait-and-see" attitude was openly mocked by writers like E. Günther Gründel.

Contrary to expectations, the party did not often need to intervene in academic affairs because the universities submitted voluntarily. The handful of professors directly appointed because of party pressure, such as the philosophers Alfred Baeumler, named to a chair at the University of Berlin in 1933, and Krieck, at the University of Frankfurt am Main, stand out as exceptions. Of the distinguished academic figures who welcomed the regime, like Johannes Haller (history), Martin Heidegger (philosophy), and Carl Schmitt (jurisprudence), none had been members of the NSDAP before January 1933.

The vow of allegiance taken by German university teachers, organized and published in three languages by the Saxon branch of the Nationalsozialistische Dozentenbund (National Socialist League of University Assistants) in 1933, contained an "appeal to the intelligentsia of the world" and was accompanied by statements from distinguished representatives of German scholarship, among them Heidegger; Eugen Fischer, rector of the University of Berlin and director of the Kaiser Wilhelm Institute for Anthropology, Human Heredity, and Eugenics; and the art historian Wilhelm Pinder. Elaborately staged as a public act of voluntary support for the National Socialist revolution, the taking of the "vow" was supposed to be evidence not of politicized scholarship endangered by National Socialism but of an expressly guaranteed autonomy—indeed, ironically, a testament to the "freedom of scholarship."

Intellectual fealty to National Socialism required not so much ideological consistency as an ethos or a willingness to adhere to the precepts of the party's worldview, which was sufficiently vague and indistinct to embrace a variety of related perspectives. Determining the true evolution of the Nazification of the universities is difficult because of the fine line between "Nazi ideology" and the many modes of accommodation and participation adopted by the academic community. The 100 percent Nazi was a phantasm who actually exonerated the equally fictional majority of so-called unpolitical sympathizers who, as the term suggests, occasionally distanced themselves silently from one or another aspect of the regime.

What was important was not the coherence of the worldview per se but its role as a unifying principle and public affirmation of loyalty. Whether "race" or "*Volk*" was defined biologically, culturally, anthropologically, or philosophically mattered less, at least for a time, than public affirmation. Even in the natural sciences, where "Jewish physics" and "Jewish mathematics" were declared anathema, many areas of study were permitted to develop with little or no coercion by the regime. The noteworthy point is not that compulsory concepts were decided upon, but that such questions were discussed.

Direct interventions in these debates by political authorities—such as the Rosenberg Office, the Reich Education Ministry, or the Dozentenbund—were rare, leading to competition among academic elites over the restructuring of the disciplines by the professors, who relied on a lexicon of available concepts to ease the Nazification of their subjects.[1] The rectoral addresses delivered in 1933 reveal a deep reverence, in both tone and language, for the "revolution" of 1933, which many scholars asserted had rescued the humanities from the irrelevance and marginalization these disciplines had suffered for decades. Consequently, in the 1940s, younger professors, trained during the Nazi era and more likely to conform to its ideological precepts, were treated preferentially by the faculties.

The image of Nazism as an alien, outside power imposed on German universities was a convenient fiction adopted after 1945. In reality, save for a minority, little assistance was needed for "coordination" since the universities submitted voluntarily. While a number of scholars built careers in the party bureaucracies and organizations, most subscribed to vaguely *völkisch* or racial doctrines; many retained the illusion of intellectual independence, while far fewer refused participation. Prominent figures like Schmitt, Heidegger, and party ideologues like Krieck, Baeumler, and Gerhard Fricke saw an opportunity to influence academic politics and perhaps even have a say in party policy and in the broader discourse on politics and society. The precipitous decline in the status of figures like Heidegger, Schmitt, and Krieck, who had run-ins with party authorities in the mid-1930s, attests more to the dangers inherent in assuming too high a profile than to the risks of dissenting from the party line—as they later claimed.

The fate of German historians exemplifies how a highly venerated university discipline could become deeply entwined in a network of institutions and conceptions permeated with racial and anti-Semitic doctrines. After 1933, when German conservatives failed to offer a positive challenge to the despised Weimar Constitution and Republic, admirers of Bismarck and fierce opponents of Weimar liberalism saw Hitler as the solution. They regarded National Socialism as the only way to not only bridge the old differences but eliminate them.

At the other extreme was Kleophas Pleyer (1898–1942), author of the "Battle Song of the Nazi Party" and the ideological soldier of the newly minted Nazi historians. In contrast to the professional historians, Pleyer wanted to destroy the established academic culture of the German mandarins. To demonstrate the firmness of his National Socialist belief, he embarked on a historiography of "the deed" in his self-proclaimed "soldierly" style. To cleanse the new historical scholarship, he asserted, academic institutions needed to remove the rules of Jewish-influenced, placid, bourgeois erudition. Scholars were to raze disciplinary boundaries and create a total science of national character (*Volkstum*), whose task was to discover a common race and shared blood by conducting research on the simple rural population and the nation's industrial workers. This extended even to the citations of works by Jewish scholars. Influenced by the nineteenth-century "herald of Germanness," Wilhelm Heinrich Riehl (1823–97), historians of the early twentieth century, such as Karl Alexander von Müller (1882–1964), had embarked on a search for the simple, unadulterated life of farmers and peasants. Müller and his students initiated a branch of historical scholarship known as *Kulturraumforschung* (cultural geography) or *Landesgeschichte* (historical regional studies) that was to grow substantially during the 1920s. The success of this movement, which favored *Volkstumsgeschichte* (the history of people's traditions), provided academic legitimacy for the "battle over borders" during the war. Well established by the 1930s, academics in the field of regional studies distanced themselves from the history of states, heroes, and ideas. For these scholars of cultural geography, the goal was to historically determine the supposedly typical and authentic traits of the regionally diversified *Volk* to make them useful to the present. The politics of racial identity permeated even the writing of contemporary history, such as Johannes Haller's account of why Germany lost the world war.

Christoph Steding (1903–38) mapped out another direction of historiography during the Third Reich. His posthumously published *The Reich and the Sickness of European Culture* (1938) is a massive work of political invective against the Swiss, the Dutch, and the Scandinavians for "weakening" German political culture. Extremely promiscuous in its choice of targets—Thomas Mann, Sigmund Freud, Karl Barth, and Søren Kierkegaard but also Richard Wagner, and even Houston Stewart Chamberlain—Steding's diagnosis of a collapse of the "old Europe" reflected the views of a new generation of Führer-led historians who saw the Third Reich as the redemption of European culture.

One of the most influential figures of the German historical profession during the 1960s, Theodor Schieder (1904–84), conducted a study of "East Prussia" (1938) that interwove the traits of the new "fighting" historiography with national and ethnic precepts to promote the "Germanization of the eastern space," meaning Polish territory. Schieder was one of the younger members of the "Königsberg circle," who sought to provide a historical basis for German hegemony in areas marked by a mélange of ethnicities and languages. After 1939, all constraint was thrown overboard as the Reich took a step across the Rubicon to embrace violent policies of ethnic cleansing and undertook the military reconquest of the east, all of which was supplemented by historically and anthropologically grounded scholarship. A notorious 7 October 1939 "memorandum" (discovered by historian Götz Aly)—the minutes of a conference of racial experts produced by Schieder just days after the invasion of Poland that called for the rapid removal (*Herauslösung*) of Jews from Polish cities—is a vivid example of how historians helped formulate re-Germanizing settlement policies in areas of German conquest (see document 383 in chapter 28). As long as philosophers did not call into question the politics of National Socialism or challenge its worldview, they enjoyed relatively wide latitude to develop their own philosophical approaches to National Socialism. Apart from the banned Marxist and logical positivist schools, a spectrum of philosophical orientations from Kantianism to existentialism flourished. Among them, the Nazi worldview played a symbolic function, indeterminate yet requiring constant refinement and reinterpretation. As a result, philosophers found themselves in a special position to give shape and substance to the new political reality. At the same time, the fact that the worldview remained the final arbiter of truth created problems for philosophers because Nazism drew some of its authority from nonphilosophical sources such as biology, race theory, myth, and mysticism—sources that, in Heidegger's words, could be considered "primitive."

These and other quandaries caused uncertainty but also engendered competition for preeminence among philosophical schools. Gerhard Fricke assaulted the legacy of Enlightenment universalism and tolerance. Similarly, Krieck, heaping contempt on academic philosophy, insisted that the National Socialist worldview had brought an "end to every form of universalism and replaced it with a principle of race and *Volk*." He rejected out of hand the "epigones" of Kant, Hegel, Nietzsche, and others. Krieck also promoted his own works to the detriment of Alfred Baeumler, appointed to the University of Berlin as the party's most prestigious academic philosopher, who wanted to build a new foundation based on the notion of Nietzsche (1844–1900) as a "philosopher of the heroic." There were many difficulties with the Nazi adaptation of the Nietzsche's ideas, not in the least that he was anti-Christian, opposed to anti-Semitism, and above all, not a racist. His "Persian" myth of Zarathustra is obviously incompatible with the notion of "positive Christianity" accepted by Nazi ideologues like Wolfgang Schultz, who published a critical essay in the house organ of the Rosenberg Office that clearly distorted Nietzsche's thought by asserting that "Iranian, ancient Germanic, and German attitudes are innately related; they are racially Nordic." More absurd but no less dangerous was the argument put forward by Heinrich Härtle in his *Nietzsche and National Socialism* (1937) that Nietzsche was a forerunner of racial biology because he promoted the cultivation and breeding of a higher race of man. (Nietzsche had made no such claim; indeed, he saw the Jews as one of Europe's strongest groups because they had survived the torments of anti-Semitism.)

By far the most important German philosopher to embrace National Socialism was Martin Heidegger (1889–1976), whose international stature was established by the publication of his *Being and Time* in 1927. Heidegger's decision to join the party, and his address when he assumed the rectorate of Freiburg University in April 1933, shocked his Jewish students—among them Hannah Arendt, Herbert Marcuse, and Hans Jonas—for its strident but somewhat ambiguous message about the Greek "beginning" and its parallel with the historical mission of the *Volk* and its ringing conclusion "that all that is great stands in the storm."[2] By November of that year, there was nothing ambiguous about Heidegger's commitment to the Führer, but he was still vulnerable to attack, often by hard-liners like Krieck, who ridiculed his language as un-German (and even Jewish inspired), or from competitors like the philosopher and sociologist Arnold Gehlen (1904–76), who tried to adapt his own version of German idealism to National Socialism by juxtaposing the state with existence (*Dasein*).

Heidegger and Gehlen typified the academic adaptation of venerable German philosophical traditions to National Socialism. Scholars hoped that philosophy would emerge from its marginal status as an academic discipline of little political importance to become the guiding force of a new politics and a "new man." The belief that a "higher" National Socialism would be adopted as a guiding light for the movement, and even supplant the more vulgar rhetoric of Nazi speakers and pamphlets about the core racial doctrine, turned out to be a pipe dream. Instead of "raising" the standard of National Socialist thinking, the attempts to adapt to Nazi ideology only debased philosophy and the reputation of philosophers.

NOTES

1. The Amt Rosenberg (Rosenberg Office), established in 1934, was an official body for cultural policy and surveillance within the Nazi party, headed by Alfred Rosenberg. Its technical name was Dienststelle Rosenberg.

2. Martin Heidegger, "The Self-Assertion of the German University (1933)" in *The Heidegger Controversy: A Critical Reader,* edited by Richard Wolin (Cambridge, Mass., 1993), 39.

119

ERNST KRIECK

Renewal of the German University

First published as *Die Erneuerung der deutschen Universität,* in Die deutsche Hochschule 1 (Marburg: N.G. Elwertsche Verlagsbuchhandlung, 1933), 2–3, 5–6.

It would be impossible to assess the current state of today's university without first providing a brief historical overview. The establishment of the University of Berlin in 1810 under the direction of [Wilhelm von] Humboldt and [Friedrich] Schleiermacher inaugurated a restructuring of all universities and must be considered the single most significant turning point in the seven-hundred-year history of the Western university. The University of Berlin was able to encompass all the forms of German intellectual life in the preceding century, a century of greatness, and was thus able to establish itself as the primary organizational center for the further development of German intellectual life. The humanistic doctrine that grew from the powerful German intellectual movement of the eighteenth century and, sometime around 1800, witnessed a turn toward the German national idea is what provided a common basis for the work on the university, scientific research, and education and professional training. Once the idea of humanism had been transformed into the national idea, the common bond, the goal, the existential purpose underlying all academic subjects, all branches of research, and all areas of individual study was put in place. It was the professors and the student body, as the Paulskirche Parliament of Professors in Frankfurt attests, that paved the way for the Bismarck Reich.[1] The educational elite of the nineteenth century, which found cohesion in and was promoted by German idealism, emanated from the work of the neohumanistic *Gymnasium* and the new university. But there remained a schism because higher education and military training for German youth could not be conjoined under the same unified sense of purpose.

By contrast, the current state of affairs at German universities is characterized by the loss of an overriding common foundation, a supportive framework, a binding purpose to guide them. It is for this reason that the output waned at German universities, the intellectual stature declined, the impact diminished. In recent decades, the university became devoid of a unified foundation and a common sense of purpose. It was reduced to a collection of dozens of individual subjects acting independent of one another. There can be no doubt about the fact that, in the past few generations, the university has substantially removed itself from developments around it: it has been relegated to the sidelines of history, and the reason is that the university, in its factitious pursuit of autonomy and autarchy, has sought to insulate itself on the periphery and lead a life of leisurely contemplation on an island. This state of inner paralysis cannot be overcome by scholarship and science alone. Ultimately, even the establishment of the University of Berlin was little more than the manifestation and affirmation of the overwhelming intellectual life of the German movement that had been growing in strength ever since Leibniz. The university and scholarship, then, if they hope to keep from falling prey to desiccation and ruin, must necessarily place themselves in the current of historical life, must receive their impetus and their content from the course of history so that they can, in turn, transform these events into scientific, scholarly terms and return them as forces that manifest and shape the future. The university—and this means science and education—cannot afford to remove itself from the fray and seek to exist on the periphery of what is happening amongst the *Volk*. [. . .]

In the future, the university will be an integral component and official mouthpiece of the state. But it is important to bear in mind that not only the university but also the state is now subject to a complete overhaul. The university, as a state organ, is thus to conduct its educational mission and set its aims under the authoritative direction and within the framework of a *völkisch*-political context. This does not imply that the freedom and autonomy of the university are in any danger of being replaced by bureaucratic administration. Far more, as an organ of the organic *Volksstaat,* the university shall thus become an integral component of the overall communal fabric and will attain a greater degree of internal and external freedom, greater powers of self-administration and jurisdiction in the communal fabric of the *Volk,* than it actually possessed in the era of liberalistic disintegration and false freedom. At the same time, the problem of academic freedom comes to rest on an entirely new set of basic premises. And might we point out that intellectual freedom is ultimately not contingent on privileges or statutes in the law that are issued from above in the form of a capacious range of freedom of movement, but rather that academic freedom is deeply anchored in the character of an instructor who is compelled by his conscience to combat the opposing forces. Freedom is not free; it must be obtained in struggle. University professors will soon realize that they are much more successful at profoundly engaging students in academic work with this militant scholarship, a science that prevails in struggle, driven by an insight that wells up from the soul to stand in battle against resisting forces, than they were using the putatively objective science that has been in force in the past several years. As soon as science encompasses the *völkisch*-political needs and exigencies of the young generation, it will become an unprecedented force in the education and formation of young people.

Note

1. Refers to the Frankfurt National Assembly, the first freely elected parliament for all of Germany, held from 18 May 1848 to 31 May 1849 in the Paulskirche at Frankfurt am Main.

120

ARTHUR GÖPFERT, EUGEN FISCHER, MARTIN HEIDEGGER, AND WILHELM PINDER

Vow of Allegiance of the Professors of German Universities and Institutions of Higher Learning to Adolf Hitler and the National Socialist State

First published as *Bekenntnis der Professoren an den deutschen Universitäten und Hochschulen zu Adolf Hitler und dem NS Staat* (Dresden: W. Limpert, 1933), 29–42. (Simultaneously published in English.)

District Chief Arthur Göpfert, Leader of the Saxon Teachers

Your Magnificence! Members of my Party and Gentlemen from the Press!

I thank you for your hearty welcome. The management of the National Socialist Teachers' Association, Saxony, has the desire that the University of Leipzig take an eminent share in not only the scientific but also the political life of the nation. We therefore commence our demonstration in one of its rooms. All of German science shall, however, lend its dignity, its essence, and its noble mind to serve the grand German concern. We have therefore asked eminent men of numerous German universities to take the word today in public. The demonstration has a purely political purpose: the world is not entirely friend to this new Germany that was formed by Adolf Hitler with revolutionary spirit. Even now there are a considerable number of stirrers and slanderers prepared to defame the new Reich. Malignant adversaries and unscrupulous traitors do not shrink from misrepresenting even now the huge success of the vote to be expected as the result of terror exerted by the party. They will not admit that the leader does not require any pressure—neither by the party nor by authorities—as he has conquered the heart of the whole German people, and the entire nation is ready to follow him on the whole line in full unanimity and impressive readiness to sacrifice. We strictly decline the idea that even a single German could be influenced in giving his vote. We are not willing to allow any defamatory reproaches to be made against us. If we, being honorable characters, refrain from exerting any pressure in the voting, we defy those unheard-of reproaches that can be made only by people who think less honorably than we do. The men of the German science, who in the present demonstration wish to make their confession to Adolf Hitler and the National Socialist state, could by no power in the world be forced to do acts or to say words incompatible with the views they hold. They will speak today in full freedom of conscience. Their noble mind induces them to tell all the educated people in the world that they confess to Adolf Hitler as frank and proud men. They want to say to the whole world that this new Germany is a land of peace, of prosperity, open to comprehension. We have, for this reason, secured international resonance for this demonstration. The resolutions and speeches delivered here will be translated into foreign languages and, provided with the signatures of all competent German scientists, sent to all universities in the world. The scientists who entertain relations to professional friends in the whole world will assist us for their love to the German fatherland. All the nations of this globe will thus be cleared up by those intellectual men of their blood to whom Truth is the supreme law and who are capable of proving justice to our own nation; who will speak to them of the deep and honest desire for peace of all the spheres of the German people, of the government and the party, of the treatment unworthy to human beings that the German nation had to suffer; of the reasons of noble humanity that make all the sensible people of this globe affirm Germany's demand for equality. But they will also be able to tell the foreign countries how deeply Germany loves Adolf Hitler, her savior from Bolshevist barbarism. German scientists are only servants of Truth, and nothing, absolutely nothing, can induce them to leave the path of Truth. Their deeds and words cannot remain without influence upon all the honorable and great men of science and art of foreign countries. Viewed from the internal aspect, we may say that this is the first time that we dare to attain the high goal, to give evidence of the unity of will of German science and the political leadership of the nation. I am convinced that the German scientists will never forsake their new fatherland, not the least in the time of need.

Eugen Fischer, Berlin

The German nation has built a house for itself. In the magnificent swing of the last few months, we have seen it grow and rise. A mighty architect has designed it and is instructing us all how to help in the building. His will fills and lifts up the nation of sixty-five million, a nation reconstructing its home on the old lands inherited from their fathers. That is what the world calls a revolution. Revolution, because it has come over us like a hurricane. Revolution, because the will of one man has created new aims, has produced something new and upset the old; all this was done in a German manner; security and order prevailed, without barricades, without hostages being placed back to wall, without civil war, incendiarism, and murder. At the beginning of this summer, we held our lectures in the usual manner—student and professor alike continued their work and helped in building the new state! There is no nation that has had such an orderly and moral revolution, and no nation will ever be able to imitate it. And yet it was and still is a revolution, for it is an upheaval and regrouping of values that has broken upon us like a seething storm in spring, a fermenting new aspect trying to set itself free from the womb, a new mental current, and all this much more "world stirring" than the trivial upsetting of a constitution and the passing of new laws.

A people's state has been established, the new National Socialist state made of blood and land. A nation—under the influence of the genial personality of the leader—becomes mindful of its own, old dried-up fountains, its national resources, its blood, its race, and its soul.

Millions of people do not yet dream what we have actually experienced in the months since January and in the months and years of struggle of the Hitler movement before that time. There are still wide circles that believe that this has been a revolution of state, a mere change of constitution. The "putsches" in the year 1918 have done away with monarchy and have created republics, also revolution, and now, they go on thinking the democratic republic has been usurped by a National Socialist one. No, it has nothing to do with the form of the state; no small parties and commissions have made any constitutions on paper. A Great One has placed his hand on the spoke of the wheel of world history, has reversed the rudder and started a new development, the results of which are so far-reaching as cannot be overlooked. A people's government, in the form as existed hundreds of years ago, has been made, grouped in professions, with men who know again that they are of the same blood, that one mother tongue binds them together, that they have leaders who want the whole, but not seducers who stir up class against class, who blast a precipice between those who give and those who take, who incite avarice and promise things impossible to fulfill. An enormous billow is passing over our nation, a surprised looking up that, all of a sudden, should make two things become important, should stand up like Irmensuls [Old Saxon for "great pillar"] visible to the whole nation: national on the one hand and social on the other! The nation becomes conscious of its dignity. For the whole nation, one man, at last, says a man's word, "no." A leader says, national disgrace has an end today! He says, "no," when honor forbids him to say "perhaps" and "in future" and half a "yes" and a whole "yes." But this national spirit is not aggressive, it is not nationalistic, it does not preach revenge, not conquest; the movement does not need to lead wars for its confirmation like the Napoleons had to do in order to preserve their thrones; it does not have to, and it does not want to; it does not quarrel with the enemies of yesterday, because the man who is leading us is speaking from the soul of the nation when he says we have no disgrace to wipe out, no honor lost during all the years of battle in west and south and east and over the sea, on the sea, and under the sea, for we have gained more military honor than the victors of many wars who are being glorified in the books of history. National does not mean to us conquest and new war, not even a reconquest of that which belonged to us. For us, it means freedom from disgraceful fetters, the recognition of equality before the nations, and the state's not being disturbed when building our new house of the people. The national character, the racial kind that has created German culture, the German soul, all these are to serve as foundations of the people's state. We are being chided, ridiculed, and spoken of in bad terms if we refuse to have foreign things and if we discard them, elements that do not belong to our kind; although they have been of aid sometimes in certain achievements, the greater part of their effects were of a disintegrating nature to mental values, poison to numerous wells of national thinking, and destruction to land-linked prosperity and numerous families of old estate. They are shouting when, during the building and erection of this people's house, shavings fall from the plane; but they are quiet when the blood runs in other revolutions and hunger eradicates whole villages. All we want is security and to be masters of our own house. And to build up the nation as a people that is of one blood and that feels as such and no longer fosters strife between the classes.

The second column is a social one. A new social spirit as Hitler wants it, a spirit of which he is an example, a spirit that we sense when we see that now, as winter is approaching, large parts of the provinces are without unemployment [*sic*]. A nation in the hand of its leader wants to ban hunger and the cold of winter, threatening millions. The will of a leader is able to achieve that on one single Sunday in Berlin—Berlin the city of amusement, of dancing halls and bars, the rich and prosperous, the stranger as well as the native, renounce joint and cake, to fill the coffers of the winter aid fund with 400,000 marks by simply eating a one-dish meal. We want to become socialistic, not Communists, not Marxists, not in class differences but in Hitler's National Socialism, in a new form, and not in the stupid idea of equality and also equal rights for all persons, those who are efficient and those who are not, but in the sense that even the poorest is of the same blood, that care must be taken of all, that unlimited prosperity must cease, not by communistic confiscation but by an inner development and a growing into the new Reich and in the formation of the genuine people's state. We are building up a new socialism on a mental and psychic fundament, not by the force of workers' fists, but understood and carried through in the Hitler spirit. But we need rest in order to build up a socialist future; external security is what we need in order to carry through a gigantic work meant to give millions of hands work and the blessing of satisfaction for their souls after work done; we need equality of rights in order to get out of this sad economic state of affairs caused by war debts, reparations, moratoriums, and interests in hard work. We need justice against Jewish agitation abroad in order to continue the trade and commerce that we need for the existence of our nation. Is that too much for the German people to ask? But nearly the whole world says, "no." Is that hostile, is that warlike, is that self-raising, if at last a German chancellor says, I am tired of this bartering, of void promises and lies? Why can't they believe him when he, as an honest man and in the name of the whole nation, assures them all that he wants nothing but peace? Why do they have suspicions that our brown battalions have brought us order in the streets, and that they guarantee the security against Communist destruction? Why do they look upon them as battalions ready for a German revenge? Can there be one German man and one German woman who does not stand behind the chancellor when he proffers his hand for peace but with the dignity and the responsibility of the real leader asking for equality in rights and honor and freedom against the threatening dangers of gas and tanks! The world must see that there is only one voice in Germany; the last man must lift his voice and no one must be absent when tomorrow the whole nation gives the leader its oath of faith; as in a veritable legislative assembly that our forefathers used to hold in the open, a distinct "yes" must be heard to Hitler's question, whether he really is speaking for the whole German nation!

The leader has said we want equality of rights with other nations. We stand behind him!

The leader has said we want liberty to build our house in the way we like. We stand behind him!

The leader has said we want peace in order to build up what feuds have until now destroyed. We stand behind him!

The leader has said we want our German honor as our fathers did. We stand behind him!!

The leader has said what he means and what he wants and has asked us all, and the German nation will say "yes" tomorrow, and "yes" again, and three times "yes."

The Leader: Hail and Victory!

Martin Heidegger, Freiburg

German Teachers and Comrades! German Compatriots, Men and Women!

The German nation has been called by the leader to vote; the leader does not beg anything of the nation, but he is giving the nation the direct possibility of highest, voluntary decision—namely as to whether this nation wishes its own existence or does not wish it. The nation is voting tomorrow for no less than its future.[1]

This vote can hardly be compared with voting proceedings as have been known until now. The unique factor in this vote is the simple magnitude of the decision to be achieved by it. The inexorability of the simple and last does not suffer any sway or delay. This last decision extends to the outmost limit of existence of our nation. And what is this limit? It consists of this primitive demand of all being—namely, to retain and save its kind. The barrier has thus been erected between that which can be demanded from a nation and that which cannot. By virtue of and based on this principle of honor, the German nation retains the dignity and decisiveness of its life. The will to self-responsibility is, however, not only the basic principle of the existence of our nation, but at the same time the initial factor in the achievement of the National Socialist state. And from this will to self-responsibility, the work of each profession, in the small and on the whole, advances to the position and rank of its equally necessary destination. The work of the various professions bears and supports the living framework of the state; this work regains for the nation its ingenuity; this same work transfers this state as reality of the nation into the scope of action of all important powers of human existence.

It was not ambition, not avarice for glory, nor blind stubbornness and striving for power, but solely the flawless will to absolute self-responsibility in bearing and mastering the fate of our nation that commanded our leader to leave the "League of Nations." That does not imply a turning away from the community of the nations; on the contrary, by this step our nation submits to the natural law of human existence that every nation must obey in the first place if it wants to remain a nation. And from this parallel obedience proceeds the very possibility of taking one another seriously, and the demand for self-responsibility expresses no more than a positive attitude towards a community. The will to a true community is equally distant from a vague world fraternization as it is from a blind tyranny. This will acts beyond this extreme; it creates the open and manly relying upon one another and sticking together of the nations.

What happens if there is such a will? Is it going back to barbarism? No! It is the refusal by the simple and large demands of self-responsible action to accept void negotiations and hidden transactions. Does that mean the dawning of illegality? No! It is the clear confession to the unimpeachable independence of every nation.

Is that a denial of the creations of a spirited nation and the smashing of a historical tradition? No! It is the eruption of a refined youth that has grown back to its roots. The will of these towards the state will make this nation hard against itself and respectful of any genuine work.

What is this that is happening? The nation is regaining the truth of its will of existence, for truth is the revelation of that which makes a nation strong and clear in its actions and knowledge. And this will to know incorporates the demand to know. And from this aspect, the limits are measured within which genuine questioning and investigation must be based and approved of. And from this origin we get science. It is tied up in the necessity of self-responsible national existence. Science is, therefore, educational passion tamed in such necessity, wanting to know in order to make knowledge. To know means to us: to have power over things in reason and to be ready to act.

We have disengaged ourselves from the idolatry of bottomless and powerless thinking. We see the end of philosophy in servitude. We are convinced that the clear hardness and the original fortitude in the altercation with that which exists, and that by doing so either to grow or to break is the innermost motive of question of a national science. For pluck entices one to go forward; pluck disengages itself from all that has existed; pluck dares to do the unaccustomed and the incalculable. Questioning is to us not the frivolous game of curiosity. Questioning does not mean to us the stubborn persistence in doubt at all costs; questioning means to us, not to hide from the terror of the untamed and the dread of the dark. We ask for the sake of these questions and are not in the service of those grown tired in their lazy desire for simple answers. We know that questioning pluck to experience the depths of existence and precipices of existence is, in itself, a higher answer than cheap information derived from artificially constructed systems of thought.

And so we, who have in our keeping the "desire to know" of our nation, confess: the National Socialist revolution is not merely the taking over of an already existing power in the state by another party sufficiently large enough to do so; this revolution means a complete revolution of our German existence. From now on, everything demands decision and every action, responsibility. We are convinced: if the will to self-responsibility becomes the law of the community between the nations, then each nation can and must be a teacher of the wealth and power of all great deeds and works of human existence.

The vote that the German nation is about to take is in itself a feat, quite independent of the result, the strongest confession of the new German reality of the National Socialist state. Our will to national self-responsibility wants it, that each nation finds and keeps the magnitude and truth of its aim.

This will is the highest security for the peace of the nations, for it binds itself to the basic principle of manly respect and absolute honor. The leader has awakened this will in the whole nation and has made one single decision out of it. No one can be absent on the day when he shows his will. Hail Hitler!

Professor [Wilhelm] Pinder, Munich

German Compatriots!

History has ever been the presence, and presence has ever been history. Ever since our heart and reason have told us that nations are living beings, having mission and fate, ever since that time do we feel more vividly than before that we are responsible for the past and the future of our national community. Whatever the shameful acts may be that have been committed against Germany or by Germany's own fault, these rest like a disgrace upon him who thinks historically—who is alive in history—as if he himself bore the blame and had been present. Only he who feels this way, however, is entitled to feel the pride when he thinks of the great things that have taken place in Germany as if he had been present. Then history is presence; knowledge becomes conscience, and then also the presence is history. That which we are doing now acts upon the lifeline of our nation that runs on even after those who are alive today have passed into oblivion. We feel and know that we are the transitory foundations of our German nation.

A thousandfold more responsibility rests upon he who has learnt to consider history. He is giving all the honor of his lifework and the entire dignity of his science as a forfeit if he makes his small contribution by saying the "yes" when the leader calls. But we say yes!

I personally confess that I have waited through all the years ever since we entered the League of Nations—for this moment, which, thanks to God, has now come. A moment in which the outraged sense of justice of a kind, strong, tormented, and defamed nation eventually seeks the only possible solution—and in what manner. So peace loving, so inexpressibly decent, so pure and honorable as the unforgettable speeches of our great leader have done. All this has originated from a policy that is higher than what has been known as politics until now. This policy is a product of morality; it is a policy of the heart, based on a religious foundation, on faith. It is something new in history. Only during the time of a Bismarck has something similar occurred, so that one can say, a sound unknown to the world, this world of "politics." And to this world of "politics" belonged a language meant to hide the thoughts; but we hear now the sound coming from the heart of a whole nation, through the leader, whom it has produced as a concentration of itself in the hour of greatest need. Let this sound be heard. I wish to point out my recent experiences and say it is not quite so bad as the press wants to make us believe. I have, for instance, during a stay in England, met some real, genuine Englishmen who admired what had happened and who told me what you have done is right and proper.

If ever a crime has been committed that will bear the damnation of history, it is the deliberate, defamatory misconstruction born from the fear of a world suffering from senile decay that misunderstands, refutes, and spits upon intentions that are pure, beautiful, peace-loving, even Europhile.

If ever there were a confirmation for the correctness, for the sacred innermost right, of what we are now doing, then it is the self-betrayal, the personal stripping of lowliness and lunacy of our honesty, it is the misconstruction that we meet everywhere, the not being able to understand from all those, where it is obvious that they belong to an "inwardly inferior world." Our world wants to become new. In fact, it is already there, driven by just that power which, as one believed, did not pertain to politics, namely, the sound that comes from the heart. In order to render this possible, much had to happen; history, which finds its replica in art and just in the history of that which I, as an art historian, have to think is special.

The very age called dark by the liberalistic epoch, the Middle Ages, was the last healthy epoch of European culture. That which is forcing its way up wants to become a new middle age in the most sublime sense of the word, and it will be a title of honor if we are successful in earning it. The Middle Ages were of the last and greatest security that we call style. Style is that which we have lost. Style is beginning to live again, more in Germany than in any other country of the world. Not in creative art—not *yet* in creative art—style in art can only return after men have style. Style appears to be form and is community and faith. Style in art must come from the style of men. If we are able to complete our reconstruction that has commenced with our new movement, we will again be free as in the Middle Ages; art will then serve again, as in the Middle Ages. Art will then no longer be an egotistic purpose, in the same manner as it was not in the Middle Ages. Art will then call the artist—i.e., the life of community will set the task and will suffer only such artists to follow its call who confess themselves to it, as in the Middle Ages. The first signs have appeared. He who does not see that is blind. He who does not want to see it is a fool, is dead and lost. Our life is beginning to get style. Art has become a secondary matter, thank God. And that is health.

He who was in Munich on the 9th of November and saw the quiet procession that called back to mind the tragic happening of ten years ago, he who has seen that: the leader and his followers, bareheaded and silent; the old torn flags before the old legionaries; many a leader supporting himself on a stick; no music, only the deep sound of drums; quiet torches throwing their light into the grey November day; the long, long silence; the thousands of raised hands—swearing a silent oath and bursting into this silence the shots of commemoration—he who has seen that had to say to himself as a man of history: this has not existed since the time of the spiritual drama. That was no longer a theater; there was no longer a separation between actors and audience, stage and audience. No audience was left; here, again, was community! And now everything acts together again. That is more than a picture (the "picture" was the last shallow remainder left over from all creative art in the nineteenth century). This, now, is style—i.e., an inseparable union of the community to produce form, an involuntarily created symbol for a thought that thousands feel; the cooperation of all in the expression of the individual life; strictly speaking, something religious. Just because there was no aesthetic intention but merely a compliance, strict and dignified, with a firm faith, the cold-hearted aesthetician was forced to say, "This is beautiful!"

Beauty can be achieved only if it is not the aim. That is how the statues of Bamberg and Naumburg were created: to produce sacred feelings and not to be enjoyed, not to be looked at but to exist. Form is safe so long as the superformal, that is faith, community, desire for symbol, style of humanity express it as a matter of fact.

Such a matter-of-fact and wonderful symbol appears to me the eternal guard at the *Feldherrnhalle* in Munich. Day after day, night after night, summer and winter, two young Germans stand at attention, two hours each. The place is never vacant; I have often controlled these young men at night, quite unnoticed. As an ex-infantryman, I know one thing: we old soldiers would have "cheated," but these two here stand two hours at attention even if there is no one to watch them. The man as a statue—that is our German symbol.

I must close because the ten minutes allotted to me are over. But you know what I wish to say; I tried to show you, as viewed from my own profession, what we have lost and that which will again return, especially in Germany. It can come only if there is peace and honor. Honor also is a concept of the Middle Ages. In the Treaty of Versailles and its continuation in the form of the League of Nations, the last concept of chivalry was buried. Now it will rise again!

He who goes and says "yes" need not be a National Socialist; in that case, it is understood, but every German must go, each man is responsible in order that our nation does its duty before the leader and in order that it is justified before history. Hail Hitler!

Note

1. This meeting of the Nationalsozialistische Lehrerbund (National Socialist Teacher's Association) of Saxony occurred on 11 November 1933, the eve of the so-called plebiscite confirming Germany's withdrawal from the League of Nations (which had already occurred on 14 October).—Eds.

121

KARL ALEXANDER VON MÜLLER

The State of the University

First published as "Die gegenwärtige Lage der Universität," in *Vom alten zum neuen Deutschland* (Stuttgart: Deutsche Verlags-Anstalt, 1938), 260–63.

Our educational aim is not to train a cadre of rote academic professionals—quite the contrary, what we have in mind is the education of Germans as human beings, building well-rounded characters, intellectual, spiritual leaders, and soldiers for our *Volk*. This implies, then, a strengthening and deepening of education in general, and particularly toward national education; it implies that we awaken and foster the spirit of community. The university, on an organizational and an intellectual level, is to be more tightly incorporated into a strictly organized state—one that is at once national and social. The German university, like the Italian, is to become integrated into a vast system of state-sponsored education and training of the *Volk*, with the aim of fostering the solidly German character, strength, and self-confidence of a particular German-Führer type. And, for this type, a new political will and a new moral drive are themselves the driving forces behind science and scholarship.

We are, of course, met with the question of academic freedom in this context, and it would seem to me cowardly to seek to avoid it. This was the question the age of liberalism hoisted most boldly on its banner. To what extent can it lay claim to validity for all time?

Looking back at the whole history of the German university, we find that it has always had to come to terms with outside forces. Absolute academic freedom has never existed—because the university, as an educational site, is a political factor for any state—but there has certainly been more than one period in history in which science and scholarship have not assumed the highest rank in the project of constructing a worldview and have thus been subject to restrictions set by a higher power. History defies the notion that scholarship, at least in many fields, is no longer possible under such limitations: it has existed in all of these periods. But the same historical experience also demonstrates that in the long run even the most calculated and vigorous political policies on the part of a government administration are incapable of dominating the inner life and growth of intellectual movements in a *Volk*. A national *Volksstaat* and scholarship are not mutually exclusive. Love of the truth does not preclude love of one's own *Volk*. Even in those periods when universalism has prevailed, science and scholarship still sprang from their roots in the people. Scholarship assumes a certain national character by sheer virtue of the language in which it is written; and every great scholar, every great artist, has a hand in shaping that character. Scholarship has always been the expression of a certain unique national character trait—as reflected in its structure, its approach, its organizational infrastructure—even when, by its very nature, it transgressed those boundaries. Serving the best interests of the *Volk* is not an ideal that will destroy the autonomous life of science and scholarship: it may, in fact, provide fertile creative impetus.

For science itself, within these parameters, remains freedom's daughter and could never become the handmaid to politics without going completely to seed. Science is firmly rooted in the whole and must serve the cause of wholeness but has its own internal laws, and both the *Volk* and the state are reliant on science, a science that retains its freedom. Naked intellect can still play its tricks on us when clad in a straitjacket, but science cannot. The human spirit demands in its development the point and counterpoint, text and context, tension and resolution: life emerges, even for the human spirit, from struggle alone. And not merely from the struggle surrounding current events. Even when scholarship adequately fulfills its purpose for the immediate concerns of the *Volk,* it will always need periods of strict, contemplative silence to nourish its creative works. Deep internal passion is as much the lifeblood of intellectual insights as it is the lifeblood of every form of creativity on earth, but this passion must be reined in before it can become science—it must be tempered by the cultivation of thought and of structure, tempered by the compulsion to get at the objective truth. Neither the *Volk* nor the state can afford to go without it in the long run. No one casts any doubt on that in the field of technological developments. Whoever is intent on building an airplane or a radio is in need of technical knowledge, conscientious schooling. But is it any different for the realm of intellect, for grasping the significance of world history? And isn't there indeed much more at stake here than in the case of building a radio or an airplane? Aren't any errors made in this regard much more dangerous and more far-reaching in their implications? And I'm not referring here merely to the statesmen active in politics. The insights, be they true or false, that an entire *Volk* gains from its own history, the practical steps, be they right or wrong, that are taken based on those insights, determine to an unpredictable degree the fate of the *Volk;* they determine war and peace, the rise and fall of nations and states.

Our modern world, with its wealth of technical means of disseminating information, is nearly brought to a standstill beneath the weight of catchwords and headlines. Much as in the way that all the contemporary phenomena far outnumber those we know from all other periods in history, the dissemination of lies and untruths has never been as massive, never as organized nor as widespread, as it is in our time. We have witnessed this more than once in the malicious propaganda against our *Volk.* This is not in itself a moral judgment against the present; it is related to the fact that all the determinations of the present are so widespread. But, in the long run, the biggest struggles—struggles of the mind and all others alike—cannot, as the Führer recently stated in Erfurt, be decided on the basis of platitudes and words. Far more, they are decided based on the relevance of the matter at hand and on the moral force driving them. The task of scholarship—one that we are here to serve at this institution, each in his own humble way—is to fortify a narrow dam of factual knowledge to prevent any inundation by the raging waters of catchphrases. That may at times prove difficult. But, my dear young friends, how would we otherwise withstand it and forever maintain our happy mien? The truth, inasmuch as we are able to recognize it, is innately endowed with sovereignty and is entirely independent of the extent of mendacity that surrounds it, be it ever so great or so small. The history of the National Socialist movement itself is evidence; it is evidenced again and again in the history of peoples: even though the truth may have remained hidden just yesterday—though it may seemingly be lying in shambles and utter defeat—who knows, perhaps even today it will rise up and spread throughout the world.

When we speak of academic freedom in this context, we are speaking not about the individualistic, liberalist rights of each individual as opposed to the entire collective; on the contrary, we are speaking in terms of the overriding moral obligation to the *Volk* on the part of the researcher that transcends the scope of his individual interest. If your teachers, despite their cognizance of the degree to which they are bound to the *Volk*, the degree to which they are conjoined with the collective, were to lack the courage to speak the truth, I tell you, my dear young friends, you would have every right to despise us. The *Führerprinzip* is also binding for the development of creative intellect. No one can possibly hope to build character in others if he is not himself in possession of good character; no one can inspire courage who lacks courage himself; no one can exude faith if he is not prepared to make sacrifices on behalf of his beliefs. Many of you know that and have experienced it firsthand in politics, but the same applies in scholarship and science.

122

E. GÜNTHER GRÜNDEL

The Intellectuals and National Socialism

First published in *Jahre der Überwindung* (Breslau: Korn Verlag, 1934), 93–94, 98–99, 101–2.

German intellectuals today are faced with a decisive task—namely, with providing sufficient evidence that their existence in the nation is justified. What is their position in the new state? Where do they fit in to the whole nation of *Volk*? They are neither the leaders nor are they councilors or advisors, and they aren't among the followers. This island of whining, faultfinding, bloodless intelligentsia floating in a sea of swirling renewal and change is admittedly growing smaller by the month and far more seldom seen. Nevertheless, even if there are scarcely a hundred thousand of them left in Germany today, they are all the more numerous in foreign countries, which, for the New Germany, is perhaps as pertinent. There they are in league with German outcasts and emigrants—the sacked [*An-die-Luft-Gesetzten*]—and thus remain vicious enemies. In Germany proper, though, they have now been largely reduced to that handful of "Yes-But-lers"—as Gottfried Feder so nicely puts it—who, though most of them have already lent their voices to National Socialism, still persist in finding fault with it and thus in spreading artificially contrived malcontent.

Here we would like to briefly address at least one of the complaints most often raised by these faultfinders. There are said to be some armchair philosophers who still fail to acknowledge the value of enthusiasm as a mobilizing force and instead drench it again and again in the filthy dishwater of their derision. But what on earth can such a malicious pessimist even know about enthusiasm? What does he know of love, belief, and the power of ideas! Absolutely nothing. All he knows is hatred. As a matter of principle, he hates everything that might be in a position to undermine the very concept of his tragic-pathetic apocalyptic melodrama. Lonely aristocrats that many of them may be, they have no understanding of the masses and no understanding of what it means to follow someone else's lead. These armchair thinkers know nothing of the forces that a great leader of the *Volk* might form with his own hands, much in the way a sculptor would mold clay, nothing of the forces motivating him to act and enabling him to overcome resistance. In Hitler's case, this jubilant enthusiasm on the part of his followers is the expression of the irresistible forces of faith in the Führer and, what is more, it exerts a formidable persuasive power over outsiders who have yet to actively support the cause. But the Führer himself remains immune to its "intoxication." He conceals his enthusiasm austerely within his heart, planning and leading with a clear head. [. . .]

The few remaining German intellectuals still lingering on the periphery today will not be able to turn a deaf ear to the new spirit of the times forever. Because, upon closer examination, their compulsive faultfinding reveals itself to be a "complex"—one that must be recognized and treated accordingly. This is how the "complex" came about: the misconstrued concept of "education" (a bloodless concept, removed from the *Volk*, purely "intellectual") that has prevailed in Germany for several generations has produced a whole cadre of such "intellectuals" (in sharp contradistinction to learned scholars) who have never been sincerely committed to participating in shaping the fate or development of the *Volk*. Responsibility for the most recent and decisive exaggeration of this unhealthy state of mind and of affairs rests in the postwar German system, which was forced to take this position among German intellectuals to the furthest extreme, because at the time it would have been difficult if not impossible to get any self-respecting, pure, dyed-in-the-wool learned scholar to feel any sense of internal affinity for the "state" that this nation represented. So it was during this period that the breeding of a cadre of bloodless "intelligentsia" wholly removed from the life and limb of the *Volk* was brought to full fruition. But now, in one fell swoop, something new has emerged in Germany, and this something is so overwhelmingly magnificent and mesmerizing that even those German "intellectuals" will be powerless to resist its pull in the long run. But in many of these intellectuals, a psychological response sets in: here is something in which I, a "scholar," that is, a "born leader" of the "*Volk*," did not participate, something I had no hand in creating, did not help to initiate, was not present as midwife at its birth—something I did not even see coming. Therefore, this must not—or, to be more accurate, cannot possibly—be anything of substance, anything true, anything rational! That is what is called the "intellectual complex."[1] And it is this that explains the desire to denigrate, to nag into the ground, to find fault after fault—because, after all, it came into the world without my doing, as a "scholar," a German intellectual. So the intellectual takes on the role of some old "Auntie Emma" sulking around on the corner of the sofa, complaining any time and every time anything happens without her direct involvement. But, of course, the batty old aunt is blind to the fact that it is her own fault. Whether this is a dignified role to play—I'll leave that up to the faultfinding intellectuals to decide for themselves. [. . .]

But the case is by no means hopeless. For the German "scholar" has some grasp of modern psychology (otherwise he could not have been able to consider himself a "scholar"—not by yesterday's terms). So he is sure that his complex will lose its grip over him because he has finally seen the light and reached the maturity to overcome it. Then all that is left for him to do is to find a way to finally rid himself of the compulsion or "abreaction," and he will be fine. This all sounds suspiciously simple. First of all, today's New Order, or, for God's sake, if it is only recognized and acknowledged as such many years from now, is not some sort of "slipshod intellectual fad"—quite the contrary: it is the open admission of past mistakes and, as such, evidence of a highly commendable degree of personal courage. And the truly effective way of "abreacting" the intellectual complex is this: the whining, faultfinding intellectual who has thus far remained at the periphery must shift the emphasis from the specific inadequacies he is complaining about and focus instead on the bigger picture of the whole as a positive to be welcomed and affirmed that is so much in line with his way of thinking precisely because it is the way of thinking of every authentic German. He must concentrate the focus of his new perspective on the jubilant affirmation and—with that genuine superiority befitting of a genuine scholar—hoist himself above all the irritating little details and gloat over them with a chuckle. But with each successive transformation, he comforts himself again and again with the proverbial wisdom: "when building a table, chips are going to fly." And it is entirely unthinkable that an earthshaking upheaval the likes of our own could possibly occur without "cosmetic error." But once he has made the curve, the inner path has been forever cleared, for the intellectual is still on the periphery, and now, even though he has missed out on the opportunity in the past, he still has a chance to help us prepare for the great movement of the German revolution, to at least contribute in leading it to an ultimate and incontrovertible victory. And not only in the superficial vote count, but in the hearts and minds of the *Volk*—each in his own way, each in his own small circle, whether it be by talking to others who remain disgruntled about something or in the practical deeds of everyday life.

Note

1. Its final incarnation is the émigré complex: "Whoever kicks me out must be a bastard; or at least I have to regard him as such for my own purposes, because otherwise, I myself would be regarded as such (and, by the way, with good reason!).

123

LUDWIG GLASER

Jews in Physics

Jewish Physics

First published as "Juden in der Physik: Jüdische Physik," in *Zeitschrift für die gesamte Naturwissenschaft* (Berlin: Ahnenerbe-Stiftung Verlag, April 1939), 272–74.

Jews as students of [Hermann von] Helmholtz.

There is scarcely another branch of science in which Nordic men make up a greater percentage than in physics. But there is also no other that has the unfortunate notoriety of having been host to a Jew like [Albert] Einstein, who was stripped of his citizenship in 1933 when it was discovered that he was not just the quiet scholar many of his followers made him out to be, but rather that he was a Jewish politician, who, in a genuinely Hebraic manner, has displayed his gratitude for the host country that took him in as a guest by vilifying, mocking, and scorning it.

One might think that the Third Reich's abrupt divorce from this vermin would have been enough to give rise to a modicum of self-reflection. But the Jewish propaganda poisoning their minds already has people too confused to notice. And this was a process that found fertile ground that had long since been prepared for it. And who is at fault? Well, none other than the immortal Helmholtz himself. Seen from a *völkisch* perspective, there are some things in the life of this incontestably great scholar whose detrimental effect can only be assessed today: his refusal to acknowledge the contributions made by Robert Mayer, his weak performance as a representative of German science at international congresses, and his failure to include [Carl Friedrich] Gauß and [Wilhelm Eduard] Weber in identifying the particles with charges of true electricity and the complete and total misapprehension of one of his greatest German contemporaries, the physicist and mathematician Hermann Graßmann. Evidence of the fact that the person at fault for allowing the Jews access to physics is indeed Helmholtz may be seen in the case of the physicist and one of the earliest opponents of Judaism, Eugen Carl Dühring: his dismissal from his academic post at the University of Berlin in 1877 acted as a flaming red flag heralding the beginning of the Jews' shameless penetration of physics departments in Germany.

The Jewish half-breed Heinrich Hertz, [Michael] Wertheimer the Jew, E. Goldstein the Jew, [Leo] Grunmach the Jew, and many more—all of them, students of Helmholtz. The degree to which Helmholtz's influence was highly amenable to the Jews is apparent in the fact that the Eastern Jewish mathematician Leo Königsberger became his biographer.

A scion of Hamburg's illustrious family of trinket traders and money changers, the Jew Emil Gabriel (!) Warburg was called in from Freiburg to replace Dühring at the University of Berlin, remained in place from 1895 through 1905, and ultimately, from 1 April 1905 until 31 March 1922, occupied the most prestigious position the Third Reich has to offer anyone in the field of physics, as president of the Reich Institute for Physics and Technology, this

Jew—this Jew who was a successor to Helmholtz. Warburg worked wonders for the Jewish community. Following his appointment, the Jew in Berlin was able to settle himself comfortably into German academic posts. He was succeeded by the Jew Heinrich Rubens in 1905 after he had been appointed a professorship at the College of Technology in Berlin and in 1903 had even been accepted into the Technical Military (!) Academy. Then came the rest of the Jews, R[ichard] Börnstein, James Franck, Peter Pringsheim, Max Born, F[ritz] Reiche, [Artur] Korn, F. Grünbaum, and many more.

In addition, the destructive Jewish spirit influenced the advisors to the early German emperor, Kaiser Wilhelm II, who nevertheless became the victim of a genuinely Jewish vengeance. The establishment of the Kaiser Wilhelm Institute in Dahlem marked the onset of a new wave of Jews flooding the science of physics. The Jew F[ritz] Haber, nephew of the Jewish big-time profiteer [Leopold] Koppel, was appointed director of the Kaiser Wilhelm Institute for Chemistry and Electrochemistry. Research positions there were reserved almost exclusively for Jews: [Otto] Sackur (who died in an accident on 17 December and was embroiled in a bizarre treason affair), F. Kirschbaum (who, after his dismissal from the KWI [Kaiser Wilhelm Institute], worked in the USA and ultimately became the director of the Gold-and-Silver Refinery in Frankfurt which, at the time, was still in Jewish hands), Leyser, the Jewess Liesa Meitner, James Franck (now an émigré, member of the Prussian Academy of Sciences, went to Soviet Russia in 1933, then to Niels David (!) Bohr, where he stayed from 1933 to 1935 before moving to the USA in 1935, where he was a professor at the Johns Hopkins University in Baltimore), R[udolf] Ladenburg (son of the Jewish chemist Ladenburg, related to the Jewish-American bankers, émigré since 1933, professor of physics at the Palmer Physical Laboratory, Princeton University), H[ermann] Mark (later employed by I. G. Farben, after that, as a professor in Vienna, dismissed after the seizure of power in Austria), Michael] v. Polanzi [*sic,* Polanyi] (Hungarian Jew, émigré, now professor at the University of Manchester), and H[artmut] Kallmann (nephew to F. Haber). In 1921, F. Haber and Findlay Freundlich (Jew) ousted, under the most humiliating circumstances imaginable, then deputy director Dr. Paul Knipping, the now deceased man famous for his discovery of interference in X-rays and who had to flee to the National Award winner P[hilipp] Lenard.

The KWI, which is now the [Max] Planck Institute, was established explicitly for the Jew, A. Einstein. His assistant was his itinerant spokesman, the Jew Erwin Freundlich (originally emigrated to Ankara, later to Prague). The second director was Einstein's friend M[ax] v. Laue.

124

SECRET REPORT OF THE SECURITY SERVICE OF THE REICHSFÜHRER SS

Citing Jewish Authors in Dissertations

First circulated on 10 April 1940 as "Zitieren jüdischer Autoren bei Dissertationen." First published in *Meldungen aus dem Reich 1938–1945. Die geheimen Lageberichte des Sicherheitsdienst der SS,* edited by Heinz Boberach (Herrsching: Pawlak Verlag, 1984), 4:979.

As reports from nearly all academic circles confirm, enforcing the ministerial directive requiring that citation of Jewish authors in dissertations is to be avoided wherever possible and that Jewish and non-Jewish authors be listed separately in the bibliography has proven difficult because the authors of dissertations cannot always ascertain whether an author is Jewish or is to be categorized as a Jew. In the case of scholars from the postwar period, and even more so in the case of those from the nineteenth century, determining Jewish ancestry or affiliation is often difficult. Therefore, the suggestion has come from academic circles that the Reich Ministry of Science, Education, and National Culture compile a comprehensive list of Jewish scholars and scientists that can be consulted not only for the completion of dissertations, but also for any additional scholarly and scientific works. This would be of particular use for jurists, who often take recourse to Jewish commentary without citing the author.

125

CHRISTOPH STEDING

Disease unto Death? Disease unto Life?

First published as "Krankheit zum Tode? Krankheit zum Leben?" in his *Das Reich und die Krankheit der europäischen Kultur* (Hamburg: Hanseatische Verlagsanstalt, 1938), 27–29, 49–50.

We are concerned here with a study of old Europe—that is to say, pre-Bismarck and most certainly pre-Hitler Europe—as it stands in relation to Bismarck's Europe and Hitler's new Europe; that means that we are concerned primarily with the depiction of a world that has fallen to ruin. So this study represents the diagnosis of phenomena that must be categorized as pathological. This endeavor must be viewed as a form of "critique" inasmuch as it considers old Europe, crumbling in corruption and stricken by a "disease unto death," as the foundation for our current existence. The diagnosis of a disease must also be viewed as critique because one cannot diagnose anything as an illness without some awareness of its opposite and the antidote that would cure it—that is to say, without some awareness of health and some desire to attain good health: and the Reich is the very embodiment of a healthy Europe. So the restoration of the Reich is what constitutes the cure for Germany because this involves the activation of those forces and currents that will always build immunity and the ability to heal in the German people.

Hence our depiction of the relationship between the neutralizing tendencies of old Europe with respect to the Reich: this diagnosis of a very advanced stage of disease unto death in old Europe is possible only because that disease has already been more or less cured within the Reich, and the logical consequences are already evident.

It is only from the perspective of a healthy and regenerative world that we are able to examine the world of old Europe and diagnose it as diseased and already marked for death, thereby allowing it to point the way toward a cure.

Since we have managed, to a great extent, to "abolish" the disease within the Reich, since advancements toward a cure persist in breakneck stride, and since the disease, where it does present, disguises itself as health and only in this disguised form as something endemic to Germany, even here, the symptoms of the disease cannot be identified as conclusively as they can be beyond the borders of the Reich, in the neutral border states as well as in the rest of the world. But in order to demonstrate that even there we are concerned with indicators of deterioration and degeneracy that will be eliminated with the reinstatement of the Reich, we must repeatedly make reference to the way these same symptoms might be studied as they exist within the borders of the Reich from the last generation up until the present.

These indicators of course are most readily identifiable wherever the influence of the West and the neutral countries is evident—for example, in certain sectors of the confessional church or, in addition, where the old Reich and old Europe still have a hold on the present: in many parts of Lower Saxony, for example, especially among the sedentary peasants, in the Hansa towns; in the southwestern regions of the Reich; in the most capitalist parts of the West, etc. But the influence of the will to reinstate the Reich in a contemporary form is making itself felt everywhere; everywhere the call of the Führer is breaking down the encasing sustaining this crud-caked existence, and everywhere the blood is beginning to pulse more rapidly in the veins. The indicators—for example as present in Thomas Mann, who was a resident of Lübeck in its final stages of development and who was so firmly stricken by "degeneracy" that it was no longer possible to turn his thinking and feeling around and steer it into the surge of German consciousness—are exceptions. He and all the rest of the emigrants who migrated to the West were still confronted with the time and stage of development that was rendered historical and obsolete, transformed into a thing of the past to some extent already by Bismarck, but most decisively by the National Socialist revolution and by the Führer's actions. For this reason, this study will at times take into consideration contemporary emigrants as well as those who left during the World War (Hugo Ball, etc.).[1] These people, who often of their own volition declined the opportunity for rejuvenation and change in direction and instead decided to take upon themselves the fate of the Wandering Jew [*Ahasver*], are perhaps the purest representative samples of the spirit characterizing that world that is incapable of changing and therefore marked for extinction. They have taken as their professional vocation the task of pursuing the disease unto death of the old Europe and of the old Reich down to the last detailed extreme in a particularly classical and typically idealist fashion. So it is that they shall provide the future historian with all the stunning examples of typically idealist theories, arguments, and thought structures that he should need to exemplify the general conditions prevailing in that final stage of European development. Thomas Mann's works, above all, must be considered highly valuable historical sources for researching the condition of the most recent human generation. Any depiction of the political-spiritual-psychological attitude found in his works can be seamlessly interjected into a portrayal of the mentality that can be extracted from the prevailing attitude toward the Reich and is found in the neutral Germanic bordering countries. It is no coincidence that enemies of the Reich and of a European rejuvenation are to be found in the classic "reservation" areas of old Europe, that they prefer to gather in greater concentration in the neutral unaligned territories—where the presence of the antiquated, archaic Europe is often more unadulterated than in the Western great powers. [. . .]

If, up until now, the European disease, particularly as it is manifest in the Germanic world, could be seen as an unavoidable destiny, calamity, or as a hardship visited upon us by God; if disease can at all under any circumstance be seen as a blessing, collective or individual, because it can act as an admonition and prevent either the nation of people or individuals within it from rushing headlong into "deals" that rob them of their soul, then we have now reached the stage in which resolution, catharsis, reversal, strophe, or catastrophe must occur. The European disease will now either become a disease unto death or a disease unto life.

Note

1. Hugo Ball (1886–1927) was the founder of Dada in Zürich and an antiwar activist.—Eds.

126

JOHANNES HALLER

The Epochs of Germany History

First published as *Die Epochen der deutschen Geschichte* (Stuttgart: J. G. Cottasche Buchhandlung Nachfolger, 1936), 389–95. Translated by Timothy Nunan.

Instead of victory there came defeat. Not through the overwhelming force of the enemies; their combined strength was not insurmountable, had the German forces been applied properly. But this is just what was lacking. The German soldier did, it is true, exceed all expectations and even moved the enemies to amazement. How strong, how willing to sacrifice, how unshakably dutiful was the nation; how healthy was its core to the end—this showed itself and is inscribed in golden letters into the book of history. Even an English statesman, Winston Churchill, has attested to the fact that that which the Germans achieved in the World War sufficed for history. And yet the war went lost. [. . .]

It never would have gone so poorly had not an enemy within extended his hand to the external enemies. From the beginning of the war on, the rebellions of the misguided and abused masses threatened the Reich. So long as the army seemed to be victorious, this danger receded to the background. Yet as the hope for victory on the field began to vanish, treachery dared to come forward: the external defeat was to open the way to internal upheaval. The government of the Kaiser could not find the power to step out of the smoldering sparks while there was still time. Step by step, shying away from what was right, it handed over the tax of the *Reichspolitik* to the Reichstag, which could not understand how not to spend it in petty party bickering. When, after the flares of the flame of victory had passed since midsummer 1918, the failure in the field could no longer be concealed, when finally the military leadership itself had to avouch that it saw the war as lost, there came the outbreak of the long-prepared revolution. The 9th of November 1918 saw this revolution's victory in the Reich's capital. In front of the rebellion of the toiling masses, the Reich chancellor and minister cleared everything out, the republic was proclaimed, "granted by the nation"—although the republic had given itself its own mandate—and the new government took over, but the Kaiser, under pressure from ministers and generals, fled the country and opted for his requested resignation in order to spare the nation from a civil war. Now the victorious enemies of Germany could set their foot on her neck: on the 12th of November, the armistice came into force, which the defeated army had to abide by, since a continuation of the struggle at the same time as the revolution was impossible. It amounted to a surrender of arms. As a result of this, after seven months there came the peace that the victorious powers forced onto the German Reich.

On the 28th of June 1919, in the Hall of Mirrors at the Palace of Versailles, the very same place where the German Empire was once proclaimed, Germany's representatives were forced to sign a treaty that prepared the end of Germany's reign as a great power, a treaty that was to forever hinder the resetablishment of a German great power. Mutilated by the relinquishment of Alsace and Lorraine, Eupen, and Malmedy in the west; Pomerelia, Danzig, Poland, and Upper Silesia in the east, disarmed through restrictions on her number of troops to a pathetically small scale through the closing of her fortresses and a prohibition against defending her borderlands on the Rhine, and additionally burdened with unaffordable tributes for an unforeseeable amount of time, Germany saw herself hurtled back into a deeper impotence and defenselessness than she had ever known, surrounded on both east and west by hostile neighbors who made no secret of the fact that their goal was the appropriation of the rest of the German country. Just as in times that one had always believed long past, the German future stood under the Sword of Damocles of partition.

This Sword of Damocles will continue to threaten Germany for a long time. And yet so much has happened since then to change the situation and to strengthen our confidence that the hope for a recovery of freedom and power, a hope that from the beginning enlivened the nation, will not prove to be in vain. To dwell on this fact is not our task. History may speak only of past things, but all that which we have experienced since 1919 remains the present, even today. It has not yet been resolved, and therefore its meaning, which can only be measured by the final effect of any event, still cannot be recognized.

We may, however, already be able to establish one thing clearly today without anticipating the judgment that the future holds: the unity of the nation has stood up to this hard test. When Germany lay defeated and gagged on the ground, there existed a real danger that the enemies would succeed in driving the powers of treachery in the interior towards the dissolution of the Reich, or at least the secession of the borderlands. But they did not succeed. Separatism and particularism came to nothing, and today the unity of Germany stands more secure than ever, and just as the confident had dared to hope a few years earlier: the unity of Germany has been perfected. Bismarck's creation—let one say what one wants—has outstandingly proven its vitality. His deed was more, endlessly more, than an episode or a futile interlude: it has slammed shut the doors of the past, made an end of the times of the disunity and fragmentation of the state, and opened the new epoch of the united Germany. Is there not a stronger testimony for the value of an accomplishment than when one may say, that which was achieved in good times is asserted in times of calamity?

This could not have happened had there not lived in the people the overwhelming will to unity and freedom of the nation, the justified consciousness of its own worth, and the unshakable resolution to self-assertion, cost what it may. We experienced, to put it in a word, the victory of the national idea over all opposition and temptations.

Events have proved it. The fact that one man from the people—an Austrian by birth, a soldier in the German army, embodying in his person the national identity and unity of the nation—succeeded by himself in bringing about the improbable through the strength of his belief in Germany, the fact that under his leadership the masses of the nation, without regard for class or party, found themselves together in the struggle for Germany's honor and freedom, for the unity of the Reich and the people's community: this alone is a landmark that will shine through the centuries.

It would be baleful to sit smugly in his shine. More than ever, it is necessary to direct every step towards this star, to never become unfaithful to the great idea that the national and the social are not opposites, as the mendacious prophets of the past taught, but rather one and the same; the fact that no one who does not see and pay homage to every German, whatever class or profession he may be, above all the people's comrades, may claim to be of a national disposition; the fact that no one for whom the nation comes before all else in the world may claim to think socially. It is more necessary than ever not only to have this thought but to live it out as a deed, a deed that makes the people strong and unconquerable.

For we cannot allow ourselves to be deceived on this point: Germany is in greater danger than perhaps any great people has ever been in. The collapse of the national idea has not made her position any easier, because the sight of her regaining strength inspires distrust and suspicion. The clouds that have long covered the horizon of the future do not wish to thin out, and courage is still the first imperative. Courage and cleverness! May our own history serve us as a reminder; nowhere could we find a better lesson for where cleverness leads when it is not bolstered by courage, but also how a thoughtless foolhardiness that grabs on to what it covets without second thought, a daredevilry that scorns scrutinizing the correct means for that which is necessary and acheivable—how this foolhardiness is its own revenge. If we know how to learn this and take it to heart, and if we above all never forget that the life of all nations has from time immemorial meant a community with others, a community from which not least Germany nor the German nation today can arbitrarily break off; if we never forget that it is truer to assert oneself in this community through strength and cleverness, through self-confidence without myopia—then may fate bring what it will. The German nation will not go under, and the belief that has held until today will be proved true: the belief that the night of the present must some day give way to bright day.

The centuries of our history serve as a warning to us. But he who knows to listen to their voice knows that they also call forth with a solution:

We call you to hope!

127

KARL ALEXANDER VON MÜLLER

The Influence of the Peasantry in the National Community of the *Volk*

First published as "Die Geltung des Bauern in der Volksgemeinschaft," in his *Vom alten zum neuen Deutschland* (Stuttgart: Deutsche Verlags-Anstalt, 1938), 244–46.

Nor is it any different in the remaining rural areas of Germany's peasant community, for although the peasants in each of these areas differ in terms of their economic systems, domiciles, heritage, and customs, and in politics, they are the natural representatives of those uniquely German qualities upon which the diverse wealth of German history in particular rests—and at the same time, the unmistakably German peasant: a typical figure, with simple, wood-cut features, who in turn demonstrates an affinity for similarly simple, broad-cut, and complete creatures and creations.

By his very nature, he is the formidable picture of his people's perseverance. Why? Not for sheer love of the old-fashioned, not for sentimental reasons. He is not cut from such fainthearted cloth. But he is not content to experiment with innovations in theory, testing them out in his mind where thoughts may easily dwell side by side; he must put them to the test in the harsh, unrelenting reality of nature; nor is he content to leave others to bankroll his inventions; he must bear the costs of each innovation himself, pay from his own pocket. This is why he is naturally suspicious of dogma passed down from the ivory tower. This is why he clings to those things he knows from his own experience, with the same degree of dogged tenacity that has served him for centuries as he has wrenched his fruits from the soil, down to the very last detail. The wooden fences such as those described in the oldest-extant Bavarian statute book from twelve hundred years ago [. . .] are still to be found here in our country; the blades of straw demarcating paths that were not to be taken through the fields still mark these paths today. So even positive innovations are usually adopted by German peasants very slowly. How long did it take for the peasant to take a liking to the potatoes that now constitute his primary source of nourishment? Very often, it is only through hardship, hunger, or war that he has been forced to accept crucial economic improvements.

Oh, but the degree of stability, the degree of endurance in the whole fabric of our *Volk* is owed to the slow, deliberate nature of the peasants. Wherever the German *Volk* has remained resilient in the world and retained its stability, the peasants have been at the root of it. And here, in our own country, the poetry that is not merely created but that grows organically—we would have none of it without them. We all have hardly a clue about the vast, inestimable wealth of poetry and music and folkloric artistic productivity [that] has flourished among the peasantry for ages, growing unfettered (as someone once so nicely put it) like flowers in the field, as plentiful and as precious as clovers in the field and the blue enzian [gentian, mountain flower] and the lovely columbine [mountain flowers]—and it is but a hop, skip, and a jump from all these folkloric creations to all our great works of art. For all the creations of great individuals are not random creations that come into the world arbitrarily but rather the ultimate, perfected expression of that which the imagination of the *Volk* has created and built from generation to generation.

And yet this ancient world of German peasantry has seen the advent of a new epoch in the past century as our modern era of sciences and technology, of machines, of traffic, of lending institutions, of the urban metropolis and heavy concentrations of people and industry has encroached on every sector of life. And the ground beneath the peasant's feet is quaking and quivering today from the earthshaking upheavals of changing times in which nothing seems secure anymore. For the peasantry, as for the entire *Volk*, the changes of the past century have been greater than those of the past thousand years, and many of these changes seem to be directly aimed at the very nature of the peasants' way of life.

But the peasantry is, as we have seen, by nature a perseverant class—and change has become a sign of our times. One of the most important internal prerequisites is the opportunity to maintain a consistent, regular source of secure income; two of its greatest dangers are the sudden shift in economic conditions and the dependence of even the smallest agricultural business on a ready store of cold cash assets. Today we are experiencing the dramatic increase in precisely these dangers; this internal prerequisite seems most acutely at risk. Germany has become a predominately industrial country in the course of the past generation. For the first time in all the centuries of our history, the peasantry no longer constitutes the bulk of the German *Volk* as a whole. At the same time, modern transportation and technology threaten to suspend the geographical limitations that have thus far protected its uniqueness. Will these developments continue to wreak havoc on the German peasantry and throw it completely off its track? Will they completely destroy the thousand-year traditions of the peasantry, completely crush its thousand-year heritage? If the culture of ownership were ever to be truly shaken beneath their feet, German history would have reached its profoundest and most dangerous turning point.

For even today, the German peasantry is the ballast that keeps not only the ship of our state but indeed of our entire folkloric heritage and our *Volk* from capsizing in the storm. The need for this ballast in our German *Volk* is in fact twofold because we are still lacking the compass of a solid national instinct that guides other people through all the tides of change and upheaval. The German peasantry is the last great bulwark of nature in the fastidiously overrefined house of artifice our culture has become.

128

THEODOR SCHIEDER

East Prussia in the History of the Reich

First published as "Ostpreußen in der Reichsgeschichte," in *Volk und Reich* 14 (1938): 730–40.

The nation seemed to have forgotten about East Prussia until the tide began to turn, when the first and most decisive impulse was provided by the East Prussian battles in the Great War. The Battle of Tannenberg in 1914 was significant not only for the fact that world history was once again made on East Prussian soil in an event that would ultimately prove to be decisive for all subsequent developments in the eastern territories; with the liberation of East Prussia from Russian invasion, the psychological effect of this battle was to rekindle for the entire nation the sense of an internal reclamation of the territory. The fact that the battle was named after the events of 1410 at Tannenberg was not insubstantial in contributing to the profound sense of the historical impact felt by German military leadership that situated the victory of 1914 as a major event in the course of Prussian and German history.

In order to understand the magnitude of the 1918 catastrophe, we must bear in mind the tremendous impetus that the Battle of Tannenberg lent the German east. In 1918, the German east not only relinquished the far-reaching new opportunities that had been afforded it by the militarization of the eastern territory in the German military reich [*Kriegsreich*]; with the geographical strangulation that severed it from the mouth of the Memel River, it was also stripped of its geopolitical significance. The danger seemed all the more threatening because, as a result of the losses forced upon Germans in neighboring territories in West Prussia and the Baltic countries, there was a potential racial isolation from the *Volk*. When confronted with this situation, the people of East Prussia at least had the wherewithal to take their destiny into their own hands and to shape it according to their will in that fateful moment in which they passed the plebiscite of 11 July 1920.[1] This was an even greater accomplishment in light of the fact that the flimsy application of the right of self-determination, as outlined in the stipulations of the Versailles Treaty, certainly was not designed with considerations of German self-interest in mind. The aim was not to guarantee self-determination for the German people; it was, rather, to grant rights that were denied millions of Germans to alien, presumably oppressed racial and ethnic groups. When these stipulations that were designed as a means of defeating and dividing the German *Volk* were retooled to become guarantors of unity in the Germanic community, the Germanic people of East Prussia delivered a blow to the peacemakers of Versailles using their own weapons against them and conquering their system from within, for the main event in July 1920 was the awakening of the Germanic community—the sudden, spontaneous eruption of a new sense of community amongst the *Volk*, a new sense of national identity. If we focus primarily on the internal benefits that the referendum had, there is one feature that cannot be denied: over 350,000 Germans, despite the risks and costs involved in the effort, made their way back home in order to profess their faith in the Germanic racial identity of their homeland [by voting in the plebiscite]. The Entente Powers erroneously anticipated a mass emigration of Poles from the Reich, but what resulted from their granting the right of self-determination to anyone native to the designated zone—in a veritably symbolic contrast to the mass exodus of people they expected—was a return of German people that can be seen as the first expression of that shift in conceptual focus from the west to the east that is reflected in the life of our *Volk* today.

The true calamity of the years immediately following, in the liberal Weimar party state, was that this tremendous momentum toward internal and external recovery from Versailles was not used beyond its immediate political success and was not cultivated for its potential to help rebuild a new national order among the *Volk*. The will to go on the political offensive contained in the plebiscite gave way to a defensive stance according to which the question of East Prussia remained but a question of support and the means for solving it restricted to economic subsidies. But the empty slogans promising support and defense were not enough to lend meaning to the role that was to be played by East Prussia in the new Reich; that was a task that could be accomplished only by means of a political plan that conceived of the restructuring of the overall population as a restructuring of the east.

Here, too, the rise of National Socialism elicited change and reversal. A treatment of its current impact is not the subject of this historical overview, but its historical achievement has already been secured today: National Socialism has transformed East Prussia from a desolate, destitute region into a first-rate political sphere of Reich influence in the east. Here again, as was the case at the onset of the eighteenth and nineteenth centuries, political renewal and economic reconstruction meet head on. *Gauleiter* Erich Koch's plan for East Prussia, which forms the basis for the constructive rebuilding of the region, is an organic outgrowth of the historical exigencies of the province reaching all he way back to the feudal state [*Ordensstaat*]. But the ongoing estrangement of this region from the Reich has since become a thing of the past once and for all: East Prussia has regained its place in the fabric of the *Volk* as a whole. Already in Hitler's speech in Königsberg, on the day of the nation's awakening, 4 March 1933, East Prussia assumed a visible position in the Reich; for the first time since 1813, the call for the nation to rise was issued at this site. The historical past and political present have come full circle.

Note

1. This plebiscite was held under Allied auspices, whereby the vast majority in eastern West Prussia and southern East Prussia (more than 96 percent) voted for incorporation in the Weimar Republic as opposed to Poland.—Eds.

129

KLEO PLEYER

Volk in the Field

First published as *Volk im Feld* (Hamburg: Hanseatische Verlagsanstalt, 1943), 11–15, 184.

War is an organic element of the human community. It compels the community to form and maintain groups; it weeds out sham leadership and cultivates true leadership by natural selection. War, by allowing the strong man, the tough man, the hero to prevail over the weakling, the milksop, the coward; by spurring incentive for the development of strength and sacrifice; by demanding the utmost from every individual man and forcing him to subordinate himself to the higher order of the community, war creates values and hierarchies that are essential to the existence of *Volk,* state, and culture.

War places man at the crossroads between life and death, at the portal to the last things, at the gateway to the Kingdom of God. War is the staging ground for the profoundest virtue and for mankind's most powerful expression of morality: the spirit of sacrifice. War is where God and the world become one; it sanctifies the mortal task of killing with the divine blessing of self-sacrifice. The moral value of military service and sacrifice exists independent of the aims and justification of any given war. Whoever is willing to place his own life on the line for the sake of a greater good has acted nobly. Whoever views his own life as one of sacrifice has transcended human limitations. The man who sacrifices his life is a superman [*Übermensch*].

War is an intensifying event. It greatens the great, strengthens the strong, ennobles the noble; it debases the base. War spreads its wings to transcend the realm of mortal human existence; it dips down into the substrata of human existence and reaches into the heights of superhuman existence. The man who is more predisposed to the subhuman will be more inclined to experience the subhuman aspects of war; the man who is capable of reaching superhuman heights will achieve the superhuman in war. The strong are the ones who die in war; heroes are more likely to fall than the cowardly. But every death in the house of heroic men begets and bequeaths heroic men in future generations. The hero is immortal. [. . .]

The German *Volk,* constituting as it does the people at the geographic center of Europe, has more neighbors and is thus more at risk than any other racial group on the planet. Germany, as a result of its geopolitical position, as a result of its standing in the world of races and states, was faced with the need for tightly regimented organization within its ranks and for an aggressively offensive stance. Nietzsche's motto "Live dangerously!" was nothing new to the historically minded Germans. For the Germanic race living in the center of Europe, there was never anything but this dangerous life. But there were indeed periods of defeat in which this basic fact—and with it, the very essence of the German existence—has been misapprehended and held in contempt. The result has been a disruption of the native habitat of the German race, a rift driven through the very life force of the *Volk,* splintering it into factions that were pitted against one another in disputes. Whenever Germany's factions have joined together along a united front, this has produced periods of progress and prosperity and of exceptional historical achievement.

Germany must remain strong in order to maintain the space it needs. Germany's struggle in central European territory is and never was merely an attempt to wrestle over space sufficient to suit its needs; it has, rather, always been and remains a struggle for the power to determine the politics of its own ancestral living space, a defensive struggle against encroaching peoples and state forces, a defensive struggle against attempts at economic and ideological infiltration of foreign elements. [. . .]

Harsh words may at times be exchanged between exhausted, dead-tired, irritated men. But camaraderie, the solidarity among soldiers, remains unaffected by them. Do not ever underestimate the unrivaled value of front-line camaraderie! There are situations in life where men deceive one another, where they try to cheat one another or pit one against another. But we know who we are and we have mutual respect for one another; we've been together at the place where any appearance of feigned humanity falls by the wayside and only the essence of true manhood survives. Together we have entered the gates of death and have come back alive together. [. . .]

As we march along the roads, we are met with Polish and Belorussian refugees who have left their homes either voluntarily or involuntarily and are now returning to where the German soldier and, with him, peace, has arrived. Whereas the French refugees carry the belongings they cannot part with in vehicles, these men carry all they own in a bundle. This is how much more modest the men in the east are, how little they need. The refugees bear their wretched fate with a tremendous faculty for suffering, the faculty for suffering that is unique to the people of the east.

The marketplaces and the rural towns are teeming with Jews. Many of them have yet to grasp the fact that their time has come. "Oh, you fine men," the Jewish girls say, standing in the doorways ogling our militiamen, not at all disinclined to exchange yesterday's Red army uniform for the field gray of today. Indeed, there are Jews who would boldly declare, "We are fascists." They may as well add, "We are whatever is currently en vogue, we'll make a deal on anything, we'll even sell our souls, as long as there is no cost to us and it has already proven to yield substantial returns. We sincerely hope that the honorable National Socialist sires will be convinced of the advantageous nature of our proposition." They will not. The Jew has always been able to make a mint off of being a conservative, a liberal, a democrat, a Social Democrat or a Communist. But the masquerade is over now. The Jew is about to face the worst business deal he's ever made—and it's going to cost him his neck.

130

ERNST KRIECK

The German of the German Language Society

First published as "Vom Deutsch des deutschen Sprachvereins," in *Volk im Werden* 2 (1934), 128–29.

When [Georg Wilhelm Friedrich] Hegel published his *Phenomenology of Spirit,* he wrote a smug letter to [Johann Heinrich] Voß explaining that, in the same way Voß had taught Homer to speak German, he, Hegel, had taught him philosophy. And this in light of the book's tongue-twisting title! With the same delusional arrogance J[ohannes] Harms praised [Martin] Heidegger as a master of the language of German philosophy in his article titled "On the German Language of German Philosophers," published in the journal *Muttersprache* [Mother Tongue] (vol. 1, 1934).

Let us for the moment gloss over the fact that the whole article is but a transparent attempt at promoting Heidegger's philosophy under false pretenses; we must, nevertheless, conclude that Harms himself writes in conspicuously bad German, and the reason is that he cannot think clearly. What, for example, is "elementary-school-trained philosophical layperson" supposed to mean? It makes about as much sense as a wooden anvil! And yet this is what prompts Harms to present Heidegger's statement about "negating Nothingness" as exemplary, a statement that is unlikely to be understood by any philosopher, nor by any elementary-school philosopher, nor by any layperson or member of the German Language Society. And it is the same thing that permits Harms to praise not only Heidegger's language as exemplary but also disparage the language of the "philosopher from Berlin"—and that means the Jewish philosopher—[Georg] Simmel. In Mr. Harm's own words, "In both instances, the reason for this is use or misuse of the German language."

Harms suggests that the following statement of Heidegger's is particularly "clear": "The self-sufficient integrity of being [*Dasein*], not grounded in hidden anxiety, expresses itself in the overcoming of total existence: transcendence."[1] Statements demonstrating this degree of "clarity" and intrinsic Germanness can be plucked from Heidegger's work by the hundreds! A few randomly selected examples include: "A covered railway platform takes account of bad weather; an installation for public lighting takes account of the darkness, or rather of specific changes in the presence or absence of daylight-the 'position of the sun,' ."[2] On the south wind: "as a mere occurrence that is meteorologically accessible, the south wind is never initially objectively present at hand, sometimes assuming the function of an omen. On the contrary, circumspection first discovers the south wind in its Being by taking the lay of the land into account."[3] Splendid clarity of language! Marvelous German!

Notes

1. Martin Heidegger, *Was ist Metaphysik?* (Bonn: F. Cohen, 1931), 22.
2. Martin Heidegger, *Sein und Zeit* (Halle: Niemeyer, 1929), 71.
3. Ibid., 81.

131

ERNST KRIECK

Philosophy

First published as "Philosophie," in *Deutsche Wissenschaft: Arbeit und Aufgabe* (Leipzig: Verlag S. Hirzel, 1939), 29–31.

Since philosophy does not have its own object of inquiry, since it is not marked by clearly defined boundaries, overviews are difficult to provide: in philosophy, various areas of specialty conjoin. The only task that philosophy can fulfill is to lay the foundation for all sciences from the perspective of a given worldview.

Philosophy, in the traditional sense, is characterized by a principle of universalism. But since the National Socialist worldview, as Reich Leader [Alfred] Rosenberg recently outlined in an article published in the press, has put an end to every form of universalism and replaced it with a principle of race and *Volk,* the logical consequence for philosophy, because it clings so tenaciously to universalism, is that it be declared null and void and that it be supplanted by a racial-*völkisch* cosmology and anthropology. This, then, is the standard of measure for an array of works that have been published since 1933 under the banner of "philosophy." The bourgeois philosophy of the eighteenth century paved the way for the bourgeois revolution. The National Socialist revolution took the philosophy of its time utterly off guard and thus ran roughshod over it. The result was that in most cases a rigorous fixation on the past set in, whereby every attempt was made to disassociate philosophy and science from ideological principles. As human being and as national comrade, one was committed to the racial-*völkisch* worldview; on the other hand, philosophy and science, which had already fallen into the hands of the epigones and were already poised on the brink of ruin, were gripped by utter uncertainty, a lack of productivity, and outdatedness. One department of the philosophy of law, for example, hosted a public event in 1935 in which nearly all the schools of thought of the nineteenth century were represented—the only thing missing was the word *National*

Socialist. Most recently, an editor for an official party organ [*Bücherkunde,* the publication of the Rosenberg Office for the Propagation of Literature (Amtes für Schrifttumspflege)] announced that the rational universalism as present in the work of Fichte and Hegel, for example, should be taken as a standard for judging philosophical works. What follows from a position such as this is that contemporary philosophy, in the majority of instances, is not guided by the National Socialist worldview but rather by the antiquated epigones of Kant, Hegel, Nietzsche, etc. It would not be worth the effort to cite individual works of this nature here. What merits mention is that, with the recent publication of *On Man,* by the senile Werner Sombart, we can expect an assault from the ranks of the "humanities" camp of epigones who seek to undermine every basic premise in the National Socialist worldview (the racial principle, etc.). This school of thought is, incidentally, typical of substantial circles within philosophy, the natural sciences, and the humanities, although it is generally better camouflaged than this. And what is characteristic of this school of thought is its fixation on the epigone and its tendency to look backward.

The year 1938 brought with it substantial progress in one significant regard, even though it was hardly registered by the outside world: the attempt, which extended over several years, on the part of scientific materialism (largely in the spirit of [Ernst] Haeckel) to hold a monopoly on the racial principle—that is, to place a materialistic tack on worldview, philosophy, and the humanities—was crushed. The very attempt was doomed from the start simply by virtue of the lack of scholarly productivity on the part of its proponents. Solid scholarship does not emerge from establishing rules but rather emanates from fertile creative prowess.

In general, we suffer from the fundamental problem that fostering science and scholarship is all too often seen strictly from an organizational standpoint, even as we gloss over the fact that it is creativity that provides the impetus and constitutive force in science and scholarship just as it does in art, and if it is not actively discouraged, is simply swept under the carpet. In every other area of endeavor, even in technology, the revolution has succeeded in drawing precisely those creative forces to the surface; but in scholarship, the principle of an easily organized tractable mediocrity has prevailed. And it is philosophy in particular that has become utterly worthless and completely fruitless as a result.

In all of his major speeches in 1933, the Führer outlined the content and purpose of the National Socialist revolution again and again; for the sake of education, he demanded a corresponding portrait of the evolution of the German *Volk* and himself provided the basic outline for this historical profile in which a new conception of the world and of the human race is perfected. And the entire revolution itself emanated from an exceptional and unique sense of historical consciousness. Unfortunately, with the exception of very few contributions, one would be hard-pressed to conclude that philosophy took on this task and thus inaugurated a new epoch for itself. The works of [Ernst] von Krieck are exemplary in this regard: Völkisch-*Political Anthropology* (1936–37), *Life as Ideological Principle* (1938).

In the process, Krieck has been similarly instrumental in providing the movement with the attendant impetus in the field of education. All these things developed from within the movement itself—they were not introduced by outsiders.

An adequate treatment of the principle that dominated the bourgeois worldview for three centuries and that has placed the Germans in a position of scholarly dependency on the West can be found in Franz Böhm's work *Anti-Cartesianism, German Philosophy in Resistance* (1937); Wilhelm Classen has provided a treatment of scholasticism from the perspective of National Socialist anthropology.

[Alfred] Baeumler has heralded Nietzsche as the spiritual and scholarly leader of National Socialism, which is, at the very least, problematic; old Hermann Schwarz seeks to adapt pantheistic mysticism to the needs of the movement, and [Ernst] Bergmann takes a similar approach but ends up taking recourse to feminism, which is not surprising in the least.

There are several areas in which German intellectual history is currently being revised as an integral component of the evolution of the German race [*Volkswerdung*]. Beginning with the standpoint of the worldview, we can expect to see substantial strides being taken toward a new conceptualization of the world and of man, here as well as in the history of the natural sciences.

The composite result of a mere five years, of course, has produced but a meager and inadequate body of works on National Socialist philosophy as compared to that of the dead epigones that remains predominant and thus bars the way for the emergence of this new train of thought.

132

ARNOLD GEHLEN

The State and Philosophy

First published as "Der Staat und die Philosophie" (1935), in Arnold Gehlen, *Gesamtausgabe Bd.2,* edited by Lothar Samson (Frankfurt am Main: Vittorio Klostermann, 1980), 2:303–4, 308–10.

The relationship between state and *Volk* and these forces as they relate to the individual, in all its dimensions, has now necessarily and naturally expanded the subject of spirit and mind, and hence of philosophy: we are no longer dealing merely with the parameters of an ontological field in which the problem of God and the Platonic trope are equally subsumed but with a field that is the *true* province of philosophy. This furthermore challenges the abstract contemplative egotism of philosophical thought and relinquishes it; expressed in idealistic terms: the task becomes one of seeking to arrive at the point at which consciousness and Being intersect—that is, to point toward the possibility of an existence that is *whole.* Philosophy necessarily instructs us how to live and outlines what life itself consists of. In this context, then, *Volk* and state comprise the components of life itself, and it is here that the laws of Being that are the province of metaphysics become tangible: Plato, in his investigations of justice, did not examine the small letters of mankind but rather the magnitude of the state. Internal compulsion led him from ethical inquiries to ontological and metaphysical ones, and to answer these questions in terms of political symbolism. And now I shift the focus of the question and say: the dissolution of the state and the conception of the *Volk* that has occurred on a theoretical level in philosophy since the Enlightenment and on a practical level through its application has disabled and corrupted man's consciousness for the metaphysical, has led to false convictions about man himself and his relationship to the world, and has, in an absolute sense, debilitated man. For example, the notion of the state as an apparatus that can be fundamentally and arbitrarily altered represents a substantial deception with regard to the degree of freedom that can be tolerated, with regard to that which man is capable of doing and that which man is capable of desiring. For, in point of fact, the state is testimony to the same truth expressed by religion and by life itself: man is a creature, involuntarily hurled into existence [*Dasein*] and by virtue of this being hurled into existence already defined and characterized: for the state is the determinate force that sets the parameters for the narrow margin of decision making available to all those who are born into it; *Volkstum* and race are the predetermined constants underlying an astonishingly broad spectrum of possibilities for characteristics of existence [*Daseinszüge*] and decision making on the part of each individual. [. . .]

Philosophy has always been concerned with the study of existence at the site at which it is most intense, with making it comprehensible and thus seeking to provide testimony and itself acting as testimony. We must assume that, for contemporary purposes, this site at which existence, the belief in existence, and the realization of existence is most intense can hardly be situated in the province of religious existence but rather that of political existence, and we are thus concerned with a new and, if you will, a third form of the natural subject of philosophy. Therefore, if the National Socialist movement that has given this *Volk* new impulses for life and a new ordering of its existence should conclude that the humanities (first and foremost the field of philosophy) are sciences that are innately ours, that must be congruent with ourselves, then it would not seek to present philosophy with so-called new tasks but rather, on the contrary, would direct it to its own unique determination. But the task of philosophy certainly cannot be to approach out of nowhere the authentic, established positions that have been advanced, proved, and disseminated and to seek to determine whether they are true or false according to arbitrarily determined standards. Rather, once we have redefined that which is "most likely to be known," this is what we must ultimately conclude:

It is not only the *Volk* and the concrete order of living it gives itself (and in which it expresses as well as form itself as a *Volk*) that is the central point of all those philosophical endeavors to grasp the inherent matter of being; it is also the higher existential experience—both are necessary to enliven a philosophy that cannot be apolitical, just as it could not be unreligious in the thirteenth century. But it is only these experiences that allow for an internal organzation of the vast and extremely heterogeneous array of traditional problems in philosophy: to formulate new problems that are actually relevant, to discard those that are void of content and have become conventional, and to reevaluate the meaning behind others that have long since been forgotten and cast them in a new light. And it is not the wholly false Hegelian doctrine according to which, over time, philosophy itself preserves and indeed resolves the thought patterns, solutions, inquiries, and results that leads us to the philosophy of German idealism; we have implied that the opposite is true—namely, that a rapid disintegration of the very culture of thought, a depletion of categories and even an extreme impoverishment of jargon, a completely incomprehensible degeneration of the very organ for higher and more profound thought processes and problems has emerged over the course of at least the past one hundred years. And these are the two factors which, in my way of thinking, render the philosophy of German idealism epochal: the fact that one is forced to excavate from these buried ruins the complex, multifaceted, manifold, and content-filled categories that are so essential to our self-understanding, and that it was this philosophy that speaks not only to those who think but equally to human beings who act.

133

GERHARD FRICKE

The German of the Enlightenment

First published as "Der deutsche Mensch der Aufklärung," in *Der deutsche Mensch* (Stuttgart: Deutsche Verlags-Anstalt, 1935), 135–39.

The fact that, throughout his life, the great, enlightened Prussian king [Frederick II (the Great)] considered the French language the only adequate form of verbal and written expression for any educated man is no less coincidental than the fact that the hero of the first German humanistic drama [*Nathan the Wise,* by Gotthold Ephraim Lessing] was a Jew. The most decisive insight of the Enlightenment was, of course, that it sought to separate what was true and good from any of its false, heteronymous foundations and to elevate it, in its own internal inevitability, to an immediate, binding, universally human certainty. Truth and justice are not contingent upon historical traditions, institutions, or ecclesiastical statutes but are rather intrinsically valid in their own right. Increasingly, the term *reason* came to signify the notion that the value and eternal destiny of man were incontrovertibly secured in each individual human being.

But the Enlightenment, on its emancipatory path of dislodging truth and justice from all presuppositions, came to a uniquely German result.

Truth and justice are like a mathematical equation in that they are equal and inalterable. Every human being is in possession of the natural faculty to be internally compelled toward truth and justice. This is what calls people to the task of allowing themselves to be guided exclusively by the eternal principles of truth and justice and to overcome anything that might distract them from this unadulterated fulfillment of moral reason. What are the forces that might distract men from their obligation to fulfill their own moral destiny? In essence, anything that cannot be dissolved in abstract exigency and the purity of rational law—for example, the positivistic religions that conjoin human actions with certain specific historical events, people, and ceremonies. But justice and truth are the same in Turkey as they are in Germany. A follower of Mohammed gleans his standard for moral conduct from the Koran, a Christian gleans his from the Bible, and the professional priesthood fosters this weakness in men rather than taking seriously the internal purity of action and countenance as such, ever emphasizing the outer trappings of Christian or Islamic ceremonies, justifications, etc. Man is compelled to do the right thing because it is Christ's command—instead of recognizing that Christ commanded it only because it was the right thing to do. And the result is that others who do the same while obeying the command of Moses or Mohammed are despised and made into bitter enemies. The value of religions cannot be determined based on conflicting dogmas, sacred traditions, or historical miracles but rather on their moral achievement. Absolute tolerance follows from the conviction that the selfsame moral law of reason is the fundamental core of all religions and that anything beyond that is just an outer shell, arbitrary historical window dressing. This tolerance renders the external differences between religions worthless and hence harmless. It works to countervail against the danger of reducing faith to the superficial, "positivistic" modalities of the individual traditions and statutes and the subsequent reduction of religious aims to the fanatical opposition of other traditions and statutes. In this way, the positivistic religions are basically faced with little more than the splendid task of rendering themselves obsolete; that is, the task of purging themselves of everything but their fundamental moral rationale becomes decisive, and the remaining external elements and institutions become insignificant extraneous details.

A not insignificant resistance to the realization of humanistic pure reason is represented by the national, racial, and *völkisch* determinacy of human beings—described in *Nathan the Wise* as but a product of the "circumstance of birth"—which demonstrates a tendency toward establishing itself as absolute that is very similar to that in the historical and positivistic religions. But for Lessing, black, yellow, or white skin is merely a surface matter of skin color and not a reflection of the rational structures of the black, yellow, or white hearts that operate eternally and ineluctably in human beings. Of course, Lessing concedes that differences between religions, races, and nations cannot simply be dissolved—no one can escape his own skin—and Nathan forever remains the same Jew he was from the beginning simply by circumstance of birth. But the point then becomes one of allowing these positive determinations, which unfortunately cannot be disassociated from earthly existence, to seem as insignificant and innocuous as possible. The point becomes one of allowing one pure, inevitable, and universal rational humanism to assume so much power that everything that is positive about denominational, *völkisch,* racial determinations of human beings becomes transparent by comparison and is made to seem baseless and insignificant. [. . .]

Let us summarize the results, with a sharp focus on the basic points. Enlightened rational humanism leads to a radical devaluation and dissolution of the historical reality of men, which is determined by destiny and by nature itself. What results from the fact that, in Germany, mathematical and moral reason is wrenched from the context of men's lives, that it supplants religion and is hypostatized into an eternal and incontrovertible universal law, is the inevitable dissolution of all individual, concrete, and historical determinations of man, which is to say, however, it leads to the dissolution of life's reality itself. The fact that this essentially obliterates the *völkisch* nationalist consciousness of the Germans resulting from the course of their political history rests on a fundamental justification of this process through the maxims of moral reason.

134

ALFRED BAEUMLER

Nietzsche and National Socialism

First published as "Nietzsche und der Nationalsozialismus," in *Studien zur deutschen Geistesgeschichte* (Berlin: Junker und Dünnhaupt Verlag, 1943), 283–85, 88–294. Published in English in George L. Mosse, ed., *Nazi Culture* (Madison: University of Wisconsin Press), 97–101.

Nietzsche and National Socialism are situated beyond the traditions of the German bourgeoisie, but what does that mean? The spiritual forces that have formed the German bourgeoisie in the last several centuries have been Pietism, the Enlightenment, and Romanticism. Pietism was the last truly revolutionary religious movement on Lutheran soil. It led men from a hopeless political reality back into their own selves and gathered them together in small private circles. It was a religious individualism that strengthened the inclination toward concern with self, toward psychological analysis and biographical examination. Every apolitical anti-state tendency necessarily had to find support and nourishment in Pietistic Germany. The individualism of the Enlightenment was of an utterly different kind, but also worked in this direction. This individualism was not religious-sentimental in character; rather, it believed in reason, it was rational; it was "political" only in that it opposed the feudal system; it was unable to erect an enduring political system of its own and was capable only of preparing the path for the economic system of capitalism. Man was viewed as a wholly individual entity, independent of all original orders and relations, a fictitious subject responsible only to himself. In contrast, Romanticism saw man again in the light of his natural and historical ties. Romanticism opened our eyes to the night, the past, our ancestors, to mythos, and to the *Volk*. The movement that led from [Johann Gottfried] Herder to [Joseph] von Görres, to the brothers Grimm, [Joseph von] Eichendorff, [Ludwig Achim von] Arnim, and [Friedrich Karl von] Savigny, is the only spiritual movement that is still fully alive [bracketed inserts ours—Eds.]. And it is also the only movement with which Nietzsche chose to grapple. . . .

When we describe National Socialism as a worldview, what we mean is that not only the bourgeois parties but also their ideologies have been obliterated. Only malicious people could maintain that everything that has been created by the past must now be negated. What we are saying is, far more, that we have entered into a new relationship with our past, that our view has been cleared for what was truly forceful in this past but which was obscured by bourgeois ideology. In a word, we have discovered new possibilities for understanding the essence of German existence. Precisely in this, Nietzsche has preceded us. We hold a view of Romanticism that is different from his. But what was his most intimate and solitary asset—the wholesale negation of bourgeois ideology—has today become the property of a generation. [. . .]

The foundations of Christian morality—religious individualism, the knowledge of original sin, humility, concern for the soul's eternal salvation of the soul—all are absolutely foreign to Nietzsche. He revolts against the concept of repentance: "I do not like this kind of cowardice about one's own action; one should not leave one's own self in the lurch before the assault of unexpected disgrace and vexation. Rather, an extreme pride is in order here. For, finally, what is the use! No deed can be undone by repentance." His implication here is not a reduction of responsibility, but rather its intensification. Here speaks the man who knows how much courage, how much pride, is necessary to maintain himself in the face of Fate. Out of his *amor fati* Nietzsche spoke contemptuously about Christianity with its "prospects for salvation." As a Nordic man, he never understood for what purpose he should be "redeemed." The Mediterranean religion of salvation is alien to and far removed from his Nordic attitude. He can only conceive of man as a warrior against Fate. A mode of thought that sees struggle and work only as a penance is incomprehensible to him. "Our real life is a false, apostatic, and sinful existence, a penal existence." Sorrow, battle, work, and death are merely taken as objections to life. "Man as innocent, idle, immortal, happy—this concept of 'highest desirability' especially must be criticized." Nietzsche turns passionately upon the monastic *vita contemplativa,* against Augustine's notion of the "Sabbath of all Sabbaths." ' He credits Luther with having put an end to this *vita contemplativa.* The Nordic tenor of the struggle and of labor is resoundingly clear. The tenor with which we enunciate these words today is one whose echo was first heard in Nietzsche.

We call Nietzsche the philosopher of the heroic. But the truth of that statement is only half understood as long as he is not at the same time seen as the philosopher of activism. He saw himself as the greatest antagonist of Plato in the history of the world. Great "works" do not proceed merely from the sense of vision or perspective, from the acknowledgement of transcendent values, but rather from practice. In order to clarify this, Nietzsche takes recourse to a well-known antithesis: "First and foremost, there are the works. And that implies practice, practice, practice! The attendant articles of faith will follow on their own—of that much you can be certain." Nietzsche opposes the Christian proscriptions against the political sphere, of the sphere of action altogether, with the thesis that also overcame the contrast between Catholicism and Protestantism (the works and articles of faith): "One has to train oneself not in the strengthening of value feelings, but in action; one has to know how to do something." In this way, he re-established the purity of the sphere of action, of the political sphere.

Nietzsche's "values" have nothing to do with the "Hereafter," and therefore cannot be petrified into dogma. In ourselves, through us, they rise struggling to the surface; they exist only as long as we make ourselves responsible for them. When Nietzsche warns, "Be true to the Earth!" he reminds us of the idea that is rooted in our strength but does not hope for "realization" in a distant "Hereafter." It is not enough to point out the "this-worldly" character of Nietzsche's values if one at the same time does not want to refute the notion that values are "realized" by action. Something inferior is always attached to the "realization" of given values, regardless whether these values are of a mundane or extramundane character. [. . .]

Nietzsche's Nordic and soldierly valuation opposes that of the Mediterranean world and that of the priests. His critique of religion is a criticism of the priest, and arises from the point of view of the warrior, since Nietzsche demonstrates that even the origin of religion lies in the realm of power. This explains the fateful contradiction in a morality based on the Christian religion. "To secure the rule of moral values, all kinds of immoral forces and passions must be enlisted. The development of moral value is the work of amoral passions and considerations." Morality, therefore, is the creation of immorality. "How to bring virtue to rule: this treatise deals with the great politics of virtue." It teaches for the first time "that one cannot bring about the reign of virtue by the same means used to establish any kind of rule, least of all through virtue." "One has to be very immoral to make morality through deeds. . . . Nietzsche replaces the bourgeois moral philosophy with the philosophy of the will to power—in other words, with the philosophy of politics. If, in doing so, he becomes the apologist for the "unconscious," this "unconscious" is not to be understood in psychoanalytic terms.

The concern is not with the instinctive and unconscious drives of an individual here; rather, "the unconscious" in this context is to be understood as "perfected," "adept." Furthermore, the unconscious refers here to life itself, to the organism, the "grand rationality" of the body.

Consciousness is only a tool, one detail in the totality of life. In opposition to the philosophy of the conscious, Nietzsche asserts the aristocracy of nature. But for thousands of years, a morality that is hostile to life has opposed the aristocracy of the strong and healthy. Like National Socialism, Nietzsche sees in the state, in society, the "great mandate of life," responsible for each life's failure to life itself. "The species requires the extinction of the misfits, weaklings, and degenerates: but Christianity as a conserving force appeals especially to them." Here we encounter the basic contradiction: whether one proceeds from a natural life context, or from an equality of individual souls before God. Ultimately, the ideal of democratic equality rests upon the latter assumption. The former contains the foundations of a new policy. It takes unexcelled boldness to base a state upon the race. A new order of things is the natural consequence. It is this order that Nietzsche undertook to establish in opposition to the existing one. In the face of the overpowering strength of the race, what happens to the individual? He returns—as a single member in a community. The herd instinct is fundamentally distinct from the instinct of an "aristocratic society" composed of strong, natural men who do not permit their basic instincts to languish in favor of a mediocre average—men who know how to curb and control their passions instead of weakening or negating them. This again must not be understood from an individualistic point of view. For a long time emotions will have to be kept under "tyrannical" control. This can be done only by one community, one race, one people. [. . .]

If there ever was a truly German expression, it is this: one must have the need to be strong; otherwise, one never will be. We Germans know what it means to maintain ourselves against all opposition. We understand the "will to power"—even if in an altogether different manner than what our enemies assume. Even in this context, Nietzsche has supplied the deepest meaning: "We Germans demand something from ourselves that nobody expected from us—we want more." If today we see German youth on the march under the banner of the swastika, we are reminded of Nietzsche's "untimely meditations" in which this youth was appealed to for the first time. It is our greatest hope that the state today is wide open to our youth. And if today we shout "Heil Hitler!" to this youth, at the same time we are also hailing Friedrich Nietzsche.

135

WOLFGANG SCHULTZ

Nietzsche's Zarathustra and the Historical Zarathustra

First published as "Nietzsches Zarathustra und der geschichtliche," in *Nationalsozialistische Monatshefte,* August 1935, 687–88, 692–93.

Can we place Nietzsche, who ultimately chose to bestow upon a Persian man, Zarathustra, the honor of selecting him, his apparent antinationalism notwithstanding, as the ideal man represented in his poetic-philosophical opus [*Thus Spoke Zarathustra*], in the same category [as Paul de Lagarde]? Why does Nietzsche bestow this honor to a Persian—Nietzsche, who, as a classical philologist, certainly has uncovered so much disparaging and damaging evidence against the Persians in his study of the Greek classics? Is it simply the exoticism, the relative obscurity, the fact that there are no strings attached, that he finds so attractive? Or is there more to it than that? It is conspicuous that even Kant once considered using a Zoroaster to embody his teachings. Does this not merit casting a net in search of sources that might produce a figure that is more suited to the history of the Nordic race?

Nietzsche introduces something new to modern philosophy inasmuch as he, unlike most of the great founders of new systems of thought, does not stand under the influence of the sciences of inanimate nature—that is to say, the so-called exact sciences and mathematics—but rather, as one who is naturally hostile to systems, as a philologist, and comes from the humanities and from history. He is not methodical in dissecting the conceptual differences in both fields, even though we find in his work substantial advances in this regard—but he thinks differently from the representatives of the exact thinking that strives to establish an abstract universal validity. He thinks instead in terms of singular historical events, ever seeking to cull from them the fundamental essence slumbering beneath their surface. In that sense, even from a distance, he has an intuitive grasp on the singularity, the uniqueness, of Zarathustra and of the Iranian mind-set and disposition.

Closer examination reveals that Nietzsche had a far more profound intuition and understanding for the driving forces behind Iranian thought than has previously been presumed. Seen from the perspective of literary history, Nietzsche's ideal man actually has little more in common with the historical Zarathustra than his name. Nietzsche's declaration [expressed in a 22 February 1884 letter to Erwin Rohde] that his Zarathustra was his creation alone and "without precedent, without peer, and without precursor" is entirely correct from a literary standpoint. All of it emanates from a grand inspiration that Nietzsche describes in radiant colors. One thing led to another and Zarathustra simply came to him and came over him in one of his bouts of midday madness. But the state of affairs from a perspective of intellectual history is a different matter altogether. [. . .]

And yet one cannot underestimate how clearly Nietzsche understood Zarathustra even beyond the doctrine of recurrence and the thousand-year Reich that would thrust it into a cycle of perpetual return. An oft-cited Nietzsche citation assumes greater significance against this backdrop:

> People have never asked me, as they should have done, what the name Zarathustra precisely means in my mouth, in the mouth of the first Immoralist; for what distinguishes that Persian from all others in the past is the very fact that he was exactly the reverse of an immoralist. Zarathustra was the first to see in the struggle between good and evil the essential wheel in the working of things. The translation of morality into the metaphysical, as force, cause, end in itself, was *his* work. But the very question suggests its own answer. Zarathustra *created* the most portentous error, *morality;* consequently, he should also be the first to *perceive* that error, not only because he has had a longer and greater experience of the subject than any other thinker—all history is the experimental refutation of the theory of the so-called moral order of things—the more important point is that Zarathustra was more truthful than any other thinker. In his teaching alone do we meet with truthfulness upheld as the highest virtue—i.e., the reverse of the *cowardice* of the "idealist" who flees from reality. Zarathustra had more courage in his body than any other thinker before or after him. To tell the truth and *to aim straight:* that is the first Persian virtue. Am I understood? The overcoming of morality through itself—through truthfulness, the overcoming of the moralist through his opposite—*through me*—that is what the name Zarathustra means in my mouth. [Translation of Nietzsche by Elizabeth Förster-Nietzsche.] [. . .]

These passages—the only ones in which Nietzsche's knowledge of Persia and of Zarathustra are reasonably accessible—teach us that what appears at first blush to be his purely superficial knowledge of Iran is nevertheless extensive enough and at the same time very profound. He comprehends and intuits more of the driving forces behind Iranian thought than one would like to presume. And he does it under the auspices of his own spiritual and intellectual struggle, though this struggle admittedly takes—again, at first glance—decidedly different twists and turns. One need only call to mind the five things he most vehemently opposed: morality, Christianity, democracy, Romanticism, socialism (Marxism). [Hans] Vaihinger pointed out several additional prohibitions: against feminism, against intellectualism, against pessimism. The list could continue, and it is particularly important to add, against the Jews as well. Long stretches of this list are congruent or convergent with our National Socialist line of thought, and in fact, it only diverges decidedly from ours on two points. Our National Socialist agenda is unequivocally in favor of morality and positive Christianity. But once the reductionist comparisons have leveled themselves ad absurdum, even the immoralist Nietzsche favors a new world order and does everything in his power to hone our senses to that. And even when he is vehement in his annoyance at the Germans for still not having fulfilled what he sees as their world-historical mission in life—namely to become the first non-Christian race in Europe—he does this primarily with respect to the new world order he hopes to herald. Many excesses, much that cannot be condoned has been glossed over here. Nevertheless, this struggle for the mental and ethical position that will guide the German future will remain instructive for anyone who hopes to forge a path to a solidly German worldview. [. . .]

This doctrine [of good and evil] likely had residual influence in the later stages of ancient Germanic culture. Iranian, ancient Germanic, and German attitudes are innately related; they are racially Nordic. And the great thinker of Ephesus, Heraclitus, belongs to this community of great spirits, and Nietzsche, too, who, despite myriad historical detours, obstacles, and occasional distractions, nevertheless has followed in his footsteps and in the Iranian tradition on the most paramount points. The proponents of Spitama Zarathustra's teachings, the great Persian kings and, before them, Darejawosch, are members of the nobility; they have the new belief to thank for the stability of their world empire.[1]

Note

1. Darejawosch was a legendary Persian king who ruled in the sixth century.—Eds.

136

HEINRICH HÄRTLE

Nietzsche and National Socialism

First published in *Nietzsche und der Nationalsozialismus* (Munich: Verlag Franz Eher Nachfolger GmbH, 1938), 82–83, 162–64.

In the wake of his fateful break with Schopenhauer and Wagner, Nietzsche drifted too far into the antithesis. Above all, he sees romanticism as strictly negative. And yet our modern concept of the *Volk* has its source in romanticism, even as it transcends romanticism by leaps and bounds. The National Socialist concept of the *Volk* is formulated not only from a historical and intuitive perspective, it has equally firm footing in science and biology.

At one point, Nietzsche attempted to describe the development of a *Volk* as follows: "When human beings have lived together under similar conditions (climate, soil, danger, needs, work) for a long time, then something arises out of that which "understands itself," a people—a *Volk*.

What is lacking here is the thing that is decisive for us, race. It is only because Nietzsche—as a product of his time—did not conceive of the *Volk* as a racial entity that he was able to distance himself so much from his *Volk*.

But for us, the *Volk* is not just a race. We acknowledge the "perpetual mutation" [*Dauermodifikation*] of our inherited racial stock through space and history, geography and fate. But the emphasis is on the racial. A Jew may reside for a thousand years within the community of shared destiny and space of the German people, but he will never become a *Volk* comrade. But the Huguenots, with their Nordic predisposition, did become full-fledged *Volk* comrades.

To speak in terms of race as the basic foundation of the *Volk* is not to imply racial purity in the biological sense. And yet our conception of the *Volk* does include a specific degree of racial miscegenation, whereby a racially inherited chromatic strain predominates, as, for example, the Mediterranean strain does in the Italians or the Nordic-Germanic strain does in the German *Volk*.

Any people that is in this sense a genuine *Volk* comprises a natural synthesis, an organic community of geopolitically, historically, biologically related men who are bound by a common destiny. A physical, psychological, spiritual, and intellectual community of people: a *Volk* is a community of people that is of one body, one soul, one spirit, and one mind. The National Socialist concept of the *Volk* conjoins the natural sciences and the humanities, feeling and fact, instinct and insight, experience and appraisal. The *Volk* is the most modern of political concepts.

This clarification seems to me the necessary prerequisite for understanding why Nietzsche was almost inevitably destined to fall short of grasping the concept of *Volk*. A half century of cataclysmic historical, ideological, and biological development lies between him and us. That which was heroically ahead of its time was necessarily a product of its time. And that is why it was bound to end in tragedy.

[. . .] As its greatest adversary of the nineteenth century, Nietzsche ruthlessly opposed the Second Reich; undeceived by its superficial successes, he exposed the bourgeois culture of corruption, the Christian-patriotic and liberal-Marxist compromise. And yet his overly brazen conceptualization of Europe hindered him in adequately honoring what Bismarck accomplished. [. . .]

One of the greatest moments in the world of Nietzsche's thought is the ingenious way in which he anticipates knowledge of the racial prerequisites underlying all values. And yet he fails to come to positive conclusions in this regard. He considers the bastardization of Europe inevitable and can only hope for a new master "race." This has a detrimental effect on the whole of his political thought. His racial instinct is unerring only in the depths of valuation.

The assumption that racial miscegenation is inevitable seduces him into advocating an assimilation of the Jews. Nor does he do justice to then-contemporary anti-Semitism. But when he recognizes the Jewish at the level of values, that is when he charges them with the greatest abomination, expressing the most overwhelming protest against two thousand years of racial desecration and the fraudulent transmogrification of values.

There has not been a more serious racial hygienist philosopher than Nietzsche since Plato. Inasmuch as his philosophy calls for the annihilation of any illusions concerning the purpose and meaning of existence, he establishes that the real task of human existence is the cultivation and breeding of a higher race of man. But he does not manage to take this a step further and clearly identify this task in concrete terms of improving the qualities of a *Volk* within the context of its natural proclivities; his demands remain universally applicable because he is lacking any organic concept of the *Volk*.

Despite many attempts, he is unable to establish a positive relationship to the *Volk*. The assumption of the inevitability of racial miscegenation compels him to reckon with a need to transcend the boundaries of nation and *Volk*. This leads him to become an adversary not only of formal nationalism but also of *völkisch* nationalism.

Throughout his life, he grappled with grasping the intrinsic nature of the German. Critical of national weaknesses in the Germans and then contemporary "things German," he became one of the most ruthless enemies in the history of great Germans. *Nevertheless, up until the end, he placed his highest hopes and aspirations in the fundamental ancient Germanic values of the Germans.*

In the midst of the dynastic patriotism that characterized his times, he advocated European unity. His concrete expectations in this regard were later confounded by history. His call for Nordic-Germanic leadership in world politics was indeed prescient.

Nietzsche is brusque in his condemnation of the atrophied form of state, one in which it is reduced to a mere institution, an institution as an end in itself. This is juxtaposed against majestic praise for the Greek state. He can only go so far in his concept of a future state because he has no substance to work with; he is lacking the concept of the *Volk*. Nevertheless, he sees "hierarchical ranking" and "structures of domination" as a prerequisite to the true state.

Nietzsche is not an individualist. And yet nor is he a *völkisch* socialist. His overemphasis on the "great individuals" and the lack of an organic concept of the *Volk* leads him into a means-to-an-end relationship between the rulers and the ruled; it leads him to the aristocratic extreme.

As remedies for the world of illusion and escape from reality, Nietzsche proposes the heroic affirmation of life, the mastery of reality, and ends up thus developing the notion of "grand politics" and advocating rule by "grand politicians."

Nietzsche's political thoughts can thus be summarized to include these basic points:

1. Exaggeration of the "great individual," underestimation of the remaining masses of the *Volk*
2. False presumption of the inevitability of racial miscegenation
3. Stringent emphasis on the natural differences between men
4. Affirmation of reality, ethical virtue of struggle
5. Enhancement of life as man's purpose in life
6. Affirmation of Germanic values, negation of Jewish values.

It is important to note here that Nietzsche's inner affinity toward National Socialism is greater than the political-historical effect he has had on National Socialism thus far.

Nietzsche's political insights are tremendous. Their real significance, however, is not so much in the realm of concrete politics as it is in the realm of the ideological system of values: he is the greatest judge of values and the greatest transformer of values of our times. (In concrete political terms, [Paul de] Lagarde, [Julius] Langbehn, and above all [Houston Stewart] Chamberlain are in some ways more closely aligned with us.)

But his political judgments contain fragments of National Socialism, and his philosophical creations are thus building blocks for a coming National Socialist philosophy. This is why I believe that Nietzsche will be seen as by far the most influential precursor to National Socialism.

Nietzsche is but the prophecy, not its fulfillment. The ingenuity of his judgments must be carried out by the ingenuity of their realization. If Nietzsche is not to have grappled with these things for naught—then the man of the Great War, the philosopher from the trenches, the thinker and doer must arrive: Adolf Hitler.

Nietzsche stands at the dawn of the twentieth century. In the brilliant nimbus of the visionary, in vague outlines, he views the emerging age. We stand at the break of day in the new age. Everything around us has cooled off, but it has also become clearer, and, with a well-defined aim in sight, we march forward into the National Socialist future.

And this future will be the future that Nietzsche envisioned.

PART FIVE

. . .

THE RACIAL COMMUNITY

11

Women and "the Woman Question"

NAZI EDUCATION provided a "special" status to women as the bearers of the next generation of the "race." Women had gradually been civilly emancipated in the various German-speaking states during the nineteenth century but were permitted to vote in the Weimar Republic as of November 1918. Women entered universities beginning in 1900 and were guaranteed access to the workplace. For Hitler, all of these advances grew out of the corruption of the German spirit by the Jews. He stated in 1934, "The word *women's emancipation* is merely an invention of the Jewish intellect, and its meaning is informed by the same spirit. The German woman never has any need for emancipation during those times when Germans are truly leading the 'good life.'" This view was certainly subscribed to by party stalwarts, even those living in Switzerland, such as the pseudonymous conservative women's activist Carola Struve (actually, Carola Tilman-Siebert).

The Nazi Party's position was unambiguous: women's primary role was that of mother. But a few Nazi women supported limited emancipation and advocated equal rights *within* the *Volk* community. As Paula Siber, the deputy leader of the official Düsseldorf women's organization, noted in her 1933 volume, "National Socialism [is] charged . . . with the task of a psychological-moral rebirth of the German race [and] will first have to elevate the woman question in all its profundity and its responsibility for *Volk* and *Volkstum* in the eyes of all sectors of the *Volk*—first and foremost for the masses of women themselves—to that which it truly is: a matter of life and death for the German *Volk,* a matter of blood and of the will to the future."

In September 1934, Hitler put an end to such heretical views. The creation of a Reichsbund der Kinderreichen (Reich Association for Multiple Offspring Families), a part of the state's Rassenpolitischen Amt (Racial-Political Office), sent a strong signal that women's proper role in the Reich was to procreate. The literary tradition of National Socialism had already enthroned the image of the self-sacrificing mother as a national heroine. Hanns Johst (1890–1978), the president of the Reich Literature Chamber from 1935 to 1945, transmuted the religious figure of Mary into a good German mother in his poetry. The poet and novelist Emil Strauß (1866–1960), whose popularity in the 1920s rivaled that of Thomas Mann, pointed poetically to the question of "blood" as the link between his mother and the *Volk*.

In accordance with Goebbels's dictum that "the most glorious task [woman] can perform is to give the gift of children to her people and nation," the state further created the Mother's Cross of Honor (*Ehrenkreuz der Deutschen Mutter,* popularly known as the *Mutterkreuz,* or Mother's Cross) on 21 May 1938 in imitation of the soldier's Iron Cross medal for bravery. The Mother's Cross bore the inscriptions "To the German Mother" and "The Child Honors the Mother" and was awarded each Mother's Day in three grades: bronze for mothers with four children, silver for mothers of six, and gold for mothers of eight or more. By 1939, three million mothers had been so honored. The qualifications made the purpose clear: the number of children of Aryan pedigree was the defining factor. There could be no trace of inherited diseases, criminality, or asocial tendencies (such as alcoholism). Women who had been awarded the cross were given priority seating on the trams and could demand a "Heil Hitler" from passing Hitler Youth. The Mother's Cross quickly came to be known as the "rabbit award" (*Karnickelorden*).

In many ways, the exemplary German woman under the Nazis was Gertrud Scholtz-Klink, born Treusch (1902–99), who was the Reich women's leader (*Reichsfrauenführerin*). A member of the Nazi Party since 1928, she was the leader of the Reichsarbeitsdienst der weiblichen Jugend (Young Women's Labor Service). When the Nazis came to power, she became the leader of the NS-Frauenschaft (National Socialist Women's Organization, NSF) and Deutsches Frauenwerk (German Women's Work), as well as becoming the de facto head of the German Red Cross in 1934. Scholtz-Klink was married three times (her first husband died in 1930 in the service of the Nazi Party); she had six children, thus earning a silver Mother's Cross.

Her organization, the NSF, had been founded in October 1931 but grew out of older Nazi organizations for women. By the end of 1932, it had approximately 100,000 members. By then, Gregor Strasser (1892–1934), who was then the party administrator (*Reichsorganisationsleiter*), had reoriented these organizations toward the political education of German women. As with all of the youth groups in Germany, the NSF amalgamated all of the existing women's organizations under the banner of German Women's Work. The NSF alone had 2.3 million members, and Scholtz-Klink was its only director until 1945. While substantial in membership, the organization had virtually no impact on policy, even toward women. The German woman was defined as "caring and reproducing," not as a political force. Conservative women writers, such as Gertrud Altmann-Gädke, pounded such lessons home. Yet surveys conducted by Nazi organizations like Kraft durch Freude (Strength through Joy) found that the vast majority of working women were not drawn to party-sponsored leisure activities and preferred "rest and relaxation" or "books" to structured leisure time. Only 25 percent found Strength through Joy offerings satisfying. When in the most austere years after the defeat at Stalingrad it was necessary to strip the home front of virtually everything for the war effort—evident in Goebbels's "total war" speech of 18 February 1943 at the Berlin Sportpalast—working women feared that they would be drafted into war-related industries. Reports by the SS Security Service registered women's resentment of this idea, noting their fears that women's sacrifice would not extend to the "well-heeled and dominant classes." Afterward Goebbels suggested that it would be necessary to close all of the beauty parlors to aid the home front, but Hitler vetoed the idea, convinced that this act alone would turn women against the war effort.

137

PAULA SIBER

The National Socialist Solution to the Woman Question

First published as *Die Frauenfrage und ihre Lösung durch den Nationalsozialismus* (Wolfenbüttel-Berlin: George Kallmeyer Verlag, 1933), 9–14.

On 31 January 1933, National Socialism was confronted with the reality of a woman question. And on 31 January 1933, the National Socialist woman's will inherited the legacy of confronting this question and undertook a complete restructuring of the question.

Today, for the vast majority of men, dependent on their character and mental predisposition, the status of the woman question is either met with a smirk of arrogance ("See to it that these women find husbands") or with brutal and even hostile rejection ("See to it that these women find their way to the cooking pot"). Only a dwindling minority of men demonstrate any willingness to confront the existence of this problem in a factual and composed manner, a willingness to acknowledge and contend with its uniquely feminine nature and necessity as determined by its very nature, rather than to dismiss it with catchphrases.

And this is not much different even amongst the women themselves. The fact that, as a result of centuries of education and habit, women's domain [*Lebensraum*] has not been defined to serve the communal interests of the National Socialist Germanic community but rather the interests of but a small sphere within it—that is, their own family unit—has led the majority of women to consider the problem of the woman question solved and to demonstrate little interest in it once their own lives and perhaps the lives of their young daughters have settled into a more or less acceptable framework.

But no problem can be solved with indifference, arrogance, or denial—now less than ever, where we look back on an entire epoch that faltered based on unsolved problems and a new epoch imperiously demands National Socialist solutions to all of the pressing matters of the present and the future that are remotely concerned with the fundamental laws governing the life of the *Volk*. The woman question, though, is a question that has the profoundest influence on the life of the *Volk* because the future of the *Volk* rests in the woman's womb. [. . .]

The problem of the woman question naturally had to be assigned a subordinate role by National Socialism in its masculine struggle for securing power over the state.

But today, when National Socialism is in possession of state power, when it has assumed leadership of the *Volk*, the task of solving the woman question has become as much a necessity as the task of solving the labor question, as much as the task of creating employment opportunities for men for the purpose of starting healthy families as the prerequisite to the preservation of the *Volk*.

But especially when the problem of creating employment opportunities for men is assigned highest priority in terms of the law for preservation of the *Volk*, it cannot be forgotten that, based on the same law for preservation of the *Volk*, in every family there stands at the side of man a woman who must be physically and psychologically sound as the mother of the *Volk*, as the bearer of blood and soul, as the purveyor of the bodily and psychological health of the *Volk*.

But if the solution to the problem of creating employment opportunities for men occurs at the expense of a renewed deprivation of women's right to work, a new generation of women will emerge that is already rendered incompetent in its youth as a result of its lack of employment. For women who spend their youth at the side of a sprightly mother as a drone in their parents' home, and are sapped of their blood and soul by idleness in their early years, can never become industrious, healthy, and exemplary mothers, educators, and wives. All of women's discontent, and thus the whole of the woman question, emanates from depriving them of their purpose and their employment.

The brutal incomprehension involved in such dismissals as "See to it that these women find husbands" or "See to it that these women find their way to the kitchen" is no way to solve the woman question today, because the course of organic development of the peoples and of the economic system has been as unequivocal as it has been brutal in decisively challenging this demand, which in itself seems natural.

The law of purpose and employment, though, is a given both for men and for women; for it is only from the sweat of the brow that the healthy blood of a Volk *can flow.*

But one of the essential goals of National Socialist *Volk* leadership must be a heroically sound German *Volk* because this German *Volk* in particular, confined as it is to the narrow straits of the European heartland, is the one race of all the peoples of this world that is faced with the most arduous path to self-assertion.

For this reason, National Socialism, charged as it is with the task of a psychological-moral rebirth of the German race, will first have to elevate the woman question in all its profundity and its responsibility for *Volk* and *Volkstum* in the eyes of all sectors of the *Volk*—first and foremost for the masses of women themselves—to that which it truly is: a matter of life and death for the German *Volk*, a matter of blood and of the will to the future.

A generation of women that has become rootless, an entire generation of female drones, but also a generation of men for whom the woman has become their personal property or plaything, must now learn, despite all the previous women's movements, that the woman question is a question of the *Volk*—and that there cannot under any circumstances be a single woman who is not aware of her responsibility and her purpose for the *Volk* and within the *Volk*.

In the grand scheme of responsibility for the National Socialist community of the *Volk*, the woman question no longer involves a small group of people with special rights that is striving to attain special rights for itself above and beyond the context of the whole; it involves, rather, a sector within the community of the *Volk* that has been marginalized according to its nature and its purpose but that can fulfill its true purpose and find fulfillment in the reciprocal workings of duty and obligation only in the context of the whole, and yet the requisite harmony of the whole can only be achieved when the needs of all its component parts find fulfillment.

Thus, the woman question in National Socialism is no longer merely a question of the right to work for unmarried women; rather, it is a question that rests at the innermost core of the *Volkstum* because it concerns woman's role as mother.

Therefore, the mother is the central focus of the woman question from a National Socialist perspective, and we are concerned here with the eternal, long-suffering, and self-sacrificing mother of the *Volk* who has always borne the burdens of the *Volk* on her heart and has always given birth to every generation of the *Volk* through the strength of her heart and who always will.

In its struggle to redeem the soul of the German *Volk* from the false doctrine of theories of degeneration [*Verfallstheorien*] that have emerged in recent decades, the struggle to redeem the German woman has become and remains as much the responsibility of National Socialism as the struggle for the soul of the German man.

138

CAROLA STRUVE

Woman's Freedom and Freedom of the *Volk* on Foundations of Camaraderie

First published as *Frauenfreiheit und Volksfreiheit auf kameradschaftsrechtlicher Grundlage* (Heidelberg: Bündischer Verlag, 1933), 6–8.

I assert the following:

1. That contemporary forms of state are wholly unnatural in terms of their most fundamental economic, cultural, and intellectual-spiritual structures and that they therefore reflect distorted growth.
2. That it never would have come to this had the woman in this system been seen as an equal colleague at man's side in all questions concerning the *Volk*.
3. That woman, by dint of her intuitive capacity for empathy [*Einfühlungsvermögen*], is the mediator between nature (God) and man.
4. That nature has placed the task of solving all ethical quandaries in the hands of woman.
5. That nature will not allow for any disobedience in the form of distancing oneself from her laws.
6. That nature fosters the principle of subservience (because it demands the intuitive capacity for empathy), while it rejects the principle of domination (since it is contrary to nature).
7. That the growth of the family and of the *Volk* is characterized by a uniform tendency for division.
8. That everything follows its own law of time.
9. That the growth of man and of *Volk* is subject to the law of the trinity.
10. That the neglect of this law is necessarily combated by and compensated for in nature.
11. That it is not the family but rather the individual human being that constitutes the unit of state.
12. That nature demands not a closed worldview but rather an open one.

139

ADOLF HITLER

Speech to the Meeting of the National Socialist Women's Organization

First delivered at the Reich Party Rally in Nuremberg, 1934. First published in *Völkischer Beobachter*, 9 September 1934.

If in the course of human history, the divisions of labor between man and woman have perhaps shifted along lines that are incongruent with nature, this has not occurred because woman sought to dominate man; rather, the reason was to be found in the fact that man was no longer in a position to complete his task in full. That is what is so marvelous about nature and providence—that conflict between the sexes and among them is impossible as long as each of them fulfills the task assigned to him by nature.

The word *women's emancipation* is merely an invention of the Jewish intellect, and its meaning is informed by the same spirit. The German woman never has any need for emancipation during those times when Germans are truly leading the "good life." She has always

FIGURE 12. "German Aristocracy of Blood throughout the World." Postcard depicting a German Labor Service leader with a swastika brooch. "R. A. D. [Reich Labor Service Leader] Führerin." Wolfgang Willrich, *Deutscher Blutadel in aller Welt* (Koblenz: Verlag A. Daehler, 1942). Collection of Anson Rabinbach.

been in possession of those gifts that nature has bestowed upon her to administer and to preserve by necessity, just as man in the best of times never need fear that he might be ousted from his position with respect to woman. [. . .]

If one says that man's world is the state, that his world is his struggle, his readiness to devote himself to the community, then one could perhaps say that the world of woman is a smaller one. For her world is her husband, her family, her children, and her home. (*Ardent applause.*) But where would the larger world be if no one wanted to care for the smaller world? How could the larger world exist if there were no one to make the cares of the smaller world their purpose in life? No, the larger world is built on this small world! The larger world cannot exist as long as the smaller world is not solid.

Providence has assigned woman the task of caring for this world of her own, and only from this world can the world of man be built and given shape. These two worlds have therefore never been in conflict. They complement each other, they belong together, like man and woman belong together. (*Applause of several minutes.*)

We do not think it proper for woman to invade the world of man, to enter his territory; instead, we think it natural for these worlds to remain separate. One is characterized by the strength of sentiment, the strength of soul! The other is characterized by the strength of vision, toughness, determination, and willingness to sacrifice! In the first case, this strength demands of woman that she be prepared to risk her life for the sake of preserving and reproducing this small unit of life, and in the second case, it demands of the man the willingness to protect this life.

Man makes sacrifices in his struggle for his *Volk*; woman makes sacrifices in her struggle to preserve that same *Volk* in individual cases. What man offers in heroism on the field of battle, woman equals with unending perseverance and sacrifice, with unending pain and suffering. Every child she brings into the world is a battle, a battle she wages for the existence of her people. (*Tremendous applause.*) And both must, therefore, mutually respect and value each other when they see that each performs the task that has been assigned by nature and Providence. Out of this separation of functions there will necessarily come mutual respect.

It is not true, as the Jewish intellect maintains, that respect depends on the overlapping of spheres of activity of the sexes; instead, respect demands that neither sex should attempt to do what rightly is in the other's sphere. In the final analysis, respect comes from each knowing that the other is doing everything necessary to maintain the whole relationship! (*Enthusiastic agreement.*)

And this is why woman has always been man's helper and, as such, his most loyal friend, and it is also why man has always been his wife's protector and, as such, her best friend. And both of them have seen in this way of life the common basis for upholding all that they hold dear and for its preservation. Woman is egotistical when it comes to maintaining her small world in order to enable man to defend the larger world, and man is egotistical in the maintenance of the larger world, because it is inseparably linked with the other. We will protect ourselves against an intellectualism of the most corrupt kind that threatens to put asunder that which God hath joined. (*Ardent agreement.*)

Because she springs from the root of life, woman is also the most stable element in the preservation of a people. When all is said and done, it is she who has an infallible sense for what is necessary if a race is not to perish, because of course her children will be the first ones afflicted by all this suffering.

Man is often far too unstable mentally to immediately find his way to these fundamental truths. Only in good times and with a good education will man also know exactly what his task is.

Accordingly, for many years we National Socialists have protested against bringing woman into political life, a life that, in our eyes, is unworthy of her. A woman once said to me, "You must see to it that women get into parliament, because only they are capable of ennobling that institution." "I do not believe," I answered, "that man should try to ennoble something that is inherently bad. And any woman who becomes involved in the workings of parliament will not ennoble it but will instead be dishonored by it. I would not want to leave something to woman that I intend to take away from man." (*Enthusiastic applause.*) Our opponents thought that this [attitude] would prevent us from ever winning women to our movement. But we gained the support of more women than all the other parties together, and I know that we would have won over even the last German woman if she had only had the opportunity to study parliament and the degrading role played by women therein.

That is why we have incorporated woman into the battle for the *Volksgemeinschaft* in the manner in which nature and Providence have determined best. Our women's movement is for us not something that inscribes on its banner a program consisting of the fight against man but something that defines its program as the common fight of woman together with man. For the new National Socialist *Volksgemeinschaft* was established on a firm basis precisely because millions of women became our most loyal, fanatical fellow combatants. (*Long-lasting applause.*) Fighting women who fought for life in its communal whole, in the service of the common task of maintaining life; fighting women who did not fix their gaze on rights that a Jewish intellectualism mirrors before their eyes but rather on duties that nature imposes on us collectively. (*Fervent applause.*)

If previous liberal intellectual women's movements contained many, many points in their programs whose openings were based on so-called intellect, our National Socialist women's movement contains only one single point, and this point is the child: that tiny being that must be born and should grow strong, for whom the entire life struggle gains its meaning. Because what would be the point of all our struggles and toils if there were no one to come in the future who would take advantage and benefit from, and later leave as his own legacy, those things we seek to accomplish today?

What else would be the purpose of the whole human struggle? Why the sorrow and the suffering? Just for the sake of an idea? For the sake of an idea alone? Only for a theory? No, that would not make it worth wandering through this vale of mortal tears. The only thing that allows us to surmount all this is the view from the present toward the future; from ourselves to those who will come after us. (*Loud approval.*) Several minutes earlier, I spoke to the youth assembled here. It is wonderful to be able to look on this golden youth; we know that they will one day be Germany after we no longer exist. (*Enthusiastic cheers.*) Youth will maintain all that we create and construct. We work for our youth. This is what our struggle is all about.

Since we recognize this simple and elegant goal that nature has bestowed upon us, the work of both sexes naturally finds its logical and proper engagement no longer in conflict but in the common struggle of real life. (*Thunderous applause.*)

You women, party comrades, you are the women who shall lead, organize, and help us in this struggle. You have taken on an honorable task. That which we seek to build in the *Volk* as a whole is what you must anchor firmly within yourselves and must constantly seek to fortify! You must provide the psychological and emotional moorings and stability for these things!

You must be man's counterpart in these, our struggles on behalf of the *Volk* for freedom, equality, and honor, and peace, so that, with this eye for the future, we may be seen as true warriors by and for our *Volk*.

Then strife or quarrels between the sexes will never again erupt because they will then join hands together and wander through this life hand in hand in mutual struggle, just as Providence so ordained it when it created both for this purpose. And then we will also reap the blessings that flow from this sort of joint labor. Then no nonsensical battle will erupt around theories, man and his wife will not be separated by false ideas but rather the blessing of the Almighty will rest on their mutual struggle for life! (*The Führer delivers these all-important concluding statements to the jubilant applause of the tens of thousands of German women assembled there, and these women, gripped by enthusiasm, break out into the second verse of the German national anthem.*)

140

HANNS JOHST

Mother

First published as "Mutter," in *Das kleine Gedichtbuch: Lyrik von Heute,* edited by Matthies Kurt (Munich: Albert Langen, Georg Müller, 1934), 38.

Father God, light the candles
in heaven on high
And Joseph, dearest man,
hold the lantern in the manger.

The pains of labor quake. I must scream.
The animals lick the sweat.
The child has a halo.
Praise the Lord and rejoice!

It is true, may the world behold
what I have always known is true.

Oh, you little child of Christ, how do you
like suckling at my humble breast?

I would rather give you golden grapes
and a sprawling stead.
But your father wanted you
to have a maid for a mother.

141

EMIL STRAUSS

The Mother

First published as "Die Mutter," in *Das kleine Gedichtbuch: Lyrik von Heute,* edited by Matthies Kurt (Munich: Albert Langen, Georg Müller, 1934), 39–41.

The pulse from which my own did grow
has had enough of this eternal ebb and flow—
but for a few dreams, be they sweet, be they sour,
this heart has dreamt its final hour,
but for a few short breaths of fear—
shall rest in peace, peace it ne'er held so dear.

Now you lie before my eyes, ivory and skin,
all that remains is a trick of air, a wisp of breath.
Your eyes, once molten hued and flaming iris,
now a hoary ice-belt blue, still and cold as ice,
Your eye, my first-born blessing in this lifetime,
delves into my own and speaks to my soul:
Peace?—My dear son, what nonsense draws you hither!
Leave me in peace with their "peace"!
For the peace that I saw in my day
will strike you dead like a bolt splits the tree:
when my own blood began to boil
forging me to steel in the floodgates of hate,
a peace for life in its most savage sense
pierced my soul like a peal of storm:
in that twinkle of an eye the stride of eternity
was felt in the most distant reaches of the galaxy.
For peace—avoiding the brands of life—not I, not ever,
I hope to be burning still in the morrow, somehow.

This blood reduced now to a bracken trickle
leapt for eighty-four years like a child
—the way it once ran through the fist veins
and burned with a thirst in pursuit of cave bears
the way it quelled in the arm that struck the enemy dead
the way it flowed with a vengeance from mortal wounds
the way it once was in the beginning, racing with desire and hatred
and even in its most passionate moment never forgot the enemy.

Many a time, overcome by the ravages of rage,
the miraculous wonder came into play:
savage and merciless, my words had their way
and the eternal agony in me was laid to rest,
and that very moment, my most ancient father broke the mortal enemy's neck
and my ancestral mother spat from the coals of the stake
in the Roman grimaces of her heretical scorn,
within me, an unknown relative came to full life
and came to my aid—I and I.

You were my blood—the most authentic part of me, you were,
abrupt, contrary, rambling, quiet, and indefatigable.
Following the call of the wild blue yonder, you tarried over land and sea,
and when you returned, you were no longer my blood;
you became the other blood, the one that whisks you
on the whorls of deception through life's storms,
the one that whirs the song of all the worldly battle cries,
that you would frolic and wonder in childhood's curiosity,
instead of basking in the slumber of the enemy's dreams!
So you drift back, a stranger to me, and solitary—
clad in leather-patched shoes, threadbare and shabby.
It could be that your madness warms your heart and satiates,
but you leave the cupboards of my heart bare!
You are no longer blood of my blood, and may my blood
run cold and freeze—till the dawn of the new day,
till one fine day another bolt of blood gushes hot
from my bosom and yet another stormy night,
till one day my purified blood bears again takes arms
and strikes squarely the brow of deception and deceit!
And then—let it circle in peace, cradled by calm—
as if with a steady wind in its sails.

142

JOSEPH GOEBBELS

German Women

First delivered on 18 March 1933 as "Deutsches Frauentum." First published in *Signale der neuen Zeit. 25 ausgewählte Reden von Dr. Joseph Goebbels* (Munich: Verlag Franz Eher Nachfolger GmbH, 1934), 118–26. Translated by Randall Bytwerk. Calvin College, German Propaganda Archive.

German women, German men!

I would like to see a happy accident in the fact that my first speech since taking charge of the Ministry for Public Enlightenment and Propaganda is before an audience of German women. Although I agree with [Heinrich von] Treitschke that men make history, I cannot forget either that women are the ones who raise our young boys to manhood. Surely you know this much: that the National Socialist movement is the only party that keeps women from direct involvement in daily politics. And, as a result, the party has been subjected to bitter criticism and hostility—all of it highly unjustified. It is not because we do not respect women that we have kept them out of the rancorous parliamentary-democratic intrigues of the past fourteen years in Germany but because we respect them too much. *It is not because we see the woman as inferior but because we see her as having a different mission, a different value, than that of man. Therefore, we believe that woman, and above all the German woman, who more than any other in the world is a woman in the best sense of the word, should rally her strengths and apply her abilities in other areas than the man.*

Woman has always been not only man's sexual companion but also his fellow worker. Just as she performed heavy labor alongside man in the field in the days of yore, just as she moved with him to the cities, she has also entered the offices and factories with him and done her part in his work, and she has done her share of the work for which she was best suited, fulfilling her purpose to the best of her abilities—with her loyalty, her selfless devotion, and her willingness to sacrifice.

Even today, the role of woman in public life is no different than it was in the past. *No one who understands the modern age would have the ludicrous idea of driving woman from public life, from work, from her profession and from breadwinning. But it must also be said that those things that belong to man must remain his. And that includes politics and the military. This is not to disparage woman, only to delegate her abilities and talents to those sectors of labor and activity that are most suited to her essential nature.*

Taking a fleeting look back at the past years of Germany's decline, we come to the frightening, nearly terrifying conclusion that the less German men demonstrated the resolve to prove themselves as men in public life, the more women succumbed to the temptation to fill man's role in his place. The feminization of men always leads to the masculinization of women. An age in which all great ideals of virtue, of steadfastness, of resolve and determination have been forgotten should not be surprised that the man gradually loses his leading role in life and politics and government to the woman.

It may be unpopular to stress this before an audience of women, but it must be said, because it is true and because it is only against this backdrop that our stance toward women becomes clear.

The modern age, with all its vast revolutionary transformations in government, politics, economics, and social relations has not left woman and her role in public life untouched. Things we thought impossible but a few years or a few decades ago are now everyday reality. Many good, noble, and commendable things have happened in recent years. But also many things that are contemptible and humiliating. Woman has been, to a great degree, deprived of her proper tasks by these revolutionary transformations. Her sights have been set on things that have nothing to do with her true nature, and the result has been a distorted public view of German womanhood that is no longer congruent with the ideal image that was once customary.

A fundamental change is needed here. At the risk of sounding reactionary and outdated, let me say this clearly and candidly: *The first, best, and most suitable place for a woman is in the family, and the most glorious task she can perform is to give the gift of children to her people and nation, children who can continue the line of generations and who guarantee the nation's immortality. Woman is the teacher of youth and therefore the cornerstone in the foundation of the future. If the family is the nation's source of strength, the woman is its core and its living center. The best place for the woman to serve the Volk as a whole is in her marriage, in the family, in motherhood. This is her highest mission.* This does not by any means imply that those women who are employed or who have no children have no role in the motherhood of the German *Volk*. They use their strength, their abilities, their sense of responsibility for the nation in other ways. We are convinced, however, that the first task of a socially reformed *Volk* must be to again afford woman the opportunity to fulfill her real task, her mission in the family and as a mother.

The national revolutionary government is everything but reactionary. It does not want to stop or slow down the pace of our rapidly moving age. Nor does it have any intention of lagging behind the times; it wants to be the flag bearer and pathfinder of the future. We fully acknowledge the demands of this modern age of upheaval. But that cannot prevent us from seeing that every age has its roots in the native soil of motherhood and that nothing more noble and exalted can spring forth from this native soil than the living mother of a family who blesses the state with her children.

Especially in recent years, a great transformation has occurred in German women. They are again coming to the realization that they are no happier as a result of being given more rights and fewer responsibilities. They already know that the right to be elected to public office at the expense of the right to life, motherhood, and her daily bread is something of a Greek gift.

One characteristic of our times is an ever more rapidly declining birthrate in our big cities. Whereas approximately two million babies were born in Germany in 1900, that number has now already fallen to one million. The most drastic decline in our population growth is most evident in the national capital itself. In the past fourteen years, Berlin's birthrate has fallen to the lowest of any European city. By 1955, without emigration, the city will have only about three million inhabitants. The government is determined to put a halt to this decline of the family and the resulting impoverishment of our blood. There must be a fundamental change. The liberal attitude toward the family and the child is partly responsible for the fact that Germany's population rate has declined so rapidly in these past few years that we must now begin worrying about the perils of an aging population. Whereas there were seven children for each elderly person in 1900, today there are only four. If the current trend continues, by 1988 the ratio will be one to one. These few statistics say it all. They are the best proof that if Germany stays the current course, it will steer with breathtaking speed unerringly toward the abyss, and we will almost be able to determine the decade in which Germany collapses altogether due to complete depopulation.

We are not willing to stand idly by and watch the collapse of our national life and the destruction of the blood we have inherited. The national revolutionary government has the responsibility to rebuild the nation on its original foundations, to transform the life and work of the woman so that it once again best serves the national good of the *Volk,* and to eliminate social inequalities so that once again the life of our *Volk,* the future of our people, and the immortality of our blood are secure.

I welcome this exhibition, whose goal is to enlighten and teach and to reduce or eliminate harm to the individual and to the *Volk* as a whole. This serves the nation and popular enlightenment, and to support it is one of the noblest responsibilities of the new government.

It is perhaps for this reason that this exhibition titled *The Woman* will represent a turning point in this regard. If the goal of the exhibition is to give the general public an impression of women in contemporary society, it does so at a time when German society is undergoing the greatest changes it has experienced in generations. I am not unaware of the significance of this task. I know about the obstacles that had to be overcome to give this exhibition a clear theme and a firm structure. It should demonstrate the significance of the woman for the family, the people, and the whole nation. Carefully curated displays are designed to give an impression of the actual life of women today and to provide the average citizen with the knowledge necessary to resolve for himself today's conflicting opinions on debates that did not first come to the fore with the contemporary women's movement.

But that is not all. The main purpose of the exhibition *The Woman* is not only to show the way things are but also to make proposals for improvement. It aims to open new doors and new opportunities. Using clear and often drastic examples, this exhibition will give thousands of German women reason to think and consider. It is particularly pleasing to us men in the new government that families with many children are given particular attention, since we want to rescue the nation from decline. *The importance of the family cannot be overestimated, especially in families without fathers that depend entirely upon the mother. In these families, the woman has sole responsibility for the children, and she must realize the responsibility she has to her people and nation.*

If this exhibition *The Woman* succeeds in revealing the causes of Germany's decline to the hundreds of thousands who view it, then it has already served the greater part of its purpose. May the thoughts that it inspires in viewers act as an alarm to German women and girls so that they might wake up and remain vigilant, that they may heed the call to fulfill their duty to the nation, that they may see the light and participate enthusiastically in the rejuvenation of our *Volk*.

For we do not believe that the German Volk is doomed by fate to decline. We have blind faith in the notion that Germany still has a great mission to fulfill in the world. We have faith that we are not at the end of our history but rather that a new, great, and noble period of our history is now beginning. This faith gives us the strength to work and not despair. It enabled us to make great sacrifices over the past fourteen years. It gave millions of German women the strength to place their hope in Germany and its future and to let their sons join in the reawakening of the nation. This faith was with the brave women who lost their husbands and breadwinners in the war, with those who gave their sons as a pledge to the future of the nation. This faith held them steadfast through the distress and desperation of the past fourteen years. And this faith today fills us with new hope that Germany will again find its place in the sun.

Nothing builds resolve and determination like battle. Nothing builds courage like defiance. During the years when Germany seemed destined to decline, a new breed of women rose from beneath the motley veneer of modern civilization. Resolute, determined, courageous, willing to sacrifice, the German women and mothers endured as stalwart companions of their men through the four years of the Great War and the fourteen years of German collapse that followed. They have borne all the bitterness, all the privation and danger, and have not faltered when struck by misfortune, worry, and trouble. As long as a nation has such a proud and noble breed of women, it cannot perish. *These women are the foundation of our race, of its blood, and of its future.*

This is where the new women's movement begins. If the nation once again has mothers who proudly and freely choose motherhood, it cannot perish. If the woman is healthy, the Volk *will be healthy. Woe to the nation that neglects its women and mothers. It has forsaken itself.*

We hope that the concept of the German woman will regain the honor and respect of the entire world. The German woman will then take her pride in her country and her people, in thinking German and feeling German. The honor of her nation and her race will be most important to her. Only a nation that does not forget its honor will be able to guarantee its daily bread.

The German women should never forget that.

I hereby declare this exhibition open to the public. May it reveal all the errors of the past and point to new paths into the future.

Then the world will once again respect us, and we will be able to affirm the words of Walther von der Vogelweide, who had this to say about the German woman in his famous poem:

> Whoever shall seek
> Virtue and proper love,
> Should come to our land.
> Here joy abounds.
> Long may I live there.

143

GERTRUD SCHOLTZ-KLINK

To Swedes and Germans

Delivered to the Swedish-German Association in Stockholm, 4 February 1937. First published as "Den Schwedischen und Deutschen Menschen. Rede der Reichsfrauenführerin Frau Scholtz-Klink vor der Schwedisch-Deutschen Vereinigung in Stockholm am Donnerstag, Dem 4, Februar 1937," in *Die Frau im Dritten Reich: Eine Dokumentation,* edited by Gertrud Scholtz-Klink (Tübingen: Grabert Verlag, 1978), 519–21.

My Dear People of Sweden and Germany! [. . .]

Again and again, you can read reports in much of the foreign press about how the German woman is the most oppressed of all the world's women. So it is clear that others have concerned themselves with the spread of propaganda on behalf of the German woman; even though it has been negative, it has nevertheless been a concern. But if there is a single group of women that should constitute the most oppressed organization of women in the world, then there would seem to be many more oppressed women; otherwise no comparison could be drawn. And in this regard, we German women are at a distinct advantage over all the other women in the rest of the world because those stalwart, resolute warriors are committed to protecting the German women throughout the world and are far more concerned with the German women than they are with anyone else. In light of these chivalrous knights of the pen and the word, I would not so much as attempt to defend the oppressed German woman; tonight, rather, I wish to address those things that we have accomplished in these three years in our state of "oppression."

Once we had made addressing the needs of mothers and working women our top concern, yet another watchword came into vogue, especially outside Germany's borders. "Great, so leaders of the Office of Women's Affairs have done their job when it comes to wives and mothers and to working women and apparently have some grasp of the social factors involved: but where does that leave the intellectual interests of women in Germany? They have been ruthlessly betrayed by this leadership. And this is sheer catastrophe." My response to that is this: I am not of the opinion that when a *Volk* picks itself up from the depths of defeat, the most solemn obligation of each person must be to set as the *primary* concern the needs of the intellectually disadvantaged over those of the intellectually privileged. If a *Volk* is host to individual members who, based on their intellectual prowess, are inclined to criticize everything they can, then I believe their most important duty in times of need would be to enlist this intellectual prowess in the service of those who are not endowed with these powers, to offer assistance and to be of use, and not to criticize. Today, in the German Women's Work, there are many people engaged in intellectual and academic work. It has been said and is still said today that any woman in Germany who was not content with the endeavors of household chores and child rearing had no other opportunity for advancement. And even those women who do get an education are unable to find work. We're familiar with that old refrain. Our response: there is nothing standing in the way of any woman in Germany who wishes to get an education. Our only stipulation is that only those women should attend German universities who are in a position to honorably represent the German nobility, pride, posture, and propriety as is befitting of the nation. We resist the notion that any German university, for men and women alike, should ever become an affair—as it was in those terrible years between 1928 and 1933—in which any son or daughter is compelled to attend simply because the father held a prestigious title or position or was a successful businessman or had otherwise amassed a fortune. We do not want that to happen again.

What we are saying today is that a *Volk* that is so systematically reliant on the deployment of forces in each individual member within its ranks and that has no resources outside itself at its disposal must retain the right to issue certain directives to individuals concerning the best use of their talents. All the German girls who attend the university should and must receive the same training as men, because science is, after all, a factual and objective field. However, once they have left the university, we tell them, please do not maintain the now outdated stance that, simply because you have followed the same path as the men during your training, you must necessarily follow in their footsteps afterward; rather, we would hope that you would give serious consideration to the way that you, as German women, might put your scientific knowledge to the greatest use. Enlist your knowledge in the service of the German nation and apply it where it is needed most.

144

DAS SCHWARZE KORPS

Fashion

A Matter for Our Women!

First published as "Das geht unser Frauen an," in *Das Schwarze Korps,* 26 July 1939, 6.

The protest we recently staged against a return to the *cul de Paris* [Paris bottom], the train [*Rüschenschleppe*], and the wasp waist was decried in some circles as a barbaric disdain for beauty on the part of goose-stepping, militant philistines. We would have been honored to bear the brunt of this charge and would not have hesitated to simply relegate it to the record had it not become necessary to address this topic anew in order to thoroughly reexamine the issues and weigh them against the true values of our bold new world.

Reich Organizational Director Dr. [Robert] Ley recently expressed his opinion on the subject of fashion at the inauguration of the House of Beauty in Berlin, where he commented on the concepts of "beauty" and what is "new." He was astute in identifying tendencies on the part of fashion designers to persistently present only the very newest fashion as that which is beautiful and to thus manipulate women's natural desire to be beautiful in order to foist their newest "creations" on women by leading them to believe these are the only fashions that are suitable to them.

Dr. Ley was also adamant in stressing that these tendencies often lead to the *senseless waste of textiles,* which is entirely incongruent with the prospective development of our economy. He stated that this fly-by-night notion of beauty promoted by contemporary fashion designs must be eliminated, and he advocated a fashion for the German woman that is truly beautiful but at the same time demonstrates enduring substance.

In principle, these words alone should suffice: they are clear and unequivocal enough. What is more, no one can contend that these statements are in any way dismissive of beauty and hence expressions of a disdain for beauty. Furthermore, in making these statements, Dr. Ley lent to our previous ideological protest an added dimension that is utterly crucial: the national economy.

After all, what is the point of the whole battle against corruption and waste when the fashion industry, with its ever-changing designs, deliberately depreciates the value of textile industry products on an almost monthly basis by forcing manufacturers either to produce second-rate trash so that the "latest rage" in the fashion world can be made available for little money or to sell off high-quality products as dirt cheap and "outmoded" because it is the only way to get women to wear them and they cannot be marketed in any other way.

The Novelty Craze

Neither the production of second-rate trash nor the depreciation of high-quality products is congruent with the economic and marketing strategies of National Socialism. It is imperative that we finally express these ideas in terms that avoid soft-soaping rhetorical flourish because we are concerned with representing the interests of the *Volk* as a whole, not merely those of certain profit-hungry industry sectors.

In one of his great speeches in Nuremberg on the subject of culture, the Führer assured us that *the pursuit of innovation simply for the sake of its newness is by no means the mark of genius* but rather that it is evidence of the contrary: innovation and newness at any cost is an index of *inner worthlessness.*

These words are applicable not only with regard to the production of great works of art and culture; they are equally valid in terms of the little things—the products we use in our everyday life, which include beauty products that should similarly serve a cultural purpose.

Every woman should be beautiful; every woman should have the opportunity to accentuate her own natural feminine charms with the flourishes of fashion so that she may bring the blessing of joy to her hardworking and dutifully fighting husband not only by fulfilling her obligations but by virtue of her very presence in his everyday life. The guiding principle of the work of [the] Strength through Joy [program] begins and ends with our women.

It is certainly no coincidence that an artist like Käthe Kollwitz is incapable of representing a single beautiful woman in her work, not even the unpretentious, simple beauty of a peasant woman in traditional dress.

Those shopworn and bedraggled woebegone figures she has made of our peasant women are designed to fan the fires of hatred in the subhuman ranks of society [*Untermenschentum*]; they are designed to demonstrate that feminine beauty and physical labor are incompatible because, essentially—and this is where the whole breadth of materialistic thought endemic to this epoch comes to light—women's beauty is merely a question of money.

Here we see the beauty of expensive apparel juxtaposed against the misery of the proletariat.

But National Socialism has pulled the rug out from beneath the foundation of materialistic thought. It is, of course, clear that this transformation is not one that can take hold overnight in our *Volk,* and that many traces of these earlier views remain, but today we have already reached a critical point in the goal we have set:

We have brought the beauty of the German mother back to the central focus of thought and understanding in our *Volk.* Whereas the humanitarian democracies elect their beauty queens, their queens of nudity, queens of gorgeous gams, etc., the New Germany rewards women with the Mother's Cross of Honor for prolific childbearing and thus honors a form of beauty that is exempt from the influence of fashion because it reflects the immortality of the German *Volk.*

In awarding the highest honor of the Reich to the mother, we thus set a standard of value that must retain its validity for everything in the realm of women's lives. And that means for fashion as well!

And one should not so much as consider arguing that contemporary fashion is in fact altogether amenable to this line of thinking inasmuch as it seeks to retrieve and revive the remnants from Grandmother's sewing chest. We have spent enough time explaining the mentality that is behind that trend in fashion. The fashion designers and propagandists of the nineteenth century have without a doubt learned from our attacks: now they are trying to lend a cultural-political undergirding to their retrospective tendencies by cloaking their arguments in erudite language to claim that the new trends in fashion take recourse to such utterly feminine touches as the ribbon, the train, pleats, and lace and thus have finally succeeded in surpassing that hideous little boys' club fashion promoted by the New Objectivity (that is: the fashion of the *Systemzeit*). The new fashion is thus said to restore authentically feminine forms of expression to the feminine charms.

Designs That Correspond to Content

[. . .] But the ideal standard of beauty today is no longer determined by the beauty of the mother and of woman as man's companion, but rather, more or less surreptitiously, *that of the handmaiden.*

This whole line of development was one of the masterstrokes of the infectious Jewish disease, and we are still suffering the consequences today. The entire Aryan world has been stricken and infected by this Jewish mind-set.

These statements are by no means to be seen as an incendiary attack against lipstick, powder compacts, and silk stockings—quite the contrary. They are merely to suggest the modest proposal that these beauty products, which are in themselves by no means to be rejected out of hand, once they begin to overshadow the inner values of womanhood and women, run the risk of misplacing priorities and allowing materialistic considerations to far outweigh the real values and concerns at issue here.

145

OFFICE OF WOMEN'S AFFAIRS OF THE GERMAN LABOR FRONT

Working Women and Leisure Time

Survey titled "Die Freizeit der erwerbstätigen Frau," in "Ein Beitrag zur Gegenwartslage der Arbeiterinnen und Angestellten. Ergebnisse einer Umfrage des Frauenamtes der deutschen Arbeitsfront an die erwerbstätigen Frauen," edited by Alice Rilke and Dorothea Goedicke, unpublished document, n.d., BKA NS 5/1, German Federal Archive, Koblenz.

Results of a Survey of Working Women Conducted by the Office of Women's Affairs of the German Labor Front

It is surprising to note that a substantial number of working women still prefer to spend their leisure time with *needlework*. This most popular hobby is equally prevalent among white-collar and working-class women. Approximately 37 percent of all women surveyed regularly state, "My favorite activity is needlework." What is included here is not mending clothing; far more, this involves actual handicrafts such as embroidery, knitting, etc.

Taking pleasure in and appreciating *the theater* has obviously been accelerated by the Strength through Joy program. But only 2 percent of those surveyed made specific mention of it.

Astonishingly little mention is given to attending *the movies.* There is no doubt about the fact that going to the movies is not seen as something that one does often or on a regular basis. It is rather something that is done occasionally out of interest in a particular film. Observations made with regard to the specific population of moviegoers allow us to ascertain that this group consists largely of housewives who attend movie matinees by themselves or who attend evening shows accompanied by their husbands.

Those who state that they have relatively little leisure time regularly tend to state that they also have little interest in anything but *rest and relaxation.* Particularly conspicuous in this category are the salesclerks who complain about spending the entire day on their feet.

Younger employed women—as a rule, those women under thirty or in their early thirties—demonstrate a marked preference for *sports,* particularly track and field, rowing, swimming, ice skating, and tennis.

There is a remarkably strong interest in *books*. The category of those indicating a tendency to read [in their leisure time] is not limited by profession or by age group. We are happy to report that they very often speak in terms of "good" books, in some cases even in specialty fields. It is astonishing to note how often reading historical or scientific books is mentioned. Working women clearly demonstrate a hefty appetite for education and cultural interests. This category further indicates that books are the most effective means of educating and influencing working women. Especially when taking into account the fact that the group surveyed consists primarily of uneducated civil servants and blue-collar workers, the percentage of 32.2 percent of women who are interested in reading must be considered substantial.

Enjoying *musical activities* seems to be restricted largely by lack of time and heavy workload, since this would entail the greatest investment of time, energy, and concentration. By contrast, the passionate interest in playing a musical instrument is relatively great. Singing, playing the piano, mandolin, guitar, etc. are extremely popular. And yet making music is an option only for those who have at least two solid hours of leisure time at their disposal.

One of the greatest options for enjoying leisure time is *nature*. The interest in nature is cited even by those who have relatively little leisure time on a daily basis. This is an indicator that every working person has an interest in "getting some fresh air" and "going for a walk." This interest is not restricted to major cities. Approximately 27 percent of those surveyed were adamant in emphasizing their desire to enjoy nature as an urgent daily need.

Only 4 percent of respondents were positive about filling their leisure time with *occupational training*. And yet, this seemingly narrow margin must be seen against the backdrop of the fact that over half of those surveyed were blue-collar working women who are generally not in need of any form of specialty vocational training. The group of respondents who emphasized vocational training as a leisure-time priority consists primarily of young civil servants expressing a clear interest in improving the nature of the work they complete and in getting promoted to better-paid positions. For this reason, the study of foreign languages is widespread. What is astonishing is that there are some individual cases of blue-collar workers who concern themselves with the study of languages. So, for example, one such worker reports that she spends her leisure time learning Italian just because it interests her.

Extracts from letters written by respondents:

From a bookkeeper, fifty-one years old, one child: "If I had more leisure time, I would like to take a whole week sleeping well and eating regularly because now sometimes I'm so exhausted I don't even bother to cook dinner."

From a stenographer: "If I had enough leisure time, I'd like to be able to just sit down and finish reading a book. Just once, I'd like to be able to sit around talking with my friends instead of with the same people I work with all day long. This is precisely the reason I don't always like the idea of comrade evenings and office parties. I'd like to have the opportunity to just have a few quiet moments to myself or to take a small child by the hand and laugh with him or take him on a walk. Or I'd like to sit around doing needlework or lie in the grass without having to think about anything else. Or at least be able to take a leisurely stroll through the streets of Berlin so I could get to know my own father city [*Vaterstadt*]. After fifteen years on the job, I'm allowed only six days' paid vacation per year. What am I supposed to do with that?"

Survey question 3: Would you like to receive suggestions and ideas for how to structure your leisure time, or would you prefer to decide for yourself how to spend your leisure time?

This question was presented in an attempt to determine the degree of interest in outside influences. Surprisingly, 81.07 percent of all survey participants responded negatively to the notion of receiving outside advice on how to structure their leisure time and stated a clear preference for managing their own leisure-time activities.

It would be erroneous to assume, based on this high number, a correspondingly vehement rejection of leisure-time activities such as those offered by the Strength through Joy program. Apparently, the question was misunderstood by a substantial portion of survey participants, and there seems to be a prevailing fear that someone may seek to "organize" their leisure time. In this regard, however, the formulation of the question itself and the attendant effect are extraordinarily interesting from a psychological perspective. They demonstrate a general human desire to retain one area of their lives over which they exercise independent control and that is not "organized" for them by outsiders. This observation seems pertinent to the psychological handling of working women (and perhaps of men as well!) in the future. Any suggestions to be made concerning the leisure-time activities made by an outside source must always assume the nature and tone of mere suggestions. Any efforts to structure leisure-time activities will undoubtedly fail as soon as people are told: You must spend your leisure time in this way or that; you are not permitted to simply stay home.

Aside from this fundamental fear, we have established the following factors as reasons for the initial rejection of structured leisure-time activities:

1. Complete exhaustion ("I'm happy to just be able to relax!").
2. Too little leisure time. ("It's simply not feasible for me, though it may make sense and be a good thing for others, I simply have too little leisure time.").
3. Children.

Only 25 percent of all respondents have thus far made use of Strength through Joy offerings in such a way as to say that their leisure time was well spent.

146

GERTRUD ALTMANN-GÄDKE

The Maternal Instinct Must Be Reinforced

First published as "Der Wille zum Kind muß stärker werden," in her *Erprobtes Haushalten: Handbuch der Hausfrauenarbeit* (Leipzig: Julius Klinkhardt Verlagsbuchhandlung, 1941), 256, 258.

The facts demand that efforts to rekindle the maternal instinct in Germany must be stepped up. It certainly must be acknowledged that the number of live births has risen from 971,000 in 1933 to 1,640,000 in the year 1939 and that the German *Volk* has truly been blessed with many more children since the assumption of power. The excess winter mortality rate and number of stillbirths have decreased by one-fifth since 1933. The infant mortality rate is now merely 6 percent. We must surpass the targeted birthrate by a healthy and sufficient margin. Otherwise, all our efforts and successes in every sector of life have been in vain because our *Volk* will be irretrievably lost as a result of its infertility.

"We had the will to political victory, and we fought for that victory. We have the will to victory in childbearing, and here, too, we will fight for that victory." It is only in the spirit of these thoughts expressed by the Reich leader of the SS that we can emerge victorious in our struggle for existence.

Note: German women, be true to your task: see to it that Germany shall not be a "*Volk* without youth," that is, without a future! You are entitled to be bursting with pride when you have blessed as many children as possible with life and a good upbringing! Only then will you have fulfilled your greatest purpose in life!

147

SECRET REPORT OF THE SECURITY SERVICE OF THE REICHSFÜHRER SS

Women's Reactions to Goebbels's "Total War" Speech

First circulated on 25 February 1943 as "Aufnahme und Auswirkung der allgemeinen Propaganda-, Presse- und Rundfunklenkung in der Zeit vom 23.2. bis 1.3. 1943." First published in *Meldungen aus dem Reich 1938–1945. Die geheimen Lageberichte des Sicherheitsdienstes der SS,* edited by Heinz Boberach (Herrsching: Pawlak Verlag, 1984), 12:4870.

The measures taken toward totalizing the war effort, above all the deployment of women's work, remain an unabated primary concern of the population. A series of reports indicates that the attitude of the working population toward enlisting nonworking women or women who have since left the workplace in these efforts sees this not so much as an "acknowledgment of the galvanization and orientation of the national community toward a common goal" but far more as a "flagrant," "often veritably malicious gloating" and "stealthy observation" on the part of members of the upper classes, and there is "profound skepticism" toward the will and capacity of the government leadership to actually carry out these measures strictly and fairly. Jealousy, suspicion, and prejudice have never been so palpably evident as they are in many places now. In countless instances, working-class or middle-class women have stipulated that their willingness to work be made contingent on the condition that the "refined ladies" or certain women whom they have named by name—for example, women living in the same apartment buildings—are also called upon to work in the factories or in similar positions. From this perspective, then, members of the lower classes would not be inclined to participate in the war effort out of an authentic sense of personal sacrifice but would rather view the deployment of their labor as a state-imposed compulsory measure, at least until their suspicions concerning the attitude of the well-heeled and dominant classes have been allayed. [. . .] A report from the Alpine regions [*Alpengauen*] stated that "the population there is annoyed" to discover that the tourist towns are "overrun by women" who "by their whole appearance certainly cannot be armaments workers in need of rest and relaxation." Especially the women "clad in pants and Indian war paint" present a major stumbling block. "In other areas, too—in Berlin, for example—these ladies running around on the streets wearing pants sewn from the finest fabrics available for men's suits and clearly leave no doubt in anyone's mind that they are not wearing these outfits for professional reasons (as, for example, a train conductress might) have again become a conspicuous eyesore." Staunch criticism has been directed particularly at classified advertisements in the paper in which hotels are looking for "receptionists, manicurists and pedicurists," or an "elderly lady [is] seeking female companionship." The working classes continue to view the attitude of the propertied classes with tense anticipation and mistrust. The ban against horse riding in Berlin's Tiergarten Park is often advanced as an argument for the notion that "again and again, the elite of the country are being handled with kid gloves." A ban on horse riding in the Tiergarten is not enough. The horse owners are still free to keep their horses outside the city and ride them there. The only proper solution would be to confiscate the horses for the Wehrmacht and to send the women who ride them directly to armaments factories. A substantial number of individuals have expressed the desire to keep the population apprised of the results produced by various programs (women in the workplace, closing of luxury spas and businesses).

12
Marriage and the Family

DURING THE FRENCH REVOLUTION, there was a systematic attempt to wrest the "sacrament of marriage"—which linked husband, wife, and God—from the prerogatives of the Roman Catholic Church. Marriage was made a contractual and legal relationship under the supervision and acknowledgment of the state. In the German lands occupied by French revolutionary forces, such civil marriages were introduced in 1798. Under Otto von Bismarck, after 6 February 1875, only civil marriages were permitted in Prussia and then in imperial Germany. Bismarck, seeing Protestant Germany in a protracted struggle with the Catholic Church and Catholic states (the *Kulturkampf*), wanted to weaken the hold of the church on the day-to-day life of all Germans, Catholic and Protestant.

The Nazis found marriage and the family to be a "natural" site for the state to intervene, especially since racial biology provided a "scientific" rationale for the micromanagement of each citizen's private life. As the SS pamphlet *Selection and Breeding* observed, "Every prudent state leadership that is consciously promoting racial demographics and racial hygiene policies must see its primary task in enforcing measures to secure the continuation of the race and for selective breeding." "Sexual hygiene" became the basis for the regulation of marriage; childbearing and child rearing became service to the state. In the Law for the Protection of the Hereditary Health of the German *Volk* (the "Healthy Marriage Law") of 18 October 1935, an entire range of marriages were forbidden. The Nuremberg Laws announced on 15 September 1935 had already banned "racial mixing." These were eugenic laws that sought to avoid the creation of degenerates (such as the morally weakened offspring of alcoholics). Individuals with mental illness (from "idiocy" to "depression"), contagious diseases (such as syphilis), or inherited disabilities (such as congenital deafness) were also forbidden to marry. Couples intending to marry had to prove their eligibility and present a semilegal document, the *Ahnentafel* (genealogical chart), to demonstrate the biological health of their forebears. If they entered into marriage surreptitiously, the marriage was null and void.

As the physician, biologist, and pedagogue Otto Steche (1879–1945) made abundantly clear, the Law for the Protection against Hereditarily Diseased Offspring (14 July 1933) "affords the national community of the *Volk* the right to exclude those men and women from reproduction" whose offspring would likely be physically, mentally, or spiritually handicapped. The fear of weakening the "race" through the creation of degenerate offspring had a long history. The possibility that "congenital syphilis," an actual but rare pathological possibility, might show up in the offspring of sexually infected individuals became the model for all other fears. With its absolutely defined physiognomy, the affliction provided a clear case for the decay of the race through "degenerate" offspring. Indeed, the protagonist in Gaston Leroux's (1868–1927) 1911 novel *The Phantom of the Opéra* evoked the horror of congenital syphilis: The Phantom's masked face had "eyes . . . so deep that you can hardly see the fixed pupils. You just see two big black holes, as in a dead man's skull. His skin, which is stretched across his bones like a drumhead, is not white, but a nasty yellow. His nose is so little worth talking about that you can't see it side-face; and the absence of that nose is a horrible thing to look at."[1] Leroux makes it clear that the Phantom can love but cannot consummate his desire because his parents cursed him with the stigmata of congenital syphilis.

As Steche pointed out, the ideal marriage could transcend even the legal definition if it served the state in producing children. One of the fears articulated in *Selection and Breeding* was that "choosing a racially well-endowed wife does not in itself constitute an improvement of the race. This is only the case if the choice of an appropriate wife leads to the production of a better-than-average number of children." The image of a dying race haunted the Nazis. Out of this came the idea for *Lebensborn*—remote SS maternity homes for "hereditarily valuable" children sired by racially "elite" men and unmarried women. The facilities were invented by the head of the SS, Heinrich Himmler (1900–45), to remedy the decline in the German birthrate from 894,978 live births in 1920 to 516,793 in 1932. Himmler saw the massive increase in abortions (he stated that 800,000 abortions had taken place during this period) as the cause of this decline. The Nazis' view of abortion was double-edged: healthy births were never to be interfered with, but the modified Law for the Prevention of Inherited Diseases of 26 June 1935 legalized abortion under certain circumstances. Pregnant women forced to undergo sterilization by order of the Erbgesundheitsgericht (Hereditary Health Court), could "consent" to terminate the pregnancy unless the fetus was already capable of independent life or unless the termination of the pregnancy entailed a serious danger to either the life or health of the woman. Bad (illegal) abortions, as we shall see in the texts on "healthy sex" in chapter 14, were regarded as the work of the Jews; good abortions rid the state of "useless life." However, during the war, abortions were criminalized. According to a decree of 18 March 1943, those who underwent or assisted in abortions could be sentenced to jail, concentration camp, or even death.

As *Selection and Breeding* explains, the cure for unhealthy, degenerate, or missing children was to breed a new generation of eugenically sound ones. In December 1935, the *Lebensborn* organization was created in Berlin under the leadership of *SS-Sturmbannführer* Guntram Pflaum and, from May 1940 to 1945, *SS-Standartenführer* Max Sollmann. The program was seen as a medical operation, and it was guided from its inception by *SS-Oberführer* Dr. med. Gregor Ebner. Breeding healthy children from and for the SS was the aim; the program was financed by a tax on SS members, and the fewer the children one had, the more one paid. To qualify as breeders of racially pure children, women had to present health and genealogical records, attest that the child was the offspring of an SS man, and give birth in one of the homes, such as the first of the *Lebensborn,* Hochland, at Steinhöring near Ebersberg (which opened in 1936 and closed at the end of the war, in April 1945). Hochland had 50 beds for mothers and 109 for children. By 1939, there were eleven such homes in Germany, and at least 770 "illegitimate" (by legal standards) children were born in them. Soon homes were built in Austria (the Ostmark), Norway, Belgium, Holland, Poland, and France. In Norway alone, almost 6,500 women (the Norwegians were "Aryan") were in the homes by 1945, having given birth to children sired by German (and Norwegian) SS soldiers. Racially suitable children were also kidnapped from non-German mothers. Healthy, racially pure children could then be raised in the homes of or given over for adoption by SS couples.

This program was the inevitable end product of the biologization of the state sanctioning of marriage. The anxiety about "healthy" children had its most horrific end point in Himmler's *Lebensborn* homes. One did not ask what happened to a child born there with visible disabilities.

NOTE

1. Gaston Leroux, *The Phantom of the Opèra,* translated by Alexander Teixeira de Mattos (New York: Harper, 1987), 30.

FIGURE 13. Nazi Party poster promoting social welfare for large families: "The NSDAP Safeguards the People's Community. Racial comrades, if you need help and advice, turn to your local party group." Collection of Alice and Leslie Schreyer, Victoria and Albert Museum, London.

148

Law for the Protection of the Hereditary Health of the German *Volk*

Announced on 18 October 1935 as "Gesetz zum Schutze der Erbgesundheit des deutschen Volkes (Ehegesundheitsgesetz)." First published in *Reichgesetzblatt* (Berlin: Reichsverlagsamt, 1935), 1:1419.

Article 1: Prohibition of Marriage

(1) No marriage shall be solemnized if:
  - (a) Either party suffers from a potentially contagious disease that might result in substantial detrimental health effects to the partner or to their offspring.
  - (b) Either party has been declared legally incapacitated or has temporarily been declared a ward of the state.
  - (c) Either party, regardless of whether he has been declared legally incapacitated, suffers from mental illness that renders the marriage undesirable for the *Volk* community.
  - (d) Either party suffers from a hereditary disease as defined by the Law for the Protection against Hereditarily Diseased Offspring.

(2) The regulation in Article 1, Section d does not restrict marriage in the event that one party is sterile.

marriage not allowed if one person has a disease

UNLESS

Article 2: Proof of Marital Eligibility

Prior to the solemnization of the marriage, both partners are obligated to provide proof of eligibility according to Article 1 by presenting certification from the Department of Health [*Ehetauglichkeitszeugnis,* Certificate of Eligibility for Marriage].

Article 3: Annulment of Marriage

(1) Any marriage solemnized in violation of Article 1, based on a Certificate of Eligibility for Marriage that has been obtained based on false testimony provided by the marriage partners with or without the complicity and cooperation of the civil service officials involved, is declared null and void. It is similarly null and void if it has been solemnized abroad with the intention of circumventing the law. A petition to nullify the marriage may be entered only by the state's attorney.

(2) The marriage shall be considered valid from the date of its solemnization should the reasons for its nullification later be deemed invalid.

Article 4: Falsification of Marriage

(1) Whoever is found guilty of entering into an illegal marriage (Article 3) shall be subject to a prison term of no less than three months. Even the attempt is subject to punishment.

(2) Criminal prosecution for the crime committed shall not begin until the marriage has been declared null and void.

Article 5: Does Not Apply to Foreign Nationals

(1) The stipulations outlined in this law are not applicable in cases in which one of the parties or the male party to the marriage is in possession of foreign nationality.

(2) Criminal prosecution of a foreigner pursuant to Article 4 shall commence only by directive issued by the Reich minister of justice in consultation with the Reich minister of the interior.

Article 6: Exceptions

The Reich minister of the interior or his authorized representative may approve exceptions pertaining to the statutes in the law.

Article 7: Implementation

The Reich minister of the interior, with the approval of the deputy Führer and the Reich minister of justice, is authorized to issue all legal and administrative ordinances necessary for the execution and amplification of this law.

Article 8: Taking Effect

(1) The law shall take effect the day after its promulgation.

(2) The date on which Article 2 takes effect shall be determined by the Reich minister of the interior. Until that time, a Certificate of Eligibility for Marriage is to be presented where there is any doubt.

149

OTTO STECHE

Guide to Racial Science and Eugenics, Fostering Congenitally Sound Progeny, and Family Science for the Intermediate Level

First published in Otto Steche, *Lehrbuch der Rassenkunde, Vererbungslehre und Rassenpflege* (Leipzig: Quelle & Meyer, 1937), 38–40, 47. Office of U.S. Chief of Counsel for the Prosecution of Axis Criminality, *Nazi Conspiracy and Aggression* (Washington, DC: U.S. Government Printing Office, 1946), 5:176–77.

It is a great fortune that the leadership of our people has not only recognized the danger of the situation, but also made a strict decision to combat it. Whoever wants to live as a member of our community is not only obliged to put all his efforts at the service of this community, but also must make sacrifices. He must tolerate encroachments on his personal rights if the need of the community demands it. One of the primary responsibilities as a member of the community is to see to it that the increasing reproduction of those who are inferior by heredity is stopped. At our stage of culture, of course, we cannot even consider extirpating them from our community, but we can easily see to it that they do not reproduce and pass their inferior genetic inheritance to new generations. To prevent this, the law exists for the Protection against Hereditarily Diseased Offspring. This affords the national community of the *Volk* the right to exclude those men and women from reproduction with whom it can be expected with certainty through knowledge of the heredity laws that their offspring will likely be severely physically, mentally, and spiritually handicapped.

Costs of welfare in comparison to average earnings

The daily cost of a	
Deaf mute	6.0 M
Cripple	6.0 M
Reform School inmate	4.85 M
Mentally disturbed	4.50 M
Criminals	3.5 M
Daily earnings of a	
Blue collar worker	2.5 M
White collar worker	3.5 M
Civil servant	4.0 M

This can be accomplished by means of comparatively simple medical intervention that will not affect the individual's well-being and ability to live at all. The law enumerates a whole series of hereditary diseases, in case of which the prevention of procreation can be carried out. Into this class belong in the first place serious physical disabilities such as hereditary blindness and deaf-muteness, but also a series of serious mental diseases, especially hereditary feeblemindedness and idiocy. Of course, in every case, before such intervention is ordered by the state, all circumstances must be thoroughly examined by a court, appointed especially for the purpose.

The results of these measures, of course, will not be immediately apparent, but in the course of many years, the health of the genetic inheritance of our people will improve and the tremendous burden that is placed today on the community by taking care of the inferior ones will continue to decrease. Actually, today it is such that the state spends more for the existence of these actually worthless compatriots than the salary for the work of a healthy man, with which he must bring up a healthy family. [. . .]

Racial Hygiene

When choosing a mate, for marriage, we also accept the obligation to keep in mind the racial composition of our national substance. The six basic races that we discussed earlier are so mixed in our national community and their participation in the construction of our culture cannot easily be separated that we cannot easily put them against each other in strong contrast. We have previously seen that the Nordic race distinguishes itself by a special leadership talent and that it has certainly played an outstanding role in the development of our national substance. The result is that today we have relatively many Nordic people among the leading strata of our people. If, therefore, an increase of these strata is helped along, the share of Nordic blood within it will become a greater one. But it is very essential that we avoid, as best as we can, the penetration of elements of alien races into our national body.

150

ANONYMOUS

Selection and Breeding

First published in *SS-Mann und Blutsfrage: die biologischen Grundlagen und ihre sinngemässe Anwendung für die Erhaltung und Mehrung des nordischen Blutes* (Berlin: Der Reichsführer-SS, 1942), 28–37, 54–62.

> If the power to fight for one's own health is no longer present, the right to live in this world of struggle ends.
>
> —*Adolf Hitler,* Mein Kampf

Every prudent state leadership that is consciously promoting racial demographics and racial hygiene policies must see its primary task in enforcing measures to secure the continuation of the race and for selective breeding. If there is no force acting to contain it, hereditary and environmental changes will, over time, allow for the development of new or subraces. Selection is the process by which nature places limits on the splintering into countless different races. In the wild, lives that are unsuitable to the preservation of the race are eliminated, whereas the carriers of particularly advantageous tendencies are preserved.

One example: amongst mammals and bird species in the polar regions, the white, long-haired specimens almost always outlive the dark-colored members of the same species. They are better protected from their enemies by virtue of their color alone.

Selection maintains the established quality of the race.

If, as a result of changes in their genetic composition, individual members of a species develop new tendencies that serve to enhance beneficial characteristics, then these organisms are at an advantage over the remaining, unaltered members of their race. They are more determined to achieve perfections and will eventually suppress and supplant those members of the species who remained at the same level of development.

Selection is progressive.

In nature, evolution of the breed for all species of life occurs only as the result of mutation and selection. Any additional possibility for the development of new races through new formations is completely irrelevant to the human species. The death of an individual member of the species has absolutely no detrimental effect on selection but is rather merely means to achieve it. What is essential to the process of elimination is that a certain genetic material is not passed on because it is no longer strong enough to survive in the next generation.

FIGURE 14. Mass public marriage of members of the German Labor Front and their brides. Collection of Foreign Records Seized, Heinrich Hoffmann (no. 242.1), box 43, item 5515, U.S. National Archives and Records Administration, College Park, Md.

It is entirely irrelevant whether the elimination occurs by way of sterilization or celibacy, by death, or however it may be brought about.

The only biologically relevant form of selection is fertility.

Any human being who does not have children, regardless of how old he may live to be, has been forever eradicated from the life of the race. Fertility alone determines the ongoing survival of the genetic material.

Choosing a Mate

Choosing a wife of superior racial quality does not in itself constitute an improvement of the race. This is only the case if the choice of an appropriate wife leads to the production of a better-than-average number of children. For what purpose would it serve to purge bad genetic material from the body of the *Volk* if this is not accompanied at the same time by the maintenance and increase in the good tendencies? If, for example, a racially well-endowed man who does not wish to have children is chosen as a mate, this could imply even a degeneration of the race because it would involve the exclusion of good genetic material from future generations.

The Triumph of Fertility and Rapid Reproductive Regeneration

An average fertility rate has a tremendous impact on the survival of a race. Where unequal rates of reproduction exist between two or three races living in the same environment, the race with the lower birthrate is marked for extinction after only a few generations. Even a small deviation from the average rate of fertility is sufficient to effect substantial shifts over a long period of time.

The age of marriage, because it has major influence on maintaining large families, is not to be underestimated. The regeneration of the generations—that is, the rapid succession of generations—is an equally essential factor determining shifts in the composition of race. The results of an early or late age of marriage become apparent after a very short time. Experience shows that the number of children is greater for early marriage than it is for late marriage. Hence, after only three generations in one hundred years, every 4 children will produce 64 offspring, and in the course of four generations in one hundred years, every 4 children will produce 256 offspring. An apt example of the necessity to increase the birthrate of racially valuable people can be seen by looking at the proportions of our own race after World War I. In the years following the world war, twice as many children were produced by illegitimate marriages than were produced by legal marriages.

151

OTTO STECHE, ERICH STENGEL, AND MAXIM WAGNER

Womb Wars

First published as "Geburtenkrieg," in *Lehrbuch der Biologie für Oberschulen und Gymnasien* (Leipzig: Quelle & Mayer, 1942), 4:3.

National Socialism has embarked on a path that has yet to be taken in the history of nations and peoples [*Völker*]. It rewards special honors to families with large numbers of children! The first step in affording special status to large families was the introduction of the Book of Honors for Large German Families. A careful selection process conducted by the Department of Health and the Racial Political Office of the NSDAP has seen to it that only those parents whose flock of children is truly a treasure to our *Volk* receive the Book of Honors. Large families that are genetically inferior or asocial are entirely ineligible. In his annual Christmas Address in 1938, the Führer introduced the Mother's Cross of Honor for mothers with multiple children. It is the Frontline-Soldier Cross in the War for the Womb! It is awarded in bronze to mothers who have blessed the *Volk* with four or five children, in silver to those who have blessed us with six or seven, and in gold to mothers with eight or more children. These honors are awarded by high-ranking officials in the party annually on Mother's Day. Thus, the value of large families is stressed as a moral challenge more forcefully than has ever been done by a white civilized race. [. . .]

Every young German man and every young German girl can and should learn much from these observations. Above all, they should all take from them this one thing: that the German mother has the most important job for the future of our *Volk!* Our beloved Führer once said that the mother of multiple children is worth more than an educated woman, and another time he challenged all his staff members to bow their heads in gratitude to all the mothers who have blessed the *Volk* with children since the seizure of power. For twenty, indeed thirty years, the mother of multiple children remains in service to her children. Day in, day out, with no vacation time, no Sundays or holidays, she works without interruption to meet all the little demands presented by each hour. In her heart of hearts, her only thought is that she raise her children to become hardworking, successful Germans. [. . .]

Women's employment, especially for married women, is, from the perspective of racial biology, generally full of disadvantages. It represents a dangerous form of antiselection for the future and should thus be restricted. The German woman must again be reminded of the fact that her truest calling is not to be found at the office, in the factory, or in the laboratory but rather in the family and in the family alone!

13

Eliminating "Superfluous Life"

"Asocials," Criminals, the Handicapped, and the Mentally Ill

THE EARLY TWENTIETH CENTURY was the age of eugenics: "Improve the race!" was the cry in all the nations (from Germany to the United States to Japan) that accepted the primacy of "science" as the means of improving the lives of their citizens. In 1927, in his comments on the compulsory sterilization case of the "feebleminded" Carrie Buck of Virginia, Supreme Court Justice Oliver Wendell Holmes Jr. wrote,

> We have seen more than once that the public welfare may call upon the best citizens for their lives. It would be strange if it could not call upon those who already sap the strength of the State for these lesser sacrifices, often not felt to be such by those concerned, in order to prevent our being swamped with incompetence. It is better for all the world, if instead of waiting to execute degenerate offspring for crime, or to let them starve for their imbecility, society can prevent those who are manifestly unfit from continuing their kind. The principle that sustains compulsory vaccination is broad enough to cover cutting the Fallopian tubes. Three generations of imbeciles are enough. [Buck v. Bell 143 Va. 310]

On 14 July 1933, the Law for the Protection against Hereditarily Diseased Offspring, based on the Virginia statute, officially sanctioned the generally accepted view that those seen as a danger to the body politic should be sterilized. Some people even silently considered a much more radical possibility: elimination of anyone whose infirmities drained the nation's resources. The law mandated compulsory sterilization for any citizen judged genetically deficient by the newly created Hereditary Health Court. By 1945, more than 350,000 people were victims of forced sterilization.

In the "case of Ernst G.," Kurt Daluege, the SS chief of the *Ordnungspolizei* (all uniformed police within the German Reich) argued in a similar vein that "the consciously asocial enemies of the people [*Volksfeinde*]" must be eliminated by state intervention "if it hopes to prevent the outbreak of complete moral degeneration." Criminality, homosexuality, and asocial behaviors of all types made individuals dangerous to the state not only in the present but even more so in the future if they should reproduce. As Reinhard Heydrich noted, "The enemy in disguise remains intangible within the organized framework of society. As he works undercover, we could perhaps call him the hidden apparatus behind the truly great enemies," by which he meant, of course, the Jews. And like the Jews, as Ferdinand von Neureiter argued, these degenerate types could be identified by their physical differences. Neureiter called upon the theories of the psychiatrist Ernst Kretschmer (1888–1964), who divided all human beings into three body types (asthenic, athletic, pyknic) that he linked with specific forms of psychological character. But Kretschmer refused to make an explicit connection to racial biology. Nonetheless, as early as 1922, Ludwig Stern-Piper, in a lecture that year at the Southwest German Psychiatric Conference, took Kretschmer's theory to the next step, claiming that the three constitutional types also defined the basic racial types. Kretschmer objected, saying that he saw all three body types in every race; indeed, he saw a certain contradiction between the very concept of "racial" types and body types. Stern-Piper continued the argument, emphasizing the inherent racial makeup of each individual and the links between body type, illness, and race. Kretschmer's steadfast opposition to the appropriation of his theories for racial purposes, in spite of his allegiance to the new academic regime, including signing the "Professors' Vow" (see document 120 in chapter 10), cost him promotion after promotion under the Nazis. The debate had been joined by Jewish clinicians, such as the Munich physician Moses Julius Gutmann (1894–1961), who attempted in 1926 to correlate Kretschmer's notion of constitutional types with specific mental illnesses. He noted that the supposed predominance among Jews of the asthenic body type—marked by a long, lanky body—suggested to him that they would be particularly subject to schizophrenia, but in his clinical work he found a greater prevalence of manic-depressive psychosis. All such analyses show that these thinkers considered the way the Jew looked, just as the way the criminal looked, to be scientific evidence of the Jew's inherently pathological condition. And this line of thinking was extended to the "degenerate" and the disabled.

In July 1939, Hitler met with the Reich health minister (*Reichsgesundheitsführer*), Dr. Leonardo Conti; his chief of staff, Hans Heinrich Lammers; and Martin Bormann to expand the program of the Annihilation of Worthless Lives (Vernichtung von lebensunwertem Leben), which had begun on a limited scale. Mental patients and disabled children would now be added to the list of those to be killed. In October 1939, Hitler signed a decree authorizing "involuntary euthanasia" of both children and adults whose lives were simply not worth the state's effort and finances to preserve. He backdated it, however, to 1 September 1939, at the very moment that World War II began and Germany invaded Poland, as a sign that such murders were economically necessary for the war effort. Even before, as early as 8 August 1939, doctors and midwives had been ordered to report all disabled children up to three years old. Hospitals and mental asylums became settings for murder, not only for the disabled and the mentally ill (including those suffering from dementia), but also for those exhibiting "criminal" psychopathologies.

In October 1939, the first site dedicated to euthanasia was created at the Grafeneck asylum near Marbach, and the first killings of patients took place on October 12. Five additional facilities began operation the next year: Brandenburg, Hartheim (near Hitler's home town of Linz), Sonnenstein, Bernburg, and Hadamar. The asylums used medications such as phenobarbital and also gassed inmates using truck exhaust. Labeling the program the "T4 Action" (after its Berlin office address, Tiergartenstraße 4) to keep these activities secret, the Reich instigated the murder of more than 100,000 patients. As Henry Friedlander has shown in his detailed study of "involuntary euthanasia" in the Reich, Jewish inmates of psychiatric and long-term-care facilities were murdered at a greater rate than non-Jews. Indeed, the physician Friedrich Mennecke made no effort to soft-pedal this policy in describing the selection process to his wife on 25 November 1941: "thereafter we examined further until 2:00 P.M. 105 patients; a second load of 1,200 Jews, which we didn't even bother to examine, showed up before we 'tossed in the towel' at 5:00 P.M. and punctually went to dinner." Death certificates and bills for cremation were often the first notifications that families received of the murder of children or parents. Contemporary historians have argued that this mass murder was the prelude to the Holocaust. But the public reaction to the euthanasia killings was very different.

On 3 August 1941, in the third of a series of public sermons on the state of the church under the Nazis, Clemens August Count von Galen (1878–1946) of Münster had a statement read from the pulpits of the churches in his diocese that condemned with great specificity the practice of "involuntary ethanasia." In 1932, he had condemned the obsessive focus on the present world rather than on the world to come in his treatise *Against Laicization*. There he condemned all: the secularists of the Weimar Republic as well as politicians of all ideological stripes. His conservatism inevitably put him in conflict with the Nazis, who wanted to capitalize on the religious beliefs of their followers, reenforcing their belief in the regime. His anonymous attacks on Alfred Rosenberg (1893–1946), the "philosopher of the party" after 1933, made him a direct target of their wrath. When Galen, whose parishioners called him "the Lion of Münster," learned of the T4 murders in 1941, he went to the local police and officially accused the doctors (and the state) of systematic murder. His sermon a few months later condemned the doctrine of life "unworthy of living" and charged the regime with blatant criminality. The official response was true anger. Martin Bormann suggested hanging him as a traitor to his *Volk*; however, Joseph Goebbels did not think it wise to create a "Catholic martyr" during wartime and suggested that the matter wait until victory. Galen outlived them both.

In January 1942, the officially sanctioned film *I Accuse* (*Ich klage an*), a polemic on behalf of voluntary euthanasia, was released, eliciting a mixed response. The SS Security Service noted the division among Catholics between those who viewed the film positively, such as Rudolf Frercks, and those who saw it as evidence of state-sanctioned murder, citing Galen's sermon. By the end of 1942, the regime sought to appease the church by claiming that involuntary sterilization was compatible with Christianity. In time, however, public exposure of the program—as increasing numbers of Germans learned that their relatives were being killed—prompted the Nazis to stop the murders.

FIGURE 15. Chart produced by the Ministry for Public Enlightenment and Propaganda claiming that in 1936, expenditures for 880,000 people ill with hereditary diseases totaled 1.2 billion Reichsmarks, which was almost double the 713 million Reichsmarks spent on the administration of the national, state, and local governments. Photograph no. 07672, United States Holocaust Memorial Museum Photo Archives, Washington, D.C. Courtesy of Roland Klemig.

152

Law for the Protection against Hereditarily Diseased Offspring

Announced on 14 July 1933 as *"Gesetz zur Verhütung erbkranken Nachwuchses."* First published in *Reichsgesetzblatt* (Berlin: Reichsverlagsamt, 1933), 1:1021.

Article 1: Sterilization and Hereditary Disease

(1) Any person with a hereditary disease may be rendered infertile (sterilized) if, according to the judgment of medical science, procreation by said person is likely to produce children who suffer from serious physical or mental hereditary defects.

(2) A person with a hereditary disease is defined by this law as anyone who suffers from one of the following illnesses:

1. Congenital feeblemindedness
2. Schizophrenia
3. Circular (manic-depressive) insanity
4. Hereditary epilepsy
5. Hereditary Huntington's chorea
6. Hereditary blindness
7. Hereditary deafness
8. Extreme hereditary physical deformity [. . .]

Article 11: Medical Intervention

(1) The surgical procedure required for sterilization may be performed only in a clinical facility by a physician licensed by the German Reich. The physician may not perform the sterilization procedure until the order issuing it has been finalized. The Executive Department of State shall determine the clinical facilities and physicians authorized to perform sterilization procedures. The procedure may not be performed by a physician who participated in filing its petition or who was a member of the committee presiding over the order.

(2) The treating physician shall be required to provide the administrating physician with a written report of the sterilization in compliance with the regulations stipulated by the procedure.

Article 12: Direct Compulsion

(1) Once the court order for sterilization has been finalized, [the procedure] must be performed even without the consent of the patient to be sterilized, unless said person initiated the petition himself. The administrating physician shall be responsible for requesting necessary law enforcement measures from the department of police. Should these measures prove insufficient, the use of force shall be permitted.

(2) Should circumstances arrive that merit a reexamination of the facts of the case, the Court of Hereditary Health shall reopen proceedings and temporarily halt the administration of the sterilization procedure. Once a petition has been denied, the case may enter appeal only if new evidence is entered to justify the sterilization.

153

KURT DALUEGE

The National Socialist Fight against Criminality

First published as *Nationalsozialistischer Kampf gegen das Verbrechertum* (Munich: Verlag Franz Eher Nachfolger GmbH, 1936), 9, 11, 12, 14.

Ernst G. was born on 2 October 1890. There is nothing in the record about his first sixteen years of life.

On 18 September 1906, he was placed in a foster care facility after having traveled in homosexual circles for an extended period of time and having committed blackmail.

As a result of this blackmail and a sexual offense, G. was punished by the court for the first time on 17 April 1907. He was sentenced to four months in prison. Already at that time, his extraordinary knowledge of criminal language was an indicator of his way of life, something the lower district court judge who placed him in the foster care facility had noted explicitly.

After serving his sentence, G. was released to a halfway house in Berlin but escaped one month later and returned to his previous haunts in known homosexual districts in Berlin—and, according to the police report, was soon caught and returned to the halfway house.

In August of the same year, he escaped again and again returned to the homosexual hangout, where he was again apprehended and admitted to being in possession of forged identification, which, by his own account, he had stolen.

On 21 January 1909, he was served with reprimand as a juvenile for falsifying his identity and fined one mark for stealing identification documents.

Shortly thereafter he escaped the halfway house for a third time. On 5 June 1909, he was caught in someone else's home, fully equipped with all the tools for breaking and entering. Upon his arrest, he again falsified his identity to the police.

Despite the fact that he was again placed in foster care, G. was unable to come to terms with the arrangement and fled for the fourth time on 14 October 1909. During his subsequent arrest in the same area of activity, he once again provided a false name.

Following his fifth escape in December 1909, he was arrested for breaking and entering and, for this attempted robbery and falsifying his identity, received his third court indictment, with a one-week prison sentence and three days' detention.

On 18 January 1910, he was again sentenced to one week in prison for robbery.

His fifth indictment, on 21 January 1910, landed him a one-and-a-half-year prison sentence for attempted grand larceny.

In the summer of 1911, he went back to his old ways, actively working the strip as a "rent boy" and extorting substantial sums of money from his clients.

He was found guilty on five such counts, which led to his sixth conviction, on 26 January 1912, with a sentence of three years in prison and five years' revocation of civil rights.

After his release from prison in the spring of 1915, the Association for the Rehabilitation of Ex-Convicts refused to accept him because he had already demonstrated that he was "unsuitable for rehabilitation."

In the fall of 1915, he was subject to a prison term of nine months in an aggravated sentence for relapse into larceny. In consideration of his danger to the public good, he was deported from the city of Berlin two months after his release from prison.

G. refused to comply with the order for deportation and for a time eluded apprehension. In the period that ensued, he was the prime suspect in, among other things, a major jewelry store robbery in May 1917. Once he was finally apprehended in April 1918, he was subject to a prison term of three and a half years and five years' revocation of civil rights in an aggravated sentence for relapse into larceny. [. . .]

On 1 February 1933, he escaped from police custody at the local jail in the town of Halle, where he was being held temporarily pending transport to another facility and was able to avoid detection until October 1933. It was only in October 1933 that he was again apprehended. At that time, he was found guilty of having participated in an additional six commercial break-ins committed in the period from June 1933 to October 1933, in which retail items valued at a total of 15,000 marks were stolen. This time, however, it was on 3 November 1933, and the National Socialist spirit was sweeping through the land; he was finally sentenced to six and a half years' hard labor.

Ever since he was sixteen years old, G. had been on an uninterrupted crime spree and had nineteen previous convictions. Nineteen times, warrants were issued for his arrest. His younger brother Max, who is enthusiastically following in his footsteps, is also well known as a common criminal.

• • •

Imagine the tremendous costs, in terms of labor, money, and effort this one man, but one of thousands of career criminals, has cost the authorities! Imagine the mountains of paper, the rivers of ink that have been wasted on his behalf! How many detectives have run their heels ragged, and what a lineup of judges, state's attorneys, lawyers, and expert witnesses private and professional have been mobilized on his account in the course of all these years? All this simply to prove once again that he was guilty of one of his crimes and to bring him to justice, whereby the majority of the crimes he has committed over the years have most certainly gone undetected! The uproar, vexation, and trouble this man has caused decent and honest people in his seventeen years of breaking the law as a career criminal is as impossible to estimate as the total amount of property loss to hardworking, frugal national comrades. The crimes that have led to his condemnation as a career criminal are ultimately but a small portion of his actual register of debts.

This degree of forbearance on the part of the state with regard to criminals was absolutely unconscionable to its citizens. The tremendous expenditure for materials and personnel—police, court costs, the cost of incarceration—that have been forced upon this corrupt Marxist state largely by career criminals was a complete waste of tax money. [. . .]

The state cannot be rigorous enough in drawing a line of distinction between the honorable sector of the population and the consciously asocial enemies of the people [*Volksfeinde*] if it hopes to prevent the outbreak of complete moral degeneration. The former state did precisely the opposite. It tolerated the romantic misrepresentation of the most horrendous criminal activity in the most widely circulated and influential papers and stood idly by as even dangerous murderers and thieves were made into celebrities instead of being castigated and denounced as the basest dregs of humanity.

154

REINHARD HEYDRICH

The Enemy in Disguise

First published as "Der getarnte Gegner," in *Das Schwarze Korps,* 22 May 1935, 63.

In contrast to the visible enemy, the enemy in disguise *remains intangible within the organized framework of society.* As he works undercover, we could perhaps call him the hidden apparatus behind the truly great enemies we have already identified. His aim is to destroy the unity of state and party leadership in order to preempt any possibility for fulfilling the ideological tasks of National Socialism. The *Volk* is to become distrustful and skeptical of leadership, and the leaders are to become nervous and distrustful of one another.

To this end, a network has been devised with points of intersection reaching into every aspect of the state apparatus, public life, and the movement. On the one hand, this network acts to inform the enemy of what dangers lie in store for him. He is thus forewarned about state-sponsored measures, decrees, and laws well in advance. But the same canal system, on the other hand, allows the enemy to begin preparing precautionary countermeasures.

Various organs within this system operate on a *consciously* traitorous level, while others consist of personal weaknesses that are being *subconsciously* manipulated.

The major pillars of this consciously traitorous enemy activity are *hostile elements still remaining within the state apparatus* who, with grandiose feigned enthusiasm, immediately committed themselves *100 percent* to National Socialism. They fell through the cracks in the Civil Service Law. Because we believed in the authenticity of the heartfelt ring of conviction in their professions of loyalty, they were allowed to retain their positions *as experts* within the state structure.

Whereas we, as National Socialists, understand bureaucracy in the best sense of the term to include precision perfected to facilitate the excellent and flawless operation of a business and administrative apparatus, these heartless and hostile elements manipulate that same bureaucracy as a means to hinder, hamper, and derail our National Socialist aims.

This network is atrociously intricate. It would be impossible to provide a seamless listing of all its branches here. The branches are apparent to the layman only in their ramifications:

Over here, attempts are being made to unhinge legislative measures.

Over there, attempts at throttling financial support in various areas that are essential to the life of the movement and the state are under way.

At the *universities,* attempts are being made to apply a "strictly scientific and factual" approach to skew National Socialist ideas in favor of liberalism.

In the *field of prehistoric research,* attempts are under way to slip one-sided, *unvölkische* elements into the hands of excavation directors, so that the contention that our ancestors were "lacking in culture" can be safely maintained.

Attempts at playing politics with anti–National Socialist *hiring policies* are aimed at regaining control of significant key positions in the state so that, whenever National Socialist legislation is passed, its execution is sabotaged and loopholes are created by manipulating the provisions for its fulfillment. Furthermore, attempts are made to exert influence on sincerely National Socialist men using the network of social connections (invitations to parties, clubs, etc.). In their attempts to turn these National Socialist men against the movement, they misconstrue the fervent desire on the part of high-ranking National Socialist superiors to adapt German legislation and German administrative structures to suit the nature and sensibilities of the *Volk.*

In order to undermine some measure of the Führer or one of his agents, or as a way of toppling some organization within the movement or the state that is troublesome or threatening to them, they do not hesitate to employ systematic rumormongering and to foment slanderous attack campaigns in the press. Leaks flow through thousands upon thousands of channels directly to the authoritative sources, recounting the supposed "dangers" posed by the Führer's policies or by these organizations. At the same time, a whole wave of complaints comes flooding in. *And the broad range of these complaints is often an immediate sign that the channels of the enemy's network are operative.*

The command is given by the Swiss Freemason or "German" émigré newspapers, and the systematic onslaught is orchestrated in a series of articles filled with the most baneful lies. At precisely the same time, the apparatus for exploiting the character weaknesses of the individual is mobilized. Man is all too inclined to lend more credibility to spurious, implausible rumors than to the hard cold facts. In full cognizance of these weaknesses and of the human penchant for scandalmongering, the rumors are then circulated to certain select personalities who are either sympathetic to or ill-disposed toward these organizations and who thus put a positive or negative spin on them and of their own volition see to it that they are spread further.

Before you know it, a sort of prefabricated public opinion has been formed that paves the way for achieving whatever goals the enemy has in mind at that particular moment.

This is how they are seeking to gradually dissolve the fabric of the state and to drive a wedge between the leadership and its subjects. By underscoring the tasks that have yet to be fulfilled, they seek to obliterate what has been done and accomplished in the past two years and to gradually strip the Führer and his confidants of the basis for every form of political work—to wrench from them the public trust.

We must recognize what the enemy's tactics are and what he is up to so that we can counteract them.

The following sentence taken from a secret enemy report is illustrative of the way the enemy views the situation in Germany and the course of action he thinks is the right one to take: "The situation in Germany is marked by an attempt on the part of the bureaucracy and other clandestine enemies of National Socialism to gain control of the NSDAP."

155

KÖLNISCHE ZEITUNG

"Socially Fit–Asocial–Antisocial"

First published as "Sozial tauglick–asozial–antisozial," in *Kölnische Zeitung,* no. 64, 10 December 1937.

The Racial-Political Office of the NSDAP [Rassenpolitisches Amt der NSDAP] is currently undertaking the first extensive study of a large population group concerning the question "Socially fit or asocial"?[1]

Those members of the *Volk* community who belong to the group of "socially fit" are those whom we normally like to call hereditarily healthy. By contrast, the scientists of the Racial-Political Office clearly define "asocial" as follows: asocial is in the first instance considered a behavior that does not live up to or contradicts the dominant social order. What is decisive is if the individual consistently exhibits the kind of asocial behavior that can simultaneously be assessed as the natural behavior pattern of an asocial person; asocial is not the same as someone, who, in a momentary lapse, acts asocially once, but the asocial is a person who always has an asocial character. Not the single act but the actor is the measure.

According to the definition of the Racial-Political Office, [an] "asocial" is characterized by a defect exhibiting uninhibited indifference and lack of receptivity to any appeal to honor, conscience, or morality. His transgressions exhibit the stamp of his weakness: malingering, begging, vagabondage, drunkenness, delinquency, prostitution, petty deceptions and thievery, primitive document falsification, and resistance. This is also the distinctive boundary with the "antisocial," the downright criminal. The character deficiencies of the "asocial" that are harmful to the community are also hereditary defects, even though this diagnosis obviously does not mean that the asocial who is unfit for the community is on the same level as the hereditarily ill comrade.

The Reich Association of Multiple Child Families [Reichsbund der Kinderreichen] has put itself at the disposal of the first large-scale investigation of the Racial-Political Office, inasmuch as it is convinced that the new ledger of high esteem will result only from careful and pertinent studies. Sometime in the new year a hundred thousand families will be divided into socially fit and asocial groupings. At that time, the first results will be available for further examination.

Note

1. The Rassenpolitisches Amt der NSDAP was established on 1 May 1933 by Rudolf Hess to establish guidelines for racial legislation and eugenics.—Eds.

156

FERDINAND VON NEUREITER

Body Type and Crime

First published as "Körperbau und Verbrechen," in *Kriminalbiologie* (Berlin: Carl Heymanns Verlag, 1940), 15–17.

If we are to address the question of relationships between body build and crime, we cannot do so without touching on the lessons taught by the school of criminal anthropology, despite the fact that these are primarily of historical interest today. [. . .]

If we ask ourselves what degree of validity the lessons of "criminal anthropology" still possess today, we must conclude, next to none. We can neither endorse any of the extant hypotheses about the nature of the criminal, nor can we accept any specific set of morphological characteristics as defining characteristics of a uniform criminal type. We can, at best, attach some validity to the notion of the born criminal as long as we concede that, while there are indeed some people born with innate propensities that naturally compel them to become criminals or to tend toward criminal behavior "if they are not subject to the deceptive effects of a milieu that is ideally suited to camouflaging their criminal predisposition," these people come in various types. These born criminals are more likely than the more socially inclined average man to demonstrate signs of physical deviation from the norm (*stigmata degenerationis*); these deviations, however, are not necessarily recognizable as such.

That being said, it must be clear that we are not concerned with a relapse into the lines of thought advanced by "criminal anthropology" in the case of numerous researchers conducting criminal biological examinations of prisoners in recent years who have taken recourse to [Ernst] Kretschmer's scheme of body and character types (and I trust that I can assume my readers are familiar with this scheme) in order to determine: (1) which of these types are most prevalent amongst criminals, and (2) whether there is, on the one hand, any relationship between the types of psychological constitution, and on the other, between the frequency, type, and execution of crimes. For it was by no means the intent of these studies to identify individual morphological indicators that, taken together, would lead to the diagnosis that these indicators allow for criminality or perhaps even explain the nature of criminal behavior; rather, the point was to "ascertain physical characteristics that point to human personality traits in general and that may at the same time be relevant with regard to criminal behavior."

157

ADOLF HITLER

Memorandum Authorizing Involuntary Euthanasia

Dated 1 September 1939 (signed October 1939). *Trial of the Major War Criminals before the International Military Tribunal, Nuremberg, 14 November 1945–1 October 1946* (Nuremberg, 1947–49), 26:169.

Reichsleiter [Philipp] Bouhler and Dr. med. [Karl] Brandt

are hereby instructed and authorized to broaden the powers of designated physicians to the extent that persons who are suffering from diseases which may be deemed incurable according to standards of human judgment based on a careful examination of their condition shall be guaranteed a mercy death.

Adolf Hitler

158

CLEMENS AUGUST COUNT VON GALEN

Sermon on Euthanasia

Predigt. Delivered on 3 August 1941. First published in *Galen, Clemens August von. Akten, Briefe, und Predigten: 1933–1946,* edited by Peter Löffler, Veröffentlichungen der Kommission für Zeitgeschichte. Reihe A, Quellen, vol. 42 (Mainz: Matthias Grünewald Verlag, 1988), 876–78.

For the past several months, we have been hearing reports that patients who are chronically ill or who may appear to be incurable are being involuntarily removed from mental asylums and sanatoria on the orders of Berlin. On a regular basis, relatives of these patients have been known to receive notice of the patient's death shortly thereafter, together with notification that the body has been cremated and that the ashes are available for delivery. In general, the suspicion bordering on certainty prevails that these considerable numbers of unexpected deaths amongst the mentally ill did not result from organic causes but that they have been brought about intentionally, that this involves an adherence to the doctrine that stipulates that "life unworthy of living" can be terminated, that is, that innocent men may be killed if their lives are determined to be of no value to *Volk* and state—a horrendous doctrine that would permit and justify the murder of innocents, one that legally authorizes the violent murder of incapacitated invalids, cripples, the incurably ill, the senile on principle!

I have been informed by reliable sources that lists of patients scheduled for transfer and transport as "unproductive national comrades" are currently being compiled in clinics and sanatoria in the province of Westphalia and that these patients will soon be put to death. The first scheduled transport already left the station sometime this week at the Marienthal Clinic near the city of Münster!

German Ladies and Gentlemen! Article 211 of the Reich Penal Code is still in effect; it states, "Whoever intentionally takes the life of another human being shall be sentenced to death for murder if the killing is premeditated." Clearly, the reason those poor people—members of our families—whose lives are scheduled for termination are being removed from clinics near their homes and transported to distant clinics in order to shield those who have intentionally taken their lives from criminal prosecution under this clause in the law. The cause of death cited is then some arbitrary illness. Since the corpses are cremated immediately, neither relatives nor police detectives are able to determine whether this illness was actually the cause of death or what the cause of death was.

I have, however, been assured that the Reich Interior Ministry and the head of the Reich Physicians' Chamber [Reichsärztekammer], Dr. [Leonardo] Conti, make no bones about the fact that a substantial number of mentally ill people in Germany have been intentionally killed and more shall be killed in the future. Article 139 of the Penal Code stipulates, "Whoever receives credible information concerning the intent to commit a crime against life and neglects to report it to the authorities or the person who is threatened in a timely fashion . . . shall be punished."

When I learned of the intention to transport patients from Marienthal to their deaths, I registered a formal complaint at the State's Attorney's Office at the state court in Münster and with the head of the police department in Münster by means of a registered letter, dated 26 July, which reads as follows: "According to information that I have received, in the course of this week, a large number of patients from the Marienthal Provincial Asylum near Münster are to be transported to the Eichberg asylum as so-called unproductive national comrades and will then soon be intentionally killed, as is generally believed has occurred with such transports from other asylums. Since such an action is not only contrary to the moral laws of God and nature, but is also punishable by death as murder under Article 211 of the Penal Code, I hereby bring a charge in accordance with my duty under Article 139 of the Penal Code and request that you provide immediate protection for the national comrades thus threatened by taking action against those agencies who are intending their removal and murder, and that you inform me of the steps that have been taken."

I have not been notified concerning any intervention on the part of the State's attorney or the police. [. . .]

Already on 26 July, I had submitted a serious written objection to the provincial administration of the province of Westphalia, which is charged with overseeing medical care and treatment. To no avail! The first transport of innocent people condemned to death left Marienthal despite my efforts! Furthermore, so I have heard, another eight hundred patients have already been removed from the care and treatment facility at Warstein.

Thus, we must reckon with the fact that, sooner or later, the defenseless patients will be killed.

Why? Not because they have committed any crime punishable by death. Not because they attacked their nurses or orderlies so that the latter had to resort to the justified use of force in defense of their lives against their attackers. Those are cases in which, in addition to the killing of an armed enemy in a just war, the use of deadly force is permissible and is often necessary. No, these are not the reasons that these unfortunate patients must die, but rather because, in the opinion of some department, on the testimony of some commission, their lives have become "unworthy of living," because according to this testimony they are "unproductive" national comrades. The argument goes, they can no longer produce commodities; they are like an old machine that no longer works; they are like an old horse that has become incurably lame; they are like a cow that no longer produces milk.

What does one do with such an old machine? It is thrown on the scrap heap. What does one do with a lame horse, with such an unproductive cow?

No, I do not want to continue the comparison to the end—as dreadful as its justification and its power of elucidation may be.

We are not concerned here with machines, horses, and cows whose sole purpose is to serve mankind, to produce goods for man. One may put them down; one may slaughter them as soon as they cease to fulfill their function. No, we are concerned here with human beings, our fellow human beings, our brothers and sisters! With poor people, sick people, unproductive people, if you will. But does that mean they have forfeited the right to life? Have you, have I, the right to live only so long as we are productive, so long as we are recognized by others as productive?

If we establish and apply the principle that "unproductive" fellow human beings can be murdered, then woe betide us all when we become old and frail! If one is allowed to kill the unproductive people, then woe betide the invalids who have spent, sacrificed, and lost their health and strength in service to the productive process. If one is allowed to forcibly remove unproductive fellow human beings, then woe betide all the courageous soldiers who return to the homeland seriously disabled, as cripples, as invalids! As soon as we accept the notion that people have the right to kill "unproductive" fellow humans—and even if this now applies only to the poor defenseless mentally ill—then the murder of all unproductive people has become permissible *as a matter of principle;* in other words, it is acceptable to murder the incurably sick, cripples, invalids, anyone who has been disabled by war or by work, and all of us once we have grown old, frail, and senile and therefore unproductive.

Then all that needs to happen is that a secret order be issued to mandate that the method developed for the mentally ill be extended to other "unproductive" people, that it be applied to anyone suffering from incurable lung disease, to the elderly who are senile or incapacitated, to soldiers severely wounded in war. Then there will be no guarantee for any of our lives.

Some commission can place any one of us on the list of the "unproductive," whose lives, in its opinion, have become "unworthy" of living. And there will be no police force to protect us and no court to investigate our murder and give the murderer the sentence he deserves! Who will be able to trust his doctor anymore? He might report his patient as "unproductive" and receive instructions to kill him. It is impossible to imagine the degree of moral depravity, of general mistrust, that would then spread even through families if this dreadful doctrine is tolerated, accepted, and followed. Woe to mankind, woe to our German nation if God's holy commandment "Thou shalt not kill," which God proclaimed on Mount Sinai amidst thunder and lightning, which God our Creator inscribed in the conscience of mankind from the very beginning, is not only broken but if this transgression is actually tolerated and allowed to go unpunished.

Please, God, let us all recognize today, before it is to late, what serves the purpose of peace!

Lord Jesus in heaven, driven to tears in desperation over the blindness and misdeeds of men, help us in your mercy to ever strive to do your will and to refrain from doing what you frown upon, that we might find our souls in your love and your peace. Amen.

Let us pray now for the poor children, threatened with death, pray for our priests who've been banished, for anyone who suffers hardship, for our soldiers, our *Volk,* our fatherland, and its Führer.

159

SECRET REPORT OF THE SECURITY SERVICE OF THE REICHSFÜHRER SS

On the Public Response to the Film *Ich klage an* [I Accuse]

Circulated on 15 January 1942. First published as "Zur Aufnahme des Films: 'Ich klage an' in der Bevölkerung," in *Meldungen aus dem Reich, 1938–1945. Die geheimen Lageberichte des Sicherheitsdienstes der SS,* edited by Heinz Boberach (Herrsching: Pawlak Verlag, 1984), 9:207–11.

All available reports confirm that the film *Ich klage an* has met with lavish praise throughout the Reich. One general conclusion that can be drawn is that the film has been widely recommended by word of mouth and discussed extensively. One index of the sensation this film has created in the public is that even in many cities where it has not even been shown, it is already being described as a movie one simply must see—even by unsophisticated people. The acting has been enthusiastically acknowledged as superb; the content has inspired deep reflection and provoked lively discussion in the public.

The film *Ich klage an* focuses on a twofold problematic. The main theme centers its discussion on the problem of someone suffering from an incurable hereditary disease requesting her own death. But the underlying theme is the question of putting an end to a life that is unworthy of living. All available reports from throughout the Reich indicate that, in principle, the majority of the population agrees, though with some reservations, with the film's basic premise that people suffering severely from diseases for which no cure exists should be subject to a swift, legally sanctioned death. This is also true for portions of the population with strong religious affiliations.

For the most part, the church—Catholic and Protestant—has completely rejected it. There are reports of Catholic clergy making house visits in the attempt to discourage individual national comrades from viewing the film, arguing that it is an inflammatory film directed against the Catholic Church or a state-sponsored propaganda film intended to justify the murder of the people suffering from hereditary handicaps.

The Catholic clergy has attacked the film indirectly in a variety of ways and, according to reports heard on the subject, have said that it is so good it could present a danger and be as "tempting as sin itself." Despite this unequivocal rejection of the film in Catholic circles, several reports indicate that the film has occasioned a rift in the Catholic camp, whereby one faction agrees with the notion that a person's life should be terminated, especially in difficult cases involving particularly severely diseased people who have been deemed incurable by a panel of physicians. The second faction, on the other hand, continues to speak in terms of "murder" in the context of this film.

All the reports coming from predominately Catholic sectors of the Reich refer to the fact that the widely circulated comments by Bishop Clemens August [*sic,* von Galen—Eds.] of Münster are often taken as a point of departure for discussions of the film, whereby various sources go so far as to claim that the film represents an attempt to justify the state's policies now that the bishop has attacked them.

So, for example, we made note of the following comments:

"The film is very interesting; but it's just the same thing that's going on in the insane asylums now where they're destroying all the lunatics."

"Whatever your take on it is, who's going to guarantee that it won't be abused? Once laws like this have been passed, the government can easily set up a commission to declare anyone who has fallen out of favor incurable and use that to get rid of them. And if anyone has enough money and influence to pull the right strings, it won't take much for them to have anyone they want declared incurable."

Outright opposition is not quite as prevalent in Protestant circles. While you hear people saying again and again that a life that God has given can and should only be taken by God, there have nevertheless been some positive opinions expressed by the church. So, for example, the superintendent of the evangelical church in Bautzen, for example, made the following statement: "It will be the state's responsibility to prevent abuses of the law and to ensure that it is applied lovingly to end the agony of the incurably diseased. That will be easier to orchestrate than the actual act of deliverance. As a Christian, I am compelled to agree with this film."

Reactions to the problems addressed here are known to be generally positive in *medical circles.* Especially the younger doctors, with the exception of a few people with strong religious affiliations, are in complete agreement.

Concerns and reservations—even in cases where they agree in principle—are most prevalent amongst the older physicians. The spread of this sort of propaganda in the general public is often seen by physicians as inappropriate.

In some instances, the question is being raised as to whether or not medical diagnosis can ascertain with any certainty, especially in borderline cases, whether or not a given condition is actually incurable.

So, for example, there are frequent instances of the seriously ill who see improvement many years after all the doctors have given up on them. People are emphatic in stressing that every doctor and every hospital is familiar with such cases.

Other doctors mention that, in their experience, most people, but especially the seriously ill or the elderly, only tend to express a strong desire to die once they have been driven to deep despair after a long period of severe pain. Those same patients, in periods where they are free of pain, however, have demonstrated a remarkable optimism for life and hope for a cure up until the bitter end.

Concerns have also been raised about the *medical panel* proposed by the film: Each physician on the commission would have to examine the patient independently. This would lead to an unnecessary psychological strain on the patient, who would be alerted to the pending decision by this series of examinations.

In the opinion of many physicians, the point at which one should be expected to intervene and provide assistance could just as well be left to the sense of responsibility in individual German physicians. In practice, they say, this sort of mercy killing already exists. Many doctors, when there is no prospect whatsoever of recovery and the patient is suffering severe pain, already prescribe a larger dosage of the appropriate medication with the intent of bringing about a painless death.

However, legal professionals in particular are inclined to see the urgent necessity for anchoring this type of medical intervention in law. The difficulties that arise from a legal perspective are considered tremendous, since, on the one hand, it is scarcely possible to legislate which of myriad illnesses fall under this category, and, on the other hand, the field of medicine is constantly advancing and illnesses that are defined as incurable today may be designated as curable tomorrow.

The *bulk* of the German *Volk* has responded with almost unanimous support of the issues the film raises in the film, whereby reports indicate that the following points are of primary import:

1. People consider it a necessary prerequisite that the family physician be included in the medical commission responsible for determining whether or not the illness is incurable.
2. In some cases, the question is raised as to whether mercy killing should be performed in all cases, since even people who are terminally ill are often still capable of productive work.
3. The consent of the patient is considered equally indispensable to performing euthanasia and, in the cases of mentally ill patients who have been declared incompetent, the consent of their relatives.
4. In any event, strict standards must be set to prevent any abuses from occurring. Under no circumstances should the decision rest with one individual alone.
5. Most comments indicate that the only person who should be granted the right to perform euthanasia is the physician himself.

The working classes are by far more inclined to respond positively to the changes in the law proposed by this film than are national comrades from intellectual circles. According to the reports, the reason for this is that population groups in socially less privileged ranks are naturally much more inclined to bear in mind their own financial burden. The film is often charged with displaying materialistic tendencies so that the notion of a person suffering from severe hardship liberating himself from his misery takes second place. It is only the medical profession that generally tends to interpret the film's content this way.

These negative statements about the problems the film addresses are by far in the minority and, with the exception of objections raised by the church, cannot be seen as fundamentally dismissive.

In summary, the conclusion that can be drawn from the wealth of available materials is that there is general approval for euthanasia procedures as long as a committee consisting of several physicians is involved in the decision-making process with the consent of the incurably ill patient and his relatives.

The general approval culminates in agreement with the statement made by the major in the film: if the state can demand that we accept the responsibility to die, then it also must grant us the right to die!

160

RUDOLF FRERCKS

Christianity and Sterilization

First published as "Christentum und Sterilisierung," in his *Das rassische Erwachen des deutschen Volkes. Nationalsozialistische Aufklärungsschriften,* vol. 5 (Berlin: Propaganda Verlag Paul Hochmuth, 1942), 20–21.

In order to keep the nation's genetic strain free from pathological hereditary dispositions, there is only one guaranteed method and that is the prevention of procreation through a simple surgical intervention.

Ever since Germany began moving closer to realizing this goal with the passage of the Law for the Protection against Hereditarily Diseased Offspring, the question has been raised by many as to whether or not the planned measures can be reconciled with Christian doctrine. None too few are the voices who would object by stating that, of all religions, Christianity is one of sufferers and the needy. Indeed, this is true! But this cannot possibly be interpreted to mean that we burden ourselves with the task of nurturing all that is feeble and hereditarily diseased so that it might bear plentiful fruit and that suffering thus continues to increase to the point that it ultimately puts the healthy life of the *Volk* and the race at risk! "If we have resisted this, if we have been fully cognizant of our responsibilities as human beings and of our obligation to compassion by resolving to no longer allow this wretched suffering and this wretched misery to continue to fester amongst us, perhaps to double or triple in the next generation, then we have performed a great deed, one that our children and our children's children will thank us for" (Dr. Heinrich Gross).

Nature is crueler than our civilized life; the genetically deficient and those too debilitated to sustain meaningful life are mercilessly driven into the ground. It is not congruent with the spirit of our times to imitate nature's cruel ways and to mercilessly destroy the feeble and the weak. It is precisely our moral and ethical conscience that is filled with satisfaction, just knowing that today it is possible to sustain the life of the individual while at the same time safeguarding the chain of generations against the perpetual return of chronic disease.

The National Socialist state is rooted in the realization of the national community of the *Volk*. Its work is built upon that one great voluntary act of renouncing all private interests on behalf of the well-being of the whole. Woman has fully internalized this idea of selfless community; she is by nature inclined to alleviate suffering and to help. She has always championed every form of charity and altruism without regard for the fact that this was part and parcel to the great work of the Christian organization Caritas or within the framework of public welfare services.

The new state has applied the idea of altruism as the one way of redirecting focus from the individual to the whole and to future generations of the *Volk*, and it now seeks to spare families tremendous suffering and worry with this simple and harmless medical procedure. This act of altruism, which seems to do so little to serve today's generation but benefits its children and grandchildren all the more and puts an end to the immortalization of tremendous misery, will therefore meet with widespread support. Those who are engaged in this work reap their greatest reward when one of these patients comes to them and says, "Indeed, I certainly don't want my suffering to be passed on to my children and my children's children and thus to create even more suffering." With this decision to voluntarily put an end to his diseased line of heredity, he has made a sacrifice whose full scope is acknowledged and much appreciated by the whole community of the *Volk*. The patient has thus proven his willingness to become an integral part of the myriad possibilities this state has to offer, and he is by no means stigmatized by the mark of inferiority. The state is happy to continue providing him protection and assistance in its effort to ease the burden of his cruel fate.

14
Healthy and Unhealthy Sexuality

IF RACIAL HYGIENE STOOD at the center of the Nazis' concern about how to improve the "race," then human sexuality was the means to that end. Germany was the site for some of the first modern sexual liberation movements. Nudism had its roots in the 1890s in the German youth movement and became institutionalized as Free Body Culture (*Freikörperkultur*) as early as 1913. Nudism was to be found throughout Germany as a sign of a healthy concern with the body. The body only revealed itself when nude. The writer Franz Kafka (1883–1924), when he went to a nudist camp run by a Christian health cult, insisted on wearing his swimming trunks. He was considered rather odd, but he was also aware that his circumcised body would reveal his Jewish identity to his neighbors.

In Nazi Germany, nudism was a matter of controversy. Wilhelm Stapel (1882–1954), a Christian theologian, a "national conservative," and a renowned "expert" on anti-Semitism (his *Antisemitismus und Antigermanismus* of 1928 was a canonical text), was attacked by *Das Schwarze Korps* for describing Germany's nudist culture as a destructive form of "paganism," and he was eventually forced to give up his posts in the Nazi publishing industry. In many ways, Nazi sexual morality was conservative or repressive even though it could positively evaluate the new meanings of an Aryan heterosexuality; the same periodical extolled the virtues of "healthy *völkisch*-oriented sex"and castigated those who worried more about young men's enjoyment of "beer, booze, and foolhardy girls" than about "the aberrant tendencies of youth who are attracted to members of the same sex which, if they are not discovered in time, can have a devastating detrimental effect on the *Volk* as a whole."

In the 1860s, the German lawyer Karl Heinrich Ulrichs (1825–95) had tried to provide an alternative, nonjudgmental model of "uranism," or homosexuality. In 1862, writing under the pseudonym of Numa Numantius, he published *Researches on the Riddle of Male-Male Love,* in which he argued for the existence of a third sex, "*anima muliebris virili corpore inclusa*" (a female psyche confined in a male body). Though he limited his references to male same-sex desire and activity, he saw this third sex as a natural alternative to the two sexes of male and female.

The term *homosexuality* (*Homosexualität*) was coined by the German-Hungarian Károly Mária Kertbeny (born Karl Maria Benkert, 1824–82) at virtually the same time as the term *anti-Semitism* came into use. He first used it in a letter to Ulrichs on 6 May 1868 and then again in two pamphlets published in 1869 in Leipzig, in which he argued against the Prussian Criminal Code (Paragraph 143) that made sexual contact between men a crime. The new term aimed to provide a "scientific" label for acts that had generally been dismissed as unnatural.

Ulrichs hoped this term would free homosexuals from the moral and medical taint accompanying any representation of "perverse" sexual attraction or activity in the evolving medical model. On 29 August 1867, he sought publicly to defuse the criminalization of homosexuality while avoiding the medicalization of homosexuality as a perversion. When he argued for a resolution urging the repeal of antihomosexual laws at the Deutsche Juristentag (Congress of German Jurists) in Munich, he was shouted down. Liberals such as Richard Krafft-Ebing, who argued his case in *Psychopathia Sexualis* (1886), also wished to free homosexuals from the charges of criminal sexual activity or moral depravity by medicalizing homosexuality and promoting therapy rather than mandating prison as an appropriate response. By the end of the century, physicians such as Magnus Hirschfeld (1868–1935) had begun applying the Ulrichs model of the third sex and were seeking a biological rather than a theoretical model. Of special interest to Hirschfeld were what he called the "intermediate cases" of sexuality, the model for which was the hermaphrodite, described as both female and male and thus neither. In 1897, Hirschfeld founded the Wissenschaftlich-humanitäres Komitee (Scientific Humanitarian Committee), the first homosexual emancipation movement, in response to the trials of Oscar Wilde (1854–1900) for "sodomy" in London during 1895. The association worked for the repeal of Paragraph 175 of the imperial German Penal Code that had criminalized homosexuality since 1871. In 1919, Hirschfeld created the first Institute for Sexual Science in Berlin, which had research facilities as well as a clinical component. Out of this institute came a range of changes, including the theoretical underpinnings of the first male-female transsexual procedures undertaken in Germany, which took place in 1921.

Such radical alterations in the public discussion about sexuality shocked the mainstream German public. Hirschfeld's 1919 film *Different from the Others* (*Anders als die Andern*), which portrayed a tormented homosexual (played by Conrad Veidt) blackmailed to the point of suicide, presented a sympathetic gay figure on the movie screen for the first time. The Right found this unacceptable. After the accession of the Nazis in January 1933, one of the most public events was the burning of "un-German" books in Berlin on 10 May of that year. Many of the books "consigned to the flames" were from the library of Hirschfeld's institute, but he was distinguished as the only writer whose bust was also thrown onto the pyre.

Being gay and being Jewish were suddenly seen as equally dangerous to the state, as *SS-Untersturmführer* Professor Eckhardt noted in *Das Schwarze Korps* in 1935. Homosexuals were unmanly, and Jewish men were cowards and shirkers, having avoided combat in World War I. (This was one of the powerful lies that the Nazis promulgated. Actually, Jews suffered higher casualty rates at the front than any other group.) Among the ancient Germans, according to Eckhardt, "homosexuality is equated (passively and actively) with cowardice. . . . Now that we have found our way back to our ancient Germanic perspectives on the question of mixed marriages with members of races that are alien to the species [*artfremde Rassen*], we must do the same for our assessments of the scourge of racial annihilation presented by the degenerate profile of the homosexual and return to the Nordic guiding principle of extirpating the degenerates." Male-male bonding, such as the "comradeship" of the front soldier, was good and healthy, but according to an essay on corruption in the armed services, "A few pathologically inclined leaders exploited the susceptibility of a specific age group in order to spread their viciously anti-*völkisch* tendencies. Using an exaggerated sense of camaraderie, they exalted friendship with men among these male youth, discouraging them from any dealings with women, suggesting that this was far beneath the dignity of any young man." What the nation needed was a real man who would help reproduce the race.

The new Nazi morality demanded, as Wolfgang Willrich noted, "a space . . . between the legal bounds of amorality and the primal sense of decency of a noble race." Though the Nazis abjured homosexuality, they promoted "normal" or "healthy" sex. But Germanic sex was different not only in practice but in sensibility. It was rather boring and tame, reported Hugo Hertwig in 1941: "It is more in line with the Nordic landscape for Nordic man to be more introverted than extroverted, that he be more taciturn and reserved and happy to go his own way. As I have already mentioned in the context of sexual attraction and love among Nordic people, we cannot reckon with any kind of unbridled passionate abandon. Nordic man, both male and female, is incredibly intent on production and performance and is all but born for family life." Hertwig expressed this view after the creation of the *Lebensborn*. But as the criminologist A. Aschenbrenner commented in "Incest and Hereditary Health" (1940), the achievement of racial purity might call for a form of incest: "Incest . . . has not had any measurable degenerative influence, either on the physical health of the populace or on its intelligence." So some forms of illegal sexual contact, such as incest, might turn out to be an advantage for the race. The irony, of course, was that anti-Semites in Germany had accused Jews, who practice endogenous marriages, of being an "incestuous people" since the eighteenth century.

In imperial Germany, the question of homosexuality was a matter of "don't ask, don't tell." After the Oscar Wilde trial, Germany was the site of many homosexual scandals, because people became eager to expose closeted gays. The most extraordinary one was created by the Jewish journalist Maximilian Harden (1861–1927), who in 1906 exposed members of the imperial cabinet as homosexuals, including Prime Minister Philipp Fürst zu Eulenburg und Hertefeld (1847–1921) and, by implication, Wilhelm II. Harden immediately became the target of a barrage of court cases, which he lost and for which he spent time in jail.

In the Third Reich, it was public knowledge (and he had admitted it) that the head of the Storm Troopers, Ernst Röhm (1887–1934), was a homosexual, but as one of the original members of the NSDAP, a conspirator with Hitler in the attempted putsch of 9 November 1923, and then head of the party's autonomous quasi-military force, he seemed untouchable. During the later years of the Weimar Republic, Röhm's homosexuality was the subject of a scurrilous campaign by the Left, which depicted the SA as a virtual bordello for gays. Hitler, egged on by Heinrich Himmler and others, felt that Röhm had too much power in the new state. Goebbels, too, characterized the SA as a "paradise for 175ers" (referring to the notorious antihomosexual statute). Röhm, convinced of Hitler's loyalty to him, followed his leader's orders to give all SA members a holiday on 29 June 1934 and announced that he too would go on vacation. The next day, he and the leaders of the SA were arrested by the SS and taken to the prison at München-Stadelheim, where they were systematically murdered between 30 June and 2 July during the "Night of the Long Knives." This act terrified all gay members of the party, as is clear from an anonymous letter to Ludwig Müller, the "German Christian" Reichs bishop of the Deutsche Evangelische Kirche (German Evangelical Church).

The official rationale for the murders was that Röhm had been planning a homosexual putsch against Hitler. After the fact, the political philosopher Carl Schmitt published his famous article, "The Führer Protects the Law," justifying the Exceptional Circumstances Law (Staatsnotwehr-Gesetz) to legitimate Hitler's actions. Hitler claimed to be shocked by the revelation that his close friend (he used the familiar "du" with him) was gay. Shortly thereafter, a joke began circulating in Berlin that the Führer was shocked to learn about Röhm's homosexuality but "how much greater will be his shock when he learns that Hermann Göring is fat and that Joseph Goebbels limps!" After the putsch against the SA, the enforcement of Paragraph 175 intensified. Himmler's Secret Directive on the Curtailment of Homosexuality and Abortion of 10 October 1936 led to many arrests of homosexuals in raids throughout Germany, and the "pink triangle," the badge that marked its wearer as homosexual, came to be seen more and more often in the concentration camps.

FIGURE 16. Women's magazine article, "They Think / We Think," contrasting attitudes toward sex and women in the Weimar Republic with those of the Third Reich. *On the left,* "They think: chic and fun. We think: dirty and disgusting." *On the right,* "They think: boring? We think: healthy and beautiful!" (Sie meinen Apart und Lustig; Wir meinen Schmutz und Krampf!—Sie meinen Langweilig; Wir meinen Gesund und Schön!), *Frauenwarte,* February 1940.

161

DAS SCHWARZE KORPS

Is This "Nudist Culture"? Herr Stapel Is Outraged!

First published anonymously as "Ist das Nacktkultur? Herr Stapel entrüstet Sich!" in *Das Schwarze Korps,* 24 April 1935, 12.

Now and then, it is interesting and necessary to subject what is being published in the papers today to more careful scrutiny in order to get a better idea of *precisely* the kind of field day the German press is having.

Of course, the papers in existence today run the gamut from the established, time-honored titles that are very much aware of their tradition, many of them champions of these times, and there are others that, despite their passionate commitment to other issues, nevertheless exert a contrived effort to make sense of the intellectual transformations of our times and, all too often, show their real face and thus manage to inadvertently reveal their true colors. [. . .]

The careful reader of the journal edited by [Wilhelm] Stapel, *Deutsches Volkstum,* will certainly not have missed the fact that on page 293 of the April issue, in the context of an eight-page treatment of the "New Age of Paganism," he also commented on the subject of nudist culture. Any objective reader will have taken this opinion at face value and set the paper aside, thinking to himself, "There's got to be something to it, coming from the likes of such a prominent personality as Herr Stapel." There are few who will have taken the time and effort to attempt to get to the bottom of what is at issue here.

Herr Stapel's opinion of nudist culture is based solely on specific photographs from a farmer's almanac that has been staunchly criticized in religious circles—images we have reproduced here by way of clarification so that every reader can judge for himself. Our primary concern here is to elaborate on the intellectual outlook of Dr. Stapel, who contends that these images constitute *propaganda for nudist culture.*

We don't need to elaborate on what every German was confronted with under the auspices of the term *nudist culture* during the years of Jewish domination. It was a complete denigration of the German body and the deliberate corruption of everything that is beautiful and refined—as a satirical contribution in the last issue of *Das Schwarze Korps* made clear. The whole point of this form of rabble-rousing was the wholesale annihilation of the German *Volkstum* because the Semitic masterminds behind it certainly did not have any intention of "bettering" the German *Volk.* Their concern was nothing less than the disassembly of every form of natural order, like marriage and family. And, in their no-holds-barred approach to this end, they set out to publicly annihilate everything that is well-bred and worthy in the world.

The thought that *these* images are the product of the Jewish spirit of nudist culture would *never so much as occur* to any German still in possession of a modicum of reverence when viewing them. Anyone who is not moved by the majesty of this young mother's loving embrace of her child (illustration 2), anyone who does not display utmost respect for the nobility of the whole image, must be completely void of noble impulses himself.

Either that, or he is driven by instincts that place him in the same category as those who are best locked behind the bars of an institution. Only a lascivious pervert could see anything derogatory about this image of the German mother. We can only presume that Herr Stapel would not be as quick to condemn the classic image of Venus de Milo because he would certainly meet with much more resistance than he has in this case. Nevertheless, he has revealed his innermost self. We'll leave it to Herr Stapel himself to decide whether or not he stands behind his judgment.

We realize, of course, that there are many members of the German *Volk* who can no longer tell the difference between what is dignified and what is not. Foreign doctrines have introduced a schism to our country and have shattered our women's pride. Woman has been decried as a "seductress" and a "temptress" and instructed to obey man's will as his servant. Her body is said to be unclean; her mind and spirit, shoddy; and her children, the gift of life, said to be born in sin. *The noblest things we hold dear have thus been destroyed, and anyone who dares to do something immediately has the whole horde of foreign prophets on his back.*

For us, woman is sacred in her natural role, and every man stands in awe of her divine mission in life. She is the guardian of the German race, and her nature is pure! She is not man's servant but his comrade and companion for life, and no one has done more to restore the dignity of woman's place in the world than our Führer.

When National Socialism depicts the nobility of the naked body, this has absolutely nothing to do with the inclinations of the Jewish desecrators of the *Volk*. Just as the Greeks knew how to depict the harmony of the Nordic body, our art, too, is charged with the task of doing justice to the ideals of the German *Volk* in sculpture and painting.

But we patently reject that form of prudery that has been a contributing factor in destroying the instinctual sense for the beauty and nobility of the body in our *Volk*.

And here, too, we must make reference to the Greeks, who were clearly aware of the quality of breeding in their race and whose athletic competitors performed naked in public contests, which further contributed to improving racial selection. And any race [*Volk*] that has lost its racial consciousness is doomed.

The fact that anyone can take issue with the picture of children playing on the beach (illustration 3) is even more difficult to grasp than it is in the case of the mother and child.

You really have to be something of a bookish stuffy old shut-in not to realize that our young scouts have always taken great pleasure in romping around outside in their birthday suits!

In our opinion, Herr Stapel is probably just jealous of the fact that he can't be out rollicking around in the nude like our frisky little boys. And that's probably why he takes all the more pleasure in turning over every stone he can in search of something to trample to the ground.

In the future, though, we suggest that Herr Stapel concern himself with cleaning up the mountains of filth himself, for which we would certainly be beholden to him.

It's about time these conservative old codgers finally start changing their ways and heed the old adage (surely, they are familiar with it): *mens sana in copore sano* [a healthy mind in a healthy body]!

162

DAS SCHWARZE KORPS

Sexual Indecency on Active Duty

First published anonymously as " . . . Unzucht in der Soldatenzeit," in *Das Schwarze Korps,* 5 March 1936, 8.

The reinstatement of the majesty of the German army has rekindled in many an old soldier memories of his own military service when he served the fatherland clad in the uniform of the "emperor's many-colored coat." On the surface, it seems that the circle ripped open by the disgrace of 1918 has again been closed, and yet, we would be mistaken were we to attempt to overlook the fact that many things are not the same today and necessarily cannot be the same as they were, say, in 1914. After all, we have a world war under our belt—one that has left its mark on everyone, even those who did not serve on active duty as soldiers in the field.

Today's younger generation is not the same as the one at the turn of the century. Unfortunately, this is something that is frequently overlooked. Otherwise, how could sentences like the following, taken from the town of Lage's Sunday paper, possibly be written:

> You're all thrown together as a group of young men, all bursting with health and brimming with the exuberance of youth—by that fact alone, there is a great risk of sexual indecency on active duty. Dirty jokes make the rounds. Whatever you don't get, you get from someone else. And if you don't laugh along, they'll poke fun at you. Some foolhardy, promiscuous girls show up, the beer and the booze help things along. Many a young man who began his tour of duty pure and clean comes home with dark stains on his conscience, and perhaps even with some disease in his body. Outwardly, he appears plucky as ever, but on the inside, he's lost his pluck because his courage failed him and he flunked the test of temptation. Show some respect for the great men of our German history and get yourselves under control!

Yesterday's Old-Fashioned Morals

We are convinced that these statements were made with the honest intention of trying to help. But they can hardly do any good because they speak a language that is completely foreign to the German youth of today. These words are laden with such pomposity, such "moral" indignation—things that were once part and parcel to the sensibilities of bourgeois society but that, to the contemporary ear, will at best elicit a chuckle because we're so far beyond that. This does not by any means imply that we scoff at everything the author of this article in the Lage Sunday paper has to say.

But in order to accurately assess the situation, one must be familiar with today's youth and their mentality. You can't just take yesterday's old-fashioned scheme and apply it to the year 1938. The author of the essay we have excerpted here takes the easy way out. He speaks in terms of "sexual indecency" that is prevalent amongst soldiers on active duty. But he doesn't offer any further explanation for what he means by "sexual indecency." Or does he? If you read the sentence about "foolhardy, promiscuous girls," you can see what all this is really about. This is an attempt to give word to a religious morality that views the body itself as something contemptuous, one that would consider natural processes as *sinful instincts*—a position that we, as National Socialists, adamantly oppose.

For us, a real man is not someone who, in the height of his reproductive years, seeks to suppress healthy urges for the sake of adapting to some abstract ideal, but rather one who takes great pleasure in affirming those urges and as an expression of that affirmation, forces himself to act within the bounds set for him based on his sense of responsibility toward the *Volk* community. But whoever believes that, in the hope of finding eternal salvation, he can demonstrate contempt for the worldly existence whose most sublime expression we see in the eternal rebirth of man is not one of us.

Puberty is a period of transition in man's life when a young man, because of what he is experiencing in his body, is particularly open and sensitive to all the impulses he encounters in the outside world. But solid upbringing can make short work of any of the difficulties and dangers that will always provide fodder for discussion by the stodgy, old-fashioned types. And while we're on the subject, we may as well let our views be known: we consider these girls, lumped together here as foolhardy and promiscuous, who supposedly need the help of beer and booze to increase the impact of their charms, to be of sound, rational judgment—like the majority of today's youth—and we see them as less a matter for concern than the aberrant tendencies of youth who are attracted to members of the same sex, which, if they are not discovered in time, can have a devastating detrimental effect on the *Volk* as a whole. [. . .]

And Today?

Even if this development goes against the grain of the whole fabric of our newly rekindled *völkisch* sensibility, we should not underestimate the danger that such circumstances still present to this day. Our whole system of upbringing in Germany is again strictly divided according to sex—that is to say, male youth are educated toward masculinity, while the aim of educating girls is to emphasize the maternal, the feminine. Throughout the course of their development, our youth pass from one organization to the next: from the German Boys' Clubs to the Hitler Youth to the Labor Service, and to the military service. So we must be particularly careful not to allow the conscious education of our youth toward masculinity and femininity to degenerate into indifference toward the opposite sex, which in turn provides the mental seeds for same-sex aberrations.

But this danger is not one that first came into being today or yesterday. Nor was it first created by the National Socialist movement—as malicious voices would contend; rather, it is a danger that has existed to a greater or lesser degree in every generation—it's just that it hasn't always been as fiercely combated as it is in the National Socialist state. We need only call to mind certain portions of the youth movement whose romantic illusions went so far as to stand in stark opposition to *völkisch* ideals. Here, a few pathologically inclined leaders exploited the susceptibility of a specific age group in order to spread their viciously anti-*völkisch* tendencies. Using an exaggerated sense of camaraderie, they exalted friendship with men among these male youth, discouraging them from any dealings with women, suggesting that this was far beneath the dignity of any young man.

Then, of course, there are the economic dangers—also present in our times. To acknowledge them is to eliminate them. But all of this can be effected only by clean, healthy *völkisch*-oriented education and upbringing, not by superficial moralistic drivel about beer, booze, and foolhardy girls.

163

WOLFGANG WILLRICH

The Suffocating Nobility

Des Edlen ewiges Reich. First published in his *Des Edlen ewiges Reich* (Berlin: Verlag Grenze und Ausland, 1943), 22–23, 24–25, 31–32.

The term *freedom from puritanical morality* [*Moralinfreiheit*] merits further explication here. The Roman [historian] Tacitus indicated that one salient index of moral tact amongst our ancient Germanic ancestors was the ruthless opposition to every form of amoral behavior: "the practice of seduction and of yielding to seduction is not seen as the custom of the times, nor is vice a laughing matter for them; no one is seduced by lewd and lascivious displays. Good morals have more force there than do good laws in other places." Nowadays, we have very good laws—for example, a specific cultural chamber law designed to prevent the basest forms of smut and filth of the Jewish epoch in art and literature from circulating amongst the *Volk*. Even degenerate art has been successfully eliminated. Of course, that didn't succeed until the Führer himself actually issued a personal directive for cleaning it up. As late as 1937, the need for that made itself clear, and now even those people who were first alerted to the danger of the encroaching corruption of culture by the Führer, consider it a blessing.

Where laws no longer suffice, everything hinges on the authority of good morals. In certain circles that have grown especially far removed from the simple, right, honorable customs of the ancient Germans, the standard for what constitutes "morally offensive" behavior differs substantially from the refined sense of Germanic tact. And those who revel in the world of the cosmopolitan metropolis respond with derision and ridicule to anyone who happens to be in possession of a modicum more tact and reserve. They consider him annoying and "contrived," "lacking any sense of humor," and seek to cast him in a shroud of skepticism by abusing a term originally coined with reference to moral Tartuffery and referring to him as a "puritanical moralist" [*Moralinsauer*] even though he is neither prudish nor drenched in moralistic sanctimony, but even if he is simply inclined to employ a lick of common sense when casting a *more* capricious glance at the future and, in so doing, follows the sharp outline of the proverbial "course of history" to where it leads in the future. So these live-for-the-moment people are then "free from puritanical morality"—that means that they and their kind act within the parameters of a space that exists between the legal bounds of amorality and the primal sense of decency of a noble race. And there, they waltz, just beyond the reach of the law, and put themselves and their experiences of the world on display, at times live and in living color, at times, though—and this is the dangerous part—in images; and in this way, they multiply. Were the freedom from puritanical morality to remain the life habit of but a small circle, it could be passed off with the saying from Lower Saxony, "They made their bed, now let them lie in it." Unfortunately, this "life of luxury," this "love is the child of a gypsy way of life," all the superficiality and caprice of these "exception to the rules" people have been funneled into the population by way of mechanical reproduction to the extent that this senseless outsider existence has been making the rounds between the productive classes and the asocial, luxurious lowlifes and riffraff in a thousand different guises and is widely viewed as a viable way of life and superior form of existence—one that acts as a role model to be imitated.

While all the positive forces of our movement are intently focused on efforts to curb this outdated international materialism and individualistic, egocentric descent into shallowness, while thousands of German men, women, and girls are teaching smaller portions of the population to develop racialist sentiments and honorable thoughts through their own exemplary behavior and through countless educational lectures in efforts to "bring people in line," as we are wont to say these days, there is still a pitiful lack of films and illustrated magazines dedicated to reaching millions upon millions with a healthy educational message. Instead of spreading this most frivolous form of Americanism, with all its "free-from-puritanical-morality" sensations that confuse the untutored urban and rural population with all-too-transparent images of hedonistic lifestyles, the film and motion picture industry will have to surpass the accomplishments already in its credit, rise above the stark-raving mob of pleasure-seeking gratification, and deliver works of art that are of genuine and lasting value to the masses who are dependent upon motion pictures for their entertainment and enlightenment. The interplay between the film industry and the illustrated press, especially as this applies to film and fashion magazines, is of absolutely no value to the *Volk*. The public contradiction between serious schooling and public education, on the one hand, and a form of mass influence designed merely to stupefy and dumb down the public, on the other—as lucrative as this may be—can be eliminated only once the danger, which far exceeds that of the degenerate art that has already seen its downfall, has been made clear. As we have already pointed out, we are poised at the very *beginning* of a new era. And at this point, it is absolutely urgent that we caution against underestimating the potentially demoralizing impact that this massive machinery of propaganda that would tout Hollywood's "free-from-puritanical-morality" and "to hell with tomorrow" philosophy may have on extensive sectors of the population. [. . .]

This is why the stark-raving mob of pleasure seekers continues unabated in promoting in revues, films, and in magazines, etc. the world of burlesque and the implausible "authentic virtues" of romanticized adventure, luxury, and the underworld—regardless of social class. Because it really makes no difference whether the passions are juiced up over cocktails in a luxury bar or get heated up in a gin joint where the hooch is flowing—it's still a matter of lust for life and of making an undignified living from the business of lewdness and lust. But any German living his life in the spirit of the Reich will of course understand "life" to mean something that is naturally healthy. Actors who've persistently demonstrated their willingness to appeal to the basest instincts for the sake of reaping praises are not suited to representing that. And it will be difficult at best for the film industry to find actors among the truly Nordic population who are willing to portray their own genuine and healthy nature, especially in the context of the content that is usually still presented in films today. For the Nordic person is ill disposed toward revealing his inner self and putting it on display—especially when it comes down to representing his love life to an audience—something he considers undignified or unseemly, at best. He looks down upon vagabonds and sturdy beggars with a mixed sense of disdain and clandestine envy at the capriciousness of people in the entertainment industry who, being of an altogether different race or racial mixture, can easily glisten with pleasure without being made of gold, while at the same time acting infamously without feeling like he has diminished himself in any way. "All who are not of good race in this world are chaff." This statement of Adolf Hitler reveals what we are to view as people of good race—namely, those who are "made of sterling quality." And these men are worth their weight in good intentions and dignity. It is only the chaff that is "light as a feather" and "flimsy." [. . .]

The Jewish concept of holiness—which is innately psychopathological and of a lesser race—finds the height of its expression in its derision of women, decrying them as "the greatest evil . . . gateway to hell . . . the source of sin" and the whole litany of invectives that have come from the mouths of "holy men." This was something altogether new for Nordic women, for something like this would never have even occurred to a single member of the Nordic race in the pagan period. No one in the Nordic species would have had the audacity to disparage conception as "immaculate" during the pagan period or to have accused honorable women and girls of having had perverse carnal relations with Satan and to have burned them alive after brutally torturing them. This kind of brutish, obscurantist behavior was able to assert itself only after many years of sermons from the pulpit and threats of excommunication issued after the browbeaten *Volk* had desperately tried in vain, risking life and limb, to ward off these preposterous advances of the priests. The pyres of the stake from the persecution of witches were the only "light of the Orient" that burned for the Nordic people in the Occident.

The shame of inferiority complexes and self-loathing on the part of Jews is wholly justified. Anything that is born and conceived of an inferior racial mixture certainly has every reason to be ashamed of its lineage, especially in consideration of what we know about David's mother: "Behold, I was shapen in iniquity; and in sin did my mother conceive me" (Psalm 51, 5). And it may make a plaintive plea to its God (Psalm 38) and, in accordance with its vision of God, bring a burnt offering, a whole burnt offering to God through its "broken spirit and contrite heart" (Psalm 51, 17–19). And it enlists the recipe for cruel propaganda to accuse its enemies of "godlessness," in the cowardly hope that, once it has elicited the wrath of God, it might sit back and enjoy a refreshing footbath "in the blood of the wicked" (Psalm 58).

All men of noble birth take pride in their lineage and demonstrate due respect for their ancestors; indeed, they deify them. Nordic man has respect for the woman of his race and, in times of danger, is content with the neutrality of fate. Thus, before he went into the battle of Kesselsdorf [1754], the Dessauer [Leopold I, prince of Anhalt-Dessau] prayed, "Dear God, be with us today in your mercy, and if you decide not to be, please, at least do not come to the aid of the scoundrels, our enemies, but see to it that whatever comes shall come." In other words, if we have to, we'll do it on our own! This is characteristic of the Nordic posture and the way of thinking of this father of all soldiers.

164

HUGO HERTWIG

Race and Love

First published as "Rasse und Liebe. Was wir von den Rassen und ihren Kreuzungsmöglichkeiten vor der Ehe wissen müssen," in his *Das Liebesleben des Menschen* (Berlin: Verlag für Kulturpolitik, 1941), 5, 279–80, 285–88.

In conflicts between nations, the *Volk* best able to prevail will be that which taps into the primeval fonts of nature and allows them to develop according to a natural dynamic. There is not a *Volk* on the planet that can defy the laws of nature without risking its own survival.

The sex drive, too, is subject to the basic laws of blood, soil, and race. It sleeps in the subconscious of nature, the beauty of the plant world, the untamed nature of the animal world; it creeps into man's consciousness. To suppress the power of sex by relegating it to the realm of animalistic drives is a step backward and involves a wantonly unsystematic waste of energy.

The ardent sex drive is replete with as-yet-untapped energy reserves dormant in both the vegetative and the animal world, which can be systematically directed to serve the community in the same way a systematically directed current serves to create electric energy.

Nordic peoples are perhaps the most innately inclined to comprehend the sex drive as a natural phenomenon and to employ it in a strategic, systematic fashion because the climactic conditions in these northern regions are uniquely suited to it.

Race and Sex: What We Need to Know about Race and Racial Mixing before We Marry

We have examined a whole series of phenomena—some strictly organizational in nature, others psychological, that can hinder one's sex and love life to greater or lesser degrees or perhaps even completely destroy it.

Sex education at home, at school, and in state organizations must see to it that our young people, before they get engaged or married, are adequately informed about all the most important phenomena that might endanger a normal love and sex life. Nowadays, where we practice selective breeding in man, we can no longer rely on chance in the hope that our young men and young women do not end up meeting someone and paying for the rest of their lives for the fact that they had not been adequately instructed in this regard.

Instruction in sex education goes beyond knowledge of the intimate details I have already outlined. Before we enter into any romantic relationship, we must have a proper orientation in questions of race and maintaining hereditary bloodlines. Once that is established, the next step is being informed about the most relevant regulations concerning engagement, marriage, and divorce under the new legislation in Germany.

At a time when there was little attention paid to the biological aspects of one's love and sex life, these things may have seemed less significant; they are becoming increasingly significant with regard to the consciously calculated human breeding that is under way today.

Let us first address the issue of race itself. The term *race* is a concept borrowed from the field of anthropology. [. . .]

It is no accident, but rather a biologically determined fact of nature, that the Nordic race matures slowly. At school, for example, Western types generally develop skills much more quickly than Nordic types. But Nordic people compensate for this with the depth of their emotions, their sincerity, their ability to judge, their daring, and their acumen. We often see this self-confidence in character coupled with self-discipline, which is at once a recognizable source of political talent. It is more in line with the Nordic landscape for Nordic man to be more introverted than extroverted, that he be more taciturn and reserved and happy to go his own way. As I have already mentioned in the context of sexual attraction and love among Nordic people, we cannot reckon with any kind of unbridled passionate abandon. Nordic man, both male and female, is incredibly intent on production and performance and is all but born for family life. Entering into a romantic relationship or a marriage with a Nordic person is destined to produce positive results and to be successful in every regard, including fertility.

The one flaw that has characterized Nordic man thus far is a certain degree of callousness. He would prefer that everyone else adapt to his needs. We can read in the Nordic sagas how difficult marriages sometimes were between partners with pronouncedly Nordic character traits, especially when women were occasionally not feminine enough to adapt to their husbands' needs and concede at the right moment. The Nordic female type is sometimes too firm, or the male is perhaps unable to develop any sensitivity for the female psyche. This then can lead to marital disputes. Here we can see how important premarital education and training are. [. . .]

Here in Germany, our results have been pretty good in producing racial hybrids in which the Nordic element remained dominant. So the racial miscegenation of the blood remains a natural law of life as long as the partners in cross-reproduction are not closely related. Incest always produces detrimental effects.

Nature's own reproductive process itself finds expression in this racial hybrid. We must never allow our indigenous races to crossbreed with foreign races of alien blood. It may be that, seen from a global perspective, all races ultimately bleed into one another. But this does not mean that individual races should overstep the bounds of their own designated territorial bonds so that, for example, two entirely unrelated species of plant, animal, or man might crossbreed.

These utterly preposterous, inferior, and dangerous racial crossbreeds we often see today have been made possible only by a technology that [enables us to] transcend time and space. Here we see how a technological development can be terribly harmful to all of us if we cease to monitor and regulate it according to the laws of nature. In the olden days, crossbreeding among people could never take place beyond the bounds of the territory that was within their reach. This is why it was never possible for all the races of the world to mix to form one, which is something many people would like to achieve using the most recent technological advancements in the world.

Today, though, we are well-informed about racial crossbreeds and crossbreeding. We avoid absorbing the blood of inferior races into our lines and have, therefore, banned marriages with people who are alien to the species of the German *Volk* (for example, with Jews). Such laws for the protection of the blood have also existed in previous nations, in the United States of America, for example, or in the South African Union, etc. These laws are designed to prevent arbitrary crossbreeding that violates the natural order and that is made possible only by technological advances.

The colonialist ambitions of *Völker* have demonstrated for us the results of various mixing of races. When the Europeans (whites) first began colonizing distant lands, the racial problem arose naturally from the absence of white women in the colonies. In the beginning, there were only a few women who followed the men's migrations. In practice, though, it did not matter whether or not the male colonizers took foreign girls or women as lovers or wives; the blood would ultimately become mixed in the children's generation. Colored blood mixed unfettered with the blood of the arriving master race. The resulting crossbreeds were often quick-witted, alert, and accommodating, but they were also weak willed and indecisive.

Concrete examples from the colonies of white *Völker* clearly demonstrate that a mixing of blood that is foreign and far removed from one's own can only have unfortunate results. The crossbreed will always have more respect for his white paternal race and will despise the maternal. He suffers from an ambivalence caused by the composition of his mixed blood and is by nature caught between races and is despised by both.

Surely it is possible that the incoming colonizers and the indigenous race happen to be more closely related than is usually the case and that, in those rare instances, the mixed bloods turn out to be somewhat better.

The race problem has grown particularly acute in South Africa and the United States. South Africa has instituted a strict apartheid policy to allow each race to live separate from the other—each following its own laws of blood, belief, and economics. Racial miscegenation of any kind is punishable by severe penalty of law. Some may consider this inhuman. But the experiences of our ancient Nordic ancestors, as I have outlined above, are proof that this is the right course of action. And these actions, especially measured against ancient Nordic standards, are in all respects humane. It would be inhumane to allow a mixed blood to enter the world necessarily riddled with difficulties. He is the product of a sexual union that is a violation of nature. But you will only succeed in preventing racial miscegenation entirely by appealing to those members of the race who have retained some understanding of both the negative and positive aspects of blood as a powerful force of love.

We should always keep the Nordic love life in mind. It is here that blood ties are bound in the species-specific soil of an indigenous flora and fauna. It is here that the births generated by sexual liaisons produce the very best results in physical, psychological, and mental terms.

In Cape Town, there are crossbloods between whites and blacks, between whites and Malays. But there are also Indians and Chinese there. Already, they have begun making awkward distinctions between whites, coloreds, and natives. But there is no way to do away with the tragic role played by the black man and the way the whites flee from him. Here it is blood that speaks. The best thing to do would be to separate the various races in South Africa and put them on reservations to allow each individual race to establish a sort of home territory on its own soil. It is a noteworthy suggestion, but hardly feasible, since each individual race has its own home territory somewhere in the world that is climactically and geographically unique.

One thing is for certain: races do not flourish when they are transplanted to foreign soil and will never be able to lead a normal sex and love life. They will always be drawn by the desire to return to their native soil. We may be able to bring sophisticated technology to all corners of the globe, but nothing has ever demonstrated that it is possible to arbitrarily transplant man or allow him to randomly crossbreed. It is the sex and love life that revolts against it most vehemently. It would be an altogether different matter if we were to transplant entire families to foreign soil that were similar to their original home territory. They would acclimate themselves over time, and if they were able to keep their bloodlines pure enough without practicing incest, they would easily predominate in these foreign lands. The inherited blood contains a sexual force whose power and magnitude are real. But it will never be as powerful as it was in its original homeland.

In my book, I have demonstrated that the impulse for crossbreeding in nature is always intent on improving the bloodlines. Similarly, in girls, women, and men, the sex and love life is instinctively driven toward unions that improve hereditary bloodlines with the clear intent of producing offspring with favorable genetic predispositions and not to produce anything that might represent a decline.

165

DER STÜRMER

The Abortion Trial

Jewish Doctors as Murderers

First published anonymously as "Der Abtreibungsprozeß: Jüdische Ärtze als Mörder," in *Der Stürmer,* vol. 17, no. 5 (February 1939), 1, 2.

How the Jews Came to Be Doctors and Pharmacists

In the year 1489, the king of France at the time issued a law mandating all Jews to subject themselves to Christian baptism. Anyone who refused was expelled from the country. The Jews in France were shocked and turned to the highest Jewish authority in Constantinople for assistance and advice. The head Jews, though, sent the famous "Toledo Letter" to the Jews in France. It was later published in 1583 under the title *La Silva Curiosa.*[1]

Here is a quote from that letter: "You complain that they threaten your lives, then let your children be baptized and become doctors and pharmacists so they can endanger the lives of your adversaries within the bounds of the law. Whoever can succeed in killing *goyim* publicly without endangering himself should do so. Whoever cannot do so should seek to cause their death by means of theft and trickery."

From the very beginning, the Jew has acted in accordance with this counsel and these laws. He never became a pharmacist in order to produce pharmaceutical products that cured disease in Gentiles. He became a pharmacist in order to produce poisons he could use to eliminate Gentiles with impunity. He would never become a doctor in order to help sick Gentiles. He became a doctor in order to rob Gentiles of their health and their lives. The Jew hates all Gentiles. Every year, at the time of the Jewish New Year, the Jews gather in schools and synagogues to address their God Yahweh with this prayer:

"May the bodies of Gentiles disappear from the face of the earth, may their tongues be parched, may their arrogance be humbled. May their spirit be shattered."

The Jewish doctor has never had any interest in healing non-Jewish patients. He has never had an interest in healing the German *Volk*. He has always been intent on poisoning, decimating, and infecting the German *Volk* with disease.

The Abortionist Dr. Mayer

And this is why it was the Jewish doctor who demanded the elimination of Paragraph 218, the law against abortion. The Jewish doctor would prefer that the German *Volk* not give birth to children. He would prefer that the fruit of German women's wombs be murdered. The Jewish *Volk* have been instructed as follows: "You shall multiply as the sand of the sea."

The Jewish people did not practice abortion. Yet they propagated and encouraged abortion in Gentiles. The Jewish people, on the contrary, though, are supposed to multiply as "sand of the sea."

This is why Jewish doctors have never performed abortions on Jewish women. Only on Gentiles. The abortion trial that came to an end before the State Supreme Court in Hamburg on 22 August 1938 is proof enough of that. Two Jewish and two Gentile defendants were in the docket. The two Gentiles were so Jewified and dummified that they went along with the Jews in performing the abortions. The Jews were the main offenders. Their names are Dr. Max Meyer and Dr. Wilfrid Alexander. Dr. Meyer is a converted Jew. He let himself be baptized and became a doctor so that he could "endanger the lives of Gentiles with impunity." He had a practice in the town of Altona for thirty-three years. His monthly income was 1,500 Reichsmarks. He supplemented this income by performing abortions for exorbitant fees. He had already been convicted of performing abortions and sentenced to six months in prison on 25 June 1930. He received a mild sentence that was typical during the *Systemzeit* and that was then actually reduced to four months and ultimately resulted in a fine of only 5,000 Reichsmarks. But the Jew Dr. Meyer was proved to have performed commercial abortions a second time and in seven cases. It goes without saying that this Jew has perhaps performed abortions in several hundred cases over the course of his many years in practice. It's just that the rest of them could not be proved. Dr. Meyer was sentenced to serve five years in hard labor.

The Abortionist Jew Dr. Alexander

The Jew Dr. Alexander had a practice in Hamburg (Große Bergstrasse 84). On 11 September 1936, he was sentenced to two years' hard labor for a sex offense in violation of Paragraph 176, Section 1 of the Penal Code. He forced himself upon a non-Jewish girl who came to him for an examination. At the time, there weren't any laws on the books to allow Jew Dr. Alexander to be charged with racial treason [*Rassenschande*] because the crime was committed in the summer of 1935—that is, prior to the promulgation of the Nuremberg Laws. The Jew Alexander was convicted of three instances of performing abortion for commercial gain. He was sentenced to three years' hard labor.

The Gentiles still sitting in the dock (a young, non-Jewish doctor and a non-Jewish midwife) were also sentenced to hard-labor terms. They are living proof of the old folk wisdom: if you fall in with a Jew, the Jew will take you down.

The German *Volk* can learn something from the dastardly deeds of these Jewish doctors Meyer and Alexander. The lesson is that the Jew, no matter where he is, is always but a Jew, and as such, the mortal enemy of all non-Jews. It is truly a blessing to the German *Volk* that the Jewish "doctor's" hands have been tied.

Note

1. *La Silva Curiosa* (1583; *Curious Miscellany*) is an anti-Semitic text by Julián de Medrano (1540-?) composed of two imaginary letters, one purportedly to be from the Jews of Spain to the Jews of Constantinople, and the second, the reply. In the first letter, the Jews of Spain ask for advice about what to do about forced conversion, property confiscation, and the killing of Jews by royal authorities. In the second letter, the Jews of Constantinople reply that as for the forced conversions, nothing can be done. But in the case of the confiscations, the Jews of Spain should make sure that their children become merchants, so that in the future it will be the Jews who are taking property away from the Gentiles. As for the killings, they should make sure their children become doctors, so that they will be the ones taking away the lives of others, and so on. This apocryphal text had long circulated as part of the anti-Semitic repertoire, and the format of disclosing hidden missives of the Jews continued, most notoriously in the 1903 hoax *The Protocols of the Meetings of the Learned Elders of Zion*.—Eds.

166

A. ASCHENBRENNER

Incest and Hereditary Health

First published as "Inzucht und Erbgesundheit," in *Archiv für Rassen- und Gesellschafts-Biologie* 34 (1940): 89, 90, 93, 99–100.

When laypeople speak in terms of incest, then there is usually some consensus that it is something completely perverse, for everyone knows of instances in which mentally or physically inferior children have been conceived within incestuous marriages and is inclined to put the blame exclusively on the fact that both partners in the marriage were blood relatives, since he cannot find any better explanation for the phenomenon. This perception is most often substantiated by the experiences of animal breeders, who are known to maintain that, in inbreeding between animals, the racial traits of offspring are degraded, as most often seen in diminished fertility. Without doubt, all these observations are correct. And yet that does not offer proof that inbreeding is the sole factor causing these symptoms to appear, because the signs of degeneration that have been registered could just as easily be traced to some other source. Strangely enough, scholarly research, however, was very late in addressing the matter of the biological effects of inbreeding. A survey of the available literature yields but an occasional contribution addressing this question. [. . .]

One area that is ideally suited to conducting experiments to determine the effects of inbreeding is the Franconian village of Hartenstein. Based on the conspicuously high number of residents sharing the same name, we suspected a substantial amount of inbreeding there. The first step was to create genealogical charts [*Ahnentafel*] for each individual resident so that we could construct an exact record of the scope and degree of incest present in the population. Once we had done so, one important part of the study was to conduct examinations of all potential participants. As it turned out, it was a job that one examiner alone could not possibly have managed, since there were four hundred residents who met the criteria for examination. For this reason, the student government at the University of Erlangen hosted a clinic in 1936 where a team of six completed the examinations under the direction of this author. [. . .]

It would certainly be interesting to determine the factors that caused this inbreeding.

The first of them, especially in previous centuries, may well be seen in the geographic location. Hartenstein is far from any major highway; it is surrounded on all sides by hills and not easily accessible. This geographical situation led to a certain isolation of the village from the outside world, which forced village members to intermarry because they rarely had any contact with strangers.

The second factor is religion. Hartenstein is host to a castle that has changed hands frequently since the Reformation, so the villagers have also had to change their beliefs to accommodate the whims of whatever castle lord happened to rule. The last castle lord had been Catholic, and Hartenstein became a Catholic town, but all the neighboring villages were Protestant. This religious conflict, then, was the primary factor causing the people of Hartenstein to practice inbreeding because marriages outside the village involved interfaith unions that were not permitted by the church. It would rather issue a dispensation for marriage between blood relatives. It has been only in the past few decades that interfaith marriages have emerged as a result of people marrying into neighboring villages. Hartenstein is no longer a purely Catholic village today. [. . .]

One of the more frequent charges brought against inbreeding is that it weakens the constitution and leads to infertility. But the fertility rate in Hartenstein is very high. The average number of children per family prior to the World War was between seven and eight. But the infant mortality rate was also very high. Today, there is still an average of three to four children per family. At the same time, the families assured us that they were intentionally keeping their families small to avoid economic hardship. So we see that inbreeding has had no impact on fertility here.

For a long time, one of the primary objections to incest was that it caused feeblemindedness. So we paid particular attention to cases of feeblemindedness in our study. As previously mentioned, we were able to identify only one case of feeblemindedness in Hartenstein. Nevertheless, we set out to identify the degree of intelligence in all village residents. We measured this according to their academic performance, which we were able to glean from school records. Of course, we kept in mind the fact that report cards and grades were only a highly relative basis for determining intelligence. So we also conducted personal interviews with each individual to assess the approximate degree of intelligence. Based on these two criteria, we drew our conclusions, ordering them by degree from 1 through 4, and came to an average of 2.49, which very nearly corresponds to normal intelligence. Then we performed the same calculation amongst only those residents who were the products of inbreeding. The result was 2.64. So, in this case, on the average, children who are the product of inbreeding are more intelligent than those who are not. So incest cannot be said to have any detrimental effects here. Of course, one cannot arrive at the general conclusion that inbreeding can, in some circumstances, actually produce results that are slightly better, which is certainly not the case. It is just that negative hereditary predispositions within any population group can be retained by incest. If the incestuous group of families in Hartenstein produces intellectually better endowed offspring, the only conclusion we can draw is that this group was more gifted than the group not affected by incest from the very onset.

Accordingly, we conclude that incest in Hartenstein has not had any measurable degenerative influence, either on the physical health of the populace or its intelligence.

167

ANONYMOUS

How Magnus Hirschfeld's Institute for Sexual Science Was Demolished and Destroyed

"Wie Hirschfelds Sexualwissenschaftliches Institut demoliert und zerstört wurde," in *Braunbuch über Reichstagsbrand und Hitler-Terror* (Basel: Universum Bücherei, 1933), 151–54. Reproduced in *Homosexualität in der NS-Zeit: Dokumente einer Diskriminierung und Verfolgung,* edited by Günter Grau and Claudia Schoppmann (Frankfurt am Main: Fischer Taschenbuch Verlag, 1993), 60–62. Translated by Patrick Camiller.

A trustworthy eye- and earwitness who, though not himself a member of the institute, was able to follow the events exactly as they happened, has kept the following record of the abominable destruction of this world-famous scientific center for research, education, and treatment in Berlin. Here is his report.

On the morning of 6 May 1933, the *Berliner Lokalanzeiger* reported that the purging of books with an un-German spirit from Berlin libraries would begin in the morning of that day and that students at the College of Physical Education would direct the operation at the Institute for Sexual Science. This institute was founded in 1918 by Dr. Magnus Hirschfeld at the former home of Prince Hatzfeld and shortly afterward was accepted by the Prussian government as a *charitable foundation.* It enjoyed an international reputation and clientele because of its unique collections and research, its archive and library. Above all, many foreign scholars, doctors, and writers came to Berlin to work there.

After the announcement appeared in the paper, attempts were made to move some especially valuable private books and manuscripts to a place of safety. This effort was foiled, however, when the young man carrying the books was arrested by guards, who had obviously been positioned to surround the institute during the night, and the items were confiscated. On 6 May at 9:30 A.M., several vans with roughly a hundred students and a brass band appeared before the institute. They took up a military-style position in front of the house and then forced their way inside, with musical accompaniment. Since the office was still closed, no official representative of the institute was present; only a few women from the janitorial staff and a gentleman sympathetic to the institute were there. The students tried to gain entry to all the rooms; when these were locked—for example, the ground-floor display rooms that have been out of use for quite some time and the former and present office of the World League for Sexual Reform—they smashed down the doors. After they found that the downstairs rooms did not have much to offer, they made their way to the first floor, and there, in the institute's reception rooms, they emptied the inkwells, pouring ink onto various papers and carpets, and then set about the private bookcases. They took with them what struck them as suspicious, keeping mainly to the so-called black list. But at the same time, they pilfered other books, such as a large work on Tutankhamen, and many art magazines from the private library of the secretary, Giese. Then they removed from the archive the large boards with representations of intersexual cases, which had once been prepared for exhibition during the International Medical Congress of 1913 at the Kensington Museum in London. They threw a large number of these boards out the window to their comrades standing in front of the house below.

They tore most of the other pictures and photographs of important persons from the walls and played soccer with them, leaving large piles of ruined pictures and broken glass behind. When one student objected that the material was of a *medical* nature, another replied that the real point, their real concern, was not to seize a few books and pictures but *to destroy the institute.* During a longer speech, a life-size model showing internal secretions was then thrown through the window and smashed to smithereens. In a consulting room, they used a long-handled scrubbing brush to smash a pantostat used for the treatment of patients. Moving on, they stole a bronze bust of Dr. Hirschfeld and hauled away many works of art. For now, they removed only a few hundred books from the institute library.

The whole time they kept a watch on the staff and more and more music was played so that inquisitive crowds gathered in front of the house. At twelve o'clock, the leader made a long closing speech and the squad pulled out, singing particularly vulgar smut songs, plus the "Horst Wessel Song."

The institute staff assumed this plundering and pillage would be the end of the matter, but at three in the afternoon, more vans showed up, filled with SA men, who announced that they were there to continue with the confiscations since the morning squad had not had enough time to clear out everything they were supposed to. This second squad then made a further thorough search of all the rooms and carted off with them all the books and manuscripts of any value, a total of two large vanloads. It was clear from their profanity that the students were familiar with the names of many authors represented in the special library. Not only did they refer to Sigmund Freud, whose picture they removed from the stairwell and carted off, as "the dirty Jew Freud," they also called Havelock Ellis "the pig Havelock Ellis." In addition to Havelock Ellis, some of the British authors that they were after were Oscar Wilde, Edward Carpenter, and Norman Haire; among American writers, books by juvenile court justice [Benjamin] Lindsey, Margaret Sanger, and Sylvester Viereck; and among the French, the works of André Gide and Marcel Proust, Pierre Loti, Zola, etc. The books of [Theodoor Hendrik] van de Velde and the Danish doctor [Hans] Leunbach also elicited a barrage of vituperation from the students.[1] Whole years of periodicals, particularly the twenty-four volumes of the *Yearbook of Sexual Intermediate Stages* [*Jahrbücher für sexuelle Zwischenstufen*], were hauled off. They also wanted to take completed questionnaires (several thousand) with them, and only when it was explicitly pointed out that they contained medical histories did the students back off. On the other hand, it was not possible to stop them from taking the materials of the World League for Sexual Reform, all the copies of the magazine *Sexus,* and the card catalog. Numerous manuscripts of Krafft-Ebing, Karl Heinrich Ulrichs, and others, many of them hitherto unpublished, fell victim to the intruders.

They kept asking about Dr. Hirschfeld's *return.* As they put it, they wanted to be "tipped off" about when he was due back. Already before the looting of the institute, SA men had several times come and asked to see Dr. Hirschfeld. When they received the answer that he was abroad because of an attack of malaria, they retorted, "Well, then hopefully he'll croak even without our help; we won't even need to hang him or beat him to death."

On 7 May, when the Berlin and foreign papers reported the operation against the Institute for Sexual Science, they included a telegram of protest from the presidium of the World League that pointed out that a lot of the collected material was the property of foreigners, and that the planned burning should therefore be called off. This dispatch, addressed to the minister of education and the arts, was ignored. Instead, all the writings and pictures were burned three days later on the *Opernplatz,* along with many works from other sources. The number of volumes destroyed from the institute's special library came to more than ten thousand. The students carried the busts of Dr. Magnus Hirschfeld on display in a torchlight procession before throwing them onto the burning stake.

Note

1. Theodoor Hendrik van de Velde (1873–1937) was a physician and gynecologist world famous for his 1926 book *Het volkomen huwelijk* (*The Perfect Marriage*), which included reliable information about birth control.—Eds.

168
MAGNUS HIRSCHFELD

Men's Leagues
A Psychosexual Analysis of the Röhm Catastrophe

First published as "Männerbünde: Sexualpsychologischer Beitrag zur Roehm Katastrophe," in *Pariser Tageblatt,* 20 July 1934, 1–2.

A little more than a quarter century has passed since we in Germany experienced an earth-shaking scandal that bears a certain resemblance to the Röhm case in its psychosexual context: I'm referring to the case of Count Eulenburg and his so-called Liebenberg Round Table [*Kamarilla*]. Both men were public figures who had long stood in the good graces of the highest-ranking officials in government, only to end in utter disgrace and shame, and in both cases, the men's adversaries used their homosexual predisposition against them "as means to an end" in order to effect their ruin, which would have been very difficult to achieve otherwise.

How do you explain the fact that such natural-born ruler types as Wilhelm II and Adolf Hitler so often feel drawn to homosexuals and, so we must logically conclude, not only due to sexological factors but to characterological ones as well? Undoubtedly, the reason is that, even in their fanaticism, they are obsequious, inverted personality types who resort to flattery and sycophancy and are least inclined to offer any kind of resistance, so they are the most expedient for the obstinate, self-willed Führer types bursting with energy; the inverted types, often internally undecided, bathe in the good graces of the Führer and feel a certain sense of safety there.

Typically, though, what happens is that more iron-fisted men appear on the scene, scheming adversaries, more often than not sexually aberrant themselves, who begrudge these homosexuals their favoritism. When they can't get anywhere armed with just the facts, they start firing poison darts that almost never miss their mark: they expose secret love affairs, feign moral indignation, throw stones just to keep people from noticing that they themselves live in glass houses: they bluff and bilk the public with phantasmagoric fearmongering, with fictitious intrigues and dangers, until the public is finally convinced that some sort of "plague" has broken out, when in fact it is the state body itself that is diseased.

[Edmund] Heines did not resort to political revenge killing because of his homosexual tendencies but rather because, above and beyond that, he was a ruthless opportunist.[1] Most political revenge killers have been heterosexual, not homosexual. [Fritz] Haarmann was not a mass murderer because he was homosexual but because he was a sadist, and there are, unfortunately, all too many of them amongst the women-loving male population. And if he hadn't been released from the insane asylum prematurely, as many sadists are, many human lives would have been spared the agony of a gruesome death. Neither was Count Eulenberg charged with homosexuality but rather with alleged perjury, which he felt compelled to commit after having been backed into a dreadful predicament much in the same way that the Austrian colonel Alfred Redl did not become a mole for the Russians within his own agency because of his homosexual tendencies, but rather because he found himself at the mercy of his blackmailers.

And isn't it so that many of the heroes—from Frederick the Great to Stefan George—who are still celebrated by the National Socialist rulers also displayed marked homosexual tendencies? And above all, isn't it such that even today there are many more, even within the Third Reich, who are still held in utmost esteem?

It is certainly no coincidence that the "concept of the Führer," as we know it today, was first introduced in a widely read text by the fanatical racial theorist Hans Blüher, published in 1912 under the title *The German Wandervogel Movement as Erotic Phenomenon: A Contribution to Understanding Sexual Inversion.*

Several years prior, [K.F. von] Leexow, which was actually a pseudonym for a high-ranking Prussian aristocrat, had already expressed similar ideas, though with a more tolerant bent than Blüher, in a pamphlet titled *The Army and Homosexuality.*

The authors of both of these texts cite examples from the blood brotherhoods and military alliances of antiquity, the Sacred Band of Thebes, the medieval orders of knighthood, like the Knights Templar and the Teutonic Order, whose grand master Ullrich von Jungingen was commonly known to be homosexual, alongside many additional examples of greater or lesser fraternal orders with decidedly homoerotic elements.

And it was none other than the great Friedrich Schiller who sought, in his play *Knights of Malta,* written with no roles for women, to portray the loving camaraderie that was widespread in many of these men's leagues. What we can derive from the unfinished fragments of the drama, which had concerned him for a decade and a half beginning in 1788, is that the battles surrounding the Great Siege of Malta, led by the sultan Suleiman the Magnificent, formed the background for this unfinished tragedy. The Knights of Malta defended the island. Schiller places at the center of his drama the two knights Créqui and St. Priest, who are described in the cast of characters as "two knights who love each other." In one of his footnotes, Schiller adds, "The love that two knights have for one another must include all the symptoms of sexual love. . . . "

There is yet another prominent source that could be cited here, too, one whose name strikes a high note of resonance with Hitler and his surroundings: Richard Wagner, in his text *Artwork of the Future,* commented as follows on homosexual love relationships in groups:

> This love, which had its basis in the noblest pleasures of both eye and soul—not like our modern postal correspondence of sober friendship, half businesslike, half sentimental—was the Spartan's only tutoress of youth, the never-aging instructress alike of boy and man, the ordainer of the common feasts and valiant enterprises; nay, the inspiring helpmeet on the battlefield. For this it was that knit the fellowships of love into battalions of war and forewrote the tactics of daring death, in rescue of the imperiled or vengeance for the slaughtered comrade, by the infrangible laws of the soul's most natural necessity.

And so we see that what is now taking place within the SA of the Third Reich is not altogether unusual and certainly nothing new. Nor is the assassination of unpopular opponents by exploiting their sexual predispositions politically anything new. What was perhaps new, however, was the way, in this instance, that exploitation was taken to the heights of frenzy in a cannibalistic slaughter of outrageous proportion.

Hitler, with his harsh treatment of the homosexual leader of youth, may well have succeeded in forming a new group of opponents whose numbers exceed those of the Jews in Germany. These selfsame "Uranians" [homosexuals] whom Hitler, in his tolerance toward Röhm and his comrades, lavished with praises and thus lured into his camp, are now feeling extremely disappointed and dismayed.

The analysis of the murder of the SA leader through the critical lens of sexuality thus lays bare all the salient aspects of the horrific catastrophe whose ramifications remain immediately palpable today as these pertain to the psychoanalytical assessment of these events.

Note

1. Edmund Heines (1897–1934) was a well-known SS man who joined the party in 1925. He was convicted of murder in 1929 but was given amnesty shortly thereafter. On 30 June 1934, he was assassinated as part of the Röhm purge, allegedly as a result of Hitler's direct order. In his speech to the Reichstag on 13 July, Hitler mentioned Heines as one of a "small group of elements which were held together through a like disposition."—Eds.

169

ANONYMOUS

Illusions

Written on 12 June 1935. First published in *Homosexualität in der NS-Zeit: Dokumente einer Diskriminierung und Verfolgung,* edited by Günter Grau and Claudia Schoppmann (Frankfurt am Main: Fischer Taschenbuch Verlag, 1993), 82, 83.

An anonymous letter from a gay man to the Reich bishop [Ludwig Müller], 12 June 1935

Reverend Reich Bishop,

I no longer know what to do, and so I am turning my steps directly to you. May God grant that this letter comes directly into your hands! May God grant that you do not close your mind to these lines but that you do everything in your power to put an end to the horror, by protesting at the very top and asking for help in this matter.

Reich Bishop, before I describe everything, I solemnly assure you that I have either myself experienced [what I report here] or it has been reported to me by trustworthy people who have themselves lived through the terror of it all; let me say that it is hard for me to be completely open in describing all these things, with all the hideous words as well—but that it has to be so that you can have a clear picture and take action with all the power of your exalted office.

In the past half year, in Berlin and throughout the Reich, roundups have been made of homosexuals or people suspected of being homosexual. They have either been taken from pubs (as half a year ago) or pursued at home, in the street, and so on. These roundups were arranged by the Gestapo and carried out by young SS men, mostly Bavarians and other southern Germans.

After they have been picked up and kept *standing* for twelve hours and more in the

FIGURE 17. German policemen standing watch on 5 March 1933 in front of the Eldorado Bar, a gathering place for homosexuals closed down by the Nazi regime and plastered with Hitler campaign posters. The Eldorado was located at the intersection of Motz and Kalckreuth Streets in Berlin. Landesarchiv Berlin, Barbara Schäche/Picture-Archive.

corridors of the Gestapo, without being given a chance to eat or drink anything at all, they are either released or taken to the so-called Columbia Haus (Tempelhof). Perhaps that does not sound so dreadful, but in reality the poor people under arrest have become so weak they have collapsed in the corridors of the Gestapo, suffered spasms, fallen faint, and so on. To have to stand for hours with your face to the wall is already a torture, but to do so without once being allowed to answer the call of nature is quite terrible. (Only after six hours were the detainees able to use the toilets—under guard!) The way in which the SS guards (members of the Adolf Hitler Regiment) treated the detainees was appalling. They kicked people on the shins, screaming and raging as if they had to deal with serious criminals behaving in a stubborn and troublesome manner. (In fact, everyone was so intimidated that they did not utter a word and followed all the guards' orders!) Curses such as, "You little piece of shit!" "Pathetic bastard!" "You bugger, you'll soon get a kick up the arse!" "What are you squinting like that for, you little horseshit!" could be heard all the time. A few complaints by some of the older men were answered with blows. The boss of the operation, one *Obersturmführer* [Josef Albert] Meisinger, did not do anything to stop this dreadful treatment; on the contrary, he put in some bellowing of his own from time to time and thus underlined the way his subordinates were behaving.

Such was the way people were treated at the Gestapo [jail] in Prinz-Albert-Straße. But much more dreadful (still today!!) is the treatment of those held in the so-called Columbia Haus, which is already known in Berlin as "Death Island" and the "Prussian Siberia."

The poor people there are tortured for weeks and months on end. (Mentally and physically!) Just a few examples: a very cultured middle-aged gentleman was not allowed to relieve himself, although he continually attracted attention at the door of his cell. They shouted at him from outside but did not let him out. In the end, so as not to dirty his cell, the pitiful man did it *in his mess tin*—which was punished with a long beating. Another prisoner, despite repeated requests, was also not taken to the toilet and did it in his cell; he was then sadistically told under threat to eat his excrement. But he refused and shouted out, "I won't do it! Beat me to death, rather. I won't do it!" What they then did to him I do not know, but it must have been something quite terrible. . . . Many prisoners have been beaten every day in the Columbia Haus, although they have done absolutely nothing wrong. (I could give you whole pages of examples, but these will surely suffice.)

A very large number of those held in the *Columbia Haus* are subsequently sent to the Lichtenburg concentration camp. Hardly anyone can describe what they do there to homosexuals and people suspected of being homosexuals. Not only do they use the foulest swearwords with the prisoners, they maltreat them in the most brutal way (allegedly on orders from above, although I simply cannot believe it!) It starts with the so-called sport (physical exercises that are so devised that the strongest men cannot continue, cannot climb any more steps, cannot stand up straight any more, and so on!). For example, knee bends and stretches forty at a time (!!), crawling on their elbows in a poorly surfaced yard, etc., etc. If someone cannot keep up or if they "have something" against him, he gets the so-called sport special: that is, a tougher and longer "sport." No description of that is adequate: it has to be heard from the mouth of someone who has been through it.

For *all inmates* of the concentration camp, the openly held beatings are a terrible experience. Every last man has to fall in, stand still, and watch while fifty to one hundred blows are rained on a poor creature. (The cries and the sight of flowing blood are terrible experiences for those who have to watch!) For some trivial matter or other, people have inflicted on them every conceivable punishment in which the sadistic character expresses itself. The darkness down in the so-called bunker is absolutely terrible. A number of people have already gone mad there.

Reverend Reich Bishop! These prisoners are people who have landed there because of some sexual inclination or even simply because they are suspected of it. *But not a single one has appeared before a judge!* (Some are due to be tried for the first time in the next few weeks!) A few hundred have already been released from Lichtenburg. Some of them are broken in body and soul; others have come out white haired although they are still young in years; others now suffer from persecution mania, wander about lost, and so on. Most of them have lost their jobs, although no criminal activity could be proved against them. (Suspicion was enough to put them in a bad light with their bosses.)

The tortures are continuing. As you read these lines, many hundreds are undergoing the most hideous torments. Reich Bishop, if someone has committed an offense, he should be brought before a judge where he can answer for it! That is the view of all decent Germans. But here people are being tortured and maltreated who, for the most part, have not acknowledged or committed a single punishable offense.

I beg of you, for our Savior's love of mankind, please help us! Inform the highest authorities of everything you learn from this letter and from elsewhere! Our Lord will richly reward you for this deed, which will certainly be well pleasing to him. You are our highest evangelical priest, whom we as soldiers especially revere. Please, follow every avenue you can so that relief comes to us as fast as possible.

People have said that our glorious Führer would punish such acts most severely if they came to his ears. I am of the same view, for Adolf Hitler wishes to see the realization of justice and the most heartfelt love of one's neighbor. But every day here—through these terrible deeds—*new enemies of the state* are being trained. That should not be happening. Please, make your own inquiries as soon as possible, but in such a way that you learn the whole truth! The guilty ones must be brought to account. (The 4th Company, under a Captain or *Sturmfüher* Bräuning, is especially incriminated!) *Obersturmführer* Meisinger, Inspector Häuserer, and Inspector Kanthack (who are all active in the Gestapo), and *particularly the director of the* Columbia Haus (!!!) [Karl Otto Koch] must be investigated. There would have to be a thorough *surprise* inspection in the Columbia Haus and at *Lichtenburg concentration camp,* and many prisoners would have to be heard separately; then the truth would come to light. If it is not done like that, everything will remain as before, and many hundred poor souls will continue to be maltreated and thus converted into enemies of the state.

For fear of revenge (I have my grounds!), I cannot tell you my name, Reverend Reich Bishop. Forgive me for not giving you my name, but it is not possible otherwise. Our Lord be with you. May he bless you in all you do!

Heil Hitler!
One who suffers greatly in the present state of things.

170

1935 Revision to Paragraph 175 of the Penal Code

Published in *Homosexualität in der NS-Zeit: Dokumente einer Diskriminierung und Verfolgung,* edited by Günter Grau and Claudia Schoppmann (Frankfurt am Main: Fischer Taschenbuch Verlag, 1993), 95–97.

Original text Paragraph 175 of the Reich Penal Code (1871)

An unnatural act of sexual indecency committed between persons of the male sex or by persons with animals is punishable by imprisonment; a loss of civil rights may also be imposed.

Revised version, pursuant to the amendment to the Penal Code passed 28 June1935, Article 6 [Sexual Indecency between Men]

(1) Paragraph 175 of the Penal Code includes the following provisions:
Any man who shall engage in an indecent sexual act with another man or who shall allow himself to be coerced into an act of sexual indecency by another shall be punished by imprisonment.

Where one of the participants has not yet reached the age of twenty-one at the time of the incident, the court may refrain from punishment in particularly mild cases.

(2) Paragraph 175 of the Penal Code shall be amended to include the following provisions, titled [Paragraph] 175a:
Penal servitude up to ten years or, where mitigating circumstances apply, imprisonment of not less than three months shall be mandatory in the following instances:

1. Any man who forcibly or by clear and present threat of physical or psychological violence or death compels another man to engage in acts of sexual indecency or forces him to be used for this purpose without his consent.
2. Any man who abuses a dependent relationship based on service, employment, or subordination to induce another man to engage in acts of sexual indecency or who forces him to be used for this purpose without his consent.
3. Any man over the age of twenty-one who seduces any man under the age of twenty-one into engaging in acts of sexual indecency or forces him to be used for this purpose without his consent.

4. Any man who engages in acts of sexual indecency for hire or who allows himself to be used for this purpose by other men or offers himself for the same.

(3) Paragraph 175 of the Penal Code shall be amended to delete the phrase "between persons of the male sex or" and shall be henceforth appended under the title "Paragraph 175b."

• • •

Commentary by Dr. Leopold Schäfer, Assistant Departmental Director at the Reich Ministry of Justice

Bad experiences in recent times have made it seem advisable to put into effect the pending general revisions to the Penal Code, which would tighten prohibitions against homosexual acts of sexual indecency between men earlier than originally planned. The fundamental flaw in the existing Paragraph 175 of the Penal Code was that—at least according to current case law—it applied only to acts resembling intercourse, so that public prosecutors and law enforcement were unable to intervene in cases involving overtly homosexual sex acts between men unless they were able to prove that something resembling intercourse took place. This loophole has now been eliminated by rendering any act of sexual indecency between men subject to imprisonment. However, in order to prevent the application of this provision to lesser misdemeanors, which, according to our experience, often occur particularly among younger offenders, the court is authorized to refrain from prosecuting perpetrators under the age of twenty-one in especially minor cases. If minors engage in this form of debauchery with other underage men or even with adults, this mitigating provision shall no longer be applicable as a rule. Above and beyond this basic category of actions, the following additional cases shall be punishable by penal servitude of up to ten years, under mitigating circumstances with imprisonment of not less than three months: coercing another man to homosexual acts of sexual indecency by use of force or by clear and present threat of physical or psychological violence or death; abusing a dependent relationship based on service, employment, or subordination (e.g., in the army, the police force, the SA, or Hitler Youth) to engage in acts of homosexual indecency; the seduction of a minor male by an adult and male homosexual prostitution.

Cases of bestiality (sexual intercourse with animals) previously falling under the jurisdiction of Paragraph 175 now appear under Paragraph 175b.

171

HEINRICH HIMMLER

On Homosexuality and Abortion

Secret Directive on the Curtailment of Homosexuality and Abortion

Circulated on 10 October 1936. First published as "Geheimerlass zur Bekämpfung der Homosexualität und Abtreibung," in *Homosexualität in der NS-Zeit: Dokumente einer Diskriminierung und Verfolgung*, edited by Günter Grau and Claudia Schoppmann (Frankfurt am Main: Fischer Taschenbuch Verlag, 1993), 122, 124, 125.

SS-Reichsführer and Director of the German Police at the Reich Ministry of the Interior
Top Secret! Not for publication in the *Bulletin of the Imperial Ministry for Administration* [*Reichsministerialblatt der inneren Verwaltung*]

To:
State Secret Police Bureau, Berlin
Prussian Provincial Criminal Law Enforcement Bureau, Berlin
All regional and local headquarters of law enforcement in the Reich
Re: Combating Homosexuality and Abortion

The substantial endangerment of population policy and public health represented by the relatively high number of abortions still being performed today that are a major violation of the ideological tenets of the National Socialist worldview as well as homosexual activities on the part of a not insignificant segment of the population, which pose one of the greatest threats to our youth, requires more effective measures for combating these public menaces to society than have thus far been implemented.

1. Handling the aforementioned offenses essentially lies within the jurisdiction of local law enforcement officials.
2. In order to secure the centralized and effective curtailment of these offenses according to uniform guidelines, I am hereby establishing within the Prussian Provincial Law Enforcement Bureau a Reich Office for the Curtailment of Homosexuality and Abortion.
3. In the event that state police intervention is required, the office of the Gestapo is to be notified and prompted to prosecute the necessary measures. A Special Department II S will be created within the Gestapo to handle matters of this nature.
4. In order to facilitate timely cooperation between agencies, Special Department II S within the Gestapo and the Reich Office for the Curtailment of Homosexuality and Abortion at the Prussian Provincial Criminal Law Enforcement Bureau will be placed under the direction of one and the same official. [. . .]

Speech to SS Group Leaders

Delivered on 18 February 1937. Published in *Heinrich Himmler: Geheimreden 1933–1945 und andere Ansprachen,* edited by Bradley F. Smith and Agnes F. Peterson (Frankfurt am Main: Propyläen Verlag, 1974), 93.

When we seized power in 1933, we also found that homosexual organizations were in existence. Their registered membership was over two million; cautious estimates compiled by the officers handling the case suggest that there may be between two and four million homosexuals in Germany. Personally, I don't set the figure that high because I don't believe that everyone involved in these organizations was actually homosexual. On the other hand, I am of course convinced that not all homosexuals were registered members of those organizations. My guess is between one and two million. But one million is really the bare minimum we can assume; that is the absolute minimum and most conservative estimate permissible in this matter.

Please think about the implications of this. According to the most recent census statistics, we probably have a total population of sixty-seven or sixty-eight million people in Germany; that means, taking the raw numbers into account, about thirty-four million men. So that means that there are approximately twenty million men in their reproductive years (men over the age of sixteen). This figure might be off by a million or so, but that is irrelevant.

Assuming that one to two million of these men are homosexuals, the result is that 7 to 8 percent of men in Germany are homosexual. What this means is that, should the situation remain the same, our *Volk* will fall to ruin as the result of this scourge. In the long run, no nation can sustain this degree of disruption of its sexual economy and equilibrium.

172

SS-UNTERSTURMFÜHRER PROFESSOR ECKHARDT

Sexually Indecent Abominations against Nature Are Punishable by Death

First published as "Widernatürliche Unzucht ist todeswürdig," in *Das Schwarze Korps,* 22 May 1935, 13.

In 98 C.E., the Roman historian Tacitus depicted, in that invaluable source for ancient German history, his *Germania,* the manners and customs of the ancient Germans, among other things their justice system: "Punishments vary according to the quality of the crime. Traitors and deserters they hang upon trees. Cowards, sluggards, and unnatural prostitutes they smother in mud and bogs under a heap of hurdles." Based on our cross-referencing of Tacitus's use of language elsewhere in his works, we know that what he is referring to as "unnatural prostitutes" (*corpore infames*) are bodies defiled by the sexually indecent abomination against nature that is *homosexuality.*

The Degenerate as Sacrificial Offering

We have no reason to doubt the accuracy of this report. And yet, what does seem unlikely, and understandably so, is the interpretation that Tacitus lends to the process in his ignorance of the religious context surrounding the various degrees of punishment: by his account, "in punishing of glaring iniquities, it behooves likewise to display them to sight; but effeminacy and pollution must be buried and concealed." In his famous book on the death penalty among the ancient Germans, Karl von Amira demonstrated that the purpose of the death penalty among the ancient Germans was to extirpate as vigorously as possible whatever deviated from the norms of the species: "The instinctual impulse within the *Volk* to maintain the purity of the race is congruent with the divine mandate to maintain the original God-given purity of the race. The degenerates, then, are *offered as sacrifices* so as not to provoke the anger of the gods in response to racial treason."[1]

Those hung upon trees and smothered in mud and bogs are sacrifices offered to various deities! A hanging is a sacrifice to the God of Wind, Wotan-Odin, who sends his ravens to retrieve the offering. Hanging, like beheading or being put on the rack, was a punishment originally reserved exclusively for men. Women, on the other hand, were not hung but rather smothered in bogs or buried alive in regions where there were no bogs. Even today, countless archeological finds of buried bog people reaching all the way back to Tacitus's time bear testimony to this practice as a form of punishment. All evidence points to the notion that being smothered in bogs or buried alive was a sacrifice to the mother earth goddess Freya-Frigga for whom our "Friday" has been named. As soon as the women slated for execution—primarily adulteresses—had been surrendered to Freya, apparently she was also offered the effeminate men in sacrifice, regardless of whether their emasculate degeneracy revealed itself in cowardice or aversion to war or whether they allowed themselves to be sexually used as women!!

In southern and northern ancient Germanic sources of justice alike, homosexuality and cowardliness are seen in the same light and assigned equal value. [. . .]

Cowardice and Homosexuality

Here, too, homosexuality is equated (passively and actively) with cowardice.

There is additional evidence for the fact that the offense [of cowardice and assuming the role of a woman in a sex act] was punishable by death. A twelfth-century Norwegian law classifies it among the inexpiable criminal offenses. In another Norwegian source, it is punishable by being buried alive or burned at the stake. Similarly, we could draw parallels to the act of engaging in sexual indecency with animals (which is generally seen as being on a par with homosexuality). According to Nordic and Frisian sources, this act is punishable by being buried alive. It must be seen as a diminished punishment if in twelfth-century Norway only the animal is smothered in the bog while the male perpetrator is, on the other hand, merely subject to castration. Similarly, the fact that Old Frisian ecclesiastical law allows for the choice between castration, live burial, and burning at the stake is an index of more recent developments in the justice system.

The castration we encounter as an optional punishment in Norway and in Frisian was already evident as a punishment for homosexuality and sexually indecent acts with animals in the laws of the Visigoths toward the end of the eighth century. We would not be in error were we to presume that here, too, this punishment replaced the original death sentence that we can no longer prove existed amongst the Visigoths. Much in the same vein, it is not infrequent to find evidence of castration as a punishment for rape, whereas rape, too, was originally considered punishable by death and merited the condign punishment of beheading.

From the eighth century onward, the church began, first in France, then throughout the rest of the Western world, to declare sexually indecent abominations against nature acts of heresy and thus to assert jurisdiction over these matters. The imperial decree of Charlemagne, king of the Franks, in 789, with its extensive regulation of ecclesiastical affairs, invoking the terms of the Council of Ancyra, still satisfied itself with stipulating that the ecclesiastical penitential system was sufficient for homosexuality and bestiality without requiring the intercession of civil penal code. But toward the middle of the ninth century, Benedict Levita, a known forger of capitularies, saw in the Old Testament grounds for the death penalty for sexual indecency with animals, and, in an appendix to his forged collection of pretend capitularies, demanded that sexually indecent abominations against nature of both types be punishable by burning at the stake because death by fire was the punishment set by Roman law—"the mother of all human laws."

The efforts of the church were highly effective. Already in the year 846, there is evidence of a Frankish man who had committed acts of sexual indecency with an animal being burned at the stake. The forgeries of Benedict Levita were generally considered by his contemporaries to be a genuine collection of capitularies and were even cited by the Frankish king himself as valid law (the first confirmed instance is dated 857). As a result, the notion that sexually indecent abominations against nature constituted heresy generally came to be accepted, and death by fire replaced the original penalty. We have already mentioned the fact that in the north and in Frisia, burning at the stake became an alternative punishment to being buried alive. This is similarly in evidence in England already at an early date. Throughout the German Middle Ages, we see this as the only punishment for homosexuality and sexual indecency with animals, regardless of whether this was tacitly subsumed under the crime of heresy, as for example in the Saxon Mirror, or whether it dared be named explicitly by its shameful name.

Even after Roman law successfully established itself in Germany and introduced a sweeping and, in the long run, decisive overhaul of the penal code, nothing changed in this regard. Already since the middle of the ninth century, then, criminal prosecution of sexually indecent abominations against nature fell under the jurisdiction of Roman ecclesiastical law, so that when foreign law [*Fremdrecht*] was adopted in its entirety around 1500, no revisions were undertaken in this regard; rather, the existing state of affairs was merely confirmed. Accordingly, the Bamberg Criminal Code of 1507 (*Constitutio Bambergensis Criminalis*), the Brandenburg Criminal Code of 1516, as well as the 1532 Criminal Jurisdiction of Emperor Charles V (*Constitutio Criminalis Carolina*), which would set the tone for the years to come, were unanimous in issuing the following stipulation: "If any person should commit unchaste acts with an animal, a man with a man, a woman with a woman, then they have forfeited their lives, and they should be executed by fire according to common custom."

This provision remained in effect as common law until the eighteenth century, even though in many places the milder sentence of beheading replaced the penalty of death by fire. However, the eighteenth century witnessed the onset of a transformation of perceptions on these matters and, *tellingly,* this change was brought to us by our international neighbors.

Voltaire, that brilliant mentor to Frederick the Great, whose perilous influence held the king in its grip until he finally freed himself from it in his later years, advanced the notion that homosexuality, while it may be unseemly, was not a criminally punishable offense because it was caused by a deceptive and mendacious heart and did not lead to the destruction of society. This is a notion that is still today a permanent fixture of the whole Western cultural sphere, but also one whose premise Frederick the Great never fully accepted; at the same time, though, in 1746, he did rescind the death penalty for sexually indecent abominations against nature, and in his Prussian Civil Code (published in 1794), he finally established a legal basis for imprisonment as the penalty. But Frederick's great adversary, Maria Theresa, was still able to retain death by fire as a penalty for sexually indecent abominations against nature in the Austrian *Constitutio Criminalis* of 1768, and it was only her son Joseph II who adopted the procedures promoted by the Prussian king, whom he greatly admired. Some of the remaining German states conformed earlier, others later. But it was only with the advent of the French Revolution that this Western world of ideas achieved its final victory.

What Does the Rest of the World Think?

The current position of foreign nations concerning homosexuality as a criminal offense is extraordinarily instructive. There is a stark contrast between the Nordic-Germanic and the Western-Roman nations and peoples. Homosexuality is seen more as a thing of ridicule than of censure among the Romans. Hence, in all the jurisdictions covered by Roman law, inasmuch as it is not accompanied by aggravating circumstances (such as involving forcible pedophilic acts, rape, creating a public nuisance), homosexuality is not a punishable offense; this holds true for France, Belgium, Holland, and Luxembourg; also for Italy, Spain, and Portugal; together with the majority of Central and South American colonies; and in Russia, Poland, Yugoslavia, Romania, Turkey, and Japan as well.

Particularly characteristic is the fact that the line of demarcation for criminalization runs straight through Switzerland: in the Roman cantons of Freiburg, Neuenburg, Geneva, Waadt, Wallis, Teffin, and Graubünden, homosexuality is permitted as a nonpunishable offense, while in the remaining cantons, it carries the risk of imprisonment or hard labor, just as is the case in the Germanic states.

The Germanic bloc of states, including those falling within the Germanic cultural sphere, consider homosexual activity a felony sexual offense. In Austria, as in Germany, homosexuality is subject to criminal prosecution—and in Hungary, Czechoslovakia, Bulgaria and Greece; in Denmark, Norway, Sweden, Finland, Latvia; in England (with a maximum sentence of lifelong hard labor), Scotland, British dominions; and in the United States of North America.

The Falsification of Origins

These are the conclusions we have drawn:

Twice in our history, the Nordic-Germanic position on sexually indecent abominations against nature has been falsified.

In the first instance, by the church, which justified the execution of homosexuals not for the sake of extirpating degenerates in the interest of maintaining the purity of the race, but rather execrated them as heretics in the name of God's greatest glory.

In the second instance, the falsification came with the advent of Western perceptions of homosexuality more as a species of play than as a degenerate form of the species itself, represented by deviations not present in the normal human specimen. This second foreign expropriation in portrayals of Nordic sentiment was ushered in by Voltaire, reached its first peak with the French Revolution and threatened to saturate Germany like a storm surge after the collapse of 1918. It eschewed the death penalty and classified homosexuality as a minor sexual offense, which of course brought with it a complete shift in the standards of measure. But this falsification did not succeed in breaking down the aversion of Nordic man toward homosexuality, and the Germanic states still stand firm today in a closed bloc against Western cultural circles.

It isn't any wonder that the power of racial thought should also be preserved in its purest form in the Germanic states and, for example, bastardizing the race with the blood of Negroes is considered an act of racial treason for the Germans, as it is for the Scandinavians, the British, and the Americans, whereas for the Western nations and peoples, it is not perceived as such. And it is no wonder, either, that the same French Revolution that decriminalized homosexuality is also the one that emancipated the Jews and that we are now threatened with the complete disintegration of the race as a consequence.

Now that we have found our way back to our ancient Germanic perspectives on the question of mixed marriages with members of races that are alien to the species [*artfremde Rassen*], we must do the same for our assessments of the scourge of racial annihilation presented by the degenerate profile of the homosexual and return to the Nordic guiding principle of extirpating the degenerates. Germany's rise and fall rest on her ability to maintain the purity of the race.

Note

1. Karl von Amira, *Die germanischen Todesstrafen—Untersuchungen zur Rechts- und Religionsgeschichte* (Munich: Verlag der bayerischen Akademie der wissenschaften, 1922.)—Eds.

15
The German Soul and Psyche

CERTAINLY, ONE OF THE HALLMARKS of the first half of the twentieth century was the invention (or discovery) of "interiority." To know what takes place within the soul, the mind, and heart of another individual or—perhaps more specifically—what takes place deep in the recesses of one's own psyche has been a desire of human beings since the Greeks. Sigmund Freud (1856–1939) was one of the undisputed shapers of twentieth-century thought through his discovery of the unconscious. Trained as a neurologist at the University of Vienna, he developed "psychoanalysis," which offered a threefold approach to understanding the human psyche: it was a therapeutic method, a method of inquiry (a way of collecting data and exploring a subject matter), and a theory (a scientific structure and body of knowledge). Freud was a Jew, and, while rejecting all religious belief, insisted that he remained one his entire life. When he first appeared on the public scene in Vienna, arguing for the existence of a hidden, submerged sexual drive that shaped all humans, he was damned as a quack and a perverted Jew. As is clear from the 1939 obituary by Fritz Bleiber, this anti-Semitic attitude persisted even after his death. Freud's initial followers in Vienna were primarily Jews, as were his first clients. By 1910, he had confronted his Viennese colleagues at the second Psychoanalytic Congress and stated the case bluntly: "Most of you are Jews, and therefore you are incompetent to win friends for the new teaching. Jews must be content with the modest role of preparing the ground. It is absolutely essential that I should form ties in the world of general science. . . . The Swiss will save us."[1] By this, he meant that the psychiatrist Carl Gustav Jung (1875–1961), a Swiss and a non-Jew, would help promote his new science. But Jung eventually came to see Freud's formulation of psychoanalysis as a "Jewish" science and stressed the differences between a Jewish psychology and an Aryan one as early as 1918. He criticized the rootlessness of the Jew, the fact that "he is badly at a loss for that quality in man which roots him to the earth and draws new strength from below." This view of the rootlessness of the Jew made the Jew's creativity, especially in the sphere of psychology, of value only for the Jew: "thus it is a quite unpardonable mistake to accept the conclusions of a Jewish psychology as generally valid." This statement, made in 1927, was repeated virtually verbatim in 1934, at which point he noted that it was "no deprecation of Semitic psychology, any more than it is a deprecation of the Chinese to speak of the peculiar psychology of the Oriental." He further qualified his view of the difference of the Jew (and the very meaning of a "Semitic" psychology) by paraphrasing a statement by the French philosopher Ernest Renan (1823–92) about the "Jew who is something of a nomad, has never yet created a cultural form of his own, and as far as we can see never will, since all his instincts and talents require a more or less civilized nation to act as a host for their development." Jung's private condemnation of the "essentially corrosive nature" of the "Jewish gospel" of Freud in a 1934 letter reflected his belief about the lack of value of the "Jewish point of view" that was Freudian psychoanalysis and echoed his statement of 1933 that Adolf Hitler "is the incarnation of the nation's *Volksseele* [soul]."[2]

After his break with Freud, Jung undertook the editing of a major psychotherapeutic journal from 1928 to 1939. The *Zentralblatt für Psychotherapie,* the organ of the Allgemeine Ärztliche Gesellschaft für Psychotherapie (General Medical Society of Psychopathology), was published in Leipzig and coedited by Jung and Matthias Heinrich Göring (1879–1945). In 1933, psychoanalysis was denounced as "Jewish sophistry" and as "hostile to religion" by pro-regime critics like Frank Maraun. A cousin of *Reichsmarschall* Hermann Göring and an officer in the Luftwaffe, Matthias Göring "rescued" what he called "a German form of psychoanalysis" by placing it in the service of racial theory. A trained lawyer and neurologist, he underwent analysis with the Adlerian psychotherapist Leonhard Seif in Munich as part of his training in 1928. Göring stressed "community feeling," which he defined, unlike most Adlerians, in terms of nationalism and Christian belief. His Deutsches Institut für Psychologische Forschung und Psychotherapie (German Institute for Psychological Research and Psychotherapy), founded in 1936 in Berlin, Aryanized psychoanalysis, destroying Freud's legacy in order to save psychology. If, as the Nazis argued, mental illness was a sign of the degeneracy of a race, Göring proposed that the truly German art of healing the soul (*Seelenheilkunde*), with its German romantic roots, was the only appropriate means of dealing with the mental illness of a superior race. Pragmatic to the hilt, the Göring Institute placed psychotherapy in the service of the new state. The promises were clear: to make the mentally ill quickly able to return to full function as productive members of the state, to cure homosexuality, and to generally improve the health of the race. Non-Jewish psychotherapists such as Kurt Gauger saw the mission of psychotherapy as one with the ideology of the Nazi party. In a speech at the congress of the Deutsche Psychoanalytische Gesellschaft (German Psychoanalytic Society) in Nauheim, held 10–13 May 1934, he stressed the therapeutic role of the *Volk*. In addition, Göring's followers truly believed that psychotherapy would be furthered by turning in Jewish colleagues and patients to the Gestapo. Göring led the drive to incorporate the German Psychoanalytic Society into his German Institute for Psychological Research and Psychotherapy in 1936. The German Psychoanalytic Society was officially disbanded in 1938, at which point classical psychoanalysis ended in Germany despite efforts by British psychoanalyst Ernest Jones (1879–1958), the head of the International Psychoanalytical Association, who was less concerned about the German Jewish analysts who were to be expelled from the organization than about preserving a semblance of psychoanalysis in any new organizations. In a letter to Anna Freud, Jones explained that he opposed the resignation of Gentiles from the Psychoanalytic Society in sympathy with the Jewish analysts.

Many German psychoanalysts had left Germany before and immediately after 1933. Freud himself was able, with the help of the French psychoanalyst Princess Marie Bonaparte of Greece (1882–1962), to evacuate himself and his family from Austria to England in 1938 after the Nazis annexed his home country. Some analysts, like Edith Jacobsohn (Anglicized as Jacobson; 1897–1978), became part of the organized underground opposition against the Nazis. Jacobsohn trained at the Berliner Psychoanalytisches Institut (Berlin Psychoanalytic Institute) in 1925, a much more politicized organization than the institute in Vienna. Having fled Berlin in 1933, she surreptitiously returned to organize the opposition group Neu Beginnen (New Beginnings), referred to as Org, with some of her former patients. Arrested in 1935, she was placed in a Berlin jail rather than in a concentration camp. Her supporters accused the International Psychoanalytical Association of timidity in protesting her incarceration, a charge refuted by Ernest Jones, the organization's director. As Jacobsohn recounted in her 1948 memoir, she had relatively good conditions and was able to manage an escape when a former member of her group arranged for her to be released for health reasons.

Certainly, the odd status of suicide in the Third Reich can be used as a litmus test for the changes in the Nazi understanding of mental health. In the 1890s, the Berlin police systematically began collecting investigators' reports of suicides and artifacts found at the scene. The general forensic view was that if one could understand the common thread in suicides, it should be possible to generate a model of suicide prevention. Each folder contained official reports and objects from the death scene: playing cards with suicide notes scribbled on them, pieces of clothing with messages, autopsy reports, and detailed police reports were filed away to document each death. With the gradual increase of pressure on Jews in Germany (and then Austria), the Jewish suicide rate increased, especially with the deportations in 1943, as the journalist Ursula von Kardoff observed. German Jews had fewer and fewer options. Only the Dominican Republic offered a blanket commitment to give Jews visas, and even that option was very limited. The police precisely documented each suicide; beginning in 1944, as it became clear that the war was going to be lost, suicides in the families of convinced Nazis began to show up in the files.

Suicide was a sign of the deep despair felt by those abandoned by their countrymen. When on 16 March 1938 the brilliant Jewish cultural historian Egon Friedell (1878–1938) spotted an SA car outside his Viennese apartment house and heard that the officers had come to arrest "the Jew Friedell," he leapt through a window to his death, warning those below to "watch out." Later, the very Germans who had condemned their Jewish compatriots exhibited the same despair as they watched the slow-motion collapse of the Third Reich.

On 18 February 1943, Minister of Propaganda Joseph Goebbels (1897–1945) issued a call for "total war." By the last stages of the war, suicide had become a familiar motif, inspired by the image of a Wagnerian apocalypse but also by the actions of Germany's ally, Japan. The Japanese notion of Bushido and the resultant use of suicide fliers (kamikaze) and honor suicide (seppuku) struck some Germans as an admirable model during the last years of the war. In the 1920s, the "geopolitical philosopher" Major General Professor Karl Haushofer (1869–1946) had argued that Japan was the Germany of the Pacific, pointing out that the two nations shared the need for more living space and honored parallel martial traditions. (It helped that the emperor of Japan asked imperial Germany in the late nineteenth century to modernize the Japanese armed forces.) Suicide seems to have been another shared phenomenon, at least in the two countries' notions of personal codes of honor. Suddenly, suicide, a sign of degeneracy or neurosis, a sign of desperation or failure, a sign of pathology and the need for intervention, became a "model" behavior in some circles for the end of the Reich. The anonymous author of the article "Kamikaze Panic: The Image of Japan in the German Population" admitted with some relief that the "cult of ritual suicide" was "utterly alien."

NOTES

1. Fritz Wittels, *Sigmund Freud: His Personality, His Teaching, and His School,* translated by Eden and Cedar Paul (London: George Allen & Unwin, 1924), 140.

2. *The Collected Works of C. G. Jung,* edited by Herbert Read, Michael Scott, Montague Fordham, and Gustav Adler, translated by R. C. F. Hull, 20 vols. (London: Routledge & Kegan Paul, 1957–79), 10:13, 7:149n8, 10:534, 10:165–66.

173

FRANK MARAUN

Christianity and Psychoanalysis

First published as "Wider die Psychoanalyse" in *Berliner Börsen-Zeitung,* no. 20, 14 May 1933, 1.

First it was psychoanalysis, with its claim to be a new doctrine of salvation for sick minds, that attacked Christianity, declared religion to be out of date, and chose itself as its appointed successor, as the contemporary fulfillment of the religious mission to mankind. It could point to the fact that sexuality, the focus of Freud's work, also has a place in Christian thought, as the concept of the sins of the flesh. The psychoanalyst wanted to be distinguished from the theologian only because he approaches this concept in a concrete form and searches out every path of this sin, even its most secret ways. Besides, in this context, he was able to remind us of an important verse in the First Epistle of St. John: "If we say that we have no sin, we deceive ourselves, and the truth is not in us." This means that the miracle of redemption can be fulfilled only in he who is conscious of his sins. In my therapy, says the psychoanalyst, the consciousness of conflicts is also a condition of cure.

But what does the psychoanalyst mean by cure? He means the attempt to turn the man who is withering away in neurotic isolation into a businessman capable of dealing with his fellows and living with them. For this, he has to strive for moral conduct. Human society has taken the place of the Kingdom of God as the highest principle. Not in vain has Freud been called "eighteenth century" and the scientific successor to Voltaire.

Not long ago, the apparent agreement of Christian and psychoanalytical doctrines, with their pessimistic ideas on original sin, led progressive groups of pastors to demand that special courses on psychoanalysis for Protestant ministers be set up, lecturers on mental care [be] appointed to theological colleges, and candidates for the first and second theological examinations [be] tested in psychoanalysis and other fields of psychology. This request, which occupied the regional synod of Saxony two years ago, aspired to the renewing and deepening of the ministry, which, by its own admission, could no longer cope with the enormous mental hardship and distress of the people. It became clear that the mere proclamation of the word in church services and Bible readings were no longer enough to relieve this distress, that reference to faith alone could not have the desired effect on modern man. Help had to come from a psychological deepening of theological study. Man had to be brought to the consciousness of his sins, awakened to the sentiment of his guilt, and made ready for the experience of remorse. That is the task of ministers of religion, and to accomplish it, they need the support of that science that leads them to a deeper knowledge of evil.

Here we have distinguished between diagnosis and therapy in such a way that the pastor, in his cure of souls, may use psychoanalysis only for diagnosis. But in therapy he must allow those heartening, progressive, unifying powers to do their work—those powers that the truths of Christian salvation put into his hands, and that are so obviously lacking in psychoanalytical therapy. The ministers who approved of this method probably did not see clearly how near they were to being ridiculous. Diagnosis and therapy, even if we dare to let the odor of the clinic come near to the House of God, must in one way or another exist at the same spiritual level. To separate them into two quite different, mutually exclusive worlds gives as little pleasure as a theoretical recipe. But what would the reality look like: for every complex, a truth of salvation; for every neurotic symptom, a prayer; first the knife of analysis and then the power of belief?

We have overlooked the fact that ideas that lead to consequences hostile to religion must have a nucleus hostile to religion and cannot be used simply as a tool. They cannot possibly give a more thorough and better "diagnosis" than the divine knowledge of man, penetrating into the creative depths of the soul that Christ has bequeathed to us. Here, man as a whole, in his responsibility to God; there, only a few mechanisms that set in motion the autocratic theater of the unconscious—an unconscious, what is more, that the ego can place at a distance, refusing responsibility for its machinations. The poverty of the analytical concept constantly terrifies anyone who is accustomed to regarding man as carved out of one block and is particularly oppressive in its opposition to religious experience. What does it mean to interpret God as the father projected into heaven? This explanation is not only inadequate, it is false from beginning to end. It shows that psychoanalysis has not felt even a breath of the magnification of the concept of God in Christian thought. For the essence of God is not that he is a father but that he is a heavenly father, whose son, faced with such perfection, is always and everywhere in the wrong, with whom he cannot quarrel as he can with his earthly father. Earthly father and earthly son are equal in the sight of the heavenly father, like brothers in a spiritual community and communion.

174

ANONYMOUS

The Role of the Jew in Medicine

The Psychoanalysis of the Jew Sigmund Freud

Published as "Die Rolle des Juden in der Medizin," in *Deutsche Volksgesundheit aus Blut und Boden* 1 (August/September 1933), 101.

Psychoanalysis is an impressive example of the fact that nothing good for us Germans can ever come from a Jew, even when he produces "scientific achievements." Even if he gave us 5 percent that was novel and apparently good, 95 percent of his doctrine is destructive and annihilating *for us*. His own fellow Jews and other races may derive advantage from Jewish ideas, but we Germans and all peoples with Nordic blood always find that it turns out badly for us when we eat anything out of the Jew's hand.

This may be the fate of Jewish blood and the Jewish spirit, but the better Jews themselves may be horrified at the results of the products of their race. It may be so! But it may be something quite different, and that is what we consider probable: the Jew uses medicine in his biblical struggle to dominate the world, so as to degenerate and decimate the Nordic peoples who stand in his way. The facts speak in favor of this idea.

Psychoanalysis aims to be a method of cure for certain nervous conditions (neuroses) that have occurred because of inner conflicts in the instinctual life. In the mind of man, often to an advanced age, there is a constant struggle between "good" and "evil," between the instincts of reproduction and self-preservation, on the one hand, and the divine blood-linked "ego" on the other. In racially superior people, this struggle ends quite naturally with the victory of the "ego," with the instincts overcome and controlled. For in superior people, the *conscience* watches over every false step, whether sexual or social; it points out to [the individual]: here you have done wrong, and the strong man takes this as a warning for the next time. But the weak man, who cannot master his instincts, is made neurotic by the conflict. But not incurably neurotic! A helper with experience of life—he does not even need to be a doctor—will successfully solve the conflict and give the patient both a new stability through advice on the regimen of his life and moral exhortation, explaining to him that life is a school in which we have to learn to overcome the instincts. This explanation gives the patient new strength, and instead of taking refuge in illness, he will resume the struggle with life. The "neurosis" is cured.

These facts are clear and have been known for centuries. At most, modern "materialistic" medicine, which knows no soul and no God, could forget it. Thus, it was possible for the Jew Freud, professor of medicine in Vienna, with a true Jewish sophistry, to obscure, distort, and misinterpret the facts so that there arose a new doctrine, the Freudian doctrine of the neuroses, and a new method of curing this condition, psychoanalysis, whose ultimate result is that the patient's mind, struggling to dominate instinctual life, *is robbed of its last ethical foothold* and is cast down into the Asiatic ideology of "Eat, drink, and be merry, for tomorrow we die!" And that was probably also Freud's *aim,* perhaps his task, for he duly joins the other Jewish efforts *to strike the Nordic races at their most vulnerable point, their sexual life.* [. . .]

According to Freud, the sexual instinct is the basic instinct of the mind, to which the whole content of life must be traced back. Disgust, shame, morals, aesthetics, authority, conscience, even religion, the thirst for knowledge, and the feeling for art arise only from sexuality. But Freud's filthy imagination does not derive everything from sex only in the conscious adult; he finds sexuality even in the child's mind: suckling its mother's breast or a substitute for it, uncovering its body, kicking, sucking its little hands and feet are all designated as sexual pleasure. This lasting drive must find fulfillment, in youth from onanism (masturbation), later from sexual intercourse (whether in marriage or outside it); otherwise we would become ill.

To silence the voice of conscience, which in Nordic peoples rises in onanism and extramarital intercourse, Freud builds in us an unconscious force, the "id," which is the mind itself. It is thus not *my* passion that drives me to actions designated as evil by my blood but something I am totally unconscious of, about which I can do nothing and for which I am not responsible. A neurosis, according to Freud, occurs because this "id" forces the drive into the unconscious. The drive is thus replaced by neurotic symptoms, whose meaning the patient is unconscious of. Cure is supposed to be achieved by bringing the instinct that has been driven into the unconscious back into the patient's consciousness by means of psychoanalysis (dissection of the mind).

In fact, reality teaches us that neuroses can appear through the conflicts of conscience with the lower instincts.

175

KURT GAUGER

Political Medicine

Foundations of a German Psychotherapy

Lecture delivered at the Medical Congress for Psychotherapy, Bad Nauheim, 1934. Published as *Politische Medizin: Grundriß einer deutschen Psychotherapie* (Hamburg: Hanseatische Verlagsanstalt, 1934), 7, 12–14, 16–17, 23–27, 49, 61, 63.

I have chosen as the subject of my address "Psychotherapy and Political Worldview."

It is clearly indicated that the sense of my talk will be political, since I am standing before you in the uniform of a political soldier, of an SA man.

The connection between psychotherapy and politics may appear strange to many of you, especially those who have come from abroad to participate in this congress, and you may probably look upon the relationship between psychotherapy and politics as a purely tactical matter.

Hence you might perhaps be of the opinion that a political address at an international scientific congress, as far as the participants from abroad are concerned, could only have been the purpose of winning sympathy for our new state. And our German participants may have sympathy for our new state. And our German participants may be of the opinion that such a political report signifies for them a directive to the action which we know adequately enough as coordination [*Gleichschaltung*]. [. . .]

Freud speaks of overcoming the pleasure principle. But he cannot name the value system that can be experienced only outside of every egoistic evaluation. Such a system of values is possible only as an expression of a worldview that does not have the individual and his well-being as its exclusive goal.

Hitherto, psychotherapy was largely individualistically oriented, and precisely at this point where one spoke of the relationship of the individual to the community. To us, the concept of the individual is at the outset false; it is the expression of an attitude that we call liberalistic.

For us, it is not at all the concept of personality but rather the concept of the individual as *ens existens per se* that from the outset constitutes the negation and falsification of a biological datum—namely, that of a reality that is not merely "metaphysical" but indeed biological, the German people.

As inheritors of the individualistic epoch, we know much about individual conditions of mental illnesses. What we did not hear so much about, however, before Adolf Hitler, are the general conditions of the health of the soul.

If you ask me about the connection between psychotherapy and National Socialism, I must answer that the problem of the health of our people's soul is the basic question with which National Socialism is concerned. Adolf Hitler did not start out from purely economic considerations.

He did not promise his first followers and later the whole German people "more earnings and less work," as had been done earlier by Marxist demagogues. He promised us nothing. He achieved something psychologically unprecedented, in that he made demands rather than promises.

He demanded of every individual the utmost in terms of participation and a disposition prepared for action. And precisely by so doing, he reopened the wellsprings of the healthy soul of our people, which had begun to run dry. Since the advent of Adolf Hitler, *Volk*dom and homeland, discipline, fidelity, and honor, are again words of biological value in Germany! [. . .]

The term *mental illness* requires, empirically speaking, a more exact explanation. Most people know or think they know what is meant when we speak of mental illness. A mentally ill person is someone who continuously makes senseless and illogical assertions and commits correspondingly irrational and illogical actions, or someone who no doubt thinks and acts logically, as it were, but on the basis of emotional and logical presuppositions that nobody but himself considers valid. The layman also usually includes among the mentally ill people who act and think logically but on the level of small children, while in terms of bodily development and age, they are adult human beings. It may be questionable whether the traditional designation "mental illness" is actually meaningful in connection with these cases. But under no circumstances can the sick people with whom psychotherapy is concerned be summarily designated as "mentally ill" or as "mentally ill to a lesser degree." The intelligence quotient of these patients, if measured against that of healthy people within the same walk of life, is in fact frequently higher than the average.

Soul is a designation that encompasses the whole area of individual human existence, so far as it is not of a physical nature. Sickness of soul, therefore, always designates the whole area. The line of demarcation between psychoses (insanity) and psychoneuroses (soul sickness) becomes perceptible only through a consideration of the total man.

Health of soul, sickness of soul, and *insanity* are, therefore, terms indicating the "gradations of the capacity to relate to others."

Hence, the concept of illness espoused by German psychotherapy is toward the basic premise that man is a community-building being. At the same time, community building must here be understood in the specific National Socialist or German sense of an essentially psychic process. An association of stockbrokers is in no sense a community, according to us.

Hence, the German psychotherapeutic concept of illness is "politically" determined, and this means politically in the sense of a definite decision about a worldview.

The term *relationship* implies a connection with something extrapersonal and suprapersonal. Like every other illness, mental illness can be immediately perceived in the impairment of the vital capacities. As with every other sickness, there are those who come by sickness of soul through heredity and those who come by it through accident, and in both forms there exist degrees of intensity, as in the case of every purely physical sickness. The feebleminded, the hereditarily insane, and the constitutional psychopath are to be mentioned among those afflicted with hereditary soul sickness.

Heretofore, when dealing with these patients, it was not customary to regard their capacity for forming psychic relationships as a yardstick to measure the degree of their illness. Yet everything depends on just that.

It is entirely analogous with ethnological research: blond or dark haired, slender or stout, brachycephalic or olichocephalic are of "scientific" interest only if these racial features are not evaluated as expressions. Only when racial difference also signifies a psychic difference is it of vital importance to us. [. . .]

But is the term *sickness of soul*—that is, the lack of psychic relationship—at all applicable to these near human beings? The answer is that it is, but only in consideration of their psychic possibilities, only in reference to their "worldview" can they be viewed as dangerously sick in a *Volk*-biological sense. This means that they are not dangerous because they are unable to count and write but because psychically they cannot relate.

The worldview of the feebleminded embraces his own person and other persons only to the extent they can serve the gratification of the most primitive instincts. Good-natured feebleminded persons attach themselves to those who give them food and drink and a bed. Their relationship to other people is therefore essentially of an egoistic nature, hence not a relation in the true sense.

This psychic inability to relate is even more explicit when viewed as a decisive symptom of severe illness in schizophrenics. There are lesser degrees of congenital feeblemindedness that can be so designated, not because the patient can count up to twenty instead of up to five, but because some beginnings of true psychic relationship are still at hand—that is, because the patient is still capable of being educated instead of merely drilled. The schizophrenic, on the other hand, is characterized by a total absence of a psychic capacity to relate. The world that he views and perceives is exclusively a dream world. Other persons may enter this dream world in speaking and acting roles, as they may in the normal dream of a healthy individual. But this does not yet constitute a true psychic relationship to real human beings. The schizophrenic, for instance, does not talk to someone who visits him—he talks to an apparition of unknown origin that may perhaps have been stimulated by the visit or that may have been created in his mind purely by accident and entirely independent of the visit. The schizophrenic seems to talk only to his visitor, if he speaks at all. And he may also simultaneously converse with others who are not present, such as someone long dead, or with fabulous beings that he sees.

The diseased state of mind of the constitutional psychopath is of the same kind, if not of the same degree. In contrast to schizophrenics and feebleminded persons, the psychopath is often entirely capable of truly perceiving the actual world—persons and situations. The psychopath is frequently not lacking in intelligence. Nor is his physical condition decisive. There are both physically strong and physically weak psychopaths.

Again the absence of psychic relationship to others is the decisive and sociologically important symptom of the sickness. The psychopath is the born egoist. Measured by the degree of his sickness, the psychopath, despite his intellectual endowment, is more closely related to the schizophrenic than is the good-natured half-wit. Only to a very inadequate extent is the psychopath capable of a true loving relationship of real passion, of true dedication. The talented psychopath, from a *Volk*-biological point of view, is infinitely more dangerous than the obvious severely mentally ill person, or the feebleminded person, or the psychotic. The psychopath is incapable of a true bond with a symbol, with a vital happening. But his talents may enable him to simulate such a bond.

An untalented psychopath, a liar who believes his own lies, may also believe that he has a relationship with others but only as long as he is not called upon to serve such a bond, as long as he can follow his own egoism, his ambition and desire for power.

This does not mean that ambition and desire for power should fundamentally be designated as psychopathic. They can be thoroughly manly virtues. It is a question of emphasis; the key word is *only*. *Only* ambition, *only* desire for power are the distinguishing marks of the psychopath.

For a normal human being, this distinction, once he has grasped its importance, is not difficult to make since it is not an abstract scientific matter but an emotional, spontaneous expression of his ethical capacity. At the same time, for the healthy and nonsentimental human being, there can be no doubt that the successes of the pathological egoism that marks the psychopath (just as *sit venia verbo* the successes of psychopathological nations) are only apparent. There is no injustice in the world. The final accounting always balances out if one never loses sight of the realm of the soul. In the life of the individual, as in the life of whole peoples, the final fate is the immediate expression of the attitude of psychic engagement, even if, from a materialistic point of view, the final accounting should not balance out. Here again, men differ along philosophical and political lines—namely, between those who can experience the defeat of a hero as a victory and those who are not capable of doing so. Or expressed in another way, there is a fulfillment of life, but never a gratification of egoism. Happiness is necessarily attainable on the level of egoistic gratification, since it is possible to satisfy everything but egoism itself.

Of necessity, therefore—and as the expression of an implacable inner-worldly justice—the liberalistic-materialistic worldview, with its goal of "the greatest happiness for the greatest possible number," ended in the deepest dissatisfaction, in the inferno of the deepest sickness of our people's soul.

The Third Reich has inscribed not happiness on its banners, but virtue . . . [. . .]

The road of Jung looks forward. Freud asks, whence? Jung asks, whither? Freud is the scientist, only the scientist; Jung is an ethicist. One could also call him a seer, in the deepest and most reverent sense of the word. Jung is the poet among psychologists. His subconscious is full of living forms with whom one speaks and consorts like human beings, who can give counsel and warning, with whom one tries to be on a good footing because otherwise they may become "angry." Jung's psychology is a demonology. The essence of a demon is contained in its name. Primordial wisdom has it that one can disarm a demon, even make a servant of him, if one knows his name.

This is nothing but the process of perception, which heals like any other form of cognition. While the true magician knows that his forms are always his forms, even if occasionally they overwhelm him, it can still happen to the sorcerer's apprentice that he seriously believes he can lead the German you to Tao, while we are satisfied with the choral music from the carillon of the Potsdam Garrison Church: "Always practice fidelity and honesty!"

Freudian psychology incorporates all the advantages and dangers of the Jewish spirit; Jungian psychology, all those of the Germanic soul.

Freud is atheistic; Jung, not in terms of doctrine but in terms of attitude, is marked by a Catholic piety . . .

Perception is courageous, active, clear-eyed self-responsibility—an attitude that accepts personal responsibility even for those matters for which the individual human being himself is not responsible. This in the face of the biblical saying, "Man is wicked from youth," or in the face of personal, undeserved calamity.

In such circumstances, the "ego" and the unconscious are not two different entities; they are one as horse and rider are one when the rider truly knows and understands his horse, can tell him what he wants him to do, and when the horse has understood that he has a good rider.

It is, therefore, not necessary to try to explain that mind and soul do not have to be enemies or that the destiny of man is his intellectuality, a progressive cerebration. The man who is condemned to die is mistaken if he assumes that the world is coming to an end.

We have described personality as a configuration of actualized possibilities. We can add here that . . . there may be individuals who not only have lived a full, well-rounded life, but also have been gifted with perception: they are the men whom we call the true leaders of the people, the thinkers, poets, and politicians.

176

HERBERT RUDOLF

Interview with Prof. Dr. Dr. M. H. Göring

Early Childhood Experiences Determine Development Later in Life

First published as "Auch die ersten Kindheitseinflüsse bestimmen die Lebensgestaltung," in *Völkischer Beobachter,* 14 May 1939.

The effects of emotional suffering on the body—improper child rearing can even cause sickness.

Two and a half years ago, the German Institute for Psychological Research and Psychotherapy, with its headquarters in the Budapester Straße in Berlin, began its work under the directorship of Prof. Dr. M. H. Göring, who recently celebrated his sixtieth birthday. He is credited with developing the only research institute of its kind throughout the world. Operating under the auspices of the German Office of Public Health, the institute provides an important public health service to the *Volk*.

In this interview [with Herbert Rudolf], Prof. Dr. Göring offered interesting insights into the work of modern psychology. He not only spoke about the *ideological* moorings of a science that slowly but surely thoroughly established itself as a *German* form of *psychotherapy,* but also elaborated extensively on the root causes of various forms of neuroses that are actually quite prevalent in the population and that must be seen as disorders of the unconscious psychology of the soul and in the context of early childhood education and rearing practices.

The psychotherapeutic institute sees its mission not only as a research and teaching institute but also [as] an outpatient clinic for the treatment of neuroses. The twenty instructors, as well as the administration, all work on a volunteer basis. Treatment is offered to the poor free of charge or at reduced fees, just enough to cover maintenance costs for the institute.

What Are Neuroses?

Neuroses are disorders of the unconscious psychology of the soul. Affected persons are hindered in their ability to function in varying degrees, depending on the severity of affliction.

Neuroses are caused either by improper rearing or various other unfavorable environmental influences. With the exception of a few extremely mild neuroses, in many instances, they present extraordinary difficulties, not only for those affected by them but, perhaps to an even greater degree, to their environment. But the results of experiments and clinical practice have also produced a more than voluminous body of evidence pointing to the astonishing influences the psyche can have on the body. The so-called organ neuroses, which afflict the heart or gastric organs, can lead to professional incapacitation, as can the severe psychological disorders. But even the mild cases of this form present diminished capacity in those afflicted. Since the number of neurotics now exceeds that of cancer and tuberculosis patients, it should be quite clear how utterly essential the need to combat psychological ailments is.

Worldview and Psychology

As mentioned above, the institute in question is also committed to research, whereby the search for solutions has become one of the fundamental concerns. The question is one of how it came to be that psychoanalysis, an utterly contemporary field of modern medicine, could have had such a corrosive impact at one time. Without a doubt, the church has made grave mistakes in matters of child rearing and public education. With its repression of all things sexual, it ultimately paves the way for Jews to infiltrate the field of psychoanalysis. And ever since Freud, [the field] has also been a domain reserved almost exclusively for Jewish doctors. It would have been a thing of impossibility for a Jew like Freud to have had any understanding of the unconscious; that is why he had to come up with some sort of strictly scientific scheme to frame his argument. But the German has no need for such explanations. And that is why, already decades ago, there was a purely instinctive rejection among Germans of Freud's doctrine, which is based solely on the development of the sexual apparatus. We have Leibniz to thank for our knowledge of the forces lying dormant in the unconscious; and the physician [Carl Gustav] Carus, Goethe's friend; and [Baron Ernst von] Feuchtersleben, who wrote a hundred years ago in his slim volume *On the Diathesis of the Soul* [*Zur Diätetik der Seele*], "The basis for life is the unconscious, the creative forces of emotion and of the imagination."

Clearly, the Jews were able to cultivate their corrosive influences in the fertile soil of the soul especially well in precisely this profession. For the Jews, psychotherapy became a business, the putrefaction of the soul an inevitability that required an antidotal purification as the next step. But today psychotherapy has established itself as a thoroughly German form of psychoanalysis.

Research and the Cure

Since, as we have seen, neuroses are always psychological in origin, they obviously cannot be treated with sedatives. But the ability to determine the cause requires a great deal of schooling and a certain degree of intuitive observational talent. Not until we have identified the root cause can we succeed in our efforts to restore full capacity of performance. Psychoanalytic treatment is long and tedious. The very opening of the unconscious may itself be an effective measure in combating whatever underlying neurosis is present. Professor Göring attributes no significant impact on the cure to the patient's fixation of will directly on the disorder. And yet, there must indeed be a will to return to good health and to allow for the unconscious to surface, and the basic predisposition of good character must, of course, be present in the patient for any cure of neuroses to occur. Dreams—which of course originate in the unconscious—can convey substantial clues in penetrating the depths of the unconscious. Most dreams, of course, represent an obscure picture that must first be interpreted through a maze of associations and a web of ideas. The causes of a neurosis can be identified with the help of dreams.

Now that we have determined that the greater part of neuroses can be traced to some flaw in rearing and education, we must apply particularly intense interest to prevention.

Childhood Experiences Determine Development Later in Life

With the severe damages that can be caused by neurosis and lead to a diminishment in capacity, it is particularly important to begin preventative treatment already in early childhood. [. . .] Experience has shown that the educational influences of the first eight years of life exert a decisive effect on the development of the human adult and his perspective on life. [. . .]

The role of the analyst is essential in circumventing errors in early childhood development. It is extraordinarily important that he not only make himself available to the child when symptoms are acute but that he be there to offer counsel at all times. In any case, the family physician should be able to determine on the basis of his overall assessment of the psychological and physical condition how much treatment the child is able to undergo.

A large portion of early childhood development mistakes are made already in infancy. A young mother must be aware of the fact that she should never pick up her child unless it is wet and needs changing or is in pain. Every manner of "mothering" showered on a child by elderly aunties can lead to later missteps. And any mother must also be aware of how much her children can take. She should feel free to take them to their maximum tolerable limit. If she is unsure what these limits are, the family physician may be able to help determine what they are. If a two-year-old child falls down inside the house, it won't cry and will get back up without the mother's help. But if the child falls down outside and lands in a patch of burning nettle, the mother will spring to his aid because of course a two-year-old infant is in dire need of assistance in that situation, and it provides the opportunity for it to experience his mother's love—which cannot be expressed through pampering and pandering to the child's needs.

"You're Not Old Enough for That!"

It is extraordinarily important that parents seek medical advice from their physician in matters of sex education. This should become a firmly fixed educational principle applied to every question pertaining to early childhood development and never something that is dismissed with such platitudes as "you're not old enough for that!" Sooner or later, any child who starts asking the question is going to satisfy his need for an answer one way or another. But whether or not he is steered along the right track then becomes a question of considerable debate. In any case, serious questions posed by children that remain unanswered by parents tend to weaken the relationship of trust between them.

The interest of public hygiene and health [*Volksgesundheit*] is greatly served by the work of the family physician who makes regular house visits, even when there is no immediate ailment to be treated. It is absolutely essential that the physician also receive psychotherapeutic training so that he is able to support the parents (and mothers especially) with his advice and services—providing for monitoring not only the physical development of the child but also for its psychological development. This is of particular import to preventative therapies. The family physician should be entitled to receive a fixed fee from the public health insurance agency. And if this should lead to an expansion of the demands placed on the medical profession, that should be considered one of the profession's finest moments.

For what could possibly be more satisfying than preventing illness, pain, and suffering and, with comprehensive care, to make a substantial contribution to the cultivation of a healthy generation of Germans?

177

The Case of Edith Jacobsohn

Indictment and Commentaries

Indictment issued on 5 December 1935. Commentaries written in 1936. Published in *"Here Life Goes On in a Most Peculiar Way . . ."—Psychoanalysis before and after 1933,* edited by Karen Brecht, Hella Ehlers, and Christine Trollope (Hamburg: Kellner Verlag, 1985), 111.

Office of the General Prosecutor of the Appellate Court
Berlin, December 5, 1935
Top Secret! Arrest! [. . .]
Indictment:
The neurologist Dr. Edith Jacobsohn, born September 10th, 1897 in Haynau (County of Goldberg), currently residing in Berlin-Wilmersdorf, Zähringer Strasse 3a, single; taken into temporary custody on October 24th, 1935; being held for interrogation in this matter at the Berlin-Moabit prison facility,
—extract from the criminal record—

> is charged with having participated in preparations, alone and with others, for the treasonous attempt to violate the constitution of the Reich through the use of force, whereby motive for the crime was to secure and sustain organizational cohesion in preparation for an act of high treason.

Dr. Anne Buchholtz

Appeal to All International Psycho-Analysts!

It has been eight months since Dr. Edith Jacobsohn was arrested by the secret state police in Berlin!

For the past eight months, Dr. Edith Jacobsohn has been sitting in prison and has yet been given a trial!

At the beginning of this tragic occurrence, the international Psycho-Analysts demonstrated interest and willingness to help. Sheer indolence and bad advice from that timid Berliner Gruppe kept them from undertaking any concrete measures.

I ask every analyst to take a long hard look at the facts:

The Berliner Gruppe, under the direction of von Boehm and Müller, had been *gleichgeschaltet* [consolidated—Eds.] and identified with National Socialism, despite the fact that the founders of the Psycho-Analysis they now practice were Jews, as are most of their active practitioners. Are we to allow the fear-ridden atmosphere around the Berliner Gruppe to result in Edith Jacobsohn having to sacrifice perhaps years of her life and her freedom?

Every analyst is hereby requested to reflect for but a half-an-hour on the conditions in a German prison.

With an urgent appeal on behalf of Edith Jacobsohn,
Anne Buchholtz

Ernest Jones

Letter to Anne Buchholtz, June 18th, 1936

Dear Dr. Buchholtz,

I cannot find that your action in appealing to the members of the International Psycho-Analytical Association to bring pressure to bear via me was a very friendly one. Had you done me the courtesy of first notifying me of your intention, I should have had the opportunity of correcting some serious misstatements in your *Aufruf*.

1. It is not true, as you imply, that international analysts showed interest and willingness to help only at the beginning of this tragic occurrence. You are evidently uninformed about what they are still showing.

2. It is not true that we have been kept back from concrete action by any advice on the part of the "timid Berliner Gruppe."

When I journeyed to Berlin in connection with the Edith Jacobsohn case, I interviewed her own lawyer and friends. We agreed on a plan of campaign best calculated to serve her interests, which we all have at heart. If you have any definite proposals for furthering these interests in any other way, there are many people who would be grateful to listen to them. But, speaking for all those whom I have consulted, I feel sure that any attempt at a publicity campaign in the Press would greatly worsen her chance of freedom and would seriously injure her interests at a time with they are hanging in the balance.

I greatly sympathize with you in your difficulty in supporting the thought of her unhappy position. I share the same difficulty myself, but am nevertheless determined not to ease my feelings at the expense of her interests.

Yours sincerely,
Ernest Jones

178

ERNEST JONES

Letter to Anna Freud

Written on 2 December 1935. Archives of the British Psycho-Analytical Society, London. Published in *"Here Life Goes On in a Most Peculiar Way . . . "—Psychoanalysis before and after 1933,* edited by Karen Brecht, Hella Ehlers, and Christine Trollope (Hamburg: Kellner Verlag, 1985), 114–15.

Dear Anna, [. . .]

Ad. Edith Jacobsohn: She is well treated and has her food at choice from a restaurant, can read and write everything and receive visits. I greatly wanted to visit her myself, but this would have meant staying two days longer in Berlin. The *Stadtsanwalt* [*sic;* prosecuting attorney—Eds.] has decided that all the other people concerned are to be charged with high treason before a Berlin court of law, i.e., not the severest forms, which go to Leipzig. Although he has read the *Akten* [files], he has not yet decided whether there is enough evidence to make it worthwhile to charge her as well. If not, she will be set free in a few days' time. There would then be a considerable probability of the Gestapo educating her in a concentration camp, but still a greater probability that English influence would be able to get her out of it in a few days. It would be evidently wrong to try to use any influence in a case as yet undecided that is in the hands of proper judicial authorities, i.e., no longer the Gestapo. Kussmann has purposely refrained from asking for the *Akten* and therefore knows little about the details. He has heard nothing about any question of patients (though that may of course be included), but only that she lent her rooms for meeting of politically underground people. It seems unlikely that this can be anything very serious unless she is quite crazy.

The essential point of the other business proceeds psychologically from this case, which had so shattered [Felix] Boehm's inner self-confidence that he can no longer rely on his judgment.[1] He is a man with very little actual anxiety, belonging to what I have described somewhere as an anxiety character with the anxiety bound in the character traits. In my opinion, such a case has to be dealt with by firm exhortation rather than by reassurance, and he reacts very well to such treatment.

Apart from this, the only other real matter was an increasing internal dissension of the groups in respect of the constant stream of demands, warnings, threats, etc. that constantly assail the unhappy people. These proceed in a steady stream from the most varied sources, from the policeman at the corner up to the *Kultusministerium* [Ministry of Culture], and it is naturally very hard for them to keep a cool judgment and estimate accurately the relative value to be attached to each incoming stimulus.

There were three questions before the Society. Two of them were decided on the lines of my advice, the third not. Two of them would have been decided in the same way had I not been there, but my presence was decisive in one question. I feel it was well worthwhile my going, not only for this reason, but also from the general reassurance that firmness from outside can give, and from the extensive insight I got into the actual problems and personalities. The first question was whether to dissolve the Society altogether. Only a minority was in favor of this, [Gustav Hans] Graber, curiously enough, being among them. The second question was whether to give up the affiliation of the Society with the I.P.V. [International Psychoanalytic Association]. Boehm and many others were strongly in favor of this (I must tell you why in another letter), [Carl] Müller-Braunschweig and [Harald] Schultz-Hencke being against it. I think my voice was decisive in this matter and I also laid down very firmly and strongly in definite recommendation about the general principles that I thought should guide their actions and decisions in regard to the outer world. On the third point, that of expelling the Jews, I was unsuccessful. The Society was unanimous in the matter and it was unfortunate that I used up so much energy about it, because one diminishes one's influence if one uses energy in a hopeless cause. I would not have done so had I known the facts. On the previous evening, there had been little mention of this question, it being left to my interview with the Jews, and also because on the day before a unanimous conclusion had been come to by both the Jews and Gentiles together that they were to resign at once, so that the matter was regarded as settled and not one about which to ask my opinion. Upon hearing that I was coming, however, the Jews made a complete volte face and presented me with some very good arguments about why the present moment would be a very inopportune time for such an action. I could also see certain dangers it might have for the Society itself, i.e., implying an admission that the alleged ideological world of psychoanalysis, contradicting the Nazi *Weltanschauung,* was identical with a Jewish ideology. So I proceeded to the General Meeting and put the case strongly, evidently to the great astonishment of the Jews, who thought the question had been settled. This was a part of bad staff-work on Boehm's part, who was present at my interview with the Jews and neither asked them the meaning of their change of opinion nor informed me that there had been such a change. Altogether I did not think very much of Boehm as a leader. He has neither the personality needed to manage a group nor a sufficiently quick grasp of the essentials of the strategic situation. Not that I know of anyone better who could replace him at the moment. I think also that there is a small amount of truth in the old accusation against him that whenever he is frightened, he tends to go to the authorities and suggest indirectly to them questions to which, from their side, they can only give one answer. He very indignantly denies this on every occasion, nor is the accusation by any means always true. It is also often exaggerated. Müller-Braunschweig is busy coquetting with the idea of combining a philosophy of psychoanalysis with a quasi-theological conception of National Socialist ideology, and you can imagine that this is a very busy occupation. No doubt he will proceed further along these lines, and he is definitely anti-Semitic, which Boehm is certainly not. Schultz-Hencke, whom you know all about, has an increasingly prominent voice in the society and is a good speaker. Curiously enough, he is often on the right side, and the only trouble about him is that the members are apt to exaggerate his external importance.

I suppose most of the Jews will now emigrate. Of the younger ones, Eva Rosenfeld struck me as outstanding and made a very favorable impression on me. Of the older ones, I liked all except Frau [Therese] Benedek, who I do not think is really sincere. Unfortunately, she has a considerable influence on the others.

I think that is the gist of the matter, anyhow all I have time to write at the moment.

Yours always,
Ernest Jones

Note

1. Felix Julius Boehm (1881–1958). German physician, a specialist in neurological and mood disorders, psychoanalyst and president of the German Psychoanalytic Association. Boehm was an "Aryan" member of the psychoanalytic community during the Nazi era.

179

DR. FRITZ BLEIBER

Siegmund [*sic*] Freud and Psychoanalysis

First published as "Siegmund [*sic*] Freud und die Psychoanalyse," in *Mitteilungen über die Judenfrage*, 44/45, 14 November 1939, 4–6.

Not long ago, Siegmund [sic] *Freud died in England. For this reason, we are presenting this portrait of the core features of his teachings, which is of particular interest as a display of a typically Jewish way of thinking.*[1]

These days—thank God!—the situation is such that your average thirty-year-old knows the name Siegmund Freud only from secondhand reports and rumor, and anyone under thirty rarely knows that much. And yet this Jew has been diligently engaged in efforts to secure for himself a position of conquest in the cultural life of nations, from the years following the November Revolution until the seizure of power, and as far as influence outside Germany's territorial bounds is concerned, has managed to extend his influence into more recent years. And the only reason he could succeed can be traced to the profound absence of instinct and helplessness of this period in which such vast sectors had been completely devastated in the wake of the Great War.

Before we present the specifically Jewish doctrine in which psychoanalysis is housed, especially in light of the significance of the fields of scientific endeavor that have been lured into its sphere of influence—pedagogy, sociology, ethnology—we think it important to provide a brief overview of the major themes that were the focus of Freud's investigation and, as we shall see, that were ideally suited to the purpose of obscuring the emotion and thought of broad sectors of the population and plunging them into a downward spiral of shabbiness.

First and foremost, there is the interpretation of dreams, which contends that dreams are coherent, interpretable phenomena. But Freud's basic assumption from the outset is that what a person experiences in a dream, or what is said about it afterward, does not necessarily reveal the true meaning of the dream but that its real meaning can be revealed only through interpretive analysis.

Such an interpretation is then constructed on the basis of so-called free association, which means that the psychoanalyst plucks certain elements from the dream narrative and pulls them together by establishing connections according to the rules of his secret doctrine to create a whole that then supposedly represents the real background and meaning of the dream. It is revealing to note here that a process of this nature flies scornfully in the face of every sense of sound scientific inquiry and necessarily leads to utterly incoherent results. However, two points strike us as being exquisitely crucial: first of all, the criticism expressed toward psychoanalysis by the patients themselves—one that is often enough passed off as inconsequential—about having a foreign interpretation, namely that of the analyst who is usually Jewish, foisted upon them as the only meaningful interpretation of their dreams; in the second place, the fact that the interpretation is formulated with the aid of symbols that are derived from the sphere of sexuality. In the psychoanalyst's catalog of symbols, there is nothing that does not have its correlation in some male or female private parts or that does not allude to them in some way, as is the case with the prominent role played by the realm of sexuality within psychoanalysis generally, which we will address shortly. However, aside from that, Freud's method of dream interpretation as briefly outlined here is so monstrous, if you bear in mind the sum of unknown and inexplicable factors underlying every dream, that to describe it as a swindle or an act of charlatanism would be an understatement applicable to only the least of its characteristics.

The situation is not much different in the case of Freud's second "discovery," the doctrine of the so-called parapraxis. What is meant by "parapraxis" are those everyday slips of the tongue, of the pen, of misplacing things to which psychoanalysis always seeks to attach some hidden motive. Here, too, the explanations that seem obvious as the light of day—so, for example, simple exhaustion or perhaps a tendency that goes with the territory of a certain profession (the absentminded professor), are patently denied and the utterly arbitrary assumption is unscrupulously made that the person *intended* the "slip" of the tongue or of the pen. Because even if we were to presume that there is nothing arbitrary about the life of the psyche, this premise neither allows us to conclude that a parapraxis of this nature is caused by one single thing alone nor that it was intentional, nor does it substantiate the notion that there is only one way to reveal its causes.

This aforesaid hypothesis, the notion that there is as little room for coincidence in the psychological as there is in the physical, and that all our ideas, drives, and instincts can be traced to factors that stand in a causal nexus, brings us to the third pillar upon which the house of Freudian doctrine rests, namely, the theory of neuroses. Basically, what it boils down to here is the thesis that man is able to repress thoughts that are so painful he believes he will not be able to stand them. The result of this repression, though, is a character change within the individual. If such a conclusion seems nothing if not brave when applied to neurotics, which of course involves a fundamental medical issue we will not elaborate on here, it seems utterly contrived as soon as it is applied to the psyche of the normal human being. What we are dealing with here is an utterly inadequate transfer of symptoms of anxiety that are undoubtedly present in a psychologically disturbed individual onto the psychological landscape of a healthy individual—with the aim of fomenting confusion and unrest and to generate a consciousness of helplessness and the need to be released from the "illness."

These thoroughly corrupt thought processes of psychoanalysis find their most flagrant expression in the notion of pansexuality and its expressed attempt to base the whole psychological life of the human being in sexual desire or lack thereof. Very early on, Freud began conducting extensive research into sexual deviance—an already established "field of inquiry," as it were—and yet, what is far more disturbing and detrimental is that his research was not restricted to simply identifying sexual deviations, but rather these results were taken as the foundation for knowledge into the workings of a normal sexual life.

The most glaring index of the incoherence of this method is the fact that the explicit overall basic premise underlying research into psychological processes is that, since human psychology is quantifiable and hence knowable through research, the foundation for all knowledge thereof is gleaned from comparisons between normal and pathological processes. However, and we shall now proceed to shed light on what is typically Jewish about the whole movement, the psychoanalyst is not at all concerned with dissecting and outlining the workings of psychological processes. This may have been what the non-Jewish [Josef] Breuer vaguely had in mind as a research goal when he, Freud's immediate predecessor and his colleague, set himself to the task of putting together the cornerstones for an analytic science of psychology. Freud's doctrine is another matter altogether—one that is not concerned in the least with "higher" aims. It is concerned with planning the premeditated annihilation of civilized values and sensitivities and to plunge the nations [*Völker*] of the world, who just barely escaped the clutches of shallow materialism last century, back into the depths of an abyss—depths from which a return would require nothing short of a miracle. Has there ever been, in the whole history of humanity, one single school of teachings that is more abhorrent, more abrasive and corrupt than Freud's, which ropes in the unsuspecting and drives the undecided to despair? We suggest that the answer to that question is an emphatic no!

In this system, which takes perversion as the basis for its deductions by wrenching every form of organic life from the natural order of things and twisting it, with hairsplitting, sophistic precision, into the opposite of what it is, in this system, the system of the Jew Freud, we see the despicable, evil grin on the face of the whole race [*Volk*] to which he belongs. This involves the psychological annihilation of the host peoples. The fact that a complete erosion of morality necessarily plays a substantial role in a world conspiracy of this nature is not likely to be something we need to point out to readers of this publication. At the same time, several vicissitudes peculiar to the weapon that is psychoanalysis merit mention here. What is genuinely Talmudic in this system is the way that it assigns significance to individual actions and events, even in part. Just as any rabbinical candidate is able to twist and turn a passage from the Torah any which way until he has extrapolated some sort of "hidden" meaning from it, so, too, does the psychoanalyst—heedless of any law of logic and dissecting individual thoughts and actions into essentially nonsensical parts that have meaning only in relation to his secret catalog of symbols—wring and wrangle his "material" into place until the image that confirms his interpretation springs to life. In his dogmatic fanaticism—a fanaticism that is in itself typically Jewish in that it is fanatic about the form, not about the content—he goes so far as to reject a priori any alternative answer to the mystery of psychological experience, which poses a wide array of questions by its very nature.

Indeed, any patient seeking a cure in the house of Freud will only then be able to so much as consider any prospect for healing once he has declared himself willing to first plaster himself to a worldview that is utterly alien to him, one that is utterly uncanny to him with the aura of magical thinking that surrounds it.

We can see then, as already outlined above in our treatment of the theoretical foundations of psychoanalysis, that the primary concern of psychoanalysis is not to bring a certain clinical method into circulation, but rather to *break down human beings before they even begin* so that, if necessary, they can then be "healed." No wonder that the frail, weak-willed, and sick types are the ones who fell pray to the psychoanalysis plague in particularly high numbers. The destructive spirit of this new "doctrine of salvation" is overtly apparent in its assessment of human nature in general. Even the crassest materialism seems idealistic by comparison to the nadir that is reached in this assessment of the nature of the human being; there have always been doctrines that have placed at the forefront of consideration man's descent from animals and the fact that human and animal drives are of the same species of drive. Freud, on the other hand, teaches not only that man, an animal blessed with the power of reason, is a higher species of animal. He also contends that man must see sickness, the degenerate, his own inferior subhumanity [*Untermenschentum*] as being at the very root of his being—and more horrifying than even this—that he must adjust his position in life with regard to his family and his surroundings accordingly.

One of the great contributions of the famous racial researcher H. K. Günther is the revelation that feelings of guilt are the quintessential emanation of the Jewish racial soul. This consciousness of sin that has become increasingly widespread among the Jews ever since the time of Nehemiah has found palpable expression through Siegmund Freud: just one look at him tells us it is written all over his face. When he and his movement were described as a slave revolt of amorality—a statement made, incidentally by one of his racial comrades (Egon Friedell)—then there is little more we have to add.

Note

1. While Freud was given the name "Siegmund" at birth, he chose the spelling "Sigmund," because "Siegmund" was the name given to the stock Jew in anti-Semitic jokes of the time. This "misspelling" echoes that anti-Semitic tradition.—Eds.

180

C. G. JUNG

The State of Psychotherapy Today

Written in 1934. First published in *Civilization in Transition,* vol. 10 of *The Collected Works of C. G. Jung,* edited by Gerhard Adler, translated by R. F. C. Hull (Princeton, N.J.: Princeton University Press, 1964), 166, 167.

The Jewish race as a whole—at least this is my experience—possesses an unconscious that can be compared with the "Aryan" only with reserve. Creative individuals apart, the average Jew is far too conscious and differentiated to go about pregnant with the tensions of unborn futures. The "Aryan" unconscious has a higher potential than the Jewish; that is, both the advantage and the disadvantage of youthfulness not yet fully weaned from barbarism. In my opinion, it has been a grave error in medical psychology up till now to apply Jewish categories—which are not even binding on all Jews—indiscriminately to Germanic and Slavic Christendom. Because of this, the most precious secret of the Germanic peoples—their creative and intuitive depth of soul—has been explained as a morass of banal infantilism, while my own warning voice has for decades been suspected of anti-Semitism. This suspicion emanated from Freud. He did not understand the Germanic psyche any more than did his Germanic followers. Has the formidable phenomenon of National Socialism, on which the whole world gazes with astonished eyes, taught them better? Where was that unparalleled tension and energy while as yet no National Socialism existed? Deep in the Germanic psyche, in a pit that is anything but a garbage bin of unrealizable infantile wishes and unresolved family resentments. A movement that grips a whole nation must have matured in every individual as well. That is why I say that the Germanic unconscious contains tensions and potentialities that medical psychology must consider in its evaluation of the unconscious. Its business is not with neuroses, but with human beings—that, in fact, is the grand privilege of medical psychology—to treat the whole man and not an artificially segregated function. And that is why its scope must be widened to reveal to the physician's gaze—not just the pathological aberrations of a disturbed psychic development, but also the creative powers of the psyche laboring at the future; not just a dreary fragment, but a meaningful whole.

181

URSULA VON KARDORFF

Suicide and Deportation

Written 3 March 1943. Published in *Berliner Aufzeichnungen* (Munich: Deutscher Taschenbuch Verlag, 1981), 37–39.

Frau Liebermann is dead. They actually came in here with a stretcher to pick up the eighty-five-year old woman for transport to Poland. The moment they came for her, she took Veronal and died a day later at the Jewish hospital without ever having regained consciousness. What abominable manner of evil is at work here, and why has it chosen our people of all peoples as its focus? What manner of change has allowed an otherwise mostly amicable and compassionate type of people to be transformed into such servants of Satan? It happens as a matter of coldly bureaucratic procedure where individuals easily fall through the cracks; that we have become wood ticks that have infested the body of the nation [*Volkskörper*] and thus have suddenly become a part of it.

The stage director Büssy told me today as we were moving that the blue-collar working women had complained loudly and unanimously about the Jewish transports. Fully armed SS men with raised bayonets firmly planted on their shoulders and steel helmets on their heads marched in and hauled these wretched souls from their apartment houses. Old women, children, petrified men—all were loaded onto trucks and whisked away. "Just leave the old women alone!" the crowd screamed. "Now will you get back to the front where you belong!" In the end, a new cordon of SS came in to disperse the protesters, who were otherwise unharmed.

You never saw anything like that in our neighborhood. Here, the Jews are hauled out at night. Were it not for my friend Bärchen, who has worked tirelessly to care for the Jewish family in her building, I wouldn't have a clue about what was happening. How quickly we all got used to the sight of the Jewish star.

Most of us responded with utter indifference, like the intern who recently said, "Why should I worry about the Jews? All I can think about is my brother in Rshew; nothing else matters to me." I think the common people are behaving more decently than the so-called intellectuals or pseudointellectuals. The story of a worker who gave up his seat to a Jewish woman wearing the star: "Have a seat, you ol' falling star, you!" and, when a nearby registered member of the party complained, he continued, "Hey, bub, where I plunk my ass is my business, and mine alone!"

Yesterday, there was a heavy air raid. Not far from here, in the Augsburg Street, there was a roof truss burning. People formed a human chain with water buckets. Mama and I helped. When we came home, exhausted, we were greeted by Papa standing there in his pajamas with a candle in his hand because the power had gone out and a copy of Proust's novel, *À la recherche du temps perdu,* tucked beneath his arm. Completely baffled, he asked us why on earth we had helped put out the fire. "Leave it to the AGP [?] to do," he said. He hates the party so much he deliberately refuses to use the party acronym NSDAP. I had to laugh. Today we know that there were 1,700 separate fires; the Prager Platz, not far from here, is completely destroyed. The Raths lost everything, even the photograph of the murdered Ernst and their fallen son. Throughout the city of Berlin, the rumor spread that this attack was in retaliation for the roundup of Jews.

182

DR. LEONARD REITBERGER

On the Psychology of Suicide

First published as "Zur Psychologie des Selbstmordes," in *Archiv für Kriminologie* 1–2 (January/February 1944): 8–11.

Any moderately inquisitive, run-of-the-mill backwoods judge knows a little something about suicide. So, for example, [he knows] that twice as many men commit suicide as women, which means that the suspicion of murder is double in cases of the dead women. But this does not apply when there is an existing connection between the individual's sex life and the death, for statisticians have calculated that a fifth of all female suicides are committed by pregnant women and that about a third have chosen to take their own lives either before, during, or directly while menstruating. We also know that men are more inclined to use a gun or a noose and women more inclined to take poison or drown themselves. This means that every time a woman dies of gunshot wounds, suspicion of murder is ten times greater than in the case of a man. What is more, we know that there are certain times of day and year that are typical in suicide cases: the early morning hours and the first months of spring are particularly popular times for suicide. On the other hand, suicides are more infrequent during the winter months and the noon hours. Suicide notes, whether filled with eloquent farewells or candid adieus to the world, provide us with valuable clues, especially if they can be verified as perfectly authentic, so, for example, if they tend to concern themselves with casual asides known to be preferences of their author or in the overall composition clearly reveal whose hand and disposition may have penned them. It is a foregone conclusion, of course, that we are particularly concerned with the specific circumstances allegedly surrounding the death—that is, with the physical condition of the body and any wounds or injuries. We could, if we wanted to swallow a pack of lies, ask the immediate family about possible motives; increasingly, we prefer to let the facts speak for themselves, gleaned from things that may not always be unequivocal but that are not deliberately deceptive.

These are some valuable basic facts that have been gleaned from statistics and are firmly rooted in many years of observing international trends. To some degree, they can act as indicators pointing the practitioner examining suspicious deaths in the right direction. Often enough, he still ends up being on the wrong track. Here is yet another example of the fact that theory is always fuzzy and that, much as we do not care to admit it, our business is not as much a handicraft as it is a science whose significance is often acknowledged only when one's own personal affairs are involved. Then, of course, it dawns on you: why don't those criminologists finally come out with it and admit that this is undeniably a case of murder? Or, you'd have to be able to prove that here was a mental disorder that prevented the exercise of free will and is therefore exempt from the stipulations of Section 169 of the German Compulsory Insurance Law. So it would be good if we could proceed on the basis of these established guidelines as a rule of thumb and make a precise determination: homicide or suicide?

> That afternoon, a young woman heated up the oven, pouring gasoline and kerosene on it to accelerate the fire, then crawled into the oven herself to be roasted alive.
>
> That was a few years ago, but it wasn't in early spring nor was it in the early morning hours, and this manner of death certainly can't have been painless. One might even describe it as unimaginable, and still, it is unequivocally a suicide—[borne out by] the autopsy report as well as the impeccable results of the investigations—but there could be a case in which the evidence is not as conclusive, and then what?
>
> A man in his midthirties was apprehended by the constable one winter evening on suspicion of vagrancy. Because the prison was located so far away, he spent the night in a holding cell at the station. The bird flew the coop sometime in the morning. The constable entered the premises, where he received notice that the escapee, who was aided by at least one individual in his prison break, had suddenly just died. There he was, lying in the bed, laid out in his Sunday best, holding a rosary in his folded hands. He even gave himself a fresh shave in preparation for his final journey. But there was a coffee cup on the windowsill with a suspicious sediment of grounds, there was a trace of it in his stomach, and he had a vial in his pocket. There was no evidence of murder, and the investigations ultimately ruled it a suicide.
>
> Here, too, a case that is the exception to the rule: a man and poison! Nor was it in early spring, though it did occur in the early morning hours!
>
> This November, a woman with her head wrapped in a scarf rang the bell at the local constable's office; when she removed the scarf, a horrific scene was revealed: she had been scalped. Then she told her story: she had stuck her head in a sewing machine with the intent of committing suicide—but it didn't work. After a while, she got up and tried another way: she tried to drown herself in a neighborhood pond. But that didn't work either. She kept coming back to the surface, climbed up the bank, went home, turned around, hopped on her bike, and turned herself in to the local police with a solemn vow never to do anything like this again. She died in the hospital several days later.

Cases such as these have brought practitioners a long way in seeking to distinguish murder from suicide—simply making a determination based on the method used to bring about death. This is certainly a dangerous way of proceeding, one that rarely succeeds in leading to irreproachable and conclusive findings. This is why we always look for some kind of plausible "motive." If we can find no motivation for someone to commit murder, we simply tend to believe it is suicide on this basis alone. We can dismiss the notion that there is no "reasonable motivation" to be found here strictly on the basis of statistics claiming that one-third of all suicides are committed by people who are mentally disturbed and so are in themselves "unreasonable" from the perspective of a healthy individual. And how are we to prove "motive"? Naturally, one might say, with witness testimony. But who can guarantee us that our principal witness isn't precisely the prime suspect—for example, the woman whom we assume must have known her husband better than anyone else but who may have been precisely the one who wanted to get rid of her spouse, which we can't so much as begin to presume? Even if the scenario is not this crass, how many people base their judgment on unconfirmed grounds for suspicion as long as they are lacking any concrete information? What kind of shenanigans can that lead to, especially in rural areas where people are more dependent on one another than elsewhere? And ultimately, then, so the generally widespread opinion goes, is the very fact that there has been an *apparent* suicide not proof that the deceased was somehow not "normal?" And then, what human being has lived his life without actions, words, and deeds that are not subject to multiple interpretations, some of which could be used to claim that the person is "crazy"? These circumstances are what come to the forefront, then, for the experts and authorities; this is what they tell us, and we're supposed to draw these drastic conclusions on that basis? And what is to prevent, for example, the wife of a "crazy" man from poisoning his coffee? In sum, what do "motives" actually mean anyway? They are but the subjective judgment made from the perspective of officials involved in the investigation, that this or that established fact is not considered sufficient grounds for someone to take his own life or the other way around. A student hangs himself over bad grades, a young woman drowns herself over unrequited love, an old man takes his life in light of some illness, and yet the "normal" person would say, rightly so, some of the greatest men have had bad grades, lovers come and go, there are plenty of fish in the sea, and the old man could have waited until he was released from his suffering naturally.

And with all of these erratic, unscientific, simplistic speculations, we would finally arrive at the psychology of the one who commits suicide. That is, we would arrive at the doctrine that seeks to judge the inner life of a human being who is ultimately no more than that, a human being, one about whom we should like to pass judgment, even though we didn't know him, a judgment based on statements made about him or on actions he has taken or statements he has made. And in so doing, we seek from the perspective of "normalcy"—and all of us either aspire to be normal or are in fact normal—to form a judgment about whether it was possible (or probable or even perhaps a certainty) that this human being somehow overcame his natural survival instinct to the degree that he was able to take his own life! Indeed, what kind of person is anyone who kills himself? He's been called a courageous coward: is it at all possible ever to fully figure out such a difficult psyche by means of research?

183
SECRET REPORT OF THE SECURITY SERVICE OF THE REICHSFÜHRER SS

Kamikaze Panic
The Image of Japan in the German Population

Circulated on 6 August 1942 as "Die Sicht Japans in der Bevölkerung." First published in *Meldungen aus dem Reich 1938–1945. Die geheimen Lageberichte des Sicherheitsdienstes der SS,* edited by Heinz Boberach (Herrsching: Pawlak Verlag, 1984), 11:4042–45.

But of [all the things we have seen in the press, the papers and the population about Japan] and its war strategies, the reports tell us that one image circulating widely in the population is that of the Japanese soldier, which has served to diminish the public view of our own soldiers. According to the prevailing view that the German soldier is the best in the world, great confusion would have arisen around stories about the Japanese minesweepers in the Hong Kong harbor, or the death-defying Japanese flying aces who literally descend with the full brunt of their bomb load and destroy enemy ships, or the Japanese supersubmarine fleet. The fact that there does not exist the same degree of deliberate and conscious sacrifice (for example, in order to destroy a battleship) among the German populace has generated something of an "inferiority complex" in some areas. The Japanese thus represents a so-called German times four. People think that you can see in the Japanese the same characteristics as those attributed to our own heroes in sagas many centuries ago. In addition to catchpenny platitudes circulating about a " yellow menace," a certain pessimism is spreading that includes the notion that the same forces once so characteristic of our own history are now finding fullest expression among the Japanese and that our current leadership efforts in battle do not live up to the mythological greatness of our past in the eyes of others, so that if perhaps the Christian centuries cannot ever be redeemed, perhaps the Japanese will again unleash their power against us.

From this perspective, then, Japan is often seen in the context of the degree to which it can act as a model for us. Questions about the new ideological and religious order in comparison to Japan were discussed rigorously [in the press]. There was no way of denying the palpable presence of uncertainty about the current course we are on and about the opportunities and models available to us. Various people are suggesting that we need to place greater emphasis on traditional Germanic values and on the essential racial character of our people [*Wesenszüge unseres Volks*]. It would be possible to do this without diminishing the values of our Japanese comrades if we were to explain the way that different standards must be applied to the people of Europe to accommodate their essential nature. This, then, explains differing behaviors and facilities [between Germans and Japanese], which is by no means to be seen as a differentiation in their respective value. [. . .]

There are forces dormant in the subconscious that harbor enormous power of dynamic-instinctual drives that enable us to perform deeds that inspire awe and yet that often remain very alien to us.

Or:

. . . and those air crews, pilots who saw themselves as "living bombs?"—men who actually became one with the whole death-delivering mass of steel and explosives, reduced to a pile of inert mass?!

[One] Japanese report is calling it self-annihilation! Self-annihilation!?—What a concept!

Now there's a fighting spirit! . . .

The sheer volume of stories being told about the rules governing life and death throughout the history of the samurai warriors and in the "Bushido spirit" that lives on as a code of ethics today does not bode well for the Japanese when conclusions are drawn from the following statements and examples:

For centuries, Japanese tradition has seen great shame in being taken prisoner—it is better to die . . .

But the Japanese soldier does not enter battle out of a sense of duty; rather, he does so to sacrifice his life . . .

. . . No, I'm not sending my son to battle so he can die a hero's death and never come home alive . . .

These attitudes have led people to believe:

This attitude is the real reason Japan has yet to lose a single war and the reason it is witnessing such tremendous successes in the current war in Greater East Asia. Another thing that is said in the report:

> It may be that in this current war—unlike in the past—there are certain situations in which one cannot possibly avoid being taken prisoner; it is also entirely possible to think that one need not necessarily fight to the death as long as one can be sure he has done his duty using the most developed modern weapons available, that one has given his all and would now be of far greater service to his country by staying alive and fulfilling his calling in life—be it in war or in peace. There is a certain justification to this attitude, but the Japanese soldier tends to think differently: if he is forced to live in the shame of imprisonment, this implies that he did not fight to the death, that he would have had one more opportunity to keep fighting, and he is filled with profound

regret that he did not fight to the death for the emperor, his fatherland, and his *Volk*. The soldier cannot so much as imagine returning to life under these circumstances.

This article at least has the advantage of providing other examples that tend to discourage people from seeing the attitudes of the Japanese as models we might seek to follow across the board—for example with its depiction of Corporal Takemori, who "falls into a sort of frenzy" in battle:

> Chaos! Is he even made of flesh and blood, this crazed warrior with bloodshot eyes whose savage screams will drive you crazy? Or is it a demon? The raging demon . . . fear, dread, a moment of petrified fear yields to wild panic: escape from the Empire of Demons! It turns into an escape. Takemori takes off in a run. His bayonet raised—like the lance of a seasoned samurai warrior—he goes after the next pack of enemies. He leaves the dead and wounded in his path; his is the path of death and destruction, that is the path of the solitary raging warrior, Corporal Takemori.

The question remains, though, whether to apply the notion of "heroic deed" to this sort of "running amok" in the way the article's author does. For our way of thinking, the Japanese women seemed particularly brutal and inhumane, especially in the way they bade their husbands farewell by saying, indeed, be brave in battle, be very brave, and die an honorable death!

Here, the author of the article couldn't refrain from posing the question, Is that something a woman could possibly say?

There were other characteristics and traits, though, that strengthened the image of perfection, even by our standards, so, for example:

To lie is to bring shame to oneself. Lies are not called sins but are rather signs of weakness, and that brings dishonor to the liar.

And from our perspective, the practice of ritual suicide described here in lurid detail is utterly alien, but this is what the article's author says about it:

> The education toward defiance of death and toward self-discipline finds ultimate expression in the cult of ritual suicide anchored in the belief that whoever voluntarily marches straight into death for the sake of sustaining military honor has performed the same service to the nation as any soldier fallen in battle. For the Japanese, anyone fallen in battle is conferred the same heroic status . . . and whoever dares to disembowel himself has also cleansed himself of all transgressions.

But the prevailing impression of the average person is summed up in formulations such as these:

> . . . a deeply rooted sense of religion, such as without ready comparison.

The reader is left with a strong impression of Japan's absolute inner resolve.

PART SIX

. . .

THE CHURCHES

16
The National Socialist State and Christianity

THE HISTORY OF THE RELATIONSHIP between Nazi Germany and the established German churches is complicated by the fact that the regime never clarified its relationship to Christianity. Some historians have argued that National Socialism was an anti-Christian movement that substituted its own "political religion" and pagan worldview for Christian doctrine. The view that the life of the *Volk* or the community rested on blood, race, and an active and vitalistic harmony with nature was ultimately a religious concept, even if it claimed scientific authority. Others, however, have called Nazism a pro-Christian movement, since most of the leading Nazis considered themselves Christians and since the party claimed to represent "positive Christianity" (a term that appeared in its party program of 1920), not as a cynical effort to recruit believers but as a thoroughgoing expression of Nazism's belief system. Certainly, the Nazis did not reject Christian followers, and more importantly, Christian leaders of both major churches did not regard National Socialism as inimical to their beliefs. Even the most anticlerical of Nazi leaders, like Alfred Rosenberg, who promoted a "Germanic religion," did not fully reject Christianity, only the established churches. Still others maintain that National Socialism retained many of Christianity's core ideals and rhetoric—anti-Judaism and belief in a messiah—albeit fundamentally transformed and expressed in secular and racial language. Most historians would acknowledge that Hitler's genocidal and "redemptive" anti-Semitism was distinct from traditional Christian Jew hatred in its apocalyptic desire to physically rid the world of Jews, even though Nazi theologians were able to draw on (and reprint) the anti-Semitic works of Martin Luther, such as *On the Jews and their Lies* (1543).

During the Weimar Republic, the majority of Nazi voters came from Protestant areas of Germany. Catholics tended to vote for the Zentrumspartei (Center Party), which maintained the allegiance of roughly 15 percent of the electorate until 1933. However, even in Catholic Bavaria, up to a third of the voters in some areas supported Hitler, and in predominantly Protestant northern Germany, voters were divided over Nazism. In 1933, Hitler became the head of a coalition government with the support of the Center Party. The regime was further strengthened by the Concordat between the Holy See and the German Reich (Konkordat zwischen dem Heiligen Stuhl und dem Deutschen Reich) negotiated on 20 July 1933 by the Vatican secretary of state, Nuncio Eugenio Pacelli (later Pope Pius XII), which guaranteed the autonomy of German Catholicism in return for the church's recognition of Hitler's rule. The Catholic Church was permitted to retain its ties to the Holy See, collect taxes, and keep control of schools in Catholic regions. In return, the church fully subordinated itself to the new Reich: the Center Party was dissolved, and Catholic bishops had to swear an oath to honor the state. As the party's *Völkischer Beobachter* boasted on the day of the signing, the concordat demonstrated that the regime was "not antireligious." Cardinal Michael von Faulhaber (1869–1952), the archbishop of Munich who helped negotiate the concordat, also compromised the church by taking an equivocal stance on Nazi racism and anti-Semitism. In his 1933 Advent sermons on the relation between Christianity and the German race, he asserted, "Love of one's own race must not lead to the hatred of other nations," but he also affirmed that "race and Christianity are not mutually opposed." Faulhaber remained consistent in his accommodation to the regime and never condemned the persecution of the Jews.

The pro-Nazi strand of German Protestants, the Glaubensbewegung deutscher Christen

(Faith Movement of German Christians), advocated dissolving the existing Lutheran denominations and establishing a Nazified "evangelical Reich Church," based on the belief that God's "law has become manifest in the person of the Führer Adolf Hitler and in the National Socialist State." Founded in 1928 and officially recognized as a legitimate Protestant movement in 1932, the German Christian movement drew its theology from the thought of *völkisch* ideologues like Paul de Lagarde (1827–91) and Artur Dinter (1876–1948), who wanted to give Protestantism a racial foundation and purge Christianity of all "un-German and Jewish influences" (including so-called non-Aryan converts, the Old Testament, and parts of the New Testament).

With the support of the National Socialist government, the German Christians won a majority of the church offices and gained control of numerous local congregations and church finances, and, even after they suffered a decline, influenced the teaching of theology by controlling appointments to university faculties. In November 1933, ten thousand people attended a German Christian rally in the Berlin Sportpalast, where anti-Semitic speakers exhorted the crowd to adopt a "manly" Christianity and proposed banning marriages between Christians and "non-Aryans" of mixed parentage. The movement was ultimately thwarted in its ambition to establish a national religion that would unify Protestants and Catholics. The public tirades in the Sportpalast against the Old Testament "morality of cattle dealers and pimps" by its Berlin leader, Reinhold Krause, scandalized many Protestants, and the radical wing of the movement even lost the support of the German Christian *Reichsbischof* (Reich bishop), Ludwig Müller.[1]

Cooling in his support for the German Christians, Hitler ultimately dropped them as a mechanism for the coordination (*Gleichschaltung*) of the Protestant church and as a vehicle for carrying believers into the ranks of the party. In April 1936, *Das Schwarze Korps* published a lengthy article concluding that the "National Socialist state shall refrain from intervening in truly religious affairs, as long as representatives of any given religion forgo involvement in the political arena." Nonetheless, the National Socialist Party continued to regard the churches with suspicion—if not as sources of opposition, then as competing centers of power—and it occasionally clashed with the church over issues like whether crucifixes could be displayed in schoolrooms. After 1938, clergymen could not be appointed to party offices or organizations, and church leaders became increasingly unwelcome at party rallies and public events. A 1941 SS report on the attitudes of Christian congregants about the requirement that Jews wear the yellow star is instructive: church members complained of having to attend services with Jewish converts (now identifiable as such). While some Catholics proposed creating separate Jewish Christian congregations or segregated churches, the archbishop of Breslau, Cardinal Bertram, condemned such measures as un-Christian, although he allowed that they might be acceptable under certain circumstances (when "necessary"). Lutheran congregations reacted differently to the challenge of the German Christians' demand for an "Aryan paragraph" in the church by-laws (see document 24 in chapter 2). The notion was widely discussed internally but applied in a variety of ways: some congregations discriminated against non-Aryan Christians, others tolerated them. Cardinal Faulhaber, in his 1933 Advent sermons, defended the Old Testament against German Christian calls for its elimination, stating that Israel had been "dismissed from the service of revelation" after repudiating Jesus. The pre-Christian Old Testament, he affirmed, at least in its "religious, ethical, and social values," retained ongoing significance for Christianity.[2]

Protestants alienated by the German Christians gathered around Martin Niemöller, who in 1933 founded the Pfarrernotbund (Pastors' Emergency League), which openly declared itself against purging the German Evangelical Church of converted Jews. At the Barmen Synod (May 1934), the Bekennende Kirche (Confessing Church) broke away and proclaimed itself the true Protestant Church. In their foundational document, the Theological Declaration of Barmen (1934), authored by the Swiss theologian Karl Barth (1886–1968), Confessing Protestants rejected the "false doctrine" of the German Christians, accusing them of abandoning Christ's message, especially in their conviction that race transcended the sacraments, including baptism.

The dissenting Protestants, whose main figures, including Niemöller and Dietrich Bonhoeffer, were persecuted by the Nazis, never won over more than a minority of believers. After November 1938, there was virtually no protest from either Catholics or Protestants against the outrages perpetrated on the Jews. The fate of a small-town pastor who refused to remain silent shows what consequences were in store for those who spoke out. Julius von Jan (1897–1964), a World War I veteran and official of the Confessing Church in Swabia, defied church authorities by delivering a sermon on 16 November 1938, one week after the anti-Jewish pogrom, in which he marked the Day of Atonement by condemning the crimes against Jews. Von Jan was brutally beaten by SA thugs, arrested, and sentenced to a prison term. Protests by his congregants and grudging intervention by the local Protestant authorities (who condemned his sermon) prevented him from being sent to a concentration camp. Instead, he was sent to serve on the eastern front in Russia and Ukraine, where he contracted jaundice and survived the war. By contrast, the bishop of Thuringia, Martin Sasse (1890–1942), published his enthusiastic justification of the so-called Reichskristallnacht in the form of a widely distributed pamphlet titled *Martin Luther on the Jews: Get Rid of Them.*

Followers of the major Christian denominations, Protestant and Catholic, had to make choices during the Third Reich about how close to or how distant from official state policy toward religion they wanted to be. Smaller evangelical groups, such as the American-based Jehovah's Witnesses, with their strict pacifism and committed refusal to join any state organization, were even more systemically persecuted and imprisoned by the Nazis than they had been in the Weimar Republic. At least ten thousand members of the Jehovah's Witnesses were imprisoned after the official banning of the church in 1934, and at least twelve hundred died in prisons and concentration camps, where they were forced to wear the purple triangle. They were given the choice to give up their fundamental beliefs, but few did.

The impact of Nazism on important Christian rituals was contradictory. Funerals of SS men were staged according to solemn rites and symbols drawn from Nazism's political religion. But families of party members—including those of SS and Storm Trooper officers—held church services. Rosenberg's attacks on Christianity, and his claim that Jesus was "Nordic," prompted a number of conservative and by no means anti-Nazi Protestant theologians like Walter Künneth (1901–97) to claim that theological and historical sources showed "the Jewish lineage of Jesus to be historical fact." The most notorious defender of the "Aryan Jesus" was Walter Grundmann (1906–76), a member of the NSDAP and the German Christian movement and, after 1936, head of the Institut zur Erforschung und Beiseitigung des jüdischen Einflusses auf das deutsche kirchliche Leben (Institute for the Study and Eradication of Jewish Influence on German Life) at the University of Jena, where he was appointed professor of theology. In *Jesus of Galilee and the Jews* (1940), Grundmann argued that Galilee was a Gentile region and that Jesus's goal of destroying Judaism was drawn from his Aryan roots. Though their influence was hard to assess, the German Christians were never able to gain the allegiance of the majority of German Protestants. However, Rosenberg's neo-paganism never received official sanction either. When Hitler's secretary, Martin Bormann (1900–45), a virulent anticlericist and arguably the most influential man in wartime Nazi Germany, issued a 1941 memorandum stating that "our National Socialist concept of the world is on a far higher plane than are the ideas of Christianity, whose essential points have been taken over from the Jews," he had to withdraw it after Hitler and Goebbels deemed it inflammatory, or perhaps just inopportune.

In 1941, when the deportations of Jews, including converts, began, Viennese Cardinal

Innitzer is reported to have called on "all priests to pray for the Jewish comrades in faith." Neither the Protestant Church nor the Catholic Church officially protested or publicly acknowledged what was happening to the Jews. The sole exception was Dietrich Bonhoeffer (1906–45), who helped establish the Confessing Church. An opponent of Hitler since 1933, Bonhoeffer spoke out against the persecution of the Jews and was arrested in 1943 for helping a group of so-called non-Aryans escape to Switzerland. After he was discovered to have been in contact with the conspirators of the failed 20 July 1944 attempt to assassinate Hitler, he was hanged along with other conspirators at Flossenburg concentration camp on 9 April 1945, just one month before the collapse of the Reich. "Resistance and Resignation," which Bonhoeffer wrote in Berlin-Tegel prison, was published in his posthumous *Letters and Papers from Prison* (1951).

NOTES

1. Reinhold Krause, *Rede des Gauobmannes der Glaubensbewegung Deutsche Christen, in Groß-Berlin Dr. Krause* (Berlin: Glaubensbewegung Deutsche Volkskirche, 1933).

2. Michael von Faulhaber, *Judaism, Christianity and Germany,* translated by George D. Smith (New York: Macmillan, 1934).

184

Concordat between the Holy See and the German Reich

Announced on 20 July 1933 as "Konkordat zwischen dem Heiligen Stuhl und dem Deutschen Reich vom 20. Juli 1933." First published in *Reichsgesetzblatt* (Berlin: Reichsverlagsamt, 1933), 2:679ff.

His Holiness Pope Pius XI and the president of the German Reich, moved by the common desire to consolidate and promote the friendly relations existing between the Holy See and the German Reich and wishing to regulate lastingly, in a manner satisfying to both parties, the relations between the Catholic Church and the state for the entire territory of the German Reich, have decided to conclude a solemn agreement supplementing the concordats concluded with individual German states and also ensuring for the remaining states a fundamentally uniform treatment of the questions to which it pertains.

For this purpose:

His Holiness Pope Pius XI has appointed as his representative his eminence the distinguished Cardinal Eugen Pacelli, his state secretary; and the president of the German Reich has named as plenipotentiary the vice chancellor of the German Reich, Herr Franz von Papen.

Who, having exchanged their respective credentials and found them to be in good and proper form, have agreed on the following articles:

Article 1

The German Reich guarantees freedom of the profession and public practice of the Catholic religion.

It recognizes the right of the Catholic Church, within the limits of the law that applies to all, to regulate and administer her own affairs independently and, within the framework of her competence, to publish laws and ordinances binding on her members.

Article 2

The concordats concluded with Bavaria (1924), Prussia (1929), and Baden (1932) remain in force, and the rights and liberties of the Catholic Church recognized in them remain unchanged within the territories of the respective states. For the other states, the agreements reached in the present concordat apply in their entirety. The latter are also binding for the three states named above insofar as they deal with matters not regulated by the state concordats or supplement the regulations previously adopted.

In the future, the conclusion of concordats with individual states shall be effected only in accord with the government of the Reich.

Article 3

In order to foster good relations between the Holy See and the German Reich, an apostolic nuncio will as heretofore reside in the capital of the German Reich and an ambassador of the German Reich at the Holy See.

Article 4

In its relations and correspondence with the bishops, the clergy, and other members of the Catholic Church in Germany, the Holy See enjoys full freedom. The same applies to the bishops and other diocesan officials in their relations with the faithful in all matters pertaining to their pastoral office.

Instructions, ordinances, pastoral letters, official diocesan gazettes, and other enactments regarding the spiritual guidance of the faithful issued by the ecclesiastical authorities within the framework of their competence (Article 1, Section 2) may be published without hindrance and brought to the notice of the faithful in the forms hitherto customary.

Article 5

In the exercise of their spiritual activity, the clergy, in the same manner as the officials of the state, enjoy the protection of the state. The latter will proceed in accordance with the general laws of the state against offenses to their persons or their character as clergy, as well as against interference with the execution of their official duties, and in case of need, will provide official protection.

Articles 6–10

[These govern the state protection of the clergy and members of orders in the exercise of state offices.]

Article 11

The present organization and demarcation of dioceses of the Catholic Church in the German Reich are to remain in force. Establishment of a new bishopric or province of the church or other changes in the demarcation of the dioceses that may seem advisable in the future, insofar as new arrangements within the boundaries of a German *Land* are involved, remain subject to agreement with the competent *Land* government. New arrangements or changes extending beyond the boundaries of a German *Land* require agreement with the Reich government, to whom it is to be left to obtain the consent of the *Länder* governments in question. The same applies to the establishment of new provinces of the church or changes in existing provinces, in the event that several German *Länder* are concerned. The foregoing conditions do not apply to changes in ecclesiastical boundaries that are made solely in the interest of local pastoral work.

In the event of reorganization within the German Reich, the Reich government will communicate with the Holy See for the purpose of changing the organization and demarcation of the dioceses.

Article 12

Without prejudice to the provisions of Article 11, ecclesiastical offices may be freely established and changed, provided expenditures of state funds are not required. Governmental cooperation in the establishment and alteration of parishes is to take place in accordance with the principles agreed upon with the diocesan bishops and the Reich Government will try to influence the *Länder* governments to make them as uniform as possible.

Article 13

Catholic parishes, parish and diocesan associations, episcopal sees, bishoprics and chapters, religious orders and congregations, as well as institutions, foundations, and property under the administration of ecclesiastical authority, shall retain or acquire legal competence in the civil domain according to the general prescriptions of the law of the state. They shall remain corporations under public law insofar as they have been such hitherto; the others may be granted the same rights under the law that applies to all.

Article 14

In principle, the church has the right to make appointments freely to all church offices and benefices without the participation of the state or the civil communities, insofar as other arrangements have not been made through the concordats mentioned in Article 2. With respect to the filling of episcopal sees, the regulation applying to the metropolitan see of Freiburg (ecclesiastical province of Upper Rhine) shall be similarly applicable to the two suffragan bishoprics of Rottenburg and Mainz, as well as to the bishopric of Meissen. The same applies, in the two suffragan bishoprics named, to appointments to the Cathedral Chapter and the regulation of the right of patronage.

Furthermore, there is agreement on the following points:

1. Catholic clergy who hold an ecclesiastical office in Germany or who exercise pastoral or educational functions must:
   (a) Be German citizens
   (b) Have obtained a diploma entitling them to study at a German institute of higher learning
   (c) Have finished at least three years of philosophical and theological study at a German state university, a German ecclesiastical academic institution, or a pontifical institution of higher learning in Rome.
2. The bull for the nomination of archbishops, bishops, of a coadjutor *cum jure successionis,* or of a *praelatus nullius* will then be drawn up only after the name of the person selected has been communicated to the Reich governor [*Reichsstatthalter*] in the appropriate *Land,* and after it has been confirmed that there are no objections of a general political nature against the person.

With the consent of church and state, the requirements listed in Section 2, figure 7, (a), (b), and (c) may be waived.

Article 15

Orders and religious associations are subject to no special restrictions on the part of the state, with regard to their foundation, establishment, the number, and—subject to Article 15, Section 2—the characteristics of their members, their activity in pastoral work, in education, in nursing and charitable work, in the ordering of their affairs and the administration of their property.

Superiors of orders who have their official residence in the German Reich must have German citizenship. Superiors of provinces and of orders whose residence is outside the territory of the German Reich have the right of visitation with respect to their establishments in Germany.

The Holy See will endeavor to ensure that the provincial organization is so arranged for the establishments of the orders within the German Reich that the subordination of German establishments to foreign provincial superiors is eliminated as much as is feasible. Exceptions to this may be permitted in agreement with the Reich government particularly in cases in which the small number of establishments makes the creation of a German province impracticable or in which there are special reasons why a provincial organization that has become historic and proved efficient should be retained.

Article 16

Before the bishops take possession of their dioceses, they shall take an oath of allegiance either before the *Reichsstatthalter* of the appropriate province or before the Reich president as follows:

"I swear and promise before God and on the Holy Gospel, as befits a bishop, loyalty to the German Reich and to the *Land* of. . . . I swear and promise to respect, and to have my clergy to respect, the constitutionally constituted government. In dutiful solicitude for the welfare and interest of the German state, I shall try, in the exercise of the spiritual office entrusted to me, to prevent any injury that might threaten it."

Article 17

The rights of ownership and other rights of the corporations under public law, institutions, foundations, and associations of the Catholic Church in their property are guaranteed according to the general laws of the state.

Buildings used for religious services may not be destroyed for any reason whatsoever without the previous agreement of the ecclesiastical authorities concerned.

Article 18

In case those payments to the Catholic Church by the state that are based on law, treaty, or special legal titles should be commuted, an amicable agreement will be reached in good time between the Holy See and the Reich before working out the principles to be laid down for the commutation.

Usage based on law is numbered among the special legal titles.

The commutation must accord to the party entitled to commutation appropriate compensation for the loss of previous government payments.

Article 19

Catholic theological faculties in state institutions are to be retained. Their relation to the ecclesiastical authorities is to be based on the stipulations set forth in the pertinent concordats and the supplementary protocols appended to them, with due regard to the relevant ecclesiastical regulations. The Reich government will interest itself in assuring a uniform practice, in accordance with all the pertinent regulations, for all Catholic faculties of Germany in question.

Article 20

The church has the right, insofar as other agreements do not exist, to establish for the training of the clergy, philosophical and theological institutions entirely dependent on the ecclesiastical authorities, provided no state subsidies are requested.

The establishment, direction, and administration of the seminaries for priests as well as of the church-maintained hostels shall, within the limits of the law that applies to all, be left exclusively to the ecclesiastical authorities.

Article 21

Catholic religious instruction in the primary schools, vocational schools, secondary schools, and higher educational institutions is a regular subject of instruction and is to be taught in accordance with the principles of the Catholic Church. In religious instruction, special emphasis is to be placed on the inculcation of a patriotic, civic, and social sense of duty in the spirit of Christian religious and moral law, just as is done in all other instruction. The subject matter of instruction and the selection of textbooks for religious instruction are to be determined in agreement with the ecclesiastical authorities. The ecclesiastical authorities are to have an opportunity, together with the school authorities, to examine whether the students are receiving religious instruction in accordance with the tenets and requirements of the church.

Article 22

In the appointment of Catholic teachers of religion, agreement is to be reached between the bishop and the *Land* government. Teachers who have been declared by the bishop unsuited for further teaching of religion because of their teachings or moral conduct may not be employed as teachers of religion as long as this obstacle exists.

Article 23

The retention of Catholic denominational schools and the establishment of new ones is guaranteed heretofore. In all parishes in which parents or guardians request it, Catholic elementary schools shall be established, if, with due regard for local conditions of school organization, the number of pupils allows a regular school operation, in accordance with the standards prescribed by the state, to appear feasible.

Article 24

In all Catholic primary schools, only such teachers are to be employed as belong to the Catholic Church and guarantee to fulfill the special requirements of the Catholic denominational school.

Article 25

Orders and religious congregations are entitled to establish and conduct private schools, within the framework of the general laws and conditions fixed by law. These private schools confer the same rights as the state schools insofar as they meet the requirements in effect for the latter with respect to the curriculum.

With respect to the admission of members of orders or religious associations to the teaching profession, and their appointment to elementary, secondary, or senior schools, the general requirements are applicable.

Article 26

Subject to more comprehensive regulation later on questions of marriage law, it is agreed that in addition to the case of a critical illness of a betrothed person admitting of no delay, also in case of serious moral emergency, the existence of which must be confirmed by the appropriate Episcopal author, the consecration of marriage by the church may precede the civil wedding. The pastor is obliged in such cases to notify the Registry Office without delay.

Article 27

The German Reichswehr is granted exempted pastoral care for the Catholic officers, officials, and enlisted men belonging to it, as well as for their families.

The army bishop is responsible for the direction of military pastoral care. His ecclesiastical appointment is made by the Holy See after the latter has put itself in touch with the Reich government in order to designate the terms of agreement for a suitable candidate.

The ecclesiastical appointment of the chaplains and other military clergy is made by the army bishop after prior agreement with the competent authorities of the Reich. The army bishop may appoint only such clergy as have received from their competent diocesan bishop permission to enter upon military pastoral work, and an appropriate certificate of qualification. The military clergy are to have pastoral rights with respect to the troops and members of the army assigned to them.

More detailed regulations concerning the organization of Catholic pastoral work in the army are to be set forth in an apostolic brief. The regulation of the relationship as it applies to the civil service is to be done by the government of the Reich.

Article 28

In hospitals, penal institutions, and other public establishments, the church is permitted to make pastoral visits and hold divine services, subject to the general rules of these institutions. If regular pastoral care is established in such institutions, and if clergy must be engaged as state or other public officials for this purpose, this is to be done in agreement with the ecclesiastical authorities.

Article 29

In matters concerning the use of their mother tongue in divine services, religious instruction, and church organizations, the Catholic members of a non-Germanic national minority residing within the German Reich will be placed in no less favorable a position than that which corresponds to the legal and actual position of individuals of Germanic descent and language within the territory of the foreign state in question.

Article 30

On Sundays and religious holidays, a prayer is to be offered up for the welfare of the German Reich and nation in the episcopal churches, chapels, and abbey churches of the German Reich following the main service, in accordance with the precepts of the church liturgy.

Article 31

Those Catholic organizations and societies that serve exclusively religious, purely cultural, and charitable purposes and, as such, are subordinate to the ecclesiastical authorities, will be protected in their establishments and their activity.

Those Catholic organizations that, in addition to their religious, cultural, and charitable purposes serve other purposes, such as social or professional interests, will without prejudice to a possible future inclusion in state associations, enjoy the protection of Article 31, Section 1, provided they guarantee to carry on their activity outside any political party.

It is reserved to the government of the Reich and the German episcopate to determine by joint agreement which organizations and associations fall within the scope of this article.

Insofar as the Reich and *Länder* have in their charge sports and other youth organizations, care will be taken that the members of the same are enabled regularly to perform their church duties on Sundays and holidays and that they will not be required to do anything irreconcilable with their religious and moral convictions and obligations.

Article 32

On the basis of the special conditions existing in Germany, and in view of the guarantees created by the stipulations of this concordat of legislation protecting the rights and freedoms of the Catholic Church in the Reich and its *Länder,* the Holy See will publish stipulations that exclude the clergy and members of orders from membership in political parties and activity for such parties.

Article 33

The matters pertaining to ecclesiastical persons or ecclesiastical affairs that have not been dealt with in the foregoing articles will be regulated for the ecclesiastical sphere in accordance with applicable canon law.

Should any difference of opinion occur in the future regarding the interpretation of application of a stipulation to this concordat, the Holy See and the German Reich will effect an amicable solution by mutual agreement.

Article 34

This concordat, whose German and Italian texts have equal force, is to be ratified, and the instruments of ratification are to be exchanged as soon as possible. It enters into force on the day of their exchange.

In witness hereof, the plenipotentiaries have signed this concordat.
Vatican City, 20 July 1933
Eugenio Cardinal Pacelli
Franz von Papen

185

VÖLKISCHER BEOBACHTER

Comments on the Meaning of the Concordat

First published as "Die Bedeutung des Reichskonkordats 20.7.33," in *Völkischer Beobachter,* 20 July 1933, 1.

The fact that the Vatican has concluded a contract with the New Germany means that the Catholic Church recognizes the National Socialist state.

This contract makes clear, and unambiguously so to the whole world, that the charges of National Socialism being antireligious are a lie, invented for the sake of fomenting political scandal. [. . .]

In the concordat, the church forbids priests from any sort of participation in party politics. Furthermore, the Catholic Church instructs its priests to support the new state, what is now the German Reich. In the future, then, the pulpits and confessionals can no longer be misused against the National Socialist state as they have been in the past, unfortunately; instead, servants of the church in Germany are obligated to support this state and its principles in the same way as every other German citizen. The German state retains the right of veto over the appointment of politically incompatible bishops. Bishops pledge a solemn oath of allegiance to the new state.

The church agrees to abandon existing Catholic political associations.

And with that, the dangerous meddling of the Center [Party] that has thus far manipulated ecclesiastical authorities for the sake of advancing political causes has finally had the rug pulled out from it.

186

CARDINAL MICHAEL VON FAULHABER

What Is the Stance of Christianity to the German Race?

First published as "Wie sich das Christentum zur germanischen Rasse stellt," in *Judentum, Christentum, Germanentum: Adventspredigten gehalten in St. Michael zu München 1933* (Munich: A. Huber, 1934), 116–18.

From the church's point of view, there is no objection whatever to racial research and race culture. Nor is there any objection to the endeavor to keep the national characteristics of a people as pure and unadulterated as possible and to foster their national spirit by emphasizing the common ties of blood that unite them. From the church's point of view, we must make only three conditions: first, love of one's own race must not lead to the hatred of other nations. Second, the individual must never consider himself freed from the obligation of nourishing his own soul by the persevering use of the means of grace that the church provides. The young man who is always hearing about the blessedness of his own race is apt too easily to conceive that he is no longer bound by duties to God and his church, duties of humility and chastity. Third, race culture must not assume an attitude of hostility to Christianity. What are we to say of the monstrous contention that Christianity has corrupted the German race, that Christianity—especially because it is tarnished with Old Testament ideas—is not adapted to the genius of the nation and that therefore it is an obstacle in the way of the national consciousness?

What is the relation between Christianity and the German race? Race and Christianity are not mutually opposed, but they do belong to different orders. Race is of the natural order; Christianity is a revealed religion and therefore of the supernatural order. Race implies union with the nation; Christianity implies primarily union with God. Race is nationally inclusive and exclusive; Christianity is a worldwide message of salvation for all nations. The concepts of revelation and redemption, of the supernatural and grace, must not be watered down. The fourth gospel makes a net distinction between those who are born of blood and those who are born of God (John 1:13). Christ also clearly distinguished between what flesh and blood had revealed and what was revealed by the Father in heaven (Matt. 16:15 ff.). We are Christians not because we are born of Christian parents; we are Christians because after our birth we were reborn and made a new creature by baptism in Christ (2 Cor. 15:17).

No nation ever insisted more on race and ties of blood than the Israelites of the Old Testament. But in the fullness of time, the dogma of race was eclipsed by the dogma of faith. Around the cradle of Bethlehem there were Jews and pagans, shepherds from the land of Judah and wise men from the East. In the kingdom of this child, according to the words of his apostle, "there is no distinction of the Jew and the Greek, for the same is Lord over all." (Rom. 10:12).

What is the relationship between Christianity and the German race? The Christian, so long as he observes the above conditions, is not forbidden to stand up for his race and for its rights. It is possible, therefore, without divided allegiance, to be an upright German and at the same time an upright Christian. Hence, there is no need to turn our backs upon Christianity and to set up a Nordic or Germanic religion in order to profess our nationality. But we must never forget: we are not redeemed with German blood. We are redeemed with the precious blood of our crucified Lord (1 Pet. 1:9). There is no other name and no other blood under heaven in which we can be saved but the name and the blood of Christ.

187

Declaration of the German Christians

Declared as "Das Bekenntnis der 'Deutschen Christen,'" 1 December 1933. Published in J. Beckmann, ed., *Kirchliches Jahrbuch für die Evangelische Kirche in Deuschland 1933–1934* (Güttersloh, 1948), 32.

1. We German Christians believe in Jesus Christ our Savior, in the power of his cross and his resurrection. The life and death of Jesus Christ teach us that the way of battle is the way of love and the way of life.

We have been placed in the community of common blood and destiny with the German *Volk* by the hand of God, the Creator, and we accept responsibility for the future of this destiny we hold in our hands.

Germany is our mission, Christ is our strength.

2. The source and confirmation of our faith are the Holy Word of God in the Bible and the testimonies of the church fathers. The New Testament functions for us as the divine witness of our Redeemer, the Lord Jesus Christ and his Father's Kingdom.

The Old Testament is for us an example of divine education of the people. Its primary value for our faith is that it helps us to understand the life, crucifixion, and resurrection of our Savior.

3. As he does for every *Volk*, the everlasting God has created a species-appropriate law to govern our existence. This law has become manifest in the person of the Führer Adolf Hitler and in the National Socialist state that he has formed.

This law speaks to us from the history of our *Volk* as this has emerged from its blood and soil. Fidelity to this law requires that we fight for our honor and freedom.

4. The way to fulfill the German law is through a devout community of Germans governed by Christ, the Lord, in his mercy and forgiveness. It is in this community that the flame of divine sacrifice burns. It is only here that the Redeemer shall greet the German

Volk and bless it with the power of faith. In Adolf Hitler's National Socialist state, the German Christians will form the nucleus of a community that shall grow to encompass the entire nation and its people in the German Christian National Church [Deutsche Christliche Nationalkirche].

One *Volk*!—One God!—One Reich!—One Church!

188

KARL BARTH

Theological Declaration of Barmen

"Barmer Theologische Erklärung." Announced 29–31 May 1934 in Wuppertal. First published in *Die Bekentnisse und grundsätzlichen Äußerungen zur Kirchenfrage,* vol. 2, edited by Kurt Dietrich Schmidt (Göttingen: Vandenhoeck & Ruprecht, 1935), 92–95. Published in English in Arthur C. Cochrane, ed. and trans., *The Church's Confession under Hitler* (Philadelphia: Westminster Press, 1962), 237–42.

Written by Karl Barth and the confessing church in Nazi Germany in response to Hitler's national church. Its central doctrines concern the sin of idolatry and the lordship of Christ.

I. An Appeal to the Evangelical Congregations and Christians in Germany

8.01 The Confessional Synod of the German Evangelical Church met in Barmen, May 29–31, 1934. Here, representatives from all the German Confessional Churches met with one accord in a confession of the one Lord of the one, holy, apostolic Church. In fidelity to their Confession of Faith, members of Lutheran, Reformed, and United Churches sought a common message for the need and temptation of the Church in our day. With gratitude to God, they are convinced that they have been given a common word to utter. It was not their intention to found a new Church or to form a union. For nothing was farther from their minds than the abolition of the confessional status of our Churches. Their intention was, rather, to withstand in faith and unanimity the destruction of the Confession of Faith, and thus of the Evangelical Church in Germany. In opposition to attempts to establish the unity of the German Evangelical Church by means of false doctrine, by the use of force and insincere practices, the Confessional Synod insists that the unity of the Evangelical Churches in Germany can come only from the Word of God in faith through the Holy Spirit. Thus alone is the Church renewed.

8.02 Therefore, the Confessional Synod calls upon the congregations to range themselves behind it in prayer, and steadfastly to gather around those pastors and teachers who are loyal to the Confessions.

8.03 Be not deceived by loose talk, as if we meant to oppose the unity of the German nation! Do not listen to the seducers who pervert our intentions, as if we wanted to break up the unity of the German Evangelical Church or to forsake the Confessions of the Fathers!

8.04 Try the spirits whether they are of God! Prove also the words of the Confessional Synod of the German Evangelical Church to see whether they agree with Holy Scripture and with the Confessions of the Fathers. If you find that we are speaking contrary to Scripture, then do not listen to us! But if you find that we are taking our stand upon Scripture, then let no fear or temptation keep you from treading with us the path of faith and obedience to the Word of God, in order that God's people be of one mind upon earth and that we in faith experience what he himself has said: "I will never leave you, nor forsake you." Therefore, "Fear not, little flock, for it is your Father's good pleasure to give you the kingdom."

II. Theological Declaration Concerning the Present Situation of the German Evangelical Church

8.05 According to the opening words of its constitution of July 11th, 1933, the German Evangelical Church is a federation of Confessional Churches that grew out of the Reformation and that enjoys equal rights. The theological basis for the unification of these Churches is laid down in Article 1 and Article 2 (1) of the constitution of the German Evangelical Church that was recognized by the Reich Government on July 14th, 1933:

Article 1. The inviolable foundation of the German Evangelical Church is the gospel of Jesus Christ as it is attested for us in Holy Scripture and brought to light again in the Confessions of the Reformation. The full powers that the Church needs for its mission are hereby determined and limited.

Article 2 (1). The German Evangelical Church is divided into *Landeskirchen* [member churches].

8.06 We, the representatives of Lutheran, Reformed, and United Churches, of free synods, Church assemblies, and parish organizations united in the Confessional Synod of the German Evangelical Church, declare that we stand together on the ground of the German Evangelical Church as a federation of German Confessional Churches. We are bound together by the confession of the one Lord of the one, holy, catholic, and apostolic Church.

8.07 We publicly declare before all evangelical Churches in Germany that what they hold in common in this Confession is grievously imperiled, and with it the unity of the German Evangelical Church. It is threatened by the teaching methods and actions of the ruling Church party of the "German Christians" and of the Church administration carried on by them. These have become more and more apparent during the first year of the existence of the German Evangelical Church. This threat consists in the fact that the theological basis in which the German Evangelical Church is united has been continually and been systematically thwarted and rendered ineffective by alien principles on the part of the leaders and spokesmen of the "German Christians" as well as on the part of the Church administration. When these principles are held to be valid, then, according to all the Confessions in force among us, the Church ceases to be the Church and the German Evangelical Church, as a federation of Confessional Churches, becomes intrinsically impossible.

8.08 As members of Lutheran, Reformed, and United Churches, we may and must speak with one voice in this matter today. Precisely because we want to be and to remain faithful to our various Confessions, we may not keep silent, since we believe that we have been given a common message to utter in a time of common need and temptation. We commend to God what this may mean for the interrelations of the Confessional Churches.

8.09 In view of the errors of the "German Christians" of the present Reich Church government who are devastating the Church and also therefore breaking up the unity of the German Evangelical Church, we confess the following evangelical truths:

8.10–1. "I am the way, and the truth, and the life; no one comes to the Father, but by me." (John 14.6). "Truly, truly, I say to you, he who does not enter the sheepfold by the door, but climbs in by another way, that man is a thief and a robber . . . I am the door; if anyone enters by me, he will be saved." (John 10:1, 9)

8.11 Jesus Christ, as he is attested for us in Holy Scripture, is the one Word of God that we have to hear and which we have to trust and obey in life and in death.

8.12 We reject the false doctrine, as though the church could and would have to acknowledge as a source of its proclamation, apart from and besides this one Word of God, still other events and powers, figures and truths, as God's revelation.

8.13–2 "Christ Jesus, whom God has made our wisdom, our righteousness and sanctification and redemption." (1 Cor. 1:30)

8.14 As Jesus Christ is God's assurance of the forgiveness of all our sins, so, in the same way and with the same seriousness he is also God's mighty claim upon our whole life. Through him befalls us a joyful deliverance from the godless fetters of this world for a free, grateful service to his creatures.

8.15 We reject the false doctrine, as though there were areas of our life in which we would not belong to Jesus Christ, but to other lords—areas in which we would not need justification and sanctification through him.

8.16–3 "Rather, speaking the truth in love, we are to grow up in every way into him who is the head, into Christ, from whom the whole body [is] joined and knit together." (Eph. 4:15, 16)

8.17 The Christian Church is the congregation of the brethren in which Jesus Christ acts presently as the Lord in Word and sacrament through the Holy Spirit. As the Church of pardoned sinners, it has to testify in the midst of a sinful world, with its faith as with its obedience, with its message as with its order, that it is solely his property, and that it lives and wants to live solely from his comfort and from his direction in the expectation of his appearance.

8.18 We reject the false doctrine, as though the Church were permitted to abandon the form of its message and order to its own pleasure or to changes in prevailing ideological and political convictions.

8.19–4 "You know that the rulers of the Gentiles lord it over them, and their great men exercise authority over them. It shall not be so among you; but whoever would be great among you must be your servant." (Matt. 20:25, 26)

8.20 The various offices in the Church do not establish a dominion of some over the others; on the contrary, they are for the exercise of the ministry entrusted to and enjoined upon the whole congregation.

8.21 We reject the false doctrine, as though the Church, apart from this ministry, could and were permitted to give itself, or allow to be given to it, special leaders vested with ruling powers.

8.22–5 "Fear God. Honor the emperor." (1 Peter 2:17)

Scripture tells us that, in the as yet unredeemed world in which the Church also exists, the State has by divine appointment the task of providing for justice and peace. [It fulfills this task] by means of the threat and exercise of force, according to the measure of human judgment and human ability. The Church acknowledges the benefit of this divine appointment in gratitude and reverence before him. It calls to mind the Kingdom of God, God's commandment and righteousness, and thereby the responsibility both of rulers and of the ruled. It trusts and obeys the power of the Word by which God upholds all things.

8.23 We reject the false doctrine, as though the State, over and beyond its special commission, should and could become the single and totalitarian order of human life, thus fulfilling the Church's vocation as well.

8.24 We reject the false doctrine, as though the Church, over and beyond its special commission, should and could appropriate the characteristics, the tasks, and the dignity of the State, thus itself becoming an organ of the State.

8.25–6 "Lo, I am with you always, to the close of the age." (Matt. 28:20) "The word of God is not fettered." (2 Tim. 2:9)

8.26 The Church's commission, upon which its freedom is founded, consists in delivering the message of the free grace of God to all people in Christ's stead, and therefore in the ministry of his own Word and work through sermon and sacrament.

8.27 We reject the false doctrine, as though the Church in human arrogance could place the Word and work of the Lord in the service of any arbitrarily chosen desires, purposes, and plans.

8.28 The Confessional Synod of the German Evangelical Church declares that it sees in the acknowledgment of these truths and in the rejection of these errors the indispensable theological basis of the German Evangelical Church as a federation of Confessional Churches.

It invites all who are able to accept its declaration to be mindful of these theological principles in their decisions in Church politics. It entreats all whom it concerns to return to the unity of faith, love, and hope.

189

Statement of the Confessing Church

Announced as "Botschaft der 'Bekennenden Kirche,' " 19–20 October 1934. First published in J. Beckmann, ed., *Kirchliches Jahrbuch für die Evangelische Kirche in Deuschland 1933–1934* (Güttersloh, 1948), 32.

I

1. The first and most basic article in the Constitution of the German Evangelical Lutheran Church of 11 July 1933 states, "The inviolable foundation of the German Evangelical Lutheran Church is the Gospel of Jesus Christ as recorded in the Holy Scripture and confessed in the ecumenical creeds and Lutheran confessional writings. All powers bestowed on this church in fulfilling its mission are determined and limited on this basis." This article, however, has been eliminated by the dogmas, laws, and measures of the Reich Church government. The Christian foundation for the German Evangelical Lutheran Church has thus been removed.
2. The motto being promoted by the Reich bishop as the goal of establishing a national church—"One State—One People—One Church"—implies that the authority of the Gospel has been revoked for the German Evangelical Lutheran Church, and the church's message is at the mercy of secular forces in this world.
3. The exclusive executive authority that the Reich bishop has usurped along with his state commissioner of the church [*Rechtswalter*] has led to the establishment of a papacy that is unsustainable by the Evangelical Lutheran Church.
4. Driven by the spirit of a fraudulent, nonbiblical revelation, the sovereign determination of the church has punished obedience to Scripture and Confession as a disciplinary offense.
5. The introduction of the secular principle of the Führer to the church violates Scripture, and the attendant demand for unconditional obedience binds church officials to the word of the sovereign determination of the church regiment rather than to the word of Christ.
6. The exclusion [*Ausschaltung*] of the synods has disenfranchised and silenced the voices of the faithful in the congregations in direct defiance of biblical and Lutheran reformist teachings about the priesthood.

II

1. All of the objections we have raised in our protests based on Scripture and Confession, all of the warnings and admonitions have been for naught. Even worse, the Reich Church government has invoked the authority of the Führer, rallied political forces, and collaborated with them in the ruthless pursuit of their continued destruction of the church.
2. With the rape of the southern churches in Germany, we have been robbed of the last possible opportunity to restructure the church order in conjunction with any existing conditions.
3. These circumstances merit the invocation of an ecclesiastical state of emergency, which we are compelled to put into effect as of today.

III

1. We hereby conclude: The Constitution of the German Evangelical Lutheran Church is in tatters. Its legal institutions no longer exist. The men who have assumed ecclesiastical leadership positions in the Reich and the *Länder* have divorced themselves from the Christian church by virtue of their actions.
2. On the basis of this state of emergency facing those churches, parishes, and clergy that adhere to Scripture and Confession, the Confessional Synod of the German Evangelical Lutheran Church has seen it necessary to create new offices of leadership [*Organe der Leitung*]. It is appointing the Brotherhood Council [*Bruderrat*] of the German Evangelical Lutheran Church and one of its members, the Council of the German Evangelical Lutheran Church, to direct and represent the German Evangelical Lutheran church as a League of Confessing churches, and to conduct their business affairs. Both offices [*Organe*] have been called together and structured according to the precepts outlined in the Confessions.
3. We hereby demand that Christian parishes, their pastors, and elders [*Ältesten*] take no further orders from the Reich Church government and its authorities and refrain from collaborating with anyone who still wishes to obey the dictates of this church authority. We are requesting that they adhere instead to the stipulations set by the Confessional Synod of the German Evangelical Lutheran Church and to their affiliated offices.

IV

We are presenting this declaration to the Reich government with a request that it acknowledge receipt of the decisions outlined herein, and we are demanding that it acknowledge that the church retain the exclusive right to make judgments and determinations in matters concerning the church, its doctrines, and structures unimpeded by the supervisory jurisdiction of the state.

190

JULIUS VON JAN

A Sermon on *Bußtag* (Day of Atonement)

"O earth, earth, earth, hear the word of the Lord!"

First delivered on 16 November 1938 as "Bußpredigt vom 16. November 1938, Dorfkirche zu Oberlenningen: 'O Land, Land, Land, höre des Herren Wort.'" Published in Eberhard Röhm and Jörg Thierfelder, eds., *Evangelische Kirche zwischen Kreuz und Hakenkreuz : Bilder und Texte einer Ausstellung* (Stuttgart: Calwer, 1982), 127–29.

Dearly Beloved!

The prophet cries out, O earth, earth, earth, hear the word of the Lord! [Jer. 22: 29] Upon first hearing these few words, we have no way of knowing what manner of trials and tribulations occasioned Jeremiah to utter this plea. He is a member of a *Volk* to whom the Lord has long since revealed himself as Father and Savior, as Leader and Comforter in his strength, his mercy, and his glory. But the people of Israel, first and foremost its kings and princes, have trampled God's law to the ground. Jeremiah has staged a tough battle against this injustice in the name of God and in the name of righteousness. For nearly thirty years, he has been delivering the Lord's word to the people, contradicting the lies set forth in sermons by those who would declare victory and salvation in the false fervor of nationalism, but no one has heeded his words. The loyal servant of God becomes increasingly isolated and alone. Then comes the great moment when God calls out to his prophet, "Go down to the house of the king . . . and speak there this word" (Jer. 22:1–9). But the king callously disregarded the word of God and was suddenly taken prisoner by his enemies; his successor heeded the words of the prophet and died after a brief reign; and the third king was at the helm for only three months before he was captured by the Babylonians! This is what we are told in this passage from the Scripture. The glory of Jerusalem was quickly demolished by the deeds of but three impenitent kings. In his utter despair over these developments, Jeremiah cried out to his people: O earth, earth, earth, hear the word of the Lord!

Why have you been unfaithful to the God of faith? Why have you ceased to follow his commandments? Don't you see what befell your kings as a result of having done the same? O earth, beloved German homeland, hear the word of the Lord! These days, there is a question circulating amongst the populace: where in Germany is the prophet who shall be sent to the house of the king to speak the word of the Lord! What man, crying out in the name of God and of righteousness, shall cry out as Jeremiah did: Execute judgment and righteousness, and deliver the spoiled out of the hand of the oppressor! Do no wrong and do no violence to the stranger, the fatherless, nor the widow, neither shed innocent blood in this place.

Men like this are sent to us by God! Today, they are either in concentration camps or have been silenced. But those who now enter the houses of princes and are allowed to execute divine acts there are false prophets, just like the nationalistic zealots of Jeremiah's times, who are quick to proclaim salvation and victory but incapable of preaching the word of the Lord. . . . If there are some then who have been *forced* into silence and others who do not *want* to speak, then today we truly do have every reason for a day of atonement, *a day of mourning* over our sins and the sins of our people.

A crime was committed in Paris. The murderer will be punished accordingly because he has violated the law of God. We mourn with the entire nation over the victim of this criminal act. But who would have thought that the consequence of this crime in Paris would be so many crimes committed in Germany? This is retribution for the masses who have fallen from the grace of God and Christ, for the organized presence of anti-Christendom.

Passions have been unleashed, God's commandments have been snubbed, houses of God, sacred to others, have been burned to the ground with impunity, the property of strangers plundered or destroyed. Men who have faithfully served our German *Volk* and conscientiously fulfilled their obligations have been thrown into concentration camps simply because they are members of a different race! Even though the people at the top will not admit to these injustices, the healthy public sentiment of the nation clearly knows, even though no one dares to talk about it. And we as Christians can see how this injustice weighs heavily on us in the eyes of God and that Germany must receive the full brunt of his wrath borne upon her in retribution. For it is written in the Scripture, Be not deceived; God is not mocked! Whatsoever a man soweth, that he shall also reap. And indeed, the horrific seed of hatred once again has been sowed. What horrific harvest will we reap from this seed if God does not grant mercy on us and our nation in our sincere repentance?

And when we speak in terms of the wrath of God, we know that many are quietly thinking to themselves, How can you speak in terms of the wrath of God and punishing Germany today when things are obviously improving and this year at least ten million Germans have been unified in the Reich? Is that not proof enough of God's blessing of our nation? Indeed, the hand of God presides over us with an astonishing degree of patience and mercy. But that is precisely why we heed the words, O earth, earth, earth, hear the word of the Lord! Finally hear it! Can you hear the God in his goodness guiding you to repent? In this chapter, the prophet is instructed by God to say, As I live, saith the Lord, though Coniah the son of Jehoiakim king of Judah were the signet upon my right hand, yet I would pluck thee thence; and I will give thee into the hand of them that seek thy life! God can lift a nation and a people to the highest heights of honor—but when it closes its heart to the word of the Lord, it is suddenly plunged to the depths. The excesses of joy, the excesses of success all too easily lead to arrogance in men, arrogance that defiles the whole of divine grace and always ends in a precipitous fall from grace. For this reason, this day of atonement is a day of mourning over our sins and the sins of our nation, sins that we confess before God, and it is a *day of prayer:* Lord, in your mercy, let us and our nation again learn to hear your word, let us again learn to respect your commandments and let it begin with us [. . .]

Standing today with you and with our nation before God in judgment, this confession of guilt we thought could not be spoken about has been, for me at least, like throwing off a huge burden! Praise God! It has been spoken before God and in God's name. Now let the world do with us what it will. We are in God's hands. God is true to his word! But you, o earth, earth, earth, hear the word of the Lord! Amen.

191

SECRET REPORT OF THE SECURITY SERVICE OF THE REICHSFÜHRER SS

The Churches' Attempts to Undermine Anti-Jewish Sentiments in the Populace

First circulated on 24 November 1941 as "Versuche der Kirchen, die judengegnerische Haltung der Bevölkerung durch die konfessionelle Gegenarbeit zu untergraben." First published in *Meldungen aus dem Reich 1938–1945. Die geheimen Lageberichte des Sicherheitsdienstes der SS,* edited by Heinz Boberach (Herrsching: Pawlak Verlag, 1984), 8: 3020–23.

The police ordinance issued by the Reich Ministry of the Interior on 1 September 1941, which forbids Jews from appearing anywhere in public without visibly displaying the Jewish star in the upper left-hand corner of the outermost piece of clothing they are wearing, has taken not only the population of large cities, where there are a large number of Jews living, by surprise, it has also attracted the attention of church members, who point to the countless numbers of converted Jews who regularly attend Sunday services.

Complaints were lodged with local clergy by church members attending services in the Sundays directly following the issuance of the ordinance. They demanded that Jews no longer be permitted to attend services and that they could not be expected to receive Holy Communion while standing in the same line as a Jew.

The attitude of the clergy of the confessional persuasion is characterized by a flyer drafted by the local vicar in Breslau and distributed throughout various regions of the Reich:

> The Christian duty is to refrain from excluding them [the Jews] from services based on their identification [through the Jewish star]. They are entitled to the same right of domicile in the church as are the remaining members of the congregation and are particularly in need of the comfort provided by God's word.
>
> The congregation is at risk of being misled by elements that are not truly Christian, it is at risk of endangering the Christian church through behaviors that are not Christian. Pastoral care must be provided here, perhaps with reference to Luke 10:25–37 ("And who is my neighbor?") or to Matthew 25:40 ("Inasmuch as ye have done it unto one of the least of these my brethren, ye have done it unto me").

At the same time, practical advice is offered for solving the problem:

> It might be worth considering whether or not church officials, pastors, etc. ought not attend to those members of the congregation identified [by the Jewish star] as a special group and, if necessary, set aside special seats for them; special seats could be set aside before each service in order to guarantee that they will not be ousted by unchristian elements.
>
> However, in order to ensure that this not be seen as a form of segregation that is not evangelical, it is necessary that trusted members of the congregation (e.g., members of the church council, of the women's counsellorship, of the rectory) also take their seats in these pews, sitting beside and amongst the non-Aryan Christians. We should also consider whether or not to have these Christians identified [by the Jewish star] picked up from their homes by members of the congregation to attend services.

The Evangelical Lutheran Consistory of the church province of Silesia has since been forced by negative reactions on the part of the populace and the official party position to distance itself from this statement, which was allegedly distributed without its prior approval. Similar determinations concerning the "treatment of Jewish Christians" has not yet been forthcoming in other areas of the Reich.

In the Catholic parishes in larger cities, a plan has surfaced whereby Jewish Catholics would be brought together in a separate Jewish Christian congregation with its own services in order to avoid any burden to the rest of the Catholics. This solution, suggested by certain sectors of the population as well as by several individual clerics, prompted the archbishop of Breslau and president of the Fulda Bishops' Conference, Cardinal Bertram, to comment explicitly on the subject of Jews' presence in churches and church facilities as well as in a newsletter (17 September 1941):

> The ramifications of the police ordinance concerning the conduct of Catholics in response to Catholics of Jewish descent present at mass are bound to differ from place to place, specifically contingent on the greater or lesser influence of attitudes that are widespread in the general populace.
>
> 1. It is therefore imperative that hastily formulated policies that may be seen as offensive to Jewish Catholics be avoided, such as introducing special pews for Jews only, segregation in the dispensation of Holy Communion, the introduction of segregated mass services for Jews only.
> 2. The officially sanctioned segregation and special handling of non-Aryans violates the notion of Christian brotherly love. It is therefore to be avoided for as long as possible. Pastors are to recommend that these Catholics seek to attend the early mass if at all possible.
> 3. Reminders concerning brotherly love and avoiding every form of denigrating treatment of any Catholic non-Aryan marked by the star are to be issued [to members of the congregation attending mass] only when and if disturbances arise.
> 4. Only if and when more substantial difficulties arise (if civil servants, party members, and others begin staying home or ostentatiously leaving mass in protest) should the step be taken of suggesting to Catholic non-Aryans that special Jewish-only masses be held.
> 5. If a reminder should prove necessary, the following text may be used:
>
>   In light of the difficulties that have arisen for Jews living in Germany as a result of the police ordinance of 1 September 1941, all Catholics are hereby reminded to demonstrate toward Christians of Jewish descent the same degree of consideration due every Christian according to the principles outlined by St. Paul: no one who believes in Christ shall be put to shame. For there is no difference between the Jews and the Greek; for the same Lord over all is rich unto all who call upon him.

> For all of you who have been baptized into Christ have assumed the mantel of Christ. There is neither Jew nor Greek, there is neither bond nor free, for you are all one in Jesus Christ.

[Theodor] Cardinal Innitzer, archbishop of Vienna, addressed the clergy of the Ostmark [Austria] along similar lines. He too rejects identifying markers for Jews, even though this corresponds to medieval Christian tradition, just as he rejects grouping together Jewish Catholics into special Jewish Christian congregations with their own churches and church services, because that measure could be interpreted to be a concession to the National Socialist racial doctrine. Any calls made by the faithful to the offices of the clergy requesting that the Jews be removed are to be strictly dismissed, and the petitioners are to be instructed that the church cannot make racial distinctions in matters pertaining to worship services. At the same time, making reference to the deportation campaign, the cardinal called on all priests to pray for their Jewish comrades in faith who will soon be forced to leave Vienna. Accordingly, despite the fact that the number of Jews flocking to the church at the moment is very great, as if they were dispatched in the manner of a delegation, apparently in the attempt to arouse pity among churchgoers, based on the opinions issued by these two cardinals, it is not likely that the church will go along with a segregation of the Jews in worship services or in the administration and receipt of the Blessed Eucharist.

192

ALFRED ROSENBERG

Theses on the Worldview

First published as "Weltanschauliche Thesen," 12 July 1941, in *Das politische Tagebuch Alfred Rosenbergs aus den Jahren 1934/34 und 1939/40,* edited by Dr. Hans-Günther Seraphim (Göttingen: Musterschmidt Verlag, 1956), 197–212.

[I]

Worldview: that means a certain way of viewing the world. Worldview is therefore a position, not a dogma.

A position with respect to the world: that is, to the outer limits of destiny and to the instincts of the soul.

A position can either be brave or cowardly, proud or subservient, the position of a freedman or that of a slave.

The brave man acts in accordance with the species of his own conscience, the coward responds to potential dangers; the proud man confronts his destiny head-on, the subservient man does the bidding of destiny's command; the freedman follows his own nature, while the slave waits for orders from above.

To invoke courage and pride and freedom is to educate in the ancient Germanic-German tradition; to teach subservience and to inspire fear is the basic educational principle of the Christian churches. A worldview encompasses religion, science, and art. These primeval human occupations are the fountain of all the remaining tributaries of human influence in the world. Harmony between *Volk* and life can then be established only when religion, science, and art assume the same position and when all their forms of expression are determined from that same point of view.

We have witnesses, Jewish-Asiatic denominations fraudulently going by the name of religion. We have witnessed science raped by biblical dogma. We saw the way art was permissible only in glorification of the Bible and the Roman Catholic Church. Germanic man has exploded the bounds of these forms. He has established a standard for the epitome of beauty equal only to himself; today it has become the conscious ideal of every German. Europe struggled hard against biblical dogma to pursue freedom of research into nature [*Naturerforschung*]. Europe today is purging itself, first and foremost among the German *Volk,* bidding good riddance to the Syrian-Jewish ecclesiastical dogma and its oriental ceremonies. Perfecting the alignment, in position and in expression, of a Germanic unity of religion, science, and art will become the very essence of the ideological shift in worldview of the twentieth century.

II

Religion and denomination have since become distinct categories of their own.

Religion: the bounds of the human soul or the soul of a *Volk* toward a divine being presiding over this life. Religion, then, is one component of the overall ideological position of a worldview. A confession of faith is inherent in any belief in God or in any deity, just as it is for any belief in prophecies. And *this* confession of faith is an essential component of religion.

The term *denomination,* though, refers to the sum of compulsory doctrines (dogmas) issued by the authority of a certain church.

One of these denominations demands belief in the Bible, in enduring ecclesiastical traditions, in the infallibility of the pope, in the so-called sacraments, in a racially homogenous universal humanity, in the power of priests in the afterlife. The other denomination demands belief in the Bible, in the so-called one and only revelation as outlined in the New Testament, in the doctrine of Martin Luther or Calvin.

But since there are *two* major denominations—and hundreds of sects in Germany—they no longer represent the overall religious foundation of the whole German nation. Christianity was once an absolute power, but with the emergence of these many denominations, it has become fragmented and localized.

The once absolute power collapsed because its effects were anti-Germanic and became increasingly anti-German. A new, Germanic-German position could not be attained by any sort of new Protestant interpretation to render the Bible binding.

Therefore, for anyone who strives to assume a unified religious position for all Germans, the prerequisite is necessarily that the existing denominations are overcome. For thousands of years, despite protestations from Rome, man set out in search of the "doctrinal purity of the gospel." And yet even to this day, not a trace of it has been found, so it either never existed, or simply cannot be recovered, or, perhaps, if it does exist somewhere, it is simply not conducive to producing any great awakening in the essential nature of Germanic man.

And this is why the New Testament can no longer serve as a decisive foundation for sustaining the formation of a new soul for the community. To attempt once again today, after a thousand years of unsuccessful efforts [to find this trace of purity], would be to recommence with a fruitless task.

Evaluating the stories of the New Testament is a purely personal matter. *Researching* these stories and *examining* this epoch no longer have anything to do with religion today, but have since become the concern of historical research instead. The New Testament is not a thing of the present but rather the matter of a dying past. This past is honorable by virtue of its duration. The only nobility due any spiritual power of the past is that determined by whether or not Germans have believed in it. It does not matter whether the object of a great faith was worth thousands of years of human investment; what is decisive is the strength of the faith that facilitated and fueled that investment.

The contemporary absence of such faith, though, is the real reason for the internal, and to some extent for the onset of the external, collapse of all churches today. The renunciation of will at the very appearance of will is the profoundest cause of death for the churches today.

Any culture, any religion, is only as strong as the will of its proponents to defend it. At a decisive historical moment, Christianity failed to come through with enough life-giving force. Throughout the world, it crumbled before Judaism and Marxism: in Moscow, in Berlin, in Budapest, in Rome, and in Madrid . . . the churches do not have the prayers of their priests nor the courage of their bishops to thank for the fact that the churches still exist—only the triumphant sacrifices of newly emerging worldviews.

Christianity itself was a revolution, later it became a European power; today it has been reduced to a bone-dry reactionary reflex. [. . .]

Whoever strives to pursue the noblest of causes fulfills a metaphysical, religious purpose. His sense of purpose in life is attached to the most exalted phenomena in the world of existence and not ecclesiastical/man-made organizations, dogmas, and ideologies. The untiring service to the most exalted causes is the mark of a genuinely *Germanic* religious genius. Religion is not a matter of renouncing the will but rather the development of will in the service of the intrinsically noble species of soul. And this realization puts an end to the influence of all previously existing religions of the Orient. The chaos of denominational divisions has provided the fertile ground from which a German religion could be born.

We could not possibly submit to the spiritual and psychological leadership of anyone on the planet who has betrayed the German *Volk* to its enemies. We vehemently reject the possibility that the soldiers of the *Volk* fighting for their honor could possibly appear in the "afterlife" as the defendants while these priestly race traitors, on the other hand, appear as judges.

Anyone who engages in racial or national treason here on earth certainly is in no position to govern in heaven. [. . .]

Religion is the tie that binds to some divinity—but also to human beings whose traditional values must find expression and stand the test of time. The new national community of the *Volk* (National Socialism) is predestined, prefigured, but not yet formed. In order to assume form, vast, all-encompassing form, kith and kin from many different families will have to extend their hands to one another.

The first inklings of this new way of life were apparent in the voluntary willingness to sacrifice seen in the simple SA man, in the stalwart demeanor of the National Socialist woman, in the passionate enthusiasm of the Adolf Hitler Youth, in the highly developed visionary scope of our revolution's early pioneers. We cannot today underestimate the Führer's will and his visionary strength if we hope to participate in the same. The integrity of the pronounced instinctive will to sacrifice is what generated the integrity of our worldview and, with a firm grasp on the future, conquered the fragmentation of the old denominations. Future generations will march in droves paying homage to the graves of the fallen from this Great War and our movement, just as the people made pilgrimages to the graves of Christian saints. Not bent over in shamefaced contrition but bursting with pride at the products of its exalted, noble soul.

The Eternal Guard [Ewige Wache, on the Königsplatz in Munich] is the parabolic example of all graves. Here beneath the open sky, the bronze-cast sarcophagi of those comrades tragically doomed to fall in our first grasp for power lie in wait for the final reveille like an ancient megalithic grave. Every year, during the annual journey to the Eternal Guard on 9 November, the names resound of all those who did not lose faith in Germany's heart and soul in one of her darkest hours, those who refused to throw in with traitors and their Christian associates. Some day, the other soldiers will be lying in their graves too, but their life's work will be a reminder to the future to be eternally prepared, at any hour of day or night, to come to the defense of the Reich these men fought so hard to secure, of the perspectives on life and destiny they fought so hard to advance, and to defend it as valiantly as they did.

Communities can be sustained only as genuine reflections of the soul. Faith can be established only when the human representatives of this hard-won community prove themselves worthy of its founders. Values that are not embodied by leaders' actions will not be upheld by community either. That is the ironclad law of selection as it applies to moral-religious life. [. . .]

The Oriental view of labor as a curse has been replaced by a view of labor as an honor. The new work ethic is a revolt against the monastic ideals of the Roman Catholic Church. The raised spade of the German Labor Service has vanquished the Rosary. The greatest danger for a new worldview is often not presented by the residual traces of the old ideologies but rather by sectarian members of the new movement. The sectarian is rigidly focused on but one element that leaves him hypnotized; he places this at the center, and his equilibrium of discernment is thrown off balance by unfettered imagination. He overdraws his arguments, exaggerates, flies into a rage over any sign of rebuff, poses as a stark-raving unacknowledged genius—and if a movement is lacking in stable and reliable, hardened men, then the growth of a grand idea can be thwarted for centuries by a bunch of unrestrained sectarians running around. The political sectarians are to be reined in and kept from espousing ideology, and this is the task of all political leaders; pandering to flamboyant sectarians for fear of hindering the development of some potential genius is the product of the same subaltern subservience as the worshiping of ancient idols just because they are old. Death is not the price we have to pay for our sins. Death is not the opposite of life in any way; it is, rather, subordinate to life. *Individuals* are born and die, not life itself. Birth and death are but *features* of life itself.

The person who can muster faith in the fact that his death is an instrument in the service of life, a transition into a form of life that we cannot know in this life—that person could be said to be deeply religious. But the prerequisite to this kind of faith is that the Christian doctrine of hell intrinsic to all denominations be vanquished; all the fearmongering methods that have been used for centuries to artificially inseminate dread in the imagination must be abandoned. [. . .]

Tolerance was never basic to Christianity. Religious tolerance is an ancient Germanic-European position. It was only able to prevail in a thousand-year struggle against the Christian churches. And the Protestant pastors are just as intolerant as the Catholic priests, the only difference being that they are lacking the format and the power to assert themselves.

When the Christian churches invoke the notion of tolerance, they are praying to an ancient Germanic entity to look kindly upon them at a time when things are beginning to go badly for them as a result of their own doings. Christianity has forfeited the *right* to tolerance by virtue of its own dogmas and deeds. Tolerance on our part is an undeserved gift granted by a noble revolution to an opponent that has made the extermination of the entire Germanic essence into its purpose in life.

We practice religious tolerance not out of respect for the *churches* but rather out of respect for the *Germans* who still believe in the teachings of their priests. The right that we reserve for ourselves is one we also grant them. But we certainly cannot expect our youth to sit piously at the feet of those who betrayed the German *Volk* at its darkest hour or those who still today endeavor to present the parasitic Jewish race as standard-bearers for an exalted concept of God.

We are one *Volk,* and the whole must rule over its parts; "public need goes before private greed" must be the religion that presides over all denominations, just as the nation presides over all professions, classes, and tribes. Our revolution will never allow the education of our youth toward the whole to be wrenched from our hands. We view the religious beliefs of all Germans with tolerance, and we will continue to defend traditional Germanic values in this life ruthlessly and without restraint as long as they remain untainted. [. . .]

True religion cannot be proved by discoveries in nature, nor can it be toppled by them. Religion is the result of *inner experience,* not the consequence of some arbitrary scientific evidence of God or some legend of resurrection; it has absolutely nothing to do with miracles and magic tricks.

The more someone believes in miracles, the less religious he is. That is why the Jew is absolutely irreligious; and the Jewified Christian conceals his religious poverty with a wealth of tales from the Old Testament and magical legends from the New Testament.

The real miracle is the fundamental laws of the universe. The existence [Da-Sein] of matter is as incomprehensible as the existence [Da-Sein] of life. The exploration and representation of these universal laws constitute the very essence of Germanic science, following the noble commands of the soul the very essence of Germanic religion.

193

WALTER KÜNNETH

Jesus: Aryan or Jew?

First published as "Jesus Arier oder Jude?" in his *Antworten auf den Mythus: Die Entscheidung zwischen den nordischen Mythus und dem biblischen Christus* (Berlin: Wichern Verlag, 1936), 103–7.

Rosenberg describes his assessment of "Christianity" as an "altogether earnest attempt to cleanse the personality of Christ from its non-Christian Pauline and Augustinian ingredients." Foremost in this cleansing campaign must be the reinstatement of the opinions long since expressed in *völkisch* circles, above all by Artur Dinter, about the Aryan lineage of Jesus. "As far as Jesus's lineage is concerned, as [Houston Stewart] Chamberlain and [Franz] Delizsch both stressed, there is not one compelling reason to assume that Jesus was of Jewish descent despite the fact that he was raised in an environment characterized by Jewish thinking." Emil Jung's 1924 study on the "Historical Person of Jesus Christ" provides some interesting research results. According to the Christian theologian Ephraim the Syrian (fourth century), Jesus's mother was from the Tribe of Dan (that is, born in Dan), and his father was Roman. Ephraim sees nothing dishonorable in that and adds, "Jesus was descended from two of the world's greatest and most famous nations of *Völker,* the Syrians on his maternal side and the Romans on the paternal." Ephraim assumes this to be common knowledge. What is more, Rosenberg says, "Jerusalem was founded by the Amorites, and they formed the northernmost group in what was later called Galilee, the 'pagan province' from which Jesus is said to have come." Another factor that would justify the assumption of Jesus's roots in the Nordic race is the portraits of him as Savior depicted in the paintings of great artists. "Almost all the great European painters have stripped the face and figure of Jesus of all characteristics of the Jewish race. Forced by the teaching of Jesus as the Lamb of God to distort their paintings, all the great painters of the northern occidental world see Jesus as slender, tall, blond, with an angular forehead and a narrow head. Nor did the great artists of the south have any appreciation for a flat-footed, hook-nosed savior. Even in the resurrection as depicted [on the right wing of the Isenheim Altarpiece, 1512–16] by Matthias Grünewald, Jesus is blond and slender. The blond Jesus gazes out into the world from the Madonna's Sistine breast with a look that is "veritably heroic." This interest in a Nordic figure of Jesus is altogether understandable, for if the intent is to arrive at a synthesis between the Nordic mythos and Jesus—with the exception of Paul and completely independent of the Old Testament—then this endeavor makes sense only if Jesus was himself an Aryan. Otherwise, in terms of "mythos," species-incompatible [*artfremd*] elements would have to be added and thus render any genuine synthesis impossible. So the outcome of the battle over Jesus's Aryanism is very crucial. As a Jew, Jesus cannot be an inspiration to Nordic man; he cannot function as a symbol for the most intimate life of the Aryan soul. You could put it another way: Jesus can be salvaged only for the Nordic mythos—we can speak only in terms of a species-compatible "positive Christianity"—if Jesus was an Aryan. If he wasn't, then the basic premise is missing from all the other statements Rosenberg makes about Jesus. For Rosenberg, though, it is clear that the doctrine of Jesus's Jewish racial heritage is a fraud and that the truth is that Jesus was of Aryan descent.

The first step in clarifying this problem is to pose the decisive question of whether there are sources (and where they are) confirming with certainty, or at least great likelihood, that Jesus was of Aryan descent. Two statements—neither of which can be considered a reliable "source"—merit mentioning in this context. One, the opinion of the Jewish Christian Ephraim (d. 373) as cited by Rosenberg. How do we evaluate the reliability of this as a source? Catholic criticism has already established that there are also forged writings attributed to Ephraim and that the above-mentioned comment is derived from a pseudo-Ephraim manuscript, because in Ephraim's authentic writings Mary is glorified as the "Virgin" and Jesus as the "Son of God" and as such are far removed from any speculations about a Latin descent. More important than even this revealing aspect of the matter is the fact, overlooked by the Catholics, that these statements were not made until the second half of the fourth century, which is extraordinarily late in history, and for that reason alone, they are disqualified from being categorized as sources.

The second literary expression, apparently unknown to Rosenberg, is to be found in the "true word" of the philosopher Celsus around 179. Celsus, an opponent of Christianity, tells it like this: Maria was banished by her husband, a carpenter, for adultery. Panthera, the father of Jesus, was actually a pagan soldier. However, this hypothesis leaves open the question of whether or not Panthera may be identified as an Aryan. As far as this speculation itself is concerned, it first appeared at a very late date, toward the end of the second century, and seems suspiciously characteristic of a Jewish invention, one that never found much overall resonance even among Jews. Hence, nor can this assumption serve as a basis for a serious study.

If there are definitively no reliable sources to confirm that Jesus was an Aryan, then the question that gains paramount importance is whether the fact that Jesus came from Galilee might suggest that the assumption of Aryan blood heritage in Jesus is justified. It is possible that Jesus's parents belonged to the Galilean population, which undeniably comprised a pronounced mixture of peoples [*Volksmischung*]. After 732 B.C., Galilee had become an Assyrian land host to a predominately pagan population. It was not until the time of the Maccabee in 104 that a process of purging set in that forced residents to live according to Jewish rituals and Jewish law or be forced by law to emigrate. It was during this same period that many Jews from Judea in Galilee returned, and the ancestors of Jesus coming from Bethlehem were probably amongst them. Nevertheless, a certain distrust of Galileans lingered in Jerusalem, and they were often seen as being less than equal. This is the basic outline of conclusions we can draw about the race and peoples [*Rasse und Volk*] of Galilee. They are by no means sufficient evidence to a truly conclusive confirmation of Jesus's Aryan descent. Even if we are to concede that there was Aryan bloodstock present in Galilee at the time, there is absolutely nothing to affirm that Jesus's ancestors or his parents descended from them. What speaks against this extremely vague hypothesis is, on the other hand, the fact that Jesus's genealogy is clearly traceable to a tribe in Judea and that those ancient Jews [*Altjuden*] who migrated to Galilee were particularly strict in their prevention of racial mixing. Hence, the fact that there was racial mixing in the population of Galilee does not provide a shred of evidence to confirm the Nordic lineage of Jesus.

A third conjecture leads from the realm of whimsical hypothesis directly to statements in the New Testament taken as the single primary source. New Testament sources across the board take the Jewish lineage of Jesus to be self-evident. Jesus is considered the "Son of David," as heir to the royal throne of Bethlehem as the "City of David" and of David's tribe (Rom. 1:3, 9:4ff.; Luke 1:32). The two distinct family genealogies of Jesus (Matt. 1:1–17, Luke 3:24–38) substantiate the claim of Jewish lineage. These assertions are all the more plausible in light of the fact that they have never been contested by the Jews in their hatred of Christianity; indeed, even the Talmud, at the beginning of the fourth century, acknowledges that Jesus was connected to the kingdom. If that is not sufficient evidence to confirm that Jesus's family tree is purely Jewish, then we have reached the limit of what can be said about anything here. Because if you explain that "even the Israelites and the Jews must be seen as mongrels, the Jewish nose is not to be found in pure Semitic races or in Arabs," when you say that David is described in the Old Testament as "reddish," which could also mean "blond," this does not lead to any conclusions; it serves only to confirm the ambiguity of any notion of a racially thoroughbred descent and thus represents an utter trivialization of the whole racial question or to contend that the ruling class in the nation of Israel was also Nordic, which would render all the basic prerequisites of Rosenberg's criticism of the Old Testament utterly superfluous. If, however, we restrict our consideration to the facts as presented in the statements from sources, then we must consider the Jewish lineage of Jesus to be historical fact.

Finally, one more principal aspect to consider. Christ's mission was always seen, both by him and by Early Christianity and equally so by the Jews, as one of zealous animosity toward Judaism intimately related to the salvation of Israel and the prophecies of the Old Testament. Jesus is the Messiah, the end of the Law, the fulfillment of Old Testament prophecy. This established fact must be the basis for a definitive answer to the question "Aryan or Jew?" Applying the perspective of racial biology to the problem involves a transfer of modern standards to a period in which there was no possible means of applying them as they were intended, and this is a dead-end street. The whole angle of the question "Aryan or Jew?" is itself false in principle. The question cannot yield any fruit nor can it be solved from a perspective of racial biology. Rather, this whole series of questions can be adequately addressed only from the perspective of fundamental religious tenets. This biblical determination is clear and unequivocal: the "real person" of Jesus Christ is a member of a certain people, the people of Israel, because he is clearly not uprooted from the people nor is he a stranger; he is a member of a specific race—the Jewish-Semitic race; his world of belief and his profession of faith emerge from the world of the Old Testament. He represents the Son of God only in the form of this real human being, bound as he is by his race, ethnicity, history, culture, and times; he is the divine revelation fulfilled as it explodes all racial, ethnic, historical, and temporal boundaries—the one "true God." That is the profession of faith for the Christian church, the one and only true basis for understanding the person of Jesus Christ.

194

WALTER GRUNDMANN

Jesus of Nazareth and Jewry

First published in *Jesus der Gaililäer und das Judentum* (Leipzig: Verlag Georg Wigand, 1940), 1–3.

The question of Jesus's relationship to Judaism and the Jews is not one that first arose in contemporary Germany or first came to life here. Far more, it is an essential question deeply anchored in the foundations of a historical development. From the very beginning, Christ's cross has stood between Christians, as believers in Jesus of Nazareth, and the Jews. And his

Crucifixion, at the behest of the Jews, must have had historical roots in the nature and person of Jesus himself, who distinguished himself in such crass contradiction to the Jews—as drastically different from the Jews as even his persecutors—that their only defense against him was to destroy him. Otherwise the Crucifixion makes no sense. His Crucifixion is the manifestation of the Jews' contemptuous renunciation of Christ. And the history of modern Christianity attests that people have always been aware of these contradictions and have always seen in the Jew the real enemy of Christianity. These observations invite us to delve deeper, to question the degree of greatness by comparison. The question then becomes one of whether the contradiction is supposed to be some sort of irony of world history, because its basic premise is that the contradiction is somehow constructed from the same basic assumptions—or does the contradiction have deeper roots and spring from an internal exigency? That is the question that needs clarification.

The need for this clarification is rendered all the more urgent by virtue of the fact that the following utterly astonishing historical findings have been gleaned from a consideration of statements made in Jewish circles concerning the life of Jesus Christ, as well as the relationship between Christianity and Judaism throughout the course of history: (1) It was only over the course of the eighteenth century that Christianity abandoned its fundamental resistance to the Jews. Under the auspices of the ideas fueling the French Revolution, the Jews emerged from the ghetto and entered Western society as civilly competent fellow citizens. What made this possible was that the Christian idea of human equality in the eyes of God was seen as synonymous with a fundamental universal equality between everything that bears a human face, and the notion of brotherly love was seen as an all-encompassing love for humanity. So the motives and the motif of Jewish emancipation did not emerge from Christianity per se but rather were an offshoot of rational humanism. (2) In the centuries immediately following Christ's first appearance, Judaism defiled and opposed him and the Christianity that grew out of his appearance; and to this day, Orthodox Judaism still assumes the same stance in this regard. On the other hand, though, assimilationist Jews in the Western world have been seeking, to an ever-greater degree, to develop a positive attitude toward Christ's appearance and in fact to see in him the most splendid fruit on the tree of Jewish history. But this attitude stems from the same motifs as those we have identified as operative for the changing stance of Christians, motifs that were cleverly manipulated by the Jews as a means of gaining entry into modern society and of balancing out the contradictions. It is more camouflage than conviction. (3) However, this development cannot have rested solely on the roots of the rational humanism shared [by Christianity and Judaism] but was also facilitated by the Christian churches, not least of all in the fact that, over the course of history, specifically Jewish views have been adopted in the cloak of Christianity to an ever-increasing measure and have thus left their mark. The contradiction was no longer a question of disparate essential nature but instead became a question of history. At the present moment, now that the innate *völkisch* contradictions between Judaism and Christianity have become a pressing question of destiny not only for the German *Volk* but are becoming a question facing all the peoples of the world, these observations force us to subject the problem of the relationship between Christianity and Judaism to articulation in the context of a new historical and structural paradigm. This exigency forms the basis for our preliminary examination of the relationship between Jesus and the Jews.

195

DAS SCHWARZE KORPS

The German Faith

Where Do We Stand?

First published anonymously as "Wie steht es um den 'Deutschen Glauben'?" in *Das Schwarze Korps,* 23 April 1936, 1–2.

One of the most important questions of our time is that of religious behavior. In recent years, an extraordinarily large number of German national comrades, pressed by the conscientious need to follow a clear path that is compatible with the National Socialist worldview, have spontaneously concerned themselves with this difficult issue and have come to very different conclusions.

It is not our task to make any sort of judgments for or against one or the other of the arrangements that have been proposed. And yet we do consider it our duty to clarify, without taking sides, what is at issue in this whole complex of questions.

The religious experience can never seek all of its content and its center of gravity solely from its opposition to the tenets of some other faith. A basic premise of this nature is better suited to a partisan political agenda, and that offends our sense of propriety. And so, in our consideration of the whole problem, we must always be mindful of the fact that it is not our place as National Socialists to take an interest in the substance of one set of teachings or the other; our interest is in the question of whether and to what degree it is compatible with that basic principle of our worldview that states that religion is a *private matter.* There are two fundamental statements in which the new state has expressed its opinion with regard to the religious question. On the one hand, Article 24 of the party program states, "We demand freedom for all religious denominations in the state, so far as they are not a danger to it and do not militate against the moral feelings of the German race." The ultimate standard for religious affiliation, then, is explicitly our inborn, species-compatible, racially determined feelings.

The National Socialist state has clearly stated, already in the so-called freedom of conscience decree, the way this is to be interpreted: "[religious] belief is a highly personal matter, unique to each individual, and it is the responsibility of individuals to make this decision based on his own conscience." This means that "the National Socialist state shall refrain from intervening in truly religious affairs, as long as representatives of any given religion forgo involvement in the political arena."

The true motivation behind this policy is the acknowledgment that it is only in this manner that every Catholic or Protestant Christian or any adherent of another religious persuasion may be equally entitled to lead his religious life within the party and within Germany as long as his acts are conscionable on the basis of his *own* inner conviction and insight.

This, of course, is not to imply that this high degree of freedom be subject to maliciously negative interpretation by persons who do not share our worldview.

The *SS-Reichsführer* lent persuasive, unequivocal expression to this in a speech addressing the whole range of tasks assigned the SS: "We will not stand for people flagrantly misusing the term *pagan* to decry us as atheists just because we refuse to come to a common consensus as a community for this denomination or the other, to adhere to one dogma or the other, nor to allow any one of our men to demand that we do."

We are in favor of religious sentiment and the revival of religion, and that means that we will have nothing to do with the materialistic perspective of history that rejects any form of religiosity on principle simply because, from the narrow confines of its ties to the things of this world, it denies the very existence of the metaphysical. To cite the heartfelt words of the *SS-Reichsführer,* we consider anyone who doesn't believe in something "arrogant, megalomaniacal, and dumb."

Accordingly, our current position on this subject does not apply to people who are left up in the air after having had a falling-out with one of the existing denominations. The Confessing Churches are not altogether wrong in asserting that we cannot expect a religious awakening and revival to come from these circles, because the negation of something else does not constitute a solid foundation for the emergence of new ideas. The emergence of a truly new religious experience can proceed only from a positive constitutive political will that attempts to create a new content for belief.

But this, according to the laws of nature, can only be the work of an individual—a human being who has what it takes to become a great reformer or prophet even though he has no need to flaunt himself as such.

From this perspective, then, the current status of the "German Faith Movement" is of particular interest to us.

As we all know, a few days ago Professor [Wilhelm] Hauer and [Ernst] Graf zu Reventlow resigned from their leadership posts [in the German Faith Movement], and in light of this, the decision was made to operate no longer under the direction of one personally accountable leader but rather under the auspices of a "board of directors." This presents the danger that the "German Faith Movement" will begin to function along the lines of an organized association and that seems to us, for the reasons just outlined, as abhorrent as it is dangerous.

What is more, the increasingly anti-Christian stance assumed of late by the Bund [for German Christianity] and its current recruitment campaign seems incongruent with its purpose, which is supposed to be to awaken religious sentiment.[1]

A large number of people who have recently joined the "Faith Movement" are adamantly opposed to this change in objectives, and this is what Hauer and Reventlow could not condone because it has nothing to do with the original goals of the Faith Movement.

This movement was first founded on the basis of a desire to mobilize as many *like-minded* individuals as possible under the auspices of one organization to consolidate them as an ideological force. It was for this reason that, for a good two years, we restricted our efforts to including in this umbrella organization only those many small regional churches (comprising the Bund) that professed to practicing some form of "Aryan" religiosity. Originally, then, the whole thing was designed to offer a "pagan" religious community as an alternative to the three Christian Confessing Churches and the four recognized Christian sects. This was supposed to enable its members to overcome the disadvantages in the public sector stemming from their status as "pagans."

The basic idea behind the movement was without doubt a good one. We don't see any reason why those Germans who want nothing to do with Christianity primarily because they refuse to subject themselves to the stipulations of those portions of Christian moral law whose dictates are alien to their very nature should not be entitled to some form of organization as a public-legal entity.

This would be desirable even for no other reason than that it is probably the only way that the persons involved and their families will ever have the chance to achieve the equality before the law that they so desperately need.

The need for [practitioners of pagan religions] to be free from ongoing discrimination based on external forms plays a role here. Even today, it is rather unpleasant, when filling out official forms, to have to leave the column for religious denomination blank because it leaves the impression that one is thus seeking to identify oneself as a dissident, merely attempting to lend expression to a negation. Furthermore, one is thus suspected of being an atheist or a materialistic monist even though this is the furthest thing from his intent.

It is for these reasons that we believe, in the long run, it is too much to ask of our national comrades who cling loyally and truly to the innate moral law unique to our race that their little children should forfeit the right to every form of so-called solemn initiation into the human community, that they should deny themselves the public sanctification of their marriages, that their burials be void of ritual. But we also know that any new form, if it is not to be reduced to a mere mockery, can develop only gradually and organically from those authentic ancient customs still in existence today and thus cannot suddenly be "created" by some organization.

Above all, though, we are of the opinion that these customs—which are the only things that justify and make necessary such an organization—can never be the sole foundation for an "organization devoted to a religious worldview." [This is] because the absence of prescriptive regulations or collectivistic determinations is precisely the characteristic that is typical of truly Germanic religious behavior.

For the ancient Germans, religion was and remains a private matter. That is why the ancient Germanic heads of households were their own priests and would not tolerate the ecclesiastic class.

So despite our support for many of their goals, we have other concerns regarding the "German Faith Movement." Hauer has proposed—understandably so, in consideration of his professional perspective as an Indologist—that we resurrect those aspects of ancient Hindu belief systems that are congruent with our race and combine them with a "Germanicized" version of ancient medieval ideas. The end result, then, has been a wild mix of pseudoscientific medievalism and misconstrued romanticism for the world of ideas of German antiquity. We think that this sort of rehashing of antiquated and, to some degree, completely obsolete ways of thinking is absolutely incapable of meeting today's religious needs. Because what we need now is an entirely new, reality-based, coherent system that consciously seeks to avoid every form of romanticism—*not a second or third recasting of the same.*

The guiding principle for Hauer's group was, "The German Faith Movement seeks a spiritual renewal of the *Volk* on the basis of the primordial hereditary legacy of the German race; the divine origin of the German race rests in its contract with the Eternal, whose laws we shall loyally obey." We wholeheartedly support the first part of this profession of faith, but the second part is cause for concern. We prefer to have nothing to do with formulations of this nature when it comes to speaking in terms of a return to the original, primordial source of our religious experience.

What we need is not some vaguely romanticized enthusiasm for a cultic, sectarian form of pseudoreligiosity but rather an open and honest profession of faith in the religious, *and above all the ethical* views of our forefathers.

One of the most ill-fated mistakes made by all the small Bund associations seeking to rejuvenate religion in our race is that they have attempted to approach the issue by connecting with the point at which Christianity was able to forcibly thwart further developments [in living religion].

It is impossible to eliminate a thousand years of human and *völkisch* development and treat it as though it never existed.

Wotan and Thor are dead—and those sentimental enthusiasts who slaughtered a white steed at the sacrificial site a good dozen years ago were sorry fools who needlessly compromised a good thing. Neither the preliterate religious customs nor the ideas upon which they were based are applicable for us today. If any attempt is to be made to lend expression to the ethical consciousness that is congruent with our race in concrete religious forms, then the best we can hope to do would be to take recourse to the sacred book of our ancestors, the Edda, in the same way that modern-day Christianity takes recourse to the Old Testament. One can allow the poetic beauty and especially the ideological passages to have a direct impact and, if so desired, to build a sort of moral law on that basis. But one should not attempt to aim for anything beyond that.

Religion is an affair of the spirit and can thus be based only on the spiritual. Our task is merely to see to it that any German who has rejected all Oriental doctrines and is striving to reclaim the inherited ethical legacy of our race from within himself is not thwarted in his efforts.

Note

1. The Bund für deutsches Christentum (Organization of German Christianity) was an alliance of regional church leaders and members of the German Christian movement that formed in November 1936 to promote a national "Jew-free" proto-Nazi church.—Eds.

196

MARTIN BORMANN

National Socialism and Christianity Are Irreconcilable

Confidential memorandum circulated on 6 June 1941. First published in *The Trial of the Major War Criminals before the International Military Tribunal, Nuremberg, 14 November 1945–1 October 1946,* document 075-D, XXXV (Nuremberg, 1947–49), 7–13.

National Socialist and Christian concepts are irreconcilable. The Christian churches build upon man's ignorance and endeavor to keep the greatest possible number of people in a state of ignorance. For it is only in this fashion that the churches can maintain their power. National Socialism, on the other hand, rests on scientific foundations. Christianity has certain unalterable principles, established nearly two thousand years ago, which have petrified into a system of dogma that is ever further removed from reality. National Socialism, on the other hand, if it is to fulfill its purpose, must forever be brought in harmony with the latest results of scientific inquiry.

The Christian churches have always recognized the dangers that threaten their existence from the exact discoveries of science. They have therefore tried to suppress or falsify scientific research using a fraudulent science, i.e., theology, and dogma. Our National Socialist concept of the world is on a far higher plane than are the ideas of Christianity, whose essential points have been taken over from the Jews. For that reason, too, we have no need for Christianity. [. . .]

When we National Socialists speak of a belief in God, we do not mean the same thing as naive Christians and their clerical exploiters have in mind—some anthropoid creature sitting around somewhere in the spheres. Instead, our intent is to open people's eyes to the fact that, aside from this small planet earth, which is relatively insignificant with relation to the vast universe, there is an unimaginably great number of other celestial bodies in the universe, an infinite number of bodies surrounded as is the sun by planets and, like these planets, in turn, similarly surrounded by smaller bodies, moons. The power of nature's law that propels these infinite bodies through the universe is what we call the omnipotent force, or God. The claim that this universal force could somehow care for the fate of each individual, of each bacillus here on earth, that it might be influenced by so-called prayers or by other astounding things, rests to a great degree on the naiveté or on profit-minded impertinence.

We National Socialists, on the other hand, demand of ourselves that we live as naturally as possible—that is to say, in accord with the natural laws of life. The more precisely we understand and observe the laws of nature and of life and the more closely we adhere to them, the more we correspond to the will of that omnipotent force. The more we understand that will, the greater our successes shall be.

The logical conclusion that flows from this basic incompatibility between National Socialist and Christian views is that we must reject any increase in existing support for and any sponsorship of emerging Christian denominations. For this reason, we have definitively abandoned the idea of establishing an Evangelical Lutheran Reich Church formed from a conglomeration of the various denominations of the Evangelical Lutheran Church because the Protestant Church is as hostile to us as the Catholic Church. Offering any form of support to the Protestant Church would ultimately work against us. [. . .]

For the first time in German history, the leadership of the nation rests consciously and completely in the hands of the Führer himself. In creating the party, its organizations, and subsidiaries, the Führer has devised an instrument for himself and thus for the whole of German national leadership that renders him independent of the church. All influences that might impair or even harm the leadership exercised by the Führer with the aid of the National Socialist Party must be eliminated. More and more, the people must be wrested from the clutches of the churches and their ministries. It is obvious from their point of view that the churches shall and must resist this loss of power. But never again are the churches to receive any measure of influence over the leadership of the nation. That influence must be broken, completely and forever.

Only the nation's government—and by its order, the party, its organizations and subsidiaries—exercises the right of governance over the people and the nation. Just as the harmful influences of astrologers, fortune-tellers, and other swindlers are being systematically eliminated and suppressed by the state, so too must the very possibility of ecclesiastical influence be removed. Only when that has occurred will the nation's leadership be able to exert complete control over the individual citizen. Only then will *Volk* and Reich be secure in their existence for all future times.

197

DIETRICH BONHOEFFER

Resistance and Resignation

Written in 1945 and first published in 1951. Reprinted as *Dietrich Bonhoeffer Widerstand und Ergebung: Briefe und Aufzeichnungen aus der Haft,* vol. 5 of *Dietrich Bonhoeffer: Werke,* edited by Christian Gremmels, Eberhard Bethge, and Renate Bethge in cooperation with Ilse Toìdt (Gütersloh: Christian Kaiser, 1998), 20–24.

The grand masquerade of evil has thrown all notions of ethics into disarray. The fact that evil should appear in the form of light, of benevolence, of historical exigency, of social justice is simply confusing to us from the perspective of our traditional, long-standing world of ethical ideas; for Christians leading their lives according to the Bible, it confirms precisely the inscrutable malice of evil.

[. . .] Who can stand up to it? Only the man who is not bound by the standard of his reason, his principles, his conscience, his freedom, his virtue, but who rather is prepared to sacrifice all of this when he feels called to act, obediently and responsibly following his faith in God alone, the responsible man whose life is singularly intent on answering God's question and his call.

Where are these responsible men?

What is actually behind complaints about the lack of civil courage? We have seen much bravery and sacrifice in these years but almost no civil courage, not even amongst ourselves. It would be psychologically naive to attribute this lack simply to personal cowardice. There are very different reasons behind it. We Germans, over the course of a long history, have had to learn the necessity and the power of obedience. We have seen the purpose and greatness of our lives in the subordination of personal thoughts and desires to the mission that became ours. Our eyes have been on heaven, not in slavish fear but in sovereign trust that has seen in our mission a profession and in our professions a calling. The willingness to privilege the orders from "above" as opposed to our own discretion necessarily involves a certain degree of justifiable mistrust toward one's own heart. Who would ever contest the notion to any German that he has always delivered utmost courage and placed his life on the line in obedience, in his mission, his calling? The German has always seen his freedom vested in his ability to break free from his own will in the service of the collective whole—and where in the world has anyone ever spoken more passionately of freedom than in Germany, from Martin Luther to the philosophy of idealism? Vocation and freedom appeared to him as two sides of the same coin. But this involved a misapprehension of the world; he never reckoned with the notion that his willingness to subjugate himself, to put his life on the line for the mission, could be abused for the purposes of evil. Were this to occur, the very practice of a calling would itself be called into question; all of Germany's foundational moral principles would begin to falter. We had to conclude that the German was lacking one decisive fundamental piece of knowledge: the knowledge of the necessity to take voluntary, responsible action even in defiance of one's profession and mission. What took its place was, on the one hand, the irresponsible scrupulousness and, on the other, the self-suffering scruple that never led to any action. Civil courage can emerge only from the freely elected sense of responsibility of a free man. Only today are Germans beginning to discover what it means to exercise a freely elected sense of responsibility. Responsibility rests in a God who demands that we act responsibly on a daring leap of faith [*freie Glaubenswagnis*] and one who promises forgiveness and comfort to anyone who becomes a sinner in the process.

PART SEVEN

. . .

NATIONAL SOCIALISM AND THE ARTS

17

Literature

Official Culture and Its Outcasts

IF *BILDUNG* (education, self-cultivation through culture) was one of the defining qualities of German society, then literature was its keystone. Before imperial Germany was created in 1871, the literary text was the strand that knit together Germans as a cultural, if not political, entity. Plays by Gotthold Lessing (1729–81) and Friedrich Schiller (1759–1805), novels by Johann Wolfgang von Goethe (1749–1832) and Theodor Fontane (1819–98), and poetry by Novalis (1772–1801) and Annette von Droste-Hülshoff (1797–1848) reached into every town and principality and provided a common cultural vocabulary and quasi-national identity. In Wilhelmine Germany, culture was defined by a rigid canon of dead and living writers. Certainly, membership in the Literature Section of the Prussian Academy of the Arts was the definitive measure of who belonged and who did not.

On 21 February 1933, the chair of the Literature Section, the prorepublican and left-leaning novelist Heinrich Mann (1871–1950), quietly packed a single suitcase, took his umbrella, and left for France. Six days later, the Reichstag burned. His brother, Nobel Prize winner Thomas Mann (1875–1955), found himself in France lecturing on the "Suffering and Greatness of Richard Wagner" and then decamped for Switzerland. Neither returned to Germany until after 1945.

The Prussian Academy was stripped of its literary elite. Its conservative president, the anti-Semitic composer Max von Schillings (1868–1933), demanded that all members take oaths swearing loyalty to Hitler. Thomas Mann and the novelists Alfred Döblin (1878–1957) and Ricarda Huch (1864–1947) resigned in protest. A further ten, including the world-famous authors Franz Werfel (1890–1945) and Jacob Wassermann (1873–1934), were excluded from the academy after the Enabling Act of 23 May 1933 placed the organization under Goebbels's control. Hanns Johst (1890–1978), who had dedicated his drama *Schlageter* (1933) to Adolf Hitler (see document 9 in chapter 1), replaced Heinrich Mann as head of the Literature Section. But even writers on the right found such changes unsettling. Goebbels immediately proposed replacing Mann with Ernst Jünger (1895–1998), the most important novelist of the "conservative revolution," whose novel *In the Storm of Steel* (first published in 1920 but republished in ever-altered form throughout the Weimar Republic), a fictional diary about comradeship in the trenches of World War I, became a best seller upon its publication. Jünger, however, who had been disenchanted with the Nazis since the mid-1920s, refused membership, stating that he saw himself as a writer, not as a member of a collective.

A wave of major literary figures on the left fled during this period that signaled the collapse of Weimar culture: Bertolt Brecht (1898–1956) departed for Prague, Paris, Denmark, and eventually California; the poet Karl Wolfskehl (1869–1948), for New Zealand; and Arnold Zweig (1887–1969), for Palestine. Some were not quite quick enough: Anna Seghers (1900–83) and Egon Erwin Kisch (1885–1948) were arrested and expelled, while Willi Bredel (1901–64) and Ludwig Renn (1889–1979) spent years in prison. The poet and critic Erich Mühsam (1878–1934), who had been minister of culture in the Bavarian Soviet in 1919, and the Communist novelist Klaus Neukrantz (1895–1941) were beaten to death in concentration camps. The list of literary talents persecuted by the Nazis was huge and not at all random. On

23 August 1933, the Nazis promulgated a list of writers and intellectuals who had been stripped of their citizenship, including Heinrich Mann; the dramatist Ernst Toller (1893–1939), who had been a central figure of the Bavarian Soviet; the satirist Kurt Tucholsky (1890–1935); and the celebrity novelist Lion Feuchtwanger (1884–1958). By 1939, more than nine thousand individuals could be counted among the authors (Jewish and non-Jewish) proscribed by the party.

In September 1933, Goebbels's Ministry for Popular Enlightenment and Propaganda oversaw the creation of the Reichskulturkammer (Reich Chamber of Culture), with its seven sections for literature, the press, broadcasting, theater, music, film, and the fine arts. The "Editors' Law" of 4 October 1933 brought all publications under the direct control of Goebbels's ministry.

The new definition of literature as the lifeblood of the nation fulfilled the desire of many conservative writers, including some Jewish ones, who had advocated this stance in the Weimar Republic. Hugo von Hofmannsthal's (1874–1929) programmatic essay of 1927 titled "Literature as the Intellectual Locus of the Nation" decried the disease of internationalism and evoked a new literary world in the service of the nation. It was this abstract idea of a transcendent national literature that the poet Stefan George (1868–1933) called for in his 1928 volume *The New Reich*. Hofmannsthal was of Jewish ancestry, and his work was excluded from the Nazi's literary canon in spite of his conservative politics. Joseph Goebbels, who had a doctorate in German literature and was a published, if dreadful, novelist, wanted George to be the figurehead for his new literary order but failed to persuade the poet to take on this mantle. George withdrew to Switzerland and decided never to collaborate with the Nazi's "New Reich."

The racialized concept of the *Volk* contrasted with the negative image of the threat of the "Jew," who became the embodiment of "cosmopolitanism," "asphalt literature," "internationalism," and "degenerate literary experimentalism." Any literature produced by a Jew—no matter the genre, voice, or approach—was by definition unacceptable to the *Volk*. This view of culture had its antecedents in the work of populist and racist critics such as Adolf Bartels (1862–1945), who spent most of his career writing books that charted the racial and, therefore (in his mind), intellectual pedigree of German-language writers. (His conclusions about who had Jewish ancestry were wrong often enough that his works became a bit of a joke, although the Reich initially used his lists to determine which works would be removed from German bookstores and libraries.) In Vienna, the academic literary historian Josef Nadler (1884–1963) wrote a "literary history of German lands and tribes" in which he attempted to determine the anthropological nature of the Germanic contribution to European letters. His major disciple, the theater historian and theorist Heinz Kindermann (1894–1985), looked at the role of tribal identity as defined by race and remained an important figure in postwar Austrian culture. Among the Nazi specialists on literary culture, Johannes Alt (1896–?) of the University of Würzburg turned to racial biology to define the "Jewish" aspect of German culture, with an eye to isolating it and destroying its presence.

On 10 May 1933, the Nazis staged one of their most symbolic public acts to mark the transition from the older notion of culture to that of Nazi culture. In the plaza adjacent to the Opera in Berlin, twenty thousand volumes—mainly stolen from Magnus Hirschfeld's Institute for Sexual Science (see document 167 in chapter 14) and the library of the University of Berlin—were publicly burned to the accompaniment of martial music by members of the SS, the Storm Troopers, and the Nationalsozialistischer Deutscher Studentenbund (National Socialist German Students' League) under the leadership of Oskar Stäbel. In more than a dozen university towns throughout Germany, the Deutsche Studentenschaft (German Student Association) orchestrated similar events, announced by a poster decrying works promoting the "un-German spirit." Not to be cowed, a small group of anti-Nazi students distributed a clandestine leaflet proclaiming "All Anti-Semitic students are assholes!"

The entire scenario was orchestrated by Goebbels as a great public spectacle of cultural purification. Among the books that went up in a "fantastic display of light," as the *Deutsche Allgemeine Zeitung* described the bonfire, were those of named "Jewish authors" such as Karl Marx, Heinrich Heine, Kurt Tucholsky, and Sigmund Freud. Among others, books by Bertolt Brecht, Lion Feuchtwanger, Ernst Toller, and Franz Werfel were burned. Erich Kästner (1899–1974), the Jewish satirist and famous writer of children's books, stood in the crowd unnoticed, watching his own books go up in flames. He quickly went underground but never left Germany during the Nazis' rule. The conservative novelist of the Bavarian countryside Oskar Maria Graf (1899–1967), who was on a lecture tour when the Nazis took power, demanded in an open letter from his temporary refuge in Vienna that his works be included in the bonfire. The official blacklists were promulgated by Goebbels's propaganda ministry, and the guidelines for their preparation were widely circulated to libraries and bookstores. After the book burnings, quasi-official blacklists of leftist, democratic, and Jewish writers also began to circulate. Libraries and bookstores were cleansed of these works by "un-German" authors. Liberal professors and critics of the regime were summarily dismissed from the universities. Within weeks, hundreds of writers and artists had fled abroad. Lion Feuchtwanger registered his anger in a sarcastic letter to the "resident" of his former home, and Thomas Mann wrote a searing defense of fellow exiles—as well as those likeminded writers who chose to remain in Germany—in a letter to the Swiss writer and cultural editor of the *Neue Züricher Zeitung,* Eduard Korrodi (1885–1955).

Public exhibitions with anti-Semitic themes justified these measures by showing how "Judeo-Bolshevism" had permeated and corrupted European culture since the French Revolution. The burning of the books left a huge gap in the literary culture of the New Germany. Older writers such as Gottfried Benn (1886–1956), who had loudly and publicly heralded the Nazis' arrival and denounced the first literary émigrés, like Klaus Mann, were quickly dumped as "swinish" because of their use of modernist literary forms. Mann, shocked by Benn's stance, wrote a blistering open letter from his exile in France. Benn's response was a clear indication that even a few radical members of the Weimar avant-garde could and did become fervent ideological supporters of the new order, at least at its very beginning. Hans Grimm (see document 73 in chapter 6), who had coined the phrase *Volk ohne Raum* (people without space) in his 1926 novel of the same name, was found to be too ideological in his demand for the Nazis to consider returning to Germany's lost colonies. Grimm's view, that Germany needed resources greater than its limited geographic space provided, was rejected, but his literary model of a colonial space provided the Nazis with a way of justifying their eventual eastward aggression and expansion into central Europe.

Nazi Germany was able to fill the gaps left by its literary purges with a generation of older nationalist writers and a series of younger writers who evolved a style of obeisance to the new order after 1933. Typical of the regime's enthusiasts was Ernst Bertram (1884–1957), whose polemics against humanism provided Nazism with a perverse historical justification in the battles of the Germanic tribes against Rome. Novelists such as Joseph Georg Oberkofler (1889–1962) glorified the peasant and damned city dwellers in his 1933 novel *The Forest Preserve.* Josefa Berens-Totenohl's (1891–1969) 1934 book *The Secret Court,* with its mixture of sex and mysticism, not to mention its villainous and clandestine antinational Jew, became popular overnight and remained a best seller for several years. Poets such as Josef Weinhaber (1892–1945), who was seen as Stefan George's natural heir, became flacks singing the crudest glorifications of the heroism of the Nazi state. (Weinhaber committed suicide in 1945.) Heinrich Anacker (1901–71), Hans Baumann (1914–88), and the head of the Hitler Youth organizations, Baldur von Schirach (1907–74), represented a new generation of Nazi poets and novelists, although their careers abruptly ended with the collapse of the Third Reich. Others tried to work certain anti-Nazi motifs into their literary endeavors.

Friedrich Reck-Malleczewen (1884–1945) attempted to outwit the censors by disguising his fiery allegory of Nazi tyranny in a Reformation setting in his novel *Bockelson*. Reck-Malleczewen, whose clandestine memoir was posthumously published as *Diary of a Man in Despair,* was eventually arrested and shot in the Dachau concentration camp. Werner Bergengruen's (1892–1964) 1935 novel *Der Großtyrann und das Gericht* (The Great Tyrant and the Court of Justice, published in English as *A Matter of Conscience*) is set in the Renaissance era, but the story of a merciless tyrant playing with the weaknesses of his underlings was widely read as an allegory of Hitler's rule. Some young poets who came of age under National Socialism, such as Franz Fühmann (1922–84), became much-praised young writers in the Soviet Zone and, after 1949, in the German Democratic Republic (GDR). Fühmann, one of the most liberal and creative writers of the GDR, never acknowledged his earlier involvement in German culture under the Nazis, even though his role was self-consciously apolitical.

After the famous 20 January 1942 meeting at a villa on the Wannsee in Berlin announcing the Final Solution to a handpicked elite of Nazi officials, literature, too, was deported to the camps. The poet Nelly Sachs (1891–1970), who would go on to win the Nobel Prize in 1966, was rescued from a concentration camp by the intervention of the Swedish government in 1940. Gertrud Kolmar (1894–1943), Arthur Silbergleit (1886–1943), and Gertrud Kantorowicz (1876–1945), among many others, were not so fortunate and were murdered.

FIGURE 18. Nazi students unloading confiscated materials for the public book burning that is to take place on the Opernplatz in Berlin, 10 May 1933. The banner on the back of the truck reads, "German students march against the un-German spirit." Photograph no. 45032, U.S. National Archives and Records Administration, College Park, Md. / Akademie der Künst, Historisches und Verwaltungsarchiv AP / Wide World Bildarchiv Preussischer Kulturbesitz.

198

GERMAN STUDENT ASSOCIATION

Down with the Un-German Spirit!

Circulated on 13 April 1933 as a poster titled "Wider den undeutschen Geist!" First published in *Die Bücherverbrennung. Zum 10 Mai 1933,* edited by Gerhard Sauder (Munich: Carl Hanser Verlag, 1983), 93–94.

1. Language and literature have their roots in the *Volk*. The German *Volk* bears the responsibility for making sure that language and literature represent the pure and unadulterated expression of the *Volk* culture.
2. Today there is a gaping contradiction between literature and German *Volk* culture. This is a shameful state of affairs.
3. Maintaining purity of language and literature is up to *you!* Your *Volk* has entrusted *you* with the faithful preservation of language.
4. *Our most dangerous adversary is the Jew and anyone who does his bidding.*
5. The Jew can think only in Jewish terms. When he writes in German, he tells lies. Any German who writes in German but whose thinking is un-German is a *traitor!* Any student who speaks and writes in an un-German way is furthermore completely *thoughtless* and untrue to his task.
6. *We seek to eradicate lies, we seek to denounce treason, we seek to erect sites of discipline and political education for our students, not sites of thoughtlessness.*

7. We seek to respect the fact that the Jew is a stranger, and we seek to take the culture of the *Volk* seriously.
   We therefore demand of the Office of Censorship the following:
   — Jewish works must appear in the Hebrew language. If they appear in German, they are to be identified as translations.
   — Rigorous action is to be taken against any abuse of the written word in German.
   — The German written word is the exclusive province of Germans.
   — The un-German spirit shall be eliminated from all public libraries.
8. *We demand* that German students demonstrate the will and the capacity for independent thought and discernment.
9. *We demand* that German students demonstrate the will and the capacity for maintaining the purity of the German language.
10. *We demand* that German students demonstrate the will and the capacity for vanquishing Jewish intellectualism and the attendant symptoms of liberal decline in German intellectual life.
11. *We demand a process of selection for students and professors designed to secure sound thought in the German spirit.*
12. *We demand that the German university become the sanctuary for the German* Volk *culture and the site of struggle emanating from the German spirit.*

199

ANONYMOUS

To the German Student Association

All Anti-Semitic Students Are Assholes!

First published in *Die Bücherverbrennung. Zum 10. Mai 1933,* edited by Gerhard Sauder (Munich: Carl Hanser Verlag, 1983), 94–95.

To the German Student Association!

I. All anti-Semitic students are assholes!

II. Assholes do not belong at the university, they belong in the shithouse.

III. Anti-Semitic students are cowards. They are afraid of the competition of the Jewish intellect.

IV. Anti-Semitic students are frauds! They eliminate high-caliber intellectual achievement only so they can comfortably remain in first place.

V. The Jews were already a royal nation of people back when the ancestors of anti-Semites were at best warthogs foraging in the mire of the Teutoberger Forest.

VI. Germans are comprised of the Wends, the Slavs, the Romans, Celts, etc., plus a whole humongous pile of other crap! There isn't a trace of the Aryan or Germanic to be seen.

VII. Back when the embryos of the current generation still closely resembled those of a pig, we were at war. At that time, we were able to ascertain that the Jews of Galicia and Russia were the standard-bearers for the Old High German language. If this generation of embryos had reached the human stage of human development, they would know this! This is how things are when they don't make it past the pig stage.

VIII. With the theses printed on the poster penned by the German Student Association, the international community is certainly getting an accurate picture of the intellectual level of today's German students. In the end, this, too, shall be blamed on the Jews!

IX. Long live the German convictions and fighting spirit.
X. Every decent human being is ashamed to say that this is the German way.
XI. If this is indeed the nature of the German way, then no one wants to be German.
XII. The international community has been notified!

200

ASSOCIATION OF GERMAN PEOPLES LIBRARIANS

General Guidelines for Compiling Blacklists

Published as "Grundsätzliches zur Anfertigung von Schwarzen Listen," in *Börsenblatt für den Deutschen Buchhandel, 16 May 1933,* 356–58.

1. The standards for compiling blacklists are of a literary-political nature. The fundamental underlying question intrinsic to any political decision is equally applicable here: Who is the real enemy? Who are we fighting against?
2. The fight is directed against the symptoms of subversion of the ways of life and of thought unique to our species—that is, against the "asphalt" literature written primarily for people residing in major urban areas as a way of affirming and bolstering his detachment from his environment, from his *Volk,* and from any sense of community, as a way of completely uprooting him. It is the literature of intellectual nihilism.
3. This literary genre is represented primarily, though not exclusively, by Jewish authors. Nor is every Jewish writer necessarily an asphalt author: so, for example, the criticism of literature by assimilated Jews written by the Zionist E[manuel] Bin-Gorion represents the principles of a Jewish *Volk.*
4. Not every Russian writer is a cultural Bolshevist. Dostoevsky and L. Tolstoy do not belong on the index (without Dostoevsky we would have no Moeller van den Bruck). New acquisitions of Russian authors are not necessary, nor do we need to destroy all the works of contemporary Russian authors (e.g., Fadejew, Tarassow-Rodionow).
5. It is recommended that *one copy* of every book always be retained, even the most dangerous books in the *poison cabinets* of the large city and university libraries, pending the coming altercation with the "asphalt" literati and the Marxists.
6. Technically, the purging should be completed *in stages* calibrated according to the ability of new acquisitions to fill the resulting gaps with German literature.
7. Books that are blocked from checkout can practically be divided into *three groups:*
   Group 1 is to be destroyed (auto-da-fé) (e.g., [Erich Maria] Remarque).
   Group 2 [is to be] deposited in the poison cabinet (e.g., Lenin).
   Group 3 contains dubious cases requiring future assessment as to
   whether they belong to group 1 or group 2 (e.g., [B.] Traven [Ret Marut]).
8. More important than the purging is the restocking of holdings in accordance with the new Germany.
9. The restocking of nationalistic and socialistic holdings definitely does not include *patriotic kitsch.* Blacklists are being compiled of such works. Examples of patriotic kitsch: P.O. Höcker, P. Hoch!

201

GERMAN STUDENT ASSOCIATION HEAD OFFICE FOR ENLIGHTENMENT AND PUBLICITY

To the Individual Student Associations

Circular distributed on 9 May 1933 as "An die Einzelstudentenschaften" (circular P, no. 4). Published in *Die Bücherverbrennung. Zum 10 Mai 1933*, edited by Gerhard Sauder (Munich: Carl Hanser Verlag, 1983), 77–78.

The following listing is to be used as the basis for the symbolic action represented by the act of burning and is to be followed as literally as possible by the student representative. Since it is not likely to be feasible in most instances to burn all of the books, throwing to the flames just those texts included in the following listing is a practicable alternative. This does not in any way prevent a huge pile of books from nevertheless being burned. Local organizers are to be given free rein in this regard.

1. *Against* the class struggle and materialism
   For the community of the Volk and an idealistic view of life
   Marx, Kautsky
2. *Against* decadence and moral decay
   For disciplined breeding and manners in family and state
   Heinrich Mann, Ernst Glaeser, Erich Kästner
3. *Against* moral laxity und political treason
   For devotion to *Volk* and state
   F. W. Förster
4. *Against* the soul-shredding overestimation of the basic instincts
   For the nobility of the human soul
   the Freudian school, the journal *Imago*
5. *Against* the falsification of our history and the degradation of its great figures
   For the reverential treatment of our past
   Emil Ludwig, Werner Hegemann
6. *Against* the democratic-Jewish brand of journalism that is alien to our *Volk*
   For the responsible collaboration in the project of nation building
   Theodor Wolff, Georg Bernhard
7. *Against* the literary betrayal of the soldiers of the World War
   For education of the *Volk* in the spirit of military defense
   Erich Maria Remarque
8. *Against* the fatuous butchering of the German language
   For the preservation of the precious treasures of our *Volk*
   Alfred Kerr
9. *Against* insolence and impudence
   For respect and reverence of the indomitable spirit of the German *Volk*
   Tucholsky, Ossietzky

Heil Hitler!
President of the German Student Association
[Gerhard] Krüger
Director of the Central Office
[Hans Karl] Leistritz

202

DEUTSCHE ALLGEMEINE ZEITUNG

The Public Burning of Outlawed Works

First published as "Die öffentliche Verbrennung der geächteten Schriften," in *Deutsche Allgemeine Zeitung,* 12 May 1933, 179–81.

Reich Minister Dr. Goebbels Addresses the Students [10 May 1933]

The student rally against the outlawed written works turned into a mass demonstration, attended by participants from seemingly all sectors of the population. Despite pouring rain, huge crowds of spectators gathered in front of the student dormitory in the Oranienburg Street. The transport vehicles carrying the books of blacklisted authors were covered with posters. At the last minute, while reviewing the extensive amount of material collected at the dormitory, a large number of books were set aside and spared, including works by Lasalle and Engels. The torches were distributed at the dormitory between 9:00 and 10:00 P.M. At ten o'clock sharp, the SA leader sounded the command: "Attention! Forward, march!" The parade made its way toward the Oranienburg Gate accompanied by the sounds of a marching band. An uninterrupted human chain formed cordons on both sides.

At the Kaiser Franz Joseph Platz, between the opera house and the auditorium, spectators had already begun gathering around 8:00 P.M., so that by 9:00 P.M., the area designated for the book burning was surrounded by throngs of people. The students had stacked wood for the stake at the center of the square. Seven spotlights stood poised to disperse light bright as day as soon as the event began. You could see throngs of people approaching from as far as the Brandenburg Gate, which lent the whole affair the impression of a *Volk* festival.

Strains of the chanting choirs echoed through the streets, attracting curious onlookers from everywhere. The crowd carried a bust of Magnus Hirschfeld, founder and director of the Institute for Sexual Science. The head was removed from the bust that had been housed at the institute. An SA officer hoisted it high on a stick for all to see. The torchlight parade meandered through Luisen and Karl Streets toward the Königsplatz. A substantial number of nonstudents had joined the marchers by then. Mounted police stood waiting for the approaching torchbearers in the middle portal of the Brandenburg Gate so that they could head up the parade from there and clear the route along Linden Boulevard [Unter den Linden]. The lorry trucks loaded with the despicable books rumbled noisily along the middle promenade. As soon as the head of the parade reached the wood stack that had been erected atop a pile of sand, several men began pouring gas on it. The torchbearers marched past the wood stack and threw their torches onto the burning stake, rapidly setting the wood stack ablaze. A tremendous flame leapt up in a brilliant burst and showered the faces in the crowd of spectators in a fantastic display of light. The flames were reflected in the windows of the national opera house and the auditorium, giving the many photographers and cameramen who were present at the scene more than their money's worth. However, the blaze grew quickly and threw off such intense heat that the crowd had to *stand back*. Besides, burning chunks of wood were churned up and hurdled through the air. Several workers had to be enlisted to toss the burning billets back onto the wood stack.

The heat was so hot that the vehicles with the despicable books could not drive directly up to the fire, so a long human chain had to be formed to pass the books to be burned into the flames. The director of the Region 10 Berlin-Brandenburg branch of the German Student Association, [Herbert] Gutjahr, said a few words as he threw to the fire works by those men identified as being particularly un-German. Some of the names he mentioned were, among others, Karl Marx, Kautsky, Heinrich Mann, Sigmund Freud, Emil Ludwig, Theodor

Wolff, Georg Bernhard, Alfred Kerr, Peter Panter, Erich Maria Remarque, and Karl v. Ossietzkis [*sic*]. In the course of this demonstration, *Reichminister Dr. Goebbels* was greeted enthusiastically when he appeared at the Kaiser Franz Joseph Platz. The minister explained that extremist Jewish intellectualism had finally come to an end in Germany. With the revolts in November of 1918, materialism had made its breakthrough, and ever since then, for the past fourteen years in Germany, an inconceivable material and intellectual disgrace has prevailed as a consequence, and even the students sensed this.

What is more, though, the minister continued, the movement that sought to take the state by storm has since marched right into the offices of the state; indeed, even better, it has become the state itself. And with this development, opportunities for the German spirit to flourish have changed drastically—the revolutionary tempo, the revolutionary vigor, and the revolutionary momentum that have animated the German youth for the past fourteen years have thus become the tempo and the vigor and the momentum of the state itself. Make no mistake: authentic revolutions are unstoppable. There are no revolutions that solely reform or overthrow the economy, politics, or cultural life. Revolutions are *new worldviews*. We intellectual people are clear about this; power political revolutions must be intellectually prepared. At their beginning stands the idea, and only when the idea merges with power will the historical miracle of transformation rise up.

Goebbels continued, "You young students are the bearers, the pioneers, and the defenders of the young revolutionary idea of this state and so, just as it was your right in the past to storm the un-state and throw it down, just as you had the right to deny this un-state your respect and your honor, you now have the responsibility to enter into the state, to be the bearers and the authorities of this state and its shining new glory and greatness.

"A revolutionary has to be everything. He must be just as good at tearing down what is blameworthy as he is at building up what is praiseworthy. If you students exercise your right to throw this intellectual flotsam and jetsam to the flames, you must also accept responsibility for paving the way for a genuinely Germanic spirit to take its place."

203

OSKAR MARIA GRAF

Burn Me!

First published as "Verbrennt mich!" in *Volksstimme* (Saarbrücken), 15 May 1933.

Like most left-leaning, decidedly socialist intellectuals in Germany, I, too, have felt the blessings of the new regime: recently, while I happened to be out of town, the police showed up at my apartment in Munich to arrest me. They confiscated mostly irreplaceable manuscript materials: carefully collected notes from primary sources, all my business and financial documents, and a great many of my books—all of it likely to be burned. So I had to leave behind my house, my work—and what is perhaps the worst of it—the land I call home, in order to escape deportation to the concentration camp.

But it's only now that I'm getting hit with the biggest surprise: according to the *Berliner Börsencourier,* I'm on the *white list* of authors for the new Germany, and all my books, with the exception of my most important work, *We Are Prisoners* [*Wir sind Gefangene*], are being *recommended!* So I am being invited to join the ranks of exponents of the "new" German spirit!

I ask myself in vain, to what do I owe this great disgrace?

The Third Reich has banished nearly the whole body of significant German-language writing, has disassociated itself from real German literature, has hounded the most essential writers into exile, and made it impossible for them to publish their works in Germany. The reckless vandalism of the powers currently holding office, working along with the ignorance of a few pompously sensationalist pen pushers, is seeking to eliminate every bit of our literature and art that is of worldwide repute and to substitute the concept of what is "German" with a narrow-minded model of nationalism that would order my decent socialist comrades to be followed, incarcerated, tortured, murdered, or driven by desperation to suicide!

And the proponents of this barbaric nationalism, which has nothing, absolutely nothing at all, to do with what it means to be German, have the nerve to claim me as one of their own in "spirit," to place me on their white list, a list that can only be a blacklist in the eyes of the world's conscience!

I have not earned this dishonor!

After all that I have lived and all that I have written, I have the right to demand that my books be relegated to the flames of the burning stake so they don't end up in the blood-spattered hands and pernicious minds of those brown bands of murderers!

Burn all the products of the German spirit! That spirit will live on for as long as your days of infamy!

(All respectable newspapers are requested to print this protest.)

204

JOSEPH GOEBBELS

The Tasks of the Ministry of Propaganda

Speech delivered to members of the press on 15 March 1933. First published as "Rede vor der Presse über die Errichtung des Reichspropagandaministeriums," in *Goebbels-Reden,* vol. 1, *1931–1939,* edited by Helmut Heiber (Düsseldorf: Droste Verlag, 1971), S. 90, 94, 95, 106–7. Published in English in David Welch, *The Third Reich: Politics and Propaganda* (London: Routledge, 1933), 136–45.

I see in the newly established Ministry for Popular Enlightenment and Propaganda a link between government and people, the living contact between the national government as the expression of the popular will and the *Volk* itself. In the past few weeks we have experienced a growing political coordination [*Gleichschaltung*] between the government and the whole people. I do not believe that we have reached our goal when, if I may use one of those old-fashioned expressions, we have a 52 percent majority in parliament. A government faced with the great and far-reaching tasks that the present government faces could not survive for long and could not find the popular support it needs from these far-reaching measures if it were satisfied with this 52 percent majority. It must, rather, see its task as making all the necessary propaganda preparations to win the whole people over to its side in the long term. If this government is now resolved never to yield—never under any circumstances—then it has no need for the dead power of the bayonet: it will not be satisfied for long with the knowledge that it has 52 percent behind it while terrorizing the other 48 percent, but will, by contrast, see its next task as winning over that other 48 percent to its own cause.

That will not be accomplished by objective work alone. Rather, the objective work of the government must also be made clear to the people. The task of the press cannot be merely to inform; rather, the press has, above and beyond that, the much greater task of instructing. It naturally has the task of making clear to the people why the government is doing what it does and why the government is forced to act in a certain way and no other. If we were to take over the legacy of the past fourteen years without explaining to the German people the causes of Germany's decline, I am convinced that our partisan opponents, with all the shrewdness they possess in their sphere, would very soon succeed in holding the new government responsible for the legacy that it has inherited. But that cannot be the case: we shall have to make clear to the German people what we have inherited, how we have inherited it, and what measures we must take and shall have to take to reform this legacy.

The name of the new ministry tells us quite clearly what we mean by this. We have established a Ministry for Popular Enlightenment and Propaganda. But these two terms do not convey the same thing: popular enlightenment is essentially something passive; propaganda, on the other hand, is something active. We cannot, therefore, be satisfied with just telling the people what we want and enlightening them as to how we are doing it. We must, rather, replace this enlightenment with an active government propaganda, a propaganda aimed at winning people over. It is not enough to reconcile people more or less to our regime, to move them towards a position of neutrality towards us; we want, rather, to work on people until they are addicted to us, until they realize, in the ideological sense as well, that what is happening now in Germany not only can be permitted, but must be permitted. [. . .]

Propaganda—a much-maligned and often misunderstood word. The layman uses it to mean something inferior or even despicable. The word "propaganda" always has a bitter aftertaste. But if you examine propaganda's most secret causes, you will come to different conclusions; then there will be no more doubting that the propagandist must be the man with the greatest knowledge of souls. I cannot convince a single person of the necessity of something unless I have gotten to know that person's soul, unless I understand how to pluck the string in the harp of his soul that must be made to sound. It is not true that propaganda presents merely a rough blueprint; it is not true that the propagandist does no more than administer complex thought processes in rough form, in a raw state, to the masses. Rather, the propagandist must not just know the soul of the people in general but must also understand the secret swings of popular sentiment from one end to the other. The propagandist must understand how to speak not only to the people in their totality but also to individual sections of the population: to the worker, the peasant, the middle class; he must understand how to speak to both the southern German and the northern German; he must be able to speak to different professions and to different faiths. The propagandist must always be in a position to speak to people in the language they understand. These capacities are the basic prerequisites for success.

The methods of propaganda cannot be subject to aesthetic judgment. The only judgment that can be passed is based on the success of the method. For propaganda is not an end in itself but rather a means to an end. We are establishing here a Ministry for Propaganda, which does not exist for its own sake and thus represents an end in itself, but which is rather a means to an end. If we achieve our end through this means, then the means is good; in any case, whether or not it meets strict aesthetic requirements is thus terribly irrelevant. But if this end is not achieved, then this means will have been a bad one. The purpose of our movement was to mobilize the people, to organize the people, and to win them over to the idea of the National Revolution. That end—and even the most ill disposed person cannot argue with this—has been achieved, and so the verdict has been passed on our propaganda methods. The new ministry has no other purpose than to place the nation firmly behind the idea of National Revolution. If that end is achieved, people can condemn me: that would make absolutely no difference if the ministry and its workers had achieved their purpose. But if that end is not achieved, then I could prove that my propaganda methods have satisfied all the laws of aesthetics, but in that case I ought to have been a theater director or the director of an art academy rather that the Minister for Popular Enlightenment and Propaganda. [. . .]

The people are not as unreasonable as is generally supposed. The people only become unreasonable when they do not understand something, and they have a right to be unreasonable because they realize that they will have to bear the burden but that nobody will tell them why they must do so.

This is where our work will have to begin. We have inherited a terrible situation. There is complete disarray in every field of public life. It is a fearfully difficult and responsible task to rectify this situation. In clearing all this up we shall not be able to shrink from unpopular measures. The incisions, however painful they may be, will have to be made. The government of National Revolution has no intention of misleading or swindling the people over certain situations but will give the people a clear and unvarnished picture of the state of affairs. That is where our work begins: we must explain to the people why the situation is as it is and why we must take steps to change it.

In this respect we shall lay claim to all the opportunities for and methods of mass influence. The new ministry will, seen as a whole, comprise five departments: Radio, Press, Active Propaganda, Film and the Department for Theater and Popular Education. [. . .]

Now I come to a field that you yourselves represent: the press. I make no secret of it: I do regard the banning of newspapers as neither a normal nor ideal state of affairs. On the contrary, I am of the opinion that the press must help the government. The press may also criticize the government, but it should not do so in order to misrepresent the government to the people. The government will employ all possible measures against such attempts. They simply will not arise. No one need be in any doubt that we will recognize them straightaway. We shall know the right time to act.

As I have already said, the press must not merely *inform:* it must also *instruct.* I turn first of all to the explicitly national press. Gentlemen! You too will consider ideal a situation in which the press is so finely tuned that it is, as it were, like a piano in the hands of the government on which the government can play, a situation in which it is an enormously important and significant instrument of mass influence that the government can make use of in the work for which it is responsible. It is quite possible that the government and the press can work with and through each other in mutual confidence. I see it as one of my principal tasks to achieve that aim. [. . .]

The essence of propaganda is simplicity: we must reject all forms of flourish and decoration in explaining to the people our ideas in all their primitivity. But we must also drum these thoughts into the public mind with such force and punch that in the final analysis, even the lowliest man in the street will know what it is all about. The task of propaganda is not to say as much as possible, but rather to gather completely confused, complex, and composite ideas into a single catch phrase and then to instill this into the people as a whole.

205

JOSEPH GOEBBELS

Speech at the Opening of the Reich Chamber of Culture

Delivered 15 November 1933. First published as *Rede des Reichsministers Dr. Goebbels bei der Eröffnung der Reichskulturkammer am 15. November 1933* (Frankfurt am Main: Brönner's Druckerei, 1933), 21–24.

As with any genuine revolution, ours also seeks to initiate a drastic overhaul of our collective cultural capital and intellectual creative production. None of the charges against us in the past has hit us as hard as the claim that National Socialism is a form of intellectual barbarism and would ultimately lead to the annihilation of the cultural life of our *Volk.* We have again set free the creative forces of the German nation; may they develop unhindered and bear abundant fruit on the tree of our newly risen *Volkstum*.

This is also the spirit of the Reich Chamber of Culture, which we solemnly inaugurate and establish today in accordance with the law. It represents the consolidated alliance of all creative artists in one unified cultural entity. It eliminates the need for those remnants of organizations still remaining from the past but functioning only at a mechanical level and serving only to stand in the way of the free development of our cultural and artistic life. Creative artists in Germany shall once again view themselves as one uniform entity; they should be relieved of that sense of disconsolate barrenness that has thus far separated them from the nation and its driving forces. We have no intention of restricting the development of art and culture; rather, we seek to promote it. The state hopes to lay its protective hand on its development. German artists should feel safe and secure in this patronage and regain the blissful feeling of being as indispensable to the state as anyone who contributes to the value of its material existence. Those who labor with their minds and those who labor with their fists shall reach out their hands to one another now in an alliance that shall remain indissoluble for eternity. The community of all creative men shall become reality, and each man in his own place shall bless the nation and its future with those gifts he is determined to give.

The newly established Reich Chamber of Culture transcends the anachronistic concepts of modernity and reactionary. Its work shall be as averse to the modernist megalomania of great men, which is merely a front to conceal artistic incompetence, as to the reactionary retrogression that seeks to place obstacles in the path of our youth and the healthy forces within them. German art needs fresh blood. The time in which we live is young. Its representatives are young. The ideas it seeks to manifest are young. They no longer have anything in common with the past behind us. And any artist who wishes to lend expression to these times must also feel young and shape things that are new. Nothing could be more erroneous than to assume that the establishment of the Reich Chamber of Culture, which is designed to serve the purpose of development, would somehow seek to open the door to lowbrow philistinism and to block the way to the top for our youth.

Whatever charges may or may not be brought against these, our times, no one will ever be able to contend that they were boring. These times are averse to every form of fustiness and pharisaic formality; they do not shrink in fear before boldness and daring, nor do they see in the bourgeois notion of leisure and repose the ultimate wisdom. Ulrich von Hutten's famous statement is operative here: "O century, o sciences, it is a lust for life therein! Get thee to the hanging tree, barbarism, and prepare; thy name shall be anathema!"

The new state has its own laws. Everyone is subordinate to the state, from the first to the last. And the artist, too, is obligated to acknowledge the state and to allow the state to become the guiding principle of his artistic production. Beyond that, though, he remains free and unfettered; his imagination is again free to venture forth into the eternal reaches of infinity. So long as he remains firmly rooted in the solid ground of his *Volk*, he may take pride and self-confidence in boldly stretching the head on his shoulders toward the stars. Nothing but the best shall suffice as food for the soul of the German *Volk* in its misery and despair. The state's only obligation in this regard is to promote, to nurture, and to clear the path for what is new. In the context of the Reich Chamber of Culture, every form of trendy commercialism shall be excluded from the outset. We seek to forge a new breed of German artist, one who, with pride and individuality, consciously and openly serves the purposes that time has bestowed upon us. Have no fear: this is not intended to become a breeding ground for attempts to weed out certain attitudes or perspectives. We have the courage to be magnanimous, and we hope that our magnanimity will be rewarded in kind with the same magnanimity on the part of the artistic world that we hope to lavish with all our loving care and nurturing. The new national art of Germany will only then enjoy worldwide renown and extend beyond the borders of our territory, bearing witness to the vigilant cultural will of young Germany if it is firmly and inextricably rooted in the fertile native soil of the *Volk*.

206

Law Establishing the Reich Chamber of Culture

Announced on 22 September 1933 as "Reichskulturkammergesetz vom 22. September 1933." First published in *Reichsgesetzblatt* (Berlin: Reichsverlagsamt, 1933), 1:661.

Article 1: Public Corporations

The Reich Minister for Popular Enlightenment and Propaganda is ordered and authorized to organize those branches of activity that affect his sphere of competence into public corporations.

Article 2: Establishment of Chambers

Pursuant to Article 1, the following chambers shall be established:

1. Reich Chamber of Literature
2. Reich Press Chamber
3. Reich Radio Chamber
4. Reich Theater Chamber
5. Reich Chamber of Music
6. Reich Chamber of Visual Arts

Article 3: Corresponding Law Concerning Film Chamber

The regulations and supplementary regulations already issued for the film industry by the Law Establishing a Provisional Film Chamber of 14 July 1933 shall be applicable to the establishment of the chambers listed in Article 2.

Article 4: Guidelines for the Structure of the Professions

The establishment of the chambers shall proceed within the guidelines set by the Reich government for the structure of the professions.

Article 5: Combination with Provisional Film Chamber

The corporate bodies listed in Article 2, together with the Provisional Film Chamber, referred to as the Reich Film Chamber, will be combined to form the Reich Chamber of Culture. The Reich Chamber of Culture is under the supervision of the Reich minister for popular enlightenment and propaganda with its headquarters in Berlin.

Article 6: Conformity to Trade Laws

The Reich minister for popular enlightenment and propaganda and the Reich minister of economics are authorized to issue a joint directive that will bring trade regulations into line with the regulations of this law.

Article 7: Implementation

The Reich minister for popular enlightenment and propaganda is authorized to issue legal directives and general administrative regulations as well as any necessary amendments for the purpose of enforcing this law. The laws and general administrative regulations affecting the financial or trade interests of the Reich require prior approval from the Reich minister of finance, in agreement with the Reich minister of economics.

Signed,
Adolf Hitler
Reich Chancellor

Joseph Goebbels
Reich Minister for Popular Enlightenment and Propaganda

207

KLAUS MANN

Open Letter to Gottfried Benn

Written from Le Lavandou, France, on 9 May 1933. First published in Klaus Mann, *Briefe und Antworten 1922–1949,* edited by Martin Gregor-Dellin (Munich: Spangenburg im Ellermann-Verlag, 1975).

Dear Dr. Benn,

May an ardent and faithful admirer of your writings approach you with a question justified solely by this concern with your intellectual existence? [. . .] Several times in the past weeks I have heard rumors about your attitude toward "the German events" that would have shocked me if I could have brought myself to believe them. I absolutely refused to lend credence to these rumors, but now I have learned for a fact that you—as indeed the *only* German author we were counting on—have *not* resigned from the academy. [. . .] What kind of company do you keep there? What could possibly induce you to put your name, a name that we regard as the epitome of high standards with an all but fanatical purity, at the disposal of men whose lack of standards is unmatched in European history and from whose moral contamination the world recoils in disgust? How many friends do you stand to lose by endeavoring to collaborate with the likes of such intellectually despicable men—and what friends do you ultimately stand to gain by aligning yourself with something that is so wrong? Is there anyone there who even understands you? Who there has so much as an ear for your language, whose radical pathos must sound terribly foreign, if not like sheer cultural Bolshevism, to those men? Your young admirers, I know, are sitting in cheap hotels in Paris, Zurich, and Prague—while you, their idol, continue to play academician to *this* state! If you are not concerned with your own admirers, then please have a look at where those people stand whom you have admired so enthusiastically. Heinrich Mann, whom you worshipped more than anyone else ever did, was booted out of that same organization in disgrace, and yet you still remain a member; my father, whom you so much loved to quote, has become nothing more than a target for billingsgate in the country whose worldwide stature he did everything in his power to elevate—though his efforts were certainly no match for the degree of damage now being done by its new masters. Great minds throughout the rest of the world, people who once mattered to you, are busy outdoing one another in protest—think, for example, of André Gide, who was certainly never one of those vapid "Marxists" you found so dreadfully repulsive.

And this brings us to the crucial point, I suppose. How well I always understood your resentment of the German "Marxist" literati types (most baneful example, [Siegfried] Kracauer)—and how often I shared it. How stupid and awful it was whenever these gentlemen scrutinized the sociological content of their own works in the *Frankfurter Zeitung,* in the *Börsencurier,* or in a diverse array of *Linkskurven* [left-leaning] publications.[1] It was enough to make you puke, and no one suffered it more than I. And yet, for years now, it has worried me to see the way your dislike for these bloated blockheads has driven you, Gottfried Benn, to seek refuge in an increasingly grim *irrationalism.*

This attitude remained purely intellectual and exerted a great deal of attraction for me, too, I admit—but that never prevented me from sensing its dangers. Recently, while reading the article in *Weltbühne* about you and the way you have sought "refuge amongst the common horsetails," I could not, for all the will in the world, completely disagree with the author's polemics against you: in fact, when I thought about it, it occurred to me that I had once written very similar things about you long ago. Today it seems almost a law of nature that strong, irrational sympathies lead to political reaction if you don't pay strict attention. First comes the grand gesture against "civilization"—a gesture that, as I know, is only too attractive to intellectuals; then, suddenly, you've reached the cult of force, and before you know it, the next step is Adolf Hitler. Isn't it indeed a little bit like the way a brilliant author (not a "Marxist") living on this coast recently said: "Benn simply got so worked up over Alfred Döblin that he finally turned into a Nazi himself"? I can completely understand how someone might get thoroughly worked up over Döblin, but not to the extent that you would completely betray your intellect itself.

. . . No Kracauer, no [Herbert] Ihering could drive me to that point. On the contrary: while Mr. Ihering might today find ways and means to dress himself up in the trappings of fascism—and maybe tomorrow, we'll find him writing "the nation" where "class struggle" stood only yesterday—I know my place now as clearly as never before. Vulgar Marxism can no longer irritate me. For I know I need not be an obtuse "materialist" to want what is reasonable and to hate hysterical brutality with all my heart.

I have addressed you uninvited; that is improper, and I must once again beg your pardon. But you must know that for me—and for several others—you are one of the few whom we would not under any circumstances want to lose to "the other side." But whoever remains ambiguous now will be lost to us now and forever. Surely you must know what you are getting in exchange for our love and what great substitute you are being offered for it over there; unless I'm a bad prophet, it will ultimately be ingratitude and derision. For one thing is clear: even if a few great minds still are not sure where they belong, those folks over there on the other side know precisely what does not belong in their ranks: the mind itself.

I would appreciate any response you may care to provide.

Klaus Mann

Note

1. *Linkskurven* is a pun on *Die Linkskurve,* the literary magazine of the German Communist Party from 1929 to 1932.—Eds.

208

GOTTFRIED BENN

Answer to the Literary Emigrants

Radio broadcast aired on 24 May 1933. First published in the *Deutsche Allgemeine Zeitung,* 25 May 1933. Published in *Der neue Staat und die Intellektuellen* (Stuttgart: Deutsche Verlagsanstalt, 1933), 24–34. Gottfried Benn, *Sämtliche Werke* (1933; repr. Stuttgart: J. G. Cotta'sche Buchhandlung Nachfolger GmbH, 1989), 6:24, 33. Translated by E. B. Ashton.

You are writing to me from the neighborhood of Marseille. In the little resorts along the Gulf of Lyons, in the hotels of Zurich, Prague, and Paris—you write—the young Germans who once admired me and my books are now sitting as refugees; from the papers, you have to see that I hold myself at the disposal of the new state, that I defend it in public, and that as an academy member I do not eschew its cultural plans. You call me to account, as a friend, but very sharply. You write, What could induce you to make your name, which to us has been the epitome of high standards and of an all but fanatical purity, available to those to whom this very rank is denied by all the rest of Europe? What friends will you gain in exchange for the old ones you lose? Who will understand you there? You will remain the intellectual—that is, the suspect—and no one will welcome you. You call me to account, warn me, demand an unequivocal reply: "He who does not declare for us in this hour will henceforth and forever cease to belong to us." So hear my reply, please, which must, of course, be unequivocal.

First, I have to tell you that many experiences in the past weeks have convinced me that German events can be discussed only with those who have witnessed them in Germany. Only those who have passed through the tensions of those months, who have experienced them continuously at close range, from hour to hour, from news to radio broadcast—even those who did not jubilantly hail all this but suffered it rather—all those can be talked with, but the refugees who went abroad cannot. For they have missed the opportunity to feel the concept of "the people"—a concept so alien to them—grow within themselves, not as a thought but as a living experience, not as an abstraction but as condemned nature. They have missed their chance to perceive the concept of nationalism—which your letter, too, employs so derogatorily and scornfully—in its true motion, as a genuine, convincingly expressed phenomenon; they have missed seeing history, form laden, image laden, at its conceivably tragic but surely fated work. And here I do not mean the spectacular side of events, the impressionistic fascination of torchlight and music, but the inner process, the creative impact that tended to cause a goading, human transformation even in the initially restive observer.

For this reason alone we shall hardly understand each other. But understanding founders also on another problem—for years a theoretical issue between your group and me—which has suddenly become so bluntly acute as to demand from everyone a direct, outspoken decision. Our best approach to it will be to consider the word *barbarism,* repeatedly used in your letter and also in others that have come to me. You put it as if what happens in Germany now were threatening culture, threatening civilization, as if a horde of savages were menacing the ideals of mankind as such. But let me ask you in turn, how do you visualize the movement of history? Do you regard it as particularly active at French bathing beaches? How, for example, do you envision the twelfth century, the passage from the Romanesque to the Gothic way of life—do you think that was *discussed?* Do you think that in the north of the country from whose southern part you are writing, somebody *thought up* a new architectural style? The people *voted* on round or pointed arches, *argued* about apses, whether round or polygonal? I think you would get further if you discarded this novelistic notion of history and viewed it more as elemental and impulsive, an inescapable phenomenon; I think you would come closer to the German events if you stopped looking at history as the bank statement rendered to creation by your bourgeois nineteenth-century brain—oh, it owes you nothing, but you owe it everything; it knows neither your democracy nor your perhaps laboriously maintained rationalism; it has no method, no style, other than at its turning points to emit, from the inexhaustible womb of the race, a new human type that has to fight its way, has to work the idea of its generation and its kind into the texture of time, unwavering, acting and suffering as the law of life commands. Of course, this view of history is not enlightened and not humanistic. It is metaphysical, and even more so is my view of man. And there we have come to the core of our old dispute—when you accuse me of fighting for irrationalism.

Your letter puts it this way: "First one professes irrationalism, then barbarism, and already one stands with Adolf Hitler." This you write at the moment when your opposite progressive concept of man has gone bankrupt far and wide, for all to see; when it is obvious that it was a vapid, frivolous, pleasure-seeking concept, that no truly great epoch of human history has ever interpreted the human essence otherwise than irrationality—for *irrational* means close to creation and capable of creation. Will you not finally realize, on your Latin shore, that the events in Germany are not political tricks, to be twisted and talked to death in the well-known dialectical manner but are the emergence of a new biological type, a mutation of history, and a people's wish to breed itself? True, the view of man beneath this breeding idea considers him, though rational, primarily as mythical and deep. True, his future is contemplated in terms of grafting way down at the trunk—for man is older than the French Revolution and has many more strata than the Enlightenment believed. True, he is felt largely as nature, as proximity to creation—after all, we are witnessing his being far less free, far more painfully bound to existence, than it would have seemed from the no more than two-thousand-year-old antithesis of idea and reality. In fact, he is the eternal Quaternary, [he is] a horde magic of feuilletonistic decking even the late Ice Age, [he is] a fabric of diluvial moods. Tertiary bric-à-brac; in fact, he is eternally primal vision: wakefulness, day life, reality—loosely consolidated rhythms of hidden creative intoxications. Will you amateurs of civilization, you troubadours of Western progress, not realize, at last, that what is at stake here is not forms of government but a new vision of the birth of man—perhaps an old, perhaps the last grand concept of the white race, probably one of the grandest realizations of the cosmic spirit itself, preluded in Goethe's hymn "To Nature"? And will you absorb this, too: no success, no military or industrial result, will decide about this vision—if ten wars should be unleashed from East and West to crush this German mankind, if the Apocalypse approached by land and sea to break its seal, we should still have the vision of man; and he who wants to realize it must breed it; and your philological inquiry into civilization and barbarism becomes absurd before so much legitimate historic existence.

But let us leave philosophy and turn to politics; let us depart from the vision and face the facts of experience. So you sit at your beaches and call us to account for our cooperation in building a state whose faith is singular, whose seriousness is stirring, whose internal and external situation is so grave that it would take Iliads and Aeneids to tell its fate. Before all foreign countries your [stated] wish was the destruction, collapse, downfall of this state and its people. It is the nation whose whose citizenship you possess, whose language you speak, whose schools you attended, to whose cultivation of science and art you owe all your intellectual property, whose industry printed your books, whose stages presented your plays, which gave you fame and reputation, by whose members you wished to be read in the greatest possible number, and which would not have done you much harm even now, had you stayed. So you cast a glance on the sea that stretches toward Africa—perhaps a battleship happens to cruise on it with Negro troops from those six hundred thousand colonial soldiers of the notorious French *forces d'outremer* that are to be committed against Germany; others may look upon the Arch of Triumph or Hradcany Castle as they vow vengeance to this country that has no political aims but to safeguard its future and that the bulk of them, spiritually, have only exploited.

You write in your letter that you have become a "true Marxist" only now, but now wholly—that no charge of "vulgar Marxism" or "materialism" can still keep you from fighting our "hysterical brutality"—that you are on the side of "the spirit" and going to war against "political reaction." I do not quite know what you really mean by these words, which sound to me as from another geological age; I might ask you also, whether you spoke of hysterical brutality when the state in which your Marxism won out killed off two million of its bourgeois intelligentsia. But I will assume that you mean socialism, and indeed in the past years, the rights of German labor have often been defended by the foremost German intellectuals now living abroad—mostly sincerely, visibly, and repeatedly by Thomas Mann. To these, I would say that the German worker is better off now than before. You know that as a doctor, I am in touch with many circles; as a social insurance practitioner, with many workers, including former Communists and Social Democrats. There is no doubt—since I hear it from every one of them—that they are better off than before. They get better treatment in their shops; the supervisors are more cautious, the personnel chiefs more courteous; the workers have more power, are more respected, work in a better mood, a citizen's mood, and what they never obtained from the Socialist Party has been given them by this new national form of socialism: a motivating sense of life. Be sure, too, that the conquest of labor by the new power will go on, for the German national community is no chimera, and the First of May was no capitalist trick in disguise. It was more impressive, it was genuine; labor had suddenly shed the stigma of a yoke, the punitive character of proletarian suffering that it bore in the past decades; instead, it stood as the base of a newly forming, class-dissolving community. No one who saw it can doubt that this year of 1933 has put a new, definite face on a lot of the socialisms that have been in the European air for decades. This year has newly proclaimed a part of the rights of man, and in case your term *political reaction* means that you wish to fight for the rights of labor, you would have to join the new state, not disparage it.

Lastly, however, you also address my own person. You ask me questions, warning, searching questions about the peculiarity of my radical sense of language that would earn me nothing but jeers and sneers on the other side, and about my reverence for certain literary figures who are now on *your* side. My answer is this: I shall go on revering what I have found exemplary and educational for German letters; I shall revere it even in Lugano and at the Ligurian Sea—but I personally declare for the new state, because it is my people whose trail is being blazed here. Who am I to exclude myself? Do I know better? No. I can try to guide it, as far as lies in my power, in the direction I should like to see followed; but if I failed, it would still be my people. The *Volk* means much! My intellectual and economic existence, my language, my life, my human relations, the sum total of my brain—all this I owe to my people. From the people come our forebears; to the people our children return. And as I grew up in the country, with the herds, I still know what "homeland" means. Big city, industrialization, intellectualism, all the shadows cast on my thoughts by the age, all the powers of the century I met in my work—there are moments when this tortured life fades away and nothing remains but the wide plain, the seasons, the earth, simple words: the people. This is how I came to put myself at the service of those to whom, as you say, Europe denies all rank. This Europe! It may have values—but where it cannot bribe and shoot, it does look pitiful! Now it whispers in your ear that the people are not behind Hitler—only his "sheep," as Lady Oxford just wrote in the *News Chronicle.* A great mistake! It is the people. Just compare the two great minds, Hitler and Napoleon. Napoleon was surely the outstanding individual genius. Nothing drove the French as a people to conquer the pyramids and cover Europe with their armies; they were driven by that immense military genius alone. But here, today, you hear the question time and again: did Hitler create the movement, or did the movement create him? The question is significant, for it shows that the two cannot be distinguished. They are identical. Here we really find that magical coincidence of individual and generality that [Jacob] Burckhardt, in his [lectures entitled] *World-Historical Observations* [*Weltgeschichtliche Betrachtungen*], ascribes to the great men of the world's historic course. The great men—it is all there: the perils of the beginning; the appearance, almost always only in terrible times; the tremendous endurance; the abnormal facility of all functions, notably including the organic ones; but also the impression of all thinking persons that here is the one to accomplish what is necessary and yet possible to him alone. Note that I said all thinking persons—and you know I place thought above all. "It is a great and creditable obstinacy to refuse ideological consent to anything not justified by thought"—with this word of Hegel's, I have always tested my political emotions. Believe me, therefore, and do not deceive yourself, whatever Europe may whisper to you: standing behind this movement, loving peace, willing to work, but also ready to perish, if need be, is the whole people.

I close with something that you abroad, if you read this, will certainly want to know about: I am not in the party, have no contact with its leaders, and do not count on new friends. It is my fanatical purity, which your letter honors me by mentioning, my purity of feeling and thought, that determines my attitude. Its foundations are the ones you find in all thinkers of history. One said, "World history is not the soil of happiness" (Fichte); another, "Nations must bring certain great living traits to the fore, regardless of individual happiness or the greatest possible collective happiness" (Burckhardt); a third, "Man's increasing diminution is the very force that makes him think of breeding a stronger race." And, "A masterly race can grow only from terrible and violent beginnings. Problem: where are the barbarians of the twentieth century?" (Nietzsche). The liberal and individualistic era had completely forgotten all this; nor was it intellectually capable of accepting it as a demand and envisioning its political consequences. But suddenly dangers arise, suddenly the community tightens, and everyone, the man of letters included, must stand up and choose: private hobby or direction toward the state. I choose the latter, and I must accept it for this state if you, from your shore, bid me farewell.

209

LION FEUCHTWANGER

Open Letter to the Current Occupant of My House in Berlin (Mahler Street 8)

First published as "Du sollst in Häusern wohnen, die du nicht gebaut hast," in *Pariser Tageblatt* 463, 20 March 1935. Published in English in M. Lincoln Schuster, ed., *A Treasury of the World's Great Letters from Ancient Days to Our Own Time, Containing the Characteristic and Crucial Communications, and Intimate Exchanges and Cycles of Correspondence, of Many of the Outstanding Figures of World History, and Some Notable Contemporaries* (New York: Simon and Schuster, 1940), 511–13.

Dear Sir,

I do not know your name or how you came into possession of my house. I only know that two years ago the police of the Third Reich seized all my property, personal and real, and handed it over to the stock company formed by the Reich for the confiscation of properties of political adversaries (chairman of the board: Minister Göring). I learned this through a letter from the mortgagees. They explained to me that under the laws of the Third Reich, confiscations of property belonging to political opponents concern themselves only with credit balances. Although my house and my bank deposits, which had also been confiscated, greatly exceeded in value the amount of the mortgage, I would be obliged to continue paying interest on the mortgage, and my German taxes as well, from whatever money I might earn abroad. Be that as it may, one thing is certain, you, Herr X, are occupying my house and I, in the opinion of the German judges, must pay the costs.

How do you like my house, Herr X? Do you find it pleasant to live in? Did the silver-gray carpets in the rooms upstairs suffer too much from the plundering of the SA officers? My houseman sought shelter in these upper rooms, as, I being in America at the time, the gentlemen seemed determined to take it out on him. Those carpets are very susceptible to staining, and red is a dark color, hard to remove. And that rubber coating on the floors in the hallway was not exactly designed with the boots of SA officers in mind either. If it has been too severely damaged, the best place to go is the company Baake—the flooring is the same as the one on the stairs at the "Europa" and the "Bremen," and Baake is where it was purchased.

Do you know why I had the half-covered terrace built on the roof? Frau Feuchtwanger and I used it for our morning calisthenics. Please see to it that the pipes in the shower don't freeze.

I wonder what you've decided to do with the two rooms that used to house my library? Books, so I have been told, are not very popular in the Reich in which you live, Herr X, and whoever has anything to do with them can easily run into difficulties. I, for example, read your *Führer's* book and innocently ascertained that his 140,000 words contained 140,000 offences against the spirit of the German language. As a result of this observation, you are now sitting in my house. Sometimes I wonder to what uses bookcases can be put in the Third Reich. In case you should decide to have them ripped out, be careful not to damage the wall. And did they tear out the sectional bench in the loggia of the library while they were plundering? At any rate, Herr X, there is a lot in this house that is in need of renovation and repair. May I recommend that you contact the architect Sobotka in this regard? It's doubtful, however, whether or not this gentleman is still allowed to practice his profession in Berlin; there weren't many architects there who were allowed to build, but many national party comrades who wanted to build. Please, if your contacts allow you this much, please do not hire one of the party comrades, but rather some outside expert. It would be such a shame for the house.

I would really like to know what is going on with that circular saw over at the arboretum in Grunewald. That noise sometimes ruined my enjoyment of the house, and it was only with great effort that I was able to see to it that the disturbance stopped. Today, of course, one can hardly be upset by the noise in Berlin. It would nevertheless be very kind of you if you would respect the victory of my pitched battle and wouldn't give in without putting up a fuss in this regard. By the way, is our street still called Mahlerstrasse? Have the masters of your Reich overlooked the fact that the composer, Gustav Mahler, for whom the street is named, was a Jew, or has Richard Strauss brought this fact to their attention?[1] And what have you done with my terrarium, which stood at one of the windows in my study? Did you actually kill my turtles and lizards because their owner was an "alien"? And were the flowerbeds and the rock garden damaged much when the SA officers, shooting as they ran, pursued my sorely beaten servant across the garden into the woods beyond?

Doesn't it sometimes seem odd to you that you should be living in my house? Your Führer is not generally considered a friend of Jewish literature. Isn't it astounding, therefore, that he should have such a strong predilection for the Old Testament? I myself have heard him quote with great fervor "An eye for an eye, a tooth for a tooth" (by which he may have meant, "confiscation of property for literary criticism"). And now, through you, he has fulfilled an Old Testament prophecy—"Thou shalt dwell in houses thou has not built,"

With many good wishes for our house,

Lion Feuchtwanger

P.S. By the way, do you think my thesis that your Führer writes bad German has been proven wrong by the fact that you are now living in my house?

Note

1. The composer Richard Strauss (1864–1949) was head of the Reichsmusikkammer (Reich Music Chamber) from 1933 until 1935.—Eds.

210

Editors' Law

Announced on 4 October 1933 as "Schriftleitergesetz." First published in *Reichsgesetzblatt* (Berlin: Reichsverlagsamt, 1933), 1:1085.

The Reich government has passed the following law, which is hereby promulgated.

Part One: The Editorial Profession

ARTICLE 1: THE PUBLIC TASK OF THE EDITOR

The collaboration, as primary employment or based on appointment to the position of executive editor, in shaping the intellectual content of newspapers and political publications published in the territory of the Reich, through word, news reports, or pictures, is a public service profession whose rights and obligations are regulated by the state through this law. The name of this profession is "editor." No person who is not authorized by the terms of this law shall identify himself as an editor.

ARTICLE 2: PERIODICAL PUBLICATIONS

(1) Newspapers and periodicals are printed matter that appear in regular sequence at intervals of a maximum of three months without limiting circulation to any one group of people.

(2) All reproductions of writings or illustrations slated for mass distribution are to be considered printed matter.

ARTICLE 3: APPLICATION OF THE LAW

(1) The provisions of this law for newspapers are also applicable to political publications.

(2) Newspapers and periodicals edited and issued by the authorities are not subject to the stipulations of this law.

(3) The Reich minister for popular enlightenment and propaganda will determine which publications are to be considered political by the terms of this law. If the publication is dedicated to a specific subject, then this decision is to be made in consultation with the highest Reich or regional authorities concerned.

ARTICLE 4: EXTENSION OF THE LAW TO AGENCIES

Even if the activity is completed outside the offices of a newspaper, but rather in an establishment concerned with the distribution of newspapers with intellectual content (written word, news, or pictures), it is still considered cooperation in the shaping of the intellectual content of German newspapers.

Part Two: Admission to the Profession of Editor

ARTICLE 5: PREREQUISITES FOR ADMISSION

Only those persons may be become editors who:

1. Are in possession of Reich citizenship
2. Have not been denied civic rights and the qualifications for assuming public office
3. Are of Aryan descent and are not married to a person of non-Aryan descent
4. Are at least twenty-one years of age
5. Are fiscally competent
6. Are trained in the profession
7. Have the qualities required for the task of exerting intellectual influence on the public.

ARTICLE 6: ARYAN DESCENT

The requirements for Aryan descent and Aryan marriage shall be determined pursuant to Article 1a of the Reich Law for Civil Service Employees, and the provisions issued for its implementation are applicable here. [. . .]

ARTICLE 8: APPLICATION FOR ADMISSION

Admission to the editorial profession is by application and is confirmed with registration in the professional editors' roster. The roster is maintained by the offices of the regional associations [*Landesverbände*] of the German press agency (Article 23, Section 2). The decision to grant registration is made by the director of the regional association. He is required to approve the registration if the requirements set forth in Article 5 have been met. He must deny the registration if the Reich minister for popular enlightenment and propaganda contests it. [. . .]

Part Three: Application of the Law

ARTICLE 12: EXERCISE OF THE PROFESSION OF EDITOR

With registration in the professional roster, the editor becomes entitled to exercise his profession with German newspapers and with German enterprises of the kind described in Article 4. If he relocates to a different regional district and association, he will be transferred to the respective professional roster without further examination.

ARTICLE 13: TASKS OF THE EDITOR

Editors are charged with treating the subjects of their topics truthfully and to judge them according to the best of their knowledge.

ARTICLE 14: DUTIES OF THE EDITOR

Editors are especially obligated to refrain from publishing anything that:

1. Is in any manner misleading to the public and confuses personal motive with public aims
2. Tends to weaken the strength of the German Reich, domestically or internationally, to weaken the common will of the German *Volk,* the German defensive capabilities, its culture or economy, or that is offensive to the religious sentiments of others
3. Offends the honor and dignity of Germany
4. Illegally offends the honor or the welfare of another, damages his reputation, ridicules him, or expresses contempt for him
5. Is immoral for other reasons. [. . .]

Part Four: Legal Protection Afforded the Editorial Profession by Affiliation with Associations

ARTICLE 22: OVERSIGHT

The editors as a collective will provide oversight regarding the fulfillment of obligations on the part of colleagues and will look after their rights and their welfare.

ARTICLE 23: REICH ASSOCIATION OF THE GERMAN PRESS AGENCY

Editors are legally incorporated in membership to the Reich Association of the German Press Agency. Every editor is a member by virtue of his registration on the professional roster. By the terms of this law, the Reich Association becomes a public corporation with its seat in Berlin.

ARTICLE 24: ORGANIZATIONAL STRUCTURE OF THE REICH ASSOCIATION

(1) The minister for popular enlightenment and propaganda shall appoint the director of the Reich Association, who shall issue a charter for the Reich Association, which will require the approval of the minister. The director of the Reich Association shall appoint an advisory councilor.

(2) The Reich Association is organized by subdivisions into regional associations, whose bylaws are stipulated by the charter.

ARTICLE 25: PURPOSES

(1) The purposes of the Reich Association are:
1. To establish educational, advanced training, and social service facilities for the editors
2. To give expert advice to Reich and regional authorities
3. To cooperate in setting stipulations for terms of employment for editors
4. To negotiate among editors at the request of one party and to settle differences between the parties
5. To maintain professional courts for the press.

(2) The Reich Association may perform additional duties in the execution of obligations listed in Article 22.

(3) The Reich Association is authorized to impose fees upon its members to be applied to organizational expenses. Regulations governing this must have the approval of Reich minister for popular enlightenment and propaganda. Dues shall be collected in the form of a public levy.

211

ERNST BERTRAM

Against Humanism

First published in *Deutsche Gestalten: Fest—und Gedankreden* (Leipzig: Insel-Verlag, 1935), 305.

"Rome was built not only under the sign of the wolf, but also of the Goddess Athena. The Germanic world must be seen in the context of this Roman reality. This Roman world has been, as if by some sort of Teutonic frenzy, persistently pushed deeper into the recesses of repression. Rome must again set its intellectual legions to the task of fending off the barbarian hordes. The Roman world must absolutely prevail."

And thus one of our fellow humanists goes so far as to invoke this Latinate hot air in order to get it into the heads of Germans that it might be time for the *Homo Europaeus* to emerge. Even here in this country that was established so late, so that then we might all finally be able to speak in the same Latinate terms. There can be no reconciliation with this species of humanism—that much is clear—not now, nor ever. And it is the worst enemy of such forms of German classicism that is at issue here, because it contaminates the capacity for German dedication to the true values of antiquity. And with that, it becomes the twofold mortal enemy of German nature itself, and we will fight it as such.

Examples such as these—this is but the first in a long litany—demonstrate at least this much: that the vigorous intuitive mistrust on the part of our new youth toward a certain species of Occidental-humanist intellectualism seems justified. We cannot conceal these things from ourselves and from others; they teach us what humanism—something we cannot do and would not want to do without—must guard against and which direction its transformation should take. It cannot turn a blind eye to the God-given right of Germans to resist the Roman "Occident" because we are not a part of it, do not want to be part of it, and never will be part of it.

212

RICARDA HUCH

Letter to Max von Schillings, President of the Prussian Academy of the Arts

Written on 9 April 1933. First published in *Literatur und Dichtung im Dritten Reich,* edited by Joseph Wulf (Gütersloh: Sigbert Mohn, 1963), 26–27.

Dear Mr. President,

Allow me to begin by thanking you for the heartfelt interest you have taken in my continued affiliation with the academy. I am concerned with making clear to you why I cannot fulfill your request. I would almost like to consider it self-evident that any German sees himself as being German, but there are many different views concerning what it means to be German and how what is German manifests itself. I consider all this centralization, this coercion, these brutal methods, this defamation of dissidents, this boastful self-congratulation to be un-German and disastrous. In consideration of the degree to which my position deviates from that prescribed by the state, I consider it impossible to remain a member of a state academy. You say that the written statement I have been provided by the academy would not restrict my freedom of expression. Despite the fact that any "loyal collaboration in the national and cultural tasks assigned to the academy by law in light of the altered historical situation" requires an agreement with the government's agenda that I do not share, I would never be able to find a newspaper or periodical willing to publish oppositional opinions. So my freedom of expression would remain strictly theoretical in nature.

You mention Mr. Heinrich Mann and Dr. Alfred Döblin. It is true that I do not agree with Mr. Heinrich Mann, nor do I always agree with Mr. Döblin, though we do agree on many things. In any case, I would prefer that all non-Jewish Germans would seek to see and do the right thing as conscientiously as he does and would be as open, honest, and respectable as I have always considered him to be. In my opinion, in light of the witch hunt against Jews, he did the only thing he could have done. The fact that my resignation from the academy is not to be seen as an expression of affinity for the above-mentioned gentlemen, despite the particular respect and admiration that I have for Herr Dr. Döblin, should be apparent to anyone who knows me personally or is familiar with my books.

I hereby submit my resignation from the academy.

Ricarda Huch

213

JOSEF NADLER

Nation, State, and Literature

Published as "Nation, Staat, und Dichtung," in *Deutscher Geist/Deutscher Osten: Zehn Reden* (Munich: R. Oldenburg, 1937), 11–27.

The question is one of grave import. The fate of the world has always hinged on this question. What we mean when we say "literature" is the whole of intellectual life reflected in one specific case. And that compels us to determine the manner and degree to which the community of the nation and the state are contingent on intellectual life.

Nation is related to *nasci,* to be born, and, for the Roman thinkers, originally meant birth lineage, genealogical descent, blood ties to ancestors and collateral relatives within a specific group. Nation is the human community created along the lines of procreation and birth. Both the term and the concept have been inserted through Western European constitutional perspectives into an ideological framework in which they have no place. In the European West, the word is equated with the sum of citizens. How much misfortune has descended upon the people of Europe as a result of the Westernized misinterpretation of the word *nation?* The [. . .] involuntary citizens of arbitrarily gerrymandered states are lumped together into a nation, and no distinctions are made between them concerning the obligations that can be inherited only by birth. As with all aspects of life, the deepest roots of the essential nature of the nation are not accessible to the rational mind or epistemological inquiry. Nation is destiny, nature, and it lies beyond the reach of individual will. The only process that is truly essential to the nation's existence is the ever-recurring renewal of connections through the succession of births. For every one hundred marriages, let us say, ninety of them will be consummated between Germans and or between French. So nation is more or less a tightly woven fabric of ancestral relations. And what distinguishes one nation from another is the degree to which these ancestral relations remain close-knit. Accordingly, the only epistemological foundation for the nation is its genealogical history. If race and nation were to coincide, this would be precisely what constitutes a nation. But they don't coincide, and so we can consider only the different races to be the basic pillars on which the nation rests. Generally, then, *nation* consists of a certain ratio of racial amalgams, and, within the broad limits of genealogical connections, of common blood relations. Everything else that is proffered as a characteristic trait of the nation is extraneous. For all these supposedly characteristic traits that are cited as essential to the nation are arbitrary in nature; they are the province of personal choice and cannot be counted as essential. [. . .]

The nation is thus the maternal foundation for existence of the sum of experiences that we call intellectual life [*geistiges Leben*]. But a word of caution is directly in order here to preempt any confusion of the thought process with misunderstandings. Genius is itself a great mystery. And no rational explanation will ever succeed in unlocking the secret of creative genius inherited by blood or through particularly felicitous circumstances of birth. The fact that Dante or Shakespeare or Goethe appeared in this earthly manifestation is an event that simply must be taken as fact beyond the reach of scholarly inquiry. But in their intellectual appearance, in the way that their comportment is commensurate with their nature, indeed, in the sum of their physical features, they are compatible with the union of racial blood from which they are descended. So it is not the *degree* of achievement that stems from the maternal depths of the nation but rather the *species* of achievement. Hence, the natural law governing the unique life of the nation reveals itself in a trinity: the individual according to his own nature, the transpersonal blood relationship to entire groups of humans, and the subconscious commonalities between them that transcend time and space.

Everything underlying the writer's primordial nature, life's instincts, and demons, all that lies beyond the control of his will and frequently beneath the surface of his consciousness, springs from the primordial origin of the nation, from somewhere in its nether regions, even though we have no access to reliable empirical knowledge about them. That tremendous capacity for vision of Goethe's, already apparent in the formidable power of his eyes, that capacity for a grasping insight of things and their context in life at their root, for simplifying life's vicissitudes to their most basic forms through the filter of reason, for painting pictures with his words rather than creating concepts—that capacity was instinctive and not acquired by experience. [Heinrich von] Kleist's horror at life's inexplicable complexity, at the inexorable intervention of some otherworldly force, is instinctive to such a degree that this man, perpetually driven by others to the narrow precipice, was persistently able to take the leap into the unknown world of what is beyond the reach of research, and [he] ultimately took that leap in the blissful confidence of one last hope. [Franz] Grillparzer's precipitous shifts between the burning fever of creative confidence and the cold chill of the inadequacy of completed works, the pitched shots at success, and the incapacity to withstand his own success were entirely instinctive and immune to any sort of remedy. [Gottfried] Keller's desire to allow at least a trace of the fool's bells to ring, even during the most solemn and serious actions, was instinctive and not a way of obeying appeals to his artistic sentiment. Wherever we see experience and acquired knowledge, where will and rationality, tradition, and law make their mark in works of art, we discover the congenital nature and daemon of bloodlines in blood that can be traced through hundreds of ancestors in the family to the common womb of the nation. When we speak in terms of a common language and culture, we have barely scratched the surface. It is truly the realm of mothers from which all individual life flows and that comes to life before our eyes in all the artistic portraits and products of the mind. And it remains the realm of the mothers even if we are only able to penetrate half its depths. And how vehemently it bars us access as long as we seek to unlock the secret of personality.

214

HEINZ KINDERMANN

The New Literary Values

First published as "Die neuen Wertgrundlagen," in *Dichtung und Volkheit: Grundzüge einer neuen Literaturwissenschaft* (Berlin: Junker und Dünnhaupt, 1939), 56–71.

In the era of objective research, one purported to proceed as though there were no set ideological standards to apply. Some standards did, however, nevertheless tacitly prevail that, promoted as they were by a certain faction, intentionally endeavored to elevate un-German literary products to the same level of merit as exalted classical art and at the same time, just as intentionally cast aside uniquely *volkhaft* traditional values. These shifts in favor of what is un-German were propitiously furthered, especially during the impressionist period, by claims that the standards people sought to set were not ideological in nature but rather aesthetic. The "artistic value" of literature was at issue and was taken seriously only when it met certain, very high formal standards with respect to style, rhythm, and composition. No reasonable human being would suggest dispensing with setting criteria to determine what constitutes excellence in production. However, the unilateral application of this aesthetic standard of measure has led to grotesque distortions in the annals of literary history.

Mere artistry was taken seriously, even though it was merely "manufactured," not pulsing with the lifeblood of experience; the literature of the *Volk* [*Volksliteratur*], on the other hand, firmly ensconced as it was in experience and paid for dearly with heart and soul, was ignored because it did not quite meet these standards for artistic measure that so often overemphasized formalistic requirements. And under the mantel of tolerance, content, meaning, and the perception of man were elevated to the level of ends in themselves in a rather unseemly fashion. Many a work of literature not deserving of the name *German* has gained entry into the hallowed halls of German artistic renown precisely because this exaggeratedly artistic standard of measure was applied. How many literary enthronements in recent decades must be attributed to this type of more or less deliberate confusion and reversal! That spurious artistry of the writers is what tipped the balance. They were willing to subject all manner of content, of meaning and perceptions of man, to all things un-German—dangerous things, unhealthy, corrosive things. The process was akin to assessing the value of a whole house based solely on its glamorous façade and being happy as a lark to accept the faulty, indeed dangerously so, inner construction of the building for the sake of its façade, even though it is precisely this inner construction that is pivotal to the house's everyday utility and functionality and to its hospitality and comfort. Our biological perspective has taught us to first examine internal structures and only then to consider the external; to first turn our attention to the health effects, to the physical and psychological benefits, and only then to focus scrutiny on the perfection of form. However, even the ideal standard we have set out to strive for can then succeed only when the external and internal aspects of literature are unanimous in their perspective, in their style, in their construction, because they both issue from one and the same outpouring of the soul, the same racial, *völkischen,* and characterological perspective. But the operative term is *unanimous,* and that presupposes that especially the internal aspect of literature—its psychological-intellectual content, its *völkisch* orientation, its worldview, and its view of mankind—be healthy.

So we must distinguish ourselves from the recent past by establishing and acknowledging literary criteria that do not merely take formalistic, artistic concerns as their point of departure but that pertain to psychological-intellectual content, to the ethnic-ideological perspective, to a racially determined view of mankind and that accordingly are pulsing with this lifeblood in their final production. [. . .]

Of course, we do not believe that artistic literature and the ethnic literature of the *Volk* [*Volksdichtung*] can continue in perpetuity to occupy two completely separate spheres in the life of the *Volk*. Rather, we are convinced that artistic literature of the *Volk* and true-to-life literature of the *Volk* necessarily and intrinsically stand in a relationship of mutual interaction. Is it by sheer coincidence that the greatest works of artistic literature that represent the ideal simultaneously become great works of literature of the *Volk*—for example, Schiller's *Wilhelm Tell* and Goethe's *Faust*—and also happen to have their origins in the literature of the *Volk*? An example from lyric poetry perhaps best illustrates what we are attempting to say here. In the case of the folk song [*Volkslied*], as is also the case, incidentally, for the popular drama and the prose chapbook [*Volksbuch*], we see again and again that the original version—that is, the earliest known version—is related to that preformation of its prototype that is derived from an exalted realm, indeed the courtly realm of the art song, the court drama, or the courtly epic. But since in this particular case the prototype involves a work that at the same time contains elementary elements derived from the *Volk* [*volkhafte*], it is adopted by the creators of the folk song or the popular drama or the chapbook, and that is where the centuries-long process of ever-changing versions, the perpetual transformation and resurrection of the original material begins. The liberal era described this process as one of "sinking cultural capital" and called an old art song, which was transformed while making its way through the *Volk*, a "mutilated" song.

215

JOHANNES ALT

Foundations and Suppositions of the Scholarly Editing of German-Language Jewish Literature

First published as *Grundlage und Voraussetzungen der wissenschaftlichen Bearbeitung der deutschsprachigen jüdischen Literatur* (Hamburg: Hanseatische Verlagsanstalt, 1937), 1:141–49.

The development of German-language Jewish literature occurred in three phases:

The first period was characterized predominantly by assimilation, in which the attempt was made to conform to Germanic forms of thought and representation. It is in this context that the eldest daughter of Moses Mendelssohn, more commonly known to us as Dorothea Schlegel, seeks to present a genuinely romantic work in her 1801 novel *Florentine*. [. . .]

We now have in our possession a biography of Heinrich Heine written by Max Brod. Brod explicitly claims Heine as a Jewish writer. Without further ado, he attributes uniquely Jewish features to Heine's language; indeed, he attempts to demonstrate that that which is considered negative in Heine actually reveals itself to be of great value when Heine is seen as a Jew. Of course, the question that immediately comes to mind for us with this approach is, what matter of concern is this Jewish Heine to us? Brod's rebuttal is that all attempts laying claim to his Jewishness notwithstanding, [Heine] is, on the other hand, still a great German poet. How has he managed to pull off this masterwork of magic? Very simply. The realm of all that is bound by race is subordinated to that free-floating realm of the intellect that is not bound by any consideration of species kinship and that situates the poet only in consideration of his own individual relationship to the language in which he writes. Hear Brod himself:

> How could such a time-bound, Jewish text inherently and universally capture all, even those from alien tribes? It would be incomprehensible if there were not a strange, often observed relationship—that the situation of the Jews represents a symbolic, generally comprehensible, if sharpened, representation of the human condition. The Diaspora Jew is lonely, ruthless, restless. But is not every person in his inner depths lonely? Does not every relationship, every moment of quiet reveal itself as useless in the light of the infinite, flowing eternal? In a certain realm of the feelings that can be sometimes circumscribed, (I do not claim that this is the last, best, and final) every human being is a Diaspora Jew. "All of us are strangers on earth—and that which connects us dies" (Werfel).

Certainly no one is ever going to believe that taking refuge in the "universally human situation" represents a serious answer to the question of [Heinrich] Heine. We would be better served to remain focused on precisely that aspect "bound in time" that is behind Brod's own approach. Was not Heine in possession of the potential for particular attraction solely by virtue of the fact that, with the full force of the capacity and training for assimilation afforded to him by race and circumstance, he took up the romantic song form at precisely the moment the genre had reached full maturity and therefore presented hardly an opportunity for progress solely based on the developments of Germans? Heine, on the other hand, had something to contribute. Something different—something Jewish. But it is precisely this internal difference in species, the inevitable contradiction it presents in relationship to the actual content of the romantic *Lied* that lends [Heine's work] its singularly seductive and at the same time insidious polish. [. . .]

This situation itself gave rise to the transition into the third phase in the development of German-language Jewish literature. The original willingness to assimilate increasingly gave way to a feeling of power based on their [the Jews] own literary position. Literature became a world unto itself and gradually severed itself from German life [*Volksleben*]. Literature thus became a weapon in the war for a worldview, one that was no longer inextricably bound by language and sensibility to the German fate but rather sought to build a world of its own; apparently, a world of universal standards, universal humanity—but truthfully, a world that reflects the expressive literary intent of its primary purveyors, the Jews.

These developments entered the decisive final stage, of course, precisely at a time in Germany when the whole situation was experiencing a state of complete upheaval as the result of war and the war's end. When the war called the bravest and the best of men to the front, a process of selection also occurred that allowed an uprooted type to prevail, one particularly susceptible to generalized theories, far from the front, where he was able to flourish particularly well.

The front soldier experienced a completely altered reality. Hardly one among them immediately found words to describe that frightening insight into the future. When he finally returned home, lending his voice to alleviating privation took precedence, and that was his reason for keeping silent about this insight. The Jew, because he is of a different race, was not in any position to understand the profound inexorability of this German fate at a deeper level, and so it was at this time that he was first able to take full advantage of his unique literary developments. He could disseminate all his universal utopian doctrines throughout his literary world and triumphantly proclaim that he knew the way out of every form of deprivation and misery. Of course, one could no longer conceal the fact that these doctrines were feasible in practice only if one were to first dissolve and destroy all ties and bounds of blood hierarchy and order.

216

THOMAS MANN

Letter to Eduard Korrodi

"An Eduard Korrodi." Written on 3 February 1936. First published in *Neue Züricher Zeitung,* 3 February 1936. Published in *Letters of Thomas Mann 1889–1955,* selected and translated by Richard and Clara Winston (New York: Alfred A. Knopf, 1971), 244–49.

Dear Dr. Korrodi,

Your article, "German Literature in the Exile's Mirror," which appeared in the Second Sunday edition of the *Neue Zürcher Zeitung* of January 26 has been much noticed, much discussed and much quoted—not to say exploited—by the press of various political opinions. Moreover, there was a connection, though a rather loose one, between it and the statement, which a few friends and I issued in behalf of our old literary home, the S. Fischer Publishing House. May I therefore now make a few comments, perhaps even raise a few objections?

You are right; it was a distinct polemical error on the part of the editor of the *Neue Tagebuch* to assert that all or virtually all of contemporary literature has left Germany, or as he puts it, "has transferred abroad." I fully understand that such an exaggeration would arouse the ire of a neutral such as yourself. Leopold Schwarzschild is a brilliant political publicist, a good hater, a forceful stylist; but literature is not his field, and I suspect that he—perhaps rightly—regards the current political struggle as far more important, honorable, and decisive than all the realms of gold.[1] In any case, his statement demonstrated a lack of knowledge of the field and a lack of artistic fairness, which provoked you as a literary critic to object, and the fact that some of the writers you name are still inside Germany indubitably refutes him.

It remains to be asked, however, whether some of these writers would not prefer to be outside if it were possible. I do not want to call anyone to the Gestapo's attention, but in many cases purely mechanical rather than intellectual reasons may be decisive, and thus the boundary between exiled and non-exiled German literature is not so easy to draw; it does not coincide so precisely with the boundaries of the Reich. It seems to me that the German writers living outside those boundaries should not indiscriminately look down on those who have chosen or have had to remain at home. The exiles should not tie their artistic judgments to the question of "inside" or "outside." They are suffering, but there is suffering inside as well; and they ought to stand guard against that self-righteousness which is often a product of suffering. Let them be more charitable also to colleagues whose belief in Europeanism and conception of Germanism has prompted them to renounce home and country, prestige and property; who have ignored broad hints that they would be welcomed back and their transgressions overlooked for the sake of their incomprehensible but nevertheless established international reputations; who have remained where they were, preferring to wait out the rise and fall of the Third Reich in freedom; but who still, whether the present German regime is to hold on or pass away, do not wish to destroy all bridges to their country and all possibility of their influencing it. Let the exiled writers refrain from instantly denouncing such a colleague as a scoundrel and renegade as soon as he disagrees with him about the relocation of German intellectual life, perhaps for good reasons they cannot fully see.

But enough of that. It is impossible to equate exile with German literature, if only because Austrian and Swiss writing also belongs to German literature. Of living men writing in German, two are especially dear to me personally: Hermann Hesse and Franz Werfel, both of whom are poets as well as novelists. They are not exiles, for the one is Swiss, the other a Czech Jew. But neutrality remains a difficult art even for people who have such long practice in it as you Swiss! How easily the neutral, in combating one injustice, falls into another. The moment that you raise objections to the identification of exile literature with the whole of German literature, you yourself set up an untenable equation. For, curiously, it is not the error itself that angers you, but the fact that it is committed by a Jewish writer; and even as you conclude from this fact that once again literature of Jewish origin is being confounded with German literature (the old complaint of the Fatherland fanatics), you yourself confound exile with Jewish literature.

Must I say that this will not do? My brother Heinrich and I are not Jews. Nor are Leonhard Frank, René Schickele, the soldier Fritz von Unruh, that authentic Bavarian Oskar Maria Graf, Annette Kolb, A.M. Frey or talented younger writers such as Gustav Regler, Bernhard von Brentano, and Ernst Glaeser.

It is in the nature of things that the Jewish contingent should be numerically strong in the exile movement; that fact follows both from the sweeping nature of National Socialist racial philosophy and from the revulsion which the Jewish spirit feels for certain state institutions of your times. But my list of writers (which I would never have thought of compiling of my own accord and which does not pretend to be complete, not any more than yours does) shows that one cannot speak of the literary exiles as being even predominately Jewish.

I add to it the names of Bertolt Brecht and Johannes R. Becher, who are poets, because you say that you cannot name a single emigrant poet. How can you make such a statement, since I know that you regard Else Lasker-Schüler as a true poet? You say that those who have emigrated are chiefly in the "novel industry," along with a "few novelists with creative talent." Well, industry implies industriousness, and certainly uprooted people who are everywhere barely tolerated by an economically fearful and distinctly uncharitable world must be industrious if they are to earn their bread and butter. It would be harsh indeed to find fault with them for that. But it is harsh enough to ask them whether they imagine that they represent the national wealth of German literature. Truly, it occurs to none of us, neither the industrialists nor the creators, to think so.

Of course, there is a historical treasury of German national literature, which is precious to all of us. And I grant that little of what is produced today will be considered worth including in that treasury. In comparison with earlier ages, many current works, the products of living human beings, may be unimpressive. This is true everywhere in the world. But again, as throughout the world, the *novel* plays a special and indeed dominant part in German writing today—a part to which you are not entirely just when you say that it is not poetry, but at best prose, the novel, which has emigrated. This in itself would not be surprising. Pure poetry—"pure" insofar as it holds itself handsomely aloof from social and political problems (which, by the way, poetry has not always done)—is governed by different laws from those of the modern prose epic. The novel, because of its analytical spirit, its consciousness, its innate critical attitude, is forced to flee social and political conditions in which poetry may continue to flower quietly on the fringes, undisturbed and sweetly oblivious to the world. But these very prosaic qualities of consciousness and critical attitude, along with the wealth of means at the novel's disposal—its free and flexible control of creation and investigation, music and knowledge, myth and science, its human scope, its objectivity and irony—make it what it has become in our state of history: the representative and dominant form of literature. Compared with the novel, drama and poetry are archaic genres. It takes the lead everywhere in both Europe and America. It has done so for some time in Germany; and therefore, my dear sir, your statement that the novel has emigrated is somewhat incautious. If this were true—and you are saying it, not I—then the political commentator Schwarzschild would surprisingly prove to have been right and you, the literary critic, wrong; for it would mean that the principal branch of German literary life has been transferred abroad.

Recently, in connection with the [Marta] Karlweis biography of [Jacob] Wassermann, you discussed the process of Europeanization of the German novel with your customary perceptiveness and subtlety.[2] You spoke of the change in the type of German novelist wrought by such gifted writers as Jakob Wassermann, and you remarked that by virtue of the international qualities of Jews, the German novel had become international. But look here: My brother and I have had as much share in this "change," this "internationalization," as Wassermann, and we are not Jews. Perhaps it was the drop of Latin blood (and Swiss blood from our grandmother) that enabled us to do that. The "international" qualities of Jews are nothing more nor less than their Mediterranean-

European qualities. And these are at the same time *German:* without them, Germanism would not be Germanism, but a totally useless sluggishness. That is precisely what the Catholic Church—which today is in straits that make her revered once again even by a product of Protestant culture—is defending inside Germany when she declares that only after the Germans accepted Christianity did they enter the company of civilized nations. Being *völkisch* is not being German. But the Germans', or the German rulers', hatred of the Jews is, in the higher sense, not directed toward the Jews at all, or not toward them alone: it is directed against Europe and all loftier Germanism; it is directed, as becomes increasingly apparent, against the Christian and classical foundations of Western morality. It is the attempt (symbolized by the withdrawal from the League of Nations) to shake off the ties of civilization. That attempt threatens to bring about a terrible alienation, fraught with evil potentialities, between the land of Goethe and the rest of the world.

Countless human, moral, and aesthetic observations support my profound conviction that nothing good can possibly come of the present German regime, not for Germany and not for the world. This conviction has made me shun the country in whose spiritual traditions I am more deeply rooted than the present rulers who for three years have vacillated, not quite daring to deny me my Germanism before the eyes of the world. And I am certain, down to the bottom of my conscience, that I have acted rightly in the eyes of my contemporaries and posterity to join with those to whom the words of a truly noble German poet (August von Platen) apply:

> But one who baseness in his heart despises
> From hearth and home by baseness will be banned
> Whenever a servile nation baseness prizes.
> Far wiser to renounce the Fatherland
> Than to endure in all its childish guises
> Blind hatred and the rabble's heavy hand.

Notes

1. Leopold Schwarzschild (1891–1950), editor of the anti-Nazi *Neue Tagebuch,* published in Paris.
2. Bracketed inserts ours.—Eds.

217

FRIEDRICH PERCYVAL RECK-MALLECZEWEN

Diary of a Man in Despair

Written on 9 September 1937. First published as *Tagebuch eines Verzweifelten* (Stuttgart: Goverts, 1966). Published in English as *Diary of a Man in Despair,* translated by Paul Rubens (New York: Collier Books, 1970), 42–44.

My friends have taken the occasion to give me a warning about my own writings. Driven as I am by my own inner necessity, I must ignore the warning and continue these notes, which are intended as a contribution to the cultural history of the Nazi period. Night after night, I hide this record deep in the woods on my land . . . constantly on the watch lest I be observed, constantly changing my hiding place.

And this is how we now live, my vanished friends. Do you, who left Germany four and more years ago, have any idea of how completely without legal status we are, of what it is to be threatened with denunciation at any time by the next hysteric who comes along?

Strange to think of you, strange now to hear your voices through the ether and over the ocean depths, coming from a world so long since barred to us! Strange to happen into places where just a few years ago we used to talk. I miss you, miss you even though, as was true for most of you, you were opponents of mine and politically on the other side—oh, believe me, finally it is the lack of all opposition and any dissension whatsoever, and the deadly monotony that results that makes life here so unbearable.

And yet you will at first no longer understand us, who were your friends, when you come back to take up again the threads of our former ties. Or will you actually be able to understand that flight into civilization was more comfortable than remaining at the dangerous outpost, an illegal watcher among the barbarians? Will you be able to grasp what it has meant to spend these long years with heart filled with hate, hate at lying down, hate at rising, hate through the long hours of bad dreams—and all of this without rights under the law, without the smallest compromise, without a single "Heil Hitler," a single attendance at a meeting—while through it all the stigma of illegality sits upon one's brow? Will we still speak the same language when this is over? Will you, surrounded as you have been all these years by all the appurtenances of civilization . . . grasp that deathlike loneliness of our lives and the misery-laden air of the catacombs that we have been breathing for so long that has made our eyes terribly clear-sighted? May it not be, in the first moments of your return, that the visions these eyes can now see in the distance will frighten you?

What about the world of ideas of 1789—the world which surrounds you, and which is still the basis for your lives and thought, as self-evident to you as the fact that a crab has its protecting shell? Understand me: we, here, know full well that all of this—enyclopedism, the whole process begun with the Renaissance of divesting man of his gods—was once a vital way of life. Let no one do me the injustice of holding my visions to be the nightmares of a *homo temporis acti* [a man stuck in the past—Eds.], or the hallucinations of one feverish with the plague that surrounds him! But isn't what we are enduring here simply the final consequence of 1789? Hasn't the bourgeoisie, which in 1790 began to conceal its seizure of the heritage of power left by the kings with a cry of "*vive la nation,*" shown itself to be a most unstable phenomenon? Didn't Balzac foretell the Russian, as well as the German, tragedy when he said that "there will come a day when the bourgeoisie will hear its *Marriage of Figaro* played?" Didn't St. Just long ago announce the coming of this insane totalitarianism of the state? And doesn't Girondism reach its final flower in the Krupps, the Vögelers, Röchlings and Associates, as, cynically, throwing aside every restraint, they make themselves the center of all things German, the focal point of German society—militant Girondism, devoid of all basic ethical content, the sworn enemy of men of faith, the ideological victor of Waterloo even though defeated on the battlefield?

As far as National Socialism is concerned, I am sure that there will be agreement in seeing in it the arch-destroyer of a nation which has always tended toward the magical and unknown, and none of you, my old friends, will argue with me when I say that in 1500 there was a German nation, but no nationalism, whereas today, when our eyes are supposed to light up at every pants button "Made in Germany," we have the reverse: nationalism, and not nation. We will certainly be in agreement that this plutocratic government with its Hitler placed in the saddle by Herr Thyssen and his friends reveals itself, in its complete demoralization of the masses, to be nothing more than one last desperate attempt to prolong the nineteenth century . . .

Oh, no, there will be no lack of agreement when we again meet on a total rejection of the German present! But will we still be in agreement when we come to talk about the future? You will have just returned from a civilization that is securely based for the present; will you still understand, or will you turn violently away from us when we tell you what we now see:

That Hitlerism is only a symptom, indicating a deep disturbance of cosmic proportions in the world; that we have now come to the end of five centuries of rationalism and free thought; that in the area occupied by mankind, a new factor, the irrational, has again made its appearance.

218

WERNER BERGENGRUEN

A Matter of Conscience

First published as *Der Großtyrann und das* Gericht (Hamburg: Hanseatische Verlagsanstalt, 1935). Published in English as *A Matter of Conscience,* translated by Norman Cameron (London: Thames and Hudson, 1952), 257–60.

The Grand Tyrant, who did not return until three days later, had himself admitted into Sperone's cell within a few hours of his arrival. The hour was late, and the servant who accompanied him set the Florentine dark lantern on the table. The servant then withdrew, and the two men were alone together in the utter stillness of the night. It was cool behind the thick stone walls, and the disturbed atmosphere of the outside world did not penetrate here.

Sperone had not yet slept, but had been sitting on his bed. He did not immediately stand up at the Grand Tyrant's entry, for the glare from the lantern had prevented him from recognizing the newcomer. When he did so, he rose and bowed rather awkwardly.

The Grand Tyrant motioned to him to resume his seat. He took his seat and brought his chair close to the table, crossed his forearms and rested them on the table.

He very carefully studied Sperone's face, which seemed calm and composed. For the attacks of faint-heartedness from which Sperone had suffered during the long and unexpected period of waiting had now left him.

"I hear you have made a confession," the Grand Tyrant began. "But I do not wish to talk about that now. What sort of a man are you, dyer? For I prefer to make that my first question, so that the second question 'What have you done?' can be answered more easily and at the same time more profoundly."

Sperone's expression revealed a slight astonishment, which passed into a smile like that of a perplexed child. Finally he said, "I am an unknown man who dyes cloth. What more should I tell you of myself, your Highness?" [. . .]

"You were once denounced to me," the Grand Tyrant began again. "I do not propose to pay any heed to that, but I am glad to take this opportunity of asking you about the matter. It was said that you told the people about you that you wished to make them fishers of the Lord—*piscatores domini;* and it occurred to one of my right-minded but not especially deep-minded servants that this expression might contain a reference to myself. How did you mean it? Or did you in fact not use the expression at all?"

"I can well believe that I used it," Sperone answered. "But if I spoke of the Lord, I certainly did not mean you, but your Lord and mine. And if this is the fish we hope to catch, we must be sure to get all of Him in our net. We must fish for him as we would fish for the mystic fish. We must catch him in the net of our love and our desire. He must be the captive of our love, imperfect though it is."

"So you do not yet love him perfectly?" the Grand Tyrant asked.

"If I loved him perfectly, I should have the power to change the world—the power to bid Monte Torvo: 'Rise up and cast thyself into the sea.'"

"If I remember the Scriptures rightly, this is said not of love, but of faith. Must I then assume that your faith is also imperfect?"

"My faith is not yet the size of a grain of mustard seed," the dyer said softly and with downcast eyes.

Then, as if he had forgotten the ruler's presence, he whispered passionately, with closed eyes: "Increase our faith. Strengthen our hope. Kindle our love."

He crossed himself. His movements as he did so had nothing habitual about them; it was as if he were performing each of them for the first time, and as if each were a nail, so to speak, with which he fastened himself to the Cross of his own bodily frame.

"You pray for the three heavenly virtues," said the Grand Tyrant. "They should certainly be prayed for. But to me it would seem almost more praiseworthy to believe and love without hope. This would be Lucifer's attitude, were he able to love—for he can certainly believe, aye, he *knows!* And perhaps it is the attitude of many men on earth."

He had spoken these words more to himself than to Sperone. Now, however, growing more spirited, he again turned towards the dyer. "Are you not forgetting that the Church's doctrine of the virtues recognizes, in addition to these three supernatural virtues, also four natural ones? Amongst them is that single most important virtue: the virtue of moderation. It is perhaps not the virtue most highly esteemed in Heaven, but it is the virtue most necessary on earth. For it is the virtue which establishes that equilibrium in which the other virtues are saved from becoming vices."

"Forgive me, Your Highness," Sperone replied. "You are certainly right. But I, for my part, have striven, even though in an imperfect manner, to acquire the heavenly virtues."

"And, I am prepared to believe, not in vain," said the Grand Tyrant. "They say that you can perform all kinds of uncommon acts. There is talk of miraculous healings."

"I have never boasted of such matters," Sperone answered. "But as to what people say, His Highness must ask them and not me."

"I cannot entirely accept what you said concerning the smallness of your faith; for I know that you are one of those religious people who seek their salvation in humility. I therefore suppose that certain things may perhaps be possible for you that are denied the rest of us. I know well that you are one of God's chosen Ones, and you know it, too. Am I not right?"

219

FRANZ FÜHMANN

Wartime Poems

First published in *Jugendliches Trio: Gedichte junger Menschen* (Hamburg: Heinrich Ellerman, 1942). Published in English in John Flores, ed. and trans., *Poetry in East Germany: Adjustments, Visions, and Provocations 1945–1970* (New Haven, Conn.: Yale University Press, 1971), 317–20.

DEPLOYMENT TO GREECE

Our ship set sail to the south with three hundred soldiers aboard.
Shimmering sparkles on their helmets glistened in the sun.
On land's distant shore a thousand people waved, bidding jubilant farewell,
and all of us, drenched in delirium on deck, scoffed at the dangers lying ahead.
The waves caressed the ship's planks in a whisper.
We drank and caught fish glittery as driven snow,
our cheeks and brows burnished by salt on the wind.
Just for laughs we made bets with our pending death.
We had already seen the island flickering from afar.

We clenched the formidable spears firmly in our fists.
The godhead had sent us a shining victory sign.
We embraced once more and everything seemed indescribably splendid.
Then our ship hit the shore with its three hundred men.
We held our lances high in the air,
then grappled with the dreaded opponent
and our god angrily turned away from us.
The mountains echo with the piercing screams of war.
Many sank to the ground, and blood ran hot from their hearts.
Beside me, my comrade, writhing in paroxysms of pain.
We marched all day long, then night came, black as lead.
Of the three hundred soldiers, only twenty returned to the ship.
We hauled up the anchor and sailed off into the night.
Our helmsman let out a savage laugh.
We ran aground on a reef—forsaken by good fortune.
The gods had no interest in our solemn sacrifice.
Morning came and the ship broke up in pieces.
The howling storm suffocated the harrowing whimpers.
The waves roiled to foam. The eddies swelled. We sank in the sea.
The sun rose high against a steel blue sky.
Our ship lay dead with shattered keel and planks.
Three hundred stalwart soldiers fought and sank.
The tide lay still. The gods were silent.

EVERY NIGHT NEW STARS BEGIN TO GLOW

Every night new stars begin to glow.
Again and again, new suns are born.
New worlds burst forth from the distance.
New gods speak to deaf ears.
New gods have wedded themselves to new worlds.
And day is broken with a tuba's fanfare.
Hardened hearts are forged anew in the sun.
New men grow, slender and smartened.

Every night a new light begins to shine.
The exchange between life and death is eternal.
And the light of love eternal speaks—
A new sun burns above the world.

18

The Visual Arts

German Art vs. Degenerate Art

ONE OF THE GREAT DEBATES in nineteenth-century aesthetics was whether music or the visual arts were the greatest expression of the human spirit. This ancient struggle between ear and eye, as the thinkers of the nineteenth century framed it, rested on which medium could best present the abstractions of human thought and feeling. The supporters of music, such as the Viennese critic Eduard Hanslick (1825–1904), argued that music could represent the world both abstractly and realistically in the form of "program music." Art, especially the newest art of photography, seemed limited to mirroring the world. Suddenly, from William Turner in England (1775–1851) to Claude Monet (1840–1926) in France, form gave way to color, and then by the 1900s, with the cubists in France, to pure abstraction, offering the sort of aesthetic quality that only music had been able to claim before then.

Against abstraction, modernism, experimentation, and eventually film and photography, representational art (art that has an immediate reference to experience) came to be regarded as old-fashioned, and in Germany, it became an ideological weapon of the nationalist Right. This tradition was embraced by the Nazis in the early 1920s. In his *Art and Race* (1924) and *Struggle for Art* (1932), Paul Schultze-Naumburg (1869–1949) advocated a "healthy" German art (and architecture) that would place art in the service of the racial improvement of the *Volk*. Art was the space in which one could regenerate the "German spirit" and reconnect the alienated to their aesthetic roots well planted in German soil. Thus, the Kampfbund für deutsche Kultur (Militant League for German Culture), the organization of Nazi arts led by Alfred Rosenberg (1893–1946), struggled to establish a canon of "pure" German art, unsullied by the presence of the Jews, which went back to medieval sculpture and the art of the Renaissance. The organization's 1928 manifesto characterized the "German" arts as a life-and-death struggle against "the bastardization and niggerization of our existence" (Verbastardisierung und Vernegerung unseres Daseins). All modern art, no matter who created it, was their enemy. Indeed, Wilhelm Frick (1877–1946), then the Nazi minister of popular education (*Volksbildungsminister*) of the state of Thuringia and later Hitler's minister of the interior (1933–43), formulated a law forbidding "nigger culture for the German people" (Wider die Negerkultur für deutsches Volkstum) on 5 April 1930.[1] In the end, the "healthy" and the "unhealthy" in art was defined by blood, as Rosenberg wrote in his *Myth of the Twentieth Century* (1930): "Art is the creation of a specific blood, and the formal nature of art can be understood only by individuals who share the same blood."[2] Art is biology, and biology is destiny.

Yet some artists, such as Otto Andreas Schreiber (1907–78), one of the young *Der Norden* ("North") painters and cofounder of the periodical *Kunst der Nation,* wished to amalgamate expressionism with the new national fervor. Their model, ironically, was Lenin's successful exploitation of Russian modernism (from avant-garde cinema to constructivism) in the service of the Bolshevik Revolution and the building of the USSR. (After Lenin's death in 1924, Stalin established much more conservative boundaries for acceptable art.) In Mussolini's Italy, the radical modernists, such as the futurist Filippo Tommaso Marinetti (1876–1944), were firmly on the Fascist bandwagon, as Marinetti made clear in his manifesto of 1924, *Futurism and Fascism.* The German poet Gottfried Benn (1886–1956), himself an expressionist as well as a supporter of the New Order, saw the need to merge the new political and social revolution with the avant-garde in his *Art and Power* (1934; see document 208 in chapter 17). Marinetti was the honored guest at a Berlin futurist exhibition in March 1934, where he was eulogized by Benn. In an odd way, this view was initially supported by Joseph Goebbels, who saw a propaganda advantage in expropriating the moderns to the benefit of the party.

In the end, Rosenberg's antimodernism held sway, but not in all respects. Clearly, it was Hitler, himself a failed painter and self-proclaimed art critic, whose views carried the day. Indeed, he attributed much of his inability to realize his artistic ambitions to the forces of modernism that had dominated the art schools in Germany and Austria and caused them to refuse to admit him to the art school in Vienna in 1907 and again in 1908. Throughout his career, he felt compelled to comment on the visual arts and architecture of the Third Reich. In 1933, when the illustrious design school the Bauhaus was closed, its director, the architect Ludwig Mies van der Rohe, confronted the evasive Rosenberg with the Bauhaus's innovative program. Regime-friendly architects, like Paul Schmitthenner (1884–1972), condemned the entirety of modern architecture as "stylistically barren." Still, Hitler was equivocal in resolving the conflict between Goebbels's pragmatic exploitation of modernism and Rosenberg's ideological fundamentalism. In his decisive speech on cultural policy at the 1934 Reich Party Rally in Nuremberg, Hitler condemned those artists whose commitment to tradition seemed out of place in the modern world: the "feigned internalization of the Gothic does not sit well in the age of steel and iron, glass and concrete," he proclaimed.

In October 1936, the contemporary art galleries of the National Gallery in Berlin were shut, and the artworks they had contained were sold abroad or destroyed. Goebbels banned all art criticism. The painter Adolf Ziegler (1892–1959), ironically called "the Reich's pubic hair painter" (*Reichsschamhaarmaler*) because of the number of female nudes among his works, was then president of the Reichskammer der bildenden Künste (Reich Chamber of Visual Art) in the Ministry for Popular Enlightenment and Propaganda. He ordered all German museums in 1937 to cull their contemporary art and to reserve some of the works for a planned exhibit. Some sixteen thousand works of art were removed from German museums as a result.

On 19 July 1937, the Degenerate Art Exhibition (Entartete Kunst Ausstellung) opened in Munich with a talk by Ziegler. The show presented 650 works of art confiscated from thirty-two German museums. This was Goebbels's response to having lost the ideological struggle with Rosenberg; he would become an even greater opponent of modern art. The exhibition toured twelve more German cities between 1937 and 1941 and was attended by at least three million people. Certainly, the vast majority visited the exhibit for the frisson of horror it provoked, as can be seen in the newsreels of the day, though a minority, like the publisher Richard Piper, knew he was witnessing a cultural outrage. Works of art that had recently hung in major art galleries were paired with works painted in asylums (and collected by the psychiatrist Hans Prinzhorn in the 1920s to prove that mental illness gave rise to a specific form of art). "Primitive" sculptures from the ethnographic museums were juxtaposed with works by major living artists. Works that had sold for large sums and hung in the major museums of the land were suddenly part of a freak show; the ugly, the grotesque, the horrific, the Jewish were on show in this world of "degenerate art." The works were the biological products of the corrupt, and therefore corrupting, minds of the Jews. Whether the artists were ardent anti-Nazis on the left, such as George Grosz (1893–1959), or were members of the Nazi Party in the 1920s who wished to resuscitate "Germanic art," such as Emil Nolde (1867–1956), their works were hung cheek by jowl as representative of modernism. Accompanied by vulgar slogans and price stickers, the "sick," "Jewish-Bolshevist" art by "racially valueless" and "political opponents" was on show. As the broadsheet that circulated with the exhibition stated, the works on exhibit were "tortured canvases, the rotting souls, the sick fantasies, the mentally ill incompetents heralded by the Jewish clique of critics, praised by them, and bought for millions of the people's money while German artists starved! See it yourself. Children under 18 not admitted!"[3]

Ernst Barlach's (1870–1938) sculpture *The Reunion* (*Das Wiedersehen*), which represented the moment when doubting Thomas acknowledged Christ, was labeled "Two Monkeys in Nightshirts." Attacked as a modernist and pacifist, Barlach saw the great public sculptures he had created to help Germans in the Weimar Republic come to terms with the horrors of World War I regularly condemned by the Right. His war monument in Magdeburg showing three soldiers—one German, one Russian, and one French—suffering the horrors of war was dismantled in 1934; his cenotaph of the angel of history in Güstrow was melted down in 1937. One of the great works of twentieth-century art, his *Grieving Mother with Child,* was removed from the Hamburg War Memorial in 1938. That same year, he was expelled from the Prussian Academy, to which he had been elected in 1919, and forbidden to exhibit any further works of art. He died of a heart attack in 1938, having rationally tried to contest Goebbels's ban of his work.

The assault on modernism was not limited to painting and sculpture. The architecture of the Weimar Republic, especially buildings embodying the "New Objectivity" of rationalization, functionalism, practicality, and Americanism, was excoriated as the "rape of objectivity at the hands of international dilution." This demand for a new Nazi view of the city was articulated by major figures of the time, such as the engineer Fritz Todt, who created Organization Todt in 1938 as an alliance of state and private enterprises to build many of the public spaces and defenses of the Third Reich. Until his death in 1934, the architect Paul Ludwig Troost was Hitler's choice for the party's first commission, the Haus der Deutschen Kunst (House of German Art) in Munich. Subsequently, the monumental, neoclassical architecture of the regime was exemplified by the renovation of the Reich Chancellery, completed by Hitler's court architect, Albert Speer, in 1939. Speer's most ambitious project was his plan to transform the Reich capital, Berlin, with grand boulevards, a reorganized railway system, and the monumental Volkshalle (People's Hall).

Coinciding with the Degenerate Art Exhibition, the Great German Art Exhibition (Großen deutschen Kunstausstellung) opened at the House of German Art in July 1937. Some sixteen thousand works had been submitted, but only six hundred were shown. Monumental sculpture glorifying the German body and paintings revealing the close bond between the German peasant and the land, the bravery of the German soldier, and the beauty of the German landscape dominated. Works by Arno Breker (1900–91), Fritz Erler (1868–1940), Ferdinand Spiegel (1879–1950), Josef Thorak (1889–1952), Ivo Saliger (1894–1987), and, of course, Adolf Ziegler were admired by Hitler, who purchased a number of works for his private collection. In particular, Breker and Thorak, Hitler's court sculptors, were lavished with expensive commissions and, during the war, exhibitions in the occupied countries. A focal point of the show was a portrait of Hitler that Heinrich Knirr (1862–1944) had painted specifically for the exhibition. Hitler did not purchase it, but he imagined a huge museum of "German" art gracing his hometown of Linz after the war was successfully ended. Throughout the war, the Nazis stole artworks owned by Jews deported to "the east" and hoarded the works in depots and museum cellars. Despite increasing complaints by artists who resented the harsh strictures on their creations, the show was held annually until 1944. By then, the museums that housed "healthy" art, the buildings that represented the "healthy German spirit," and the plan to create a cityscape that would be an architectural monument to the Third Reich—as stated in 1939 political manifesto for Nazi urban planning—as well as to redesign the cities conquered by the Reich, were in ashes. Such destruction had been part of the Nazi plan for terror, as Heinrich Himmler observed in his order to destroy the Warsaw ghetto in 1943; now, it was experienced on the home front.

NOTES

1. Wilhelm Frick, "Erlass Wider die Negerkultur für deustsches Volkstum," cited in Markus Fleischhauer, *Der NS-Gau Thüringen 1939–1945: Eine Struktur- und Funktionsgeschichte* (Köln Weimar: Böhlau, 2010), 66.

2. Alfred Rosenberg, *Der Mythus des 20. Jahrhunderts: eine Wertung der seelisch-geistigen Gestaltenkämpfe unserer Zeit* (Munich: Hoheneichen Verlag, 1930), 120.

3. This poster is reproduced in the exhibition catalog Stephanie Barron, ed., *"Degenerate Art": The Fate of the Avant-Garde in Nazi Germany* (New York: Harry N. Abrams, 1991).

220

OTTO ANDREAS SCHREIBER

The Continuation of Expressionism

First published as "Fortsetzung des Expressionismus," in *Kunst der Nation* 2, no. 7 (1 April 1934): 1.

The question as to what role, if any, is to be played by the artistic movement called "expressionism" has again become one of central interest with the current exhibition of works by Emil Nolde, Lyonel Feininger, and Karl Schmidt-Rottluff in Berlin. Furthermore, the Fascists, acting under the auspices of Prime Minister Hermann Göring, opened a Futurist Exhibition in Berlin on 28 March.

Here we are confronted with the fact that the casual observer judges works of art from an entirely different perspective than the painter. The layperson might recoil from the expression of the human figures appearing in this portrait or the other, or from the portrayals of nature that are too "interpretive" for his tastes. And it should be stated from the outset that this latter point is precisely what hinders his understanding. Painting is never an imitation of nature but rather always an "interpretive" translation of nature into color and form. [. . .]

The exhibitions of today's young painters demonstrate that the legions of painters parroting and pursuing the tradition of expressionism have disappeared from the scene. National Socialism has eradicated the last remnants of those who, with the enthusiastic support of the academies, would seek to attach didactic value to the "new style" in the form of the "decorative." And it was precisely this "decorative effect" that was one of the very worst perversions to have emanated from this artistic persuasion. Furthermore, expressionism never developed into a finished product; it was but a beginning, and when you attach didactic value to beginnings, you have already bottled them up and expropriated them from their original purpose.

The young painters see and judge expressionism differently than casual observers and even art historians. [. . .]

The new beginning that was needed at the turn of the century was inaugurated by the expressionists. It approached like a train bearing down with such vehemence that the casual observer could barely follow its tracks. But that need not serve as an argument against the historical necessity of this upheaval, and even if twenty years of efforts in contemporary art remain incomprehensible to the lay observer, that is little compared to a guarantee for centuries of new developments in German art.

The consequences of expressionism for the overall perception of art remain to be seen, and the future alone will tell whether these consequences do not turn out to be even greater and more significant than the new beginning itself. In that case, expressionism will have fulfilled the important purpose of testing the rudiments of painting for their viability as elements of the great art of the future.

How do today's young painters stand with regard to the expressionists? The answer is simple: what the young painters consider to be tradition is acknowledging the values of the past, and what they consider to be painting is lending expression to one's own personality in images. So they continue *sine ira et studio* to build on extant artistic experiences in the field of color and form. This organic continuity offers hope for a higher development in German painting. What is more, [these young painters] aren't the types to be taken in tow by any single painter, neither past nor present, nor by any school, any "style"; they are consciously autonomous in the advances they make so that painting itself will be advanced.

221

ALFRED ROSENBERG

Revolution in the Visual Arts?

First published as "Revolution in der bildenden Kunst?" in *Völkischer Beobachter,* 7 July 1933.

First of all, the political revolution of National Socialism is the most important step of the movement. This is true, however, only because it signifies the externalization of a *socialist-spiritual* revolution in the German people. The great uprising is not self-contained but rather is directed towards certain goals, driven by certain wills. Therefore, ever-new areas of life are engulfed by the coursing waves of the movement, and millions of souls are excited anew and spurred on towards organization.

Bitter clashes of opinion have prevailed in the visual arts for a long time, and it is completely understandable that *politically* like-minded National Socialists have very differing opinions when it comes to art and—even with regard to passing judgment on certain artists—often engage in lively controversy.

We can all agree that the mendacious pseudobaroque of the nineteenth century was just as unbearable as the "engineered art" of today. In judging the helpless protest against this, the *Jugendstil,* one opinion predominates. All National Socialists are certainly of one mind with regard to that great exhibition of men's fashion over the centuries called the *Siegesallee.* However, a temperamental clash has broken out over such men as Nolde and Barlach. One group of National Socialist artists wants to exclude them from the ideological foundations of the coming art, while another group, which calls itself *revolutionary,* bears them on its shield.

If we attempt to rise above all subjectivity and arrive at a judgment that conforms with the *collective* thought of National Socialism, we will have to ascertain that in spite of all differences in fashion and dress, in spite of the passage of a thousand years, in spite of every political upheaval, the Nordic artist has been dominated by a well-defined ideal standard of beauty. Nowhere is this powerful, and powerfully natural, ideal as striking and prevalent as it is in Greece. But it predominates in Titian as well, and in Palma Vecchio, Giorgione, and Botticelli, who painted Gretchenesque figures. This ideal surface in Holbein, too, as, for example, in his painting of Gudrun, and in Goethe's *Hermann und Dorothea.* It stands out in the face of Pericles as well as in that of the [medieval statue of the] Bamberg Horseman.

It doesn't matter whether a given *individual* corresponds completely to the ideal, as long as a *longing* for that ideal is alive, and the nation is in proximity to it and united in nature. It is this *intuitive quality* that, combined with figure and form, prepares the way to the future in the field of painting and the plastic arts. If, on the basis of *this* viewpoint, one now asks what our attitude toward Nolde and Barlach must be, we will be able, or at least I personally believe I can say for myself, that there can be little doubt that both artists display outspoken talent. For example, there is a Nolde seascape hanging in the crown prince's palace that has been painted masterfully and forcefully. However, there are also some representative samples of portraiture alongside it: negroid, lacking piety, raw, and devoid of true inner strength of form. Barlach, for his part, has mastered his materials like a virtuoso, and no one would ever deny that his woodcuts are momentous. But whenever he sets out to portray a human form, the result is alien, utterly alien—characterized by a temperament enslaved to the limitations of mortal existence and by exuberance over the burdensome weight of sheer matter. These are no "Mecklenburg peasants." Oh no, the latter stride across the fields in a *completely different* way than those figures we see in Barlach's depictions of humanity! And finally, we gaze upon Barlach's Magdeburg War Memorial, which was completed for the church there: these puny, half-imbecilic mongrels, crosses between indeterminate human types wearing Soviet helmets, are supposed to represent fighting men! I believe that any healthy SA man would draw the same conclusion about this as any conscious artist. In any case, I have found the Noldes and the Barlachs of the world to be self-appointed "revolutionaries," most of whom have very little genuine relationship to the fine arts but who now believe they must suddenly become active in this field.

By the way, it is no accident that Nolde and Barlach were so enthusiastically pushed into the foreground by that band of November gentlemen, people who openly berated the work of both artists as an aberration of German art, not unlike Otto Braun, who was an aberration of German politics.[1]

Note

1. Otto Braun (1872–1955) was a Social Democratic politician who intermittently served as prime minister of Prussia between 1920 and 1932.—Eds.

222

ADOLF HITLER

Art and Its Commitment to Truth

First delivered as "Kunst verpflichtet zur Wahrhaftigkeit" at the 1934 Reich Party Rally in Nuremberg. First published in *Reichsparteitag in Nürnberg 1934* (Dresden: Völkischen Verlag, 1934), 72–75.

Style and stylistic laws are the artistic crutches upon which most average men rely to hobble behind the great spirits of creative men. And this is as it should be! For it is better to rely on an already existing solution than to invent a bad one that only leads backwards in time. What remains singularly decisive is that the *Volk* avail itself of the aura of its own inherited aspect and not some foreign one. So it is wrong, when constructing a new culture, to incorporate elements that were once artificially introduced to the cultural ideology but that are not anchored by blood in the *Volk*).

It is hence all too easy to understand why, for any artist who is truly an artist of the *Volk* whose creative production proceeds from the contingencies of blood, the works of those artists who are racially related in spirit must necessarily stand in closer proximity to his own and convey much more meaning for him than the artificial products of an alien infection that has spread amongst his *Volk*. So it is no coincidence that the spark of Hellenistic art immediately spread as soon as it came in contact with advanced Nordic cultures, allowing Germans, Danes, Englishmen, Italians, French, etc. to create in a spirit that may have found different forms of *völkisch* expression in each of these populations but that stemmed from the same blood root. After all, what are but two or three thousand years in the history of man? Peoples come and peoples go, but the great racial roots remain. Both language and the constructs of state have always been suited only to spreading confusion, to obscuring the traces of common heritage and building walls between people whom nature has created from one and the same fabric and spirit over many millennia. And the written word in particular, with its mechanical fixation of the sounds of language, has contributed more than any other factor not only to obscuring the common roots of peoples beyond recognition but also to separating languages according to their respective phonetic articulations.

Therefore, the first task for any development of German art is to relax stylistic restrictions and to promote with particular vigor the notion that one should never fall prey to a wholly affected artistic mania—far more, rather, it is better to liberate the creative force of the nation from this sort of mannered affectation. This is not to be seen as some sort of formula by which any run-of-the-mill worm can become a great artist; it is merely the basic prerequisite to assuring that true innate genius is not left to waste away in the Procrustean bed of archaic stylistic laws.

Today, then, the National Socialist movement must overcome two dangers:

[One,] it is threatened by the possibility that those destroyers of art [*Kunstverderber*] who believe that a new truth cannot be expressed in any terms that have thus far been in widespread use will enthusiastically step up. These are stammering cowards whose motto for artistic production follows but one commandment: "Innovation at any price." But since there is no innovative insight that does not build on the experiences and contributions of the past, there can also be no new art without taking recourse to the finest and best knowledge of form developed by genetically related predecessors of the same species. A third-rate bungler will not be able to build a modern church like a Greek temple. The impotent but conceited coward shakes in his boots at the mere thought of using a classical column in new construction. But the sovereign spirit reaches deep into the sum total of related cultural achievements of his species throughout millennia and still manages to resolutely lend expression to his own artistic will and intent.

The whole stammering stream of what these cubists, futurists, Dadaists, and others have to say about art and culture is neither racially sound nor is it is it tenable from the point of view of the *Volk*. At best, it can be seen as the expression of a worldview that concedes, of its own volition, that the greatest aim of its guild of intellectual founders and leaders is the dissolution of all existing concepts, the mixing and corruption of all peoples and races. This cultural supplement to the political destruction they have wrought attempts, with an innately guileless naiveté, to bless the new state with the bounties of its prehistoric culture as if nothing had happened. The task of National Socialist art education cannot be to cultivate geniuses who can offer the peoples [*den Völkern*] only some prophetic prospect of the future, rather than offering to actively preserve and protect not only existing cultural assets but also the healthy instincts of our movement from these thieves and burglars breaking in here with their foreign ideas about state and culture, if they might not even be described more aptly as swindlers. And this much must be made loud and clear: the people who will determine not only the political but also the cultural lines of development in the Third Reich will be the ones who created it, and these charlatans are deceiving themselves if they think the founders of the new Reich are foolish or frightened enough to be bamboozled, much less intimidated, by their drivel. They are about to witness the way that what may be the greatest cultural and artistic mission of all times is about to pass right by them to quickly become the order of the day, as if they never existed. The second thing the National Socialist state must guard against is the sudden appearance of those backward bumpkins who think it is somehow their solemn duty to provide the National Socialist movement with the binding legacy of "ancient Germanic art" drawn from the muddled world of their own romantic preconceived notions. These people were never true National Socialists. They either remained recluses in the haunts of an ancient Germanic dream world that was always subjected to ridicule by the Jews or they trotted along, solemn and staid, within the ranks of those hordes of crusaders for the renaissance of the middle class. It was never worth the effort to them to acquaint themselves with National Socialist ideas. On the contrary, perched on the loftiest limbs of their bourgeois haunts, they looked down in pity on the unpleasant, tumultuous life and doings of the lowly National Socialist rabble-rousers.

This is why they completely missed the point that National Socialism is based on solid knowledge, with its foundations in blood and not in antiquated traditions. When they hastily climbed down from their ladders shortly after our victory to proffer their services as political masterminds and strategists for the National Socialist movement, which of course had been mobilized only by the fanfare of propaganda, they were lacking any comprehension whatsoever of the magnitude of the upheavals that had taken place amongst the German *Volk*. And so it is that today they offer train stations built in a renaissance of genuine Germanic style, street signs and typefaces in authentic Gothic font, songs loosely adapted from Walther von der Vogelweide, fashion trends in the manner of Gretchen and Faust, paintings in the manner of [Viktor von Scheffel's romantic poem] *Trumpeter von Säckingen,* two-handed swords and crossbows, perhaps as weapons for protection. They have no clue that the way to be German might mean to be clear; otherwise, it would be better for them to retreat as fossilized artifacts in the museums than for them to strive to take the world around them by storm as persevering great spirits. Just because we have the profoundest respect for the sum total of accomplishments of the past, they like to pretend that everything we have planned for the future is similarly a thing of the past.

Oh no, dear sirs! We know that our ancestors, in their times, were already plagued by the same malevolent spirits whose last remnants hound us to this day. But just as we gave the German spirit free rein in its development in every other aspect of our lives, so too must we refrain from raping modernity in order to privilege the medieval in the field of art. Your feigned internalization of the Gothic does not sit well in the age of steel and iron, glass and concrete, the age of women's beauty and men's strength, of heads held high and of a sense of defiance.

What has been bound in shackles for a thousand years shall now be released in the service of our nation's salvation and health. The nobility of the human body has cast off the bane of rape and deformity. A whole new world of beauty is emerging. But the people don't want to seem any less grateful to God for all that he has created just because they now seek to once again place the magnificence and eternal wisdom of his works on display for all to see.

National Socialism does not thrive on the dark shadow of your prejudices, and we are happy enough just knowing that there is an obvious congruency to be seen between the stylistic sensibilities of the Greek alphabet and the runes of our ancestors. We are once again looking to the great ancient peoples with wonderment, admiring their accomplishments in the field of human culture and especially in art. They may be far removed from us as nations [*Völker*], but as members of the ancient Indo-Germanic racial community, they are eternally close to us.

We scoff in rebuttal at the contention that this kind of thinking is unchristian. For, beginning with the cultural world of antiquity and continuing throughout the romantic and Gothic periods and beyond, Christianity was an element of Renaissance, baroque, and rococo and today spreads its gospel in so-called modern temples in which we National Socialists often see little more than a mockery of God's eternal beauty, even though that doesn't seem to have visibly shaken Christianity in any way.

No, there is absolutely no basis for the cultural guardians of art to justify their attack against the current Reich. And whatever is applicable to the cultural Bolsheviks is equally applicable to them. The future Reich will be marked by the traits of those who created it, not of those who can neither grasp nor understand it.

The artistic creations of a productive period are not restricted by style. Their ties to ancient blood relations, or ideologically related periods and a few assimilated foreign eras, form the bridge they cross to new tasks, new materials and motifs, new hygienic exigencies, as well as to the driving insights of the time. People blessed by God with the gift of creative genius are the ones who shape the forms that finally lead, after a centuries-long development, to the totality of expression of cultural and artistic life, which may well appear to a subsequent, creatively impotent world of posterity to be viewed as style that was unique to that particular time period or people.

But these geniuses—and they alone have been charged by Providence to herald beauty and dignity to humanity—do not require dictates imposed upon them nor formulaic prescriptions. They will prevail in their aims. And it is our responsibility in the National Socialist Reich, whenever God's grace manifests itself in one of these men, that we not satisfy ourselves with acknowledging this fact, then move on, but rather that we place the tasks of the nation in his hands.

They will express their profound gratitude in their works, works that are an honor to our essential nature and our spirit. It is through them that art is brought back into the most vital relationship to the *Volk*, to its laughter, its worries, and its desires. From the theater, they will craft a stage for the great tragic and comical characterization of life. In their statues, they will demonstrate to us an inkling of the perfection of the most splendid living substances we share and of what should be taken as a model to be emulated. They will deliver our cities from the clutches of confusion spread by the thousandfold blows at the hands of foreign spirits of the past and present, and they will leave the overwhelming mark of power and our will on these cities. Symbolically, they will elevate the temples of God and the edifices of the community far above the domiciles of the individual! They will allow the strains of the soul to resound in the notes they produce, and they will immortalize our spirit in stone.

Then they will be able to sing and to speak of a time that was great because it endeavored to do great things, and what may seem to our smaller-minded contemporaries like an illusory, impossible purpose and intent will one day be rewarded by the love of the gods, who will bow down to those who bravely and wholeheartedly dared to demand what seemed impossible. Long live our German *Volk*, and long live our German art!

223

JOSEPH GOEBBELS

Ban on Art Criticism

First published as "Anordnung des Reichsministers für Volksaufklärung und Propaganda über Kunstkritik vom 27. 11. 1936," in *Völkischer Beobachter*, 28 November 1936. Published in Joseph Wulf, ed., *Die bildende Künste im Dritten Reich. Eine Dokumentation* (Gütersloh: Sigbert Mohn, 1963), 119–20.

In the context of the reconstruction of German cultural life, art criticism is one of the most pressing but also one of the most difficult questions to solve. Since the seizure of power, I have given German critics four years to conform to National Socialist principles. The increasing number of complaints about criticism, both from the ranks of artists themselves and from other sections of the population, prompted me to summon the critics to a conference. At this conference, I gave German critics the opportunity to discuss in depth with the most prominent German artists the problem of art criticism, and at the end of the conference, I once again expounded my own views on criticism in unequivocal terms. Furthermore, I have banned all reviews [*Nachkritik*].

Since the year 1936 still did not produce a satisfactory improvement in art criticism, today I am finally and definitively placing a ban on the pursuit of art criticism in its present form.

The previous art criticism, which, in a complete distortion during the period [of] Jewish cultural hyperalienation has perverted the concept of "criticism" into a sort of artistic judiciary empire [*Kunstrichtertum*], shall henceforth be replaced by the "art report"; the arts editor will take the place of the art critic. The art report will be less of an evaluation of art and more a description and thus also a demonstration of appreciation. It provides the public the opportunity to make its own judgment and encourages people to form their own opinions about works of art on the basis of their own intellectual and emotional responses.

In taking such an incisive measure, I base it on the point of view that only those who have a genuine understanding of the area they are criticizing should express criticism. Anyone who is himself creatively gifted will be less concerned with criticism and will be much more motivated by the urge to tend to his own creative achievement. Let me remind you that the greatest critics of the past century—Lessing, Kleist, Tieck, Brentano, Fontane, Gustav Freytag, and many others—had already completed many great creative works before they began writing criticism. The form their art criticism assumed serves to this day as a good example for our time. The great critics of the past wanted only to serve art. They were respectful of the achievements of others and did not position themselves as the infallible judges of anyone else's work. This was left to the Jewish literati, from Heinrich Heine to [Walter] Kerr, and the form of art criticism still prevailing today can in part be traced back to them.

Prerequisite to the art report of the future is respect for the artistic production and artistic achievement. It requires training, tact, a respectable outlook, and respect for artistic intent. In the future, only those editors who undertake this task honorably and wholeheartedly and in the spirit of National Socialism will be permitted to comment on artistic achievements. That is why we have always demanded, and rightly so, that any report or review of art cannot be completely anonymous.

Therefore, I herewith declare:

In the future, every art review must be signed with the full name of the author. Registration as arts editor on the professional roster of the German press shall be contingent upon special authorization, which may be acquired upon presentation of evidence of sufficient background in the area of the arts pertaining to the writer's subject matter. Since professional involvement with artistic works presupposes a certain degree of maturity and life experience, arts editors must be at least thirty years of age before they can be authorized to enter this branch of the German press.

224

ERNST BARLACH

Letter to Joseph Goebbels

Written 25 May 1936. Published in *Ernst Barlach und die nationalsozialistische Kunstpolitik: eine dokumentarische Darstellung zur "entarteten Kunst,"* edited by Ernst Piper (Munich: R. Piper, 1983), 159–62.

The fact that I am compelled personally to demand a decision from you in this matter stems undoubtedly and immediately from the details outlined here concerning the confiscation by the Bavarian political police of my book, *Drawings* [*Zeichnungen*], recently published by R. Piper & Co.

The court order calling for the confiscation was issued on 24 March 1936, and, with reference to Article 7 of the Decree of the Reich President for the Protection of *Volk* and State of 4 February 1933 [the so-called "Desk Drawer Order," which limited press and publishing freedom], justified the confiscation on grounds that "the content is amenable to the endangerment of public safety and order."[1] Herr Reich Minister, I cannot believe that a law for the protection of the German *Volk* mandates the invocation of this law in response to the illustrations at issue here. Indeed, I cannot bring myself to take seriously the charge that my illustrations might be seen in the context of endangering public safety, and it is easy for me to express my primary objection to the court order of 24 March by stating that I am of the opinion that the authorities who issued this law were intent on suppressing the entire category of publications in word, text, and graphic arts to which this volume of illustrations I have drawn also belong, and that the belief on the part of the Bavarian political police that they should need to protect the public by applying such heavy artillery is by no means commensurate with my work as an artist.

This is not the place for me to elaborate on the explanation for these actions I have arrived at in my consternation, for speculations are not relevant here. With all the more confidence in your inclination to review this matter, I can point only to the severe ideological and other forms of damage that I have sustained and to the consequences that this incident and others like it are bound to have for me, sooner or later, with publishers, theater directors, and the whole broad circle of my admirers.

Despite the absence of a detailed justification of the actions taken against me, I must assume that only a portion of my work has been targeted, not all of it, and so it is now a matter of determining which of the fifty-six illustrations reproduced in this volume have been cause for concern on the part of the political police. For my obligation here is not, Herr Reich Minister, to assert my so-called interests but rather, now that I have been forced to defend my moral integrity, to erase the grave stain that has been placed upon it. I must do everything in my power to have this confiscation overturned.

Note

1. Barlach confuses the date and provisions of the law. He apparently means the Decree of the Reich President for the Protection of *Volk* and State of 28 February 1933. Paragraph 2 refers to "measures necessary for the restoration of public security and order." (See document 20 in chapter 2.)—Eds.

225

ADOLF HITLER

Speech at the Opening of the Great German Art Exhibition

Delivered on 18 July 1937. First published as "Hitlers Rede zur Eröffnung des Hauses der Deutschen Kunst, München, 18. 7. 1937," in *Mitteilungsblatt der Reichskammer der bildenden Künst* (1 August 1937), 4. Republished in Peter-Klaus Schuster, ed., *Nationalsozialismus und entartete Kunst: Die Kunststad München 1937.* (Munich: Prestel Verlag, 1988), 242–52.

As we all know, the collapse and overall demise of Germany was not only economic and political, it was also, to perhaps an even greater degree, a cultural collapse. And this process could not be attributed to the military defeat alone. Catastrophes of this nature have always befallen nations and states and, not infrequently, have been precisely the catalyst for purging them and thus ultimately for inner renewal. The whole flood of mire and rubbish that spewed forth to the surface of our lives with the year 1918 was not the result of losing the war—that defeat only triggered its release. It is only through its utter demise that an already thoroughly corrupt body confronts the full extent of its inner decay. [. . .]

Normal common sense and human instinct were replaced by certain catchwords that, thanks to their constant reiteration, gradually left a large number of people who concern themselves with artistic things or with the world of art feeling insecure, or at the very least intimidated enough that they no longer dared to seriously resist or oppose the constant stream of these catchphrases exerted. Beginning with general contentions such as, for example, saying that art is international and continuing through analyses of artistic production based on certain essentially meaningless assertions, the attempt to confound common sense and basic human instinct persisted. By touting art, on the one hand, as little more than an international human experience, thus killing off any sense of understanding for its grounding in each individual *Volk,* and increasingly viewing art in terms of periods or ages, that is, suddenly there was no such thing as the art of individual *Völker,* or better, the art of individual races, any more, merely the arts of a certain period. According to this theory, then, Greek art

FIGURE 19. Organizers of the 1937 Great German Art Exhibition presenting artworks to Hitler for his approval. Hitler is flanked by Adolf Ziegler, head of the Reich Chamber of Visual Art, on his right, and his personal photographer, Heinrich Hoffmann, on his left. "Opening of the House of German Art," *Die Weite Welt,* no. 29, 18 July 1937, 1.

was not the product of the Greeks but a product of a certain time. The same, of course, applies to Roman art, whose rise just happened to coincide with the rise of the Roman Empire. Similarly, subsequent epochs in art were not shaped by Arabs, Germans, Italians, French, etc., but rather were merely products of the times, and that is why even today there is no distinctly German art, French art, Japanese or Chinese art; there is simply "modern" art. Accordingly, then, art as such is not only utterly stripped of any sense of stemming from racial impulses but instead becomes an expression of a certain period—one that is now described as "modern" and, of course, will be considered old-fashioned tomorrow because it will have become obsolete.

But this theory serves, then, to place art and art theory on a par with mere craftsmanship such as we might find in a modern tailor shop or fashion studio operating on the principle of introducing something new every year. One year it is impressionism, the next it is futurism, cubism, or perhaps Dadaism, etc. And, of course, a thousand different expressions will have to be invented to describe even the most horrendous of these monstrosities. If it weren't so tragic, it would be almost amusing to sit down and calculate how many catchwords and phrases the so-called artistically inclined have produced to describe and interpret the pathetic products of their art in recent years. [. . .]

Up until the National Socialists assumed power, there was so-called modern art in Germany—that is, as implied by the term itself, something new nearly every year. But National Socialism advocates the return to a specifically "German art" and—like all the creative values of any nation of people—this art shall and must be eternal. Anything devoid of this eternal relevance for our *Volk* is of no value to us today either.

When the cornerstone for this building [the House of German Art] was laid, it was to signal the building of a temple to house not only so-called modern art but also genuinely and eternally German art—better yet, a building to house the art of the German *Volk* and not a place for the international artwork from the year 1937, or 1940, 1950, or 1960. Art is not a product of the times; it is the product of peoples [*Völker*]. So the artist's task is not so much to memorialize his time but to memorialize his *Volk*. For time is ever changing; the years come and they go. Anything that springs exclusively from a certain given time will pass into oblivion as quickly as the time itself. But not only those things created before our time, even the things we create today or what might first take shape sometime in the future, would similarly fade into oblivion.

But we as National Socialists are concerned with only one past, and that is the past of the *Volk* itself. And we know what the causes are. But the one thing that remains an immovable constant throughout all manner of fluctuations is the *Volk*. It is the essence of life and of permanence. And art, as an expression of this living being, thus also becomes the essence of life and of permanence—an eternal monument.

Hence, our standard of measure has nothing to do with yesterday or today, with modern or unmodern; the only standard, rather, is what is "of value" and hence what is either "eternal" or "ephemeral." And this eternity is tied to the life of nations and people as long as these continue to exist.

So when I speak in terms of German art—the very reason this building was constructed—I want to see the standard as set by the German *Volk*, its essence and its life, its sentiments, sensibilities, and its development reflected here. The standards for the value or lack thereof in our cultural life, and thus of our artistic production, also rests within the expanses of the *Volk*'s very existence.

We know from the history of our *Volk* that it is comprised of several more or less distinct races, which, in the course of thousands of years, as a result of the formative influence of a certain racial core, have produced the composite we see in the current makeup of our *Volk*. This racial force at the center of our development in the past thus continues to shape us now and is evident here today in the same Aryan race of men in whom we recognize not only the bearers not only of our own culture but of all the civilizations of the ancient world. It is this composite nature of our race that accounts for the tremendous diversity of our own cultural developments and for the resulting natural blood relation between peoples and cultures derived from the same racial core in other European families of people. Nevertheless, we who see in the German *Volk* the gradual emergence of the end result of this historical development have hopes for a German art that reflects the ever-increasing racial homogeneity of this racial fabric and itself becomes one with it.

The question as to what it actually means to be "German" has often been posed. Of all the definitions that have been proposed over the centuries by men of every stripe, those I find most praiseworthy are the ones that have not even attempted to define the term in the first place and have instead established a law. There is one law that I would find most fitting as the law for my people to adopt as their purpose in life to fulfill, [and it] was already issued by a great German man: "To be German is to be clear." But that would also imply that to be German is thus to be logical and, above all, to be true. It is truly a magnificent law, but it is one that everyone must follow and serve in order for it to take force. And this law also provides us with a standard for measuring the value of art because it is congruent with the natural laws and essence of our *Volk*.

This deep inner desire for a genuinely German art that reflects this law of clarity has always been present in our *Volk*. It has inspired our great painters, our sculptors, our architects, our thinkers and poets, and above all our musicians. On that terrible day in June 1931, when the Glaspalast [the 1851 exhibition hall in Munich, modeled after the London Crystal Palace] went up in flames, an immeasurable treasure trove of this genuinely German art perished with it. [The creators of the destroyed artworks] were called the romantics, and as such, they were the very finest representatives of that uniquely German pursuit of the authentic and genuine nature of our *Volk* and the pursuit of a respectable, upstanding expression of this internalized law we know by intuition.

Because it wasn't just an issue of the subject matter portrayed that was decisive in [these works'] characterization of essential German nature, it was also a matter of the clarity and simplicity with which these sensibilities were rendered.

It is therefore no coincidence that these masters were the most Germanic of people.

These masters were and shall remain immortal, even now when many of their works no longer exist in the original, and only in copies and reproductions, if at all. But how far removed the influence and works of these men were from that pathetic marketplace of so many of our so-called modern artistic creators, with their abominable paint smears and droppings on canvas that could be bred, propagated, and applauded only by equally unconscionable and unscrupulous literary activity, but that nevertheless always remained completely alien to the German *Volk* in accordance with their inner instinct, which in fact seemed horrific to them. It never once occurred to our great German masters of the past to be or strive to be ancient or modern. They considered themselves German, they felt like Germans, and hence could reckon with enduring respect for their work, for as long as the German *Volk* continued to exist. What a tragedy, then, that their works of all things should have perished in that fire, while at the same time the products of these manufacturers and marketers of modern art, which are consciously promoted as products of their times, have remained intact for far too long already. Still, we should like to preserve them as documentation of the depths of decay in our *Volk* and our culture. This purpose is also served by the exhibition of works from the period of decadence [*Verfallszeit*] that we have made open to the public and recommend to all national comrades at the same time as this exhibition. It should serve as an eye-opening lesson to us all.

Over the many years of planning, which included shaping the spiritual orientation and organization of a new Reich, I was often concerned with identifying the tasks that would be incumbent upon us in the rebirth of the nation, especially in the field of cultural cleansing. For Germany's resurrection was to be not only political or economic but first and foremost cultural. Indeed, I was and remain convinced that the latter will have greater significance for the future than the other two. I have always fiercely opposed and rejected the opinions of those small-minded proponents of the "November time" who dismissed every single great cultural agenda, indeed every great construction project, based on the argument that it was too great a burden to place on the shoulders of such a politically and economically devastated nation as our own. [. . .]

One of the many and varied plans that came to my mind during the war and in the period directly following the collapse, especially in light of the utterly abysmal condition of the old building, was the idea for a new exhibition palace in Munich—the one city with by far the most illustrious history of artistic exhibitions. Even the site that has since been selected was precisely what I had in mind years ago. But when the old glass palace suddenly came to such a tragic end, I was afraid that, in addition to the terrible pain of this irretrievable loss of the finest German cultural capital, those representatives of the most egregious desecration of art in Germany would ultimately succeed in prohibiting me from fulfilling this task that I had already identified years earlier as one of the most pressing concerns for the new Reich. [. . .]

And so it is that a building has now taken shape that is worthy of housing the greatest achievements in art and providing the German public the opportunity to see them. The construction of this building, then, should at the same time represent a turning point that marks the end of the chaotic bungles in construction we have since put behind us. This first bit of new construction shall be the glorious inauguration of the immortal achievements of our German art.

You must understand, however, that it is not enough to give the German fine arts this building—as respectable, clear, and genuine as it is and thus clearly worthy of the name House of German Art; rather, the exhibition itself must mark a turning point that signals the end of the decay we have just experienced in the realm of the arts, of sculpture and of painting.

If I may be so presumptuous as to pass judgment, to express my opinions, and to act accordingly, then I reserve the right to do so based only on my position with regard to German art in general, but, above all, based on my own contributions to the restoration of German art.

Because the state as it exists today—the state that I have struggled together with my compatriots so hard to establish in a long and arduous battle against a whole world of adversaries—is the only thing that has provided the basic prerequisites for a strong and innovative renaissance of German art.

It was neither the Bolshevik art collectors nor their literary cohorts who established the foundation for a new art or even the conditions for existing art to continue: this was accomplished by those of us who built this state and who have made substantial resources available to German art—resources it needs to survive and to produce. Above all, this is to our credit because we are the ones who in fact assigned new and important tasks to the field of art. [. . .]

And so it is imperative that any artist who ever hopes to be exhibited in this House of German Art or to have any exposure whatsoever in Germany from now on must be in possession of great ability. The desire to create great art is not enough and is taken as a given from the outset. Because it would be an absolute outrage for a man to burden his fellow men with tasks they ultimately have no desire to fulfill. But when these blathering windbags seek to render their works more attractive by presenting them as expressions of a new age, all you can say to them is that it is not art that creates new ages of men but rather the life of the people overall that changes shape and thus often seeks new forms of expression. Even critical discussions of the new art in recent decades in Germany have failed to apprehend the spirit of the new German age. Because the literati are not the ones who usher in new epochs—revolutionaries do; the fighters go down in history as founders, as movers and shakers, and as leaders of nations and people. But these pathetically confused and befuddled paintbrush pushers and scribblers are not likely to be included amongst them. Furthermore, it is either an act of abject audacity or of nearly incomprehensible folly to proffer up to the people of our time works that could have been completed by any caveman ten or twenty thousand years ago.

They speak in terms of primitivism in art, and yet what they completely forget is that it is not the purpose of art to distance itself in reverse teleology from the *Volk* but rather that its only purpose can be to symbolize this dynamic process of development.

The new age of today is working to create a new type of man. Overwhelming efforts are being made in countless sectors of life to elevate the nation's people, to make better, stronger, and more beautiful men of our people, of our youth and our boys, our women and girls. And this strength and beauty exudes a new lust for life, a sense of joy in life!

Man has never been more similar in appearance and in sensibilities to the men of antiquity than he is today. Millions of young people are steeling their bodies through participation in competitive sports, contests, and tournaments and, increasingly, are putting these bodies on display in a form and constitution that has not been seen, much less imagined, in perhaps a thousand years. There is an absolutely stunning new type of man emerging, one who pays homage to the old adage: hard work makes for happy festivities.

This new type of man who, in all his glistening, glorious human strength, made his spectacular debut at the Olympic Games last year—this, dear sirs of prehistoric artistic stammering, is the model of man for the new age, and what do you continue manufacturing? Deformed cripples and cretins, women whose image can but elicit disgust, men who look more like animals than humans, children who would be considered a curse from God if they were to actually live the way you portray them! And these despicable dilettantes in our midst today would present this as the art of our times—that is, as the expression of what these times produce and what bears the mark of our time.

And let us not say that this is just the way these artists see things. Among the many paintings that were submitted to this exhibition, I have seen some that would lead one to conclude that certain men do indeed see things differently from the way they actually are—that is, that there are indeed men who can see in the contemporary state of our *Volk* nothing but deformed cretins, who truly do see blue meadows, green skies, and sulfur yellow clouds, or, as they would say, "experience" them as such. I am not about to engage in a discussion about whether these people indeed see or experience these things in this way. My only interest is in preventing, in the name of the *Volk,* these pathetic unfortunates, who so obviously suffer from defective vision, from attempting to foist the results of their faulty observations on their fellow man as reality or to somehow present them to the world as "art."

No, there are only two options here: either these so-called artists actually do see things this way and therefore firmly believe in what they portray—in which case, the only thing left to do would be to ascertain whether this defect in their eyesight is attributable to a mechanical malfunction or whether it is hereditary in nature. In the case of the former, this is truly unfortunate for them, but in the case of the latter, it becomes a matter for the Reich Ministry of the Interior, which would be charged with the task of preventing the perpetuation of these horrific diseases of the eye in future generations. Or perhaps they do not themselves believe that their impressions reflect reality, and they have other motivations for pestering the nation with this humbug, and that would place their actions under the jurisdiction of the criminal courts.

In any case, this building was neither planned nor constructed to house the works of this sort of artistic incompetent or malfeasant. A thousand workers did not labor for four and a half years on this building only to have the works of people who are brazen enough and lazy enough to stand for five hours spattering the canvas with paint in the self-assured hope that the audacious price tag attached to it will produce the desired effect and result in the work being hailed as a great stroke of genius. No, the diligence and hard work of those who built this house and all their collaborators shall be commensurate with the diligence and hard work of those whose work is on display here. And I am not the least interested in whether or not that whole gaggle of pseudoartists chooses to continue going goo-goo eyed over the crap they produce amongst themselves!

Because the artist does not create for other artists but rather, just like everyone else, for the *Volk.*

And we shall see to it that from here on out, the *Volk* will again be called to pass judgment on its own art.

Let us not contend that the *Volk* does not have any appreciation for what is truly a valuable enrichment of its cultural life. Long before the critics did justice to the genius of Richard Wagner, he had the *Volk* on his side. On the other hand, the *Volk* has had absolutely no affinity for the works that have been touted as so-called modern art in recent years. The people could not relate to it in any way. The masses have visited these art exhibitions with a sense of complete indifference, or they have simply not even bothered to attend. Their healthy, intuitive sensibilities led them to perceive all these smears and smatterings for what they are—the by-products of an impudent, unabashed arrogance, or a simply shocking lack of skill. Millions of people have instinctively sensed that the artistic stammerings of recent decades, which have been on a par with the maladroit bungling efforts of eight- or ten-year-old children completely lacking in talent, must not under any circumstances be regarded as expressions of our time, and certainly not as expressions of the German future.

Since we now know that the development of millions of years is reflected in each human individual, condensed in the span of a few decades, we can take this as proof of the fact that artistic production that does not go beyond the level of what eight-year-old children might produce cannot be seen as "modern" or "future oriented" but rather that it is, on the contrary, highly archaic, for it is most likely less developed than the art of the Stone Age, when people were etching their impressions of their environment on the walls of caves. So these bungling amateurs are not at all modern but rather utterly archaic, deplorable retards who have no place whatsoever in our modern times.

And this is why I know that as the German public passes through these galleries, I will be acknowledged as its speaker and counselor, because the public will recognize that this is the first time in many decades that genuine artistic excellence, and not an artistic swindle, has finally been dignified here.

Just as the public has expressed its approval of the buildings we have constructed, so too will it heave a heavy sigh of relief in enthusiastic affirmation of this cleansing of the art world.

And that is decisive, for any art that does not resonate with the enthusiastic, heartfelt affirmation of the healthy masses of the *Volk* but that instead relies only on the support of a few small cliques—some sincerely interested, others merely in it for the prestige—is absolutely untenable. It is one that seeks to confound the healthy, instinctual certainty of public sentiment in a *Volk* instead of seeking enthusiastically to confirm it.

It only serves to generate trouble and strife, and so these sniveling little welterweights cannot defend themselves by claiming that the great masters of the past were not understood in their own times either. It was merely the quibblers, the so-called literary types, who stood apart from the *Volk* as the torturers and tormentors of these geniuses. But we are also convinced that the German *Volk* will one day again be able to wholeheartedly welcome and enthusiastically appreciate the truly great German artists of the near future. And the day will come again when not only the quality of work and rhetorical flair is valued but equally so the effort to speak from the deepest depths of public sentiment and to accommodate and serve the sensibilities of the *Volk*. This too must be the task of our artists. They cannot distance themselves from their people, not without quickly finding themselves lost in isolation.

This exhibition, then, is but a beginning. I am convinced that this is necessarily the only beginning with any promise for success in the endeavor to usher in that felicitous turning point in the arts that we have already seen come to fruition in so many other areas. For there should no longer be any doubt about one thing: that National Socialism has set itself to the task of eliminating from the German Reich, and thus from the life of its *Volk*, all those influences that are detrimental to our existence. And while this cleansing cannot take place in one day alone, no one and nothing that contributes to or participates in this detriment should delude himself into thinking that the hour of his elimination will not come sooner or later.

But the opening of this exhibition also marks the beginning of the end for the stultification of German art and thus for the annihilation of culture.

226

ADOLF ZIEGLER

Speech at the Opening of the Degenerate Art Exhibition

Delivered on 19 July 1937. First published as "Rede des Präsidenten der Reichskammer der bildenden Kunst, Prof. Adolf Ziegler am 19. 7. 1937 anlässlich der Eröffnung der Ausstellung Entartete Kunst," in *Mitteilungsblatt der Reichskammer der bildenden Künst,* 11, 12. Republished in Peter-Klaus Schuster, ed., *"Nationalsozialismus und entartete Kunst: Die Kunststat München 1937.* (Munich: Prestel Verlag, 1988), 217, 218.

Today we all stand here still reeling from the profound impression left by the festivities surrounding the inauguration of the House of German Art. Everything that the contemporary masters of the fine arts have created in the values and works of visual art was put on

FIGURE 20. Guide to the 1937 Degenerate Art Exhibition in Munich. Collection of Anson Rabinbach.

display for the public in this glorious new temple of German art. But before we leave the city of Munich after these days, we, we German artists and comrades, we have one more tragic obligation to fulfill; we must also show the German *Volk* that up until just a short while ago, forces that saw in art neither a natural nor a crystal-clear expression of life exerted substantial influence over the production of art, forces that consciously relinquished what was healthy and instead promoted what was diseased and degenerate—celebrating this as the highest revelation.

What we can enthusiastically glean from the Führer's words in yesterday's speech is that this form of artistic engagement is finally done with and gone. And it is also over for anyone who during the *Systemzeit* acted as a walking billboard for this so-called art—the art of downfall and degeneracy; it is over for those who abused the power of their pens to take what their racial and ideological comrades offered them for the sake of commerce and to pass this off to the German people as genuine revelation, as the most modern of innovations.

We are in the midst of a show that represents but a fraction of what has been purchased by museums from the nest egg of the German *Volk* as art and placed on exhibit as such. All around us you see these miscreants of madness, the mutant by-products of impudence, of ineptitude, and of degeneracy. What this show has to offer elicits from all of us the same revulsion and utter dismay. Many of our museum curators do not have a shred of the sense of accountability to the *Volk* and the country that is the primary prerequisite to curating an art show. With this show, I used one particular example to illustrate the tendency on the part of museum curators to exhibit things that are pathological or degenerate. In this artist's case, we witness the way interest in his older works, which had been rejected for as long as he remained healthy and continued to create from the depths of the landscape from which he originated, suddenly surged after he suffered his second stroke, at which point everything he produced amounted to pathological or unintelligible scribbles. It is for the same reason that I have included in this show works by a series of artists that were created very late in life, or in a period of mental decline or disability, works that were hanging in our museums up until just a brief while ago, and, at the same time, one could search entirely in vain for any healthy works by these same artists. So painting had been reduced to something that served a purpose for museum curators as collectors and no longer served the interests of the people.

In order to execute my duty to gather together every bit of documentation of artistic decline and artistic degeneracy, I visited almost every museum in Germany. It was clear from the onset that the number of acquisitions in recent years would be tremendously large. But I was utterly taken aback by the fact that, up until just a few days ago, these documents of art's demise that we have brought together here in Munich were still on exhibit in public museums and collections throughout Germany, which means that the directors of these institutions have been subjecting the viewing public to these works. The products on display here, however, represent only a portion of what still remains in the inventory of the above-cited institutions. Even with several freight cars at your disposal, you wouldn't be able to clear out all that rubbish from the German museums. That task is yet to be completed, and it will be done very soon. It is a sin and a shame that the walls of these institutions have been cluttered up with this junk and that local artists, fine upstanding German artists, were denied the opportunity to have their works exhibited particularly in these shrines of great art.

I can spare you the details concerning my own personal reaction to discovering these works. I hope that your reactions will be the same on the tour we are about to make.

An old front-line soldier cannot help but be struck with horror at the sight of the way a German front-line soldier is spat upon and spattered in blood here, or at the way the German mother is portrayed as a sex-starved whore or as an elemental force, and when she is mocked by these pigs who would depict her face with such dull expressions of stupidity; horror at the notion that, at a time when the government was the very center of life, public agencies could afford to purchase those so-called works of art that ridicule Christian symbols in such an inimitable way. In essence, you'd have to say, everything that is sacred to decent, upstanding Germans simply had to be dragged through the dirt here. I do not have the time, dear *Volk* comrades, to outline in detail all the crimes committed against German art by these fellows at the behest of and as frontrunners for international Jewry. The menial and the base were elevated to high ideals. The most hideous standard of ugliness became the epitome for standards of beauty. Accordingly, this is the underlying assumption when you hear these people say things like "You cannot possibly destroy enough culture on behalf of culture. You cannot possibly destroy enough works of art on behalf of art. Enough of this respect for all this bourgeois culture. Shatter all these blasphemous old images in the name of the coming proletarian culture. Go ahead and set all the libraries on fire. Open the canals and flood the museums. Let them float down the rivers, these glorious images."

What those literati wrote, dear German *Volk* comrades, is about to become reality. We are going to throw out their old blasphemous images, if we haven't done so already. We will make clear to these gentlemen that, even in the realm of the fine arts, the days are long since over in which these poseurs can hoist their banners of "We would rather live in filth than be clean and go down with the ship. We will leave the task of being incompetent but upstanding to pigheaded individualists and old maids. We aren't afraid of ruining our reputations."

During the whole period directly preceding the seizure of power, while the German worker struggled to piece together his existence with the paltry support of unemployment compensation, these Jewish helots were busy squandering outrageous amounts of tax revenues on so-called art that was nothing but a mockery of the *Volk* and stripped the nation of its honor and dignity in the eyes of other nations. The artists are grateful to their German national comrades for the fact that, just as the cultural Bolsheviks were primed to try and pass off their grimy scrawl on the so-called class-conscious worker, the national comrades felt more innately German in every respect than ever. They simply didn't fall for the swindle. They were and remain healthy. All they could do was shake their heads, uncomprehending, whenever these products were applauded up and down with catchphrases and clichés in their old partisan presses. Naturally, what happened was that these forms of expression you see all around you were then presented as works that were only for the so-called educated class—things that were beyond comprehension for the mind of the average man. Unfortunately, even during the previous bourgeois period, for a whole series of national comrades, it was seen as a sign of good form to have enough money in the bank to go out and buy stuff like this just to be in step with modern times.

We realize that it is the seducers, not the seduced, who must be taken to task for these things. That is why we did not take stock immediately following the seizure of power but rather four years later. We have given it four years' time. Now our patience is finally at an end for all those who have not fallen in line with National Socialist reconstruction efforts in the field of the fine arts in the course of these past four years; may they be judged by the German *Volk,* and let us not hesitate to let that verdict stand. Here, as in every other sector of our lives, we will see that we can place unconditional faith in the man who is our Führer today, the man who knows the best direction for German art to take in order to fulfill her great purpose of heralding German art and the essence of German character. I hereby declare the exhibition Degenerate Art free and open to the public. German *Volk,* come and judge for yourselves!

227

REINHARD PIPER

A Visit to the Degenerate Art Exhibition

Written 28 July 1937. First published as "Brief an Barlach," in *Ernst Barlach und die nationalsozialistische Kunstpolitik: eine dokumentarische Darstellung zur "entarteten Kunst,"* edited by Ernst Piper (Munich: Piper, 1983), 196–200.

Letter to Ernst Barlach:

Of course the Degenerate Art Exhibition currently here in Munich in the Galeriestraße has feelings running high. I visited it a few days ago already. It is drawing extraordinary crowds. The paper reports that it was attended by three hundred thousand visitors last week on Tuesday alone. The same day, there were only six thousand visitors to the House of German Art. That is, of course, related to the fact that there is no admission fee for the Degenerate Art Exhibition and that many people are expecting a sensation. The lines extended far into the street, and people were being admitted in batches. Since there have been several changes made to the exhibition since I last visited it, I went back to see it again today. There are about six large rooms altogether, containing perhaps five hundred paintings and graphic illustrations. There is a display case on the ground floor that contains, among other things, your illustrations, accompanied by a large placard containing the following text: "Desecrator of culture. The dereliction of duty on the part of the literary pimps of the publishing industry, the museum directors and curators who have foisted this abominable spirit on the German public and to this day would still pass off this stuff as art is just as bad as the diseased by-products of these evil or pathologically disturbed 'artists.'"

Your book is lying open for viewing in this display case, whereby the words "Munich 1936" have been underlined on the title page and pages 26, 41, and 45 placed beside them as individual pages, but without their titles, so that the public could assume that in the case of the illustration *Animal-Man* [*Tiermensch*], for example, you have attempted to portray in these figures your idea of ideal standards. That's all there was to see of you and your work. There are several other books from the "Young Art" [*Junge Kunst*] series in the same display case—among others, volumes about Rohlfs, Hofer, Schmidt-Rottluff, Pechstein, Grossmann, Klee, Feiniger, and Hötger. There is a caption to accompany these books that reads, "This is how Professor Beiermann helped spread artistic Bolshevism throughout Germany."

The following artists are listed on a poster that reads "Art Critics of the *Systemzeit*": Paul Fechter, Meier-Graefe, Wilhelm Hausenstein, W. Niemeyer, C. G. Heise, among others. As far as paintings are concerned, there are between twenty and thirty paintings by each of these artists: Nolde, Kirchner, Otto Müller, Heckel, Pechstein, and Schmidt-Rottluff—all taken from public collections, from the National Gallery, the Hamburg Kunsthalle, from the museums in Cologne, Lübeck, Mannheim, Barmen, Essen, Frankfurt, Dresden, and elsewhere. In addition to Nolde's paintings of figures, which one need not necessarily find appealing, there are some very beautiful landscapes and still-life paintings of flowers. There are about a dozen paintings by Beckman and Kokoschka, which means that even these artists have apparently been utterly purged from the public collections. There are also six paintings of figures by Karl Hofer, which are completely harmless in my view. Marc's *Blue Horses* [*Blaue Pferde*] are there, as well as Lehmbruck's famous *Kneeling Figure* [*Kniende*].

In addition to the artist's name and the title of the painting, each work of art includes a notice indicating how much was paid for it, and beneath the price tag, there is a fairly large red note attached with the following text: "Paid for with hard-earned tax revenues by the German *Volk*." But these seemingly exorbitant prices mostly turn out to be inflated and are in fact very low. Furthermore, there are many citations from art critics—for example, one of Däubler's comments on Archipenko, one of Karl With's on Rohlf.

In the second-to-the-last room, there are seven paintings by Lovis Corinth: three Walchensee landscapes from the National Galleries in Munich, Hamburg, and Mannheim; the portrait of Grönvold from the art center in Bremen; and the utterly incredible *Ecce Homo* from the National Gallery, a very important and truly distressing image, masterfully crafted despite the artist's much-discussed stroke. Then there was also the painting the *Trojan Horse,* and *Child in a Playpen* [*Kind im Laufställchen*], etc. Here you find a sign reading, "These paintings were on exhibit to this day!" What is conspicuous is this: while the artist is identified for all the remaining paintings, here, in the case of these Corinth paintings, the name has been covered up so that viewers who wouldn't recognize Corinth's signature are not aware of the fact that these paintings are his. Why is the name concealed here? There is a glass display case featuring photographs of some of Corinth's diligently detailed early paintings, and the caption reads, "The artist when he was still young and upstanding." But even here, Corinth's name is not mentioned.

In the last room, which was open to the public only for a few days and has since been closed, there are three paintings by my friend who is a professor at the academy here, Karl Caspar: his *The Resurrected* [*Auferstandenen*], *St. John at Patmos* [*Johannes auf Patmos*], and *Spring Landscape* [*Frühlingslandschaft*] depicting his daughter Felicitas—paintings from the state collection of national treasures in Munich that are absolutely beyond reproach and that have never elicited any form of objection before. Written in large print on the wall below them, "Masters like this were permitted to teach our German youth up until just recently!" There were works by other academy professors hanging in the same room—for example, an utterly normal landscape by [Hans] Purrmann.

You have to bear in mind the fact that the whole exhibition is primarily the project of another academy professor here, Professor Ziegler, that is—one of Caspar's *colleagues.* And Ziegler succeeded Hoenig as president of the Reich Chamber of Art, after all.

When my son tried to enter that last room, one of the visitors said, "You can't go in there; there's a painting by Munch in there; the Norwegian delegation objected to it. [. . .]

Goebbels mentioned in his speech that it was obvious to the public how much *enormous effort* was needed to dispose of this art in order to make way for the eternal Germanic art. But in fact all that was required was that someone lay down the law, and the paintings were taken down.

As far as the exhibition at the House of German Art is concerned, I went there sincerely intent on enthusiastically embracing all that was of genuine value. But one cannot by any means speak of this show in terms of a significant exhibition of exemplary German artists or act as if it had something to offer that hasn't already been seen in every art exhibition for the past twenty years and nothing that hasn't been given its due by the critics. You get the feeling you're at an exhibition not unlike any other that might have been on display in any given year at the Glaspalast . Three-quarters of the paintings are diligently crafted but artistically inconsequential. They've been completed by the same kind of run-of-the-mill artists that have existed for all time. One clearly does not need to "liberate" them! It would be interesting to see the paintings that were not included, since the number of entries was supposedly extremely high.

228

ROBERT SCHOLZ

Vital Questions of Visual Art

First published in *Lebensfragen der bildenden Kunst* (Munich: Zentralverlag der NSDAP, 1937), 61, 62, 65, 66.

Schopenhauer once put it this way: "There is no such thing as the happy life, only the heroic one." So the simple, dispassionate heroic life is worthy of depiction in art and should serve to exemplify for us life's higher calling. And thus, the point is not to seek to mandate that the subjects of art today conform to a certain pathos or to violently foist upon them some contrived monumentality. The realm of the heroic and of German art is much greater in scope than that, and heroism and genuine monumentality in art are much more a question of inner outlook than they are of any particular subject matter. We are entirely justified in placing certain demands on artists with regard to the selection of motifs, but it would be a big mistake to equate a representation of the times with the spirit of the times. This is why the heroic outlook and evidence of internal identification with the times are not restricted to a narrowly defined thematic scope in art. Albrecht Dürer's profoundly moving portrait of his mother, where he has inscribed her life struggle in every single line and furrow of worry and woe on her face—this is a work of art that exemplifies the heroic character in the finest sense of the word. When a contemporary artist depicts a worker and a peasant with his calloused hands on the plow or the anvil, this is, for our times—times in which we have attached the same value to the heroism of the soldier and that of the worker—this image is the genuine epitome of the heroic. For our time, the mark of monumentality in art must be sought not in contrived pathos and theatrical gesticulation but rather in the greatness of perspective. [. . .]

Here we come up against the oft-discussed problem of the relationship between the *Volk* and its art. This question is rarely addressed without some set of preconceived inner prejudices. In artistic circles especially, the tendency is to view the problem of drawing *Volk* and art into a closer relationship with a substantial degree of skepticism. But it merits pointing out that the experiences of creating art and that of receiving art have always been multi-layered, that great works of art have always been understood only by a select circle of people, that the great masses of the *Volk* have always sought to satisfy their need for art in what is easily accessible and comprehensible. There is de facto no such thing as "everyman's art," except in the form of the antithesis of art. All these sorts of objections emerge from a conscious misapprehension of the fact that the demand for drawing *Volk* and art into a closer relationship involves an attempt to work toward an ideal, and the people who have established this ideal are entirely conscious of the fact that bringing any ideal to fruition is not only something that requires time but also something whose fulfillment is always limited by the natural constricts of human imperfection. But no one seriously doubts the necessity of these ideals and this ideal in order to maximize the potential for what is possible. It is a foregone conclusion that an understanding for art always bound by certain prerequisites and capacities will never be uniformly present in all human beings. And there will always be a certain remainder of uninspired people for whom art will never have existed and never will. The mistake of the past, however, was that the circle of participants in the world of art was consciously limited by theories that frightened most away. The demand for strengthening the relationship between art and *Volk* is targeted primarily at combating this kind of conscious limitation placed on the radius of artistic production. But this does not require of artists any sort of self-sacrifice in the form of stooping to the tastes of the masses, who have no understanding for art. National Socialism in particular, with its staunch rejection of the intellectually annihilating Marxist dogma of equality between all men and their respective capacities, will never promote a form of "everyman's art" in the sense of an art that has been ratcheted down to conform to the basest dictates of taste. These new times do not applaud a simplified or dumbed-down art, merely a form of art that is not situated fundamentally beyond the realm of the *Volk*'s experience. The *völkisch* flavor that we demand for the art of our times can be based only on the desire to restore the essential Germanic nature to art so that it again reflects a distinctly Germanic character in both content and form. The conscious "understanding" of art as was promoted by the intellectualist artistic period of the past is always an intellectual construct, and an understanding of art of this nature is therefore always necessarily contingent on the natural intellectual predilections of the individual. But today it is much less a matter of this sort of understanding and more a matter of a visceral affirmation of art as such by the *Volk*. And if this sort of visceral relationship to masterpieces of ancient Germanic art does indeed still exist among substantial sectors of the population, as no one would deny, based on the number of visitors to the old museums, then this indicates that the possibility exists for an affirmation of a similarly distinct national character and traditional *völkisch* values that can always be emotionally grasped.

229

WERNER RITTICH

Contemporary Architecture and Architectural Sculpture

First published in *Architektur und Bauplastik der Gegenwart* (Berlin: Rembrandt, 1938), 140–48.

A great number of sculptural works commissioned in conjunction with new construction for the air force, the marines, and the navy are worthy of consideration, although they are often difficult to access by the general public. Even the regulation stipulating that the national

FIGURE 21. Josef Thorak working on some of his massive sculptures in his atelier. Kurt Lothar Tank and Wilfrid Bade, eds., *Deutsche Plastik unserer Zeit* (Munich: Raumbild-Verlag Otto Schönstein), card no. 110.

emblem shall be prominently displayed at all sites of new construction, and in an innovative, nonconventional form, have presented and continue to present a wealth of opportunities for commissions. But even these works completed for military installations—with the exception of the enormous eagles, for example, created by W. E. Lemcke for the honor court [*Ehrenhof*] of the Reich Ministry of Aviation—are the smaller commissions. Up until now, the most monumental of all renderings of the national emblem could be found in the bronze eagles created by Kurt Schmid-Ehmen for the pillars at either end of the Luitpold Arena on the Reich Party Rally grounds and for the House of Germany [Das Deutsche Haus] at the World Exposition in Paris.

The purpose of sculpture and its relationship to architecture finds its clearest expression to date in this work: it is here that what can emerge from one and the same idea is most conspicuous. The national emblems and both larger-than-life groups of figures by Josef Thorak were already conceived during the planning stages of construction. The building was designed to embody security, pride, self-confidence, clarity, and discipline and, as such, the very essence of the New Germany. The motifs of camaraderie and family formed the cornerstones of the building, accentuating the driving forces of the Reich, symbolically crowned by the building and its pillars. The external harmony of the structure was also such that no single element could have been lacking without disrupting the overall composition. The groups themselves, taken as a whole, are a reflection of the entire building's overall structure; taken individually, they highlight the majestic glory of the structure as a whole, its self-confidence and nobility.

In the honor court of the new Reich Chancellery in Berlin, two bronze sculptures by Arno Breker, *The Party* [*Die Partei*] and *The Army* [*Die Wehrmacht*], may be seen as a symbolic introduction for an entire series leading into a given space, as an expression of the external and internal forces influencing political life in contemporary Germany; combined with the magnificent architecture, they leave the impression of grandeur.

230

SECRET REPORT OF THE SECURITY SERVICE OF THE REICHSFÜHRER SS

The Great German Art Exhibition in Munich, 1940

First distributed on 2 July 1940 as "Große Deutsche Kunstaustellung 1940 in München." First published in *Meldungen aus dem Reich 1938–1945. Die geheimen Lageberichte des Sicherheitsdienstes der SS,* edited by Heinz Boberach (Herrsching: Pawlak Verlag, 1984), 5:1340, 1341.

According to the 18 March 1940 number of *Reports from the Reich,* [. . .] over the course of the past few months of war, views critical of the Munich Artistic Doctrine [*Münchener Kunstrichtung*] have become conspicuously more vocal.[1] The reports are unanimous in perceiving the selection of artworks for the exhibition in Munich as a prescriptive and confining "doctrine" to which there is increasing resistance, though this is often more a matter of general sentiment than a palpable expression of public opinion. Whereas in the Ostmark [Austria], the rejection of the Munich Artistic Doctrine remains restricted to relatively small circles; reports from Munich, Berlin, Stettin, Hamburg, and elsewhere confirm that there is staunch criticism for the Munich Artistic Doctrine in the artistic communities there. The opinion is that the Munich Artistic Doctrine is constrictive and places undue restraint on young artists who are more daring and exploratory in their art. Many artists, for example, as reports from Dresden indicate, have consciously begun adapting their approach in the hope of being exhibited at the House of German Art in Munich. Everyone "is doing impasto painting and seeking to conform to the thematic trend in Munich as well." Reports from Liegnitz and Hamburg complain that many artists from northern Germany could not paint in the "Munich style" without having their works seem unauthentic. At the same time, the need to set stringent standards is accepted as an effective means of rejecting the corrupt art [*Verfallskunst*] that, to some extent, still continues to flourish beneath the surface. And yet, in many artistic circles, the comparison is being made between the current situation for certain individual artists whose works have not been accepted for exhibition at the House of German Art in Munich and that of artists from previous centuries, such as Rembrandt and C[aspar] D[avid] Friedrich. Friedrich, for example, with his newfangled art, was considered artistically incompetent during his lifetime, much like many of the artists who are not being admitted in Munich now.

According to available reports, this growing opposition stems primarily from left-leaning circles but is also being fueled by regional forces that would like to see a "loosening" of restrictions and more freedom of expression of ideas that do not conform to the expressly "southern" German ideals of the Munich Artistic Doctrine. Accordingly, repeated requests coming from artistic circles suggest that explicitly "northern" German exhibitions be organized as a way of complementing the Munich exhibition with a more "northern" focus that is either indifferent to or expressly opposed to the Munich Artistic Doctrine. This year, the greatest evidence of concrete measures being taken to loosen or defy the standards set in Munich could be seen at exhibitions in Berlin, the Rhine Valley, central Germany, and even Munich. These efforts have been received with unanimous enthusiasm in artistic circles.

According to available reports, many people in artistic circles hope to draw upon the war experience itself to find strong new impulses for artistic production, and at the same time, they are hoping to see a relaxation of restrictions and an increase in the means available for artistic production. In this context, the rumor that the Führer himself will seek to take art in a completely different direction at war's end is gaining popularity.

Note

1. "Munich Artistic Doctrine" is shorthand for the artistic norms governing the art displayed at the annual exhibition of "Great German Art" in Munich.—Eds.

231

SECRET REPORT OF THE SECURITY SERVICE OF THE REICHSFÜHRER SS

Masterpieces of German Art in Private Jewish Collections

Distributed on 11 February 1940 as "Meisterwerke deutscher Kunst in jüdischem Privatbesitz." Published in *Meldungen aus dem Reich 1938–1945. Die geheimen Lageberichte des Sicherheitsdienstes der SS,* edited by Heinz Boberach (Herrsching: Pawlak Verlag, 1984), 3:768.

Artistic circles in Berlin are reporting that some masterpieces of the German fine arts remain in possession of private Jewish collectors. These circles are advocating that Jews be forced to register their artistic holdings, and the matter is being reviewed by experts. If Jews are found to be in possession of works of national significance, the works must be relinquished to the state or to national museums.

232

ROBERT SCHOLZ

The Mission of the New German Sculpture: On the Arno Breker Exhibit in Paris

First published as *Die Sendung der Neuen Deutschen Plastik: Zur Arno Breker-Kollektivausstellung in Paris,* in *Die Kunst im Deutschen Reich,* edition A, 6:7 (July 1942), 173.

The exhibition of works by the preeminent German sculptor Arno Breker, currently on display at the Orangerie in Paris, has met with greater success than almost any previous exhibition of German fine arts outside of Germany. Not only was the exhibition viewed by an extraordinary number of visitors, the Parisian art world took an astonishing degree of interest in Breker's work and in the artistic intent of the New Germany. The tone for this series of highly laudatory assessments was set by the publication of a book by Charles Despiau at the time of the exhibition's opening in which the renowned French sculptor expressed his heartfelt appreciation for Breker's work. But it was not only Despiau, who had already established a personal relationship with Breker during Breker's frequent stays in Paris between 1927 and 1933, but rather a great number of prominent personalities from the French arts and cultural scene who expressed in countless essays and public statements their sincere appreciation of Breker and his work as the preeminent representatives of the new German sculpture. Particularly noteworthy is the fact that the French art world acknowledged not only the universal, absolute artistic qualities of Breker's works but also their underlying ideological content as expressions of a new German intellectual outlook.

The efforts on the part of the French public to grasp the ideological-political content and its constitutive significance for Breker's work enhanced the exhibition's ability to present the opportunity for following the logical progression of Breker's work from the early works still rooted in the traditions of the nineteenth century to an increasingly pronounced monumental style strongly influenced by the ideas and mission of these times. Needless to say, even Breker's early works reveal not only his extraordinary skill as a sculptor but also the fundamental impulse toward formalistic grandeur. But this impulse was constrained by subjectivist perceptions of sculpture in the nineteenth century and is shackled by the moment of a unique individual experience of nature. Developments in European sculpture at the end of the nineteenth century and into the twentieth, which followed on the heels of historicizing stylistic experimentation, were influenced by a profound skepticism concerning any and all stylistic

FIGURE 22. Postcard with an image of Arno Breker's *The Guardian (Head)* (*Der Wächter [Kopf]*). Photograph by Charlotte Rohrbach. Film, Foto, Verlag, Berlin, SW 68. Collection of Anson Rabinbach.

tendencies in sculpture; by dint of resignation, they were fundamentally opposed to all forms of ideological, abstract, and formalistic efforts in the world of sculpture. The sculpture from this period had fallen prey to the disquiet of a seemingly futile search; the only alternative left for sculpture was seen in lending expression to a feeling of cosmic connectivity in the form of sensitive manifestations of what was a strictly individual perception of nature. The style of this sculpture was the indeterminacy of form designed to reflect inner and external forces. The changes in surface appearance produced by the play of light assumed stylistically constitutive significance. This sculptural style was lacking in architectonic moorings and an overarching impersonal principle as determinate forces.

Breker's beginnings, too, can be seen as belonging to this realm of sculptural utilitarianism in all its sentimentality and limitations. But the fact that this was so clearly brought to the fore at the exhibition in Paris is what rendered the turn to the monumental form in Breker's work visible and revealed that its impetus stemmed from the acceptance of an overarching impersonal principle. By comparing his earlier works with today's, any visitor to the exhibition became immediately conscious of the fact that the turn to the monumental style in Breker's work was precipitated by the fact that his immense natural capacity for sculptural expression was able to develop its full potential only within the parameters of new tasks set by the new German architecture combined with an ideal that extended far beyond the realm of the individual and its limits. The impersonal clarity of a stringently architectonic formalistic will for extreme sculptural precision replaced the reproduction of certain moments in the modified expressions of sensibilities on randomly selected natural objects. And with that,

Breker made the move from an expressive form of individual representation to a monumental one. This move, however, also initiated a historically significant developmental turn in European sculpture because this model is what opened the door to formalistic ideals and paved the way for an architectonically precise formalism.

Based on his adherence to the law of architectonics and his experience of the impersonal content of our contemporary political ideals, Breker's will to form reached monumental proportions that lent his work that classically impersonal style that no artist or art epoch can set out to devise but that can emerge only when the overall expressive intent of the times converges with an ability to grasp the ideological tendencies of a certain epoch in the person of great artistic talent. And that kind of artistic style represents the complete fusion of form and content.

Anyone who enters the main gallery of the exhibition in Paris and finds himself face-to-face with the formalistic dramatics in the relief *Comradeship;* with the figures of *Prometheus, Dionysus,* or *Berufung* [*Calling*], which exude superhuman dignity and intellectual prowess; and beside them, the symbolic representations of a new psychological and physical ideal, the figures of *The One who Dares* [*Der Wager*] and *Psyche;* in addition to the bust of Wagner and the exquisite depiction of the wounded warrior, in which the value of individual personality finds splendid expression, cannot help but conclude that he is standing before works of art that are again filled with power and the breath of life, works of art that embody a new epitome for the standard of beauty and nobility and that fulfill the greatest purpose of sculpture as expressed by Goethe, "to represent human dignity in human figures."

233

PAUL SCHMITTHENNER

Tradition and New Design in Architecture

First published as "Tradition und Neues Bauen," in *Deutsche Kultur-Wacht: Blätter des Kampfbundes für Deutsche Kultur* (1933). Published in *Architektur im Dritten Reich 1933–1945,* edited by Anna Teut (Berlin: Ullstein, 1967), 121–23.

The danger to the whole fabric of public culture inherent in abandoning sensible traditions is perhaps most evident in the field of architectural design, which is always the ultimate expression of the cultural totality [*Gesamtkultur*] of any given period. The demise of German architectural design began with the abandonment of tradition and coincided with the onset of the technological century, which at the same time marked the end of the last self-contained epoch that can be summed up by invoking the name of "Goethe." Architectural design begins to disintegrate with the development of technology, although that is not the fault of technology but rather of the inability to harness technology in the service of culture. The architectural accomplishments of the past fifty years are a shocking mirror image of our state of cultural advancement. Not even the Thirty Years' War wreaked as much havoc on cultural values in Germany as has the senseless construction of the last fifty years. The various architectural epochs in our history display a tremendous amount of diversity. All the things that each architectural epoch has created throughout the generations have been new and have been the ultimate expression of the intellectual life of those respective epochs, but they have been new only in the sense that tradition itself is the eternal font of innovation from which new life springs. The magnificent ancient German cities upon which centuries have been built join together to form a harmonic melody. The Germanic *Volk* and its culture carry the main melody through a series of beautiful variations in the symphony of the splendid cities of Germany, from the north to the south, from the east to the west. But the

FIGURE 23. Albert Speer's German Pavilion at the 1937 Paris World Exhibition ("Turmbau des Deutschen Ausstellungsgebäudes auf der Pariser Weltausstellung 1937"). Albert Speer, ed., *Neue Deutsche Baukunst* (Prague: Volk und Reich Verlag, 1943), 24.

progression of the tradition of German spirit in design stopped in the suburbs of the years just beyond 1870. Apartment buildings, tenements in all their jerry-built artifice, the spirit of unchecked entrepreneurialism—these documented indices of social misery are what gave rise to these faceless cities without souls. There is no evidence of any intent to shape the face of the times here in these cities, and what has emerged instead is a caricature, a grimace, a travesty.

Karl Friedrich Schinkel once said, "Whatever is useful and sufficient, as good as it may be in principle, will go bad as soon as it manifests itself stripped of any decency and dignity, and the only way to cloak it in decency and dignity is through beauty—which is why beauty is so fundamental and must be given as much consideration as utility and sufficiency."

The way beauty, decency, and dignity are defined is an identifying characteristic of any human individual or nation of people and plays a decisive role in its culture.

Beauty, decency, and dignity are frivolous things that spring not from the mind, not from the intellect, but from the heart alone. Our thinking has been far too heavily influenced by the ever-calculating intellect of the times. Decency and dignity have all too capriciously sacrificed to the intellect, and not just in the field of architectural design. We are seeing the same phenomena appear in literature, in theater, and in politics. Whatever generated a profit was permissible and considered socially acceptable. But what this intellect of calculation left out of the equation was the human factor. The most illustrative example of this new kind of thinking, this exaggerated intellect, is evident in the so-called New Objectivity [*Neue Sachlichkeit*] in design. There is no such thing as a "new" objectivity, there is only objectivity, and this notion of "New Objectivity" is, in fact, just lacking in objectivity. The architecture of the 1870s didn't intend to forgo beauty for the sake of utility and sufficiency; hollow pathos was mistaken for decency and dignity. The misery of the tenements was not alleviated by covering them up with façades in German Renaissance style, and post office buildings draped in Gothic are and shall forever remain a sheer absurdity. The more absurd architectural concepts became during this period, the more sensible the construction of machines became. Here we see designs reduced to their very simplest form, of highest quality and self-evident beauty. Around 1900, a new consciousness of healthy architectural design began to set in and slowly but surely gained ground. There were various different avenues taken along the path to new design, but they all shared the same aim: to cleanse architectural design of hollow and therefore un-German pathos. Signs of a will to pursue a Germanic concept of design were already apparent in the fact that people sought to pick up where development has stopped. This development of healthy design, for all its progressiveness, remained rooted in tradition and thus remained Germanic, was unsettled and staunchly opposed by the so-called New Objectivity. A concept of architectural design that was nationalistic in the best sense of the word was confronted with internationalist interests. The triumph of the new style in architectural design was heralded boldly, and its international currency was established immediately. Whereas during the period of stylistically barren style-architecture, machines were adorned with the ornamentation in keeping with the times, and factories were dressed in the garb of the Middle Ages or the baroque; in the New Objectivity, the peculiar characteristics of engineering and industrial design were applied equally to the construction of churches, schools, and residential buildings. The most salient expression of this tendency in design could be seen in the concept of the "machine house." Whereas it may have been difficult to distinguish between a judicial palace and a brewery around 1890, now you could find many a church that might be confused with a granary, and there was barely anything distinguishing a school from a shoe factory. The basic idea underlying this New Objectivity is "intellectual acumen honed at the expense of the heart," which Schiller once declared was no longer sacred to him. Every sense of obligation to tradition, to the landscape, to heaven and earth was abandoned. One need only call to mind those all-too-familiar housing developments that have been propagated by the New Objectivity: Weißenhof-Stuttgart, Dammerstock-Karlsruhe, Breslau, and others. Future generations will never understand, but it is also a sign of the confusion that characterized those postwar years, especially if you recall that people dared to package these creations in the wrap of housing reform. These buildings are nothing but documented evidence of the rape of objectivity at the hands of international dilution. This international architectural design is the other side of the same coin as that unfounded arrogance of style-architecture after 1870 that passed itself off as nationalistic architectural design. It is inspired by the same spirit; only the form is different. The products of this new impulse in design were often fondly described as belonging to the new spirit of the times. And this spirit—the spirit of the 1918 revolution—has found permanent expression in the designs of the New Objectivity.

The national government under the direction of Adolf Hitler has taken on the task of cleansing every sector of life from the spirit of 1918. It shall be replaced by the German corporate state [*Ständestaat*]. But then the various components of its corporate structure must work together like a team of laborers on a major construction project in a way that was once undermined by political parties. But in order for that to occur, every individual must be in the place he belongs according to his talents, his ability, and his character. But he can be assigned this place only by the Führer, who wants nothing more than for him to act responsibly. This is a path that can be pursued only by a nation of people in which each individual is prepared to assume his proper place so that he can serve the whole and serve the nation with his work.

234

LUDWIG MIES VAN DER ROHE

Conversation with Alfred Rosenberg, April 1933

First published as "Gedächtnisprotokoll Mies van der Rohes (12 April 1933)," in *Architektur im Dritten Reich, 1933–1945,* edited by Anna Teut (Berlin: Ullstein, 1967), 140.

I asked Rosenberg the question, "As the cultural *Führer* of the new Germany, what is your position regarding the new questions concerning design that are raised by technological and industrial developments? Do you consider addressing these issues a matter of cultural significance?"

Rosenberg: Why do you ask?

Mies: Because addressing such issues is the primary agenda for the Bauhaus, and I would really like to know whether there is any point in continuing our work.

Rosenberg: Aren't these questions being addressed at the polytechnical institutes?

Mies: No. At polytechnical institutes, these subject areas have been divided up into too many specialized disciplines when the opposite is what is actually needed. These design issues can be adequately addressed only in relationship to one another. Besides, serious work needs to be done in this area. But that is impossible at the polytechnical institutes, where there are a hundred to one hundred and fifty students to every professor.

Rosenberg: So why are you seeking to rely on political support? We have no intention of outlawing private initiatives. If you are so sure of the matter, you will prevail.

Mies: Every form of cultural work requires peace and quiet, and I would like to know whether we are going to be left in peace.

Rosenberg: Have you been hindered in your work?

Mies: Hindered is not exactly the word for it. Our building has been shut down, and I would greatly appreciate it if you would attend to the matter.

Rosenberg promised that he would.

235

ADOLF HITLER

The Reich Chancellery

First published as "Die Reichskanzlei Adolf Hitlers," in *Die Kunst im deutschen Reich* 3, no. 9 (September 1939): 277–81.

While the chancellors of the Reich prior to 1918 sought to make more or less tasteful improvements to the Reich Chancellery, the building gradually fell into decline after the revolution. When I decided in 1934 to nevertheless move into the building, not only had large sections of the roof's timber framework begun to rot, but the attics and turrets were also beginning to deteriorate. The police had passed an ordinance restricting the number of people allowed to occupy the congress chamber designed for receiving diplomatic guests to a maximum of sixty people at one time because any more than that would have presented the risk of collapse. When the floorboards were torn out in preparation for the reception for Reich President von Hindenburg, with a good one hundred guests in the same room just a few months prior, we discovered that the supporting beams had been reduced to kindling that readily crumbled at the touch of a bare hand. During heavy storms, the water came in not only from above but also from below. Rooms at the ground level were inundated with a steady stream from the Wilhelmstrasse that was made much worse by leaks that began springing from every imaginable opening in the building, including the toilet. Since all of my predecessors could generally never have reckoned with a period in office longer than three, four, or five months, they rarely felt compelled to clean up the mess left by whoever lived in the building before them, nor were they particularly inclined to leave the place in better condition for their successors than they found it. They were not burdened with any foreign diplomatic obligations because the international community barely took note of their existence. So the building was a complete shambles in 1934, its roof and turrets rotting, its wallpaper and floors in ruin, the whole place filled with an awful, nearly nauseating stench of decay. The reconstruction that has since been completed to convert the Chancellery to a modern office building on Wilhelmsplatz leaves the impression of a warehouse or municipal fire department from the outside, and the interior looks like a sanatorium for tuberculosis patients, which actually is not an unapt descriptor for the illness afflicting the people who were tending to their affairs in this building at the time.

In order to make the building at least moderately serviceable, I decided in 1934 to subject it to an overall renovation. This first conversion was not financed by state funds but rather out of my own pocket. The renovations were based on the previous work of Professor Paul Troost,[1] and their purpose was:

1. To relocate as many of the residential and reception rooms as possible to the ground level, and
2. To reconfigure the second story to accommodate the routine daily business of the Reich Chancellery.

Because up until then, the office of the Reich chancellor was situated in a room that was much too close to the Wilhelmsplatz and that, both in size and in design, more closely resembled the tasteless office of a sales representative for cigarettes and tobacco in a midsized firm. The heat in this room with the windows closed made it impossible to work here, and with the windows open there was too much noise. Since, up until then, all the official receptions of the Reich chancellor were conducted here, and since, at the time, the old Reich president was temporarily housed in the same space while the Imperial Presidential Palace was undergoing renovation, so that all the presidential receptions were also being held at the Reich Chancellery, the upper rooms were laid out for this purpose. However, this also meant that they stood empty and had no practical purpose for most of the year. This was my reason for relocating the reception rooms to the ground level and transforming those rooms facing the garden on the second floor to office space. The congress chamber, which was similarly left unused most of the year, was made into a conference room for cabinet meetings.

Since there was no room at all designed to accommodate large diplomatic receptions and state visits, I decided to commission the architect Professor Leonhard Gall with the task of building a grand hall with a capacity to receive two hundred people. It would at least allow for a modest accommodation of these needs while the renovations to the lower level were ongoing. But the increasing overlapping of the offices of the Reich presidency and the Reich chancellorship since 1934 not only demanded that we create new rooms for the presidential chancellery and the adjutant general's offices but also that we provide an appropriate backdrop for state visits. The first move we made in an attempt to accommodate this need was the acquisition of the Borsig Palace, a building that was stylistically perhaps incongruent with the times but nevertheless towers above the miserable interior design of the Reich Chancellery of the 1890s.

This is how Professor Albert Speer received the contract for rebuilding the Reich Chancellery. [. . .]

So on 11 January 1938, I commissioned national building inspector Professor Speer to design a new Reich Chancellery in the Voßstraße and set the deadline for its completion for 10 January 1939. The official opening of the building was set for that day. Even though we had already discussed the theoretical outline for the project in countless conversations on the matter, the task was nevertheless enormous, the deadline unimaginably tight, especially since we could not even begin construction on 11 January because the buildings in the Voßstraße had to first be demolished and removed, which meant that the actual construction could not get under way until the beginning of March at the earliest. That left about a nine-month period for the construction work. The fact that this project ever came to fruition in the way that it did was attributable exclusively to this ingenious architect, his innate artistic abilities and his unprecedented organizational skill, together with the diligence of his coworkers. The workers of Berlin outdid themselves on this construction project. Even from the perspective of the sheer labor involved, I don't believe there is any example of this kind of achievement in the world.

The basic outline of the building is sufficiently clear and handsomely scaled to reflect its purpose using the space allotted to it. The layout of the whole overwhelming length of the building along the Voßstraße is artistically exceptional and extremely functional. The arrangement of interior rooms, everything from the honor court [*Ehrenhof*] to the innermost chamber, is not only functional and ideally suited to its practical purposes but is also genuinely splendid in its aesthetic effect. The artistic appointments of the individual rooms are truly exquisite, thanks to the efforts of excellent interior designers, sculptors, painters, etc. They are worthy of consideration as great achievements in German art. Work on the surrounding park grounds is now complete, with the exception of the area that is still set aside for construction. In the end, the limited amount of time available for construction prevented us from completing the banquet hall located at the far end of the great hall in its ultimate scope and grandeur. So this hall is to be seen as a provisional solution that renders the building serviceable for the time being. That space will not be completely finished for another two years. The Reich Chancellery building, which, incidentally, is slated to assume an entirely different purpose beginning in the year 1950, thus represents a crowning achievement, not only from a technical but also from an artistic standpoint. It is a testimony to the greatness of its ingenious architect and master builder, Albert Speer.

Note

1. Paul Ludwig Troost (1878–1934) was an architect who joined the Nazi Party in 1924. Hitler regarded him as one of the greatest German architects and chose him for the party's first commission, the

House of German Art in Munich. Troost's monumental, neoclassical buildings became the signature style of the regime's public architecture. He died in 1934 and was replaced by Albert Speer.—Eds.

236

HANS KIENER

Germanic Tectonics

First published as "Germanische Tektonik," in *Die Kunst im deutschen Reich* 1, no. 2 (1937): 48–64.

There is a common thread running through the artistic style of Paul Ludwig Troost's work. He was rich and open-minded enough to reject anything foreign or alien to his nature and to persevere in following his own line of development. And when that architectural Bolshevism that was so alien, so lacking in form, so lacking in vision, and so corrupt to this highly sensitive man began tyrannizing architectural industrialists and master builders in Germany, Troost refused to give in—he was a man of character. He preferred the onus of being decried as "untimely" or "unmodern" rather than betraying his art and his calling. So it was a stroke of fate that when the Führer first met Troost and was so enthralled by his artistic work and taken by the mark of good character involved in rejecting artistic Bolshevism, he decided to share with this man his far-reaching architectural vision and found his architect in Paul Ludwig Troost.

One of the first fruits of the conceptual collaboration between the Führer and his architect can be seen in the renovation of the Brown House [Braunes Haus, Munich] to house the party offices. [. . .]

Thus, in intimate contact with the Führer, over years of quiet, creative work, the "House of German Art," the Führer's office building, and the administrative building in the Arcisstraße, together with the two Temples of Honor [*Ehrentempel*], were conceived. One can do justice to the historical significance of these buildings only by bearing in mind the prevailing politics of art at the time. Certainly, the genuine tradition of German art was never entirely obliterated. Munich was still the only major outpost for artistic perception and architectural sensibilities in all of Germany. But there was a pitched battle under way, with the threat of chaos bearing down from all sides: there was no shortage of instances in which utter formlessness managed to seep through. Were it not for the Führer's highly refined sense of cultural awareness, we never would have succeeded in stemming the tide of corruption through architectural Bolshevism and the odious monotony of its technomania—nor would the salvation of the German nation through National Socialism have succeeded in banishing the ever-increasing threat of evil inherent in this architectural Bolshevism. And, despite the rigors of these times and all its technomaniacal shenanigans, [it was able] to reestablish the value of clear representation of functionality in design, of transparency, of beauty in proportions, of a coherence in outline and surface effect using the finest materials.

The Führer has described Troost's buildings as works of "the noblest Germanic tectonics." And this is true in the altogether obvious sense that there is a conspicuous sensibility for clear configuration of construction, an awareness of the basic principles of supporting forces and distribution that is always evident wherever the ancient Germanics, the Indo-Germanics, have built, to the extent that clarity of construction may be seen as the shining light of the Aryan spirit, as opposed to the stultifying, muddled massive construction apparent in the buildings of non-Aryan nations of people.

237

FRITZ TODT

The Meaning of the New Building

Speech delivered to the Bridge Building Engineers and Architects of the Autobahn in Nuremberg on 4 October 1937. First published as "Der Sinn des neuen Bauens," in *Die Strasse* 4, no. 21 (1 November 1937): 616–17.

We stand at the beginning of a turning point in German spiritual life, German artistic productivity, and in particular, German architecture. For the first four years of the National Socialist revolution, the emphasis lay in the political arena. This time was spent securing political power, forming the party-political *Volk* community and building up political organizations and associations. Those who have had the good sense to correctly understand this construction recognize how in these first years Adolf Hitler erected a solid basis and foundation for his work in its initial phase, making the Reich secure and capable of resistance through his foreign policy.

The master architect of the Third Reich planned to further expand the fortified Reich. The spiritual and cultural edifice of the Reich would emerge from the first years of political construction; spiritual content would assume external form. This spiritual revolution would be exactly as thorough, complete, and purposeful as the political revolution.

We are experiencing the beginnings of new spiritual life, first and foremost in the visual arts. In 1933, the brownshirts passionately chased out the Jews and Communist pack, eliminating the representatives of an artistic tendency no longer compatible with our political beliefs. We readily admit that those who might be counted masters of the visual arts today are few in number, that a great deal of mediocrity is occupying space that might be filled by better works. But already in the achievements of the best, the future success of a more noble conception has been clearly heralded. In the field of music, the "marching community" of the German *Volk* found expression worthy of its time and type in the songs of the Hitler Youth and the Labor Service. On the other hand, the development of a new writing is still in its beginnings. That need not concern us further. At the Reich Party Rally in 1937, Hitler declared with a certain satisfaction that our times have required so many men for political activity that it is not surprising so few turned to the area of the poetic arts. In the first four years of the National Socialist revolution, the poet was in the first instance also a fighter for the movement.

In the domain of architecture, the shift is in full swing. Here we do not need to wait until the times bring forth a master. Adolf Hitler himself provided the first models, not only as an architect but also as an enterprising and energetic builder. The first major examples of a new German architectural spirit are the House of German Art and the structures on the Königlichen Platz [*sic*] in Munich and on the Party Rally grounds in Nuremberg. Here, too [in Nuremberg], are the partially built Congress Hall and the athletic field, where work has just begun. The House of German Art in Munich was built according to the first designs by Professor [Paul Ludwig] Troost. It is an example of how, in the aftermath of the chaotic style, a clear, convincing design triumphed. The broad façade of the building demonstrates this turn away from chaos to composure and grandeur. Under the strong and direct guidance of the Führer, the complex on the Königlichen Platz in Munich brings about for the first time the disciplined articulation of individual elements and shows how everything has been carefully thought through to the smallest function.[1] The structures of the Reich Party Rally grounds reveal to us the unique characteristic of the Führer's architectural aesthetic, which consists of architecture that is no longer an end in itself but the meaningful frame for the action that occurs within these constructions. The structures of the Party Rally grounds [in Nuremberg] are the great frame for the festive hours of the nation. The terraces and wings of the Luitpold Arena are no mere architectonic facades.[2] Their proportions and dimensions are, like the proportions and dimensions of the ancillary streets, determined by the number of SA flags displayed there in the hour of commemoration and carried for the consecration of the dead.[3] The whole complex of the Party Rally grounds, including its structures, is the meaningful solution to the difficult traffic problem created by the mass processionals of the nation.

This essential characteristic of the Führer's architectural aesthetic reveals itself to an even greater degree in the new plans for the expansion of Berlin, Hamburg, and Munich. It is totally absurd for small-time contemporaries with no perspective on the future to describe them with the term "window dressing streets." The wide streets planned for the large urban centers of the Third Reich are essential to problem-free traffic management, which will develop in the next fifty to one hundred years. The proportions of the Reichsautobahnen are also developed according to this conception. These roads must be wide enough to serve not only today's but also tomorrow's high-speed traffic as best and as practically as possible.

The turn away from the past is also evident in the details of the Führer's architectural aesthetic. Besides form, the demands placed on the construction of buildings for our times require that the material and the way it is handled be equal to the task of this great undertaking and suited to the purpose of the structure. The Congress Hall in Nuremberg, with space for sixty thousand persons, was originally designed in reinforced concrete, then redesigned with reinforced concrete and a granite façade, and finally, the structure was built, at the behest of the Führer and befitting his task to build for eternity, out of pure granite and brickwork.

The Sports Forum in Nuremberg is a stadium that will fundamentally differ from the one in Berlin, first and foremost through its open side, so that larger formations can march in and out simultaneously.[4] Consistent with the spirit of its dedicated purpose, the Sports Forum will also be built entirely of granite and brickwork.

Contemporary road construction is represented in our times above all by the Reichsautobahn workers called to participate in this project are not at liberty to simply develop another new style. We are obliged to create in the spirit of our times, which must find its expression in our structures. Whoever is called to this task and is capable of fulfilling it must dutifully find his proper place in the newly emerging community of our *Volk* to create and express his work in a spirit and manner so that coming generations will recognize it as the work of our time, just as we admire the works of the great masters of bygone times.

We concede that not all structures that have come into being in the first years of our construction will withstand contemporary criticism. We admit that there is much that might better exist not at all. This is no reproach, since we can only accomplish our work on the basis of that which has developed. Perhaps it will become necessary after the completion of our work to replace some of the buildings constructed in the first years. Above all, nothing should emerge in the future that cannot withstand the criticism of those who come after us. The best way to achieve something exemplary is to recognize that many things are lacking, so as to be all the more consequential in taking all necessary measures. We must have a more circumspect and stricter conscience. The responsibility for our deeds is infinitesimally great. We must never be satisfied with performing our tasks strictly by the book. In our work we must be the authentic bearers of culture. Few have the fortune to have an impact beyond their own life span. But great are those who can leave permanent works behind for their people through their efforts. We have to erect an architecture to last a thousand years. We have nothing but contempt for those who have no understanding for this new meaning of our life and work; those who would dare to leave something deficient as an eternal legacy.

The standard for all our deeds and actions are therefore the words of the Führer from the cultural address at the Party Rally of Labor in Nuremberg in [September] 1937:

Our enemies will suspect, but our followers must above all know: these buildings have come into being to strengthen our authority. This authority will be useful for that which you see being raised up in this city, for what in Berlin and Munich, in Hamburg, and in other places is already planned and in part ripe for realization, or even finished and standing before you! This is the attitude that lies behind these buildings! And since we believe in the eternity of this Reich—as far as we can reckon in human measurement—these works should also be eternal—that is, they should be adequate to an eternal requirement not only in the greatness of their conception but also in the clarity of their foundations, in the harmony of their proportions. Minor daily necessities have changed throughout the centuries and will continue to change for eternity. But the great cultural documents of humanity in granite and marble remain fixed for centuries. And they alone are a truly unmoving center in the flux of all other phenomenon. In them humanity has always sought and ever again found the eternal magic that enables it to become the master of confusion and create a new order out of chaos. These structures should not be conceived for the year 1940, or even for the year 2000. Like cathedrals of past epochs, they should tower over us for centuries to come.

And if God today turns poets and singers into fighters, he also gave to fighters the master architect, whose trust it is to take care that the triumph of this struggle will find its inalterable substantiation in the documents of a uniquely great art!

Lesser minds will not be able to understand this, but they have never understood anything of our struggle. This may embitter our enemies, but up to now, their hatred alone has not been capable of obstructing our success. Once and for all, we understand with utmost clarity how great is the blessing that radiates from the powerful architectural works of this history-making era across the centuries. It is precisely they that will be able, more than ever, to help unify and politically strengthen our people: socially, they will create for the Germans a component of the feeling of proud belonging; they will demonstrate how ridiculous mortal differences appear when opposed to powerful gigantic witnesses to our community; psychologically, they will fill the citizens of our people with an infinite self-consciousness, namely this: to be a German!

These powerful works will at the same time become the most sublime justification for the political strength of the German nation. This state shall neither be a power without culture nor a force without beauty. For the arming of a people is morally justified only when it is the sword and shield of a higher mission. We strive therefore not after the raw power of a Genghis Khan but after the treasure of a force in the service of creating a stronger, social, and protected community, as the bearer and guardian of a higher culture!

Notes

1. The structures on the Königsplatz in Munich, erroneously referred to above as "Königlichen Platz," which Hitler considered to be the most beautiful square in the Reich, consisted of the Führer Building, the administrative headquarters of the party, and two Temples of Honor. [All notes by translator.]

2. The Luitpold Arena in Nuremberg, a crescent-shaped tribune in classical style was designed to hold one hundred twenty thousand people.

3. Each year the SA honored those members who died in the struggle for power with a solemn ritual of commemoration.

4. The comparison is to the Olympic Stadium built for the 1936 Olympic games in Berlin.

238

ALBERT SPEER

Redesigning the New Capital of the Reich

First published as "Neuplanung der Reichshauptstadt" (January 1939), in *Der Deutsche Baumeister* (Munich, 1939), book 1. Published in *Architektur im Dritten Reich, 1933–1945*, edited by Anna Teut (Berlin: Ullstein, 1967), 196–200.

Surveying the expressions of the architectural impulses of our times, we can see that new construction in German cities and in the German countryside is increasingly coalescing into a better-balanced overall picture. This picture reflects the self-confidence and strength of this epoch we are experiencing firsthand and are indeed forming with our own hands.

The things our Führer committed to paper already in 1924 in his book, his thoughts on architectural aesthetics and urban planning, have in large part already become reality today.

The enormous network of superhighways on the Autobahn already spanning a good three thousand kilometers of the Reich to establish connections between various regions and municipalities is an enduring symbol of our times that has completely transformed the thoughts and emotions of an ever-growing nation of *Volk* in just a few years. With the construction of this extensive network of superhighways on the Autobahn, the beginnings of a new type of urban planning are beginning to appear in cities both large and small.

Here, too, it was the Führer himself who took the initiative and made the decision to subject several large cities within the Reich to comprehensive reconstruction. On 30 January 1937, the Führer announced to the Reichstag that the rebuilding of Berlin to make it a truly genuine imperial capital for the German Reich should be at the forefront in expressing the model of urban planning for our times.

Drawing on the ideas already developed by the Führer many years ago, I have drafted a plan for the capital of the Reich whose center will be formed by the point of intersection between the two axes that traverse the city of Berlin from east to west and from north to south, and which connect the city center to the ring of superhighways on the Reichsautobahn. Whereas the East-West Axis is already a fairly prominent feature of the city that will only require substantial expansion and must be extended to connect with the Reichsautobahn to the east and the west, the North-South Axis—which is actually slated to become the representational centerpiece of the new Reich capital—will involve a complete reconstruction of the very heart of the city.

The primary focus of this incredibly impressive new boulevard, spanning 38.5 kilometers from one Reichsautobahn to the other, will be an approximately 7-kilometer-long stretch on which the greatest and most representative buildings of the German Reich shall be erected. At each end of this North-South Axis running through the city center—to the north and to the south—two major railway stations shall be built to replace no fewer than ten existing, outdated rail stations serving Berlin today. This will also entail a thoroughgoing renovation of the entire railway system, and with it, the hideous freight yards and storage facilities of the German rail will be moved out of the city center. One of the largest of these freight yards, located south of Potsdam and the Anhalter train station, will be the place for the new axis and its surrounding area.

Near the point where the two axes intersect in the heart of the city, Berlin's most ambitious construction project will tower above all, the Great Hall of the German *Volk*.

The whole orientation of the city plan is drastically transformed by the two axes, directing traffic through the heart of the city from all four directions—especially with the addition of the new North-South Axis. Because the streets won't be lined just with these imposing public buildings, space will also be allotted for new industrial construction undertaken by private developers, and this will enhance the atmosphere of state-of-the-art urban planning in Berlin's city center. In the future, then, neither private nor public industrial construction will be situated arbitrarily somewhere in the urban landscape but rather will be integral components of the city plan and become part of the city's new crowning glory at its center that sets the tone for the entire city landscape.

The construction zones, however, will not be oriented in relationship to the rings but rather to the axes. That is to say, the height of buildings will not, as has been the case up until now, decrease in concentric circles emanating from the city center; instead, the whole intersection of the axes becomes the center, and the height of the buildings will decrease axially from there, with shorter buildings and open spaces ultimately leading to vast open recreational areas. Some of the already-existing major arterial roads leading into the city will be retained and will assume the same function as these major axes in the zoning plan. This will allow for the eventual introduction of large sections of concentrated park areas as close to the city center as possible. To this end, existing park areas that cannot be incorporated now without hindering ongoing construction will be integrated gradually. At the same time, corrections will be made to the existing urban rail network to accommodate newly constructed buildings and adapt them to fit the new radial scheme of development. One of the most important tasks I see in redesigning Berlin is in residential housing. Before we can begin rehabilitation work in the older sections of the city, interlocking sectors of new development must be completed. With the expansion of the major axes, especially in the south, large swaths of space will be freed up in the immediate vicinity of the city center to allow for the construction of several hundred thousand new apartments.

Today, two years after the Führer's decree, not only is the basic planning already complete; the reconstruction is also in full swing in countless areas of the Reich capital. The first major building, the new Reich Chancellery in the Voßstraße, is already up and running and has already been inaugurated. We have already doubled the width of the East-West Axis, and it will only be a few months before it extends all the way from the Brandenburg Gate to Adolf Hitler Platz—a distance of seven kilometers—and is open to traffic. With the reconstruction of the Military Technological Institute [Wehrtechnische Fakultät], the new college campus quarter of the city has gotten under way. Last year, on 14 June, both the pace and the intensity of reconstruction picked up with the start-up of industrial construction projects at sixteen separate sites.

239

GERMAN LABOR FRONT

Urban Planning

A Political Task

First published as "Gemeindeplanung—Eine Politische Aufgabe," in *Städtebild und Landschaft* (Berlin: Verlag der DAF, 1939), 1, 2, 4, 13, 14, 18.

In terms of its ability to enhance and support the cultural achievements of our *Volk*—especially as it pertains to the development of residential districts and the expansion of existing ones, though not to representational architecture—urban planning needs much longer to reach full maturity because, above and beyond the obvious aesthetic demands to be met, political, topographical, and economic considerations ultimately have a decisive impact on solutions to these issues. When a balance is struck between all these individual demands in urban planning and design, that is when there is organic unity in creativity.

This places particular demands on our cities and towns as they revise their centuries-old plans for expansion. The policies of expansion at any price and in any which way must give way to a thorough investigation of the topographical features of the site allotted and its relationship to the surrounding landscape.

Even though there has been an increasing tendency to focus on the design of individual buildings in recent years, the ever-expanding development in the proximity of human settlements is destroying the landscape as we know it. The state and regional building administrations have not been any more successful in effecting substantial improvement of this situation in the field of residential housing and development than have the participating financial and artistic institutions.

This is a clear index of the fact that the political breakthroughs that have found expression in other sectors of life have not taken place in the course of the Residential Development Program [Wohnungsbauprogramm].

In recognition of the preeminence of space [*Raum*] for the German *Volk* and Reich, the basic prerequisite for a healthy recovery for residential housing and development has been set by the National Socialist state in a decree issued on 26 June 1935 with the establishment of the Organization for Reich and Rural Planning [Reichsarbeitgemeinschaft für Raumordnung].

For the first time ever, the concept of regional planning [*Raumordnung*] has been assigned overarching value as a matter of public good to everyone in the German living space and landscape, but this at once implies an attendant responsibility to lay the foundation for all our political, economic, social, and cultural aims combined with a systematic study of the living space. [. . .]

We started by addressing the overriding importance of regional planning as absolutely essential to the National Socialist state. If this task begins with the study of spatial relationships and ends with planning and design, in the broadest sense of the terms, that is, with regional planning and design implemented in the municipalities, then it is already at this level that the task begins for a central, party-sponsored office for regional planning—by offering consultation and input into the selection of residential districts in accordance with its insights into the vicissitudes of rural and urban landscapes and by assuming responsibility for the course of continued development of the urban landscape, of the individual construction projects, as well as for agricultural and economic planning and interior design, in close collaboration with all the parties involved and with the private architects. Not until we have succeeded in establishing an organized system of order to residential development and settlement to accompany the remaining efforts to improve upon conditions for public life can we anticipate any form of a truly far-reaching restoration of health to our urban and rural architecture.

240

HEINRICH HIMMLER

Order for the Destruction of the Warsaw Ghetto

"Befehl des Reichsführers-SS Heinrich Himmler zur Zerstorung Warschaus 16. February 1943." First published in *Architektur im Dritten Reich, 1933–1945*, edited by Anna Teut (Berlin: Ullstein, 1967), 361.

SS-Reichsführer Field Command
Top Secret!
To All High-Ranking SS Officers and Chiefs of Police, East *SS-Obergruppenführer* Krüger, Cracow

For reasons of security, I hereby order that the Warsaw ghetto be razed as soon as the concentration camp has been relocated: anything that can be salvaged from the buildings should first be removed, together with any salvageable materials of any kind prior to the demolition.

It is imperative that the ghetto be razed and the concentration camp relocated because there is no other way we will ever quell the upheaval there, nor will we ever be able to eliminate crime as long as the ghetto remains standing.

You are to submit to me a comprehensive plan for the destruction of the ghetto. At the very minimum, the living quarters—utterly unfit for occupancy by Germans as they are—currently allotted to these five hundred thousand subhumans must be wiped from the face of the earth, and the size of this city of millions that has always been a hotbed of corruption and revolt must be drastically reduced.

19

Music

The Wagner Cult vs. Degenerate Music

"GERMAN MUSIC, especially that of the nineteenth century, celebrated the greatest victories in the whole world; it was this branch of the arts that secured the exemplary international reputation of German art and German artists in a way that no other branch of the arts did." Apart from the redundant use of the word *German,* it is hard to dispute these words spoken by the distinguished composer Richard Strauss (1864–1949) at the opening of the Reichsmusikkammer (Reich Music Chamber) in February 1934. However, the same cannot be said for his admiration of Hitler or the new regime's attitudes toward music that followed. It is hard to explain why Strauss, who had no previous connection to the Nazis and was not under any overt political pressure, accepted the presidency of the chamber when Goebbels named him to the post in November 1933. Goebbels no doubt scored a major propaganda triumph with the appointment of the world-famous sixty-nine-year-old composer. Even before he took office, Strauss took over the Berlin Philharmonic from the Viennese Jewish conductor Bruno Walter, who had fled to Austria, and in July, he stood in for Arturo Toscanini at the 1933 Bayreuth Festival when the anti-Fascist Italian maestro remained in the United States. Strauss apparently was under the illusion that he could improve German musical culture by raising professional standards and adequately compensating serious composers. Nonetheless, in 1935, Joseph Goebbels demanded Strauss's resignation when the Gestapo revealed that the composer had refused to remove the name of his Jewish coauthor, Stefan Zweig, the librettist of their opera *The Silent Woman* (*Die schweigsame Frau,* 1935), from the playbill. Strauss's letter to Hitler reveals both the composer's sycophancy and his naïve forthrightness in protesting his dismissal.

Even more controversial is the case of Wilhelm Furtwängler (1886–1954), the most distinguished conductor in Germany and the director of the Berlin State Opera. In 1933, Furtwängler elicited a sharp reproach from Goebbels when he challenged him on behalf of Jewish conductors and directors such as Bruno Walter, Otto Klemperer, and Max Reinhardt by arguing that as genuine artists they should be exempted from the otherwise acceptable "fight against the Jews." Goebbels's response, which contains the notable phrase "Politics too, is an art form—perhaps the most exalted and all-encompassing one there is," politely but firmly rebuffed Furtwängler. The following year, Furtwängler presented a work by the modernist composer Paul Hindemith, *Matthias the Painter* (*Mathis der Maler,* 1934), based on the life of the Gothic painter Matthias Grünwald. Though the symphony (not yet an opera) did not violate the cultural requirements of the regime—it was more conventional than modernist in its style—Hitler himself and the Rosenberg cultists in the National Socialist cultural establishment attacked Hindemith. Furtwängler defended Hindemith in print as "entirely German" (and was supported by Strauss). Goebbels, calling Hindemith's work "dance music," removed Furtwängler from his permanent post as director of the Berlin State Opera. Furtwängler eventually capitulated, and in 1936, he resumed his position, continuing to conduct (on one notable occasion for Hitler's birthday) and to exercise an imperious influence over German musical life—occasionally helping Jews or controversial composers like Hindemith—until the end of the war. As Klaus Mann aptly remarked, figures like Strauss and Furtwängler played a crucial symbolic role: by 1936, German culture and National Socialism were no longer distinguishable.

That Adolf Hitler revered the composer Richard Wagner (1813–83) is well known. In *Mein Kampf,* he described his first encounter with Wagner's music, attending a performance of *Lohengrin* in Linz at age twelve: "I was captivated at once. My youthful enthusiasm for the Master of Bayreuth knew no bounds. Again and again I was drawn to his works."[1] He insisted that the theme from Wagner's *Rienzi* be played each year at the opening of the cultural session of the Reich Party Rally in Nuremberg. After meeting Wagner's daughter-in-law, Winifred, in October 1923, Hitler was a frequent guest at the family villa, Wahnfried, and virtually became a member of the family. In a letter to Wagner's son, Siegfried, Hitler wrote that nothing had given him greater satisfaction than to visit Bayreuth, "where first the Master and then [Houston Stewart] Chamberlain [Wagner's son-in-law] forged the spiritual sword with which he fights today."[2] Prominent Nazis—Dietrich Eckart, Rudolf Hess, Joseph Goebbels, Hermann Göring, Freikorps leader Hermann Ehrhardt—were frequent guests at Wahnfried during the 1920s. It "stinks of swastika and reaction," noted a contemporary musicologist.[3]

Welcoming Chancellor "Wolf" (as she called Hitler) to the Bayreuth Festival had been Winifred's dream since his first visit. "Now there is a chancellor who loves Wagner, understands German culture, and who will not be afraid to deal with the Jewish Question," declared the Wagnerite house organ, *Bayreuther Blätter,* in 1933.[4] Hitler reciprocated by arranging the bulk purchase of tickets to rescue the financially strapped festival. Since the year 1933 coincided with the jubilee fiftieth anniversary of Wagner's death, the festival celebrated the "Year of Wagner." Over three thousand complimentary tickets were distributed to students and young visitors—not all of them equally devoted to the Master. As Siegfried Scheffler noted in a newspaper supplement published for the occasion, Hitler attended the opening performance of the *Meistersinger,* and Wagner was celebrated as one of the "staunchest allies" of the *Volk* and the nation. The annual Bayreuth Festival became, in the words of the *Manchester Guardian,* a "Hitler festival," with Führer-kitsch memorabilia on sale in the shops and adoring crowds lining the streets. But the quality of the performances of *Meistersinger* and *Parsifal* suffered, as the writer explained, because Toscanini, the eminent Italian conductor and vocal anti-Fascist, had been forced to withdraw from the festival.

Too much can be made of Hitler's Wagner obsession and his self-appointed role as the Reich's number one fan of the composer. Was National Socialism only a crude popularization of Wagner's esoteric philosophy? Was Hitler the disciple and Wagner the prophet of the Reich? Did Hitler translate Wagner's operas into a unique "reconciliation of art and politics, the discovery of the artist-man, which would bear fruit in the process of the healing of German people," as one Nazi writer claimed in 1933?[5] And did Hitler make Wagner's image of the artless Jew in his *The Jews and Music* (1850) the leitmotif of his own virulent anti-Semitism? Even today, musicologists heatedly debate whether Wagner's music and operas contain anti-Semitic motifs and figures. Despite Hitler's obvious affinity for the music, there is surprisingly little direct evidence that he was influenced by the mythology in Wagner's operas. Hitler never acknowledged the impact of Wagner's ideological message nor commented on his anti-Semitism. Rather, it was Houston Stewart Chamberlain, the composer's son-in-law, who promoted Wagnerian philosophy as the source of Germanic "regeneration." Only one story about Hitler's thoughts in this area may have some credibility (though it was not told by Hitler himself): after attending a performance of Wagner's *Rienzi* in 1905, Hitler reportedly remarked that like the hero, he was destined to lead his people to greatness.[6] Hitler's single-minded passion for Wagner notwithstanding, a number of leading members of the Nazi elite—Alfred Baeumler and Alfred Rosenberg—were anti-Wagnerians. Musicologists like Herbert Birtner (1900–42), author of "On the German Interpretation of Beethoven Since Richard Wagner," preferred to allow Nietzsche's condemnation of Wagner stand for his own. Thus, many defenses of Wagner as the spokesman of a true Germanic spirit for the Third Reich, such as that of Curt von Westerhagen, had to counter the underlying critical views of him stemming from Nietzsche.

Anti-Nazi refugees, notably Thomas Mann and Theodor W. Adorno, developed the theme of Hitler's demonic Wagnerism. Mann caused a sensation in 1933 when he delivered his commemorative address "The Sorrows and Grandeur of Richard Wagner" in the Great Hall of the University of Munich. Driven to what Mann later called "a transport of rage," forty local dignitaries and Wagner cultists signed "A Protest from Richard Wagner's City of Munich," condemning him for defaming the memory of the German Master by daring to invoke Freudian psychoanalysis and labeling Wagner a dilettante. Above all, the letter condemned Mann's remark that Wagner's music was "a blend of the Germanic and the modern"—"accessible to the larger world"—which was a direct affront to the "national" Wagner of the Third Reich. Mann claimed that this reaction to his speech "determined my emigration, or, more correctly, my failure to return to Germany."

Oskar Loerke (1884–1941), an expressionist poet whose writings were banned by the Reichsschrifttumskammer (Reich Literature Chamber), registered his despondency at the protest in his private diary. But even Wagner was not safe from the racial ideologues: Fritz Stege pointed out that from a racial standpoint, some authors considered even Wagner less qualified than, for example, Bach, who was "the ultimate incarnation of Nordic music."

By 1938, Mann no longer hesitated to condemn "the intricate and painful interrelationships that undeniably exist between the Wagnerian sphere and the National Socialist evil." In his 1938 essay "Bruder Hitler," Mann interpreted Nazism as perverted Wagnerism. And in a letter to *Common Sense* magazine in 1940, commenting on an essay by Peter Viereck, he wrote, "I find an element of Nazism not only in Wagner's questionable literature, I find it also in his 'music,' in his work, similarly questionable, though in a loftier sense—albeit I have so loved that work that even today I am deeply stirred whenever a few bars of music from this world impinge upon my ear."[7]

After 1936, when Strauss was replaced by Heinz Drewes as head of the Reich Music Chamber, Goebbels's efforts to promote "German music" and proscribe so-called degenerate music were undermined by the impossibility of defining what those terms meant, as well as by the decentralization of musical activity in Germany. Atonality (like abstraction in painting) was excoriated and banned or redefined, especially after 1938, when Arnold Schönberg (1874–1951) and twelve-tone music were vilified at the shaming Degenerate Music Exhibition in Düsseldorf, which opened on Wagner's birthday. Jazz was far more difficult to control, especially in live venues where, as the Gestapo reported in 1942, bands from Belgium, Holland, and even some indigenous groups like the Willy Artelt Band played for enthusiastic young audiences, sometimes made up of "swing kids"—jazz aficionados. Jazz records could be ordered from catalogs and, of course, were traded in the youth culture of the Reich. Though jazz was nominally banned from the airwaves because of its "Negroid characteristic of syncopation," Goebbels permitted "acceptable" dance music on the radio, and some critics even tried to distinguish between jazz and radio music, which was, of course, geared toward German sensibilities. Jazz, even though recognized as stemming from "Negroid" (i.e., African-American) culture, was labeled as a tool of international Jewry, a means of undermining the aesthetic sensibilities of the German *Volk*. During the war, jazz was "alive and well," as Ilse Deyk wrote, but she hoped that once the war ended, it would finally be erased. Tellingly, one argument by the pseudonymous author and radio commentator Wulf Bley (actually W. H. Hartwig) against jazz was that "a musically inclined person simply cannot dance to it and just stumbles hopelessly over his own feet."

NOTES

1. Adolf Hitler, *Mein Kampf*, translated by Ralph Manheim (New York: Houghton Mifflin, 1943), 17.
2. Hitler to Siegfried Wagner, 5 May 1924; reprinted in Michael Karbaum, *Studien zur Geschichte der Bayreuther* Festspiele, *1876–1976* (Regensburg: Bosse, 1976), 66.

3. The musicologist is Heinz Stuckenschmidt, cited in Frederic Spotts, *Bayreuth: A History of the Wagner Festival* (New Haven, Conn.: Yale University Press, 1994), 157.

4. *Bayreuther Blätter,* Summer 1933, 117. Cited in Spotts, *Bayreuth,* 165.

5. Cited in Eric Michaud, *The Cult of Art in Nazi Germany,* translated by Janet Lloyd (Stanford, Calif.: Stanford University Press, 2004), 59.

6. The source of this story is a memoir by Hitler's boyhood friend August Kubizek (1888–1956); *Adolf Hitler, mein Jugendfreund* (Graz: L. Stocker, 1954), 140.

7. Thomas Mann, "To the Editors of *Common Sense,*" *Common Sense,* January 1940. Response to an article by Peter Viereck titled "Hitler and Wagner," *Common Sense,* November 1939, 3–6.

241

RICHARD STRAUSS

Speech at the Opening of the Reich Music Chamber

Delivered on 2 February 1933. First published in *Bücherei der Reichsmusikkammer,* Bd.1, *Kultur-Wirtschaft-Recht* (Berlin, 1934), 9, 10.

Dear Sirs!

I am here to open the first conference of the Reich Music Chamber—a hearty welcome to you all.

The Reich Music Chamber—which for decades has been the ultimate dream and goal of all German musicians—was established on 15 November 1933, and with it, the first step on the way to revitalizing the whole fabric of musical life in Germany was taken.

I feel compelled, on behalf of all musicians in Germany, to take this opportunity to express my heartfelt appreciation to Reich Chancellor Adolf Hitler and to Reich Minister Dr. Goebbels for having passed the legislation establishing the Reich Chamber of Culture.

I repeat that this, for the moment, is only the first step on the path to our ultimate goal: to once again establish an intimate relationship between the German *Volk* and its music such as that which existed, for example, in the sixteenth century or which was even more evident than it is now in the first few decades of this century.

German music, especially that of the nineteenth century, celebrated the greatest victories in the whole world; it was this branch of the arts that secured the exemplary international reputation of German art and German artists in a way that no other branch of the arts did. But one side effect that the overall cultural, economic, and technical development of the past forty to fifty years has had, despite the great individual advancements it has wrought, has been a gradually increasing estrangement of the German *Volk* as a whole from the fine art of music. And that was closely related to the deterioration of the economic situation for German musicians and, on the other hand, to a decline of the level of taste in music that in turn could not possibly occur without having a lasting detrimental effect on cultural production overall.

The fact that so much has changed in Germany, not only politically but also in the realm of culture, since Adolf Hitler's seizure of power—the fact that the National Socialist government was able to breathe life into such an entity as the Reich Music Chamber proves that the New Germany is not inclined to allow artistic developments to more or less simply come as they may and stand on their own, but rather that there is a desire to pursue targeted means and methods for intervention that will provide new impetus for the life of our musical culture.

242

RICHARD STRAUSS

Letter to Adolf Hitler

Written on 13 July 1935. First published in Joseph Wulf, ed., *Musik im Dritten Reich* (Frankfurt am Main: Ullstein, 1983), 198, 199.

My Führer!

I received in today's mail Herr Reich Minister Dr. Goebbels's approval of the request to relieve me of my position as president of the Reich Music Chamber. As per the instructions provided by Herr Reich Minister Dr. Goebbels, I returned this request after he had it hand-delivered to me by special delivery. I consider the circumstances surrounding my removal from the Reich Music Chamber a matter of such grave importance that I feel obliged to provide you, my Führer, with a brief outline of the affair.

The impetus for my dismissal seems to be a private letter addressed to my last collaborator, Stefan Zweig, which was opened by the state police and turned over to the Ministry of Propaganda. Admittedly, the content of this letter—taken out of the context of the long-standing artistic correspondence [between me and its intended recipient], with no knowledge of the background and spirit in which it is written—readily lends itself to misinterpretation and could easily be misunderstood. However, in order to fully understand the spirit in which it was written, one must, above all, seek to put himself in my position—that is, to take into consideration the fact that as a composer, I, like most of my colleagues, suffer constantly from the fact that, despite concerted ongoing efforts, I am unable to find a well-reputed German writer to pen texts for my operatic compositions.

The letter in question includes three passages that have been called into question and interpreted to mean that I have little sympathy for anti-Semitism or understanding of the concept of the *Volk* community or of the significance of my position as president of the Reich Music Chamber. Unfortunately, I was not afforded any opportunity whatsoever to provide a personal explanation for the spirit, content, or meaning of the letter, which, to put it bluntly, was simply shot out without further reflection in a moment of annoyance toward Stefan Zweig himself.

In light of the series of works that I have created as a German composer in the course of my lifetime, I sincerely would hope that I need not provide any further assurance that this letter and all its quickly thrown together statements cannot be seen as a characteristic representation of my ideology or my true outlook.

My Führer! I have dedicated my whole life to German music and the indefatigable struggle to elevate German culture—I have never been a politician, nor have I ever been politically active, and so it is that I hope to find a sympathetic ear in you, the great architect of German life: I beg you, with all due respect, to understand how profoundly disturbed I am over the process of my dismissal as president of the Reich Music Chamber and ask only that I may be allowed to serve the purest and most exalted aims and ideals for those few years I have left to live.

With enduring confidence in your sense of justice, I humbly beseech you, my Führer, to grant me audience, that I might have the opportunity to justify my actions to you personally before I take leave of my office as president of the Reich Music Chamber. I remain respectfully yours, Herr Reich Chancellor, and in expression of my utmost admiration,

Forever faithfully yours,
Richard Strauss

243

FRITZ STEGE

Future Tasks of Musicology

First published as "Zukunftsaufgaben der Musikwissenschaft," in *Zeitschrift für Musik* 15 (May 1933): 489–90.

The study of race is undoubtedly one of the newest sciences. But the seriousness that has been applied to this problem as the object of scientific experiments has already produced a great number of standard works on the subject whose scholarly and scientific value cannot be denied. First and foremost amongst them are Prof. Dr. H F. K. Günther's *Racial Science of the German Volk* [*Rassenkunde des deutschen Volkes*], *Race and Style* [*Rasse und Stil*]; [Paul] Schultze-Naumburg's *Art and Race* [*Kunst und Rasse*], [Ludwig] Schemann's *Race in the Humanities* [*Die Rasse in den Geisteswissenschaften*], [Ludwig Ferdinand] Clauß's *Race and Soul* [*Rasse und Seele*], [Hermann] Brunnhofer's *Prehistory of the Aryans* [*Urgeschichte der Arier in Vorder- und Centralasien*], as well as works by [Richard] Müller-Freienfels, Kurt Gerlach, Walther Darré, and many more.

It seems appropriate that these insights also be applied to the field of music history, for the stylistic diversity of developments in music must present the racial researcher with a virtually inexhaustible source of new impulses. However, it has only been very recently that racial studies have begun addressing the issue as it relates to music. The pioneer for this new research approach is Richard Eichenauer, who recently made his debut with a lecture on this topic and who has recorded the results of his research in the authoritative volume *Music and Race* [*Musik und Rasse,* 1937].

The difficulties posed by this sort of racially oriented consideration of musical life are enormous, and it is to the author's credit that he affords ample room for a detailed clarification of the methodology underlying his approach, lending credence to the seriousness of his scholarship. Rather than elaborate further on the basic assumptions underlying the work, we shall let this statement suffice in order to proceed directly to the practical implications of its research results.

When we read, for example, that Bach was "the ultimate incarnation of Nordic music," that Mozart and Haydn demonstrate Nordic-Dynaric composite traits, that Bruckner was Dynaric with an element of Eastern blood, that Pflitzner, on the other hand, was more "Nordic" than Wagner—we must first ask ourselves what these characteristics mean in practical terms.

But just as there are individual master musicians who conform precisely to the racial type, there are entire musical periods throughout the history of music marked by the influence of specific racial factors. Richard Eichenauer is ingenious in his presentation of evidence of the way the Nordic spirit invigorates the polyphonic form while Oriental elements find expression in Gregorian chants. The monumental composition of polyphony leads to the preeminence of purely Nordic essence in the centuries from the great Dutch contrapuntal tradition. Whenever "racial boundaries" are transgressed, it is the result of individual personalities who are possessed of Nordic spirit but who break with a principle that has become too one-sided and venture into uncharted stylistic territory.

From this perspective, we are in a much better position to understand and assess the racial implications of various currents running through contemporary musical life. The introduction of Middle Eastern racial characteristics to the spirit of our musical aesthetics contributed to the gradual dissolution of the Occidental understanding of harmony. There is nothing essentially Nordic about "atonality." So it would be wrong to condemn the representatives of this style. They cannot help but conform to the tasks assigned to their own race. "For us, on the other hand, to follow suit in this regard would be to commit a transgression against the spirit of our race."

One need not necessarily agree with every detail of Eichenauer's analysis, which is sometimes based more on emotion than reason, in order to recognize nevertheless that ground has been opened here for a broad new area of inquiry that must be taken very seriously and that has the potential to produce astonishing results in the wake of this pioneering and felicitous attempt by Eichenauer.

244

WILHELM FURTWÄNGLER AND JOSEPH GOEBBELS

The Case of Wilhelm Furtwängler

Wilhelm Furtwängler to Joseph Goebbels

First published in *Vossische Zeitung,* 11 April 1933.

Dear Herr Reich Minister:

In light of the many years that my work has resonated with the German public and of my inner bond with German music, I am taking the liberty of drawing your attention to certain incidents within the world of music that, in my opinion, need not necessarily go hand in hand with the restoration of our national dignity, which all of us welcome with gratitude and enthusiasm.

My feelings in this matter are strictly those of an artist. The function of art and artists is to unite, not to divide. In the final analysis, I recognize only one line of distinction: that between good art and bad. However, when, as now, the distinction between Jews and non-Jews is being drawn with relentless, all-but-doctrinaire stringency, even when the political outlook of the person in question provides no grounds for complaint, that other line of distinction—which is so central to the world of music and in the long run decisive—that between good and bad, is sorely neglected.

Musical life today, already weakened by the world crisis, by radio, etc., cannot afford any more experiments. One cannot impose rations on music the same way you would on other staples in life like potatoes and bread. People will not go to concerts that have nothing to offer them. This is why the quality of music is not an idealistic question but a matter of life and death. This is just fine as long as the fight against the Jews is directed primarily at those artists who in their own lack of roots and in their destructivity seek to leave their mark by producing nothing but kitsch, dry virtuosity, and the like. The fight against them and the spirit they represent—which, incidentally, also has its Germanic representatives—cannot be emphatic or consistent enough. However, when this fight is directed against genuine artists, the interests of cultural life are not served, if only because genuine artists are far too few and far between no matter where you go. There isn't a country in the world that can afford to dispense with their work without sustaining a loss to its culture.

We must therefore clearly establish that men like Walter, Klemperer, Reinhardt, etc. are able to express themselves artistically now and in the future.

Therefore, I repeat, let us fight to combat the rootless, subversive, corrosive, destructive spirit but not the genuine artist who, by his very nature, will forever remain creative and therefore constructive—regardless of how his art is viewed.

It is in this spirit that I appeal to you, in the name of German art, to prevent anything from happening that might not be put right again.

Very respectfully yours,
Wilhelm Furtwängler

Joseph Goebbels's Response to Wilhelm Furtwängler

First published in *Berliner-Lokal-Anzeiger,* 11 April 1933. Later published in Joseph Wulf, ed., *Musik im Dritten Reich* (Frankfurt am Main: Ullstein, 1983), 85–89.

Dear National Director of Music:

I am grateful for the opportunity your letter affords me to offer you some insights into the position of those forces in Germany driven by nationalism, both in general and with specific regard to music. I am particularly thrilled to see, at the very beginning of your letter, that you emphasize—on behalf of all German artists—the fact that you welcome the restoration of our national dignity enthusiastically and with gratitude.

Nor had I ever assumed this could not be the case, for I believe our struggle for Germany's reconstruction is not only a passive concern of the artist but an active one. I should like to call to mind here something the Reich chancellor said three years before our seizure of power: "If German artists knew what we planned to do for them one day, then they would not fight us, they would join us in the fight."

It is your right to see and feel things strictly from the perspective of an artist. But that need not imply that you adopt an apolitical stance with regard to the developments that have set in throughout Germany. Politics, too, is an art form—perhaps the most exalted and all-encompassing one there is. It is not the task of art and the artist to unite; far more, it is [the task of the artist] to shape, to lend form, to eliminate what is diseased and to make way for what is healthy. So, as a German politician, I cannot acknowledge only one line of distinction as you suggest, that between good and bad art. Art must not only be good, it must also emerge from the *Volk,* or, better, only an art that draws inspiration from the whole of the *Volk* itself can, in the final analysis, be deemed good and have meaning for the people for which it was created. There can be no art as an absolute value as it is promoted by liberal democracy. Any attempt to serve this kind of art would ultimately result in the people no longer having any intimate relationship to art and in the artist isolating himself, severing himself from the driving forces of his times in the vacuum of a *l'art pour l'art* perspective. Art must be good, but beyond that, it must also have a sense of responsibility, must be professional, must be popular with the *Volk,* and aggressive. I readily concede that art cannot afford any more experiments.

But it would be more appropriate to protest against artistic experiments at a time when the whole world of German art was being dominated almost exclusively by the addiction to experimentation on the part of racially and genetically alien elements who have tainted and compromised the reputation of German art throughout the world.

You are altogether right in contending that the quality of music is not an idealistic question but a matter of life and death. Even more, you are right in joining our struggle to combat artistic productivity that is lacking in roots, that is destructive kitsch based on dry virtuosity. I freely admit, too, that Germanic representatives also participated in those abysmal practices; that just goes to prove how deeply the roots of these threats had penetrated the very core of our *Volk* and how imperative it is, on the other hand, to form a united front against them. Genuine artists are a rarity. They must therefore be promoted and supported. But they must indeed be genuine artists.

You will always be able to express yourself artistically in Germany—now and in the future. To complain about the fact that now and then such men as Walter, Klemperer, Reinhardt, etc. have been forced to cancel concerts seems to me all the more inappropriate in light of the fact that over the course of the past fourteen years, so many genuine German artists have been completely condemned to silence, and the events of the past few weeks, which we did not endorse, were but a natural reaction to this fact. At any rate, I am of the opinion that every genuine artist amongst us should be given free rein in exercising his creativity. But he must be, as you have said yourself, a constructive and creative individual, not one who is aligned with those whom you have properly censured as rootless, corrosive, subversive, and destructive professionals whose skills are merely technical in nature.

Please rest assured that any appeal made in the name of German art will always resonate in our hearts and minds. Artists who are truly able to have an impact and whose impact beyond the world of art does not transgress the fundamental norms of state, politics, and society will always be entitled to our heartfelt support and encouragement—in the future just as they have in the past.

Please allow me, Herr National Director of Music, to express my appreciation for the many hours of truly uplifting, great, and at times heart-wrenching art that you have created for many of my political friends and hundreds of thousands of good Germans. It would be a great pleasure to know that I have found an open ear and understanding for my stance.

With great respect,
Yours sincerely,
Dr. Goebbels

245

SIEGFRIED SCHEFFLER

Bayreuth in the Third Reich

First published as "Bayreuther Festspiele 1933," in *Bayreuth im Dritten Reich: ein Buch des Dankes und der Erinnerung,* in *Sonderdruck der Hamburger Nachrichten zu den Festspielen* (Hamburg: Alster, 1933).

The year 1933 has become a year of crucial significance to the work of Richard Wagner and his educational, artistic impact at the *Festspiele* in Bayreuth. The Festspielhaus [Festival Theater], built upon the indefatigable will, upon the profound belief in its necessity, built upon the strength of Richard Wagner, the willingness of his friends to help, from the noble compassion of a king, today this Festspielhaus opens it doors not only to a certain select social class—long-standing friendships, admirers, the artistically and economically privileged circles of their heirs—but rather to the *Volk* itself and to its youth, the bearers of its future. This is the first time in the history of the *Festspiele* that a German government has acknowledged the didactic and ethical value of Wagner's works for the *Volk* and unconditionally enlists them in the effort to instill these values in the *Volk* organism, so that they will have an impact and will live on in the people. Whoever has recognized Wagner's life and work as an artistic, individual, creative, and predestined crystallization in the development of German history, whoever has understood its form, its expression, and its necessity in this context, witnesses today the most magnificent testimony to this ineluctable connection in the fact that the Year of Wagner 1933 is synonymous with the rejuvenation of nationalist Germany, with the breakthrough of those forces galvanizing the *völkisch* consciousness, nationalist strength, honor, and capacity for life in Germany. Wagner's work itself has remained one of those bulwarks that allowed the nation to persevere ideologically through a materialistically and intellectually difficult period [in its history]; it is one of those reserves that helped put an end to the onslaught of cultural Bolshevism. The New Germany thanks its German poets and musicians for their contributions to this effort.

Richard Wagner and Adolf Hitler: Two *Führers* Meet in the Fateful Year of 1933

The chancellor of the German Reich honors Richard Wagner as the most ingenious manifestation of German art and the German spirit, one of the staunchest allies in the enormous task of forging lasting bonds between the tribes and the *Volk*, between the *Volk* and the nation, welding them together like the joints of a sword. "Today I understand why, of all people, Wagner and his destiny spoke to me more than any other great German man. His is the same perilous, eternal struggle against hatred, envy, and ignorance. His concerns are the same as mine." These are the words Adolf Hitler used to acknowledge the bond of common destiny [*Schicksalsgemeinschaft*] that has never suffered as mercilessly and never been pursued as passionately anywhere else in the world than it is in Germany!

Bayreuth, the city of hospitality in Upper Franconia, welcomes its visitors to the *Festspiele*. Dress rehearsals are under way at the Festspielhaus, the final dispositions are being made in stage and musical direction. In the electrifying atmosphere of these days, in the hustle and bustle of organizational preparations and in the onslaught of final rehearsals, in anticipation and preparation of everything directly or indirectly related to the spectacular production, the one thing everyone is conscious of throughout is this: the content of the *Festspiele*, its purpose, to become—in accordance with Wagner's own will—the property of those for whom it was created in the first place; their aim, to unite everything that genuine and responsible people have in common without regard for class or social distinctions in the German *Volk*.

The amphitheater in the Festspielhaus is not designed to serve purely acoustical needs: it symbolizes the equality of all people before the work of art; it represents the relinquishing of personal ambition in exchange for concentration and obedience. And the Festspielhaus, towering over the city from the hilltop with its massively forceful yet functional architecture, is not there to serve the public, the season-ticket holders (or the "patrons" as we might care to term them!), but rather to serve all those who know that great art does not come to you, it must be sought out, that it cannot be "disseminated" but rather must be gathered, that it demands community and creates it. And so the lesson we have to learn from the *Festspiel* rests in the acknowledgment that true art must be demanding in order to persevere throughout time, that it requires obedience in order to blossom. And, in the age of talking film and radio, this reminder does not seem superfluous.

The rigorous support of the Reich government has made it possible for even those of our national comrades who are without means to attend the Bayreuth *Festspiele*. It made 3,300 complimentary tickets available to youth, with travel and accommodations paid; 10,000 students are expected to attend who have been offered a discount rate to experience the great pleasure of the Wagner festivities in Bayreuth. Reich Chancellor Adolf Hitler and prominent representatives of the government are scheduled to attend the opening performance of the *Meistersinger* on 21 July 21. It is safe to say that this year's German *Festspiel* will embrace and be brimming with all that lends name and rank to the new Germany. The international community remains reticent; a certain degree of mistrust has always been attached to the decisive facts that were first hammered out in Germany to serve the interest of the whole world's welfare. The horrific propaganda campaign orchestrated by racially alien un-Germans and never-to-be-Germans in the effort to secure their "interests," propaganda with nary a word about Bolshevik brutalities, which only then exposed any form of infamy that seemed more beneficial than the truth, this insidious, faint-hearted horrific propaganda is also aimed at the Bayreuth *Festspiele.* But we need not worry: consider the source—it's the same source that has been hurling destructive propaganda at German culture for ages under the honorable mantle of "Enlightenment." Nevertheless, Bayreuth is also anticipating many friends from outside this country and guarantees them that the *Festspiel* of Richard Wagner and of nationalist Germany will be a memorable experience. The case of Toscanini—a typical parallel to that scandalous affair in Milan—might be enough to prevent several personal admirers of the conductor [from attending].[1] The great and incomparable artist Toscanini has not become Germany's enemy based on ideological considerations but rather on a stubborn insistence of individuality. It is simply grotesque that he should have cancelled his scheduled return to the Bayreuth *Festspiele* to protest the fact that his friend Bruno Walter had been slighted. Toscanini, Bayreuth's most contemporary honorary citizen, decided to take measures that clearly demonstrate how far removed he is from the reality of the challenges presented by the total work of art [*Gesamtkunstwerk*],indeed, from any understanding of what is true German nature. And Italy has been even more critical of Toscanini's critique in this matter than has Germany, for Italy is an official participant in the *Festspiele* and expresses its amicable relationship to Germany in this manner.

Note

1. A reference to the events of 14 May 1931, when Toscanini refused to conduct the Fascist anthem *Giovinezza* at La Scala in Milan.—Eds.

246

MANCHESTER GUARDIAN

The Bayreuth Festival: August 15, 1933

"Featuring" Herr Hitler

First published in the *Manchester Guardian,* 15 August 1933.

It would have been a pardonable error on the part of any casual visitor to Bayreuth to have mistaken this year's Wagner festival for a Hitler festival. For previous festivals every shop, no matter what its wares, managed by hook or by crook to display a photograph or at least some reproduction of Wagner's face. From the windows of china shops, dozens of ceramic Wagners used to gaze into space. Booksellers displayed Wagner's autobiography. This year the china shops are full of Hitler plaques and *Mein Kampf* has displaced *Mein Leben* [*My Life,* Wagner's autobiography—Eds.]. From every flagstaff and nearly every window, a Swastika flag is flying. Brown shirts are almost de rigueur, and passing "Café Tannhäuser" and "Gasthof Rheingold" one hears nothing but the Horst Wessel Lied.

Herr Hitler attended the first six performances of the festival and the behavior of the audience gave one the impression that for them "this was a Hitler festival, and since Hitler likes Wagner's music, we are here, too." Thousands of people lined the streets from his house to the Festspielhaus and, with the exception of the foreign visitors, the audience waited outside the theater to cheer him as he arrived, and then rushed into their seats to gaze admiringly, almost reverently, at his box until the lights were lowered. At the end of each act, the center of attraction changed immediately from the stage to the Chancellor's box. And when business detained Herr Hitler in Berlin, two thousand people were made to wait an hour and a half for their opera until he should take his seat in the theater.

It would be idle to pretend that this outward display of national politics increased the pleasure of the international music-lover whose only interests were artistic. But, unfortunately, Hitler's influence over Bayreuth was not confined to outward show. Through his policy we were deprived of the presence of Toscanini, and consequently the performances of *Die Meistersinger* and *Parsifal* were considerably inferior to those that most of us expected when, five or six months ago, we bought our tickets. The fault is not on Toscanini's side—no one can blame him for his withdrawal.

Musical Protectionism

Toscanini's wire announcing his decision not to conduct at Bayreuth undoubtedly gave Hitler unpleasant food for thought. I am informed that the publication of that news practically stopped foreign bookings, and was followed by hundreds of cancellations from all parts of the world. The national pride that gave birth to the Nazi shibboleth "Only German art performed by German artists" must have been deeply wounded; but what is national pride? Conversations I have had with prominent German musicians of Nazi persuasion have convinced me that the actuating motive is fear. The German performers have seen with dismay that in nearly every instance the finest interpretative artists are foreign, and that the few of the first class who are German are also Jewish.

247

OSKAR LOERKE

Diary Entry

Written on 10 April 1933. First published in *Oskar Loerke: Tagebücher 1903–1939*, edited by Hermann Kasack (Heidelberg: Lambert Schneider, 1955), 270–71.

Hailstorms, as I step out into the garden. Loneliness. Almost all my friends are dead, gone, missing. Thinking is forbidden, as is thinking of human beings in humane terms. Neither the great godlike men of the past nor the idols: the city of Munich wages war on Thomas Mann's splendid treatment of Wagner. The protest has been signed by Richard Strauss, [Hans] Pfitzer, [Olaf] Gulbransson, [Siegmund von] Hausegger, [Hans] Knappertsbusch, and others. How can it be? Could it be that none of them bothered to read the text? Should highly skilled artists who have put Germany's name on the map throughout the world be struck dead because some idiosyncratic deviation in their way of thinking does not suit the tastes of the ruling elite? Even during the witch trials, our fellow men did not turn on one another this viciously! Yesterday while I was at the publishing house, I was profoundly and painfully moved by the news. To live and not be left to live, it is sheer hell. I gathered my academic files and packed them up today. I cast them aside—that too is a closed chapter in my life. Banished from the present—and if you're wallowing in the bellows of reminiscence, you're not allowed to admit it. Rivulets of joy bleed themselves dry. What is a human being?

248

A Protest from Richard Wagner's City of Munich

First published as "Protest der Richard-Wagner-Stadt München," in *Münchener Neueste Nachrichten,* no. 105, 16 April 1933. Published in English in Thomas Mann, *Pro and Contra Wagner,* translated by Alan Blunden (Chicago: University of Chicago Press, 1985), 149–51.

Now that the uprising of Germany as a nation has assumed stable institutional form, it can no longer be regarded as an unwarranted diversion if we now address the public at large in order to protect the memory of that great German Master, Richard Wagner, against defamation. We regard Wagner as the musical-dramatic embodiment of the deepest German sensibilities, which we will not permit to be insulted by the kind of aestheticizing snobbery that finds such arrogant and pretentious expression in the commemorative addresses on the subject of Richard Wagner delivered by Herr Thomas Mann.

Having had the misfortune to forfeit his erstwhile national sentiments at the time of the establishment of the Republic, exchanging them for cosmopolitan-democratic views, Herr Mann has failed to draw from this the lessons of a modest and decent reticence, but has elected to make a name for himself abroad as a spokesman for the German spirit. In Brussels and Amsterdam and elsewhere he has described Wagner's figures as a "fertile field for Freudian psychoanalysis," and characterized his work as "a case of dilettantism that has been monumentalized by a supreme effort of the will." His music, we are told, is not music in the pure sense, nor are the texts of his operas pure literature. It is the "music of an oppressed soul, lacking the élan of dance." At bottom (he says) there is an element of the philistine about him.

If this in itself must be accounted as an ignorant presumption in the context of a commemorative address, the critical affront is made quite insufferable by the lukewarm and patronizing praise that Wagner's music is accorded on the grounds that it is "made for the larger world, and accessible to the larger world," and represents a blend "of the Germanic and the modern."

We are not disposed to tolerate such disparaging treatment of our great German musical genius from anyone—and most certainly not from Herr Thomas Mann, who has furnished the most telling critique and revelation of his own true nature by revising his *Reflections of a Non-Political Man* after his conversion to the republican system in such a way that the meaning of key passages was completely reversed. Any man who has shown himself to be so completely unreliable and unknowledgeable in his published works has no right whatsoever to criticize German intellectual giants of enduring merit.

Max Amann, publisher and Member of the Reichstag

Dr. Arthur Bauckner, Directer of the State Theater

Prof. Hermann Bauer, President of the United Patriotic Association of Bavaria

Dr. Alexander Berrsche, musicologist

Prof. German Bestelmeyer, Privy Councillor and President of the Academy of Fine Arts

Prof. Bernhard Bleeker, sculptor

Prof. Gottfried Boehm

Prof. Reinhard Demoll, Privy Councillor and former Director General of the Bavarian State Gallery (retired)

Friedrich Franz Feeser, Major General (retired)

Karl Fiehler, Chief Burgomaster

Clemens von Franckenstein, General Manager of the Bavarian State Theater

Prof. Walther Gerlach

Hermann Groeber, Full Academic Professor
Olaf Gulbransson, Full Academic Professor
Hermann Hahn, Privy Councillor and Full Academic Professor
Prof. Siegmund von Hausegger, Privy Councillor and President of the Academy of Music
Julius Hess, Full Academic Professor
Dr. Ludwig Hoeflmayr, Senior Public Health Officer
Angelo Jank, Privy Councillor and Full Academic Professor
Franz Klemmer, Full Academic Professor
Prof. Hans Knappertsbusch, Director of the Bavarian State Opera
Dr. Hans Küfner, Privy Councillor and Burgomaster elect
Friedrich Langenfass, Dean
Wilhelm Leupold, publisher of the *Münchner Zeitung*
Carl von Marr, Privy Councillor, former Director of the Academy (retired) and painter
Wilhelm Matthes, musicologist
Karl Miller, Full Academic Professor
The Board of the Musical Academy: Eduaard Niedermayr, Michael Uffinger, Hermann Tuckermann, Emil Wagner
Fred Ottow, Editor of the *München-Augsburger-Abendzeitung*
Josef Pschorr, Privy Councillor of Commerce and President of the Chamber of Commerce and Industry
Prof. Hans Pfitzner, Musical Director
Christoph Röschlein, First President of the Upper Bavarian Chamber of Trades and Crafts
Hans Schemm, Minister in the Bavarian State Government
Adolf Schiedt, Editor of the *Münchner Zeitung*
Adolf Schinnerer, Full Academic Professor
Dr. Hans Schmelzle, Councillor and President the Bavarian Higher Administrative Court
Prof. Georg Sittmann, Privy Councillor
Dr. Richard Strauss, Musical Director
Adolf Wagner, Minister in the Bavarian State Government
Fritz Westermann, First Chairman of the Bayreuth League

249

THOMAS MANN

Response to City of Munich Protest

"Erwiderung auf den 'Protest der Richard-Wagner-Stadt München.'" First published in *Vossische Zeitung,* 21 April1933 (evening ed.). Published in English in Thomas Mann, *Pro and Contra Wagner,* translated by Alan Blunden (Chicago: University of Chicago Press, 1985), 152–53.

"A passion for Wagner's enchanted *oeuvre* has been a part of my life ever since I first became aware of it and set out to make it my own, to invest it with understanding." That sentence is a quotation from an extended critical essay which I published in the April number of the *Neue Rundschau* under a title that says a good deal about the approach and the spirit of the work—"The Sorrows and Grandeur of Richard Wagner." The piece contains many such sentences; but this has not prevented it from becoming the target of a violent protest, which, issued in the name of a large number of Munich dignitaries, has not only been published in the *Münchener Neueste Nachrichten,* but also broadcast over the Munich radio station.

The text of this document, filled as it is with grave slurs on my character and my opinions, does not refer explicitly or directly to the original essay. It does not quote it by name, nor does it state where it was published, thus making it difficult for the reader to check the validity of the charges made against me. The protest speaks of lectures I have given in a number of foreign cities, in which I have allegedly disparaged the name of the German Master abroad. To prove his point, the author has taken a number of quotations out of their original context in the *Rundschau* essay and dished them up to a mass radio audience in a manner calculated to jeopardize a just appreciation of my intentions and stir up the wrath of the nation against me.

The truth of the matter is that I drew on that fifty-two page essay, which is a passionately written summary of all that Wagner has come to mean to me, for the substance of a public lecture that I have so far delivered on four separate occasions in connection with the recent anniversary. While the original essay was conceived as a definitive literary statement, full of nuances and shades of meaning, the lecture was intended for a specific festive occasion, and as such, of course, it eschewed a good deal of psychological cut and thrust that might have run counter to the spirit of such an occasion. I delivered if for the first time on February 10th in the Great Hall of the University of Munich, at the invitation of the Munich Goethe Society—to enthusiastic applause from an audience of some five hundred persons, and without exciting any hint of protest or disagreement. I delivered it again on the fifth anniversary of Wagner's death in the *Concertgebouw* in Amsterdam, and then again, in French, in Brussels and Paris. On each occasion it was followed with the most attentive interest by an audience of ardent Wagner lovers. The official representatives of the German Reich in the various capitals were present at these gatherings, and they expressed to me their thanks for the service I had thereby rendered the German name. Yet the protest issued by "Wagner's Own City of Munich"—as the signatories collectively describe themselves—accuses me of the exact opposite.

I owe it to the German public and to myself to state that this protest proceeds from a gross misunderstanding, and that its content and tone do me a grave and bitter injustice. Hardly any of the honorable, not to say highly distinguished men who appended their names to this document can even have read my essay "The Sorrows and Grandeur of Richard Wagner," for only a complete ignorance of the role that Richard Wagner's gigantic oeuvre has always played in my life and work could have persuaded them to associate themselves with this malicious attack on a German writer.

I therefore urge all those in Germany who look with quiet favor on my work not to doubt for one moment my loyalty to German culture and tradition—or my loyalty to them.

250

HERBERT BIRTNER

On the German Interpretation of Beethoven Since Richard Wagner

First published as "Zur deutschen Beethovenauffassung seit R. Wagner," in *Beethoven und die Gegenwart: Festschrift des Beethovenshauses Bonn* (Berlin: Ferdinand Dümmlers Verlag, 1937), 21, 22, 23.

At the same time that this heated, internalized battle is for Beethoven and serves to identify his historical mission, this battle [for Nietzsche] is the battle for the genuine German essence and for genuinely Germanic music. During his period of revaluation [*Umwertungszeit*] [Nietzsche] managed to see in the German music of the nineteenth century nothing but a "stunning, multifaceted, educated form of decline." However, it was during the seventeenth and eighteenth centuries that Germany reached the height of expression in the art form that is most intrinsic to its nature, music. But these "good old" days are gone; "in Mozart they sang themselves out." Beethoven "was, in fact, only the final chords of a stylistic transition, a break in style, and not, like Mozart, the final notes of a great, centuries-long European taste."

> Beethoven is something that happens between an old crumbling soul that is constantly breaking up and a very young soul of the future that is constantly advancing. In his music, there lies that half light of eternal loss and of eternally riotous hoping—that same light in which Europe was bathed when it dreamed with Rousseau, when it danced around the freedom tree of revolution, and finally almost worshipped before Napoleon.
>
> What has come into German music since then belongs to the romantic period—that is, historically considered, to an even shorter, even more fleeting, even more superficial movement than was that great interlude, that transition in Europe from Rousseau to Napoleon and to the arrival of democracy. (Nietzsche, *Good and Evil,* paragraph 245)

Mozart—the end! And Beethoven, "something that happens between an old crumbling soul"—the great interlude between Mozart and the romantic period. And what comes after him is the "decline," and both he and Wagner are unanimous in calling it blasphemous. So Beethoven remains what he was, although with many ambiguities. He is the last European event in German music. However—Mozart was the same, but to a far greater degree—he, the "utterly impeccably good German," was the "intermediary" who worked as a "European." And from this perspective, Nietzsche turns his gaze to the older Germanic art, to "the Germans of the stronger race" who have since gone extinct: Schütz, Bach, and Händel. The maestro Heinrich Schütz, though, is one of the most authentic and German musicians, German in the old sense of the word, not merely belonging to the German empire." And it is the experience of and the impression left by this "old" German music that ultimately arouses his distrust "even if the completely innocent Beethoven is called a classic everywhere." Then he sees in Beethoven "the first great romantic, in the sense of the French romantic, as Wagner is the last great romantic . . . both are instinctual opponents of classical taste, of the strict style—not to speak here of 'greatness.' " This marks the great reversal of the Wagnerian view of Beethoven that Nietzsche was finally able to achieve. Beethoven and Wagner are situated differently in relationship to one another, in a relationship of blasphemy, because their relationship is sublated in a historical context. Just as Nietzsche was able to overcome Wagner, he was able to overcome Wagner's interpretation of Beethoven. However, it would be a grave misapprehension of the situation to attempt to make a connection between what is going on in Nietzsche's campaign against Wagner and his century and the partisan political conflicts of that time while at the same time seeing Nietzsche himself as some sort of successor to the

Beethoven bashers of old and, ultimately, to believe that Wagner ruined his appreciation for Beethoven. His position is consistent and always unequivocal. It is apparent in his citation of Aristotle to contradict D[avid] Fr[iedrich] Strauß on Mozart: "only to praise him, is not permitted the bad" [*ihn nur zu loben, ist den Schlechten nicht erlaubt*].

Finally, Nietzsche's perspective on Beethoven requires that we distinguish between his grappling for a historical perspective within the context of the constraints placed upon him by his battle against his own century and that which Beethoven was to him and nevertheless so remained for him, for him—who suffered so over the fate of music, as though "from an open wound"; for him—who was himself too much of a musician at heart to not be a romantic. "In Goethe, Beethoven, and Bismarck," he saw "a stronger future" laid out than he did in Wagner and Schopenhauer, these "miscreants of the race." Beethoven, though, was for him the "main event of the last century, along with Napoleon's appearance"—and we all know what Napoleon the Great means for Nietzsche in modern history; to take the measure of what it means for him to mention Napoleon together with Beethoven, the half barbarian.

251

CURT VON WESTERNHAGEN

Richard Wagner's Struggle against Foreign Domination of the Soul

First published as the foreword to his *Richard Wagners Kampf gegen seelische Fremdherrschaft* (Munich: J.F. Lehmanns Verlag, 1935).

This book is based on an essay titled "From the Polyphonic German Soul" [*Von der vielstimmigen deutschen Seele*] which was in turn inspired by the performance of the *Meistersinger* on the Day of Potsdam [see document 18 in chapter 2], that rare moment in the life of a *Volk* in which a great historical event coincides with a great artistic experience. The context was an allegory for the essence of German nature itself, which incorporates the unity of the will to act with the depth of inner reflection; and it was at the same time testimony to our proximity of presence to Richard Wagner that sprang from the narrow confines of the stage and burst into the life of the nation.

Imperiously, the publication assumed the task of daring to ask what this great master has to say to the German people today with regard to the questions that move them and concern them emotionally: what he has to say about the German meaning of revolution and the resurrection of myth; about the eternal significance of the Greeks and of universal works of art; of a people's celebrations and genius as the voice of the people; of religious revival from the spirit of Germanic myth and German mysticism; and about the heroic sages of German history.

My intent was to convey and interpret, in a very limited space, the *answers that Wagner* provided in his works, his writings, his letters, conversations, in his deeds so that his voice would remain ever present and his presence ever visible. In the interest of fielding potential misunderstandings from the onset: it is not a matter of determining whether Wagner was right in holding this opinion or another. What is the point of being right? *What matters is that one provides direction!* The fact that, for example, in his relationship to the Greeks, he did not follow the Asiatic-Dionysian principle but rather the Nordic-Apollonian; that in his religion, he neither became slave to Jewish-Roman doctrine nor did he subordinate himself to any sort of theological letter of the law but instead promoted the Germanic freedom of conscience—that is the essence of the kind of direction he provided by example.

I had to clear up many of the erroneous opinions about Wagner in these two areas—especially with reference to the way they can be traced back to Nietzsche. In the process, I heeded the philosopher's own warning against seeking to mediate between two thinkers who were each very set in their own views, because seeing these kinds of parallels is an index of poor eyesight. The publications of recent years—specifically the diaries of Cosima [Wagner] that were made accessible by Du Moulin-Eckart's biography and the works of Alfred Lorenz on the form of Wagner's work—were well suited to the cause of sharpening the eye for the true content [of his work]. Furthermore, Karl Otfried Müller's study, *History of the Doric Race* [*Die Dorier,* 1824], which had a decisive influence on Wagner his whole life, gave me my first insight into the broader picture with regard to [Wagner's] Nordic understanding of the Hellenic world.

Regardless of the relationship any individual has to the art of Wagner, the German *Volk* and the educators of the German *Volk* should become conscious of the fact that there is no other genius in possession of the same power to deliver art from the seduction of abstraction and to introduce it to the heart of the life of the nation as Richard Wagner; that all other attempts, however well intentioned, to unify art and *Volk,* will necessarily fall short unless they are guided by the light of *his* torch! Our most ardent concern is to present a vibrant, living example of the challenge put forth by Heinrich von Stein: to translate the sensibilities of art into facts of life.

252

THOMAS MANN

Letter to the Editor of *Common Sense*

First published in *Common Sense,* January 1940.

Sir:

I am very grateful to you for your kindness in sending me the November issue of your magazine, containing the article on *Hitler and Richard Wagner* by Peter Viereck. Since I am an avowed admirer of the art of Richard Wagner, you assume that I must have many objections to this essay and might even be minded to protest against it. I must disappoint you. Such is not the case. I read Mr. Viereck's piece with very nearly complete approval and regard it as extraordinarily meritorious. For the first time in America, as far as I know, the intricate and painful interrelationships which undeniably exist between the Wagnerian sphere and the National Socialist evil here undergo a sharp and inexorable analysis, which will put an end to much sentimental innocence. The dismay, confusion, and disillusion this is likely to strike in many well-meaning heads and hearts are no different from the effects that spring from the first impact of knowledge generally. They must be accepted for the sake of the service thereby rendered truth.

I can well understand the bitter laughter that overcame your contributor on the occasion of that fashionable Wagner concert, when he heard the speaker solemnly distinguish between the Germany of Hitler and the Germany of Wagner—the latter a Germany of creative freedom, racial tolerance, and democracy. Creative freedom—I can still let that stand. They were indeed exceedingly free, those sensuously intellectual masterpieces by a musician-dramatist, a genius in the art of the theater. Braving scorn and opposition, they embarked upon their triumphant course in a world still dominated by the classic ideals of humanism. It is certain that, had the word existed in Wagner's time, he should have been called a *Kultur*-Bolshevik.

But racial tolerance? Democracy? There the outlook is gloomy. Nietzsche had not yet openly broken with Wagner—indeed, he may still have believed himself a disciple of Wagner—when he noted down: "*Meistersinger*—a lance against civilization. The German against the French." That is a mere statement of fact, not yet a taking of issue. But it is a sort of transition from purely critical appreciation to repudiation of Wagner's Germany. It lends significance to the fact that the *Meistersinger* was destined to become the favorite opera of our wretched Herr Hitler.

If two people like the same thing and one of them is inferior, is the object of their affection inferior too? One ought to read the incomparable piece of prose that Nietzsche dedicated to the prelude to the *Meistersinger.* One ought to reread his famous page on *Tristan* in *Ecce Homo.* Baudelaire was one of the earliest Wagnerians. Another favorite of his, aside from the creator of *Lohengrin,* was Edgar Allan Poe. The juxtaposition is bewildering, almost incomprehensible to German ears (if "German" is taken to be synonymous with a complete lack of psychological insight). Yet it shows who and what Wagner really was—disregarding the fact that he was a "German master craftsman" and "against civilization." He was a European creative artist who knew every last trick of his trade. He had soaked up all the romantic wiles of seduction to console, delight, and enchant long-suffering worldly-wise souls. It was no accident that his works had a worldwide effect, such as was never before the lot of any German of stature. The creator of the most overwhelming dramatic spectacles offered by the West in modern times was a shrewd and soul-stirring stage director of ancient legends. His boundless urge and enthusiasm swept into their orbit all the emotional elements of his century—the democratic-revolutionary as well as the nationalist. Later and on a smaller scale, d'Annunzio became an imitator of this system.

Nietzsche spoke of the "twin optics" that dominated Wagner's enormous talents—his ambition to win the finest as well as the coarsest. He succeeded, and the result is a certain sense of discomfort felt by the one section of his admirers in the presence of the other. A further consequence of the ambitious ambiguity inherent in this artistry is a corresponding ambiguity inherent in all higher criticism of which it becomes the object. Such criticism will always have an element of discord and passionate irony. It will be a curious blend of abandon and distrust, calling to mind the philosopher's love of "life" which Nietzsche called the love for a woman who "fills us with doubt."

Wagner is one of the most complex phenomena in the history of art and intellect and one of the most fascinating, because he offers the most profound challenge to one's conscience. I am somewhat taken aback by the fact that Mr. Viereck, in his excellent article, gives the impression that I had proved rather unresponsive in the face of the gravity of this phenomenon, as though I had contributed to the over-simplified notion that Wagner is an unmistakable representative of the "good" Germany, in contrast to the "evil" of Herr Hitler. He quotes a lecture of mine on Wagner's essays on the philosophy of art—quotes it inaccurately, or at least incompletely. I described Wagner's essays as astonishingly acute writings by an artist, though having the character of propaganda on his own behalf and being far removed from truly great essay writing. Consideration kept me from commenting on the style of these "essays"—a style which, regarded as purely prose and apart from all content, doubtless has a strong National Socialist element. This was, after all, a memorial address requested of me by foreign societies in Amsterdam and Paris on the occasion of the 50th anniversary of Wagner's death.

What Mr. Viereck does not know or has forgotten is that it was this very speech in 1933 that determined my emigration, or, more correctly, my failure to return to Germany. Its enthusiasm was so faint that it put the Nazis into a transport of rage. This vermin is affected by shades of difference as is a bull by a red rag. Yet it is these very nuances of difference that are the most indispensable element in any discussion of Wagner.

May I say that I miss ever so slightly a sense of nuance in Mr. Viereck's revealing characterization of Wagner? I mean the nuances of love, of passionate personal familiarity with this artistry, which is, after all, admirable and gifted beyond measure. Wagner was full of such naive wonder at his own works that he spoke of them as miracles [*Wunderwerke*]. And in the end—this is the proper word. No term better fits these unexampled manifestations; nothing in the history of creative art does it fit better—even though we, on our part, may not necessarily use that term as the absolute superlative. We were never similarly tempted to describe as "miracles" other precious and indispensable cultural properties, such as *Hamlet* or *Iphigenia* or even the Ninth Symphony. But the score of *Tristan* is a miracle—especially in its irksome affinity with the *Meistersinger,* which almost defies mental grasp. It is still more of a miracle when both of these are taken for what they really are, mere relief from the minute and gigantic thought structure of the *Ring.* Wagner's work is a veritable eruption of talent and genius, the profoundly serious yet enchanting work of a sensuous sorcerer, drunk with his own wisdom.

It is a unique case, one subject to severe intellectual criticism (this must be admitted over and over)—this combination of poet and musician in which both qualities necessarily lose their pure character, becoming something different from what they usually are, on a big scale or small. As a poet, Wagner was a musician; as a musician, he was a poet. His relationship to dramatic poetry was that of the composer; his music forced his language back into a primitive state so that without their music his dramas are only half poetry; nor was his relationship to music purely musical; it was literary or poetic to the extent that the spiritual and symbolic content of his music, its significant charm and interpretative magic, decisively influenced this relationship.

It was from this dubious mixture of talents, developed to absolute greatness, that the *Ring of the Nibelungen* grew. It is a work that stands by itself. It seems utterly beyond modernity, yet in the refinement, awareness, and deliberate recency of its technique it is extremely modern. Again, in its pathos and its romantic, revolutionary urge, it is primitive—a world-poem interlaced with music and prophetic Nature. In it the original substance of life interacts; day and night hold colloquy; the mythical prototypes of man—the fair, blithe, golden-haired, and those that brood in hate, grief, and rebellion—engage each other in profound fairy-tale plot.

The tremendous thing about all this is a certain epic radicalism for which I shall never lose my enthusiasm. It is the radicalism of *beginning,* of going back to the first and original source of all things, the primeval cell, the first E-flat of the prelude to the overture. It is the obsession to rear a musical cosmogony, indeed, a musical cosmos, to be endowed with a meaningful life of its own—the ringing pageant of the world's beginning and end.

This blend of drama and music is often called impure, the work of a charlatan. I admit the charge. These are the cases in which admissions of all kinds may be made—and still, something overwhelming remains. The parallelism between music and the creative world of things places the epic birth of the world in coincidence with the birth of music. The mythology of music is interwoven with that of the world. A mythical philosophy, a musical poem of Creation, grow up before our senses and proceed to unfold into a richly joined world of symbols rising from the E-flat major triad of the deep-flowing Rhine.

We are dealing with a work that is intensely German to an exemplary degree. This conclusion is disquieting when we remember the relationships uncovered by Mr. Viereck. It leads to identifications that we today are profoundly interested in repudiating. But the truth is that such a work could only spring from the German spirit. Perhaps—though this is not certain—Jewish blood did its share. Certain qualities of this art—its sensuousness and intellectualism—speak in favor of the assumption. But first and foremost it is German. It is the German contribution to nineteenth-century creative art in the monumental tradition—the type of contribution which in other nations preeminently took the form of the great social novel. Dickens, Thackeray, Tolstoy, Dostoyevsky, Balzac, Zola—their works, heaped up with the same urge for moralizing grandeur, constitute Europe's nineteenth century, constitute the world of literary and social criticism. The German contribution, the form that this greatness took in Germany, has no social element nor desires to have anything to do with it. Society is not musical; indeed, not even capable of creative art. The roots of creativeness go down into the pure humanity of the mythical age, into the timeless, non-historical proto-poetry of Nature and of the heart. That is what the German spirit desires. That was its instinct, long in advance of any conscious decision. So far as time and mind are concerned, the *Ring des Nibelungen* has a great deal in common with the Rougon-Macquart series. The essential and characteristic national distinction is that between the social instinct of the French work and the mythical, primitive, poetic spirit of the German. With the appreciation of this difference, the intricate old question: "What is German?" perhaps finds its tersest answer. Essentially the German spirit lacks social and political interest. Deep down, that sphere is foreign to it. But its accomplishments do not permit a purely negative evaluation of such a fact. Still, one is fully entitled to speak here of a vacuum, a failure, a deficiency. And in so decidedly social and political time as ours, this often so productive deficiency may truly take on a fateful, indeed, a disastrous character. In the face of the problems of the times it may lead to efforts at solution which are poor evasions and which are by way of being mythical substitutes for truly social solutions. But that brings us to National Socialism.

National Socialism means: "I do not care for the social issue at all. All I want is the folk-tale." This formulation, to be sure, is the mildest, the most intellectual. The fact that in reality National Socialism is also filthy barbarism springs from the other fact, that in the realm of politics fairy-tales become *lies.*

National Socialism, in all its ineffable empirical vileness, is the tragic consequence of the mythical political innocence of the German spirit. You see, I go a little farther than Mr. Viereck. I find an element of Nazism not only in Wagner's questionable literature, I find it also in his "music," in his work, similarly questionable, though in a loftier sense—albeit I have so loved that work that even today I am deeply stirred whenever a few bars of music from this world impinge upon my ear. The enthusiasm it engenders, the sense of grandeur that so often seizes us in its presence, can be compared only to the feelings excited in us by Nature at her noblest, by evening sunshine on mountain peaks, by the turmoil of the sea. Yet this must not make us forget that this work, created and directed "against civilization," against the entire culture and society dominant since the Renaissance, emerges from the bourgeois-humanist epoch in the same manner as does Hitlerism. With its *Wagalaweia* and its alliteration, its mixture of roots-in-the-soil and eyes-toward-the-future, its appeal for a classless society, its mythical-reactionary revolutionism—with all these, it is the exact spiritual forerunner of the "metapolitical" movement terrorizing the world today. This is the movement that must be beaten if a really new order is to arise in Europe.

Let us not deceive ourselves. National Socialism must be beaten. In practice this means, unfortunately: Germany must be beaten. It is meant, however, in a very definite sense—a spiritual sense, too. For there is but *one* Germany, not two, not a good and an evil. And Hitler, in all his wretchedness, is no accident. He could never have become possible but for certain psychological prerequisites that must be sought deeper down than in inflation, unemployment, capitalist speculation, and political intrigue. Yet it is true that nations do not always show the same face, that it depends on time and circumstances how their constant qualities appear. Germany today makes a frightful appearance. It torments the world—not because it is "evil," but because it is at the same time "good"—a fact with which Anglo-Saxon humor is fully familiar, as evidenced by the words of the estimable Harold Nicolson: "The German character is one of the finest but most inconvenient developments of human nature."

Germany must be beaten. That means it must be compelled to reactivate all the constructive social elements in its fund of tradition from earlier centuries. It must do so in order to fit into the European Confederation, the comity of nations for which Europe is ripe. Such federalism will require sacrifices in national sovereignty and selfishness from *every* nation. This war is waged in Germany's interest. It would be asking too much, of course, for Germany to see this at the moment. But the war is waged to bring about a state of affairs that will free Germany from the curse of power politics, more depraving for her than for any nation. It is waged for a pacified, depoliticized Europe that alone can provide an atmosphere conducive to Germany's greatness and happiness. Such an atmosphere will restore political innocence to the works of German and a clear conscience to those who admire them. They will no longer have to sigh: It is great, it is splendid, but it is "against civilization."

Yours very sincerely,
Thomas Mann

253

MOSER'S DICTIONARY OF MUSIC

Atonal

First published as "Atonal," in *Hans Joachim Moser: Musiklexikon* (Berlin: Hesse, 1943).

Atonal is the term used to describe a musical style that has abandoned any point of reference to a functional tonal center in the overall harmonic fabric of composition; strictly speaking, the artistic quality cannot be achieved using this method for longer intervals because the listener will always tend by default to seek an underlying logical order to the music. [. . .] The intellectual history of the atonal style can be traced to its attempt at a radical, constructivist liberation from the oppressive legacy of the romantic period, with all the demands it placed on musical content, and at the same time, as the culmination of an intensity of dissonance that had increased consistently with each passing epoch, as a reflection devastating postwar experiences of revolution and inflation, as a symptom of cultural decay. [. . .] Fortunately, already now most of these symptoms have been overcome through a return to basic tonalities much in the same way that these appear in the fine arts as "New Objectivity." Central European representatives of atonal style were Arnold Schönberg and his protégés Anton von Webern, Alban Berg, A. Hába, and with some reservations and only momentarily, P. Hindemith, Bartók, Stravinsky.

254

DEGENERATE MUSIC EXHIBITION

The Theoreticians of Atonality!

Poster from the Entartete Musik [Degenerate Music] Exhibition, 1938.

The Theoreticians of Atonality!

The oldest of them all is the Jew Arnold Schönberg, author of the theory of harmony (1910).

The most "modern" of them is Paul Hindemith, creator of the theory of composition (1937).

We see in these frontrunners of the atonality movement—alongside parallel figures participant in the process of disintegration in the fine arts and in literature—the fundamental intellectual property holders for intellectual constructivism and the most dangerous destroyers of our racial instincts as a *Volk*. Our instinct is to see what is clear, what is pure, genuine, and organically grown; and we will oppose these driftless, rootless charlatans from the highest posts in the nation!

255

The Hindemith Affair

Exchange between Wilhelm Furtwängler and Joseph Goebbels, 1934

Wilhelm Furtwängler to Joseph Goebbels

First published as "Joseph Goebbels zum Fall Furtwängler-Hindemith," in *Berliner Lokal-Anzeiger,* 7 December 1934. Published in Joseph Wulf, ed., *Musik im Dritten Reich* (Frankfurt am Main: Ullstein, 1983), 373–78.

In certain circles, a campaign has been launched against Paul Hindemith based on the charges that he is "not tenable" for the New Germany. Why? What are the charges against him?

First of all, things of a purely political character: he is said to be of Jewish lineage and for years helped to found and has played as violist in the Amar Quartet, which has at times consisted exclusively of Jewish members. Furthermore, even after the National Socialist revolution, he recorded an album of live concerts with two Jewish émigrés. At issue here is a string trio that was formed years before the overthrow and whose remaining members were not "émigrés" but rather the first violinist for the Berlin Philharmonic Orchestra—[Simon] Goldberg, who left the orchestra a few months ago with the intent of devoting himself fully to a career as soloist, and the highly respected Austrian [Emanuel] Feuermann, who worked for many years at the National College of Music [Staatlichen Hochschule für Musik] in Berlin and is widely acknowledged to be the best European cellist there is. What is more, these recordings involved the fulfillment of commitments made according to a previous contract.

Even Hindemith's opponents know that their objections cannot rest exclusively on these types of things. They seek primary justification for their position in those of his works that seem impeachable for ideological reasons: above all, in a portion of those works for which he has written musical scores. Admittedly, the material for the three one-act plays *Murder, Women's Only Hope* [*Mörder, Hoffnung der Frauen*], *Nusch-Nuschi,* and *Sancta Susanna* is rather dubious, as is the piece *News of the Day* [*Neues vom Tage*], which is perhaps best described as contemporary cabaret. However, one must take into account that the three one-act plays are actually best seen as juvenilia: at the time of their writing, Hindemith was not yet certain that he wanted to become a composer. And, without seeking to compare them in any other point, is the degree of perversity in these one-act plays any greater than, say, in the mature work of the master Richard Strauss, *Salome?* But who would censure Richard Strauss simply on the basis of the *Salome* text? So much for the textual content of the works. As far as music is concerned, even in the three one-act plays cited above, the scores are to some extent full of life and talent. On the other hand, *News of the Day,* a later piece, contains—despite the technical mastery that can never be denied in Hindemith—no small amount of purely mechanical, relatively hollow "revue music," so it would be understandable if the prevailing theory of the time (the "theory of objectivity" or "antiromanticism" originally inaugurated by Stravinsky) would be readily identified with Hindemith's works. To go after both at the same time today, in the context of an entirely different ideological perspective, and to hold the composer accountable for the theoretical excesses of his critics, while it may be convenient, is wrong. All the more so if you consider the fact that the works from this particular period of the composer's development are almost all hastily completed occasional works, whereas the bulk of Hindemith's productivity in this period—the years directly preceding the collapse—had seen an increasing tendency to shift his emphasis from purely compositional work to the immediate practical concerns of musical life. In addition to Hindemith the concert violist, this period witnessed Hindemith the music teacher stepping into the limelight. The impeccable ethics of craftsmanship—reminiscent of the old German masters—that characterizes Hindemith seems to have virtually predestined him for the teaching profession: what is more, he has a rare innate capacity for understanding youth and making himself feel like one of them. An entire generation of students is being trained with and by him—no one else in Germany today enjoys this much support from the musically inclined youth. Music education in the schools has particularly benefited from his efforts: he is untiring in his attempt to bridge, in his own way, the precipitous gap between popular music and music as a fine art. His intentions in this regard are marked by tendencies that are particularly characteristic of our most recent developments—that is, of National Socialist Germany.

If one were to attempt to create a profile of Hindemith the composer based on his works, one would have to describe him as being a decidedly "German" type, since his genealogy is, after all, purely Germanic. The solid craftsmanship and native sterling quality of his work, as well as the modesty and reserve apparent in his relatively rare emotional outbursts, are entirely German. His most recent work, the symphony to the opera *Mathias the Painter* [*Mathis der Maler*], reconfirms this impression of his work. It has had tremendous impact everywhere that it has been performed since its premiere in March 1934 and has found resonance even with those who haven't exactly been his friends. This reflects, as I have already stated, not a sensationalist "turn" in Hindemith's work but rather far more—if you will, a return to his beginnings, a return to himself. When this work first made its debut eight months ago, no one really paid it any mind—perhaps there was a subconscious reticence to intervene in cultural development as an outsider. Today, in retrospect, even though he has not produced anything new since then, people are making up for lost time, seeking to publicly defame him in order to—because this is what it ultimately boils down to—run him out of Germany. And there are no lengths they will not go to: they are ruthless enough in this context to go so far as to occasionally call to light some parodies of misinterpreted Puccini and Wagner—as if Hindemith hadn't a clue as to who Wagner was! Of course, with any composer who has written as much as Hindemith and whose work has been published so that it is easily accessible, there will be certain "sins of youth" one could drag out of the closet. Hindemith was never politically active: what on earth could we possibly gain from employing political denunciation in the broadest sense to the field of the arts?

One thing is certain: no one in the younger generation has contributed more to establishing the reputation for German music internationally. What is more, there is no way to assess today the significance Hindemith's work may have in the future. But that is not the issue in this debate. What is at issue here is far more than the specific "Hindemith case," it is a fundamental question of principle. Furthermore, and we must be clear about this, in a world as utterly bereft of genuinely productive musicians such as our own, we cannot necessarily afford to casually dispense of a man like Hindemith.

Goebbels Responds

First published as "Joseph Goebbels on the Furtwängler—Hindemith Affair," in *Berliner Lokal-Anzeiger*, 7 December 1934.

A densely packed throng of thousands welcome Dr. Goebbels with the Nazi salute.[1] Under the blare of fanfare, the horns in the state orchestra strike up the tone of celebration. Ably conducted by Peter Raabe, the Philharmonic Orchestra heralds, with strains of Beethoven, the powerful words of the Führer in *Mein Kampf* on the subject of art and the *Volk* that act to set the tone and direction. The state-sponsored actor Lothar Müthel recites these works very simply, in compelling clarity. Then comes the music again, this time from [Hans] Pfitzner's *From the German Soul* [*Von deutscher Seele*].

A cry of "Germany Awake!" thunders through the hall. Dr. Goebbels is again welcomed with greetings of "Heil!" as he steps up to the speaker's podium. The minister begins with a historical retrospective and reminds us of his previous statements about creative liberty, about art that remains forever free to develop according to its own system of laws but is nevertheless bound by the fundamental premises of propriety, the social fabric, and the nation established by the state.

"The degree of loyalty the state deserves from any creative artist," the minister continued, "is not met when the demands made by National Socialism in the spirit of a revolutionary, oppositional movement are rendered suspect and discredited—as certain circles have been wont to do. For National Socialism is not only the political and social conscience of the nation, it is also its cultural conscience."

In this context, the minister went on to discuss several fundamental issues raised by the infamous Furtwängler-Goebbels case. For those new generations of musicians, he explained, the fact that they once functioned as the mouthpiece for a bygone epoch does not grant them license to take pleasure in the paternal patronage of undisputed master artists who, however, in this instance lack the necessary political instincts. Ideological infelicities cannot be excused by dismissing them as juvenilia. You would have to abandon all logic and rationality to demand that an artist produce sensationalist work just because this is what is en vogue at the time. National Socialism would have to insist on stipulating a set time frame that should be used to determine whether the man of yesterday or the man of today is to be taken as the genuine and true reflection of his character.

"Technical mastery," Dr. Goebbels elaborated, "is not an excuse, it is a responsibility. To abuse those skills for the sake of producing purely mechanical 'dance' music void of all content is to spit derision in the face of the genius that is the guiding principle for every form of genuine art. It is thus convenient and all too easy to contend that this concerns hastily completed occasional works. This is the problem: namely, that this occasions not only thieves, it occasions atonal musicians who, in the interest of sensationalism and conformity to the spirit of the times, produce naked women to appear bathing on stage in the most obscene and basely kitschy scenes, and who, in the attempt to ridicule a generation of cowards that is too weak to offer any resistance, surround them with the bawdy strains of dissonance composed in complete musical ineptitude. As if our old German masters would be grateful for being mentioned in this context. And if Germany's youth assents to this, that just further substantiates the need for us to remain relentless and fearless in our opposition to those artistic cliques and claques dwindling on the verge of extinction, even as they employ intellectual terror as a means of passing this stuff off as the revelation of eternal genius. In any case, we do not see anything of visionary or futuristic value in it; we are vehemently opposed to seeing this type of artist identified as being German, and in our book, the fact that he is of purely Germanic blood heritage is but dramatic evidence of the depths of festering by which the Jewish intellectual infection has already penetrated the body of our *Volk*."

Furtwängler Resigns from His Offices

First published in *Deutsches Nachrichtenbüro*, 4 December 1934.

Privy Councilor Dr. Wilhelm Furtwängler petitioned Herr Reich Minister Dr. Goebbels to be relieved of his offices of vice president of the Reich Music Chamber and as conductor of the Berlin Philharmonic Orchestra. At the same time, he submitted a request to be released from his position as director of the State Opera in Berlin. Both Reich ministers approved his petitions.

Furtwängler's Regrets

First published in *Die Musik*, March 1935.

According to an official report, Reich Minister Dr. Goebbels convened a meeting with Privy Councilor Dr. Wilhelm Furtwängler on 28 February in which Dr. Furtwängler explained that he had written his widely circulated article on Hindemith on 24 November 934 as an expert reviewer in music with the sole intention of addressing a musical matter from a musical perspective. He deeply regrets the political waves and consequences that have since been attached to the article, all the more so because he did not have the remotest intention of intervening in the administration of the artistic polices and politics of the Reich, matters that, in his view are of course the exclusive province of the Führer and Reich chancellor and the ministers appointed to his cabinet.

Note

1. The heading "Goebbels Responds" was added by the editor of a later collection.—Eds.

256

WULF BLEY

Is It Jazz or Just Radio Dance Tunes?

First published as "Jazz oder Rundfunk-Tanzmusik?" in *Rufer und Hörer* 11, no. 3 (February 1934): 520–22.

The opinions about what jazz is are indeed varied. For musical reactionaries—there are about as many of them as there are ardent admirers of the latest flavor of Jewish hit tunes—the use of the saxophone is the mark of jazz. And in fact, the saxophone is one of the most versatile of all wind instruments. Hector Berlioz, to whom we are indebted for perhaps the most significant text on the subject of instrumentation, was the first to have incorporated it as a viable instrument in the orchestra. The inventor of the instrument, [Adolphe] Sax, was German. But he did not succeed in establishing the instrument he invented in Germany. The

War Ministries dismissed him out of hand, and in a not altogether civilized manner. So there was nothing left for him to do but to go outside the country, and he was quickly able to introduce his "saxophone" to Belgian military music, whose sound is unquestionably splendid. From there, the instrument made its way to the United States of America, where its construction was perfected by instrument makers there, so that its range of expression increased substantially over the original model for the instrument. That rendered it all the more useful. The most beautiful notes on the saxophone are in its soothing, mellow tones. But you can also elicit a highly unique comical, if not even caricature-like effect using a staccato not unlike that of a bassoon. Bear in mind, of course, a similar use of the bassoon already in Beethoven, where we also find liberal application of the allegedly Negroid characteristic of syncopation. But it certainly would not so much as occur to anyone to contend that Beethoven, just by virtue of the fact that he used the saxophone or syncopated time, was a jazz composer.

The muted trumpet is similarly altogether capable of producing effects that are appropriate to the aesthetic sensibilities of German music enthusiasts. The muted trumpet is nothing but a trumpet with a mute, much like the ones used on string instruments that always produce a nasal sound under exaggerated usage. A bad violin, played by a bad violinist, makes a nasal sound. And that is one reason no one would ever consider using a mute on a violin or a brass instrument. Brass instruments are often muted by placing the hand inside the bell, which is seen as a primary characteristic of Negro music. In America, where orchestra music is not so strictly bound to tradition as in Germany, brass instruments have been greatly improved to render them more versatile. This has nothing to do with the quality of German instrument manufacture. The increased rigor of competition between musicians in America placed substantially greater demands on players of horn and woodwind instruments and saxophonists, which in turn went hand in hand with the increased range of expression of the wind instruments. The American players of wind instruments were thus able to attain an extraordinary level of proficiency of artistry with wind instruments. But this does not mean that the level of proficiency of artistry necessarily stands in contradiction to aesthetic proficiency. It is more plausible to arrive at the notion that a high level of artistic proficiency should be seen for all orchestra musicians as the prerequisite for the aesthetic proficiency that they are expected to display. And wherever genuine training for orchestras is in place, this is in fact the case.

Jazz did not originate exclusively from Negro music but also could be traced in large part to the frenzied atmosphere of American big cities and to a bizarre, uniquely Anglo-Saxon propensity for self-caricature. Its primary characteristic is the haphazard and choppy fragmentation of rhythmic symmetry that runs contrary to the fundamental principles of rhythm and of the melody line—that is to say, the breaking down of an organic pattern of sound into shreds and tatters. The result is that there is no longer any rhythm but rather an anarchical chaos of disassociated rhythmic innuendos. In order to render this "music" danceable, a sort of rhythm is artificially reconstructed using the most primitive means. The drum set is not introduced to accompany the rhythm but rather carries the rhythm all on its own. But even this surrogate rhythm is intermittently interrupted here and there, but only for as long as the dancer is still able to sustain it. By way of preempting any misunderstanding: the use of syncopation alone does not by any means constitute jazz, for there is a fundamental difference between syncopation and the choppy fragmentation of rhythm. It is indeed indicative that jazz can be danced to only by people who have no sense of music. A musically inclined person simply cannot dance to it and just stumbles hopelessly over his own feet. In the Anglo-Saxon countries, where the nonmusical people of the white race live, jazz has persevered emphatically.

One particular characteristic of jazz instrumentation is the deliberate misappropriated use of instruments. Much in the same way that rhythm is fragmented or drummed to death by the drum set, the violin is consciously stripped of its enchantment, the saxophone of its mellowness, the trumpet of its appealing call, the cello of its masculine delicacy, etc. and turned into the precise opposite. The German dance bands have abandoned this misappropriation in instrumentation. In this regard, the Anglo-Saxon dance bands were quicker to embrace a compromise suitable to the British ear. It is only recently that German dance bands have gradually begun to follow suit, but only because a shift in the public has allowed for it. But this is the reason that German radio listeners don't tend to view the British dance bands as being somewhat less jazzy than the German ones.

The instrumentation for coffeehouse and hotel orchestras is built around the need for the band to drown out the sound of dance steps throughout a very large room. As soon as you put a microphone in front of [instruments], they sound "noisy." Competition between musicians keeps them and the dancers on their toes. But their style of playing as well as their instrumentation is not conducive to microphones and amplification through loudspeakers. So purely by virtue of aesthetic considerations, and particularly as regards the dance, it would seem urgent and desirable to bring together musicians—either from the existing in-house orchestras at the radio stations or from the greater population of musicians—to form an orchestra specifically for radio broadcasts. They must be exceptionally proficient dance-band musicians. Which is to say that not every orchestra musician is necessarily a good dance musician. We are dealing here with a very specific musical gift. Radio broadcast orchestras of this nature would be a tremendous help in preventing German ballroom dancing from being dominated by the so-called English style of dance.

And we must prevent it—because the English style of dance emerged from the international hotel-ballroom lifestyle the same way as the concept of the "bar," etc. But this style is not congruent with German sensibilities. Because for the Germans, dancing isn't a form of sports but rather a gala event, not a form of gymnastics but an expression of lust for life. And with that, we have established that the dance compositions we are to be playing must spring from this source—that is, from a lust for life on the part of the composer. But the primary characteristic of hit-parade music is not lust for life but rather that bizarre mix of hideous unpleasantries and off-key, unmelodic kitsch that is nothing but one long appeal to the shaken instincts of the masses that reached the height of expression under the November system. Usually, it has very little to do with music itself. A Strauss waltz goes "straight to your toes"—that is, it makes you want to dance—but the music of the hit parade speaks to very different physical needs. And the fact that the [masses] can dance to it makes the matter ever worse.

257

ILSE DEYK

Jazz Is Dead

May the Jazz Band Live!

First published as "Der Jazz ist tot—es lebe die Jazzband!" in *Zeitschrift für Musik* 109 (January 1942): 12–14.

I'm altogether serious in contending that jazz is alive and well! Or can someone seriously tell me that what is often presented as dance music today is free of the errors we thought had been safely relegated to the past? Have you ever listened closely to this dance music?

So we tried our best to keep Negroid or at least American influences out of our music. We wanted to go back to the melodic music, to a form of dance music that is congruent with our nature. And it seemed as though we had managed: everyone kicked up their heels—enthusiastically and without a word of criticism—to anything and everything coming out of the gramophones, loudspeakers, dance bands, and martyred pianos; everyone sang along to those oh-so-sweet songs in the hit parade and was obviously quite content. If we are to draw from this any conclusions, then, about the music that is most congruent with the primal essence of our nature, we would have to ascertain that every one of us with any inclination to dance has a pronounced preference for jazz rhythm but is himself so rhythmically inept that he needs to have the beat veritably hammered home by drums and cymbals. And we are so rhythmically inept that we are not bothered by the fact that even a moderately complex melody line is fragmented by the rhythm, shredded by the squeaky strains of the instruments until finally, intimidated by the clack of the wood block, it disappears. We are so limited in our sense of dance that we are not even capable of keeping step through a passage in the music that does not clearly mark the time—for example, to improvise the dance to a Beethoven waltz without the help of the "oompah-pah, oompah-pah" of dance music or a rudimentary martial rhythm. That would be the conclusion we would have to draw.

But is this in fact accurate? We can placate ourselves with knowing that, in general, this is not an accurate portrayal: there are a lot of people today who, while they may not be able to put in words what it is precisely that bothers them, still realize there's something wrong with this picture. Nor does this apply to all of our dance music but in many cases, even some in recent years, especially [that music] from the actual hit parade.

We now have time to reflect on this and intend to take full advantage of that time. But as soon as we are able to again devote ourselves to peacetime activities, one of our most noble tasks will be to become the arbiters of culture [*Kulturträger*] in areas that were previously the exclusive province of the intellectual elite.

258

CARL HANNEMANN

Jazz as a Weapon of Jewry and Americanism

First published as "Der Jazz als Kampfmittel des Judentums und des Amerikanismus," in *Musik in Jugend und Volk* 6 (1943): 49–57.

In the last scene of the jazz opera *Johnny Strikes Up the Band* [*Johnny spielt auf,* 1927] by Ernst Krenek, the son-in-law of the Jew Gustav Mahler, there is a huge, slowly rotating globe, large enough to cover most of the stage. Johnny the Negro is perched atop the globe playing his fiddle. On the ground all around the globe, at the feet of the Negro Johnny, the whole white race dances to jazz. The last refrain is "So Johnny strikes up the band. Here comes the new world across the sea, to put the dance in old Europe's knee."

This prophecy of the Jews and their sympathizers has come to full fruition.

The fact that jazz is a political weapon in the arsenal of international Jewry, that it is a form of musical Esperanto, is substantiated by this statement from the *New Book of Jazz* by Alfred Baresel: "Judging from the overall situation, it looked as though jazz had the potential for becoming exactly what it did become: a new form of international folk music, and only those countries whose musical traditions included popular elements (like Italy, with its highly accessible operas) were able to resist it for a time."

The Jew Egon Wellesz once said, with regard to the noisy instruments in jazz music, "It is an extreme attempt, comparable to certain tendencies in cubist painting, to depart from substance and to represent the noise (or color in painting) in and of itself."

What the Jew Franz Werfel preaches about jazz is this: "To be German, that means you are allowed to do whatever you want because you are not bound by any form or relationship."

The Jew Bernhard Sekles, former director of the Hoch Conservatory in Frankfurt am

Main, was the first to introduce jazz music to the college curriculum. In a newsletter, he distributed, among other things, the following justification for his actions: "Presenting disciplined study of jazz to young people is not only beneficial based on opportunistic concerns, it also has educational benefits."

259

SECRET REPORT OF THE SECURITY SERVICE OF THE REICHSFÜHRER SS

Jazz Music and Youth

First circulated on 10 August 1942 as "Jugendliche und Jazz Musik." First published in *Meldungen aus dem Reich 1938–1945. Die geheimen Lageberichte des Sicherheitsdienstes der SS,* edited by Heinz Boberach (Herrsching: Pawlak Verlag, 1984), 11:4054, 4056.

In the course of recent months, there has been an increase in reports from various "urban areas" that unanimously confirm the following: when jazz music with a decidedly British or American flair finds its way into the coffeehouses, it is no longer the fault of a few isolated dance bands. There is a minority of youth among the regulars who visit these haunts that is unequivocally boycotting any form of popular music with a respectable Germanic flavor while at the same time demanding jazz music—at times with such vehement insistence that the bands eventually "give in" to their demands, and the wilder, jazzier, and more titillating the music, the more unrestrained the enthusiastic reception from these youth.

Some examples:

1. *Report from Berlin.* As we have learned, the Belgian band Fud Candrix brought its music to Berlin with the best intentions. The appropriate administrative offices in Belgium and the band's manager removed all the British and American jazz tunes from the repertoire. During the first two-week run in "Delphi," the band played respectable music. But then we repeatedly observed the way young people in the audience approached the band and became ever more insistent in demanding American hit songs until the band finally played them.
2. *Report from Saarbrücken.* When the Café Vienna recently featured as a guest act the Dutch band Ferdinand Rikkers, with its moderate-to-heavy jazz influences, the band was not only applauded by countless numbers of youth in the audience, the crowd flew into a veritable "rage" requesting American jazz.

When the Willy Artelt Band brought its brand of supposedly British jazz to the Georg Palace in Hanover, some of the guests—party members in particular—got up and left the room in protest as soon as the jazz music began. But then the young people really went overboard in lavishing praise on the band. The crowd went absolutely wild with applause over the "Tiger Rag."

Reports from Hamburg about the same band. The bandleader seems to be working in an ecstatic trance. With his back bent and eyeballs askance, he conducts the band to the ruckus of the roaring audience. Every time a dissonant chord is struck, he is inundated with hurricane-force showers of applause. Every seat in the house was filled at the Alter Pavilion, primarily by youth from the "swing kids."

20

Cinema

Entertainment and Propaganda

A GREAT DEAL OF THE POPULAR CULTURE of Nazi Germany lacked the heavy-handed ideology, mythologizing, and pseudoclassical forms of representation embodied in the officially sanctioned architecture, painting, and music. For the vast majority of Germans, the most ubiquitous face of Nazi culture was the less overtly political entertainment offered on radio and above all in film, though these media were hardly devoid of ideological motifs. This distinction was in part an expression of class: art, theater, opera, and classical music appealed to elite tastes; cinema, radio, sports, and travel had a much broader appeal. Film was especially popular, with cinema attendance growing fourfold between 1933 and 1942, from 250 million to 1 billion viewers.

This dramatic increase cannot be credited to an interest in propaganda films. According to one study, of the 1,100 films produced in Germany between 1933 and 1945, only a fifth had manifest propagandistic and political content. Apart from war films produced after 1939, most were love stories, comedies, or crime thrillers. Propaganda films like *Triumph of the Will* (*Triumph des Willens,* 1935), *Olympia* (1938), *Storm Trooper Brand* (*SA Mann Brand,* 1934), and the notorious *Jew Süss* (*Jud Süß,* 1940) were heralded as triumphs of Goebbels's Ministry for Popular Enlightenment and Propaganda. But they were hardly the only products of the Nazi film industry.

The Nazis recognized the power of the medium before they took power, as contemporary commentators often stressed, effectively employing film during Hitler's 1932 electoral campaigns. In December 1930, Goebbels organized concerted SA movie riots (*Kinokrawalle*) against "the poisonous alien spirit" of Lewis Milestone's Oscar-winning film of 1930 based on Erich Maria Remarque's novel *All Quiet on the Western Front*—inciting protesters to disrupt the Berlin opening by mounting demonstrations and releasing stink bombs and white mice in theaters showing the movie, as Curt Belling noted in his 1936 account of the history of film in the Nazi Party. Nazi cultural policies banished Jews and political enemies from the film industry—an action justified in the scurrilous 1937 tract *Film "Art," Film Cohen, Film Corruption* (*Film-"Kunst," Film-Kohn, Film-Korruption*). In the book's opening sequence, a generic Jewish entrepreneur, "Herr Kohn," is "unmasked" as a vile exploiter and merciless calculator, controlling and contaminating the film industry and its artists to the detriment of genuine German film.

After 1933, film production was subject to the demands of the Propaganda Ministry's Film Office. But as Goebbels readily admitted in his 28 March 1933 speech to the leaders of the film industry at the Hotel Kaiserhof in Berlin, the films that made "a lasting impression" on him were not party documentaries but great films of the silent era, like Sergei Eisenstein's Soviet film *Battleship Potemkin* (1925), Fritz Lang's two-part *Die Nibelungen* (1924), and Greta Garbo's first film version of *Anna Karenina* by Metro-Goldwyn-Mayer entitled *Love* (1927). In other words, Goebbels promoted films that mimicked the Soviet, Weimar, and Hollywood successes that he admired. Goebbels understood that although film was an educational medium, the cinema was not a classroom, and entertainment was a better propaganda tool than political speeches were. At the same time, he warned against the influence of Jewish directors and encouraged the industry to make National Socialist films. Despite his claim that there would be artistic "freedom," the Reich Cinema Law of 16 February 1934 subjected film to heavy intervention and censorship, specifying prison terms and fines for violators.

Goebbels understood the power of "public taste"; the films that drew the biggest audiences were classical melodramas, comedies, and entertainment spectacles rather than explicitly political propaganda. Film expert Hans Traub (1901–43), the first to offer film studies in a German university, agreed, noting in 1933 that film "will provide primarily entertainment. But this should not be alien to the *Volk*." Indeed, in many respects, the Third Reich fostered a modern media culture, adopting the latest technology, introducing radios into almost every household, developing television, and staging political events as film spectacles—for example, by designing the Nuremberg Reich Party Rally largely around Leni Riefenstahl's cinematographic needs.

This is not to say that entertainment films with high production values and mass appeal were free of ideological motifs. As Fritz Hippler (1909–2002), one of the leading film functionaries in Goebbels's ministry, an SS officer, and after 1939, a *Reichsfilmintendant* (Reich film supervisor), argued in his appeal for more "positive" films and fewer "morbid," "negative" ones, even so-called unpolitical films had a "formative power" and could influence how viewers regarded themselves. Hippler pointed out that what was considered a "happy ending" depended on the artistic context: it might be "a passionate kiss," the reunion of two lovers in death, or, as he put it, "the hanging of the Jew in *Jew Süss*." After the German military defeat at Stalingrad in 1943, overtly political films—with the exception of Goebbels's major epic of Prussian resistance during the Napoleonic wars, *Kolberg* (released as Berlin was already in ruins)—virtually disappeared as German cinema became increasingly escapist.

Luis Trenker's drama *The Prodigal Son* (*Der verlorene Sohn,* 1934) depicted America as a site of temptation and foreboding, and Paul Martin's *Lucky Kids* (*Glückskinder,* 1936), an unabashed copy of the Hollywood romantic comedy, was on closer examination no less ideological. *Lucky Kids,* a critical remake of Frank Capra's 1934 *It Happened One Night,* was set in New York and used sexual stereotypes and exaggerated Hollywood conventions to depict Germanic virtues. Films produced with an eye toward female audiences featured actresses who embodied "sparkling wit," grace, maturity, and, of course, "vampishness," albeit in a "German tempo," along with the requisite ideals of motherhood. These films projected a feminine identity that was often at variance with the ideological tropes prescribed in the regime's hard-core racial propaganda. Even the masculinist *Das Schwarze Korps* took issue with the demeaning gender stereotypes offered by German cinema in 1937, contrasting the "long-since-outdated clichés" of women's deference in German films with the lack of submissiveness shown by women in American films.

Cinema in the Third Reich was not only popular, it often reproduced the generic conventions, conventional sensibilities, and a star system reminiscent of that of the 1920s—despite the regime's excoriation of the lasciviousness and wantonness of Weimar culture. The female lead in *Lucky Kids,* Lilian Harvey, had been a star in the Weimar Republic and had also made a number of films in Hollywood after 1933. During the Nazi years, she remained a star in the Weimar/Hollywood mode, exhibiting a "seductive sassiness" and sprightly singing, at one point in *Lucky Kids* warbling "I Wish I Were Mickey Mouse!" Harvey was the epitome of the urban, free-spirited "lucky kid," in contrast to the rural and earthy "blood and soil" incarnation of German womanhood central to Nazi ideology. Films made abroad, even in Hollywood, remained enormously popular and did not disappear overnight, as is evident in the movie magazine *Film-Kurier*'s 1935 enthusiastic description of the German premiere of Metro-Goldwyn-Mayer's *The Painted Veil* (1934) with Greta Garbo in the lead role. Nonetheless, the number of American films shown by German theaters declined in the first years of the Third Reich, increasing slightly in 1937 and falling precipitously thereafter. As late as

February 1940, the Gestapo registered some grumbling at positive press responses to the "dangerous" Shirley Temple.

Ewald von Demandowsky (1907–46), head of the film production firm Tobis and a close associate of Goebbels, complained that few films addressed the realities of the Third Reich—the Hitler salute, the SA, the SS, and the Labor Service, as well as the Wehrmacht. There is no question that filmgoers had different motivations for going to the cinema, a factor that government-sponsored public opinion surveys like "What Does the Audience Want to See on the Silver Screen?" tried to gauge. Not unsophisticated, the survey revealed that some viewers attended films with "the desire for spectatorship," others with "the desire to experience something." What moviegoers actually experienced was a mix of offerings, as Winifred Holmes, a British film journalist observed during a few hours in Hamburg, where she viewed a bit of "civic propaganda" on how to store old tins; a propaganda newsreel of Mussolini, Chamberlain, Hitler, and Göring; a variety act featuring dancing poodles; and finally, the feature *The Blue Fox* (*Der Blaufuchs,* 1938), starring the Swedish Zarah Leander, who became Germany's leading actress and Garbo's indigenous competitor, once Garbo left for Hollywood. Holmes judged Leander to be "heavy and stagey."

By far the most notoriously anti-Semitic feature film produced in Nazi Germany was Veit Harlan's commercially successful *Jew Süss,* the story of an eighteenth-century Jewish court financier whose depredations and manipulations lead to the collapse of the Duchy of Württemberg, the impoverishment of its citizens, and the suicide of the heroine (played by film star Kristina Söderbaum) after she is raped by Süss Oppenheimer (played by leading man Ferdinand Marian). The absolute antithesis of Lion Feuchtwanger's sympathetic portrait of Süss Oppenheimer in his famous 1924 novel (and a 1934 film), Harlan's story famously ends with Süss hanging in his cage as a jubilant crowd in the Stuttgart town center welcomes a proclamation expelling the Jews.

On 12 November 1938, three days after the Reichskristallnacht, German Jews were forbidden to attend cinemas in accordance with the decrees excluding them from German economic life. Hippler's *The Eternal Jew* (*Der ewige Jude*), produced at Goebbels's request in 1940, opened on 20 January 1941 in the Casino-Lichtspielhaus (Casino Movie House) in Litzmannstadt (formerly, Polish Łódź), where Jews had been ghettoized since December 1939. In a montage showing the ability of Jews to take on modern disguises and dress, the film depicts them as hordes of rats invading and infesting Europe and the world. The Jewish "actors" in the film had been recruited in the Łódź ghetto with the promise of "special treatment"; all were eventually murdered. In keeping with Goebbels's instructions, *The Eternal Jew* was designed to incite anti-Semitic feeling at home as well as to firm up the resolve of German soldiers occupying Poland. The film cynically uses footage of the sick and destitute Jewish ghetto inhabitants as evidence of the disease and danger posed by the Eastern European Jews. Along with Erich Waschneck's *The Rothschilds* (1940), this trio of anti-Semitic films (they were certainly not the only ones produced in Nazi Germany) coincided with the deportation and ghettoization of European Jewry—and were intended to incite audiences to genocide. Coinciding with newsreels and wall posters depicting the dangerous and threatening "Jewish enemy" deserving of elimination, they were a direct expression of a radical anti-Semitism that regarded winning the war and the elimination of the Jews as one and the same event. As the Reich Security Service reported after overhearing remarks at screenings, *Jew Süss* was regarded by filmgoers as a realistic and convincing portrayal of Jews, so much so, in fact, that anti-Semitic outbursts had erupted in a number of theaters. The anti-Semitic films of 1940 and 1941, though few in number, were enormously portentous, presaging the murder of European Jewry and encouraging viewers to acquiesce, if not cooperate, in the Jews' destruction.

Given a lavish spread in the 1937 *Berliner Illustrirte Zeitung,* "Germany's number one filmmaker," Leni Riefenstahl (1902–2003), was photographed at home in Munich discussing film with family members and her guests, Hitler and Goebbels. Photographs like these and other films of her 1939 visit to Poland, where she witnessed the Wehrmacht's war crimes, belie Riefenstahl's later claims to innocence of the regime's aims. In April 1935, *Film-Kurier* reported on a lecture she gave at the Lessing-Hochschule (Lessing Institute [of Adult Education]) in Berlin on her most famous film, *Triumph of the Will,* which she described as a "work of art" in which "Führer and the *Volk* represent the dramatic core of the film." The gala opening of *Triumph of the Will* at the UFA Film Palace in Berlin was a major occasion in which the elite of the Third Reich, including Hitler, joined Riefenstahl for the premiere. UFA (*Universum Film AG),* was founded in 1917 and remained the major German film studio under the Nazis; it also owned a series of cinemas throughout Germany. Similarly, *Olympia* was the highpoint of Riefenstahl's marriage of documentary film and mythology, as the contemporary review by film writer and critic Frank Maraun proposes.

Manfred Georg (1893–1965), a distinguished émigré journalist and editor of the *Aufbau* (*Rebuilding*), a German-language anti-Nazi newspaper in New York, grappled with the question of whether laughter was appropriate when it came to Hitler in his review of Charlie Chaplin's extraordinary 1940 film *The Great Dictator*—and answered in the affirmative. Oddly, George believed Chaplin to be Jewish, a common error that Nazi anti-Semites were happy to echo in Julius Streicher's notoriously anti-Semitic weekly tabloid *Der Stürmer,* which intentionally repeated the misidentification.

Nor were German refugees in the United States entirely protected from the anti-Semitism and xenophobia they had left behind. As the Hollywood Reports column in the *Aufbau* commented, in response to a frequent complaint that Hollywood was being taken over by German-Jewish refugees, only nineteen members of the Screen Actors Guild had fled Europe, and the Nazis were in fact the source for the widely believed rumor that there was "a flood of refugee actors inundating the Hollywood scene."

260

JOSEPH GOEBBELS

Speech at the Kaiserhof

Delivered on 28 March 1933 at the Berlin Imperial Court in the Hotel Kaiserhof. First published in Gerd Albrecht, ed., *Nationalsozialistische Filmpolitik: Eine soziologische Untersuchung über die Spielfilme des Dritten Reichs* (Stuttgart: Ferdinand Enke Verlag, 1969), 26–31. Published in English in David Welch, *The Third Reich: Politics and Propaganda* (London: Routledge, 1993), 149–54.

I am grateful for this opportunity to discuss the state of film in Germany and the probable tasks of the German film industry in the future. I speak as someone who has never lost contact with film in Germany: in fact, I am a passionate devotee of the cinematographic arts. For many years I have seen what great heights the German film can attain as a result of the power and ingenuity of the German mind.

We must rid ourselves of the idea that the present crisis is a material one: it is more a spiritual crisis, and it will go on until we are courageous enough to radically reform German films. For the past two weeks, I have been having discussions with representatives from every branch of the German film industry with very amusing results. These film gentlemen have the same picture of National Socialism as that given in the hostile press. These people have no real idea of the National Socialist movement and its supporters, not even in their own minds.

In every discussion, fears of an uncertain future were expressed again and again. They thought that the future for film production was uncertain. In fact, the exact opposite should be the case. At the time of Brüning and Müller, producers had every reason to feel insecure, since the concept of what was modern changed every four weeks or so.

But now we have arrived. Even the skeptical will be convinced that we are going to remain in power for at least four years. That which is here remains—we shall not leave!

With this fact as a basis, the film industry has every reason to feel secure. But at the same time, you can be sure that the National Socialist movement will assume an active role in the economy and in general cultural affairs, and, therefore, in the film industry as well. With the aid of a few examples, I want to illustrate what in films is aesthetically good and what is dangerous. A few films have made a lasting impression on me.

First of all, *Battleship Potemkin:* this is a marvelous film without equal in the cinema. The reason for this is its power of conviction. Anyone who had no firm political conviction could become a Bolshevik as a result of this film. This shows very clearly that a work of art can be tendentious, and even the worst kind of ideas can be propagated, if this is being done by an outstanding work of art.

Then comes *Anna Karenina.* Greta Garbo has proven that there is such a thing as cinematic art. This film is not substitute theater, but art in its own right as a film.

The Nibelungen is a film that is not far removed from our own epoch; it is so modern, so close to our own age, and so topical that even the old fighters of the National Socialist movement were deeply moved by it. It is not the themes themselves that are important. Themes from Greek mythology can have just as modern an effect as themes taken from the present day. The important thing is the way in which these themes are treated.

With the advent of the new era in Germany, certain attempts were made to produce so-called National Socialist films, but they were so out of touch with the spirit of the time that one shuddered on seeing them. This kind of National Socialism is simply a veneer. The new movement does not exhaust itself with marching around parade grounds and blowing trumpets.

Finally, there is a film that could even convert a National Socialist, *The Rebel.* This example illustrates that it is not only a film's convictions that make it good, but also the abilities of the people making it.

The ability to make a film is not the only important thing. The inner greatness of the ideas must coincide with external means. When this happens, German films can become a force in the world, with limitless opportunities for development. Vague, formless films are not capable of making this kind of impact on the world. The more closely a film reflects national contours, the greater are its chances of conquering the world.

If the film industry starts to exercise a dangerous influence, then it is the duty of the State to step in and exert control.

Again and again I hear the complaint that we have no subject matter. This is simply not true! What is lacking is the courage to come to grips with this subject matter. The film-producer has forgotten that he should be a pioneer of his age. Films should not take such a superior view of the experiences of the common German people at the present time. If films do not treat popular themes, then they will no longer be able to fill the cinemas. It is possible to say that the people are better than the film directors. Public taste should not be underestimated, and if it is in need of improvement, then we young people in the new movement are not too old to set about a regeneration of public taste and gradually improve it, instead of lowering it by making bad films for materialistic reasons.

The crisis in Germany has left the film industry completely unaffected: while the German nation, full of worries and desires, was going through the greatest period of suffering in history, the gentlemen of the film industry were completely ignoring the whole affair. They did not come to grips with the interesting aspects of life but remained shallow and vague.

Whoever understands our present age is aware of what dramatic situations are at the disposal of films. They occur every night, outside on our streets. German films are estranged from reality, without any contact with the actual situations of everyday life. It is indeed appalling that all the creative work in films was done in the pre-war era. Time and again the argument is heard that the kind of films that we demand would not fill the cinemas. I was told the same thing in 1926 when I first began discussing this. What is needed is imagination to bring to life the inner meaning and form of a new world. Many filmmakers still regard the seizure of power on the thirtieth as a phenomenon to which the only possible reaction is a shake of the head.

One cannot understand the spirit of the new age by means of a sudden reversal of one's own position. Only the man who lives in the mainstream of his age can mold it; the man who lives on the sidelines can never do this. So this crisis is also a personal one.

Many people today must understand, then, that if the flag falls, then the bearer must fall with it. Anyone who has not understood the age properly has neither a political nor a cultural nor a moral right to hoist another flag. The general mood in films is characterized by a lack of personal conviction and courage. "Scold me, but don't try to change me," is what the film people say, and they are just content with hoisting a new flag as similar to the old one as can be. That intellectual liberalism, which actually resulted in intellectual anarchy, is dead and buried. The objection that all art is without bias is stupid, naïve, and illogical.

Where does this absolute objectivity exist, then? The real danger lies in a complete lack of bias, and we must examine more closely those who support this idea. In reality, they want to prevent the root-and-branch reformation of the German people. But this reformation represents the common denominator of all public life.

Indeed, art is only possible if it has its roots firmly embedded in the National Socialist soil. I must strongly warn films against taking such a low view of the German people as the other branches of the arts unfortunately did before the advent of film.

We have no intention at all of allowing those ideas, which are being destroyed lock, stock, and barrel in the new Germany, to reappear in films, whether in a camouflaged or an open form. Of course, this represents interference in the production of films.

The new age does not want to inhibit the art of films; it wishes, rather, to take measures to encourage it. This does not necessarily mean just financial encouragement. The German government is also capable of promoting ideas, and I believe that soon it will occupy such a distinguished position in this respect that it will be regarded as the highest of honors to be honored by the government. The artists and producers must draw their own conclusions from this situation. They must profess their desire to create anew; the courageous approach of the new age is a precondition for this. There must not be only new ideas; new people must also emerge.

The creative artist must lead the way with a profession of faith in the new age. There is no more wonderful feeling than to be completely involved in one's age, and to be able to say for one's own modest part, "We were there!"

In any case, public taste is not as it is conceived in the mind of a Jewish director. It is impossible to gain an idea of the German people while living in a vacuum. One must take an honest look at the German people, and for this, one must have one's own roots firmly embedded in German soil. One must be a child of this nation.

It is said that the film industry lacks money! When I see some films and hear how much they have cost, I would like to say to the producer: "Get the money back that you paid out on your training!" If a government is, in its heart of hearts, kindly disposed towards the film industry, then people should be grateful to this government since it is not our intention to put the film industry in a strait jacket. We reject authoritarian dogmatism, but we do require that people should be ready to work in close contact with the new ideas and aspirations. Art is worth nothing without this direction of will or this partisan intent.

At the same time, we do not want to suppress the creation of a daily ration of small amusements designed to combat the boredom and troubles of daily life. We do not want to concentrate the attention the whole time on political attitudes. Our temperament is itself too gay and artistic for this. Art is free and should remain so, but, of course, it must adapt itself to certain norms. In any country other than Germany it would be superfluous to have to emphasize this. But in the last few years every mode of normal political thinking has been destroyed.

From the point where censorship must intervene, right up to the film, which is a model for all artistic creation, there is an ample amount of scope for all kinds of artistic talent to roam freely.

Below this point, no allowance can be made. It is here that dangerous experiments begin, which all too often can only be treated as the excesses of a sick brain. Our film producers will have to get used to the fact that gradually, new standard bearers will arrive on the scene.

If the government picks out from the production of a whole year one film, which is in complete accordance with its aims, wishes, and tasks, then the whole film industry will consequently be given a push forward which it would not have been possible to achieve by means of purely financial encouragement.

We have no intention of hobbling the film industry, or of allowing a state of insecurity to develop. In this time of great changes, films must draw closer to the genuine experiences of the people. Also, we do not want to hinder private enterprise; on the contrary, it will receive great encouragement from the national movements as a result of the firm foundation that these events have created for a new Germany.

It is not the intention of the government to interfere in the affairs of the professional organizations. These organizations will, in fact, be given more rights. The government wants to proceed in full cooperation with the creative film world and to tread a common path with it. For this, it is not necessary for the artist to be tied to the party. But he must clearly acknowledge the new basis of society, raise himself fully to the general spiritual level of the nation, and acknowledge the demands of its views on life.

You must not believe that we feel ourselves compelled to make life difficult for you. The young men who are now in the government feel very sympathetic to the problems of the German film artist. I myself have watched films on many evenings recently with the Reich

Chancellor and have found relaxation after the trying battles of the day. Believe me that we are grateful to you for this.

What we want is that you should again take pleasure in your work. It must be a great feeling for the creative artist to feel totally involved in his age and to be able to say that he has also played a modest part in events. I believe that with this new sense of conviction in films a new moral ethos will arise.

I ask for trustworthy cooperation, so that it will be possible to say of German films, as in other fields, Germany will lead the world.

261

Reich Cinema Law

Announced on 16 February 1934. First published in *Reichsgesetzblatt* (Berlin: Reichsverlagsamt, 1934), 1:95.

Preliminary Examination

ARTICLE 1: SUBMISSION FOR EVALUATION

Feature films produced in Germany must be submitted in draft form to the Reich Film Councilor for evaluation. According to the terms of this law, feature films are defined as films which present a continuous, fictional action, for the sake of which the films were made.

ARTICLE 2: REICH FILM COUNCILOR

The functions of the Reich Film Councilor are as follows:

1. to assist the film industry in all dramaturgical questions;
2. to advise on the production of films in draft form and to make recommendations for the adaptation of materials;
3. to provide a preliminary evaluation of film material of manuscripts and film scripts submitted to him by the industry in the effort to determine whether the filming of these subjects is in accordance with the provisions of this law;
4. to advise film makers whose work has been rejected on the rewriting of the material;
5. to circumvent, in a timely fashion, any treatment of themes contrary to the spirit of the times.

The Reich Film Councilor will maintain a register of all film titles submitted to him for review.

ARTICLE 3: FILM CENSORSHIP OFFICE

The Reich Film Councilor will keep the film Censorship Office informed of all the draft films and film scripts he has approved.

The Examination of Films

ARTICLE 4: PERMISSION BY CENSORSHIP OFFICE

Films may only be shown publicly, or circulated for the purposes of public showing, if they have been licensed by the official Censorship Office. Showings in clubs, associations and other closed venues are treated as public showings. No permission is required for the public showing of films for artistic or educational purposes in recognized public, educational or research institutes. Films consisting exclusively of written text, as well as foreign-language translations (versions) of films produced domestically are also subject to the provisions of this law.

ARTICLE 5: FORBIDDEN FILMS

For films that have been rejected, a petition may be submitted for a license to show them abroad. Exceptions to this are films that have been rejected on the ground that they endanger the vital interests of the state or public order and security, or because they are offensive to National Socialist, religious, moral or artistic sentiments, or because they jeopardize Germany's reputation or its relations with foreign countries.

ARTICLE 6: APPLICATION FOR LICENSING

License for a film is issued by application only. In the case of domestic feature films, the Censorship Office must deny the application if the evaluation pursuant to Paragraph 1, Section 1 is not included in the application.

ARTICLE 7: REJECTION OF LICENSING

The license will be denied if the examination reveals that showing the film is liable to endanger the interests of the state or public order or security, or to offend National Socialist, religious, moral or artistic sentiments, or to have a brutalizing or immoral effect, or to jeopardize Germany's reputation or its relations with foreign countries.

A film is regarded as having jeopardized Germany's reputation if it has been shown abroad with an anti-German bias; the Censorship Office may, in this case, make the granting of a license contingent upon an examination of the film in the form in which it was shown in the country of origin.

ARTICLE 8: SCOPE OF EXAMINATION

The examination of a film by the Censorship Office must also determine whether the film is valuable from a political, artistic, education or cultural point of view and, in the case of feature films, whether it is a film of any particular worth.

Upon application, the Censorship Office is also charged with determining whether the film is suitable for use as an instructional film for teaching purposes.

ARTICLE 9: PARTIAL GROUNDS FOR DENIAL

Films that have been denied application for license based on only a portion of the material submitted may be licensed if the banned sections are edited out and turned over to the Censorship Office, together with the assurance that the banned sections will not be circulated. The license can be denied if the banned sections represent the major part of the film's content.

ARTICLE 10: RESTRICTED SHOWINGS

Films that have been denied license for unrestricted showings pursuant to Paragraph 7 may be granted license for viewings by specific groups or with particular restrictions placed on the showing. The restricted nature of the performances must, however, be guaranteed in both instances.

Paragraph 1 is not applicable to films that have been denied license based on the endangerment of vital interests of the state or public security or because they offend National Socialist or religious sentiment.

ARTICLE 11: YOUTH BAN

Films that are not licensed for viewing for audiences of children or youth under the age of 18 years may not be shown in front of these persons. The Censorship Office decides ex officio on the granting of all licenses; if this is contingent upon the editing out of certain sections, then the permission of the applicant is required. [. . .]

Provisional and Penal Regulations

[. . .]

ARTICLE 25: DETERMINING PENALTIES

The penalty of up to one year's imprisonment and a fine, or one of these two penalties shall be imposed upon:

1. whoever willingly shows or circulates, in contravention of these regulations, films or parts of films which have not been licensed by the competent authorities, or the showing of which has been suspended, or the license of which has been revoked;
2. whoever willingly shows films to children or young people that are not licensed for showing to children or young people (11), or whoever willingly allows children or young people to see a preview of such films;
3. whoever willingly shows films that are licensed for showing to special groups of persons, or which are licensed with other conditions, disregarding these particular regulations;
4. whoever willingly allows children under the age of six years to attend cinema performances, without particular provision being made for this by the Reich Minister for Popular Enlightenment and Propaganda;
5. whoever willingly uses or circulates for the purpose of public use an advertisement that has not been licensed;
6. whoever willingly announces a film or the appropriate advertisement under a title other than that licensed by the Censorship Office;
7. whoever willingly submits to the Censorship Office a film, the license for which has already been refused or revoked, and knowingly suppresses this fact (Article 15). If the offender acts negligently, then a fine is imposed.

ARTICLE 26: LICENSE CARD AND FORBIDDEN ADVERTISEMENTS

A fine of up to RM 150 is imposed on:

1. whoever does not present his license card on demand to the official in charge of supervising cinema performances (Article 21, Section 2).
2. whoever displays or distributes an advertisement that has not been given a license stamp (Article 21, Section 2).

ARTICLE 27: FORBIDDEN VISITS TO FILM SHOWINGS

A fine of up to RM 150 is imposed on:

1. whoever willingly visits film showings that are licensed for performances to special groups of persons without belonging to these groups;
2. whoever takes children or juveniles to cinema performances contrary to the regulations laid down or, if the child or juvenile is in his care or protection, gives permission for or tolerates the forbidden visit to the cinema.

262

HANS TRAUB

The Cinema as Entertainment Site

First published as "Das Kino als Unterhaltungsstätte," in *Der Film als politisches Machtmittel* (Munich: Verlag Münchener Druck- und Verlagshaus, 1933), 5–7.

The effects of journalistic measures are not only psychological in nature. Certainly, their language—both in written and spoken word—images and movements elicit substantial responses from their recipients, but once they have become a permanent fixture of public life, a certain reputation becomes attached to them. And they must live up to it. So a book is going to have a different effect than a pamphlet, just because it is a book and not a pamphlet. They are both printed in the same typeface. They may not necessarily differ substantially in scope. A speech leaves a different impression than a lecture, and yet both of them employ the spoken word. Let us ask what the reputation of film is, what kinds of demands are placed on it: without a doubt, it should satisfy the need for entertainment, amusement, killing time. This, of course, is not applicable to every type of film, but it is for the movies. Film and the movies are not the same thing.

Not unlike movable type, moving-picture technology can be used for a variety of purposes. And each of these technologies leaves its own defining characteristic mark. But what do the book and the newspaper have in common? Who would buy a newspaper with the price tag of a book attached? And yet there are countless books lesser in scope and in value than the newspaper. So it's not just the form of language (in this case, the printed word) or the content itself that explains the impact, but rather, to at least the same degree, the value attached to the genres "book" and "newspaper" within the community. So it's not so much film itself that we are talking about; it is the moving picture as shown in the movie theater.

In 1932, there were an average of 9,000 movie showings, in contrast to 250 theatrical performances. But it would be premature to jump to conclusions and fault the theaters here. These statistics do not by any means present the theater as unpopular or as something alien to the *Volk* or as a luxury no one can afford. Far more, this is evidence of the influence of the major linguistic institutions of the nation, independent of what is produced and presented [on stage]. The task of the theater is not to entertain but rather to edify. Healthy instincts have always made distinctions between the theater and the operetta. Our task is to follow these instincts. The theater has again become a genuine artistic institution—not in the sense of pragmatic moral didactics, but rather in the sense of profound inner edification and amusement that can be satisfied only by truly artistic production and the creativity that is truly bound to the *Volk*. Certainly, everyone in the population can and should have access to the theater, but not everyone will visit the theater all the time, on a daily or weekly basis. Theater should remain a highlight in people's lives. And these types of highlights require leisure and internal preparation.

So the greater portion of the populace will always be drawn toward entertainment. And with its easier accessibility and flexibility in scheduling, cinema is much better suited to this end. And for that reason alone, the cinema will provide primarily entertainment. But this should not be alien to the *Volk;* rather it should, by all means, depict ideal images of people engaged in suspenseful action not necessarily possible in real life. Film, especially in its beginnings when it was still categorized more in the professional category of the variety show, was often disparagingly compared to the annual country fair. In fact, this need not be seen as derogatory because there was a time when the country fair was where the people went for entertainment, for amusement, to have fun, to learn, be educated, and in isolated instances, even for inner edification. In the old days, the country fair was the place where the visible ties within the community were put on display. So when the movies are compared to the fair, this should be seen as a comment on the significance of the movies in terms of satisfying entertainment needs. It is not "liberalistic" to praise the movies as a site for entertainment. What was liberalistic was to burden this site of entertainment with deceptive images of social conditions and relationships, to depict lifestyles that were in fact deadly, to further undermine the sense of joy and faith in one's own existence rather than provide the viewer with physical and psychological "relaxation."

There is a negative connotation to the term *entertainment*. Entertainment and the struggle for life are mutually contradictory. But today especially it behooves us to put in a good word on behalf of entertainment. It implies refreshment, amusement, rest, and relaxation in the pauses between battles. The cinema first became popular in the big cities. The daily struggle for existence was not fought most fiercely in the big cities—who amongst the city dwellers had so much as an inkling of the trials and tribulations of peasants struggling to guarantee good crops and plentiful harvest?—but it was here that this struggle took its most drastic twists and turns and surprising maneuvers. The desire to forget one's own existence, a general sense of exhaustion, and a certain indifference toward all the urges of will drove the people in the big cities to the movies. There are a variety of reasons for this; this has been documented by scholars interpreting the matter from the perspective of social ethics and to that of psychology. At any rate, this is de facto the situation we face today. We should be happy about that, for what could be more satisfying than the opportunity to present the people with pleasure and entertainment? We need only muster the courage to take a serious and healthy approach even to the unheroic.

Humor, the gay art of making people laugh even in sorrow and of moving them deeply in laughter—that would indeed be an exquisite aim in life. Not to draw on the American grotesque, but rather on the likes of Pat and Patachon [the Danish silent film stars Pat and Patachon—original Fy og Bi] or on the fine art of the old Casper theater [the *Kasperltheater*, the German Punch and Judy puppet show], taking genuine pleasure in the triumph of playful trickery, in the battle between cleverness and stupidity, in the infallibility of "cosmic coincidence." What has happened to those comic acts that go beyond life's hardships to elicit the whole spectrum of human joy from jubilation to a wistful smile? The 1933 film *Waltz War* [*Walzerkrieg*], for example, gives us a taste of its power for the future. Photography and reality have little in common. The reality we seek to capture on film is indeed real, regardless of how much reality protests against it. So let us allow the cinema to mirror these fictional realities in *fata morgana* of humanity's most secret desires. So let us then see entertainment in the sense of light fiction designed to entertain: "Stories that one would not likely read more than once but would take great pleasure in reading the first time" (Meyer). The movies are made to satisfy all too human needs.

263

CARL NEUMANN, CURT BELLING, AND HANS WALTHER BETZ

Portrait of the Unmasked Mr. Kohn

First published as "Das Bildnis des demaskierten Herrn Kohn," in *Film-"Kunst," Film-Kohn, Film-Korruption: Ein Streifzug durch vier Filmjahrzehnte* (Berlin: Verlag Hermann Scherping, 1937), 9–10.

The Man with the Cigar

This is his trademark: that malicious sneer, with a burning cigar dangling from between his bulging lips. With that blunt glimmering ember of a black stub poking out at the world and

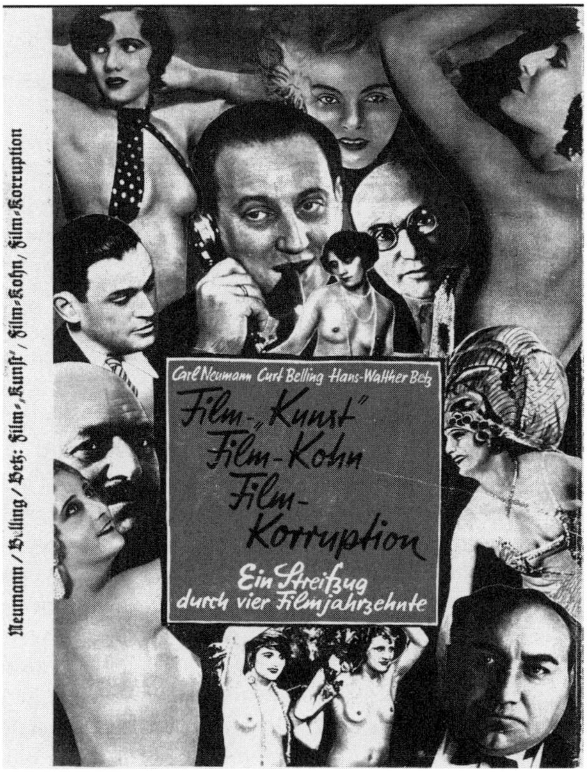

FIGURE 24. The cover of *Film "Art," Film Cohen, Film Corruption,* a 1937 film history book that attacks Jews for corrupting the German film industry. Carl Neumann, *Film-"Kunst," Film-Kohn, Film-Korruption: Ein Streifzug durch vier Filmjahrzehnte* (Berlin: Verlag Hermann Scherping, 1937).

the mouth to go with it, he scoffs at the world in a silent but unmistakable gesture that is as arrogant as it is derisive and provocative: here I am!

There's a gleam in his eyes and restlessness in their piercing gaze. They don't like the light. They don't give off a spark of spirit; if anything, rather, the mark of some wretched petty trader. Not a glimmer of soul shines forth; if anything, the lifelessness of a pathetic, nasty little peddler type. Not a thought springs from his head; if anything, a hankering for haggling and horse-trading and the fervent desire to have pulled off yet another con job on someone. These eyes don't have a clear or composed word to say to anyone. All they are good for is trying to assess how much money someone has or how much he is worth and how wily that person is in watching his wallet. The only thing they can appreciate about a woman is how she is built and how much she might churn out if she has any marketable skills. The hat casually tipped back on his head underscores the slipshod nonchalance that finds tangible expression in the following practices: unscrupulously raking in the dough, making his partners pay through the nose, swindling business associates, exploiting every loop in the law to call people's bluff, to lie, to slander, and to bribe their way into a life in the lap of luxury—to stuff their bellies full, throwing huge sums of money around without a red cent of regard for its value. There's a simple enough explanation for it: anyone who never had to work for his money but swindled himself into an ill-gotten mint, whoever has made his money by hook or by crook, and not by hard work, but has nevertheless established for himself some relationship to the value of money—that person is likely to throw his money around. Money can easily destroy people whose character is not the strongest; it can turn tenuous loyalty to betrayal. You can open many doors with money; you can create the appearance of greatness and afford yourself a lot of leeway. For money necessarily translates into power.

His hands are stuck in his pants pockets. One hand never knew what the other was up to. While one was paying Paul, the other was robbing Peter. He was up to his elbows in every shady deal he could get his hands on. These hands have wrung the neck of many an unsuspecting victim without showing any sign of mercy. These hands have demonstrated excessive dexterity in all manner of fraudulence and card sharking. And this is why we see the man with the cigar and the piercing gaze, with his hat hanging halfway down his neck, his hands in his pockets, standing in his secondhand store, in his pawnshop, his bank offices, the stock market, showing off his designer clothing collection, at the racetrack, in the executive offices of editors, of publishers, of musical and film directors. He is everywhere: he is a talent promoter in the fashion industry, in publishing, and in film. In the fashion industry, it was the attractive and admiring pinup girls; in the publishing industry, accommodating and admiring members of parliament; in the film industry, actresses who—though they may have been lacking artistic skills—were nevertheless talented and admiring—or others, who, regardless of whether they were justified in their attempts, wanted to become actresses. This man was a gambler who placed his bet by laying other people's existence on the line. He is the robber baron of modernity, the pathfinder for high finance; he is the fraudster *par excellence,* the grotesque opposite of a Count Cagliostro, of a John Alexander Dowie, of a king of Corsica, a Theodor Neuhof, or a John Law. These men were intelligent pirates but made a career of robbing people of their lives and livelihood for the sake of satisfying the most deplorable of passions, defrauding people for the basest of reasons—a wimp and a welterweight. He was just a bum characterized by a cowardly unscrupulousness, availing himself of the tricks any low-level clerk might have ready at hand but that only he has the audacity to use. He was the shabbiest kind of Apache, one who remained unscrupulous only as long as no one dared to take him seriously and threaten to take him out. Once he was finally found out, he managed to save his skin by fleeing [the country], only to stand there howling from a safe distance. A bandit completely lacking in imagination, a charlatan of paltriest proportions—the only thing that is big about him is his depravity and fraudulence—he has always been at harmony with himself and has thus always lived up to the laws of his own natural characteristics.

What a feeling it must be for him, living now in luxury villas, surrounded by innumerable servants and girlfriends, frequenting bars and casinos, where he is serviced and fawned over by jackals in tuxedos and tailcoats and half-naked hyenas in evening gowns. Oh, but the way he savored the bittersweet irony of being king of the late-night parties where the champagne flows after having been dirt poor and destitute without a penny in his pockets when he first made the trip to Germany from Galicia on the bed of a freight car! What utter grandeur ensues when the corrupter begins carousing with the corrupted, only to see the way they licked the corrupter's boots and danced around them and around him—the one who was just one decisive degree more brazen, more audacious, more irresponsible than he!

We need to deal with this man. With him and others like him who sat there in the film industry, acting as impostors and villains to commit every imaginable crime against humanity, against probity, against economic and intellectual property. The history of the first four decades of film in Germany is, for the most part and decisively so, the history of their "art"; it is the history, in every shade and nuance, of Little Mr. Cohen's corruption and every trick he has up his sleeve. It is the history of tyranny and of the demise of infinite inferiority.

Once the man with the cigar had exploited every con game in the book—economic and psychological—once he had laid the entire landscape to waste and sowed the seeds of his desolating poison, he left others to clean up the field of devastation in his wake. He moved on, often in fear of the law of retribution, to other pastures that he destroyed in similar fashion. He moved to Prague, to Warsaw, to Vienna, Paris, London, even to Hollywood, not as a thief on the run but in the celebrated greatness of one scoffing at the curses and imprecations of all the people he has deceived and destroyed.

Now, as his gruesome and hellacious Shrovetide nights draw to a close, we would like to rip the mask from his face—to expose to the public in this country and the rest of the world the magnitude of his crimes and the inglorious role he has played, and to demonstrate the full extent to which this personification of evil has dominated the face of the German film industry since at least 1918.

264

CURT BELLING

Preparatory Work of the Party until the Takeover of Power

First published in *Der Film* in *Staat und Partei* (Berlin: Verlag "Der Film," 1936), 17–19.

Moviegoers who were not too nauseated by the poisonous alien spirit in film have noticed the deterioration of the aesthetic standards in film to the level of meaningless nothingness. Film had nothing left to offer genuine Germans who, after a long day of work, just wanted some wholesome, culturally sound entertainment. The film industry was dominated by a spirit of rampant commercialism. Film was reduced to a means of generating profit, and it was obviously irrelevant whether or not the proprietors of small movie houses and their employees, whether the producers, the minor actors, the extras, or the economically weak in general, were trampled to the ground in the process.

National Socialism was familiar with and recognized the flaws and fundamental ills plaguing this branch of artistry—which is ultimately what the film industry is—which could only lead to its horrific end if it was not rescued just in the nick of time; [National Socialism] recognized that the systematic exploitation of the Jewish spirit had to be stopped in its tracks if there was to be any hope for sustaining the life of film or for creating a genuinely German film industry.

German national comrades of National Socialist persuasion were dead set against the Jewish-infested film industry and protested staunchly and unanimously against the defamation of German soldiers in the films that were shown on screens in German movie theaters.

The Case of *All Quiet on the Western Front*

Early in December 1930, National Socialists took their first unified stand against a cinematic hatchet job. In America, the Jew Carl Laemmle had produced the war film *All Quiet on the Western Front,* based on the novel of the same name by the nauseatingly pacifistic "German" author [Erich Maria] Remarque, and brought the film to Germany. The film was submitted to the Film Censorship Bureau in Berlin in November 1930. Expert reviewers from the Reich Ministry of the Army [Reichswehrministerium] clearly expressed their reservations concerning this mendacious piece of work and recommended that it not be shown because it was an affront to every German citizen.

Nevertheless, the film was released for public viewing, because the Cinema Law did not provide any basis for banning it for its political content. The Jewish directors of the so-called German Universal [Studios] breathed a sigh of relief—the objections on the part of the army and warnings from people who thought like Germans and felt like Germans were to no avail. So this scandalous film, *All Quiet on the Western Front,* was able to make its debut in the former Mozart Hall in Berlin.

What no one anticipated, however, was the way the public would respond. The showing became a historical event because the German *Volk* made clear that it would no longer stand for having the corrosive spirit of foreign-born Jewish profiteers forced down their throats. The sold-out crowd in the theater remained calm until German soldiers in the trenches were portrayed as whimpering cowards—then a hurricane-force hail of indignation broke out. The outraged audience—and the man who won the battle for Berlin, *Gauleiter* Dr. Joseph Goebbels, was amongst them—demanded that this travesty be called to a halt and that the cameras be stopped. Police were called in to clear out the theater.

Despite the events that demonstrated the opinions of the German *Volk* clearly enough, no one seemed too concerned about what the German people wanted, not even when the press in the Reich capital praised this film as an "American masterpiece"—and we certainly need not elaborate further on the makeup of the press in those days. The film remained on the bill. The only organization that took a strong stance against the film in the press at the time and rattled the consciousness of the public was Berlin's *Angriff* [*Attack*, Goebbels's newspaper].

The propaganda against this film and the aversion on the part of anyone with a Germanic mind to the shameless insults against German soldiers drove those members of Berlin's population who remained untainted by the Jewish virus to march to the Nollendofplatz, and Berlin's chief of police should not have been surprised when, the next day, a huge crowd of some forty thousand National Socialist Berliners converged before the Mozartsaal for a highly impassioned rally. The federal government of the republic at the time had ordered police to break up the protests with truncheons and clubs. But some members of the police force could not quite countenance enforcing an order of this nature because eyewitness reports say that a whole series of officers stood idly by and waited for the event to come to an end.

Despite all the hue and cry of the Marxist and Jewish press, despite the orders given by the liberal administration, and despite all the whining from Jewish film directors, the rally succeeded in getting the film banned.

This people's referendum, of course, did not sit well with the gentlemen of Universal and their lust for profits: they looked for ways to influence the censorship board. The Austrian Jew Sam Spiegel was contracted expressly for the purpose of conducting negotiations about the film with the proper government offices. He quickly figured out how to put just the right Jewish "twist" on it to find a loophole for continuing to poison the *Volk* with this masterful travesty. He was able to exploit his relationship with then Reich Chancellor [Wilhelm] Marx to receive a permit to show the film to the Marxist unions in private showings—which would nevertheless take place in public theaters and not in specially designated viewing rooms. As if this fact alone were not enough, the theaters—most of them in Jewish hands or managed by Jews—were not too particular about making the distinction between members of the unions and the general public. No one had any problem procuring a ticket, regardless of whether they were union members or not, and, unfortunately—due to all the hullabaloo surrounding this film—many of our national comrades took advantage of that. The Jewish spirit once again made its mark!

265

CURT BELLING

The Beginning of National Socialist Film

First published as "Der Anfang des nationalsozialistischen Films," in *Der Film* in *Staat und Partei* (Berlin: Verlag "Der Film," 1936), 18, 19.

National Socialists were well aware of the power of film, but the party did not have a lot of money and had to use what it had wisely. There was a film department within the propaganda office, but it was more or less condemned to doing nothing. When the Reich director of propaganda appointed Arnold Raether to be director of the Party Film Agency in 1930, the agency stood charged with two important tasks. Film was to be used as an instrument of propaganda and enlightenment in the party struggle. In addition, though, the path was to be paved for the seamless, completely unhindered takeover of the Germany film industry so that it could be transferred to National Socialist hands as soon as the seizure of power was complete. In the beginning, the film department of the party had to restrict itself to producing propaganda films for the National Socialist worldview. A huge effort was made to borrow enough money to produce the first election campaign films. Building the party film organization from less than scratch was not an easy task. Everything that was accomplished in this regard happened without a cent, not the slightest bit of aid, from outside sources. The only thing that allowed for the creation of this massive organization as it exists today was the selfless diligence and willingness to sacrifice on the part of all the National Socialist fighters and workers who made it happen.

The first fruits of the party propaganda apparatus became evident during the 1932 election campaign, when the subdivision of the cultural political agency of the NSDAP [. . .] was in a position to print 182 copies [of a film] for the election campaign and for election propaganda and was able to use motion-picture footage to reach even our national comrades living in outlying areas with the speeches of the Führer, Dr. Goebbels, Göring, and other National Socialist pioneers. The real success was that the film agency was thus able to continue expanding its scope, and before long, it was no longer possible to manage all of the propaganda film activities from one central office in Berlin.

266

FRITZ HIPPLER

The Formative Power of Film

First published as "Die formende Kraft des Films," in *Betrachtungen zum Filmschaffen* (Berlin: Max Hesses Verlag, 1942), 102–7.

In addition to establishing a personal relationship between the viewer and the leading actor in the course of the action, the film at the same time generates the desire to be just like him. The way [the actor] clears his throat or spits phlegm, the way he dresses, the way he behaves, whether he drinks and what he drinks, whether he smokes and what he smokes, whether he is a philistine or a playboy—all these things not only have an impact in the film itself, they influence the viewer in real life. An action-packed movie of triumph leaves the audience changed in a different way than a tragedy or comedy. After seeing a Hans Albers, even a hairdresser's assistant suddenly becomes a Hans Albers; one should not dare to so much as approach him.[1]

Similarly, there can be no denying that the epitome for the standard of beauty in women that is portrayed in film has an influence on the masses. For this reason, casting decisions in film cannot be subjected to enough scrutiny. It is not just that this or that woman should be particularly well suited to this film or that. No, any woman who has been selected on the basis of her outward appearance as well as her inner qualities and attributes can have—with repeated successful performances in various films—a subliminal but emphatic positive influence on the general standards for taste and the epitome of beauty for a great number of men and can thus make a valuable contribution not only in terms of her "political impact on the populace" but also in terms of a qualitative elevation of standards.

And this is no different when it comes to representing children on screen. Under no circumstances whatsoever is it sufficient for the audience to accept a child or children more or less as *quantité négligible* or, at best, to consider them "very nice." No, both casting and role assignments as well as direction can and must also serve to fuel a passion for and desire to have children in the hearts of viewers, even though it's not as though you could win the heart of a hardened misanthropic bachelor who can't stand children this way! But there are a number of psychological and emotional processes that are entirely subject to intense intervention and influence in this regard—for example, a mildly negative or undecided position.

Finally, what about the depiction of the family in film? Is there any example of a family in German film that does not meet the unhappy end of its existence without tensions, jealousies, squabbles, tragedy, murder, inheritance hunting, and the like? Whenever you pose this question to writers and directors, the answer you usually get is that [the film is] this way because if it were done any other way, there would be no dramatic tension—an argument that, as I have often attempted to point out, is not entirely watertight or compelling. Furthermore, it would be entirely conceivable from a purely dramaturgical perspective to deploy the family as a unified organism for the purposes of dramatic contrast. Thinking along these lines need not necessarily imply that there should be absolutely no more representation of familial tension and strife in the movies. In many instances, there is no way to avoid this development of the story line without potential detriment to the essential core of the whole. On the other hand, though, the same considerations as outlined above must be taken into account regarding the formative power of film.

No one would dispute the notion that the ongoing depiction of quarrelsome families in film does not at least have a less than positive effect on the desire to start families—and the opposite can also be said to be true. Or would anyone seriously contend that any film's aesthetic value is contingent upon the depiction of a good old-fashioned family feud? I am familiar, for example, with a number of recent Czechoslovakian films that portray an extremely harmonious family life and are "nevertheless" still considered to be of great aesthetic value; by contrast, many films with decidedly disharmonious marriages are "nevertheless" simply bad and unaesthetic.

One might perhaps object by saying that these observations about types and casting, about women and children, about family, etc. stem from considerations outside the realm of aesthetics. The clear and simple rebuttal is that film has been a folk art since time immemorial and will always remain so. And the masses as well as the heart of the *Volk* are not as easily moved by films with a fundamentally negative outlook as they are by those with a positive one.

There is no doubt that there are an extraordinarily large number of films that demonstrate absolutely negative and morbid elements and yet, from a purely aesthetic perspective, are worthy of recognition as great works of art. But no one would seriously seek to maintain that their greatness is rooted solely in this [negativity]. These films, however, are simply not "pleasurable." There are certainly particular circles in which these films are seen as the ultimate divine revelation. But the vast majority of people—the so-called petty bourgeoisie, office employees, blue-collar workers, and peasants—do not take any pleasure from these types of films. What is more, it is a well-known fact that there are great works of art in film with a positive outlook that have become some of the most successful movies ever.

In recent years, several films have been produced in France that have won both national and international awards, but, based on their pessimistic basic outlook, had to be banned even by the absolutely liberalistic French government when the war broke out, despite the fact that the outlook of these films did not demonstrate any political tendencies whatsoever. Let us note, as an aside, that France lost the war, surely not because of these films. But the fact that they could be produced in such a way and in such large numbers is certainly utterly symptomatic of the general attitude from which they emerged and upon which they had an influence.

One might be inclined to counter the critique of these films with a decidedly morbid, pessimistic, basic outlook by pointing to the fact that there are many world-renowned literary works that would definitely be worthy of providing the foundation for film adaptation but that, even though this may not be their intent or their overall tendency, are in point of fact simply amoral, though not amoral in the sense that fault might be found in their lack of solid bourgeois or strictly religious morals or the absence of a just measure of censure and praise or some visionary guiding light. Very often, however, the lives and destinies, as well as the manifest reactions and actions of the "actors," are not in harmony with that overall sense of order that is fundamental to the spirit of all men and all religions. Of course, this is not an artistic criterion; on the contrary, the purely artistic value of this type of presentation is acknowledged and affirmed independently of these considerations.

But it is the writer's prerogative, for example, to portray the characters he has created as vividly, as interestingly, as intricately or, on the other hand, as innocent and kindly, as childish and as pious as he pleases; or, for example, to present the ideas that enter the mind of his characters in measured doses so that the resulting action that would formally be considered criminal is simply accepted as an inevitable and entirely justified consequence that might even merit approval, without necessarily requiring that the question of crime and punishment even be addressed. This often leaves the impression of particularly harsh realism in the framework of plot development in such a work: the good guy suffers, the bad guy is happy, the crime goes unpunished, etc. But all this ultimately has nothing to do with artistic production; it is merely the object of that production, which only then becomes a glamorous thing of prestige in the literary work itself; otherwise, it would be reduced to yet another component of some hodgepodge of trashy literature. Furthermore, when considering the effect of a literary work on the reader, one must take into account the fact that the reader is left with far greater opportunity to bring his own impressions and personal imaginative craft into the overall aesthetic effect of the work, especially with regard to the characters.

But this is entirely different in the case of film, which will never be able to offer this type of profound, nearly analytical psychological portraiture, or such a compelling imbrication of the internal and external world, without suffocating in dialogue or seeming tortured and unsatisfactory. This is not to diminish its artistic character (just as one cannot fault the fine arts, for example, simply because film is capable only of reproducing fixed events in time with no reference to what came before or after). It is, however, a restriction of its aims since this is where the limits of its representational means lie; on the other hand, these means also extend into areas that the writer cannot reach with the means available to him.

The question of the "happy ending" is to be seen in the same context as outlined above. Much has already been said and written on this subject, and many overzealous critics have taken this as a strong indictment of the artistic nature of film. But this is ridiculous in every regard, although the actual formulation of any given "happy end" could admittedly be an artistic failure. Furthermore, though, the possibilities for drafting content around a "happy end" are much more extensive than is often thought; so, for example, it might consist of a passionate kiss between two lovers or in the death of "Annelie" who is reunited with her husband in death, or the hanging of the Jew in *Jew Süss,* etc.

Film is and remains the most intensely effective, and still to this day, the form of art most produced for the masses. The example it sets and its effect are too readily internalized by millions. Above and beyond the arguments based on artistic considerations as outlined above, it does seem advisable for purely pedagogical and psychological reasons that the film's ending should be constructed such that everyone can wholeheartedly applaud it—for example, by allowing selfless love to prevail and be requited or by punishing crime in the end. Even if the film would not necessarily conform to life's cruel reality, this flaw would be more than compensated for in the resulting life-affirming power the film would convey.

Note

1. Hans Albers (1891–1960) was the most popular male star of Weimar-era cinema. Despite his reluctance to demonstrate public support for the Nazis, he remained the most sought-after leading man until 1945. His career continued to thrive in postwar Germany.—Eds.

267

FILM-KURIER

We Lucky Kids

First published as "Wir Glückskinder," in *Film-Kurier,* 19 September 1936.

Bravo! Bravo! Whatever Americans do, we can do better. Maybe no one wanted to believe that the German language was capable of being a match for American slang when it comes to screwball comedy. *Lucky Kids* [*Glückskinder*] proves this is not the case. Curt Götz has arrived, and already it's curtains for any [George Bernard] Shaw play. Suddenly, the dialogue sparkles and sparks fly in a contemporary comedy. Set in New York, a story about madcap journalists trying to outmaneuver each other—you have to see it with your own eyes to believe it.

Amazing how much meaning can reside in just one "exactly." The philosophy of "as if" has hardly packed more meaning into these two words than the volumes that can be said by the word "exactly" coming from sassy, sensuous lips. For example, a young man tries to justify his scatterbrained behavior by proudly boasting, "I'm a poet." And there's no better response a poet can get than "exactly." There's no need to get defensive about it and, in the effort to circumvent potential misgivings about one's own idealism, emphatically reiterate, for God's sake, one's appreciation for poetry. . . . And then, when the only response you get is an even more emphatic "exactly," wouldn't it bring the strongest man in the world to admit he's met his match? That's what you'll see and hear in *Lucky Kids.*

Lucky Kids is brimming with this kind of high jinks, wordplay, and laughs by the dozen in the dialogue. Native Berliners will be tickled pink by it. Or isn't the description of the last radish slice left on the plate as a "red tail ender" just the thing for the colorful dialect of Berlin? All this humor and nonsense brought to you by three journalists. One of them is an apprentice with ambitions of becoming a poet, who is giving it his best shot as a court reporter when, before you know it, he finds himself married to one of the defendants. The others: two quick-witted reporters who go through thick and thin with the poet. After they're all fired from their jobs, they get together with the young bridal couple to form a foursome and celebrate a wedding, where they do all the cooking and catering themselves, right down to the music and song; and what a job they do . . . making the cake, mixing the dough, spices and all, baking it . . . taking an occasional break in between to kick up their heels on the dance floor . . . everything orchestrated in perfect rhythm, in step with the time. Peter Kreuder wrote the snappy jazz score for the film, and Paul Martin arranged a lively, upbeat version of "Singing before Breakfast" that was every bit as good as the original American Broadway melody.

Suddenly, the men we need to pull something like this off on stage are there. Willy Fritsch, Paul Kemp, Oskar Sima . . . Fritsch as a lovable, nice guy, naïve and tall, a lover of poetry. He doesn't put on too much of an act, keeps himself nicely under wraps, not as in previous films, where far too much revolved around him. Because here [Oskar] Sima and [Paul] Kemp have at least just as much to say—Sima with prolific sarcasm and materialistic candor (!) and Kemp with a disarmingly heartwarming naïveté, which cannot be taken seriously—not even as an insult.

A marvelous trio! Add to the mix Lilian Harvey, whose frailty becomes the object of frivolous mockery in the film, sprightly stepping in time to an upbeat tempo, punctuating the dialogues with a seductive sassiness and a simply enchanting manner of puckering her sweet little lips into a mousy pout, only to break out in song with "I Wish I Were Mickey Mouse!"

There is also a powerful executive publisher in the film who doesn't let himself be browbeaten into submission by empty platitudes but instead exerts his infinite superiority and callousness and passes out the pink slips; Otto Stoeckel plays the part superbly. Paul Bildt, playing a night-court judge, delivers a young couple into marriage more quickly than they expected. One could envision someone other than Erich Kestin doing a better job in the role of the drunken screwball journalist, though. Albert Florath plays a white-haired but childish oil magnate who plays with his electric train set; Kurt Seifert, with his classically Berlin-style wit, deserves special praise for his role as the restaurant proprietor who lands in front of the judge for being all too quick with his hands. Minor roles are played by Fred Goebel, Thomas Cziruchin, Jac Diehl, Arno Ebert, Max Hiller, Fred Koester, Hermann Meyer-Falkow, Carl Merznicht, Paul Rehkopf, Walter Steinweg. Director Paul Martin's skillful hand succeeds in bringing lustrous polish to the many, many punch lines. He has created a comedy that is worth seeing and, above all, hearing more than once. Cameraman Konstantin Irmen-Tschet stood faithfully at his side throughout the production, and Erich Kettelhut's stage-set design accurately replicates the milieu. Excellent film editing by Karl-Otto Bartning. Peter Kreuder's hit song, the fox trot "I Wish I Were a Chicken" [Ich wollt', ich wär' ein Huhn] and the slow fox trot "Miss Nobody" [Fräulein Niemand] are ably rendered in the impeccable sound editing of Fritz Thiery and Dr. Erich Leistner.

Overall, a film that leaves many of its predecessors in the dust, one that elicited a storm of gleeful enthusiasm throughout yesterday's premiere and closed to thunderous applause showered on the leading actors who appeared on the stage. The best comedy in years!

268

FILM-KURIER

The Latest Greta Garbo Triumph

First published as "Der neue Garbo-Triumph," in *Film-Kurier,* 28 March 1935.

Metro-Goldwyn-Mayer's major production of the film *The Painted Veil,* starring Greta Garbo, has already arrived in the Reich. The premiere showing in Berlin is scheduled for 5 April at the Capitol am Zoo [movie theater]. The pinnacle of success achieved by the new group at Metro-Goldwyn-Mayer is reflected in the tremendous rush for advance ticket sales at the Capitol am Zoo.

Munich, where the film had its German premiere, immediately sent a gushing cable: "Garbo premiere smashing success. Audience and press thrilled to the nines. Stop. Sold-out house despite inclement weather, congratulations on this magnificent film—Maly Motta Atlantik Palace Theater Munich."

Hamburg followed suit with the following telegram: "Yesterday's Garbo premiere smashing success. Ticket sales thirty-five percent more than the Christina premiere. Stop. Congratulations on this great film and huge success.—Waterloo Theater."

And the sentiment in these telegrams is underscored by rave reviews in papers throughout the country.

> Greta Garbo, this woman who is always such a lovely sight to behold, gives a no less stunning performance in this new psychologically challenging role than in her previous film *Queen Christina. (Münchner Neueste Nachrichten)*

> This woman [Garbo] is likely to have far greater impact than the queen of Sweden herself. The film's action is so interesting that it would be of value even without Greta Garbo and her screen partner, Herbert Marshall. And yet—what she brings to this film! (*Münchner Zeitung*)

> It wasn't easy for Greta Garbo to sustain the same level of sensational interest generated by the sweeping success of her role in *Queen Christina.* And yet, she's succeeded in so doing—in every way. (*Deutsche Filmzeitung*)

With this kind of reception from the press, it is no wonder, then, that the 28 March issue of *Film-Kurier* reports that "the success of *The Painted Veil* in Munich has even managed to surpass the theater's previous record sales brought in by *Queen Christina.*"

Hamburg is reporting the same results and Dresden as well. The same is true for locations in and around Düsseldorf, where the film has also been shown.

269

FILM-KURIER

This, Too, Is Worldview!

First published as "Auch das ist Weltanschauung!" in *Film-Kurier,* 16 February 1937.

How do you define "worldview"? Easier said than done. In any case, it is "something" that these days, with the best intentions, is increasingly being associated with film. For now, it still remains something that is imposed more by external forces than by an organic internal development. "Worldview" still often appears in film in a sort of claptrap interpretation in the context of a far too narrow and far too superficial political perspective, making its intent noticeable and annoying.

In order to get beyond this claptrap character of cultural demands whose opacity all too easily confounds filmmakers, it would behoove us, instead of speaking in terms of "worldview," to speak more distinctly and to the point in terms of demanding a *healthy modern-day understanding of existence and unadulterated vital consciousness.*

Perhaps this would be more effective in clarifying what is really at stake. By setting such broad aims, it is more likely that films will be permeated by an uncontrived and compelling portrayal of human character and action that is congruent with our times. It is, after all, from this healthy modern-day meaning of existence and unadulterated vital consciousness that great political ideas are ultimately born, the most famous of which even superficial coordination [*Gleichschaltung*] efforts believe they can exhaust in paying ideological tribute to contemporary film. Even in overtly political films, whose necessity in our current international culture war cannot be denied, "platitudes" will not suffice, but rather, here too, the intended effect must emerge as the self-evident organic result of the story line and the actors' roles.

Above all, we demand that events and character roles be developed based on the healthy vital consciousness of our contemporaries, especially for the so-called entertainment films. It will not suffice to tack little "ideological floral" decals on the lapels in retrospect; modern subject matter must be drawn from natural sources.

Let us compare American films and German films with regard to the following theme that is so often a plot element: a rich man falls in love with a pretty little poor girl . . . In German films (Reich German and Austrian), it is not infrequently the case that the poor girl suffers from a nearly debilitating inferiority complex in relation to the rich man. She bats her eyes in deference, flattered that this great man would lower himself to her level, looks up at him in awe; as if that weren't enough, she goes so far as to express her concerns about her paltriness and insignificance. Not so in America! When the big boss stoops to his employee's level, she suddenly considers herself his equal. The girl in American films suffers from no such inferiority complexes; on the contrary, very often she triumphs over the economic powerhouse. In real life, especially today in Germany, where girls from modest and wealthier families alike stand side by side as men's comrades in the professional struggle for existence, the German girl, like her American counterpart, does not harbor these kinds of inferiority complexes with respect to her lover, no matter how much better off he is in terms of social status. It is only in film that we see such stubborn adherence to the remaining traces of these long-since-outdated clichés. Real men are often embarrassed for these girls who are forced to feign this kind of deference in films. Admittedly, some of these films are set in earlier periods when the real-life situation may have been quite different. But when these bygone eras are called back to mind, this can also be done with an ironic grin. But the packaging of these things as past events that are better laughed off or scoffed at is missing. Whereas the bureaucratic types in these nostalgic films are caricatured in all their ossified glory, the deferent gesticulations of these young women are portrayed as though they were entirely contemporary. It is a well-known fact that when talking about German women abroad, many people used to claim that German women were much too inclined to reduce themselves to being mere servants to their husbands. But, in this case, the German woman's knack for economic efficiency has often been completely misunderstood by these superficial foreign observers. But as long as German entertainment movies shown abroad still continue to portray German girls in this demeaning way, the foreign prejudices against the German woman that still persist today will only be fortified.

Another concrete example is worth mentioning in this context: in a recent, overall well-made film that was very close to real life, a young ticket taker at the subway station, who boldly succeeded in challenging all the prejudices of the world of the bourgeoisie, is invited by one of his colleagues to attend a lively gala party with his bride. While he is attending the big ballroom bash, he is suddenly overcome by feelings of inferiority, and, with great apprehension, asks his bride, a member of the upper class by birth, whether she's having a good time, and he is happy when she says yes because, as he adds, everything is so modest and simple, and he says this in such a way as to imply that these subway workers couldn't possibly stage parties that would appeal to a white-collar employee from the upper class.

These and similar scenes are to be found every now and then in entertainment films. Especially in portrayals of everyday life, there is still much improvement to be made. Because here is where the roots of the worldview lie. We must become more honest, healthier, and more natural, and that means more modern, especially with regard to these seemingly minor details. If, then, filmmakers and writers ever hope to quit speculating about just what a "worldview" is and instead would simply set themselves to the task of adequately incorporating the healthy modern-day understanding of existence and unadulterated vital consciousness of today's generation into their character roles and the subject matter of their films, we would make much better progress and, in this manner, the desired worldview would become self-evident.

270

EWALD VON DEMANDOWSKY

Film as I See It

First published as "Film, wie ich ihn sehe," in *Völkischer Beobachter,* 1 February 1939, no. 32, 6.

People have finally begun remembering the German landscape and are now shooting films where they should have long since been filmed in the first place.[1] We've had films set in Hamburg, in the East Prussian countryside, in the Ore Mountains, the Rhine Valley, and in the course of the coming weeks, films are scheduled for release from Central Germany and Thuringia, from the Pfalz region, and from the Baltic Sea coast.

These attempts were worthy of recognition and particularly worthy of praise when they went beyond mere attempts to be particularly compelling. The first film to emerge from the working-class milieu, set on the Reichsautobahn, is soon to be released. There is a film about the German Wehrmacht in the works, and it will address a few very topical and contemporary issues. All too often, the most elegant tuxedos and evening gowns, bars and cocktail parties predominate in film, and all too often, an illusory fantasy world that exists only in the imaginations of foreign filmmakers is presented.

Enough of This Anachronistic Slacking Off

While we're on the subject of the "topical and very contemporary," it is not enough to show a shot with the date 1938 on a calendar or the insignia of the Third Reich in a scene from a motion picture. The people who appear in these films, too, must be people who reflect this spirit and who act in a manner that we are accustomed to.

We have no need to forgo the German salute in film. We cannot simply circumvent our state organizations like the SA, the Labor Front, Labor Service, etc. without subjecting ourselves to the charge that we are participating in anachronistic slacking off. And why should these issues that concern us every day—matters of clan, family, race, and state—not also be addressed in our films and work to deepen our relationships to one another? What could be more self-evident than showing films with children and families, all the way from the oldest to the youngest generation? There is such an endless series of themes lying dormant here; it is time that we keep our eyes out for this and express our appreciation for films that give birth to and sustain who we are and those that teach us and help us to grow.

Note

1. Ewald von Demandowsky (1906–46) was Reich film director (*Reichsfilmdramaturg*) and the producer of major propaganda films, including the 1942 *Ich klage an* (*I Accuse*). (See document 159 in chapter 13.)—Eds.

271

WALTER PANOFSKY

What Does the Audience Want to See on the Silver Screen?

First published as "Was will das Publikum auf der Leinwand sehen?" in *Film-Kurier,* 24 September 1938.

In its 17 September issue, *Film-Kurier* published recommendations on the subject matter of film in which they demand that film once again focus on individual professions. "What is lacking are films portraying people who find complete fulfillment in their work" was the subheading.

And with that, a problem that has often been addressed, but rarely with any satisfactory outcome, was once again opened to debate. Because the decisive question of whether the events portrayed in film can and should be drawn from everyday life of the common man is, on the one hand, answered with an emphatic yes, but it is just as often laughed off, usually with some reference to the so-called public taste.

The audience doesn't want daily routine. After a hard day's work, [film viewers] want to see something that consciously transports them into a fictional world; they want to be able to "be someone else in these few hours they spend at the movies"—these are the kind of answers you'll get, and more often than not, underscored by allusions to American films. Very frequently, people will cite the fact that American film producers have studied audience psychology very thoroughly, and their selection of subject matter and production were very heavily influenced by these psychological factors.

In many instances, people have automatically assumed that factors that are perhaps valid for the American mentality are equally applicable to German (and more generally for European) film production. The oft-cited "public taste" has been accepted as a factor that simply must be taken at face value without any regard to voices warning of the dangers involved.

What follows are the results of several studies of "public taste" drawn from many years of thoroughgoing and ongoing studies involving the public itself. To date, there has been hardly any truly comprehensive and extensive attempt to compile and evaluate public opinion concerning content, form, and acting in film. The producers believe—and it can't be denied that there is something to this—that studies of this nature don't produce any conclusive results. They still contend that the best way to interpret public taste is to measure box office success and that, therefore, any subject matter or actor that has been well received once will also succeed in a similar role a second or perhaps even a third time.

Fortunately, though, the notion that this kind of calculation also involves a number of uncertainties is gradually gaining ground, especially with regard to German film. As soon as one seeks, on the one hand, to accommodate the vast variety of wants and needs expressed by the public in terms of what is portrayed in film—and this is done in Germany just as it is done in the United States—one is already indirectly conceding that public taste cannot necessarily be easily pressed into one single scheme. [. . .]

The intellectual background and therefore the demands placed on film will be different for a streetcar conductor than for a university professor—and thank God they are—but, and my selection of this example is not arbitrary, a professor will expect a resurrection of antiquity in film and will defend his idea of "what a film is supposed to accomplish" on this basis.

It seems impossible to arrive at any answer to the question as to whether any viewer of film demands a fantasy world or a realistic portrayal of life. In the opinions expressed in these studies, there are various audience groups, some leaning one way and some leaning the other. In general, we were able to establish that female viewers are more inclined to demand a fantasy world than men. Especially in midsized and small theaters, we were able to conclude that the episodic portrayal of a housewife keeping the apartment in order—engaged, that is, in the routine of daily chores—was generally rejected with comments like "Why bother! Ain't nothing I don't see every day!"

On the other hand, there were a whole series of subway workers who were very sympathetic to the portrayal of their profession in the film *Gleisdreieck Station, Alarm on Track B* [*Gleisdreieck (Alarm auf Gleis B)*]. A characteristic of their expressed responses: "I gotta say, I was s'prised by how much excitement we got in our job. Never thought 'bout what was so pretty 'bout jus' driving a train into the ground, not till I saw it in that film. Some 'o dat stuff seemed a little far-fetched, but most of it wasn't so far-fetched after all, you know? When you's in the business, hey, it bugs you every time the rules gets broke, even if it's just in a film."

Of about twenty voluntary respondents among the subway employees, only four of them stated that they didn't go see the film simply because [according to the study] "that's what they see every day on the job." And when they do go to the movies, then the last thing they want after work is to be reminded of what they do on the job every day. One respondent rejected the film for this reason even after he had seen it.

If you apply these statements made by audience members to a decidedly American revue film—a film with a dream sequence completely removed from reality—making distinctions between individual tastes becomes easier in many ways. The simple experience of watching—the pleasure taken from lavish stage sets, from catchy hit tunes—is decisive here. Almost without exception, these types of films tend to attract an audience of regulars who are expecting passive entertainment and who have no desire whatsoever to be bothered with thoughts about their daily routine when they go to the movies in the evening, no desire to be burdened by serious matters or to be reminded in any way of their own daily life, restricted as it so often is to a very narrow realm of experience, by events portrayed in film.

A whole series of statements were gathered in which the revue film was rejected without providing any further explanation, "What a bunch of nonsense!" "Only in the movies!" "Wish I had it that good!" "People making these movies don't have a clue about real life," etc. On the other hand, there is ample confirmation for clear approval, expressed at the psychological level of humming the hit tunes and in explicit comments to this effect: "After seeing a film like this (revue film), I was able to forget how difficult my own life is. I'd like to experience something like this in real life for once. I don't like films that are too serious or tragic because they make me think too much about my own fate" (temporary office clerk, twenty-two years old, with a slight limp in her foot). "For my money, I want to go to the movies to have fun and to forget about my daily routine. I'm going to get up the next morning anyway and go back into the office where I don't have these kinds of diversions" (twenty-four-year-old typist). "I like going to operettas and revue films best—where you get something to see. I always go to period films, but I don't like serious films" (thirty-two-year-old female, manual laborer).

These statements can by no means be seen as a perversion of taste on the part of the German moviegoer. The desire for spectatorship and the desire to experience something—those are the two opposing psychological reasons audiences give for going to the movies. And the simple desire for spectatorship, the "lust for images," does not always counterbalance the desire to experience something, the will to participate cathartically in someone else's tragic fate. In addition to our demands for true-to-life subject matter and genuine, unadulterated, realistic portrayals for the German public, we must also take into consideration their desire to escape from their everyday lives, as clearly expressed in these statements, and we must respect this as a natural propensity on the part of viewers. [. . .]

In conclusion, one more additional factor merits mention: a perversion of taste rarely stems from any given action but more often rather from the way that action is handled in the film. Any film that is clearly based on incidents from everyday life can be terribly kitschified, just as a story that is basically sentimental can be framed in tolerable terms. The audience's taste remains basically intact in all its diversity. If the films of the past have violated public taste, then the German production of films in recent years sees as one of its primary aims the attempt to compensate for these damages. Regardless of whether the content involves an event from the distant past or a contemporary one, decisive is the manner of treatment and this will always remain, just as there will always be two main reasons for going to the movies: the desire to experience something or simply for the sake of entertainment. Film audiences have a right to demand that we attempt to accommodate both.

272

WINIFRED HOLMES

Hamburg Cinema

A Typical German Program

First published as "Hamburg Cinema: A Typical German Programme Described by Winifred Holmes," in *Sight and Sound* 8, no. 29 (Spring 1939): 18–20.

The train from Copenhagen gets into Hamburg at 7 P.M. I have four hours to wait until my sleeper even enters the station. What shall I do with myself until eleven? [. . .]

Leaving the dark waters of the Alster behind, I walk along a wide main street and at last see UFA Palast written up in lights, with the usual film posters outside.

Der Blaufuchs [*The Blue Fox*—Eds.] seems to be the name of the feature, starring Zarah Leander . . . Zarah Leander, Swedish, called the second Garbo of course, and the most popular film star of Germany today.

Evidently the UFA Palast is very grand. I enter its vast portals timidly and buy myself a two mark ticket as I can't say the number of pfennigs for anything less. Two marks is a lot out of the thirty I have been allowed to bring into the country and out of which I will have to pay for my sleeper to Cologne, but I can't help it. I shall have a "*jour maigre*" and miss out dinner; there's still a ham roll left among my luggage, I remember; I will eat it when I get into the train at 11 P.M.

The young men attendants are very polite and pleasant—as I found all the officials on my journey through Germany—and I am shown up the broad staircase into a balcony seat. The program evidently isn't continuous as all the lights are on and the curtain down. Will it be long before it begins? I wonder, as I have only three hours left, or rather two and a half to allow for my walk back to the station and for getting out my luggage. To my horror the huge auditorium has no clock visible anywhere in it. And I have no watch. Perhaps the public clocks are considered prehistoric and unnecessary in Germany, where everyone has a watch that keeps perfect time as part of his or her punctual-to-a-minute personality. Anglo-Saxon vagueness in these matters has no place here.

Looking round before the lights go out and I find the balcony three-quarters full of the more prosperous-looking bourgeoisie. No one is really dressed smartly, and no one is shabbily dressed. Not a single girl or woman is made up, and I can see no face with even a trace of Jewish blood in it. Most of the men wear the little round enamel Swastika badge in their buttonholes. Next to me sit a young couple—perhaps just married; they hold hands in the dark. She is a plump, kind-looking housewife. Perhaps I shall dare to find out the time from her later on . . .

The lights go out, the curtains are rolled away and the doors are firmly shut. Not a soul comes in after the program begins.

First we see advertising films such as we come across sometimes in our own provincial cinemas. Then a propaganda film—what the householder should do with empty tins. You shouldn't take them away surreptitiously in a sack and throw them into the river, lake, or sea for a fair bather to tread on and cut her feet; you shouldn't stack them up like a miser in your study for scientific experiments so that they all fall down and show you to be just a crazy old professor; you shouldn't attempt to hammer or chop them up and so injure your plump and important cooking arm . . .; no sir, . . . you should place them in a separate dust- or tin-bin—from which two stalwart geniuses will remove them in super modern vans to be melted down and reborn as new and better tins. Nothing is wasted in Germany today.

After that spirited little bit of civic propaganda, there is an instructional film made by a professor of natural history on the subject of the increasing stages of intelligence in nature from a toad to a monkey. This turns out to be a superb film. Excellently planned, beautifully photographed and well cut and edited. [. . .]

A newsreel follows. Rather heavy fare it seems—three actuality films together. Later I found out the reason. The government remits part of the entertainment tax when cinemas show a certain proportion of the instructive films in their programs.

Now at last—the newsreel. I shall be able to put my finger for a moment on the pulse of the ordinary folk of Germany, judging as one can here in England by the emotion of the audience displayed whenever a public figure or event comes on the screen—the boos, cheers, hissing, and clapping that always accompany a newsreel when it deals with politics.

But to my surprise, there is silence. Silence while Mussolini and Chamberlain smile and bow and wave to the crowd and shake hands in Rome. Silence while Field-Marshal Göring thanks the guard of honor who has come to congratulate him on the birth of his daughter. A few discrete laughs when the said daughter pats Herr Hitler's face, and silence again when pictures of the new and magnificent Reich Chancellery in Berlin are shown, in front of which a wildly cheering crowd surges. Up roll the ambassadors in their cars to celebrate the opening of this super-Roman building, followed by the *Führer,* who later receives them in a glittering and vast room. Longest receiving shot is in a glittering and vast room. Longest receiving shot is of the Japanese ambassador, next the Hungarian; no mention of the British envoy.

Still there is silence in my cinema, in spite of the acclamation of the crowds outside the building, who surge forward and break through the police cordon when the *Führer* appears on the balcony and cheer him over and over again. The good citizens in the cinema just watch the spectacle as a spectacle and take no active part in its emotion. I attempt no supposition or judgment, but merely record. And I must also record that the photography of the newsreel is superb, and that the propaganda for the greatness of the Reich is as *éscrasant* and as stupefyingly well done as in the Nuremburg Conference [Rally] film.

Now comes the intermission. My neighbor's man goes out to buy chocolate. I take courage and by means of nods and beckons and idiotic grimaces I ask her the time. She is intelligent enough to understand me—a remarkable feat—and I find there is still plenty of time to stay and see most of the feature. But I am wrong. As soon as the interval is over and the doors are again shut firmly, we are treated to a long variety program. There's a cinema organ; then a troubadour with a guitar singing in American; then a trapeze and tight-rope act—almost a strip tease—and lastly sixteen performing poodles. My chances of seeing the feature are rapidly diminishing, but the poodles are fun—we all love their act, especially enjoying the poodle who runs round virtuously with the others in line, pretends to jump the hurdle but in reality just sneaks round it every time unnoticed by the trainer. The audience is wide awake now and amusing itself hugely and audibly.

I look uneasily at my neighbor's watch and murmur something about the *Hauptbahnhof.* She understands vaguely that I have a train to catch and after that looks at her watch every five minutes. This makes me so nervous that soon I sneak out after seeing a short of the feature film. Is it taboo to go out between intervals, I wonder, looking at the shut doors. Well, I will pretend to feel ill if anyone tries to stop me. Of course, nothing of the sort happens.

I have far too much time in which to catch the train, due to the kind German lady's anxiety on my behalf, and I could have seen more of the long film. But I don't mind as I already can tell it is bad. The scene is feudal Hungary of semi-modern times—the protagonists rich and romantic *châtelaines* or dashing and equally rich young men. Zarah Leander is beautiful, there's no denying it; but to my tastes she overacts in this film and is affected. Certainly, from what I see of it, the film bears out another contention—that while Germany's documentary and instructional films are super today, its feature films are of a less high standard—too heavy and stagy.

Four companies produce them for a home market, of which Ufa and Asa are chief. Several hundreds are turned out each year because the home market is a large one—80 million people to be catered for. Some so-called French films are made in Germany in two versions. Later I see one in Paris—*Adrienne Lecouvreur*—with Yvonne Prentemps starring. And thoroughly bad and stagy I find it too.

But others are good, of course. I have news of a fine film of which much has been shot in the jungles of Brazil. Current ideologies make it difficult for German films to have been circulated outside Germany, except in the Scandinavian countries, which are free from controversy. Not very many American and English films can be shown in Germany either. So it seems as if the two worlds of political thought—dictatorship and democracy—will have to remain separated even in the universal medium of the screen.

273

SECRET REPORT OF THE SECURITY SERVICE OF THE REICHSFÜHRER SS

Shirley Temple

Enemy of the Reich

First circulated on 7 February 1940 as "Beurteilungen im Filmwesen." First published in *Meldungen aus dem Reich 1938–1945. Die geheimen Lageberichte des Sicherheitsdienstes der SS,* edited by Heinz Boberach (Herrsching: Pawlak Verlag, 1984), 3:741.

Reports from Munich say that many are disgruntled over the fact that these films with Shirley Temple are currently being shown because this actress is at the forefront of American oppositional propaganda. People took particular issue with articles in the press that responded positively to this "Little Miss Winnetou" [Fräulein Winnetou] in the film [*Susannah of the Mounties,* 1939].

274

LICHT BILD BÜHNE

Hitler Youth Quex

First published as "Hitlerjunge Quex," in *Licht Bild Bühne,* 12 September 1933.

UFA [Universum Film AG] has selected a magnificent, distinctive venue for its film *Hitler Youth Quex* [*Hitlerjunge Quex*]. And this Munich premiere, with the chancellor of the German *Volk,* Adolf Hitler, perched high above a singularly spectacular auditorium, punctuates the magnitude of the event for circles reaching far beyond the film world and fields of specialty.

The occasion is a work produced by UFA that obviously seems utterly suited to be called to such a momentous task. Germany's biggest film studio has rallied all its uniquely qualified technicians, all its material and artistic resources, to take a huge and extraordinary leap of faith and create this film about our fighting German youth—this paean to youthful enthusiasm of the passionately inflamed standard bearers for the national revolution.

UFA did not set out to produce a film for whiling away a pleasant evening of entertainment here but rather sought to paint an epic portrait of our times, an enduring document of the human and social circumstances, the spiritual and psychological impulses that have led to these changes in Germany's history. It is not enough to simply employ extraordinary ma-

FIGURE 25. Brochure for the 1933 film *Hitler Youth Quex* (*Hitlerjunge Quex*), a mythologized version of the life of Herbert Norkus, a Hitler Youth member killed by German Communists in 1932. *Illustrierter Film-Kurier* (Berlin: Verlag Illustrierter Film-Kurier, 1933).

terials and means to this end; these must be accompanied by extraordinary respect for the unique responsibility this subject matter entails. A passionate commitment to what the film reflects must shine through in everyone who has participated in its production.

It is a marvelous work, a film of far more than average importance. Many of the things a critic might object to from one perspective or another are absent from this film. The fact that the film, in its attempt to fulfill the very difficult task of representing the ideological conflicts of the past decade, relies all too heavily on rhetoric in the dialogue, to the detriment of the film's rhythm. This can never be convincing in its effect because it is but a limited shortcut facilitated by the technology of sound film. The psychological effect of this emphasis on dialogue forces a juxtaposition of these conflicting ideologies and results in an overexaggeration of the contrasts.

The actual plot is built around the tragic destiny of the Hitler Youth Herbert Norkus and so is set in a narrowly restricted context that proves to hinder the action in many instances. The characters slip out of their everyday lives and are pressed into systematic, preprogrammed roles.

The plot: . . . the distant sound of a drum roll. Germany's youth, the Hitler Youth, stand at attention beside their comrades in the SA.

In the north of Berlin, in the Beusselkietz District, the center for communism, there is tremendous unrest among the workers. Desperate people who need very little provocation to set off their inner discontent. A riot—precisely the excuse the Communist agitators need to go berserk. Windows are shattered. Rubber clubs are flying. The unemployed worker Völker gets a blow to the head and staggers home with the help of his Communist Party comrade Stoppel.

His home: a dark tenement, a half-starved, emaciated wife. The husband, chronically unemployed, blowing all his money drinking with others in the same boat. Völker can barely hold himself together; he needs money to quench his thirst (again). He can't find any anywhere. His rage knows no limits; he hauls off and hits his wife. At that moment, Heini Völker appears. He quickly slips the mark he had gotten as a tip into his mother's hand. And Papa Völker goes out drinking. Booze is what he dreams of most.

The Communist Stoppel tries to enlist Heini Völker for the Communist Youth. By coincidence, he runs into him at the nearby Rummelplatz one day while out looking for a universal pocketknife—the kind he has yearned for ever since childhood. But he doesn't ever get around to fulfilling this childhood dream. Stoppel keeps pressing Heini Völker until he finally gives in and joins [the Communist Party].

The next day, a meeting at the train station. The hordes of Communists are undisciplined, but the Hitler Youth are crisp and poised in their uniforms. Heini begins to have his doubts: he feels drawn to the others. Secretly, he steals away from the Communist camp. He can hear the song of the Hitler Youth:

> Our flag it flutters forward,
> forward man for man
> we march forward for Hitler
> through thick and thin.

While he is standing there eavesdropping, he is caught and cast from the camp as a spy. Back at home, he pours his heart out to his mother. As he is singing the Hitler Youth song with great gusto, his father shows up suddenly, slaps him across the head to teach him a lesson about the "Internationale."

On the way to school, he meets a new friend from the Hitler Youth, Fritz Doerries, who invites Heini to join him that evening at the new Hitler Youth center on Beussel Street. He promises to do so, but then Stoppel gets his hands on him again and tries to win him over to his cause. Stoppel tells Heini that people are planning to blow up the Hitler Youth center. Heini manages to inform the Hitler Youth center people of the plan, but in so doing becomes a traitor in the eyes of the Communists, who vow to take revenge. That night, in her desperation, the mother, who knows about all this, turns on the gas, determined to spare her son and herself this terrible fate and to take her beloved son with her into the afterworld. The wonders of medicine are able to keep Heini alive, but the doctors cannot save his mother. While he is in the hospital, members of the Hitler Youth group from the Beusselkietz District, who have recognized Heini to be one of their most loyal friends, pay him a visit. They drape his bed with the coat of honor he has been yearning for for so long, and, after he has recovered, he finds his home away from home at the Hitler Youth center. He is the most diligent of all his comrades and, because he is as nimble as quicksilver, he is nicknamed "Quex" (Quick).

In the heat of the campaigns leading up to the elections, there are flyers to be distributed. Quex always volunteers for the most difficult jobs, but in vain. Finally, he is given the opportunity to actively intervene in this struggle, but the Red Front has vowed to exact revenge upon him—the one who counts amongst their greatest threats. One day, while he's busy doing his work, he is surrounded by the commune with no escape route in sight; he is not even safe in the shooting gallery on the Rummelplatz where he has sought refuge. Like hunted, entrapped wild game, little Quex is cornered and pays for his loyalty to his flag and his

Führer with his life. But in the shadow of his martyr's death, millions more new fighters are born and brought to life. From now on, it is no holds barred, and there is no going back, and the song that once so ardently inspired little Quex resounds triumphantly through the night. The scenes that are played out on the Rummelplatz are represented quite realistically and naturally—not so, however, the attack on the barracks of the comrades. The dramatic portrayal of Hitler Youth Quex is exquisite: free and natural—a Hitler Youth could not hope to find a better representation. Both Ulla, the BDM [League of German Girls] girl, and Gerda (Rotraut Richter) are a bit too girlish in their representation. Claus Clausen is good as the *Bannführer Kaß,* admired and loved by all his comrades. Excellent acting and dramatic expression by Bertra Drews in the role of Mother Völker—her love for her son and fear of her husband is breathtaking. Heinrich George, in his role as the father, ably personifies the typical misery of the drunk without failing to demonstrate the kernel of human goodness at his core. Hermann Speelmans's performance in the role of Stoppel is unsurpassable, and the same applies to Karl Meixner as Wilde. Fritz Doerries as the lead comrade, Grundler as a Hitler Youth, and Hans Richter in the role of Franz contribute substantially to the success of the film *Hitler Youth Quex.*

The UFA, the author [of the novel, Karl Aloys Schenzinger, who cowrote the film with Bobby E. Lüthge], Karl Ritter [producer], Hans Steinhoff [director], and everyone else involved in this production are deserving of praise for their efforts. The film *Hitler Youth Quex* being shown in Munich today will be a tremendous experience tomorrow and for a long time throughout Germany.

275

FILM-KURIER

Leni Riefenstahl Spoke

First published as "Leni Riefenstahl sprach," in *Film-Kurier,* 4 April 1935.

Long before 9:00 P.M., the large hall of the Lessing Institute [Lessing-Hochschule] was already packed; throngs of listeners were crowding into the seats to hear Leni Riefenstahl speak, with an introduction by Prof. Dr. von Arnim on the production work behind *Triumph of the Will.*

The hour becomes an experience in itself because Riefenstahl is a highly refined, sensitive human being with a sincere nature, and the experience is doubled by the way that one is gripped by her retelling of the experience and utterly taken by the idealism of such great work and because one relives the experience of this work, its sentiment, its creative power, its accomplishment. It is not a personal achievement that is at the center of her soft-spoken, simple report but rather it is the work that shines through—a work that speaks for itself and is in no need of palliative glosses. It consists solely of the self-evident nature of an obligation, the fulfillment of a great task one has been presented.

Just as she recently did for the foreign and German press, Leni Riefenstahl outlines the tremendous amount of work this film required that is virtually unimaginable to the outsider. She discusses the preliminary stages, the organizational structure, the artistic and technical demands that were placed on each individual collaborator, and describes the way the work inspired in everyone the will to do his very best, the way they were all caught up in the contagiously impassioned atmosphere of Nuremberg and thus driven to superhuman levels of achievement. She describes the way that, in the midst of this atmosphere, she was suddenly struck by the idea of the way she wanted to shape the face of the film—and this would become the overriding principle behind the filming and subsequent editing and cuts—to have the Führer and the *Volk* represent the dramatic core of the film.

There were times when she thought she would be crushed by the enormity and magnitude of the work, when she thought she could not get through it, but then her loyal coworkers who believed in her, the raw power streaming from this strip of film itself helped her back on her feet. Instinctively, then, she sensed that the editing had to incorporate a whole new complex of ideas in order to emphasize the depth and profound meaning of the short sentences in the Führer's speeches, in order to use the images and the musical score to emphasize in the faces and words the political sentiments of the *Volk*. She knew how to transform the truth of those days in Nuremberg into a work of art.

At the conclusion of her speech, which was met with appreciative applause, she answered a few questions from members of the audience. The Führer gave her free rein over everything—because, as he said, artists need freedom to create. She readily admits to having been plagued by terrible fear and heart palpitations while watching the film four days before it was scheduled to be shown to the Führer at a commemorative preview—and there was not a meter she wanted to have cut. And the costs? Barely 400,000 Reichmarks: the amount it would take to produce any good feature film and one that would be far exceeded by any more elaborate production.

276

FILM-KURIER

Triumph over the Heart—*Triumph of the Will*

First published as "Triumph über die Herzen—'Triumph des Willens': Festvorstellung des Weihefilms im Beisein des Führers," in *Film-Kurier*, 29 March 1935.

The gala showing of *Triumph of the Will* was such a big event that it attracted hundreds of Berliners to the vicinity of the UFA Palast already in the late afternoon hours. Arriving early was the only way to guarantee a spot as an uninvited guest. As showtime approached, the crowd swelled to many thousands, packed in lines on the curb lining the street to see the invited guests and, above all, the Führer arrive. A whole host of police units had their hands full with attempts to keep people behind the barricades and keep the entrance clear for the arriving guests. People climbed every available structure; they were standing on the chairs and tables in the coffeehouses, the awnings, planks and boards, and lampposts. There wasn't a single window in the surrounding buildings that wasn't packed with spectators. And above it all, the mighty flags that hung from the housefronts flew, the massive golden eagle, symbol of power and will, rose above the portal in the glistening light of the floodlights! The gleeful atmosphere of anticipation, the bustle of happy people, filled the foyer and auditorium of the UFA Palast.

The walls of the foyer were graced with the most splendid pictures the world has ever seen of the Führer and his loyal inner circle.

The auditorium is decked out with green garlands and the symbol of the movement, the swastika banner, gleams resplendent from the side of the stage. The orchestra pit is overflowing with brightly colored flowers.

The seats in the main floor and the balconies fill up long before the start of the show. In the theater lobby, all the way up the stairs and along the corridor center box, hundreds of guests are lined up behind the cordon formed by the Hitler Body Guard Spalier—all waiting to greet the Führer upon his arrival.

FIGURE 26. Illustrated supplement devoted to the 1934 Nuremberg Reich Party Rally showing Leni Riefenstahl (next to eagle sculpture) during the filming of *Triumph of the Will. Berliner Illustrirte Zeitung,* 13 September 1934.

Chief of Staff Lutze, Reich Press Secretary Dr. Dietrich, Reich Organizational Director Dr. Ley, Sports Leader von Tschammer-Osten, *Gauleiter* Streicher, *Gauleiter* Görlitzer, Reich Minister of Labor Seldte, General Ritter von Epp, and Reich Ministers Darré and Dr. Frank take their seats in the government box. In the remaining boxes, there are, in addition to numerous representatives of the diplomatic corps, high-ranking officers of the army and the marines. Then Leni Riefenstahl appears and, a few minutes later, shouts of "Heil!" from the streets announce the Führer's arrival.

A few minutes later, accompanied by Reich Ministers Dr. Goebbels and Rudolf Hess and *Obergruppenführer* Brückner, he enters the box. The crowd stands mesmerized, silently greeting the Führer with raised arms. The Führer greets Leni Riefenstahl before taking his seat. Slowly, the lights are lowered, the curtain is raised, and the floodlights focus on the drum corps of the Hitler Body Guard "Adolf Hitler." Under the direction of musical director Müller-John, the band strikes up with the "Fanfare for Crusaders" [Kreuzritterfanfare] and "Here Good Brandenburg Everywhere" [Hie guet Brandenburg allewege], and the strains of the Badenweiler March resound through the house. The band is showered with appreciative applause.

There is a curtain raiser before the show. Then the symbolic eagle appears—the title etched in stone—then the clouds, and the Führer's plane gliding through them to the Reich Party Rally at Nuremberg. And then, the experience of Nuremberg—depicted in artistic perfection, in images of overwhelming beauty, in electrifying design. The applause blaring from the loudspeakers is contagious, and the audience breaks out in cheers of jubilation again and again. Everyone has the feeling that the Führer's presence amongst us is doubled. The magnitude of these hours is immense. When the "Horst Wessel Song" strikes up in the closing frames, the crowd rises from its seats, deeply moved, and sings along; it sounds like a vow to loyally follow the Führer, who is with us in the audience. When the lights go up, thundering shouts of "Heil!" rise repeatedly in the direction of the Führer's box.

The Führer expresses his gratitude, then gives Leni Riefenstahl, the servant to this great work, a big bouquet of white lilacs. A crowd remains gathered before the theater long after the Führer has left, waiting for Leni Riefenstahl, expressing its gratitude in an enthusiastic chorus of "Heil!"

277

FRANK MARAUN [FRANZ GOELZ]

Olympia

First published as "Olympia," in *Der Deutsche Film,* no. 11, May 1938. Translated by John Hanhardt.

A triumph of the documentary film. In Los Angeles, the Americans tried at the time to produce a film of the Olympic Games. They filmed a great deal, but the film was never seen. It was a failure. In Germany, the place of cultivation and the stronghold of the documentary film, [the film *Olympia*] has succeeded in the most convincing manner. It had to succeed here because Germany had created, for the Eleventh Olympic Games in Berlin, such a grandly perceived, symbolic framework that from the outset lifted the event out of the sphere of a mere sports report for the creatively reproducing camera and because here we already have a tradition of not only copying reality with film but also of revealing the idea that animates and illuminates. This is not only an action of the film. It is a result of National Socialism, which is penetrating the total life of the nation into its most detailed ramifications, with its idea-based directional force, and which has accustomed us to see reality and idea together. Only in the ideological structure of National Socialism could this great documentary film have come into being as an artistic achievement. Indeed, it had never existed previously.

Only the eye that has been rendered keen to the self-revelation of the idea within reality, that found present a reality permeated with idea-based content, could be inspired to artistic imagination by reality. Only this eye could see more than an accumulation of beautiful and interesting pictures—that is to say, the configuration of the event irradiated by a spiritual energy. The camera regained the vision of the spiritual eye, which recognizes the mythical content of things. It is the same vision that inspired Goethe to say it is wrong to look for theories behind things; the things themselves express these theories (a statement that defines the entire secret of the film and the intrinsic character of its effect). In this competence of vision of the camera there is based the avant-garde mission of the documentary film. The documentary film leaves ample space for free development; it does not restrict, as does the feature film in most cases, by means of cheap and convenient dialogue and the communication method of the spoken word. The documentary film leads the film back to its elementary means of expression, which today, as always, is the dynamically moving symbol language of pictures.

Leni Riefenstahl makes use of this means of expression in her *Olympia* films [*Olympia Part 1—Festival of Nations (Fest der Völker)* and *Olympia Part 2—Festival of Beauty (Fest der Schönheit)*] with imposing effect. Especially gripping and directly pleasing are the prologue and the masterful creation of the marathon. When from out of the statues of the Acropolis, out of the images of gods and heroes, the vision of the Greek human form arises, as if its combination of strength and charm radiates through the centuries, when out of the *Discus Thrower* by Myron the form of the athlete of today, from out of the idea hewn in stone, the living reality of our time is brought into focus, when the machine-like uniform beat of the legs of the marathon racers lets the track recede from a vertical angle—so these are only a few of the most beautiful examples of the creative initiative with which the potentiality of the film is here utilized to permit an idea to become an intense imaginative experience.

This is not reporting; it is a real creative effort. A happening of reality becomes an artistic event that offers entirely new impressions and experiences, more intensive, more stirring than the summer days of 1936 themselves could offer. Everywhere, the camera approaches more closely than the eyes were able. It obtains settings and focal points that were attainable by no spectator, as, for example, when it follows from closest range, during the 4 × 400meter relay race for men, the hard-fought shoulder-to-shoulder contest of two runners over approximately 200 meters. The camera is everywhere: in the arena, in the air, in the camera pits under the grass. It is present everywhere where it is most interesting: close to the most tense, relaxed, nervous faces at the starting line; at the collapses beyond the finish lines; at morning training and in the sauna in the Olympic Village; in the Führer's box; and it reveals in slow motion the beauty of movement, swimming style, and the technique of the dive. The contests of sixteen days are concentrated here into a few hours. Each contest is a drama in itself, full of suspense, full of surprise, full of tragic situations: not too imposing a word considering the supreme effort that the best athletes of the world wrest from their bodies—every single one not only he himself but also the representative of his country and of his race. There is no lack, therefore, of gripping moments. For here it becomes clear that the athletic victory is not only a victory of moral energy; that the *Olympia* film reveals these ethical values of sports; that it, over and beyond the outward tenseness of the contests, brings out the value of the idea absolutely and clearly that is inherent in the Olympic Games, that may be considered to be, perhaps, the decisive argument for the film's success.

The incomparable and ever-exciting beauty of the pictorial creation is obvious with grandiose extravagance and with the use of the half a hundred of the best German camera artists and specialists. Leni Riefenstahl had enough material to select in such a manner that no shot and no idea in the editing process was repeated. What is more, she proves herself to be a master of moderation in the face of this abundance. No overloading, no accumulation of shots in short sections. The clarity of delineation, the uncluttered buildup of the event, the exactly measured sequence of events, and the well-balanced spacing of the points of rest and of the points of intensification are an outstanding achievement of cinematic structural skill. It is supported in an exemplary manner by the impressive and flexible handling of the soundtrack, which—with the masterfully controlled musical background of Herbert Windt and the effectively placed speakers—lets the atmosphere of the stadium become alive in a contagious manner with speaking choruses, shouts of encouragement and discouragement of the national groups, and the roaring shouts of joy of the entire stadium over the great achievements.

It is really a "Festival of Nations" and a "Festival of Beauty" that a person experiences in both of these *Olympia* films. It is one of the greatest works of art that German film has produced up to now—filled with a spirit which we sense not only as the spirit of Olympia but also as the spirit of the German reality of today.

FIGURE 27. Photo spread showing director Leni Riefenstahl at work and at home. *Berliner Illustrirter Zeitung,* 15 July 1937, 1028.

278
BERLINER ILLUSTRIRTE ZEITUNG
Leni Riefenstahl
Germany's Number One Filmmaker

First published as "Leni Riefenstahl: Deutschlands Filmschaffende Nr 1," in *Berliner Illustrirte Zeitung,* 15 July 1937.

Top left: Leni Riefenstahl cutting and editing the *Olympia* film. No less than 400,000 meters of film footage was shot at the most sensational sports event of the year 1936. Viewing this footage, organizing, and cutting it is an enormous task that, according to Professor Lehnic, president of the Reich Film Chamber, is scheduled to be completed by the end of January 1938.

Top right: The artist's new home in Dahlem. View of the west side of the white house in the woods.

Bottom left: One of the cozy corners Leni Riefenstahl has furnished according to her exquisite artistic taste.

Bottom right: Guests at the artist's house. *From right,* the Führer and Reich chancellor; 1935 National Film Award [*Filmpreisträgerin*] winner, Leni Riefenstahl; Reich Minister Dr. Goebbels; Frau Dr. Ebersberg; Frau Ilse Riefenstahl, sister-in-law of the artist; *in the background.* mother and brother, Heinz Riefenstahl.

279
FILM-KURIER
Jews No Longer Permitted to Attend the Cinema—All Forms of Participation in Representations of German Culture Forbidden!

First published as "Teilnahme an Darbeitungen deutschen Kultur," in *Film-Kurier,* 14 November 1938.

Dr. Goebbels, in his capacity as president of the Reich Chamber of Culture, has forbidden all theater directors, concert and lecture organizers, proprietors of theaters, owners of artistic venues, organizers of dance events and public exhibitions involving cultural matters to allow Jewish persons to attend their events, effective immediately.

Infringements will result in severe punishment for the organizers and especially for the Jews.

The text of the ordinance reads as follows: [. . .]

> Pursuant to Article 25 of the First Ordinance Concerning the Execution of the Reich Chamber of Culture Law of 1 November 1938, I hereby issue the following ordinance:
>
> Now that the National Socialist state has already allowed the Jews over five years' time to create and maintain their own cultural life within the context of special Jewish organizations, it is no longer feasible to continue to allow them to participate in representations of German culture. Therefore, Jews are hereby forbidden entrance to events of this nature, especially theaters, cinemas, concerts, lectures, artistic events (variety shows, cabarets, circuses, etc.), dance events, and exhibitions involving cultural matters, effective immediately.

Berlin, 12 November 1938
President of the Reich Chamber of Culture
Dr. Goebbels

This ordinance represents one of the harsh measures in response to the Jewish assassination in Paris and, together with the ordinance issued by General Field Marshal Göring to exclude Jews from German economic life, is designed to result in a thoroughgoing segregation of Jews from people of German blood.

Immediately following the seizure of power, the Jews were already excluded from active participation in film production, from appearing on stage or in concert. From now on, they are also banned from the audience.

With that, a clear line of demarcation has been drawn between the community of the German *Volk* and the Jewish population, even in terms of free time—and the basic prerequisites for this have long since been established by the creation of Jewish cultural organizations permitted by the state to produce representations of their own culture.

In the context of yesterday's event at the Germania Hall, where five hundred male and female volunteers of the Winter Relief Program were gathered for the Sunday soup pot [*Eintopfsonntag*], Dr. Goebbels made reference to the ordinances passed by the National Socialist state leadership on Saturday: "It is a disgrace to our German artistic life to expect that a German should have to sit in a theater or cinema next to a Jew."

280

DER STÜRMER

Charlie Chaplin

The Jewish Chimp in America

First published as "Charlie Chaplin: Der Affenjude in Amerika," *Der Stürmer,* no. 18, May 1940, 3.

After the war, when the Jew was allowed to play first fiddle in Germany, millions of non-Jews could no longer see the way the descendants of Abraham were pulling the wool over their eyes, and they danced to the tune just the way the Jews wanted them to.

At that time, it also came to pass that Germans at the cinema applauded the likes of a certain Charlie Chaplin and, in fact, couldn't get their fill of this chimp in human clothing. Well, National Socialism has put a swift end to this monkey business.

But while we were in the midst of restoring our health, it is a good thing to remind ourselves of those times that are barely imaginable from today's perspective. Charlie Chaplin is neither a Frenchman nor an Englishman; he is a 100 percent full-fledged Jew living in America. Only a Jew has the oh-so-telling flat feet and other physical deformities that allow a human being to mimic a chimp the way Charlie Chaplin is still doing to this day. He's still alive and has recently let the world know that his next film is called *The Great Dictator* and that he will donate net profits from this film to the fund for Jewish emigration from Central Europe.

The Jewish chimp Charlie Chaplin has also been "famous" for his Talmudic knowledge of non-Jewish women. He has been married seven times and plans to "marry" an eighth time now. And of course he has no intention of taking any old Jewish sweetheart as his wife: it's always the beautiful blondes, not the Jewish girls, that he makes his own for any given time.

281

ANONYMOUS

The Eternal Jew
Film of a 2,000-Year Rat Migration

First published as "Der ewige Jude," in *Unser Wille und Weg,* vol. 10, 1940, 54–55. Translated by Randall Bytwerk. Calvin College, German Propaganda Archive.

The Eternal Jew is the first film that not only gives a full picture of Jewry but also provides a broad treatment of the life and effects of this parasitic race using genuine material taken from real life. It also shows why healthy peoples in every age have responded to the Jews with disgust and loathing, often enough expressing their will to defend themselves in action.

Just like rats, two thousand years ago the Jews left the Middle East to invade Egypt, at that time a flourishing land. Even then, they had all the criminal traits they display today; even then, they were the enemies of hardworking, creative peoples. In large hordes, they migrated from there to the "Promised Land," flooded the entire Mediterranean region, broke into Spain, France, and southern Germany, then followed the German colonists as they moved into the countries of the east. Along the way, they remained eternal parasites, haggling and cheating. Poland, above all, became the enormous reservoir from which Jewry sent its agents to every leading nation of Europe and the world.

The self-portrait Jewry offered the world was disgusting from the beginning. But all that is surpassed by the powerful examples in this new and most valuable film, *The Eternal Jew.* This film, with its persuasive power, must be shown everywhere where anti-Semitism is still questioned. No one will fail to shudder at the sneaking servility and dirty bartering of the Jew from the very beginning of his existence; at the perfidy, insidiousness, and vulgarity of his methods; at the brutality and all-devouring hatred he exhibits when he reaches his goal and is in possession of the power of money.

The most revolting scenes show Jewish slaughtering methods. These customs, which cast a particularly vivid spotlight on the so-called Jewish religion, are so horrific that it is hard to watch the film as the grinning Jewish butchers carry out their work. It is illuminating to see how stubbornly Jewry holds to its method of slaughter and the casuistry with which it defends it against the horror of the civilized world. Rarely will people be more horrified than from watching the desperate and horrible death throes of these slaughtered animals. Long before the seizure of power, the NSDAP fought against Jewish slaughter. National Socialist representatives in parliament repeatedly introduced legislation to abolish this form of animal torture through a ban on Jewish slaughter. Such proposals were always rejected, since the entire Jewish and Jewish-influenced press ran long articles against them and the so-called German parties refused to support National Socialism in its battle against this evil.

Not only in this regard but in other areas too are we reminded with a shudder of what once was reality in Germany: the power of the Jews in the economy, finance, culture, theater, film, publishing, press, radio, education, and politics. All these Jewish leaders of the Weimar era had their home or their origin in the filthy ghettos of the east.

One has a deep sense of salvation after seeing this film. We have broken their power over us. We are the initiators of the fight against world Jewry, which now directs its hate, its brutal greed, and destructive will toward us. We must win this battle for ourselves, for Europe, for the world. This film will be a valuable tool in that struggle.

FIGURE 28. Advertisement for the 1940 anti-Semitic feature film *The Eternal Jew* (*Der Ewige Jude*), directed by Fritz Hippler. *Illustrierter Film-Kurier* (Berlin: Verlag Illustrierter Film-Kurier, 1940).

282

FILM-KURIER

Review of *The Eternal Jew*

First published in *Film-Kurier,* 20 January 1941.

Last Friday, at the Casino cinema in Litzmannstadt, the documentary film about world Jewry was shown for the first time in the presence of prominent men in state government and the movement—at a site that has a certain degree of symbolic significance for this film. For here in Litzmannstadt—what was once the Polish city of Łódź—is where much of the film's footage was shot. Here in the ghetto, the camera captured those types of Judaism that are the most conspicuous personifications of world Jewry. In all the corners, corridors, and caves of the Jewish quarter, but also in the opulently cluttered, pompous palaces that today serve different and better purposes, is where those creatures wreaked their havoc, and it was here that those wretched faces shown in the film were discovered. At that time, before the German administration intervened to establish order and clean the Augean stables, the film camera wandered through the streets of the Litzmannstadt ghetto to preserve a factual, unadulterated picture of this stinking cesspool that provided an endless stream of replenishment for world Jewry.

The figures and faces shown in the film once meandered through the streets of this city like parasites hawking their wares. They felt at home here, protected by the Polish authorities, who let them flourish and in many ways even promoted their interests. Here, largely due to their shockingly high numbers in the population, they controlled almost every aspect of economic and cultural life—inasmuch as one can even speak in terms of cultural life under Polish leadership.

The film left a very strong impression.

283

GERHARD STARKE

Review of Jew Süss

First published in *Deutsche Allgemeine Zeitung*, 26 September 1940, 6.

Jew Süss [*Jud Süß*], a film produced by Terra, was presented to the public in a gala performance at the UFA Palast am Zoo in Berlin. Reich Minister Dr. Goebbels was in attendance at the show. In addition, Dr. Meißner, along with many other men from the party, the state, and the army, as well as artists from Berlin and throughout the Reich, attended. Actors in attendance, in addition to director Veit Harlan, were Kristina Söderbaum, Ferdinand Marian, and Malte Jäger.

The film was rated "artistically and politically very valuable." On 4 February 1738, a Jew named Joseph Süss Oppenheimer, an official financial adviser, "was hanged wearing a scarlet red caftan in a cage on iron gallows," explains a copper engraver who was his contemporary in a brief chronicle of the gallows specifically constructed for the occasion, as an aside in his commentary on his "faithful and accurate depiction of the Jew Süss as well as of the iron gallows and the cage." It was a long way from the artistic efforts of this copper engraver from Stuttgart who etched in copper the sensational end and unscrupulous rise [of the Jew Süss] and Veit Harlan's filmic portrayal of the life of the court Jew Süss. Nevertheless, despite the two-hundred-year interval separating them, they have many an astonishing thing in common. The film adheres so faithfully to historical sources that one could just as easily describe it, too, as a "faithful and accurate depiction." History is not glossed over and polished with a thin veneer; the outline of events as they played out in the middle of the eighteenth century at the court of Duke Karl Alexander von Württemberg is ably and conscientiously traced here.

Already immediately following its world premiere in Venice, the film began reaping high honors for overall production, and particularly for the great achievement of all the artists involved. But its political accomplishment is equal to its artistic [one], and this demands that we comment extensively on the milestone this represents.

The film resembles the old copper engraving in other ways, too. Here, too, the leading figures are outlined in biting precision, sharp and angular, without a trace of blurring or fuzziness in their contours: engraved with a steel stylus. But there is one group that especially stands out from the others: three Jews. These three profiles are enough, and yet the incontrovertible nature of their species is anchored as law in the lines of their contours. The scenes of savagery we see written on their faces can reveal themselves only from the perspective of chaos that is intrinsic Jewish nature. The film captures the essence of world Jewry and all its problems in one fell swoop in the figures of Süss Oppenheimer, his secretary, Levy, and Rabbi Loew.

They are completely different types but cut from the same cloth, the basic types of Jews invading the life of other peoples. It is the same creature, just projected onto different surfaces and subjected to different fragmentation of its energies through different mediums. Its moral compass point is permanently fixed on the same point set by the Talmud: "Because you have made me the lone ruler of the world, so shall I make you the lone ruler of the world!" This is seen here from three different perspectives, three different spiritual paths, all leading to the same goal: the one may see certain ways and means that remain hidden to the others. Süss, Levy, and the rabbi are individuals but at the same time representatives of the teeming army of their comrades—and they see themselves as their pathbreaking pioneers: "I shall open the gate for you!" The whole race is condensed in each of these three individuals, and each of these condensations demonstrates certain characteristics of the race so that each is a unique but at the same time general representative. Ferdinand Marian as the Jew Süss and Werner Krauß as Levy and Rabbi Loew are fanatical and ardent in their portrayal of these strange figures they depict. Their facial expressions and physical gestures exude the inner essence of these figures.

Jew Süss is the pull-yourself-up-by-your-bootstraps-to-transcend-the-ghetto type of Jew; clever and crafty, he uses his cleverness only to satisfy and give free rein to the base instincts that drive him. He remains true only to himself in his malfeasance, thinking and acting accordingly. He has a thousand tricks up his sleeve, and these are made all the more effective by his intimate knowledge of the other's soul and capacities, his nearly fanatical knowledge of his weaknesses and inhibitions. He does not have the slightest inkling about the thirty pieces of silver and what they imply. He deceives, robs, tortures, and kills, obeying the categorical imperative of his being. Cocooned in his own web of notions of good and evil, he would fall into a bottomless abyss if the web should ever give way. The Jews themselves have summarized the basic essence of their nature in the concepts of "Cain" and "chutzpah." In Marian's *Jew Süss,* it is the nature of Cain that predominates: he is slippery as a snake, and this finds various forms of expression depending on the situation: at times in wit and cleverness, at times as underhanded treachery, contrived endearment, or feigned fawning and flattery.

Levy's chutzpah represents the polar opposite. A Jew who does not possess the wherewithal to leave the ghetto, not even in his outward appearance, even when he does get the chance to go off to "see the world," he remains clad in his caftan and Jewish beard. He is incapable of pretending, cannot put on a mask. His arrogance, cruelty, lack of respect, and cowardly lust for vengeance are written all over his face. Süss is too clever to publicly pose as the judge himself, but Levy does so, and his loins are aflame with *Schadenfreude* when he succeeds in toppling the basic premise of ancient Germanic law: *Judex stat pro deo, quod juaeus ex sese nequit.* Jew Süss is instinct plus intellect, but Levy's type is sheer instinct, all greed, all lust. The way Werner Krauß portrays this character and the rabbi as well has a certain ghastliness that is simply beyond words. It's not just his garbled Jewish gibberish, the stupid look on his face—despite all manner of cleverness—Krauß's performance exudes a certain aura of unidentifiable origin.

The third type we see portrayed here is that of the highly erudite, unkempt rabbi—the living embodiment of Talmudic dogma. There is no doubt about it: this character is a "*chacham godol ha Israel,*" a great wise man of Israel. He is "knowledgeable," but his knowledge is a demonic knowledge whose sole purpose is to provide a fabricated legal justification for the actions of types like Süss and Levy. And it's amazing how much latitude there is in the ensuing dialectic, which could certainly just as easily provide proof of the precise opposite of what it sets out to prove. He creeps along at a spider's pace, looking like an evil goblin unleashed upon a morbid world to hasten its demise. Two souls eternally conjoined in one heart: the one is beholden to God and the law, prophetically wise, and the other, a slave to the idolatry of gold as God—a soul that will even sell itself.

The film masterfully portrays the way these types mutually complement one another, masterfully portrays the common bond between them characterized by one more particular feature: the common bond of malice. The closing scene, as the announcement that the Jews have been banished rings through the estates of Württemberg, is symbolic: a nightmare is over, a spook has left.

284

SECRET REPORT OF THE SECURITY SERVICE OF THE REICHSFÜHRER SS

The Popularity of *Jew Süss*

First circulated on 28 November 1940 as "Zum laufenden Filmprogramm." First published in *Meldungen aus dem Reich 1938–1945. Die geheimen Lageberichte des Sicherheitsdienstes der SS,* edited by Heinz Boberach (Herrsching: Pawlak Verlag, 1984), 6:1811, 1812.

According to unanimous reports from throughout the Reich, the film *Jew Süss* continues to glean extraordinarily resounding approval. Opinions concerning any film have rarely been as unanimous as in the case of *Jew Süss,* which goes to uncommon extremes in its realistic portrayal of certain horrific episodes that are nevertheless utterly compelling in their artistry and aesthetic treatment, with a dramatic sense of suspense that "won't let you go." The film's overall sentiment is perhaps best expressed in this spontaneous remark: "You just want to wash your hands." Reports from Leipzig, Breslau, Oppeln, Salzburg, Potsdam, Reichenberg, Karlsruhe, Troppau, Dortmund, and elsewhere indicate that parents and educators asking whether it is a good thing for children to see the film have almost all said "no" in light of the extraordinarily severe psychological impact it would have.

Reports everywhere indicate that, in contrast to the majority of feature films currently in circulation, this film is being discussed primarily in terms of the dramatic performance of the actors, which—so says a report from Nuremberg—are "frightfully real" with regard to its portrayal of the Jews. In this particular regard, *Jew Süss* is disproportionately more effective and convincing than the film *The Rothschilds* (Berlin). The scenes that concern the general public the most—aside from the rape scene—are the ones in which the Jews march in with house and home and take over the city of Stuttgart. This scene in particular has repeatedly led to open outbursts of anti-Jewish sentiment in the audience during the film. In Berlin, for example, [members of the audience] started shouting, "Run the Jews off the Kurfürstendamm! Drive every last Jew from the streets of Germany!"

There is no general consensus of opinion in the populace on the character of the duke of Württemberg. From what we have thus far observed, opinions tend toward seeing the duke as being almost just as opprobrious as the Jew Süss himself and [seeing] his death [as] just punishment, except that it comes too early for him to have ever been taught to see through the Jew Süss and through the Jews and Jewry.

285

MANFRED GEORG

Charlie Chaplin in *The Great Dictator*

First published as "Charlie Chaplin in 'The Great Dictator,'" in *Aufbau,* 18 October 1940, 8.

Outrage, hatred, scorn—as long as we haven't perished by fire from this earth, this is what we will spew at that barbarism currently intent on trampling us beneath their [the Nazis'] jackbooted feet. Outrage, hatred, scorn—every day the chambers of our heart are filled with it. There are others, though, who simply removed themselves completely from these times, fleeing to some corner of the earth where they cower in fear and try to keep their wits about them. They don't want to see, hear, nor speak because they feel as though being any part of these times would be the end of them—they would go under.

Outrage and escape: both possibilities exist. But is laughter a possibility? The French may have put stock in the saying that comedy kills. But only in France. And not anymore today in any case. Otherwise, a character like [Marshall Philippe] Pétain [chief of state of Vichy France] could never have come into existence. But to kill someone with comedy necessarily requires that one be able to laugh in the first place. Laugh at the horror, joke about the horror, and be wise enough to let this suffice—to see that profound comedy immanent in every extreme form of existence. It is manifest in the bloodiest, most exaggerated passion. Even a monstrous murderer can be made into a comical figure when cast in the naked, revealing light of that profound comedy. If you do too much killing, scream too much—indeed, even if you love too much—all it takes is a little nudge to reduce your grandiose airs and aims to a hilarious mockery. Anyone familiar with the classics will be reminded of the proverbial "one step [from the sublime to the ridiculous]."

What Charlie Chaplin has accomplished in this film is so stupendous, one has to wonder how and if the masses will be able to grasp it. He subjects the horror of war, the atmosphere of pogroms, the inhuman cruelty to the corrective mechanism of laughter and thus suddenly balances out the scales. Chaplin is not the first Jew to take on the world as a Jew in his public performances and to thus win the hearts and minds of all non-Jews. For he goes straight to the heart of universal humanity. In this film, he literally picks up the pieces of a world left with nary a leg to stand on, puts them back together, and sets the world right again.

What a tremendous feat of psychological and dramatic achievement—to play the role of the dictator and at the same time his alter ego, the little Jewish barber. Hitler and Charlie—the great gruesome grimace and the picture of innocence, perfidy paralyzed by paroxysm and the pitiable personified—the more you think about the two sides of this double figure, the greater your enthusiasm for the metaphysics of acting.

Hitler once said to [Hermann] Rauschning, "If the Jew hadn't existed, we'd have had to invent him." What he meant was that there must always be a certain type that can be blamed for everything—in Hitler's case, there is something of this type within him, something he wants to get rid of: Hitler's Jewish complex is a sort of exorcism of all his own base instincts that he has banished from himself and projected onto someone else in order to free himself of them. And that's why he hates the Jews so much; it is his own self-hatred directed at miscreants of his own making.

Chaplin's Hitler represents, in this sense, an unmasking of unparalleled intensity. Whether he is imitating the language, parodying the spectacle of facial contortions, or [performing] his daily "life in poses," the portrayal is always laced with nuanced finesses that can make even this hard-core monster into a forlorn clown forsaken by the world who is destiny's idea of a joke. The dictator's dance with the globe, for example, is likely to become as famous as the dance of the dinner rolls in *Gold Rush*—with its ballet-style arabesques, its unencumbered caprice and symbolic implications. This exposé is simply so ingenious one doesn't know whether to laugh or cry.

And that's what is so great about this film in general: it makes you laugh and cry at the same time. Only rarely does one of these emotions overpower the other. One has to laugh at the hilarious barbershop scene in which Chaplin is dancing around a customer, soaping him up, and shaving him to the tune of the Hungarian Rhapsody, and one must cry over a few of the ghetto scenes that are punctuated with moments of great power.

The emotional ambiguity is there from the start: Chaplin rescuing a German fighter pilot in the World War. Their plane goes down together, he is brought to the field hospital and doesn't recover from his amnesia until twenty [years] later, to discover his old barbershop covered in cobwebs with a sign on his shop window in the form of "Jude," like an SA calling card. The focal point of the film is that, just when the dictator is preparing to invade another country, the barber winds up being confused with the dictator as the result of a strange coincidence, and this makes up the better part of countless hilarious and deeply moving scenes, all leading precipitously to the final climax: the barber-dictator is scheduled to announce his plan of attack to the world [in a radio address], and instead gives a speech addressing humanity [in a plea for human rights].

We've heard a lot of speeches at the ends of films these days: Abraham Lincoln's famous proclamation, the social philosophy of Ma Joad's closing speech [in *The Grapes of Wrath*], or one of the somber and determined beer-drinking songs sung by the typical American in *The Ramparts We Watch.* And this dramatic ending is what catapults this Chaplin film into the real world of today. It is a spectacular success.

You can't say enough about this film: from the character of Benzino Napolini (wonderful acting by Jack Oakie) and the meeting of the dictators that is a cross between a circus grotesque and sublime satire, to the "Last Supper" scene, where the five little Jews determine who is destined to sacrifice himself as the "nation's salvation" based on whoever finds a coin in his pudding, or the scene with Field Marshal Herring's ting-a-linging medals as he romps through the palatial corridors, or Paulette Goddard's enchanting portrayal of Hannah, who in her sweet nature and melancholy seems to have been composed from the faces of Chaplin's dreams.

As I said, not enough can be said about this film. Every minute of it is exquisite. But, ultimately, films are meant to be seen.

286

ANONYMOUS

Hollywood Reports

On the Situation of Refugees in Hollywood

First published as "Hollywood meldet: Zur Situation der Refugees in Hollywood," in *Aufbau,* 25 October 1940, 9.

Based on complaints filed by several of its members concerning the current flood of refugee actors inundating the Hollywood scene, the Screen Actors Guild, as we reported, has joined the Producers Association to undertake a thorough investigation of the matter. The results of that study reveal that of the 19,151 people under full-time employment contract by the eight major studios, there are, believe it or not, only eighteen refugees, and only four of them are actors. The contradiction between the persistent claims that there is a "flood of refugees inundating the scene" and the facts is so crass that the FBI has since taken on the task of identifying the men who are behind these rumors. The assumption is that this involves an orchestrated Nazi propaganda campaign—in some cases deliberately disseminated disinformation; in others, disseminated by unsuspecting Americans.

As small as the numeric participation of refugees in the Hollywood film industry is, the rate of success is diametrically disproportionate to the same. So-called preview polls keep a monthly running tab on the best performances of each month in the run-up to the upcoming Academy Awards scheduled for December, and in the September poll, of ten names listed, we find no fewer than four refugees: Henry Koster (Kosterlitz) for best director, Felix Jackson (Joachimson) for best screenplay, and Szöke Szakall for best acting, all for the film *Spring Parade;* the fourth name on the list is Albert Bassermann for Best Supporting Actor in *Foreign Correspondent.* This is the third time that Bassermann has been marked with this level of distinction in the monthly preview polls; the other two instances were for his performances in *Dr. Ehrlich* and *A Dispatch from Reuter's.* The "great old man from Germany," as Bassermann is referred to in these parts, is once again a candidate for no fewer than three positions in the immediately forthcoming October preview poll: for his roles in *Escape* (Metro), in *Moon over Burma* (Paramount), and in *Knute Rockne, All American* (Warner Brothers).

21

Politics and Entertainment

Theater, Radio, and Television

THE CURSE OF HIGH CULTURE was that its favorite medium, drama, already seen by Friedrich Schiller (1759–1805) as a means of educating the sensibilities of the public, could reach only a very limited audience. In 1889, the Berlin theatrical critic Otto Brahm (1856–1912) created the Freie Volksbühne (Free People's Theater) to make available to the masses very inexpensive theater tickets for the new "naturalistic" dramas. Even with this (limited) attempt, at best thousands of urban dwellers visited a given "serious" play. The theater attempted to become part of mass culture, but it rarely succeeded. Only the more popular forms—the revue theaters with their musical shows featuring half-clothed dancers, the cabarets with their political satire, and the varieties, much like the American vaudeville houses—had a mass base, but that, too, was limited to the urban areas.

All this changed on 13 March 1933 when Goebbels's Ministry for Popular Enlightenment and Propaganda centralized all aspects of culture, establishing control over newspapers, literature, art, film, theater, and music. Politically suspect plays were removed; even the popular plays of social criticism by the Anglo-Irish dramatist George Bernard Shaw slowly vanished from the repertoire. But Goebbels knew that the elite and relatively limited audiences of the classic theater were not representative of the masses.

Something else happened on the stage: it became a site for celebrating the Nordic ideal. No longer confined to the traditional enclosed theater, drama came to be played out in open-air amphitheaters set up as ritual *Thingstätte* (Thing places), hailed as a Nazi innovation. The *Thing* was a Nordic ritual celebration of the seasons, the sunrise, the leader, meant to replace the rituals of the church, whatever the denomination. In fact, these mass celebrations simply Aryanized some of the more ritualized Communist mass demonstrations of the 1920s. With hundreds of actors and tens of thousands of participant-observers in the audience, *Thing* plays were akin to other mass demonstrations, such as those documented in Leni Riefenstahl's films of the Nuremberg Reich party rallies or the 1936 Olympics. They presented in ritual form (with a chorus and leader) the eventual success of the Nazi revolution. Among the best-known authors of these dramas was Richard Euringer (1891–1953), a cultural commentator for the Nazi Party paper *Völkischer Beobachter*. His *German Passion* (*Deutsche Passion*) appeared in December 1933 and was awarded the first German National Prize for Drama by Goebbels. By 1936, however, the impact of such activities had diminished and *Thing* plays had virtually disappeared from the Nazi cultural landscape, performed, if at all, by the Hitler Youth for their own events. Yet it was state policy for the theater to remain a vehicle for party propaganda, as the dramatist and critic Hermann Wanderscheck noted in 1939.

Goebbels realized that true mass media would reach well beyond the plays' audiences to establish Nazi ideology in the smallest villages as well as in Germany's sprawling cities: "The radio will be for the twentieth century what the press was for the nineteenth century." Moreover, he said, the Reich would waste no time in establishing radio policies that would capitalize on the power of the medium: "faster than is generally believed, we will clearly and resolutely introduce the Führer principle." As Franz Hartung quite boldly noted, "In the total National Socialist state, there is no such thing as 'apolitical'; everything is subsumed under this one and only notion of the state. As a result, all the topics that were permissible—for example, as treated from a 'purely scientific' perspective—must now necessarily be subject to examination of whether there is a place for them in the broader framework of the National Socialist scheme of cultural values." Radio began to take on the collective and religious overtones once offered by the *Thing* play, as Ferdinand Eckardt observed: "Here we would like to draw the comparison to those kinds of ceremonial rituals that might be most deserving of being called a commonly understood folk art tradition: the religious service."

Not only did the party control radio content; the licensing of inexpensive radios called *Volksempfänger* (people's receivers)—designed by engineer Otto Griessing—spread radio ownership in the early years of Nazi rule. And millions listened. Radio was already ubiquitous in the Weimar Republic, with nine regional networks beginning operation in 1924. But the Nazis produced *Volksempfänger* so cheaply that everyone could listen to Großdeutscher Rundfunk (Greater German Radio), the national network of long-wave broadcast stations controlled by the Ministry of Propaganda from 1 January 1939 to 1945. The *Volksempfänger* were designed to receive only the long-wave national stations of the Deutschlandsender (Reich Broadcast Agency) and the regional stations of the Reichs-Rundfunk-Gesellschaft (Reich Broadcasting Company), so that sanctioned domestic broadcasts could readily be heard while foreign stations could not.[1]

Not surprisingly, Nazified radio encompassed a wide range of programming, most of it "light" entertainment and broadcasts aimed at women or children, as regular surveys of listeners showed. If the regime decried the "star cult" and commercial radio, it did not hesitate to use the same techniques for its own purposes. In part, the programs on the radio were as much a creation of survey research, which revealed a strong preference for music and radio plays—especially among women—as they were vehicles for heavy-handed propaganda. Certainly the Führer's speeches were broadcast into every living room during *Hour of the Nation [Stunde der Nation],* but even the extremely popular music request programs were political in that they sought to create a sense of normalcy during the war and were therefore tinged with ideological implications. Anti-Semitic content, though only rarely presented in crass form, was nonetheless present, being slipped into innocuous contexts; the Jews were the source of all corruption, and hearing such on the radio meant that it had to be true. In 1943, Heinrich Himmler proposed an illegal English-language anti-Semitic broadcast for England and America. Goebbels, for his part, asserted in 1942 that even the language heard on the radio was to be "pure," not sullied with dialect or slang; any such language, despite the Nazi's professed populism, was excised from programming.

There was another medium that had just begun to become available: television. Philo T. Farnsworth had shown the first experimental television broadcast on 7 September 1927 in San Francisco, and D. von Mihály broadcast the first German experimental program in Berlin on 11 May 1928. Television was the great hit of the Fünfte Große *Deutsche Funkausstellung* (Fifth German Radio Exhibition) in 1928. As of 22 March 1935, the select few who had access to a television could watch actual programming, as the *Film-Kurier* reported. Large cities had "television rooms" where up to thirty people could watch the programs on a tiny 7×8 inch (18×22 cm), flickering black-and-white screen. The viewing experience was very primitive compared to that in the luxurious movie palaces, where the images on the silver screen were of a much higher quality. And the content was often the same, with film travelogues and music dominating the airwaves. In May 1945, television and radio went off the air, and Greater German Radio marked the end of the Third Reich by playing Wagner's *Götterdämmerung (Twilight of the Gods).*

NOTE

1. Großdeutscher Rundfunk was created in 1926, and its broadcasts were heard throughout Europe. After 1939, it was the sole long-wave broadcaster in Germany. The Reichs-Rundfunk-Gesellschaft, founded in 1925 as a ring of regional stations, was used exclusively for party propaganda after 1933. After 1939, Reichs-Rundfunk-Gesellschaft and Deutschlandsender were part of the Großdeutscher Rundfunk.

287

LUDWIG MOSHAMER

The *Thingstätte* and Its Meaning for the Future of German Theater

First published as "Die Thingstätte und ihre Bedeutung für das kommende deutsche Theater" in *Bauwelt* 26 (1935), 1–8.

Even though the official position on the *Thingstätte* designates it as the site of celebration and spiritual edification for the unified German *Volk*, many people are now going beyond this and seeing in the *Thingstätte* the beginnings of a rejuvenation of the German theater. Whether these views are correct is something only time will tell; my only aim here is to attempt to demonstrate the possibilities the *Thingstätte* presents by way of substantiating these views and, of course, to simply express my own opinion in this matter.

The following factors were primary considerations in creating the *Thingstätte:*

1. Best possible integration into natural surroundings
2. Intimate, seamless connection between the audience area and the staging area
3. Accommodating the needs of modern stage production to meet the needs of individual actors and mass choruses
4. Solving traffic issues resulting from the arrival and departure of large numbers of people
5. Making sure that the axis of the facility is facing the right direction
6. Ensuring that the site is sufficiently far away from major traffic arteries and railroad tracks to not be bothered by the noise.

Best possible integration into natural surroundings: Here one must take into account the needs shared by every *Thingstätte*—that is to say, needs that are common to all *Thingstätte.* These are, for one thing, the separate, secure audience area and the raised stage area opposite. So the most ideally suited site for a *Thingstätte* is an area with two sloping sides. If there is only one sloping side available, the elevation needed for the stage areas must be created artificially by landfill, which, however, does allow for the possibility of building the dressing rooms and stage areas needed for the actors, choruses, and directors in the landfill. Building a facility on a flat surface requires the artificial creation of the two-sided slopes through excavation and landfill. All *Thingstätte* facilities have this same need for the audience terraces and stage terraces, and these must be met regardless of which of the three basic surface areas is used.

Intimate, seamless connection between the audience area and the staging area: The latest link in the two-thousand-year line of development of the amphitheater, opera houses, and theater houses is the so-called chariot-and-pole system, which separates the audience from the actors, with the stage lighted and the house lights dimmed; the curtain falls after every act and thus interrupts the flow of action and the artistic experience, only to replace it with social interaction, inserting the profane workaday reality between these hours of celebration . . .

The *Thingstätte* has a sloping audience arena with its broad corridors leading through it and up to it, on the one side, and, on the other side, stage areas with staggered terraces at varying heights, loosely joined by stairs. These stage areas swing back to connect with the corridors in the audience arena and form an integrated architectural whole. The actors and choruses can emerge from within the audience to flood the stage areas, and the actors can carry the whole action directly to the audience, thereby escalating the dramatic tension in the audience to the point that they are wholly and intimately involved in the action and have the feeling they are a part of it. And this is the major difference between the *Thingstätte* and the Greek theaters of antiquity, which, while the orchestra pit did protrude into the audience in an arc, still did not include the spatial, architectural integration of stage and audience. Unlike the Greek theater, which sharply separated the spectators from the stage with vertical, balus-

FIGURE 29. The Heidelberg Thingstätte amphitheater where *Thing* plays were performed, ca. 1934. Postcard ca. 1960. Collection of Anson Rabinbach.

traded terraces, the *Thingstätte* terraces encircle the spectators. This distinction is magnified even more when one compares the actual stage layout of these two forms of theater: the antique Greek theater has a two-tiered stage that separates the audience from the action at an angle. Such a stage on which the action is performed from above does not integrate the audience architecturally, whereas the *Thingstätte* stage consists of open terraces that are organic extensions of the audience arena.

288

RICHARD EURINGER

The German Passion 1933

Radio Play in Six Acts

First published as *Deutsche Passion 1933: Hörwerk in Sechs Sätzen* (Oldenburg: Gerhard Stalling, 1933), 33–36.

Act IV

(*Storming masses.*)
(*Extremely upbeat pace. In rapid succession.*)

THE BEGGAR: That's not a German! Where'd he come from?
THE PROLETARIAN: He just wants to stick us back in the military! He wants another war! He's a capitalist!
LEARNED SCHOLAR: I know that man, he is the Antichrist!
He makes a fool of the Redeemer, of the Virgin Mother born!
Makes a mockery of the crown of thorns!

THE INTELLECTUAL: What has he contributed to science?
RACKETEER: What does a dead man know of world economics?
BIG-WHEEL BOSS: He'll terminate the contracts!
He's not fit for those acts!
But you'll see there's hell to pay
when he shakes up the currency some day!
LEARNED SCHOLAR: He'll plunge you into inflation!
With no regard for your salvation!
THE PROLETARIAN: Enough with all these trickeries,
get thee back to the factories.
Today the state provides.
But you'll be slaving away for ages
when he comes after your wages!
THE BEGGAR: Useless parasites! Milksops! Charge!
Beggars take the lead!

(*Violent ruckus.*)

THE MOTHER: Children of the street! I am but a wife.
A mother shields him with her life.
EVERYONE: Get outta there! Power to the masses!

(*Hue and cry.*)

Ahhhhhhhh!!!!!!!
He is not to be had.
THE MOTHER: He'll slip through your hands.
CHILD: I saw it: he climbed out of the mass grave!
RACKETEER: Well, go and get the knave!
BIG-WHEEL BOSS: What? He can't be gotten, can't be bought or sold?
CHILD: Blood dripping from his wounds, still he remains whole!
CRIPPLED WAR VETERAN: Comrades, let him speak!
He comes with revenge to wreak.
THE PROLETARIAN: Just shut your mouths and get in line.
MANY VOICES: Hey, dead man, let the program be assigned.

(*Tremendous silence.*)

THE UNNAMED SOLDIER: (*There is an audible echo from the crowd as these words are spoken.*) You, peasant, do not curse the city
because it's robbed you blind!
Don't escape into the bliss of misery!
Kiss the ground that rejects you!
I'll say it to your face, aristocratic class,
do not despise your noble heritage!
The peasant farmers were a disgrace for the foreigners.
But you have a peasant class of your own.
You, citizen, go to it! It's not enough to reap alone
if you want to dignify the dead.
Do not break your pride, break your gloom instead.
To serve, Lord, is a divine right!
From you, you German youth,
one virtue I request:
your life and limb are not your own.

Die a mortal death and immortality is yours!
And you, you who are beggars here today,
you in the class struggle and proletariat,
step down from the clouds!

(*With arms outstretched,*)

Rejoin the *Volk* of *Volk!*
Extricate yourself from the madness of politics!
Do not curse the jobs and the factories!
Work, work is not drudgery.
Work is comfort. Work brings its own reward. Work, work is what will save the nation.
Where is the man? The man amongst you is not a member of the working class?

THE EVIL SPIRIT (*eerily*): I am the man. Look at me! Pallid and ashen,
glowing like an ember in the flames! I am the one, hatred in person!
Despicable, incorrigible hatred.
I, hatred, am the one who devours the world.
Forward, march! By the column into death!
I am the red dawn of despair!

MANY VOICES: A spirit! In scarlet! Pallid and ashen.

THE MOTHER: Here there is love, there there is hate.
The spirit of good. Of evil.
Now you decide which of them shall be your Redeemer!

THE UNNAMED SOLDIER: People, get down to work! You have the choice.
Now make up your minds, once and for all.

(*Muffled murmuring.*)

289

HERMANN WANDERSCHECK

The Transformation of the Theater in the Third Reich

First published as "Die Verwandlung des Theaters im Dritten Reich," in *Deutsche Dramatik der Gegenwart* (Berlin: Bong & Co., 1939), 1–5.

The transformation of the theater that has been achieved and perfected today is the result of distinct and very clear National Socialist political policy regarding the theater. A government cannot "make" art. It can only provide the basic necessities for creative people to complete their artistic work. In the field of theater, this has been accomplished in large measure. The state provided a great degree of economic and cultural security. With the ratification of a new and modern theater law, the internal relationships between the *Volk* and the theater, between the theater and the leadership of the *Volk* have been reestablished.

With the creation of the Reich Guidelines for Dramaturgy, the state has expressed its unerring will to exert lavish influence over the organic development of the spiritual and artistic, and its firm and generous resolve to become the cultural conscience of all aspects of the theater world. The total exclusion of Jews and all things Jewish from the cultural life of the *Volk* guaranteed that the German stage would again become the "moral institution" of Schiller and the platform for the political and social morality of the times. After having thus removed these decadent elements, the German theater program was reconfigured. The Reich Theater Chamber served as an umbrella organization for the various professional groups and rankings in the theater. Setting up a social security retirement and health insurance system for performing artists inaugurated the beginning of tremendous strides in social security for all German artists. With the establishment of the Reich Academy of Theater, we can be assured of the systematic training and cultivation of new generations of artists to perform on German stages.

There has never been a state government in Germany that has so passionately and vigorously supported the theater as the National Socialists. National Socialism has restored life and liveliness to the German theater. The various stations in the process of reclaiming the theater for the national culture are recorded in the Reich Theater Festivals. The crowning achievements and pinnacles of development in the will to reconstruct are reflected here. In 1934, the first signs of this will toward transformation, this readiness to act, this will to meet the aim were seen in Dresden. In 1935, with its Dietrich Eckart performances, Hamburg took the first steps toward the realization of a distinctly National Socialist German national theater. In 1936, Munich set a groundbreaking benchmark in contemporary political drama: the plays of Hanns Johst, Friedrich Bethge, and Eberhard Wolfgang Möller set the tone for the direction that would ultimately determine the calling and lasting endurance for German drama. By 1937, the German dramatic play had clearly emerged as a poetically sound and morally cultivated form. In 1938, the first Reich Theater Festival for Greater Germany was held in Vienna to stage a spectacular display of German dramatic arts. In addition to the Reich Theater Festivals, the theater festivals of the Hitler Youth, and the cultural festivals of the individual *Gau* throughout the Reich have become veritable weeklong dramaturgical training camps for contemporary drama.

Dramatic theater, after all the years of turbulence, despair, and upheaval, has restored faith in new creative works of art. The finished product is never in evidence at the onset of such a complete, top-to-bottom reformation as German theater has experienced. Many of the literary and dramatic impulses are only now beginning to emerge in rough outline. The transformation of the theater is now a fact of life, a felicitous fact of the drama of our struggle in the future.

The actor becomes the megaphone for the new political rhythm. His pathos is transformed. The dramatic performance is no longer determined by the superficial talent for mime and mimicry, nor by the stylistic artistry of donning masks; instead, dramatic form is now the driving force behind indefatigable rigor in all aspects of the dramatic performance. It is a magical process that the actor goes through with his own literary will to persevere: putting himself in the dramatist's shoes, making his mark in a new literary signature. Recreating the dramatic tension—that is one of the arduous tasks the actor must take on in the struggle for the Third Reich. Even the greatest of actors and performers are adherents and activists, in service to the writer and to the nation. [. . .]

The community-oriented dramatist is not positioned below the *Volk* but rather is part of the *Volk*. The singular force of unity that emerges from this bond is overpowering: it is the destiny that fuels his resolve to create dramatic works of art. The man who is rooted in and flourishes amongst the *Volk* is the hero of a new art that not only illustrates the problems but also overcomes them. The dramatist has deposed daring [as a virtue] and replaced it with duty, has deposed prescriptive standards for what "should" be and replaced them with cultivated morality and faith, has deposed intent and replaced it with insight. The dramatist who accepts responsibility for his *Volk* is the unerring herald and narrator of the German soul and the German spirit.

The original source is always the *Volk,* and the idea that is paramount is that the community-oriented dramatist will always draw his strengths from adherence to this belief. The theater is not driven by any political or any other manner of ulterior motive; it is merely the designated poetological space for theater that is an unmitigated expression and creative product of the *Volk*. Thus, Hanns Johst concludes that it is not so much a matter of the didactic power of a dramatist inspired by a high-handed, self-appointed task of educating the *Volk*, but rather that it is a matter of the formative and constructive power of the *Volk* itself that gives rise to and elevates the new dramatist.

> Which presupposes, of course, that the drama is not created in some academic cubicle, distanced by education, distanced by isolation, but rather that it is created from the common struggle for existence with one's fellow man, who clearly senses the immediate overall resemblance to his own life; and with that, the drama at once becomes an exemplary reflection of the totality of the *Volk*.

Drama is currently engaged in a reclarification of its basic premises. The political morality of National Socialism is forming the basis for a new *völkisch* mythology in drama. The direction it takes is subordinate only to the grandeur of an ideological worldview, not to the vicissitudes of workaday life. This implies always thinking and feeling as part of a whole and on behalf of a whole.

> What art can do and what it should do is this: glean from the midst of arbitrary circumstances and events that problem that transcends the limits of time that can be depicted to have a didactic effect, to make sense of the moment in light of eternity, and to point toward the future from the prospect of the present. If the drama is not to end up in mere dialogue, every manner of artistic production must be indirect. In this sense, the period play is not only legitimate, it is necessary: you could go so far as to ask whether every piece of strong drama should not be categorized as a period play. The only thing that can ever be of interest to us about long-bygone periods and peoples is that which has meaning for us and offers us insights into ourselves. We designate a work as having an impact when it really does have an impact, and the much-touted timelessness of a work is nothing more than its power to capture the life of a certain period and to thus preserve it so well that it remains alive for all eternity. (Dr. Rainer Schlösser)

290

SECRET REPORT OF THE SECURITY SERVICE OF THE REICHSFÜHRER SS

On Performances of Works by [George] Bernard Shaw

First circulated on 10 March 1941 as "Zur Aufführung der Werke von Bernard Shaw." First published in *Meldungen aus dem Reich 1938–1945. Die geheimen Lageberichte des Sicherheitsdienstes der SS*, edited by Heinz Boberach (Herrsching: Pawlak Verlag, 1984), 6:2096.

According to reports here, performances of works by the Irish writer [George] Bernard Shaw have increased in recent months. Reports from Berlin, Weimar, Düsseldorf, Karlsbad, Munich, Oppeln, Dresden, and Karlsruhe indicate that these performances have been somewhat successful, although theatergoers continue to ask themselves why, in wartime, the works of an Irish-English author currently living in England are being performed on German stages in a translation by the Jew [Siegfried] Trebitsch. The public was somewhat surprised to learn, for example, that Shaw's *Saint Joan* was featured at the gala performance on 30 January 1941 in Chemnitz. Reports indicate that public opinion sees Shaw first and foremost as an Englishman, especially since he has so often been given a high profile as an Englishman in literary scholarship and in the press. In theater circles you often hear the question as to whether the royalties for the translations are still going to the Jew Trebitsch. Since performances of works by Shaw are being subjected to this form of criticism, it would seem that a clarification of this matter is in order.

291

JOSEPH GOEBBELS

Radio as the Eighth Great Power

Delivered on 18 August 1933 as "Der Rundfunk als achte Großmacht." First published in *Signale der neuen Zeit: 25 ausgewählte Reden von Dr. Joseph Goebbels* (Munich: Zentralverlag der NSDAP, 1938), 197–207. Translated by Randall Bytwerk. Calvin College, German Propaganda Archive.

My fellow citizens!

Napoleon spoke of the press as "the seventh great power." Its significance became politically visible with the beginning of the French Revolution, and it maintained its position for the entirety of the nineteenth century. The century's politics were largely determined by the press. One can hardly imagine or explain the major historical events between 1800 and 1900 without considering the powerful influence of journalism.

The radio will be for the twentieth century what the press was for the nineteenth century. Applying Napoleon's words to our age, we could adapt this statement to speak in terms of the radio as the eighth great power. Its discovery and application are of truly revolutionary significance for contemporary community life. Future generations may conclude that the radio had as great an intellectual and spiritual impact on the masses as the printing press had before the beginning of the Reformation.

The November Regime was not able to understand the full significance of the radio.[1] Even those who claimed to have awakened the people and gotten them involved in practical politics were without exception almost blind to the possibilities of this modern method for influencing the masses.

At best, they saw it as an easy way to distract the masses from the difficulties of our national and social life through games and entertainment. Only reluctantly did they think of using radio for political purposes. As in all other things, they viewed radio through the mildew of an ostensible objectivity. They left the radio and its development to its technical and administrative experts, limiting their own use of it for partisan purposes to times of particular domestic crises.

It goes without saying that the National Socialist revolution, which is modern and intent on action, as well as the popular upheaval we have led, must change abstract and lifeless methods in the radio. The old regime was content simply to fill empty offices or change the faces, without, however, changing the spirit and content of public life. We, on the other hand, intend a principled transformation in the worldview of our entire society, a revolution of the greatest possible scope that will leave nothing out, changing the life of our nation in every regard.

This process, which has been visible to the layman in the past six months, was naturally not random. It was systematically prepared and organized. We have used our power in the past six months to carry out this transformation. We spent the period before 30 January in winning power, having then the same goals that we have carried out in the six months since we seized power.

It would not have been possible for us to seize power or to use it in the ways we have without the radio and the airplane. It is no exaggeration to say that the German revolution, at least in the form it took, would have been impossible without the airplane and the radio.

FIGURE 30. Hitler inspecting a model of the people's receiver (*Volksempfänger*), a basic mass-produced radio to facilitate listening to propaganda broadcasts. *Unser Führer: zum 50. Geburtstag Adolf Hitlers am 20. April 1939* (Munich: Verlag Franz Eher Nachfolger GmbH, 1939), 31.

It is, in fact, a modern revolution, and it has used the most modern methods to win and use power. It therefore goes without saying that the government resulting from this revolution cannot ignore the radio and its possibilities. To the contrary, it is resolved to use them to the fullest extent in the work of national construction that is before us and in ensuring that this revolution can stand the test of history.

That means a series of important reforms in the organization and content of the radio. On the one hand, these reforms will assure the organic continuation of the radio and its further development both in the near and long term. They will also mean a transformation of its whole nature, bringing it in tune with the modern community of our people.

As in all other areas, the changes are primarily spiritual in nature. The radio must be brought out of the stubborn emptiness of its technical limitations into the lively spiritual developments of our age. It is not possible for the radio to ignore the times. More than any other form of public expression, it has the duty to meet the needs and demands of the day. A radio that does not seek to deal with the problems of the day does not deserve to influence the broad masses. It will soon become an empty playground for technicians and intellectual experimenters. We live in the age of the masses; the masses rightly demand that they participate in the great events of the day. The radio is the most influential and important intermediary between a spiritual movement and the nation, between the idea and the people.

That requires a clearly expressed direction. I have spoken of this often with regard to various areas of our spiritual life. There can be no lack of direction, neither for people nor for things. The moral value or lack thereof depends not on words but on content. The direction and the goal always determine whether something is good, useless, or even harmful for our people.

A government that is determined to bring a nation together so that it is once more a center of power in the scales of great world events has not only the right but the duty to subordinate all aspects of the nation to its goals, or at least ensure that they are supportive. That is also true for the radio. The more significant something is in influencing the will of the broad masses, the greater its responsibility to the future of the nation.

That does not mean we want to turn the radio into a spineless servant of our partisan political interests. The new German politics rejects any partisan limitations. It seeks the totality of the people and nation, and the reconstructive work it plans or has already begun includes all who are of good will. Within the framework of these great tasks, the radio, if it is to remain living, must hold to and advance its own artistic and spiritual laws. Just as its technical methods are modern and distinct, so too are its artistic capacities. It is only distantly related to the stage and film. It is rarely possible to bring a powerful stage or film presentation to the radio without making adaptations. There is a style of speaking on the radio, a style of drama, of opera, of radio show. The radio is in no way a branch of the stage or film but rather an independent entity with its own rules.

It faces particular demands to be topical. It works with the tasks and needs of the day. Its duty is to give immediate events lasting meaning. Its actuality is both its greatest danger and its greatest strength. It gave impressive evidence on 21 March and 1 May of its ability to reach the people with great historical events. The first event acquainted the entire nation with a major political event, the second with an event of social-political significance. Both reached the entire nation, regardless of class, standing, or religion. That was primarily the result of the tight centralization, the strong reporting, and the up-to-date nature of the German radio.

Being up-to-date brings one close to the people. We call our revolution a popular one for good reason. It came from the depths of the people. It was carried out by the people and done for them. It dethroned absolute individualism and put the people once again at the center. It broke with the weary skepticism of our intellectual leadership, which in the end turned out to be only a thin layer of morbid big-city intellectualism that left the masses alone in their hopeless misery.

The problems that we in the government face today are the same problems facing the man in the street. The problems we treat over the ether in plays, speeches, addresses, and dramas are the problems that directly concern people. The better the radio recognizes them and treats them in fresh and varied ways, the better it will fulfill its tasks and the more the people will resolve to deal with these problems.

Before we reach this ideal situation in our radio policies, there are a series of preparations and problems to deal with. These are primarily organizational. It was apparently characteristic of the period directly preceding us that it, for lack of any significant spiritual or political purposes, restricted its focus to administrative governance, which then burgeoned far beyond any tolerable limit. The disease of that period infected radio stations as well. Here, too, one organized not what had to be organized but whatever *could* be organized. Just as a hundred cooks spoil the soup, a hundred bureaucrats will spoil any measure of spiritual success. The more committees, review committees, bureaucrats, and higher offices there were in the German radio system, the fewer its political accomplishments. Here more than anywhere else, there were no personalities who took pleasure in responsibility. The spiritual energy, the flexibility necessary to reach the people in changing times, may not be the responsibility of boards, commissions, or committees. They only get in the way. Here too, faster than is generally believed, we will clearly and resolutely introduce the Führer principle.

Excessive organization can only get in the way of productivity. The more bureaucrats, the more obscure the internal structures, the easier it is for someone to hide his inability or incompetence behind some committee or board. And not only that: excessive organization is always the beginning of corruption. It confuses responsibility and thus enables those of weak character to enrich themselves at public expense.

That is what formerly happened in the German radio system. There were huge salaries that lacked any justification given what was accomplished, outrageous expense accounts, generous insurance policies, usually inversely disproportionate to any positive achievements. There are some today who claim to have been the "fathers of radio." One can say to them only that they were not the ones who developed radio but rather that they made no productive use of it in hard times. They knew only how to exploit it for their own benefit. It would surely be good for those who really built the German radio if they did not have to stand beside these fortune hunters with their fat wallets and empty consciences. As the saying has it, "Tell me your friends and I'll tell you who you are."

I need not say that the government of the National Socialist revolution will not be moved in its resolve to bring order here. We will eliminate excessive organization as quickly as possible, replacing it with spartan simplicity and economy. We will also systematically increase productivity in all areas. We will bring to the microphone the best spiritual elements of the nation, making radio into the most multifaceted, flexible means of expressing the wishes, needs, longings, and hopes of our age.

We do not intend to use radio only for our partisan purposes. We want room for entertainment, popular arts, games, jokes, and music. But everything should have a relationship to our day. Everything should include the theme of our great reconstructive work, or at least not stand in its way. Above all, it is necessary to clearly centralize all radio activities, to place spiritual tasks ahead of technical ones, to introduce the leadership principle, to provide a clear worldview, and to present this worldview in flexible ways.

We want a radio that reaches the people, a radio that works for the people, a radio that is an intermediary between the government and the nation, a radio that also reaches across our borders to give the world a picture of our life and our work. The money generated from fees paid by radio listeners should, in general, go back into radio. If there are surpluses, they should be used to serve the spiritual and cultural needs of the whole nation. If the stage and publishing industries suffer from the rapid growth of radio, we will use the revenues not necessary for the radio to maintain and strengthen other areas of intellectual and artistic life. The purpose of radio is to teach, entertain, and support people, not to gradually harm the intellectual and cultural life of the nation. One of my main tasks in the near and more distant future will be to keep a reasonable balance in this regard. I am convinced that the radio, as well as theater, publishing, and film, will benefit.

With the opening of this [annual German Radio] exhibition, a systematic campaign to advertise for new radio receivers begins. We will use the knowledge of propaganda we gained in the past years. Our goal is to double German radio listenership. That will result in a financial foundation that will not only enable radio to carry on its mission but also support the entire intellectual and cultural life of the nation. We will strengthen the stage, film, music, and publishing, providing a firm financial foundation.

This year's radio exhibition opens in this spirit. Its keynote is the people's receiver. Its affordable price will enable the broad masses to become radio listeners. Science and industry have done what they could, earning the thanks of the government and of the whole nation. May the radio leadership now do its part. Then we will together accomplish our goal. If science, industry, and intellectual leaders work hand in hand, and if their common efforts are supported by a steadfast sense of the highest political responsibility, then we will leave behind the many mistakes and errors of the past and open a new era of German radio. It will open new paths not only for Germany's political life but also for the work of radio throughout the world.

This exhibition stands in the shadow of this great task. It is a start, a beginning, an expression of German courage and German confidence.

It is our dearest wish that science, industry, and the intellectual leadership of German radio from now on will follow a new path, at the end of which stands our common, great goal:

One *Volk,* one Reich, one will, and a glorious German future!

In this sense, I declare the Tenth German Radio Exhibition open.

Note

1. The so-called November Regime began on 9 November 1918 when Philipp Scheidemann announced the existence of the new Weimar Republic from a balcony at the Reichstag building in Berlin.—Eds.

292

FRANZ HARTUNG

Radio and Politics

First published as "Rundfunk und Politik," in *Rufer und Hörer* 8, no. 3 (November 1933): 355–57.

Politics in Radio

In the total National Socialist state, there is no such thing as "apolitical"; everything is subsumed under this one and only notion of the state. As a result, all the topics that were permissible—for example, as treated from a "purely scientific" perspective—must now necessarily be subject to examination of whether there is a place for them in the broader framework of the National Socialist scheme of cultural values. Every form of activity in the state must be examined in terms of its utility and benefit to the political needs of the state; this utterly obliterates any notion of the apolitical because the only measure of value is in terms of political relevance. This is why politics is the determining factor in radio: it resembles the center axis of a wheel whose spokes are the driving force behind everything else.

Political Radio

The situation is an entirely different one for political radio. Political radio is an instrument employed consciously by the state as an active force to achieve a desired goal. Radio's role as a reflector of events is transformed into one of a vehicle for prescriptive and prosperity-driven propaganda promoting a specific political state structure. This "messenger" [as it were] becomes a town crier of sorts and a signpost or guide whose influence, power, and creative force take marching orders from an outside source that is ruled by the law of the moment or deployed as a preliminary organism in the interest of reaching some praiseworthy goal. The framework for any task determined in this fashion (which may occur in various fields and be approached from various angles) will always leave enough latitude and room for interpretation for radio to always develop from its own creative impulses. Certain shifts within the broadcast agency relating to the scope of each individual thematic focus play an altogether minimal role because we are concerned here with temporary circumstances. Once the goal that has been set is reached, an adjustment must and will take place that avoids any stagnation of the organic growth. The following example perhaps illustrates both functions of radio. When the Führer addresses the nation on all the German broadcast channels, then that is political radio—that is to say, an instrument employed to serve the interests of the state. The Führer's statements form, at the same time, the basis for the political life of the nation; they are political guidelines that must also determine the direction of future work in radio. Within the framework of these guidelines, broadcast media can develop programming at will; they must only adhere to the same standard that is applied to everything else: that politics is a necessary element of radio.

Politics through Radio

The word *politics* is to be understood here in the very broadest sense to mean the highest level of politics: foreign policy. Since other countries are governed by different laws concerning radio broadcasting, the political policies of German radio have perhaps not been understood and been staunchly criticized outside our national borders. Whoever has fully grasped the ideologies and the idea of the total state in all its ramifications must necessarily acknowledge the primacy of politics in radio broadcasting as a state organism and see in radio the means to transmit every aspect of national political and national cultural life. The political radio outlined here makes sense only from the perspective of the total state with an eye for the internal political policies of the National Socialist state. This function is to be strictly distinguished from our foreign policy goals. That may often prove a difficult task, understandably enough, in light of the fact that the impact of wireless frequencies is not bound by any national boundaries. Political radio directs its broadcasts into the political living space of its own people and is tailored specifically to the mentality of the German listener. And this is the only foundation for any critical assessment from outsiders. Employing radio systematically in the framework of foreign policy is politics through radio: by virtue of its technical capacities for impact, radio has become an invaluable instrument that is a whole new modern form of communication. That is how it is seen by outsiders, and that is how it should be received by listeners. (One could object by saying it's not a form of communication, it's an instrument of propaganda!) If that is the case, then every broadcast station anywhere in the world is an instrument of propaganda, whether it promotes its message through oratory or through the power of a musical masterpiece. In that sense, every form of cultural production is propaganda by simple virtue of its inherent content, without any targeted intent. A little over a year ago, leaders of various countries were still considering the telephone the most modern mode of communication (and were in awe of it, even though every private citizen had already been using it for similar purposes for decades as a matter of course); today these telephone conversations are broadcast publicly for the political public of the participating or affected nations to hear: that is politics through radio! This function of radio is anything but an invention of the German Reich or of any form of state structure. (Italy, for example, is proof that this is not the case, because here there is very little use of radio in foreign policy. That can only be understood in the context of the way radio is structured and used in general in Italy.) No, this is a function assigned to radio in all modern, advanced technological states. The abhorrent deployment of radio in Russia's foreign policy that has been sharply criticized by all the nations of Europe is a form of "propaganda" that has nothing in common with cultural advertising and understanding based on the mutual exchange of ideas.

293

FERDINAND ECKHARDT

No More Stars!

First published as "Los vom Star!" in *Rufer und Hörer* 8, no. 3 (November 1933): 351–53.

The star is beyond a shadow of doubt one of the most baneful, calamitous by-products of the liberalistic-individualist arts industry, whether on the stage, in film, music, literature, fine arts, and finally also in radio. During the age of superficial "education," everyone had to have at least a few catchwords to say for every topic, even if he knew nothing else about it; in every field of art, you had to know at least a couple of names, just the bare minimum, extraneous knowledge that was not the least bit essential to the subject, and this is what led to a flagrant overestimation of the individual, which in turn gave rise to the star. All too predictably, then, the masses formed their understanding of what was representative for each individual field [of art] based on the most tired old clichés. The spirit of unscrupulous opportunism then bolstered these platitudes to the hilt and ruthlessly exploited the misguided public for its own interests. Based on the pretext of offering "quality," everything that was truly of value was destroyed. For in showering certain individuals who were, for the most part, not overly talented in the first place with fame and fortune, perhaps in order to fuel their ambitions and their lust for material goods so that they would intensify their performances to the heights of so-called virtuosity, people engaged in an almost criminal neglect of that class of people that could be called the "arbiters of culture," thus rendering not only every form of spectacular achievement utterly impossible in the future, but even every form of good achievement.

However, what we do know is that not only in every period of history that has enjoyed a genuine folk art such as we again strive to establish today in the spirit of the National Socialist state, but also in every field where there still exists today a form of folk art that is understood by everyone—for example, in church music—the spectacular achievements are not what is decisive, but rather solid average achievements. Similarly, in all periods that have been host to a genuine folk art, the name of the producer [of that art] has never played anything but a practical role. Far more, those works that could be described as "popular" in the finest sense of the term—from the *Song of the Nibelungs* to the medieval cathedrals, from the simplest of folk songs to *Doctor Faust*—were created anonymously. All too often, though, when the name of the artist is cited in conjunction with a work of art, people fall back on responding to superficial, extraneous details. Instead of appreciating the genuine, intrinsic value, precedence is given to outward appearances. This is how it could ultimately come down to a situation in which people are willing to pay much more for a simple signature on a painting than for another sterling-quality artistic achievement, or in which the actual work involved in lectures, books, etc. is no longer compensated but that instead names become worth their weight in gold.

This is not an attempt to explore whether or not the speculative exploitation of a name in the service of certain business interests is what created this superficial intellectualism or whether the ground for this was already laid in the latent tendency of the masses to gravitate toward unconscionable exploitation of catchphrase education by shameless, petty thinkers; it is more likely that the one fed and fueled the other. One thing is certain—that this intellectualism was veritably cultivated by the existing arts industries. Honest, hardworking men in theater and in film have long since recognized the baneful problem and have attempted repeatedly to fight it—in vain, unfortunately. Even the attempt to attack the beast by going after the practice of naming prestigious names just for their advertising value is futile whenever the business interests of the company are impinged upon; this includes listing the names of individual famous actors, singers, conductors, or names of sound equipment manufacturers, labels in films, or the instrument manufacturers in concerts. All these cases involve one-sided advertising that promotes one thing at the expense of all others, which, as we have outlined above, comprise the class that has been the arbiter of culture all along. No wonder, then, that previously existing methods, especially in intellectual and artistic matters, have led to the formation of a corporate alliance that has been at least as devastating in its effect on culture as it has in economics.

If there is any area of cultural and intellectual life that, any short-term self-interest notwithstanding, is in a position to make an uncompromising break with something that has been unequivocally declared wrong, and in fact destructive, then it is radio. We see in radio the one cultural organization that, because it rests securely in the hands of the state, is young enough not to be as set in its ways as, for example, the National Theater or museums that have been devastated by the star cult not only in their outstretched branches but that have been gutted at their very root. For it is not merely a matter of shutting down those few world-famous tenors and prima donnas in all their attention-seeking airs; it must necessarily imply the elimination of everything that might foster the development of similar habits of thought in the future. Therefore, the suggestion is that the names of announcers, actors, and speakers or authors be withheld from radio broadcasts, at the very least on a trial basis and in select areas.

We do not see the point in subjecting the audience of a radio play to a whole list of collaborators beyond the author and director. At best, we might make note of one or the other names of individual actors or perhaps remember that we have seen or heard this or that one on some other occasion. But what does that have to do with the content of the radio play? We do not understand either why it is necessary to list the names of all the musicians on a piece of music played by a seven-member band. Here we would like to draw the comparison to those kinds of ceremonial rituals that might be most deserving of being called a commonly understood folk art tradition: the religious service. Who could so much as imagine listing the names of every individual involved with the altar and even members of the liturgical staff before a church service or, before a choral element, announcing the name of the composer and musicians? Justifiably, this would be seen as a completely unnecessary distraction from the intended spirit of the religious ceremony. And the same, of course, also applies to any political ceremony. In this context, it would be unthinkable to announce the name of the conductor or the singer. It is only in a certain form of art, or of music, one that is devoid of any ritual significance—and is therefore far removed from any higher purpose—[that] a form of art that exists but for its own sake, for the sheer "pleasure" of it, that the name of the artist does not seem like an intrusion. But this form of art—severed from life, "abstract" in the fullest sense of the term, and catering to an ever-smaller class of "educated" people who are "in the know"—this form of art cannot be the art of the new state; it cannot represent a *Volk* of people unified as one nation; therefore, it cannot be the art of radio, which is something that belongs to the *Volk* as one nation. [. . .]

Responsibility for citing the authors of intellectual property does not play any role in this matter, for it is the responsibility of the author or speaker to ensure that the radio broadcast cites his authorship. But the radio station bears sole responsibility for the quality of the broadcast and the reliability of its guests, and he cannot excuse a bad or less than average broadcast by saying that some sensational expert—the provost of some university, member of the National Theater, etc.—did all the talking. It is far more pertinent that the radio station permit only such programs to be broadcast as are of such sterling quality that they represent the very best in their field—or, more appropriately, that are the most amenable to radio broadcast. The station itself must accept full responsibility for the quality of each individual program.

294

LISA PECK

Women and Radio
The Numbers

First published as "Die Frau und der Rundfunk—in Zahlen," in *Rufer und Hörer* 4, no. 2 (May 1934): 65, 71, 72, 75.

The material presented in this article is taken from statistics gathered in a survey of 500 German women between the ages of twenty-five and seventy-five. These 500 women were categorized in five separate groups:

100 housewives

100 farmwives

100 laborers

100 office employees and officials

100 freelance, self-employed women [. . .]

As was to be expected, the survey reflects all women's natural love of music. Women continue to find opera music particularly attractive. Countless respondents in each of the groups repeatedly asked why contemporary radio programming has such a limited offering of opera recordings and emphasized that they would very much like to see more of this.

The question that is always hotly debated not only amongst producers of radio broadcasts but also among listeners as to whether serious or popular music is preferable was answered by survey respondents as follows.

laborers: prefer popular music only

farmwives: prefer classical and popular music

housewives: prefer classical and popular music

office employees/officials: prefer classical and popular music

freelance, self-employed women: half prefer classical music only, the rest popular music only

However, a very different picture emerges when it comes to concerts on phonograph records:

laborers: prefer concerts on phonograph records

farmwives: love concerts on phonograph records but only those by first-rate artists

housewives: love concerts on phonograph records but only those by first-rate artists

office employees/officials: love concerts on phonograph records but only those by first-rate artists

freelance, self-employed women: reject the very notion of concerts on phonograph records

Particularly noteworthy is the degree of political engagement equally evident in all groups—the Führer's speeches, reports on national holidays, etc. This raises the question we have already posed as to whether it would not make sense to introduce a weekly program *Ten Minutes of Politics for Women.*

Opinions about radio plays are divided. Many of the survey questionnaires indicate that they are especially popular. But at least as many also note, "no radio plays because they're too hard to understand," or, at the very least, "not so many radio plays." It is conspicuous that this is especially true of laborers, a portion of the office employees and officials, and the freelance, self-employed women—women, that is, who have little free time for listening to music during the day and therefore would prefer to hear music in the evening.

The question of the opera, of serious versus popular music, of phonograph records, politics, and radio plays are of general interest to all the women surveyed. However, the women are naturally more concerned with the women's hour [*Frauenstunde*] because these issues pertain exclusively to them. A rather odd picture emerges with regard to programming in the two major subject categories of home economics and art and culture. (Please note, in the interest of avoiding potential misunderstandings, that arts and culture programming is understood to include all scholarly and scientific lectures, radio plays, lectures on the lives of famous women, vocational training for women, programs about child rearing and education, fashion, etc.; home economics programming includes the housewife's hour, bill of fare, practical tips, recipes, new products and services for the household.)

laborers: strong preference for home economics, little interest in arts and culture programming

farmwives: no interest in home economics but strong interest in arts and culture programming

freelance, self-employed women: the same

housewives: equally interested in home economics and arts and culture programming

office employees/officials: the same

The surprising result is the almost unanimous rejection of home economics issues by farmwives. And yet there is a logical explanation. The farmwives feel they are proficient enough in matters of home economics that they would prefer to spend what free time is available to them with the arts and culture programming for which they have a far greater passion. [. . .]

In general, women's expectations for radio are situated somewhere between two extreme poles: rest—relaxation and stimulus—education. It is understandable that all the laborers and a portion of the freelance and self-employed women—amongst them, a number of prominent artists and film actresses—are interested only in rest and relaxation. But there is no single group that is interested exclusively in stimulus and education. Radio as an instructive medium is patently rejected by women—vehemently so. Because the office employees and officials, and to an even greater degree, the farmwives—who have expressed a desire for this kind of programming—concede at the same time that they look for rest and relaxation in radio programming to balance out the more strenuous programming. For housewives, the interest in both types of programming is about equal. And yet, in their case, the perspective is somewhat skewed by the fact that they comprise by far the largest consumer group, measured on the basis of number of listening hours. For them, unfortunately, the loudspeaker often serves as background noise. They listen to anything that is broadcast whenever they are at home in the apartment. The demand for an increase in the frequency and intensity of the women's hours is likely to be based primarily on the rural women's interest in arts and culture in radio.

295

A. WULFF

500 Schoolchildren in Berlin Tell about Radio

First published as "500 Berliner Volksschulkinder erzählen vom Radio," in *Rufer und Hörer* 3, no. 4 (June 1934): 176, 177, 178, 179, 182, 183.

Hour of the Nation and Hitler's Speeches

All children across the board report that they listen to Hitler's speeches and to those of the other government officials. The same is true of the *Hour of the Nation* [*Stunde der Nation*]. It seems that the *Hour of the Nation* has in fact established itself as standard fare everywhere. Gathering around the radio every evening to listen to the *Hour of the Nation* seems to have become a set ritual. Children report on a regular basis, "My parents listen to the *Hour of the Nation* every night at 7:00 P.M." Or "*Hour of the Nation* is always very interesting. I particularly enjoy listening to the old village music when the program is broadcast from Bavaria. There should be more programs like this. I like to hear some shepherds from the Alm speak." This child is apparently especially taken with programming designed to generate better understanding between rural and urban populations. But this is the only one to have made specific reference to this program in particular; the others are apparently far too urban-oriented to take much interest in rural life. Very often, children report that what they like best about *Hour of the Nation* are the radio plays. Some children conclude that the *Nation* programs are often very good but sometimes hard to understand. What they like best is when radio plays whose protagonists are from the working class are broadcast. This opinion is interesting from a psychological perspective. Everyone likes to hear material derived from his own life. The listener wants to see himself. His life is what should be depicted. One girl has stated, "I especially like the *Hour of the Nation* because it connects us to people from all walks of life; it offers information about the manners and customs of the ancient Germanics."

The children have even more to say about the Führer's speeches. That only stands to reason since they listen to the major speeches in school. It is clear to them from the very outset that a Hitler speech is something special because regular classroom instruction is preempted to accommodate it. But the same degree of interest in the Führer's speeches is reflected even at home. Everyone everywhere gathers around the radio to be sure they don't miss a single word of a speech. When Hitler speaks, everyone else automatically falls silent because everyone wants to hear what he has to say. "My father is especially glad that the Hitler speeches are always rebroadcast in the evening; that way, you can sit down and listen to every word at your leisure." "We all sit around the radio when the Reich chancellor is speaking." "When Hitler speaks, we all sit around listening with heartfelt passion." One eight-year-old admits, "I like to listen to Adolf Hitler speak, but really it's not for me." Apparently, this child sees being allowed to listen to the radio as a sign of adulthood—he doesn't really understand any of it but [listens] since all the adults are listening! One twelve-year-old explains, "But the best part is Adolf Hitler's speeches—they are so full of power, of trust in God and faith in his *Volk*."

You can see from this broad palette of opinions that indeed all age groups already have some grasp of the significance of great political speeches. But the full scope of the overriding importance of the *Hour of the Nation* can be understood only in light of what else people listen to, or, better, prefer not to listen to. What people expect first and foremost from radio is relaxation, and this has been substantiated again and again. [. . .]

Summary:

One child wrote a report that included a listing of everything that his family listened to at home, and this is a typical list of priorities:

When there are lectures or opera, we turn the radio off. But when our Führer is speaking, we turn it on. But we also tune in to variety shows, gramophone records, military or dance music. Sunday afternoons, there is always a nice children's hour broadcast from *Königs Wusterhausen*. I always listen to that while I'm doing my handicrafts. One boy lists the following priorities:

> I like to listen to fairy tales on the radio, and to [the Silesian humorist Ludwig Manfred] Lommel, and I like the handicrafts hour. I also like Otto Kermbach and the military marching songs. I like to listen to folk songs, I like to listen to the daily news. I like to hear Adolf Hitler speak. My mama likes to listen on Thursdays because she likes Otto Kermbach and [Johann] Strauss. She also likes to listen to Lommel. My papa likes to listen to the *SS-Standarte,* Adolf Hitler, and Lommel. I don't like to listen to chamber music, and neither does my papa.

These listings are interesting not only for what they contain but perhaps even more for what they leave out—that is, what seems to play no role whatsoever. In general, one gets the impression that the children's statements reflect the general sentiment of the population when they say, "My parents like radio just the way it is now. They say it is a lot better now than it was before, and we listen to it a lot now." Radio has since become a permanent fixture and major factor in rest and relaxation for a substantial portion of the populace. Furthermore, it is used as a means of staying abreast of major political developments. The *Hour of the Nation* demonstrates that there is a demand for information concerning the complexities of the overall cultural framework, but in programming that should not be all too demanding for the listener. This is certainly a better method for cultural education than the attempt to influence the listener through isolated lectures or to present them with good music in long concert evenings.

296

HEINZ GOEDECKE AND WILHELM KRUG

Soldiers of the German Army, Lend Us Your Ears!

First published as "Soldaten der deutschen Wehrmacht! Einmal herhören!" in *Wir beginnen das Wunschkozert für die Wehrmacht* (Berlin: Nibelungen-Verlag, 1941), 34, 35.

For four weeks now, you Eastern Front soldiers have been marching from one victory to another. For the past four weeks, the soldiers of the Western Front have been loyally defending Germany's border in the bunkers of the West Wall. For four weeks now, the proud German air force has been making decisive contributions to crushing an opponent that once advertised to the whole world that it would do us in at the Battle of Berlin. And at the same time, our boys in blue [in the navy] have been doing great honor to the German name, sailing the seven seas, or the harbors, and in the coastal batteries protecting Germany's shores from any form of attack.

You soldiers on the Western Front, and on the coast and the high seas, get news of your comrades' victories in the east and what is happening on the home front from the radio. In the past few weeks, while you soldiers on the Eastern Front were engaged in your stormy advance and the "letters to the front" [*Feldpostbrief*] couldn't reach you, the radio was your only contact to home. How often have you gathered together around the radio to listen for news of the homeland and so to remain in touch with your great German fatherland through the ether? From somewhere on the Bzura, on the San, on the Weichsel or Narew Rivers, you heard the Führer addressing the nation of German *Volk,* and in that moment you were filled beyond measure with pride and bliss. So it is no wonder that German radio has been a particularly good friend to you these days.

This is why so many of you have written us letters from the front in the past several weeks, and what we take from these field post letters is always the same thing: you'd like to hear more music. Many of you made requests for us to play your favorite song. We will be glad to accommodate these requests—to the extent that we are able.

297

SECRET REPORT OF THE SECURITY SERVICE OF THE REICHSFÜHRER SS

Armed Forces Radio Request Program Well Received

First circulated in September 1940 as "Aufnahme der Wehrmachtswunschkonzerte bei der Bevölkerung und bei den Soldaten." First published in *Meldungen aus dem Reich 1938–1945. Die geheimen Lageberichte des Sicherheitsdienstes der SS,* edited by Heinz Boberach (Herrsching: Pawlak Verlag, 1984), 5:940–41.

Countless reports from all areas of the Reich are unanimous in stating that, while the *Armed Forces Radio Request Programs* [*Wunschkonzert für die Wehrmacht,* broadcast every Sunday afternoon at 3:00 PM] have lost some of their "novelty," they still remain among the most popular and widely listened to radio programs at the front, in the garrisons, and throughout the civilian population. According to reports from the Palatinate, especially for soldiers in the bunkers whose entertainment options are severely limited, the radio request program is greatly appreciated. Soldiers from around Aachen report that on their Sunday leaves, they often seek out locales or families where they know they won't miss the program. This statement in a letter from a navy radio dispatcher is typical: "We look forward to the request program for days in advance." From ethnic German [*volksdeutschen*] regions of the protectorate and from the southeast, there are reports that the request programs are particularly popular amongst the "strewn" Germans [*Streudeutschen*] because they offer ethnic Germans a highly profound way of participating in the national community of the German *Volk* in the greater German Reich.[1]

What is most appreciated about the program's concept and design is the fact that, despite the repetition of the same format each week, the program still manages to offer surprises and variety by always coming up with new programming ideas. One report from Karlsruhe states, "In general, you hear only good things about the inventiveness of the programmers of the radio request concerts." One point of disagreement in public opinion about the radio request program is without doubt the question of whether more serious and heavier musical compositions should be aired. There are far more people in all areas of the Reich who firmly believe the principle should be "the lighter the fare in the request program, the better"—which is not to imply that more serious musical compositions are not welcome and not well liked, especially at the beginning of the program, as a way of accommodating the wishes of those listeners who prefer this type of music. There is special appreciation for the fact that most of the individual numbers are performed by first-class musicians and presenters. Appearances by famous artists in every field of art or noteworthy public personalities are particularly well received because they lend an especially interesting and topical note to each individual broadcast of the show. The appearance of these "prominent" personalities is appreciated all the more when there is no immediately apparent "self-promotion" involved. The sequence of numbers in the program is praised and appreciated for its variety, as is the balanced presentation of musical and spoken numbers. Countless soldiers and vacationers agree that they most enjoyed the appearances of truly excellent, genuine comedians, because, as the old saying goes, a soldier is always up for a good laugh.

There are countless laudatory statements about the Soldier's Voice [*Stimme des Soldats*, short for the *Wunschkonzert für die Wehrmacht*].

Reports confirm that the reading of these [soldiers'] names by the thousands kindles the shared experience of the *Volk* community, even though there are some who consider the listing of names and financial contributions inappropriate. Many soldiers' statements point to the fact that the individual units directly at the front can hardly expect their names to be read, especially when there are extended delays covering several broadcasts in the series.

The contributions are widely discussed even outside the context of the request concert series and are applauded all the more when it is obvious that the donor is truly making a sacrifice, but if the presentation so much as smacks of advertising, it is sharply criticized.

Almost all areas of the Reich report, independent of one another, suggest that the request program be rescheduled later in the evening during the summer months because the civilian population and a large number of soldiers are not in their apartments or workplaces during the late-afternoon hours.

Note

1. *"Streudeutsche"* was the nickname for German ethnic communities in Central and Eastern Europe.—Eds.

298

HEINRICH HIMMLER

Illegal Broadcasts for England: Memo to Ernst Kaltenbrunner

Written on 19 May 1943. First published in Peter Dahl, *Radio: Sozialgeschichte des Rundfunks für Sender und Empfänger* (Reinbek bei Hamburg: Rowohlt Verlag, 1983), 172, 173.

Top Secret
Field Command Post

Dear Kaltenbrunner!

I have ordered large quantities of the book *The Jewish Ritual Murders* [*Die jüdischen Ritualmorde*], which I am having sent to everyone all the way up to the rank of colonel in the SS.[1] I am sending you several hundred copies so that you can distribute these to your mobile command [*Einsatz-Kommando*] units, especially to those men who are more involved with the Jewish Question.

My orders for this book are as follows:

Investigations everywhere are to be initiated immediately into ritual murder by Jews who have not yet been evacuated. Any incidents of the same are to be singled out and presented to me. We will have to conduct any number of proceedings in this regard.

Think about whether we might not want to work with the Foreign Office to create an illegal, purely anti-Semitic radio broadcast for England and America. It would have to be fed with materials that cater to the British and Americans—much like *Der Stürmer* during the time of struggle [*Kampfzeit*]. In this case, I think a highly sensationalist manner of presentation is important. Please be in touch with *SS-Gruppenführer* Dr. Martin to see if you can't get one or the other of the folks at *Der Stürmer* behind this.

Furthermore, you must immediately call upon those people who are following and looking into the court reports and police notices about missing children so that we can provide updates in our broadcasts about children missing in town X, Y, or Z and report that it probably involves a Jewish ritual murder.

In general, I think that we could stimulate worldwide anti-Semitism tremendously with a major anti-Semitic propaganda campaign in the English language, perhaps even in Russian, with heavy emphasis on propaganda concerning ritual murder.

Please discuss these things with your colleagues and begin making preparations so that you can offer me some recommendations.

Yours,
Heinrich Himmler

Note

1. Frederik Gaste, *Die Wahrheit über die jüdischen Ritualmorde* (Berlin: P. Hochmuth, n.d.).—Eds.

299

JOSEPH GOEBBELS

No Dialect in Radio Broadcasts

Circulated on 13 April 1942 as "Vorlage . . . für Goebbels." Published in *Die Rückseite des Hakenkreuzes. Absonderliches aus den Akten des Dritten Reiches,* edited by Beatrice and Helmut Heiber (Munich: DTV, 1993), 244, 245.

In conjunction with the *More Manners* [*Mehr Höflichkeit*] program, recent radio broadcasts have included scenes written in dialect. The Reich minister of propaganda has reiterated that the Führer does not under any circumstances wish to foster dialect. If it hadn't been for the war, even the theaters performing in dialect would have already been closed. But because of the war, we have had to put this task off until after the war. Just as Luther's Bible translation established clear guidelines for a standard German orthography and just as the concept of the Reich has established itself, the broadcasters of Greater Germany must accept the task of speaking a more or less classical German.

300

FILM-KURIER

First Television Broadcast Launched

First published as "Fernsehen Gestartet," in *Film-Kurier,* 23 March 1935.

Last night—and the date 22 March 1935 will be recorded as a memorable day for posterity—the Greater German Radio [Großdeutscher Rundfunk], after years of ongoing experimental broadcasts transmitted from the circular ultra-short-wave antenna at the top of the TV broadcast tower in Berlin-Witzleben, launched the world's first operating German television broadcast to offer regular programming. Every week on Mondays, Wednesdays, and Saturdays it will broadcast image and sound and television programming on two ultra-short-wave frequencies.

A bold and magnificent dream of a lifetime has thus taken its first step on the path to becoming reality. Just as was the case in the early days of radio, there are still only very few people who have television sets and can experience with their own eyes what the airwaves have to offer, but the number is sure to grow, and just as radio now has the ear of the whole nation in its hands, so, too, will the optical expansion that has now begun soon be there for all eyes to see.

The significance of the moment was palpable last night at the broadcast center, where the press had gathered to watch the screens of seven industrial television receiver sets with one loudspeaker set up especially for this event to allow for the common viewing of this first official transmission of image and sounds by the television broadcast station [*Fernsehsender*] "Paul Nipkow" [named after the inventor of one of the early technical developments that led to television] at Berlin-Witzleben. This first station will remain in operation until the plans and intentions for improving on this innovation can be fully realized.

Dr. Bachmann, director of the Press Department of the Reich Broadcasting Company [Reichs-Rundfunk-Gesellschaft, RRG], welcomed invited guests to this gala event. Dr. Hübmann, technical director of the Reich Broadcasting Company, was out of town and yet still present—he greeted guests in a broadcast on the television screens. Chief Engineer Dr. Hofmann from the RRG [and] Senior Postal Director Dr. [Friedrich Wilhelm] Banneitz from the Central Reich Post Office discussed the current status of technical developments in television, and, after Director of the Reich Broadcasting Company [Eugen] Hadamovsky finished his address, the broadcasts of image and sound began.

Director Hadamovsky first thanked his colleagues, above all Secretary of State [Karl Wilhelm] Ohnesorge, for vigorous support of television, also the Tobis Sound Film as well as the [film studios of] UFA for the use of equipment.

The director of the Reich Broadcasting Company elaborated extensively on the relationship between television and the film industry.

The television industry should not be seen as competition for film, and he wanted to be sure to rigorously repudiate any fears of this nature right from the outset. On the contrary, he said, television promises to significantly enrich the film industry, bringing fresh impetus and stimulus—to an ever-increasing degree as it becomes more and more a household fixture for the *Volk*.

Owners of cinemas need not entertain any fears of this nature either: the cinemas will be precisely the ones who benefit from these television broadcasts because they will be thrust to the center of popular interest as a result.

The third point in the very thoroughgoing comments of the director of the Reich Broadcasting Company was to emphasize that it was the job of exhibitors at the German Radio Exhibition in Berlin, then under the Propaganda Ministry, to draw on all available experience and expertise to develop a functional television receiver that is so advanced in terms of craftsmanship and quality that it leads the way for the development of television internationally. He recommended that the industry collaborate to produce such a product. This will also promise to give amateur home mechanics a boost as well, not only individual hobbyists but also the group as a whole.

Finally, he said, television will generate innovative ideas in art and will galvanize the community in a common political experience; the future goals of television will involve not a proletarianization of cultural production but rather its aristocratization. Director of the Reich Broadcasting Company Hadamovsky presented two telegrams, one to the Führer and Reich chancellor and one to Minister of Propaganda Dr. Goebbels—and with that, the first German broadcast channel was launched!

For the first time ever, one could actually see the broadcast announcer; following the director of the Reich Broadcasting Company address (the whole program was broadcast with sound), a series of images were shown, including mass rallies from the years 1933–34, the veterans memorial service of 1935, the UFA cultural film *On the Cruise Ship Königsberg at Sea* [*Mit dem Kreuzer 'Königsberg' in See*], and an animated cartoon film also by UFA, *Look Out! Fire!* [*Vorsicht! Es brennt!*]. Gramophone records were played between programs.

The broadcast was transmitted with a 180-line roster system over two ultra-short-wave transmitters (16 megahertz), one for the images and one for sound. [. . .]

The sound quality of the reception was, of course, the same quality one would expect from a loudspeaker, and the picture reception was riddled with the typical flickering and unsteadiness. But these flaws that still need to be worked out in television are in principle the same that characterized early cinematography or the beginnings of radio—and it is not likely to take as long to fix them in this case as it did for the others.

22

Jewish Culture under Nazi Persecution

The Jewish Cultural League

ZIONISM, WHICH HAD ALREADY BECOME A POTENT FORCE in Germany by the 1910s, argued that only a return to a Jewish homeland (and Palestine was eventually the only option accepted) would assure the Jews the stability of a "peoplehood" as well as a national state. After the first months of the Nazi "revolution," German Zionists accurately predicted that there was no future for Jews in Germany. One of these, Robert Weltsch (1891–1982), editor of the *Jüdische Rundschau,* the journal of the Zionistische Vereinigung für Deutschland (Zionist Organization for Germany), published his admonition of 1 April 1933—the day of the anti-Jewish boycott—to "wear the yellow badge proudly," a reference to the requirement that all Jewish businesses affix a yellow sign with a Jewish star to their exteriors.[1] (The official dictate requiring all Jews in Germany to wear the "yellow star" did not take effect until 1 September 1941, well after the star had been introduced in occupied Poland in 1939.) Weltsch's article criticized German Jews for their lack of self-awareness: "Because the Jews did not display their Jewishness with pride, because they wanted to shirk the Jewish question, they must share the blame for the degradation of Jewry." His use of the yellow star metaphor was sadly prescient. Before the war, German anti-Semites imagined a "Germany without Jews," but what would happen if Jews, now no longer accepted into the German body politic, did not "vanish"?

Between 1933 and 1935, the Jews were increasingly isolated. Jews' civil rights, which had taken over a century to acquire, were stripped from them, and they were "encouraged" to emigrate, as is noted in the official description of Jewish structures in Germany in 1935. It was still possible to leave Germany, but there was an older law (1931) on the books that taxed anyone leaving the country with valuables of 50,000 Reichsmarks or more, with some assessments reaching 25 percent of the value. The Nazis took advantage of this law: driving the Jews out would not only permit the "Aryanization" of large areas of the economy but also provide a source of income for the state. Many of the Jews who were able to get visas to enter other countries brought, as one of the most valuable things they owned, their libraries of the German classics with them. The door finally closed on 23 October 1941, when all further Jewish emigration from Germany was forbidden.

The Jews who remained were to be reshaped into a separate people, a Jewish *Volk,* and for them (as Germans and as Jews), *Bildung* (a concept that now embraced culture as well as education) remained central to their self-definition. In July 1933, the Kulturbund Deutscher Juden (Cultural League of German Jews) was created by the young opera director Kurt Baumann (who later immigrated to the United States and created the Ithaca Opera) and the neurologist and amateur musician Kurt Singer (1885–1944) "to create a haven for unemployed Jews here on this scantly fertile, highly constricted ground." Creating the league was initially a pragmatic move designed to find employment for Jewish artists and musicians who had suddenly become unemployable by the state orchestras and opera houses. Self-financed, the league did not at first think of itself as propagating a "Jewish" cultural presence. The Nazis quickly disabused the organizers of this distinction and refused to allow them to have an organization that was deemed both "Jewish" and "German." One rationale the Nazis gave for segregating the Jews from Germany's cultural world was Jews' supposed overrepresentation in the arts: "consider the unbelievable degree to which the theater scene in Germany at the time was infiltrated by alien Jewish elements." This unfounded argument had been made also about the so-called free professions such as medicine and law. One model for the separation of the "races," according to *Reichskulturwalter* Hans Hinkel (1901–60), the Reich administrator of culture, was Jim Crow America: "it is entirely self-evident that German people do not attend Jewish concerts or comedy acts, etc.; no American would ever, under any circumstances, go to a Negro theater—and there should be no doubt whatsoever that National Socialists will support only German art and culture." The first play performed under the auspices of the Cultural League of German Jews, opening on 1 October 1933, was Gotthold Lessing's *Nathan the Wise* (*Nathan der Weise*), the great Enlightenment drama of religious toleration written by a non-Jew.

By April 1935, the Jüdischer Kulturbund (Jewish Cultural League), as it was now called due to Goebbels's desire to eliminate any suggestion that these Jews were also Germans, had thirty-six regional branches with approximately seventy thousand members (though it never reached more than 10 percent of Germany's Jews). It put on as many as two hundred monthly performances, concerts, exhibitions, and lectures in over one hundred cities. In August 1935, Goebbels forced all of these branches to join the Reichsverband der jüdischen Kulturbünde in Deutschland (Reich Organization of Jewish Cultural Leagues in Germany), which became part of the Ministry for Popular Enlightenment and Propaganda, reporting to the extremely anti-Semitic Hans Hinkel.

The Gestapo censored everything the Organization of Jewish Cultural Leagues planned. Some members complained about the "spooky" collusion of the league's leaders with Hinkel and the Nazi authorities. By July 1937, one hundred twenty organizations had been coalesced into this group, with the greatest weight in urban areas. Thus, the original organization in Berlin had nightly concerts, lectures, or cinema. Though these events perpetuated the culture of German Jewry under Nazism, they also provided a living experience of the isolation of the Jews in the middle of German society. No non-Jews could perform in productions mounted by the league, and no non-Jews could attend these events. The organization rarely was allowed to perform non-Jewish plays or non-Jewish music and could not exhibit non-Jewish art or publish books authored by non-Jews. And the Gestapo defined what was "Jewish," albeit on an ever-sliding scale: foreign works could be "Jewish" even if written or composed by non-Jews; "German" music was never permitted in Jewish venues with their Jewish audiences. Thus, the music of Johann Sebastian Bach (1685–1750) could not be performed, but the music of Felix Mendelssohn-Bartholdy (1809–47), who rediscovered and championed Bach in the nineteenth century, could be performed only for these Jewish audiences. Raised a Christian and baptized, Mendelssohn-Bartholdy was too Jewish for the Nazis under the biological rules of the day, [being] considered a "full Jew" because his parents were Jews. In 1935, the league could offer Friedrich Hebbel's *Judith* (by a non-Jewish and German author, albeit with a Jewish theme), George Bernard Shaw's play *You Never Can Tell* (a political drama by a non-Jewish and English author), and Perez Hirschbein's *Green Fields* (by a Jewish author and with a Jewish theme). The group even had its own publishing house (Verlag Jüdischer Kulturbund), which printed not only Jewish classics (such as works by the Jewish writer Heinrich Heine, himself a convert to Christianity) but also a number of Jewish writers of the day who wrote novels about the extraordinary lives that they and their Jewish compatriots had in Nazi Germany.

As a countermeasure to the anti-Semitic hate campaign, the Philo-Verlag of the Central-Verein deutscher Staatsbürger jüdischen Glaubens (Central Association of German Jewry) in Berlin, run by Ludwig Holländer (1877–1936), produced well-researched and beautifully illustrated lexicons and carefully edited texts. Anyone who wanted an accurate presentation of historical facts or information about the contributions of Jewish artists, writers, and thinkers could consult them. The Nazis closed Philo in 1936, along with most other Jewish publishing enterprises. By 1937, all "Jewish" authors were removed from German publishers' lists, and their works could be acquired only though the Jüdischer Buchverlag (Jewish Book House). After the murderous attacks on Jews and Jewish institutions during the Reichskristallnacht of 1938, all of the branch organizations of the Jewish Cultural League were closed except for the original one in Berlin, which remained open for propaganda purposes. The organization was officially closed on 11 September 1941, when it was dissolved "for the protection of people and state." On 5 November 1939, Rabbi Leo Baeck held the last public lecture under the auspices of the Jewish Cultural League. The organization then existed in a shadow landscape until 11 September 1941, when the Gestapo dismantled it, abandoning all pretenses that the Jews had an autonomous cultural life in Germany.

On 18 October 1941, the first thousand Berlin Jews were deported to the ghetto at Łódź. German and Austrian Jews were deported: but even in the ghettos of the east, such as Vilna, the official organization regularly reported on cultural activities in the ghetto, and the best-known one in Terezin (Theresienstadt—the ghetto created to impress the International Red Cross), culture was part of the mechanism for retaining one's sense of identity. The journalist Oskar Rosenfeld (1884–1944) wrote in his dairy from the Łódź ghetto on 5 March 1943, "The contradiction: on the one hand, as punishment [the Jews are] isolated because [they are] harmful to the 'people's body' and parasitic—on the other hand, [they are] creative. Achievements demanded out of nothing, and reached. In this case, the German coercion had a favorable effect."[2] For most of the deported, death was the end; most of the leaders of the Jewish Cultural League, including its founder, Kurt Singer, were deported to the east and murdered.

NOTES

1. *Jüdische Rundschau (Jewish Review)* was published from 1902 to 1938, when it was banned by the Nazis.

2. Oskar Rosenfeld was a Viennese writer who kept detailed notes on his experiences and observations in the Łódź ghetto before his deportation to Auschwitz, where he perished. Here, Rosenfeld comments ironically on the contradiction between Nazi racial ideology and the remarkable cultural productivity and personal dignity of the Jews, even when confronted with hunger, disease, degradation, and physical violence.

301

KURT SINGER

Let's Get Started!

First published as "Fangt an!" in *Monatsblätter* 1, no. 1 (October 1933): 1.

At this hour—one of the most difficult times of recent decades but also a time that has galvanized us as German Jews to one great community sharing the same fate [*Schicksalsgemeinschaft*]—at this hour that demands at once sacrifice, hope, and the will to rebuild, it is time for us to pursue our own path of cultural production. We flee the reality of life, escaping to the appearances of the stage and the illusions of music. Left strictly to our own devices now, we seek to avoid letting our own creative activities run on idle; we seek to create a haven for unemployed Jews here on this scantly fertile, highly constricted ground, seek to establish a home for many who expect to find intellectual and spiritual instruction, musical training, dramatic stimulus at the Cultural League of German Jews.

At the moment, we are still standing here empty-handed but showered with good wishes and a welcoming reception on the part of all those who came to us in response to our first call. Laying the groundwork for this project has been hard work; the last, the best, and most decisive task lies ahead: the *delivery*.

We are not begging for leniency, not seeking to curry favor, nor courting commendation. All that we ask for is faith in our work and our idea. But this implies and must include a profession of faith in Judaism, fortified by the consciousness of being inextricably bound for centuries to the cultural capital of Germany. The word of the Bible, the ethics of the prophets, the wisdom of Talmudic and rabbinical religious scholars anchored as firmly in our hearts and souls in the same way as the world of Kant and Humboldt, Goethe and Beethoven, has become part of us. Our work should be guided by no other principle, by no other tendency than the desire to continue to administer and create the crown jewels of art to the extent that we remain able.

We do not want to compete with the artistic endeavors of other theaters, other orchestras that have established themselves through years of successful work, nor do we have any intention of racing to stay ahead of the shadow cast by outdated forms that have become tradition. We do not want to experiment. Immortal works and contemporary art certainly go hand in hand in our programming: the elders hope to pass their experience on to the young, and the young hope older generations will have a share in their youthful enthusiasm. But the outlines of a coherent plan should also be evident in the diversity of artistic design. A felicitous task: to train a staff of assistants who have yet to be shaped by any degree of world fame to become a highly effective ensemble presenting performances of exquisite quality.

We have just begun. We are all inspired by a profound sense of responsibility. As yet, not a single note has been played by an orchestra, not a single scholar has presented his work, no protagonist stolen our hearts, no poet moved us to tears. Nevertheless, we know already now: the resonance—born of the will and the power to create—will be there the day we open our ears and our hearts to the music, the scholarship, the play on the world stage. The authorities have given us a vote of confidence. We shall not disappoint them.

We sincerely hope that we will pass the test and live up to your expectations as members of our association. We would also like to thank you for coming to us, for your hard work, endurance, enthusiasm, and we hope you will be able to thank us for enhancing your well-being and reinforcing your zest for life. And now we will get to work. The times are hard, and yet we cannot rebuff them. For any work is worth its salt only when it has had to persevere tediously and tirelessly to resist adversity. When the urgent call first came—"Let's get started!"—we hesitated for a long time at first. But now the stage is set. In proud deference, we answer the call filled with optimistic hope!

Let the show begin!

302

KURT SINGER

Speech at the Opening of the Cultural Conference of the Reich Organization of Jewish Cultural Leagues in Germany

Delivered on 5 September 1936. First published as "Eröffnungsrede zu Beginn der Kulturtagung," in *Geschlossene Vorstellung: Die Jüdische Kulturbund in Deutschland 1933–1941*, edited by Akademie der Künste (Berlin: Edition Hentrich, 1992), 266.

5–7 September 1936
Right Honorable Herr Reich Administrator of Culture!
Ladies and Gentlemen!

I hereby open the conference of the Reich Organization of Jewish Cultural Leagues [Reichsverband der jüdischen Kulturbünde].

We are in attendance at this working conference to assess what has been done in the past and to lend an ear to the future; I would like to think that the speeches and lectures presented at this conference are likely to have less impact than the actions that result from them.

The fact that I have the pleasure and the honor of officiating, together with our friend Benno Cohn, over this gathering of organizations and of Jewish men and women, is for me and for all of us symbolic of the unity that prevails in the platform of the Cultural Leagues and of the fact that there are no differences between the Zionist and non-Zionist wishes. The presence of Reich Administrator of Culture [Hans] Hinkel greatly underscores the importance of this conference. I welcome him and the remaining gentlemen from state offices here today.

I also welcome the delegates of the Jewish Representation in Germany, of the Zionist Union, the Central Organization of Jews, the Reich League of Jewish Veterans, the Association for Liberal Judaism, the Jewish Women's Organization, and the Freemasons; I welcome representatives of the Jewish communities as well as Herr Director Hauser from the conservatorium in Jerusalem and representatives of the Jewish press. Special thanks are due representatives of the Jewish artistic community who have been working diligently with us for forever and a day.

What we have here is a unified Jewish labor front, and we work in the spirit of solidarity. And at the moment we have, as a model of this solidarity for all things Jewish, Palestine as a shining example before our eyes.

We are watching the course of developments in the land of our fathers with great anticipation and great expectations—where Jewish people have been engaged for years on end, not just recently, in the attempt to defend and preserve the Holy Land—and that means to defend and preserve us—risking all their worldly wealth and even life and limb. As a sign of our common bond with Eretz Israel and its people, and above all with the arbiters of Jewish culture in Palestine, I will, providing you are in agreement, be sending telegrams to the Hebrew national theater, Habima, as well as to the Jewish Palestine Orchestra Hubermann.

In anticipation of a productive and successful conference, I hereby open the Cultural Conference of the Reich Organization of Jewish Cultural Leagues.

303

HANS HINKEL

The Policy of Purging Jews from the Theater

First published as "Die judenreine Theaterpolitik in deutschen Reich," in *Ziel und Weg* 21 (1936): 587–88.

In accordance with the demands of National Socialism, I had already purged all state and municipal arts organizations, especially the theaters, of all representatives of the Jewish race in the summer of 1933 in my capacity as director of the official Prussian Theater Committee, which was established at the time by the Prussian prime minister in conjunction with the Prussian Ministry of Culture. These special provisions made up less than one of hundreds passed at the time.

If you consider the unbelievable degree to which the theater scene in Germany at the time was infiltrated by alien Jewish elements, you can imagine how many artists were necessarily confronted with the question of where they would find work in the future. All I can recall is that in the capital city of the Reich alone, over two-thirds of private theaters operating at the time were in the hands of Jewish directors, that the Marxist cultural policies of that *Systemzeit* fostered the Jewification of our theaters, and that, for all these and many more similar reasons, November Germany increasingly became a site of asylum for these Jewish clowns. So it is no wonder, then, that as we came to political power in 1933 and began the process of de-Jewifying our German cultural and artistic life, the question of what to do with all these Jewish artists who could not be persuaded to emigrate and, at the moment, who saw no options for resettlement in another country, above all Palestine . . .

On 18 July 1933, I was able to inform a number of well-known Jewish artists who had addressed us with this question that my superiors—in their shrewd foresight and with the utmost sense of responsibility—had approved of my proposal to allow for Jews to create a *Jewish cultural organization of their own.* The "Jewish Cultural League" was thus established. I appointed the previous director of the former municipal opera in Berlin, Dr. [Kurt] Singer, to be director of this organization, which will limit its activities to Berlin for the time being.

Since the number of Jews excluded from the German theater industry was larger, for example, than the number of musicians or painters, it seemed utterly self-evident that Dr. Singer should immediately set himself to the task of laying the groundwork for a future theater for Jews.

Certain stipulations were placed on the Jewish Cultural League that were not, however, intended to prevent Jewish artists in all sectors of artistic production from performing for exclusively Jewish audiences, which must also be members of the same organization. Already at the beginning of the winter 1933–34 theater season—on the stage of the former Berlin Theater—the theater company of the Jewish Cultural League was presenting plays. The program could include operas, operettas, and plays. Prominent Jews who had not found or sought employment outside Germany's borders immediately found employment here. Only a few months passed before the Jewish cultural movement also spread to other big cities in Prussia. By 1 April 1934 there were already about two hundred viable local groups in operation. Agreements with the political police allowed the Jews to pursue their work undisturbed in their own closed circles when they were busy tending to their artistic culture. By the winter of 1934–35, in Berlin alone five hundred thousand visitors had attended the Jewish theater, Jewish concerts, and Jewish lectures. The leadership of the Jewish Cultural League left no stone unturned in its attempts to remind the majority of economically well-situated Jews of their more or less *völkisch* obligations, but, sadly, the Jews soon realized for the most part that those Jews who did support the efforts of the Jewish Cultural League were those whose lives weren't exactly a bed of roses. By sheer coincidence, in 1935, again on 18 July, in recognition of the urgent need for a resolute solution to the decisive Jewish Question, Dr. Goebbels assigned me the task of monitoring the cultural and artistic activities of all the Jews in the Reich so that in this manner all of the existing Jewish cultural organizations, including the Jewish Cultural League, could be brought together under one umbrella organization or "Reich league." So, in the course of the past year, then, the Reich Organization of Jewish Cultural Leagues developed into the only Jewish cultural organization whose members today include all associations of Jewish artists and similar organizations. Directorship of this Reich league was assumed by the former director of the Jewish Cultural League in Berlin and, in accordance with wishes expressed by large numbers of Jews, increasingly supplemented by so-called political personalities within the Jewish community—that is, influential personalities in the Zionist movement.

What may have seemed inexplicable, perhaps even superfluous, to some has since proven itself—even for more unsympathetic Germans—to be justified and organic: the Jews in Germany can cultivate the cultural life they purport to have within their own circles, and we will tolerate the so-called programming agenda within the local affiliates of the Jewish Cultural League as long as it does not seek to exert direct or indirect influence on German cultural life and its manifold forms of expression.

The Jews themselves have seen the pragmatic benefit of this work in the past three years, whenever they were forced to avail themselves of anything that was not ethnically Jewish in the fields of music, theater, or literature. It was only through this experience that they became aware of the grave consequences of so-called assimilation; they have seen the way that only a few of their poets, composers, or playwrights have limited themselves to specifically Jewish problems and Jewish themes without making concessions to accommodate non-Jewish expectations. These are the questions that rigorously concern the leading men within the Reich league, and, not infrequently, they have led to sharp tensions between individual Jewish political factions, between the Zionists, the liberals, the Orthodox, etc. But as precipitous as these tensions may have seemed at times, we National Socialists have always found in the Jews a unified voice of Jewry whenever it comes to representing their interests in the state or whenever some supposed danger lay ahead for Jews and Judaism.

For a long time following 30 January 1933, numerous observers and critics of Germany in other parts of the world did not want to so much as see that this Jewish cultural organization existed, or they sought to trivialize the whole operation as a diversionary maneuver on the part of National Socialists. It was only after tens of thousands of Jews in Germany had joined the Reich league, only after quite a number of prominent Jews found work as artists there and the directors of the Jewish Cultural League issued a vote of confidence for our decisions—only then did anyone take note of these highly significant developments, and even that was ever contingent on the degree of willingness to see the New Germany for what it really is. People simply did not want to believe that an established Jewish theater existed in the National Socialist Germany so many liked to peg as being "barbaric"—that there were Jewish touring companies visiting Jewish communities, that Jewish orchestras could travel from city to city to play for audiences of their racial comrades, that every single week, throughout the Reich, in dozens of evening lectures, cabarets, etc., Jews were given the opportunity to develop their own style amongst members of their own race. If you ask us why we decided to carry out all these de-Jewification measures and to consign all the Jews excluded from German cultural life to their own Jewish organization, the answer to that question—above and beyond the fundamental demands posed by National Socialism in matters of race—is quite simple: we wanted to reinstate the Germans' domiciliary rights in the ever-so-decisive realm of cultural life, and we would no longer stand for our intellectual and artistic life to be determined by elements alien to its nature. Today, the National Socialist state, as the formal organ of the will of the *Volk*, is in possession of all rights of sovereignty pertaining to cultural life.

We recognize the existence of a distinct Jewish *Volk*, but we also insist upon strict recognition of the distinctive character of our German *Volk* and can only afford pure-blooded representatives of the race the opportunity to tend to the cultural and political needs of our national comrades here in our homeland. There is no room for disseminators of the Jewish-Bolshevist poison and no possibility for them to work with our German national comrades. And this is why we have drawn the line and are closely guarding it so that no foreign elements from this race cross it. Anyone who has the best interest of our *Volk* in mind will therefore support the efforts of those for whom life isn't exactly a bed of roses.

304

ROBERT WELTSCH

Wear the Yellow Badge with Pride!

First published as "Tragt ihn mit Stolz, den gelben Fleck," in *Jüdische Rundschau,* April 1933, 1. Translated by Harry Zohn, in Lucy S. Dawidowicz, ed., *A Holocaust Reader* (West Orange, N.J.: Behrman House, 1976), 147–50.

The first of April 1933 will remain an important date in the history of German Jewry—indeed, in the history of the entire Jewish people. The events of that day have not only political and economic aspects, but moral and psychological ones as well. The political and economic implications have been widely discussed in the newspapers, although the requirements of agitation have frequently obscured an objective understanding of them. To speak about the moral aspects is our task. For no matter how often the Jewish question is discussed these days, we ourselves are the only ones who can express what is going on in the hearts of German Jews, what can be said about events from the Jewish point of view. Today Jews can speak only as Jews; anything else is utterly senseless. [. . .]

The first of April 1933 can be a day of Jewish awakening and Jewish rebirth—*if the Jews want it to be;* if the Jews are ripe for it and possess the requisite magnanimity. If the Jews are not as they are depicted by their adversaries.

Having been attacked, Jewry must avow its faith in itself.

Even on this day of electrifying tension, when the most tempestuous emotions fill our hearts in the face of the unprecedented phenomenon of the entire Jewish population of a great civilized country being universally outlawed, the one thing we must maintain is our composure. Even though we are staggered by the events of recent days, we must not be dismayed, but must take stock without self-deception. What should be recommended at this time is that the work, which witnessed the infancy of Zionism, Theodor Herzl's *The Jewish State,* be disseminated by the hundreds of thousands of copies among Jews and non-Jews alike. If there still remains any shred of greatness and nobility, gallantry and justice, then every National Socialist who looks into this book is bound to shudder at his own blind actions. Every Jew who reads it would also begin to understand and would be consoled and uplifted by it. Page after page of this pamphlet, which first appeared in 1896, would have to be copied to show that Theodor Herzl was the first Jew dispassionate enough to examine anti-Semitism in connection with the Jewish question. And he recognized that an improvement cannot be affected by sticking one's head in the sand like an ostrich, but rather only by dealing with the facts frankly and in full view of the world. [. . .]

We Jews who have been raised in Theodor Herzl's spirit want to ask ourselves what our own complicity is, what sins we are guilty of having committed. At times of crisis throughout its history, the Jewish people has faced the question of its own guilt. Our most important prayer says, "we were expelled from our country because of our sins." Only if we are critical toward ourselves can we do justice to others.

Jewry bears a great burden of complicity because it failed to heed Theodor Herzl's call and even mocked it in some instances. The Jews refused to acknowledge that the "Jewish question still exists." They thought the only important thing was not to be recognized as Jews. Today we are being reproached with having betrayed the German people; the National Socialist press calls us "enemies of the state," and there is nothing we can do about it. It is not true that the Jews have betrayed Germany. If they have betrayed anything, they have betrayed themselves and Judaism.

Because the Jews did not display their Jewishness with pride, because they wanted to shirk the Jewish question, they must share the blame for the degradation of Jewry. [. . .]

The leaders of the boycott gave orders that a sign "with a yellow badge against a black background" be affixed to the boycotted stores. Here is a powerful symbol. This measure is intended as an act of stigmatization, of disparagement. We accept it and propose to turn it into a badge of honor.

Many Jews had a devastating experience last Saturday. Suddenly they were Jews—not out of inner conviction or out of pride in a magnificent heritage and contribution to mankind, but through the affixing of a red slip and a yellow badge. The squads went from house to house, pasting them on storefronts and business signs and painting them on windows; for twenty-four hours German Jews were in a pillory, as it were. In addition to other marks and inscriptions one frequently saw on the shop windows a large *Magen David,* the Shield of King David. This was supposed to be a disgrace. *Jews, pick up the Shield of David and wear it with honor!*

For—and this is the first task of our spiritual stocktaking—if today this shield is stained, it has not been entirely the work of our enemies. There have been many Jews whose undignified self-mockery knew no bounds. Judaism was regarded as something outmoded; people did not give it their serious attention; they wanted to free themselves of its tragic aspects by smiling. Today, however, there is a new type of Jew: the new, free Jew, a kind as yet unknown to the non-Jewish world. If today the National Socialist and German patriotic newspapers frequently refer to the type of the Jewish scribbler and the so-called Jewish press, if Jewry is held responsible for these factors, it must be pointed out again and again that they are not representative of Jewry, but at most have tried to derive a financial profit from the Jews. At a time of bourgeois self-righteousness, one might expect these elements to be applauded by Jewish audiences if they lampooned and made light of Jews and Judaism. These circles preached to us nationally-oriented Jews often enough the ideals of an abstract cosmopolitanism in an effort to destroy all deeper values of Judaism. Self-respecting Jews have always expressed indignation over the raillery and caricature Jewish clowns and comedians have directed at Jews to the same degree, at times even greater, than they have aimed them at Germans and others. Jewish audiences applauded their own degradation, and many attempted to create an alibi for themselves by joining in the mockery. [. . .]

As recently as thirty years ago it was considered objectionable in educated circles to discuss the Jewish question. In those days, the Zionists were regarded as troublemakers with an *idée fixe.* Now the Jewish question is so timely that every small child, every schoolboy as well as the man in the street has no other topic of conversation. All Jews throughout Germany were branded with the word "Jew" on the first of April. If there is a renewed boycott, the new directives of the boycott committee provide for a uniform designation of all shops: "German business" in the case of non-Jews, the simple word "Jew" for Jewish establishments. They know who is a Jew. There is no longer any evading or hiding it. The Jewish answer is clear. It is the short statement of the prophet Jonah: *Ivri anokhi,* I am a Hebrew. Yes, a Jew. The affirmation of our Jewishness—this is the moral significance of what is happening today. The times are too turbulent to use arguments in the discussion. Let us hope that a more tranquil time will come and that a movement which considers it a matter of pride to be recognized as the pacemaker of the national uprising will no longer derive pleasure from degrading others, even though it might feel that it must fight them. As for us Jews, we can defend our honor. We remember all those who were called Jews, stigmatized as Jews, over a period of five thousand years. We are being reminded that we are Jews. We affirm this and bear it with pride.

305

C.-V. ZEITUNG

The Reich Representative Council of German Jews in Germany after the Nuremberg Laws

First published in *C-V. Zeitung,* 16 September 1935. Published in English in Lucy S. Dawidowicz, ed., *A Holocaust Reader* (West Orange, N.J.: Behrman House, 1976), 162–64.

The laws passed by the Reichstag at Nuremberg have most adversely affected the Jews in Germany.[1] But they are intended to create a basis on which a tolerable relationship between the German *Volk* and the Jewish *Volk* will be possible. The Jewish Representation in Germany is prepared to commit all its energy to this end. The prerequisite to a tolerable relationship is the hope that the end of the boycotts and defamation will permit Jews and Jewish communities in Germany to sustain their moral and economic existence.

Establishing order for Jewish life in Germany requires that the government recognize autonomous Jewish leadership. The Reich Representative Council of German Jews in Germany is the authoritative agency responsible for this. With few exceptions, it is supported by the whole of Jewry and Jewish communities, particularly all the provincial and metropolitan communities, as well as unaffiliated Jewish organizations: Zionist Union of Germany, Central Committee of Jews in Germany, Reich League of Jewish Veterans, Association for Liberal Judaism, Organized Orthodox Community, Union of Jewish Women, Reich Commission of Jewish Youth Organizations.

The most pressing tasks of the Reich Representative Council of German Jews in Germany that shall be pursued energetically and with full commitment along the lines it has already established are:

1. Our own Jewish educational system must serve to train our youth to become religiously secure, self-respecting Jews who draw strength from their conscious commitment to the Jewish community, from their work on the Jewish present and their belief in the Jewish future to meet the formidable demands placed upon them in life. The Jewish school must go beyond the mere transmission of knowledge and systematically prepare [its students—Eds.] for their future occupation. With an eye for emigration eligibility, particularly to Palestine, primary emphasis will be placed on developing manual labor skills and learning the Hebrew language. Education and vocational training for girls must prepare them for fulfilling their obligation to preserve the family and as the mothers of future generations.

   The independent rejuvenation of culture must provide Jews in the artistic and cultural professions with employment opportunities and serve the interests of independent Jewish cultural life in Germany.
2. The increased need for emigration is to be met with grand-scale planning, especially with regard to youth, which includes first and foremost Palestine, but also other coun-

tries that may be under consideration. This also includes increasing opportunities for emigration, training in professions that will facilitate emigration, especially in agriculture and manual labor and creating opportunities for mobilizing and liquidating the assets of financially independent persons as well as expanding existing options for money transfers and creating new ones.

3. Support and care for the needy, the sick, and the elderly must be guaranteed through the ongoing systematic expansion of Jewish welfare services provided by the communities to supplement government social services.
4. An impoverished community is not prepared to cope with these varied and difficult tasks. The Reich Representative Council of German Jews will use every available means in the attempt to strengthen the economic capacities of the Jews by guaranteeing that existing employment opportunities remain in place. The economically disadvantaged shall be supported through further development of measures for economic aid, financial counseling, and issuing personal or mortgage loans.
5. The spirited progress in reconstructing a Jewish Palestine offers us strength in the present and hope for the future. In order to involve German Jewry to an even greater degree in these developments, the Reich Representative Council of German Jews will become an organizational member of the Palestine Foundation Fund [Keren Hayesod—Eds.] and emphatically urges remaining Jewish communities and associations to follow its example. The Reich Representative Council of German Jews is prepared to establish organizational links between Jewish institutions in Germany and the Foundation Fund in Palestine.

In full cognizance of the magnitude of responsibility and the difficulty of the task, the Reich Representative Council of German Jews summons all Jewish men and women and all Jewish youth to unity, to a Jewish morale, to strictest self-discipline, and to the highest degree of self-sacrifice.

Pursuant to a motion advanced by the Reich Representative Council of German Jews's executive board, the Reich Representative Council of German Jews itself, and the provincial organizations and the individual communities are requested to undertake, promptly and in close cooperation, such organizational and personnel measures as are required within Jewish organizations to assure vigorous and consistent execution of the agenda by all Jewish agencies.

Note

1. The publication in which this article appeared, *C.-V. Zeitung,* was the weekly newspaper of the Centralverein deutscher Staatsbürger jüdischen Glaubens (Central Association of German Citizens of Jewish Faith), founded in 1922.—Eds.

306

KONGRESS-KORRESPONDENZ

Interview with Hans Hinkel

Must the Jews in Germany Starve?

First published as "Staatskommissar Hinkel: Müssen die Juden in Deutschland verhungern?" in *Kongress-Korrespondenz,* 28 August 1935, 1–4.

Ever since the nationwide all-out boycott of Jews in the revolutionary year of 1933, there has been unrest surrounding the race issue: every conscientiously German person knew how he was expected to behave. Even the smear campaigns abroad gradually abated. It was only the Jew himself who continued to speak out again and again. That's just the way it is: he may have lost some of what he had, but it's never long before he's got twice or three times what he had.

And in those days the papers, both in Germany and abroad, were again abuzz with the Jewish Question. At first, they concentrated solely on the events that transpired on the Kurfürstendamm in Berlin. Many a foreign visitor is said to have gone so far as to cancel plans to visit Germany; well, we don't really care about those kinds of visitors who can't seem to see beyond their own little personal corner of the world! And, as far as the international press is concerned, once again the papers are dripping with fairy tales of horror, and one gets the sneaking suspicion that they've just been on the lookout for some opportunity to forget about their own weal and woe—if only for a moment.

Then one day State Commissioner [*Staatskommisar*] Hinkel was appointed by Reich Minister Dr. Goebbels to the post of special commissioner for the Jewish Question. Everyone suddenly took notice. Shortly thereafter, guidelines developed by State Commissioner Hinkel and the Secret State Police concerning activities of the Jews in Germany were published. What these guidelines reveal—irony of ironies for the lies being reported by the international press—is that the opportunities for Jewish citizens have actually increased substantially in the Third Reich.

Public interest in this whole complex of questions prompted the special commissioner, State Commissioner Hinkel, to ever so kindly permit Berlin editor Dr. Scharpin to pose the following questions about his new duties. Here are his answers:

Question: Herr State Commissioner, what actually is your new job?

Answer: This special appointment involves monitoring the Jewish organizations in conjunction with the cleansing of our cultural life.

Question: Why was it necessary to issue standardized guidelines for the activities of Jewish cultural organizations?

Answer: Already in the Wilhelmine Era the Jew managed to surreptitiously poison German cultural life. His influence was perhaps greatest during the Weimar period [*Zwischenreich*]. It goes without saying that the kind of liberalistic morass we found when we arrived on the scene in 1933 can never again befall our culture in the Third Reich. German soil is a healthy soil, and we will keep it free from alien species of growth. The need to actively intervene arose when some of the Jews attempted to again spread out. When the people start avoiding those theaters that employ Jews and thus imperil the existence of these establishments, then something has to be done—to protect the German *Volk,* the German artists, and to protect even the Jews themselves. For the Jews should not be deprived of the opportunity for active participation in the arts. While the National Socialist state insists on strict segregation between German and Jewish cultural life, it is not opposed to the Jews developing and practicing their own art amongst themselves.

Question: What is the practical impact of this National Socialist perspective on the Jews?

Answer: It was this attitude in the Third Reich that made it possible for the "Jewish Cultural League" to be established in Berlin already in 1933—which has thus far been free to operate as it chooses—within the context of certain stipulations, of course.

Question: How many Jews have joined this association?

Answer: Hardly three months after it was established, the association already had 13,000 enrolled members in Berlin. From 1 October 1933 to 30 September 1934, it hosted 538 events, and from 1 October 1934 to 31 July 1935, an additional 311. These were attended primarily by the 18,500 active members currently enrolled in the association in Berlin.

In April 1935, the [Jewish] Cultural League was listed in the official roster of organizations. This fact is evidence of the degree to which the Third Reich has shown its fidelity in its treatment of the Jews. As long as the Jews keep to themselves, they are free to do as they please. The only condition is that they do not disturb the German *Volk* community and that they conduct themselves in a manner that is befitting of any guest: reserved and inconspicuous.

Question: So it's not true that the Jew in artistic and intellectual professions in Germany today has to "starve"?

Answer: Even though unscrupulous émigrés living abroad make that contention, the available facts clearly demonstrate the untruth of this claim. One example from the field of medicine: at present, the percentage of non-Aryan physicians in Berlin is 38.2 percent; the percentage of non-Aryan physicians working for the state insurance program is 43.79 percent. The percentage of Jewish physicians in the state insurance program is substantially higher than that of non-Aryan physicians in all of Berlin. While the total number of Jewish physicians in Berlin decreased by 3 percent last year, the number of non-Aryan physicians in the state insurance program fell by only 2.3 percent. Jewish artists, too, would benefit—they would be better paid and have more employment opportunities—if all their Jewish racial comrades would attend Jewish events. Of the well over 160,000 Jews in Berlin, only 18,500 are members of the Cultural League—that is a sign of too little racial consciousness amongst the Jews. Wealthy Jews—and the majority are indeed wealthy—would definitely be in a position to pay more for their theater and concert tickets than those who are not wealthy, but that's an issue for the Jews themselves to address.

Question: What is the situation with regard to cultural independence for the Jews throughout the Reich? Up until now, you've talked only about Berlin.

Answer: The idea for a cultural association has also gradually taken hold in other major cities. Berlin is the model. According to the statistical record, from 1 September 1934 through 30 April 1935, 1,070 Jewish events took place in sixty-one German cities. Cologne, for example, has received a second Jewish theater, and in Frankfurt am Main, the Cultural League even has its own professional orchestra.

Question: Isn't it difficult to monitor the activities of every individual Jewish Cultural League?

Answer: In order to facilitate oversight, we have created the umbrella organization, the so-called Reich Organization of Jewish Cultural Leagues. By 15 August 1935, ninety-two organizations with a total of 60,000 members had joined. That is, however, still not very many when you take into account that, according to the Jews' own figures, there are still 500,000 Jews remaining in Germany (499,683 to be precise, 238,747 men and 260,936 women), 303,000 of them employed. Even the "converted" Jews who still cannot ever become Germans should go ahead and join their local cultural association. We will not tolerate this kind of "disguise"—oftentimes undoubtedly intentional—and all its consequences in the Third Reich. And we will investigate, uncover, and put an end to all cases that have not yet been scrutinized.

In conclusion, one more thing:

It is entirely self-evident that German people do not attend Jewish concerts or comedy acts, etc.; no American would ever, under any circumstances, go to a Negro theater—and there should be no doubt whatsoever that National Socialists will support only German art and culture.

307

PHILO-LEXIKON: HANDBOOK OF JEWISH KNOWLEDGE

Encyclopedia Entries

Emigration, Distinctions, Emancipation, Military Service

First published in *Philo-Lexikon: Handbuch des Jüdischen Wissens* (Berlin: Philo Verlag, 1937), 59–60, 60–61, 174–75, 478–80.

Emigration. Following the mass expulsions of Jews during the Middle Ages, ever since then, the only major movements of Jews have been in the defeated, underpopulated German states after the Thirty Years' War.

1830–71, the first voluntary wave of emigration, in response to political and economic pressures, particularly in Bavaria and Posen (approx. 20,000), mostly petty traders and tailors, to France, England, and the United States.

1843–71: Jewish emigration from Prussia = 36 percent of the natural growth rate; dwindling rate of Jewish emigration since the establishment of the Reich in 1871. Sharply increased rate of emigration in response to political upheaval in Germany since 1933. By the end of 1936, approximately 110,000 Jews, or 22 percent, emigrated: 18,000 (18 percent) of these Jews resettled in Central and Eastern Europe, 38,000 (34 percent) in Palestine, 23,000 (22 percent) in Western Europe (Belgium, England, France, Holland), 3,000 in Central and Southeastern Europe (Switzerland, Austria, Italy, Czechoslovakia, Yugoslavia), 1,000 in Nordic countries, 2,000 in Southwestern Europe (Spain, Portugal), 400 in other European countries, 25,000 (25 percent) have gone overseas (9,500, United States; 9,100 South and Central American countries), 3,000 to South Africa, and 400 to other overseas countries. The Refugee Commission of the League of Nations investigated the possibilities for permanent relocation (James G. Macdonald, later Sir Neill Malcolm, assisted by Professors Norman and Bentwich). By the end of 1934, 5.5 million [Reichsmarks—Eds.] in aid had been spent, 95 percent of which was raised by Jews themselves. The Jewish Agency, in collaboration with the Association of Emigrés in Palestine [Hitachdut ole Germania], established a special "German Department" to assist with integration in Palestine.

Distinctions. Available material is sketchy; therefore, the following distinctions are to be seen only as examples:

1. *Pour le mérite:* (a) for wartime activities: Simon Kremser 1812, Wilhelm Frankl 1914; (b) for peacetime actitivies: E. A. von Baeyer, G. H. F. Bendemann, C. G. Hitzig, J. Jacobi, M. Joachim, F. Liebermann, G. Mendelssohn, A. Meyerbeer, R. Rubenstein, Wilstätter.
2. *Goldnes Militärverdienstkreuz* (Golden Cross for Military Service) for an "extraordinary act of courage in the face of the enemy," awarded 1,760 times in the Great War, among others, to the following individuals: Alexander (Breslau), Wilhelm David (Grebenstein), Viktor Frey (Beuthen), Ernst Noah, Max Pappenheim (Mergentheim).
3. *Adlerschild des Deutschen Reiches* (Eagle Shield of the German Reich): Robert Kronfeld, Max Liebermann.
4. *Schwarzer Adlerorden* (Order of the Black Eagle): Heinrich von Friedberg, Walter von Mossner, Eduard von Simson.
5. *Elefantenorden* (German Colonial Medal) (under Lettow-Vorbeck): Theodor Freudenberger.
6. *Eisernes Kreuz* (Iron Cross): (a) first class: C. Guttfeldt, L. Lang, J. Nußbaum, I. Rawitz, 1870; awarded to hundreds of Jews 1914–18; (b) second class: awarded to sixteen Jews

1812–13 (among others Luise/Grafemus), to many thousands between 1914–18. A total of approximately 35,000 German Jews were decorated for their service in the World War, approximately 23,000 promoted (2,000 of them officers). See also: pilots, war statistics, military service, Nobel Prize laureates.

Emancipation. (Lat.–jur. term for liberation from paternal authority), as it pertains to the Jews, refers to the promulgation or enforcement of legislative acts designed to guarantee equality for Jews. Although the Enlightenment and natural law provided the intellectual impetus, [the] first practical implementation [of an act of emancipation—Eds.] came in the context of the fight for independence in the United States of America, with the passage of the Virginia Declaration of 1776 (freedom of religion and moral authority). In the wake of the French Revolution, the National Assembly (1791) declared the equality of Jews under law. In Prussia, Jews were recognized as German citizens under the Emancipation Edict of 11 March 1812, which was later subject to legal and practical restrictions. By 1869 or 1871, the emancipation was complete in Germany: since 1933, limitations have been put in place by the Aryan laws. Efforts for group emancipation have been under way since 1933.

Military Service. There is ample evidence of Jewish military service from biblical times to antiquity and in the Middle Ages, but these materials have not been compiled. From the beginning of the nineteenth century onward, with the advancement of emancipation efforts, increased active participation of Jews in their home countries. In Germany's wars of independence in 1812–13, 800 Jews (561 of them volunteers), 15.5 percent of the Jews fit for military service, served in the military; one woman was among them, Luise Grafemus; Tobias Eltzbacher and Philipp Veit were in Lützow's Freikorps; among the 21 officers, Meno Burg and Simon Kremser (*Pour le mérite*), Lt. Meyer Hilsbach; 20 fallen [. . .]; a memo from the Prussian minister of the interior substantiate for 1847 the exceptional military skills of the Jews; in 1864, there were 195 Jews, already by 1866, 1,025 (amongst them, First Lt. Karl Henle), and by 1870–71, 4,500 Jews were enlisted as soldiers in military campaigns. During China's Boxer Rebellion, there were 35 Jews in the German units, there were 20 Jews during the Herero-German War, and 16 (7 fallen, 6 wounded) under General Lettow-Vorbeck in German Southeast Africa in the World War; 1914–18, a total of 96,000 Jews enlisted in all branches of military service. [. . .] As Houston St. Chamberlain wrote in 1915, "It was as if they were simply swept up in the powerful events of the time; there was nothing left of the "Jews" to find, for they were all busy serving their country as Germans, either at home or against the enemy." Ever since 1812, German Jews have participated in the military, even though, with few exceptions [. . .], they were barred from advancing in rank up until the Great War. As a result of the Aryan laws, 34 enlisted men and 5 officers were discharged from the army, 9 enlisted men and 2 officers from the navy (50 in all); the compulsory military service law of 21 May 1935 exempts Jews from active duty (though not from military service altogether). [. . .]

Approximately 60,000 English Jews (including 18 commanding officers) were enlisted [in the British army] during the World War; 2,325 were killed in action, 6,000 wounded, and 1,000 decorated with honors (6 with the highest-ranked medal, the Victoria Cross). [. . .]

Approximately 7,800 Jews fought in the American Revolutionary War in the United States (1773–74); in the Civil War, General Frederic Salomon and Admiral Uria Phillipps Levi (1796–1862) were decorated with honors.

308

CULTURE DEPARTMENT OF THE VILNA GHETTO JUDENRAT

Cultural Activities in the Vilna Ghetto

Report (1942) in YIVO Archives, New York, translated from the Yiddish by Adah B. Vogel. Published in Lucy S. Dawidowicz, ed., *A Holocaust Reader* (Orange, N.J.: Behrman House, 1976), 208–13.

The number of cultural events in March [1942] was exceptionally high, because all existing suitable premises in the ghetto, like the theater, gymnasium, youth club, and school quarters, were used. Every Sunday six to seven events took place with over two thousand participants. At the end of the month, the Culture Department had to give up to the incoming out-of-town Jews a number of premises like the gymnasium, School No. 2, Kindergarten No. 2, and part of School No. 1. This will greatly affect the work of the schools, the sports division, and also the theater, which had to take into its building the sports division and the workers' assemblies.

1. School Division

A disruption in the regular school activity occurred on March 24th because of the occupation of the above-mentioned part of the school premises. School No. 1 had to shift its two upper grades (6 and 7) to afternoon session. School No. 2, which occupied the upper story of the school building on 21 Niemeck Street, also had to shift two classes (both 6th grades) to afternoon session. Kindergarten No. 2 moved into the quarters of the Children's and Youth Club. School No. 3 gave up half of its quarters to School No. 2 and shifted all five high school classes to afternoon session. All these changes are an impediment to the work of the schools and if at all possible, the schools should be returned to their premises as soon as possible. At the start of the month, the schools conducted several more morning programs (see report for previous month). On March 7th, School No. 3 invited all parents to a school program in the theater. School No. 1 presented a morning program by the younger classes in its own quarters on March 14th. On March 21st (Purim), special children's celebrations were held in all classes without exception. The children received a gift from the food supplies department—*hamantaschen*. Kindergarten No. 1 and School No. 2 presented morning programs that day for the parents.

The Children's and Youth Club, besides its regular activities, organized special projects every Sunday. The History Circle presented a trial of Flavius Josephus, which was on a high scholarly level, the Literary Circle, a Yehoash evening with a rich program. Besides that, the club prepared a Purim entertainment and recitation contest. In connection with the Yehoash program, the Club set up a Yehoash exhibit, which later remained open to the public for two weeks. The older classes of the schools also visited the exhibit with their teachers.

High school teachers have completed their work on the curriculum of the high school classes in the ghetto.

On March 1st, a discussion evening was held at the Ghetto Chief's on the education of the young people in the ghetto. Several dozen teachers, writers, and communal leaders were invited.

On March 12th, an [Avrom] Sutzkever evening was held at the Teachers' Association. The poet read his latest poem, "*Kol Nidre.*" The Music School continues regularly.

2. Theater Division

Two important premieres took place in the theater this month. On March 13th, the symphony orchestra, under the baton of W. Durmashkin, presented its fifth program: Beethoven's Leonore No. 3, Chopin's Piano Concerto in E. Minor, and Tchaikovsky's Fifth Symphony.

The youthful orchestra surmounted the great difficulties of the program and the performance was satisfactory. On March 27th, the opening of D. Pinkski's *The Treasure* took place. The play's text was significantly abridged and considerably revised by the director, I. Siegel. His conception was to turn the play into a musical comedy. Original lyrics were written by Leib Rosenthal. Musical accompaniment was by M. Wechsler. Opening night was a great success. A number of writers, teachers, and cultural leaders attended a general rehearsal (a day before the opening), of which they spoke favorably.

Because of preparations for the two openings, there were only twelve events during the month. There were four performances of *The Treasure,* two of *The Man Under the Bridge* (for the fifteenth and sixteenth times, the play is still a success), two performances of the review *You Never Can Know* (the nineteenth and twentieth times, a special matinee performance for residents of the Káilis blocks); the program of the symphony orchestra was repeated three times, and a literary-musical evening was held once, with a mixed program . . .

On March 30th the theater celebrated the fortieth anniversary of actress Esther Lipovska's stage career. *The Treasure* was presented and appropriate speeches made. The guest of honor was awarded all receipts.

The theater's gross receipts for March totaled over 4,300 marks. Of this, the Communal Relief Committee and the Winter Relief received about 2,000 marks.

For April, fourteen events in the theater are planned. Because of the small number of events in March (only Saturdays and Sundays), there was no free performance. In April, one free performance is being planned for the Brigadiers Council and one free concert for the Social Welfare.

3. Library, Reading Room, Archives

During the month, the library lent 13,500 books (an increase of 2,800 over the previous month), 65 percent of which were for adults and 35 percent for children. In March, 100 subscribers were added and by April 1st, the library had 2,592 readers. On March 12th, the Ghetto Chief ordered the ghetto population to return to the library all books (except textbooks and prayer books) by the end of the month. By the end of the month, 1,750 books had been returned. On March 25th, the ghetto court tried 15 readers who had not returned books. The court sentenced them to one day of conditional arrest and a fine.

An average of 206 persons visited the reading room daily (155 in February), as hitherto, a maximal number.

During the month the Archives collected 101 documents. Besides that, 124 folklore items were assembled.

4. Sports Division

The Sports Division, which resumed its activity only at the beginning of February in the room at 7 Rudnicka Street, had to give up the space on March 24th and is once again without quarters. This is a great loss, because in a short time the Sports Division had attracted 415 active members, acquired considerable equipment, and developed exemplary activities. When the premises were closed, two groups had been organized for gymnastics, aerobics, running and jumping games, and boxing, with 637 members (many members are registered in two or even three groups). Besides the usual program of the sports groups in March, sport competitions were held every Sunday, namely, a contest of running and jumping games between the "Káilis" and the ghetto teams; a five-player team for men and a three-player game for women, and a basketball tournament. In the mornings the ghetto schools held their gymnasium classes on the sports premises.

In April it is expected that the Sports Division will move to the lobby of the theater. The quarters are small and the Sports Division will have very few program possibilities.

5. Art Exhibit

On March 29th an art exhibit of paintings, sculpture, graphics, etc., opened in the lobby of the theater. Fifteen artists are represented with a variety of works. Besides the noted Vilna artists Rachel Sutzkever (oils and watercolors), Jacob Sher (part of the album, *Vilna Ghetto*), Uma Olkenicka (graphics), and Yudel Moot (sculptures and an album of papier-mâché), a number of young artists participated. N. Drezin exhibited twelve satires and caricatures of well-known ghetto figures; four members of the Plastic Plan of Vilna showed carved medallions and miniatures of the Great Synagogue, cathedral, etc. Engineering architect F. Rom made miniatures of her own designs for office furniture; G. Sedlis exhibited three paintings (watercolor and pencil). Of special note are the works of three children in the exhibit. S. Wolmark and Z. Weiner sketched ghetto themes (gates of the ghetto, etc.). Nine-year-old S. Bock is considered by the jury to be extraordinarily gifted, and the jury selected thirty of his drawings to show.

Award-winning works in the art contest (see February report) were also shown. The exhibit was extremely successful and visited daily by the hundreds. Children of the ghetto schools visited the exhibit together with their teachers. The exhibit will remain open until April 4th. The Ghetto Chief intends to purchase several of the exhibited works, which have ghetto themes.

6. Support for Writers and Artists

During the month the Literary Association continued to submit works of its members in order to obtain honoraria from the Ghetto Chief through the Culture Department. Dr. Gordon completed the first chapter of a philosophical work, *Apriorist Foundations of History,* and received another advance on his honorarium; Jacob Sher submitted to a jury his album, *Vilna Ghetto,* from which the jury selected ten sketches. Leib Turbowicz completed the first four chapters of a large work on the history of the Jews in Vilna, receiving a substantial honorarium (500 marks). The board of the Literary Association has strict standards for submission and at its last meeting rejected various works of six authors. In the April budget the sum of 1,000 marks is expected to be assigned to the support of writers and artists.

7. Workers' Assemblies

The workers' assemblies, organized by the Brigadiers' Council in cooperation with the Culture Department, are attracting ever larger audiences. In March they covered these topics: (1) Award-winning writers (outside and inside the ghetto), (2) the ghetto court, (3) Itzik Manger. After every lecture there is entertainment (recitations, singing, etc.). Last Sunday no assembly was held because the premises were taken over for sports. From April 4th, the assemblies will be resumed on Sunday mornings in the ghetto theater.

Vilna Ghetto, April 2nd, 1943
signed
G. Jaszunski
Director

PART EIGHT

. . .

WORK, INDUSTRY, MODERNITY

23

Industry and Labor

The Four-Year-Plan, Beauty of Labor, and Strength through Joy

DURING THE WEIMAR REPUBLIC, nationalists were divided between romantic anticapitalists who yearned nostalgically for a preindustrial, premodern past and the wing of the German Right that embraced technology, total mobilization, and the figure of the soldier of labor (the "Worker" in the famous essay by the novelist Ernst Jünger). The Nazis incorporated both of these elements, combining attacks on the corrupting influence of commercial civilization with the promotion of "German" labor, technology, and "rationalization" (a catchword of the 1920s meaning "scientific" approaches to management and efficient production). Typical of the regime's fetish for productivity was the Four-Year Plan, announced in August 1936, which aimed to speed up the economy, increase efficiency, and above all, rearm the German military machine to prepare for a war against Bolshevism. In a secret memorandum, Hitler stressed the aim of "developing the German Army as quickly as possible into the best army in the world." The rearmament and military mobilization of German society was to be based on intensive economic nationalism: bolstering the Reichsmark against foreign currency, increasing fuel production, improving the development of synthetic rubber, and stepping up the production of iron. All of this was to be achieved by private industry, which would improve industrial output by modernizing its methods. And, Hitler pointed out, not only would this expanded productivity serve the Reich's military ends, but it would also satisfy consumer desires.

To achieve this aim, after 1936, workplace authoritarianism, exemplified by Karl Arnhold's campaign to make work more "meaningful," blended with scientific management and innovative consumer design, concepts once maligned by Nazi ideologues as Weimar-era "New Objectivity." These efforts now became symbols of the modernizing thrust of Nazi industrial policy. The emphasis on streamlining everything from canteen service to automobiles and trains reveals a good deal of continuity between the modern designs of the 1920s and the industrial policies of the Nazis. One difference, of course, is that under National Socialism, as Hitler's August memorandum warned, failure to comply could lead to prison and under the Reich, "the whole of Jewry [was] liable" for "economic sabotage."

Architectural journals distinguished between the monumental style of public buildings and the more practical style necessary for the factory. According to Hitler's chief architect, Albert Speer, the modern plant had to reflect the unadorned functional style appropriate to a powerful industrial society. Architect Emil Rudolf Mewes wrote in a comprehensive article that industrial architecture had to be "subordinate to the laws of utility." Speer established a division of the pseudo–trade union Deutsche Arbeitsfront (German Labor Front) called the Amt für Schönheit der Arbeit (Bureau of Beauty of Labor), to be headed by Karl Kretschmer. The bureau's slogan, "The German everyday shall be beautiful," combined propaganda with a modernizing thrust in architecture and design. Sports and gymnastics in factories promoted the National Socialist cult of the body, emphasizing the link between physical well-being and the overall health of the nation. The Beauty of Labor program borrowed modernist Bauhaus-like designs (and Bauhaus designers) for factory canteens and mounted campaigns to transform the interiors and exteriors of German plants. In Hamburg, for example, the 1936 World Congress for Free-Time Culture and Recreation of the Worker offered pictures, models, and designs to popularize these efforts, including a "More Beautiful Germany" exhibit, models of a "community-room," a workers' canteen, and photographs of a recently remodeled factory. German factories that modernized according to plans provided by the Bureau of Beauty of Labor received tax abatements and recognition as a "National Socialist Model Plant." Beauty of Labor campaigns like "Clean People, Clean Factories" also promoted better lighting and warm meals and emphasized cleanliness and order as external signs of the worker's inner attitude. The clandestine report by the Social Democratic Party in exile (Sopade) on the impact of these efforts to produce social cohesion noted the "alarmingly positive results" of these measures. As the Sopade pointed out, all of the measures they introduced, "whether for or against the workers, are always designed to extinguish any thought of the need for acting in solidarity."

Another division of the German Labor Front was Kraft durch Freude (Strength through Joy), one of Nazi Germany's most successful programs. Under Labor Front leader Robert Ley (1890–1945), sometimes referred to as the "party's bullfrog" and according to Albert Speer "a vulgar drunkard," Strength through Joy was primarily a travel and hiking organization dedicated to "offering visitors the blessings of culture and customs."[1] It was also a profitable venture. Its main purpose was to affect the private lives of workers and employees by organizing day trips, weeklong outings, communal activities, theatrical productions, and the popular outings offered by the Travel, Hiking and Holiday Department. For a few carefully selected voyagers, Strength through Joy offered ocean cruises at reduced prices on one of its eight steamships (including trips to Lisbon, Madeira, and Norway). In her (in all likelihood officially encouraged) diary of her trip around Italy, Gertrud Meyer described a day on the *Wilhelm Gustloff* (later a troop ship that sank on 31 January 1945 while filled with 9,400 refugees, which is the subject of Günter Grass's 2002 novel *Crabwalk*). Her account offers a glimpse of the exhausting round of political and cultural activities demanded of the cruise's participants.

These programs were clearly part of Nazi Germany's attempt to instill pride in the workplace and to acknowledge that working-class Germans needed to enjoy their leisure hours. The popularity of Strength through Joy demonstrated that a revolution in status and self-esteem could be effective, especially in lieu of material rewards. But mass working-class tourism also created problems for more conventional affluent vacationers. As Sopade reported, "The big mass trips are for the proletariat. People now look for places where there are no Strength through Joy visitors. 'Not visited by Strength through Joy' is now a particular asset for summer vacations."

NOTE

1. On Ley, see Albert Speer, *Spandau: The Secret Diaries,* translated by Richard and Clara Winston (New York: Pocket Books, 1976), 236.

309

ADOLF HITLER

Secret Memorandum on the Four-Year Plan

First circulated in August 1936. First published in *Documents on German Foreign Policy, 1918–1945, Series C (1933–1937)*, vol. 5, *The Third Reich: The First Phase* (Washington D.C.: U.S. Government Printing Office, 1966), 853–62.

Politics are the conduct and the course of the historical struggle for the life of peoples and nations. The aim of these struggles is the assertion of existence. Even the idealistic *Weltanschauungskämpfe* [struggles over the worldview—Eds.] have their ultimate cause and are most deeply motivated by *völklich* [determined by the *Volk*—Eds.] purposes and aims of life. Religions and ideologies are, however, always able to impart particular harshness to struggles of this kind, and therefore also to lend them immense historical urgency. They leave their imprint on the content of centuries. In such cases it is not possible for peoples, nations and states surrounded by such ideological or religious conflicts to dissociate or exclude themselves from these events. Christianity and the migration of peoples determined the historical content of centuries. Mohammedanism, too, shook the Orient, and with it the Western world, for half a millennium. The Reformation caught up the whole of Central Europe in its way. Nor was it possible for individual States—either by dint of skill or by strategic non-participation—to steer clear of events. Since the outbreak of the French Revolution, the world has been moving at an ever increasing rate of speed towards a new conflict, the most extreme solution to which is called Bolshevism, whose essence and aim, however, is solely the elimination of those elements in human society that have thus far provided leadership so they can replace them with worldwide Jewry.

No state will be able to withdraw or even remain at a distance from this historical conflict. *Ever since Marxism, with its victory in Russia, established one of the greatest empires in the world as a forward base for its future operations, this question has become a menacing one. Against a democratic world ideologically rent within itself stands a unified aggressive will founded upon on authoritarian ideology.* In the meantime, the military power at the disposal of this aggressive will continues to increase rapidly from year to year. One has only to compare the Red Army as it actually exists today with the assumptions of military men 10 or 15 years ago to realize the menacing extent of this development. Just think about what conditions will be like if these developments continue at the same rate for the next 10, 15 or 20 years!

Germany

Germany will always be seen as the epicenter of the Western world when it comes to confronting Bolshevist attacks. I do not see this as a pleasant mission, but rather as a handicap and encumbrance upon our life, regrettably resulting from our position in Europe.

We cannot, however, escape this destiny.

Our political situation results from the following:

At present, Europe has only two States which can be seen as standing firm in the face of Bolshevism: Germany and Italy. The other countries have either been shattered by their democratic lifestyles, infected by Marxism and thus on the verge of imminent collapse, or ruled by authoritarian governments whose only strength lies in their military power; however, this means that, being obliged to secure the existence of their leadership in face of their own peoples by means of the armed hand of the Executive, they are unable to direct this armed hand outwards for the preservation of their States. All these countries would be incapable of ever conducting a war against Soviet Russia with any prospect for success. In any case, apart from Germany and Italy, only Japan can be regarded as a power standing firm in the face of this world peril.

It is not the aim of this memorandum to prophesy the time when the untenable situation in Europe will become an open crisis. My sole intent in these lines is to set down my conviction that this crisis cannot and will not fail to arrive and that it is Germany's duty to secure her own existence by every means in the face of this catastrophe and to protect herself against it, and that from this exigency, a series of conclusions arises pertaining to the most important tasks that have ever been set for our *Volk*. *Because Bolshevism's victory over Germany would not lead to a Versailles Treaty but to the final destruction, indeed, the annihilation of the German* Volk.

The consequences of such a catastrophe are entirely unforeseeable. How, indeed, would the whole of densely populated Western Europe (Germany included)—in the aftermath of a collapse into Bolshevism—survive probably the most gruesome human tragedy that has been visited upon mankind since the downfall of the states of antiquity? *In light of the urgency of this threat, all other considerations must recede into the background as being utterly irrelevant.*

Germany's Defense Capabilities

Germany's defense capabilities are based on several factors. I would give pride of place to the intrinsic value of the German *Volk* itself. The German *Volk*—with impeccable political leadership, a solid ideology and a thorough military organization—certainly constitutes the most valuable factor of resistance which the world of today can possess. Political leadership is guaranteed by the National Socialist Party; since the triumph of National Socialism, ideological solidarity has burgeoned to a degree never before attained. It must be constantly fortified and galvanized on the basis of this content. This is the aim of the National Socialist education of our people.

The expansion of the military is to be effected through the new Army. *The extent and pace of military exploitation of our resources for the sake of expansion cannot be too great nor can it happen fast enough!* It is a capital error to think that there can be any argument on these points or any comparison to other vital necessities. However much the general pattern for the life of a people ought to be a balanced one, it is nonetheless imperative that at particular times certain disturbances of the balance must be adopted, to the detriment of other less vital concerns. *If we do not succeed in developing the German Army as quickly as possible into the best army in the world—in training, in the number of troops, in armaments, and above all, in mind and spirit—Germany will be lost!* The operative principle here is that the omissions of peacetime cannot be made up for in centuries.

All other wants and needs must therefore be unconditionally subordinated to this task. For this task is life and the preservation of life, and all other wants and needs—however understandable they may be in other periods—are of no account by comparison, and in fact may even be a mortal threat and must therefore be rejected. Nor will posterity ever ask us by what prevailing methods or by what concepts, views, etc. we achieved the salvation of nations, but only *whether* we achieved it. Nor would we be able to one day make excuses for our downfall by pointing to the measures which had nevertheless unfortunately caused that downfall, be they ever so well-intended.

Germany's Economic Position

Just as the political movement in our *Volk* knows only one goal—to make good the claim to life for our *Volk* and our Reich, that is to say, to secure all the spiritual and other pre-requisites for the self-assertion of our people—so, too, does the economy share this same single purpose. The *Volk* does not live for the economy or for economic leaders or economic or financial theories; on the contrary, finance and economy, economic leaders and theories must all exclusively serve this struggle for self-assertion in which our *Volk* is engaged.

Germany's economic position is, however, in the briefest outline, as follows:

1. We are overpopulated and cannot feed ourselves from our own resources.
2. When our nation has 6 or 7 million unemployed, the food situation improves because these people are deficient in purchasing power. It naturally makes a difference whether 6 million people have 40 marks a month to spend or 100 marks. It should not be overlooked that a third of all who earn their living is involved, that is to say that, taken as a proportion of the total population, through the National Socialist economic policy about 20 million people have been afforded an increase in their former standard of living of, on an average, from at most 50 marks a month to at least 100–120 marks. This means an increased and understandable run on the foodstuffs market.
3. But if this rise in employment fails to take place, then a higher percentage of people must gradually be deducted from the body of our nation as having become valueless through undernourishment. It is, therefore, in spite of our difficult food situation, the highest commandment of our economic policy to see to it that, by incorporating all Germans in the economic process, the precondition for normal consumption is created.
4. In so far as this consumption applies to articles of general use, it is possible to satisfy it to a *large* extent by increasing production. In so far as this consumption falls upon the foodstuffs market, it is not possible to satisfy it from the domestic German economy. For, although numerous branches of production can be increased without further ado, the yield of our agricultural production can undergo no further substantial increase. It is equally impossible for us at present to manufacture artificially certain raw materials that we lack in Germany, or to find substitutes for them.
5. It is, however, wholly pointless to keep noting these facts, i.e., stating that we lack foodstuffs or raw materials; what is decisive is that we take those measures which can effect a *final* solution for the *future* and a *temporary* easing for the *interim period.*
6. The final solution lies in expanding the living space of our *Volk* and/or the sources of its raw materials and foodstuffs. It is the task of political leadership to one day solve this problem.
7. The temporary easing can only be brought about within the framework of our present economy. In this context, the following must be noted:
   a. Since the German *Volk* will be increasingly dependent on imports for food and likewise, whatever happens, must import at least a portion of raw materials from abroad, all means must be employed to facilitate this import.
   b. An increase in our own exports is theoretically possible, but in practice hardly likely. Germany does not export to a political or economic vacuum but to areas where competition is stiffer than it has ever been. Our exports, compared with the overall international economic decline, have sunk not only *not more* but in fact *less* than those of other peoples and States. But since imports of food have, on the whole, hardly dropped at all, but if anything are on the rise, an adjustment must be found in some other way.
   c. It is, however, impossible to use foreign currency allocated for raw materials to import foodstuff without inflicting a heavy and perhaps even fatal blow to the rest of the Germany economy. *But above all it is utterly impossible to do this at the expense of national rearmament.* I must at this point vehemently reject the view that, by restricting national rearmament, i.e., the manufacture of arms and munitions, we could bring about an "enrichment" in raw materials that might then benefit Germany in the event of war. Such a view is based on a complete misconception—to not use a harsher expression—of the tasks and military requirements with which we are faced. For even a successful conservation of raw materials by reducing, for instance, the production of munitions, would merely mean that we should stockpile these raw

> materials in times of peace so as to manufacture them only in the event of war; that is to say, we should be depriving ourselves, during the most critical months, of munitions, in exchange for raw copper, lead or possibly iron. But in such a case it would nonetheless be better for the nation to enter the war without one kilogram of stocks of copper but with full munitions depots, rather than with empty depots but so-called "enriched" stocks of raw materials.

War makes possible the mobilization of even the last supplies of metal. For it then becomes not an *economic problem* but solely a *question of will.* And the National Socialist State leadership would possess the will, as well as the resolve and the toughness, to solve these problems in the event of war. But it is much more important to prepare for war in times of peace! In addition, however, the following must be stated:

There can be no stockpiling of a reserve of *raw materials* for the event of war, just as there can be no stockpiling of foreign currency reserves. The attempt is sometimes made today to represent matters as though Germany had gone to war in 1914 with well-prepared stocks of raw materials. This is a lie. It is not possible for any State to assemble beforehand the quantities of raw materials needed for war if the war lasts any longer than, say, a year. If any nation were really in a position to assemble the quantities of raw materials needed for a year, then its political, economic and military leaders would deserve to be hanged. For they would in fact be setting aside the available copper and iron in preparation for the conduct of a war, instead of manufacturing munitions for that war. But Germany entered the World War without any reserves. What was available at that time in Germany by way of apparent peacetime reserves was abundantly counterbalanced and rendered worthless by the miserable war-stocks of ammunition. *Moreover, the quantities of raw materials that are needed for a war are so large that there has NEVER in the history of the world been a real stockpiling for a duration of any length!* And as regards preparations in the form of piling up foreign currency, it is quite clear that:

1. War is capable of devaluing foreign currency at any time, unless it is held in gold, and
2. There is not the least guarantee that gold itself can be converted in time of war into raw materials. During the World War Germany still possessed very large foreign currency assets in a great many countries. It was not, however, possible for our shrewdly competent economic policymakers to bring to Germany, fuel, rubber, copper or tin in any sufficient quantity in exchange for these assets. To assert the contrary is ridiculous nonsense. For this reason and for the reason that we must safeguard the feeding of our people, therefore, the following task presents itself as imperative:

It is not sufficient merely to draw up, from time to time, raw material or foreign currency balances, or to talk about the preparation of a war economy in times of peace; on the contrary, it is essential to ensure peacetime food supplies and above all those means which can be mobilized by human energy and activity for conducting a war. And I therefore propose the following program for a final solution to a dire predicament:

I. Like the military and political rearmament and mobilization of our *Volk,* there must also be an economic one, and this must be effected in the same tempo, with the same determination, and, if need, be, with the same degree of ruthlessness.

   In the future, the interests of individual gentlemen can no longer be allowed to play any part in these matters. There is only one interest and that is the interest of the nation, and there is only one single view, which is that Germany must be brought into a state of self-sufficiency, politically and economically.

II. To this end, in every sector that allows us to satisfy our needs through domestic German production, foreign currency must be saved so that it can be applied to those needs which cannot under any circumstances be met by any means but by import.

III. Accordingly, German fuel production must now be stepped up as quickly as possible and be brought up to full speed within the next eighteen months. This task must be attacked and executed with the same determination as required for waging a war; for the way we conduct any future war is contingent on our solution to this problem, and not on stockpiling petroleum.

IV. It is equally urgent that the mass production of synthetic rubber be organized and secured. The contention that the processes are perhaps not yet fully determined and similar excuses must cease from now on. It is not a matter of discussing whether we want to wait any longer, for that would just cost us time and the hour of peril would take us all unaware. Above all, it is not the task for the state economic institutions to rack their brains over the means of production. This has nothing to do with the Ministry of Economics. Either we possess today a private industry, in which case, it is its task to rack its brains over the means of production, or we believe that it is the task of the state to determine the means of production, in which case we no longer need private industry.

V. The question of the cost of these raw materials is also quite irrelevant, since it is in any case better for us to produce in Germany expensive tires which we can actually use than for us to buy cheap tires for which, however, the Ministry of Economics cannot allocate any foreign currency and which therefore, are of no use to us at all. If we are in any case compelled to build up a large-scale domestic economy on the lines of autarky—which we are, because lamenting and harping on our foreign currency plight will not solve the problem in any case—then the price of raw materials in and of itself no longer plays any decisive role.

It is further necessary to maximize the German production of iron. The objection that we are not in a position to produce from the German iron ore with a 26 percent content as cheaply as pig-iron from the 456 percent content Swedish ores, etc. is irrelevant because we are not in fact faced with the question of what we would *rather* do but only of what we *can* do. The objection, moreover, that in the event all the German blast furnaces would have to be converted is equally irrelevant; and, what is more, this is not a concern of the Ministry of Economics. It is for the Ministry of Economics simply to set the national economic tasks, and it is for private industry to carry them out. But should private industry believe that it is not able to do this, then the National Socialist State will succeed in carrying out this task on its own. In any case, for a thousand years Germany had no foreign iron ores. Even before the war, more German iron ores were being processed than during the period of our worst decline. *Nevertheless, if we still have the possibility of importing cheap ores, well and good. But the future of the national economy and, above all, of the conduct of war, must not be dependent on this.*

It is further necessary to prohibit forthwith the distillation of alcohol from potatoes. Fuel must be obtained from the ground and not from potatoes. Instead, it is our duty to use any arable land that may become available, either for human or animal foodstuffs or for the cultivation of fibrous products.

It is further necessary for us to make our supplies of *industrial* fats independent of imports as quickly as possible and to meet them from our coal. This task has been solved chemically and is actually just crying out to be done. The German economy will either grasp the new economic tastes or it will prove itself quite incapable of surviving in this modern age when a Soviet state is setting up a gigantic plan. *But in that case it will not be Germany that goes under, but, at most, a few industrialists.*

It is further necessary to increase Germany's output of other ores, *regardless of cost,* and in particular to maximize the production of light metals to act as a substitute for certain other metals.

Finally, it is necessary even now for rearmament, too, to make use whenever possible of those materials which must and will replace high-grade metals in time of war. *It is better to consider and solve these problems in times of peace than to wait for the next war, and only then, in the midst of a multitude of tasks, to try to undertake these studies of the economy and methodology such as these!*

In sum: I consider it necessary that now, we must pursue one hundred percent self-sufficiency with iron-clad determination in whatever sectors are feasible, and not only should the national requirements in these most important raw materials be made independent of other countries, but we should also save the foreign currency that we require for our imports of foodstuffs in peacetime. *Here I would emphasize that in these tasks, and not in the throttling of armament industries in peacetime in order to save and stockpile raw materials for war, do I see the only true economic mobilization.*

But I further consider it necessary to make an immediate investigation into the outstanding debts in foreign currency owed to German business abroad. There is no doubt that the outstanding claims of German business today are enormous. Nor is there any doubt that behind this in some cases there lies concealed the contemptible desire to possess, whatever happens, certain reserves abroad which are thus withheld from the grasp of the domestic economy. I regard this as deliberate sabotage of our national self-assertion and of the defense of the Reich, and for this reason I consider it necessary for the Reichstag to pass the following two laws:

1. A law providing the death penalty for economic sabotage, and
2. A law making the whole of Jewry liable for all damage inflicted by individual specimens of this community of criminals upon the German economy and thus upon the German *Volk*.

Moreover, only the performance of these tasks in the form of a Multi-Year Plan for rendering our national economy independent of foreign countries will make it possible for the first time to demand sacrifices from the German people in the economic sphere and the sphere of foodstuffs, for in that case the people will have a right to demand of their leaders, in whom they place blind trust, that they tackle the problems in this sphere too with unprecedented and resolute action and do not merely discuss them, but that they solve them and not merely put them on record!

Nearly four precious years have now passed. There is no doubt that by now we could have been completely independent of foreign countries in the area of fuel supplies, rubber supplies, and partly also iron ore supplies. Just as we are now producing 700,000 or 800,000 tons of petroleum, we could be producing 3 million tons. Just as we are today manufacturing a few thousand tons of rubber, we could already be producing 70,000 or 80,000 annually. Just as we have stepped up the production of iron ore from 2.5 million tons to 7 million, so we could be processing 20 or 25 million tons of German iron ore, and if necessary even 30 million. There has been time enough in four years to discover what we cannot do. Now we need to state what we can do.

I thus assign the following task:

I. The German army must be operational and ready to deploy within four years.
II. The German economy must be capable of sustaining a wartime economy within four years.

310

KARL ARNHOLD

Senseless Work Is Un-German

First published as "Sinnloses Arbeiten ist undeutsch," in *Mensch und Arbeit* (Berlin, 1936), 25–27.

The German working man must know and be convinced that there is a sense of purpose to whatever he does. He will always inevitably falter as soon as he realizes that there is no point to any task he has been assigned. It goes without saying that any modern-day business would not demand [that its workers complete] pointless tasks, but it happens again and again that, as a result of excessive bureaucratization or of a predominately rationalistic approach to business operations, the work performed by a certain individual seems pointless. The consequences, as previously stated, include workers showing signs of being tired before they should, lack of desire to work, even a pronounced hatred toward work itself. Just one cold, calculated intellectualist and rationalist on the job can manage—often unwittingly—to plunge a whole cordon of followers into despair in this manner! Anyone with a competitive spirit will feel to a certain degree at the mercy of this kind of rationalist behavior, because the weapons are not distributed equally here. People who are fighters will always *instinctively* know whether their job or the tasks they are assigned have a purpose or not, whereas the business manager who is "trained" to run things from a purely rationalistic point of view will often lack the healthy common sense for the organic structuring and organic development of work.

Noncompetitive work is contrary to German nature. One might ask, Can there be such a thing as competitive work on the job today? The answer is, of course! One need only call to mind the difference between an hourly wage and payment based on performance and output, the difference between personal investment and bureaucratic dispassion, between "doing something" and "just getting it done." Competitive work is always a personal confrontation with a task; it is the struggle toward a goal and striving for perfection, to the degree that this is within the means of the individual completing it.

Idle work is alien to our nature and at the same time detrimental to business because this is precisely what strips the competitive person of the very thing that marks him as a fighter—the will to perform. It is no coincidence that digging up sugar beets from fields that seem to go on forever is one of the most detested jobs of German farmworkers; it is no coincidence that carting sand from one site to another with no apparent planning—and with no apparent prospect for a successful end to the task—is one of the most wretched jobs you can give a German worker. The aversion to pointless work is in fact highly characteristic of Nordic—that is, of Indo-Germanic—peoples in general. There are enough examples of this to be found in the ancient Greek sagas (the leaky jars of the Danaides or the myth of Sisyphus, etc.).

The psychological absurdity of pointless, noncompetitive, aimless work mandates certain inevitable and inalterable consequences: businesses are to do everything in their power to make sure that everyone who works there knows the purpose of what he is doing; special efforts are to be made—if necessary, by mandate—to ensure that there are objective standards for evaluating and monitoring performance levels. Finally, every German business undertaking must set certain goals for itself—competitive aims that will sufficiently challenge the fighting spirit of the competitive worker.

There is one more aspect of this psychological trait of the German worker: there is no other worker in the world who is more sensitive to injustices as the German worker. We should like to attribute this heightened sensitivity to injustice to inborn propensities ultimately rooted in the ancient Germanic loyalty to the *Volk*. You can subject the born soldier to just about anything else, but when you do him an injustice, something will well up within him in rebellion that cannot be suppressed, not even by armed force. And exactly the same is true for the German worker: a business manager can get him to perform the most grueling work if need be, but his willingness to perform drops to nil once he sees himself as being treated unjustly. One is perhaps reminded in this context of the struggles for wages in recent decades: we are convinced that in many cases what spurned the workers on to these struggles was none other than precisely this feeling of having been treated unfairly. They were convinced that they had performed valuable services and were thus entitled to a decent wage for their work; the fact that "labor leaders" of every stripe exploited this otherwise essentially healthy characteristic to serve their own interests does not change that fact. The only way to explain the degree of determination with which these struggles were pursued is through this struggle for justice. Today we have the possibility of examining time and motion studies to determine the basis for a fair working wage that would of course be staggered according to job performance. One of the simplest prerequisites for ensuring that the wage is *perceived* as being just is that the calculation of those wages is transparent for the worker. If it isn't—if a worker must sift through an intricate and confusing array of calculations for compensation in order to gain a clear understanding of how wages are calculated—then he falls prey to the sins of the past and begins to suspect that hard-earned money is being withheld from him. Every well-managed business, too, must have a policy of rewarding excellent performance unconditionally and lavishly, and the system of rewards must be structured to maximize its psychological impact.

311

SOPADE

On Recruiting Workers through Compulsory Membership and Social Bribery

Report first appeared in November 1935. First published in *Deutschland-Berichte der Sozialdemokratischen Partei Deutschlands (Sopade)* (Frankfurt am Main: Verlag Petra Nettlebeck, 1980), 2: 1375.

All National Socialist mass organizations have the same mission. Whether it be the Labor Front, Strength through Joy, the Hitler Youth, or the Rewarding Labor [*Arbeitsdank*] program, all these organizations serve the same purpose: to "register" national comrades, or to "care for" them, not to let them fend for themselves and certainly not to give them any time to reflect or to think.[1] Just as any idle activity will eventually exhaust any possibility for serious work, the National Socialists are spreading an overzealous sense of industriousness with the explicit intent of preventing any genuine sense of community or any form of voluntary alliances. [Robert] Ley recently admitted as much publicly: the "national comrade" shall have no private life, and the first thing he should give up is his private bowling club. This organizational monopoly is designed to keep your average man on the street completely lacking in independence, to extinguish in him any form of initiative toward building even the most primitive alliances, to separate him from anyone who may share his views or his voice, to isolate him and make him dependent on state organizations. And this has not been without impact. Now and then one of the workers in the Strength through Joy program expresses a word of praise by saying something like "no one ever bothered to worry about us before!" Indeed, but nor did the state used to consider it its job to send its workers to the movies on a regular basis in their free time. In the past, workers took pride in being able to make these kinds of arrangements on their own. And yet none too few workers are likely to prefer the state-organized leisure and "relaxation" activities simply because they are more convenient. Obviously, with things as they are, the motivation for these practices cannot be simply to casually demonstrate to the workers that one individual success or the other is the result of their ability to "stick together"; rather, these practices place an activity in the realm of work that is essentially illegal.

Compulsory membership in organizations, on the one hand, and atomization, on the other, are at the very essence of fascist control of the masses.

The National Socialists are very well aware of the fact that a sense of solidarity is the source of impetus for the workers, and, consequently, all of the measures they introduce, whether for or against the workers, are always designed to extinguish any thought of the need for acting in solidarity. All of the changes for the worse they are foisting upon the workers in terms of wages, taxes, social security insurance, etc. are always set up so they never have the same impact on any two or more major sectors of the population. Otherwise, if the changes for the worse become more general, they might also spurn more general resistance efforts. These political policies of the National Socialists have produced alarmingly positive results, not least of all because the destruction of the sense of solidarity had already set in with the economic crisis. The economic crisis caused many workers to pay little mind to the most valuable product of acting in solidarity—union wages—and to seek work wherever they could get it. Now the National Socialists have pushed the workers so far that one of them often runs to the supervisor on his own and, on the condition that he doesn't tell his coworkers about it, [and] makes some kind of deal to avert a decrease in wages—especially when piece-rate pay is involved. Especially among younger workers, you often get the impression that it wouldn't so much as occur to them that they might lend more weight to their demands by acting collectively—even if only in the most insignificant points.

Note

1. The *Arbeitsdank* program was set up in November 1933 to compensate Labor Service members who had suffered work-related injuries or illness—Eds.

312

KARL KRETSCHMER

On the Tasks of the Beauty of Labor Program

First published as "Über die Aufgaben des Amtes für Schönheit der Arbeit," in *Die Form,* July 1934, 161–65.

In any National Socialist business, validation of the honor in work and human dignity must also find clear outward expression. It is only in a healthy, orderly workplace that workers can work with enthusiasm and élan. Whoever takes pleasure in his work will perform well.

Director of the Beauty of Labor Program

If the structural mistakes of the past few decades have produced anything of use for us, it was the knowledge of how important every single thing in our environment is because it influences our lust for life through its language. The Marxists, faithful adherents to the theory of environmentalism, have apparently overlooked this bit of truth, which we see confirmed each spring; otherwise, they wouldn't have allowed so much misery, emptiness, and desolation to arise. Not unless it was their conscious aim to structure the environment so hideously as to force any German citizen to despair, dissatisfaction, and nihilism . . .

Today the young National Socialist Germany stands before the task of restructuring the environment according to its new worldview: in tune with nature, life affirming, noble, and

FIGURE 31. Leisure organization Beauty of Labor gymnastics in German workplaces. "The fitness wheel and smokestacks—an unusual combination! There's quite the bustle out on the sports areas of this factory." Werner Rittich, *Architektur und Bauplastik der Gegenwart* (Berlin: Rembrandt, 1938).

strong. Testimonies to our decline still surround us in the superficial façades of Wilhelmine architecture and the functionalist tenement blocks of the republic. It will take centuries for them to disappear altogether. But as long as they act as a warning, reminding us that when a nation of people falls apart, its culture dies with it, but that then no amount of some hidden beauty nor fanatical search to salvage something useful will be of help.

The beginning of new concepts in construction! We don't want to get bogged down drawing up elaborate plans but are already doing whatever possible to restructure daily life in Germany to make it more pleasant. One of the primary priorities is in putting a better face on the workplace because it is here that millions of German national comrades spend most of their time. Does this serve the interest of sober and serious concentration on the job? Certainly, but one should not forget that all forms of labor are in turn of service to our lives, and these lives always need periodic bursts of impetus and pleasure in order to be strong enough for serious commitment on the job.

Tens of thousands of workplaces are in miserable condition. Greed and lack of forethought were their godfathers from birth onward and have stood by them for all their lives. The machines were kept well maintained, built with the finest materials and lavished with painstakingly loving care because people knew that they would otherwise fail to operate properly. Unfortunately, the most valuable labor assets—the workers themselves—were not afforded the same degree of attention. Apparently, they weren't assumed to react as sensitively as the machines. It took a series of laws, legislation, law enforcement, and other agencies before any transformation of this situation could occur. But laws can be effective only if they reflect the general will of the people [*Volkswillen*] and this will has not been there in Germany in the past; so workplaces were left in disarray, in whole or in part. Only the most sensible business manager has always known that sites of production are sites of life, places where human beings are active—human beings who must be healthy and happy in order to produce anything of value. So from the very beginning, he structured his business with the welfare of his employees by making sure there was enough light and fresh air, that the place was clean and healthy, and that everything possible was done to provide a relaxing environment that was pleasing to the eye. He knew that the architecture of his enterprise would have to symbolize the spirit of the people working inside the building and that it would have a major influence on the appearance of the landscape or street in which it was situated and which was the property of all. And this is why he also refrained from using his factory as a billboard for advertising. He told himself that the good reputation of his business would be worth more than any form of advertisement. And the result was that he garnered the respect of all his employees, who helped him maintain it and spoke in terms of "my factory" and "my workplace," and that people living in the immediate neighborhood looked upon the factory with pride.

But the businesses of those harebrained money sacks present an altogether different picture. All you will find there are things that make work utterly unpleasant and therefore ultimately despised. Danger and illness prevail in them—filthy, cramped, with stifled air and a stifling atmosphere, clutter piled high in the yards, and instead of pleasant pictures, there are only placards hanging on the walls that read *Verboten . . . Verboten*. Here, behind the dark and dingy windowpanes, surly employees work in cold inhospitable rooms just because they must. "Dumps" is what such places of employment are called in the vernacular, and no kitschy sign hanging at the entrance is going to change that.

These businesses are a task that the Beauty of Labor program must tackle. The first and most pressing item on the agenda is to transform these miserable, unhealthy battle sites into places that are home to happy workers. We will begin with a propaganda campaign that will be drilled into every business, every office, and every factory or shop until our message has become a binding imperative for every last place of employment. Clean up the workplace! We don't need any legislation or guidelines for execution in this regard; in the final analysis, everyone knows what is meant, and if there is a boss around who doesn't know, then his employees would gladly explain it to him.

Furthermore, our job will be to enlist all available competent forces available to join in this great work, which will be a cultural task. Only when the concept of the "Beauty of Labor" has come to life in the whole of the population can insights gleaned from the science of industrial hygiene [*Betriebshygiene*] have a broad-based effect so that laws and regulations may be passed that will be of benefit to every last business and ultimately form the basis for a dignified and pleasant structuring of the workplace, in new projects that will give German urban planners, engineers, architects, physicians, sculptors, and landscapers their due.

The structure of workplaces is multifaceted, so the aesthetic possibilities for design are also multifaceted and manifold. It goes without saying that the citadels of cast-iron style will have as little chance of being resurrected as that old familiar static concrete and steel steam-engine style you still encounter here and there. Just as the workplaces must be there to serve the people, raw materials and construction are there to serve the purpose of design. The profile of the workplace will be sleek and noble in some cases, more ornate or more natural in others: the nature of the work itself will set the tone. The uniformity, for example, of our present-day office buildings, interior and exterior, will disappear. At present, people are still talking about the architectural construction of the factories in terms of the world of machines and their "stylistic laws." But consider how brief the life span of any given modern phenomenon in construction is and how quickly it fades from view compared to the eternal laws of the human eye. And taking the machine as the point of departure for a new sensibility in form can apply only to dynamic things. Where would we be if we sought to lend every building a "dynamic form" because that form moves something within us! Engineers in particular would have every reason to reject the idea on technical grounds alone. In the meantime, the scope and form of machines is being constantly scaled back; their appearance is becoming less busy. So it seems that industrial architectural design is bound to become an architectural task that is increasingly independent of the "world of machines," and not just as it pertains to human beings. The material and construction of buildings is increasingly being enlisted in the service of genuine design. The sleek new face of the factories certainly has no room for frivolous ornamentation, inside or out, but that does not imply that it will have to subordinate itself entirely to the whims of a concrete lover.

The interior of a plant floor can be either cold and expressionless or strong and imposing in its design. Building owners, in their calculating precision, and often even engineers, in their technical calculations, but above all, all those who simply believe they must appreciate anything that is sober and cold always keep forgetting to bear the human being and the human eye in mind.

But before these last questions in design can be solved, the first thing that needs to happen is what should have long since happened without further debate: pleasant places of work must be built!

313

WILHELM LOTZ

Reconstruction Work in German Factories

First published as "Reconstruction Work in German Factories: 'Beauty of Labour' on the 'World Congress for Free-Time Culture and Recreation of the Worker,'" in *Schönheit der Arbeit* 1, no. 3 (July 1936): 109, 110. Original text in English.

The aim of the "World Congress for Free-Time Culture and Recreation of the Worker," to be held at Hamburg from July 23rd to 30th, is to give our international as well as German guests an impressive idea of the mental forces that, derived from each nationality, strive to make the working-man's life richer and more beautiful.

Much preparatory work was indispensable here for a great General Display of the new Germany's efforts in that direction. "Beauty of Labor" had a prominent part in this, for without work that gives full satisfaction, no really enjoyable rest-time is imaginable!

In the weeks preceding the Congress, the Head Office of "Beauty of Labor" had sent out a collaborator who—with the aid of first-class photographers—was to collect material showing truly representative examples of new and reformed working places of today. For in spite of the close contact existing with all factories, etc., it was certainly only by this place that a genuine collective idea of the great change effected in the outer appearance and the installations of German industrial plants was conveyed. Even if there still remains much to be done, and in our progressive times of technique and economy a final stage will never be attained in that regard, we know today that the leaders of German industrial life have offered their wholehearted cooperation to the promoters, in a way never thought of before when, three years ago, Dr. Ley, leading genius of the Deutsche Arbeitsfront (German Labor Front) for the first time announced his inspiring directives for "Beauty of Labor!"

It is certain that the German workman never regarded the embellishment of the conditions under which he has to work as a mere trifle or simple maneuver to distract his attention from more important things, but is today firmly convinced that this new movement constitutes a necessary ingredient essential for German reconstruction. In innumerable cases the German community of all employed [*Betriebsgemeinschaft*] has proved its merits in this great, uplifting task.

A selection made of the most striking results of the zealous efforts displayed for a "More Beautiful Germany" will likewise be seen in pictures, models, and designs at the Congress Exhibition at Hamburg; it has also been provided with ample material by the Bureau of Beauty of Labor. The central figure of the whole will always be the creative German worker who is master of, not slave to, the Machine!

It was not intended to show a representative collection of good factory equipment, as for instance, laundry-equipment, wardrobes, bicycle stands, etc. These were minor details. On the contrary, a small laborers' canteen, completely outfitted with furniture designed by the department, it is shown in order to emphasize the importance and value of the "community-room" in factories.

In the three main sections entitled "The Working Place," "The Recreation Facilities," and "The Community Room," the first order of priority is to show not new constructions but well rebuilt ones of older factories. As the latter are by far in the majority, they consequently play a more decisive role. Of special interest in this respect are two models, one representing a 70-year-old factory at Leipzig where—by contrasting the former and present state of affairs—the results of well-planned reconstruction are convincingly shown to everyone.

The building and shipping trades receive special treatment. In models and snap examples, good methods of housing are exhibited and of the kind all German shipping companies nowadays endeavor to introduce.

For men employed in the Building Trade, the construction-camp labeled "Beauty of the Workplace" will be of particular attraction, in addition to the pictures of the Reich Motorway [*Reichsautobahn*].

Since, however, even the very best exposition can never be as convincing as practical life itself, different Hamburg factories will be also shown to the visitors. There, in cooperation with the above-mentioned department and reputed artists, much good has been done. We shall be able to see here a number of "comrade-assembly-houses" [*Kameradschaftshäuser*] in the course of erection.

During the whole Congress, leading German personalities will deal with the fascinating problems of a "More Beautiful Germany" and "Beauty of the Workplace." Artists as well as technical and economic experts will be heard.

Exposition, tours, and speeches are to show that National Socialism has thus awakened a profound feeling of responsibility all over Germany, and that the communal work done here accomplished something that the dead letter of the Law would never be able to achieve in a disunited Nation!

314

EMIL RUDOLF MEWES

Thoughts on Architecture in Industrial Construction

First published as "Gedanken über Architektur im Industriebau," in *Schönheit der Arbeit* 4, no. 3 (August 1938): 155, 156, 159.

The tremendous construction projects of the Third Reich include, not least of all, the industrial building construction. The Four-Year Plan, with the overwhelming demands it places on German technology in terms of skills and performance, includes the construction of innumerable industrial plants that will perhaps leave their mark on the environment for centuries to come. There is a binding obligation to everyone to allow those buildings to lend expression to the sensibilities in construction of our times; the responsibility for enlisting the proper forces to this end must be weighed carefully. Not every engineer or every architect will be well suited to industrial construction. Only those who have fully appreciated the need for collaboration between the architect and the engineer in all its profound implications are called to industrial construction and capable of bringing us closer to the goals we have set. What we must achieve, even while meeting the highest demands stipulated by operational concerns, is that these works lend expression to a culture of design that is inspired by the spirit of our times.

There is no other form of art that leaves so much room for imagination and reason as architecture and yet, at the same time, is entirely and immediately subordinate to the laws of utility. And the very essence of industrial construction is anchored in this statement. The architect has at his disposal only a certain limited number of possibilities for combining certain geometric surfaces in such a way as to effect the intended harmonious integration of light and shadows in his work, yet look at the tremendous effects he is able to produce with these very limited means! The more modest these means are, the greater the effect, for the highest aim of art, especially in the field of industrial construction, is to lend expression only to the very essential.

Anything that is nonessential has no place in art. But it is apparently rather difficult to discern between the essential and the nonessential, to sort and single out. Any masterpiece is necessarily a modest thing, containing only what is essential. As long as the *Volk* retains its appreciation for simplicity, it will continue to appreciate the masterpieces in every field. The only immutable law there is for us is the one governing the relationship between light and shadows enabling us to bring these two contrasts together in harmony. And at the same time, this represents to us the play between movement and stillness also evident in the cubic capacity of a project. But there is something mysterious about work: it offers much to the patient and the modest men but not to the zealots and self-absorbed social climbers; it may often satisfy the apprentice but will fail the student, and then one day, something miraculous enters the world at the hands of a humble worker. If he is to master the tasks demanded of him by our times, the architect must therefore eavesdrop carefully on the voices of nature and the *Volk*—in a persistent, deferent, and passionate effort.

Industrial construction is one of the most salient tasks in the development of style. The architect must accept responsibility for bringing the technical, operational, and engineering requirements to resonate in the context of a clearly defined and designed organism and [ensuring] that the rhythm of their respective functions finds expression in the construction project and its cubic capacity. Only in this manner can we guarantee that the monumental industrial buildings will not be disruptive to the urban or rural landscape but rather will be proudly cited right alongside other monuments to cultural achievement by every national comrade.

What is essential to the success of collaboration between the engineer and the architect is that the collaboration begin at the very onset of the project.

315

ROBERT LEY

On the Anniversary of the Establishment of Strength through Joy

First delivered as "Zum Jahrestag von Kraft durch Freude," 11 November 1934. First published in Robert Ley, *Durchbruch der sozialen Ehre: Reden und Gedanken für das schaffende Deutschland,* edited by Hans Dauer (Berlin: Mehden Verlag, 1935), 167.

It was the Führer who, as usual, set the tone for this. He said, "I want every worker to be guaranteed sufficient vacation time and I want not only this vacation but all his free time to be genuinely relaxing. And the reason I want this is that I need a *Volk* with nerves of steel, because only with a *Volk* that won't lose its nerves can one develop truly great political policy." This will of the Führer was like a sacred command! [. . .] Even if we were to embellish them with the patina of state-incorporated endorsement, we cannot allow the instruments of class struggle of the Marxists and bourgeoisie—the old associations—to remain in existence. This is why we have undertaken a systematic and thoroughgoing organization of the entire society of gainfully employed, the owners and the workers alike, into the Labor Front. The essence of life cannot be reduced to a simple matter of bread and butter or to one of wage issues nor even of dividends; we have learned, rather, and the *Volk* has firmly grasped this too: life is a sum of many things—an attitude of basic decency, investment, and participation in culture, taking in the sights of splendor that our fatherland has to offer, the design of the workplace, keeping the body physically fit, awakening folkloric customs, traditions, and sensibilities, and much, much more. [. . .] Never before in history has an upheaval of this overwhelming magnitude been achieved without the people making demands of a material nature. And yet this is the miracle of what we have done. And so it is that, after not even two years in existence, [Strength through Joy] is a smashing success. The Labor Front is the public square where the community gathers daily to practice drills to stay in shape, and Strength through Joy is the program that fills the agenda after the exercises have been completed. [. . .]

The crown jewel in the program is the Department of "Travel and Hiking." [. . .] According to reports from the individual *Gaue* and the central office, a total of 2,168,032 workers were sent on vacation through this program, 1.75 million of them for vacations of seven to ten days [. . .]. The economic impact of our trips can be seen in the following statistics: around 40 million Reichsmarks were spent by all the waves of vacationers. The Reich Railroad alone took in an additional 7 million Reichsmarks or so. Prices for the individual fares were kept sensationally low by the exquisite organization of the program. For example, a seven-day trip from Berlin to the *Riesengebirge,* food and lodging, round-trip train fare, and event tickets included, cost around 28 Reichsmarks. [. . .] Our cruise vacations enjoyed special popularity. No less than approximately 80,000 national comrades from throughout Germany sailed on cruise vessels to the Norwegian fjords and the English coast. The cost of a trip like this, from Berlin and back, including lodging and ship passage, was 42 Reichsmarks. Finally, let us not forget to note the many thousands of events offering visitors the blessings of culture and customs. In the first year, Strength through Joy hosted 66,739 in all the *Gaue* in Germany. In Berlin alone, 500,000 workers were given the opportunity to visit the *Theater des Volkes* and other theater productions and concerts of sterling quality for the admission fee of only 70 cents. Baden hosts a highly modern theatrical touring company that travels to the villages and towns. The Ministry of Propaganda has fourteen film and radio vehicles, [*Film- und Funkzüge*] some of which are also equipped for theatrical productions, running through all the *Gaue.* At the moment, these are being managed and maintained by the workers on the Autobahn and emergency disaster relief areas.

316

HORST DRESSLER-ANDRESS

Travel, Hiking and Holiday Department

First published as *Three Years of the National-Socialist Community "Kraft durch Freude": Aims and Acheivements* (Berlin, 1936), 17–19.

In Germany there is now not only a right to a holiday but also the moral obligation to spend it suitably, i.e., briefly expressed, a holiday without travel is no holiday. The German worker is to travel, relax properly for once in the year, and accumulate fresh strength for the coming working year. The Travel, Hiking and Holiday Department performs a gigantic task in carrying out these journeys. Everyone will be surprised to learn that the gigantic total of three million "Strength through Joy" travelers in 1935 was *more* than doubled this year. *The total number of people dealt with by this Department in 1936 was more than six million.* This included nearly five million "Strength through Joy" travelers on longer holiday and week-end trips on land, one million hikers and about 150,000 persons who went on cruises. In addition, there were several hundred thousand who made trips on steamers on inland lakes and rivers.

Particularly satisfactory results were achieved by the "Strength through Joy" hiking movement, which increased by 150% compared with the previous year. This shows that the idea of hiking in their homeland is constantly gaining more adherents among the German workers. There is no doubt that considerable further developments in this sphere of the work of the National Socialist community "Strength through Joy" are to be expected in the course of the next few years.

The year 1936 was marked by a whole series of triumphs for the Travel, Hiking and Holiday Department. In March and April, a total of eight large overseas steamers made cruises to Lisbon and Madeira with German workers, which represents an almost threefold increase as compared with last year's Atlantic cruises. As a start, on the first of May, the keels of the first two new steamers of the "Strength through Joy" fleet were laid in Hamburg.

317

GERTRUD MEYER

Around Italy

The Great Travel Experience

Written in 1939. First published as "Rund um Italien: Das große Reiseerlebnis," in Heinz Schön, *Die KdF-Schiffe und Ihr Schicksal: Eine Dokumentation* (Stuttgart: Motorbuch Verlag, 1987), 95, 98–99.

Gertrud Meyer was one of the few people selected for participation in the 28th Voyage of the Strength through Joy ship *Wilhelm Gustloff,* the Ninth Sail around Italy Tour, scheduled to begin in Genoa on 15 February 1939, led by Captain Heinrich Bertram, and to end on 25 February in Venice. Here is her description of the trip:

[. . .] This ship is a place to celebrate and be happy. Five dance floors, a concert stage, cinema, everything on board. The walls are hung with pictures, German landscapes, and figures in traditional dress. Light reflects off the exquisitely polished wood of the walls. Every room has its own peculiarities, its own beauty. There is a smoking lounge, a room for comfortably lounging around surrounded by walnut-paneled walls and leather inlays on the front and rear walls. Here, a portrait of the Führer; there, one of Robert Ley. Throughout the room, there are comfortable sofas arranged around tables, and there are even incredibly comfy overstuffed upholstery chairs to nod off in after dinner. I consider it all very interesting, even from a professional perspective, because I'm an interior designer.

Then there is the theater: walls with a flat varnished finish, Gobelin draperies, dance floor, stage, everything very bright, upbeat, festive, even the mural of Mediterranean seascapes on the front, rear, and side walls.

Still reeling from the impression left by what I've just seen, I enter the grand hall that encompasses four different rooms: the Hall of Traditional Costumes with figures dressed in traditional costumes from every German *Gau,* followed by a connecting room with writing desks to the starboard and port sides, leading to the next room which takes on a very special note with its lively wall murals of German landscapes. The paintings fill the entire wall space between the windows, so you are surrounded by the German countryside, with the seascape shining in through the big windows. This spectacular hall is appropriately called the "Germany Hall."

This leads then to the Music Hall. There is a dance floor here, too, but nevertheless the atmosphere is rather somber with large, colorful landscape reliefs, some of which are particularly expressive. [. . .]

On Tuesday, 21 February, we were told to get up early because we were to pass the Stromboli volcano around 6:15 A.M. And who would want to miss seeing that? The whole day is filled with spectacular sights on board and it is worth staying on deck all day, because at 10:20 we pass Cap Dell Armi on the port side. Unfortunate that the weather is somewhat overcast, the sea is slightly choppy.

There are program offerings in almost every room onboard the *Gustloff* today: At 9:00, in the auditorium, a lecture from the board reporter Fincke on "Looking Back: Genoa—Naples—Palermo"; beginning at 10:30, a "100-kilometer march" around the lower promenade deck, and the ship's band is giving a concert on the sunning deck, followed by another lecture in the auditorium at 1:15 P.M., "The Development and Significance of German Overseas Shipping."

Around 5:00 P.M., the programs continue with an event in the Music Hall: the Hitler Youth Radio Choir Königsberg, directed by Herbert Gudschun, singing "The Songs of Germany's *Gaue.*" Around 8:30, the masquerade and costume ball begins, celebrated throughout the ship, and it isn't until an hour after midnight that there is quiet on the ship.

On Wednesday, 22 February, there is yet another day of programming on board to keep everyone from getting bored. Around 10:15, there are a lot of passengers on deck as we pass the island of Corfu and at 11:50, the North Corfu Straits. At 9:00, there is a lecture in the auditorium titled "Our Former German Colonies"; at 10:30, the "Olympics on the High Seas 1939"—that 100-kilometer walk around the lower promenade deck—comes to an end with an award ceremony and distribution of medals; at 1:15 P.M., the onboard lecturer gives the lecture "Everything You Ever Wanted to Know about the KdF [Strength through Joy] ship *Wilhelm Gustloff,*" and the event in the Music Hall scheduled for 5:00 P.M. is called "Singing and Laughing Can Do No Wrong—You're All Invited to Sing Along," hosted by the Hitler Youth Radio Choir Königsberg, under the direction of Hans Joachim Paris, and the day draws to a close with an "Italian Evening" beginning at 8:30 P.M. in the Music Hall, featuring the soprano Hilde Schellenberg and pianist George Gericke together with the board orchestra of the MS *Wilhelm Gustloff,* conducted by G. A. Wiessenborn. The concert will be broadcast live in the auditorium, in the Germany Hall, in the Hall of Traditional Costumes, and in the winter garden.

Afterwards, beginning at 10:00 P.M. there will be dancing throughout the ship.

We are gradually nearing the end of our "Sail around Italy" tour.

318

SOPADE

On "Strength through Joy"

Reports first published in *Deutschland-Berichte der Sozialdemokratische Partei Deutschlands* [*Sopade*] (Paris: Sozialdemokratische Partei Deutschlands, 1938 and 1939), 1938, 172; 1939, 472. Published in English in Jeremy Noakes and Geoffrey Pridham, eds. and trans., *Nazism 1919–1945: A Documentary Reader,* vol. 2, *State, Economy, and Society 1933–1939* (Exeter, England: University of Exeter Press, 1984), 353.

Berlin, February 1938

Strength through Joy (KdF) is very popular. The events appeal to the yearning of the little man who wants an opportunity to get out and about himself and to take part in the pleasures of the "top people." It is a clever appeal to the petty bourgeois inclinations of the apolitical workers. For such a man it really means something to have been on a trip to Scandinavia, or even if he only went to the Black Forest or the Harz Mountains, he imagines that he has thereby climbed up a rung on the social ladder . . .

Bavaria, April 1939

On the group tours there is a sharp social differentiation. The "top people" only go on big trips where there will be a more select clientele. The big mass trips are for the proletariat. People now look for places where there are no KdF visitors. "Not visited by KdF" is now a particular asset for summer vacations. A landlord in a mountain village in Upper Bavaria wrote in his prospectus, "Not visited by KdF tourists." The Labor Front, which was sent the prospectus by someone, took the landlord to court. He had to withdraw the prospectus and was not allowed to receive summer guests. Nevertheless, information about summer pensions that are not used by KdF is becoming more widespread . . .

Rhineland-Westphalia, April 1939

For a large number of Germans the announcement of the *Volkswagen* [People's Car] came as a pleasant surprise. There developed a real KdF-Car psychosis. For a long time the KdF Car was a big talking point among all classes of population . . . With the KdF car, the leadership of the Third Reich has killed several birds with one stone. In the first place, it removes, for a period of several years, money from the German consumer that he would otherwise spend on goods that cannot be supplied. Secondly, and this is the most important thing, they have achieved a clever diversionary tactic in the sphere of domestic politics. This car craze, which has been cleverly induced by the Propaganda Ministry, keeps the masses from becoming preoccupied with a depressing situation. Hitler has acquired domestic political credit with the car savers and the delivery of the car. For it is well known that, while they are saving up for a particular commodity, people are prepared to make quite a lot of sacrifices. Another aspect must not be overlooked. Despite all the export subsidies paid by other countries for their cars, the KdF car will be a least half the price of an equivalent car from the other exporting countries. In all the markets of northern and southern Europe, Asia, South and Central America, everywhere where the market is open, the KdF car will beat all the other mass produced cars.

24

Modernizing Germany

The Autobahn and Americanism

BEFORE 1933, ADOLF HITLER could be counted as something of an admirer of the United States for its productive power and size. As a continental power, America represented for him the ideal ratio of population and territory; he attributed American productivity not to industrial output per se but to the economic potential afforded by its size and living space. At the same time, he reiterated his statement in *Mein Kampf* that the Jews were "the controlling masters of the producers in a nation of one hundred and twenty millions; only a single great man, [Henry] Ford, to their fury, still maintains full independence."[1] Ford, in Hitler's and in the world's eyes, was not only the preeminent American industrialist but the leading American anti-Semite, whose newspaper, the *Dearborn Independent* (1919–27), with the second largest circulation in the United States, ran regular, vitriolic attacks on world Jewry as the cause of World War I and reprinted the forged *Protocols of the Elders of Zion*. Material from the newspaper was translated into German in four volumes in the 1920s and voraciously read by Hitler.

Though Hitler could not drive, the automobile played an important role in his conception of German modernization. As he said in his speech to the International Automobile Industry Exhibition in Berlin, just days after assuming the chancellorship, "In the past, one attempted to measure a people's standard of living in terms of track kilometers; in the future, road kilometers for motorized traffic will replace this yardstick."[2] One year later, on 7 March 1934, Hitler announced the development of an affordable "people's car." The plan was to create economies of scale that could keep production costs, factory overhead, raw materials, and maintenance costs of the car within a manageable relation to income, as he claimed was the case in America. Indeed, Henry Ford's River Rouge plant in Detroit served as the model for the production of the people's car.

The automobile industry, though initially attracted to the idea, eventually declined to participate, and the project was transferred to Robert Ley's German Labor Front. With great fanfare, Ferdinand Porsche's design for a people's car that he called the "Strength through Joy" car, or *KdF-Wagen,* was promised to all Germans for under 1,000 Reichsmarks. However, as the Sopade noted, the system that allowed workers to put aside 5 Reichsmarks per month for the new car in the form of savings book stamps kept money out of the economy that could have fueled the production of more consumer goods for them to buy. By 1938, the Strength through Joy organization trumpeted the plant at Fallersleben that was slated to produce the car (now rebranded the Volkswagen) as the greatest and most beautiful automobile manufacturing plant in the world. Yet the new factory remained unfinished, and not a single car had been manufactured. Though more than one hundred thousand workers contributed to the scheme, the "car craze" surrounding the Volkswagen turned out to be what the philosopher Ernst Bloch called "a swindle of fulfillment"—the anticipation of happiness in the hope of future delivery. The Volkswagen proved to be an empty promise: only a few prototypes were produced and none were delivered. In 1940, the Fallersleben plant was quietly diverted to producing military vehicles.

Whatever the fate of the people's car might have been, the Reichsautobahn, an ambitious network of roads that Hitler announced just days after assuming power, was in many respects the regime's most potent technological symbol. It was in fact the realization of a dormant project begun in 1926 to link Hamburg, Frankfurt, and Basel with a single highway known as the Verein zur Vorbereitung der Autostraße Hansestädte–Frankfurt–Basel (Association for the Preparation of the Motorway Hanseatic Cities–Frankfurt–Basel *[HaFraBa]*). The Autobahn concept was revived on 28 June 1933 when Hitler appointed Fritz Todt (1891–1942), an engineer and longstanding member of the NSDAP, to the post of inspector general for German roadways (*Generalinspektor für das deutsche Straßenwesen*) and made him head of the project. Given considerable funds and latitude at the national level, Todt was the incarnation of the "reactionary modernist," able to tout the virtues of "Nordic man" while simultaneously rejecting antimodernist and antitechnological attitudes as atavistic: "I would much more prefer to believe that especially these two most recently developed modes of transportation—the automobile and the airplane—do not serve to further dilute the effect of this ancient predisposition common to Nordic man but allow it to again come into bloom." In response to the Nazi claims that there was such a thing as a "German" technology, Eugen Diesel, also an engineer and the son of Rudolf Diesel, inventor of the engine that bears his name, pointed out that there were "a whole series of significant technological achievements and inventions in which, try as one may, one cannot ascertain a trace of dependence on geographically or ethnically specific factors."

For the Third Reich, the Autobahn project was more symbol and spectacle—an ode to the regime's aesthetic of technological modernity—than it was a practical achievement, since there were only 1.5 million private automobiles in Germany in 1931 and just over 2 million in 1935. Among the exaggerated claims made for the Autobahn was the pronouncement by Friedrich Tamms in *Die Strasse* (a magazine to promote motoring) that it was both an "engineering marvel" and a "cultural monument." Todt attempted to take the hyperbole a step further by claiming that the Autobahn made the German homeland more accessible: rather than destroy the landscape, it fit into the natural environment and brought towns and villages closer. Financed in large part by unemployment insurance, the Autobahn was planned to extend seven thousand kilometers, but it remained unfinished as the demands of war ended construction in 1942.

Perhaps even more significant than the propaganda value of the technological fetishism of the Third Reich was its promotion of the idea that war would advance German science and engineering. As Jakob Korn wrote in 1940, "This war to determine who will prevail concerns not only our national existence but, far more, the lasting impact our vision will have; it is also a war to determine the future direction of science."

For Hitler and for the Nazis, modernity, technology, and "America" were intertwined for good and for ill. America functioned as a polyvalent concept in Nazi Germany, its status changing dramatically from envied economic competitor in the early 1930s to "Jewish enemy" during the war. In 1934, a German report on the American West, "Felix versus USA: A German Takes On America," reiterated the clichés of Weimar conservatives, describing small-town life in the American West as "mass manufactured," dull, lifeless, and monotonous. In turn, an obviously pro-Nazi group of Americans visiting Germany in 1934 could not understand why so many non-Germans found it incomprehensible "that this unified *Volk* would cling so enthusiastically to its Führer."

By the mid-1930s, National Socialist propagandists spoke less of American success in promoting efficiency and rationalized industry than of the "authentic rationalization" of the German economy. While some observers cautiously remarked on the apparent similarities between Roosevelt's New Deal and National Socialism, the Nazis quickly refuted this parallel; the official view was that the United States lacked Germany's grand goals and national focus: a "revolution without a plan and without a strong revolutionary party or a popular majority was completely unthinkable." Roosevelt, according to some German writers who professed familiarity with the United States, "had expressly Jewish sympathies" and was hardly favorably disposed to the new Germany. Even before Germany declared war on the United States in December 1941, *Das Schwarze Korps* attacked Superman and his real-life creator, Jerry Siegel, as a Jewish invention. It also warned that "like anything that is promoted by the Jews, Americanism's lack of culture and morality, its freedom-promising 'Century of the Child,' is nothing but a concealed way of ruining the youth." Giselher Wirsing's (1907–75) *Unbounded Continent: Roosevelt's Struggle for World Domination* (1942), a book distributed by the Ministry for Popular Enlightenment and Propaganda, was itself an exercise in unbridled anti-Semitism combined with an anti-Americanism that focused on "degenerate Puritanism." This view clearly echoed Henry Ford's *Dearborn Independent* and its desire for a new, pure, Aryan America. Copies of the essays from the defunct newspaper (closed after a succesful lawsuit for libel by one of its Jewish targets in 1927) continued to circulate well after America entered World War II in 1941. But by then, the Ford Motor Company was deeply engaged with the war effort against the Axis.

NOTES

1. Adolf Hitler, *Mein Kampf* (1927), translated by Ralph Manheim (Boston: Houghton Mifflin, 1943), 639.
2. Max Domarus, *Hitler Speeches and Proclamations 1932–1945: The Chronicle of a Dictatorship* (London: I. B. Tauris, 1990), 1:251.

319

WILFRID BADE

The Führer and the Automobile

First published as "Der Führer und der Kraftwagen," in *Das Auto erobert die Welt* (Berlin: Verlag Wilelm Anderman, 1938), 309–11.

Just a few days after the Führer assumed power, the International Automobile Industry Exhibition opened in Berlin on 11 February 1933. The Führer himself opened the exhibition. He used this opportunity to speak out on a topic that had quietly concerned him again and again over the many years of struggling for power. The Führer—one who has traveled hundreds of thousands of miles in the automobile, driving from place to place, from city to city; one who knows every major street or highway in the Reich, who has traveled them through fair weather and driving rain, by day and by night; one who has had the opportunity to study in exact detail the condition of all the German streets and roads and the current state of affairs in the German automobile industry—he was able to construct a precise, intricately well-thought-out and flawless plan that he was determined to immediately put in place as soon as he was able to seize power in Germany. He spoke about this plan repeatedly with his close circle of collaborators, charged them again and again with executing new studies, research, construction designs, and solutions. By the time the year 1933 arrived, all their plans were already laid out in crisp detail and in the Führer's hands. They were designed to achieve two primary aims: to motorize Germany and build the autobahns.

The Führer was brilliantly keen in recognizing that no nation of people could be competitive in today's world without being substantially equipped with the world's most modern form of transportation, the automobile, just as those nations that could not lay claim to their own reliable and extensive rail system in the second half of the last century fell into decline and were left behind.

He also recognized that a radical break had to occur with the idea that existing roads were sufficient for traffic, that the automobile would require roads built specifically to allow the technology to develop to its fullest potential in terms of horsepower and speed. But it was not just the tremendous economic potential of motorization that he recognized as essential to guaranteeing Germany's future in transportation and in competitiveness, he also understood that it would provide effective relief in the fight against unemployment by giving a sudden, significant, and decades-long boost, making it a key industry whose success or failure does not leave any other industrial sector untouched.

The Führer also saw what escaped the eye of everyone else who was involved professionally with the automobile industry and mobilization: that motorization was not just an economic issue, regardless of whether it was viewed from the perspective of the industry or consumers: it was just as much a profoundly ethical issue because having an automobile promised to make human beings more independent and free again from the collective constraints placed on them by the rigid schedule of the rail; it would return to man the spontaneity of travel, allowing him to experience and explore the world firsthand. The Führer understood precisely how much this would mean, especially to a *Volk* like the Germans, and he decided to give every single German comrade this opportunity.

320

GERHARD ENGEL

Adolf Hitler on the Reichsautobahn

Diary entry from 5 September 1938. First published in *Heeresadjutant bei Hitler 1938–1943. Aufzeichnungen des Majors Engel,* edited by Gerhard Engel and Hildegard von Kotze (Stuttgart: Deutsche Verlags-Anstalt, 1974), 35.

On a recent walk, the Führer elaborated quite extensively on the problems with transportation in the world and predicted that, with the development of the automobile and the increase in production, within the next ten years none of the roads anywhere would still be capable of handling the traffic. He said he had very specific ideas concerning the building of the [Volkswagen] plant. It should not only become a good source of income for the country but also should replace the bicycle [as a mode of transportation], especially for the working class. He said he would not rest until production had increased so steadily over the years that a time would come, one he would hope to live to see, in which at least every skilled worker had his own Volkswagen. A time would come, he said, in which the bicycle would even be completely supplanted, first by the motorcycle (which, incidentally, he does not hold in high esteem), then by the passenger vehicle. Bicycles would be ridden only by boys and little girls.

He told me he thought the expansion of the Autobahn was proceeding too slowly for his tastes but there was no way to accelerate the process without neglecting the steel and armaments industries. Up until now, there was only one other country that recognized the transportation problem, and that was the United States. There, they have already begun building major bypass roads around the outskirts of the cities. Above all, they've built multilane highways, whereas here in Germany, entire companies of foot soldiers within the rural district councils are fighting like crazy for the preservation of the unpaved bridle paths to accommodate the prehistoric mode of transportation they call "the horse." He said he would put a swift end to this ridiculous point of view and has already sent instructions in this regard to all the *Gauleiter*. In fifty years, he said, the horse would be a showpiece for the army to parade about or put on display at the zoo or the circus where children would marvel at it the same way they do now at camels and elephants.

321

FRITZ TODT

Nordic Man and Transportation

First delivered on 21 June 1937 as "Der nordische Mensch und der Verkehr" at the Fourth Conference of the Nordic Society in Lübeck. First published in *Die Strasse,* 2 July 1937, 394, 398.

What is the driving force motivating these pioneers in transportation, all of whom hail from Nordic societies? What drives these men, each and every one of them, to invest far more than he can ever hope to regain from his efforts? What is the secret source spurring these men to such overwhelming levels of achievement, particularly as regards overcoming the limits of distance and space? What secret source [is] lending them the predisposition and capacity to perfect this level of achievement? [. . .]

Whoever concerns himself with this question will be increasingly struck by the degree to which this genetic propensity and predisposition prevails in Nordic man. It drives the individual to boldly embark upon an adventure of discovery and turns him into a pacesetter leading the way in the development of progress, but it similarly influences the attitudes and proclivities of his entire *Volk*.

To this day, [. . .] the boldest discoverers, inventors, and researchers are still born of these societies, and this ancient, genetically inherited drive toward exploration and open spaces is at work throughout the entire *Volksgemeinschaft,* diluted perhaps and somewhat diffused, but nevertheless clearly apparent. One might object by saying, "It is entirely possible that in the ancient races of Vikings, living as they did in isolation at the time, a genetic predisposition of this kind was passed down to and retained in the next generation or two. Developments in transportation today, though, are influenced not by these kinds of emotional tendencies but rather by entirely different factors, first and foremost amongst them—the modes of transportation that are developed." Furthermore, one might add that genetic predispositions of this nature, which may well have been factors at a time when people lived in isolation, are becoming increasingly obscured or entirely eliminated as a result of the far greater density of population and the much more extensive interaction amongst races and peoples in this day and age.

But I am of a different opinion: I would much more prefer to believe that especially these two most recently developed modes of transportation—the automobile and the airplane—do not serve to further dilute the effect of this ancient predisposition common to Nordic man but allow it to again come into bloom. The airplane and the hydrogen balloon open up new opportunities for the explorer, and I am convinced that Nordic societies will, accordingly, make bold forays into uncharted territories in the coming decades, aided precisely by the airplane and the hydrogen balloon. The precursors are already there: as early as 1897, the Norwegian [*sic*] [S. A.] Andrée attempted to reach the North Pole in a hydrogen balloon that was still in its nascent stages of development. Captain [Hermann] Köhl, Colonel Lindbergh, and the many others who were the first to make transcontinental flights in the spirit of the ancient pioneers in exploration already laid the groundwork ten or fifteen years ago for the trans-Atlantic air travel that has since been developed based on their pioneering work. Whereas the airplane offers opportunities primarily for individual accomplishments and innovation, the automobile, a mode of transportation that has been in existence for only fifty years, is virtually tailor-made to satisfy that dream of unlimited, independent travel to and exploration of faraway places that is so widespread in the Nordic *Volk* and resurfaces again and again from that ancient genetic predisposition. Not everyone can be a Viking, a [Fridtjof] Nansen, or a [Roald] Amundsen, but the automobile puts even the "little man," whose genetic inheritance and destiny were insufficient to make him a bold conqueror, in a position to embark on his own private adventures in exploration of faraway places. With the automobile, he is no longer limited to exploring the confines of a thirty-kilometer radius in his immediate vicinity, nor is he bound by rails and the train schedule, and he can even leave the main highway to explore and discover places that are off the beaten path. Without taking recourse to this strong inner disposition, there would be no way to explain the fact that at least half of all automobile owners are willing to spare themselves no amount of effort, of cost, and sacrifice when it comes to the costs and burdens involved in acquiring and maintaining a vehicle of this type. This behavior surrounding the purchase of an automobile is—from a material perspective—irrational and can be explained based only on this ancient Nordic predisposition. And we can see that it is equally operative in our great forebearers as it is in these little people who are similarly endowed with it and are thus willing to invest much more than they stand to gain simply for the sake of satisfying this internal drive to travel and explore, freely and independently.

I know that this idea seems new and surprising and will perhaps be ridiculed by some. But, in my opinion, these considerations are at least as important and probably at least as correct as the strictly scientific ones when it comes to the future development of transportation. And I would like to contend that, once the automobile has been around longer—it's been in existence for only fifty years, after all—the number of people who own automobiles will be substantially greater amongst Nordic peoples than it is in territories inhabited by other races of people. [. . .]

The driver of a passenger vehicle wants to be free of train tickets and schedules. The increase in the number of passenger vehicles is not contingent on the transportation needs of those people who need to reach a given destination at a given time because these people will continue to use the train. In Nordic countries, the increase in the number of automobiles is contingent on the standard of living and income of the *Volk*. As soon as a Nordic man and his family are able to afford, based on his income and the sacrifices he is happy to make in other areas, the amount it costs to purchase and maintain a vehicle for an annual mileage of ten thousand kilometers, he will purchase his own automobile. This is not motivated by any material need for transportation but rather by that last drop of Viking blood at work within him.

322

FRIEDRICH TAMMS

The Reichsautobahn as All-Encompassing Architectural Marvel

First published as "Die Reichsautobahn als architektonische Gesamterscheinung," in *Die Strasse* 2 January 1937, 32–33.

Engineers and architects are working together on the construction projects surrounding the Reichsautobahn. Even though these are essentially engineering projects, the contributions of architects are being given particular consideration here. The purpose of this collaboration is not by any means to provide employment opportunities for the architects; it is far less personal than that. It does not revolve around the individual personalities involved in the collaboration but is rather an attempt to perceive the countless and trendsetting artistic structures of the Reichsautobahn exclusively, not only as functional buildings but also as buildings that are designed such that they so far exceed the capacity to serve their intended purpose, that they could be ranked alongside the great monumental buildings of the past. The Autobahn is a cultural monument. But if that is what it is, every part of it must be so.

It would be mistaken to assume that the work of the engineer is not cultural in nature while at the same time assuming that cloaking great feats in engineering in the "mantel of architecture" would elevate them to the realm of great works of art. At first glance, it seems misleading even to place the concept of "architecture" in conjunction with the structures of the Reichsautobahn. These are not architectural buildings in the generally accepted sense of the term. The buildings of the Reichsautobahn differ substantially in their very nature from those of skyscrapers. Whereas those are designed with an external shell to enclose a given space, and space then becomes the top concern, these engineering marvels are not designed to enclose any sort of space but rather merely to bridge distance. So the only means available for these projects to achieve architectural expression are those needed to serve this purpose. The prevailing principle is and remains that of construction, and the most important thing is to think this principle through to its ultimate end, simply, clearly, and single-mindedly.

But there is always more than one road leading to any given destination, more than one way to achieve any goal, and this is the point at which careful deliberation alone will not suffice. Determining whether or not any given structure fits a given landscape or a given system is a decision that can be made based on reason inasmuch as it pertains to the decision to build the structure at all. But any structure should blend in with nature, and that means that the standards applied to the structure must be appropriate to the landscape in which it is to be built. A

FIGURE 32. Propaganda for the "Munich-Berlin" stretch of the Reichsautobahn, a showpiece of the Nazi regime. Albert Speer, ed., *Neue Deutsche Baukunst* (Prague: Volk und Reich Verlag, 1943), 93.

different structure will be required for a shallow valley, which needs a bridge of moderate height, than will be required for a deeper valley, which needs a bridge placed at a much higher altitude. Whereas in the first case, one would seek to keep the height at a very minimum and rely on many supporting beams, one would seek to get by using only two supporting beams set at a greater distance and height on a viaduct designed to cross a larger valley.

There are also several ways of designing construction. Here, too, it is essential from the very outset to keep in mind solutions that are not purely design oriented but that at the same time also take into consideration the way the chosen construction design can stand on its own and still blend in with its environs. Nor is it secondary to take into consideration when a steel structure, whose primary support system is constructed from fully walled sheet metal plates, is involved that the remaining components are developed in the same way—that is, that a structure should not be built using a combination of eclectic and self-contained architectural design elements or a combination of riveted and wrought-iron steel components. It is also necessary to take into account the proportions of each individual component in relationship to the whole with the intent of allowing the "weight-bearing" elements to seem light and to lend to the "supporting" elements an air of strength so that people can trust that the structure has the strength it needs to support the weight it bears. The purpose of the work must be to lend vivid expression to the very process of transferring weight from one place to another, using the proper selection of building material, of design and forms, measurements of individual components, their relationships and proportions. The internal consistency that is especially characteristic of the engineering marvel is very accommodating to this end. Nothing is without meaning here, nothing arbitrary, and yet there is always enough freedom in all of it to allow room for creative powers to find the right form of expression. A powerful, genuinely vital, and thus harmonious architecture cannot exist without internal consistency. That means that we don't seek to build anything that is "architecturally sound," so to speak, that is not at the same time structurally sound. On the other hand, nor do we want to build anything that is structurally sound whose form is not at the same time beautiful and good.

These exigencies, or, better yet, these insights, are what led us to enlist the services of the engineer and the architect jointly in this great task. Developments in recent years have made "specialists" of them both. Each has gone his own way, and each step in the work has widened the distance between them. While one of them lost himself to the arbitrary world of forms, the other barricaded himself behind the insular uniformity of "abstractions." This new task forces the two of them together, forcing them to balance each other out in their separate worlds. Already today any number of major and minor engineering marvels have proven the viability of this thought. But it also proves just how enthusiastically this idea was received by everyone involved and how they charged ahead into this uncharted professional territory, into the new world. The architect again learned to properly perceive structures and to recognize and acknowledge their internal consistency without necessarily seeing them as contradictory to his own work but rather to see that, on the contrary, they may enrich it in unforeseen ways. The engineer again realized that there are values outside the limits of his conceptual world that cannot be neglected and that are not at all a hindrance to his work, but rather that they lift it from its insular uniformity and elevate it to the level of genuine cultural monument. Now that the ice has been broken, it is delightful to see that neither of them has cowed himself rigidly into his own corner but rather that the joy of the enrichment, of mutually complementary collaboration, allows many an architect to think more in terms of structure and design than the engineer, and many an engineer to be more beholden to "pure form" than his architect. Which is not to say that their roles are reversed. That would not be a positive outcome. This is just to point out where the mutual conflation begins to take hold to the extent that it gives reason to believe in the ultimate goal, which is to transcend the dualism between two individuals, who together master all that is required to erect such all-encompassing engineering marvels. The immediate goal, however, is that from this at times rather contrived friendship, works emerge that conform not only to the laws of reason but also to the laws of pure and expressive form—structures that thus exude an air of unity and internal consistency, not of individual aims and arbitrariness. But a unified position such as this with regard to these questions of engineering and architectural design is possible only when the state places the value of cultural goals at the forefront of overall reconstruction to the degree that the Third Reich has done. It is only then that the efforts of each individual can transcend the realm of the personal to become truly a culture-shaping force.

The engineering marvels of the Reichsautobahnen have made considerable progress in this regard. They are already a perfect example of the impact this approach can have, though not yet in every aspect. Nevertheless, one can already see in them the unity and the concern for pure form, for clean construction and design, the concern for what materials are used and for their proper use, for properly blending into the landscape, and for much more. One can already speak in terms of an "all-encompassing architectural marvel," especially in the new sense of "architectural" implied here. They are a forceful expression of a higher order governing all that is viable and valid in life.

323

ANONYMOUS

Five Years of Strength through Joy

First published as "5 [Fünf] Jahre 'Kraft durch Freude,'" in *Leistungsbericht NS-Gemeinschaft "Kraft durch Freude" zum 27. Nov. 1938* (Berlin: Verlag der Deutschen Arbeitsfront, 1938), 38–39.

The "Strength through Joy" car is the work of the Führer. Organizing to meet the prerequisites of production and distribution is a task that the NS Association Strength through Joy and the German Labor Front are honored to fulfill.

FIGURE 33. Dr. Ferdinand Porsche, Robert Ley, and Hitler inspecting a model of the Strength through Joy car in 1936. Collection of Anson Rabinbach.

The Volkswagen Production Plant

The Volkswagen production plant near the town of Fallersleben will become the greatest and most beautiful automobile manufacturing plant in the world. Ever since the Führer first laid the foundation stone for this plant on 26 May of this year, enormous buildings have since sprung up in this half year alone. Already, several production facilities are so near completion that only the roof remains to be installed; the gigantic steel girders for the electrical power plant are already in place, and the separate harbor with a direct connection to the *Mittellandkanal* is almost finished. Four thousand workers, with two thousand Italians amongst them, are working diligently day after day to complete enough of the grandiose plans within one year so that production of the Strength through Joy car can commence.

In the immediate proximity of the construction site, there are barracks to house German and Italian workers who are living together in an exemplary model of disciplined camaraderie. The accommodations are the very best, the food is excellent, and the NS Association Strength through Joy provides a variety of leisure-time activities in the evening. All of the barracks' inhabitants are often brought together under one roof for festive events in the grand edifice of the Cianetti Hall. There are also ample opportunities to participate in sports activities. This barracks facility can be seen as an exemplary model for exquisitely executed attention to every single detail.

[. . .] The second greatest task involved in implementing the introduction of the Strength through Joy car consisted of establishing a system of sales that would make the car accessible to the broadest sectors of the populace, in accordance with the Führer's will. The Strength through Joy program's savings plan that has been in place since August has found tremendous resonance in all social strata of the *Volk*. Even though no one had so much as seen the Strength through Joy car, and no one knew the precise details, a veritable flood of applications was submitted to the German Labor Front and the NS Association Strength through Joy. This was marvelous testimony to the *Volk*'s faith in the Führer and in the German Labor

Front. The savings plan—with its minimum weekly installment of only 5 Reichsmarks—is allowing hundreds of thousands of people to fulfill a dream they have long held dear, and we know that within just a few years, there will be millions.

The Strength through Joy car is not only affordable, it is far superior to anything else that has been produced thus far in terms of comfort and performance. Two and a half million test miles attest to the fact that it has "gotten past the 'growing pains'"; the results that have since been produced continue to amaze not only laypeople but experts as well. The Strength through Joy car is a "wonder car"—as anyone who has ever driven it once or who has encountered it on the road while driving in another car will attest.

The aim of the men of the German Labor Front and the NS Association Strength through Joy is to see to it that the whole *Volk* is able to enjoy the benefits of this great technological achievement of the car's designer, Dr. Porsche, who was awarded the National Prize by the Führer.

324

FRITZ TODT

Foreword to *Adolf Hitler's Roads and Buildings*

"Foreword," Reichsautobahn. First published in Georg Fritz, *Strassen und Bauten Adolf Hitlers* (Berlin: Verlag der deutschen Arbeitsfront, 1939), 13–14.

One fundamental idea of National Socialism is its insistence on seeing life whole. Only he who feels this wholeness in himself will look upon life as a calling. Only the nation that acknowledges and professes wholeness will be capable of a great mission and be able to give expression to that mission in all departments of its life by a strong national will. In art, this unity of life becomes visible, and most convincingly, in architecture. Architecture, as a German romantic writer once aptly said, is "frozen music," is the queen of the arts. German architecture of today is an art of conviction, the mirroring and embodiment in stone of that conception of the state realized by Adolf Hitler in the Third Reich! If heroism be an attribute of the race to which we belong, and if we wish to live according to the laws of our blood, then heroic conviction and a sacred spirit of fellowship must be impressed also upon the documents of stone that we erect in our generation, the generation of National Socialism!

The Reichsautobahnen that now traverse the soil of Germany from one end to the other have nothing in common with what had hitherto been realized in this regard. They are more than just new traffic connections linking up the big towns and industrial centers of the Reich upon which automobiles can be made to put forth the utmost of which they are capable. They are more than just technical marvels, piercing space like arrows and ignoring the obstacles the ruthless landscape rears against them in their course; for technology herself, however highly we may esteem her as our handmaid and instrument in the fostering and unfoldings of life, does not possess a living soul. Motorways can, after all, be built by any nation, but that we should have been the first to span our fatherland with these ribbons of light, and that they are looked upon and felt by everyone in the nation as being throughout a work of National Socialism, is no mere chance. They are to be comprehended from the very center of our being; they stand at the very axis of our mental life. These roads bear witness to the unity of the Reich that has made it possible for the human beings traveling upon them to speed ceaselessly along in a glorious rhythm to the song of the motor from east to west, from north to south, over heath and moor, uphill and down dale, leaving towns and villages behind. They have a message that brings joy to the heart, going infinitely beyond the "aesthetic" rapture that a few of the "initiated" may in former times perhaps have felt upon the contemplation of works of art. They are not smoothly spic and span, not "beautiful" in the current sense of the term, but willful and defiant, if need be, even passionately moved, and therefore personalities of stone to whom content means more than form. They are understood by the whole German people, thus enabling us to share anew together, in a national community of art, to experience such as had been lost to us for generations. These roads, however, are not only signs of the might and greatness of present-day Germany in the making of which a vast host was wrought with head and hand; they are not only monumental symbols of national pride, as they flow broad and silent like the great streams of the lowland through the plains, mounting in light curves into the midmost heights to devour their way at last, defiant and challenging, over precipice and gorge aloft among the mighty Alpine peaks and compelling them to mingle their life with theirs. They have also a mediatory role! They open up to Germans wide areas of their homeland of which hitherto they had known practically nothing. They educate them to see! Nor for nothing do parking places, provided with benches, invite the traveler to break his journey and tarry awhile, nor for nothing do Adolf Hitler's roads lead again and again past stretches of landscape that the railways and the old highways were unable to reveal. Mountain range, forest, bush, pastures, hills, lakes draw into view, fall away, call and beckon to the voyager to stop, to stay awhile, to rest and think. And there is no need always to seek only grandiose and impressive prospects like those that present themselves on trips through the Swabian Alps, on the great German Alpine road, or when passing by Duisburg and Oberhausen. A cluster of hedge roses at the roadside, a field of lupines, forget-me-nots by the water's edge, a few deer at the edge of a wood, a pair of pheasants—all that is food not for the eye alone, the heart too needs sustenance! Who thus looks out upon the world will find a response in every created thing; even the very tiniest, will find his inmost soul, the inmost soul of his people, Germany!

325

EUGEN DIESEL

Is Modern Technology National?

First published as "Technik, Nation und Welt," in *Das Reich im Werden* (Frankfurt am Main: Verlag Moritz Diesterweg, 1934), 34, 35, 37, 38.

We recognized that we have the very nature of man and of his environment to thank for everything that is ethnic and national. Preindustrial technologies were conspicuously marked with a nationalist imprint because they sprang not only from the subconscious will of the people and the essential character of man but also from the landscape and the history of the *Volk*. Modern technology, on the other hand, is almost entirely derived from the achievements of a whole series of nations and peoples woven together, and mechanical engineering can be sustained in its development only with the ongoing participation of all nations and peoples in their respective countries, for any industrialized nation is dependent on many raw materials, fuels, and inventions from all over the world. Mechanical engineering is no longer determined or inspired primarily by forces within national boundaries. [. . .]

There is certainly a whole series of significant technological achievements and inventions in which, try as one may, one cannot ascertain a trace of dependence on geographically or ethnically specific factors. Let us take, for example, the development of the diesel engine: a German working in Paris, Berlin, and Augsburg on the invention of an engine, compelled simply by his own inner drives, by intellectual and practical goals. He is far removed from any oil-producing territory that is sure to be heavily influenced by this invention; indeed, he's never even seen an oil-producing landscape. But he works within an "intellectual territory" in which the many threads of Europe converge. The intellectual pedigree of the resulting engine traces its lineage to three different countries: to Germany, where [Nikolaus August] Otto invented the internal combustion engine and [the technical engineer Gustav Anton] Zeuner; to France, with the Carnot cycle [studied by Nicolas Léonard Sadi Carnot]; and to the Englishmen James Watt and Lord Kelvin.

In light of all this, could one not perhaps conclude that, while the significance of the national environment may have diminished, this is precisely the reason that an even greater role must be assigned to the internal national sentiment in man than it has ever been assigned before? In a certain sense, this question can be answered in the affirmative without reservations, although it is important to point out the great difficulty involved in joining the internal and intellectual essence of nation in man together in one technological achievement. Any number of such relationships between national forces and technological achievements are available and can be identified, but on the other hand, these relationships often enough fall completely apart. We have to be honest about this, and one should not attempt to interpret nationalist phenomena in such a way as to render them meaningless to the *Volk*, the nation, and its culture. Many inventions were made by citizens of several nations at roughly the same time. American engineers visiting the German Museum in Munich are surprised to see the names of so many European inventors attached to countless machines and devices that have been known to them since childhood as American inventions. If Daimler and Benz had not built the internal combustion engine–powered automobile in the 1880s, it would have been built somewhere else in Germany or in France or in America, because the internal combustion engine was already in existence, and sooner or later, someone was bound to try using it to power an automobile. Understanding the relationships between technology and national character is fuzzy and inexact, but there would be much insight to be gained if one were to undertake a study of national character as it relates to the various technological achievements of respective nations. There is no doubt whatsoever that there are utterly fascinating relationships and connections between individual inventions and the essential national character of the inventor; no doubt that the character and construction of manufacturing facilities, of industry, the appearance of machines, their design, the formulation of patents, which problems are addressed and how they are solved are all things that can be seen as uniquely national. Automobiles, ships, locomotives all have uniquely national characteristics, and even the rigid objectivity of technology, while it has often managed to erase that national imprint, has never succeeded in removing it altogether. Even engineering blueprints will differ according to whether they are completed by an Englishman or a Japanese man. Despite the ruler, the drawing board, and the slide rule, Japanese engineering blueprints still carry an undeniably Asiatic or Japanese mark. Above all, though, there are myriad indices of national characteristics in all the technological and industrial conditions as they stand in relation to everything else about the *Volk* and the state—even though, as previously stated, these characteristics are no longer necessarily tied to the geographic landscape and the culture. But taken together, industry, science, scholarship, and the technology of a *Volk* all form a rhythm, a structure, an organization, and achievement that must be assigned a national color, a national spirit, a national life. These relationships, these facts of life, of spirit, of will are, however, in any case decidedly different from the traditional national image.

There most certainly exists a connection between the most significant achievements in modern technology that points to peoples and races [*Völker und Rassen*]. One country is always host to far more technological and scientific achievements than another. Great Britain, Germany, America, France are leading the way at the top, and Scandinavia, Switzerland, Austria, and Northern Italy are also of great importance. Modern technology finds its home primarily in Nordic territory; the whole field of mechanical engineering originated in Central, Northern, and Western Europe. The creative contributions of southern Italy, southern France, and the Slavic countries have remained minimal to this day. But, of course, these modern technological developments cannot be traced exclusively to race. The consistency of the terrain in any country, its climate, and the influences of its own unique history cannot be left out of consideration.

326

JAKOB KORN

The War Experience and Renewal of Science

First published as "Kriegserlebnis und Wissenschaftserneuerung," in *Zeitschrift für die Gesamte Naturwissenschaft,* 1940, 319, 320.

Ours has been the first period in history to allow science to manifest itself visibly in the public and private life of the *Volk,* and we will continue to make it ever more manifest. For the first time ever, the forces shaping political life are also taking a direct role in reshaping science. The question of this new order of things has long since become a political problem, and it will be resolved politically. One can safely say that it is at precisely this point—in the assessment of these new circumstances—that the intellectual parting of ways becomes final: whoever is still today cowering in the attempt to construct some sort of "apolitical science" for himself is as far removed from our political aims as he is from our scientific ones.

Hence, one's perspective on the history of innovations in science will always be intricately bound to political history, particularly to racial political history, and political revolution has virtually become a springboard to the great debates that heralded the scientific revolution. *Do we need to provide any further evidence to prove that the current war will be of great import for the renewal of science, that the seeds of change are already planted?* This war to determine who will prevail concerns not only our national existence but, far more, the lasting impact our vision will have; it is also a war to determine the future direction of science. And war in a double sense: the outcome of the war will present, in international and domestic politics, new opportunities to establish the standards of new scientific ideals once and for all, and it will, above all, be a final death blow to all these opposing ideological forces; in the souls of many German scientists, the war experience, on the other hand, has already served as the final, profound affirmation of their search for a new scientific ideal! For the war, this elemental acid test for what is genuine and what is forgery will be an ordeal by fire in which the will and the spirit of all who are engaged in the struggle will be purified and cleansed.

The test that war thus poses is to force the individual to become someone he is not and to place himself in a completely different setting than he is used to. Torn from his familiar surroundings, internal and external, the soldier in wartime is able, at the very least, to observe and to judge against the toughest standards the world around him and perhaps even to observe and judge himself.

We cannot expect that this war will bring about the crucial transformations that occurred in the German people in a way that was perhaps unique in history during the World War: it wasn't just that it purged us of then-prevailing views—the views themselves were not entrenched enough for that—but it was in the fires of the World War that a new worldview was born. For us, it is merely a matter of making one last check of and securing the same position we held going into war the first time.

327

HANSJÜRGEN WEIDLICH

Felix versus USA

A German Takes on America

First published in *Felix contra U.S.A. Ein Deutscher haut sich mit Amerika* (Berlin: Buch- und Tiefdruck, 1934), 115–17.

Finally, they come upon a town. Gray wooden barracks with corrugated steel roofs. A dusty main street running from east to west. Perpendicular to it, side streets void of people. Warm air glistening with dust in the sun. Eleven faint strokes peal from the whitewashed church. The only sign of traffic in the whole place, a woman tanned brown and trotting into a butcher's store. Bang! the screen door slams shut behind her. Shiny blue flies buzz around the mesh of wire.

There's an Indian squatting on the wooden stairs to the café. Wrinkled face, with a long gray mane hanging down. No doubt he's scalped a paleface or two in his day. Now he's drinking soda pop in a color that doesn't even exist. Even drinking it through a straw—just like you're supposed to. Holding the bottle infirmly in both hands. It's probably Coca-Cola. That fizzy dishwater hooch you see those two old men sitting around drinking in the advertisements. There was a silver watch dangling from a chain against the red gentleman's tattered vest. His dusty jacket was alive with the reflections of light it cast.

Next to the gas station, the general store. A stack of aluminum pots at the center of the display window. A few neckties are hanging from the top pots on the stack. Back in the far left corner, a blue housedress with white dots. Next to it, brown work shirts. Right in front, directly behind the glass, six loaves of white bread. Stacked in twos. A row of cigarette packs stretching all the way to the right side. Right up to the teddy bear sitting there in a circle of stuffed animals. Behind him, there is a pyramid of canned goods. You can hardly imagine the clutter—ugh! There was everything. Everything a cowboy, an Indian, or anyone else might need. From chewing gum to a button for your pants.

Suddenly, the owner comes out and asks Felix if there is something he would like to buy. He squints his eyes in the blinding sun of the steaming hot main street.

There's a vacant lot just before the last house on the edge of town. The scorched brown grass, littered with broken bottles, shards of glass, and empty aluminum cans. Two cowboys are working on a banged-up Ford. One is under the car draining the oil—checking to get the last drop. The other one is taking a shot with the engine. He's got a cowgirl helping him out. The only way to tell she's a girl is by looking at her feet. High-heeled oxfords. And by the silk stockings that are visible only as far as her calves in the rolled-up pants. Otherwise, she is dressed just like the man. With a broad-brimmed hat. Red-and-black–checkered bandanna. A dark blue mechanic's jacket covering a green short-sleeved shirt. Worker's pants. Leather belt.

You see the same thing in every town. The cowboys always in a Ford. Never on horseback. Not a lasso in sight. The towns, too, are all the same. Only an occasional tavern. An occasional school. Or there is a school situated between two towns where it's easy to get to from both.

But it's always inevitably the same: Main Street, the church, the gas station, and the general store. The towns leave the impression of having been mass manufactured in a factory. As if they are products off an assembly line: serial number 2020. Wyoming has ordered twenty towns. To be assembled on the conveyer belt. To be delivered to highway 20 and set up twenty miles apart.

There they stand. Mass manufactured. There is no life in them. Because even the people living here could not breathe life into them. On the contrary: rather than live up to the norm, they've been crushed by it. The unique character of each individual crushed by the monotony of it all.

328

DR. J. F. E. RASCHEN

Germany—As Seen by Americans

First published as "Deutschland—von Amerikaneren gesehen," in *Volk und Welt,* February 1935, 15–17.

An impression of Germany, in four weeks! Don't let anyone say it's impossible to see enough to so much as come close to a complete picture. [. . .]

But it would be impossible to describe in words the impressions [left with American academics on this four-week exchange program]. And it seems almost superfluous to note that the opinions on political, economic, and social issues differ in their specifics. But it would be wrong to conclude, these qualifications notwithstanding, that the general opinion of Germany was unfavorable or even averse. Certainly, some of the guests embarked on the trip with piqued interest, afforded the situation insightful observation. The wealth of experiences gave rise to new insights and lasting impressions. Thanks to the heartfelt and welcoming words of Dr. Max Ilgner encouraging us to "see the Third Reich for what it really is," we were blessed with the opportunity to gain insights that are rarely afforded foreign visitors.[1] We realized what a lot of other guests have also seen: that law and order prevails in the new Reich. Furthermore, that the German *Volk* is concerned with improving itself; [Germans] are unified in investing all their intellectual and economic resources to serve the common good heedless of all obstacles. Especially for foreigners living outside this country who have no way of imagining it, this completely new social fabric, so utterly different from what was here not so long ago, is extremely strange. What is worse is when this lack of knowledge translates into wholly inaccurate and screwball preconceived notions or judgments. One is reminded of Goethe's words, "The old foundations must be honored, but one cannot ever relinquish the right to build anew." Without seeking to privilege National Socialism or any other political system, however, the objective observer would be remiss in condemning any system as innovative in its structure as National Socialism as a failed attempt or even as evil. Discerning judgment requires that the basic position, as well as the exigencies of the country itself, be taken into consideration. And yet, these powers of discernment relating to the internal motivations, as well as to the trials and tribulations imposed by the outside world that are steering the German ship of state on a surprisingly new and—from the perspective of a foreign observer—completely unexpected, perhaps even undesirable course, are absent in the foreigner. And wherever these powers are present, a well-organized propaganda campaign has deflected attention from assessments or any form of recognition of the movement's essence or its successes to focus instead on ridiculing all the secondary issues, the missteps and—a favorite subject—the suppression of freedom of speech, especially in the press. To this author, it seems like precisely the injection of ill will on the part of foreign readers that is needed to inflect their view with the desired degree of psychosis for the event that developments in Europe suddenly take an unanticipated denouement. And no one who is afforded so much as a glimpse at the situation in modern-day Germany will be able to deny this conclusion. The facts that follow are observations from personal, firsthand experience. A newspaper in New York reported a story also carried by its Paris edition about how it was uncertain when we landed whether we would even be able to carry out our plans and whether the difficulties encountered at the Polish border weren't part of some plot! What a mendacious twisting of facts! Furthermore, upon our return to New York, the first question some reporter blurted in our faces was whether we had witnessed any torture or cruelty with our own eyes and whether the Nazis had tried to prevent us from entering Jewish businesses!

It is entirely incomprehensible to foreigners that the Germans have been so blessed with that unity—that "best laid plan of German men" as [Joseph Victor] von Scheffel put it [in his famous epic poem, *The Trumpeter of Säckingen*]—for which they have been praised in song for centuries. *It is equally incomprehensible to them that this unified Volk would cling so enthusiastically to its Führer.* Naively, it is usually assumed that the mass rallies with crowds in the hundreds of thousands are just people driven together in fear. As if they had ventured out to hear the voice of a preacher in the wilderness. Precisely these mass rallies, as well as the tremendous participation in southern Germany's Olympic Games, which Nuremberg has the pleasure of hosting, are opportunities for foreigners to witness *just how deeply this movement has taken root in the German* Volk.

Well-meaning acquaintances speculated that we would only be allowed to get a very superficial look at things; that the real situation would be hidden from view. Nowhere did we encounter such hindrances and restrictions. Our hosts and their deputies permitted us unfettered access to any information we requested. And it goes without saying that the various participants paid careful attention to those things relating to their fields of interest, that they asked questions and got answers. Everyone was especially pleased with the willingness to help. [Our hosts] even lent an ear to criticisms and responded—which does not exactly testify to the suppression of freedom of speech.

Note

1. Max Ilgner was a German industrialist and manager of I. G. Farben.—Eds.

329

DAS SCHWARZE KORPS

Jerry Siegel Attacks!

Superman the Jew

"*Jerry Siegel* greift ein!" First published in *Das Schwarze Korps,* 25 April 1940, 8. Translated by Randall Bytwerk. Calvin College, German Propaganda Archive.

> Once there was a man who was so strong that he could stop a speeding locomotive with his ring finger, but he didn't do it.
>
> —*Folk tale from Des Moines, Iowa, USA*
>
> *Siegellack stinks!* [literally "Sealing wax stinks," but also a pun on Siegel's name].
>
> —*Proverb from Massachusetts*

Jerry Siegel, an intellectually and physically circumcised chap with his headquarters in New York, is the inventor of a colorful figure with an impressive appearance, a powerful body, and red swimming trunks, who can fly through the air with the aid of a white cape.

The inventive Israelite named this pleasant guy, whom the powers that be had blessed with an overdeveloped body and underdeveloped mind, "Superman." Superman's sense of heroism and justice was touted widely throughout society and in advertisements ideally suited to entice the youth into emulating him.

As you can see, there is nothing the Sadducees won't do for money!

Jerry looked about the world and saw things happening in the distance, some of which alarmed him. He heard of Germany's reawakening, of Italy's revival—in short, of a resurgence of the manly virtues of Rome and Greece as they have flourished again and again in Europe. "That's fine," thought Jerry, and he decided to import the idea of manly virtue and disseminate it among young Americans. Thus was born this "Superman." On this page, we present you with several particularly unusual examples of his activities. We see Superman, lacking any strategic sense or tactical ability, storming the West Wall with bare legs in his shorts. We see several German soldiers in a bunker, who, in order to receive the American guest who just popped in, have borrowed old uniforms from a military museum. Their faces are filled at once with desperation and cheer. We see this bicepped wonder in a rather odd pose, wrapping the Krupp-steel gun barrels around his bulky arms like spaghetti dough. "What's a little concrete?" he shouts in another picture as he slams his fist into the bunkers and they explode like overripe tomatoes. His real strength, however, shows itself only in flight. He leaps into the air to tear the propeller from a passing German airplane with his fist. As we can see from the next frame, however, Superman has apparently made a mistake, since he seems to have encountered a Yid pilot. No German would say what the pilot says: "Himmel! Vos is diss?" The American answer, "Well, here it is," seems to us not quite right. The right response would be something like, "Laff if ya likes, I'm Simple Simon!" [*Se wern lachen, jach bin der kleine Moritz!*].

A triumphant final frame shows Superman, the conqueror of death, dropping in at the headquarters of the chatterboxes at the League of Nations in Geneva. Although the rules of the establishment probably prohibit people in bathing suits from participating in their deliberations, Superman ignores them as well as the other laws of physics, logic, and life in general. He brings with him the evil German enemy, along with Soviet Russia.

Well, we really ought to ignore these fantasies of Jerry Israel Siegel, but there is a catch. The daring deeds of Superman are those of a Colorado beetle. He works in the dark, in incomprehensible ways. He cries "Strength! Courage! Justice!" to the noble yearnings of American children. Instead of using the chance to encourage really useful virtues, he sows hate, suspicion, evil, laziness, and criminality in their young hearts.

Jerry Siegellack stinks. Woe to the American youth, who must live in such a poisoned atmosphere and don't even notice the poison they swallow daily.

330

DAS SCHWARZE KORPS

The Danger of Americanism

First published as "Die Gefahr des Amerikanismus," in *Das Schwarze Korps,* 14 March 1944, 1–2. Translated by Randall Bytwerk. Calvin College, German Propaganda Archive.

When we speak of young Europe and its young nations, we contrast them to the senile world of dying liberalism, which, under the leadership of Jewry, is once more gathering all its material resources in an attempt to forever subject the world to the power of money under the domination of those who have it. They want to perpetuate the social injustice they find so comfortable. But the contrast involves more than differences between ages and generations.

Our camp includes not only those who are young enough to topple the old and build a new world. It includes all those spiritual forces that see the new in the collapse of the old, that want to build a new future with new ways and means.

The triumph of the Copernican worldview over the unfruitful dogma of the past, the triumph of science over empty faith, was a victory of the youth. They followed the shining examples of their predecessors. The youth have always been the battering ram that helped bring the national idea to fruition. The discovery of the laws of inheritance has been the occasion and guidepost of a new youth movement that builds on the eternal culture-building values of race and blood. They lead from the deadly and destructive lethargy of materialism to the new world of tomorrow.

Our situation today is the same as it has always been in times of revolution. Those fighting for the new have more to offer the youth than those who are living in a world of yesterday, who hold to what they have grown accustomed to, even after it has long since become rigid, empty, and stifling. We offer our youth the freedom to develop as a nation of people, the right, even in the case of smaller nations of people, to develop the full potential of one's race. We offer them room for creative fantasy, the opportunity to transform great thoughts to reality outside the lecture hall. We offer the realization of dreams on a world scale, a common Germanic will, a common European will. We fill the spiritual vacuum left by liberalism with the magic of a worldview that draws self-confidence and meaning to life from race and the blood of one's ancestors.

What does stodgy old England have to offer its youth to justify the war's requirements? It cannot even begin to solve its own social problems, much less offer anything to other peoples. Where are there healthy youth who are on fire for Bolshevism? It was a danger only during the spiritual interregnum that followed the World War. In the face of an inadequate immediate past, it was the only force, the only revolutionary movement available, and anything was better than nothing.

Today, Bolshevism may have reached its material and organizational pinnacle on the bent backs of its devotees, but as a spiritual movement it is finished. The crass incompetence of its methods and goals has proven it to be the very epitome of capitalist slavery.

The only remaining alternative is Americanism. As strange as it may sound, it is the only serious competition to National Socialism's racial worldview in the struggle for the youth, in the struggle for the future of humanity. In the end, however, it is only a forerunner of Bolshevism.

Americanism is certainly not a spiritual movement, nor is it a worldview that can be opposed at the intellectual level. Its political beneficiaries have tried in recent years to give it, if not a face, at least a program or a goal: "the American Century." It is a collection of empty promises of the type democratic orators have always made—but this time on a world scale. There is nothing in them to excite a reasonable man. But that is exactly the point of Americanism! The key is not what it promises but what it cannot promise. The key is not what it demands of men but what it gives them.

That would not matter if the world's youth were of the sound character that develops from racially conscious lines, tradition-rich families, good upbringing, and close camaraderie. But that is not the way things are. The good fairy will not give young people the values they will need in life. The racially sound youth can be inspired by virtue of his blood. But the blood does not tell him what should inspire him. He can be misled into serving a bad cause. He can squander his enthusiasm if he matures in a spiritual vacuum. One should not underestimate the danger of Americanism or its seductive power. It offers devotion to a culture of nothingness, independence, lack of restraint, a freedom from all obligation, from all honor, from all consideration.

We do not wish to deny this culture of nothingness its right to exist. It can even, rightly used, be good, just as it is sometimes a pleasure to do nothing. Should a German soldier happen to find a portable record player and jazz records in the deserted quarters of British or American soldiers, he does not smash them against the wall. Instead, he takes them along and considers them a great treasure. We don't want to suggest excessive cultural disaster here. There are times when he wants a vacation from himself, from us, from the whole world. He needs to relax and certainly does not wish to ponder intellectual matters. Nothing is better suited to take him out of the normal world than the complete nonsense of this hot music, this cacophony of animal howls, wild instruments, and foot-stomping Negro lust. It takes him away from human concerns back to the depths of prehuman apedom, returning him to the time when people did not need to think because there was no past and no future. Its effect is like that of alcohol, which turns normally rational men into shouting, destructive children. That can sometimes be good for serious and intelligent men. And the soldier certainly does not forget his German mission, nor does he lose his character or honor when he occasionally spends an hour relaxing to entertaining music. He is immune to the danger of confusing this rhythmic pig grunting with good music, much less art or culture. It cannot meet his higher standards.

Others, however, are not as immune. That is what those who deny any appeal of Americanism forget.

Certainly there is no danger that our young boys and girls will fall into sexual frenzy while listening to some Jewish lout blowing on a saxophone. One can introduce them to the high priests of the American jitterbug with no worries at all. At most they will laugh. Our young *Luftwaffe* aides and working girls would hardly join in a dance marathon. And the winning couple running through the arena in tattered, sweaty clothes would receive not applause but a beating. But that is our youth. They are made of different stuff and grew up in a world in which dignity comes from doing one's duty, and both are seen not as a burden but as the joy of life.

That may be self-evident to us, but it is not so to others. Whole nations behave in ways not guided by clear tasks. They are only individuals, parents, teachers, tribes, and groups, able to lead them out of error and confusion into a clear world of meaning. We may not forget that during the tragic years following the First World War, a significant part of our youth too fell under the appeal of Americanism, waving their limbs in the Shimmy and the Charleston because there was nothing else to do.

We sometimes fail to see that there are young people in Europe today—often from the so-called better classes—who not only do not stand within the camp of young Europe but also even mock or scorn it. Many of us simply cannot understand how there can be a mass meeting at a Norwegian university protesting those who are risking their lives in the east for the freedom and security of their native land, or how Swedish students, even if they do not jump to the side of their Finnish brothers, do not at least follow their struggle with respect.

These young men surely are not consciously supporting the plans of Stalin and Roosevelt. Thank God, this small part of Europe's youth is not a politically aware counterpart to the European youth defending young Europe in the east. Those who think politically and act from conviction demonstrate it through their actions. The others have followed the comfortable path that leads from political thinking to Americanism.

That is the political danger of Americanism. It leads those who fall prey to it away from political thinking, away from responsibility, even to their nation, away from decency, even from national decency.

The American lad may use fine phrases to say that the nationalist is his political enemy. In reality, however, he fights a man who makes uncomfortable and difficult demands on him, the man who recognizes the fate of the nation as his fate, who respects the woman who will become the mother of his children, who wants to be a role model, who always acts as if the eyes of the nation were upon him. The American lad feels his "freedom" restricted by such behavior. He wants to keep the hot music spinning on the record player, not be reminded that he must work as well as relax, that he must not only enjoy but also honor the dignity of his nation.

That is neither comfortable nor pleasant. It is pleasant to talk slang and enjoy a loose moral life with those of like mind. Americanism has its delights, and whomever they captivate not only has his head stuck in the sand but also has a good time. It is nice to be able to dismiss all criticism of a too-hearty enjoyment of life with the claim that one is defending human rights against Nazi brutality.

Americanism is not a logical development of the Americans. It certainly does not spring from the descendants of the Virginia colonists with their Prussian sense of honor and duty, nor from the healthy farmers and citizens of the Midwest. It did not triumph easily against the often-overdone moralism of Puritan circles. It spreads in direct proportion to the growth of Jewish power. And like anything that is promoted by the Jews, Americanism's lack of culture and morality, its freedom-promising "Century of the Child," is nothing but a concealed way of ruining the youth.

Americanism is a splendid instrument of depoliticization. The Jews have used jazz and movies, magazines and smut, gangsterism and free love, and every perverse desire to keep the American people so distracted that they pay no attention to their own fate. Even in politics, they are no longer influenced by the head, only by what is under the belt.

The Jews would not be Jews if they did not want to apply such tested methods to the entire world. Nearly every nation in the world faced or is facing the need to combat Americanism, a generally pleasant retreat to a barbaric lack of culture.

The logical consequences of Americanism will help the world combat it. The fact that 60 percent of American crimes are committed by children thirteen years old and under and that rapes increased threefold between 1942 and 1943 proves that Americanism has reached its limits. It will provoke a countermovement that, just as in Europe, can only be political.

Americanism is not merely a moral-cultural form of degeneration, nor can it be combated by nonpolitical means. It has already been defeated when one digs it up by its roots and sees there plainly the words, "Made in Israel."

331

GISELHER WIRSING

Unbounded Continent: Roosevelt's Struggle for World Domination

First published in *Der Masslose Kontinent: Roosevelts Kampf um die Weltherrschaft* (Jena: Eugen Diederichs Verlag, 1942), 426–32.

We have demonstrated throughout this book various reasons why America, in its present state of existence, is an ideal breeding ground for Jewry. Its role is ideally suited to ruthless exploitation of the chaotic lack of any sense of direction that currently characterizes the state structure, the economy, and the society of the USA. Jewish intellectuals are doing exactly what was so typical for them throughout Europe: privileging debate over concrete action and confusing analysis with active intervention and deed. Disdain for the European revolution and its racial thinking could easily rest on American doctrines because, of course, when you mechanically transfer this idea to the racial mosaic of the USA—a completely different context—it explodes like dynamite on impact. This is how the Jews came to be the real masterminds behind the American pseudorevolution and how they came to be the only sector of society that profited greatly from the immediate crisis precisely because they were able to adapt so quickly. The almost wholesale control the Jews exert over the press, radio, and film was complicit in preventing any discovery of the real roots of the American crisis from occurring. This went so far, for example, that there wasn't a single major publisher who dared to publish an incendiary book by the author Lawrence Dennis, so it had to be printed privately, and that Theodore Dreiser fell victim to a conspiracy of silence when he once inadvertently dared to go against the grain.[1] While [Dreiser] was being showered to high heaven with laurels and praise in the Soviet Union, his warning against the mad rush to war was immediately subject to a boycott. Anti-Semitism in America today is a force that has again gone underground, as it was up until Theodore Roosevelt's era. What was previously a strictly instinctive anti-Semitism is now fully conscious. And the Jews know this. Already in 1938, Bernard Baruch, speaking on a visit to London—we got wind of it at the time only through an English source—admitted that he had his assets invested in almost every country on earth because he wanted to be sure there would be a place where he could retire in peace when life became impossible for the Jews in the United States. The Jew is not capable—not even in the United States—of learning from the mistakes he has made everywhere else in the world. Here, too, he's taken it to the extreme, stretched everything to the limit, and it is only a matter of time before it snaps. No one can say when and how. But there is consensus among everyone who can be seen as a serious observer of America—and even, at least under the table, among a number of Americans who are otherwise of a very different mind on most things—that it will come down to this. The Jewish domination that resulted from the crisis of Americanism is far too flagrant and far too triumphant to ever avoid ultimately getting the tide to turn against it and bring on a wave of hatred all by itself. Unless all the signs have been wrong, our generation will have the pleasure of witnessing this spectacle as it occurs. [. . .]

In the second chapter, we pointed out similar roots and results evident in Judaism and in Puritanism. The crisis in Americanism of our times is ultimately also the result of a *degeneration of the Puritan spirit.* [. . .]

Degenerate Puritanism is second only to Judaism in terms of America's unique internal threat. The Puritans promoted the repression and suppression of human sexuality in a two-hundred-year campaign against human nature, which led to a complete reversal of relationships between the sexes and thus to the kind of promiscuity that is so typical of American college campuses. As long as the religious foundations of Puritanism remained intact, the threats presented by these repressed complexes were kept in check. But now that puritanical morality and self-righteousness have long since lost their binding force, and now that the current relationship Americans have with religion—with the exception of Catholicism—is not unlike the one in most European countries, now the Puritan perspective can only be one of a hypocrisy that desecrates both soul and character. [. . .]

America is the only one that can free itself from its puritanical tyranny that has suffocated any genuine sense of arousal for so long now. There are enough Americans who are keenly aware of this. No one can help them from the outside; they must conduct this battle over life and death on their own, in accordance with the exigencies of our times. And this battle will likely be conducted on a social front. But the Roosevelt era thus far has had precious little to do with it. On the contrary, here again we see the whole ball of prejudices that degenerate Puritanism has foisted upon the American people all rolled together in the Roosevelt era. This is why Americanism—at present still a dominant, legitimate force—has become a threat to the world.

[. . .] This "save the world" complex forms the psychological foundation from which Roosevelt's Americanism strikes against every country under the sun, and thus the new imperialism of the United States emerged. This joins forces, then, with that utterly self-righteous Puritanism that causes Americans to categorize people as good or evil based on naive moral judgments. In light of the national character of America, at least for the moment, a Crusades mentality of this sort is liable to ignite at any given time, and this has been seen as the refuge of last resort to escape the crisis of Americanism. But that is not going to solve the crisis. It will just make its effects deeper and more devastating. But we are completely baffled by the way Americanism has somehow attained international stature.

Note

1. Lawrence Dennis (1893–1970) was an isolationist and Axis sympathizer. His *The Coming American Fascism* (1936) argued that capitalism would be replaced by global collectivism. Theodore Dreiser (1871–1945), author of *Sister Carrie* (1900) and *An American Tragedy* (1925), was a successful novelist and strong critic of American capitalism. His *Dreiser Looks at Russia* (1928) and his pro-Communist views were anathema to the political right.—Eds.

PART NINE

. . .

BODY CULTURE, SPORTS, PUBLIC AMUSEMENTS

25

The 1936 Olympics and the World of Sports

IN 1933, ALL INDEPENDENT SPORTS and free-time associations were subject to "coordination" (*Gleichschaltung*) to implement their complete Aryanization and subordination to the Führer principle. After 30 January 1934, sports were overseen by the Nationalsozialistischer Reichsbund für Leibesübungen (German Reich League for Physical Education), headed by the *Reichsportführer* (Reich sports leader), Hans von Tschammer und Osten—though other Nazi organizations like the Deutsche Arbeitsfront (German Labor Front) and the Hitler Youth had competing sports associations. After a brief period during which "wild" (unaffiliated) sports groups continued to exist, the reorganization of German sports led to the disbanding and prohibition of all sports associations that could not be brought into line with the law. This primarily affected Jewish, Christian, and proletarian sports associations. Jews were expelled from the remaining organizations. However, in keeping with the Nazi view that Jews were a separate people who should have a separate culture, until 1938, Jewish athletes were permitted to belong to Jewish associations such as the Maccabi and its major German competitor, Schild (Shield), both of which had flourished during the Weimar Republic.[1] In 1933, both of these groups had over forty-five thousand member athletes in three hundred regional groups throughout Germany.

The Olympic Games were scheduled to be held in Berlin in 1936, a decision made by the International Olympic Committee (IOC) in 1931. Though some members of the committee initially doubted whether the National Socialists would be interested in holding the games, Hitler, who, after the death of President Hindenburg on 13 November 1934, saw an opportunity to gain foreign prestige, assured Theodor Lewald, president of the Olympic Organizing Committee, that he would assume the position of patron of the Olympic Games. As sports writer Max Ostrop argued, "[The] German people have been said to have a unique understanding of the Hellenic nature," and a Berlin Olympics would bear out this perception.

Germany's tourist industry geared up for the event, establishing tight control over the advertising to ensure that it downplayed the more egregious aspects of Nazi rhetoric, as Friedrich Mahlo noted. Anti-Semitic signs and posters were temporarily removed from public spaces near the Olympic Village. In 1933 and 1934, the American and British members of the IOC, concerned that a German Olympics would violate the principle of equality of "all races and creeds," demanded assurances from the German government that Jewish athletes would be able to train and participate as part of the German team. At the same time, a strong and vocal opposition to the "Nazi Olympics," especially in the United States, demanded that the IOC support a boycott of the games. To appease the IOC, *Reichssportführer* von Tschammer invited the 1928 Olympic champion fencer, Helene Mayer (1910–53)—officially a "half Jew"—then teaching in California, to participate. Mayer's letter to Avery Brundage, the American representative on the IOC and a strong proponent of the Berlin Games, reveals the hesitation with which she accepted this offer. Even some American publicists supported the games once the "Jewish Question" was "settled," as Harry Hirsch noted in the American news magazine *Literary Digest*.

During 1935, the boycott movement reached international proportions. A seventeen-year-old Austrian swimmer, Judith Deutsch, withdrew from the Games, writing, "As a Jew my conscience prohibits me from participating in the Olympic Games."[2] In the same year, *Das Schwarze Korps* was outraged that Richard Kalischer, a Jewish member of the college swim team in Berlin, could take first place at the university diving championships.

Supporters of the boycott in the United States were not satisfied with the German response or with the IOC's claim that the boycott intruded politics into sports. As the Committee on Fair Play in Sports wrote in its statement, "The issue is not whether American athletes should refuse to participate in the Games in Nazi Germany because the Nazis are seeking to destroy the German Jews, or because they are persecuting German Catholics, or because they have virtually enslaved the German working man, or because of their oppression of Masons, pacifists and all independents, or even because they are threatening the peace of the world by the construction of a gigantic military machine paid for largely at the expense of Germany's creditors in this and other countries. The issue is rather whether Nazi policies and activities in the realm of sports and in connection with the Olympic Games themselves are of such a character as to make it impossible for the Games to be held in Nazi Germany in the true spirit of sportsmanship and of the Olympics."

By the end of 1935, however, the IOC had decided against supporting the boycott by a small majority, and the Games went forward in August 1936. Among those who lobbied the IOC against the boycott was Germany's most internationally famous athlete, the heavyweight boxer Max Schmeling (1905–2005). On 9 June 1936, Schmeling won his most legendary bout, knocking out the undefeated American champion, Joe Louis, the "Brown Bomber," in the twelfth round. The Nazi propaganda machine misused the fight—Schmeling was not a Nazi—touting it as "Max Schmeling's Victory—A German Victory" in the press and newsreels.

Physical training increasingly combined ideology and science in keeping the *Volk* fit and "rejuvenated," promoting scientific methods of enhancing physical constitution and performance level. While this approach had been part of a German nationalist ideology since the mid-nineteenth century, it flew in the face of Pierre baron de Coubertin's 1894 vision for a new Olympiad that would answer the new European nationalism. Physical training became, as Dr. A. Mallwitz observed in 1936, the means of preserving and enhancing the race. While the rhetoric remained "*mens sana in corpore sano*" ("the healthy body as the prerequisite to a healthy character"), as was stated in a 1941 commentary on Hitler's speech on body training, notions of what was healthy and what was character had radically shifted since this classical phrase was used by German nationalists such as Friedrich Ludwig Jahn (known as "*Turnvater,*" father of gymnastics) in the mid-nineteenth century. Even advocates of nudism, like Wilm Burghardt, employed the rhetoric of "conscious, disciplined reproduction and breeding," in his short-lived pamphlet series *Spirit and Beauty* (*Geist und Schönheit*). As Count Wolf Baudissin (1907–93), later a champion of a peace army for postwar Germany, noted, "The aim of sports in the military is to enhance the level of physical performance and emotional fortitude in the soldiers to make them fit for battle."

NOTES

1. Letter from Judith Deutsch to the International Olympic Committee, 26 June 1936. Cited in Reinhard Rürup, ed., *1936—Die Olympischen Spiele und der Nationalsozialismus: eine Dokumentation* (Berlin: Argon, 1996), 63.

2. Maccabi was part of the World Maccabi Union, which was founded in 1921 but had roots in a number of Jewish athletic organizations that were established in the late nineteenth century. Maccabi had branches in twenty-seven countries. Schild, founded in 1919, grew out of the Reichsbund jüdischer Frontsoldaten (Reich Federation of Jewish Front Soldiers).

332

MAX OSTROP

Olympic Games: German Style

First published as "Olympische Spiele deutschen Gepräges," in *Westermanns Monatshefte* 159 (October 1935): 194–97.

The German people have been said to have a unique understanding of the Hellenic nature. The grandfather of German gymnastics, [Johann Christoph Friedrich] Guts-Muths and its father, [Friedrich Ludwig] Jahn, had already drawn on Greek gymnastics, and it was, after all, German archaeologists—with [Johann Joachim] Winckelmann and Ernst Curtius at the forefront—who salvaged not only Troy and Pergamon but also ancient Olympia from the miles-deep layers of quicksand and ruins in which they had found a final resting place; it was they who offered to humanity clearer insights into that sunken world and its spiritual-intellectual ways. So when the German Olympic Committee for the eleventh Olympiad suggested enhancing the opening ceremonies for the event with a relay run of torchbearers from [the site of the ancient games] in Olympia to Berlin, it did so believing it was acting as faithful steward of the Olympic ideal. We Germans are thus taking recourse to the ancient cultic, ceremonial custom of passing a lit torch from one man to another until it reaches the site of the ceremony. With this torch relay, we will retrieve the flame from the very source of the Olympic idea, from Olympia itself, and with it, we will light the Olympic flame that must remain burning atop the Marathon Tower at the site of the Olympic Games throughout the duration of the Olympiad. It is a wonderful idea that not only symbolizes the connection to the origin of the games but that at the same time touches thousands of young people with the spark of that Olympic flame—and they bear the torch proudly, for it is an honor to actively participate in this international festival that they might otherwise never experience—an idea that brings together people of so many different nationalities in the spirit of community that is the standard for the Olympic ideal. Runners from seven countries—Greece, Bulgaria, Yugoslavia, Hungary, Austria, Czechoslovakia, and, finally, Germany—will cover the approximately three-thousand-kilometer course of this unprecedented, first-of-its-kind relay run in which the Olympic torch will be carried by three thousand different runners until, ten days later, it arrives in Berlin to herald the festive opening of the eleventh modern Olympic Games.

Another powerful symbol that has been added to the ceremony by the German Olympic Committee is the Olympic bell inscribed with the words "I summon the youth of the world." This motto already speaks to everyone from the printed programs and promotional materials, but very soon, it will hang—cast in bronze—directly from the Führer's Tower, where its powerful voice will ring, heralding the festive opening of the Games and welcoming all those youthful sports enthusiasts from around the world who have come here in answer to the bell's call.

German art will make its mark in every area of design for the surrounding activities and events. A separate committee has been formed for the various artistic-design needs to host such an event as an Olympiad—the musical theme of the games, the ceremonies and festivities, and the first of the German artists have already been commissioned. A series of artistic events will run parallel to the games so that they become not only a meeting of great masters in the field of sports but rather a meeting of all cultural enthusiasts gathering in a peaceful exchange between nations. The Olympic Art Exhibit that is scheduled for installation in an exhibition hall next to the Olympic Village will include, in addition to the works submitted to the artistic competition, a section for German art that is not entered in the competition and another section with the most beautiful works of antiquity—on the one hand, items from German excavations that we have in our possession, and on the other, items on loan from other countries or reproductions.

333

FRIEDRICH MAHLO

German Tourism and the Olympic Year

First published as "Vortwort," in *Deutsche Werbung,* March 1936. Later published in *1936—Die Olympischen Spiele und der Nationalsozialismus: Eine Dokumentation,* edited by Reinhard Rürup (Berlin: Argon, 1996), 84.

The year 1936 will be a landmark year for the German Foreign Tourism Office. The Tourism Office had been on a steady incline ever since the advent of National Socialism. [. . .] The Olympic advertising is the best benchmark for measuring the efficacy of this reorganization of order. There was a time when advertisements, posters, and other promotional material would have been haphazardly produced and distributed by any number of different offices, but today there is a targeted, centrally organized campaign of advertising and a stringent consolidation of resources. The concept of the Olympics has been well received by the German populace: even in the most remote towns and villages, people know about the greatest sports event of the year 1936 and the possible effect this will have on Germany's international relations. We can proudly contend that we are well prepared for the Olympiad. It hardly needs to be said that it was not easy to convince many countries that Germany was in a position to host the Games in accordance with Olympic protocol. If there is no longer any international objection to holding the Games in Germany today, then this is primarily the result of the exquisite work that the Foreign Tourism Offices of the Central Reich Rail System conducted through its propaganda and information services promoting German tourism along the lines developed by the Propaganda Committee for the Olympic Games to spread word of the Olympic Games throughout the world.

334

HARRY HIRSCH

The Playing Fields of Nazi Germany

First published in *Literary Digest,* 17 November 1934, 22.

After lengthy deliberation, it has been decided that American athletes will invade Nazi Germany to take part in the next Olympic games. It is interesting to survey the playing fields of Germany, to discover now what thousands of athletes may expect when they go to Berlin, where the Eleventh Olympic Games will be held in August 1936.

Germany wasn't as sports-minded before the war as it is today. Of course, she had tennis, soccer, track and field, swimming and rowing twenty years ago, but all those sports were carried on only by hundreds and thousands of people, not by millions as they are today. The war, which opened the eyes of every German to the values of physical education, started the era of prosperous years for sport; which began in 1920, and has not yet come to a standstill. Developed from the year 1920, there are now several millions of Germans who are banded together in various sports organizations, some small and many large sport-clubs.

The most popular sport in Germany is soccer. Next to soccer, track and field finds the most enthusiastic followers. Both men and women have their championships every year and about 650,000 men and women take part. They rank first in Europe, both the men and the women.

No Professionalism in Sport

One might think that the outcome of the last war, the disillusionment, the hardening, might have opened the way for professional sports in Germany. But that is not the case. Sports in Germany are all strictly amateur. Even the coaches—at least 90 percent of them as far as track and field, swimming and soccer are concerned—are also amateurs.

Sport in Germany is carried on differently from sports in America. Sports in the United States are built up primarily in universities, colleges and high schools. Sports in Germany are carried on 99 percent in clubs, which are absolutely private.

The private clubs are the organizations that develop the German boys and girls into the internationally known athletes. Most of the clubs have departments for all kind of sports, usually soccer, track and field, field hockey, and handball. Most German sports clubs have as many as 3,000 or 4,000 members, and most all of them have either large or small stadiums. My former club, the Sport Club Charlottenburg, especially known to all American track and field teams that visited Berlin during the last few years, has a stadium that can hold 30,000 spectators; a quarter-mile track circles a soccer field, and five tennis courts are just outside of the stadium. Two fields for hockey and two others for soccer are also owned by this one club, which has about 2,000 members. Eight hundred of them are women.

Athletes in Germany can be found most among the working class of people. When boys and girls want to go in for serious competition, and intend to accomplish something, they have to pack their things, and go out to the fields after office hours, when they are tired from their day's work or, as it has been for quite some time now, when they don't have a job, and must start their 100-meter-dash with an empty stomach. That's the main reason why German athletes cannot keep up with the marvelous showing of the Americans.

Consider that nearly all of the German sport-youngsters have been born and brought up during and after the World War. Most of those boys have been unlucky enough never to find a job. Their parents have been without work too. Latest dispatches from Germany say that the Reich Sport Leader gave better jobs to those who have been picked for special training for the Olympic Games, so they may be able to turn in a better performance in the Olympics.

Today, a different point of nationwide interest has arisen. Since the Hitler government came into power, most of the boys joined the Nazi army, and, of course, had to attend, most of their free time, to a different kind of sports education than they were given in their respective sport clubs. The boys find it difficult to combine their training in the sport clubs with the duties of a Nazi Storm Trooper. The consequence is that the sport clubs are very badly off today. They have a hard time, for instance, trying to coach a relay team for meets, since usually one or two of the team have to be away on just that day to march with their comrades through the woods.

Of course, this government wants to do its best and I am glad to say that the German Government encourages sport. Only our "old-fashioned" ideas conflict sometimes with those of the new Nazi style.

The Universal Language

The Olympic Games of 1936 will be carried out, no matter what's going on. The Jewish question is settled. The Reich Sport Leader promised to give placement to any German-Jewish athlete who is considered good enough to make the German Olympic team. There is no doubt that this promise will be fulfilled as Germany fears that America and England may not participate if she handles the situation otherwise. The German people themselves are no more anti-Semitic than they used to be.

German athletes never wanted the race question to be brought into sport. As a matter of fact, when [Ralph] Metcalfe—the great American colored sprinter—traveled with an American track and field team through Germany last summer, he was the most applauded athlete on the team. The spectators yelled for Metcalfe all the time. He was the hit of the whole season. The Olympic ideal knows no creed or color. Like music, it is a universal language.

335

COMMITTEE ON FAIR PLAY IN SPORTS

Preserve the Olympic Ideal

First published in *Preserve the Olympic Ideal: A Statement of the Case against American Participation in the Olympic Games at Berlin* (New York: Committee on Fair Play in Sports, 1935), 5–10, 20, 24.

The Issue Is Whether America Should Participate in the XI Olympiad If It Is Held in Germany

The American Olympic Committee seeks to make it appear that those who disagree with them are trying to deprive American athletes of the opportunity of competing in the Olympic Games. This is one of the ways in which they attempt to arouse the resentment of American athletes against those who oppose American participation, and thus to prevent consideration of the matter on its merits.

This is a gross misrepresentation of the issue. The issue is not whether America should take part in the Eleventh Olympiad, but whether America should participate in it if it is held in Germany; and these are two entirely different questions.

In 1932 the International Olympic Committee awarded the Games to Berlin, which was then in Republican Germany. Republican Germany no longer exists; and if the Games are held in Germany, they will be held in a Berlin and a Germany that are Nazi. In sports, as in almost every other way, Nazi Germany is a very different country from Republican Germany.

Sports in Republican Germany were democratically organized and privately conducted, just as they are in America. Sports in Hitler's Germany, including all activities in connection with the Olympics, are dominated and controlled by the Nazi Government and the Nazi Party and have entirely lost their private, their democratic and their independent character.

Under the Olympic regulations, the International Olympic Committee "fixes the place and dates of meetings according to needs and circumstances." It has full power to take the Games away from Nazi Berlin in Nazi Germany, to which they were never awarded, and to give them to some other country in which it is possible to hold them in the true spirit of sportsmanship. If the International Olympic Committee, at the instigation of the American Olympic Committee, should nevertheless refuse to remove the Games from Nazi Germany, it will be these Committees and not those who oppose holding the Games in Germany, who will have deprived American athletes of their opportunity to take part in the Eleventh Olympiad.

In their enthusiasm for holding the Games in Nazi Germany, the proponents of American participation misrepresent the issue in other ways. They seek to make it appear that the issue is what they like to call a political one involving Germany's internal and private affairs which, they say, do not touch the Olympic Games and with which, therefore, athletes are not concerned and have no right to meddle.

This, too, is a misrepresentation of the issue. The issue is not whether American athletes should refuse to participate in the Games in Nazi Germany because the Nazis are seeking to destroy the German Jews, or because they are persecuting German Catholics, or because they have virtually enslaved the German working man, or because of their oppression of Masons, pacifists and all independents, or even because they are threatening the peace of the world by the construction of a gigantic military machine paid for largely at the expense of Germany's creditors in this and other countries.

The issue is rather whether Nazi policies and activities in the realm of sports and in connection with the Olympic Games themselves are of such a character as to make it impossible for the Games to be held in Nazi Germany in the true spirit of sportsmanship and of the Olympics. If that is the case, American athletes ought to refuse to participate in the Games in Nazi Germany and the International Olympic Committee ought to remove the Games from Nazi Germany.

In the pages that follow we shall show that that is the case; that Nazi Germany has violated her pledge not to exclude German Jews from the German team solely because they are Jews, by denying them the opportunity to train and compete for the German team; and has violated her pledge to observe the Olympic Code not only by her treatment of her Jewish athletes, but by her treatment of her Catholic and Protestant athletes and by her misuse of the Games to serve the interests of the Nazi regime rather than the interests of sport.

By her treatment of her Jewish athletes, Nazi Germany has introduced *race* into the Olympics; by her treatment of her Catholic and Protestant athletes, she has introduced *religion* into the Olympics; and by her exploitation of the Games she has introduced *politics* into the Olympics.

To say that Nazi Germany's violation of her pledges given to the International and American Olympic Committees is Nazi Germany's private affair is, of course, to speak nonsense. It is as if a debtor should say to his creditor: "You have no right to complain of my failure to keep my promise to repay you what I borrowed from you, for that is my private affair."

And in what follows we shall also show that to hold the Games in Nazi Germany would be to give the moral and financial support of the sports world to what is perhaps the most cruel, the most despotic and the most barbarous government of modern times.

Germany Has Failed to Keep Her Pledge Not to Exclude Jews from the German Team [. . .] Thus, on April 1st, 1933, the German Boxing Federation forbade Jewish boxers or referees to take part or officiate in German championship contests, and as early as April 26th, 1933, Jews were barred from membership in German sports associations. On June 2nd, 1933, the German Minister of Education issued instructions that Jews were to be excluded from youth, welfare and gymnastic organizations and that the facilities of these organizations were to be closed to them. Moreover, Dr. Theodore [*sic*] Lewald , a Christian who was then the President of the German Olympic Committee, was threatened with the removal from his office because one of his grandparents was a Jew.

International Olympic Committee Acts

Disturbed by these and similar events, the International Olympic Committee threatened on June 6th, 1933 to remove the Games from Germany unless the German representatives on the Committee guaranteed that Dr. Lewald would be permitted to retain his office and that Germany would not discriminate against her Jewish citizens in the realm of sports. The demand for these guaranties was made largely at the instigation of General Charles H. Sherrill, Colonel William May Garland and Commodore Ernest Lee Jahncke, the American representatives on the Committee.

Whatever his present opinions may be, General Sherrill was not then of the opinion that

Germany could comply with the Olympic Code at the eleventh hour by the gesture of inviting one or two Jews to compete, or that it was enough to justify and excuse German violation of the Olympic Code that some American clubs do not admit Jews to membership and that Negroes do not engage in sports with white persons in our southern states.

Evidently, General Sherrill's opinions have, in the meantime, undergone radical alteration.

The German Pledges

In any event, as the result of the demand of the International Olympic Committee, Dr. Lewald stated on June 7th, 1933, that with the consent of his Government, he was authorized to declare:

1. The German Olympic Committee has delegated the mandate that has been entrusted to it to a special Organizing Committee, composed of Dr. Theodore Lewald, President; the Duke of Mecklenburg-Schwerin; Dr. Ritter von Halt; Captain von Tschammer-Osten; Dr. Sahm, the Mayor of Berlin; and Herr Diem, Secretary of the German Olympic Committee.
2. All the laws regulating the Olympic Games shall be observed.
3. As a principle, German Jews shall not be excluded from German teams at the Eleventh Olympiad.

Thus it is only as the result of the International Olympic Committee's threats to remove the Games from Germany that Dr. Lewald, who is not even a Jew but a Christian with a single Jewish grandparent, was permitted to retain his position. And yet the American Olympic Committee have not seen fit to disclose that fact to American athletes although they are careful to point out to them that the "Chairman of the German Organizing Committee is of Jewish descent."

Is it possible that the American Olympic Committee are attempting to mislead their best friend, the American athlete?

Or is what was right in 1933 wrong in 1935?

Nazi Government Controls Sports and Olympics

The German pledges have three interesting features. In the first place, the representatives of the German Olympic Committee were unable to promise fair play until they had consulted and obtained the consent of the German Government. In the next place, never before in the history of the Olympics has it been necessary to obtain such a pledge from a country in which the Games were to be held. Finally, the German Olympic Committee abrogated its functions and delegated them to a special committee of which Captain von Tschammer-Osten was made a member. Von Tschammer-Osten, as we shall see, was then and is now the Reichssport-Kommissar and, as such, in absolute control of sports in Germany.

Thus, as early as June 1933, the International Olympic Committee was furnished with conclusive proof that the Nazi Government dominated and controlled both German sports and the German Olympic Committee, and was given clear notice that the Eleventh Olympiad was likely to be used, as it is in fact being used, to serve the aims and necessities of the Nazi regime rather than the interests of sports and of the Olympics.

Pledges Given in Bad Faith

The giving of these pledges is typical of the duplicity which has characterized the dealings of the politically dominated German Olympic Committee with the International and American Olympic Committees and of its studied efforts to deceive the sportsman of other countries.

The German pledges seem clearly not to have been given in good faith with the intention that they should be kept, but in bad faith for the purpose of appeasing sportsmanship and fair play. Five days after these pledges were given, von Tschammer-Osten testified to their spurious character. Addressing a group of Nazis in Germany on June 12th, 1933, he declared: "You are probably astonished by the decision in Vienna, but we had to consider the foreign political situation." And almost in the next breath, he expressed gratification for the numerous anti-Semitic resolutions that had therefore been adopted by the German athletic and sports clubs. [. . .]

Germans Admit Inequality of Training for Non-Aryans

But it may be assumed that Dr. Lewald, Herr Gaertner and Dr. Karl Ritter von Halt, whom they themselves quote, are as well informed about the matter as the editors of German Jewish newspapers and that they have greater freedom in stating what they know. Although there are about 35,000 Jewish athletes in Germany, Messrs. Lewald, Gaertner and von Halt together can name precisely *four* who have been admitted to the special Olympic training groups and precisely *three* who have been permitted to participate in the elimination trials.

They say that there are no German Jewish athletes of Olympic caliber.

But they do not tell American athletes that Germany has driven a number of German Jewish athletes of Olympic caliber to their deaths or into exile, such as Prenn the tennis player, Seelig the boxer, and Nathan the long-distance runner. Nor do they explain how they can know that among the 35,000 German athletes of Jewish blood none of Olympic caliber would have been discovered or developed had they been given the same opportunity for training and competition that has been given the more fortunate Aryan athletes.

German Pledges Not Confined to Miss Mayer

They say that Helene Mayer, a Jewess, has been invited to join the German team without a tryout in recognition of her known ability as a fencer.

But, although they quote from General Sherrill, they do not tell American athletes that the General says that it took him *two years* of hard work to induce the Nazis to invite Miss Mayer to join the German team although her skill as a fencer is so great and so well known to them that they have at last put her on the team without a tryout.

Of course, we do not know why Miss Mayer has conditionally accepted the Nazi invitation, but we suspect that her acceptance is not unrelated to the fact that her mother and other members of her family still live in Germany and are still subject to Nazi brutality and Nazi vengeance. We suspect that fear rather than love of Nazi Germany is responsible for accepting this belated invitation. [. . .]

De Courbertin Would Be Horrified

This position would, we think, have horrified Baron Pierre de Coubertin, through whose efforts the ancient Greek Olympic Games were revived, and Professor William M. Sloane, the historian of the modern Olympics and a former member of the International Olympic Committee.

As far back as 1908, Baron de Coubertin said that the Olympic idea is the conception of physical strength united with the spirit of chivalry or fair play. And long ago Professor Sloane stated that fair play for all, even the weakest, was the essence of the Olympic idea. It would be strange doctrine to these men that the Olympic requirements of chivalry and fair play apply only to the conduct of the elimination contests, as Dr. Lewald and General Sherrill seem to believe, or only to the conduct of the Games themselves, as the American Olympic Committee seem to believe.

In a pamphlet that the International Olympic Committee issued just before it exacted the

German pledges, it is said that without fair play there is no beauty in sport and that the spirit of chivalry is the ennobling feature of sport.

Who can find the beauty of fair play or the nobility of chivalry in Germany's treatment of her Jewish athletes?

336

HELENE MAYER

Letter to Avery Brundage

"Brief von Helene Mayer an Avery Brundage." Written on 26 October 1935. First published in *1936—Die Olympische Spiele und der Nationalsozialismus: Eine Dokumentation,* edited by Reinhard Rürup (Berlin: Argon, 1996), 57.

My Dear Herr Brundage,

Ever since July of 1935, your words have been cited with regard to the German Olympic Committee's extension of an invitation to Helene Mayer, and I might have long since written you to inquire as to whether this was true [. . .]

About two weeks ago, I received the invitation from Herr von Tschammer, and already I am finding the most unbelievable statements being made [about it] in the papers; therefore, I think that you, as the president of the American Olympic Committee, should know the truth. I am sending you a copy of my response, which is currently en route to Germany, together with an English translation. On October 24th, I responded to the telegram I received from His Excellency Lewald . . . . "Have you received von Tschammer's invitation?" . . . as follows: "Answer to you and von Tschammer delayed due to illness. Conditional acceptance sent yesterday." I do not know whether a copy of my letter will assist you in your difficult task, but please show it to General Sherrill as well. Personally, I am very distraught over the fact that my name has been drawn into these dreadful controversies, and I am greatly disheartened by the many insults that I have done nothing to deserve. But that is surely of no interest to you, and I, as an individual, am truly insignificant in the greater scheme of these things! I am writing you these things because I consider you a friend. His Excellency Lewald has spoken and written about you and Mrs. Brundage often. [. . .] I sincerely hope to meet you in Berlin.

Yours sincerely,
Helene Mayer

337

VÖLKISCHER BEOBACHTER

Schmeling's Knockout Victory over Louis

And the Match Goes to the Opponent

First published as "Schmelings k.o.-Sieg über Louis: Die größere Kampfeskraft fällte den Gegner," in *Völkischer Beobachter,* 21 June 1936.

Max Schmeling took down a decisive win in New York. But where were the technical reports from the training camps? Where was the Negro's murderous right—where was his "killer instinct"? What did these people think they were pulling over on us? They bragged about this boxing wonder, this "Brown Bomber" who could make mincemeat of anyone. Max Schmeling got in the ring with him and beat this boxing wonder with no problem whatsoever. He defeated him because he is the better fighter; Louis was crushed by Schmeling's strength as an opponent.

Schmeling is within reach of doing what none of his predecessors could and what everyone thought was impossible: making a comeback. He is closer to it now than he has ever been because the general consensus is that the current world champion [James J.] Braddock is no match for this Louis, whom he just took down in a knockout.

New York, the city that has hosted the biggest and most brutal boxing matches in the world, had not witnessed the kind of attraction of a major heavyweight fight that is gripping from the first blow to the last for many years before this fight. Not since the days of [Jack] Dempsey and [Gene] Tunney ten years ago have two men entering the ring together created such a sensation that captivated the masses this way. From the moment he arrived over there, Schmeling has demonstrated impeccable sportsmanship and fairness in the ring and enjoyed enormous popularity, thanks not least of all to his tremendous technical skill, but after he was defeated by the Americans [Max] Baer and [Steve] Hamas, he was pretty much relegated to the "scrap iron" heap. No one thought he had so much as a shot at the highest honor a professional boxer can aspire to, the world championship. But the New World started to pay attention when they saw the results of the matches against [Walter] Neusel and [Steve] Hamas, which ended in decisive victories for Max, and when they heard about his record defeat on points of Paolino Uzcudun. Now, after this young Negro had swept everyone who dared to get in the ring with him, and for the most part, within very few rounds, there was only one man left—the German Max Schmeling—with a chance to break the Brown Bomber's winning streak.

338

DAS SCHWARZE KORPS

Jewish Victor in the German College Championships

First published as "Jüdische Sieger bei deutschen Hochschulmeisterschaften," in *Das Schwarze Korps,* 3 July 1935, 3.

Yesterday, the Jewish press reported, triumphantly, "Richard Kalischer, a member of the college swim team in Berlin, took first place in diving at the college championships held by the Association of German Students in the Kurmark Gau." And the date was not June 1920 but rather 28 June 1935.

Everywhere these days you can hear men who are concerned with the well-being of the *Volk* preaching about how the "Jews are our misfortune!" And we have decades of evidence attesting to the fact that this statement is all too true. The state passes racial laws. The Jew is excluded, and rightly so, from serving in the military and the Labor Service—both schools of German honor. But members of a so-called German student association allow Jews to participate in their college championship, measuring their mettle in competition against alien races and thus sabotaging all those healthy efforts aimed at liberating the German *Volk* from the Jew and his influence. If there are still German comrades who, after years of being under the spell of the Jew, still spend their money at Jewish department stores, we still have hope that these comrades will someday be cured. However, when we see the younger generation still cavorting with Jews like this—and to top it off, in German universities—then it seems to us that something is truly afoul here. So afoul that it must be righted.

339

COUNT WOLF BAUDISSIN

Sports in the Army

First published as "Sport im Heere," in *Westermanns Monatshefte* 161, no. 965 (January 1937), 409–10.

The goal of military service is to train the soldier for battle. The automatic weapon and motor are what shape the face of the battlefield and are what have allowed the individual warrior to emerge as the personification of today's soldier type. His physical characteristics are speed, agility, strength, and endurance and his emotional ones are resolve, decisiveness, and ambition. Any soldier who does not have those characteristics is not fit for battle, no matter how well-trained he is in combat techniques and weapons.

The aim of sports in the military is to enhance the level of physical performance and emotional fortitude in the soldiers to make them fit for battle. So it serves the purpose of military training. The compulsory sports requirement in the military reads as follows: "Sports contributes to the education of the soldier to become a battle-ready fighter."

The purpose of sports in the army is not to manufacture "heavy hitters," but one does have to have role models: the German officers, petty officers, and enlisted men who excel in sports are role models for the whole nation. They are always seeking to push the limits of achievement to the extreme and to take their own initiative in training body and character far beyond the call of duty.

In military sports—here and in other countries—a special space is reserved for the pentathlon—modeled after the ancient Hellenic version that includes "running, discus throw, jumping, javelin throw, and wrestling." It is clearly and consciously a sport designed to train the career soldier, first and foremost the military officer; you have to think in terms of an adjutant charged with the order to deliver a message from one heavily besieged place to another. He jumps on the best horse he can find, which is exhausted after the first five kilometers or so. Now he must continue on foot, armed only with his pistol and forced to rely solely on that to get through. He is stopped in his tracks by a body of water. Sheer muscular strength is his last refuge. He swims across the river, but there are still nearly four kilometers to go running on foot.

From time to time, military leadership will mandate official pentathlons. These are adapted to include horseback riding, fencing, shooting, swimming, and cross-country running. For the most part, the layman vastly underestimates the difficulties involved in training for the pentathlon. There is hardly another sport that presents as many obstacles in the various events: in the shooting event, the officer must train incessantly so that he can fire off one round after another in 2.6 to 2.9 seconds. Just as he must learn to handle his pistol even in rain and wind, he must be prepared to run cross-country in any weather. Depending on one's general constitution, anywhere between one and three cross-country runs are needed per week, in addition to aerobics and jump roping. In the fencing contest, the only option was to practice the basic steps and ripostes one had learned in training school. It's the same thing with swimming—if you weren't a born swimmer, it took years to become one. Finally, as far as riding is concerned, in order to train for covering five kilometers in just under eight minutes you need a fast, seasoned horse during training so you can learn to jump, to climb, to judge your speed, and to judge the course.

340

JOHANNES ÖHQUIST

Physical Pedagogy

First published as "Leibeserziehung," in *Das Reich des Führers: Ursprung und Kampf, Weltanschauung des Nationalsozialismus geschildert von einem Ausländer* (Bonn: Ludwig Röhrscheid Verlag, 1941), 211–12.

Already in his book, *Mein Kampf,* Adolf Hitler said, "Not a day may go by on which a young person does not complete an hour of physical training each morning and night, and that includes every form of sports and gymnastics."

What used to be considered "gymnastics" in Germany was everything that involved any sort of physical training: equipment exercises, free exercises, field games, swimming, fencing, walking, etc. Over the years, gymnastics became more specialized. Clubs and leagues were formed specifically for "track and field"; others, specifically for soccer, boxing, etc. Even within these organizations, we saw increasing specialization: while one runner became a sprinter, the other a marathon runner, one swimmer specialized in the backstroke, etc. There were "bourgeois" sports clubs and "proletarian" sports clubs. The competition between clubs often generated mutual animosity between them: in sum, in this area, too, the "free play of forces" has led to a state of affairs in which the actual purpose more or less took a backseat to all manner of other incidental purposes.

This actual purpose—namely, to elicit understanding and interest in all-around fitness and high-performance physical skill—is what National Socialism sees and promotes as the primary purpose of sports. National Socialism does not view sports in terms of setting records but rather in terms of the healthy body as the prerequisite to a healthy character. Certainly, National Socialism does not oppose efforts on the part of individuals toward outstanding achievement. But it sees these merely as testimony to the strength of will, for the dexterity of spirit and the endurance of nerves. It is not as interested in world records and "heavy hitters." It does not underestimate the "national" and "political" significance of the Olympic Games. But the first order of priority is to tend to widespread performance on the part of average people. Exceptional achievements can emerge from a strong, healthy community working together quite naturally, without the need for excessive training. Physical achievements should go hand in hand with an impeccable character and purity and tenacity of will.

341

DR. A. MALLWITZ

Sports Hygiene

First published as "Sporthygiene," in *Westermanns Monatshefte* 160, (July 1936): 466, 469.

The decisive importance of racial grooming and following biological heredity laws can be touched upon only briefly in this context, despite the fact that a conscious program of physical fitness, of sports and gymnastics, plays a very specific role in that, one that has yet to be fully understood.

On the other hand, it is absolutely necessary to stress, emphatically, that today more than ever before it is every Germany's *duty*—as an expression of gratitude to the state and the movement—to keep himself fit and to lead a healthy lifestyle. So it is incumbent upon us to present the *Volk* with a broad palette of prospects that place the principle of performance in the foreground and are thus ideally suited to providing inspiration and guidelines for each individual national comrade who is fully committed to supporting his family, his profession, his state, and his Führer. [. . .]

And why this now? Because the athletically active person is already very accustomed to knowing what the most important considerations must be in making everyday decisions concerning a healthy, active lifestyle—even though his experience derives from a different but nevertheless related and equally valid context. What is at the center of this research is not a natural type of exhaustion but rather each individual's different tendency to suffer from rapid exhaustion of body and mind; it is not the necessary respite taken after work but a physical, mental, and emotional reaction that can be described as a capability for recovery, a resilience while facing greater-than-usual strain, a hardening off caused by atmospheric and climatic influences. And the matter at issue here is less being able to recognize inefficient means of, say, lifting, carrying, or throwing weight and more one of physical constitution and condition. And the question of whether one is in top form is as pertinent to his performance in sports or gymnastics as it is to his performance in his profession. Because sports trainers and physicians are now in possession of highly sophisticated stopwatches and other instruments of measure, countless observations have already been evaluated by science to yield results that confirm an intimate connection between physical constitution and performance levels. The relationship between constitution and character, between temperament and performance, is sure to provide fruitful insights into the field of labor psychology.

342

GEIST UND SCHÖNHEIT

Rejuvenating Life, Enthusiasm for Life, Rejuvenating the *Volk*

First published as "Lebenserneuerung, Lebensbejahung, Volkserneuerung," in *Geist und Schönheit* [pamphlet series], no. 2, edited by Wilm Burhardt (Dresden: Verlag Geist und Schönheit, 1936), 9, 10, 15, 16.

The greatest purpose in life is to rejoice in life. The will to greater achievement resides in this enthusiastic affirmation of life, inspiring us to ever-greater, ever-more-spectacular, ever-more-perfect things. Works that burgeon beyond the bounds of what is decrepit, aging, or even negating in its effect spring from the fortitude of eternal youth. Fortitude is what shapes beauty, but beauty—like everything that is alive—is ever changing: "maturing, in order to stay pure" and yet young, forever young.

The immortal works of the ages have all been born of the exuberance of youth and the wisdom of age and experience.

It is the works of these creative men that are at the center of all artistic and historical epochs; these works have allowed nations to emerge from the will of racial inheritance.

We, the living, those who are experiencing the German nation in her youth, we know that the *Volk* is abloom with the consciousness of rejuvenation and that this is the spring of her life. But today every German knows what many did not know before: that this birth, this rebirth, was precipitated by an unbridled will for rejuvenating life, for rejuvenating the *Volk;* that this affirmation of meaningful life was decisive.

And for us, this was one of the magnificent prophetic deeds of our Führer, who emphasized, in word and deed, that the most important thing is to prevent our *Volk* from ever growing old and to constantly renew life with this affirmation of life. "After all, we have you, the children!" And being able to build our future on this foundation—letting them mature to their full potential in the same will and purity that the creator of the Third Reich used to rejuvenate his *Volk*—this education and preservation of our youth is itself a form of rebirth in the noblest sense of the term—it is an affirmation and enhancement of life.

But we must realize that this rebirth can occur only in the context of conscious, disciplined reproduction and breeding as the most sensible ideal for human and cultural evolution, for racially conscious culture, fostered by a connection to nature, emotion, and the perspective on life that develops naturally from them.

This is what is behind the will to preserve future generations; indeed, it is what is behind the will to perform, the principle of achievement itself. This is what allows the German working in any profession to take pleasure in performing his life's work—regardless of whether this is in the field of art or science, in commerce or skilled labor, in farming or any other area of engagement.

Is it not such that everyone, regardless of his position in life, honors himself with his performance and thus expresses public recognition of labor, and doesn't this serve to conjoin the purpose of one's actions with the purpose of life in a way that even the simplest of men amongst us can understand?

Life visibly renews itself in spring when the fields are freshly sown, when plants and the animal world are budding with freshness, vigor, and cheer; man's renewal of life is not as apparent—the community of the *Volk* in the new buildings, the little things they say and do to contribute, whether in art or in skilled labor.

But we can bring renewal to the workday only if this goes hand in hand with the renewal of individual human energies. And if we single out the tremendous recreational program of the Third Reich, Strength through Joy, that is because there is no better example to demonstrate how sorely the working population was in need of physical respite born of biological necessity and the way this stupendous program was thrown together to meet that need. This recreational program has since become one of the most important of all recreational activities—a resource we can no longer do without.

Recreational activities: each individual finds his own way of relaxing, depending on his own predispositions—in the form of physical exertion, perhaps in sports or gymnastics, team sports, water sports, hiking; taking a trip; or going to the theater or to concerts for relaxation; learning new things in new areas of expertise; relaxing by reading a good book. What matters most here, though: relaxation as a community activity; this alone is enough to inspire in every individual the great spark of life that is joy. In that most rejuvenating, relaxing expression in the hour of joy, the community rewards itself with leisure, which is just as imperative of the rewards gleaned from having done one's duty in the workaday life on the job.

26

"Amusmang": Laughter in the Third Reich

The Berliners had a slang word for it, an adaptation of the very high-class French word *amusement,* pronounced in the working-class neighborhoods of Berlin as "*amusmang.*" Certainly, the master of *Amusmang* in the 1920s was the popular artist Heinrich Zille (1858–1929), whose caricatures of working-class Berliners at play was a source of amusement for all. Zille's take on the world was funny, and most people who saw his work got the point: being poor did not make you less than human; indeed, it gave you a certain ironic way of seeing the world. The annual "Zille Ball" at the Große Schauspielhaus (Great Theater) in Berlin's Friedrichstraße found bohemians as well as middle-class Berliners dressed in the costumes of the working-class characters in Zille's drawings. This amusement was led by the cabaret singer Claire Waldoff, at a substantial cost of 12.5 to 50 Reichsmarks a ticket, much more than the working class could afford. "Berlin—watch out," warned the posters on every corner in the late 1920s, "You are dancing with Death."[1] But it seemed that the desire for all types of amusement defied such warnings, at least in the public perception of life in Weimar Germany—persisting in spite of, or perhaps because of, economic collapse and hyperinflation.

Decried by the Nazis as degenerate and Bolshevist, Zille's works vanished after 1933, and Claire Waldoff (1884–1957) fled Berlin with her life partner, Olga von Roeder, surviving by living anonymously in Bavaria. The SS put all performers on alert: "we [have] put those times behind us in which the primary index of artistic excellence was, to some degree, to be seen as conforming to a certain asocial attitude—times in which scandals, perversities, and criminal behaviors were part and parcel of the artist's profession. It was seen as a liberation from bourgeois constraints—so-called artistic freedom." The party demanded more rigid artistic standards, and as *Das Schwarze Korps* reported, Goebbels "banned various stage and cabaret artists from membership in their local chamber of culture and thus prohibited them from further performances." Yet public laughter continued to define Germany, contradicting the image of the dour National Socialists, albeit in ever-more-censored form.

For the Nazis, having a sense of humor was both necessary and dangerous. *Das Schwarze Korps* noted in 1936, "People who have no sense of humor are like a punishment from God. They come in all shapes and sizes. They're the ones who strut around like little demigods and who consider themselves above weakness and superior to everything and anything, even their fellow men." But, unlike in the Weimar Republic, the arbiters of humor in the Third Reich defined appropriate and inappropriate targets for humor. "Out of sheer malicious desire and the opportunity to complain, [people who like political humor] are always on the lookout for certain topics that allow them to craft their idea of a joke, but in reality this is a means of poisoning confidence and making a mockery of a healthy outlook on life." The SS warned against targeting the party and its authorities. "Our ideals are not an amusement park for comedians' overactive imaginations," complained a writer in *Das Schwarze Korps.* Of course, jokes sprang up about both, but these were told in a whisper (*Flüsterwitze*) rather than spoken loudly in public. When the Bavarian-dialect comic Weiß Ferdl (1883–1949) introduced a family of pigs in his act as "Sohn [Son] Mann, Tochter [Daughter] Mann, Frau [Madam] Mann, and Herr Mann," the unmistakable reference to the obese Field Marshal Hermann Göring, nicknamed *Der Dicke* (Fatso), earned him a term in prison. People learned quickly when and where to tell jokes about the party.

But jokes about shortages of basic commodities still circulated and sometimes even appeared in the newspapers, much to the discomfort of the authorities. Rarely were food riots, such as one protesting the shortage of coffee in Berlin, reported locally, though they were amplified by anti-Nazi organizations abroad. But the SS also found topics that amused its members, such as the images of Hitler and Göring used to sell clothing: "But our question is, when are we going to see the Führer and Hermann Göring as mannequins in the shop windows rotating on the magical platform of a nickelodeon disk? But please, can we put wipers on the windows just in case anyone feels the need to retch?" To the Nazis, fawning attention was as deserving of punishment as critical humor. Yet swastika-shaped crossword puzzles with clues to the names of Nazi leaders appeared in the daily papers.

Of course, the leadership could be a source of public embarrassment, as when the notoriously profligate Reich minister of labor, Robert Ley, gave a speech advocating sobriety while himself obviously inebriated. Or when Hermann Göring swore in public on 9 August 1939, "*If* ever a *bomb* falls on *Berlin,* you may call me Meier," and the locals quietly began to refer to him with this Jewish-inflected name as the bombs fell on the city.

NOTE

1. Wolf Von Eckardt and Sander L. Gilman, *Bertolt Brecht's Berlin: A Scrapbook of the Twenties* (New York: Doubleday, 1975), 74.

343

DAS SCHWARZE KORPS

What Will Santa Bring?

First published as "Was bringt der Weihnachtsmann?" in *Das Schwarze Korps,* 12 December 1935, 10.

The long December night has already descended upon the cities in the early hours of evening, and the sparkling rays of light streaming from the shop windows dissolve into nothing when they reach the middle of the sidewalk. The city streets are bustling with life. Fretting housewives carefully inspect the treasures on display, quietly calculating whether or not there's enough in the Christmas budget to cover it.

What does Old King Cole really have in his bag? Inquisitive, bright-eyed children wonder. We've asked ourselves the same question and taken a careful peek in the bottomless bag of treasures, and we promise we'll never do it again because it has ruined our Christmas surprises.

Give practical gifts! It's been the battle cry of the recent years. Oskar is in the SA [Sturm Abteilung, Storm Troopers] and would certainly be happy to get a uniform. But who knows anything about uniforms? What color are the lapels, are the pants supposed to have piping or satin strips, or nothing at all?

But then, as coincidence would have it, the fashion pages of the *Rundschau* with the latest patterns appear on the table. The riddle has been solved! A delighted cry of "Eu . . . " leaps from the throat—but the " . . . reka" never escapes the lungs because the model in the sketch artist's overimaginative design for the uniform of the *SA-Gruppenführer* is none other than the Führer himself! Who then would so much as dare to question the authenticity of this as a standard-issue brown suit? Aside from the fact that the epaulets are wrong, as well as the cap, and the waist belt, not to mention the fact that the Führer has never worn boots with shafts as stiff as that—but that's how the sketch artist saw him; that was his vision of Adolf Hitler.

We won't call him a sensationalist, fly-by-night artist: we can see from his rendering of Minister President Göring published alongside his portrait [of the Führer]—that he is a member of the "Old Guard" because here the *SS-Gruppenführer* is wearing the swastika armband that was standard issue in 1923.

What manner of simple-minded, unbridled, fawning devotion screams from these images? They are symbols of the sanctimonious brain of a fashion designer who is apparently so obsessed day and night with National Socialism that he cannot forget about his heroes even while he is at work and uses his idols as fashion models!

But our question is, When are we going to see the Führer and Hermann Göring as mannequins in the shop windows rotating on the magical platform of a nickelodeon disk? But please, can we put wipers on the windows just in case anyone feels the need to retch?

"Give practical gifts!" is the resounding demand of the times . . . "and sensible!" the industry shouts after the roving shoppers. As its promotional brochure attests, J. M. Jäckel in Schwenningen, manufacturers of Black Forest cuckoo clocks, has gotten the message loud and clear:

> During the National Socialist revolution, the German people reflected deeply on the energies found within themselves. And this idea is the source for the design of the Trumpeter Clock "People Take Arms!" The Germanic spirit guards over and resides in the Germanic house. And this is the house that every German young person, the whole German *Volk,* dreams of having. The ancient warrior lets his trumpet sound: "People take arms!" The door opens on the hour and the half hour, and the bugler blows his horn to mark the hour or the half hour before the door closes again.

The old familiar Black Forest clock has been recrafted into a Germanic brick frame house; to the left and right of the clock face, SA men in knapsacks wrangle impatiently at the door where the cuckoo used to quickly pop out, until the helmeted Germanic warrior, armed with a spear and his trumpet, emerges to announce his powerful call to arms: "People take arms!" Everything exquisitely handcrafted, available in your choice of stains. May that cuckoo some day catch up with those National Socialists who shot his job to hell!

People stare in reproach at Santa Claus standing there shrugging his shoulders. He digs into his bottomless bag one more time, and the hairs on his beard stand on end, horrified, as if he were pulling the accoutrement of the man with the cloven foot out of the sack. And we turn to stone, too, even without looking Medusa in the face or being bitten by a rabid dog.

Of course, the greeting card industry has issued its own "German salute" Christmas cards. A cute little angel with a candle; in the background, the swastika appears in the foreground as a sort of fata morgana. The Christ child—notice the pair of wings, attributes of heavenly beings—is portrayed as some kind of Diogenes, "I come in search of Nazis!"

But for us mortal infants whose hearts grow fond in winter but for whom the fine art of letter writing has lost its charm, there is the greeting card. This tidal wave of romantic magic was unleashed by the perfection of photographic technology. Around 1913, photographs in the size of a postcard began to appear, picturing a soldier and a girl gazing dreamily into each other's eyes beneath a lilac tree, accompanied by some scintillating sentimental verse. These were sent back and forth, with the stamp placed askew in the corner as a way of affirming a mutual burning desire to be together and looking forward to talking at the dance on Saturday. This time, though, the image personifying a man bursting with brute masculinity is not a pioneer from the first guard regiment, but rather—let us hope that the turntable does not collapse—an SA man. Demure and deferring, his bride stands at his side, and you'd almost half expect her to offer him the marriage certificates from generations of her maternal ancestors as a dowry instead of daisies. If there's one thing the man decked out in warrior paint attests to, it is that any business-savvy photographer can get his hands on a uniform quicker than a member of the NSDAP can get a party badge if he doesn't have the proper credentials.

What, you say what you've seen of Santa's gift leaves your feet sleeping? Well, there's a solution for that: "Serving your *Volk!*" And, just above the inscription, there is an eagle bearing the swastika flag in his claws. Too bad the bird resembles a ringdove more than an eagle. There's a board-certified pedicurist selling his cure for ingrown toenails, bunions, calluses, and various and sundry as a noble service to the *Volk,* but he still doesn't understand that what really sticks in our craw is that we no longer want to see any more of this shameless abuse of the symbols of our worldview, and it makes us want to puke to know that there is a certain class of people who are more drawn to a bunion bandage with a swastika seal than they are to a simple "Have a nice day!" [*Lebewohl*].

Lest we forget: there are also some reading materials under the tree. Let us not forget either that we are a warrior *Volk*. So line up for the drill! The publisher Paul Müller in Munich offers some reading on this subject: *Boy Scout Stories from God's Country,* one of which is called "Come Lord Jesus, Be Our Guest." Letters home from a child at camp. Roman à clef for the Rural Labor Service. Quotations? No need. Buy the book! This book is simply a must-have! It's about a girl, obviously depicted as a National Socialist, who plays an almost despicable role. The only one who comes out clean is the brave little lad who peels potatoes on a wing and a prayer and writes his father about the Pharisees in search of their kith and kin—covered in a flour-white sprinkling of innocence. If we were to so much as suggest producing texts of this nature, a crimson tide of indignation would break out, leaving men from here to Rome shaking their heads in outrage.

That's what Santa has to bring. And a dozen other things. But this alone ought to be plenty—don't you think?

344

AMERICAN COMMITTEE FOR ANTI-NAZI LITERATURE

Humor à la Nazi

From American Committee for Anti-Nazi Literature, *Underground News,* no. 87, 12 May 1939, 2.

The cynicism with which the Nazis deal with the needs of the German people is adequately expressed in a so-called "joke" printed in the Nazi *Hamburger Tageblatt:*

Woman customer in grocery store, "It's simply terrible. We have no butter, no vegetables, no coffee—one might just as well turn on the gas . . ."

Nazi standing nearby, "Well, my dear woman, go right ahead! I have heard that it won't be long before we've run out of gas, too . . . !"

345

AMERICAN COMMITTEE FOR ANTI-NAZI LITERATURE

Drunken Nazi Leader Speaks against Liquor and Tobacco

First published in American Committee for Anti-Nazi Literature, *Underground News,* no. 88, 23 May 1939, 1.

When Dr. Robert Ley, leader of the Nazi German Labor Front organization, recently opened the Congress on Hygiene in Frankfurt, he delivered a speech in which he warned the German people against drinking and smoking. This speech received international publicity through the press.

Dr. Ley has a past record of drunkenness that received wide publicity during the Republican regime. On one occasion, he attacked the president of the Social Democrat Party, Mr. Wels, whom he injured with a wine bottle.

An eyewitness at the Hygiene Convention in Frankfurt reports that Dr. Ley was under the influence of alcohol while delivering his speech, which resulted in frequent interruptions by stuttering and belching.

The high point in Dr. Ley's speech occurred when he stated that he had become a teetotaler at great personal sacrifice. The entire audience burst into a roar of laughter, making it impossible for Dr. Ley to continue his discourse.

346

DAS SCHWARZE KORPS

We're Not So!

First published as "Wir sind nicht so!" in *Das Schwarze Korps,* 23 July 1936, 1.

People who have no sense of humor are like a punishment from God. They come in all shapes and sizes. They're the ones who strut around like little demigods and who consider themselves above weakness and superior to everything and anything, even their fellow men. For others of these moribund types who just can't take a joke, life is just a vale of tears, a solemn procession, a necessary evil. In mordant self-ridicule, they wallow in self-pity for their own inadequacy. Or they tyrannize everyone around them with their garrulous, holier-than-thou chatter—hypersensitive curmudgeons and malcontents. [. . .]

But on a more serious note, there are "political jokes" in which we fail to see any humor. And not because we don't have any sense of humor! These fairy tales of cruelty have lost their charm and are no joking matter. Their tendency is destructive by design and targeted at everything we seek to keep pure and strong: our ideals, our outlook. In their maliciousness and their insidious trickery, they twist all our weaknesses, however great or small, all the missteps and mistakes we ourselves hope to redress, and consciously misconstrue them to form a willfully tendentious view of the movement. Out of sheer malicious desire and the opportunity to complain, they are always on the lookout for certain topics that allow them to craft their idea of a joke, but in reality this is a means of poisoning confidence and making a mockery of a healthy outlook on life.

These "comedians" are as cowardly when it comes to expressing constructive criticism as they are when it comes to responsible collaboration. They overstep the bounds of tact, of inner decency: they're just trying to rid themselves of their own psychological complexes. Just as we require of any man who fights with us for our ideals and who has proven where he stands that he subject himself to self-scrutiny in exchange for his right to exercise healthy, constructive criticism of us, we are not well disposed to the notion of looking the other way when it comes to those covert opponents, who, operating under the veil of anonymity, would believe they could camouflage their scandalous breaches of decorum as "jokes."

As tempting as it may be to some to invent jokes, if only for the pleasure of getting a charge out of people, well, our ideals are not an amusement park for comedians' overactive imaginations. The only people who can and should participate in our laughter and our joy are those who work together with us with an honest heart, an open mind, and the best of goodwill. And these are the only people who are entitled to occasionally crack a good joke about those little weaknesses that we acknowledge and seek to correct. We know how many times laughter has gotten us through difficult times. And it's not something we hope to forget. But to all those dry-as-dust people who are lacking any sense of levity, we strongly suggest that they carefully study *Das Schwarze Korps*. We aren't as glum as people think!

347

DAS SCHWARZE KORPS

Fool's License for Artists

First published as "Narrenfreiheit für Künstler," in *Das Schwarze Korps,* 16 February 1939, 1.

Reich Minister Dr. Goebbels, in his capacity as president of the Reich Chamber of Culture, recently banned various stage and cabaret artists from membership in their local chamber of culture and thus prohibited them from further performances.

This decision was precipitated by the artists' own behavior, one of whom had already been given a warning about his political tomfoolery. The artists involved are too insignificant to merit careful consideration of this particular incident, but we do think it important—especially in light of the Führer's major speech on 30 January 1939, in which he outlined the scope of responsibility incumbent on all Germans to conform to the laws of German nature in the *Volk*—to elaborate on the symptomatic aspects of this individual case.

There has never been a government at the helm of the German ship of state that has elevated the value and meaning of art for the *Volk* to the level of a constitutive principle as the administration of Adolf Hitler—that is, of the Führer himself. There has never been a party or a movement with a coherent worldview that has challenged, without prejudice, the artists to this degree of participation as has the National Socialist movement.

An Emphatic Reminder

But considering how forgetful many people are, an emphatic reminder is in order concerning the way that, just a few years ago in Germany, the prevailing atmosphere in the arts was that of an arts industry manufactured and devised by Jews and decadent snobs who exercised a kind of dictatorship over artistic production that could not have been more brutal.

Anyone who refused to conform to the prevailing tendencies was starved out of existence by being excluded from the arts industry.

And it hasn't been that long since we put those times behind us in which the primary index of artistic excellence was, to some degree, to be seen as conforming to a certain asocial attitude—times in which scandals, perversities, and criminal behaviors were part and parcel of the artist's profession. It was seen as a liberation from bourgeois constraints—so-called artistic freedom.

The World as Loony Bin

It is entirely understandable that, in a period that was utterly unproductive and dominated by certain elements whose primary characteristic was criminal incompetence, this fundamental outlook would lead to a process of negative natural selection so effective as to be virtually unimaginable. Moneymongering and unbridled carnal indulgence were the things that made the artistic profession seem so attractive to many. And these kinds of characters necessarily developed, then, a worldview in art that is reflected in the horrendous legacy of "degenerate art"! The world as loony bin and cathouse!

Not only in our times, but wherever and whenever people live healthy, performance-oriented lives, a consensus of opinion has prevailed concerning these degenerate creations, and the German vernacular has aptly summed it up in the notion of "fool's license."

348

AMERICAN COMMITTEE FOR ANTI-NAZI LITERATURE

Coffee Shortage Announced

First published in American Committee for Anti-Nazi Literature, *Underground News,* no. 80, 24 March 1939, 2.

Berlin—(by special cable from Paris to ACANL)

The Reich League of Coffee House Owners issued a secret communiqué in which it was announced that "there will be a shortage of coffee all throughout 1939."

It is strictly prohibited to serve "mocha" (a demitasse of particularly strong coffee). The authorities furthermore "expect all restaurants to discontinue serving coffee in coffeepots. Coffee must be served in cups only."

The communiqué advises that cocoa as well will be obtainable in insufficient quantities only. Berlin coffee dealers were ordered by the police to introduce a card system for rationing coffee to their customers.

Strong protests against the government's "coffee policy" were made at several meetings of the League of Coffee House Owners. They claimed that the government's policy is ruining the trade.

Clashes between the people and the police took place in the Berlin suburb of Marienfelde when the police tried to break up the lines of women who were waiting before the shops for their ration of coffee.

349

ILLUSTRIERTER BEOBACHTER

Swastika Crossword Puzzle

First published under "Rätsel," in *Illustrierter Beobachter,* 17 March 1934, 366. Answers first published as "Lösungen der Rätsel in Folge 10," in *Illustrierter Beobachter,* 18 March 1934, 409.

Fill in the following letters in the figure below (a, e, e, e, e, e, e, e, e, e, e, e, g, h, h, i, i, i,, l, l, l, m, n, o, o, r, r, r, r, r, r, s, s, s, s, s, s, w, w, w) so they yield answers to the following:

Down: 1. German statesman (answer: Hitler); 2. President of the Reich Association of the German Press (answer: Weiß); 5. *Reichsstatthalter* (answer: Roever); 6. Prussian minister (answer: Kerrl)

Across: 2. Old Guard fighter for the movement (answer: Wagner); 3. Reich minister (answer: Roehm); 4. Bavarian minister (answer: Esser); 7. Hero of the movement (answer: Wessel)

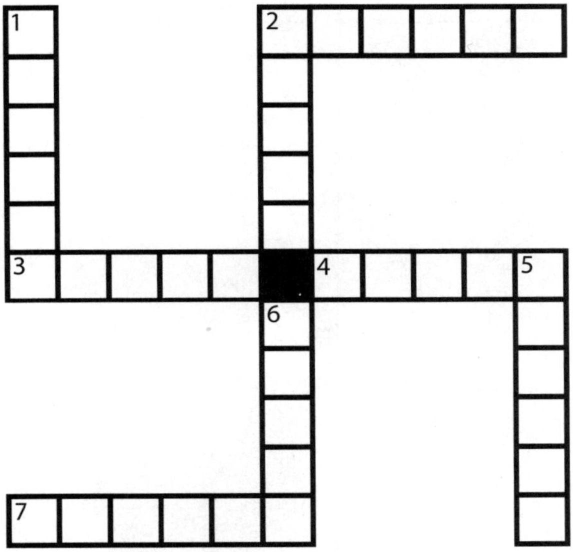

FIGURE 34. Swastika-shaped crossword puzzle with clues showcasing Nazi leaders. *Illustrierter Beobachter,* 18 March 1934, 409.

PART TEN

. . .

WAR, CONQUEST, AND THE ANNIHILATION OF THE JEWS

27

The Holocaust Begins

Violence, Deportation, and Ghettoization, 1939–1942

NAZI IDEOLOGY CONCEIVED of the opposition between Aryans and Jews as a world-historical battle for racial supremacy. A racially pure Germany demanded, as Hitler's chief ideologist Alfred Rosenberg (1893–1946) wrote in his 1930 *Myth of the Twentieth Century,* the radical removal, indeed elimination, of the Jews. Only through such an apocalyptic event could Germany again become a "healthy" nation. Upon reading Rosenberg in 1942, the Jewish philologist Victor Klemperer, living with his non-Jewish wife, saw the tract as an almost comic commentary on the time: "Only Nordic man has true religion, true artistic genius, true science, is truly able to observe nature. Inner freedom of the soul. (Jews without religion—materialistic. Jehovah's arbitrary power—magic)." The ravings of Rosenberg became the policies of the Reich.

From the Nuremberg Laws of 1935 to the confiscation of Jewish property in August 1938, Jews were systematically deprived of all rights—from new laws that forced all Jews to take the same middle names (Sarah and Israel) to the banning of pet ownership. The threat level rose precipitously after Reichskristallnacht in November 1938, when synagogues and Jewish shops were destroyed and as many as four hundred Jews were murdered. In a speech to the Reichstag on 30 January 1939, Hitler declared that "the annihilation of the Jewish race in Europe" would be his response if a new world war commenced. From that point, elimination of the Jews—whether by exile or forced immigration—became ever more central to the Nazi vision of a New Aryan German (and then, a New European) Order.

With the occupation of France in May 1940, the Nazi press unleashed a full-scale campaign against "the Jewification of Europe" and framed the war as a worldwide struggle against Jewish (a synonym for British and American) finance capital, as Rosenberg stated in 1941. After 1942, Hitler returned often to the "prophecy" he had made in the Reichstag speech, which he wrongly dated to the actual beginning of the war on 1 September 1939. This view was echoed by Goebbels when he declared the Jews "guilty" for the war in an article published in the periodical *Das Reich* in November 1941.

On 1 September 1939, the German Wehrmacht attacked across the German-Polish border with overwhelming air power to support massive movements of troops and tanks across multiple fronts. The initial intent of the Germans was to clear the *Reichsgau* Wartheland—the western part of Poland to be annexed to the Reich—of all Jews, unleashing a radicalization in the practices of violence as the war progressed. Whatever inhibitions might have forestalled full-scale racial annihilation no longer obtained. On 23 August 1939, Joachim von Ribbentrop, the German foreign minister, and Vyacheslav Molotov, his Soviet counterpart, had agreed to a nonaggression pact and divided Poland. The Soviet Union helped the Nazis dismember Poland, invading its eastern part on 19 September 1939. In a matter of weeks, independent Poland, which had existed for barely twenty years, vanished.

The conquest of Poland brought with it unprecedented violence. In the notorious "Operation Tannenberg," more than fifteen thousand Polish civilians, designated as "intelligentsia," as well as thousands of Jews, were shot by *Einsatzgruppen* (death squads of the SS Security Police) under Heydrich's control. These units were attached to the Wehrmacht. In his candid lecture notes, General Johannes Blaskowitz (1883–1948), commander in chief of the Polish invasion army, expressed his antipathy to this slaughter and predicted that it would make the Polish population more, rather than less, sympathetic to the Jews. He presciently warned of "the rampant brutalization and moral decrepitude that will rapidly spread like a plague throughout the fabric of the German *Volk*." His protests enraged Hitler, who relieved him of his command on 29 May 1940. The lesson was clear: by the time Hitler launched ""Operation Barbarossa," the invasion of the Soviet Union on 22 June 1941, the Wehrmacht had become a Nazified organization that its leaders, like Field Marshal von Reichenau, expressly saw as the instrument of the war of annihilation. "The soldier in the eastern territories is not merely a fighter according to the rules of the art of war but also a bearer of ruthless national ideology and the avenger of bestialities that have been inflicted upon German and racially related nations."

Occupied Poland, with its 1.7 million Jews, the largest Jewish population in the world, quickly became a land of ghettos and camps. On 21 September, Heydrich instructed the *Einsatzgruppen* commanders to concentrate the Jews from the countryside in ghettos in the larger towns and cities, in preparation for mass deportation to a Jewish reservation (*Judenreservat*). Just one month later, on 26 October 1939, decrees were issued mandating forced labor for Jews resident in the *Generalgouvernement,* the rump part of Poland occupied by the German military under the brutal anti-Semite Hans Frank (1900–46). Heydrich made no bones about distinguishing these short-term measures from "the final aim," which was to remain secret. Polish-speaking middle-class Jews were rounded up and placed in the ghetto at Warsaw or in the city of Łódź, now renamed Litzmannstadt.

Julius Streicher's rabid *Der Stürmer* charged the Jews with conducting a war "against non-Jewish peoples." The image of the "Jewish enemy" dominated wartime propaganda, even seeing the use of "black" soldiers (mainly from North Africa) in the French army during World War I as part of a Jewish conspiracy. In addition to Jews, all non-German ethnic groups were to be "racially cleansed," deprived of education, and recruited as forced laborers. Sinti and Roma (so-called Gypsies) were segregated and sent to concentration camps. Jews not fortunate enough to flee to Soviet-occupied Poland were deported as late as February 1940 to the *Generalgouvernement.* Nazi ideologues conjured up solutions to what was euphemistically called "the final solution to the Jewish Question." For example, a plan suggested in June 1940 and openly discussed by such regime zealots as Karl Baumböck, proposed that Jews could be eliminated from Europe through exile to the French colony of Madagascar, but this scheme was ultimately judged impracticable.

With the invasion of Poland, as Himmler observed in 1940, it was vital to set the ethnic groups found in the east against one another and especially against the Jews. The racist ideology was extended to eliminate "the Asiatic-Jewish danger," as Field Marshal von Reichenau ordered after the invasion of the Soviet Union on 22 June 1941. Göring had already set the groundwork for mass annihilation in a letter to Heydrich on 31 July 1941. On 12 December 1941, the day after Germany declared war on the United States, Goebbels recorded in his diary that Hitler said, "The world war is here, and the destruction of the Jews must be the necessary consequence."[1] Even earlier, gas vans had been used at the Chelmno extermination site, and the construction of gas chambers had begun at the extermination camp at Belzec. All of this culminated in Heydrich's convening of a high-level conference to discuss the scope and administration of a systemic "evacuation to the east"—understood as the murder of all European Jews—among a select group of high-ranking officials at the Wannsee conference in Berlin.

NOTE

1. Cited in Peter Longerich, *Holocaust: The Nazi Persecution and Murder of the Jews* (Oxford: Oxford University Press, 2010), 306.

350

ADOLF HITLER

Speech to the Great German Reichstag

Delivered 30 January 1939. First published in *Hitler: Reden und Proklamationen, 1932–1945*, vol. 2, edited by Max Domarus (Wiesbaden: Löwit, 1973), 1057–58.

The German *Volk* has no desire to have its affairs settled or governed by an alien people. France to the French, England to the English, America to the Americans, and Germany to the Germans!

We are determined to put an end to the way this alien people is infiltrating our society, taking control of every leading institution in the country, and to eliminate this alien *Volk* once and for all. For we are intent on educating our own people to assume these positions.

We have hundreds of thousands of the most intelligent sons of peasants and workers. We will educate and train them, as we have already begun to do, and we hope that they will someday occupy the leading positions of state and society, together with members of our own educated elite, not with these racial aliens.

Above all, though, German culture—as its name implies—is a Germanic culture, not a Jewish one, and, accordingly, its care and administration will be placed in the hands of our own people. And when the rest of the world works itself into a frenzy of hypocritical hue and cry over this barbaric expulsion of such indispensable, culturally superior elements from Germany, then we can only shake our heads in amazement at the conclusions they draw from these actions.

For how thankful must people be to us for liberating these august bearers of culture and making them available to the rest of the world. Based on their own expressed views on the subject, the rest of the world would have no excuse for refusing to welcome these extremely high-caliber people in their own countries.

There is no plausible explanation for why the Germans of all people should be burdened with members of this race, while in those countries that so enthusiastically laud them as "splendid people," their applications [for immigration] are suddenly rejected on the flimsiest of pretexts.

Because there can be no peace in Europe until the Jewish Question is out of the way.

It is entirely possible that, sooner or later, this very problem will be the one to produce an agreement in Europe between nations that might not have easily come together otherwise. There is enough territory in the world for everyone, but the first thing that needs to happen is that this notion that the Jews were somehow entitled by the hand of God to be beneficiaries of a certain set percentage of the body and productive labor of other nations must be dismissed once and for all.

The Jews are just going to have to adapt themselves to the rigor of solid, constructive activity, just as all other peoples do; either that, or they will succumb, sooner or later, to a crisis of unimaginable magnitude.

And on this day—one that is perhaps memorable not only for us Germans—I would like to add one more thing: In my lifetime, I have very often been a prophet and have mostly been ridiculed for it. In the period of my struggle for power, it was primarily the Jews who laughed off my prophecies that I would one day assume leadership of the German state and the entire German *Volk* and that the Jewish problem would be among the many I would finally solve. I believe, however, that German Jewry is now choking on its resounding laughter.

Today I will again be a prophet and say, if international finance Jewry in and outside Europe succeeds in plunging nations into another world war, then the end result will not be the Bolshevization of the planet and thus the victory of the Jews—it will be the annihilation of the Jewish race in Europe.

The era of propagandistic defenselessness among non-Jewish nations and peoples is over. National Socialist Germany and Fascist Italy are in possession of the means to make clear to the world, in no uncertain terms, the nature of this problem that so many people recognize instinctively but cannot explain scientifically.

At the moment, it may be possible for the Jew to conduct his unscrupulous campaigns in other countries under cover of the press, film, radio advertising, theater, literature, etc.—all of which are in his control. If this people again succeeds in leading masses by the millions into war that only serves these utterly senseless Jewish interests, then there will be a campaign that will be so effective as to have completely bagged the beast in just a few years in Germany alone.

People are tired of dying on battlefields just so that this international race may profit from the business of war and satisfy its Old Testament thirst for revenge. The Jewish slogan "Proletarians of the World Unite!" will be trumped by a higher calling, "Productive Nations of the World—Know Your Common Enemy!"

351

JULIUS STREICHER

Bolshevism and Synagogue

First published as "Bolschewismus und Synogoge," in *Der Stürmer,* no. 36, 1941. Translated by Randall Bytwerk. Calvin College, German Propaganda Archive.

The Jews do not like people talking about them. They want the public to hold the opinion that they are innocent adherents of a religion. They do not want non-Jews to learn the truth. Thus, Jewish newspaper writers and their bribed non-Jewish friends have done all they can to make the world forget what the Jews did in Spain from 1936 to 1939. To divert attention from Jewish blood guilt, the Jewish makers of public opinion speak of the Spanish "Civil War." In reality, what happened in Spain was identical to what has happened in the Soviet Union since 1917: *a war by the Jews against non-Jewish peoples!* The Jews wanted to achieve in Spain what they had long since accomplished in the east: they wanted to seize control of the Spanish nation and add as the symbol of their victory the Red Star and the hammer and sickle to the Spanish flag. The fact that the Jews were able to secure the help in Spain of confused non-Jews may not mislead us into viewing the event as simply the Spanish "Civil War." If the events of our time are to be a useful warning to coming generations, historians must make this clear: the war in Spain was an act of the Jewish world conspiracy to enslave the Spanish people. This Jewish war in Europe's southwest, they planned, would spill over from a Jewish-dominated Spain into France and the rest of Europe. They expected that Stalin's army, standing ready to the east, would complete Jewish domination of Europe.

The fact that the Bolshevist war in Spain was a Jewish war was made evident in some striking events: Christian churches were set afire, priests murdered, and the bones of holy nuns were removed from their crypts and given over to the scorn of subhumans. *But the synagogues were spared destruction, and not a single rabbi lost his life in the Bolshevist mass slaughters.* What happened in Spain is happening today in the land of the Soviets, in the land once named Russia. Stalin's order to burn down everything to keep it from falling into German hands extends to everything but the synagogues. Even at the beginning of the Bolshevist revolution, Christian churches were destroyed or turned into movie theaters or warehouses and Christian priests bestially murdered.

But the synagogues, called dens of thieves in the New Testament of the Bible, were preserved, and the rabbis could continue to pray their prayers of hatred and curse Christianity in the name of their god Yahweh. Is that not clear proof that the battle of Bolshevism for godlessness is aimed only at non-Jews? And is it not clear proof that what presents itself to the world as Bolshevism is nothing other than an outright Jewish cause?! Never before has the world seen so clearly the realization of the Talmudic law: *Each Jew has the duty to work to burn down and exterminate Christian churches. The saints must be insulted and the priests killed* (Schulchan-aruch, Jore be'ah, page 146, 14. Aboda zarah and Hilschoth). The end of the battle against the Bolshevist army in the east is German victory and therefore the victory of non-Jewish humanity over the most dangerous instrument of the Jewish world destroyers. The cause of the world's misfortune, however, will be forever eliminated only when Jewry in its entirety is annihilated.

352

Four Decrees Issued in Occupied Poland, 1939–1941

First published in Lucy S. Dawidowicz, ed., *A Holocaust Reader* (West Orange, N.J.: Behrman House, 1976), 65–68.

Decree on the Introduction of Forced Labor for the Jewish Population of the *Generalgouvernement,* October 26th, 1939

Pursuant to Article 5, Section 1, of the Decree of the *Führer* and Reich Chancellor on the Administration of the Occupied Polish Territories, of October 12th, 1939, I hereby issue this ordinance:

Article 1: Effective immediately, forced labor shall be instituted for Jews resident in the *Generalgouvernement.* For this purpose, the Jews will be concentrated in forced-labor teams.

Article 2: Directives required for the execution of this ordinance shall be issued by the Higher SS and Police Leader. He may designate areas east of the Vistula in which the execution of this ordinance is suspended.

Warsaw, October 26th, 1939
Governor General for the Occupied Polish Territories
Frank

Decree on Identification of Jewish Men and Women in the *Generalgouvernement,* November 23rd, 1939

Pursuant to Article 5, Section 1, of the Decree of the *Führer* and Reich Chancellor on the Administration of the Occupied Polish Territories, of October 12th, 1939, I hereby issue this ordinance:

Article 1: All Jewish men and women in the *Generalgouvernement* who are over ten years of age are obliged, beginning December 1st, 1939, to wear a white band, at least 10 centimeters wide, with the Star of David on the right sleeve of their inner and outer clothing.

Article 2: Jewish men and women must themselves procure these armbands and provide them with the appropriate distinguishing mark.

Article 3:

1. Violations will be punished by imprisonment

2. The Special Courts will have jurisdiction for judging such cases.

Article 4: Regulations for the execution of this ordinance will be issued by the Internal Administration Division in the *Generalgouvernement*'s office.

Cracow, November 23rd, 1939

Governor General for the Occupied Polish Territories

Frank

Decree on Establishing Jewish Councils, November 28th, 1939

Pursuant to Article 5, Section 1, of the Decree of the *Führer* and Reich Chancellor on the Administration of the Occupied Polish Territories, of October 12th, 1939, I hereby issue this ordinance:

Article 1: In each municipality a body representing the Jews will be formed.

Article 2: This body representing the Jews shall be known as the Jewish Council. In communities with up to 10,000 inhabitants, it will consist of 12 Jews, and in communities with more than 10,000 inhabitants, of 24 Jews, drawn from the resident population. The Jewish Council will be elected by the Jews of the community. If a member of the Jewish Council ceases to serve, a new member is to be elected immediately.

Article 3: The Jewish Council will elect a chairman and a deputy from among its members.

Article 4:

1. After these elections, which must be completed no later than December 31st, 1939, the Jewish Council roster is to be reported to the appropriate senior district official (*Kreishauptmann*), in urban districts to the senior municipal district official (*Stadthauptmann*).

2. The respective district or municipal district official will decide whether the Jewish Council roster reported to him should be approved. He may direct changes in the roster.

Article 5: The Jewish Council is obliged to accept the orders of German agencies through its chairman or his deputy. It is answerable for conscientious execution of orders to their full extent. The directives it issues to implement these German decrees must be obeyed by all Jewish men and women.

Cracow, November 28th, 1939

Governor General for the Occupied Polish Territories

Frank

Decree on the Restriction of Residence in the *Generalgouvernement,* October 15th, 1941

Pursuant to Article 5, Section 1, of the Decree of the *Führer* and Reich Chancellor on the Administration of the Occupied Polish Territories, of October 12th, 1939, I hereby issue this ordinance:

Article 1: In the Decree on Restrictions of Residence in the *Generalgouvernement* September 13th, 1940, as amended by the Second Decree on Limitations of Residence in the *Generalgouvernement,* of April 29th, 1941, the following Article 4 (b) is to be inserted following Article 4 (a).

Article 4, Section b:

1. Jews who, without authorization, leave the residential district to which they have been assigned will be punished by death. The same punishment applies to persons who knowingly provide hiding places for such Jews.

2. Abettors and accomplices will be punished in the same way as the perpetrator, and any attempted act will be treated in the same way as an accomplished one. In less serious cases the sentence may be penal servitude, or imprisonment.

3. Cases will be judged by the Special Courts.
This ordinance takes effect on the day of promulgation.

Warsaw, October 15th, 1941
Governor General for the Occupied Polish Territories
Frank

353

DER STÜRMER

The Eternal Shame

Black France Enlists Negroes as Cannon Fodder for the Eternal Jew

First published as "Das Schwarze Frankreich marschiert. Neger als Kanonenfutter Alljudas," in *Der Stürmer,* no. 5, February 1940, 1, 2.

The Jews have taken over France. They have completely corrupted a substantial portion of the French populace with their filthy press, their lewd books, films, and plays. Ever since the Jew assumed power in France, it has been a *dying* nation of people. The population rates in this country are sinking at an alarming pace. Now, in the effort to prop up this ailing populace that once had such a glorious past, an increasing number of Negroes are being introduced to France at the behest of the Jews.

Advertisement for the Negro

But there are still decent men and women living in France who raise objection to this inundation of their fatherland with Negroes. In the attempt to now eliminate the last remaining shred of racial consciousness in the French people, the Jew is currently engaged in an elaborate advertising crusade to glorify the Negro. The Negro vocalist Josefine [*sic*] Baker tingle-tangles from town to town parading her black "allure" to French people, who have had enough of it. Negro bands play in the music cafés. Black-skinned "film stars" make appearances in the cinemas. In the theaters, Negro songs are sung, and the audience is "entertained" by the black belly dancer's gyrations.

France's thoroughly Jewified press repeatedly prints laudatory articles about the Negro race with the intent of convincing the French that all races are equal. So, for example, the Parisian magazine *France Magazine* recently published a picture of a Negro clad in the uniform of a French soldier. The caption reads, "The savagely proud facial expression of this gunner testifies to his loyalty to the fatherland. It is France's glory, its pride, a cornerstone to French confidence."

So this is how the Jews think they can convince the French people of the "value" of the black race. This is how they want to present the Negro to the French people—as a "loyal fellow citizen." They are lying through their teeth to the French people, trying to pass this off as a "laurel leaf" in the history of France.

What Do the Negroes Have to Say about It?

It's interesting to see how the Negroes respond to the Jews' paeans to their greatness. It is, in fact, true that most black soldiers set sail for France with a certain degree of pride. But the Frenchman would be mistaken to believe that the Negro troops go to battle in their enthusiasm for France's aims. That is not the case! The Negroes go to battle in the conviction that they are fighting and dying for the liberation of African peoples. And it is precisely this consciousness of a community of all Negroes engaged in a war of liberating their race from the white peoples that inspires confidence and enthusiasm for battle in the black troops. [. . .]

The Eternal Stain

Jewified France will bear the eternal stain for the way this Negro race was viciously unleashed on their neighbors in Germany. But the day is soon to come when the Negro troops get wise. The day is soon to come when the Negroes realize that they have just been used as instruments of the Eternal Jew. And the day will come when the black troops in France will raise their bayonets against the Jews and their servants. History will have to be the one to tell the story of the way the Negro people took revenge on the Jewish oppressors who enslaved and abused them.

354

ALFRED ROSENBERG

The Jewish Question as World Problem

Speech delivered on 28 March 1941. First published in Office of U.S. Chief of Counsel for the Prosecution of Axis Criminality, *Nazi Conspiracy and Aggression* (Washington, D.C.: U.S. Government Printing Office, 1946), 5:554–57.

At the concluding ceremony for the opening of the Institute for the Study of the Jewish Question in Frankfurt on the Main, Reich leader Rosenberg spoke from Berlin over the radio on the theme "The Jewish Question as World Problem." This speech was listened to jointly by the participants of the session. Reich leader Rosenberg stated essentially the following:

The war that is being waged today by the German armed forces under the supreme command of Adolf Hitler is therefore a war of inestimable import. The fate not only of European nations, but of others as well, hinges on its outcome. The fronts in this war, though they may not have been clear to some at the outset of the war, have become firmly established by the dynamic of forces in this past year and a half. And the fronts are nearly the same as they were in 1914, it's just that some of the partners have switched sides and taken a different position in this struggle for a new future according to their respective national interests.

The war of encirclement of Jewish-British finance was a plan long in the making and already well underway by 1914. The Zionist movement first founded by Theodor Herzl witnessed substantial growth especially during the World War. It was, like the advance regiment, sent in ahead of those few Jewish finance magnates who were still cautiously hesitant, and it thus had precisely the effect its founder hoped. In the diaries of this Theodor Herzl, there is an actual memorandum he sent to Lord Landsdowne in which he offers Great Britain the services of all the Jews in the world. Herzl explains that there are ten million Jews in the world. While they may not be permitted to openly carry England's flag, they would certainly all carry England in their hearts if the [establishment of the Jewish State] would become reality and facilitate the protection of the Jewish people.

"In one stroke England would gain over ten million secret but loyal subjects, active in all possible occupational branches throughout the world. They sell twine and needles in many small villages in the East: but they are also active in large-scale commerce, in industry, in finance, and they are also scholars and artists and journalists and much else. As if a signal were given, they will put themselves in the service of a courageous Nation that offers them the long-desired assistance. England gains ten million agents for its greatness and for its influence. . . . Might the English government recognize what value it would be to win over the Jewish people?"[1]

This form of consolidating all the stock market forces with the powerbrokers of Jewish finance was political policy in the decades preceding the World War. Today we are convinced that many nations of people will gradually begin to see, if they haven't already, that the victory of 1919 as solidified by the Versailles Diktat was ultimately not a blessing for them but instead led to a slow hemorrhaging, and that this attempt on the part of Jewish finance and others in high finance to enslave 80 million Germans was ultimately a crime committed against all of Europe and almost unprecedented in history.

Today, now that Jewish high finance has again enlisted many nations in its war against Germany, it is essential that we remind people of a few facts—if only because they are the symbolic manifestations of a historical condition. As is congruent with their nature, the Jews of course stood behind Great Britain to a man. Herzl's hopes became reality on November 2nd, 1917 with the so-called Balfour Declaration, in which the Zionist leader Professor [Chaim] Weizmann assumed responsibility for establishing a Jewish homeland in Palestine and to see to it that Jewish rights in other countries were not adversely affected by the existence of this "Jewish State." The necessary financial relationships in the United States were set up for the British by the Rothschilds, and the Jewish press was unanimous in championing the cause of victory for Jewish-British high finance. In France, Georges Mandel (whose given name was actually Jerobeam [*sic*] Rothschild) served on the personal staff of [Premier Georges] Clemenceau and was relentless in his ongoing efforts to foment hatred of Germany. Mandel himself assumed a crucial ministerial post in 1939 as Minister of the Interior under Raynaud and persecuted all the French people of *völkisch* persuasion who sought to promote a sensible political agenda in France. The condemnation of French pacifists in the World War came at the hands of the Jew Ignace and, when he later died, the French government and all the Jews expressed their sincerest gratitude for his having thousands upon thousands of French pacifists incarcerated and executed. North America entered this war because the capitalist financiers around Morgan and his cohorts were apparently inextricably bound to those in England. Now, on Wilson's order, all of the major Jewish and non-Jewish banks and businesses are now being joined in one conglomerate group of Jewish bosses under the kingpin Bernard Baruch. He was in control of the entire industrial infrastructure of the United States; he could send his spies into any business operation of the so-called free Americans and enlisted his Jewish minions to develop a press agency for international Jewry in a process that was as dictatorial as the world has ever seen. Wilson himself, whose interest was supposedly to secure peace and who was elected as an apostle of peace, was unduly pressured to act. And when the *Lusitania* carrying contraband munitions was torpedoed, it was considered a battle cry against German barbarism and America was hastened to war in Europe for the sake of sustaining the dictatorship of world finance. When Wilson later attended the Paris Peace Conference at Versailles, he was accompanied by no fewer than 117 Jews. Once the Conference was underway, headed by the council of the so-called Big Three or Big Four, a number of participants did not master all the languages, and the Jews then managed to slip their Jewish Professor Mantoux in as interpreter and to use him as an agent to access all the details of the secret negotiations.

Under these circumstances, then, it was entirely self-evident that all of German Jewry would support and defend the so-called policy of appeasement and that the German *Volk* would be doomed for decades to laboring in indentured servitude and slavery for the Jewish and non-Jewish financiers and world bankers.

The Struggle against Jewish World Finance

We have seen it with our own eyes and seen it for what it is. And we could hardly believe that German history could possibly end in this manner of filth, moral decrepitude, and political disaster, and so, all German men, women, and children who were of sound character gradually joined together in an increasing awareness of the fact that the so-called rule of Jewish finance can only last as long as it never meets resistance from formidable forces not bound by financial interests. We have been unconditionally committed to this political struggle and others and have, in any case, succeeded in running this hideous specter of corruption and filth out of town on a rail; we have succeeded in destroying, within days, the Jews' position that had seemed so unshakeable, and now, after a century of ever-increasing Jewish domination of Germany, Germans alone are deciding the fate of the Reich. That was already accomplished in 1933.

The Nuremberg Laws set a worldwide historical and revolutionary precedent, and the National Socialist Movement is charged—today and forever—with the task of ensuring that there will never again be a November 9th, 1918 and that there will never again be anything so much as resembling that kind of Jewish domination in Germany. Never again shall any state have at its disposal, as Herzl himself prophesied, millions of "loyal servants," informants and Jewish spies living as "German citizens" on German land, and there certainly shall never again be such a brazenly offensive monument erected to the likes of someone like Douaumont. We are battle-hardened enough that we can prosecute this policy of war without showing a single sign of weakness.

The war being waged today under the high command of Adolf Hitler is therefore a war of immense reform. Not only does it far exceed the French Revolution in its ideas; it immediately eliminates all the hereditary contaminated and infectious germ cells that have been able to flourish unchecked for over a hundred years right at the center of European nations. The Jewish question, which Europe has been charged with solving for two thousand years without success, will now be solved by the National Socialist Revolution—for Germany and for all of Europe!

And our answer to anyone who asks what form this solution will take is this: In recent decades, there has been much talk of the Jewish State as the solution to the Jewish Question, and to some innocent simpletons, Zionism may still look like an honest attempt on the part of Jews to contribute to the solution of the Jewish Question.

In reality, though, there has never been, nor will there ever be, such a thing as a Jewish State.

In contrast to every other nation of *Völker* [people] on earth, Judaism is not organized vertically to encompass all professions, but has always formed a horizontal strata of society within other nations, a strata that pursues intermediate material and intellectual trade. Secondly, the proposed territory in Palestine is by no means suitable to host a Jewish State. It is too small to accommodate the 10 to 15 million and counting Jews; in other words, it is not a solution to the Jewish Question. The purpose of Zionism, after all, was never to solve the Jewish Question by bringing all the Jews together in one place, it was something else altogether.

The goal was to build a purely Jewish center in Palestine, a perfectly legitimate Jewish State, at first so that Jews could be represented as Jewish nationals with full rights at diplomatic conferences. Secondly, the goal was to make Palestine into a gigantic economic staging area to go against the entire Middle East. Thirdly, this Jewish State was to provide asylum to all those Jewish adventurers in the world who have been expelled from the countries they were in. In Palestine, they would be given new names and new passports before they were sent back to continue their corrosive handiwork in other countries they hadn't yet hit. And no one so much as considered even slightly limiting the so-called civil rights of Jews in Germany, England, America, or France. The Jews were to retain the same rights as Germans, Englishmen, Frenchmen, etc., and the Jewish world state without territory would come increasingly close to realizing its goal of an all-Jewish center with no non-Jewish presence whatsoever, and Jewish finance would be at the rudder in every country in the world.

But that dream is over now!

Now, just the opposite is true, we have to figure out how and where to put these Jews. Like

I said, they cannot be put in a Jewish state, but rather only in what I would call the Jewish *reservation.* We can only hope that future statesmen will have the wherewithal to gradually introduce a settlement of Jews who will work under experienced police supervision to complete the necessary jobs that non-Jews have been doing.

So we have a relatively clear view of the Jewish question before our eyes. It is as simple as a question of national hygiene. It requires that all nations who still value culture and the future defend their native national traditions. And it is an economic problem for all those who are so crippled by Jewish financial dictatorship that they cannot solve their social problems. It is a problem of political power as well because many states still have not found the will to shatter this financial dictatorship of Jewry. And ultimately, it is a historical-ideological problem that has been the charge of Europeans ever since the days when the first Jews immigrated to Rome. These problems must be solved in full. We as National Socialists, however, have but one unequivocal answer to give: for Germany, the Jewish question will not be solved until the last Jew has left greater German territory.

At this first working conference hosted by a scientific institute to research the Jewish Question, there was, in addition to the many German participants, a large number of important political leaders and researchers from a wide array of European states—also as a sign of tremendous political and ideological upheaval. Since it was Germany, with its blood and its *Volkstum,* that finally put a definitive end to this Jewish dictatorship for Europe and is now charged with keeping Europe as a whole free from the Jewish parasites, I believe we can also speak for all Europeans and say: the Jewish question will not be solved until the last Jew has left Europe altogether.

And it doesn't matter whether this program takes five, ten, or twenty years to complete. The transportation facilities of our times are such that a large-scale resettlement could be easily organized and executed if all nations work together. But the problem must be addressed and solved in this way—as we have envisioned it from the first days of our struggle, when we were decried as utopian for suggesting it—today we present it as pragmatic politics. All nations have an interest in solving this problem ,and we must be passionate in declaring today that not even Mr. Roosevelt, with his Baruch and his trophy Jews, will be capable of hampering us in [our efforts to cleanse Europe of Jews]; on the contrary, it is precisely the proclamation that this parasitic Jewish spirit is supposed to somehow represent world freedom today that will rile the spirit of resistance in the German character to its full potential, and the most powerful military instrument the world has ever seen—the German armed forces under Adolf Hitler—will see to it that an end is put to this last desperate attempt to let the masses of the white race march to war against Europe for the sake of Jewish financial domination once and for all.

We believe that this great war also constitutes a world revolution in biological cleansing, and that even those nations still opposed to us today will realize by war's end that Germany's cause is today not only the cause of the whole European continent and the cause of the whole white race, but also the cause of all other civilized races throughout the world who fight to secure their own native cultural life and governance. So we hope the world can one day, with a sensible distribution of territories, live and work in peace and prosperity that has been disrupted by these untiring parasitic activities. We see the Jewish question as one of the most important problems in the context of overall European politics—a problem that must be solved and will be solved, and we hope—indeed we know—that ultimately all the nations of Europe will join the march for this cleansing.

Note

1. Arguing for British assistance for a Jewish settlement in Palestine, Herzl included these remarks in an exposé written on 24 October 1902.

355

VICTOR KLEMPERER

Reading Rosenberg's *Myth* in 1942

Written on 13 June 1942. First published in *I Shall Bear Witness: A Diary of the Nazi Years,* translated by Martin Chalmers (New York: Random House, 1998), 77, 78.

LTI [*Lingua Tertii Imperii/The Language of the Third Reich*].
The couple of pages of notes I had made on the *Myth* were torn up. I shall attempt to outline in a few words what sticks in my mind as important. As a student I made fun of the author of the Shakespeare monograph (Sieper?) [Ernst Sieper, *Shakespeare und seine Zeit,* 1907—Eds.], who counts the drums, trumpet blasts, and pipes; now I had prepared a sheet of paper to record the use of *blood,* in all its substantive, adjectival, verbal combinations, ditto of *species* and *race. Earthbound* should be checked for use as praise and rebuke. When Phoenicians, Etruscans, etc., it is a rebuke = materialistic.—The ironical quotation marks (the Jewish "nation") should be counted. The use of foreign words to give oneself a scholarly air [. . .].

Three parts: I: The conceptual and historical foundation. II. The art of Nordic man. III. Program of the National Socialist state. (The work was first published in 1930 [. . .], my edition dates from 1934. When the program was already beginning to be realized.) Much of what Rosenberg demands has by now long been taken for granted. In some respects he is more aristocratic than the present line (but in no way less brutal), in foreign policy he arranges the pieces in a pattern different from the current one. (He still places hopes in England, he is no friend of the yellow race.) He frequently repeats himself, for he knows only *one* sentence: The Nordic race, Nordic blood is the bearer of *all* culture, of *all* that is good—every mixing of blood produces something inferior.—Close relationship to [Houston Stewart] Chamberlain, whom he often paraphrases and greatly admires. But goes far beyond him. Race research is more differentiated and self-confident now. And everything is incomparably more politicized, topical and fanatical than in Chamberlain.—Extensive discussion of matriarchy ("earth-bound," "Phoenician," etc.) and patriarchy, the Nordic sun-worshipping mentality (cf. *sunny!*). [. . .] Polemic against Spengler's cultural crisis.—The Jews for Chamberlain: not a people, but—the phrase is a quotation, but from whom?—a parasitic "antirace," which must be extirpated, at least driven out of Europe. But the main thrust of the opus, repeated over and over, is against the Roman Church, against Pope and Jesuits. "Jesuits," "humanity," "Pope" are red rags to Rosenberg. The figure of the Nordic Jesus (No brown Jew boy with flat feet and a hooked nose! I think that's literally what it says) is venerated, everything Pauline, Jewish is forbidden. Protestantism also comes off badly, also Luther. Religion should build on Meister Ekkehard (viewed through Kant), have no dogma [. . .]. It should hark back to Odin, press forward as far as Emperor Frederick II. Its innermost essence, its "supreme value": honor. In contrast to Christian *love.* Love is not "character building." Love is often weakness, and in church policy it stands for universalism, just like "humanity," and equals hypocrisy!—Religion, including the Christian religion, is to be free—*but:* the "so-called Old Testament" [. . .] will be forbidden, Pauline doctrine (i.e., "Jewish" doctrine) will be rewritten, prominence given to a blond, blue-eyed Christ—*blond* is a favorite word, once *blond blood!* Ban on the Catholic bishops' oath to combat heretics.—*Two* positions with regard to the family: (1) paterfamilias prevails over matriarchal sexuality. (2) The family is not the basis of the state, only male bonds (classical antiquity, officers, SA).—Only Nordic man has true religion, true artistic genius, true science, is truly able to observe nature. Inner freedom of the soul. (Jews without religion—materialistic. Jehovah's arbitrary power—magic.)

356

HEINRICH HIMMLER

Some Thoughts on the Treatment of Racial Aliens in the East

Position paper dated 15 May 1940 and presented to Hitler. Published as "Einige Gedanken über die Behandlung der Fremdvölkischen im Osten 15.5.40," in *Deutsche Geschichte 1933–1945: Dokumente zur Innen- und Aussenpolitik,* edited by Wolfgang Michalka (Frankfurt am Main: Fischer, 1993), 238–40.

In our treatment of racial aliens in the east, we must be sure to recognize individual ethnic groups to the extent that this is possible; that is, in addition to the Poles and Jews, we must also acknowledge the presence of Ukrainians, Belorussians, Gorals, Lemkos, and Kashubians. If other small and isolated national groups can be found in other places, they should be treated the same way.

What I mean to say is that we have great interest not only in merely preventing the population of the east from unifying, but also, on the contrary, in splitting them up into as many parts and fragments as possible.

But even within the ethnic groups themselves, we haven't the slightest interest in leading these to unity and greatness, or perhaps gradually arousing in them a national consciousness and national culture; we seek, rather, to dissolve them into innumerable small fragments and particles.

Naturally, we want to install members of all these ethnic groups, especially the smaller ones, in positions of police officials and mayors.

Only the mayors and local police authorities will be allowed to head those ethnic groups; as far as the Gorals are concerned, the individual chieftains and tribal elders, who are constantly feuding amongst themselves anyway, should fill these positions. There can be no centralization toward the top, because only by dissolving this whole conglomeration of peoples of the *Generalgouvernement,* amounting to fifteen million, and of the eight million of the eastern provinces, will it be possible for us to carry out the racial sifting that must be the basis for our considerations: namely, fishing out of this conglomeration the racially valuable elements and bringing them to Germany and assimilating them there.

Within a very few years—I should think about four to five years—the name of the Kashubes, for instance, must be unknown, because at that time there won't be a Kashubian people any more (this also goes especially for the West Prussians). I hope that the concept of the Jew will be completely eliminated by the possibility of a large emigration of all Jews to Africa or some other colony. Within a somewhat longer period, it should also be possible to make the ethnic concepts of Ukrainians, Gorals, and Lemkos disappear in our area. What has been said for those fragments of peoples also applies on a correspondingly larger scale for the Poles.

A basic issue in the solution of all these problems is the question of schooling and thus the question of sifting and selecting the young. For the non-German population of the east, there must be no higher education available than the four-grade elementary school. The sole aim of this school shall be to teach:

Simple arithmetic up to 500 at the most; writing one's name; the doctrine that it is a divine law to obey the Germans and to be honest, industrious, and good. I don't think that reading is necessary.

Apart from this school there are to be no schools at all in the east. Parents, who from the beginning want to give their children better schooling in the elementary school, as well as later on in higher education, apply to the higher SS and police leaders. The first consideration in dealing with this application will be whether the child is racially perfect and conforming to our conditions. If we acknowledge such a child as being German by blood, the parents will be notified that the child will be sent to a school in Germany and that he will permanently remain in Germany.

Cruel and tragic as every individual case may be, this method is still the mildest and best if, out of inner conviction, one rejects as un-German and impossible the Bolshevist method of physical extermination of a people.

The parents of such children of good blood will be given the choice of either giving their child away—in which case, they will not likely produce any more children so that the danger of this subhuman people of the east obtaining a class of leaders that, since it would be equal to us, would also be dangerous for us, will disappear—or the parents pledge themselves to go to Germany and to become loyal citizens there. The love toward their child, whose future and education depends on the loyalty of the parents, will be a strong weapon in dealing with them.

Apart from examining the applications made by parents for better schooling of their children, there will be an annual sifting of all children of the *Generalgouvernement* between the ages of six and ten years in order to separate the racially valuable from the nonvaluable. The ones considered racially valuable will be treated in the same way as the children who are admitted on the basis of the approved application of their parents.

I consider it a matter of course from an emotional as well as from a rational viewpoint that the moment children and parents come to Germany, they are not to be treated like lepers in the schools and in everyday life but rather that, after having changed their names, they should, in full confidence, be incorporated into the German life, although attention and vigilance must be exercised with regard to them. The children cannot be made to feel like they are outcasts, because, after all, we believe in this, our own blood, which, through the errors of German history has flowed into an alien nationality, and we are convinced that our ideology and our ideals will strike a chord of resonance in the racially equal soul of these children. Here, teachers and Hitler Youth leaders especially must be thorough in their jobs, and the mistake that has been made in the past with the people from Alsace-Lorraine must never be repeated; namely, that on one side, one wants to win the people as Germans, and on the other side, one constantly assaults and repudiates their human value, their pride, and their honor through distrust and insults. Insults like "Polack" and "Ukrainian" or anything of the sort must not be permitted.

The children will have to be educated in an elementary school, and after those four grades, it can be decided whether the children should continue to go to the German grammar school or should be transferred to a national political institution of education.

The population of the *Generalgouvernement* during the next ten years, by necessity and after a consistent execution of these measures, will be composed of the remaining inferior population supplemented by the population of the eastern provinces deported there and of all those parts of the German Reich that have the same racial and human qualities—for instance, parts of the Sorbs [Sorben] and Wends [Wenden].

This population will, as a people of laborers without leaders, be at our disposal and will furnish Germany annually with migrant workers and with workers for special tasks (roads, quarries, buildings): they themselves will have more to eat and more to live on than under the Polish regime; and, though they have no culture of their own, they will, under the strict, consistent, and just leadership of the German people, be called upon to help work on its everlasting cultural tasks and its buildings and perhaps, as far as the amount of heavy work is concerned, will be the ones who make the realization of these tasks possible.

357

Persecution of the Sinti and Roma
Three Decrees

I. HEINRICH HIMMLER, Combating the Gypsy Plague

Issued 12 December 1938. First published in Hans Joachim Döring, *Die Zigeuner im nationalsozialistischen Staat* (Hamburg: Kriminalistik Verlag, 1964), 197.

1. Previous cumulative experiences in combating the Gypsy plague and the knowledge gained through racial biological research appear to indicate that control over the Gypsy question can be achieved through racial principles. Experience shows that those of mixed race [*Mischlinge*] are involved in most of the Gypsy criminality. On the other hand, it has been shown that the attempt to make Gypsies sedentary, especially among the racially pure Gypsies, has failed as a consequence of their strong nomadic drive. It is necessary, therefore, to separate the racially pure Gypsies from those of mixed race in the handling of the final solution of the Gypsy question.
2. For the achievement of this goal, it is first advisable to determine the racial membership of individual Gypsies living in the German Reich and those vagabonding in Gypsy style.
3. I therefore decree that all sedentary and nonsedentary Gypsies, as well as those vagabonding about, be registered by the criminal police office (Reich Central Office for Combating the Gypsy Trouble).
4. The police authorities must consequently report all persons who, by their appearance, their morals, and practices, can be regarded as Gypsies or Gypsies of mixed race, as well as all vagabonds, to the appropriate criminal police post and the criminal police post of the Reich Criminal Office for Combating the Gypsy Trouble.

II. REICH COMMISSAR FOR THE REUNIFICATION OF AUSTRIA WITH THE GERMAN REICH, School Attendance of Gypsy Children

Issued 15 November 1939. First published in Romani Rose and Documentary and Cultural Centre of German Sinti and Roma, *The Nazi Genocide of the Sinti and Roma* (Heidelberg: Documentary and Cultural Centre of German Sinti and Roma, 1995), 52–53.

At the beginning of the current school year, I ordered that Gypsy children no longer be accepted in the schools. At a time when many schoolteachers have been called up and many school buildings claimed for military purposes, no school place can be placed at the disposal of this scum.

Now the Ministry for Internal and Cultural Affairs has received a decree from the Reich Minister for Science, Education, and Public Pedagogy (Decree Zl. E II e 624/79), which states:

"The acceptance of Gypsy children who do not possess German citizenship and therefore are not required to attend school is completely forbidden. Given the fact that these children are not schooled, and therefore endanger public security and public order, it is a matter for police administration to respond with corresponding measures, and if need be, can be implemented by the expulsion of these elements.

"Gypsy children who are German citizens and are required to attend school will not be affected by the fundamental refusal of acceptance. Given the number of Gypsy children so affected, it will not be possible to create special schools. Insofar as such children pose a danger for their fellow students of German blood in moral or other respects, they can be removed from the school. In such cases, it is advisable to inform the police authorities accordingly."

III. REINHARD HEYDRICH, Confinement Decree

Issued on 17 October 1939. First published in Romani Rose and Documentary and Cultural Centre of German Sinti and Roma, *The Nazi Genocide of the Sinti and Roma* (Heidelberg: Documentary and Cultural Centre of German Sinti and Roma, 1995), 92.

1. The local police authorities and gendarmerie are henceforth advised to inform those Gypsies and Gypsies of mixed race that from this moment forward they are forbidden to leave their places of residence or of domicile. The penalty for disobeying this order is confinement in a concentration camp. . . .
2. Roundup days for the collection and enumeration of Gypsies and Gypsies of mixed race are October 25, 26, and 27, 1939. This order will be carried out by the local police and gendarmerie.

358

JOHANNES BLASKOWITZ

The Military and the Slaughter of the Jews

"Vortragsnotiz es generaloberst Blaskowitz für einen Vortrag beim Oberbefehlshaber der Heeres in Spala." Notes for a lecture delivered on 15 February 1940. First published in *Der Weg zur Teilung der Welt. Politik und Strategie von 1933 bis 1945*, edited by Hans Adolf Jacobsen (Bonn: Wehr und Wissen, 1977), 33.

On the military and political situation:

In the industrial sector of Kazierna, we have established the first evidence of a widespread resistance and sabotage organization. Primary proponents of the organization are members of the former Polish army. The materials confiscated from numerous requests are currently under investigation. The Gestapo have decided to refrain from making any additional arrests so as not to jeopardize plans for the complete destruction of the entire organization. The threat that is emerging here requires that we address the question of how to treat the Polish population in general.

It would be a mistake to continue with the slaughter of ten thousand Jews and Poles that is currently under way because this does nothing to squelch the idea of a Polish national state in the masses nor does it serve to eliminate the Jews. On the contrary, the nature of this slaughter does irreparable damage, complicates the problems, and makes them even more dangerous than they would be if we were to act on the basis of a calculated and well-thought-out strategy. The impact that this slaughter is having includes:

(a) Feeding oppositional propaganda with material that could hardly be more effective. What the foreign press has reported is of course but a fraction of what has actually happened. We must reckon with the fact that international outcry will increase steadily and result in substantial political damages, especially since the atrocities actually did occur and cannot be refuted.

(b) The acts of violence being committed publicly against Jews not only serve to arouse profound aversion on the part of religious Poles, they spark sympathy for the Jewish population in equal measure, whereby up until now, the average Pole has been more or less ill disposed toward them. It will be a matter of only a very short time before our archenemies in the east—the Pole and the Jew—will have the active support of the Catholic Church and will be able to mobilize their hatred in widespread opposition to Germany.

(c) I need not reiterate the fact that the military, forced as it is to stand idly by and witness this crime, will suffer irreparable damage to its reputation, particularly among the Polish population.

(d) The most devastating damage, however, that will be sustained by the body of the German *Volk* under these circumstances is the rampant brutalization and moral decrepitude that will rapidly spread like a plague throughout the fabric of the German *Volk*.

When high-ranking officials in the SS and the police advocate and publicly condone acts of violence and brutality, then before long the only ones who respond to them will be violent people. Like-minded people and pathologically disturbed characters are surprisingly quick to rally together and, as is the case in Poland, to give free rein to their bestial, pathological instincts. There is hardly anything that can be done to restrain them because they, of course, see their behavior as authorized and consider themselves justified in committing any act of cruelty.

The only possibility that exists for preventing the spread of this sort of plague is to quickly see to it that the guilty parties and their ilk are brought before the military leadership and brought to justice.

359

JOSEPH GOEBBELS

The Jews Are Guilty!

Delivered as "Die Juden sind Schuld!" on 16 November 1941. First published in *Das Eiserne Herz: Reden und Aufsätze aus den Jahren 1941/42* (Munich: Zentralverlag der NSDAP, 1942), 85–91. Translated by Randall Bytwerk. Calvin College, German Propaganda Archive.

The historic responsibility of world Jewry for the outbreak and spread of this war has been proven so clearly that it merits no further discussion. The Jews wanted war, and now they have it. But the Führer's prophecy of 30 January 1939 to the German Reichstag is also being fulfilled: if international finance Jewry in and outside Europe succeeds in plunging nations into another world war, then the end result will not be the Bolshevization of the planet and thus the victory of the Jews—it will be the annihilation of the Jewish race in Europe.

We are seeing the fulfillment of this prophecy. The fate that is befalling the Jews is certainly harsh but more than deserved. Pity or even regret is entirely unmerited here. World Jewry erred completely in its calculation of the forces at its disposal for instigating this war and now is gradually experiencing the process of annihilation that it planned for us and would have carried out without a second thought if it had possessed the ability. It is perishing according to its own law: "an eye for an eye, a tooth for a tooth."

Every Jew is our enemy in this historic conflict, regardless of whether he sits vegetating in a Polish ghetto, or carries on his parasitic existence in Berlin or Hamburg, or blows the trumpets of war in New York or Washington. All Jews, by virtue of their birth and their race, are part of an international conspiracy against National Socialist Germany. They want its defeat and annihilation and do all in their power to bring it about. The fact that they can find little opportunity to do so within the Reich is hardly a sign of their loyalty, but rather results from the fact that we took the measures we deemed appropriate against them.

One of these measures is the introduction of the yellow star that each Jew must wear on visible display. We wanted to make them identifiable as Jews on sight, particularly for the event that they should make even the least attempt to harm the German community. It is a remarkably humane measure on our part, a hygienic and prophylactic measure to be sure, that the Jew cannot infiltrate our ranks unseen to sow discord.

As the Jews first appeared several weeks ago on the streets of Berlin graced with their Jewish star, the initial reaction of the citizens of the Reich capital was surprise. Only a few knew that there were still so many Jews in Berlin. Everyone suddenly found someone in the neighborhood who seemed like a harmless fellow citizen, who perhaps complained or criticized a bit more than normal, and whom no one had thought to be a Jew. He had concealed himself, mimicked his surroundings, camouflaged himself to fit the background, adjusted to the environment in order to wait for the proper moment. Who among us had any idea that the enemy was beside him, that a silent or clever auditor was attending to conversations on the street, in the subway, or in the lines outside cigarette shops? There are some Jews one can hardly recognize by their outward appearance. These are the most dangerous. It always happens that whenever we take some measure against the Jews, English or American newspapers report it the next day. Even today, the Jews still have secret connections to our enemies abroad and use these not only in their own cause but in all military matters of the Reich as well. The enemy is in our midst. What makes more sense than to at least make him clearly identifiable to our citizens?

In the first days after the introduction of the Jewish star, newspaper sales in Berlin went through the roof. Each Jew on the street bought a newspaper to conceal his mark of Cain. When this was banned, one began to see Jews on the streets of the west side of Berlin in the company of non-Jewish foreigners. These Jewish lackeys actually should wear the Jewish star themselves. The excuse they give for their provocative conduct is always the same: the Jews are, after all, human beings too. We never denied that, just as we never denied the humanity of murderers, child rapists, thieves, and pimps, though we never felt the need to parade down the *Kurfürstendamm* with them! Every Jew is a decent Jew who has found a dumb and ignorant Goy who thinks him decent! As if that were a reason to give Jews a kind of honorable escort. What nonsense.

The Jews gradually are having to depend more and more on themselves and have recently found a new trick. They know there's a good Samaritan in each of us—one who is always ready to forgive the injustices inflicted on him at the drop of a single sentimental tear. One suddenly has the impression that the Berlin Jewish population consists only of little babies whose childish helplessness might move us, or else fragile old ladies. The Jews are putting their most pathetic people on parade. They may confuse some harmless souls for a while, but not us. We know exactly where we stand with them.

For their sake alone, we must win the war. If we lose it, these harmless-looking Jewish chaps would suddenly become raging wolves. They would attack our women and children to exact revenge. There are enough examples in history. That is what they did in Bessarabia and the Baltic states when Bolshevism marched in, even though neither the people nor their governments had done anything to them. There is no turning back in our battle against the Jews—even if we wanted to, which we do not. The Jews must be removed from the German community for they endanger our national unity.

That is an elementary principle of racial, national, and social hygiene. They will never give us rest. If they could, they would drive one nation after another into war against us. Who cares about their difficulties, they who want only to force the world to accept their bloody financial domination? The Jews are a parasitic race that feeds like a foul fungus on the cultures of healthy but ignorant peoples. There is only one effective measure: cut them out.

How stupid and thoughtless are the arguments of the backward friends of the Jews in the face of a problem that has occupied mankind for millennia! How they would gape if they could ever see their dear Jews in power! But that would be too late. That is why it is the duty of a national leadership to take all necessary measures to keep such a thing from happening. There are differences between people, just as there are differences between animals. Some people are good, others bad. The same is true of animals. The fact that the Jew still lives among us is no proof that he belongs among us, just as a flea is not a household pet simply because it lives in a house. When Mr. Bramsig or Mrs. Knöterich feel pity for an old woman wearing the Jewish star, they should also remember that a distant nephew of this old woman by the name of Nathan Kaufmann sits in New York and has prepared a plan by which all Germans under the age of sixty will be sterilized. They should recall that a son of her distant uncle is a warmonger named Baruch or Morgenthau or Untermayer who stands behind Mr. Roosevelt, driving him to war, and that if they succeed, a fine but ignorant U.S. soldier may one day shoot dead the only son of Mr. Bramsig or Mrs. Knöterich. It will all be for the benefit of Jewry, to which this old woman also belongs, no matter how fragile and pitiable she may seem.

If we Germans have a fatal flaw in our national character, it is forgetfulness. This failing speaks well of our human decency and generosity but not always of our political wisdom or intelligence. We think everyone else as is good-natured as we are. The French threatened to dismember the Reich during the winter of 1939–40, saying that we and our families would have to stand in lines at their field kitchens to get something warm to eat. Our army defeated France in six weeks, after which we saw German soldiers giving bread and sausages to hungry French women and children, and gasoline to refugees from Paris to enable them to return home as soon as possible, only to [see them] spread at least some of their hatred against the Reich as soon as they got there.

That's how we Germans are. Our national virtue is our national weakness. We do not want to change all that much, and as long as our world-famed good nature does no great harm, why should we? Klopstock gave us some good advice, however: don't be too good-natured, since our enemies are not noble enough to overlook our mistakes.

If this advice applies anywhere, it apples to our relations with the Jews. Carelessness here is not only a weakness, it is dereliction of duty and a crime against the security of the state. The Jews long for one thing: to reward our foolishness with bloodshed and terror. It must never come to that. One of the most effective defenses is an unforgiving, cold hardness against the destroyers of our people, against the instigators of the war, against those who would benefit if we lose, and therefore also against the victims if we win.

Therefore, we must say again and yet again:

1. The Jews are our undoing. They are the ones who instigated and brought on this war with the intent of annihilating the German Reich and our people. This plan must be foiled.

2. There is no difference between one Jew and another. Every Jew is a sworn enemy of the German people. If he does not make his hostility plain, it is only from cowardice and slyness, not because he loves us.

3. The Jews are to blame for each German soldier who falls in this war. They have him on their conscience and must also pay for it.

4. If someone wears the Jewish star, he is marked as an enemy of the people. Anyone who deals with him is the same as a Jew and must be treated accordingly. He earns the contempt of the entire *Volk*, for he is a craven coward who leaves them in the lurch to stand by the enemy.

5. The Jews enjoy the protection of our enemies abroad. That is all the proof we need to show how harmful they are for our people.

6. The Jews are the enemy's agents among us. Whoever stands by them is a traitor who aids and abets the enemy in war.

7. The Jews have no right to claim equality with us. If they wish to speak on the streets, in lines outside shops, or in public transportation, they should be silenced, not only because they are simply wrong but because they are Jews who have no right to a voice in the community.

8. If the Jews appeal to your sentimentality, realize that they are banking on your forgetfulness; immediately let them know that you see through them and hold them in contempt.

9. A decent enemy will deserve our generosity after we have won. The Jew, however, is not a decent enemy, though he tries to seem so.

10. The Jews are at fault for this war. The treatment they receive from us is hardly unjust. They have deserved it all.

It is the job of the government to deal with them. No one has the right to act on his own, but each has the duty to support the state's measures against the Jews, to defend them with others, and to avoid being misled by any Jewish tricks.

The security of the state requires that of us all.

360

HERMANN GÖRING

Order to Heydrich to Begin Preparations for the Final Solution to the Jewish Question

Issued on 31 July 1941. First published in Office of U.S. Chief of Counsel for the Prosecution of Axis Criminality, *Nazi Conspiracy and Aggression* (Washington, D.C.: U.S. Government Printing Office, 1946), document 710-PS, 3:525–26.

To *Gruppenführer* Heydrich:

Complementing the task that was assigned to you on 24 January 1939, which dealt with the carrying out of emigration and evacuation, a solution of the Jewish problem, as advantageous as possible, I hereby charge you with making all necessary preparations in regard to organizational and financial matters for bringing about a total solution of the Jewish question in the German sphere of influence in Europe.

Wherever other governmental agencies are involved, these are to cooperate with you.

I charge you furthermore to send me before long, an overall plan concerning the organizational, factual, and material measures necessary for the accomplishment of the desired final solution of the Jewish question.

Göring

361

FIELD MARSHAL WALTER VON REICHENAU

Orders for Conduct in the East

Crushing the Jewish-Bolshevist System

Issued on 10 October 1941. First published in Office of U.S. Chief of Counsel for the Prosecution of Axis Criminality, *Nazi Conspiracy and Aggression* (Washington, D.C.: U.S. Government Princeton Office, 1946), 8:585–87.

Army H.Q., October 10, 1941

Subject: Conduct of Troops in Eastern Territories.

Regarding the conduct of troops towards the Bolshevistic system, vague ideas are still prevalent in many cases. The most essential aim of war against the Jewish-Bolshevistic system is a complete destruction of their means of power and the elimination of Asiatic influence from the European culture. In this connection the troops are facing tasks that exceed the one-sided routine of soldiering. The soldier in the Eastern territories is not merely a fighter according to the rules of the art of war but also a bearer of ruthless national ideology and the avenger of bestialities which have been inflicted upon German and racially related nations.

Therefore, the soldier must have full understanding for the necessity of a severe but just revenge on subhuman Jewry. The Army has to aim at another purpose, i.e., the annihilation of revolts in the hinterland, which, as experience proves, have always been caused by Jews.

Combating the enemy behind the front line is still not being taken seriously enough. Treacherous, cruel partisans and degenerate women are still being made prisoners-of-war, and guerilla fighters dressed partly in uniform or plain clothes and vagabonds are still being treated as proper soldiers and sent to prisoner-of-war camps. In fact, captured Russian officers talk even mockingly about Soviet agents moving openly about the roads and, very often, even eating at German field kitchens. Such an attitude of the troops can only be explained by complete thoughtlessness, so it is now high time for the commanders to clarify the meaning of the pressing struggle.

The feeding of the natives and of prisoners of war who are not working for the armed forces from Army kitchens is an equally misunderstood humanitarian act as is the giving of cigarettes and bread. Things which the people at home can spare under great sacrifices and things that are being brought by the command to the front under great difficulties should not be given to the enemy by the soldier even if they originate from booty. It is an important part of our supply.

When retreating, the Soviets have often set buildings on fire. The troops should be interested in extinguishing fires only as far as it is necessary to secure sufficient numbers of billets. Otherwise, the disappearance of symbols of the former Bolshevistic rule, even in the form of buildings, is part of the struggle of destruction. Neither historic nor artistic considerations are of any importance in the Eastern territories. The command issues the necessary directives for the securing of raw material and plants vital to the war economy. The complete disarming of the civilian population in the rear of the fighting troops is imperative considering the long, vulnerable lines of communications. Where possible, captured weapons and ammunition should be stored and guarded. Should this be impossible because of the battle situation, the weapons and ammunition will be rendered useless. If isolated partisans are found using firearms in the rear of the army, drastic measures are to be taken. These measures will be extended to that part of the male population who were in a position to hinder or report the attacks. The indifference of numerous apparently anti-Soviet elements, which originates from a "wait and see" attitude, must give way to a clear decision for active collaboration. If not, no one can complain about being judged and treated a member of the Soviet system.

The fear of German countermeasures must be stronger than threats of the wandering Bolshevistic remnants. Regardless of all future political considerations, the soldier has to fulfill two tasks:

1. Complete *annihilation of the false Bolshevist doctrine of the Soviet state and its armed forces.*

2. *The pitiless extermination of foreign treachery and cruelty and thus the protection of the lives of military personnel in Russia.*

This is the only way to fulfill our historic task to liberate the German people once and for all from the Asiatic-Jewish danger.

Commander-in-Chief
(signed) von Reichenau
Field Marshal

362

KARL BAUMBÖCK

Jews Practice World Politics

First published in *Juden machen Weltpolitik* (Berlin: Propaganda-Verlag Paul Hochmuth, 1942), 28–31. Translated by Randall Bytwerk. Calvin College, German Propaganda Archive.

Jewish World Policies—Jewish World Leadership

We have discussed the centers of world Jewish power. The unified plan is clear. That leads necessarily to the question, Is there some form of worldwide Jewish leadership that carries out this plan?

There are a series of international Jewish organizations to indicate that there is: the Alliance Israélite Universelle, the Independent Order of B'nai Briss [*sic*], the various Zionist agencies (e.g., the Jewish Agency), the international Jewish boycott organizations against Germany, the American Jewish Joint Consultative Council—to name only a few. All of these organizations promote Jewish world power policies in some way. How they relate to each other, which are the most significant, and whether there are secret connections and a central leadership and where that leadership might be, are subordinate questions. Whether or not there is an organized Jewish government recognized by all the Jews is less important than the fact that there is a unified and conscious Jewish desire for world power. This is proved by a variety of political events that are taking place in plain sight today.

What Does World Jewry Want Today?

We have already outlined in detail the fundamental aims of world Jewry. Its present activities are determined by the tactical situation. What does the situation look like today? Under the leadership of National Socialism, the German people have eliminated one of Jewry's three pillars. In many other countries, people are also beginning to wake up and see through the Jewish plans for domination. Jewry is therefore doing everything in its power *to defeat these awakening nations and to force them to give up their new racially oriented policies.* World Jewry is more united today than ever before. They [the Jews] foment hatred toward the awakening peoples with all the resources at their disposal. They depend most heavily, as we have shown, on world Bolshevism and world democracy. With ice-cold, diabolical calculation, they unleashed a new world war that they hoped would defeat the national-authoritarian nations. After defeating these nations, the way would once again be open to establish Jewish domination of the remaining nations. The immutable and lunatic goal of world Jewry is and remains: ruling all the nations by controlling their government organs, their territory, their money, and all their goods.

Jewry will not bring these awakening nations to their knees; rather, the example of these nations will finally awaken the people who are still being lulled into sleep by "democratic" or Bolshevist rule. That will be the time for a *final solution to the Jewish Question.* As *Reichsleiter* Alfred Rosenberg said in his speech on the Jewish question to diplomats and the world press on 7 February 1939, this can only occur by removing the Jews from every nation where they have lived as parasites and transporting them to a sufficiently large, uninhabited area suitable for colonization.

How little Jewry has understood the gravity of its situation, threatened by the racial awakening of nations, is evident in its reaction to the emigration question. Jewry wants Palestine. In order to make it possible for the Jews of every nation to move to one place? Not at all. Such a thing is impossible. Palestine could hold only a small percentage of the

Jews. The four hundred thousand Jews who currently live in the midst of nine hundred thousand Arabs (with more than thirty million Arabs in surrounding countries!). Even if, in violation of all principles of justice, the Palestinian Arabs now living there were forced out to make room for the Jews, it would be impossible for a significant part of the world's Jews to move there.

As Alfred Rosenberg pointed out in his speech, Jewry is promoting the Palestine project for entirely different reasons. It wants to establish a center of power that will provide Jews remaining in those other countries a valuable legal and governmental base. A relatively small, purely Jewish state in Palestine would provide the powerful Jewish groups in other nations with the status of a respectable minority, the right of asylum, diplomatic representation, and similar benefits. It is not a satisfactory solution to the Jewish Question, since it leaves the Jews to continue their parasitic existence among the other nations and indeed gives them new advantages.

The Jews have no serious intention of establishing colonies. That would not be difficult for a people of seventeen million, or perhaps twice that number if one includes all who are racially Jewish. They have vast resources and have already made major strides toward their goal of dominating the nations. It would not be difficult for them to secure a suitable territory. That would be a worthy goal for world Jewish capital. But the rich and powerful Jews of the Bolshevist clique of despots, or in the huge trusts in the United States, or the international banks in England and many other countries, feel too comfortable to undertake such a difficult, economically unfeasible endeavor. It hardly seems necessary to go to the trouble of bringing all Jews together in one place.

Developments will force them in that direction, however. One day there will be only one escape, a single honest way to solve the Jewish Question. Then for the first time in three thousand years, the Jew will have his own land, which—in the words of his own creation story—he can "cultivate by the sweat of his brow," the same sweat he has always disdainfully dismissed as being beneath him.

There is enough room on the earth for the Jews. A number of possibilities have already been mentioned: Kenya in the British Empire is two and a half times the size of England, and only 18,000 whites, some Indians, and Arabs, and 3.1 million blacks live there. Rhodesia is three times as large as England, but only 10,000 Europeans and 1.5 million blacks live there. British Guyana is a large and fertile land the size of Yugoslavia. It is still almost entirely unsettled. Large parts of Australia are still uninhabited. French Madagascar is another possibility, and there are others as well. Without going into all the details, it is clear that the question of finding a suitable place for the Jews depends only on their own desire and that of their protectors. That desire is lacking. The future of world Jewry depends on its bowing one day to the pressures of the situation.

The Decisive Battle Has Begun!

Our goal is not to predict the future. We see things as they have developed so far and evaluate the forces currently in motion. These forces, however, already exclude certain "solutions" to the Jewish question. The Jews can no longer hope for a halt to the awakening of nations or for a defeat of the authoritarian states.

> If international finance Jewry in and outside Europe succeeds in plunging nations into another world war, then the end result will not be the Bolshevization of the planet and thus the victory of the Jews—it will be the annihilation of the Jewish race in Europe!

The *Führer* gave the Jews a clear warning in these words on 30 June [*sic*] 1939 [see document 350 in this chapter]. International Jewry has succeeded in plunging humanity into another world war, but the results of the tremendous battle so far have made it clear that the Jewish string pullers have miscalculated this time. Jewish domination of Europe has been broken and will never return. Jewish world politics in the old manner is no longer acceptable to the rest of the world. They must fail. The result of the violent current conflict will not be the establishment of Jewish control over the world but *rather a just new order in which all constructive nations will build.*

28

The Annihilation of European Jewry, 1942–1945

HITLER PROBABLY NEVER COMMITTED to paper an explicit order to exterminate European Jewry. However, the decision to murder all Jews under Nazi control was likely made between September 1941 and January 1942. On 12 December 1941, the day after Germany declared war on the United States, Hitler gave a speech to the leaders of the Nazi Party in Berlin, some of which Goebbels recorded in his diary. "In respect of the Jewish question, the Führer has decided to make a clean sweep. The world war is here, the annihilation of the Jews must be the necessary result. This question is to be regarded without sentimentalism. We are not here to have sympathy with the Jews, but rather with our German people. If the German people have sacrificed 160,000 dead in the eastern campaign, so the authors of this bloody conflict will have to pay for it with their lives."[1] By then, more than a million Jews had already been murdered by death squads, the SS *Einsatzgruppen,* together with local irregulars, mostly in Poland, the Baltic countries, and in the Soviet Union (after the German invasion on 22 June 1941). One of the first systematic mass murders of the Jews occurred on 30 November 1941 at Rambula (Latvia), an action carried out by local Latvian auxiliaries as well as the SS. Others died in large numbers in the Polish ghettos as a result of mass starvation and draconian deportations to the east in the fall of 1941. The use of gas vans as a method of killing was introduced in Chelmno at the beginning of December 1941; even earlier, this method had been used to murder Jews declared unfit for work in the Belzec extermination camp. (The gas vans were first used in "Action T4," the *euthanasia* program that killed the mentally ill and disabled between 1939 and 1941. Even after the cancellation of the program, the practice continued unofficially until 1945. Jewish patients were disproportionately murdered in this action.)

The first invitations to the (subsequently postponed) Wannsee Conference, at which Nazi leaders discussed the extermination plan in some detail, were printed in early December, and the meeting eventually took place on 20 January. The Wannsee Protocol summarizing the meeting was marked "top secret" and was made available to a select group of Nazi administrators to inform them of the decisions already taken and to clarify problems arising from their implementation in different countries. Once the war began, it became evident that Hitler intended to make good on his 30 January 1939 promise that the Jews were responsible for the war and would suffer the consequences. Moreover, in early 1942, the killing process accelerated dramatically; the policy of deportation, ghettoization, and even mass shootings was replaced with a comprehensive approach to the annihilation of European Jewry. After the invasion of the Soviet Union on 22 June 1941 and the declaration of war by Nazi Germany against the United States in December, the Nazi elite viewed the war as an existential struggle between Germany and the forces of world Jewry. In appropriating the concept of *Lebensraum,* or living space, the Nazis expanded the notion of territorial expansion to include economic and racial hegemony. By 1942, military planners were aware that the conquered territories had to supply German troops and civilians with food; to do so, they were willing to sacrifice the Slavs, if need be, and most certainly the Jews, who were marked for extinction. This became the mantra of German anti-Semitic propaganda, exemplified in a 1943 pamphlet from the Central Office for Racial Policy: "The Führer's words at the beginning of the war will be fulfilled: the German people will not be annihilated in this war but rather the

Jew." The most explicit statement by any Nazi leader about the "annihilation of the Jewish people" was *SS-Reichsführer* Heinrich Himmler's secret speech to the SS and high party functionaries in Posen on 4 October 1943. Its most infamous lines, "Most of you must know what it means to see a hundred corpses lie side by side, or five hundred, or a thousand. To have stuck this out, and—excepting cases of human weakness—to have kept our integrity, that is what has made us hard," is a candid statement starkly presenting the "ethic" of the ideal SS man.

By the end of 1943, the murder of the Jews was an open secret. In February, a report circulated by the Security Service described broad support for Hitler and for the notion that the "war against the Jews shall be prosecuted unremittingly." Dr. Walter Gross (1904–45), head of the Rassenpolitisches Amt der NSDAP (Racial-Political Office of the NSDAP), published his *Racial Political Prerequisites for the Solution of the Jewish Problem,* which speaks of the "final elimination" of the Jewish problem. Hitler assured Hans Frank that the *Generalgouvernement* would not have to absorb the Jews being sent to Poland in ever-greater numbers because Poland would eventually be made free of Jews (*Judenfrei*).

The expansion of the German-occupied lands in Eastern Europe created a constant stream of new deportations to the ghettos of Poland and beyond. Fifteen-year-old Dawid Sierakowiak described the conditions for Jews in Łódź in his diary: "We are returning to the Middle Ages. The yellow patch once again becomes a part of Jewish dress. Today, an order was announced that all Jews, no matter what age or sex, have to wear a band of 'Jewish-yellow,' 10 centimeters wide, on their right arm, just below the armpit. In addition, Jews are forbidden to leave their apartments between five in the afternoon and eight in the morning."[2] By 30 April 1940, more and more Jews had been forced into the ghetto, which was hermetically sealed off from the rest of the city. Soon there were 160,000 Jews in a ghetto with no sewage system. Reeking carts roamed the streets daily to take human waste to Marischin, which doubled as the ghetto's cemetery and waste pit. The "houses" were for the most part wooden shanties, regularly prone to fires. Only 757 of the 30,000 buildings had running water.

The war radicalized both rhetoric and reality. As Goebbels publicly stated in 1940, "Every Jew is our enemy in this historic conflict, regardless of whether he sits vegetating in a Polish ghetto or carries on his parasitic existence in Berlin or Hamburg or blows the trumpets of war in New York or Washington" (see document 359 in chapter 27). Until the ghettos were liquidated in 1944, they became, at least on their surface, places of employment that "made the Jews work." In each Jewish community, a Judenrat (Council of Jewish Elders) was set up and, as Reinhard Heydrich laid out in a policy statement about the treatment of Polish Jews, "made *fully responsible,* in the literal sense of the word, for the exact and prompt implementation of directives already issued or to be issued in the future." In Łódź, the second-largest ghetto, the visible face of the Judenrat was that of the "King of the Ghetto," Mordechai Chaim Rumkowski (1877–1944, murdered in Auschwitz), the former director of the Jewish orphanage in Łódź and one of the most controversial figures in the history of the Holocaust. He was an older, distinguished-looking man who strongly believed he had a mission to rescue as many Jews as possible.

Though he was closely watched over by the Nazi official Hans Biebow, Rumkowski exerted inordinate power in the ghetto, using his autocratic style of leadership to create an enormous manufacturing complex to produce goods on behalf of Germany, in an effort to stave off deportation and destruction. Nevertheless, starvation and disease, combined with the ever-more-irrational behavior of Rumkowski—who even had currency and postage stamps printed with his visage—fueled dissatisfaction, which he then stifled by means of the Jewish police. If the Jews of the ghetto were productive, he argued, they could counteract the Nazi (and Polish) stereotype of the Jew as an idler who avoided work at all costs, whether it was physical labor in the fields, factory work, or war service. Rumkowski played on this myth of the unproductive Jew and told his fellow residents that the ghetto had to be seen as valuable to the German war effort. His model was Jewish productivity in the economy of Łódź, now transferred to the example of Jews' hard work in the ghetto. In the Litzmannstadt ghetto, everyone had to work according to Rumkowski's "survival through work strategy."

The brutal treatment of the Jews in the ghettos naturally frightened other victims of the brutal Nazi occupation of Poland, Ukraine, and western Russia. As Frank noted in his diary on January 1943, Poles worried that "after the Jews have been destroyed, then they [the Nazis] will employ the same methods to get the Poles out of this territory and liquidate them just like the Jews." Many pious Jews, among them Hillel Zeitlin and Dr. Israel Milejkowski, recognized that no good could come out of the ghetto but believed that "our salvation lies only in an inner religious awakening capable of working miracles." Still, some Jewish leaders clung for a time to the illusion that they could continue to negotiate for the survival of the Jewish inhabitants in the Polish ghettos. At the end of July 1942, Adam Czerniaków (1880–1942), the president of the Warsaw Ghetto Council, was confronted with the German demand that he provide orders for the deportation of thousands of ghetto inhabitants to the east, including the elderly and children in orphanages. Rather than submit, Czerniaków committed suicide as an act of protest, as Stefan Ernest recorded in his secret diary of the time. By contrast, in Łódź on 4 September 1943, the Germans demanded that children up to age ten, the elderly, invalids, and those unable to work be handed over. Despite the panic that ensued, Rumkowski declared the measure to be "necessary" and announced that "nothing could be done to prevent it." He ordered the Jewish police to round up the people chosen by ghetto leaders, an event recorded with sober bitterness by Józef Zelkowicz (1897–1944). Rumkowski's compliance was controversial—the Łódź ghetto was the first established and the last liquidated—but, as Zelkowicz wrote, "the bloody page of this history should be inscribed with black letters for all those officials who petitioned to have some role in this action."

The questions of how the Jews in the ghetto were able to organize resistance and whether their actions were too little too late are extremely difficult to answer. Certainly the events surrounding the "summons to resistance" in the Vilna ghetto (Lithuania) by partisan leader Abba Kovner (1918–87) demonstrate that a great deal of Jewish acculturation and longstanding strategies of accommodation had to be overcome in a very short period of time for Jews to act in concert, despite their knowledge that they faced almost certain death. In marked contrast to Łódź, where there was no uprising, Warsaw was the scene of the most famous revolt of European Jewry. In early 1943, as Stanislaw Sznapman recounted in his diary, those Jews who had been fortunate enough to survive the deportations well knew that they were being sent to their deaths, and on 19 April, they mounted armed resistance against the Germans, astonishing the world by holding out for four weeks until 16 May, when the "bloody glow" witnessed by Stefania Staszewska, a member of the Polish Workers Party, was extinguished, and the ghetto was razed by General Jürgen Stroop (1895–1952). Stroop's report to Heinrich Himmler gave a chilling description of the extensive preparation for resistance, the tenacity of the Jewish combatants, and the retaliatory measures taken by the SS against the ghetto residents once the fighting had ended.

In the spring of 1944, the Czech ghetto Theresienstadt, or Terezin, designated a "model ghetto" for the outside world, was purged of the sick, the aged, and the infirm to prepare for a visit by the Red Cross. Egon Redlich (1916–44), who witnessed the orchestration of the visit, the staging of the ghetto inhabitants' responses to questions, and the "embellishment" of the ghetto for the now-infamous 1944 propaganda film *The Führer Gives the Jews a City,* cynically registered the "beautification of the city."

Auschwitz has become a metaphor for the Holocaust. But in 1944, the word was almost unknown. In fact, it comprised two main camps, Auschwitz and Birkenau, in addition to several factories, including the Buna rubber complex and two facilities belonging to the

Krupp and Siemens firms. Despite his denials at his Nuremberg trial, Albert Speer, named minster of armaments in February 1942, was instrumental in the expansion of the camp and its use for armaments production, as noted in the minutes of the meeting held on 15 September 1942. A report published in November 1944 and authored by two Slovak Jews, Alfred Wetzler (1918–88) and Rudolf Vrba (1924–2006), who escaped from Auschwitz on 7 April 1944, was the first to reveal to the world the details of the site's operation as an extermination camp and to attempt an accounting of its victims. Zalmen Gradowski (1910–44), a member of the Sonderkommando (Special Command) unit (a group of inmates forced to prepare and clear the Auschwitz gas chambers and crematoria) meticulously recorded and buried his chronicle of the suffering and disorientation of those who died—including his own family—in "the murder of the children of our people." Gradowski himself was killed leading the Sonderkommando revolt in October 1944.

NOTES

1. Cited in Peter Longerich, *Holocaust: The Nazi Persecution and Murder of the Jews* (Oxford: Oxford University Press, 2010), 306.

2. *The Diary of Dawid Sierakowiak: Five Notebooks from the Łódź Ghetto,* edited by Alan Adelson, translated by Kamil Turowski (New York: Oxford University Press, 1996), 63.

363

REINHARD HEYDRICH

Policy and Operations Concerning Jews in the Occupied Territories

Issued 21 September 1939. Published in English in Lucy S. Dawidowicz, ed., *A Holocaust Reader* (West Orange, N.J.: Behrman House, 1976), 59–64.

The Chief of the Security Police

Berlin, September 21, 1939
Schnellbrief [Express Mail]
To *Chiefs of all Einsatzgruppen of the Security Police*
Subject: *Jewish Question in Occupied Territory*

I refer to the conference held in Berlin today, and again point out that the *planned total measures* (i.e., *Endziel* [the final aim]) are to be kept *strictly secret.*

Distinction must be made between:

1. the final aim (which will require extended periods of time) and
2. the stages leading to the fulfillment of this final aim (which will be carried out in short periods).

The planned measures require the most thorough preparation with regard to technical as well as economic aspects.

It is obvious that the tasks ahead cannot be laid down from here in full detail. The instructions and directives below must serve also for the purpose of urging chiefs of the *Einsatzgruppen* to give practical consideration [to the problems involved].

I

For the time being, the first prerequisite for the final aim is the concentration of the Jews from the countryside into the larger cities.

This is to be carried out speedily.

In doing so, distinction must be made

(1) between the zones of Danzig and West Prussia, Poznan, Eastern Upper Silesia, and

(2) the rest of the occupied territories.[1]

As far as possible, the areas referred to under (1) are to be cleared of Jews; at least the aim should be to establish only a few cities of concentration.

In the areas under (2), as few concentration centers as possible are to be set up, so as to facilitate subsequent measures. In this connection it should be borne in mind that only cities which are rail junctions, or are at least located on railroad lines, should be selected as concentration points.

On principle, Jewish communities of *less than 500 persons* are to be dissolved and transferred to the nearest concentration center.

This decree does not apply to the area of *Einsatzgruppe* 1, which is situated east of Cracow and is bounded roughly by *Polanice, Jaroslaw,* the new line of demarcation, and the former Slovak-Polish border. Within this area, only an approximate census of Jews is to be carried out. Furthermore, Councils of Jewish Elders (*Jüdische Ältestenräte*), as outlined below, are to be set up.

II

Councils of Jewish Elders

(1) In each Jewish community, a Council of Jewish Elders is to be set up which, as far as possible, is to be composed of the remaining authoritative personalities and rabbis.

The Council is to be composed of up to 24 male Jews (depending on the size of the Jewish community).

The Council is to be made *fully responsible,* in the literal sense of the word, for the exact and prompt implementation of directives already issued or to be issued in the future.

(2) In case of sabotage of such instructions, the Councils are to be warned that the most severe measures will be taken.

(3) The Jewish Councils (*Judenräte*) are to carry out an approximate census of the Jews of their areas, broken down if possible according to sex (and age groups): (a) up to 16 years, (b) from 16–20 years, and (c) above; and also according to the principal occupations. The results are to be reported in the shortest possible time.

(4) The Councils of Elders are to be informed of the date and time of the evacuation, the means available for evacuation, and, finally, the departure routes. They are then to be made personally responsible for the evacuation of the Jews from the countryside.

The reason to be given for the concentration of the Jews in the cities is that the Jews have taken a decisive part in sniper attacks and plundering.

(5) The Councils of Elders in the concentration centers are to be made responsible for the appropriate housing of the Jews arriving from the countryside.

For reasons of general police security, the concentration of the Jews in the cities will probably call for regulations in these cities that will forbid their entry to certain quarters completely and that—but with due regard to economic requirements—they may, for instance, not leave the ghetto, nor leave their homes after a certain hour in the evening, etc.

(6) The Councils of Elders are also to be made responsible for the suitable provisioning of the Jews during the transport to the cities.

There is no objection to the evacuated Jews taking with them their movable possessions insofar as that is technically possible.

(7) Jews who fail to comply with the order to move into cities are to be given a short additional period of grace where there was sufficient reason for the delay. They are to be warned of the most severe penalties if they fail to move by the later date set.

III

All necessary measures are, on principle, always to be taken in closest consultation and cooperation with the German civil administration and the competent local military authorities.

In the execution [of this plan], it must be taken into consideration that economic requirements in the occupied areas do not suffer.

(1) Above all, the needs of the army must be taken into consideration. For instance, for the time being, it will scarcely be possible to avoid, here and there, leaving behind some trade Jews who are absolutely essential for the provisioning of the troops, for lack of other possibilities. But in such cases the prompt Aryanization of these enterprises is to be planned and the move of the Jews to be completed in due course in cooperation with the competent local German administrative authorities.

(2) For the preservation of German economic interests in the occupied territories, it is obvious that Jewish-owned war and other essential industries, and also enterprises, industries and factories important to the Four-Year Plan, must be maintained for the time being.

In these cases also, prompt Aryanization must be aimed at, and the movement of the Jews completed later.

(3) Finally, the food situation in the occupied territories must be taken into consideration. For instance, as far as possible, land owned by Jewish settlers is to be handed over to the care of neighboring German or even Polish farmers to work on commission to ensure the harvesting of crops still standing in the fields and replanting.

With regard to this important question, contact is to be made with the agricultural expert of the Chief of the Civil Administration.

(4) In all cases in which it is not possible to coordinate the interests of the Security Police on the one hand and the German civil administration on the other, I am to be informed by the fastest route and my decision awaited before the particular measures in question are carried out.

IV

The Chiefs of the *Einsatzgruppen* are to report to me continuously on the following matters:

(1) Numerical survey of the Jews present in their areas (according to the above classifications, if possible). The numbers of Jews evacuated from the countryside and of those already in the cities is to be listed separately.

(2) Names of the cities that have been designated as concentration centers.

(3) The dates set for the Jews to move to the cities.

(4) Surveys of all the Jewish [owned] war and other vital industries and enterprises, or those important to the Four-Year Plan in their areas.

If possible, the following should be specified:

(a) Type of enterprise (with a statement on possible conversion to truly vital or war-important enterprises or ones of importance to the Four-Year Plan);

(b) Which factories should be most urgently Aryanized (in order to forestall possible losses);

What kind of Aryanization is proposed? Germans or Poles? (the decision contingent upon the importance of the enterprise);

(c) The number of Jews working in these factories (specify those in leading positions).

Can operations at the enterprise be continued without difficulty after the removal of the Jews, or will it be necessary to allocate German or possibly Polish workers in their place? In what numbers?

If Polish workers have to be used, care should be taken that they are drawn mainly from the former German provinces so as to begin to ease the problem there. These matters can be carried out only by means of coordination with the Labor Offices which have been set up.

V

In order to reach the planned aims, I expect the fullest cooperation of the whole manpower of the Security Police and the SD.

The Chiefs of neighboring *Einsatzgruppen* are to establish contact with each other immediately in order to cover the areas in question completely.

VI

The High Command of the Army; the Plenipotentiary for the Four-Year Plan (attention: Secretary of State *Neumann*), the Reich Ministry for the Interior (attention: State Secretary *Stuckart),* for Food and the Economy (attention: State Secretary *Landfried*), as well as the Chiefs of Civil Administration of the Occupied Territories have received copies of this decree.

signed Heydrich

Note

1. The areas of Danzig, West Prussia, Posen, Eastern Upper Silesia were to be incorporated into Germany, whereas the rest of the occupied territory of Poland would comprise the *Generalgouvernement.* —Eds.

364

Wannsee Protocol

Minutes taken on 20 January 1942. "The Wannsee Protocol." U.S. government translation prepared for evidence in the Nuremberg trials, published in John Mendelsohn, ed., *The Holocaust: Selected Documents in Eighteen Volumes,* vol. 11, *The Wannsee Protocol and a 1944 Report on Auschwitz by the Office of Strategic Services* (New York: Garland, 1982), 18–32.

Stamp: Top Secret
Minutes of discussion.

I

The following persons took part in the discussion about the final solution of the Jewish question, which took place in Berlin, am Großen Wannsee No. 56/58 on January 20th, 1942.

Gauleiter Dr. Meyer and *Reichsamtleiter* Dr. Leibbrandt, Reich Ministry for the Occupied Eastern Territories

Secretary of State Dr. Stuckart, Reich Ministry for the Interior

Secretary of State Neumann, Plenipotentiary for the Four-Year Plan

Secretary of State Dr. Freisler, Reich Ministry of Justice

Secretary of State Dr. Bühler, Office of the General Government
Under Secretary of State Luther, Foreign Office

SS-Oberführer Klopfer, Party Chancellery

Ministerialdirektor Kritzinger, Reich Chancellery

SS-Gruppenführer Hofmann, Race and Settlement Central Office

SS-Gruppenführer Müller and *SS-Obersturmbannführer* Eichmann, Reich Central Security Office

SS-Oberführer Dr. Schöngarth, Security Police and SD Commander of the Security Police and the SD in the General Government

SS-Sturmbannführer Dr. Lange, Security Police and SD Commander of the Security Police and the SD for the General-District Latvia, as deputy of the Commander of the Security Police and the SD for the Reich Commissariat "Eastland."

II

At the beginning of the discussion, Chief of the Security Police and of the SD, *SS-Obergruppenführer* Heydrich, reported that the Reich Marshal had appointed him delegate for the preparations for the final solution of the Jewish question in Europe and pointed out that this discussion had been called for the purpose of clarifying fundamental questions. The wish of the Reich Marshal to have a draft sent to him concerning organizational, factual and material interests in relation to the final solution of the Jewish question in Europe makes necessary an initial common action of all central offices immediately concerned with these questions in order to bring their general activities into line. The *Reichsführer-SS* and the Chief of the German Police (Chief of the Security Police and the SD) was entrusted with the official central handling of the final solution of the Jewish question without regard to geographic borders. The Chief of the Security Police and the SD then gave a short report of the struggle that has been carried on thus far against this enemy, the essential points being the following:

(a) the expulsion of the Jews from every sphere of life of the German people,

(b) the expulsion of the Jews from the living space of the German people.

In carrying out these efforts, an increased and planned acceleration of the emigration of the Jews from Reich territory was started as the only possible present solution.

By order of the Reich Marshal, a Reich Central Office for Jewish Emigration was set up in January 1939 and the Chief of the Security Police and SD entrusted with the management. Its most important tasks were

(a) to make all necessary arrangements for the preparation for an increased emigration of the Jews,

(b) to direct the flow of emigration,

(c) to speed the procedure of emigration in each individual case.

The aim of all this was to cleanse German living space of Jews in a legal manner.

All the offices realized the drawbacks of such enforced accelerated emigration. For the time being they had, however, tolerated it on account of the lack of other possible solutions of the problem.

The work concerned with emigration was, later on, not only a German problem, but also a problem with which the authorities of the countries to which the flow of emigrants was being directed would have to deal. Financial difficulties, such as the demand by various foreign governments for increasing sums of money to be presented at the time of the landing, the lack of shipping space, increasing restriction of entry permits, or the canceling of such, increased extraordinarily the difficulties of emigration. In spite of these difficulties, 537,000 Jews were sent out of the country between the takeover of power and the deadline of October 31st, 1941. Of these

approximately 360,000 were in Germany proper on January 30th, 1933

approximately 147,000 were in Austria (Ostmark) on March 15th, 1939

approximately 30,000 were in the Protectorate of Bohemia and Moravia on March 15th, 1939.

The Jews themselves, or their Jewish political organizations, financed the emigration. In order to avoid impoverished Jews remaining behind, the principle was followed that wealthy Jews have to finance the emigration of poor Jews; this was arranged by imposing a suitable tax, i.e., an emigration tax, which was used for financial arrangements in connection with the emigration of poor Jews and was imposed according to income.

Apart from the necessary *Reichsmark* exchange, foreign currency had to be presented at the time of landing. In order to save foreign exchange held by Germany, the foreign Jewish financial organizations were—with the help of Jewish organizations in Germany—made responsible for arranging an adequate amount of foreign currency. Up to October 30th, 1941, these foreign Jews donated a total of around 9,500,000 dollars.

In the meantime, the *Reichsführer*-SS and Chief of the German Police had prohibited emigration of Jews due to the dangers of an emigration in wartime and due to the possibilities of the East.

III

Another possible solution of the problem has now taken the place of emigration, i.e. the evacuation of the Jews to the East, provided that the *Führer* gives the appropriate approval in advance.

These actions are, however, only to be considered provisional, but practical experience is already being collected which is of the greatest importance in relation to the future final solution of the Jewish question.

Approximately 11 million Jews will be involved in the final solution of the European Jewish question, distributed as follows among the individual countries:

Country	Number
A. Germany proper	131,800
Austria	43,700
Eastern territories	420,000
Generalgouvernement	2,284,000
Bialystok	400,000
Protectorate Bohemia and Moravia	74,200
Estonia—free of Jews	
Latvia	3,500
Lithuania	34,000
Belgium	43,000
Denmark	5,600
France/occupied territory	165,000
Unoccupied territory	700,000
Greece	69,600
Netherlands	160,800
Norway	1,300
B. Bulgaria	48,000
England	330,000
Finland	2,300
Ireland	4,000
Italy including Sardinia	58,000
Albania	200
Croatia	40,000
Portugal	3,000
Rumania including Bessarabia	342,000
Sweden	8,000
Switzerland	18,000
Serbia	10,000
Slovakia	88,000
Spain	6,000
Turkey (European portion)	55,500
Hungary	742,800
USSR	5,000,000
Ukraine	2,994,684
White Russia, excluding Bialystok	446,484
Total	over 11,000,000

The number of Jews given here for foreign countries includes, however, only those Jews who still adhere to the Jewish faith, since some countries still do not have a definition of the term "Jew" according to racial principles.

The handling of the problem in the individual countries will meet with difficulties due to the attitude and outlook of the people there, especially in Hungary and Rumania. Thus, for example, even today the Jew can buy documents in Rumania that will officially prove his foreign citizenship.

The influence of the Jews in all walks of life in the USSR is well known. Approximately five million Jews live in the European part of the USSR, in the Asian part scarcely 1/4 million.

The breakdown of Jews residing in the European part of the USSR according to trades was approximately as follows:

Agriculture	9.1%
Urban workers	14.8%
In trade	20.0%
Employed by the state	23.4%
In private occupations such as medical profession, press, theater, etc.	32.7%

Under proper guidance, in the course of the final solution the Jews are to be allocated for appropriate labor in the East. Able-bodied Jews, separated according to sex, will be taken in large work columns to these areas for work on roads, in the course of which action doubtless a large portion will be eliminated by natural causes.

The possible final remnant will, since it will undoubtedly consist of the most resistant portion, have to be treated accordingly, because it is the product of natural selection and would, if released, act as the seed of a new Jewish revival (see the experience of history).

In the course of the practical execution of the final solution, Europe will be combed through from west to east. Germany proper, including the Protectorate of Bohemia and Moravia, will have to be handled first due to the housing problem and additional social and political necessities.

The evacuated Jews will first be sent, group by group, to so-called transit ghettos, from which they will be transported to the East.

SS-*Obergruppenführer* Heydrich went on to say that an important prerequisite for the evacuation as such is the exact definition of the persons involved.

It is not intended to evacuate Jews over 65 years old, but to send them to an old-age ghetto—Theresienstadt is being considered for this purpose.

In addition to these age groups—of the approximately 280,000 Jews in Germany proper and Austria on October 31st, 1941, approximately 30% are over 65 years old—severely wounded veterans and Jews with war decorations (Iron Cross I) will be accepted in the old-age ghettos. With this expedient solution, in one fell swoop many interventions will be prevented.

The beginning of the individual larger evacuation actions will largely depend on military developments. Regarding the handling of the final solution in those European countries occupied and influenced by us, it was proposed that the appropriate expert of the Foreign Office discuss the matter with the responsible official of the Security Police and SD.

In Slovakia and Croatia the matter is no longer so difficult, since the most substantial problems in this respect have already been brought near a solution. In Rumania the government has in the meantime also appointed a commissioner for Jewish affairs. In order to settle the question in Hungary, it will soon be necessary to force an adviser for Jewish questions onto the Hungarian government.

With regard to taking up preparations for dealing with the problem in Italy, SS-*Obergruppenführer* Heydrich considers it opportune to contact the chief of police with a view to these problems.

In occupied and unoccupied France, the registration of Jews for evacuation will, in all probability, proceed without great difficulty.

Under Secretary of State Luther calls attention in this matter to the fact that in some countries, such as the Scandinavian states, difficulties will arise if this problem is dealt with thoroughly and that it will therefore be advisable to defer actions in these countries. Besides, in view of the small numbers of Jews affected, this deferral will not cause any substantial limitation.

The Foreign Office sees no great difficulties for southeast and western Europe.

SS-*Gruppenführer* Hofmann plans to send an expert to Hungary from the Race and Settlement Main Office for general orientation at the time when the Chief of the Security

Police and SD takes up the matter there. It was decided to assign this expert from the Race and Settlement Main Office, who will not work actively, as an assistant to the police attaché.

IV

In the course of the final solution plans, the Nuremberg Laws should provide a certain foundation, in which a prerequisite for the absolute solution of the problem is also the solution to the problem of mixed marriages and persons of mixed blood.

The Chief of the Security Police and the SD discussed the following points, at first theoretically, in regard to a letter from the chief of the Reich chancellery:

(1) Treatment of Persons of Mixed Blood of the First Degree. Persons of mixed blood of the first degree will, as regards the final solution of the Jewish question, be treated as Jews. From this treatment the following exceptions will be made:

(a) Persons of mixed blood of the first degree married to persons of German blood if their marriage has resulted in children (persons of mixed blood of the second degree). These persons of mixed blood of the second degree are to be treated essentially as Germans.

(b) Persons of mixed blood of the first degree for whom the highest offices of the Party and State have already issued exemption permits in any sphere of life. Each individual case must be examined, and it is not ruled out that the decision may be made to the detriment of the person of mixed blood.

The prerequisite for any exemption must always be the personal merit of the person of mixed blood. (Not the merit of the parent or spouse of German blood.)

Persons of mixed blood of the first degree who are exempted from evacuation will be sterilized in order to prevent any offspring and to eliminate the problem of persons of mixed blood once and for all. Such sterilization will be voluntary. But it is required to remain in the Reich. The sterilized "person of mixed blood" is thereafter free of all restrictions to which he was previously subjected.

(2) Treatment of Persons of Mixed Blood of the Second Degree. Persons of mixed blood of the second degree will be treated fundamentally as persons of German blood, with the exception of the following cases, in which the persons of mixed blood of the second degree will be considered as Jews:

(a) The person of mixed blood of the second degree was born of a marriage in which both parents are persons of mixed blood.

(b) The person of mixed blood of the second degree has a racially especially undesirable appearance that marks him outwardly as a Jew.

(c) The person of mixed blood of the second degree has a particularly bad police and political record that shows that he feels and behaves like a Jew.

Also in these cases exemptions should not be made if the person of mixed blood of the second degree has married a person of German blood.

(3) Marriages between Full Jews and Persons of German Blood. Here it must be decided from case to case whether the Jewish partner will be evacuated or whether, with regard to the effects of such a step on the German relatives, [this mixed marriage] should be sent to an old-age ghetto.

(4) Marriages between Persons of Mixed Blood of the First Degree and Persons of German Blood

(a) Without Children. If no children have resulted from the marriage, the person of mixed blood of the first degree will be evacuated or sent to an old-age ghetto (same treatment as in the case of marriages between full Jews and persons of German blood, point 3.)

(b) With Children. If children have resulted from the marriage (persons of mixed blood of the second degree), they will, if they are to be treated as Jews, be evacuated or sent to a ghetto along with the parent of mixed blood of the first degree. If these children are to be treated as Germans (regular cases), they are exempted from evacuation, as is therefore the parent of mixed blood of the first degree.

(5) Marriages between Persons of Mixed Blood of the First Degree and Persons of Mixed Blood of the First Degree or Jews. In these marriages all members of the family (including the children) will be treated as Jews and therefore be evacuated or sent to an old-age ghetto.

(6) Marriages between Persons of Mixed Blood of the First Degree and Persons of Mixed Blood of the Second Degree. In these marriages both partners will be evacuated or sent to an old-age ghetto without consideration of whether the marriage has produced children, since possible children will as a rule have stronger Jewish blood than the Jewish person of mixed blood of the second degree.

SS-*Gruppenführer* Hofmann advocates the opinion that sterilization will have to be widely used, since the person of mixed blood who is given the choice whether he will be evacuated or sterilized would rather undergo sterilization.

State Secretary Dr. Stuckart maintains that carrying out in practice of the just mentioned possibilities for solving the problem of mixed marriages and persons of mixed blood will create endless administrative work. In the second place, as the biological facts cannot be disregarded in any case, State Secretary Dr. Stuckart proposed proceeding to forced sterilization.

Furthermore, to simplify the problem of mixed marriages possibilities must be considered with the goal of the legislator saying something like: "These marriages have been dissolved."

With regard to the issue of the effect of the evacuation of Jews on the economy, State Secretary Neumann stated that Jews who are working in industries vital to the war effort, provided that no replacements are available, cannot be evacuated.

SS-*Obergruppenführer* Heydrich indicated that these Jews would not be evacuated according to the rules he had approved for carrying out the evacuations then underway.

State Secretary Dr. Bühler stated that the *Generalgouvernement* would welcome it if the final solution of this problem could be begun in the *Generalgouvernement,* since on the one hand transportation does not play such a large role here nor would problems of labor supply hamper this action. Jews must be removed from the territory of the *Generalgouvernement* as quickly as possible, since it is especially here that the Jew as an epidemic carrier represents an extreme danger and on the other hand he is causing permanent chaos in the economic structure of the country through continued black market dealings. Moreover, of the approximately 2 1/2 million Jews concerned, the majority is unfit for work.

State Secretary Dr. Bühler stated further that the solution to the Jewish question in the *Generalgouvernement* is the responsibility of the Chief of the Security Police and the SD and that his efforts would be supported by the officials of the *Generalgouvernement.* He had only one request, to solve the Jewish question in this area as quickly as possible.

In conclusion the different types of possible solutions were discussed, during which discussion both *Gauleiter* Dr. Meyer and State Secretary Dr. Bühler took the position that certain preparatory activities for the final solution should be carried out immediately in the territories in question, in which process alarming the populace must be avoided.

The meeting was closed with the request of the Chief of the Security Police and the SD to the participants that they afford him appropriate support during the carrying out of the tasks involved in the solution.

365

SECRET REPORT OF THE SECURITY SERVICE OF THE REICHSFÜHRER SS

Battle against the Jews

First circulated on 22 January 1942 as "Kampf gegen die Juden." First published in *Meldungen aus dem Reich 1938–1945. Die geheimen Lageberichte des Sicherheitsdienstes der SS,* (Herrsching: Pawlak Verlag, 1984), 9:3196, 3197.

The recent denunciation of the Jews and the attendant invocation of the Old Testament logic of an "eye for an eye, tooth for a tooth" has been interpreted to refer to the notion that the Führer's war against the Jews shall be prosecuted unremittingly to its end and that it will not be much longer before the last Jew has been driven from European soil.

Reports are unanimous in confirming that what interests people most is the part of the Führer's speech in which he addresses the situation in the east. The German *Volk* listened to the Führer in profound gratitude when he reported that the shift in strategy from an offensive to a defensive position was successful and that the Bolshevists would no longer be able to use the opportunity presented by the coming winter to their advantage. The Führer's reassurance that the worst part of the war against Bolshevism was already behind us left a particularly lasting impression. Many people were deeply moved and inspired with the confidence of victory upon hearing those portions of the speech in which the Führer declared his willingness to accept full responsibility—the same responsibility that compelled him to occupy the position of commander in chief—and it only served to strengthen their faith in the Führer. The entire German *Volk* was sincerely impressed by the unconditional certainty of victory expressed by the Führer. The Führer repeatedly reassured listeners of his willingness to accept full personal responsibility for the Eastern Campaign and thus succeeded in defusing rumors that were still in limited circulation in conjunction with the scandal surrounding [Walther von] Brauchitsch.[1]

The Führer's description of his experience as an infantry soldier, as the first musketeer of the Reich, was received with enthusiasm and only further solidified confidence in the Führer because it was seen as reassurance that the Führer would be familiar with the concerns and suffering of soldiers from his own experience and that he would therefore do everything in his power to improve their situation and—to the degree that it was possible—to make their lives tolerable. The Führer's comparison between the contemporary situation in Germany and the one that Frederick the Great had to overcome was described as particularly "apt and felicitous" and served to bolster confidence about a final victory amongst the German people.

The Führer's statements about his not being able to tell people when exactly the war will be over elicited disappointment from only a few individuals; the rest of the German people had resigned themselves to the thought of a long war.

Note

1. Field Marshal Walther von Brauchitsch (1881–1948) was relieved of his command in December 1941, after the failure of the German army to take Moscow.—Eds.

366

REICH LEADER SS/SS MAIN OFFICE

The Jew

First published as "Der Jude," in *Rassenpolitik, Der Reichsführer SS, SS-Hauptamt* (Berlin: Der Reichsführer SS/SS-Hauptamt, 1943), 7. Translated by Randall Bytwerk. Calvin College, German Propaganda Archive.

It was primarily Jews who first formulated and subsequently expanded upon the teachings of equality in the church, liberalism, and Marxism and who were the most fanatic proponents of the idea. The Jew Paul spread the Christian doctrine of equality. Freemasonry dominated the intellectual world of the French Revolution, and liberalism grew out of Freemasonry, whose direction has always been influenced by the Jew. The Portuguese-born English Jew [David] Ricardo, the "father of classical national economics," is the prophet of the liberal economic theory of free trade and economic piracy. The foundation of Marxism and Bolshevism is *Das Kapital,* by the Jew Mardochai ([Karl] Marx).

How did the Jew gain this destructive power over the European peoples? The Jews are a mixed race. The essential characteristic that separates them from all other races and peoples is the instinct for parasitism. This has been expressed most clearly by members of the Jewish race themselves. Karl Marx, the author of *Das Kapital,* says, "What is the essential trait of Jewry? Practicality, self-interest. What is the culture of the Jew? Haggling. What is his god? Money." The Jewish philosopher Spinoza said, "What we require is simple: that we control everything necessary for our own good."

The parasitic instinct of the Jew is clear in his ability to adjust to the host peoples. A characteristic example is the relationship of the Jew to language: Even before the beginning of the common era, the Jewish people had changed their language several times. Wherever they went, they took on the host language, though most of them were unable to conceal the racial accent in their speech.

Yet, the Jews are one of the most racially conscious peoples. The laws of the Old Testament and the Talmud strongly prohibit marriage with non-Jews. Leading Jews have always stressed the importance of race and racial purity. Even the Soviet Union, otherwise opposed to race, had passed measures to protect Jewish blood. The best-known statement comes from the Jew Benjamin Disraeli (originally d'Israeli, later Lord Beaconsfeld), the longtime British prime minister: "No one may be indifferent to the racial principle, the racial question. It is the key to world history. History is often confusing because it is written by people who did not understand the racial question and the aspects relevant to it . . . Race is everything, and every race that does not keep its blood from being mixed will perish . . . Language and religion do not determine a race—blood determines it."

His parasitic instincts led the Jew to hold his own race pure and to strike other races at the core of their being, their racial nature. Only when a people's racial purity has been destroyed is the Jew able to develop freely and without restraint. Disraeli's political policies prove that many Jews consciously work to destroy racial purity. He made Queen Elizabeth [*sic,* Victoria] empress of India, creating an opening in England for Oriental lifestyles. He misled the English people with the notion of an Oriental empire, thereby dulling and falsifying English racial instincts. The Jew also betrayed the peoples of Russia with images of heaven on earth, leading to widespread race mixing, greatly accelerating a process of decay already in progress. The Jew could realize his plans for world domination only when Russia had become weak, without instincts, without culture. That is how we understand [Theodor] Mommsen's description of the Jewish people as the "ferment of decomposition." As a result, there can never be peace, but only combat, between the Jew and racially aware peoples. Europe will have defeated this threat only when the last Jew has left our part of the planet. The Führer's words at the beginning of the war will be fulfilled: the German people will not be annihilated in this war but rather the Jew.

367

HILLEL ZEITLIN AND DR. ISRAEL MILEJKOWSKI

Evaluating the Ghetto

Interview in Warsaw, 1941

First published in *Bleter far geschikhte* 1, no. 2 (1948). Published in English in Lucy S. Dawidowicz, ed., *A Holocaust Reader* (West Orange, N.J.: Behrman House, 1976), 218–25.

Hillel Zeitlin

Q: *Do you see any positive factors in the ghetto?*

Unfortunately I see only negative ones: hunger, epidemics, mass mortality. The area of culture is precisely where something positive could be created. Within the ghetto walls a Jewish culture of our own, a Jewish life, could emerge, but Jews are a contrary people. They speak Polish with such ardor. Polish has become the holy language of the ghetto, the holy tongue of the ghetto Jews.

This is something simply paradoxical. They packed us into the ghetto so they could forcibly isolate us from other peoples, cultures, and languages. Yet we insist on speaking a foreign language and spit on our own language, our own cultural and spiritual values. We see something similar with the Sabbath. For years Jews in Poland fought against Sunday observance laws, but now that Jews in the ghetto can observe the Sabbath and do business on Sundays, they insist on doing business just on the Sabbath.

A misfortune has occurred. Assimilation has made its way from Snob Hill to the ghetto and influences the whole Jewish quarter.

Q: *How do you explain the odd liberalism and tolerance with regard to converts in the ghetto?*

Jews are a compassionate people. As long as the apostates were in the camp of our persecutors, we hated them. But now that they are together with us in the camp of the persecuted,[1] we pity them. "Toleration" even goes so far that the converts among us now find themselves in a privileged position. There are good public kitchens run by the Żydowskie Towarzystwo Opieki Społecznej (Jewish Society for Public Welfare, after 1940, ŻTOS) especially for converts and the meals there are much better than those in the regular kitchens. Such is the concern of the converts. It has already come to the point that people rush to convert so as to get a better meal.

While speaking of converts, we ought to mention the deplorable role of the Kehilla, which shows favoritism to the converts, provides them the best jobs, and puts them in the forefront in our communal life in the ghetto.

Q: *What is the source of this love our community leaders have for converts?*

It springs from the fact that there are in the Kehilla concealed, disguised assimilationists who have contempt for Yiddish, Jewish culture, and the Jewish populace.

Q: *How can you explain the decline and weakening of religious life in the ghetto? History teaches us, after all, that always when the trials of the Jews increased, religious faith increased and the people clung more firmly to their faith, to Torah.*

Yes, it is unfortunately a sorrowful fact that religious life in the ghetto has declined considerably. The Sabbath is vanishing. Of the 220 families in the building where I live barely two or three observe the Sabbath. If our enemies would persecute our religion, forbid Sabbath observance, forbid Jews to pray, resistance would be strengthened and religiosity would grow. When there are no hindrances, people grow indifferent to a religion.

At the start our enemies had indeed tried to persecute religion, attacking synagogues and prayer houses. But right away they realized that these were wrong tactics because thereby they would only strengthen religiosity and consequently the spiritual resistance of the Jewish people as well. Therefore they straightaway changed their tactics.

Characteristic is the rebellion against God, against Heaven, which is noticeable among many religious Jews who no longer wish to declare that God's judgment is right.

Religious leaders in Poland regrettably did nothing before the war to strengthen religiosity among the populace. They fought for kashrut. But what was this kashrut propaganda? Did it explain just what kashrut should be observed? No, they did not explain. The Sabbath observers made scandalous scenes in the streets, fighting with the carters. Was this "propaganda"? They explained nothing, they did not enlighten people as to what the Sabbath was, its meaning, its significance, its sacredness.

They continue to do nothing for religious enlightenment, these religious officials of ours. They content themselves with begging from the Joint Distribution Committee.[2] One must admit that unfortunately the Jews have shown themselves to be much weaker, much less able to resist than we had supposed. The Jews have shown themselves to be unable to withstand the least hardship, as we saw before the war, for instance, in the struggle against prohibiting ritual slaughter and on behalf of kashrut. People ate non-kosher meat even when the difference in price was only a few pennies. We observed this too in the struggle to keep the Sabbath as a day of rest.

Corruption, demoralization, and thievery in the ghetto are terrible. Their cause—the extraordinary misfortunes. Evil traits and base instincts are now revealed in all their nakedness. But if 400,000 Gentiles were locked up in such a ghetto, who knows if the picture would not look much worse. They would probably just slaughter one another.

Jews in the provinces turn out to be better. The old Jewish feeling of compassion has not yet been eradicated from them. Jews in the provinces are self-sacrificing, renouncing a bit of food to send packages to relatives, acquaintances, and even to strangers in Warsaw.

It is also sad that there are no visions of the Messiah in the ghetto, no visions of redemption in the spiritual sense. People think in purely materialistic terms, the redemption means return to an easy life, fancy resorts, fleshpots. Perhaps there is a perception of the travail before the Messiah's coming, but people do not want to draw the necessary conclusions and therefore do not respond and prepare themselves for messianic redemption.

Q: *What is the outlook for the Jewish people, especially the Jewish masses in Poland?*

Without a religious awakening, with a messianic idea, the Jews will not be saved. Why? The political outlook is not promising. The Poles will say that the Jews made the best deal with the Germans, received autonomy from them, and Jew-baiting will continue to thrive. The optimistic hopes Jews direct toward England are also naïve and ridiculous. It is clear to me as two and two make four that England will once again fool us, betray us, as she does other small and weak peoples, by not giving us Palestine. I say, therefore, that our salvation lies only in an inner religious awakening capable of working miracles. No one can rob us of Heavenly Jerusalem, the spiritual Jerusalem, and with the force of the spirit we will finally conquer also politically . . .

Dr. Israel Milejkowski

. . . I head up the public-health service in the program to combat epidemics and also the hospital department. Besides, I also direct the medical board here in the ghetto, where over 800 doctors are concentrated. All these activities leave me very little free time and my remarks will therefore be based on my daily practice in my own field, but I will try, as far as possible, to give my conclusions a general character . . .

The root and source of all evil in our miserable existence at the present moment lie in the very fact that we have been locked up in a ghetto. This gives rise to degenerating and demoralizing consequences in our community life. This is the cause of our physical and moral collapse.

The ghetto and life in the ghetto have no future in themselves, because we have been locked up behind its walls against our will, because this was done by brute force which was impervious to any human feelings. We must not let ourselves be persuaded for a moment that the ghetto way of life can be adapted to our needs, that it can solve any of the vexing problems of our gloomy existence . . .

For us the ghetto is only a temporary residence which has been forced upon us. It is a sort of roofless *sukkah,*[3] utterly unfit for human habitation, only a makeshift dwelling, a passing stage in our communal life, and the source of all our troubles and hardships at this time. The ghetto, which has hit us so murderously, is our greatest affliction and calamity, for the generality as well as for the individual: moral insanity. All other troubles and afflictions vanish when compared with the ghetto.

The chief curse of the ghetto is that there we cannot be creative. We were creative before the ghetto, when we created cultural values for ourselves and for all mankind, for we are capable of creative work, but only under more or less free conditions. In the ghetto, however, that is impossible. Under brutal outside pressure we have lost the possibility and also the qualities of creativity.

Here in the ghetto we must now make every effort to survive this terrible period in our existence. Endurance and perseverance—this must now be our slogan in the ghetto.

From the foregoing I derive my negative attitude to the whole ghetto setup which I perceive as the most painful event in our entire history. No good will come to us out of the ghetto. Quite the contrary—the ghetto brings more demoralization and more corruption to the locked in, tightly squeezed masses.

I can explain this better by using two medical terms, endogeny and exogeny. Internally we must do everything to enable us to persevere and endure. But externally the oppressor's whip cracks over our heads, forcing us to do work beyond our weak capacities, The oppressor's attitude to us can be stated in the words of the Jewish foremen to Pharaoh: "There is no straw given unto thy servants and they say to us: 'Make bricks.'" We are ordered to do many things that we are in no position to perform under ghetto conditions, precisely because of these difficult conditions themselves.

Bearing this in mind, I therefore always try to act in the area of my competence, so that "their" authoritarian orders may for a while be tempered by my instructions for their discharge and that the lash of the whip will thus be eased. Under the present terrible conditions I cannot and do not wish to be creative because this would be a wasted effort and an impossibility.

In order to get a true picture of ghetto life we cannot judge on the basis of what we see in the street. I differentiate between two strata in the ghetto. I would express it graphically as follows: The whole Jewish community in the ghetto is as if it had been thrown into a huge pot of seething water on a big fire, the fire of our afflictions. In the seething water we can distinguish an upper layer and a lower one.

The upper layer seethes and boils and many bubbles appear on its surface. The second layer also boils, but more quietly, more slowly. The upper layer is more conspicuous, though it is not the more numerous or more important, but because it is more visibly astir. If we want to see the true face of the ghetto, we must acquaint ourselves with the lower layer.

At first glance what is most obvious is the benumbed sense of compassion among Warsaw Jews. Without any pity for the desperate plight of thousands of our brethren whom want has forced from their hovels out onto the streets, we pass almost indifferently the barely living unfortunates and the paper-covered corpses of those who died of hunger. Savagery has begun to rule our minds and, accordingly, also our actions. It is worth mentioning that "They" have condescended to note this tragic phenomenon in our lives.

The life of the first layer is not, however, the true one. That is represented by the lower layer . . . in which we find modest but very important happenings, luminous, vigorous, cheering: the sense of compassion as manifested by the work of the basic cells of organized Jewish life, the tenement committees,[4] thanks to which the true Jewish trait of compassion and of charity has been fulfilled.

In addition, there is the quiet, modest work, which has only a temporary life, being done in other areas, for example, in setting up public kitchens of various kinds, medical courses, and vocational training for Jewish adolescents. Intensive medical research on starvation and typhus is also being done. All the clinical materials, unfortunately so bizarrely voluminous, are carefully being researched and the studies are being prepared for their definitive medical conclusions.[5] This is our ambitious and prestigious undertaking!

But this is by no means an original, creative ghetto culture. Afterwards, after the cataclysm, we want to be able to show the world that even horrible persecutions could not crush us. Right now, a small scientific meeting devoted to the ghetto is being held at the hospital. Here (!) problems and scientific presentations, responses and discussions. The results of the research will be published later and I hope that they will interest a broad audience.

These attempts at constructive work in the ghetto, in relation to the negative happenings, are small comfort to us, because one thing is terribly clear: the ghetto demoralizes! What is a blessing for the ghetto—smuggling, for example—is from the national standpoint a curse.

If, for a moment, we discount the utilitarian factor involved in smuggling, if we can forget that thanks to those Jewish smugglers who risk their lives to provide the ghetto with all sorts of delicacies, many Jews can supply themselves with the finest and best meals, and if we ponder instead on what sort of generation will grow out of these smugglers, good-for-nothing scamps—is the ghetto not a curse? Or take, for instance, vocational courses, medical and others. The courses will produce nothing but bunglers, though neither the teachers nor supervisors are at fault. At fault are only the harsh and abnormal conditions of the ghetto. This is not progress or advancement. This is degeneration and brutalization.

Under such harsh conditions of our communal life in the Warsaw ghetto, to return to our simile of the pot of seething water, people from the very bottom rise to the surface of our pot. Blackmailers, informers, bribe-takers of all sorts, and influence-peddlers. This layer of underworld characters, antisocial elements are always found in every society. They increase and multiply in wartime, just as if inhuman living conditions were the best subsoil for the disorderly development of these human hyenas.

I do not at all wish to deny the fact that this type of person is, in the present circumstances, to a certain extent necessary and useful for outside purposes. The authorities demand dirty work from us which, under pressure from those in power, must be done. Not everyone is capable of doing it and willy-nilly we are beholden to the underworld. In this case I realize the positive role these elements play in community life. I think that this is also the situation in the provinces.

People complain that our ghetto smells worse than any other place. This is certainly true and derives from the fact that our substance is finer, more delicate and therefore spoils more quickly. With regard to corruption this is frightfully conspicuous. At fault, once again, are the conditions in which we live. These conditions breed corruption and the fight against corruption is a hard, hopeless one. To fight corruption means to fight the ghetto. Cursed is our vegetation within the ghetto walls, a curse hovers over the work of our leaders and officials. What is ugliest in the Diaspora comes to light in the ghetto in concentrated form . . .

Our present educational work here in the ghetto ought to be aimed at inculcating the tradition in the hearts and minds of the young generation, that they absorb it so that it becomes part and parcel of their inner being. From this standpoint I take an altogether positive attitude to the religious values of our people. I have realized that the will to survive of the Jewish people, their stubbornness and persistence—"a stiff-necked people"—really come from the traditional religious approach to the problem of our survival. In the religious Jew I see this wholeness. He is without the self-reproachfulness and the doubts that totally consume the mind of the enlightened Jew and thus empty it of its essence.

The mind possesses a whole series of attributes among which faith occupies a prominent place. Deep faith is an antidote for the poison which comes with our daily terrible life. To close the chasm that opens up before the modern Jew's eyes and to enable him to overcome the strongest temptations, his religious feelings must be awakened.

Notes

1. The Germans regarded Jewish converts to Christianity and their children as racial Jews, in accordance with the Nuremberg Laws. These apostates lived in the ghetto and attended two Catholic churches located within ghetto boundaries. Because of expertness or high reputation in their fields, some held prestigious posts in the ghetto bureaucracy.
2. The American Jewish Joint Distribution Committee—JDC, the leading American Jewish philanthropic organization serving needy Jews throughout the world.
3. A booth with a roof of branches and leaves which serves as a temporary residence during the festival of Sukkot.
4. The tenement committees were a ŻTOS [the name of the Jewish Society for Public Welfare after October 1940—Eds.] spinoff. Each building was organized for self-help activities and ghettowide philanthropic fundraising.
5. The study was completed October 1942 after the mass deportations from the Warsaw ghetto. It appeared in Warsaw in 1946, published by the JDC under the title, *Maladie de Famine: Recherches cliniques sur la famine executes dans le ghetto de Varsovie en 1942.*

368

Warsaw Diary of Adam Czerniaków

First published in *The Warsaw Diary of Adam Czerniaków: Prelude to Doom,* edited and translated by Raul Hilberg, Stanislaw Staron, and Joseph Kermish (New York: Ivan R. Dee, 1979), 384, 385.

July 22, 1940 [*sic*]—In the morning at 7:30 at the Community. The borders of the Small Ghetto surrounded by a special unit in addition to the regular one.

Sturmbannführer Höfle and associates came at 10 o'clock.[1] We disconnected the telephone. Children were moved from the playground opposite the Community building.

We were told that all the Jews irrespective of sex and age, with certain exceptions, will be deported to the East. By 4 P.M. today a contingent of 6,000 people must be provided. And this (at the minimum) will be the daily quota.

We were ordered to vacate a building at 103 Zelazna Street for the German personnel who will be carrying out the deportation. The furniture was kept where it was. As the Council staff with their wives and children are exempted from deportation, I asked that the JSS [Żydowska Samapomoc Społczna, Jewish Social Self-Help Committee, ZSS, until October 1940—Eds.] personnel, crafts-men, and garbage collectors, etc. also be excluded. This was granted.

I requested the release of Gepner, Rozen, Sztolcman, Drybinski, Winter, Kobryner, which was approved. By 3:45 P.M. everyone but Rozen is already back in the ghetto.

In the afternoon Lejkin sent a message that a piece of glass had allegedly been thrown at a police car. They warned us that if this were to happen again our hostages would be shot.

The most tragic dilemma is the problem of children in orphanages, etc. I raised this issue—perhaps something can be done.

At 5:30 one of the officials Forwort (?) drove in and demanded that Jozef Ehrlich should be named Lejkin's deputy. Ehrlich is already wearing 3 stars.

Sturmbannführer Höfle (*Beauftragter* [plenipotentiary] in charge of deportation) asked me into his office and informed me that for the time being my wife was free, but if the deportation were impeded in any way, she would be the first one to be shot as a hostage.

July 23, 1942—In the morning at the Community. Worthoff from the deportation staff came and we discussed several problems.[2] He exempted the vocational school students from deportation. The husbands of working women as well. He told me to take up the matter of orphans with Höfle. The same with reference to crafts-men. When I asked for the number of days per week in which the operation would be carried on, the answer was 7 days a week.

Throughout the town a great rush to start new workshops. A sewing machine can save a life.

It is 3 o'clock. So far 4,000 are ready to go. The orders are that there must be 9,000 by 4 o'clock. Some officials came to the post office and issued instructions that all incoming letters and parcels be diverted to the Pawial [prison].

Notes

1. SS-Major Herman Höfle headed a 20-man *Aussiedlungsstab* [Resettlement Staff]. Although subordinated to SS and Police Leader Globocnik of the Lublin district, Höfle's detachment handled roundup and loadings in several *Generalgouvernement* districts.
2. SS-1st Lieut. (later Capt.) Hermann Worthoff, on Höfle's staff.

369

STEFAN ERNEST

Warsaw Ghetto Diary

Written in July 1942. First published in Micha Grynberg, ed., *Words to Outlive Us: Eyewitness Accounts from the Warsaw Ghetto,* translated by Philip Boehm (New York: Metropolitan Books/Henry Holt, 2002), 99, 289–91.

The President's suicide was an act of protest. Or did he want to teach the dying ghetto to assert its right to choose its own death? But in this the President committed a major error, possibly even an act of cowardice. Perhaps at the very last moment he lost the courage, the strength, the nerve to give his *no* a greater voice, to turn private reaction into public expression. Believe me, in our circumstances nothing was easier than choosing to die; deciding to survive was harder by far. Czerniaków should have lived and led the rebellion. And if at the age of sixty he felt so worn out by his three years of struggle that he truly lacked the necessary strength, he should have at least told people what was in store for them before he took his leave. For the sake of honor he should have let them assume responsibility for shedding their own blood. Because Czerniaków now knew the whole truth. In the end, though, the people went to their death leaderless, submissive and ignorant of the fate awaiting them. The man who had been raised on parliamentarian, democratic, and pacific traditions—the modern humanism of a passing era—was simply unable to grasp the need for a course of action that required bloodshed. He shied away from the necessary sacrifice, which he would have had to help direct.

Throughout the deportations, the ghetto was plastered with announcements of his death—Adam Czerniaków / Licensed Engineer / President of the Jewish Council of Warsaw / sixty years—the black-rimmed notices a symbol of the demise of the district he had led with such devotion. But Czerniaków was not a man of active resistance. [. . .]

The war's "third front" was finally broken after another few days' resistance, from Monday to Saturday (19–24 April). The cleanup action is still going on; anyone caught is sent to the Befehlsstelle or to Umschlagplatz.

The final act of this tragedy is coming to a close, behind a curtain that was never raised, a thick cordon of army and police at a distance from the walls. According to the decree of 24 April, trespassing in the former Jewish district is punishable by shooting. The liquidation of the ghetto is to be kept shrouded in secrecy. Only the din, the smoke, and the fires attest that it's still not over.

There are stories going around about Jewish fighters wearing German uniforms and helmets, about a decisive battle at Muranów, about the Germans storming the hospital on Gęsia Street and massacring all inside, about the Polish flag flying from the Carmelite Church—exaggerated enemy losses numbering in the hundreds.

A thick cordon of police and army units are strictly guarding the secret of what has actually happened. But even now we know for a fact there are some who, armed only with a revolver or a grenade, or perhaps with nothing at all, managed to break through the columns of fire and smoke, through the walls, through the cordon of police and soldiers. And they will tell what happened. They will preserve the memory of the last days of the Warsaw Ghetto, when resistance atones for previous submissiveness. They will testify to the heroism of those who fell and those who are dying still—the last of the last—to salvage the honor, courage, and dignity of all who died earlier, without fighting, and of all who were saved earlier, also without fighting, on the other side of the wall.

They died in glory for those who yet survive, who are being hunted down like animals, who are hiding and waiting for the war to end or plodding along from day to day pretending to be Aryans. May these people remember what they owe to those who died, so that those fortunate enough to spend the war in Allied or neutral countries will know what happened. May they remember what they owe. And may they fight on.

They died for other nations, as a testimony of their own right to exist. They died for Poland, whose banner they raised in their last battle, in honor of a shared tragedy of enslavement and persecution and in the hope of a better coexistence in the future. They died to bridle the Nazi beast.

On 19 April, at five in the morning, the same beast commences the final liquidation. Because they're expecting resistance, the Germans are employing special equipment: tanks, light artillery, flamethrowers, howitzers, grenades, and machine guns—even reconnaissance planes.

The main points of defense are Muranowski Square and Muranowska Street itself, the hospital on Gęsia, and the brushmakers shop. The district is bombarded, the buildings burned or reduced to rubble. The organized resistance breaks, with smaller pockets remaining. The soldiers move in to ferret out those in hiding. With tried and true methods they finish off anyone they find. Supposedly the beast is avenging the loss of some hundred soldiers—as well as a tannery, burned down inside the ghetto, and a few other places producing for the German war effort. People talk about prisoners escaping from Pawiak.

To this day the former Jewish District is heavily cordoned off, and trespassing is still punishable by death. News comes by way of the firefighters or occasional escapees. The fact that SS men and Ukrainians continue to hunt them down proves beyond doubt that there are some Jews left hiding in the ghetto, fated to die of starvation.

370

[ABBA KOVNER AND OTHERS]

A Summons to Resistance, Vilna Ghetto

Circulated in January 1942. Published in English in Lucy S. Dawidowicz, ed., *A Holocaust Reader* (West Orange, N.J.: Behrman House, 1976), 224–336.

Let us not be led like sheep to the slaughter!

Jewish youth!

In a time of unparalleled national misfortune we appeal to you!

We do not yet have the words to express the whole tragic struggle which transpires before our eyes. Our language has no words to probe the depths to which our life has fallen nor to vociferate the anguish which strangles us.

It is still too hard to find the proper definition for the state in which we find ourselves, for the extraordinary cruelty with which the annihilation of the local Jewish population has been carried out.

The community of the Jerusalem of Lithuania numbered 75,000.[1] On entering the ghetto, 25,000 were already missing, and today only 12,000 remain. All the others have been killed! Death strolls in our streets; in our tents—powerlessness. But the anguish at this huge misfortune is much greater in the light of the ignorable conduct of the Jews at the present time. Never in its long history of martyrdom has the Jewish people shown such abjectness, such a lack of human dignity, national pride, and unity, such communal inertia and submissiveness to the murderers.

The heart aches even more at the conduct of Jewish youth, reared for twenty years in the ideals of upbuilding and halutz [pioneer] defense, which now is apathetic, lost, and does not respond to the tragic struggle.

There are, however, occasions in the life of a people, of a collective, as in the life of an individual, which seize you by the hair of your head, shake you up, and force you to gird up all your strength to keep alive. We are now experiencing such an occasion.

With what can we defend ourselves? We are helpless, we have no possibilities of organizing any defense of our existence. Even if we are deprived of the possibility of an armed defense in this unequal contest of strength, we nevertheless can still defend ourselves. Defend ourselves with all means—and moral defense above all—is the command of the hour.

Jewish youth!

On none but you rests the national duty to be the pillar of the communal defense of the Jewish collective which stands on the brink of annihilation!

I. *Let us defend ourselves during a deportation!*

For several months now, day and night, thousands and tens of thousands have been torn away from our midst, men, the aged, women, and children, led away like cattle—and we, the remainder, are numbed. The illusion still lives within us that they are still alive somewhere, in an undisclosed concentration camp, in a ghetto.

You believe and hope to see your mother, your father, your brother who was seized and has disappeared.

In the face of the next day which arrives with the horror of deportation and murder, the hour has struck to dispel the illusion: There is no way out of the ghetto, except the way to death!

No illusion greater than that our dear ones are alive.

No illusion more harmful than that. It deadens our feelings, shatters our national unity in the moments before death.

Before our eyes they led away our mother, our father, our sisters—enough!

We will not go!

Comrades! Uphold this awareness and impart to your families, to the remnants of the Jerusalem of Lithuania.

Do not surrender into the hands of the kidnappers!

Do not hand over any other Jews!

If you are caught, you have nothing to lose!

Let us defend ourselves, and not go!

Better to fall with honor in the ghetto than to be led like sheep to Ponary!

II. *On guard over national honor and dignity*

We work for Germans and Lithuanians. Everyday we come face to face with our employers, the murderers of our brothers. Great the shame and pain, observing the conduct of Jews, stripped of the awareness of human dignity.

Comrades!

Don't give the foe the chance to ridicule you!

When a German ridicules a Jew—don't help him laugh!

Don't play up to your murderers!

Denounce the bootlickers at work!

Denounce the girls who flirt with the Gestapo men!

Work slowly, don't speed!

Show solidarity! If misfortune befalls one of you—don't be vile egoists—all of you help him. Be united in work and misfortunes!

Jewish agents of the Gestapo and informers of all sorts walk the streets. If you get hold of one such, sentence him—to be beaten until death!

III. *In the presence of the German soldier*

Instead of submissiveness and repulsive bootlicking, you are given the possibility in daily encounters with German soldiers to perform an important national deed. Not every German soldier is a sworn enemy of the Jews, not every German soldier is a sworn Hitlerite. But many have false ideas about Jews. We, the youth, by our conduct, in word and deed, can create in the mind of the German soldier another image of a Jew, a productive one, a Jew who has national and human dignity.

Comrades, show the Jews with whom you work and live together that this is the approach to the German soldier.

IV. *To the Jewish police*

Most tragic is the role of the Jewish police—to be a blind tool in the hands of our murderers. But you, Jewish policemen, have at least a chance to demonstrate your personal integrity and national responsibility!

Any act which threatens Jewish life should not be performed!

No actions of mass deportation should be carried out!

Refuse to carry out the orders which bring death to Jews and their families!

Do not let service in the police be turned into national disgrace for you!

Jewish policemen, sooner risk your own life than dozens of Jewish lives!

Comrades!

Convey your hatred of the foe in every place and at every moment!

Never lose the awareness that you are working for your murderers!

Better to fall in the fight for human dignity than to live at the mercy of the murderer!
Let us defend ourselves! Defend ourselves until the last minute!

Note

1. Vilna was called "the Jerusalem of Lithuania," an epithet attributed to Napoleon, when he passed there in 1815 in the retreat from Moscow.

371

HANS FRANK

Diary Entry

Written 25 January 1943. First published in Office of U.S. Chief of Counsel for the Prosecution of Axis Criminality, *Nazi Conspiracy and Aggression* (Washington, D.C.: U.S. Government Printing Office, 1946), 4:891–92.

Warsaw, 25 January 1943

Present: Dr. Hans Frank and others [. . .]

State Secretary Krueger: When we settled about the first 4,000 in Kreis Zamosc shortly before Christmas I had an opportunity to speak to these people. [. . .]

(State Secretary Krueger) It is understandable that in resettling this area . . . we did not make friends of the Poles. [. . .]

(State Secretary Krueger) In colonizing this territory with radical Germans, we are forced to chase out the Poles. [. . .]

(State Secretary Krueger) We are removing those who constitute a burden in this new colonization territory. Actually, they are the asocial and inferior elements. They are being deported, first brought to a concentration camp, and then sent as labor to the Reich. From a Polish propaganda standpoint this entire first action has had an unfavorable effect. For the Poles say: After the Jews have been destroyed then they will employ the same methods to get the Poles out of this territory and liquidate them just like the Jews. [. . .]

(State Secretary Krueger) As I have mentioned a great deal of unrest in Polish territory has resulted because of this resettlement. [. . .]

Dr. Frank: We will discuss each individual case of resettlement in the future exactly in the same manner as in the case of Zamosc, so that you will, Mr. State Secretary, appear before me and render a report. [. . .]

Dr. Frank: Gentlemen, be assured that this composite structure of General Government, on which all who are gathered around this table have worked so splendidly, really has the power to endure over this period. The great task which is given us will grow more difficult. No one will help us; we are fully and entirely dependent on ourselves. The Führer can only help us as a kind of administrative island or administrative pill-box. We must defend ourselves from all sides. To all criticism of methods which we have heard—you know my basic principle, I don't need to say it in this circle—I would like to stress one thing: we must not be squeamish when we learn that a total of 17,000 people have been shot. These persons who were shot were nothing more than war victims. If we compare this number against the irreplaceable blood sacrifices which the German people uninterruptedly day by day and every hour are making, then it weighs as nothing in the balance. We are now duty bound to hold together. Each must bring with him understanding for the other, he must be convinced that he is doing his best. The main thing is that we do not allow any personal slackness to arise. We must remember that we, who are gathered together here, figure on Mr. Roosevelt's list of war criminals. I have the honour of being Number One. We have, so to speak, become accomplices in the world historic sense. Just because of this we must hold together, and be in agreement with one another, and it would be ridiculous if we were to let ourselves get involved in any squabbles over methods.

372

WALTER GROSS

Racial Political Prerequisites for the Solution of the Jewish Problem

First published as *Die rassenpolitischen Voraussetzungen zur Lösung der Judenfrage* (Munich: Hoheneichen-Verlag, 1943), 31–32.

Summarizing the results of our observations and attempting to ascertain what can be said about the future European solution to the Jewish problem from the perspective of racial biology and racial politics, we see that the following requirements must be met:

1. The Jewish race is equally alien to all European races in the same degree. Its historical and intellectual/spiritual danger cannot, therefore, be averted by any form of assimilation. The only way to eliminate from Europe the threat it poses by virtue of its very existence is to completely remove it from the territory.
2. The Jewish race, as a result of the peculiar circumstance of interbreeding, has become a permanently mongrelized cross-breed, and as such, is also alien to the so-called Semitic races.
3. Therefore, for racial political reasons, it can neither be relocated to a European country nor to any land in possession of the Arabs outside of Europe.
4. In establishing which persons are to be considered Jewish for the purpose of actions taken in this regard, the sole criteria must be racial considerations, without regard for religious affiliation, social standing, nationality, or other factors.
5. The first-degree mixed bloods, the so-called half-Jews must be dealt with as thoroughly as Jews.
6. Reproduction of the remaining second-degree mixed bloods in the European races is to be kept at a very minimum.
7. Regardless of the existing laws or transitional solutions, as well as of future legislation in various countries, it is absolutely imperative and urgent that all European nations reach an agreement on fundamental anti-Jewish policies in solving the Jewish problem, based on the basic principles of racial politics.

We are convinced that if we continue to handle the Jewish problem according to the basic principles outlined here, the new order of Europe will arrive at a final elimination of that ever-so-catastrophic Jewish problem. And with that, a dangerously gaping wound in the history and culture of Europe—indeed, we might even say, of the world—will be closed. And for the first time ever, the path will be cleared for all nations to develop freely for themselves and for humanity, each according to its own unique racial character without having to worry about intellectual and spiritual forgery, racial degeneracy, or political abuse and exploitation by a power that is equally alien to all peoples—a dangerous power, one that one great German man rightly described as the very personification of the demon of human decline.

373

JÓZEF ZELKOWICZ

Diary of the Łódź Ghetto

Written in September 1942. Published in *The Chronicle of the Łódź Ghetto, 1941–1944,* edited by Lucjan Dobroszycki, translated by Richard Lourie, Joachim Neugroschel et al. (New Haven, CT: Yale University Press, 1984), 249–55.

Litzmannstadt Ghetto September 14, 1942

The period of September 5–12, 1942, will leave indelible memories among that portion of the ghetto's population on whom fate smiles and who survive the war.

One week, eight days that seem an eternity!

Even now it is difficult to grasp what has occurred. An elemental force has passed through the ghetto and swept away some 15,000 people (no one knows the exact number yet) and life appears to have resumed its former course.

In his speech of September 4, 1942 (at 4:00 P.M.), the Chairman announced that, by order of the authorities, about 25,000 Jews under the age of 10 and over 65 must be resettled out of the ghetto. Those were the instructions received by the Resettlement Commission which is composed of the following: commandant [of the Order Service, Leon] Rozenblat, [Szaja-Stanislaw] Jakobson, [Henryk] Neftalin, the attorneys, commissioner [Zygmunt] Blemer, Grynberg, a legal trainee, and a clerical staff. The commission was located on the third floor at 4 Kosielny [Church] Square (on the premises of the Main Trade Commission), while the preparatory work was done on the second floor, on the premises of the Department of Statistics, and consisted of copying out the names and exact ages of families on separate cards, going through the 19 volumes of the population records, building by building, apartment by apartment. The work was initially done in two 12-hour shifts; later, the 38-person crews (two people for each volume) were changed every eight hours. The preparatory material, arranged by streets, then went up to the third floor from which it was sent to individual Order Service precincts for execution.

In accordance with the Chairman's proclamation on the 4th of this month, pedestrian traffic after 5 P.M. has been suspended until further notice since the 5th of this month, and it was then that the Jewish police's action to round up all persons subject to resettlement began. The arrest of persons to be resettled proceeded on the basis of lists supplied by the Resettlement Commission, which in turn received information from the above-mentioned commission on population records. Upon receiving the cards, the Jewish police collected people in different parts of town and delivered the children, the elderly, and the ill—on foot or by wagon—to the assembly points. It was said that had this action encountered any difficulties or resistance, the German authorities would have stepped in. The action, however, had scarcely begun when on Monday, the 7th of this month, there was talk that the German authorities, who were not relying on lists but were guided solely by visual impressions, had taken the initiative.

In point of fact, the operation proceeded as follows—block after block was surrounded by the Jewish police and then each building surrounded by a host of police and Jewish firemen and entered by a representative of the authorities (the Gestapo). A shot was fired as the signal to assemble, and then all the residents of a given building were assembled in the courtyard, arranged in two rows, and subjected to inspection by representatives of the authorities. In the meantime, the Jewish police were searching the apartment and bringing out anyone who had been hiding or people who were ill. In the smaller buildings, this operation often took only a few minutes. The deportees and those who were to remain were separated into two groups. Those selected for resettlement were sent by wagon to the assembly points. The hospital on

FIGURE 35. Jews standing in line to get food in the Łódź ghetto. "Food may be given out only on clean dishes," reads the placard on the wall. Photograph no. 99977, United States Holocaust Memorial Museum Photo Archives, Washington, D.C. Courtesy of Benjamin (Miedzyrzecki) Meed.

Drewnowska Street was the assembly point for the left side of the ghetto, while the hospital on Lagiewnicka Street served the right hand side. Since this operation took place at an extremely rapid pace and wagons were constantly leaving from and arriving at the hospital, the clerical workers sent to the assembly points to make lists of the deportees were unable to list all the people brought there and only a portion were included in their lists, while others were taken from the ghetto by vehicle and their personal data was not, and may never be, established.

In light of these incidents, the work of the Resettlement Commission and the work done in conjunction with the commission on population records have proven entirely superfluous, even though that work continued without interruption throughout the entire resettlement action. The entire population has been listed on some 60,000 cards, which remain in the commission's hands and may possibly serve as a point of reference when the next census is taken.

To carry the weak and the sick to the wagons, the so-called white guard, i.e., the porters from the Department of Food Supply, headed by Jankiel Rozenberg (*Chmol*) were mobilized; the porter's families were exempted from resettlement.

When the wagons were being loaded, there were incidents in which people, either because of a misunderstanding or intentionally, attempted to join the group that was remaining here; retribution was very swift in such cases (such people were shot without warning), and took place right before the eyes of the assembled tenants of a building. That, however, did not prevent people from escaping from the wagons or while en route, or from being rescued from the hospital by means both legal and illegal. For the most part, it was people employed in workshops who were rescued legally. In such cases the appeals were sent from a representative of workshop to Aron Jakubowicz, who during the operation played a very active role in exempting the so-called workshoppers, finding positive solutions in many cases.

To encourage the Jewish police and the firemen to conduct the operation conscientiously, promises that their closest relations would be spared had been made. Thus, their children were placed in a hospital and isolated from the rest of the population, and an isolation ward was set up in Marysin for those relations who were elderly or under special protection. There were some 1,500 of these lucky ones who in spite of their age and infirmity, were spared resettlement. Of course, these were not people who were making any contribution to society, not even people able to perform any especially valuable work in the ghetto but were, we repeat, people with connections.

But if being loaded onto a wagon did not block off every avenue of escape, being loaded onto a 5-ton truck whose trailers have high plank siding meant that every hope was crushed. These vehicles would leave the ghetto at once and return in less than an hour. From this one may conclude that the deportees were let off somewhere not too far from the ghetto.[1]

Dramatic scenes were played out in the hospitals. Escape attempts came to a bloody end. Anyone who attempted to save himself by fleeing and was spotted by the authorities had to pay for that attempt with his life. Because the operation proceeded so rapidly, the authorities gave no thought to the motives or causes for any particular act. At 38 Zgierska Street, an elderly woman from Sieradz did not understand if she had been ordered to go to the left or the right and, instead of going to a wagon, she walked over to a group of "remainers." This the authorities interpreted as an escape attempt. The woman was shot to death on the spot. At 3 Zgierska Street, Rozenblum, a 13-year-old boy, attempted to hide in a dustbin; he was seen and shot dead. There were many such victims but even more numerous were cases of people who were wounded when a crowd was fired on.

On Wednesday, the 9th of this month, the operation seemed to have concluded on the left side of the ghetto and people had even been permitted to come out in groups to be given bread. People rushed to the co-ops, but not all the distribution points had bread in their stock rooms and orders were rushed to the bakeries. On the whole, things ran rather smoothly here. But it was another matter with the collection of the 8-kilogram potato ration, the lion's share of which the ghetto had not managed to obtain before the *szpera* [the German *Gehsperre,* curfew, became *Szpera* in the ghetto—Eds.]. People were simply starving. They had no bread, no potatoes, there had been no deliveries, and it is understandable that when potatoes and cottage cheese began to be distributed in the dairy stores—on the Bazar [Square], and on Wesola and Rybna streets—enormous lines formed. Suddenly, a few representatives of the authorities drove up from the direction of Limanowski Street. Seeing crowds of people on the street when the szpera had not yet in fact been rescinded, they opened fire; the crowd quickly scattered to the adjacent buildings and hid in apartments. Among these people were some who had already been "commissioned" and exempted from deportation. The authorities, however, summoned everyone outside from the buildings on Rybna Street. And here, again, people were lined up in twos on the street, separated into groups, and some earmarked for deportation. Those attempting to flee were shot. Apparently, 17 people were wounded. At another part, on Wesola Street, people were driven from the line-up to the old Jewish cemetery, while those on Bazarna Street were brought to a building at 10 Bazarna Street where, through an opening in the fence, they were also told to go on to the cemetery. Suddenly, five representatives of the authorities came running up from the direction of Krótka Street and seized three [women] escapees. The crowd assembled at the cemetery was called on to hand over any escapees under threat that they would all be shot if they refused to obey. Since that was purely a random gathering of people, there was no question of determining who the guilty parties were.

Those people were kept at the cemetery for about two hours. Many were selected for deportation, and five were shot dead. Those who were present at the scenes played out at the cemetery have had much to say on the subject.

After the conclusion of the regular operation, a so-called random verification took place. It was not carried out in the courtyards of buildings this time, rather, all residents (on the smaller streets) were called out to the street and, again, many people who had formerly been exempted were taken away to the wagons. There were many victims among those who, in disregard of the curfew, found themselves by chance in a neighborhood that was being checked. On the whole, however, the repeated inspections did not produce much of a yield, and there were buildings from which not a single person was seized.

The criteria for specific inspections varied greatly, as is demonstrated by what occurred at 38 Zgierska Street. This building, which has many outbuildings, is inhabited by more than 200 families. One of the outbuildings on the right-hand side also has an exit and windows that face No. 40. The inspection of 38 Zgierska Street was already completed, while the one in the neighboring building was still in progress; the inhabitants of the first outbuilding who had been exempted from resettlement returned to their apartments and, out of curiosity, looked out their windows at the operation in progress in the building next to theirs. This was noticed by the inspecting officers, who then ordered everyone out into the courtyard. During this new inspection, 40 of the 50 people present were selected for deportation. It was only due to intervention by A[ron] Jakubowicz that many of these people, workshop employees for the most part, were released. A few, however, did fall victim to chance.

Intervention was possible on the spot, and, in many cases, actions taken by our police proved effective. A person could be rescued before the loading took place or after; everything depended on the individual [German] police officer. There are known cases of direct personal intervention. A 40-year-old woman employed by the Community, when selected for deportation, asked the inspecting police officer, in good German, why she, a woman in her prime, was being deported. The officer thought for a moment, glanced over at her, and ordered that she be allowed to remain in the ghetto. There were cases of quite haggard people being allowed to remain because representatives of our police stated that they were good, useful ghetto workers, and in other cases it sufficed for a Jewish policeman to claim a deportee as a relative. Clearly, all this was a matter of chance, the exception, not the rule. In many cases, however, outward appearance was the deciding factor in obtaining an exemption. It was observable that people who looked better, and particularly those wearing clean clothes, were not taken. There were cases of people over 70 being allowed to remain, while middle-aged and even young people were taken if their appearance betrayed weak health.

As we have already seen, names were not listed when people were seized in the buildings, and they were often taken so quickly to the trucks at the assembly points and driven away that the officials assigned to draw up the lists were barely able to record a small percentage of those being resettled. Since no other list had been drawn up—at least no such lists have been sent to the ghetto—it is impossible to speak with any accuracy about individuals or about the number of people who have been resettled out of the ghetto. The figure 14,432 has been mentioned, but it does not seem likely that such an exact number could be determined. It may be possible to determine the total resettled after another census is taken, but none are under consideration at the moment. Besides, it is doubtful whether the authorities would agree to an interruption of work, without which a census campaign is unthinkable.

No one knows what will happen next. Things have to be put into some sort of order because many families have been using, and continue to use, ration cards belonging to resettled family members, while in other instances, deportees have inadvertently taken an entire family's food ration cards with them. People are talking about horrific incidents in this regard; in one case, a wife who was resettled along with her three children took all their cards with her and her husband starved to death after five days of nothing whatsoever to eat. The people seized by the authorities from the potato lines on Bazar and from in front of the dairy co-ops had their [vegetable] coupons and food cards in their possession, so here again families were left without rations. The Ration Card Department has had enormous work to do in connection with these cases, but only after a new census is taken will it be possible finally to determine who is entitled to rations.

This could not be of less concern to the populace itself, for it is still under the effect of the shock it has experienced and, moreover, is accustomed to associating every new development with yet another calamity. So it was wise to let things stand as they were until people regained a certain calm.

Incidentally, the populace's strange reaction to the recent events is noteworthy. There is not the slightest doubt that this was a profound and terrible shock, and yet one must wonder at the indifference shown by those—apart from the ones who were not directly affected and who returned to normal life at once—from whom loved ones had been taken. It would seem that the events of recent days would have immersed the entire population of the ghetto in mourning for a long time to come, and yet, right after the incidents, and even during the resettlement action, the populace was obsessed with everyday concerns—getting bread, rations, and so forth—and often went from immediate personal tragedy right back into daily life. Is this some sort of numbing of the nerves, an indifference, or a symptom of an illness that manifests itself in atrophied emotional reactions? After losing those nearest to them, people talk constantly about rations, potatoes, soup, etc.! It is beyond comprehension! Why this lack of warmth toward those they loved? Naturally, here and there, there are some mothers weeping in a corner for a child or children shipped from the ghetto, but, as a while, the mood of the ghetto does not reflect last week's terrible ordeal.

Sad but true!

Note

1. The 5-ton trucks took deportees to a railroad station outside of Łódź, where the victims were loaded onto railroad cars and sent via Kutno to Kolo, and from there taken directly by vehicle to the death camp in Chelmno (Kulmhof), a distance of 14 kilometers.

374

DAWID SIERAKOWIAK

Notebooks from the Łódź Ghetto

Written 4 September 1942. First published as *The Diary of Dawid Sierakowiak: Five Notebooks from the Łódź Ghetto,* edited by Alan Adelson, translated by Kamil Turowski (New York: Oxford University Press, 1996), 215–18.

Friday, September 4. Łódź. Yesterday's tragic news has turned out to be unfortunately true. The Germans are demanding all the children up to age ten, the elderly over sixty-five, and all other sick, swollen invalids, people unable to work, and those without employment. The panic in the city is incredible. Nobody's working anywhere; everyone's running to secure work assignments for those in their family who are unemployed; parents of the unfortunate children are trying to save them by any means. The Registration Office was sealed after the lists were made, so that all rescue attempts by falsifying birth certificates, registration books, and other documents, or making up death certificates, etc. are failing.

Incredible scenes were taking place in our *Arbeitseinsatz.* Work assignments were issued in great haste, even though they already say that our efforts don't matter because there will be a general *Szpera* [curfew], during which medical commissions will examine everyone to decide on their ability to work.

Today, despite incredible difficulties, I managed as a clerk to get a work assignment for Mom in the furniture workshop. Even so, I am very worried about Mom because she's terribly emaciated, shrunken, and weak. Nevertheless, she still works in the garden most of the time, is not sick, and even cooks, cleans, and, if there's need, does laundry at home.

Early in the morning, the office of the School Department was registering eight- and ten-year-old children for work, but at twelve it was announced that the lists had been invalidated.

At 2:00 P.M. our office was closed, and we were all ordered to go home until further notice. Similarly, except for food-supply people, "fecesmen," police, firefighters, and various guards; all other departments, offices, administration agencies, etc. have been closed.

The mood of panic is intensifying by the second. All kinds of rumors are repeated from lips to lips that we should expect the worst. At four, Rumkowski and [Dawid] Warszawski, the supreme director of a number of workshops, gave speeches on Firemen's Square (13 Lutomierska Street). They said that "the sacrifice of the children and the elderly is necessary," that "nothing could be done to prevent it," and asked us "not to hinder carrying out the deportation action."[1] It was easy for them to say that because they managed to secure from the Germans exemption from the deportation for children of workshop directors, firemen, policemen, doctors, instructors, the *Beirat,* and the Devil knows who else. In addition, all kinds of connections will be set in motion now (thousands of the well-connected elderly, the sick, and children will receive in their place completely different persons who, though able to work, will nevertheless be sacrificed to make up for the "connected" children and elderly).

Father's cousin, who has a three-year-old girl and wants to save her, came to us in the evening. We've agreed to let her stay with her child, and even to let her whole family come down. They were afraid to stay at their home, not to be taken hostages for the child. As a result of the heat outside and stuffiness at home, which is caused by the presence of so many people, I could hardly fall asleep.

Note

1. Sierakowiak's quotations are basically paraphrasings. For the verbatim text of Chaim Rumkowski's staggering speech, see *Łódź Ghetto: [Inside a Community Under Siege]*, edited by [Allan] Adelson and [Robert] Lapides [New York: Viking, 1989], pp. 328–31. "They are asking us to give up the best we possess . . . . I never have imagined that I would be forced to deliver this sacrifice with my own hands . . . . I must stretch out my hands and beg: Brothers and sisters, hand them over to me! Fathers and mothers, give me your children! . . . I must perform this difficult and bloody operation—I must cut off the limbs in order to save the body itself!—I must take children because, if not, others may be taken as well, God forbid! . . . My duty is to preserve the Jews who remain. . . . The part that can be saved is much larger than the part that must be given away."

375

STANISLAW SZNAPMAN

Warsaw Ghetto Diary

Written in 1943. Published in Micha Grynberg, ed., *Words to Outlive Us: Eyewitness Accounts from the Warsaw Ghetto,* translated by Philip Boehm (New York: Metropolitan Books/Henry Holt, 2002), 191–95.

Only about 40,000 Jews are left in Warsaw, out of the approximately 400,000 who were there before the deportation.

Once again there are dark clouds looming over us. Once again the Germans are planning to crush us. They never give us a moment's peace, never let us stay in one place. This is one of their special tactics, another way to torture us. And once again there is unrest; people sell off their last clothes, their sheets, so they can be ready to move at a moment's notice. We have nothing left but what we can carry—and, of course, our naked lives. But this is exactly what our oppressors are after, as they lie in wait and scheme. Now they tell us we're being moved to Poniatów or Trawniki in the Lublin district, since Warsaw must be "*judenrein.*"[1] They tell us to expect forests and fresh air; we'll sleep on bunks and live out the war there. But we already know there's nothing there for the deportees but empty countryside, heavily fenced with barbed wire, and guarded by SS. The local population was deported some time back. Hunger and disease are rampant. So far they've starved about 20,000 Russian prisoners to death there, burying them in the nearby forests. We realize they're trying to tempt us to leave—it's much easier to get rid of everybody all at once, without commotion, without witnesses. That's why no one is eager to go. They prefer to die where they are. But the Germans force them to leave "voluntarily" by using armed thugs to surround the workshops and send people away on the spot.

From the papers it's clear that the situation on the front is getting better day by day: The Russians are bravely crushing this plague, and England and America are preparing to pounce, in order to free the world from this horrible monster. Hope is beginning to stir in our hearts. Perhaps we will live to see a miracle after all. We want to survive so much, to see the pogrom turned on the beast. We want to live to see light triumph over darkness, justice over tyranny, and freedom over oppression and terror. We yearn to live to build a better world. But will we make it? Is it not too late?

Until October 1942, the Jews didn't know where people were being deported. They held on to the illusion that at least some might survive, so they took their last savings, the last bits of jewelry that even the poorest people keep stashed away for some bleak moment—such as their wedding bands—and hid everything, stitching it into the most secret folds inside their clothing, deluding themselves that these things would help them survive. But they were ordered to undress and shower, and after the shower they either went into the ground or into the ovens, and the clothes with the rings and wedding bands, the diamonds and money, wound up in the hands of the SS. It's no exaggeration to say that the booty taken from those 400,000 murdered Jews from Warsaw was worth tens of millions of dollars, and the value of the property and equipment left in their apartments—which also went to the SS—was similar. Moreover, the valuables, money, and other items the Gestapo and the gendarmes took over the course of the previous year was worth the same amount. And what about the people murdered in other towns throughout Poland, or of those from France, Belgium, Holland, or Czecho-Slovakia? What about their possessions? And how many millions of dollars were in the warehouses that were plundered? The SS men, Gestapo officers, and gendarmes divvied up the booty, quietly and unofficially, lining their pockets with cash and jewelry and amassing huge fortunes, which they buried and hid. And after the war, the same SS men, Gestapo officers, and gendarmes will travel to America, Africa, or Australia and use that money to buy up plantations, where they will retire in comfort following their arduous labors.

You English and Americans! Know that, after the war, when the Germans come to your colonies and start buying up land, know that they murdered our mothers and wives, children, fathers, sisters, and brothers. They robbed them of their possessions, their money, their wedding bands, and their jewelry. Their money comes from theft and murder; it is stained with the blood of our dearest. Remember that every one of these Germans was once an SS man, Gestapo officer, or gendarme. Take the money away from them and put it in the hands of the law. Let me repeat myself! You must do this, because what happened here was mass theft and murder, monstrous and horrible. They would have done the same to you and your children, to your wives and mothers had you been under their rule. This is what justice demands, the justice currently being fought for, the justice for which so much blood is now being shed.

The deportation happened gradually, in spurts. The first group was sent off, and the people left behind deluded themselves into thinking there would be no more; some miracle might end the war. The deadline for the second transport approached relentlessly, and afterward those who had survived thought *they* would not be taken. But their date came too, and if not enough people showed up of their own accord, others were "volunteered" with the help of military cordons and pistols aimed at their heads. Then they herded whoever was left into a new location, packing them in even tighter so the workshop would take up less space. Everyone was ordered to move from Walicǿw Street to Prosta, so they began running around looking for apartments. The next moment a new order declared the reverse, so now everyone ran from Prosta to Walicÿw. Because the Germans were ordering everyone to move, people reasoned that they must be interested in decreasing the size of the factories but not in liquidating the shops completely—and they happily concluded that the transport to Poniatów must have been called off for the moment. Then, out of the blue, 800 people were ordered to the transport.

Sometimes people who already have a place to live don't want to take in others who need one, and the newcomers sometimes try to force themselves in, which leads to fights and quarrels. There are also those who simply break down in despair at the idea of being deported. As the factory grounds are reduced, new walls are built and old ones torn down.

It's a vicious circle: walls built and torn down, relocation, deportation. Behold the twentieth century. Ordinary people, innocent and free, are placed behind walls, imprisoned, beaten, kicked, robbed, killed, enslaved, and freighted off to their destruction. Bravo cultured, civilized Germany!

The Germans have conceived and planned the extermination with exactitude, precision, and devilish shrewdness. Now and then they seem to let up a little and pursue a gentler course, using propaganda to steer the masses to one particular spot. Then they surround the spot, capturing and liquidating everyone in their snare. They act like cats toying with a mouse—except cats are driven by instinct, while here everything is carefully thought out and planned in advance, because these particular beasts of prey are equipped with reason.

Note

1. The two camps mentioned functioned variously as training camps for the SS, prisoner of war camps for captured Soviets, and forced labor camps for Jews.

376

STEFANIA STASZEWSKA

Warsaw Ghetto Diary

Written 19 April 1944. First published in Micha Grynberg, ed., *Words to Outlive Us: Eyewitness Accounts from the Warsaw Ghetto,* translated by Philip Boehm (New York: Metropolitan Books/Henry Holt, 2002), 263–65.

It's already started inside the big ghetto. We can hear the sound of fighting. Here on Leszno Street things are still quiet. It's warm; the sky is clear, studded with stars. I'm standing in the courtyard, listening. The shooting intensifies, then grows quiet. When will it be our turn?

The authorities posted their decrees all over the streets early in the morning: The last transports for the Többens and Schultz factories (Leszno—Nowolipie—Nowolipki) will take place tomorrow at 7 A.M. Anyone who stays will be shot.

Outside the ghetto, army units are cordoning off the walls. Gendarmes have been called in to reinforce the sentries. We make our final preparations and set up our chain of contacts. Lots of running around. On the street I meet up with Bernard—he's in the bunker with Różka. We talk for a minute, then shake hands with heartfelt emotion. I ask myself whether we'll ever see each other again. Before evening I make the rounds of my friends. We say our farewells; they have decided to report for deportation.

Today no one will be able to get out. Suddenly the streets are empty but for the sound of the gendarmes' boots beating the cobblestones. I turn around. They're marching straight toward us, and the way back has been cut off. The Germans are rounding up everyone waiting to pass through the checkpoint, including me. They aren't letting any of the off-site workers through. I'm furious at myself for not making it back to my people in time.

The Germans shout, "You're trying to escape! We'll take care of you bandits right this minute." They line us up—thirty to forty people—in ranks of four. They lead us outside the ghetto and herd us down Żelazna Street to the Befehlsstelle. That's bad. We know what they do to people there. I'm too mad at myself for getting caught to be afraid. How could I be so stupid? One boy tries to escape and takes a series of bullets in the stomach. He runs a few more meters, curling up like a cat. He's writhing with pain; the Germans order us to carry him by his arms and legs to the Befehlsstelle. We wait next to the wall for the end, men on one side, women on the other. The wounded boy is howling with pain; his brother asks the Germans to put him out of his misery but they just laugh. "You'll all look like that in a minute."

The day is hot, the sunlight stings our eyes. I stare at the walls and listen. I can make out shots from around Nowolipie. There are only a few dozen meters between me and the wall, but they are insurmountable. Some armored cars drive up. The Germans unload ammunition, set up their heavy guns, ready themselves for the siege. All these tanks and cannons, their whole army armed to the teeth—all mobilized against our pistols, grenades, and fire bombs.

I know our side won't give up easily; our people are ready to fight to the last, their only thought is to fell as many Germans as possible, to do their little part in the struggle for freedom, for human dignity.

I'm standing on Żelazna waiting to be executed, completely numb, surrounded by barking Germans. Some are yelling to shoot us right away; others want to take us to the transport. I hear the words *Lager Poniatów*. And all of a sudden we're marching in double step along the walls, down the Aryan side of Lezno and Karmelicka. I see the Poles' horrified faces; the Germans chase them away.

We pass through the space between the ghettos, and finally we're in the big ghetto, which is full of army troops, gendarmes, shooting, and, in some places, fires. Near Niska Street we see a burned-out German tank. Hurrah! It's worth being alive just to see that. The Germans are cowering, they're creeping along the walls; they're afraid, afraid of the "Jewish bandits." Angrily they prod us on with their rifle butts, shouting "*Schnell, schnell!*" We're already at Umschlagplatz. The freight cars are packed, they load us on. We stand, jammed together, and listen. The sound of the fighting grows louder and louder.

Later, during the night, as the train carries us into the unknown, we see a light above Warsaw, a great bloody glow. The ghetto is fighting; the ghetto is burning. Does the world see that glow?

377

GENERAL JÜRGEN STROOP

Report on the Destruction of the Warsaw Ghetto

Issued 16 May 1943. Published in *Trials of War Criminals before the Nuremberg Military Tribunals under Control Council Law No. 10, Nuremberg, October 1946–April 1949, Germany 1949–1953* (Washington, D.C.: U.S. Government Printing Office, 19XX), 26: 628–98.

"THE WARSAW JEWISH QUARTER IS NO MORE!"
GENERAL STROOP'S REPORT: MAY 16, 1943

I

For the Führer
and for their country

the following were killed in action during the destruction of Jews and bandits in the former Jewish quarter in Warsaw [15 names with date of birth and rank, arranged by date of death].

In addition, the Polish Police sergeant Julian Zieliński, born November 13, 1891, 14th Commissariat, was killed on April 19, 1943, while carrying out his duties.

They ventured their utmost, their lives. We shall never forget them [. . .]

Units Used in the Action	*Average Number of Personnel Used per Day*[1]
SS Staff and Police Leaders	6/5
Waffen-SS	
SS Armored Grenadier Training and Reserve Battalion No. 3, Warsaw	4/440
SS Cavalry Training and Reserve, Unit, Warsaw	5/381
Police	
SS Police Regiment 22	
1st Battalion	3/94
3rd Battalion	3/134
Engineering Emergency Service	1/6
Polish Police	4/363
Polish Fire Brigade	166
Security Police	3/32
Army	
Light Anti-Aircraft Alarm Battery, III/8, Warsaw	2/22
Engineers Detachment of Railway Armored Trains Reserve Unit, Rembertow	2/42
Engineers Reserve Battalion 14, Gora-Kalwaria	1/34
Foreign Guard Units	
1 Battalion Trawniki men	2/335[2]

II

. . . Security considerations made it necessary to remove the Jews entirely from the city of Warsaw. The first large resettlement action took place in the period from July 22 to October 3, 1942. In this action, 310,322 Jews were removed for resettlement. In January 1943, a second resettlement action was carried out, comprising 6,500 Jews in all.

In January 1943, the Reichsführer SS, on the occasion of his visit to Warsaw, ordered the SS and Police Leader in the District of Warsaw[3] *to transfer to Lublin the armament factories and other enterprises of military importance installed within the ghetto, including their personnel and machines.*[4] The execution of this order proved to be quite difficult, since both the managers and the Jews resisted the transfer in every conceivable way. The SS and Police Leader therefore decided to effect the transfer of the enterprises by force, in a large-scale action to be carried out in three days. My predecessor had attended to the preparation and orders for this large-scale action. I myself arrived in Warsaw on April 17, 1943, and took over the command of the large-scale action on April 19, 1943, at 0800 hours, the action itself having started the same day at 0600 hours.

Before this large-scale action began, the boundaries of the former Jewish quarter had been blocked by an exterior cordon to prevent the Jews from breaking out. This cordon was continually maintained from the start to the end of the action and was especially reinforced at night.

When the ghetto was first invaded, the Jews and the Polish bandits, by a well-prepared concentration of fire, succeeded in repelling the participating units, including tanks and armored cars. In the second attack, at about 0800 hour, I deployed the forces separately through previously defined fighting zones, so as to have the whole ghetto combed out by the different units. Although the firing was repeated, the blocks were now successfully combed out according to plan. The enemy was forced to retreat from roofs and elevated bases to basements, bunkers, and sewers. To prevent escapes into the sewers, the sewer system beneath the Jewish quarter was promptly closed off and filled with water, but this move was for the most part frustrated by the Jews, who blew up the turn-off valves. Late the first day, rather heavy resistance was encountered, but was quickly broken by a specially assigned raiding party. Further operations succeeded in expelling the Jews from their prepared resistance bases, sniper holes, etc., and, during April 20 and 21, in gaining control of most of the so-called residual ghetto, to the extent that resistance within these blocks could no longer be called major or considerable.

The main Jewish fighting group, which was mixed with Polish bandits,[5] retreated as early as the first and second day to the so-called Muranowski Square. There it had been reinforced by a considerable number of Polish bandits. Its plan was to maintain itself in the ghetto by every means in order to prevent us from invading it. Jewish and Polish flags were hoisted on top of a concrete building as a call to arms against us. These two flags, however, were captured as early as the second day of the action by a special raiding party. In this skirmish with the bandits, SS *Untersturmführer* Dehmke was killed when a grenade he was holding in his hand was hit by the enemy and exploded, injuring him fatally.

After the first few days, I realized that the original plan had no prospect of success, unless the armament factories and other enterprises of military importance scattered throughout the ghetto were dissolved.[6] It was therefore necessary to require these enterprises to evacuate their quarters and move immediately, within an appropriate deadline. One enterprise after another was dealt with in this way, and thus in minimal time the Jews and bandits were deprived of the opportunity to take refuge, again and again, in these enterprises, which were under the supervision of the Army. Thorough inspections were necessary to decide in what length of time these enterprises could be evacuated. The conditions observed in the course of these inspections are indescribable. I cannot imagine that greater chaos could have existed anywhere than existed in the Warsaw ghetto. The Jews had control of everything, from chemical substances for manufacturing explosives to Army clothing and equipment. The managers knew so little of their own enterprises that the Jews were able to produce arms of every kind, especially hand grenades, Molotov cocktails, etc., inside these shops.

Moreover, the Jews had managed to set up resistance bases in these enterprises. One such resistance base, in an enterprise serving the Army's Quartermaster's Office, had to be combated as early as the second day by deploying an engineers' unit with flame throwers and by artillery fire. The Jews had installed themselves so firmly in this enterprise that it proved impossible to induce them to leave the shop voluntarily. I therefore resolved to destroy the enterprise by fire on the next day.

The managers of these enterprises, even though usually supervised by an Army officer, were in nearly all cases unable to provide concrete information about their stocks or the locations where stocks were stored. The statements they made as to the number of Jews employed by them did not check out in a single case. Again and again it was found that rich Jews, under cover as "armament workers," had found accommodations for themselves and their families in the labyrinths of buildings attached to the armament concerns as residential blocks, and were leading cushy lives there. Despite all orders to make the Jews leave those enterprises, it was repeatedly found that managers shut the Jews in, expecting that the action would last only a few days and that they then would go on working with the Jews remaining to them. According to statements by arrested Jews, owners of businesses arranged drinking parties with Jews. In these, women were said to have played a prominent part. The Jews reportedly endeavored to maintain good relations with Army officers and men. Carousals are said to have been frequent; and, in their course, business deals allegedly were concluded between Germans and Jews.

The number of Jews taken out of the houses and apprehended during the first few days was relatively small. It turned out that the Jews were hiding in the sewers and in specially constructed bunkers. Whereas it had been assumed during the first days that there were only isolated bunkers, it appeared in the course of the large-scale action that the whole ghetto had been systematically equipped with cellars, bunkers, and passageways. In every case these passageways and bunkers had access to the sewer system. Thus, undisturbed subterranean traffic among the Jews was possible. The Jews also used this sewer network to escape underground into the Aryan part of the city of Warsaw. Continually, reports were received of Jews attempting to escape through the sewer holes. Under the pretext of building air-raid shelters, the bunkers had been constructed in this former Jewish quarter since the late fall of 1942. They were intended to house all Jews during the new resettlement action, which had long been expected, and the resistance against the task forces was to be organized from here. Through posters, handbills, and whispering campaigns, the Communist resistance movement[7] in the former Jewish quarter had in fact managed to have the bunkers occupied as soon as the new large-scale action started. How far the Jews' precautions went was demonstrated by many instances of bunkers skillfully laid out with accommodations for entire families, washing and bathing facilities, toilets, arms and munition-storage bins, and ample food supplies for several months.

... To discover the individual bunkers was extremely difficult for the task forces, due to camouflage, and in many cases was possible only through betrayal on the part of the Jews.

After only a few days it was clear that the Jews no longer had any intention to resettle voluntarily, but were determined to fight back by every means and with the weapons at their disposal. Under Polish Bolshevik leadership,[8] so-called combat groups had been formed; they were armed and paid any price asked for available arms.

During the large-scale action it was possible to capture some Jews who had already been evacuated to Lublin or Treblinka, but had broken out from there and returned to the ghetto, equipped with arms and ammunition. Time and again Polish bandits found refuge in the ghetto and remained there virtually undisturbed, since no forces were on hand to penetrate this maze. Whereas at first it had been possible to capture the Jews, who normally are cowards, in considerable numbers, apprehending bandits and Jews became increasingly difficult during the second half of the large-scale action. Again and again, battle groups of 20 to 30 or more Jewish youths, 18 to 25 years of age, accompanied by corresponding numbers of females, kindled new resistance. These battle groups were under orders to put up armed resistance to the last and, if necessary, to escape capture by suicide.

One such battle group managed to climb from a sewer basin in the so-called Prosta[9] onto a truck and to escape with it (about 30–35 bandits). One bandit, who had arrived with this truck, exploded two hand grenades, which was the signal for the bandits waiting in the sewer to climb out of the basin. The bandits and Jews—there frequently were Polish bandits among them, armed with carbines, small arms, and one with a light machine gun—climbed on the truck and drove away in an unknown direction.[10] The last member of this gang, who was on guard in the sewer and was assigned to close the sewer-hole cover, was captured. He gave the above information. The search for the truck unfortunately proved fruitless.

During the armed resistance, the females belonging to the battle groups were armed in the same way as the men; some were members of the *Halutzim* movement. Not infrequently, these females fired pistols with both hands. Time and again it happened that they kept pistols and hand grenades (Polish "pineapple" hand grenades) concealed in their drawers up to the last moment, to use them against the men of the Waffen-SS, Police, or Army.

The resistance put up by the Jews and bandits could be broken only through energetic, indefatigable deployment of the patrols day and night. *On April 23, 1943, through the office of the Higher SS and Police Leader of the East, at Cracow, the Reichsführer SS issued an order to effect the combing of the ghetto in Warsaw with the greatest severity and ruthless tenacity.* I therefore decided to carry out the total destruction of the Jewish quarter by burning down all residential blocks, including the blocks attached to the armament factories. One enterprise after the other was systematically evacuated and immediately destroyed by fire. Nearly always the Jews then came out of their hiding places and bunkers. Not infrequently, the Jews stayed in the burning houses until, because of the heat and the fear of being burned to death, they chose to jump from the upper floors after having thrown mattresses and other upholstered articles from the burning houses into the street. With bones broken, they still would try to crawl across the street into blocks of houses which were not yet in flames, or only partly so. Often, too, Jews changed their hiding places during the night, by moving into the ruins of buildings already burned out and taking refuge there until they were found by the individual patrols. Their stay in the sewers also ceased to be pleasant after the first week. Frequently, loud voices, coming through the sewer shafts, could be heard in the street. The men of the Waffen-SS or Police or Army engineers would then courageously climb down the shafts and bring out the Jews, and not infrequently they stumbled over Jews already dead, or were shot at. It was necessary to use smoke candles to drive out the Jews. Thus, one day 193 sewer entrance holes were opened and at a fixed time smoke candles were lowered into them, with the result that the bandits, fleeing from what they believed to be gas, assembled in the center of the former Jewish quarter and could be pulled out of the sewer holes there. Numerous Jews, who could not be counted, were taken care of by the explosions in the sewers and bunkers.

The longer the resistance lasted, the tougher the men of the Waffen-SS, Police, and Army became; here as always, they tackled their duties indefatigably, in faithful comradeship, and constantly held their own in model, exemplary fashion. Their duty often lasted from early morning until late at night. At night, search patrols with rags wound around their feet remained at the heels of the Jews and kept up the pressure on them without interruption. Not infrequently, Jews who used the night for supplementing their stores of victuals from abandoned bunkers or for making contact or exchanging information with neighboring groups were apprehended and taken care of.

Considering that the men of the Waffen-SS for the most part had had only three to four weeks' training before being assigned to this action, the mettle, courage, and devotion to duty which they showed deserves special recognition. It may be stated that the Army engineers, too, executed their work of blowing up bunkers, sewers, and concrete buildings with indefatigable devotion to duty. Officers and men of the Police, a large part of whom already had front-line experience, again proved themselves through exemplary daring.

Only the continuous and untiring deployment of all forces made it possible to apprehend or verifiably destroy a total of 56,065 Jews. To this figure should be added those Jews who lost their lives in explosions, fires, etc., but whose numbers could not be ascertained.

Even while the large-scale action was going on, the Aryan population was informed by posters that entering the former Jewish quarter was strictly forbidden, and that anybody found in the former Jewish quarter without a valid permit would be shot. At the same time, the Aryan population was once more instructed by these posters that anybody who knowingly gave refuge to a Jew, especially anyone who housed, fed, or concealed a Jew outside the Jewish quarter, would be punished by death.

The Polish police were authorized to turn over to any Polish policeman who arrested a Jew in the Aryan part of the city of Warsaw one third of the Jew's cash property. This measure has already produced results.

The Polish population by and large welcomed the measures taken against the Jews. Toward the end of the large-scale action, the Governor[11] addressed a special proclamation, which was submitted to the undersigned for approval before publication, to the Polish population, enlightening the Poles about the reasons for destroying the former Jewish quarter and calling them to battle against Communist agents with reference to the assassinations lately carried out in the territory of the city of Warsaw and to the mass graves in Katyn.[12]

The large-scale action was terminated on May 16, 1943, with the blowing up of the Warsaw synagogue at 2015 hours.

At this time, there no longer are any industrial enterprises in the former Jewish quarter. All the objects of value, raw materials, and machines there have been moved and stored elsewhere. Whatever buildings, etc., existed have been destroyed. The only exception is the so-called Dzielna Prison[13] of the Security Police, which was exempted from destruction.

III

Inasmuch as one must reckon with the possibility, even after completion of the large-scale action, that a few Jews still remain among the ruins of the former Jewish quarter, this area must remain firmly shut off from the Aryan quarter during the near future, and must be guarded. Police Battalion III/23 has been assigned to this duty. This Police Battalion has instructions to keep watch over the former Jewish quarter, particularly to see that no one enters the former ghetto, and immediately to shoot anybody found there without authorization. The Commander of the Police Battalion will continue to receive further instructions directly from the SS and Police Leader. In this way, the small remnants of Jews, if any, must be kept under constant pressure and destroyed. By the destruction of all buildings and hiding places and the cutting off of the water supply, the remaining Jews and bandits must be deprived of any further chance of existence.

It is suggested that the Dzielna Prison be made into a concentration camp and that the inmates be used to salvage the millions of bricks, scrap iron, and other materials, collect them and make them available for reuse.

IV

Of the total of 56,065 Jews apprehended, about 7,000 were destroyed within the former ghetto in the course of the large-scale action, and 6,929 by transporting them to T. II,[14] which means that altogether 14,000 Jews were destroyed. Beyond the number of 56,065 Jews, an estimated 5,000 to 6,000 were killed by explosions or in fires.

The number of destroyed bunkers amount to 631.

Booty: 7 Polish rifles, 1 Russian rifle, 1 German rifle; 59 pistols of various calibers; several hundred hand grenades, including Polish and homemade ones; several hundred incendiary bottles; homemade explosives; infernal machines with fuses; a large amount of explosives, ammunition for weapons of all calibers, including some machine-gun ammunition.

Regarding the booty of arms, it must be taken into consideration that the arms themselves could in most cases not be captured, as the bandits and Jews would, before being arrested, thrown them into hiding places or holes which could not be ascertained or discovered. The smoking out of the bunkers by our men also often made the search for arms impossible. As the bunkers had to be blown up at one, a search later on was out of the question.

The captured hand grenades, ammunition, and incendiary bottles were at once reused by us against the bandits.

Further Booty Taken: 1,240 used military tunics (part of them with medal ribbons—Iron Cross and East Medal); 600 pairs of used trousers; other equipment and German steel helmets; 108 horses, 4 of them still in the former ghetto (hearse).

Up to May 23 [sic], 1943, we had counted: 4.4 million zloty; furthermore, about 5–6 million zloty not yet counted, a large amount of foreign currency, among others, $14,300 in paper money and $9,200 in gold, besides jewelry (rings, necklaces, watches, etc.) in large quantities.

State of the ghetto at the termination of the large-scale action: Apart from 8 buildings (police barracks, hospital, and accommodations for housing the factory police), the former ghetto is completely destroyed. Only fireproof walls are left standing where no explosions were carried out. But the ruins still contain a vast amount of stones and scrap material which could be used.

Notes

1. Officers and men are shown separately; 4/440 means four officers, 440 men.

2. Totals: 36 officers, 2054 men.

3. Ferdinand von Sammern-Frankenegg (1897–1944) was for a short while SS and Police Leader in the Warsaw District. He was replaced by General Stroop on April 19, 1943.

4. On January 9, 1943, Himmler, astonished that his orders (of July 19 and October 9, 1942), to clear the *Generalgouvernement* of Jews by the end of 1942 had not yet been complied with, gave Sammern-Frankenegg until February 15 to do so and to transfer the industrial enterprises to Lublin.

5. No non-Jews participated in the fighting in the ghetto. By predicating a Polish presence, Stroop could portray the Jews as cowards, unable to fight without outside help.

6. Most of the units of the Jewish Combat Organization were based in the factories, where both fighters and civilians worked and slept.

7. The Jewish resistance movement was in fact Zionist and Bundist, with the Jewish Communists playing only a modest role.

8. Stroop falsely attributed Polish, that is non-Jewish, and Communist initiative to the organization of Jewish resistance.

9. A street that ran from inside the ghetto to beyond its confines.

10. In this case, a few members of the Communist Polish (non-Jewish) underground cooperated with the Jewish combatants, picking up, by truck, those who had managed to escape through the sewers and taking them to safety.

11. Governor Hans Frank.

12. A reference to the mass graves of Polish officers found in 1943 in a forest near the village of Katyn near Smolensk in the Soviet Union. The Germans charged that the Russians had murdered the Polish officers during the Russian invasion and occupation of Eastern Poland in 1939. In 1990 the Russian government finally admitted that in 1940 the NKVD (predecessor of the KGB) had shot more than 6,000 Polish officers in the back of the head in the Katyn Forest.—Eds.

13. The prison was more commonly known as Pawiak, because it was located on Pawia Street, with its main entrance on Dzielna.

14. A code for the death camp of Treblinka.

378

HEINRICH HIMMLER

Speech at Posen

Delivered 4 October 1943. Published in *Trial of the Major War Criminals before the International Military Tribunal* (Nuremberg, 1947–49), doc. no. 1919-PS, 29:110–73.

Summation, October 4, 1943

. . . In 1941 the Führer attacked Russia. This was, as we probably can assert now, shortly—perhaps three to six months—before Stalin was winding up for his great push into Central and Western Europe. I can sketch this first year in a very few lines. The attack cut through. The Russian army was herded together in great pockets, ground down, captured. At that time we did not value this human mass the way we value it today, as raw material, as labor. In the long run, viewed in terms of generations, it is no loss, but today, because of the loss of manpower, it is regrettable that the prisoners died by the tens and hundreds of thousands of exhaustion, of hunger . . .

Good Nature in the Wrong Place

It is a basic mistake for us to infuse our inoffensive soul and feeling, our good nature, our idealism, into alien peoples. This has been true since the time of Herder, who must have written *Stimmen der Völker* in a boozy hour,[1] and who thereby brought such immeasurable sorrow and misery on us later generations. This has been true since the case of the Czechs and Slovenes, to whom, after all, we gave their sense of nationality. They themselves were not capable of achieving it; we invented it for them.

One basic principle must be absolute for the SS man: we must be honest, decent, loyal, and comradely to members of our own blood and to nobody else. What happens to the Russians, what happens to the Czechs, is a matter of total indifference to me. What there is among the nations in the way of good blood of our kind, we will take for ourselves—if necessary, by kidnapping their children and raising them among us. Whether the other nations live in prosperity or croak from hunger interests me only insofar as we need them as slaves for our culture; otherwise, it does not interest me. Whether 10,000 Russian females drop from exhaustion while building an anti-tank ditch interests me only insofar as the anti-tank ditch gets finished for Germany's sake. We shall never be brutal and heartless where it is not necessary—obviously not. We Germans, the only people in the world who have a decent attitude toward animals, will also take a decent attitude toward these human animals. But it is a crime against our own blood to worry about them and to give them ideals that will make it still harder for our sons and grandsons to cope with them. If someone were to come to me and say, "I cannot build the anti-tank ditch with women and children; it is inhuman, they will die in the process," then I would have to say, "You are a murderer of your own blood, for if the anti-tank ditch is not built, German soldiers will die and they are sons of German mothers. They are our own blood." This is what I want to instill into the SS and what I believe I have instilled into them as one of the most sacred laws of the future; Our concern, our duty is to our people and our blood; it is for them that we have to provide and to plan, to work and to fight, and for nothing else. Toward anything else we can be indifferent. I wish the SS to take this attitude in confronting the problem of all alien, non-Germanic peoples, especially the Russians. All else is just soap bubbles, is a fraud against our own nation and an obstacle to the earlier winning of the war . . .

Foreigners in the Reich

We must also realize that we have between six and seven million foreigners in Germany, perhaps even eight million by now. We have prisoners in Germany. They are none of them dangerous so long as we hit them hard at the smallest trifle. Shooting ten Poles today is a mere nothing when compared with the fact that we might later have to shoot tens of thousands in their place, and that the shooting of these tens of thousands would also cost German blood. Every little fire will immediately be stamped out and quenched and extinguished; otherwise—as with a real conflagration—a political and psychological fire may break out among the people.

The Communists in the Reich

I do not believe the Communists could risk any action, for their leading elements, like most criminals, are in our concentration camps. Here something needs saying: After the war it will be possible to see what a blessing it was for Germany that, regardless of all humanitarian sentimentality, we imprisoned this whole criminal substratum of the German people in the concentration camps; and for this I claim the credit. If these people were going about free, we would be having a harder time of it. For then the subhumans would have their NCO's and commanding officers, they would have their workers' and soldiers' councils. As it is, they are locked up, and are making shells or projectile cases or other important things, and are very useful members of human society . . .

The Evacuation of the Jews

I also want to make reference before you here, in complete frankness, to a really grave matter. Among ourselves, this once, it shall be uttered quite frankly; but in public we will never speak of it. Just as we did not hesitate on June 30, 1934, to do our duty as ordered, to stand up against the wall comrades who had transgressed, and shoot them,[2] so we have never talked about this and never will. It was the tact which I am glad to say is a matter of course to us that made us never discuss it among ourselves, never talk about it. Each of us shuddered, and yet each one knew that he would do it again if it were ordered and if it were necessary.

I am referring to the evacuation of the Jews, the annihilation of the Jewish people. This is one of those things that are easily said. "The Jewish people is going to be annihilated," says every party member. "Sure, it's in our program, elimination of the Jews, annihilation—we'll take care of it." And then they all come trudging, 80 million worthy Germans, and each one has his one decent Jew. Sure, the others are swine, but this one is an A-1 Jew. Of all those who talk this way, not one has seen it happen, not one has been through it. Most of you must know what it means to see a hundred corpses lie side by side, or five hundred, or a thousand. To have stuck this out and—excepting cases of human weakness—to have kept our integrity, that is what has made us hard. In our history, this is an unwritten and never-to-be-written page of glory, for we know how difficult we would have made it for ourselves if today—amid the bomb raids, the hardships and the deprivations of war—we still had the Jews in every city as secret saboteurs, agitators, and demagogues. If the Jews were still ensconced in the body of the German nation, we probably would have reached the 1916–17 stage by now.[3]

The wealth they had we have taken from them. I have issued a strict order, carried out by SS-Obergruppenführer Pohl, that this wealth in its entirety is to be turned over to the Reich as a matter of course. We have taken none of it for ourselves. Individuals who transgress will be punished in accordance with an order I issued at the beginning, threatening that whoever takes so much as a mark of it for himself is a dead man. A number of SS men—not very many—have transgressed, and they will die, without mercy. We had the moral right, we had the duty toward our people, to kill this people which wanted to kill us. But we do not have the right to enrich ourselves with so much as a fur, a watch, a mark, or a cigarette or anything else. Having exterminated a germ, we do not want in the end, to be infected by the germ, and die of it. I will not stand by and let even a small rotten spot develop or take hold. Wherever it may form, we together will cauterize it. All in all, however, we can say that we have carried out this heaviest of our tasks in a spirit of love for our people. And our inward being, our soul, our character has not suffered injury from it.

The Bearing of the SS Man

In giving, I might almost say, an accounting before and on behalf of all of us of what we have done this year, there is one thing I must not overlook or pass over: the significance of the SS man's bearing . . .

We have come into being through the law of selection. We have made our selection from a cross section of our people. This people came into being by the throw of the dice of fate and of history—eons ago, through generations and centuries. Alien peoples swept over this people and left their heritage behind them. Alien bloodlines merged into this people; yet, in spite of the most terrible hardships and the most terrible blows of fate, this people in essence of its blood has had the strength to win through. Thus this whole people is permeated and held together by Nordic-Falic-Germanic blood, so that one could and can, after all, still speak of a German people. From this people, multifariously mixed in its hereditary tendencies, as it emerged from the collapse after the years of the fight for freedom, we have consciously tried to select the Nordic-Germanic blood, for we could most fully expect this portion of our blood to be the bearer of the creative and heroic, the life-preserving qualities of our people. We have gone partly by outward appearance, and for the rest have verified this outward appearance through constantly renewed demands, constantly renewed tests—physical and mental—of the character and the psyche. Again and again we have sifted out and cast aside what was unfit, what did not belong with us. As long as we have the strength to do so, this brotherhood[4] will be healthy. If we were to forget for one moment the law of our basis as a people and the law of selection and of severity toward ourselves, in that moment we would have the seed of death in us; in that moment we would perish just as every human organization just as every blossom in this world perishes at some time. To make this blossoming and bearing of fruit as beneficial as possible for our people, to make it continue as long as possible, even—don't be alarmed—for thousands of years if possible, must be our endeavor, our inner law. That is why, whenever we meet and whatever we do, we are obligated to be mindful of our guiding principle: blood selection, severity. The law of nature, after all, is this: What is hard is good; what is vigorous is good; whatever wins through in the struggle of life, physically or in terms of the will or the spirit, that is what is good—always taking the long view. Of course, occasionally (and this has often happened in history someone may get to the top by fraud and deceit. To nature, to the fate of the earth, to the fate of the world this makes no difference. After some time, reckoned not in generations of man but in historical eras, reality (that is, nature) and fate depose the imposter. Never to deceive ourselves but always to remain genuine, that must be our endeavor; that is what we must continually preach and instill into ourselves and into every boy and each of our subordinates . . .

The Virtues of the SS Man

I will speak now of the most important virtues which I began years ago to preach to, and impress on, this brotherhood, this whole General SS[5]—for they are the basis of the brotherhood and just now, in the fifth year of the war, are of such decisive significance and importance.

(1) *Loyalty*

So far, I am glad to say, we have not had a single case in our ranks of a prominent SS man becoming disloyal. Let this be your guideline: If within your purview anyone should ever be disloyal to the Führer or the Reich, even if only in thought, it is up to you to see to it that this man departs from the brotherhood, and we will see to it that he departs this life. For anything—I have said this before, and I repeat it today—anything can be forgiven in this world, but one thing cannot be forgiven among us Germanic people, and that is disloyalty. It would be unforgiveable and *is* unforgiveable. Cases like the Badoglio[6] case in Italy must not and will not occur in Germany. In the future, the name Badoglio will be the name for bad dogs, the epithet for four-legged mongrel curs, just as in antiquity the name Thersites was an epithet for traitors. We can say only this and preach it constantly: Let the German people as embodied in each of its men and each of its women, show by means of matchless and unconditional loyalty that it was worthy to live in the time of Adolf Hitler, and to have this leader arise for its sake, who has dedicated his life of care, of responsibility, of toil, to our German, Germanic people

(2) *Obedience*

In the soldier's life, obedience is demanded and given, morning, noon, and night. And the man of low rank obeys all or most of the time. If he does not obey, he is locked up. The question of obedience is more difficult where it concerns higher-ranking officials in the state, the party and the armed forces, and here and there in the SS as well. I would like here to state clearly and unequivocally: It is a matter of course that the man in the ranks must obey; it is even more a matter of course that all high-ranking leaders of the SS—the whole Gruppenführer corps,[7] that is—are models of unconditional obedience. If someone believes that an order rests on a misconception on the part of his superior, or on a false basis, it goes without saying that he—that is, each of you—has the duty and responsibility to bring the matter up for discussion, and also to state his reasons truthfully, like a man, if he is convinced that such reasons speak against the order. But once the superior concerned or the Reichsführer SS—it will be he in most cases where the Gruppenführer corps is concerned—or the Führer himself has made a decision and given the order, it must be carried out, not only according to the word and the letter, but also in spirit. Whoever executes the order must do so as a faithful steward, as a faithful representative of the authority that gives the command. If you thought initially that something was the right thing to do, and something else was not right, or was actually ill-advised, then there are two alternatives. If a man believes he cannot take on the responsibility for obeying an order, he must candidly state: "I cannot take the responsibility; I beg to be excused." Probably in most cases, an order will come through, saying: "You must carry it out anyway." Alternately, one may think: "His nerves are shot, he's weak." In that case, one can say, "Very well, retire on a pension." But orders must be sacred. When generals obey, armies obey automatically. This sacredness of orders applies the more, the larger our territory grows. To enforce an order in our little Germany was not difficult at all. To enforce an order once we have—and I am convinced that we will have—garrisons in the Urals, that's a bit more difficult. There it will not always be possible to verify whether the order has been carried out. With us, the verifications must not, must never be left to a commissar, as it is in Russia. The only commissar we have must be our own conscience, devotion to duty, loyalty, obedience. If you lead the way with this example, gentlemen, every subordinate will follow. But you will never be able to demand obedience of your men if you do not give the same obedience to the authority above you, and give it unconditionally and without reservation.

(3) *Bravery*

Bravery, I think, requires the least exhortation among us, for our leaders and our men *are* brave . . .

Within our ranks we live by our Germanic laws, among which a particularly beautiful one reads: "Honor is compulsion enough." To the alien people we will apply Asiatic laws. We will never confuse this issue. When we are dealing with someone of our own blood, a Norwegian or Netherlander of good race, we can win his allegiance only by way of our—that is, his and our—pan-Germanic laws. When we are dealing with a Russian or with someone who, in terms of blood, is a Slav, we will never apply our sacred laws to him, but will use the proven Russian laws of the commissars . . .

(4) *Truthfulness*

I now come to a fourth virtue, which is very rare in Germany: truthfulness. One of the greatest evils that have spread during the war is untruthfulness in information, reports, and statements which subordinate agencies in civilian life, in the state, the party, and the armed services send to the agencies above them. The information, the report, is the basis of every decision. It is a fact that during the present war one can assume in many spheres that 95 out of 100 messages are lies, or only half true or partly correct . . .

While on the subject of truthfulness, I come to another matter. In war and in peace—in peacetime especially this will be an educational task—we SS men must get to the point where we will no longer conclude written agreements; where among us, as was customary in former days, a man's word and handshake constitute a contract, and where the handshake of one SS man will, if necessary, be binding for a million or more. We must get to where the handshake or the word of an SS man is proverbially more reliable than a mortgage on someone else's most valuable property. That's how it must be.

If we enter contracts, we must keep them. If I enter a contract with an agent, even with a disreputable type, I keep the contract. I take my stand unconditionally on this point of view. When I announce in the Generalgouvernement that anyone informing against a Jew who has sought shelter and gone into hiding is to have a third of the Jew's property,[8] it very often happens that some Secretary Huber[9] or Untersturmführer Huber—who takes illegal trips when he can, who orders a new telephone or new pencils without a moment's thought, in short who never saves—suddenly begins to save for the German Reich. He will say, for instance: "This Jew has 12,000 Reichsmark. Why, that means I'd have to pay out 4,000 RM to the Pole who denounced him. I'd rather save that for Germany. The Pole will get only 400."

In this way, a little man goes and breaks the promise of a whole organization. That sort of thing should be impossible . . .

The Future

. . . When peace has become definitive, we will be in a position to tackle our great work for the future. We will colonize. We will indoctrinate the younger people with the laws of the SS brotherhood. I consider it inescapably necessary for the life of our people that we teach the concepts of ancestry, posterity, and the future not just in a superficial way, but feel them to be part of our being. Without any talk about it, without our having to make use of prizes or suchlike material things, it must be a matter of course that we have children. It must be a matter of course that the most numerous progeny comes from this brotherhood, this racial top stratum of the Germanic people. Twenty to thirty years from now, we actually must be able to supply the leading echelon for all of Europe. If the SS together with farmers—we with our friend Backe[10]—will then carry on the colonization in the East, on a grand scale, without any inhibition, without any concern about traditional ways, with elan and revolutionary impetus, we will within twenty years push the ethnic boundary 500 kilometers eastward.

I requested of the Führer today that the SS—provided we fulfill our task and our duty up to the end of the war—be granted the privilege of holding Germany's extreme eastern frontier as a defense frontier. I believe this is the only privilege for which we have no competitors. I believe not one person will dispute our claim to this privilege. Out there, we will be in a position to give each year's crop of young men practical training in the use of arms. We will force our laws upon the East. We will charge ahead and push our way forward, little by little to the Urals. I hope our generation can still succeed in having each year's age group fight in the East, and in having each of our divisions spend a winter in the East every second or third year. If so, we will never grow soft; we will never have wearers of our uniform who join us only because it is classy and because the black coat naturally will be very attractive in peacetime. Each one will know: "If I join the SS, there is the possibility that I might be shot dead." He has it in writing that every other year he will not be dancing in Berlin or celebrating carnival in Munich, but will be stationed on the Eastern frontier in an icy winter. In this way, we will have a healthy elite for all time. With it we will create the conditions under which the whole Germanic people and the whole of Europe—guided, organized and led by us, the Germanic people—will be able to prevail generations hence in its fateful struggles with an Asia that is sure to surge forward again. We do not know when that will be. When that human mass lines up on the other side with 1 or 1½ billion, then the Germanic people, numbering, I hope, 240 to 300 million, together with the other European peoples, making a total of 600 to 700 million—and with an outpost area stretching as far as the Ural or, a hundred years from now, beyond the Urals—will have to prevail in its struggle for existence in Asia. Woe betide if the Germanic people were not to prevail! It would be the end of beauty and civilization, of the creative power of this earth. That is the distant future. It is for this that we fight, pledged to hand down the heritage of our ancestors.

We look into the distance because we know what it will be. That is why we are doing our duty more fanatically than ever, more devoutly than ever, more bravely, obediently, and honorably than ever. We want to be worthy of having been permitted to be the first SS men of the Führer, Adolf Hitler, in the long history of the Germanic people which stretches before us.

We now direct our thoughts to the Führer, our Führer, Adolf Hitler, who will create the Germanic Reich and will lead us into the Germanic future.

To our Führer Adolf Hitler:

Sieg Heil!

Sieg Heil!

Sieg Heil!

Notes

1. Johann Gottfried von Herder (1744–1803), German philosopher and poet, has been called the father of German nationalism. He published an anthology of folk songs of various peoples called *Stimmen der Völker* (Voices of the Peoples).

2. A reference to the purge of the SA and the murder of its top leaders by SS officers and men. (See chapter 2.)

3. The reference is to the time when the tide of the First World War began to turn against Germany. German nationalists and rightists then attributed Germany's losses and ultimate defeat to the *Dolchstoß*, the "stab in the back" by the Jews.

4. The German is *Orden*, a monastic or military order. Himmler tried to organize the SS along the line of a medieval religious/military order.

5. The *Allgemeine SS* (General SS) denoted the general body of SS members, as distinct from special groups with the SS, like the *Totenkopfverbände* (Death's-Head units), assigned to the concentration camps or the *Waffen-SS*, fully militarized combat formations that participated in military campaigns alongside the Armed Forces.

6. Field Marshall Pietro Badoglio (1871–1956) took over the leadership of the Italian government, formed in July 1943, after the overthrow of Mussolini. He later joined the Allies in the war against Germany.

7. The ranks of lieutenant-general and above.

8. Cf. Stroop's report, part II. [See document 377 in this chapter.—Eds.]

9. The average man, "Huber" is the German equivalent of "John Doe."

10. SS Obergruppenführer (General) Herbert Backe (1896–1947) had been the Secretary of State in the Reich Ministry of Food and Agriculture and, since 1943, Reich Minister of Food and Reich Peasant Leader.

379

EGON (GONDA) REDLICH

Theresienstadt Diary

Entries written between 11 April and 2 August 1944. Published in *The Terezin Diary of Gonda Redlich*, edited by Saul S. Friedman, translated by Laurence Kutler (Lexington: University Press of Kentucky, 1992), 145–50.

April–August

[Diary editor's note] *Another spring in Terezin, with a different emphasis from the Nazi authorities. Heydrich's "Paradise Ghetto" for the elderly was to be purged of the aged, the sick, and overcrowding to impress a Red Cross delegation scheduled to arrive in June. Redlich's fear that Terezin might serve as a Potemkin Village became a reality after several months of Embellishment.*

April 11, 1944. They took down the fence that surrounded the city square. But it is forbidden to walk in the square. We are awaiting an important commission and want to show the city in its beauty.[1]

A tale of a man who brought contraband into the city. They wanted to search among his belongings and asked him what he was carrying. He answered that in his pack was the excrement of people who had typhus. He was bringing it to the station in order to send it to the university in Prague for testing. The police were afraid of this contagious disease and allowed him to pass.

April 17, 1944. Two children arrived from Lublin. The children spent a year in a monastery with their Christian grandmother who brought them to the ghetto, then returned to Lublin.[2]

We aren't living in the ghetto, but in the Jewish *Siedlungsgebiet* (settlement).

April 23, 1944. The German commandant [Rahm] toured the park. Children followed him and called out: "Pane Rahm. Pane Rahm!" He smiled and swelled with pride: "You see how famous I am"[3]

April 27, 1944. They have handed some mothers from the infants' house, who did not want to work outside the shelter, over for judgment. I was called as an expert. It's hard to decide. On the one hand, it's hard for the childcare people to get along with the mothers. On the other hand, perhaps we should understand the mothers who don't want to give over the care of their children to caretakers because such care isn't good enough. Sometimes, the caretakers are too lax.

They are beautifying and improving the city. They fixed two children's homes and they look like nice sanitoriums.

May 3, 1944. A new hall has opened.[4] Festive speeches. Music, song. Two Germans stand on the gallery and look at the proceedings.

May 9, 1944. Barbed-wire fences have been forbidden. The password today is *Stadtverschönerung* [beautification of the city].[5]

June 1, 1944. Transports have gone. How many times already? Seventy-five hundred people traveled. Most had worked here for two years . . .[6]

A commission will be coming to inspect the city. They have been working for more than two months in order to improve the city.

The Germans took out two hundred craftsmen from the transport. Jews from Germany left, from Austria, and the Protectorate. There were many arguments among the *Landsmannschaften* [regional groups].[7]

June 6, 1944.[8] The story of a young man: his mother died a while ago and a woman who did not like her wanted to assume custody of the child. Before her death, the mother asked that the son not agree to have this woman as a guardian. Very well and good, but this woman is the lover of an influential man who could exempt him from a transport. What to do?

June 12, 1944. A cripple wants to get something from a medical orderly.[9] The orderly says: the thing isn't available. I can't get it for you. The cripple gives the orderly a can of sardines. Suddenly the thing is found in storage. Suddenly it can be obtained.

June 14, 1944. An incident with a doctor: the doctor is a young Jew who loves his profession. He married a girl sixteen years his junior. The girl was rich and spoiled. After the wedding, she helped him in his surgery. The doctor did not permit her to go and have a good time in the coffee houses. They did not have any children because her husband did not want any.

When they came here, the wife was happy that she was not living with her husband. Then, finally, she and her husband got an apartment together. Then all hell broke loose. The doctor became very involved in his work. He was the only one who was loved by all the mothers in the infants' house. The wife saw the doctor taking care of all the other children. Her husband loved her passionately.

After a while, the doctor became ill with typhus. The disease lasted several months. The wife was left alone in the house because her husband was lying ill in the hospital. She was free.

During the same period, she got involved with a conductor and had sex with him. When the doctor was restored to health, she returned to him. Meanwhile, she became pregnant, and the doctor tried to force her to have an abortion. There were many reasons: it is forbidden to give birth in the ghetto, no security for the future, and the fear that the child she was carrying was not his. But the wife refused to listen to him. He urged her until, in desperation, she attempted suicide. Her husband did not want to save her. Instead, he wanted to join her. By chance, her father saved her. She went to the hospital, and there they performed an abortion. Afterwards, she refused to sleep with her husband. Her parents were put on the last transport. The doctor succeeded in saving them, and as a reward she slept with him. A few days ago, she left him for good.

June 18, 1944. Inspections by high-ranking officials (State Minister Frank).[10] They permitted the reconstruction of the school.[11] Jewish *chutzpah* [gall] is really too much. One Jew changed his name from Cohen to Coma twenty years ago. Now a package of sardines has arrived with the name Cohen and he wants it. Suddenly his name is Cohen, not Coma.

June 19, 1944. All events center around one thing: the visit of the commission. They rain down order after order. Kindergarten children are to sing during the visit, the workers are to return home. Plays and cultural events and sporting activities must take place. Even the few labs left here roam about on the grass around the city. The children, the workers, the sheep—a perfect idyll.[12] An argument whether to teach Hebrew as a mandatory subject or an elective.

June 22, 1944. A sign "school for boys and girls. Now, in vacation time!" Such is the teaching permitted. It is forbidden to smoke in the city. This is a permit to smoke.[13]

June 25, 1944. "Do not smoke, gentlemen. Mr. Eppstein has imposed a ban on smoking."[14] The Germans told this to the Red Cross Commission.[15]

July 6, 1944. Today, two weeks after the committee's visit, they ordered the firing of the administrators of houses L417 and L318. These are people who have worked with me for more than two and one-half years. No one knows the reason for the firing.[16]

August 2, 1944.[17] A woman has arrived in the ghetto, bringing with her one thousand crowns of ghetto money. She bought them in Prague and paid over thirty thousand Czech crowns for them.[18]

Notes

Notes edited for length. Bracketed additions ours.—Eds.

1. To impress the Red Cross, some of the barriers segregating the Jews from German personnel [. . .] were eliminated. As the visit of the international commission drew near, concerts were given twice daily from the pavilion in this idyllic setting.

2. [H. G.] Adler, [*Theresienstadt 1941–1945: das Antlitz einer Zwangsgemeinschaft. Geschichte, Soziologie, Psychologie* (Tübingen: Mohr, 1955)], 699, reports some four thousand Jews of mixed ancestry in the ghetto at this time.

3. Leo has left a sketch showing the ghetto commander in a different time, when the barriers were up. The commandant, replete with jackboots and a riding crop, is strutting through the wooded yard, while on the other side of a flimsy wooden barricade, Jews crowd by in despair.

4. While the post office and bank were merely refurbished, the *Sokolovna,* which had served as a hospital for encephalitis patients, was transformed into a community center. There were carpeted meeting rooms for the *Ältestenrat* in *the Haus der Jüdischen Selbstverwaltung,* Hebrew signs posted over the morgue, a library, a stage for cultural performances. And after all the aggravation about sharing space for religious services with other activities, the gymnasium became a prayer hall.

5. Adler and Lederer concur that the process had been ongoing for several months, but the best testimony comes from Rena Rosenberger, who wrote: "For the children, a playground was laid out with sandboxes and swings, a 'children's pavilion' was built and painted from inside with big wooden animals as toys. Behind a glass veranda you could see a dozen kribs [*sic*]. It was like a story book—but children were only allowed to enter this little paradise on the say the commission visited Theresienstadt. . . . That was it. Only bluff! The barracks and all the houses were painted from outside and inside. Only that part was painted where the Commission was supposed to make their inspection. Gazons [*sic?*] were laid out, an eating hall was opened which was only used during the time of the Commission's visit. There you were served by girls with white aprons and you were served on a plate. Forks and spoons you had to bring yourself. At the day of the Commission's visit, the tables were set with white tablecloths and flowers. The city now had a restaurant. . . . The windows of the stores also got another look with displays of things you couldn't buy and you could see suddenly sugar, margarine and vegetables in the foodstores. The butchers carried sausages, canned meat and liver sausages. Everybody looked with amazement at the windows"

6. Transport Dz left on May 15 with 2,503 persons bound for Auschwitz. In July, this group underwent selections and 119 survived. Transport Ea left for Auschwitz on May 16 and Eb followed on May 18, both with 2,500 persons. Some of the Hungarians (80 in the first group) and some musicians were spared. Most were gassed in the July selections of the Birkenau Family Camp. There were 5 survivors of Ea, 261 of Eb. The arrival of so many more Jews from Terezin probably hastened the end of the Family Camp.

7. It was during the registration of these May transports that Otto Zucker, his face bandaged, confronted Commandant Rahm and insisted that a number of personnel crucial to ghetto operations not be deported. Rahm was furious, but ultimately got his way sending most of those who had temporarily been exempted to their deaths ([Zdenek] Lederer, [*Ghetto Theresienstadt* (London: E. Goldston, 1953)], 112–14). The transports included 511 children, 3,601 persons between the ages of fifteen and sixty, and 3,391 over sixty-one. They were divided among 3,125 Germans, 2,543 from the Protectorate, 1,276 Austrians, and 559 Ditch Jews. When it was all over, the ghetto population was a manageable 28,090 (Adler, [*Theresienstadt 1941–1945*], 699).

8. Redlich was aware of the Allied invasion of Normandy on this date. See entry for June 23, 1944, in [the diary he kept after the birth of his son] Dan [in March 1944].

9. Almost as amazing as the availability of sardines (which arrived in special Red Cross parcels via Portugal) was the existence of a lame and handicapped person (1,398 cripples, 333 blind) in the ghetto after the May transport (Adler, [*Theresienstadt 1941–1945*], 699).

10. Obergruppenführer Karl Hermann Frank was Heydrich's successor as Protector of Bohemia and Moravia. He was executed in Prague in 1946.

11. Lederer tells how Commandant Rahm placed a sign "Boys' School" over the entry to a former hospital. The rooms were furnished with blackboards on which was written "closed for the holidays." See entry June 22, 1944.

12. There were numerous rehearsals before the commission arrived. In contrast with earlier visits. Terezin's Jews were told to answer questions put to them. Dr. Eppstein was supplied with an auto and a chauffeur. On June 23, the commission made up of Frants Hvass of the Danish Red Cross, Dr. Juel Henningsen of the Danish Foreign Ministry, Dr. M. Rossel from the Swiss Red Cross, and D. Heidenkampf of the German Red Cross were accompanied by Everhard von Thadden of the German Foreign Office, Günther, and Commandant Rahm. Their tour, through specific areas of the ghetto, was, writes Theodor Möbs, very successful: "It [the commission] saw a soccer game with excited onlookers, exemplary rock gardens, interiors of buildings, the children's rest home, the steam laundry, sun-browned children singing and laughing with shovels on their shoulders, white gloved bread distributors, the white bread bakery and the pharmacy. In the dining hall, it saw how well the camp inmates were fed and how they were served by white-approved waitresses.

"During the noon hour, the guests were fed and the sightseeing quickly continued. They were shown the central swimming pool, the butcher shop, the fire department, the hospital and the boys' home. Then there was a long discussion with Dr. [Erich] Springer, the Surgical Director, and then they saw the steam kitchens, and the children's pavilion. The tour lasted six hours and it is no wonder that the individual commission members were extraordinarily influenced and had not the slightest suspicion of any deception" (Dr. Theodor Möbs, *Theresienstadt: Eine Philatelistische Studie* [Frankfurt: Philipp Kohler, 1965], trans. Dr. Carl Praeger, 6–7).

13. Redlich's comments are etched in sarcasm. After interfacing with any semblance of an organized school curriculum, the Nazis furnished a building with benches and other materials to create the illusion that education was continuing in the ghetto. As for smoking, even the possession of cigarettes was punishable.

14. The charade would not last much longer. With more deportations looming that fall, Dr. Eppstein advised his colleagues on September 19: "We are like a ship that sees the long-awaited harbor from a distance. We can recognize our friends on the shore. But we still must steer through unseen reefs. We should not be deceived by premature celebrations" (Adler, [*Theresienstadt 1941–1945*], 814). Eight days after making that speech, Eppstein was arrested by Rahm and thrown into the Little Fortress [prison]. He was shot there in October (Lederer, [*Ghetto Theresienstadt*], 148–50).

15. How much the Red Cross delegates were influenced by this sham is difficult to tell. In their reports, Hvass, Hennigsen, and Rossel described Terezin as an *Endlager* (final camp) where conditions were "relatively good." After the war, representatives of the International Red Cross explained they had not been deceived and that their very presence had eased conditions for the Jews. In fact, the IRC never made a formal representation on behalf of the Jews in concentration camps who, it agreed in Nazi parlance, were *Schutzhäftlinge* (common criminals). See Arthur Morse, *While Six Million Died* (New York: Random [House], 1967), 325; *Report of the International Committee of the Red Cross on Its Activities during the Second World War*, XVIIth International Red Cross Conference (Geneva, 1948), Vol. I, p. 19; and Jean Claude Favez, *Une Mission impossible? Le CICR, les deportations et les camps de concentration Nazis* (Lausanne, 1988). This particular visit led directly to the May deportations from Terezin, which in turn prompted the destruction of the Family Camp in Auschwitz. That the survivors in Terezin were not overjoyed, see July 6, 1944 entry. Apparently Hans Günther was delighted with what had occurred, for he now ordered the filming of a documentary on this so-called Jewish health spa. As noted previously,

only forty yards of this film, labeled "Aktion Z" has survived. See Lederer, [*Ghetto Theresienstadt*], 119–21.

16. The Embellishment was, said Edith Ornstein, "irrisinnig Vorbereitungen, irrsinniger humbug" (insane preparations, insane humbug) [Ornstein report, Beit Terezin Archives, p. 9]. "We wanted so much to believe," wrote Resi Weglein, "that the terrible hunger would be past. But we saw our hopes dashed to the ground. Two days after the commission disappeared, our meals were stripped back for two weeks. The common cry resounded: 'Nie wieder Kommissionen!' (never again commissions)" (Weglein memoir, Beit Terezin Archives, p. 45).

17. Redlich's last entry in his own journal.

18. Ghetto *Krone* were useless outside of Terezin. Possession of large sums of Czech currency inside the ghetto was dangerous. Thus, the desperate exchange.

380

OSWALD POHL

Expanding Auschwitz

Memo to Heinrich Himmler written on 15 September 1942. First published by Susanne Willems, www.susannewillems.de/buch_speerdokumente.php (accessed 12 April 2011).

To the
SS-Reichsführer
Berlin SW 11
Prinz Albrechtstr. 8

Reichsführer!

Yesterday the meeting took place with *Reichsminister* Prof. Dr. Speer.

Present were:

Reichsminister Prof. Speer,

SS-Obergruppenführer Pohl,

SS-Brigadenführer Staatsrat Dr. Schreiber,

Dipl. Ing. [diploma in engineering] Bauer

Ministerialrat Steffen

Ministerialrat Dr. Brisse

SS-Brigandenführer Dr. Ing. Kammler,

Themes:

1. Expansion of the Auschwitz barracks camp due to the influx from the East
2. Larger-scale takeover of closed industrial tasks by the KL [concentration camps]
3. Bomb-damage assistance by the KL
4. Light-metal smelter at Fallersleben.

The results of the meeting were as follows:

Re 1. *Reichsminister* Speer has approved the expansion of the barracks camp Auschwitz in full measure and made available for the increase in building volume up to 13.7 billion Reichsmarks.

This building volume includes the construction of about three hundred barracks with the necessary facilities and space for expansion.

The necessary raw materials will be delivered in the fourth quarter of 1942, as well as in the first, second, and third quarters of 1943.

When this additional construction program is completed, a total of 132,000 men can be continuously housed.

Re 2. All present were in accord that the labor available in the concentration camps must be deployed for large-scale armaments production. We have constantly tried in the past to achieve this in the Economic-Administration Main Office (W.-V. Hauptamt) but have failed due to resistance, which to my great surprise I discovered yesterday in the camp of *Reichsminister* Prof. Speer himself.

I reported about this in passing verbally once. Hans Sauer plays a strange role here.

The assumption of larger closed armaments tasks by us assumes, of course, that we proceed from a principle [illegible]. We no longer have to narrow-mindedly insist that all the production must be situated in our camp. As long as we are preoccupied with so-called fiddling about with our previous work, as a consequence of its small scale, as you, *Reichsführer,* already completely correctly indicated, we can rightly make this demand.

If tomorrow, however, we want to take over a closed armaments works with five or ten or fifteen thousand inmates, that is impossible to achieve quickly. We have to do this, as Prof. Speer noted, in the open countryside. Then an electrical fence has to be set up around the empty works, and then the inmates have to be selected by us. . . . [. . .]

SS Armament Works

The totality of these SS armaments works would then make a contribution to the armaments program and, as *Reichsminister* Prof. Speer himself emphasized, can only be announced by you to the Führer. If free works are not available. armaments works, which, because of their inadequate personnel, don't up to now fulfill their full capacity, should be completely emptied and filled 100 percent with our inmates.

The German and foreign workers who would be freed from these plants should be used to fill gaps in the labor in similar armaments works. *Reichsminister* Prof. Speer, will in this way, temporarily make possible the deployment of almost fifty thousand Jews capable of work in closed available plants with housing possibilities.

We will siphon off the necessary labor power for this purpose in the first instance from the east migration to Auschwitz, so that our existing productive facilities will not be disturbed in their productive capacity and construction by permanent changes in the labor power.

All travel of Jews capable of work chosen for east migration will be halted, and they must be used for armaments work.

I have urged that deployment of labor by these Jews in the areas from which they have migrated cease immediately in any case.

It is clear that the SD must cooperate with this labor deployment. I will guarantee this.

We will therefore no longer accept smaller armaments tasks in the future. Insofar as such work is running from an earlier time, I propose to carry it through, until it exhausts itself. [. . .]

Heil Hitler!

Pohl

SS-*Obergruppenführer* and General of the Waffen SS-B

381

ALFRED WETZLER AND RUDOLF VRBA

Auschwitz Protocols

First published by the Executive Office of the United States War Refugee Board, 25 November 1944, as Alfred Wetzler and Rudolf Vrba, "German Extermination Camps—Auschwitz and Birkenau." Published in Lucy S. Dawidowicz, ed., *A Holocaust Reader* (West Orange, N.J.: Behrman House, 1976), 110–19.

On April 13, 1942, our group of 1,000 men was loaded onto railroad cars at the assembly camp at Sered. The doors were sealed, so that nothing would reveal the direction of the journey. When they were opened after a long while, we realized that we had crossed the Slovak frontier and were in Zwardoń.[1] Until then the train had been guarded by Hlinka men,[2] but it was now taken over by SS guards. After a few cars had been uncoupled from our convoy, we continued on our way, arriving at night at Auschwitz, where we stopped at a siding. . . . Upon arrival, we were counted off in rows of five. There were 643 of us. After a walk of about twenty minutes with our heavy packs—we had left Slovakia well equipped—we reached the concentration camp of Auschwitz.

We were led at once into a huge barracks, where we had to deposit all our luggage on one side and on the other undress completely, leaving our clothes and valuables behind. Naked, we then proceeded to an adjoining barracks, where our heads and bodies were shaved and disinfected. At the exit, every man was given a number, beginning with 28,600. With this number in hand, we were then herded to a third barracks, where so-called registration took place. Here the numbers we received in the second barracks were tattooed on the left side of our chests. The extreme brutality with which this was done made many of us faint. The particulars of our identity were also recorded. Then we were led by hundreds into a cellar and later to a barracks, where we were issued striped prisoners' clothes and wooden clogs. This lasted until 10 A.M. In the afternoon our prisoners' outfits were taken away from us and replaced by the ragged and dirty remains of Russian uniforms. Thus equipped, we were marched off to Birkenau.

Auschwitz is a concentration camp for political prisoners under so-called "protective custody." At the time of my arrival, that is, April 1942, about 15,000 prisoners were in the camp, the majority Poles, Germans, and civilian Russians under the categories of criminals and "work-shirkers."

Auschwitz camp headquarters also controls the labor camp of Birkenau as well as the farm-labor camp of Harmense. All the prisoners arrive first at Auschwitz, where they are provided with prisoners' registration numbers and then are kept there, or are sent either to Birkenau or, in very small numbers, to Harmense. . . .

There are several factories on the grounds of the camp of Auschwitz: a war production plant of *Deutsche Ausrüstungswerke* (DAW), a factory belonging to the Krupp works, and one to the Siemens concern. Outside the camp's boundary is a tremendous plant covering several square kilometers named Buna.[3] The prisoners work in all the aforementioned factories.

The prisoners' actual living quarters, if such a term is at all appropriate, covers an area approximately 500 by 300 meters, surrounded by a double row of concrete posts about three meters high, interconnected, inside and out, by a dense netting of high-tension wires fixed into the posts by insulators. Between these two rows of posts, at intervals of 150 meters, there are five-meter-high watchtowers, equipped with machine guns and searchlights. The inner high-tension ring is encircled by an ordinary wire fence. Merely to touch this fence is to draw a stream of bullets from the watchtowers. This system is called the "small" or "inner ring of sentry posts."

The camp itself is composed of three rows of houses. The camp thoroughfare lies between the first and second row. A wall used to stand between the second and third row. Up to mid-August 1942, the over 7,000 Jewish girls deported from Slovakia in March and April 1942, lived in the houses separated by this wall. After these girls had been removed to Birkenau, the wall was removed. The road into the camp bisects the row of houses. Over the entrance gate, always, of course, heavily guarded, stands the ironic inscription: "Work brings freedom" [*Arbeit macht frei*].

At a radius of some 2,000 meters, the whole camp is encircled by a second ring called the "big" or "outer ring of sentry posts," also with watchtowers every 150 meters. Between the inner- and outer-ring sentry posts are the factories and other workshops. The towers of the inner ring are manned only at night when the high-tension current is switched into the double row of wires. During the day the garrison of the inner-ring sentry posts is withdrawn, and the men take up duty in the outer ring. Escape—and many attempts have been made—through these sentry posts is practically impossible. Getting through the inner-ring posts at night is completely impossible, and the towers of the outer ring are so close to one another that it is out of the question to pass unnoticed. The guards shoot without warning. The garrison of the outer ring is withdrawn at twilight, but only after all the prisoners have been ascertained to be within the inner ring. If the roll call uncovers a missing prisoner, sirens immediately sound the alarm.

The men in the outer ring remain in their towers on the look-out, the inner ring is manned, and hundreds of SS guards and bloodhounds begin a systematic search. The siren brings the whole surrounding countryside to a state of alarm, so that if by miracle the escaping man has succeeded in getting through the outer ring, he is almost certain to be caught by one of the numerous German police and SS patrols. The escapee is furthermore handicapped by his clean-shaven head, his striped prisoners' outfit or red patches sewn on his clothing, and the passiveness of the thoroughly intimidated population. The mere failure to give information on the whereabouts of a prisoner, not to speak of extending help, is punished by death. If the prisoner has not been caught sooner, the garrison of the outer-ring sentry posts remains on the watch for three days and nights, after which it is presumed that the fugitive succeeded in breaking through the double ring. The following night the outer guard is withdrawn. If the fugitive is caught alive, he is hanged in the presence of the whole camp. If he is found dead, his body—wherever it may have been located—is returned to camp (it is easily identifiable by the tattooed number) and seated at the entrance gate, a small notice clasped in his hands, reading: "Here I am." During our two years' imprisonment, many attempts at escape were made, but except for two or three, all were brought back dead or alive. It is not known whether those two or three actually managed to get away. It can, however, be asserted that among the Jews who were deported from Slovakia to Auschwitz or Birkenau, we are the only two who were lucky enough to save ourselves.

As stated previously, we were transferred from Auschwitz to Birkenau on the day of our arrival. Actually there is no such district as Birkenau. Even the word Birkenau is new in that it has been adapted from the nearby Brzezinki.[4] The existing camp center of Birkenau lies four kilometers from Auschwitz, though the outer borders of Birkenau and Auschwitz adjoin. . . .

When we arrived in Birkenau, we found only one huge kitchen there for 15,000 people and three stone buildings, two already completed and one under construction. The buildings were encircled by an ordinary barbed-wire fence. The prisoners were housed in these buildings and in others later constructed . . . . All are built according to a standard model. Each house is about 30 meters long and 8 to 10 meters wide, [divided into tiny cubicles] . . . too narrow for a man to lie stretched out and not high enough for him to sit upright. There is no question of having enough space to stand upright. Thus, some 400–500 people are accommodated in one house or "block." . . .

After three days I was ordered, together with 200 other Slovak Jews, to work in the German armament factories at Auschwitz, but we continued to be housed in Birkenau. We left early in the morning, returning at night, and worked in the carpentry shop as well as on road construction. Our food consisted of one liter of turnip soup at midday and 300 grams of bad bread in the evening. Working conditions were inconceivably hard, so that the majority of us, weakened by starvation and the inedible food, could not endure. The mortality was so high that our group of 200 had 30–35 dead every day. Many were simply beaten to death by the overseers—the *Kapos*[5]—during work, without the slightest provocation. The gaps in our ranks caused by these deaths were replaced daily by prisoners from Birkenau. Our return at night was extremely painful and dangerous, as we had to drag, over a distance of five kilometers, our tools, our firewood, heavy cauldrons, and the bodies of those who had died or had been killed during the working day. With these heavy loads we had to maintain a brisk pace, and anyone incurring the displeasure of one of the Kapos was cruelly knocked down, if not beaten to death. Until the arrival of the second group of Slovak men some fourteen days later, our original number had dwindled to 150. At night we were counted, the bodies of the dead were piled up on flat, narrow-gauge cars or in a truck and brought to Brzezinki, where they were burned in a trench several meters deep and about fifteen meters long. . . .

Until the middle of May 1942, a total of four convoys of Jewish men from Slovakia arrived at Birkenau and all were given treatment similar to ours.

From the first two transports 120 men—90 Slovak and 30 French Jews—were chosen, including myself, and placed at the disposal of the administration of the camp of Auschwitz, which needed doctors, dentists, intellectuals, and clerks. As I had in the meantime managed to work my way up to a good position in Birkenau—being in command of a group of fifty men, which had brought me considerable advantage—I at first felt reluctant to leave for Auschwitz. However, I was finally persuaded to go. After eight days, eighteen doctors and attendants as well as three other persons were selected from this group of 120. The doctors were used in the so-called *Krankenbau* ("patients building," infirmary) at Auschwitz. . . . The remaining 99 persons were sent to work in the gravel pits where they all died within a short time.

Shortly thereafter a *Krankenbau* was set up. It was destined to become the much dreaded Block 7, where I was first chief attendant and later administrator. The "infirmary" chief was a Pole. This building actually was nothing but an assembly center of candidates for death. All prisoners incapable of working were sent there. There was no question of any medical attention or care. We had some 150 dead daily and their bodies were sent for cremation to Auschwitz.

At the same time, the so-called "selections" were introduced. Twice weekly, Mondays and Thursdays, the camp doctor indicated the number of prisoners who were to be gassed and then burned. Those selected were loaded onto trucks and brought to Brzezinki. Those still alive upon arrival were gassed in a big barracks erected near the trench used for burning the bodies. The weekly contingent of dead from Block 7 was about 2,000, 1,200 of whom died a "natural death" and about 800 by "selection." For those who had not been "selected," a death certificate was issued and sent to the central administration at Oranienburg, whereas a special list was kept of the "selectees" with the indication "S.B." (*Sonderbehandlung*—special treatment). Until January 15, 1943, up to which time I was administrator of Block 7 and therefore in a position directly to observe the events, some 50,000 prisoners died of "natural death" or by "selection."

As previously described, the prisoners were numbered consecutively, so that we can reconstruct fairly clearly their order of succession and the fate which befell each individual convoy on arrival.

The first transport of Jewish men reaching Auschwitz for Birkenau was composed, as mentioned, of 1,320 naturalized French Jews bearing approximately the following numbers: 27,400–28,000.

28,600–29,600	In April 1942 the first convoy of Slovak Jews (our convoy).
29,600–29,700	100 men (Aryans) from various concentration camps.
29,700–32,700	3 complete convoys of Slovak Jews.
32,700–33,100	400 professional criminals (Aryans) from Warsaw prisons.
33,100–35,000	1,900 Jews from Cracow.
35,000–36,000	1,000 Poles (Aryans)—political prisoners.
36,000–37,300	In May 1942—1,300 Slovak Jews from Lublin-Majdanek.
37,300–37,900	600 Poles (Aryans) from Radom, a few Jews among them.
37,900–38,000	100 Poles from the concentration camp of Dachau.
38,000–38,400	400 naturalized French Jews with their families.

This whole convoy consisted of about 1,600 individuals, of whom approximately 200 girls and 400 men were admitted to the camp, while the remaining 1,000 persons (women, old people, children, as well as men) were sent without further procedure from the railroad siding directly to Brzezinki, and there gassed and burned. From this moment on, all Jewish convoys were dealt with in the same way. Approximately ten percent of the men and five percent of the women were assigned to the camps and the remaining members were immediately gassed. This process of annihilation had already been applied earlier to the Polish Jews. During long months, without interruption, trucks brought thousands of Jews from the various ghettos directly to the pit in Birkenwald. . . .

48,300–48,620: 320 Jews from Slovakia. About 70 girls were transferred to the women's camp, the remainder, some 650 people, gassed in Birkenwald. This convoy included about 80 people who had been transferred by the Hungarian police to the camp at Sered. . . .

49,000–64,800: 15,000 naturalized French, Belgian, and Dutch Jews. This figure certainly represents less than ten percent of the total convoy. This was between July 1 and September 15, 1942. Large family convoys arrived from various European countries and were at once directed to Birkenwald. The *Sonderkommando,* employed for gassing and burning, worked day and night shifts. Hundreds of thousands of Jews were gassed during this period.

64,800–65,000: 200 Slovak Jews. Of this transport, about 100 women were admitted to the camp, the rest were gassed and burned. . . .

65,000–68,000: Naturalized French, Belgian and Dutch Jews. Not more than 1,000 women were "selected" and sent to the camp. The others, 30,000, at the least, were gassed.

71,000–80,000: Naturalized French, Belgian and Dutch Jews. The prisoners brought to the camp hardly represented ten percent of the total transport. A conservative estimate would be that approximately 65,000 to 70,000 persons were gassed. . . .

Number 80,000 marks the beginning of the systematic annihilation of the Polish ghettos.

80,000–85,000: Approximately 5,000 Jews from various ghettos in Mlawa, Makóv, Ciechanów, Lomża, Grodno, Bialystok. For fully thirty days truck convoys arrived without interruption. Only 5,000 persons were sent to the concentration camp; all the others were gassed at once. The *Sonderkommando* worked in two shifts, twenty-four hours daily, and was scarcely able to cope with the gassing and burning. Without exaggeration, it may be said that some 80,000–90,000 of these convoys received *Sonderbehandlung.* These transports also brought in a considerable amount of money, valuables, and precious stones.

85,000–92,000: 6,000 Jews from Grodno, Bialystok, and Cracow, as well as 1,000 Aryan Poles. The majority of the Jewish convoys were directly gassed and about 4,000 Jews daily were driven into the gas chambers. During mid-January 1943, three convoys of 2,000 persons each from Theresienstadt arrived. . . . Only 600 men and 300 women of these 6,000 persons were admitted to the camp. The remainder were gassed.

99,000–100,000: End of January 1943, large convoys of French and Dutch Jews arrived; only a small proportion reached the camp.

100,000–102,000: In February 1943, 2,000 Aryan Poles, mostly intellectuals.

102,000–103,000: 700 Czech Aryans. Later, those still alive were sent to Buchenwald.

103,000–108,000: 3,000 French and Dutch Jews and 2,000 Poles (Aryans). During the month of February 1943, two contingents arrived daily. They included Polish, French, and Dutch Jews who, in the main, were sent to the gas chambers. The number gassed during this month can be estimated at no smaller than 90,000.

At the end of February 1943, a new modern crematorium and gassing plant were inaugurated at Birkenau. The gassing and burning of the bodies in Birkenwald were discontinued, the whole job being taken over by the four specially built crematoria. The large ditch was filled in, the ground leveled, and the ashes used, as before, for fertilizer at the farm labor camp of Harmense, so that today it is almost impossible to find traces of the dreadful mass murder which took place.

At present four crematoria are in operation at Birkenau, two large ones, I and II, and two smaller ones, III and IV. Those of type I and II consist of three parts, i.e.: the furnace room, the large hall, and the gas chamber. A huge chimney rises from the furnace room around which are grouped nine furnaces, each having four openings. Each opening can take three normal corpses at once, after an hour and a half the bodies are completely burned. Thus, the daily capacity is about 2,000 bodies. A large "reception hall" adjoins, so as to give the impression of the antechamber of a bathing establishment. It holds 2,000 people and apparently there is a similar waiting room on the floor below. From there, a door and a few stairs down lead into the very long and narrow gas chamber. The walls of this chamber are also camouflaged with simulated entries to shower rooms in order to mislead the victims. The roof is fitted with three traps which can be hermetically closed from the outside. A track leads from the gas chamber to the furnace room.

The gassing takes place as follows: the unfortunate victims are brought into the reception hall where they are told to undress. To complete the fiction that they are going to bathe, each person receives a towel and a small piece of soap issued by two men in white coats. Then they are crowded into the gas chamber in such numbers that there is, of course, only standing room. To compress this crowd into the narrow space, shots are often fired to induce those already at the far end to huddle still closer together. When everybody is inside, the heavy doors are closed. Then there is a short pause, presumably to allow the room temperature to rise to a certain level, after which SS men with gas masks climb on the roof, open the traps, and shake down a preparation in powder from out of tin cans labeled "Zyklon—For use against vermin," manufactured by a Hamburg concern. It is presumed that this is a cyanide mixture of some sort which turns into gas at a certain temperature. After three minutes everyone in the chamber is dead. No one is known to have survived this ordeal, although it was not uncommon to discover signs of life after the primitive measures employed in Birkenwald. The chamber is then opened, aired, and the *Sonderkommando* carts the bodies on flat trucks to the furnace rooms where the burning take place. Crematoria III and IV work on nearly the same principle, but their capacity is only half as large. Thus the total capacity of the four gassing and cremating plants at Birkenau amounts to about 6,000 daily.

On principle only Jews are gassed; Aryans very seldom, as they are usually given *Sonderbehandlung* by shooting. Before the crematoria were put into service, the shooting took place in Birkenwald and the bodies were burned in the long trench; later, however, executions took place in the large hall of one of the crematoria which has been provided with a special installation for this purpose.

Prominent guests from Berlin were present at the inauguration of the first crematorium in March 1943. The "program" consisted of the gassing and burning of 8,000 Cracow Jews. The guests, both officers and civilians, were extremely satisfied with the results and the special peephole fitted into the door of the gas chamber was in constant use. They were lavish in their praise of this newly erected installation.

At the beginning of 1943, the political section of Auschwitz received 500,000 discharge certificates. We thought, with ill-concealed joy, that at least a few of us would be liberated. But the forms were simply filled out with the names of those gassed and filed away in the archives. . . .

Cautious estimate of the number of Jews gassed in Birkenau between April 1942 and April 1944, by country of origin

Poland (transported by truck)	ca. 300,000
[Poland] ([transported by] train)	[ca.] 600,000
Holland	[ca.] 100,000
Greece	[ca.] 45,000
France	[ca.] 150,000
Belgium	[ca.] 50,000
Germany	[ca.] 60,000
Yugoslavia, Italy and Norway	[ca.] 50,000
Lithuania	[ca.] 50,000
Bohemia, Moravia, and Austria	[ca.] 30,000
Slovakia	[ca.] 30,000
Various camps for foreign Jews in Poland	[ca.] 300,000
[Total]	ca. 1,765,000

Notes

1. Zwardoń was on the Polish side of the Polish-Czech frontier.

2. These were members of the Hlinka Guard, the paramilitary arm of the Hlinka People's party, a right-wing Catholic nationalist party, the only legal party in Slovakia after March 1939. The Hlinka Guard collaborated with the SS.

3. *Deutsche Ausrüstungswerke* (German Armament Works) was an SS enterprise founded in 1939. It was administered by the SS WVHA [Wirtschafts-Verwaltungshauptamt (SS Main Economic and Administrative Department)—Eds.] [. . .] Krupp and Siemens were among Germany's largest industrial manufacturers, with plants all over Europe. The Buna plant at Auschwitz, part of the vast network of I. G. Farben industrial enterprises, produced synthetic rubber.

4. "Birch tree" in Polish is *brzezina;* in German, *Birke. Brzezinki* is the plural diminutive, hence, a wood of small birches: the German equivalent was Birkenwald.

5. *Kapo* (sometimes *Capo*) was concentration-camp slang for a foreman of a labor gang, who was himself a camp inmate. The origin of the word is obscure. It may be an abbreviated form of the French *caporal,* a term used in the German army during the Second World War. *Kapo* was also used long before the war among carpenters as a German slang word for foreman. Another hypothesis is that Kapo is a borrowing from the Italian *capo,* "head" or "chief."

382

ZALMEN GRADOWSKI

The Czech Transport

A Chronicle of the Auschwitz Sonderkommando

Written in March–April 1944. Published in David Roskies, ed., *The Literature of Destruction: Jewish Responses to Catastrophe* (Philadelphia: Jewish Publication Society, 1989), 548–64.

The Convoy

Wednesday, March 8, 1944, Purim Night, when those Jews lucky enough to be in countries that still allowed them to exist went to their synagogues, study houses and other places to celebrate the glorious festival of the national, eternal miracle of Purim and to pray that our new Haman might soon meet his end . . .

On that same night in Auschwitz-Birkenau 140 Jews of the *Sonderkommando* were also marching to a certain destination, but not to a synagogue, not with the intention of celebrating the festival and commemorating the Purim miracle.

They walked like mourners, like heads sunk deep in sorrow, and the profound sadness that emanated from them spread to all the Jews in the camp. For the road on which they marched was the road to the crematorium, to the hell of the Jewish people. And soon they would see not a celebration of the Jewish people's past delivery from death to life, but festivities of another sort—of a nation of betrayers who on this night were carrying out the ancient Purim decree, which their god had revived with still greater brutality.

Soon we would bear witness. With our own eyes we would have to watch our own destruction, as five thousand Jews, five thousand vibrant, thriving souls, women and children, young and old, would pass under the truncheons of civilized brutes. At the authorities' disposal would be rifles, grenades and automatics, as well as their constant four-footed companions, their vicious dogs; these would chase and savagely attack the Jews, who, distracted and confused, would run blindly into the arms of death.

And we, their own brothers, would have to help with this, help unload them from the trucks and lead them to the bunkers, help strip them mother-naked. And then, when all was ready, accompany them to the bunker—to the grave.

When we came to the site of crematorium 1, the representatives of the regime were already there, spread out along the field. Several SS men were among them, ready for battle, with rifles loaded and grenades at their sides. These well-armed soldiers completely surrounded the Crematorium, so that if anything were to go wrong they could respond immediately. Cars with searchlights were set up in every corner to illuminate the battlefield. And there was also a special ammunition truck, in the event that they should run out of bullets to use against the enemy, the mighty one . . .

If you, citizen of the free world, could have seen this, you would have been struck with wonder. You would have thought that in that enormous building with the towering chimneys were giantlike men who could fight like demons, so well-armed they must have been. They could have wiped out entire worlds, mighty armies, in an instant. You would have thought: these men must certainly be great heroes, preparing to do battle with an enemy that coveted their land, their people, their wealth.

Imagine your shock when, after waiting a while, you actually beheld this terrible enemy, the source of this great hatred, the target of this brutal force.

Again whom were they preparing to do battle? Against our people Israel. Soon Jewish mothers would arrive, pressing their babies to their breasts and leading the older children by the hand, and they would stare, frightened and helpless, at the chimneys. Vibrant young girls would leap from the trucks and wait for a mother or a sister to accompany them to the bunker. And men, too, young and old, fathers and sons, would arrive at this inferno and be driven to their deaths.

So this was the great enemy against whom the villain was prepared to conduct battle that night. They were afraid, these brutes; perhaps not every one of the thousands of victims would drop like flies, perhaps one would have the courage to take a stand before dying. And it was because of that one, the unknown hero, that they were so afraid and hid behind their civilized guns. All was ready. Seventy men from our squad were also assigned to guard the area of the fenced-in crematorium. And behind us, outside the fence, they stood with their rifles aimed at the doomed.

Cars and motorcycles raced back and forth. There was much activity to make sure that things were in order. A deathly silence reigned in the camp. Every living thing must have disappeared, escaped into the wooden graves. The silence was suddenly disturbed by footsteps. Soldiers in helmets, with weapons loaded, marched by as though they were coming onto a battlefield. Never before had military personnel entered the camp at night, when everything was sleeping behind the barbed wires. The camp was prepared for battle.

Now every living thing remained motionless, frozen in the cages, even though everyone knew that many times, and especially in the recent past, victims had gone to their deaths in broad daylight, for all to see. Only tonight, out of fear and dread, did the authorities operate in this way. Only the night sky with its stars and bright moon could not be deceived by the devil: They alone would bear witness to what the devil had carried out.

In the silence, the secret silence of the night, trucks were heard approaching. Already they were bringing victims into the camp. Dogs howled ferociously, eager to attack. The voices of drunken officers and soldiers rang out.

German and Polish prisoners also came, having freely offered to help with the festivities, and all of them, this gang of devils and the murderers, went to meet the trucks, load the victims and send them on to the crematorium.

The victims were still in the barracks, stifled by the fear of death, their hearts pounding. The suspense was maddening as they listened to the activity outside the boarded-up doors. Through the crevices they could see the murderers, the robbers who were waiting in trucks to steal their lives. They knew that it could not last long, that they would not be allowed to remain even in this dismal place, where they wished they could stay forever. They would be dragged out forcibly and taken somewhere else—to hell.

A dreadful trembling suddenly seized the despairing crowd, and they remained silent, in paralyzing suspense. Like corpses, they turned to stone in their places. Now, as they heard the approaching footsteps, their heart stopped beating. The board was torn from the door. This board, which had entombed them, had also protected them. As long as it was nailed in place it had set them apart from death, and they had secretly hoped that they could remain in this cage indefinitely—until they were freed.

And now the door burst open, and the victims, still motionless, nervously eyed their brutal oppressors and instinctively drew back, as from a ghost. They wanted to escape to a place where the barbaric eyes could not see them.

They were frightened, coming face to face with these who intended to take away their lives. But the angry dogs began to howl savagely and threw themselves on the nearest victims, and a club wielded by the hand of a brute—a Pole or German—came down on a young Jewish girl. And the crowd, which had clung together in a solid mass, poured out of the barracks in single file and gradually began to disperse—to fall apart. Hopeless, baffled, crushed, they began to run to the trucks, dodging the snapping of the dogs and the blows of the enraged brutes. And more than one fleeing woman fell with her child, so that the accursed earth already drank warm blood from young Jewish skulls.

The victims stood on the trucks, waiting to depart, looking around as if for something they had lost. It seemed to a young wife that her beloved husband might come to her out of nowhere. A mother peered into the tragic night; perhaps her young son would appear. And a girl looked around desperately; perhaps her lover was with the people in the trucks, over there.

They looked nervously at the beautiful world, at the sky with the stars and the moon moving majestically within it. They looked at the barracks, the tomb that they had just left. If only they could go back! They knew, they sensed that the truck—this precarious coach—would not help them for long. Their eyes wandered over the wires to the camp where they had just been. The frightened Czech families were standing there, looking through the crevices at their brothers and sisters who were about to be taken away. In the glare of the light their gazes met. Their hearts beat rhythmically, full of fear and foreboding. In the night silence hovered the farewells of the sisters and brothers, the friends and acquaintances who remained in the camp waiting for the end, to the sisters and brothers, the fathers and mothers about to be carried in trucks to their deaths. And so the second stage had already succeeded; the devil had brought his victims to the second step of the grave.

They Are Here

They had already arrived, the unfortunate victims. The trucks pulled up. Their hearts froze as they stood stricken with terror, helpless and despondent, and looked toward the building in which they, their young lives, their vibrant bodies, would soon vanish forever.

They could not understand what they wanted—all of these officers with their silver and gold epaulets, their shining revolvers and grenades hanging at their sides. And why were they, the victims, standing here like condemned thieves, watched by helmeted soldiers, while from between the trees and wire, gleaming in the light of the moon, the black barrels of rifles pointed at them? For what purpose? Why were all the searchlights shining? Was the night too dark? Was the moonlight too faint?

They stood baffled, unarmed and resigned. They had already perceived the truth. The void gaped before their eyes; they were sinking in it already. They felt that everything, earth, life, field, trees—everything that lives and exists—was vanishing and sinking with them right into the deep abyss. The stars went out, the sky darkened, the moon stopped shining, the world descended with them. And they, the unfortunates, wanted only to sink, to disappear quickly into the abyss.

They threw down their parcels—everything they had brought for the "journey." They no longer wanted or needed anything. Passive, unresisting, they let themselves be removed from the trucks and fell, almost fainting, like cut stalks into our arms. Take me by the hand, brother, and lead me to the stretch of road that is all that remains of my life. We led them, our dear, beloved sisters; we held them under their arms, walking quietly step by step, our hearts beating together rhythmically. We suffered with them, bled with them, and we felt that each step we took was a step away from life, toward death. At the entrance to the sunken bunker, before they took the first step into the grave, they looked for the last time at the sky and the moon—and a moan escaped instinctively from deep in both our hearts. In the moonlight a tear would glisten in the eye of each sister who had been led here, and another would form in the eye of the brother who had led her.

In the Disrobing Room

In the center of the deep, vast room flooded by harsh electric light stood twelve posts that supported the weight of the building. Around the posts and against the walls, benches had been placed with hangers attached for the victims' clothes. A placard fixed to the first post stated that this was the entrance to a "bathhouse," and clothes had to be removed for disinfection.

We met them, looked at their glazed eyes. They knew everything, understood everything, that this room was not a bathhouse, but the corridor that led to the grave.

The room filled with people. Trucks arrived with fresh victims, and the room swallowed them all. We stood as if confused, unable to speak to them. Even though this wasn't the first time. We had already received many transports and witnessed many scenes like this one. But still we felt as weak as if we would faint together with these doomed women.

We were stunned. Their clothes, already old and tattered, covered bodies full of grace and charm. From heads covered with hair—black, brunette, blond, and even gray—large, deep-set eyes looked bewitchingly at us. We saw before us fresh, lively women, all in their prime and full of vitality, all nurtured from the wellspring of life, like roses growing in the garden, satiated by rainwater and the morning dew. In the brilliant light the teardrops in their flowerlike eyes sparkled like pearls.

We didn't have the daring or brashness to tell them, our dear sisters, to strip themselves naked, for their clothing was the armor that shielded their lives. The moment they took off their clothes and stood mother-naked, they would lose their last foothold. And therefore it was impossible to tell them to hurry and undress. Let them remain just a moment, just an instant, in their armor, in the mantle of life.

The first question on their lips was if their men had already been there. Each wanted to know if her husband, father, brother, or lover still lived, or if his corpse already was burning in flames that would leave no trace, and she herself a widow with an orphaned child. Perhaps she already had lost her father, brother or lover forever. Then why should she remain alive? "Tell me, brother," said one, who in her mind had long ago given up on life and the world forever—she asked frankly and boldly, "Say, brother, how long does it take to die? Is it easy or hard?"

They weren't let alone for long. The murderous beasts could not restrain themselves. The air was torn by the cries of the drunken criminals, who couldn't wait to satisfy their bestial, thirsting eyes with the nakedness of my dear, beautiful sisters. Clubs came down on shoulders and heads, and clothes quickly dropped from the bodies. Some of the women were embarrassed, wanted to disappear somewhere where their nakedness could not be seen. But there was no hiding place here, no room for shame. Morality and courtesy passed with life into the grave.

A few passionately threw themselves into our arms and asked us with bashful glances to strip them naked; they wanted to forget everything now, to think of nothing. They had given up all thought of their previous life, with its moral principles and ethical considerations, when they took the first step into the grave. Now, on the threshold of doom, they thought only about the basic needs of life and of the body—the body alone still felt and sensed and desired. They wanted to give it everything, everything, to satisfy the last pleasure that life still offered the body before its death. And so they wanted their bodies, still pulsing with life's blood, to be touched, to be fondled by the hands of the strangers, who were the only ones present to receive their love. And in this way each would feel the hand of her lover or husband, stroking and fondling her body consumed by passion. They wanted rapture, my beautiful, beloved sisters, and their burning lips drew lovingly toward us, wanting to kiss passionately, to stay alive.

Several new trucks arrived and move victims entered the big room. Many broke from the line and fell wildly, weeping and crying; naked children recognized their mothers and kissed, embraced, rejoiced that they had been reunited here. And a child felt lucky to have a mother, a mother's heart, accompany him to the grave.

They all stripped themselves naked and stood straight in the line. Some cried, while others were stonily silent. One tore her hair and talked madly to herself. When I approached her, I heard only the words: "Where are you, my love, why don't you come to me? I'm certainly young and pretty enough." Those standing near told me that she had lost her mind in prison the day before.

Others spoke to us quietly and calmly: "We're still young. We want to live, just a little more life." They weren't pleading with us, for they knew that we were victims just like themselves. They simply spoke, spoke just like that, because their hearts were heavy and before they died they wanted to tell their sorrow to those who would survive them.

A group of women sat embracing and kissing. These were sisters, who had met here and clung together.

There a mother sat naked on the bench, holding her daughter, a girl not yet fifteen, on her lap. She pressed her head to her breast and kissed all her limbs. And streaming hot tears fell on the young flower. Thus the mother mourned for her child, whom she would soon lead to death with her own hand.

More light now poured into the room, into their giant grave. On one side of this hell the women were now lined up, their white bodies waiting, waiting for the doors to open and admit them to the grave. We the men, still dressed, stood opposite them and motionlessly looked on. We could no longer grasp if this scene was real or only a dream. Had we fallen into a world of naked women who were soon to be the victims of a demonic game? Or had we fallen into a museum or artist's studio where these women, of different ages and with faces contorted in every way, weeping softly and moaning, had been brought specifically to serve as models for the artist?

For we wondered why they, unlike many other transports, were on the whole so calm, many even brave and carefree, as though nothing could happen to them. They faced death so heroically, so calmly, that we were deeply moved and surprised. Could it be that they didn't know what awaited them? We regarded them with pity, because already there came to us a new, dreadful realization of how all these vibrant souls, even the noise and chatter that rose from them, would in a few hours be stilled by death, their mouths silenced forever. The sparkling eyes, now so bewitching, would gaze fixedly in one direction—seeking something in the deadness of eternity.

These same women who now pulsed with life would lie in dirt and filth, their pure white bodies smeared with human excrement.

From the pearly mouths—teeth and flesh would be torn out together and blood would flow.

From the noses, so finely shaped—two streams would trickle, red, yellow and white.

And the faces, white and pink, would turn red, blue and black from the gas. The eyes would fill with blood, so that it would be impossible to know if this was the same face we were looking at now. The head, now covered with wavy hair, would be shaven by cold hands, and ears and fingers would be stripped of their earrings and their rings. And then two strangers would pull on gloves or lay strips on their hands, because the snow-white figure, so dazzling now, would by then be so repulsive that they would not want to touch her with bare hands. They would drag her—this same beautiful young flower—across the cold, filthy cement floor, and the body, after sweeping all the dirt in its path, would be flung aside like a carcass, to be lifted by pulley to the inferno above and fed to the fire that in minutes would reduce it to ashes.

Already we saw their inevitable end. I watched them, these vibrant souls who filled such an enormous room; entire worlds were represented here—and in only minutes from now . . . A second image appeared before my eyes, of a fellow prisoner steering a wheelbarrow filled with ashes to the mass grave. I was standing now near a group of ten or fifteen women and thought now all their bodies, all their lives, would soon fill a wheelbarrow. No trace would remain. All of them, who had occupied entire cities, who had had a place in this world, would be effaced, uprooted, as though they had never been born. Our hearts ached with sorrow. We felt through them, suffered through them the anguish of passing from life to death.

Our hearts filled with pity. If we could only have given them pieces of our own lives, sacrificed ourselves for our sisters, how happy we would have been! We wanted to press them to our sorrowful hearts, cover their limbs with kisses, imbibe the life that soon would vanish. To etch in our heats their living images, to carry their portraits in our hearts forever. We were all in the grip of these nightmarish thoughts, while they, our beloved sisters, wondered why we were so shaken when they were so calm. They wanted very much to know what would be done with them when they were dead, but none of them dared ask, and the secret was never revealed to them.

The enormous, naked crowd now stood looking fixedly in one direction, and it could be that a single dark thought wove through all their minds.

There on the other side all the clothes and articles that they had just discarded lay in a pile. These things troubled them now. Although they realized they would no longer need them, they had been strongly bound to these possessions, which still retained the warmth of their bodies. Here they lay cast off—a dress, a sweater that had clothed someone and kept her warm. If they could only put them on once more, how good, how happy they would feel. Was it really so—their situation so hopeless that they would never wear these things again?

Was it possible that these clothes would just be left there? That their owners would never return to them?

Clothes abandoned like orphans. Like witnesses or testimonies to the approaching death.

Ah! Who knew who would wear these things after them? A girl stepped out of place to retrieve a strip of silk from under the food of a companion. She took it quickly and stepped back into the line. I asked her why she needed this kerchief. "For a keepsake," the girl replied in a low voice. She would take it with her to the grave.

The Death March

The doors burst open. Hell gaped wide before its victims. In the little room that led to the grave, the representatives of the regime stood in full regalia, as if for a military parade. The entire Political Section had turned out for the celebration. High-ranking offers were there, whose faces we had never before seen during our sixteen months in the camp. Among them stood a woman, an SS officer, the director of the women's camp. She too had come to witness the "national" festival, the murder of the children of our people.

I stood aside and observed both groups—the terrible murderers and their hapless victims, my sisters.

The march, the death march, had begun. The victims walked proudly, boldly, with firm steps, as though they were marching toward life. Nor did they break down on seeing the place where the final scene of their lives would be played. They kept their footing even when they realized that they were captives in the heart of hell. They had settled all accounts with the world and with life before coming here. All ties with life had been broken in captivity. That was why they walked so peacefully, so calmly, approaching their end without breaking down. Without a pause, these vibrant, naked women marched. It seemed to go on for an eternity, an eternity.

It seemed as though entire worlds, entire worlds, had been stripped naked and brought here for a devilish soul.

Mothers passed with small children in arms; others were led by the hands of their little ones. They kissed their children—a mother's heart cannot be bound—kissed them all along the way. Sisters walked arm in arm, clinging together, wanting to face death together.

All glanced scornfully at the line of officers, not wishing to grace them with direct gazes. No one pleaded, no one sought mercy. They knew there was no spark of human conscience in those hearts. They didn't want to give them the pleasure of watching them beg for their lives in despair.

Suddenly the naked procession came to an abrupt halt. A pretty girl of nine, whose long, intricately plaited braids hung in golden strips down her childish shoulders, had approached followed by her mother, who now stopped and boldly addressed the officer: "Murderers, thieves, shameless criminals! Yes, now you kill innocent women and children. You blame us, helpless as we are, for the war. As if my child and I could have brought this war upon you."

"You think, murderers, that with our blood you can hide your losses on the front. But the war is already lost. You know very well what beatings you take every day on the eastern front. Remember! Now you can smooth everything over, but there will come a day—a day of revenge. Russia will be the victor, and she will avenge us! You will be carved up alive. Our brothers all over the world will not rest until they have avenged our innocent blood."

And then she turned to the woman and said, "She-beast! Have you also come to look on our misfortune? Remember! You too have a child, a family, but you will not enjoy them for long. You will be torn into pieces, and your child won't live much longer than mine. Remember, murderers! You will pay for everything—the whole world will take revenge on you."

Then she spat in their faces and ran into the bunker with her child. The officers stood silent, stunned. They couldn't look at one another. The terrible truth they had just heard tore into their bestial souls. They had let her speak even though they knew what she would say, compelled to listen to this Jewish woman on her way to die. Now they stood gravely, deep in thought. This doomed woman had torn the blinders from their eyes and revealed the future that loomed before them. None of this was new to them; many times dark thoughts had clouded their minds, but now it was a Jewish woman who spoke the truth. Unashamed, she had forced them to see reality.

They were afraid to think too long, for the truth might penetrate too deeply. And then what would they live for?—But no! The *Führer,* their god, had claimed something completely different, that victory was not to be won on the battlefields of the east and west . . . but here in the bunker. This was where victory lay—here where the terrible enemy, the cause of German blood being spilled on the battlefields of Europe, was now marching past. These were the hated enemy; for their sakes English airplanes dropped bombs night and day, killing young and old. It was because of these naked women that they were so far from home, because of them that their sons had to lay their heads down in the east. No, the *Führer,* the god, was correct. They must be exterminated, destroyed. Only then, when these naked women and children lay dead, would victory be assured. Ach, if only it could happen faster, if only all the Jews could be gathered and driven from the world more quickly, stripped naked and driven into the inferno like these women here! How good it would be. The cannons would cease thundering, the airplanes would stop dropping bombs, the war would be concluded. Peace would reign over the world. Their scattered children would return home to begin new and happy lives. Only one obstacle remained—these naked women—there were members of their nation still in hiding, who had not yet been brought here to be stripped naked like these who were marching past. And a brutal hand stretched out a whip and mercilessly beat the naked bodies.

Run faster, our enemies, faster into the bunker, into the grave, for every step you take brings us closer to victory. And victory must come more quickly, more swiftly! We have paid too dearly for you on the vast battlefields—now run faster, children of devils, and don't stop along the way, because that would hinder our victory.

They marched on—rows of young, naked women. And again the marching came to a halt. Another woman, this time a lovely, blond girl, had addressed the officers: "Wretched murderers! You look at me with your thirsty, bestial eyes. You glut yourselves on my nakedness. Yes, this is what you've been waiting for. In your civilian lives you could never even have dreamed about it. You hoodlums and criminals, you have finally found the right place to satisfy your sadistic eyes. But you won't enjoy this for long. Your game's almost over, you can't kill all the Jews. And you will pay for it all." And suddenly she leaped at them and struck Oberscharführer Voss, the director of the crematoria, three times. Clubs came down on her head and shoulders. She entered the bunker with her body covered with wounds, and the warm blood caressed her body lovingly; she laughed for joy, for her hand still tingled from the blow she had dealt the notorious killer's face. She had achieved her final goal, and proceeded calmly to her death.

Pouring in the Gas

Two pairs of footsteps disturbed the night's silence. In the moonlight two figures appeared. They put on masks, in preparation for pouring the poisonous gas that they carried in two cylinders, enough to kill the thousands of victims who waited there. They walked now in the direction of the bunker, treading softly. They walked calmly, cold and assured, as if called upon to perform some sacred duty. Their hearts ice, their hands never even trembling, they guiltlessly moved to each "eye" of the sunken bunker, poured in the gas, and covered the "eye" with a heavy lid so that no gas could escape. Through the peepholes they could hear the deep, agonized groan of the mass of people struggling with death, but they remained unmoved. Deaf and dumb, they moved on to the second "eye" and again poured in the gas. Then, after taking care of the last one, they removed the masks. Proud, calm, at peace with themselves, they walked away, having performed a great service for their people and country, having brought them a step closer to victory . . .

The Second Front

Everyone now moved "over there," to the second crematorium—the officers and guards, as well as ourselves. Again, a front was established. All was tense, in readiness for combat. Even more security measures were taken now than before because, even though the first reception of prisoners had proceeded smoothly and without any kind of resistance or casualties, the present group consisted of strong, young men, and so anything could happen. Before long we heard the familiar sound of the trucks. "They are coming!" shouted the Commandant. This was a signal to get everything ready. In the silence, one heard the rifles and machine guns being positioned for the last time before battle, so that they could function properly if called upon to do their "duty."

The enormous searchlights once again illuminated this place of death. And in their light and the light of the moon, several rifle barrels glittered once more, wielded by the "Great Regime" that now stood ready to do battle against the defenseless, hapless people for Israel. Faces peered wildly through the trees and barbed wire. In the moonlight the "death's head" gleamed frightfully from the helmets of "heroes" who wore it with pride. Like demons, like murderers, they huddled in the silent night, waiting, waiting in fear and hunger for their prey.

Devastation

We were all tense—both "us" and "them." The representatives of the regime stood frightened, apprehensive. They were trembling. Perhaps this group of desperate men would go down like heroes on the threshold of the grave. In such a case, a "misfortune" could strike one of the guards. Each one wondered who it might be; perhaps he himself was marked.

We too were tense, our hearts pounding as we removed them from the trucks. We hoped, believed, that it would happen tonight, that tonight would bring the redeeming moment for which we had been impatiently waiting, when the desperate throng on the edge of the grave would pull out the flag of resistance. And we would go with them, side by side, into the unequal battle. At that moment we would not think about the futility of our struggle or whether it would gain us life and freedom. Our best hope would be for a heroic end to this dismal life, an end to this terrible tragedy.

But what actually happened shattered our hopes; instead of fighting like wild animals, the victims for the most part came down from the trucks peacefully and passively, looking nervously at the vast area around them. Their final glances lingered on the building, the giant hell, and with arms dangling and heads bowed in resignation they proceeded quietly to the grave. All of them asked if their women had already been there. Their hearts beat only for them; thousands of unbroken threads still joined them. Flesh and blood, hearts and souls were still bound together into single organisms. It was not yet known by these fathers, husbands, brothers, bridegrooms and friends that their wives and children, sisters and brides, the thousands of souls whom they still thought of as alive and connected to their own lives, already lay dead in that gigantic building, that deep grave. They didn't want to believe it when we told them that the thread that bound them to the women was already severed.

A few threw their parcels violently to the ground. They recognized only too well this building whose chimneys every day spewed forth corpses to the high heavens. Others stood still, or whistled a little tune while looking wistfully and dreamily at the moon and the stars, and then, moaning, descended directly into the deep bunker. Before long all the naked men had gone peacefully, without struggle or resistance, to their deaths in the bunker.

She and He

It was a heartrending scene when a number of women who had been unable to fit into Crematorium 1 were brought over to the men. Naked men ran frantically to the women, each seeking his wife, his mother, his child, sister or friend. The few "lucky" couples who were reunited here clasped each other firmly and kissed passionately. In the middle of the big room one saw unbearable things—a naked man holding his wife in his arms: a brother and a sister standing embarrassed, kissing through tears, and passing "happily" together into the bunker.

There were several women who remained miserably alone. Perhaps a husband, brother or father was already there in the bunker. Perhaps he was thinking about his wife and child, mother or sister, not realizing that she was in the same bunker, naked among strange men, seeking his beloved face in the crowd. And so, yearning, searching, her gaze wandered wildly.

In this crowd of men a woman stretched upwards, yearning and searching, her body facing the throng. Even as she was drawing her last breath, she looked for her husband.

And there on the edge of the crowd, by the wall, he stood restlessly, on the tips of his toes, looking for his wife. And when finally he saw her, his heart began pounding furiously, and he stretched out his arms toward her, trying to make a path, to shout her name. That was when the gas entered the room, and so he remained transfixed in that position—arms outstretched, mouth open, eyes insanely frozen. His heart had given out, his soul departed, with her name still on his lips.

Their two hearts had beaten together with one pulse, and, yearning and searching, together they expired.

"Heil Hitler!"

Through the little window in the gas chamber's door, they, the authorities, could see for themselves how the mass of men lay dead, stiffened from the poison gas.

Happy, assured, with victory in their grasp, they emerged from the place of death. Each of them could now go home relaxed and confident. Effaced and annihilated was the great enemy of their people, of their country. And now, everything was possible once more. The *Führer,* the great god, had said it himself: "Every dead Jew—a step toward victory." And here, here were five thousand at once, killed off in just a few short hours. Such victory, such triumph, without one loss or sacrifice! Who, who else but they, these brilliant officers, could claim such a glorious deed?

They parted with the raised-arm salute and, after hailing their "holy one," climbed contentedly into their cars.

They drove quickly, exhilarated and full of daring, leaving behind a triumph that assured them heroic stature. Soon telephones would start ringing, spreading the news.

Until word of the great victory secured tonight would reach him, "the *Führer* and god." "*Heil Hitler!*"

In the Place of Death

It had become quiet in the area of the crematorium. No guards, no cars with grenades, no searchlights. Everything had suddenly vanished. A fatal stillness resumed its pacing over God's world, as if all the death contained in that deep hell would gather into a silent wave and inundate the world—would cradle and lull the entire world into the eternal sleep of death. The moon continued her peaceful stroll. The stars glittered enchantingly in the deep, blue sky. The night flowed in calm silence through eternity, as though nothing could have happened in the world below. Night, moon, sky and stars had swallowed up the secret that the devil had prepared for them, leaving no sign or vestige of cruelty for the world to perceive.

In the moonlight the only things discernible in this place were little hills of shadows, of discarded parcels—witnesses to lives that were no more. A few silhouetted human figures were dragging a heavy load along the ground; they passed the load—a corpse—through an open door. They went back with quiet steps and retrieved another one, this time disappearing with it behind the door. Through the night silence came the sound of a bolt being turned; the brothers, the wretches who had to dispose of the dead, were not locked in. Again footsteps were heard in the quiet night. This was the guard circling the death house, watching over those who worked in that hell among the corpses of their brothers and sisters; and he made sure—this guard—that none of them could escape from that place of death.

In the Bunker

Hands trembling, brothers removed the screws and lifted the four bolts, opening the two doors to the giant tombs. A sickening wave from that scene of violent death washed over us. We stood stark still and could not believe our eyes. How long? How long had it been since we had seen them alive? They still hovered before us—the vital young men and women. Their last words still echoed in our ears. The gaze of their tear-filled eyes still accused us.

And what had become of them now? Thousands, thousands of spirited, bustling, singing beings now lay stiffened by death. No word or sound was heard, their mouths silenced forever. Their gazes were fixed, their bodies motionless. In the deadened, stagnant stillness there was only a hushed, barely audible noise—a sound of fluid seeping from the different orifices of the dead. That was the only movement in this vast, dead world.

Our eyes were glued to this sea of naked corpses. We were viewing a naked world. They lay as they had fallen, contorted, knotted together like a ball of yarn, as though the devil had played a special game with them before their deaths, arranging them in such poses. Here one lay stretched out full length on top of the pile of corpses. Here one held his arms around another as they sat against the wall. Here part of a shoulder emerged, the head and feet intertwined with the other bodies. And here only a hand and a foot protruded into the air, the rest of the body buried in the deep sea of corpses. The surface of this naked globe was made up entirely of parts of human bodies.

Here and there heads broke through this sea, clinging to the surface of the naked waves. It seemed that while the bodies were submerged in the vast sea, only the heads could peer out from the abyss. These heads—dark, fair, brown—were the only parts that broke through the universal nakedness.

Preparation for the Inferno

One must deaden the feeling heart, dull its capacity for pain. One must suppress that anguish that sweeps like a storm over every limb. One must turn into an automaton, unseeing, unfeeling, uncomprehending.

Hands and feet set to work. Every member of the squad is assigned a specific task. We pull, vigorously pry apart the knot of intertwined bodies, one of us taking a foot, the other a hand—how convenient it all is. It seems as though we will tear the corpses to pieces with our systematic prying. Each one is then dragged along the filthy, cold cement floor, the beautiful, clean body sweeping up all the dirt and filth in its path like a broom. Then it is laid facing upwards, eyes fixed in a stare that seems to ask, "What are you going to do with me, brother?" Frequently one recognizes an acquaintance. Three prisoners prepare the body of a woman. One probes her pretty mouth with pliers, looking for gold teeth, which, when found, are ripped out together with the flesh. Another cuts the hair, the woman's crown, while the third quickly tears off earrings, often drawing blood in the process. And the rings, which do not come off the fingers easily, must be removed with pliers.

Then she is given to the pulley. Two men throw on the bodies like blocks of wood; when the count reaches seven or eight, a signal is given with a stick and the pulley begins its ascent.

In the Heart of Hell

On the upper level, by the pulley, stand four men. The two on one side of the pulley drag corpses to the "storeroom"; the other two pull them directly to the ovens, where they are laid in pairs at each mouth. The slaughtered children are heaped in a big stack, they are added, thrown onto the pairs of adults. Each corpse is laid out on an iron "burial" board; then the door to the inferno is opened and the board shoved in. The hellish fire, extending its tongues like open arms, snatches the body as though it were a prize. The hair is the first to catch a fire. The skin, immersed in flames, catches in a few seconds. Now the arms and legs begin to rise—expanding blood vessels cause this movement of the limbs. The entire body is now burning fiercely; the skin has been consumed and fat drips and hisses in the flames. One can no longer make out a corpse—only a room filled with hellish fire that holds something in its midst. The belly goes. Bowels and entrails are quickly consumed, and within minutes there is no trace of them. The head takes the longest to burn; two little blue flames flicker from the eyeholes—these are the eyes burning with the brain, while from the mouth the tongue also continues to burn. The entire process lasts twenty minutes—and a human being, a world, has been turned to ashes.

We watch, stunned. Two more are laid out. Two people, two worlds, who have occupied a place in the human scheme, who have lived, existed, acted and created. Who have labored for the world and for themselves, laid a brick on the great edifice, woven a thread for the world, for the future—and in only twenty minutes no vestige of them remains.

Two more lie there now; they have been washed thoroughly. Pretty young women—how splendid they must have been! In life they made up two entire worlds—what happiness and joy they brought; their every smile was a comfort, every glance a delight, their every word charmed like heavenly music. Wherever they went they brought joy and gladness with them. Once loved by many, now they wait on the iron board. Soon the mouth will open, and within twenty minutes no trace of them remains.

Now there are three. A child pressed to its mother's breast—what happiness, what joy its birth brought to its parents! They built a home, wove a future, lived in an idyllic world and in twenty minutes no trace of them will remain.

The pulley moves up and down, lifting bodies without end. As in a giant slaughterhouse, stacks of bodies lie here waiting to be removed.

Thirty hellish mouths blaze now in the two huge buildings and swallow countless bodies. It won't be long before the five thousand people, the five thousand worlds, will have been devoured by the flames.

The ovens blaze furiously, like waves in a storm. This fire was ignited long ago by the barbarians and murderers of the world, who had hoped to drive darkness from their brutal lives with its light.

The fire burns boldly, calmly. Nothing stands in its way, nothing puts it out. Sacrifices arrive regularly, without a number, as though this ancient, martyred nation was created specifically for this purpose.

If you who are free should chance to notice this great fire; if some evening you should raise your eyes to the deep, blue sky and see that it is covered by flames, then you will know that this is the same hellfire that burns here endlessly. Perhaps your heart will feel its heat, and your hands, as cold as ice, will extinguish it. Or perhaps, your heart bolstered with courage, you will exchange the present victims of this never-ending inferno for those who first ignited it, that *they* may be consumed by its flames.

29
Total War
1939–1945

HITLER ANNEXED THE AUSTRIAN REPUBLIC to Austrian popular acclaim and jubilation in March 1938. His next domino, Czechoslovakia, proved something of a disappointment since Britain and France acceded to his wishes in order to avert the war he desired. Neville Chamberlain and Eduard Daladier met with Hitler and Mussolini in Munich on 29 September 1938 and agreed to the occupation of the Sudetenland. The word *Munich* has since become a synonym for appeasement—a foolhardy surrender to Hitler's blackmail. But after German troops marched into Prague in March 1939, in violation of the agreement, Stalin dropped his policy of "collective security" and support for the Western democracies against "fascism." Hitler, for his part, regarded a rapprochement with the Soviet Union as a crucial stepping-stone to attacking Poland. On 23 August 1939, Soviet Foreign Minister Vyacheslav Molotov (1890–1986) concluded a pact with German Foreign Minister Joachim von Ribbentrop (1893–1946) that committed the two nations to remaining neutral in case of war, participating in future trade agreements, and agreeing to a secret protocol dividing Eastern Europe into Soviet and German spheres of interest. The Soviets acquired the Baltic states (Latvia, Estonia, and part of Lithuania), and Germany agreed to a division of Poland, with the Soviets taking control of the eastern areas.

On 3 September, the German army unleashed *Blitzkrieg* against Poland, reaching Warsaw in less than a week and defeating Polish resistance in less than a month. Even some members of the Wehrmacht's general staff were outraged and ashamed by the level of brutality and slaughter, as Major General Hellmuth Stieff demonstrated in a letter to his wife.[1]

After the military conquest, "scientific" surveys were undertaken to assist the occupation by developing a comprehensive plan for urgent re-Germanizing settlement policies in areas "that have now fallen to the Reich." The October 1939 memorandum by Theodor Schieder exemplifies how readily historians and social scientists anticipated and identified with the goals and ideals of the regime, including the "de-Jewification of residual Poland and the establishment of a healthy ethnic order." Germanization—including an official ban on learning Polish by German settlers in Poland—was aggressively pursued, and the non-German population was denied basic health and welfare services to encourage a decline in the population. At the same time, programs promoting racial hygiene for Germans in the Reich and the occupied territories and civilian measures geared toward assisting mothers and "fostering births of genetically sound progeny" played an important role, given the labor shortages and structural weakness of the war economy. During the night of 27–28 January 1944, Hitler revealed to his private secretary, Martin Bormann, his greatest fears for Germany even after the victory he still believed certain. Consistent with his belief that race and demography were the driving forces in history, he proposed that the deaths of German males and the consequent low wartime birthrate be offset by a campaign to encourage women (even without husbands) to have as many children as possible. He proposed that the word *unmarried* be expunged from the vocabulary and that children born "out of wedlock" be legitimized along with "marriagelike" relationships—essentially advocating the official sanction of a cult of motherhood.

The period from 1939 to May 1940, when Britain and France were only nominally at war with Germany, allowed Hitler to prepare for attacks on Holland, Belgium, Luxembourg, and France, which he launched on 10 May. The German army then went on to occupy Norway and Denmark in the spring of 1940. On 25 June, Marshal Philippe Pétain, the French hero of World War I, signed an armistice with Germany and became head of the pro-German Vichy government in the south of France, while Paris and northern France were under German control. After the fall of France, Paris was depicted in *Der Stürmer* as a city plagued by race mixing, attributed to the "Jewish democratic system." At the end of 1940, only Britain remained independent; Spain, Sweden, and Switzerland were neutral, and Germany, Italy, and Japan were united by the Tripartite Pact. On 26 October 1940, Goebbels addressed the leaders of the National Socialist Party in Vienna, declaring, "When this war is over, we hope to be masters of Europe."

Hitler's decision to invade the Soviet Union, code-named Operation Barbarossa, fulfilled a longtime ideological goal but also grew out of strategic considerations of Soviet military weakness and above all timing: Hitler planned a six-month war. He instructed his generals to fight the war on the Eastern Front with extreme ruthlessness. The infamous secret "Commissar Order" of 6 June 1941, signed by Field Marshal Wilhelm Keitel, instructed the Wehrmacht to treat political commissars (captured Soviet political indoctrination officers) not as soldiers but as civilian leaders to be "liquidated" on the spot. Field Marshal Hermann Göring declared in October 1942 that unlike World War I, "this war is the great race war. Whether here the German and Aryan will stand or the Jew will rule the world . . . that is why we are fighting abroad."[2]

By the winter of 1942, the German army had penetrated one thousand miles in from the Polish-Soviet border, and the Africa Campaign was under way in Egypt. However, there was a great deal of trepidation in Germany, as is evident in Security Service reports citing rumors about the general staff and the conditions on the Eastern Front—the cold, insufficient provisions, and lack of equipment—that began to filter back to the home front. Propaganda depicting the Russians as "subhuman" was apparently undermined by more nuanced, even positive impressions recorded by some of the occupiers. In other areas, propaganda was more effective, as in the campaign surrounding the massacre of thousands of Polish officers at Katyn, which (accurately in the case of the Soviets) assigned "responsibility for the slaughter to the Soviets, the British and the Jews."

During the fall of 1942, Soviet forces launched a major counterattack, and at the end of January, the Wehrmacht suffered its most decisive defeat when General Friedrich Paulus surrendered the Sixth Army at Stalingrad. With the hope of German victory shattered, Joseph Goebbels responded on 18 February 1943, delivering a defiant speech at the Berlin Sportpalast, his favorite pulpit. Resounding with the refrain "Do you want total war?," the speech—titled "Now, People, Rise Up and Let the Storm Winds Blow!" but later simply called the "Sportpalast speech"—was delivered amid frenetic cheering aimed to firm up the resolve of the radio audience and those in attendance. Goebbels later mocked his audience in private as idiots, stating that if he had told them to jump out of a third-floor window, they would have done it. Among the changes announced in the speech was the military conscription of men and women between sixteen and sixty-five (though the plan to draft women was never carried out). Despite the cheering that could be heard on the radio, the Security Service noted in a secret report that the speech made many Germans aware for the first time of the "terrible gravity of the situation," and Goebbels's refrain "Do you want total war?" left some people wanting more detail than the Ministry for Popular Enlightenment and Propaganda was prepared to offer. Thomas Mann, the voice of anti-Hitler Germany, also reacted to the speech in a radio address a few days later. He charged that the cynical leaders of the Third Reich were using their so-called candor about the tragic defeat in Russia to mobilize fears of the "Red Menace" and, worse, "to abuse the forces of elementary patriotism in the nation and its *Volk* to save the regime and to mobilize every last reserve into a *levée en masse* [mass conscription]." The "total war" that Goebbels urged was turning into total defeat. From July 1943, when the Soviet military defeated the Germans at Kursk, to May 1945, the Wehrmacht retreated steadily toward Berlin, where it capitulated on 8 May.

NOTES

1. Stieff was arrested on 21 July 1944 and interrogated under torture. He held out for several days against all attempts to extract the names of fellow conspirators. Tried by the Volksgerichtshof (People's Court), he was sentenced to death on 8 August 1944 and executed the same day in Plötzensee prison in Berlin.

2. Cited in Jeffrey Herf, *The Jewish Enemy: Nazi Propaganda during World War II and the Holocaust* (Cambridge, Mass.: Harvard University Press, 2006), 169.

383

THEODOR SCHIEDER

Notes on Settlement and Population Surveys in the Reclaimed Eastern Provinces

Written as "Aufzeichnung über Siedlungs- und Volkstumsfragen in den wiedergewonnen Ostprovinzen" on 4–7 October 1939. First published in *1999* 1, no. 92: 84, 85–86, 87–88, 90–91.

The complete triumph of the German military over Poland marks the moment of restitution for the injustice served upon the German order and the German population in 1919. In those territories that have now been returned to us, we are confronted today with the results of twenty years of brutal policies of eradicating everything German from the Polish population that have led to an unprecedented annihilation and expulsion of ethnic Germans, of their living space and their territory in these areas. In the provinces of Posen and West Prussia that were ceded from the Reich in 1919, there were 1.1 million Germans living in 1910. In 1935, in the region of what was formerly Wojewodschaft Pomerellen, there were 102,000 ethnic Germans, and in eastern Pomerania and Posen combined, 325,000. There is no way to estimate today's numbers to reflect the most recent loss of German population in the area. [. . .]

So the return of German territory and restoration of German population may be seen as reparation for a blatant political injustice. But a reparation of this nature cannot occur on an individual basis, according to which the right of title to land and property is restored to individuals; rather, it must be a reconciliation between one nation of people and another in which reparations are made to the entire German people that are commensurate with the exigencies of their future and that are to be placed in the hands of trustworthy stewards.

The gold standard for a new order must be securing ethnic German territory in the east by establishing a coherent German population that includes all classes of people in a healthy social order, a healthy balance between urban and rural groups, and that is borne by people who possess the strength of their own initiative to fight the nationalist struggle on even the smallest fronts against the ethnic Poles. The first prerequisite is to make a clear distinction between ethnic Poles and ethnic Germans in order to avert the dangers presented by ethnic and racial crossbreeding as well as infiltration. In this context, it is a question of establishing a clear border between the German Reich proper and the [territories of the] Polish residual state. The contemporary constellation of ethnic groups, however, still leaves the prospect of drawing ethnic borders along lines that correspond to actual ethnic groupings unrealistic. Germany, however, has national, ethnic, and historical political claims that can be taken as the basis for such decisions in the future. [. . .]

It would seem imperative that the following preliminary measures be taken immediately:

1. Authorizing the state to confiscate rural and urban properties from Poland. In this context, the immediate registration of all properties that were in German possession in 1918. This would include the immediate confiscation of all properties owned by Poles who have escaped or who have been indicted on charges of participating in anti-German agitation.
2. The deportation of all Poles who have immigrated to Posen–West Prussia since 1919. In addition, as a temporary measure, the registration of addresses for the Polish population resident there in the year 1914.
3. The immediate mobilization of economically disadvantaged ethnic Germans in order to bolster the economy in urban and rural areas. Allotment of land parcels to the heirs of indigenous ethnic Germans' farms and to German rural workers.

4. Preventing the Poles from exiting the reclaimed territories and flooding the border areas of the Old Reich, whose ethnic composition is at risk.
5. Mandatory registration of all persons born in the reclaimed territories who are currently living in the Old Reich or as German citizens in other countries.

The following questions must be addressed in the interest of future planning:

1. What means are available within the whole fabric of the German *Volk* for deployment in Posen–West Prussia, and are these means sufficient for the complete Germanization of these territories?
2. As pertains the timetable and nature of German repatriation of these territories, which territories should have priority?
3. What should be done with Poles displaced from the reclaimed east German territories?

Particular urgency is to be afforded the clarification of the problem of directing the anticipated flood of Polish émigrés from Posen–West Prussia. Here, it is important to note that overseas emigration is always preferable to emigration into the Polish residual state and should be encouraged under all circumstances. An increase in immigration to residual Poland [*Restpolen*] would seem merited when the following two conditions are met: (1) the removal of all Jews from the Polish cities, (2) an intensification of agricultural production that will ease the nutritional crisis in Poland and at least ease the problem of rural overpopulation through a thoroughgoing process of amelioration and segregation. The question of what happens to the displaced Polish population is by no means irrelevant to the Reich: the de-Jewification of residual Poland and the establishment of a healthy ethnic order requires the deployment of German means and forces and brings with it the threat that a new Polish leadership elite develops from the Polish middle class. If these things are left to develop without intervention, there is concern that the body of the Polish *Volk* will degenerate and become a dangerous breeding ground for unrest.

384

MAJOR GENERAL HELLMUTH STIEFF

Letter from Poland

Written to his wife on 31 October 1939. First published in Wolfgang Marienfeld, *Konferenzen über Deutschland: die alliierte Deutschlandplanung und -politik, 1941–1949* (Hanover: Verlag für Literatur und Zeitgeschehen, 1962), 9.

The masses of millions in that city's (Warsaw) population have fallen somehow and some way into a vegetative state, though no one can say why. It is an unspeakable tragedy that is playing itself out there. [. . .] It is a city and a population that is doomed. The situation is so horrific that one cannot enjoy so much as a moment of life spent in this city where one does not move with a sense of victory but rather with the burden of guilt! And I'm not the only one who feels this way—the men forced to live there feel the same. To top it off, there are all these unbelievable things happening on the periphery, and all we can do is stand by with our arms crossed and watch! Even the most vivid fantasies of cruelty spread by propaganda pale by comparison to the crimes being committed by an organized band of murderers, thieves, and plunderers—supposedly with unrestrained approval. You can no longer speak in terms of "righteous indignation over crimes against ethnic Germans." This extirpation of entire lineages [*Geschlechter*], including women and children, can be committed only by a subhuman breed of humans that is not worthy of being called "German." I am ashamed to be a German! This minority that is sullying the German name with its murdering, plundering, and pillaging will bring ruin to the entire German *Volk* if we do not soon put an end to their handiwork. For the things that have been described by reliable sources and proven cannot help but call forth the wrath of nemesis. That, or perhaps this riffraff will one day turn against decent people the same way and terrorize even their own *Volk* with its pathological passions.

385

SECRET REPORT OF THE SECURITY SERVICE OF THE REICHSFÜHRER SS

Bilingualism as Means and Expression of German Superiority in the East

First circulated on 27 March 1940 as "Zweisprachigkeit als Mittel und Ausdruck deutscher Überlegenheit im Osten." First published in *Meldungen aus dem Reich 1938–1945. Die geheimen Lageberichte des Sicherheitsdienstes der SS,* edited by Heinz Boberach (Herrsching: Pawlak Verlag, 1984), 4:920.

The idea of encouraging reliable Germans to learn the Polish language for their deployment in the east was again rejected by the central authorities. The opinion is that Germans have no business concerning themselves with the rather difficult language of an inferior race; the Poles should learn enough German to be able to understand orders given to them. Germans who have been assigned various tasks in Polish-speaking territory for months now, however, are finding this negative stance increasingly difficult to reconcile with the practical tasks of German leadership in the east. In practice, bilingualism has proved itself an expression and an instrument of German superiority for those Germans deployed in the east who speak Polish. The opinion is that it is a strategic error to allow Poles who are not so easily assimilated to learn German, but [it is] much more important that the German understand Polish so he can circumvent the need for employing foreign interpreters. The fact that hardly a single administrative office in the east can do without a Polish or Ukrainian interpreter—independent of the security risks involved—is not conducive to the needs of German leadership. If the authorities of the Reich maintain their negative stance, we cannot anticipate any change in the situation for the future either. What is more, students have demonstrated only very minimal interest in learning Eastern European languages.

It is in this context that Germans in the east point out the opportunity this provides to encourage learning the Ukrainian language. One could consider accepting Ukrainians into certain select German institutes of higher learning throughout the *Generalgouvernement* and at the same time introducing Ukrainian to the curriculum. On the one hand, this would establish in the Ukrainians a stronger connection to German culture (just as it did in eastern Galicia before the war), and, on the other, it would offer Germans the opportunity to learn the language of these 40 million people—a matter that is not insignificant in terms of the future.

People who concern themselves with these problems advocate devoting considerable attention to the question of Polish-language courses (at universities, administrative academies, and other institutions) and to the problem of learning Eastern European languages in general, especially with regard to aims in the East.

386

JOSEPH GOEBBELS

Address to Leaders of the NSDAP in Vienna

Delivered on 26 October 1940. First published in "Zweiter Weltkrieg," in *Bulletin des Arbeiterkreises* "Zweiter Weltkreig," no. 3 (1969): 39.

Everything in the life of the state is replaceable but the substance from which the *Volk* is made, the value of its blood, which, of course, must be deployed during wartime. This is why the foremost principle guiding our prosecution of this war has been extensive preparation and planning for short wars—not long wars with little planning and preparation. [. . .] And, of course, this is a matter of life and death, a question of to be or not to be; of course, we have put a lot on the line, but we took these risks at a time when there was maximum prospect for making them worthwhile. No one can fault German and Austrian policy prior to the World War for having entered the war in 1914; one can only fault them with not having done so six years earlier, at a time when their situation was by far more advantageous [. . .]

I get the impression that the world is being redivided at this very moment, and in a way that it has never been before. And since we've come out on the short end of the stick every time the world has been divvied up and doled out, our only battle cry can be, On your mark, forward march! And when anyone asks me, "What do you really want?" I can't give him a precise answer. It all depends on the circumstances. Depending on how much we want and whether we can get it. What we want is living space. Indeed, but what does that mean? We'll define the term when the war is over. [. . .] When this war is over, we hope to be masters of Europe. [. . .] Then we will finally rank among the wealthy nations, we will own raw materials and resources, and a great colonial empire shall be ours. [. . .]

We National Socialists have always promoted the same position: the war was not over in 1918. That was just the end of the first act, followed by a long interlude. The final act is now in progress. The drama ends with a German victory, and there is no tragedy here.

387

DER STÜRMER

Africa in Paris

First published as "Afrika in Paris," in *Der Stürmer,* no. 46, 14 November 1940, 9.

Before the outbreak of this war, there were three hundred thousand French colonials living in Paris alone, most of them working in the factories. We visited several quarters in the city that were inhabited primarily by coloreds. What we saw there was horrific. Negroes clad in conspicuously modern clothing cavorting jovially with pretty Parisian women. Young, wet-behind-the-ears girls strolling arm in arm with nappy-headed southern Negroes. Our faces turned red with shame. This, then, is modern Paris!

The grungy, narrow streets were lined with miserable tenement buildings. Crumbling mortar and the fusty odor of mold were signs of the misery and disease prevailing here. In the dark courtyards behind the buildings, hollow-cheeked children played on the dank, naked ground. Their nappy heads wobbled atop their skinny, emaciated bodies, and their black eyes peered at us timidly. Mixed bloods! Pathetic creatures burdened with the curse of racial defilement [*Rassenschande*]. There was a small fire burning in the corner of one of the courtyards. A group of adolescent Negro boys in tattered clothing was standing around it, frying up potatoes. Africa in Paris!

In another narrow street, Oriental whites caught our ear. They'd emerged from a dank and dirty locale where Algerian women were gathered around the entrance, taking care of "business." In another street, there were dark-skinned Tunisians loitering around. We struck up a conversation with one of them. He informed us that the Tunisians left their wives at home because there were enough women to go around in Paris. He was referring to the white Parisian women who offered up their services.

Africa in Paris! That's an altogether different Paris from the Paris of the Concordia Square or the Elysian Fields! Here we found the other face of Paris, the "stud farm on the Seine." Here is where the "blessings" of the Jewish democratic system were revealed. Here, the savage tribal peoples of Africa were imported to Paris to serve the interests of a Jewish economy. Here, racial defilement was official policy. And the result was a horrendous societal breakdown.

388

Guidelines for the Treatment of Political Commissars

"Richtlinien für die Behandlung politischer Kommissare ('Kommissarbefehl')." Circulated on 6 June 1941 and signed by Field Marshall Wilhelm Keitel. First published in *Anatomie des SS-Staates,* edited by Martin Broszat, Hans-Adolf Jacobson, and Helmut Krausnick (Olten: Walter-Verlag, 1965), doc. NOKW-1076, 2:178.

Staff Command Secret Document
Chief Only
[Transmit] Only via Officers
High Command of the Wehrmacht
WFST [Armed Forces Operational Staff] Div. L (VI/Qu)
No. 44822/41 g.K Chiefs

In the fight against Bolshevism, it is *not* to be expected that the enemy will act in accordance with the principles of humanity or international law. In particular, the *political commissars* of all kinds, who are the real bearers of resistance, can be expected to mete out treatment to our prisoners that is full of hate, cruel and inhumane.

The army must be aware of the following:

1. In this battle, it would be mistaken to show mercy or respect for international law toward such elements. They constitute a danger to our own security and to the rapid pacification of the occupied territories.
2. The barbaric, Asiatic fighting methods are originated by the political commissars. Action must therefore be taken against them *immediately,* without further consideration and with all severity. Therefore, when they are picked up in battle or resistance, they are, as a matter of principle, to be finished immediately with a weapon.

In addition, the following regulations are to be observed:

Operational Areas

(1) Political commissars operating *against our armies* are to be dealt with in accordance with the decree on judicial provisions in the area of "Barbarossa." This applies to commissars of every type and rank, even if they are only suspected of resistance, sabotage or incitement to sabotage.

389

MARTIN BORMANN

To Alfred Rosenberg

On the Treatment of Non-German Populations in the Eastern Territories

Issued on 23 July 1942. First published as "Reichsleiter Martin Bormann Grundsätze für die besetzen Ostgebieten, 23.7.1942," in *Das Dritte Reich und seine Denker,* edited by Léon Poliakov and Joseph Wulf (Berlin: Arani, 1959), 517.

The Führer requests that I inform you that you see to it that the following principles are observed and executed in the occupied eastern territories:

1. We are all too happy to see girls and women in the occupied eastern territories abort their children; German jurists should therefore not, under any circumstances, seek to intervene in these matters. In the Führer's opinion, we should even allow for vigorous trade in contraceptives in the occupied eastern territories, for we have absolutely no interest in any increase in the non-German population.
2. The risk that the birthrate in the non-German population will increase even more steadily than before is great, for the overall standard of living for the non-German population is of course much better and much more secure. For this reason especially, we must take the necessary prophylactic measures to prevent an increase in the non-German population.
3. Therefore, under no circumstances shall German health services be provided for the non-German population in the occupied eastern territories. So, for example, under no circumstances shall immunizations and similar preventative medical services be so much as considered.
4. The non-German population shall not be afforded any form of higher education whatsoever. If we were to make this mistake, we would in fact be planting the seeds of future resistance. So, the Führer is of the opinion that it is more than sufficient that the non-German population—including the so-called Ukrainians—learn to read and to write.
5. Under no circumstances should any of our policies foster a mentality of superiority in the non-German population! Precisely the opposite is what is needed!
6. The Cyrillic alphabet currently used in schools should be replaced by the standard alphabet in the future.
7. The Germans absolutely must be stationed outside the Ukrainian cities; even housing them in barracks just outside the cities is better than housing them in the cities. Russian (Ukrainian) cities should not be subject to any form of urban renewal or improvement whatsoever, for the population should not experience any improved standard, and the Germans will live in cities and towns yet to be built in which the Russian (Ukrainian) population will be strictly forbidden to enter. Therefore, the buildings designed to house Germans should bear absolutely no resemblance to those of the Russians (Ukrainians) (no roughcast walls, thatched roofs, etc.).
8. The Führer stresses that far too many things in the Old Reich are regulated and controlled; we cannot under any circumstances make the same mistake in the occupied eastern territories. Not under any circumstances shall too much be regulated for the non-German population; we must restrict ourselves to the absolute bare necessities in this regard. This means that the German administration absolutely must be kept at a minimum; the regional commissar must work closely with local authorities; and yet nor can there be, under any circumstances, a uniform Ukrainian administration reaching all the way to the rank of commissar general or Reich commissar.

390

SECRET REPORT OF THE SECURITY SERVICE OF THE REICHSFÜHRER SS

Rumors and Murmurings

First circulated in January 1942 as "Beeinträchtigung der öffentlichen Führungsmittel." First published in *Meldungen aus dem Reich 1938–1945. Die geheimen Lageberichte des Sicherheitsdienstes der SS,* edited by Heinz Boberach (Herrsching: Pawlak Verlag, 1984), 9:3196, 3197.

Countless rumors remain in circulation saying that General Field Marshall von Rundstedt has been dismissed and replaced by General Field Marshall von Reichenau and, furthermore, that General Field Marshall von Bock no longer holds his position either.[1] People were therefore extremely surprised at news of the operation that von Brauchitsch recently underwent and the Führer's heartfelt wishes for a speedy recovery.[2] The reference to the length of the leave of absence General von Brauchitsch would still need for his recovery immediately gave rise to speculation that he would indeed be returning to the job at some point. The same applies to the news that General Field Marshall von Rundstedt would be representing the Führer at the state funeral for General Field Marshall von Reichenau—and that, just after von Reichenau had taken over command from General Field Marshall von Rundstedt—according to rumors. The surprise is complete, then, when General Field Marshall von Bock makes appearances with the Führer shortly after his return from sick leave. The populace "could see neither rhyme nor reason" in collecting woolen goods and winter clothing and why it was necessary. Above all, they wondered who was responsible for putting our soldiers in the situation they are in now. Alternately, people speculate about why—as rumor would have it—the "sacked general field marshalls" were suddenly being treated so well and, as in the case of Bock, even being invited back. The national comrades say that, between what you "hear" and what you read in the papers, you can hardly make any sense of the conflicting stories.

We have gathered ample confirmation of the fact that the opinions expressed before, during, and after the woolen goods and winter clothing collection were strongly influenced by letters from the front and reports from soldiers. Many soldiers did not hesitate to send home their harrowing, indeed hair-raising, stories about the strain they were under, the cold, insufficient provisions, lack of equipment, etc. Soldiers who were less forthright in talking about their hardships because they know the people at home would never understand it anyway, and it would only make them sad, were less likely to be believed. Very often, they are told, "with the way you're talking, I'd say you've never even been to the front." One petty officer, decorated with the Medal of Honor [*Ehrenkreuz*], avoided the gory and gruesome details to provide a positive report of his war experiences and was told many times, "We don't understand why you got the Medal of Honor." And yet, in many instances, precisely those soldiers who served farthest from the front or behind it or even in their home base were the ones who tended toward gross exaggeration.

Soldiers seeking a sense of celebrity status are known to go about boasting exaggerated war stories. At home, men like this are revered as frontline soldiers, and their horror stories are taken to represent truth and reality. This situation greatly diminishes the efficacy of the press and radio and especially of the weekly newsreels. In various parts of the Reich, we have observed that the citizenry no longer believes what is being shown and openly states their belief that the images they are being shown are highly selective. So, for example, at the cinema in Aachen recently, when one of the newsreels showed images of preparations being made to send fur coats and clothing to the soldiers in the time between Christmas and New Year and of the soldiers slaughtering a pig, there was grumbling in the audience: "that's not right, our soldiers are freezing and all they have to eat is horse meat" and the like. It works the other way too, as we have often seen—namely, that families, wives especially—outline in minute, overblown detail every one of their travails in letters to the front, and the party is held responsible and staunchly criticized for even the most trifling problems. Frontline soldiers home on leave were astonished at the relatively good overall conditions here at home—especially with regard to the food supply situation, which—though it couldn't be described as plentiful—was much better organized now than in the Great War. From reading the letters they got from home and which were passed from comrade to comrade [at the front], one would have expected the place to be a complete shambles, and they'd been determined to come home on leave and "put their foot down."

Notes

1. General Field Marshall von Rundstedt (1874–1953) was relieved of his command by Hitler in November 1941, after the retreat of Army Group South from Rostov. He was replaced by General Field Marshall von Reichenau (1884–1942), who died of a heart attack in January 1942.—Eds.
2. A similar fate awaited General Field Marshall Walther von Brauchitsch (1881–1948), who also suffered a heart attack and whom Hitler replaced in December 1941. General Field Marshall Fedor von Bock (1880–1945) was also relieved of his command after the Army Group South was forced to retreat from Moscow in the winter of 1942.—Eds.

391

SECRET REPORT OF THE SECURITY SERVICE OF THE REICHSFÜHRER SS

The Image of Russia in the Populace

First circulated in August 1942 as "Das Russlandbild in der Bevölkerung." First published in *Meldungen aus dem Reich 1938–1945. Die geheimen Lageberichte des Sicherheitsdienstes der SS,* edited by Heinz Boberach (Herrsching: Pawlak Verlag, 1984), 11:4084–86.

Recently, we have received from various areas through the Reich and from all social classes countless individual reports indicating that the entire population is making an effort to form an increasingly coherent opinion about the Soviet Union, the country, its internal constitution, its people, their emotional and material existence. What is most often expressed is that all previous notions about the Soviet Union have shifted in the course of the war against this country, and that a series of contradictions exist for which no satisfactory explanation can be found.

1. Our previous propaganda against the Soviet Union established that the Communist-Bolshevist system was erected by the Jews as a system of tremendous oppression and deprivation for the entire Russian population. Particular emphasis was placed on the difference between Bolshevist ideology and agitation and the reality of the Soviet Union. This propaganda generated the ideas that were aptly and accurately substantiated and underscored in the recent exhibition, "The Soviet Paradise." The soldiers in particular repeatedly stressed the accuracy of these images in their depictions. The image of the Soviet Union and its people was portrayed here in all its black-and-white depredation and horrific deprivation. And yet, you do often hear from the general populace such things as, "And German people are supposed to be relocated to this terrible country after the war!" "There's nothing in the world that would make me want to go there!" "And even if they were to force me to go there, there's no way they'd get me to go!"
2. This image of the Soviet Union is the source of great confusion. One may recall the many years of imposing reports over the disorganization, for example, in the fields of agriculture and transportation, the failures of the Five-Year Plan in industry, etc. Already in the first few months of the war against the Soviet Union, people were starting

to get the impression that we had fallen prey to a certain degree of deception. The huge stockpiles of weapons, their technical sophistication, and the massive industrialization were the first signs of illusion that were used as a primary argument to counter the previously held opinion of the Soviet Union. And the soldiers, too, reported from their own experience that, in addition to the primitive conditions and in the midst of terrible misery, there were massive architectural projects, huge industrial plants similar to those we find in America, that power plants, etc. had been built. One had to wonder how Bolshevism was able to accomplish all this? "There have to be positive forces at work here, too, or not?"

3. The people of the Soviet Union were seen as animalistic, herd-like, beastly. To the political commissars and the *Politruk,* they are the very personification of "subhumans." Reports provided about the atrocities that were committed in the first few months of the Eastern Campaign served to solidify the opinion that members of the enemy army are "beastly." People began asking themselves how we might best deal with these "animals" in the future. Many of our national comrades envisioned the need to radically eradicate them. Together with the reports about violent acts committed by Russian prisoners of war who'd escaped, there is a growing sense of fear that these characters and types could begin entering the Reich in greater numbers and might even find employment.

Today, this stands in stark contrast to the impression on the part of many national comrades about the intellect and character of thousands of workers from the east. Especially amongst workers, we have ascertained that the opinion of the Russians is that they are intelligent, skillful and clever, and quick to learn how to operate even the most complicated mechanical procedures. Many of them were very quick to learn the German language and are obviously not all that poorly educated. These experiences have lent a degree of ambiguity to the image of people from the east.

392

HERMANN ERNST GROBIG

Why Racial Hygiene in Wartime?

First published as "Warum Rassenhygiene im Kriege?" in *Archiv für Rassen- und Gesellschaftsbiologie* 37, 1944, 175–79.

I remain to this day of the opinion that of all the circumstances that surround us, marriage is and must forever remain the one that is the source of our whole racial, eternally self-rejuvenating life. The family is the smallest unit in the state. And it is only a biologically born and bred fabric of state such as this that will last. Therefore, I consider the promotion of all things related to the institution of marriage between genetically superior, healthy human beings and of all things related to the reproductive output of these people as being essential to the postwar effort and, as such, as essential to the war effort. And the postwar effort, of course, does not begin after the war; rather, the racial politics of wartime must sustain everything that comes after the war. The degree to which we can best use our victory is entirely dependent on the genetic and racial quality of our densely populated state.

[. . .] The state has done a very good job of providing economic incentives for marriages that further our racial-hygienic planning. I'm thinking, for example, of provisions for allowing early marriage in the student population, a program that benefits precisely that group which promises to supply us with the talented young people we will need for future generations. Then there are the extended regulations concerning the marriage loan program, which provides every genetically sound German with a financial basis for newly married couples.

Enthusiasm for marriage has increased as a result of these and other state-sponsored measures since 1933, and people welcome the opportunity for early marriage for genetically sound Germans. The number of births in these new marriages is felicitously high. However, especially now, the "will to reproduce" must be encouraged; pride in the newborn child must be evoked. So, for example, I know of certain formations in the military who welcome the birth of any one of their most distant comrades as a child born to the whole formation. May this someday be the case everywhere—that the newborn son of a soldier becomes an enduring source of pride—for the moment and for all the hours and days to come.

In this context, the very serious problem of insufficient living space arises. Already, in the last years of peace, we were in dire straits concerning apartments that were too small and in some cases simply not available at all, but the events of war have also taken their toll on our homeland and will continue to do so, and the lack of new residential construction has created a serious housing shortage. At this juncture in the war, of course, we cannot expect a solution to the problem to be found.

Whether it concerns the mother with children bombed out of her home who can afford to secure only very confined quarters, whether it concerns the newly wedded daughter forced to live with her parents, we must seek in any way we can to help each other through this reduction of our living space. We must keep any ensuing loss in human reproductive output for future generations at an absolute minimum. This is an area in which leaders of the regional districts and their colleagues can have great impact. These things cannot be regulated by statutes; they are matters of the heart!

One additional wartime task for which planning is already well under way is providing apartments for families with multiple children that will be needed in peacetime. The will to produce multiple children will not emerge unless there is sufficient living space to accommodate them. This is one of the most urgent programs we must initiate after the war.

Our detractors persistently object to the argument that these programs are necessary to countervail against losses at the front; objections are raised by our detractors by saying, "It doesn't matter who's carrying the weapons—whether they are talented men or untalented—genetically sound or suffering from hereditary defect." In the first place, this certainly does make a difference on the front, and secondly, the children being born today should no longer need to arm themselves with weapons twenty years from now but rather with ideas.

Many believe (not necessarily in the interest of National Socialist racial politics) that another way of compensating for these losses would be to encourage the production of illegitimate children. [. . .] For us, the question does not ultimately boil down to whether any child is legitimate or illegitimate but merely whether one has a child or does not. We need not stress that this, of course, refers exclusively to genetically sound children who are free from hereditary defect. There was a time in Germany when concerns issuing from mistaken ideas about the social fabric or from egotism caused the birthrate to drop.

But the most recent drop in the birthrate—war-related factors notwithstanding—primarily concerns the future of the new lives one would be putting into the world. And here, too, I see another task for those of us thinking in racial-hygienic terms. Belief in victory is the basic prerequisite to gaining support for all these state-sponsored and civilian measures toward fostering births of genetically sound progeny.

Fortunately, the protective measures and relief programs for mothers-to-be are extensive in this war. Above all, though, the entire population must be prepared to bend over backward for mothers-to-be and mothers with children who've been bombed out of their homes. We must circle the wagons to protect our mothers-to-be and our war children. They will come if their mothers know that they are in good hands.

Especially in wartime, then, all active measures in eugenic intervention taken by the state or the civilian population are to be strongly promoted, especially those that focus on genetically sound German marriages as their goal. So, for example, marriage counseling [should be] tailored to the needs of our current situation, and particular emphasis should be placed on what is called "matchmaking." This should not be arranged to occur from one central location but rather from various offices organized according to the same guidelines. Furthermore, employees of these matchmaking offices must have excellent judgment about people and must be particularly adept at emotional empathy. Above all, one must avoid offering this matchmaking service as a mechanical procedure, since this diminishes the likelihood of success. It is advisable to coordinate these services, even the private initiatives, with offices that provide racial-hygienic and eugenics testing and genetic counseling.

Any and all remaining means of fostering births—such as state-funded child support contingent on racial-hygienic restrictions, educational programs for the gifted and talented, allowing gifted and talented members of the *Volk* to further enroll in higher education without the necessary educational prerequisites—also merit special emphasis during wartime and should be carried out in consideration of the incontestable demands of racial hygiene we have outlined.

From this perspective, then, racial hygiene and racial politics are not issues that must be set aside in favor of others that are vital to the war effort. Precisely the opposite is the case! The war is requiring ever more effort and presents us with ever more challenges. It is not just the outcome of the war that hinges on our ability to master these challenges; it is the success of our victory.

393

JOSEPH GOEBBELS

Now, People, Rise Up and Let the Storm Winds Blow!

Speech delivered on 18 February 1943. First published as "Nun, Volk, steh auf, und Sturm brich los! Rede im Berliner Sportpalast," in *Der steile Aufstieg* (Munich: Zentralverlag der NSDAP, 1944), 167–204. Translated by Randall Bytwerk. Calvin College, German Propaganda Archive.

I am firmly convinced that the German *Volk* has been deeply moved by the blow of fate at Stalingrad. It has looked into the face of hard and pitiless war. It now knows the awful truth and is resolved to follow the Führer through thick and thin. (The crowd rises and like the roaring ocean chants, "Führer command, we follow! Heil our Führer!" The minister is unable to continue for several minutes.)

The English and American press in recent days has been writing at length about the attitude of the German people during this crisis. The English seem to think that they know the German people much better than we do, its own leadership. They give hypocritical advice on what we should do and not do. They believe that the German people today are the same as the German people of November 1918 who fell victim to their persuasive wiles. I do not need to disprove their assertions. That will come from the fighting and working German people.

To make the truth plain, however, my German comrades, I want to ask you a series of questions. I want you to answer them to the best of your knowledge, according to your conscience. When my audience cheered on 30 January, the English press reported the next day that it was all a propaganda show that did not represent the true opinion of the German people. (Spontaneous shouts of "Pfui!" "Lies!" "Let them come here! They will learn differently!") I have invited to today's meeting a cross-section of the German people in the best sense of the word. (The minister's words were accompanied by stormy applause that increased in intensity as he came to the representatives of the army present at the meeting.) In front of me are rows of wounded German soldiers from the Eastern Front, missing legs and arms, with wounded bodies, those who have lost their sight, those who have come with nurses, men in the blush of youth who stand with crutches. Among them are fifty who bear the Knight's Cross with Oak Leaves, shining examples of our fighting front. Behind them are armaments workers from Berlin tank factories. Behind them are party officials, soldiers from the fighting army, doctors, scientists, artists, engineers and architects, teachers, officials and employees from offices, proud representatives of every area of our intellectual life that even in the midst of war produce miracles of human genius. Throughout the Sportpalast I see thousands of German women. The youth are here, as are the aged. No class, no occupation, no age remained uninvited. I can rightly say that before me is gathered a representative sample of the German population, both from the homeland and from the front. Is that true? Yes or no? (The Sportpalast experiences something seen only rarely even in this old fighting locale of National Socialism. The masses spring to their feet. A hurricane of thousands of voices shouts "Yes!" The participants experience a spontaneous popular referendum and expression of will.) You, my hearers, at this moment represent the whole nation. I wish to ask you ten questions that you will answer for the German people throughout the world, but especially for our enemies, who are listening to us on the radio. (Only with difficulty can the minister be heard. The crowd is at the peak of excitement. The individual questions are razor sharp. Each individual feels as if he is being spoken to personally. With full participation and enthusiasm, the crowd answers each question. The Sportpalast rings with a single shout of agreement.)

The English maintain that the German people have lost faith in victory.

I ask you, Do you believe with the Führer and us in the final, total victory of the German people?

I ask you, Are you resolved to follow the Führer through thick and thin to victory, and are you willing to accept the heaviest personal burdens?

Second, the English say that the German people are tired of fighting.

I ask you, Are you ready to follow the Führer as the phalanx of the homeland, standing behind the fighting army and to wage war with wild determination through all the turns of fate until victory is ours?

Third, the English maintain that the German people have no desire any longer to accept the government's growing demands for war work.

I ask you, Are you and the German people willing to work, if the Führer orders, ten, twelve, and if necessary, fourteen hours a day, and to give everything for victory?

Fourth, the English maintain that the German people are resisting the government's total war measures. They do not want total war but capitulation! (Shouts: "Never! Never! Never!")

I ask you, Do you want total war? If necessary, do you want a war more total and radical than anything that we can even imagine today?

Fifth, the English maintain that the German people have lost faith in the Führer.

I ask you, Is your confidence in the Führer greater, more faithful, and more unshakable than ever before? Are you absolutely and completely ready to follow him wherever he goes and do all that is necessary to bring the war to a victorious end? (The crowd rises as one man. It displays unprecedented enthusiasm. Thousands of voices join in shouting, "Führer command, we follow!" A wave of shouts of "Heil!" flows through the hall. As if by command, the flags and standards are raised as the highest expression of the sacred moment in which the crowd honors the Führer.)

Sixth, I ask you, Are you ready from now on to give your full strength to provide the Eastern Front with the men and munitions it needs to give Bolshevism the death blow?

Seventh, I ask you, Do you take a holy oath to the front that the homeland stands firm behind them and that you will give them everything they need to win the victory?

Eighth, I ask you, Do you, especially you women, want the government to do all it can to encourage German women to put their full strength at work to support the war effort, and to release men for the front whenever possible, thereby helping the men at the front?

Ninth, I ask you, Do you approve, if necessary, the most radical measures against a small group of shirkers and black marketeers who pretend there is peace in the middle of war and use the need of the nation for their own selfish purposes? Do you agree that those who harm the war effort should lose their heads?

Tenth and lastly, I ask you, Do you agree that above all in war, according to the National Socialist Party platform, the same rights and duties should apply to all, that the homeland should bear the heavy burdens of the war together, and that the burdens should be shared equally between high and low and rich and poor?

I have asked; you have given me your answers. You are part of the people, and your answers are those of the German people. You have told our enemies what they needed to hear so that they will have no illusions or false ideas.

Now, just as in the first hours of our rule and through the ten years that followed, we are bound firmly in brotherhood with the German people. The most powerful ally on earth, the people themselves, stand behind us and are determined to follow the Führer, come what may. They will accept the heaviest burdens to gain victory. What power on earth can hinder us from reaching our goal? Now we must and will succeed! I stand before you not only as the spokesman of the government but as the spokesman of the people. My old party friends are here around me, clothed with the high offices of the people and the government. Party comrade Speer sits next to me. The Führer has given him the great task of mobilizing the German armaments industry and supplying the front with all the weapons it needs. Party comrade Dr. Ley sits next to me. The Führer has charged him with the leadership of the German work force, with schooling and training it in untiring work for the war effort. We feel deeply indebted to our party comrade [Ernst Friedrich "Fritz"] Sauckel [1894–1946], who has been charged by the Führer to bring hundreds of thousands of workers to the Reich to support our national economy, something the enemy cannot do. All the leaders of the party, the army, and government join with us as well.

We are all children of our people, forged together by this most critical hour of our national history. We promise you, we promise the front, we promise the Führer, that we will mold together the homeland into a force on which the Führer and his fighting soldiers can rely on absolutely and blindly. We pledge to do all in our life and work that is necessary for victory. We will fill our hearts with the political passion, with the ever-burning fire that blazed during the great struggles of the party and the state. Never during this war will we fall prey to the false and hypocritical objectivism that has brought the German nation so much misfortune over its history.

When the war began, we turned our eyes to the nation alone. That which serves its struggle for life is good and must be encouraged. What harms its struggle for life is bad and must be eliminated and cut out. With burning hearts and cool heads we will overcome the major problems of this phase of the war. We are on the way to final victory. That victory rests on our faith in the Führer.

This evening I once again remind the whole nation of its duty. The Führer expects us to do that which will throw all we have done in the past into the shadows. We do not want to fail him. As we are proud of him, he should be proud of us.

The great crises and upsets of national life show who the true men and women are. We have no right any longer to speak of the weaker sex, for both sexes are displaying the same determination and spiritual strength. The nation is ready for anything. The Führer has commanded, and we will follow him. In this hour of national reflection and contemplation, we believe firmly and unshakably in victory. We see it before us, we need only reach for it. We must resolve to subordinate everything to it. That is the duty of the hour. Let the slogan be, Now, people, rise up and let the storm break loose!

(The minister's final words were lost in unending stormy applause.)

394

THOMAS MANN

Response to Joseph Goebbels

Broadcast on 23 February 1943. First published in Thomas Mann, *Deutsche Hörer: Radiosendungen nach Deutschland aus den Jahren 1940–1945* (Frankfurt am Main: Fischer Taschenbuch Verlag, 1987), 89–92.

German Listeners!

History will one day be divided over what was more repulsive, the Nazis' words or their deeds. And it will be difficult to decide when this riffraff was more offensive to humanity: when they were lying or when they were telling the truth. Because in their mouths, even truth becomes a lie, an instrument of deception—and there is no more disgusting way to lie than by manipulating the truth. Goebbels and his ilk were recently languishing in a love affair with the truth. The heartfelt candor with which they reported the disaster in Russia to the German *Volk*—an event that, incidentally, ranks amongst the most egregious strategic failures in military history—was indeed monumental and overwhelming. They spared none of the gruesome details about the end of the siege on Stalingrad—except perhaps that they neglected to mention the fact that Hitler alone was personally responsible for this particular catastrophe. The song played to accompany the news in the radio broadcast was not the party hymn, the "Horst Wessel Song," which may have at least given cause for some feeling of unease; instead it was, "I Once Had a Comrade." Four days of national mourning were declared for the Reich, a period of mourning over the disastrous misdeeds of the Nazi regime—a mockery of the real grief that has descended upon the people as a result of the senseless waste of the lives of tens of thousands of their sons. Whatever potential there was for outrage, desperation, or rebellion is left buried beneath this mourning. We all want to mourn together, the Führer and his fawning followers, join together in song: "I Once Had a Comrade."

The nauseating aftertaste of honesty came from the fact that it was used as a means to an end. Its purpose was, in the first place, to abuse the forces of elementary patriotism in the nation and its *Volk* to save the regime and to mobilize every last reserve into a *levée en masse*—whereby the men in charge of the conscription are less concerned with the dubious results of the final challenge than they are with the distraction the attendant emotion provides. Second, though, and particularly noteworthy, is the fact that the victories of the Russians and the Nazi losses were portrayed so openly and honestly and possibly even exaggerated in order to thrust the Anglo-Saxon world into fear of the "Red Menace," fear of the European continent being flooded by Bolshevism. The incoherent message Hitler delivered in his speech on the tenth anniversary of the seizure of power is replete with extortionist warnings of this nature, replete with rhetorical Rudolf Hess flights over the canal, undertaken in the obstinate hope of still getting England and the United States to join him in opposing "Central Asia" (meaning Russia). "East Asia"—Japan, that is, his ally—is good, but "Central Asia"—that is, Russia, the country he stupidly and brazenly invaded—is the world's enemy. Hitler himself is the personification of the finest, most noble, most endearing and cultivated Europe has to offer; but the land of Pushkin, Gogol, and Tolstoy is Hun territory, whose hordes are about to plunge Hitler's budding continent into "unimaginable barbarism."

It is a noble swindle, one that will produce no results. It behooves the Nazis to play the role of the socially respectable ones, allowing Göring to drop hints more heavyset than he is: "We are perfectly willing to enter a peace accord with gentlemen but never with the Soviets!" Haven't they figured out yet that it is entirely presumptuous of them to so much as consider speaking in terms of a peace accord? That no one is interested in reaching a peace agreement with them, neither the democracies nor the socialist states? That peace will come *after* they are gone? But as far as the Red Menace is concerned, Stalin, in his speech of 6 November 1941, states, "Our primary goal is to liberate Russian soil and its inhabitants from the Nazi yoke. Our military aims do not include imposing our will and our form of governance on the Slavic Balkans or any other European nations." And he sent word through his ambassador [Ivan] Maisky that "The Soviet Union defends every nation's right to independence and the inviolability of its territory . . . as well as its right to establish that social order and to elect that form of government which it considers necessary and best." But with regard to Germany, he said, "Hitler will come and go, but the German nation and the German State shall remain." Surely he has some desire to punish the people who have inflicted such infinite suffering on his country, but nary a word of threat or intent to annihilate the German *Volk* has crossed his lips. Was it Russia that attacked Germany or the other way around? The day is perhaps not far off when the German *Volk* will see in Russia a level-headed ally.

395

SECRET REPORT OF THE SECURITY SERVICE OF THE REICHSFÜHRER SS

Reactions to Goebbels's Speech

First circulated on 22 February 1943 as "Die Rede des Reichsministers Dr. Goebbels am 18.2.1943." First published in *Meldungen aus dem Reich 1938–1945. Die geheimen Lageberichte des Sicherheitsdienstes der SS,* edited by Heinz Boberach (Herrsching: Pawlak Verlag, 1984), 12:4831.

According to reports on hand, Reich Minister Dr. Goebbels's 18 February 1943 speech was listened to by a substantial portion of the population despite the fact that it was announced unexpectedly and on rather short notice. The speech reached many more sectors of the population through its rebroadcast on radio, through transcripts published in the press, and through the spirited discussion of its content in the public. Reports are unanimous in confirming that the effect of the speech was unusually great and overall positive. Following recent developments on the Eastern Front, above all the alarming news of the evacuation from Charkov, national comrades were again plunged to a low point in morale and were hungry for a clear explanation of the situation. People say that Reich Minister Goebbels's speech was reassuring despite its very candid depiction of the gravity of the situation, and it served to again reinforce confidence and faith in military leadership and war strategy. Dr. Goebbels succeeded in generating an enthusiasm and "fighting spirit" at the Sportpalast that was transmitted over the airwaves to radio listeners.

The thesis of "imminent threat" confirmed the fears of many national comrades that no stabilization of the Eastern Front was in sight, the series of defeats was nowhere near an end, and the war still had the potential to take a serious turn [for the worse]. In some cases, it was only through this speech that people became aware of the "terrible gravity of the situation." They were shocked but not despairing. The people are grateful to leaders for finally speaking candidly and "coming clean" with the truth. However, many have expressed the desire to also receive more concrete details concerning the military situation—inasmuch as this does not involve revealing military secrets. A few individuals remarked that they thought Dr. Goebbels portrayed the situation "more pessimistically than it was" in order to stress the need for totalitarian measures. In his discussion of these measures, Dr. Goebbels addressed the public "from the heart," even though various people pointed out that his statements on those measures that have thus far been introduced did not provide information beyond what was already available and once again mentioned only that the total war would be prosecuted "very late in the game." The announcement of radical implementation of these measures met largely with strong approval throughout the Reich.

There was little consensus of opinion concerning the last part of the speech. While, in general, the cogency of the ten questions was highlighted, there were national and party comrades everywhere who stated that the propagandistic intent of these questions and answers was all too apparent to listeners.

The populace continues to discuss with deep concern the questions of where the front will ultimately end, why Stalingrad had to happen, what these retreats will cost in terms of lives sacrificed, munitions, materials, and for the provision of important territories, and what kind of success can be expected from the spring offensive. As the reports make clear, most of the population is almost afraid to see any optimism in the military situation, lest they be disappointed. The opinion that the current retreats could be incorporated into the upcoming spring offensive and therefore be less matter for concern would be "too good to be true." Only a few people speculate about the prospect of luring the Bolshevists as far as possible from their supply bases so that they can be surrounded in the spring and then annihilated completely.

396

SECRET REPORT OF THE SECURITY SERVICE OF THE REICHSFÜHRER SS

Reactions to the Katyn Forest Massacre

First circulated 16–19 April 1943 as "Aufnahme und Auswirkung der allgemeinen Propaganda-, Presse- und Rundfunklenkung in der Zeit vom 16. Bis 19. 4. 1943." First published in *Meldungen aus dem Reich 1938–1945. Die geheimen Lageberichte des Sicherheitsdienstes der SS,* edited by Heinz Boberach (Herrsching: Pawlak Verlag, 1984), 13:5416, 5147.

The way the mass murder at Katyn has been presented in the press has been well received throughout the populace.

[. . .] Above and beyond the facts of the case as reported, the vast majority of the populace has gleaned from this that the discovery of the mass graves has been a "gift from heaven" in terms of effectively confirming our views of Bolshevism and the Jews from the standpoint of German propaganda abroad. Most people hope that this material will allow us to finally succeed in influencing the remaining neutral or hostile forces abroad in our favor. So the propaganda campaign has been unleashed in which the details of the way the "dead of Katyn" died is affirmed, and it is assumed that it will be "headlined by all the news agencies" in reports assigning responsibility for the slaughter to the Soviets, the British, and the Jews equally. In some instances, one might say with "a twinkle in the eye" that the propaganda campaign doesn't necessarily have to be "entirely accurate." And yet the widespread coverage in the foreign press, the on-site observations of Poles, the participation solicited from the Red Cross, and the response on the part of Bolshevists, the British, and the Polish government in exile in London all indicate that "very concrete" documents are in evidence concerning the massacre at Katyn.

397

MARTIN BORMANN

Safeguarding the Future of the German People

Written on 29 January 1944. Published in Jochen von Lang, *The Secretary—Martin Bormann: The Man Who Manipulated Hitler,* translated by Christa Armstrong and Peter White (New York: Random House, 1979), 276.

Führer Headquarters
January 29, 1944

Note Re: Safeguarding the Future of the German People

1. During the night of January 27–28 the Führer had a conversation with us on the problem of our future as a people. The upshot from this and earlier discussions and reflections is here recorded:

Our racial situation will be *disastrous* after this war, for our people is now experiencing the second massive bloodletting within a span of thirty years. There can be no doubt that we will win the war militarily, but we will lose it racially unless we make drastic readjustments.

The loss of blood is not something that just happens once; rather, it has effect year after year, way into the distant future.

A single example:

How many more children would have been born during the war if it had been possible to give our front-line soldiers leave from the army entirely or more frequent home leave?

We are shown what frightful political consequences a war can have by the Thirty Years' War: at its start the German people numbered over 18 million, and by the time it ended, a mere 3½ million. The consequences of this spilling of blood have not yet been made up and compensated for to this day, for we lost that world leadership which at the beginning of the Thirty Years' War the German people seemed first in line to assume by predestination; our dismemberment as a state persisted until 1870, and as a people, looking at the big picture, until 1933; the sectarian religious disunity is not yet mended to this day.

2. On previous occasions I have pointed out again and again the condition that will prevail after the war is over: we must hold before our eyes the population map of Europe and Asia as of 1850, 1870, and 1900 and 1945: *The Asiatic peoples are multiplying at a much faster rate than the* Nordic peoples, some of whom are not increasing their population at all any more. If this ratio persists, then it will do our Nordic peoples no good at all if we win this war, for in a hundred years at the latest, they will still be overwhelmed by the tremendous masses of Asiatic peoples. The present struggle is already made infinitely difficult by the waves of ever fresh masses of troops the Russians are able to keep throwing in.

3. As the Führer stressed, after this war we will have 3 to 4 million women who either no longer have husbands or will not get any. The drop in the birth rate resulting from that would be impossible to put up with for our people: how many divisions—the Führer emphasized—would we be short in twenty to forty-five years and beyond that!

4. The future and life of a people are the more secure, the higher the birth rate of that people.

The calculation of many parents to keep down the number of their children in order to assure the future of those children already born is basically wrong-headed: the reverse is true! With sufficient insight all women, therefore, who have *one* child, should insist that not only they themselves but all other women have as many children as possible, since these children's future is that much more secure, the greater their number. This is a completely cool-headed calculation.

5. Now, it is a fact that women who find themselves without a man after this war cannot have children by the Holy Spirit but only by men who have survived. Increased propagation by the individual man is—obviously from the standpoint of the good of the people—only desired in the case of a portion of these men. Good men with strong character, physically and psychically healthy, are the ones who should reproduce extra generously, not the ones warped in body and mind.

6. If the dead of the past world war and the present are not to have died in vain, we must secure the victory with all means at hand. Every woman whose husband or brother or father or other relative was killed in one of these struggles must wish that! This means that every woman must wish that *every* healthy woman capable of doing so after the war's end will have as many children as possible, to secure the victory and to secure the future of our people and the future of her own grandchildren.

7. Now, government regulations alone, particularly in this ticklish area, serve no purpose whatever. Here only a very serious conviction borne along by the Movement can lead to the required attitude. The question is too serious for wisecracks and cheap jokes; here what is truly at stake is the safeguarding of the future of our people.

8. After this war we cannot command women and girls to have babies. What is called for is the most intelligent enlightenment possible—and here the much overused superlative is used advisedly.

9. This [enlightenment] must in my opinion not be carried out by men who might too easily be considered personally interested parties, [sexual] profiteers. In my opinion only older men should be allowed to speak on this theme, and above all, our women's organizations must perform the necessary job of enlightenment.

10. These needful actions involve not only convincing the women who have lost husbands or will never get one, but what is needed first of all is the enlightenment of the old folks, the mothers and fathers, who grew up among quite different attitudes in the past.

11. Still more necessary is the enlightenment of the wives, who in many cases turn into fanatical [advocates] of respectability only after their marriage.

12. When we reflect on what is necessary to bring this so vitally important problem for our people to a successful solution, then we must make the situation clear for the individual case. At first many women—want of logic is something women are born with—will affirm the appropriateness [of the new order of things], but in the individual case, applied to their personal lives, they will fanatically reject it.

13. The public, i.e., general, enlightenment [campaign] can, for obvious reasons, only get under way after the war. To mention only one reason: we cannot yet appeal today to the women whose husbands might become casualties in the future, and also out of consideration for our soldiers we cannot begin our enlightenment campaign; that would assume that we would have to get this line of thinking across to our men now serving as soldiers, but not every soldier will readily accept the prospect of his wife or bride bearing children by another man after his own death.

14. Meanwhile *we* must be fully cognizant of the steps that can be taken while the war is still on, and of those to be introduced immediately after war's end.

15. We must begin immediately to remove all impediments to the attainment of our objective; in particular, the point is to orientate contemporary poets and writers. New novels, short stories and stage plays based on marriage and divorce are no longer to be permitted, and by the same token [we will allow] no poems, writings, motion pictures that treat the child born out of wedlock [*unehelich*] as of diminished worth, as a bastard.

(The word "unehelich" must, as I pointed out long ago, be expunged [right out of the language]. The prefix "un" generally denotes something to be rejected.

Examples:

ehelich [in wedlock, legitimate], *unehelich* [illegitimate]
Frieden [peace], *Unfrieden* [strife]
Ehre [honor], *Unehre* [dishonor]
frei [free], *unfrei* [in bondage]
sympathisch [likable], *unsympathisch* [unpleasant]
appetitlich [appetizing], *unappetitlich* [unappetizing]
hold [lovely], *unhold* [unfriendly]
Heil [salvation], *Unheil* [ruin]
Glück [luck, happiness], *Unglück* [disaster]
Glaube [faith], Unglaube [infidelity].)

In other words—we must begin right away to reject anything that presents this problem in a way that partly or fully harms the future of our people! Neither on the stage nor in the world of literature can we allow conflicts between a "lawful wife" and her "unlawful rival" to be introduced anymore.

On the contrary, we must cleverly and unobtrusively point out that, for instance—as has come to light in tracing ancestry—many family trees of famous scholars, artists, statesmen, industrialists and soldiers show evidence of children born out of wedlock. To put it another way: how many famous men who performed the greatest services for our people would not have been born if their mother or female forebear had not brought her child into the world.

16. Now, the antipathy toward illegitimate children undoubtedly has a reason behind it, which we—more precisely *we of all people*—must recognize.

No more than anyone else, we don't want our sisters or daughters to have children casually by just any man, or first by one and then by another. What we should strive for is to get the women in our country who are unable after the war to get married in the way that has prevailed up to the present to commit themselves to a man who really suits them and have children by him.

When I observe that in animal husbandry only animals that can tolerate each other are bred to each other, then I must hold to the rules that govern all mammals in the case of humans too: if I want children with a pleasant disposition who are never disturbed, then I must let it be known that only people who really suit each other should beget children.

In other words, we must not wish that a woman—even by means of so-called remote conception—should get children from just any man; it is much more desirable that only people who are really attached to one another should conceive children.

17. Conclusion: It is desirable that wherever possible, women who do not have or find a husband after the war enter into a marriagelike relationship which will produce as many children as possible.

It is of course possible that not all such relationships will last through a lifetime; rather, it is natural, as many marriages also are terminated in divorce after long or short duration. Moreover, I am convinced that two people who are bound together in friendship but do not see each other all that often can stay together for a lifetime more easily than others; this is particularly true when the bond is strengthened by children of love and friendship.

18. As I mentioned above, any defamation directed at relationships that are desirable from the viewpoint of the people must be stopped. Whoever insults a woman who has children without a husband (in the current sense) must be severely punished. Whoever—this will hit many pastors—speaks out against propaganda that is for needs of the people is likewise to be punished severely.

19. In many cases, the resistance on the part of married women will be due to material

considerations: for the sake of her own children, the wife would not want to share her income or her husband's inheritance with another woman and her children.

This is understandable! But since the people and the state want to secure their future, they must use every means, hence also material means, to ensure the greatest possible increase in numbers of births; hence the state must provide adequate subsidies.

20. Should the state fail to do so, the most important capital would be irretrievably lost: the productivity of many age groups consisting of millions of women.

21. Many women and young girls would be glad to have children—many children, in fact—if they only knew that they would be taken care of for the rest of their lives. They do not want to have children and then find that one day, because the father of these children dies, becomes impoverished or leaves her [sic], she and her children are left unprovided for, having to depend on the mercy and compassion of charitable institutions.

22. It is quite obvious that women who work at a job and have children should be paid proportionately, and further, that such women should be allocated housing commensurate with the number of family members in the household.

23. After the war I would like to have this kind of housing built in Sonnenwinkel for female employees of the Party Chancellery who have children born to them.

24. The number of state-run boarding schools (public schools—boarding schools, upper classes of elementary schools with boarding, and preparatory schools, upper schools with boarding and preparatory schools) must be increased considerably so that all women with any reason for not being able to bring up their children part or all of the time can let them be brought up without difficulty in the state-run boarding schools. This should be the case for [both] boys and girls.

These state boarding schools are also needed because the best and most capable men are usually real wild ones in their youth and cannot be controlled by their mothers alone.

25. Meanwhile, these women should not have to wait until their children are of mandatory school age before they can send them to state boarding schools; rather, according to Führer decree the NSV [National Socialist People's Welfare, *Nationalsozialistische Volkswohlfahrt*], as pointed out earlier, should build the best maternity homes and also the best children's homes, where children can be raised from infancy to school age. The upbringing in these children's homes must be far better than it can be in the general run of family households. *This* is the great task for the future for the future for the NSV!

26. We must—for the sake of the future of our people—get a singular motherhood-cult going, and in it there must be no difference between women who have children by a man to whom they are bound in friendship! All these mothers are to be honored alike.

(Obviously this would not be the case, for instance, for those asocial elements who don't even know who the fathers of their children are.)

27. When two young people go to the registrar's office to make their intended union for life known to and legitimized by the state, this [act] has chiefly the following purposes:

(a) The marriage partnership, together with the progeny, is placed under the protection of the state and its powers and its codes of civil and criminal law.

(b) Both partners are thereby aware that one is obligated to the other, and that one is not free to leave the other for no good reason.

(c) Moral security: Extramarital relations are taboo according to hypocritical bourgeois attitudes. Marital sexual relations are, however, considered respectable beyond any question!

(d) Material security: A man who gets a divorce must take care of his wife as long as she is not at fault.

28. These statements illustrate what inhibitions we must eliminate and what preconditions we must create in order to attain the increase in births needed for survival:

(1) For mothers who have not been married in the hitherto acceptable way we must also

create a quite similar encompassing moral as well as material security. That includes among other things that the children must in every case get their father's name without any difficulty.

(2) Additionally: On special petition, men should be able to enter into a binding marital relationship not only with one woman, but also with another, who would then get his name without complications, and the children automatically getting the father's name.

(3) The idea of a man letting himself be sued for nonpayment of alimony ought to be an exception; any man who behaves that way without a compelling reason deserves to be disgraced for it, because in general, his conduct is outrageous.

(4) As mentioned before, it is necessary that we abolish the terms for relationships currently in use, having a more or less disreputable overtone, and forbid them. Instead, we must coin good, positive-sounding terms. We must also think about what to call the relationship between a woman and a man whom she cannot marry in the usual sense; we must think about what the children of such a friendship union are to be called, etc.

The more felicitous the designations we come up with, the easier it will be for us to get rid of the existing inhibitions. But these inhibitions must be eliminated, for otherwise all the sacrifices of the previous war and of this war will be in vain because our people *must* [inevitably] fall victim to the coming onslaught. In twenty or thirty or forty or fifty years we will be lacking the divisions that we absolutely need if our people is not to perish.

(5) After the war, childless couples and single men must be taxed much more severely than hitherto. The taxes on bachelors imposed up to now will seem like child's play compared to the tax burdens to be laid on them in the future.

The revenue from these bachelor taxes will serve to support the mothers who have children, i.e., for the material support of our efforts on behalf of the coming generation.

I ask you to give close attention to the entire problem and then let me have your opinion.

[signed] M. Bormann

PART ELEVEN

. . .

RESISTANCE

30
Communists, Socialists, Youth, and the Conservative Resistance

MANY GERMAN MEN AND WOMEN resisted Nazism for a variety of reasons, some of them noble and heroic, others less so. Before 1933, the Communists and the Social Democrats were Nazism's most visible opponents. During 1932, street battles between Nazi brownshirts and members of the Communist and socialist militias were a daily occurrence, though in November, the Communists cooperated with the Nazis during the Berlin transportation strike. Otto Wels (1873–1939), chairman of the Social Democratic Party of Germany since 1919, was the only member of the Reichstag to speak against Hitler's Enabling Act (Law to Remedy the Distress of People and Reich) during the last constitutional session of the Reichstag, on 23 March 1933. The Communists were outlawed immediately thereafter, and the party leaders fled to Paris and Prague. The Social Democrats were permitted to remain a legal party until the summer of 1933. Once the party was declared illegal, rank-and-file SPD members were beaten, arrested, and sent to concentration camps. Subsequently, many sought to adapt to the regime or withdraw into private life, while others formed clandestine underground anti-Nazi groups. Prominent Social Democrats, notably Rudolf Breitscheid, went into exile and participated in the anti-Hitler emigration. Though Communists claimed to be the only authentic "anti-Fascists," the Communist International did not cease to concentrate its propaganda on the Social Democrats (whom it derisively called "social fascists") until July 1935, when it officially adopted the policy of the Popular Front. Anti-Fascism was an ambiguous ideology, especially during the Hitler-Stalin Pact, when Communists suddenly were no longer permitted to be anti-Fascists (or to criticize Nazism), provoking a number of dedicated anti-Fascist intellectuals to become anti-Communists.

The *Brown Book of the Reichstag Fire and Hitler Terror,* published in Paris in August 1933 by a group of Communist exiles, convinced much of the world that the ruthless and diabolical Nazis had conspired to burn the Reichstag as a pretext for establishing a dictatorship on the eve of the March 1933 elections. Proclaiming an imminent Communist uprising against the regime and charging that the arson plot was a homosexual conspiracy, the book and the campaign that accompanied it were the creations of Willi Münzenberg, the renowned international Communist impresario and Reichstag deputy. In the Weimar Republic, he had earned the nickname of the Red Hugenberg for his organizational empire that included the International Red Aid and a host of dailies, periodicals, and the highly successful illustrated weekly the *Arbeiter-Illustrierte-Zeitung.* As an example of what Münzenberg called "counterpropaganda," the *Brown Book* became a best seller, was translated into some twenty-four languages, and was published in more than fifty-five editions, including miniaturized camouflaged books smuggled into Germany.

Even after the National Socialists had been in power for more than a year and after the purge of the SA on 30 June 1934, the German Communist Party press continued to call the regime a dictatorship of monopoly capital and to regard its base of support as the German "petit bourgeoisie." Its exile press interpreted the purge as foreshadowing a collapse of the Nazi regime. Nonetheless, the parties of the Left had conflicting visions of what had happened in Germany and, more importantly, what alternatives remained to remove the regime from power. Among the anti-Nazi émigrés who gathered in Paris, Prague, and elsewhere in non-occupied Europe were intellectuals like Heinrich Mann who were dedicated to upholding humanism and the values of civilization and culture. After 1933, some small groups of dedicated anti-Fascists were disillusioned with the failure of both the Communists and the Social Democrats to prevent Nazism from taking power or to mount any effective resistance. One of these was Neu Beginnen (New Beginning), a group of former members of the SPD who took their name from a pamphlet of that name written by Walter Löwenheim and published in August 1933 under the pseudonym of Miles. New Beginning provided a realistic assessment of the failure of the organized parties and their illusions, remaining underground until it was penetrated and broken up by the Gestapo in 1935.

A few nonconformist intellectuals tried to go beyond the clichés of the organized Left to provide a more incisive analysis of the appeal of the Nazis. Wilhelm Reich's *The Mass Psychology of Fascism* (1933) was one the first attempts by a left-wing psychoanalyst to explain the psychodynamics of Nazism, which, he argued, could be explained by sexual repression that produced false satisfactions as substitutes for suppressed desires. Reich's work prefigured a wide-ranging set of studies of the psychopathology of Nazism and anti-Semitism by exile writers like the novelist Hermann Broch and the Nobel Prize–winning writer Elias Canetti, as well as by philosophers like Theodor W. Adorno, all of whom saw Nazi ideology as a pathology of mass psychology. Outside of the left-wing organizations were some forms of disgruntlement that did not fit neatly into any political rubric. One might include the ordinary Germans who stayed away from the newsreels after the defeat at Stalingrad, as was noted by the Reich Security Service, or those who passed around poems ridiculing Hitler, or simply those who made anti-Hitler remarks, sometimes within earshot of the Gestapo. Others belonged to the youth underground—some of whom were jazz enthusiasts, called "swing kids," and others who called themselves the Edelweiss Pirates—who refused to perform "their obligations within the *Volksgemeinschaft* or the Hitler Youth," as Heinrich Himmler noted in his 1944 memorandum warning of these youth gangs. A quite different youth resistance movement was the White Rose, a group of Munich students that included Sophie Scholl (1921–43), Hans Scholl (1918–43), Willi Graf (1918–43), Christoph Probst (1919–43), and philosophy professor Kurt Huber (1893–1943). In 1942–43, the White Rose distributed leaflets calling for passive resistance—withholding public signs of support—against the Nazis. Though somewhat equivocal about anti-Semitism, the White Rose called what was happening to the Jews "a crime that is unparalleled in the whole of history." Arrested in February 1943, the members of the White Rose were murdered for their courage. By then, those found guilty of making disparaging remarks were subject to special people's courts and capital punishment.

The most serious threat to Hitler's power was the conservative nationalist opposition drawn from the upper-middle and upper classes. This resistance movement consisted of small, interlocking circles, including the intellectuals of the Kreisau Circle around Helmuth James von Moltke (1907–45) and Peter Graf Yorck von Wartenberg (1903–44), civilian leaders such as Carl Goerdeler (1884–1945), former civil servants like Ulrich von Hassell (1881–1945) and Johannes Popitz (1884–1945), former trade union leaders, and younger senior military officers, like Ludwig Beck (1880–1944) and Claus Schenk von Stauffenberg (1907–44) who carried out the failed assassination attempt on Hitler. Characterized by different shadings of Christian, antiliberal, and German national aspirations, these figures shared an aristocratic contempt for mass society and for the radical, vulgar, and chaotic oligarchy of the Nazi parvenus. As is evident in the notes by the diplomat Ulrich von Hassell, there were also differences in temperament and ideology among the conspirators. For example, Beck, as a senior military officer, was skeptical of the wisdom of Hitler's war plans as early as 1937.

The Kreisau Circle proposed a religious-inspired reconstruction of Germany within the framework of the manageable communities of "family, parish, and *Land*." At the same time, these elites were motivated by a profound sense of the moral, military, and political disaster that awaited Germany, especially once defeat appeared inevitable after 1943. Von Hassell's diaries record their consensus that "it is most earnestly to be desired that we get, as head of the government, a man whose name will be considered both as a deliverance and a program." The man chosen, Carl Goerdeler, mayor of Leipzig, was a national conservative who had supported the Nazis in the early years of the Reich until his proposals for an economic rapprochement with the West fell on deaf ears. An implacable foe of the regime, Goerdeler prepared a speech to the nation, which remained undelivered, in anticipation of a successful coup, in which he decried the "injustice, despotism, every manner of crime, self-interest, and lies" perpetrated by the Nazi leaders. The chief obstacle facing all groups large and small in mounting resistance was the loyalty of the German population to the Führer and the consensual nature of the Nazi regime, which became even more evident with the rise in Hitler's popularity after the unsuccessful assassination attempt on 20 July 1944.

398

THE BROWN BOOK

The Road to Power

"Der Weg zur Macht." First published in *Braunbuch über Reichstagsbrand und Hitlerterror* (Basel: Universum Bücherei, 1933), 9–10, 27–28, 33–34.

The "German Workers' Party" was founded in Munich in January 1919. In July of that year Adolf Hitler, at that time "education officer" in the Reichswehr, joined this party. He was the seventh member of what later developed into the National Socialist German Workers' Party.

Who were the founders and first members of this party? From what sections of the population did they come, and what interests did they represent? In the first place, they consisted of soldiers and officers who had come back from the war completely disillusioned. For four years they had honestly believed in the chauvinist slogans with which they had been fed. They had staked their lives in the struggle for a Greater Germany. They believed in the legend that pacifist and Social Democratic traitors had stabbed the German army in the back and brought about its defeat. These men who came back were deeply embittered by what they thought was the weakness of the ruling class, the treachery and flight of the Kaiser and of the deposed princes, and the failure of the generals of the Great War to strike down the "November criminals."

These deeply disillusioned soldiers and officers could no longer find a place for themselves in civil life. To a great extent the professions that they had once practiced now no longer existed. This was true particularly of the professional soldiers, military cadets, and a number of categories of officials. They were joined by members of the uprooted nobility, by students who had been torn from their studies by the war, and by declassed and radicalized members of the middle classes who now began to feel the ground giving way under their feet. All of these elements, who at that time also flocked into the many other military bodies which arose at that time—the *Einwohnerwehr,* the Stahlhelm, and the Ehrhardt Brigade—formed the first basis of the young National Socialist German Workers' Association [Nationalsozialistischen Deutschen Arbeitervereins], as the party first officially called itself.

For two years after its formation, the National Socialists were quite an insignificant group. The November Revolution of 1918 had been beaten down, and the capitalist system had got a new lease on life. The Social Democrat Friedrich Ebert became the first president of the Weimar Republic. The old forces of finance capitalism consolidated their rule again. The trade union leaders had concluded an agreement with the employers, based on negotiations in November 1918 between Hugo Stinnes and the president of the General Committee of the trade unions, the Social Democrat Carl Legien. What, at that time, could Hitler do for the leading groups of German capitalists? At that period, they were not yet in need of the National Socialists. Hitler's association therefore remained without any significance. He himself continued in the service of the Reichswehr until 20 April, giving political lectures to the soldiers. On instructions from the Reichswehr, he also "observed" political organizations and meetings, bringing in reports and information. This was how Hitler first came into contact with the "German Workers' Party."

Not long afterward, the political importance of the party began to grow. The political situation in Germany began to change rapidly under the effect of the dictated Peace of Versailles and the losses of the war. Billions of marks were demanded in reparations and had to be paid. Important industrial areas were lopped off: Alsace-Lorraine, Upper Silesia, the Saar territory, Posen, and West Prussia—the so-called Polish Corridor—Danzig, and Eupen-Malmedy. The German market was still further restricted by the loss of a considerable portion of its European and overseas connections in addition to the German colonies. The cost of demobilization and of moving the war industries to a peacetime basis was a terrific burden on the smaller taxpayers, as the dominant circles of German monopoly capital were continuously devising new methods of transferring the reparations payments and all other losses onto the shoulders of the workers and the middle class.

This development reached its highest point in the inflation that had begun during the war but was only widely felt among the population in the course of 1921 and 1922. In the autumn of 1923, it reached the point of catastrophe. It had brought about still further impoverishment of the workers and had transformed a considerable section of the middle classes into proletarians. Millions of the poorer sections of the middle class were literally robbed of everything they had by the inflation. The state paid the banks and heavy industry concerns 600 million gold marks as compensation for the occupation of the Ruhr by the French, and these concerns also made enormous profits.

The economic chaos produced far-reaching political disturbances. [Matthias] Erzberger and [Walther] Rathenau fell victims to the bullets of nationalist murderers. Among the working class, a process of radicalization was taking place. The Spartacus struggles in Berlin in January 1919 were followed by the rising of the workers in the Ruhr during the Kapp Putsch of March 1920 and the workers' revolt in March 1921. The workers began to leave the Social Democratic organizations, making their way first to the Independent Social Democrats, then, after the autumn of 1920, to the Communist Party. Great demonstrations culminated in the Hamburg rising of October 1923. [. . .]

The Papen-Schleicher Era

The Papen-Schleicher government was a further stage on the road to a Hitler dictatorship. Its emergency decrees were models for Hitler to follow: the death penalty for high treason; the death penalty for "political acts of violence"; the establishment of emergency courts that imposed long sentences of imprisonment for minor "offenses." But this government of big capitalists, Junkers, and generals had no mass following. The Stahlhelm and the German National People's Party were entirely inadequate. Papen's much-advertised economic program of September 1932 laid new burdens on the workers and gave new millions to the rich. Powerful anti-Fascist demonstrations under the leadership of the Communist Party, which was carrying on the only serious extra-parliamentary fight against Fascism, were broken up. These reached their highest point in the Berlin traffic strike of November 1932, which demonstrated the helplessness of the government in face of the determination of the workers.

At this period, too, National Socialism was passing through a serious crisis. In the November elections, it lost almost two million votes. The total vote for the Communist Party reached six million.

At the end of November, Papen fell, and Schleicher succeeded him early in December. Behind-the-scenes negotiations were carried on, in one direction with the trade unions and also with a view to the drawing in of Hitler. No government can sit on bayonets. Schleicher hesitated, did nothing, and merely modified some of Papen's emergency degrees. On 22 January, the National Socialists staged a provocative demonstration in front of the Communist Party headquarters, the Karl Liebknecht House. General Schleicher sent the whole police force to protect the Nazis from the workers' counterdemonstrations.

The situation grew more and more acute. General Schleicher was considering the immediate proclamation of a military dictatorship. Papen worked against Schleicher's plan by negotiating with Hitler and Hugenberg. At last, the ruling groups of Germany, as the *Deutsche Allgemeine Zeitung* put it, tried a leap in the dark. On 30 January 1933, Hindenburg, the candidate for the presidency who had been supported by the Social Democrats, appointed Hitler chancellor of the German Reich. [. . .]

The chancellorship fell into Hitler's lap, but not as the fruit of some heroic struggle. January 30 was not the culmination of a "national revolution" that had conquered power by a bold attack. Adolf Hitler was given the post of chancellor when the leading sections of the ruling class wanted not only to strengthen their power against the working class but also to smother the smell of the *Osthilfe* scandal.

On the evening of 30 January, the Storm Troopers and the Stahlhelm marched with flaming torches along the Wilhelmstrasse, cheering Hindenburg and Hitler. The Storm Troopers and the Stahlhelmers knew nothing of what had been going on behind the scenes, and when they acclaimed "the day of national awakening," they did not know the corruption and the lust for profit that were its godparents.

The Wave of Resistance Rises

On 30 January 1933, the Communist Party made an official proposal to the executive of the Social Democratic Party and to the General Council of the Trade Unions under Social Democratic leadership and also the Christian trade unions, that they should jointly organize a general strike for the overthrow of the Hitler government. Social Democracy and [the] trade unions answered, "Hitler has come to power legally." It was necessary to wait, they said, until he violated legality. No fight should be put up now. The general attitude of the Social Democratic press was that Hitler would soon be finished with.

Considerable sections of the German workers accepted these statements. The Communist Party was unable as yet to bring the majority of the working class into action. The hastily formed Hitler government would have been unable to cope with the united assault of the working class in those first days of February. The Nazi Storm Troopers had just been passing through a severe crisis and in some places lost half their membership. The police apparatus could not yet be relied upon by the new government. It would also have had difficulties with Schleicher's Reichswehr. But the refusal of the general strike gave the Hitler government the time it needed.

Nevertheless, the resistance of the workers was growing in Berlin, in Hamburg, in the Ruhr, in the Lower Rhine area, in Central Germany, and in all parts of the Reich. The Hitler dictatorship was opposed by a working class whose fighting strength was as yet unbroken. On 22 January, they had refused to allow themselves to be provoked; now a wide movement was developing for united action against the raging Fascist terror. Social Democratic, Christian, and Communist workers united to defend newspaper and trade union buildings. Hitler could prohibit papers, refuse to allow demonstrations, and send his Storm Troopers into the working-class quarters—but the working-class answer was the rise of a broad anti-Fascist movement in which all sections were united.

The Need for a Provocative Act

Hitler had held power for some weeks, but the situation was far from favorable. The new cabinet had dissolved the Reichstag and ordered new elections. Papen's terrorist decrees were again brought into force in sharpened form, and the *Osthilfe* scandal was buried in a secret commission. Hitler proclaimed on the wireless his nonexistent "Four-Year Plan." But the millions of his voters who were looking forward to "German socialism" could not be put off merely with a couple of emergency decrees and vague promises.

At the end of January, Hitler had been compelled to enter the government on the restricting conditions imposed by Hindenburg. There were many reasons why he was ready to compromise: the discontent among his members and supporters, crisis, and numerous resignations from the National Socialist Party, besides the enormous debts of the party. In bourgeois circles, a number of former Nazi voters had already begun to show a tendency toward the German Nationalists. On 6 November 1932, the Communists had won eleven seats in the Reichstag, while Hitler lost thirty-five. In the new government, there were three National Socialist ministers opposed by eight representatives of the German Nationalists and of the Stahlhelm. There could be no change in the cabinet without Hindenburg's consent.

In view of the growing anti-Fascist sentiment among the workers, Hitler's election prospects were not good. Hugenberg and the German Nationalists held all the economic posts of vantage in the cabinet, and masses of the people were beginning to realize that Hitler was carrying out the policy of the worst firebrands among the capitalists. The disillusionment of the masses would show itself in an increased Communist vote on 5 March. It had become an imperative necessity for the National Socialist leaders to change the situation by an act of provocation planned on a grandiose scale. Then the elections could be carried out while the pogrom feeling against the Communists and Social Democrats was at its height. At the same time, the position of the National Socialists within the cabinet could be strengthened.

Goebbels provided the plans for the most outrageous of all the acts of provocation that a ruling class has ever used against the insurgent working class. Göring, president of the Reichstag and commander of the Prussian police, was responsible for the exact carrying out of the plan. The original plans of the National Socialist leaders, to bring all the Storm Troopers to Berlin for the night of 5–6 March, had been shattered by the threat of their allies to bring out the Reichswehr against them; but the new plan of provocation provided the means to satisfy the National Socialist demand for complete governmental power and also to prepare the way for an unrestrained Nazi terror.

The National Socialist leaders moved into action. The German Nationalist police president of Berlin, Dr. [Kurt] Melcher, was transferred to Magdeburg, and his place in Berlin was filled by the National Socialist retired admiral [Magnus] von Levetzow. On 24 February, the Karl Liebknecht House, the headquarters of the German Communist Party, was once again searched by the police. Although the Karl Liebknecht House had already been in the possession of the police for some weeks and was only left by the police after a thorough search that produced no results, now, suddenly, "seriously incriminating" material was found.

The day before the Reichstag fire, gigantic headlines in the whole bourgeois press told readers of the "secrets" of the Karl Liebknecht House, of "subterranean passages," "treasonable material," and "plans for a Bolshevistic revolution." The press also reported an alleged Communist bomb outrage on the railway in East Prussia (this outrage was never mentioned again!) On 25 January, there was a small fire in the Berliner Schloss, which was announced sensationally as a "Communist act." In this way, public opinion was carefully prepared, from paper to paper, from day to day, for the "great *coup*."

The Communist Party received reliable reports that the government had planned an act of provocation. The deputy, Wilhelm Pieck, spoke of it in the Sportpalast in Berlin. He mentioned a Nazi plan for a faked attempt to assassinate Hitler on some other act of provocation that was to take place some days before election day and lead to the prohibition of the Communist Party. The Communist f action in the Reichstag made a similar statement at a conference of foreign press representatives.

The Hitler press, following instructions, raised the campaign against the revolutionary workers to boiling point. Everyone who was following the political situation realized that a crisis was imminent. Everyone felt that "there was something in the air." Then, on the night of 27–28 February, all German wireless stations broadcast the message "The Reichstag is in flames!"

[. . .] In the middle of February, Marinus van der Lubbe left Leyden. Before his departure, he had a new suit and new shoes. The *Vossische Zeitung* of 2 March reported that he spent the night at Glindow, near Werder, on 17 February; and that he went on to Berlin on 18 February. In Berlin, he met the National Socialist friends whose acquaintance he had made through Dr. Bell. [. . .]

Van der Lubbe, the Tool

On 27 February, Van der Lubbe was arrested in the burning Reichstag. The flames were the background of the hoax in which Van der Lubbe for a few hours played the leading role. Then he passed from the stage. The searchlights of truth have pierced the fog of deception and mercilessly shown up Göring and Goebbels, who made use of Van der Lubbe as their tool. Why did the murderer Heines and his associates, who had been entrusted by Göring and Goebbels with the technical carrying out of the incendiary act, choose Van der Lubbe as the tool?

Van der Lubbe's homosexual connections with National Socialist leaders and his material dependence on them made him obedient and willing to carry out the part of the arsonist.

Van der Lubbe's Dutch nationality was a further advantage. It enabled Göring and Goebbels to represent the burning of the Reichstag as an international plot.

The leading figures in the plot were:

Dr. Goebbels: concocted the plot for setting fire to the Reichstag, also the fanatical lies and provocation.

Captain Göring: a drug fiend, directed operations.

Edmund Heines: a murderer; was entrusted with the leadership of the incendiary group.

Marinus von der Lubbe: the tool.

When the Chicago police in 1886 staged a bomb explosion carried out by paid provocateurs—an explosion that killed a large number of the police—it was seven years before the act of provocation was established. The tools had been well chosen. After the burning of the Reichstag, it took only three days to make the whole world certain that the National Socialists had set fire to the Reichstag. The tool Van der Lubbe was too ill chosen.

399

The Bloody Thirtieth of June in Germany

First published as "Das blütige 30 Juni in Deutschland," in *Rundschau über Politik, Wirtschaft und Arbeiterbewegung,* no. 39, May–July 1934, 1541–42.

The thirtieth of June revealed the extreme depths of crisis facing the fascist dictatorship, and the thirtieth of June marks the beginning of the end of fascist dictatorship in its National Socialist manifestation.[1] The forces of economic, social, domestic, and international crisis came to blows on the thirtieth of June, but this thirtieth of June also represents a desperate, last-ditch effort on the part of German monopoly capital to rescue its fascist dictatorship and reconstruct an overtly terrorist dictatorship. [. . .]

Once it had assumed power, the Hitler regime put the dictatorship of monopoly capital in effect, and this is precisely why it inevitably clashed with its own popular base. All the more so because the fascist dictatorship never succeeded and never could succeed in infiltrating the working-class masses. Our proud, heroic German working class—crowned by its Communist Party—stood firm as granite against the stormy maelstrom of fascist dictatorship swirling around it. All the waves of fascism came crashing in on this granite rock. And since the fascist dictatorship had worsened conditions not only for the proletariat but also for employees of every stripe by plunging the country into economic, social, domestic, and international catastrophe, it necessarily also lost the support of its middle class and rural base. The enthusiasm displayed by these groups early on soon turned to a critical wait-and-see attitude, then to disappointment, and ultimately into outrage.

The crisis that came to a head on the thirtieth of June is just the reverse side of the momentum building in the working class, which is very much on the verge of winning the outraged urban middle classes and the rural peasant masses over to their side.

The SA was a kind of Praetorian Guard, a politically partisan army in the service of finance capital. After Hitler's seizure of power, hundreds upon thousands flocked to join the ranks of the SA, which soon numbered between 2.5 and 3 million. The monopolizing upper echelon of the bourgeoisie was forced, in preparation for its civil war against the proletariat and for its imperialistic war, to appeal to the broad masses. But the flocks of millions brought with them to the ranks of the SA all their disillusionment, their dissatisfaction, their outrage, the rebelliousness of the lower middle classes, the plebian classes, and even certain recalcitrant sections of the proletariat. Röhm, Ernst, Heines, and the remaining Condottieri of fascism dreamt of Hitler's demise, of the establishment of an SA state. They sought to take advantage of these dissatisfied voices in the outraged masses—even if they had to distort them to do so. Of course, they could not comprehend that there was no clearly self-evident role for them to play between the two millstones of modern society, between bourgeoisie and proletariat during the period of monopoly capitalism in which they stood under pressure from the petit bourgeoisie, the plebeians, the lumpenproletariat, the underclasses—this even despite their mercenary character.

The monopolistic upper bourgeoisie managed to put a bloody end to the rebellion of the petit bourgeoisie—at least in the manifestations found in the upper ranks of the SA—availing themselves of the Reich army, the police, and the SS. And the reason they were able to defeat the rebellion was that the mass mobilization efforts of the proletariat did not succeed in establishing leadership in these strata of society. Hitler, Göring, and Goebbels were just the lackeys of reactionary finance capital in this operation. They were the decoy figureheads designed to obscure from view the bloody, repugnant mug of big capital and the Junkers.

Hitler was in Neudeck and humbly accepted the orders of Oldenburg-Januschau, and the East-Elbian Junkers as delivered to him by Hindenburg. From Neudeck, he went to Krupp, where he humbly received the joint orders of heavy industry and the corporate elite of German industry. After Neudeck and Essen, he went to Munich. In Munich and Berlin, he promptly executed the orders he'd received from Neudeck and Essen.

The thirtieth of June is index of the fact that the fascist dictatorship has once and for all lost the support of the petit bourgeoisie base—more aptly put, of the remnants that remained—because it simply could no longer contain these masses. The industrial elite, the Junkers, the generals, and the upper echelons of bureaucracy left the dirty work to Hitler, Göring, Goebbels, and Himmler. Monopoly capital and the Junkers are cynical enough to let their lackeys play the dirty role of henchmen and to do so in such a way as to at once effectively thwart a "second revolution" and any "backlash." They allowed Goebbels and Göring to once again stage a Reichstag-fire-like provocation, to construct a harebrained conspiracy between Röhm and Schleicher and to spin mysterious fabrications about some "foreign power." Like knights in shining armor, they allowed General Schleicher and his wife to be shot dead and allowed Papen to be put into police custody. All of this can be attributed to the machinations of the Hitler-Goebbels machine, just as can the exposure of the way the upper ranks of the fascist elite were utterly corrupted by Hitler himself.

Note

1. The thirtieth of June marked the purge of the SA, conducted between 30 June and 2 July 1934.—Eds.

400

MILES [WALTER LÖWENHEIM]

Socialism's New Beginning

First published as *Socialism's New Beginning: A Manifesto from Underground Germany* (New York: League for Industrial Democracy, 1934), 17–21.

The National Socialist Party is today not only in sole possession of power, but also the only organized force in the political life of the nation. It is the sole arbiter of the education of children, and it is the sole arbiter of what expressions of opinion shall reach the public. In a period of less than eighteen weeks, a transformation has been effected in the political structure of society and in the form of the state, which, for its rapidity and the radical nature of its results, is without parallel in history.

To the socialist labor parties this lightning development has come as a bolt from the blue. They have fallen pray to the fascist onslaught without any attempt at, nay, with nary a thought of, serious resistance, and the remaining few, reduced to a state of hopeless confusion and complete bewilderment, are increasingly falling prey to the terrorist power of the state, which is being consolidated steadily. The great working-class organizations, which once appeared to be so powerful, and which were organized only for open mass agitation under conditions of legal democracy, are proving completely incapable of adapting themselves to the new conditions of illegal struggle under fascism. This might have led merely to a serious but temporary suspension of the struggle for socialism. What was of far greater import, however, was the fact that they were completely incapable of comprehending the social events leading up to the fascist revolution that had taken place in their midst, and the fact that, uncomprehending and bewildered as they were, they regarded the victory of German fascism only as a short episode in a society which could, fundamentally, only be democratic and which was bound, therefore, after a shorter or longer period of fascist dictatorship, to return to democratic conditions on its own.[. . .]

What position, then, have the socialist parties in Germany taken up since the victory of fascism? Up until now the communists have not even deigned to take cognizance of the historical changes. Germany is, for them, still in the stage of "revolutionary uprising." Their party, it is true, has been destroyed, and developments have been quite contrary to their political expectations and predictions. So much the worse for history! Incapable of reasoning otherwise than according to their dogmas and theses, they believe with positively religious fervor in spontaneous revolutionary forces that, they maintain, lie dormant in the proletariat and owe their origin to its class position. They are firmly convinced that fascism is bound by the pressure it exerts to liberate these forces, and that the German working class is only waiting to be led on by the communists to the "final struggle for freedom." If, however, the proletarian masses have not yet drawn the logical conclusions from these convictions, it can only be the fault of the Social Democrats and other groups, who, in demagogic fashion, restrain the masses from proclaiming the Communist Soviet Republic. The communists, therefore, need only proclaim "the truth" in hand-bills and newspapers in order to hold back the masses from the wrong path; they need only tell the proletariat, which, of course, desires the communist revolution, that the "general staff" for this uprising is already in existence in order to incite the masses of the people to overthrow the brutal fascist rule. The Communist Party of Germany is today nothing but a decimated machine for the distribution of illegal hand-bills; and, owing to the methods of its work and its attitude to the tasks in hand, it is becoming useless for any genuinely effective anti-fascist struggle and is destroying life from day to day. The communists are fundamentally creatures of bourgeois democracy. With amazing fortitude and extraordinary devotion to their cause, they hurl themselves with bared breasts against a vastly superior enemy, shouting, "kill me, but I still believe in my cause!" This is the kind of courage that leads to the destruction of one's own forces.

German Social Democracy has taken up no united position. A distinction must be made between the utterances of leaders and refugees of the old party, which has been able to create, while in exile, a wide forum for the promulgation of its views, and the standpoint of the socialists, who are carrying on the struggle in Germany itself. The latter have been able to win through to greater clarity owing to the conditions of their struggle, but because of their participation in the struggle, they have been more or less prevented from advocating their views before the democratic public abroad and in getting them accepted. The following pages should constitute at least the first step in this direction.

What, then, is the position of the social democratic refugees? They too expect that a spontaneous uprising of the masses will put an end to fascism. They too believe that they can accelerate the natural end of this "unnatural" barbarian rule by means of democratic propaganda. The only difference between them and the communists is that they carry on this propaganda almost exclusively outside Germany's borders.

On a closer examination, therefore, it is clear that the theoretical position of the two parties is by no means so far apart as first appears. The belief in a revolutionary spontaneity inherent in the proletariat forms the basis of all their judgments and actions. The social democratic refugees, however, look forward to a new Weimar Republic as the objective of this spontaneity, whereas the communists believe that it is bound to result in a Soviet Republic.

But what if this revolutionary spontaneity were to exist only in the imagination of the socialist parties and not in reality? What if the proletariat were not to be impelled of itself, that is, by natural social forces, towards the "final struggle for socialism"? Why was it that in the post-war period, precisely in that period in which the bankruptcy of world capitalism, predicted decades before by the socialists, was revealed in such a terrible way, that the process of decline in the international socialist movement set in? Why, in spite of this, did the masses follow the bourgeois leaders and not the socialists? Why was it possible for fascist parties to come into existence in large countries with enormous proletarian classes and to win and hold the masses and the power without any effort? Why did the crisis lead in Italy and Germany to fascism and not to socialism?

401

WILHELM REICH

The Mass Psychology of Fascism

First published in *Massenpsychologie des Faschismus: Zur Sexualökonomie der politischen Reaktion und zur proletarischen Sexualpolitik* (Copenhagen: Verlag für Sexualpolitik, 1933), 52–54.

Sexual repression heightens the strength of political reaction, not only through the process described here whereby masses of individuals are rendered passive and apolitical; it also generates in the structure of individual citizens a secondary force, an artificial interest that actively supports the prevailing order. Because whenever sexual repression serves to prevent sexuality from following the natural trajectories of satisfaction, [sexual urges] will always find various forms of ersatz satisfaction. So, for example, natural aggression escalates into the brutal sadism that forms a substantial component of the mass psychological foundation for any war that is orchestrated by the few in the interest of imperialistic aims. To cite another example, the efficacy of militarism has its mass psychological basis primarily in a libidinous mechanism; the sexual attraction of the uniform, the erotic stimulation emitted by the perfect rhythm of parade marches, the exhibitionist character of military presence have thus far been more apparent in their effect to a simple domestic servant or your average office worker than to our most highly educated politicians. On the other hand, political reaction consciously taps into these sexual interests. Not only does it create uniforms expressly designed to allow men to strut around like peacocks; it also follows the American model by using seductive women for recruitment purposes.

Finally, let us call to mind the recruitment posters of the warmongering powers, whose content is more or less something like this: "Would you like to travel to foreign countries? Then join the Royal Navy!"—and these foreign countries are represented by [images of] exotic women. Why are these posters so effective? Because our youth have grown hungry for sexual gratification as a result of restrictions placed on sexual expression.

The sexual mores that suppress class consciousness, as well as those forces that accommodate capitalist interests, draw their energy from repressed sexuality. And this helps us to better understand a central component in the process of ideology's retroactive effect on the economic base: sexual inhibition elicits a structural change in the economically oppressed individual, to the degree that he acts, thinks, and harbors emotions that are against his own material interests. It is tantamount to assimilating the ideology of the bourgeoisie.

Lenin's observation in this regard is thus validated and given meaning from the perspective of mass psychology. The soldiers of 1905 subconsciously saw in [military] officers their childhood fathers, concentrated in a conception of God that would deny sexual expression—men whom one was neither permitted to nor able to kill, even though they shattered all lust for life. The regrets they expressed after the seizure of power and the war stories they told were an expression of the opposite—hatred transformed into pity—which, in this manner, could not ever lead to action.

The practical problem of mass psychology thus involves activating the passive majority in the populace that persistently aids and abets political reaction to victory; and it involves the elimination of those inhibitions that act as constraints on the development of a class consciousness [that should result] from the social-economic situation. The psychological energies of an average mass of people that can follow a *soccer match* with scintillated gusto or take pleasure in a tacky little operetta—were these to be released from their shackles and channeled to serve the rational aims of the workers' movement, this would be a force that could no longer be contained.

402

WILLI MÜNZENBERG

Propaganda as a Weapon

First published in *Propaganda als Waffe* (Paris: Edition Carrefour, 1937), 272–76.

"Even propaganda is no more than a weapon, though a frightful one in the hand of an expert," Hitler conceded in his discussion of propagandistic methods in *Mein Kampf*. Throughout the course of its struggle for supremacy and power, Hitler's propaganda machine has never once failed to wield this weapon, unabashedly and unscrupulously exploiting its limits [to serve its own interests]. Propaganda was used as bait to lure the masses—the underlying assumption being their lack of education, their limited intelligence, and their lack of experience in political struggle. [The Hitler movement] used propaganda to manufacture the illusion of some "savior" and the "myth" of the movement; it seduced the "little man" with propaganda, evoked the impression that the Hitler movement had the nation's best interest in mind, that it would direct the country on the path of socialism and revolution; it fooled its opponents with propaganda, caught them off guard, ambushed them in a drumfire of propaganda; it denounced certain persons as alleged criminals, [it] spread lies; indeed, the whole organization of the state overthrow was built on the use of propaganda, and it is propaganda that glorifies the most horrific form of terror. Organizations with millions of members are being used as instruments in this propagandistic campaign, and everything the Hitler movement has thus far undertaken [is] the product of artful propagandistic strategies taken to the pinnacle of shrewdest demagoguery and bottomless mendacity.

The Hitler movement believes it has conquered Germany and the German *Volk* with the power of propaganda, and it believes propaganda will sustain its power. Hitler considers himself the inventor of "propaganda as a weapon" and thinks he can wield it to win the war he is relentlessly preparing for, the war that will turn all of Europe into National Socialists. Like some potion brewed up by Doctor Eisenbart [a character in a children's song] as an all-purpose remedy against any ailment, the Hitler system expects to wave the wand of his propaganda weapon to solve any and all of the mounting problems arising on the economic front, as well as in domestic and international policy.

The depletion of resources and the chronic hunger crisis are to be concealed from the public through "propaganda." "What we are lacking," so sayeth the Führer, "is not money, raw materials, food, but rather propaganda to make the masses believe we have all these things in abundance. We need propaganda, more and more propaganda." The SA *Gruppenführer* Schöne, at a conference in Metgethen (East Prussia), expressed the firm conviction of all the National Socialist leaders when he exclaimed, "We still haven't learned to see everything from the perspective of propaganda. Therefore, we must step up the propaganda campaigns."

The few public events that are still permitted for National Socialist organizations are all designed to serve a propagandistic purpose, to sing the praises of National Socialist economic policies, "the blessings that these four years of the Hitler regime have brought us" and all the inventions that are of "epoch-shaping" magnitude. There is an incessant stream of new and ever-more-powerful propaganda methods available, especially those tailored to influencing foreign opinion; the cadres of speakers and propagandists are in constant training and ever more awards being given for new tricks of the propagandist's trade. But something has gone awry, something is out of whack, somehow the wheels are falling off the advertising and publicity machine. The propaganda is beginning to lose its ability to rile and mobilize the public.

Because the propaganda is total, the little man is bowled over by it, but it is precisely this totality that in turn compensates for another aspect of propaganda, for the man who is dissatisfied with the slightest imperfection will necessarily be compelled to find fault with the whole system. Once he finds reason to oppose one individual measure taken by the regime, he necessarily discovers that there is something wrong with the whole system. But the time has long since passed in which mere trivialities have any enduring impression on the bamboozled adherents of the regime. The unintended consequence of the totality of propaganda has been that nothing in the life of the individual is spared; everywhere you go, you are confronted with its effect—everything is a brush with the clutches of propaganda. The propaganda is too all encompassing to guarantee that it won't be used against the very people who created it. The Hitler propagandists give too many speeches, write too many articles, make too many promises—and tell too many lies.

Hitler propaganda will necessarily, in the course of a certain time, become a weapon against National Socialism. Lies that are repeated incessantly always turn against those who spread them as soon as a ray of truth comes to light. The unfulfilled promises are working against the regime. But Hitler propaganda neither intends nor is it able to fulfill the myriad and multifaceted promises it has made, for the contradiction between the imperialistic content of the Hitler system and the social as well as nationalist demagoguery of his propaganda is too grandiose and, in the long run, not sustainable even with the most creative propagandistic strategies.

The time has come when propaganda already struggles to barely disguise the system. And this development was also foreseen by [Georgi] Dimitrov in his famous speech from the year 1935 when he explained that the fascist party was in no position to eliminate class divisions and resolve class conflicts and that one of the causes for the instability of the fascist dictatorship was to be found in "the fact that the contrast between the anticapitalist demagoguery of fascism and the policies of predatory exploitation to line the pockets of the bourgeois monopoly makes it easier to expose the inherent class-based nature of fascism and that it necessarily deals a blow to and shrinks its own mass base." And that is how we know that there is something amiss here, that the propagandists' numbers just don't add up. That is already evident in the fact that the phony peace propaganda is no longer having an effect. In order to buy itself some time, the Hitler regime, even as it was engaged in a tremendous rearmament program, carried out a flamboyant peace propaganda campaign designed to drown out the noise of war. In the years 1935 and 1936, the Hitler propaganda machine summoned tremendous resources and sought, with the most flagrant demagoguery, to put the Hitler administration on a pedestal as the great government of peace that was supposedly engaged in "limited" armament programs designed exclusively for the purposes of defense; the Hitler administration wanted nothing but peace and peace alone and was prepared to enter into twenty-five-year peace agreements with individual states. Hitler himself received countless delegations, especially veteran frontline soldiers, and repeated the demagoguery of peace and reassurances of his propaganda director. It took barely a year before the world recognized the lies and deception involved in this peace propaganda. In light of the tremendous scope of military buildup in Hitler's Germany, overtly designed for offensive purposes; in light of the ongoing attempts to solidify a fascist military alliance between Germany, Italy, and Japan; after Germany's refusal to participate seriously in any solution to all international matters within the framework of a collective system for maintaining peace and security; in light of the military support of the Spanish rebels and the barbaric excesses of German pilots in Spain—the lies of the Hitler propaganda about the Hitler regime's "peaceful intentions and the willingness to make peace" have been recognized for what they have always been and remain: camouflage to mask a major perpetrator of war and his preparations for a war of invasion.

And the social demagoguery has also begun losing its charm. The workers have waited too long for the socialist promises to be fulfilled and are beginning to doubt the sincerity of those promises. The ever-worsening economic situation is forcing them to make new demands for wage increases and other benefits, which the Hitler administration cannot deliver as a protector of world industrial power. [. . .]

The broad masses, "the little man" who was one of Hitler's most devoted followers, who looked up to him as his Savior, Messiah, Führer, has begun having doubts. Already in the winter of 1936–37, the Hitler propaganda suffered a serious blow in these sectors of society. In the early years of the regime, the masses still let their concerns for government abuse and corruption in the economy and state be placated with the explanation "The Führer doesn't know, and if he knew, this scandal would be cleared up immediately." This illusion is out the window.

The scandals are far too great and have no end, the unfulfilled promises too many, for them not to have a negative impact on Hitler himself.

The basic attitude of the "little man" has changed; already now he no longer hesitates to express criticism of Hitler, already now he considers Hitler one of the ones at fault, and before long—thanks to the system of dictatorship [Hitler has] built purely to serve his own personal interests—he will begin to see Hitler as the only one at fault. The fact that Hitler propaganda seeks to appeal only to a select circle of propagandists with a pseudoscientific education that stands in stark contrast to the truths and results of the exact sciences and is otherwise restricted to inciting the masses to propagandistic offensives certainly serves to accelerate the process. We are already seeing that happen today in the military.

403

HANS SCHOLL, WILLI GRAF, AND CHRISTOPH PROBST

The White Rose

The Second Leaflet

First circulated in January 1942. First published in *The White Rose: Munich 1942–1943*, edited by Inge Aicher-Scholl, translated by Arthur Schultz (Lebanon, N.H.: University Press of New England, 1983), 77–80.

It is impossible to engage in intellectual discourse with National Socialist Philosophy, for if there were such an entity, one would have to try by means of analysis and discussion either to prove its validity or to combat it. In actuality, however, we face a totally different situation. At its very inception, this movement depended on the deception and betrayal of one's fellow man; even at that time, it was inwardly corrupt and could support itself only by constant lies. After all, Hitler states in an early edition of "his" book (a book written in the worst German I have ever read, in spite of the fact that it has been elevated to the position of the Bible in this nation of poets and thinkers): "It is unbelievable to what extent one must betray a people in order to rule it." If at first this cancerous growth in the nation was not particularly noticeable, it was only because there were still enough forces at work that operated for the good, so that it was kept under control. As it grew larger, however, and finally in an ultimate spurt of growth attained ruling power, the tumor broke open, as it were, and infected the whole body. The greater part of its former opponents went into hiding. The German intellectuals fled to their cellars, there, like plants struggling in the dark, away from light and sun, gradually to choke to death. Now the end is at hand. Now it is our task to find one another again, to spread information from person to person, to keep a steady purpose, and to allow ourselves no rest until the last man is persuaded of the urgent need of his struggle against this system. When thus a wave of unrest goes through the land, when "it is in the air," when many join the cause, then, in a great final effort, this system can be shaken off. After all, an end in terror is preferable to terror without end.

We are not in a position to draw up a final judgment about the meaning of our history. But if this catastrophe can be used to further the public welfare, it will be only by virtue of the fact that we are cleansed by suffering; that we yearn for the light in the midst of deepest night, summon our strength, and finally help in shaking off the yoke which weighs on our world.

We do not want to discuss here the question of the Jews, nor do we want in this leaflet to compose a defense or apology. No, only by way of example do we want to cite the fact that since the conquest of Poland *three hundred thousand* Jews have been murdered in this country in the most bestial way. Here we see the most frightful crime against human dignity, a crime that is unparalleled in the whole of history. For Jews, too, are human beings—no matter what position we take with respect to the Jewish question—and a crime of this dimension has been perpetrated against human beings. Someone may say that the Jews deserve their fate. This assertion would be a monstrous impertinence; but let us assume that someone said this—what position has he then taken toward the fact that the entire Polish aristocratic youth is being annihilated? (May God grant that this program has not yet fully achieved its aim as yet!) All male offspring of the houses of the nobility between the ages of fifteen and twenty were transported to concentration camps in Germany and sentenced to forced labor, and all the girls of this age group were sent to Norway, into the bordellos of the SS! Why tell you these things, since you are fully aware of them—or if not of these, then of other equally grave crimes committed by this frightful sub-humanity? Because here we touch on a problem that involves us deeply and forces us all to take thought. Why do German people behave so apathetically in the face of all these abominable crimes, crimes so unworthy of the human race? Hardly anyone thinks about that. It is accepted as fact and put out of mind. The German people slumber on in their dull, stupid sleep and encourage these fascist criminals; they give them the opportunity to carry on their depredations; and of course they do so. Is this a sign that the Germans are brutalized in their simplest human feelings, that no chord within them cries out at the sight of such deeds, that they have sunk into a fatal lack of conscience from which they will never, never awake? It seems to be so, and will certainly be so, if the German does not at last start up out of his stupor, if he does not protest wherever and whenever he can against this clique of criminals, if he shows no sympathy for these hundreds of thousands of victims. He must evidence not only sympathy; no, much more: a sense of *complicity* in guilt. For through his apathetic behavior he gives these evil men the opportunity to act as they do; he tolerates this "government," which has taken upon itself such an infinitely great burden of guilt; indeed, he himself is to blame for the fact that it came about at all! Each man wants to be exonerated of a guilt of this kind, each one continues on his way with the most placid, the calmest conscience. But he cannot be exonerated; he is *guilty, guilty, guilty!* It is not too late, however, to do away with this most reprehensible of all miscarriages of government, so as to avoid being burdened with even greater guilt. Now, when in recent years our eyes have been opened, when we know exactly who our adversary is, it is high time to root out this brown horde. Up until the outbreak of the war, the larger part of the German people was blinded; the Nazis did not show themselves in their true aspect. But now, now that we have recognized them for what they are, it must be the sole and first duty, the holiest duty of every German to destroy these beasts.

If the people are barely aware that the government exists, they are happy. When the government is felt to be oppressive, they are broken.
Good fortune, alas! builds itself upon misery. Good fortune, alas! is the mask of misery. What will come of this? We cannot foresee the end. Order is upset and turns to disorder, good becomes evil. The people are confused. Is it not so, day in, day out, from the beginning?
The wise man is therefore angular, though he does not injure others; he has sharp corners, though he does not harm; he is upright but not gruff. He is clear minded, but he does not try to be brilliant.
Lao-Tzu

Whoever undertakes to rule the kingdom and to shape it according to his whim—I foresee that he will fail to reach his goal. That is all.
The kingdom is a living being. It cannot be constructed, in truth! He who tries to manipulate it will spoil it; he who tries to put it under his power will lose it.
Therefore: Some creatures go out in front, others follow, some have warm breath, others cold, some are strong, some weak, some attain abundance, others succumb.
The wise man will accordingly forswear excess, he will avoid arrogance and not overreach.
Lao-Tzu
Please make as many copies of this leaflet as possible and distribute them.

404

SECRET REPORT OF THE SECURITY SERVICE OF THE REICHSFÜHRER SS

Reports on the Program to Combat Criminal Subversion

First circulated on 2 December 1943 as "Meldungen zur strafrechtlichen Bekämpfung von Zersetzungsversuchen." First published in *Meldungen aus dem Reich 1938–1945. Die geheimen Lageberichte des Sicherheitsdienstes der SS,* edited by Heinz Boberach (Herrsching: Pawlak Verlag, 1984), 15:6096–98. Translated by Timothy Nunan.

With the increasing hardship of the war, the punishments against attempts at subversion on the part of a few defeatists have been considerably sharpened in the course of this year. In the first years of the war, defeatist statements were most often not prosecuted at all. In the worst cases, they were prosecuted under the law against malicious statements [*Heimtückegesetz*], which prescribed five years of imprisonment as the maximum punishment. As of late, however, one often sees in these statements a crime worthy of death; when, as a court order of the Reich justice minister put it, "they abet the major offensive of the enemy in the inner front by portraying the casualties that the total war demands from all as senseless and no longer bearable." Those who utter such statements from now on will be punished according to Section 5, Paragraph 1, Number 1 of the Military Order for Exceptional Criminal Law [*Kriegssonderstrafrechtsverordnung*], under the section "Subversion of the Military"—a breach that carries the death penalty as the normal punishment and permits prison sentences only in less serious instances.

Already with the provision for the change of the decree concerning jurisdiction from 1 January 1943, the jurisdiction for the punishment of these crimes under Section 5 of the Military Order for Exceptional Criminal Law was transferred from the extraordinary courts to the people's courts [*Volksgerichtshof*]. In doing so, the need for central oversight of all relevant cases, especially as concerned their political meaning, was satisfied. The senior Reich attorney of the people's court may render less serious cases to the appropriate general state attorney, who may then arraign the defendants before the treason senates that exist within some of the Reich's higher regional courts.

Reports from the Reich have shown that the hitherto practice of prosecuting attempts at subversion has raised two major problems:

1. A lack of unity in the penal assessment of statements that are harmful to war events or that belittle leading figures of the Reich;
2. Shortcomings in the personnel of the courts who are responsible for the punishment of such statements.

As concerns the first problem, the following becomes clear from the reports: again and again, judgments of individual extraordinary courts or penal senates become known to the higher regional courts, whose severity of punishment is disproportionate to that of the harsh penalties of the people's courts. In spite of the more or less similar personality of the perpetrator and the same circumstances of the crimes, the same kinds of utterances that merit a death sentence from the people's courts are punished in the lower courts using the Law against Malicious Speech *or even* the Military Order for Exceptional Criminal Law to (more or less) long jail sentences.

Examples:

The people's court sentenced the government advisor Dr. K. to death on 23 August 1943 on account of subversion of the military. While in a streetcar in Rostock shortly after the reformation of the Italian government, K. said, "The same must happen here; the Führer has to step down, since we surely can't win anymore, and no one wants to be burned alive."

The extraordinary court in Frankfurt am Main sentenced P., a security officer in a major plant, an active businessman, and an officer from the First World War, to one year in prison on 13 September 1943 on account of a misdemeanor under Section 2 of the Law against Malicious Statements. He made the following statement in June 1943: "By fall, at the latest November of this year, we're finished. By next year, there won't be anything here in the west anymore. Adolf is going to stand behind the Elbe; he'll give up the west in order to hold back the brutes in the east."

The sentenced also added in an objection, "What do they all want? Everyone knows that they're all nincompoops. Göring is a morphine addict, Goebbels has a venereal disease, Adolf is a hysteric and a choleric, Keitel is an old aunt—even when he was the regiment commander in Fulda, they called him the regimental auntie."

He added to this that a Mr. E. had told him that a soldier awarded the Knight's Cross with Oak Leaves had been ordered to meet with the Führer but that the man did not even have the chance to speak. Adolf talked at him for two hours, just as hysterics are known to do.

Further, P. called Field Marshall Keitel and Ambassador von Papen fools [*Hanswürste*].

(Even in this case, the state attorney's office sentenced P. to only eight months in prison. In the meantime, a proposal to reassess the judgment with the intent to declare it null and void has been introduced by the Reich justice minister.)

The people's court sentenced four employees of a Berlin welfare office to death on 4 October 1943 for subversion of the military. They had composed a political agitational and malicious poem, whose basest lines had been written by one of the defendants himself. In the poem, it is claimed that the closest associates of the Führer are not taking part in the food-rationing programs. In the pre–National Socialist era, the poem says, everything was well and good, but now one gets only bare bolts [*kahle Bolzen*] to eat. Besides this, the poem derides the *Volk*'s confession of loyalty to the Führer.

The extraordinary court in Frankfurt am Main sentenced Else W., a stenographer working for a plant in Frankfurt, to two years of prison in the middle of October 1943 on the basis of Section 2 of the Law against Malicious Statements. In August 1943, Ms. W. placed a slip of paper at the desks of three of her workmates with the following humorous poem, which she herself had authored:

He who rules like a Russian rogue
His hair curled to match what in France is vogue
Like an Englishman his mustache shorn
Himself not in Germany born

He who taught us the Roman greeting
Who our women and children dream of meeting
So virile, that not one child he turn out can
Is in Germany the leading man.

(The Public Prosecuting Office sentenced her to one year in prison.)

In the preceding instances, which are by no means isolated, the difference in the severity of punishment between charges for subversion of the military and malicious speech is conspicuous. Even in cases in which defendants were charged for subversion of the military, there were different and inconsistent results, as the following judgments of the criminal senate of the Munich Higher Regional Court show.

The fifty-one-year-old Walburga P. said the following to her housemates in the period from October 1940 to December 1942, after she received an inquiry from an office of the navy as to the whereabouts of her son, who was supposed to enlist: "They can kiss my ass! They should go find him themselves. My son doesn't put his neck into things where you don't know what's going on and for whom you're doing it . . . the poor man has to help his own children. If every mother would do this, then there wouldn't be any war; they'd have to stick their own necks out there."

Many a time she had the following to say: "I'm international, like my boy. I'm not interested in going along with the Hitlers of the world."

When she was asked by her landlady why she had not yet purchased a swastika flag for the house, she said the following in the presence of the landlady's husband: "What do the old people know about how things work in this world? They don't know a thing! We have to be rid of Hitler, and the war has to end. Bavaria is going to secede from Prussia, and you had better believe that I'm not buying a swastika flag."

When a care package of food that she had sent to her son (who was sentenced to nine years in jail for desertion) was returned to her: "Not once can you send the poor boy something to eat. My poor child is going to starve. Hitler has enough to chow down on! You see him running around with that fat head of his; of course he's not hungry." And so on and so on.

The 2nd Criminal Senate of the Munich Higher Regional Court sentenced Mr. and Mrs. P. to six months in prison on 5 October 1943 for subversion of the military.

Rosa P., wife of the engineer Mr. P., said the following in March 1943 in a store in Immenstadt: "I find that those involved in business have started to cut us some slack ever since Stalingrad went lost for us."

405

SECRET REPORT OF THE SECURITY SERVICE OF THE REICHSFÜHRER SS

Reactions to the Weekly Newsreel for 27 February 27–5 March 1943

First circulated on 4 March 1943 as "Zur Aufnahme der Kriegswochenschau vom 27. 2 bis 5. 3 1945 1943." First published in *Meldungen aus dem Reich 1938–1945. Die geheimen Lageberichte des Sicherheitsdienstes der SS,* edited by Heinz Boberach (Herrsching: Pawlak Verlag, 1984), 12:4892–95.

Reliable sources observe that the weekly newsreels [*Wochenshau*] have not yet regained the popular status as a means of persuasion they once enjoyed, despite the fact that there is some isolated recognition of the topicality and urgency of the cinematic reporting involved here. There are substantial sectors of the population that no longer consider it worthwhile to go to the cinema just to see the weekly newsreel and are no longer willing to go through the unpleasant rigmarole a visit to the cinema often involves, like standing in line to get a ticket. At any rate, spontaneous statements such as these have been known to be made on rare occasions. Getting opinions on the content of the films themselves was generally possible only by asking individual visitors to the cinema what they thought about what they had just seen.

However, while these reports may seem to indicate that the weekly newsreel "is currently no longer at the forefront in terms of influencing public opinion and national sentiment," viewers of the weekly newsreel were viscerally impressed by the filmic images of the assembly at the Sportpalast on 18 February 1943 [see document 393 in chapter 29—Eds.]. We can confirm that this cinematic report has greatly increased the lasting propagandistic impact of the assembly at the Sportpalast, even where skepticism had been the prevailing attitude. Even more reticent sectors of the population could not resist these images of the visibly enthusiastic effect and resonance this speech had on the audience present at the speech. People recognize the way the camera is able to translate the speaker's every word into an optical image and thus to transmit the "atmosphere of the Sportpalast" to the viewers of the weekly newsreel. People said that a weekly newsreel had rarely found such a penetrating and concrete resonance in the press and radio reporting. "These images really sparked a lot of things. It is very much different to be able to see everything that's going on; it has a much more persuasive effect than words coming from a loudspeaker."

406

HEINRICH HIMMLER

Decree on Youth Gangs

"Erlass des Reichsführers SS und chefs der Deutschen Polizei, Heinrich Himmler," 25 October 1944. First published in Detlev Peukert, ed., *Die Edelweisspiraten: Protestbewegungen jugendlicher Arbeiter im Dritten Reich: eine Dokumentation* (Cologne: Bund-Verlag, 1983), 123–33.

Highly Confidential!
Memorandum to all Security Services and Police

Throughout the Reich, especially in large cities, associations of youth (gangs) have been forming in ever-increasing numbers of late. In part, these gangs exhibit criminal, antisocial, or oppositional political tendencies and therefore require intensified surveillance, especially in view of the absence due to the war of many fathers, Hitler Youth leaders, and educators.

All youth associations must be watched closely and appropriate steps must be taken against them as needed . . . [. . .]

Variety and Appearance of Gangs

1. Gangs are associations of youth who are not in the Hitler Youth and who lead a separate and extraordinary existence based on principles not in accordance with National Socialist ideology. They all share a rejection of or disinterest toward their obligations within the *Volksgemeinschaft* or the Hitler Youth; this is especially evidenced in their lack of willingness to conform to the exigencies of war.
2. These gangs have made their appearance under a variety of names (clique, mob, gang, pack, the Platters, the Shufflers, the Edelweiss Pirates, and so on). A centralized organization does not, in general, exist. Outward association is often only very loose and irregular. Occasionally they wear special identifying insignia (for example, an edelweiss emblem, death's-head ring, colored pins, and the like). Membership dues are usually not collected, but in some cases identification insignia are issued. The gangs more or less have their regular meeting places and operating territories; they often go on outings together. Between certain gangs cross-communication does exist. This can be of a friendly or of an antagonistic nature. It is primarily young lads who belong to these gangs, but there are a few girls as well.
3. Formation of a gang usually involves common affiliation in a factory, school, some other organization, or simply [through] residing in the same district. Initially, such associations can be quite harmless (street friendships, standing at corners together, and so forth); later, however, depending on prevailing convictions and goals, ominous developments can ensue. It is not unusual to be able to trace this activity back to a single antisocial or criminally inclined fellow who knows how to bring the others to heel and can direct their harmless desire for adventure instead toward dangerous avenues. Generally, three different basic forms of behavior can be determined, although it must be noted that few gangs exhibit only one of these basic characteristics in pronounced form. More-

over, activity of one particular kind most often leads to activity of another kind. We have isolated the following:

a. Groups of *antisocial* orientation. This is characterized by acts of minor to serious criminal offenses (mischief, brawling, violations of police directives, petty larceny, sexual offenses—especially those involving members of the same sex, and so on . . .)
b. Gangs of *oppositional political* orientation, although not always with a well-defined program of opposition. Their orientation is marked by generally seditious behavior, rejection of the Hitler Youth and other community obligations, indifference toward the conduct of the war, engaging in disruptions of youth service obligations, attacks on Hitler Youth members, listening to foreign radio broadcasts, dissemination of rumors, maintaining the traditions, song repertoire, and the like of the prohibited federated [youth] groups or of other groups. Youth of this orientation frequently attempt to infiltrate [Nazi] Party organizations in order to provide a screen for themselves or in order to have the possibility for subversive actions.
c. Gangs of a *liberal-individualist* orientation, characterized by a predilection for English ideals, language, demeanor, dress (English casual), cultivation of fast music, jazz and swing, etc. The members of these gangs come primarily from the "upper middle class" and want to pursue their own pleasure and sexual or other excesses. They thereby soon conflict sharply with National Socialist ideology. They resist directives from the Hitler Youth, Labor Service, and military service and acquire the behavioral characteristics listed under item b.

4. The members of gangs can be differentiated, based on the degree of their participation, into leaders, active participants, and nominal members (hangers-on).

Leaders of the gangs (ringleaders) are—not that a solid leadership always exists—one or more people, often even adults or foreigners who have asserted themselves through exceptional intelligence, initiative, or brutality. Some have previous criminal records; some are former members of earlier federated (youth) or other oppositional political circles. They are only seldom members of the Hitler Youth. If, however, they are Hitler Youth members, they do not do their duties, do them only reluctantly, or have already withdrawn from the Hitler Youth due to certain offenses or loss of interest. Cases have been documented, however, where they have performed their duties flawlessly in order not to arouse any outward suspicion.

Some of the active members and hangers-on of the gangs also have previous criminal records or come from disorderly family circumstances and antisocial clans. Others, however, come from respectable families and are themselves basically still decent. In many cases, they were moved to join because of negligent parents (neglect of educational and supervisory responsibilities) or because of a misguided craving for adventure, romantic conceptions, or for other puberty-related reasons.

The members of a gang frequently exhibit identical styles of clothing, hair fashions, and behavior and often have nicknames derived from the images of their perceived world or from their approved stock of ideas. Because of the war, many youth have been left largely to their own devices. Gangs therefore exert a strong attraction on these youth and for that matter even on decent young people.

407

LUDWIG BECK

Beck's Response to Hitler's Arguments on 5 November 1937

Written on 12 November 1939. First published in *Deutscher Widerstand 1938–1944, Fortschritt oder Reaktion?,* edited by Bodo Scheurig (Munich: Deutscher Taschenbuch Verlag, 1969), 29–34.

Germany is undeniably faced with a problem of territory, primarily due to its central position in Europe and, for all times past and perhaps all times ever, as a result of the territorial changes imposed by Versailles. But one cannot overlook the fact that the "population demographics" of Europe have been stabilized for the past thousand years to the degree that sweeping changes cannot be made without anticipating serious upheavals of inestimable duration, and parallels cannot be drawn between the territorial shifts involved for Italy in Africa or for Japan in East Asia. It seems that minor changes are still possible. But they cannot lead to any renewed endangerment of the homogeneity of the German *Volk,* the Germanic racial stock.

The kinds of autarchic intentions underlying parts of the Four-Year Plan were, from our perspective, emergency measures designed for a limited time but never as permanent policy regulations. One thing is certain: every attempt at autarchy that launches an assault on one's own essential substance, thereby threatening the very future, is bound to fail as a permanent solution.

The fact that participation in the world economy restricts independence is all too true. But to glean from this fact the only remedy in the acquisition of more living space seems to me a proposition that fails to apply the foresight necessary to fully master the problem. As far as my understanding is concerned, what we need, if the German *Volk* is not to slowly fall to ruin, is the greatest possible degree of participation in the world economy for all times.

The magnitude of France and England's resistance to Germany's efforts to increase its territory and power is not to be underestimated. And yet the very notion of seeing them as incontestable or invincible seems—in light of all the fruitless attempts we have made to combat them—still nowhere in sight. Politics is the art of the possible. All three of these nations exist simultaneously, in that same part of the world that is Europe. That means that every possibility for diplomatic compromises must first be exhausted, especially in light of the respective levels of strength involved. It is further strategically more circumspect in the event of some future collapse.

To be sure, the [British] Empire is not invincible. The likelihood that it will remain a determining world power second only to America for the foreseeable future seems to me much greater. And that is also why England will not stand alone for the foreseeable future but will always have allies. The brief observations he makes about England and France—unfortunately, Russia is not afforded closer consideration as a world power here—have very little to do with the ultimate objects of the "Führer's" statements. For him, it is a matter of one question alone: where will England, France, etc. stand in 1938?

There is no historical truth to the notion that Bismarck's wars against Austria and France were wars of unprecedented risk; they were simply the best wars ever prepared by a statesman, and that is why they were won. The whole palette of historical parallels is subject to critique.

The chronological distinction is assailable in all three cases since they can be based on only some of all the factors involved—those factors that are known in advance.

In the first case, the military justification is not the province of the statesman and is better left determined and examined by the experts. The issues of military policy, of the financial, economic and spiritual foundations, are not even addressed here. The conclusion that the question of German living space must be resolved by 1943–45 at the latest is stunning simply by virtue of its lack of substance.

In the second [case], I still consider this highly unlikely—*wishful thinking.*

In the third case, France will always have enough forces in hand to oppose Germany.

Czechoslovakia and Austria may be overestimated as countries with a surplus, and even so, in the best-case scenario, we could expect a minimal improvement of our agricultural and raw material potential.

The potential military and political constellations that would arrive after an annexation of Czechoslovakia and Austria merit careful investigation.

408

ULRICH VON HASSELL

Diary Entry

Written 21 December 1941. First published in *The Von Hassell Diaries: The Story of the Forces against Hitler inside Germany, 1938–1944* (Boulder, CO: Westview Press, 1994), 230–32.

What has engrossed and disquieted me most during the past weeks are the numerous conferences on questions concerning a change of the regime. One major difficulty is Goerdeler.[1] He is too sanguine, always sees things as he wishes to see them, and in many ways is a true reactionary, though otherwise he has splendid qualities. Nevertheless, we finally agreed on the chief issues. Also, despite all doubts about his position, we agreed that the Crown Prince must come to the fore. Beck assented, although through past connections he knows the Crown Prince well.

The principal difficulty with Beck is that he is very theoretical. As Popitz says, a man of tactics but little willpower, whereas Goerdeler has much willpower but no tact(ics). [Johannes] Popitz himself often manifests a slightly professorial manner, the somewhat abstract views of an administrator. Nevertheless all three are capital men.

I was always afraid that we had too little contact with younger circles. This fear has now been realized, but only to reveal new and formidable difficulties. First of all, I had a long talk with [Adam von Trott zu Solz] Trott during which he passionately contended for the avoidance, within as well as without the country, of any semblance of "reaction," "gentlemen's club," or "militarism." Therefore, although he, too, was a monarchist, we should under no circumstances have a monarchy now, for a monarchy would not win the support of the people and would not win confidence abroad. "Converted" Social Democrats, that is, Christian Social Democrats, one of whom (a former Reichstag representative) he named, would never go along with us on the monarchy and would wait for the next group.

To these negative points he added the one positive thought that [Martin] Niemöller should be made Chancellor of the Reich. He was, on the one hand, the strongest internationally recognized exponent of anti-Hitlerism, and, on the other hand, the most popular reformer here and the one most likely to appeal to the Anglo-Saxon world.[2]

Afterward I met the alert, cultured Peter Yorck—a genuine offspring of his highly intellectual and sometimes too theoretically inclined family. He expressed similar sentiments. Finally, at his own request, I went to see Yorck again. There I met [Helmuth James Graf von] Moltke, Trott, and Guttenberg. All four, under the leadership of Trott, set to work on me furiously.

On the day of my departure, at Popitz's, Fritzi Schulenburg hammered away at the same theme. Of the five young men he was easily the most sober-minded, the most politically conscious, but, on the other hand, the most prejudiced against the Crown Prince, because his father had absolutely enjoined him to oppose any such possibility because of the stand taken by the Crown Prince in the crisis of 1918. So far as Prince Louis Ferdinand is concerned, he apparently considers himself the man of the hour, though he lacks many qualities he cannot get along without. He seems to have done so by insisting that they are part of the inheritance.

Goerdeler takes an almost completely unfavorable attitude toward the ideas of these young men, who, on their part, disapprove of him. He maintains that he himself has good relations with the Social Democrats. In the matter of the Crown Prince he is less positive in his opinion.

Beck firmly supports Goerdeler in this as he does in most questions. Popitz, more than anyone, favors the Crown Prince as an immediate solution. All three emphasize that we should not permit ourselves to be unduly influenced by passing moods of the people; but Goerdeler, of course, overestimates the degree to which people in general resent the present system and long for a liberating action.

I am trying to find a kind of connecting link with the younger men by arguing somewhat as follows: The premise "no reaction, but attempt to get popular support," was correct. Therefore, it is most earnestly to be desired that we get, as head of the government, a man whose name will be considered both as a deliverance and a program. This is important, too, in the interest of foreign policy, even if only to a limited degree. The latter qualification is necessary because the national character of this change, rising out of the peculiar will and needs of our people, can be maintained only if we do not look over our shoulder at other countries. Also because the Christian-pacifist circles among the Anglo-Saxon peoples, on whom Trott counts most heavily, are entirely useless as a dependable political factor.

In general, I am against Trott's theoretical and illusionary outlook. Unfortunately, such a personality as we hope for is not there. I am convinced that the man Trott proposed [Niemöller] has some unsuitable characteristics. He is somewhat unbending, non-political, and not a good strategist. Aside from all this, I think that, after the first effect had worn off, he would not be a successful symbol. On the contrary, he might even create opposition.

In this state of affairs there is nothing left to do but to act without such a popular personality—for act we must, and that very soon. It is clear that the situation having advanced so far, the role of a new government will be utterly thankless, one taken on in the middle of a mess—yes, a kind of liquidator's role.

We must keep in mind that we may be used only to clean up and will then be replaced by others, or that we may fail altogether. The task is to manage this as well as is humanly possible. Moreover, we shall have to fashion a government that is as free as possible of the odor of reaction, militarism, et cetera. Action, however, is the main thing.

Notes

1. Carl Friedrich Goerdeler (1884–1945), a conservative and former mayor of Leipzig, was the most prominent figure in the resistance group that included Ulrich von Hassell, Johannes Popitz, Adam von Trott zu Solz, and Ludwig Beck. Along with Claus Schenk von Stauffenberg, all participated in the abortive 20 July 1944 bomb plot against Hitler and were executed.—Eds.

2. Martin Niemöller (1892–1984) was a Lutheran theologian, pastor, and one of the founders of the Confessing Church that opposed the Nazificiation of German Protestantism. Niemöller was interned in Sachsenhausen and Dachau concentration camps until his release by the Allies in 1945.—Eds.

409

HELMUTH JAMES VON MOLTKE

Principles for the New Order (the Kreisau Circle)

Written 9 August 1943. First published as "Grundsätze für die Neuordnung (Kreisauer Kreis)," *in Deutscher Widerstand: Fortschritt oder Reaktion?,* edited by Bodo Scheurig (Munich: Deutscher Taschenbuch Verlag, 1969), 196–98. Translated by Peter Ludlow.

Draft of 9 August 1943 (note by Helmuth James von Moltke)

The government of the German Reich sees in Christianity the foundation for the moral and religious renewal of our nation, for the conquest of hatred and deception, and for the reconstruction of the European community of nations.

The point of departure lies in human sensitivity to the divine order that upholds man's inward and outward existence. This sensitivity is imperative. Only when it is possible to make the divine order the test of relationships between men and nations will we be able to overcome the moral and material disorder of our time and establish a genuine peace.

The internal reconstruction of the Reich is the basis for the achievement of a just and durable peace.

Situated in the midst of the collapse of a power structure that has lost all sanction and that is founded exclusively on technical mastery, Europeans, more than any other group of men, face this problem. The path to a solution lies open—through the determined and energetic exploitation of the Christian heritage. The Reich government is therefore resolved to fulfill the following irreducible domestic and external demands with all the means at its disposal.

1. The law, which has been trampled upon, must be restored and given authority over all orders of human existence. Under the protection of scrupulous, independent, and fearless judges, it is the keystone of any future peace.
2. Freedom of belief and conscience is guaranteed. Existing laws and regulations that infringe these principles are to be repealed immediately.
3. Destruction of the totalitarian constraint upon conscience and acknowledgment of the inviolable dignity of the human person as the foundation of the legal and international order has to be aimed at. Everyone has a full share of responsibility in social, political, and international affairs. The right of everybody to work and property, regardless of race, nation, or creed, is upheld by the public authorities.
4. The basic unit of peaceful communal life is the family. It is protected by the public authorities, who ought also to guarantee education and the external necessities of life; food, clothing, housing, parks, and health.
5. Work must be so organized that it encourages rather than stunts personal responsibility. This entails attention to working conditions and the provision of advanced professional schools. It also requires that each person should have a real share of responsibility in the individual firm, and beyond that, in the general economic sphere to which his own work contributes. This means that he is to cooperate in the development of a healthy and secure social order in which the individual, his family, and the communities can develop organically within coordinated spheres of activity. The economic authorities must guarantee these basic requirements.
6. The personal political responsibility of each individual requires that he should share in the self-government of the small and manageable communities that are to be revived. Rooted and proved at this level, he must share in the decision making of the state and the international community through his own elected representatives. In this way, he is given a strong sense of sharing responsibility for political activity in general.

7. The special responsibility and loyalty that everyone owes to his nation of origin, his language, and the intellectual and historical tradition of his people must be respected and protected. However, this must not become an excuse for amassing political power or for degrading, persecuting, or oppressing a foreign race. The free and peaceful development of national culture is incompatible with the retention of absolute sovereignty by each individual state. Peace demands the creation of an order that spans the separate states. As soon as the free consent of all nations involved is assured, the authorities in this new order must have the right to demand of every individual obedience, honor, and, in case of need, the pledge of life and property for the highest political authority in the international community.

The Structure of the Reich

The Reich remains the highest authority of the German people. Its political constitution ought to be characterized by genuine authority and real cooperation and participation by the people. It rests upon the natural divisions of the nation: family, parish, and *Land*. The structure of the Reich is based on the principles of self-government. The latter unites freedom and personal responsibility with the requirements of order and leadership.

This structure ought to assure the unity and concerted leadership of the Reich and ought to enable it to be integrated into the community of European nations.

The political will of the nation is to be exercised within limits that are still open to the inspection of the individual. Physically, economically, and culturally integrated *Länder* are to be formed on the foundation of the natural divisions of parish and county. In order to make the self-government truly effective, the *Länder* ought to have between three and five million inhabitants.

The distribution of responsibility is to be made according to the principle that every corporation is responsible for performing all the tasks that it can most sensibly carry out itself.

410

CARL FRIEDRICH GOERDELER

(Prepared) Radio Address

"(Vorbereitete) Rundfunkansprache (Entwurf von Goerdeler)." Written in 1944. First published in *Deutscher Widerstand 1938–1944, Fortschritt oder Reaktion?,* edited by Bodo Scheurig (Munich: Deutscher Taschenbuch Verlag, 1969), 282–83.

Germans!

As of today, you know what is at stake, what our motivations and intentions are. The rule of extreme self-defense and the obligation for self-preservation are our guideposts now. We did not get the state we were promised, one of solid and wise leadership; rather, we had a terrifying, tyrannical government forced upon us. The bravery of our soldiers, their courage in the face of death, and their skill has been shamefully abused; our homeland has been unscrupulously subjected to privation and destruction.

As the final link in a chain of perversions of justice and breaches of law that would have been entirely avoidable, Hitler, in his speech to the Reichstag of 25 April 1942, declared open season on all Germans by appropriating for himself the right to overturn any legal opinion whatsoever at his own discretion. And with that, he pronounced the arrival of an absolute nadir of lawlessness thus far unparalleled and unsurpassed in the history of civilized nations. He has made the Germany that proudly advocated equal rights for all into a powerless collective of slaves thrown together by necessity in which the average citizen no longer has the chance to defend himself against injustice. The highest-ranking dignitaries, including Adolf Hitler himself, have committed countless crimes against life and limb, against property and honor—and have sanctioned and ordained these crimes. Men of the highest position have shamelessly bilked the public coffers or other sources of revenue to line their own pockets—first and foremost amongst them, Hermann Göring! We will no longer stand for German honor to be sullied like this by a pack of parasites. We don't want to be led by these scoundrels, who seem incapable of distinguishing between what's mine and thine, who abuse their position to lead lives of decadent opulence even in times of war while the general populace suffers in privation, while the sons, husbands, and fiancés fight and fall in battle; and while the madness of annihilation and total war runs rampant.

An adventurous, powermongering foreign policy has placed the populace in a situation whose gravity can no longer be overlooked. We are forbidden by the exigencies of war to call a spade a spade. But you know or at least have a sense of what all this shameless lack of conscience and lunacy has brought us. We have called upon men of all social classes and from all areas of the Reich, and we shall name them by name, to conscientiously investigate everything that has happened and to inform all of you as to where we stand, based on what our investigations reveal, as soon as the situation allows for us to do so.

One thing we can tell you now, though: the ship of state that has been built upon injustice, despotism, every manner of crime, self-interest, and lies shall be torn asunder. The principles of human community will form the foundation for a new ship of state built on justice and what is right, built on sincerity, decency, cleanliness, reason, consideration for one another, and consideration for all God's creations and their best interests. If we wish to avoid repeating the experience of November 1918, the moment has come in which we must translate these intentions into action. In the coming days, we will be publicly calling those persons to account—without regard for their position—who are responsible for the crimes they have committed against the state and the people.

There is hard work before us, in every aspect of life. There is no magic panacea to act as an immediate or gradual remedy for the wanton destruction of every basic prerequisite for meaningful life we have experienced. We hope to collectively save our fatherland and restore the common fabric of community to our nation.

PART TWELVE

. . .

DEFEAT

31
Hitler's Last Will and Testament

Adolf Hitler dictated his last will and testament to his secretary Traudl Junge in his Berlin *Führerbunker* on 29 April 1945. He and Eva Braun married that day and committed suicide the following day, three days before the surrender of Berlin to the Soviets on 2 May and one week before the end of World War II in Europe on May 8. It consists of two documents, a personal will and a political testament.

Hitler's personal will states that he chose death over disgrace or capitulation and specifies that his body—and that of Eva Braun (not mentioned by name)—be cremated. It leaves his wealth to the National Socialist Party—or if it no longer exists, to the state. It also bequeaths his art collection to his hometown, Linz on the Donau.

His self-serving political testament predictably blames the Jews for the war, encourages the Wehrmacht to continue fighting, and most importantly, expels Göring and Himmler from the party for negotiating with the enemy, naming Admiral Dönitz as his successor.

411

ADOLF HITLER

Political Testament

Dictated on 29 April 1945. First published in Office of U.S. Chief of Counsel for the Prosecution of Axis Criminality, *Nazi Conspiracy and Aggression* (Washington, D.C.: U.S. Government Printing Office, 1946), 6:258–63.

Since 1914, when as a volunteer, I made my modest contribution in the World War that was forced upon the Reich, over thirty years have passed.

In these three decades, only love for my people and loyalty to my people have guided me in all my thoughts, actions, and life. They gave me the strength to make the most difficult decisions, such as no mortal has yet had to face. I have exhausted my time, my working energy, and my health in these three decades.

It is untrue that I or anybody else in Germany wanted war in 1939. It was desired and instigated exclusively by those international statesmen who were either of Jewish origin or working for Jewish interests. I have made so many offers for the reduction and elimination of armaments, which posterity cannot explain away for all eternity, that the responsibility for the outbreak of this war cannot rest on me. Furthermore, I never desired that, after the first terrible World War, a second war should arise against England or even against America. Centuries may pass, but out of the ruins of our cities and monuments of art there will arise anew the hatred for the people who alone are ultimately responsible: International Jewry and its helpers!

As late as three days before the outbreak of the German-Polish War, I proposed to the British Ambassador in Berlin a solution for the German-Polish problem—similar to the problem of the Saar area, under international control. This offer cannot be explained away, either. It was only rejected because the responsible circles in English politics wanted the war, partly in the expectation of business advantages, partly driven by propaganda promoted by international Jewry.

But I left no doubt about the fact that if the peoples of Europe were again only regarded as so many packages of stock shares by these international money and finance conspirators, then that race, too, which is the truly guilty party in this murderous struggle would also have to be held to account: the Jews! I further left no doubt that this time we would not permit millions of European children of Aryan descent to die of hunger, nor millions of grown-up men to suffer death, nor hundreds of thousands of women and children to be burned and bombed to death in their cities, without the truly guilty party having to atone for its guilt, even if through more humane means.

After six years of struggle, which in spite of all reverses will go down in history as the most glorious and most courageous manifestation of a people's will to live, I cannot separate myself from the city which is the capital of this Reich. Because our forces are too few to permit any further resistance against the enemy's assaults, and because individual resistance is rendered valueless by blinded and characterless scoundrels, I desire to share the fate that millions of others have taken upon themselves, in that I shall remain in this city. Furthermore, I do not want to fall into the hands of enemies, who, for the delectation of the hate-riddled masses, require a new spectacle promoted by the Jews.

I have therefore resolved to remain in Berlin and there to choose death of my own will at the very moment when, as I believe, the seat of the *Führer* and Chancellor can no longer be defended. I die with a joyful heart in the awareness of the immeasurable deeds and achievements of our soldiers at the front, of our women at home, of the achievements of our peasants and workers, and of the contribution, unique in history, of our youth, which bears my name.

It goes without saying that I thank them all from the bottom of my heart and that it is also my desire that, in spite of everything, they should not give up the struggle, but continue fighting wherever they may be, faithful to the great Clausewitz, against the enemies of the Fatherland. From the sacrifices of our soldiers and from my own comradeship with them, there will come in one way or another into German history the seed of a brilliant renaissance of the National Socialist movement and thus the realization of a true national community. Many very brave men and women have resolved to link their lives to mine to the very end. I have requested them, and finally ordered them, not to do so, but instead to take part in the continuing struggle of the nation. I ask the commanders of the army, navy, and air force to strengthen by all possible means the spirit of resistance of our soldiers in the spirit of National Socialism, emphasizing especially that I too, as founder and creator of this movement, have preferred death to cowardly flight or even capitulation.

May it be one day a part of the code of honor; as it is already in the navy, that the surrender of an area or of a town is impossible, and above all in this respect the leaders should give a shining example of faithful devotion to duty unto death. Before my death I expel the former *Reichsmarschall* Hermann Göring and deprive him of all the rights he may enjoy by virtue of the decree of June 29, 1941, and also by virtue of my statement in the Reichstag on September 1, 1939. I appoint in his place *Großadmiral* Dönitz as President of the Reich and Supreme Commander of the Armed Forces.

Before my death I expel the former *Reichsführer*-SS and Minister of the Interior Heinrich Himmler from the Party and all offices of state. In his place, I appoint *Gauleiter* Karl Hanke as *Reichsführer*-SS and Chief of the German Police and *Gauleiter* Paul Giesler as Reich Minister of the Interior.

Göring and Himmler, by their secret negotiations with the enemy, without my knowledge or approval, and by their illegal attempts to seize power in the state, quite apart from their treachery to my person, have brought irreparable shame to the country and the whole people.

In order to give the German people a government composed of honorable men, who will fulfill their duty of continuing the war by all available means, I, as the *Führer* of the nation, nominate the following members of the new Cabinet:

President of the Reich: Dönitz; Chancellor of the Reich: Dr. Goebbels; Party Minister: Bormann; Foreign Minister: Seyß-Inquart; Minister of the Interior: Gauleiter Giesler; Minister for War: Dönitz; C.-in-C. of the Army: Schörner; C.-in-C. of the Navy: Dönitz; C.-in-C. of the Air Force: Greim; Reichsführer-SS and Chief of the German Police: Gauleiter Hanke; Economics: Funk; Agriculture: Backe; Justice: Thierack; Culture: Dr. Scheel; Propaganda: Dr. Naumann; Finance: Schwerin-Krossigk; Labor: Dr. Hupfauer; Munitions: Saur; Leader of the German Labor Front and Member of the Reich Cabinet: Reichminister Dr. Ley.

Several of these men, such as Martin Bormann, Dr. Goebbels, etc., together with their wives, have joined me by their own free will and do not wish to leave the capital of the Reich under any circumstances, but on the contrary are willing to perish with me here. Yet I must ask them to obey my request, and in this instance place the interests of the nation above their own feelings.

Through their work and loyalty they will remain just as close to me as companions after my death, just as I hope that my spirit will remain amongst them and will always accompany them. Let them be hard, but never unjust; above all, let them never allow fear to counsel their actions, but may they place the honor of the nation above everything on this earth. Finally, may they be conscious of the fact that our task of building a National Socialist state represents the labor of the coming centuries, and this places every single person under an obligation always to serve the common interest and to subordinate his own interests. I demand of all Germans, all National Socialists, men and women and all soldiers of the Armed Forces, that they remain faithful and obedient to the new government and to their President unto death.

Above all, I charge the leadership of the nation and their followers with the strict observance of the racial laws and with merciless resistance against the universal poisoner of all peoples, international Jewry.

Given at Berlin, April 29, 1945, 4 A.M.

Adolf Hitler

As witnesses:

Dr. Joseph Goebbels
Wilhelm Burgdorf
Martin Bormann
Hans Krebs

Bibliography of English-Language Works

Hitler and the Third Reich

Aly, Götz. *Hitler's Beneficiaries: Plunder, Racial War, and the Nazi Welfare State.* New York: Metropolitan Books, 2007.

Aschheim, Steven E. *Culture and Catastrophe: German and Jewish Confrontations with National Socialism and Other Crises.* New York: New York University Press, 1996.

Baranowski, Shelley. *The Sanctity of Rural Life: Nobility, Protestantism, and Nazism in Weimar Prussia.* New York: Oxford University Press, 1995.

Bendersky, Joseph W. *A Concise History of Nazi Germany.* 3rd ed. Lanham, Md.: Rowman & Littlefield, 2007.

Berghahn, Klaus L., and Jost Hermand, eds. *Unmasking Hitler: Cultural Representations of Hitler from the Weimar Republic to the Present.* German Life and Civilization, vol. 44. Oxford: Peter Lang, 2005.

Bessel, Richard. *Fascist Italy and Nazi Germany: Comparisons and Contrasts.* Cambridge: Cambridge University Press, 1996.

———. *Life in the Third Reich.* Oxford: Oxford University Press, 2001.

Bracher, Karl Dietrich. *The German Dictatorship: The Origins, Structure, and Effects of National Socialism.* New York: Praeger Publishers, 1970.

Bukey, Evan Burr. *Hitler's Austria: Popular Sentiment in the Nazi Era, 1938–1945.* Chapel Hill: University of North Carolina Press, 2000.

Burleigh, Michael. *The Third Reich: A New History.* Basingstoke, England: Palgrave Macmillan, 2000.

Burleigh, Michael, and Wolfgang Wippermann. *The Racial State: Germany, 1933–1945.* Cambridge: Cambridge University Press, 1991.

Burrin, Philippe. *Hitler and the Jews: The Genesis of the Holocaust.* London: Edward Arnold, 1994.

Caplan, Jane. *Nazi Germany: Short Oxford History of Germany.* Oxford: Oxford University Press, 2008.

Crew, David F. *Hitler and the Nazis: A History in Documents.* Pages from History. Oxford: Oxford University Press, 2005.

Dülffer, Jost. *Nazi Germany, 1933–1945: Faith and Annihilation.* London: Edward Arnold, 1996.

Eley, Geoff. *From Unification to Nazism: Reinterpreting the German Past.* Boston: Allen & Unwin, 1986.

Evans, Richard J. *The Coming of the Third Reich.* New York: Penguin Books, 2004.

———. *In Hitler's Shadow : West German Historians and the Attempt to Escape from the Nazi Past.* London: I. B. Tauris, 1989.

———. *The Third Reich in Power.* New York: Penguin Books, 2006.

Fest, Joachim C. *Hitler.* New York: Harcourt Brace Jovanovich, 1974.

Fischer, Conan. *The Rise of the Nazis.* New Frontiers in History. Manchester, England: Manchester University Press, 1995.

Fischer, Klaus P. *Nazi Germany: A New History.* New York: Continuum, 1995.

Frei, Norbert. *National Socialist Rule in Germany: The Führer State 1933–1945.* Oxford: Blackwell, 1993.

Fritzsche, Peter. *Germans into Nazis.* Cambridge, Mass.: Harvard University Press, 1998.

Furet, François. *Unanswered Questions: Nazi Germany and the Genocide of the Jews.* New York: Schocken Books, 1989.

Geary, Dick. *Hitler and Nazism.* Lancaster Pamphlets. London: Routledge, 1993.

Gellately, Robert. *Backing Hitler: Consent and Coercion in Nazi Germany.* Oxford: Oxford University Press, 2001.

Gellately, Robert, and Nathan Stoltzfus. *Social Outsiders in Nazi Germany.* Princeton, N.J.: Princeton University Press, 2001.

Gregor, Neil. *Nazism.* Oxford: Oxford University Press, 2000.
———, ed. *Nazism, War and Genocide: Essays in Honour of Jeremy Noakes.* Exeter, England: University of Exeter Press, 2005.
Haffner, Sebastian. *The Meaning of Hitler.* Cambridge, Mass.: Harvard University Press, 1983.
Hitler, Adolf. *Speeches of Adolf Hitler: Representative Passages from the Early Speeches, 1922–1924, and Other Selections.* Edited by Norman Hepburn Baynes. New York: Howard Fertig, 2006.
Keeley, Jennifer. *Life in the Hitler Youth.* San Diego: Lucent Books, 2000.
Kershaw, Ian. *Hitler: 1889–1936: Hubris.* London: Allen Lane, 1998.
———. *Hitler, 1936–45: Nemesis.* New York: W. W. Norton, 2000.
———. *The Nazi Dictatorship: Problems and Perspectives of Interpretation.* 4th ed. New York: Oxford University Press, 2000.
———. *Popular Opinion and Political Dissent in the Third Reich, Bavaria 1933–1945.*Oxford: Oxford University Press, 2002.
Kirk, Tim. *Nazi Germany.* Basingstoke, England: Palgrave Macmillan, 2007.
Koshar, Rudy. *Social Life, Local Politics, and Nazism: Marburg, 1880–1935.* Chapel Hill: University of North Carolina Press, 1986.
Large, David Clay. *Where Ghosts Walked: Munich's Road to the Third Reich.* New York: W. W. Norton, 1997.
Leitz, Christian, and Harold James. *The Third Reich: The Essential Readings.* Blackwell Essential Readings in History. Oxford: Blackwell Publishers, 1999.
Lukacs, John. *The Hitler of History.* New York: Vintage Books, 1998.
Machtan, Lothar. *The Hidden Hitler.* New York: Basic Books, 2001.
Mason, Timothy W., and Jane Caplan. *Nazism, Fascism and the Working Class.* Cambridge: Cambridge University Press, 1995.
McElligott, Anthony, and Tim Kirk, eds. *Working towards the Führer: Essays in Honour of Sir Ian Kershaw.* Manchester, England: Manchester University Press, 2003.
Michael, Robert, and Karin Doerr. *Nazi-Deutsch/Nazi-German: An English Lexicon of the Language of the Third Reich.* Westport, Conn.: Greenwood Press, 2002.
Mitchell, Allan. *The Nazi Revolution: Hitler's Dictatorship and the German Nation.* 4th ed. Boston: Houghton Mifflin, 1997.
Moeller, Robert G. *The Nazi State and German Society: A Brief History with Documents.* New York: Bedford / St. Martin's, 2009.
Mosse, George L. *The Nationalization of the Masses: Political Symbolism and Mass Movements in Germany from the Napoleonic Wars through the Third Reich.* New York: Howard Fertig, 1975.
———. *Nazi Culture: Intellectual, Cultural, and Social Life in the Third Reich.* New York: Grosset & Dunlap, 1966.
Noakes, Jeremy, and Geoffrey Pridham. *Documents on Nazism, 1919–1945.* London: Jonathan Cape, 1974.
———. *Nazism 1919–1945.* Exeter, England: University of Exeter Press, 1998.
Overy, R. J. *The Dictators: Hitler's Germany and Stalin's Russia.* New York: W. W. Norton, 2004.
Pauley, Bruce F. *Hitler and the Forgotten Nazis: A History of Austrian National Socialism.* Chapel Hill: University of North Carolina Press, 1981.
Peukert, Detlev. *Inside Nazi Germany: Conformity, Opposition, and Racism in Everyday Life.* New Haven, Conn.: Yale University Press, 1987.
Sax, Benjamin C., and Dieter Kuntz. *Inside Hitler's Germany: A Documentary History of Life in the Third Reich.* Sources in Modern History. Lexington, Mass.: D. C. Heath, 1992.
Schmölders, Claudia, and Adrian Daub. *Hitler's Face: The Biography of an Image.* Philadelphia: University of Pennsylvania Press, 2006.
Speer, Albert. *Inside the Third Reich: Memoirs.* New York: Collier Books, 1981.
Spielvogel, Jackson J. *Hitler and Nazi Germany: A History.* 4th ed. Upper Saddle River, N.J.: Prentice-Hall, 2001.
Stachura, Peter D. *Gregor Strasser and the Rise of Nazism.* London: Allen & Unwin, 1983.
Stackelberg, Roderick, and Sally Anne Winkle. *The Nazi Germany Sourcebook: An Anthology of Texts.* London: Routledge, 2002.
Steinweis, Alan E., and Daniel E. Rogers. *The Impact of Nazism: New Perspectives on the Third Reich and Its Legacy.* Lincoln: University of Nebraska Press, 2003.
Weinstein, Fred. *The Dynamics of Nazism: Leadership, Ideology, and the Holocaust.* Studies in Social Discontinuity. New York: Academic Press, 1980.

The National Socialist Worldview: Ideology and Propaganda

Aronsfeld, Caesar C. *The Text of the Holocaust: A Study of the Nazis' Extermination Propaganda, 1919–1945*. Marblehead, Mass.: Micah Publications, 1985.

Barkai, Avraham. *Nazi Economics: Ideology, Theory, and Policy*. New Haven, Conn.: Yale University Press, 1990.

Brüggemeier, Franz-Josef, Mark Cioc, and Thomas Zeller. *How Green Were the Nazis?: Nature, Environment, and Nation in the Third Reich*. Ohio University Press Series in Ecology and History. Athens: Ohio University Press, 2005.

Burrin, Philippe. *Nazi Anti-Semitism: From Prejudice to the Holocaust*. New York: New Press, 2005.

Bytwerk, Randall L. *Bending Spines: The Propagandas of Nazi Germany and the German Democratic Republic*. East Lansing: Michigan State University Press, 2004.

Cigaretten-Bilderdienst GmbH, and Hermann Göring. *The Propaganda of Adolf Hitler*. Phoenix, Ariz.: O'Sullivan Woodside, 1975.

Friedländer, Saul. *Nazi Germany and the Jews*. New York: HarperCollins, 1997.

Goodrick-Clarke, Nicholas. *The Occult Roots of Nazism: Secret Aryan Cults and Their Influence on Nazi Ideology: The Ariosophists of Austria and Germany, 1890–1935*. New York: New York University Press, 1992.

Herbert, Ulrich, ed. *National Socialist Extermination Policies: Contemporary German Perspectives and Controversies*. New York: Berghahn Books, 2000.

Herf, Jeffrey. *The Jewish Enemy: Nazi Propaganda during World War II and the Holocaust*. Cambridge, Mass.: Belknap Press of Harvard University Press, 2006.

Herzstein, Robert Edwin. *The War That Hitler Won: Goebbels and the Nazi Media Campaign*. New York: Paragon House, 1987.

Hutton, Christopher. *Linguistics and the Third Reich: Mother-Tongue Fascism, Race, and the Science of Language*. Routledge Studies in the History of Linguistics. London: Routledge, 1999.

Jäckel, Eberhard. *Hitler's World View: A Blueprint for Power*. Cambridge, Mass.: Harvard University Press, 1981.

Kallis, Aristotle A. *Fascist Ideology: Territory and Expansionism in Italy and Germany, 1922–1945*. London: Routledge, 2000.

Kaplan, Marion A. *Between Dignity and Despair: Jewish Life in Nazi Germany*. Studies in Jewish History. New York: Oxford University Press, 1998.

Klemperer, Victor. *The Language of the Third Reich: LTI-Lingua Tertii Imperii: A Philologist's Notebook*. London: Continuum, 2006.

Koonz, Claudia. *The Nazi Conscience*. Cambridge, Mass.: Belknap Press of Harvard University Press, 2003.

Lane, Barbara Miller, and Leila J. Rupp. *Nazi Ideology before 1933: A Documentation*. Austin: University of Texas Press, 1978.

Levy, Evonne Anita. *Propaganda and the Jesuit Baroque*. Berkeley: University of California Press, 2004.

Majer, Diemut, and United States Holocaust Memorial Museum. *"Non-Germans" under the Third Reich: The Nazi Judicial and Administrative System in Germany and Occupied Eastern Europe with Special Regard to Occupied Poland, 1939–1945*. Baltimore: Johns Hopkins University Press, 2003.

Mühlberger, Detlef. *Hitler's Voice: The Völkischer Beobachter, 1920–1933*. 2 vols. Oxford: Peter Lang, 2004.

Muller, Jerry Z. *The Other God That Failed: Hans Freyer and the Deradicalization of German Conservatism*. Princeton, N.J.: Princeton University Press, 1987.

Steinweis, Alan E. *Studying the Jew: Scholarly Antisemitism in Nazi Germany*. Cambridge, Mass.: Harvard University Press, 2006.

Uekötter, Frank. *The Green and the Brown: A History of Conservation in Nazi Germany*. Studies in Environment and History. Cambridge: Cambridge University Press, 2006.

Vondung, Klaus. *The Apocalypse in Germany*. Columbia: University of Missouri Press, 2000.

Wachsmann, Nikolaus. *Hitler's Prisons: Legal Terror in Nazi Germany*. New Haven, Conn.: Yale University Press, 2004.

Welch, David. *Nazi Propaganda: The Power and the Limitations*. London: Croom Helm, 1983.

Zeman, Z. A. B. *Nazi Propaganda*. 2nd ed. London: Oxford University Press, 1973.

Nazifying German Youth

Bäumer-Schleinkofer, Änne. *Nazi Biology and Schools.* Frankfurt am Main: Peter Lang, 1995.
Blackburn, Gilmer W. *Education in the Third Reich: A Study of Race and History in Nazi Textbooks.* Albany: State University of New York Press, 1985.
Dalton, Margaret Stieg. *Public Libraries in Nazi Germany.* Tuscaloosa: University of Alabama Press, 1992.
Farías, Víctor, Joseph Margolis, and Tom Rockmore. *Heidegger and Nazism.* Philadelphia: Temple University Press, 1989.
Ferry, Luc, and Alain Renaut. *Heidegger and Modernity.* Chicago: University of Chicago Press, 1990.
Golomb, Jacob, and Robert S. Wistrich. *Nietzsche, Godfather of Fascism?: On the Uses and Abuses of a Philosophy.* Princeton, N.J.: Princeton University Press, 2002.
Hentschel, Klaus. *Physics and National Socialism: An Anthology of Primary Sources.* Science Networks Historical Studies, vol. 18. Basel: Birkhäuser Verlag, 1996.
Lacoue-Labarthe, Philippe. *Heidegger, Art, and Politics: The Fiction of the Political.* Oxford: Blackwell, 1990.
Macrakis, Kristie, *Surviving the Swastika: Scientific Research in Nazi Germany.* Oxford: Oxford University Press, 1994.
Neske, Günther, and Emil Kettering. *Martin Heidegger and National Socialism: Questions and Answers.* New York: Paragon House, 1990.
Pauwels, Jacques R. *Women, Nazis, and Universities: Female University Students in the Third Reich, 1933–1945.* Contributions in Women's Studies, no. 50. Westport, Conn.: Greenwood Press, 1984.
Rabinbach, Anson. *In the Shadow of Catastrophe: German Intellectuals between Apocalypse and Enlightenment.* Berkeley: University of California Press, 1997.
Rabinbach, Anson, and Wolfgang Bialas, eds. *Nazi Germany and the Humanities.* Oxford: Oneworld, 2007.
Remy, Steven P. *The Heidelberg Myth: The Nazification and Denazification of a German University.* Cambridge, Mass.: Harvard University Press, 2002.
Rockmore, Tom. *On Heidegger's Nazism and Philosophy.* Berkeley: University of California Press, 1992.
Rockmore, Tom, and Joseph Margolis, eds. *The Heidegger Case: On Philosophy and Politics.* Philadelphia: Temple University Press, 1992.
Sluga, Hans D. *Heidegger's Crisis: Philosophy and Politics in Nazi Germany.* Cambridge, Mass.: Harvard University Press, 1993.
Sünker, Heinz, and Hans-Uwe Otto. *Education and Fascism: Political Identity and Social Education in Nazi Germany.* Knowledge, Identity and School Life Series, vol. 6. London: Falmer Press, 1997.
Young, Julian. *Heidegger, Philosophy, Nazism.* Cambridge: Cambridge University Press, 1997.

Making the Racial Community

Baumslag, Naomi. *Murderous Medicine: Nazi Doctors, Human Experimentation, and Typhus.* Westport, Conn.: Praeger Publishers, 2005.
Bleuel, Hans Peter. *Sex and Society in Nazi Germany.* Philadelphia: Lippincott, 1973.
Bridenthal, Renate, Atina Grossmann, and Marion A. Kaplan. *When Biology Became Destiny: Women in Weimar and Nazi Germany.* New Feminist Library. New York: Monthly Review Press, 1984.
Bridenthal, Renate, and Claudia Koonz. *Becoming Visible: Women in European History.* Boston: Houghton Mifflin, 1977.
Burleigh, Michael. *Death and Deliverance: "Euthanasia" in Germany c. 1900–1945.* Cambridge: Cambridge University Press, 1994.
———. *Ethics and Extermination: Reflections on Nazi Genocide.* New York: Cambridge University Press, 1997.
Burleigh, Michael, and Wolfgang Wippermann. *The Racial State: Germany, 1933–1945.* Cambridge: Cambridge University Press, 1991.
Clay, Catrine, and Michael Leapman. *Master Race: The Lebensborn Experiment in Nazi Germany.* London: Hodder & Stoughton, 1995.
Cocks, Geoffrey. *Psychotherapy in the Third Reich: The Göring Institute.* 2nd ed. New Brunswick, N.J.: Transaction Publishers, 1997.

Crane, Cynthia. *Divided Lives: The Untold Stories of Jewish-Christian Women in Nazi Germany.* New York: St. Martin's Press, 2001.

Deichmann, Ute. *Biologists under Hitler.* Cambridge, Mass.: Harvard University Press, 1996.

Eckart, Wolfgang Uwe. *Man, Medicine, and the State: The Human Body as an Object of Government Sponsored Medical Research in the 20th Century.* Stuttgart: Franz Steiner Verlag, 2006.

Friedlander, Henry. *The Origins of Nazi Genocide: From Euthanasia to the Final Solution.* Chapel Hill: University of North Carolina Press, 1995.

Frosh, Stephen. *Hate and the "Jewish Science": Anti-Semitism, Nazism and Psychoanalysis.* Basingstoke, England: Palgrave Macmillan, 2005.

Gonen, Jay Y. *The Roots of Nazi Psychology: Hitler's Utopian Barbarism.* Lexington: University Press of Kentucky, 2000.

Grau, Günter, and Schoppmann, Claudia. *Hidden Holocaust?: Gay and Lesbian Persecution in Germany.* Translated by Patrick Camiller. Chicago: Fitzroy Dearborn, 1995.

Guenther, Irene. *Nazi Chic?: Fashioning Women in the Third Reich.* Oxford: Berg, 2004.

Herzog, Dagmar. *Sexuality and German Fascism.* New York: Berghahn Books, 2004.

Kirkpatrick, Clifford. *Nazi Germany: Its Women and Family Life.* New York: AMS Press, 1981.

Koonz, Claudia. *Mothers in the Fatherland: Women, the Family, and Nazi Politics.* New York: St. Martin's Press, 1987.

Lifton, Robert Jay. *The Nazi Doctors: Medical Killing and the Psychology of Genocide.* New York: Basic Books, 1986.

Martin, Elaine. *Gender, Patriarchy, and Fascism in the Third Reich: The Response of Women Writers.* Detroit: Wayne State University Press, 1993.

Michalczyk, John J. *Medicine, Ethics, and the Third Reich: Historical and Contemporary Issues.* Kansas City, Mo.: Sheed & Ward, 1994.

Mosse, George L. *Nationalism and Sexuality: Respectability and Abnormal Sexuality in Modern Europe.* New York: Howard Fertig, 1985.

Nicosia, Francis R., and Jonathan Huener. *Medicine and Medical Ethics in Nazi Germany: Origins, Practices, Legacies.* New York: Berghahn Books, 2002.

Proctor, Robert. *Racial Hygiene.* Cambridge, Mass.: Harvard University Press, 1988.

Reese, Dagmar. *Growing Up Female in Nazi Germany.* Social History, Popular Culture, and Politics in Germany. Ann Arbor: University of Michigan Press, 2006.

Stargardt, Nicholas. *Witnesses of War: Children's Lives under the Nazis.* London: Jonathan Cape, 2005.

Stephenson, Jill. *Women in Nazi Germany.* Harlow, England: Longman, 2001.

Thomas, Katherine. *Women in Nazi Germany.* New York: AMS Press, 1981.

Weindling, Paul, and American Council of Learned Societies. *Health, Race, and German Politics between National Unification and Nazism, 1870–1945.* Cambridge History of Medicine. Cambridge: Cambridge University Press, 1989.

Nazism and Christianity

Baranowski, Shelley. *The Confessing Church, Conservative Elites, and the Nazi State.* Texts and Studies in Religion, vol. 28. Lewiston, N.Y.: E. Mellen Press, 1986.

Bergen, Doris L. *Twisted Cross: The German Christian Movement in the Third Reich.* Chapel Hill: University of North Carolina Press, 1996.

Burleigh, Michael. *Sacred Causes: The Clash of Religion and Politics, from the Great War to the War on Terror.* New York: HarperCollins, 2007.

Conway, John S. *The Nazi Persecution of the Churches, 1933–45.* Toronto: Ryerson Press, 1968.

Dietrich, Donald J. *Christian Responses to the Holocaust: Moral and Ethical Issues.* Religion, Theology, and the Holocaust. Syracuse, N.Y.: Syracuse University Press, 2003.

———. *Human Rights and the Catholic Tradition.* New Brunswick, N.J.: Transaction Publishers, 2007.

Feige, Franz G. M. *The Varieties of Protestantism in Nazi Germany: Five Theopolitical Positions.* Toronto Studies in Theology, vol. 50. Lewiston, N.Y.: E. Mellen Press, 1990.

Gallo, Patrick J. *Pius XII, the Holocaust, and the Revisionists: Essays.* Jefferson, N.C.: McFarland & Co., 2006.

Hanf, Theodor. *Dealing with Difference: Religion, Ethnicity, and Politics: Comparing Cases and Concepts.* Baden-Baden: Nomos, 1999.

Haynes, Stephen R. *The Bonhoeffer Legacy: Post-Holocaust Perspectives.* Minneapolis: Fortress Press, 2006.
Henley, Grant Holder. *Cultural Confessionalism: Literary Resistance and the Bekennende Kirche.* Studies in Modern German Literature, vol. 102. Oxford: Peter Lang, 2007.
Heschel, Susannah. *The Aryan Jesus: Christian Theologians and the Bible in Nazi Germany.* Princeton, N.J.: Princeton University Press, 2008.
———. *Transforming Jesus from Jew to Aryan: Protestant Theologians in Nazi Germany.* Albert T. Bilgray Lecture. Tucson: University of Arizona, 1995.
Hockenos, Matthew D. *A Church Divided: German Protestants Confront the Nazi Past.* Bloomington: Indiana University Press, 2004.
Krieg, Robert Anthony. *Catholic Theologians in Nazi Germany.* New York: Continuum, 2004.
LeConte, John. *The Priest and the Nazi.* Titusville, N.J.: Hopewell Publications, 2006.
Lewis, Keith D. *The Catholic Church in History: Legend and Reality.* New York: Crossroad Publishing, 2006.
Lewy, Guenter. *The Catholic Church and Nazi Germany.* New York: McGraw-Hill, 1964. Reprinted Boulder, Colo.: Da Capo Press, 2000.
Locke, Hubert G., and Marcia Sachs Littell. *Holocaust and Church Struggle: Religion, Power, and the Politics of Resistance.* Studies in the Shoah, vol. 16. Lanham, Md.: University Press of America, 1996.
Phayer, Michael. *Protestant and Catholic Women in Nazi Germany.* Detroit: Wayne State University Press, 1990.
Spicer, Kevin P., and Center for Advanced Holocaust Studies. *Antisemitism, Christian Ambivalence, and the Holocaust.* Bloomington: Indiana University Press, 2007.
Steigmann-Gall, Richard. *The Holy Reich: Nazi Conceptions of Christianity, 1919–1945.* New York: Cambridge University Press, 2003.
Stein, Leo. *Hitler Came for Niemoeller: The Nazi War against Religion.* Gretna, La.: Pelican Publishing, 2003.

The Arts: Visual Art, Architecture, Music, Literature

Adam, Peter. *Art of the Third Reich.* New York: Harry N. Abrams, 1992.
Applegate, Celia, and Pamela Maxine Potter. *Music and German National Identity.* Chicago: University of Chicago Press, 2002.
Art and Power: Europe under the Dictators, 1930–1945. Edited by Dawn Ades. London: Thames & Hudson/Hayward Gallery, 1995. Exhibition catalog.
Bacht, Nikolaus. *Music, Theatre and Politics in Germany: 1848 to the Third Reich.* Aldershot, England: Ashgate, 2006.
Bergmeier, H. J. P., and Rainer E. Lotz. *Hitler's Airwaves: The Inside Story of Nazi Radio Broadcasting and Propaganda Swing.* New Haven, Conn.: Yale University Press, 1997.
Cernyak-Spatz, Susan E. *German Holocaust Literature.* Rev. ed. New York: Peter Lang, 1989.
Clinefelter, Joan L. *Artists for the Reich: Culture and Race from Weimar to Nazi Germany.* Oxford: Berg, 2005.
Cuomo, Glenn R. *National Socialist Cultural Policy.* New York: St. Martin's Press, 1995.
"Degenerate Art": The Fate of the Avant-Garde in Nazi Germany. Edited by Stephanie Barron and Peter W. Guenther. Los Angeles: Los Angeles County Museum of Art, with Henry N. Abrams, 1991. Exhibition catalog.
Doherty, M. A. *Nazi Wireless Propaganda: Lord Haw-Haw and British Public Opinion in the Second World War.* International Communications. Edinburgh: Edinburgh University Press, 2000.
Etlin, Richard A., ed. *Art, Culture, and Media under the Third Reich.* Chicago: University of Chicago Press, 2002.
Fox, Jo. *Film Propaganda in Britain and Nazi Germany: World War II Cinema.* Oxford: Berg, 2007.
Friedländer, Saul. *Reflections of Nazism: An Essay on Kitsch and Death.* New York: Harper & Row, 1984.
Fuller, Steven Nyole. *The Nazis' Literary Grandfather: Adolf Bartels and Cultural Extremism, 1871–1945.* Studies in Modern German Literature, vol. 62. New York: Peter Lang, 1996.
Gadberry, Glen W. *Theatre in the Third Reich, the Prewar Years: Essays on Theatre in Nazi Germany.* Westport, Conn.: Greenwood Press, 1995.

Gättens, Marie-Luise. *Women Writers and Fascism: Reconstructing History.* Gainesville: University Press of Florida, 1995.

Giesen, Rolf. *Nazi Propaganda Films: A History and Filmography.* Jefferson, N.C.: McFarland, 2003.

Gilbert, Shirli. *Music in the Holocaust: Confronting Life in the Nazi Ghettos and Camps.* Oxford Historical Monographs. Oxford: Clarendon Press, Oxford University Press, 2005.

Hake, Sabine. *Popular Cinema of the Third Reich.* Austin: University of Texas Press, 2001.

Hamann, Brigitte. *Winifred Wagner: A Life at the Heart of Hitler's Bayreuth.* London: Granta, 2005.

Hillenbrand, F. K. M. *Underground Humour in Nazi Germany, 1933–1945.* London: Routledge, 1995.

Huener, Jonathan, and Francis R. Nicosia. *The Arts in Nazi Germany: Continuity, Conformity, Change.* New York: Berghahn Books, 2006.

Insdorf, Annette. *Indelible Shadows: Film and the Holocaust.* 3rd ed. Cambridge: Cambridge University Press, 2003.

Jaskot, Paul B. *The Architecture of Oppression: The SS, Forced Labor and the Nazi Monumental Building Economy.* Architext Series. London: Routledge, 2000.

Kamenetsky, Christa. *Children's Literature in Nazi Germany: The Cultural Policy of National Socialism.* Athens: Ohio University Press, 1984.

Kater, Michael H. *Composers of the Nazi Era: Eight Portraits.* New York: Oxford University Press, 2000.

———. *Different Drummers: Jazz in the Culture of Nazi Germany.* New York: Oxford University Press, 1992.

Kleeblatt, Norman L., ed. *Mirroring Evil: Nazi Imagery/Recent Art.* New Brunswick, N.J.: Rutgers University Press, 2001.

Kracauer, Siegfried. *From Caligari to Hitler: A Psychological History of the German Film.* Rev. ed. Princeton, N.J.: Princeton University Press, 2004. First published by Princeton University Press in 1947.

Lane, Barbara Miller. *Architecture and Politics in Germany, 1918–1945.* Cambridge, Mass.: Harvard University Press, 1985.

———. *National Romanticism and Modern Architecture in Germany and the Scandinavian Countries.* Modern Architecture and Cultural Identity. Cambridge: Cambridge University Press, 2000.

Leiser, Erwin. *Nazi Cinema.* New York: Collier Books, 1975.

McBride, Patrizia C., Richard W. McCormick, and Monika Zagar. *Legacies of Modernism: Art and Politics in Northern Europe, 1890–1950.* New York: Palgrave Macmillan, 2007.

Michaud, Eric. *The Cult of Art in Nazi Germany.* Translated by Janet Lloyd. Stanford, Calif.: Stanford University Press, 2004.

Painter, Karen. *Symphonic Aspirations: German Music and Politics, 1900–1945.* Cambridge, Mass.: Harvard University Press, 2007.

Potter, Pamela Maxine. *Most German of the Arts: Musicology and Society from the Weimar Republic to the End of Hitler's Reich.* New Haven, Conn.: Yale University Press, 1998.

Reimer, Robert C., ed. *Cultural History through a National Socialist Lens: Essays on the Cinema of the Third Reich.* Rochester, N.Y.: Camden House, 2000.

Rentschler, Eric. *German Film & Literature: Adaptations and Transformations.* New York: Methuen, 1986.

———. *The Ministry of Illusion: Nazi Cinema and Its Afterlife.* Cambridge, Mass.: Harvard University Press, 1996.

Schulte-Sasse, Linda. *Entertaining the Third Reich: Illusions of Wholeness in Nazi Cinema.* Durham, N.C.: Duke University Press, 1996.

Shirer, William L. *"This Is Berlin": Radio Broadcasts from Nazi Germany.* Woodstock, N.Y.: Overlook Press, 1999.

Spotts, Frederic. *Hitler and the Power of Aesthetics.* Woodstock, N.Y.: Overlook Press, 2003.

Steinweis, Alan E. *Art, Ideology, and Economics in Nazi Germany: The Reich Chambers of Music, Theater, and the Visual Arts.* Chapel Hill: University of North Carolina Press, 1993.

Taylor, Brandon, and Wilfried van der Will. *The Nazification of Art: Art, Design, Music, Architecture, and Film in the Third Reich.* Winchester, England: Winchester Press, Winchester School of Art, 1990.

Taylor, Richard. *Film Propaganda: Soviet Russia and Nazi Germany.* 2nd ed. Cinema and Society. London: I. B. Tauris, 1998.

Winkel, Roel Vande, and David Welch, eds. *Cinema and the Swastika: The International Expansion of Third Reich Cinema.* New York: Palgrave Macmillan, 2007.
Zortman, Bruce. *Hitler's Theater: Ideological Drama in Nazi Germany.* El Paso, Tex.: Firestein Books, 1984.

Modernity: Work, Sports, Amusements

Bachrach, Susan D. *The Nazi Olympics: Berlin 1936.* Boston: Little, Brown, 2000.
Baranowski, Shelley. *Strength through Joy: Consumerism and Mass Tourism in the Third Reich.* Cambridge: Cambridge University Press, 2004.
Black, Edwin. *IBM and the Holocaust: The Strategic Alliance between Nazi Germany and America's Most Powerful Corporation.* New York: Crown, 2001.
Bonde, Hans. *Gymnastics and Politics: Niels Bukh and Male Aesthetics.* Copenhagen: Museum Tusculanum Press, University of Copenhagen, 2006.
Brenner, Michael, and Gideon Reuveni, eds. *Emancipation through Muscles: Jews and Sports in Europe.* Lincoln: University of Nebraska Press, 2006.
Erenberg, Lewis A. *The Greatest Fight of Our Generation: Louis vs. Schmeling.* New York: Oxford University Press, 2006.
Fraser, Catherine C., and Dierk Hoffmann. *Pop Culture Germany!: Media, Arts, and Lifestyle.* Popular Culture in the Contemporary World. Santa Barbara, Calif.: ABC-CLIO, 2006.
Gispen, Kees. *Poems in Steel: National Socialism and the Politics of Inventing from Weimar to Bonn.* Monographs in German History, vol. 6. New York: Berghahn Books, 2002.
Hart-Davis, Duff. *Hitler's Games: The 1936 Olympics.* London: Century, 1986.
Hillenbrand, F. K. M. *Underground Humour in Nazi Germany, 1933–1945.* London: Routledge, 1995.
Homze, Edward L. *Foreign Labor in Nazi Germany.* Princeton, N.J.: Princeton University Press, 1967.
James, Harold. *The Nazi Dictatorship and the Deutsche Bank.* New York: Cambridge University Press, 2004.
Krüger, Arnd, and W. J. Murray. *The Nazi Olympics: Sport, Politics, and Appeasement in the 1930s.* Rev. ed. Sport and Society. Urbana: University of Illinois Press, 2003.
Large, David Clay. *Nazi Games: The Olympics of 1936.* New York: W. W. Norton, 2007.
Margolick, David. *Beyond Glory: Joe Louis vs. Max Schmeling, and a World on the Brink.* New York: Alfred A. Knopf, 2005.
Mason, Timothy W., and Jane Caplan. *Nazism, Fascism and the Working Class.* Cambridge: Cambridge University Press, 1995.
Myler, Patrick. *Ring of Hate: Joe Louis vs. Max Schmeling: The Fight of the Century.* New York: Arcade Publishing, 2005.
Patel, Kiran Klaus. *Soldiers of Labor: Labor Service in Nazi Germany and New Deal America, 1933–1945.* Publications of the German Historical Institute. New York: Cambridge University Press, 2005.
Petersen, Vibeke Rützou. *Women and Modernity in Weimar Germany: Reality and Its Representation in Popular Fiction.* New York: Berghahn Books, 2001.
Tooze, Adam. *The Wages of Destruction: The Making and Breaking of the Nazi Economy.* London: Allen Lane, 2006.
United States Holocaust Memorial Council. *The Nazi Olympics, Berlin, 1936.* Washington, D.C.: United States Holocaust Memorial Council, 1997.
Walters, Guy. *Berlin Games: How Hitler Stole the Olympic Dream.* London: John Murray, 2006.

The War and the Annihilation of the Jews

Aly, Götz, Belinda Cooper, and Allison Brown, eds. *"Final Solution": Nazi Population Policy and the Murder of the European Jews.* Oxford: Oxford University Press, 1999.
Arad, Yitzhak. *Belzec, Sobibor, Treblinka: The Operation Reinhard Death Camps.* Bloomington: Indiana University Press, 1987.
Arendt, Hannah. *Eichmann in Jerusalem: A Report on the Banality of Evil.* New York: Viking, 1969.
Bankier, David. *The Germans and the Final Solution: Public Opinion under Nazism.* Oxford: Blackwell, 1992.
Bartov, Omer. *The Eastern Front, 1941–45: German Troops and the Barbarization of Warfare.* London: Macmillan, 1985.

Bauer, Yehuda. *A History of the Holocaust.* New York: F. Watts, 1982.
Bergen, Bernard J. *The Banality of Evil: Hannah Arendt and "The Final Solution."* Lanham, Md.: Rowman & Littlefield, 1998.
Bergen, Doris. *War & Genocide: A Concise History of the Holocaust.* Critical Issues in History. Lanham, Md.: Rowman & Littlefield, 2002.
Breitman, Richard. *The Architect of Genocide: Himmler and the Final Solution.* New York: Knopf, 1991.
Browning, Christopher R. *Ordinary Men: Reserve Police Battalion 101 and the Final Solution in Poland.* New York: HarperCollins, 1992.
Browning, Christopher R., and Jürgen Matthäus. *The Origins of the Final Solution: The Evolution of Nazi Jewish Policy, September 1939–March 1942.* Comprehensive History of the Holocaust. Lincoln: University of Nebraska Press, 2004.
Bullock, Alan. *Hitler: A Study in Tyranny.* Harmondsworth, England: Penguin Books, 1962.
Burrin, Philippe. *Nazi Anti-Semitism: From Prejudice to the Holocaust.* New York: New Press, 2005.
Calvocoressi, Peter, Guy Wint, and John Pritchard. *Total War: The Causes and Course of World War II.* Vol. 1. London: Penguin, 1989.
Cesarani, David. *Eichmann: His Life and Crimes.* London: W. Heinemann, 2004.
———. *Holocaust: Critical Concepts in Historical Studies.* 6 vols. London: Routledge, 2004.
Cesarani, David, and Paul A. Levine. *Bystanders to the Holocaust: A Re-Evaluation.* London: Frank Cass, 2002.
Chalk, Frank, and Kurt Jonassohn. *The History and Sociology of Genocide: Analyses and Case Studies.* New Haven, Conn.: Yale University Press, 1990.
Childers, Thomas. *A History of Hitler's Empire.* Chantilly, Va.: Teaching Co., 2001. CD-ROM.
Czerniaków, Adam. *The Warsaw Diary of Adam Czerniakow: Prelude to Doom.* Edited by Raul Hilberg, Stanislaw Staron, and Joseph Kermish. New York: Stein and Day, 1979.
Dawidowicz, Lucy, ed. *A Holocaust Reader.* West Orange, N.J.: Behrman House, 1976.
———. *The War against the Jews 1933–1945.* New York: Bantam, 1986.
Dietrich, Donald J., ed. *Christian Responses to the Holocaust: Moral and Ethical Issues.* Religion, Theology, and the Holocaust. Syracuse, N.Y.: Syracuse University Press, 2003.
Eley, Geoff. *The Goldhagen Effect: History, Memory, Nazism—Facing the German Past.* Social History, Popular Culture, and Politics in Germany. Ann Arbor: University of Michigan Press, 2000.
Fings, Karola, Herbert Heuss, Frank Sparing, and Donald Kenrick. *The Gypsies during the Second World War.* 3 vols. Hatfield, England: Gypsy Research Centre, University of Hertfordshire Press, 1997.
Fleming, Gerald. *Hitler and the Final Solution.* Berkeley: University of California Press, 1984.
Friedlander, Henry. *The Origins of Nazi Genocide: From Euthanasia to the Final Solution.* Chapel Hill: University of North Carolina Press, 1995.
Friedlander, Saul. *Nazi Germany and the Jews: The Years of Persecution, 1933–1939.* New York: HarperCollins, 1997.
———. *Probing the Limits of Representation: Nazism and the "Final Solution."* Cambridge, Mass.: Harvard University Press, 1992.
———. *The Years of Extermination: Nazi Germany and the Jews, 1939–1945.* New York: HarperCollins, 2007.
Gilbert, Martin. *The Holocaust: A History of the Jews in Europe during the Second World War.* New York: Henry Holt, 1986.
Goldhagen, Daniel J. *Hitler's Willing Executioners: Ordinary Germans and the Holocaust.* New York: Knopf, 1996.
Gross, Jan Tomasz. *Fear: Anti-Semitism in Poland after Auschwitz: An Essay in Historical Interpretation.* New York: Random House, 2006.
———. *Neighbors: The Destruction of the Jewish Community in Jedwabne, Poland.* Princeton, N.J.: Princeton University Press, 2001.
———. *Revolution from Abroad: The Soviet Conquest of Poland's Western Ukraine and Western Belorussia.* Rev. ed. Princeton, N.J.: Princeton University Press, 2002.
Gutman, Israel, ed. *Encyclopedia of the Holocaust.* New York: Macmillan, 1990.
Graml, Hermann. *Antisemitism in the Third Reich,* Translated by Tim Kirk. Oxford: Blackwell, 1992.

Grynberg, Michal, ed. *Words to Outlive Us: Eyewitness Accounts from the Warsaw Ghetto.* New York: Metropolitan Books/Henry Holt, 2002.
Harmidarow, Walter J. *The Final Solution.* Shelburne, Ontario: Battered Silicon Dispatch Box, 1998.
Hartmann, Geoffry. *The Longest Shadow: In the Aftermath of the Holocaust.* Bloomington: Indiana University Press, 1996.
Heifetz, Julie, ed. *Too Young to Remember.* Detroit: Wayne State University Press, 1989.
Herbert, Ulrich, ed. *National Socialist Extermination Policies: Contemporary German Perspectives and Controversies.* New York: Berghahn Books, 2000.
Hilberg, Raul. *The Destruction of the European Jews.* New York: Watts, 1973.
Kaplan, Marion A. *Between Dignity and Despair: Jewish Life in Nazi Germany.* Studies in Jewish History. New York: Oxford University Press, 1998.
Katz, T. Steven. *The Holocaust in Historical Context.* Vol. 1, *The Holocaust and Mass Death before the Modern Age.* New York: Oxford University Press, 1994.
Klarsfeld, Serge, ed. *Documents Concerning the Destruction of the Jews of Grodno 1941–1944.* New York: Beate Klarsfeld Foundation, 1985.
Klee, Ernst, Willie Dressen, and Volker Riess, eds. *"The Good Old Days": The Holocaust as Seen by Its Perpetrators and Bystanders.* New York: Free Press, 1988.
Kogon, Eugen. *The Theory and Practice of Hell: The German Concentration Camps and the System behind Them.* New York: Berkley Books, 1998.
Krausnick, Helmut, Martin Broszat, and Hans-Adolf Jacobsen. *Anatomy of the SS State.* London: Collins, 1968.
Laqueur, Walter. *The Terrible Secret: An Investigation into the Suppression of Information about Hitler's Final Solution.* London: Weidenfeld & Nicolson, 1980.
Levy, Evonne Anita. *Propaganda and the Jesuit Baroque.* Berkeley: University of California Press, 2004.
Lewy, Guenter. *The Nazi Persecution of the Gypsies.* New York: Oxford University Press, 2000.
Lipstadt, Deborah. *Denying the Holocaust: The Growing Assault on Truth and Memory.* New York: Free Press, 1993.
Longerich, Peter. *Holocaust: The Nazi Persecution and Murder of the Jew.* Oxford: Oxford University Press, 2010,
Lozowick, Yaacov, and Haim Watzman. *Hitler's Bureaucrats: The Nazi Security Police and the Banality of Evil.* London: Continuum, 2002.
Maier, Charles S. *The Unmasterable Past: History, Holocaust, and German National Identity.* Cambridge, Mass.: Harvard University Press, 1997.
Marrus, Michael. *The Holocaust in History.* New York: New American Library/Dutton, 1986.
Mayer, Arno J. *Why Did the Heavens Not Darken?: The "Final Solution" in History.* New York: Pantheon Books, 1990.
Mazower, Mark. *Hitler's Empire: How the Nazis Ruled Europe.* London: Penguin Books, 2008.
Megargee, Geoffrey P. *War of Annihilation: Combat and Genocide on the Eastern Front, 1941.* Lanham, Md.: Rowman & Littlefield, 2006.
Millen, Rochelle L. *New Perspectives on the Holocaust: A Guide for Teachers and Scholars.* New York: New York University Press, 1996.
Mosse George L. *The Crisis of German Ideology: Intellectual Origins of the Third Reich.* New York: Grosset & Dunlap, 1964.
———. *Toward the Final Solution: A History of European Racism.* New York: Howard Fertig, 1978.
Müller, Ingo. *Hitler's Justice: The Courts of the Third Reich.* Cambridge, Mass.: Harvard University Press, 1991.
Pringle, Heather Anne. *The Master Plan: Himmler's Scholars and the Holocaust.* New York: Hyperion, 2006.
Redlikh, Egon, and Saul S. Friedman. *The Terezin Diary of Gonda Redlich.* Lexington: University Press of Kentucky, 1992.
Rittner, Carol, and John K. Roth, eds. *Different Voices: Women and the Holocaust.* New York: Paragon House, 1993.
Rose, Romani. *The Nazi Genocide of the Sinti and Roma.* 2nd ed. Heidelberg: Documentary and Cultural Centre of German Sinti and Roma, 1995.
Roseman, Mark. *The Wannsee Conference and the Final Solution: A Reconsideration.* New York: Metropolitan Books, 2002.

Shandley, Robert R. *Unwilling Germans?: The Goldhagen Debate.* Minneapolis: University of Minnesota Press, 1998.
Sierakowiak, Dawid. *The Diary of Dawid Sierakowiak: Five Notebooks from the Łódź Ghetto.* Edited by Alan Adelson. Translated by Kamil Turowski. New York: Oxford University Press, 1996.
Spielvogel, Jackson. *Hitler and Nazi Germany: A History.* Upper Saddle River, N.J.: Prentice-Hall, 1996.
Steinweis, Alan E. *Studying the Jew: Scholarly Antisemitism in Nazi Germany.* Cambridge, Mass.: Harvard University Press, 2006.
Stone, Dan. *The Historiography of the Holocaust.* New York: Palgrave Macmillan, 2004.
Stroop, Jürgen. *The Stroop Report: The Jewish Quarter of Warsaw Is No More!* New York: Pantheon Books, 1979.
Vidal-Naquet, Pierre. *Assassins of Memory: Essays on the Denial of the Holocaust.* New York: Columbia University Press, 1992.
Wachsmann, Nikolaus. *Hitler's Prisons: Legal Terror in Nazi Germany.* New Haven, Conn.: Yale University Press, 2004.
Weiss, John. *The Ideology of Death.* Chicago: Ivan Dee, 1996.
Yahil, Leni. *The Rescue of Danish Jewry: Test of a Democracy.* Philadelphia: Jewish Publication Society of America, 1969.
———. *Sho'ah. The Holocaust: The Fate of European Jewry, 1932–1945.* New York: Oxford University Press, 1990.
Zelkowicz, Józef. *In Those Terrible Days: Writings from the Łódź Ghetto.* Translated by Michal Unger. Jerusalem: Yad Vashem, 2002.
Zuccotti, Susan. *The Italians and the Holocaust: Persecution, Rescue and Survival.* New York: Basic Books, 1987.

Resistance

Altman, Linda Jacobs. *Resisters and Rescuers: Standing Up against the Holocaust.* The Holocaust in History. Berkeley Heights. N.J.: Enslow Publishers, 2003.
Bethge, Eberhard, and Renate Bethge. *Last Letters of Resistance: Farewells from the Bonhoeffer Family.* Philadelphia: Fortress Press, 1986.
Cartarius, Ulrich, and Institut für Auslandsbeziehungen. *The German Resistance Movement 1933–1945: Information and Documentation Exhibition.* Rev. ed. Stuttgart: Institut für Auslandsbeziehungen, 1988.
Chandler, Andrew. *The Moral Imperative: New Essays on the Ethics of Resistance in National Socialist Germany, 1933–1945.* Widerstand, Dissent and Resistance in the Third Reich. Boulder, Colo.: Westview Press, 1998.
Dietrich, Donald J. *Human Rights and the Catholic Tradition.* New Brunswick, N.J.: Transaction Publishers, 2007.
Fest, Joachim C. *Plotting Hitler's Death: The Story of the German Resistance.* New York: Metropolitan Books, 1996.
Garbe, Detlef, and United States Holocaust Memorial Museum. *Between Resistance and Martyrdom: Jehovah's Witnesses in the Third Reich.* Madison: University of Wisconsin Press, 2007.
Gill, Anton. *An Honourable Defeat: A History of German Resistance to Hitler, 1933–1945.* New York: Henry Holt, 1994.
Gutman, Israel, *The Holocaust and Resistance: An Outline of Jewish History in Nazi Occupied Europe (1933–1945).* Jerusalem: Yad Vashem, 1972.
Hassell, Ulrich von. *The Von Hassell Diaries, 1938–1944: The Story of the Forces against Hitler inside Germany, 1938–1944.* Boulder, Colo.: Westview Press, 1994.
Henley, Grant Holder. *Cultural Confessionalism: Literary Resistance and the Bekennende Kirche.* Studies in Modern German Literature, vol. 102. Oxford: Peter Lang, 2007.
Hoffmann, Peter. *German Resistance to Hitler.* Cambridge, Mass.: Harvard University Press, 1988.
———. *The History of the German Resistance, 1933–1945.* 3rd ed. Montreal: McGill-Queen's University Press, 1996.
Langbein, Hermann. *Against All Hope: Resistance in the Nazi Concentration Camps, 1938–1945.* New York: Continuum, 1996.
Large, David Clay, and Goethe House New York. *Contending with Hitler: Varieties of German*

Resistance in the Third Reich. Publications of the German Historical Institute. Cambridge: Cambridge University Press, 1991.

Laska, Vera. *Nazism, Resistance & Holocaust in World War II: A Bibliography*. Metuchen, N.J.: Scarecrow Press, 1985.

Marrus, Michael Robert, ed. *The Nazi Holocaust: Historical Articles on the Destruction of European Jews*. Westport, Conn.: Meckler, 1989.

McDonough, Frank. *Opposition and Resistance in Nazi Germany*. Cambridge: Cambridge University Press, 2001.

Merson, Allan. *Communist Resistance in Nazi Germany*. London: Lawrence and Wishart, 1986.

Mommsen, Hans, and Angus McGeoch. *Alternatives to Hitler: German Resistance under the Third Reich*. Princeton, N.J.: Princeton University Press, 2003.

Niven, William John. *Facing the Nazi Past: United Germany and the Legacy of the Third Reich*. London: Routledge, 2002.

Ottaway, Susan. *Hitler's Traitors*. Barnsley, England: L. Cooper, 2003.

Scholl, Inge. *Students against Tyranny: The Resistance of the White Rose, Munich, 1942–1943*. Middletown, Conn.: Wesleyan University Press, 1970.

Shuter, Jane. *Resistance to the Nazis*. Chicago: Heinemann Library, 2003.

Siefken, Hinrich, and Hildegard Vieregg. *Resistance to National Socialism: Kunst und Widerstand: Forschungsergebnisse und Erfahrungsberichte: Third Nottingham Symposium*. Munich: Iudicium, 1995.

Steinbach, Peter, John M. Grossman, Johannes Tuchel, and Gedenkstätte Deutscher Widerstand, eds. *Exhibition, Resistance to National Socialism*. Berlin: Gedenkstätte Deutscher Widerstand, 1990.

Stern, J. P. Hitler: *The Führer and the People*. Berkeley: University of California Press, 1975.

Stoltzfus, Nathan. *Resistance of the Heart: Intermarriage and the Rosenstrasse Protest in Nazi Germany*. New York: W. W. Norton, 1996.

Thomsett, Michael C. *The German Opposition to Hitler: The Resistance, the Underground, and Assassination Plots, 1938–1945*. Jefferson, N.C.: McFarland, 1997.

Tillich, Paul. *Against the Third Reich: Paul Tillich's Wartime Addresses to Nazi Germany*. Edited by Ronald H. Stone. Translated by Matthew Lon Weaver. Louisville, Ky.: Westminster John Knox Press, 1998.

Vinke, Hermann, and Ilse Aichinger. *The Short Life of Sophie Scholl*. Cambridge, Mass.: Harper & Row, 1984.

Von Klemperer, Klemens. *German Resistance against Hitler: The Search for Allies Abroad, 1938–1945*. Oxford: Clarendon Press, Oxford University Press, 1992.

Young, Ian. *Gay Resistance: Homosexuals in the Anti-Nazi Underground*. Toronto: Stubblejumper Press, 1985.

Credits

Unless otherwise noted below, all translations are by Lilian Friedberg.

5 From "Guidelines of the German Worker's Party," in *Nazi Ideology before 1933: A Documentation,* introduced and translated by Barbara Miller Lane and Leila J. Rupp. Copyright © 1978. By permission of the University of Texas Press.

6 From "Adolf Hitler, Letter to Adolf Gemlich" (September 16, 1919), in *Hitler: Sämtliche Aufzeichnungen 1905–1924,* ed. Eberhard Jäckel and Axel Kuhn (Stuttgart: Deutsche Verlags-Anstalt, 1980). Reprinted by permission of Oldenbourg Wissenschaftsverlag GmbH.

8 From "The Founding of the Party 1920," in *Deutschland erwacht: Werden, Kampf, und Sieg der NSDAP.* Reprinted by permission of Reemtsma Cigarettenfabriken GmbH.

10 From Dietrich Eckart, "Jewishness in and around Us," in *Nazi Ideology before 1933: A Documentation,* introduced and translated by Barbara Miller Lane and Leila J. Rupp. Copyright © 1978. By permission of the University of Texas Press.

14 From Gottfried Feder, "Manifesto for the Breaking Bondage of Interest," in *Nazi Ideology before 1933: A Documentation,* introduced and translated by Barbara Miller Lane and Leila J. Rupp. Copyright © 1978. By permission of the University of Texas Press.

20 From "Hanns Johst, Schlageter, in *Nazi Culture,* George L. Mosse. © Reprinted by permission of The University of Wisconsin Press.

22 From "Hans Hinkel, One of a Hundred Thousand" (1942), in *Einer unter Hundertausend* (Munich: Verlag Knorr & Hirth, 1942). Translation © Randall Bytwerk. Reprinted by permission of Randall Bytwerk.

27 From *The Hitler Trial* (1933), in *Deutschland erwacht: Werden, Kampf, und Sieg der NSDAP,* ed. Wilfrid Bade. Reprinted by permission of Reemtsma Cigarettenfabriken GmbH.

31 From Fritz Oerter, "Our Speakers in the Anti-Marxist Struggle" (1932), in *Unser Wille und Weg* (1932, 2). Translation © Randall Bytwerk. Reprinted by permission of Randall Bytwerk.

35 From Hermann Führbach, "How I Became a National Socialist" (1934), in *The Nazi Years* by Remak, 1969. Hans Hinkel Collection, Hoover Institution Archives.

46 From Erich Ebermayer, *Denn heute gehört uns Deutschland. Persönliches und politisches Tagebuch* (Hamburg: Zsolnay, 1959). © Paul Zsolnay Verlag Wien, 1959. Reprinted by permission of the publisher.

50 From Otto Wels, "Speech against the Passage of the Enabling Act (1933), in "Die nationalsozialistische Revolution 1933," in *Dokumente der deutschen Politik,* Vol. 1, edited by Paul Meier-Benneckenstein. Translated by Thomas Dunlap. Reprinted by permission of the German Historical Institute.

58 From Carl Schmitt, *Staat, Bewegung, Volk: Die Dreigliederung der politischen Einheit* (Hamburg: Hanseatische Verlagsanstalt, 1933). Reprinted by permission of the heirs of Carl Schmitt.

59 From Ernst Forsthoff, *Der Totale Staat* (Hamburg: Hanseatische Verlagsanstalt, 1933).

62 From Alfred Rosenberg, "The Total State?" in *Völkischer Beobachter* (January 9, 1934).

63 From Carl Schmitt, "The Führer Protects the Law: On Adolf Hitler's Reichstag Address of 13 July 1934, in "Der Führer schützt das Recht: zur Reichstagsrede Adolf Hitlers vom 13. Juli 1934," in Positionen und Begriffe im Kampf mit Weimar–Genf–Versailles 1923–1939 (Hamburg: Hanseatische Verlagsanstalt, 1940). Reprinted by permission of Duncker & Humblot, GmbH.

67 From Hans Frank, "On the Position of the Judge before National Socialist Law and in the National Socialist State" (1936), in *Dokumente der deutschen Politik* (16, V), ed. F. A. Six, 16, V (Berlin, 1942).

72 From Baldur von Schirach, *Hitler As No One Knows Him* (1933), ed. Heinrich Hoffman (Berlin: Zeitgeschichte Verlag, 1933). Translation © Randall Bytwerk. Reprinted by permission of Randall Bytwerk.

74 From Rudolf Hess, "The Oath to Adolf Hitler" (1934), in *Reden* (Munich: Zentralverlag der NSDAP, 1938). Translation © Randall Bytwerk. Reprinted by permission of Randall Bytwerk.

77 From Baldur von Schirach, "To the Führer" (1935), in *Die Fahne der Verfolgten*. Translation © Randall Bytwerk. Reprinted by permission of Randall Bytwerk.

91 From "The Party Rally Day of Victory: The Victory of Faith" (1933), in *Deutschland erwacht: Werden, Kampf, und Sieg der NSDAP, Deutschland erwacht: Werden, Kampf, und Sieg der NSDAP,* ed. Wilfrid Bade. Reprinted by permission of Reemtsma Cigarettenfabriken GmbH.

95 From Victor Klemperer, *I Shall Bear Witness: A Diary of the Nazi Years 1933–1941* (Modern Library, 1999). Translation © Martin Chalmers. Reprinted by permission of the publisher.

97 From Hannes Kremer, "New Meanings for 'Inherited' Customs?" in *Die neue Gemeinschaft 3* (1937). Translation © Randall Bytwerk. Reprinted by permission of Randall Bytwerk.

134 From Carl Schmitt, "National Socialist Legal Thought" (1934), in *Deutsches Recht: Zentralorgan des Bundes Nationalsozialistischer Deutscher Juristen* (May 25, 1934). Reprinted by permission of the heirs of Carl Schmitt.

157 From Walter Gross, *Nationalsozialistische Rassenpolitik. Eine Rede an die deutschen Frauen* (Dessau: C. Dünnhaupt, 1934). Translated by Randall Bytwerk. Calvin College, German Propaganda Archive.

163 From Paul Brohmer, "Biological Studies and Völkisch Education" (1933), in *Biologie Unterricht und völkische Erziehung* (Frankfurt: Verlag Moritz Diesterweg, 1933), in *Nazi Culture,* George L. Mosse. © Reprinted by permission of The University of Wisconsin Press.

167 From G. Hecht, "Biology and National Socialism," in *Zeitschrift für die gesamte Naturwissenschaft, 3* (1937–1938). George L. Mosse. © Reprinted by permission of The University of Wisconsin Press.

169 From "Reichsführer of the SS Central Office for Racial Policy, Racial Thinking" (1942), in *Rassenpolitik* (Berlin, 1942). Translation © Randall Bytwerk. Reprinted by permission of Randall Bytwerk.

174 From Karl Haushofer, "National Socialist Thought in the World" (1933), in *Der nationalsozialistiche Gedanke in der Welt* (Munich: Georg D. W. Callwey Verlag, 1933). Reprinted by permission of Callwey Verlag.

175 From Hans Simmer, "German Territory and German *Volk*" (1934), in *Grundzüge der Geopolitik in Anwendung auf Deutschland* (Munich: R. Oldenbourg, 1934). Reprinted by permission of Oldenbourg Wissenschaftsverlag GmbH.

177 From Hans Grimm, "My Father, My Colonies" (1934), in *Lüderitzland: Sieben Begebenheiten* (Munich: Albert Langen/Georg Müller, 1934). Reprinted by permission of Klosterhaus Verlag and the family Grimm.

178 From Ernst Gerhard Jacob, "Colonial Policy As Cultural Mission," in *Deutsche Kolonialpolitik in Dokumenten. Gedanken und Gestalten aus den letzten fünfzig Jahren.* (Leipzig, Dieterich'sche Verlagsbuchhandlung, 1938). Reprinted by permission of the publisher.

185 From "Aryan and Jew," in *Mein Kampf* by Adolf Hitler, translated by Ralph Manheim. Copyright © 1943, renewed 1971 by Houghton Mifflin Company. Reprinted by permission of Houghton Mifflin Company. All rights reserved.

195 From E. H. Schulz and R. Frercks, "Why the Aryan Law? A Contribution to the Jewish Question," in *Warum Arierparagrah? Ein Beitrag zur Judenfrage* (Berlin: Verlag Neues Volk, 1934). Translation © Randall Bytwerk. Reprinted by permission of Randall Bytwerk.

200 From Martin Buber, "An Open Letter to Gerhard Kittel" (1933), in *Die Sünde und die Erkenntnis. Reden und Aufsätze* (Berlin: Schocken, 1936). © Translation Disputation and Dialogue: Readings in the Jewish-Christian Encounter. Edited and translated by Frank Ephraim Talmage (New York: KTAV Publishing House, 1975), 51–54.

202 From Wilhelm Stuckart and Hans Globke, "Civil Rights and the Natural Inequality of Man" (1936), in *Kommentare zur deutschen Rassengesetzgebung,* I (Munich, 1936), in *Nazi Culture,* George L. Mosse. © Reprinted by permission of The University of Wisconsin Press.

216 From Carl Schmitt, "German Jurisprudence and the Struggle against the Jewish Spirit," in *Deutsche Juristen-Zeitung* (41:20, Berlin). Reprinted by permission of the heirs of Carl Schmitt.

218 From Hertwig Hartner-Hnizdo, "Accident of History or Destiny of the Race?" in *Volk der Gauner: Eine Untersuchung des jüdischen Gaunertums* (Munich: Hoheneichen Verlag, 1939).

233 From Betty Scholem, "Report on Kristallnacht" (1938), in *Mutter und Sohn im Briefwechsel, 1917–1946* (Munich: Beck, 1939). Reprinted by permission of Verlag C. H. Beck.

241 From *Adolf Hitler Is Our Führer!* (ca. 1938), in *Schulbuch aus Wien.* Reprinted by permission of the S. Fluegge Collection.

243 From "Conference Minutes: Horst Wessel School in Kassel," in *Schule im Dritten Reich–Erziehung zum Tod?* eds. Gert Platner und Schulern der Gerhart Hauptmann Schule in Kassel (Munich: Deutsche Taschenbuch, 1983). Permission granted by Deutscher Taschenbuch Verlag, Munich, Germany. All rights reserved.

249 From Dietrich Klagges, "German History for Schools" (1942), in *Volk und Führer: Deutsche Geschichte für Schulen,* ed. Dietrich Klagges, Middle School Edition (Frankfurt am Main, 1942). Reprinted by permission of the Klagges family.

253 From Baldur von Schirach, "The National Socialist Youth Movement" (1933), in *Deutschland erwacht: Werden, Kampf, und Sieg der NSDAP,* ed. Wilfrid Bade. Reprinted by permission of Reemtsma Cigarettenfabriken GmbH.

255 From Reimund Schnabel, *Leadership Training Program of the Hitler Youth* (1938). Reprinted by permission of Juventa Verlag GmbH.

259 From Oberbannführer Stephan, *The League of German Girls Organization in the Hitler Youth* (1935), in *Quellen und Documenten Wir Schaffen, Jahrbuch des BDM* (Weinheim und München: Juventa Verlag, 2001). Reprinted by permission of Juventa Verlag GmbH.

261 From Erna Bohlman, "The Position of the Ancient Germanic Woman," in *Wille und Macht* (2:20, 1934; Weinhem und München: Juventa Verlag, 2001). Reprinted by permission of Juventa Verlag GmbH.

262 From Günther Kaufmann, "Faith and Beauty," in *Wille und Macht* (6:3, 1938; Weinheim : Juventa Verlag, 2001). Reprinted by permission of Juventa Verlag GmbH.

264 From Reich Directive 36/K: "Collecting Women's Hair," Gisela Miller-Kipp, " 'Auch Du gehörst dem Führer,' Die Geschichte des Bundes deutscher Madel (BDM)," in *Quellen und Dokumenten* (Weinheim: Juventa Verlag, 2001). Reprinted by permission of Juventa Verlag GmbH.

264 From Jutta Rüdiger, "The 'Eastern Deployment' of the BDM," in "Das junge Deutschland" (36, 1942). Kristel Paun, " 'Auch Du gehörst dem Führer,' Die Geschichte des Bundes deutscher Mädel (BDM)," in *Quellen und Dokumenten* (Weinheim und Munchen: Juventa Verlag, 2001). Reprinted by permission of Juventa Verlag GmbH.

265 From "Wartime Fashion Show" (1942), in *Wir Schaffen. Jahrbuch des BDM.* Kristel Paun, " 'Auch Du gehörst dem Führer,' Die Geschichte des Bundes deutscher Mädel (BDM)" in Quellen and Dokumenten (Weinheim: Juventa Verlag, 2001) Reprinted by permission of Juventa Verlag GmbH.

270 From Ernst Krieck, *Renewal of the German University* (Marburg: N. G. Elwertsche Verlagsbuchhandlung, 1933). Reprinted by permission of Rudolph Braun-Elwert, Elwert Verlag.

285 From Johannes Haller, *The Epochs of German History* (Stuttgart: J. G. Cottasche Buchhandlung Nachfolger, 1936).

288 From Karl Alexander von Müller, *The Influence of the Peasantry in the National Community of the Volk* (Stuttgart: Deutsche Verlags-Anstalt, 1938).

295 From Arnold Gehlen, "The State and Philosophy" (1935), in *Gesamtausgabe,* Vol. 2 (Vittorio Klostermann, 1980). © Reprinted by permission of Vittorio Klostermann.

298 From Alfred Baeumler, "Nietzsche and National Socialism," in *Studien zur deutschen Geistesgeschichte* (Berlin: Junker und Dünnhaupt Verlag, 1943), in *Nazi Culture,* George L. Mosse. © Reprinted by permission of The University of Wisconsin Press.

300 From Wolfgang Schulz, "Nietzsche's Zarathustra and the Historical Zarathustra," in *Nationalsozialistische Monatshefte* (August 1935), in *Nazi Culture,* George L. Mosse. © Reprinted by permission of The University of Wisconsin Press.

316 From Joseph Goebbels, "German Women" (1933), in *Signale der neuen Zeit. 25 ausgewählte Reden von Dr. Joseph Goebbels* (Munich: Zentralverlag der NSDAP, 1934). Translation © Randall Bytwerk. Reprinted by permission of Randall Bytwerk.

320 From Gertrud Scholtz-Klink, "To Swedes and Germans" (1937), in *Die Frau im Dritten Reich: Eine Dokumentation,* ed. Gertrud Scholz-Klink (Tübingen: Grabert Verlag, 1978). Translation © Randall Bytwerk. Reprinted by permission of Randall Bytwerk and Grabert Verlag.

325 From Gertrud Altmann-Gädke, "The Maternal Instinct Must Be Reinforced" (1941), in *Erprobtes Haushalten: Handbuch der Hausfrauenarbeit* (Leipzig: Julius Klinkhardt Verlagsbuchhandlung, 1941). Reprinted by permission of Julius Klinkhardt Verlagsbuchhandlung KG.

343 From Kölnische Zeitung, "Sozial Tauglich–Asozial–Anti-sozial," in *Kölnische Zeitung* (64, December 10, 1937). Reprinted by permission of Kölner Stadt-Anzeiger.

345 From Clemens August Count von Galen, "Sermon on Euthanasia" (1941), in *Galen, Clemens*

August von. Akten, Briefe, und Predigten: 1933–1946, ed. Peter Loffler, 42 (Mainz: Matthias Grünewald Verlag, 1988). Reprinted by permission of the Kommission für Zeitgeschichte.

367 From "How Magnus Hirschfeld's Institute for Sexual Science Was Demolished and Destroyed" (1933), in *Homosexualität in der NS-Zeit: Dokumente einer Diskriminierung und Verfolgung,* eds. Günter Grau and Claudia Schoppmann (Frankfurt am Main: Fischer, 1993). Reprinted by permission of Fischer Taschenbuch Verlag.

371 From "Illusions" (1935), in *Homosexualität in der NS-Zeit: Dokumente einer Diskriminierung und Verfolgung,* ed. Günter Grau and Claudia Schoppmann (Frankfurt am Main: Fischer, 1993). Reprinted by permission of Fischer Taschenbuch Verlag.

374 From "1935 Revision to Section 175 of the Penal Code" (1935), in *Homosexualität in der NS-Zeit: Dokumente einer Diskriminierung und Verfolgung,* ed. Günter Grau and Claudia Schoppmann (Frankfurt am Main: Fischer, 1993). Reprinted by permission of Fischer Taschenbuch Verlag.

375 From Heinrich Himmler, "Secret Directive on the Curtailment of Homosexuality and Abortion (1936)," in *Homosexualität in der NS-Zeit: Dokumente einer Diskriminierung und Verfolgung,* ed. Günter Grau and Claudia Schoppmann (Frankfurt am Main: Fischer, 1993). Reprinted by permission of Fischer Taschenbuch Verlag.

399 From C. G. Jung, "The State of Psychotherapy Today" (1934), in *The Collected Works of C. G. Jung, 10, Civilization in Transition* (Princeton, NJ: Princeton University Press, 1964). Reprinted by permission of © Princeton University Press.

400 From Ursula von Kardorff, "Suicide and Deportation" (1943), in *Berliner Aufzeichnungen,* © Verlag C. H. Beck, München, 1992. Reprinted by permission of the publisher.

420 From "Declaration of the German Christians" (1933), in *Kirchliches Jahrbuch für die Evangelische Kirche in Deuschland 1933–1934,* ed. J. Beckman (Güttersloh, 1948), in *Deutsche Geschichte 1933–1945: Dokumente zur Innen- and Aussenpolitik,* ed. Wolfgang Michalka (Fischer: Frankfurt am Main, 1993). Reprinted by permission of Fischer Taschenbuch Verlag.

421 From Karl Barth, "Theological Declaration of Barmen" (1934), in *Die Bekentnisse und grundsätzlichen Äusserungen zur Kirchenfrage,* Vol.2, ed. Kurt Dietrich Schmidt. Arthur Cochrane, *The Church's Confession under Hitler* (Eugene, OR: Pickwick Publications, 1976), 237–242. ISBN 978–0–915138–28–7. Pickwick Publications is an imprint of Wipf and Stock Publishers.

425 From Julius von Jan, "Sermon on *Bußtag* (Day of Atonement)" (1938), in Landeskirchen Archiv des Evangelischen Oberkirchenrats (Stuttgart) in *Die Zeit* (November 4, 1999). Reprinted by permission of Landeskirchliches Archiv Stuttgart.

429 From Alfred Rosenberg, "Theses on the Worldview" (1941), in *Das politische Tagebuch Alfred Rosenbergs aus den Jahren 1934/34 und 1939/40,* ed. Dr. Hans-Günther Seraphim (Göttingen: Musterschmidt Verlag, 1956). Reprinted by permission of Muster-Schmidt Verlag.

449 From German Student Association, "Down with the Un-German Spirit!" (1933). First appeared as a poster titled *Wider den undeutschen Geist!,* in *Die Bücherverbrennung. Zum* 10 May 1933, ed. Gerhard Sauder. © 1983 Carl Hanser Verlag, München Wien. Reprinted by permission of the publisher.

450 From "To the German Student Association: All Anti-Semitic Students Are Assholes!" (1933), in *Die Bücherverbrennung. Zum,* 10 May 1933, ed. Gerhard Sauder. © 1983 Carl Hanser Verlag München Wien. Reprinted by permission of the publisher.

451 From "General Guidelines for Compiling Blacklists" (1933), in *Die Bücherverbrennung. Zum* 10 May 1933, ed. Gerhard Sauder. © 1983 Carl Hanser Verlag München Wien. Reprinted by permission of the publisher.

454 From Oskar Maria Graf, "Burn Me!" (1933), in *Volkstimme (Saarbrücken),* May 15, 1933, ed. Gerhard Sauder. © 1983 Carl Hanser Verlag München Wien. Reprinted by permission of the publisher.

455 From "Joseph Goebbels, The Tasks of the Ministry of Propaganda," delivered on March 15, 1933, published in *The Third Reich: Politics and Propaganda* (London: Routledge, 1933), translated by David Welch. Reprinted by permission of Taylor and Francis.

457 From Joseph Goebbels, "Speech at the Opening of the Reich Chamber of Culture" (15 November 1933) (London: Routledge, 1933), translated by David Welch. Reprinted by permission of Taylor and Francis.

459 From "Law Establishing the Reich Chamber of Culture," 22 September 1933, in *The Third Reich: Politics and Propaganda* (London: Routledge, 1993), translated by David Welch. Reprinted by permission of Taylor and Francis.

462 From Gottfried Benn, "Answer to the Literary Emigrants" (1933), radio broadcast of 24 May

1933. Reprinted by permission of Gottfried Benn, *Sämtliche Werke,* Vol. VI. © 1933, 1989 J. G. Cotta'sche Buchhandlung Nachfolger GmbH, Stuttgart, Germany.

469 From Ernst Bertram, "Against Humanism," in *Deutsche Gestalten. Fest und Gedankreden* (Leipzig: Insel-Verlag, 1935). Reprinted by permission of Suhrkamp Verlag.

471 From Josef Nadler, "Nation, State, and Literature," in *Deutscher Geist/Deutscher Osten: Zehn Reden* (Munich: R. Oldenburg, 1937). Reprinted by permission of Oldenbourg Wissenschaftsverlag GmbH.

475 From Thomas Mann, "Letter to Eduard Korrodi" (February 3, 1936). Reprinted by permission of Neue Zürcher Zeitung and Random House.

480 From Werner Bergengruen, *A Matter of Conscience* (1935), translated by Norman Cameron (London: Thames and Hudson, 1952), 257–260. Reprinted by permission of Thames & Hudson.

492 From Joseph Goebbels, "Ban on Art Criticism" (November 27, 1936), in *Deutsche Geschichte 1933–1945: Dokumente zur Innen und Aussenpolitik* (Frankfurt a. M.: Fischer, 1993). Reprinted by permission of Fischer Taschenbuch Verlag.

493 From Ernst Barlach, "Letter to Joseph Goebbels" (1936), in *Ernst Barlach und die Nationalsozialistische Kunstpolitik: Eine Dokumentarische Darstellung zur "Entarteten Kunst,"* (Munich: Piper, 1983). Reprinted by permission of Piper Verlag GmbH.

500 From Adolf Ziegler, "Speech at the Opening of the Degenerate Art Exhibition" (1937), in *"Entartete Kunst:" Dokumentation zum Nationalsozialistischen Bildersturm* (Munich: Prestel Verlag, 1987). Reprinted by permission of the Adolf Ziegler family.

503 From Reinhard Piper, "A Visit to the Degenerate Art Exhibition" (July 28, 1937), in *Ernst Barlach und die Nationalsozialistische Kunstpolitik: Eine Dokumentarische Darstellung zur "Entarteten Kunst"* (Munich: Piper, 1983). Reprinted by permission of the heirs of Reinhard Piper.

532 From "Wilhelm Furtwängler and Joseph Goebbels" (1933), in *Vossische Zeitung,* April 11, 1933. Translation © J. Noakes and G. Pridham, *Nazism 1919–1945,* Vol 2. *State, Economy, and Society 1933–1939. A Documentary Reader* (Exeter: University of Exeter Press, Exeter UK, 1994). Reprinted by permission of the University of Exeter Press.

534 From "The Bayreuth Festival: August 15, 1933–'Featuring' Herr Hitler," in the *Manchester Guardian,* August 15, 1933. © Guardian News & Media Ltd, 1933. Reprinted by permission of *Manchester Guardian.*

538 From "Protest der Richard-Wagner-Stadt München," in Münchener Neueste Nachrichten," in *Müncher Neueste Nachrichten,* no. 105, 16 April 1933. Published in English in Thomas Mann, *Pro and Contra Wagner,* translated by Alan Blunden (Chicago: University of Chicago Press, 1985), 149–51.

539 From Thomas Mann, "Response to City of Munich Protest," in *Vossische Zeitung,* April 21, 1933, Evening Edition. ©Translation by Alan Blunden in *Thomas Mann, Pro and Contra Wagner* (Chicago: U. of Chicago Press 1985). Reprinted by permission of the University of Chicago Press.

541 From Herbert Birtner, "On the German Interpretation of Beethoven Since Richard Wagner" (1937), in *Beethoven und die Gegenwart: Festschrift des Beethovenhauses Bonn* (Berlin/Bonn: Ferdinand Dümmlers Verlag, 1937), translated by Alan Blunden. Reprinted by permission of the University of California Press.

560 From Joseph Goebbels, "Speech at the Kaiserhof" (March 28, 1933), in *Nationalsozialistische Filmpolitik: Eine Soziologische Untersuchung über die Spielfilme des Dritten Reichs* (Stuttgart: Ferdinand Enke Verlag, 1969). © Translation David Welch, *The Third Reich: Politics and Propaganda* (London: Routledge, 1993). Reprinted by permission of Taylor and Francis.

563 From "Reich Cinema Law" (February 16, 1934), in *Nationalsozialistische Filmpolitik,* (Stuttgart: Ferdinand Enke Verlag, 1969). © Translation David Welch, *The Third Reich: Politics and Propaganda* (London: Routledge, 1993). Reprinted by permission of Taylor and Francis.

566 From Hans Traub, "The Cinema As Entertainment Site," in *Der Film als politisches Machtmittel* (Munich: Verlag Münchener Druck und Verlagshaus, 1933).

595 From "The Eternal Jew: Film of a 2,000–Year Rat Migration" (1940), in *Unser Wille und Weg,* Number 10 (1940). Translation © Randall Bytwerk. Reprinted by permission of Randall Bytwerk.

603 From Ludwig Moshamer, "Die Thingstätte und ihre Bedeutung für das kommende deutsche Theater," (1935), from *Bauwelt* (26, 1935). Reprinted by permission of the publisher.

612 From Joseph Goebbels, "Radio As the Eighth Great Power" (1933), in *Signale der neuen Zeit: 25 Ausgewählte Reden von Dr. Joseph Goebbels* (Munich: Zentralverlag der NSDAP, 1938). Translation © Randall Bytwerk. Reprinted by permission of Randall Bytwerk.

616 From Franz Hartung, "Radio and Politics" (1933), in *Rufer und Hörer* 8, 3rd Edition (November 1933). Translation © Randall Bytwerk. Reprinted by permission of Randall Bytwerk.

626 From Joseph Goebbels, "No Dialect in Radio Broadcasts" (1942), in *Die Rückseite des Hakenkreuzes. Absonderliches aus den Akten des Dritten Reiches* (Munich: DTV, 1993). Reprinted by permission of Deutscher Taschenbuch Verlag.

632 From Kurt Singer, "Let's Get Started!", in *Monatsblätter 1:1* (October 1933). © Akademie der Künste. Reprinted by permission of the Akademie der Künste.

633 From Kurt Singer, "Speech at the Opening of the Cultural Conference of the Reich League of Jewish Cultural Leagues in Germany" (September 5, 1936), in *Geschlossene Vorstellung: Die Jüdische Kulturbund in Deutschland 1933–1941* (Berlin: Edition Hentrich, 1992). © Akademie der Künste. Reprinted by permission of the Akademie der Künste.

636 From Robert Weltsch, "Wear the Yellow Badge with Pride," in *Jüdische Rundschau,* April 1933. © Translation Lucy S. Dawidowicz. © Berhrman House, Inc. Reprinted by permission of Ruben Weltsch.

672 From Wilfrid Bade, "The Führer and the Automobile," in *Das Auto erobert die Welt* (Berlin: Verlag Wilhelm Anderman, 1938), translated by Jeremny Noakes and Geoffrey Pridham. Reprinted by permission of the University of Exeter Press..

685 From "Jerry Siegel Attacks!", in *Das Schwarze Korps,* April 25, 1940. Copyright © 1998 by Randall Bytwerk. Reprinted by permission of Randall Bytwerk.

686 From "The Danger of Americanism," in *Das Schwarze Korps,* March 14, 1944. Translation © Randall Bytwerk. Reprinted by permission of Randall Bytwerk.

724 From Julius Streicher, "Bolshevism and Synagogue," in *Der Stürmer,* 36 (1941). Translation © Randall Bytwerk. Reprinted by permission of Randall Bytwerk.

732 From Victor Klemperer, *I Will Bear Witness,* Vols. 1 & 2, translated by Martin Chalmers, translation copyright © 1998 by Martin Chambers. Used by permission of Random House, Inc.

735 From "Persecution of the Sinti and Roma: Three Decrees," in Hans Joachim Döring, *Die Zigeuner im nationalsozialistischen Staat* (Hamburg: Kriminalistik Verlag, 1967). Reprinted by permission of Verlagsgruppe Hüthig Jehle Rehm GmbH.

737 From Joseph Goebbels, "The Jews Are Guilty!" in *Das Eiserne Herz: Reden und Aufsätze aus den Jahren 1941/42* (Munich: Zentralverlag der NSDAP, 1942 Translation © Randall Bytwerk. Reprinted by permission of Randall Bytwerk.

742 From Karl Baumböck, "Jews Practice World Politics" (Berlin: Propaganda-Verlag Paul Hochmuth, 1942). Translation © Randall Bytwerk. Reprinted by permission of Randall Bytwerk.

759 From Central Office for Racial Policy, "The Jew," in *Der Reichsführer SS/SS-Hauptamt, Rassenpolitik* (Berlin: Der Reichsführer SS/SS-Hauptamt, 1943). Translation © Randall Bytwerk. Reprinted by permission of Randall Bytwerk.

764 From *Warsaw Diary of Adam Czerniakow (1940/42),* (New York: Ivan R. Dee, 1979). Reprinted by permission of publisher.

765 Selections from the Warsaw Ghetto Diary by Stefan Ernest, Stanislaw Sznapman, and Stefania Staszewska published in *Words to Outlive Us: Eyewitness Accounts from the Warsaw Ghetto,* edited by Michal Grynberg, Translation © 2002 by Metropolitan Books. Reprinted by permission of Henry Holt and Company, LLC.

771 From Józef Zelkowicz, *Diary of the Łódź Ghetto* (1942), translated by Naftali Greenwood (Jerusalem: Yad Vashem, 2002). Reprinted by permission of Yale University.

775 From "Notebooks from the Łódź Ghetto" (1942), in *Diary of Dawid Sierakowiak: Five Notebooks from the Łódź Ghetto,* translated by Kamil Turowski. © 1996 by the Jewish Heritage Project and Kamil Turowski. By permission of Oxford University Press.

791 From Egon (Gonda) Redlich, "Theresienstadt Diary" (1944), *The Terezin Diary of Gonda Redlich* (Lexington: University Press of Kentucky, 1992). Reprinted by permission of The University Press of Kentucky.

803 From Zalman Gradowski, "The Czech Transport: A Chronicle of the Auschwitz Sonderkommando" (1944). Reprinted from *The Literature of Destruction: Jewish Responses to Catastrophe,* © 1989, edited by David Roskies, published by The Jewish Publication Society, with the permission of the publisher.

821 From Joseph Goebbels, "Address to the Leaders of the NSDAP in Vienna" (October 26, 1940), in *Bulletin des Arbeiterkreises "Zweiter Weltkrieg,"* Number 3 (1969). Reprinted by permission of Fischer Taschenbuch Verlag.

828 From Joseph Goebbels, "Now, People, Rise Up and Let the Storm Winds Blow!", (February 18, 1943). First published as "Nun, Volk, steh auf, und Sturm brich los! Rede im Berliner Sportpalast," in *Der steile Aufstieg* (Munich: Zentralverlag der NSDAP, 1944), 167–204. Translation © Randall Bytwerk. Reprinted by permission of Randall Bytwerk.

855 From Hans Scholl, Willi Graf, and Christoph Probst, "The White Rose: Second Leaflet" (pp. 77–80), in *The White Rose: Munich 1942–1943,* trans. Inge Scholl (Wesleyan University Press, 1983). © 1983 by Inge Scholl and reprinted by permission of Wesleyan University Press.

857 From "Reports From the Reich, Death Penalty for Demoralization" (1943), in *Meldungen aus dem Reich, 1938–1945: Die Geheimen Lageberichte des Sicherheitsdienstes der SS,* Bd. 15 (Herrsching: Pawlak, 1984). Translation © Timothy Nunan. Reprinted by permission of Timothy Nunan.

859 From "Reactions to the *Wochenschau* (Weekly Newsreel) for 27 February–4 March 1943," in *Meldungen aus dem Reich, 1938–1945: Die geheimen Lageberichte des Sicherheitsdienstes der SS,* Bd. 12 (Herrsching: Pawlak, 1984).

863 From Ulrich von Hassell, "Diary Entry" (1941), in *The von Hassell Diaries: The Story of the Forces against Hitler Inside Germany, 1938–1944* (Boulder: Westview Press, 1994). Reprinted by permission of the Perseus Books Group.

Index

Weimar and Now: German Cultural Criticism

EDWARD DIMENDBERG, MARTIN JAY, AND ANTON KAES, GENERAL EDITORS

1. *Heritage of Our Times,* by Ernst Bloch
2. *The Nietzsche Legacy in Germany, 1890–1990,* by Steven E. Aschheim
3. *The Weimar Republic Sourcebook,* edited by Anton Kaes, Martin Jay, and Edward Dimendberg
4. *Batteries of Life: On the History of Things and Their Perception in Modernity,* by Christoph Asendorf
5. *Profane Illumination: Walter Benjamin and the Paris of Surrealist Revolution,* by Margaret Cohen
6. *Hollywood in Berlin: American Cinema and Weimar Germany,* by Thomas J. Saunders
7. *Walter Benjamin: An Aesthetic of Redemption,* by Richard Wolin
8. *The New Typography,* by Jan Tschichold, translated by Ruari McLean
9. *The Rule of Law under Siege: Selected Essays of Franz L. Neumann and Otto Kirchheimer,* edited by William E. Scheuerman
10. *The Dialectical Imagination: A History of the Frankfurt School and the Institute of Social Research, 1923–1950,* by Martin Jay
11. *Women in the Metropolis: Gender and Modernity in Weimar Culture,* edited by Katharina von Ankum
12. *Letters of Heinrich and Thomas Mann, 1900–1949,* edited by Hans Wysling, translated by Don Reneau
13. *Empire of Ecstasy: Nudity and Movement in German Body Culture, 1910–1935,* by Karl Toepfer
14. *In the Shadow of Catastrophe: German Intellectuals between Apocalypse and Enlightenment,* by Anson Rabinbach
15. *Walter Benjamin's Other History: Of Stones, Animals, Human Beings, and Angels,* by Beatrice Hanssen
16. *Exiled in Paradise: German Refugee Artists and Intellectuals in America from the 1930s to the Present,* by Anthony Heilbut
17. *Cool Conduct: The Culture of Distance in Weimar Germany,* by Helmut Lethen, translated by Don Reneau
18. *In a Cold Crater: Cultural and Intellectual Life in Berlin, 1945–1948,* by Wolfgang Schivelbusch, translated by Kelly Barry
19. *A Dubious Past: Ernst Jünger and the Politics of Literature after Nazism,* by Elliot Y. Neaman
20. *Beyond the Conceivable: Studies on Germany, Nazism, and the Holocaust,* by Dan Diner
21. *Prague Territories: National Conflict and Cultural Innovation in Franz Kafka's Fin de Siècle,* by Scott Spector
22. *Munich and Memory: Architecture, Monuments, and the Legacy of the Third Reich,* by Gavriel D. Rosenfeld
23. *The Ufa Story: A History of Germany's Greatest Film Company, 1918–1945,* by Klaus Kreimeier, translated by Robert and Rita Kimber
24. *From Monuments to Traces: Artifacts of German Memory, 1870–1990,* by Rudy Koshar
25. *We Weren't Modern Enough: Women Artists and the Limits of German Modernism,* by Marsha Meskimmon
26. *Culture and Inflation in Weimar Germany,* by Bernd Widdig
27. *Weimar Surfaces: Urban Visual Culture in 1920s Germany,* by Janet Ward
28. *Graphic Design in Germany: 1890–1945, by Jeremy Aynsley*
29. *Expressionist Utopias: Paradise, Metropolis, Architectural Fantasy,* by Timothy O. Benson, with contributions by Edward Dimendberg, David Frisby, Reinhold Heller, Anton Kaes, and Iain Boyd Whyte
30. *The Red Count: The Life and Times of Harry Kessler,* by Laird M. Easton
32. *The Dark Mirror: German Cinema between Hitler and Hollywood,* by Lutz Koepnick
33. *Rosenzweig and Heidegger: Between Judaism and German Philosophy,* by Peter Eli Gordon
34. *The Authority of Everyday Objects: A Cultural History of West German Industrial Design,* by Paul Betts

35. *The Face of East European Jewry, by Arnold Zweig, with fifty-two drawings by Hermann Struck.* Edited, translated, and with an introduction by Noah Isenberg
36. *No Place Like Home: Locations of Heimat in German Cinema,* by Johannes von Moltke
37. *Berlin Alexanderplatz: Radio, Film, and the Death of Weimar Culture,* by Peter Jelavich
38. *Berlin Electropolis: Shock, Nerves, and German Modernity,* by Andreas Killen
39. *A Concise History of the Third Reich,* by Wolfgang Benz, translated by Thomas Dunlap
40. *Germany in Transit: Nation and Migration, 1955–2005,* edited by Deniz Göktürk, David Gramling, and Anton Kaes
41. *Weimar on the Pacific: German Exile Culture in Los Angeles and the Crisis of Modernism,* by Ehrhard Bahr
42. *The 1972 Munich Olympics and the Making of Modern Germany,* by Kay Schiller and ChristopherYoung
43. *Berlin Psychoanalytic: Psychoanalysis and Culture in Weimar Republic Germany and Beyond,* by Veronika Fuechtner
44. Cinema and Experience: Siegfried Kracauer, Walter Benjamin, and Theodor W. Adorno, by Miriam Bratu Hansen
45. *Siegfried Kracauer's American Writings: Essays on Film and Popular Culture,* edited by Johannes von Moltke and Kristy Rawson
46. *Metropolis Berlin, 1880–1940,* edited by Iain Boyd Whyte and David Frisby
47. *The Third Reich Sourcebook,* edited by Anson Rabinbach and Sander L. Gilman